WORLD WAR II FRONT PAGES

THE STARS AND STRIPES

WORLD WAR II FRONT PAGES

BONANZA
New York

The Bill Mauldin cartoons on the front pages dated June 1, 1945 and June 9, 1945 are reproduced with the permission of Bill Mauldin and Wil-Jo Associates, Inc.

The front pages in this book were reproduced from material at the New York Public Library, Astor, Lenox & Tilden Foundations.

This 1987 edition is published by Bonanza Books, distributed by Crown Publishers, Inc., 225 Park Avenue South, New York, New York 10003, by arrangement with Hugh Lauter Levin Associates, Inc.

Printed and Bound in the United States of America

Library of Congress Cataloging-in-Publication Data

The Stars and Stripes.

Reprint. Originally published: New York : Hugh Lauter Levin Associates, 1985.
1. World War, 1939-1945—Sources. 2. Stars and stripes.
3. American newspapers—Sections, columns, etc.—Front pages—Facsimiles.
D735.S73 1987 071'.3 87-71.66
ISBN 0-517-64618-8

h g f e d c b a

PUBLISHER'S NOTE

The front pages of *The Stars and Stripes* gathered here tell the story of World War II from the perspective of the United States Armed Forces, which published the newspaper for its troops. Operating one step behind the front lines, the paper moved with the armed forces on all fronts. By the end of the war, it had established over thirty editions, in such places as London, Algiers, Sicily, Paris, Germany, and Shanghai.

Because space does not permit the reproduction of every front page, a representative selection was made, taking into consideration each sample's importance in relating the story of World War II. This story includes not only the progress of the fighting but also the human interest accounts of life in the armed forces and news from back home. Making the selection proved to be a difficult task, necessitating the omission of many excellent front pages. Similarly, due to the scope of the book, the fine feature articles inside the paper could not be included.

Since the paper operated so close to the front lines, stories about the fighting at hand had to be censored. As you go through the pages you will see many headlines that read "Nazis Report . . ." or "Japs Say . . ." In these cases, only the news already known by the enemy was reported. On the other hand, news of actions thousands of miles away was reported in detail. In both cases, this approach was used in the interest of maintaining security and morale.

This book would not have been possible without the aid of the New York Public Library and its extensive records of the various *Stars and Stripes* editions. The library staff made every effort to provide clear, legible copies of much-handled old newspapers. Special thanks go to Ms. Ruth Anne Stewart, of the External Services Division, Mr. William Boddie, of the Photographic Service Division of the library, and Mr. Henry Epstein, a longtime employee of *The Stars and Stripes,* who aided greatly in the development of this book and the selection of the pages.

3D. THE STARS AND STRIPES 3D.
Weekly Newspaper of the U.S. Armed Forces in the British Isles

Vol. 2 No. 1 67290 Saturday, April 18, 1942

President in 10th Year

President of the United States and Commander in Chief of all United States Armed Forces, Franklin Delano Roosevelt last month began his tenth year in the White House little changed by the heavy burden of events which has been his since his first inauguration. "Because of Mr. Roosevelt's ability to remain calm in the face of great trials," said the president's physician, "nine years in the White House have left scant mark." *(New York Times Photo.)*

Red Cross Play Halls Open Soon

By Pvt. Ford Kennedy

The first Red Cross recreation centers for American forces in Northern Ireland will be opened within 60 days, J. S. Disosway, field director, has announced.

Two centers, one in Belfast and the other at Londonderry, will be among the first ready to receive soldiers. These will be located in buildings already available and will provide rooms, showers and meals for soldiers.

Present plans indicate that a charge of half a crown will be made for one night's lodging, a shower and breakfast.

Soldiers on pass or furlough will be admitted to these and other recreation centers to be opened within the next several months.

The Plaza, which was Belfast's swankiest dance hall and amusement center until it was destroyed partly by fire last year, has been taken over by the Red Cross and

Red Cross - - -

(Continued on Page 5)

Troops Are Getting Up As U.S. Is Going to Bed

SOMEWHERE IN NORTHERN IRELAND—American troops here find themselves six or seven hours ahead of the folks at home after the latest time change which took place April 5.

Normandie Fire

WASHINGTON, D.C. (UP) — The Normandie fire was the result of "carelessness," a congressional investigation committee decided last week.

Dear Adolf,

We know your stooges will get this paper into your hands at an early date. Suggest you read at once:

Coming up in the next issue will be a story by Cecil Brown on "Heroes in Far East War." You won't get any more comfort out of it than you get from the story of United States Production from Time Magazine on Page 1 of this issue.

The Staff.

P.S.—Joe Palooka, Superman and Popeye are coming to our comic page soon.

U.S. Winning In the Battle of Production

(Reprinted from Time Magazine)

Something is happening that Adolf Hitler does not yet understand—a new re-enactment of the old American miracle of wheels and machinery, but on a new scale.

This time it is a miracle of war production, and its miracle worker is the automobile industry.

Even the American people do not appreciate the miracle, because it is too big for the eye to see in an hour, a day or a month. It is, in fact, too big to be described. It can only be understood by taking a sample.

There is no better sample than Henry Ford. Two years ago he was an earnest pacifist who refused to take an order for plane engines for Britain.

Today, like the rest of industry, he is not only working for war, but for war alone, and working as he never worked before.

A generation ago he performed the first miracle of mass production.

Today he is only one of many miracle-workers in his industry, but his part in their common job is itself greater than the greatest job he ever did before.

These things are not exaggerations, but the truth about Detroit today is not easy to believe.

* * *

A year ago Willow Run was a lazy little creek west of Detroit, surrounded by woodlands, a few farmhouses, a few country schools.

Today Willow Run is the most enormous room in the history of man: More than a half-mile long, nearly a quarter of a mile wide.

In this great room errands are run by automobile; through the flash of moving machinery and the dust of construction, no man can see from one end to the other.

The plant contains 25,000 tons of structural steel. By summer 70,000 men will work in this room; by December, 90,000.

In planning the building, Ford Motor Company's drafting room used five miles of blueprint paper a day, seven days a week, for six months.

In this enormous workroom Ford hopes eventually to turn out a four-motored Consolidated bomber every hour. The raw materials will go in at one end; from the other will emerge the 30-ton machines, coughing with life. The bombers will be born from half-mile assembly lines so fast that Ford will not try to store them.

The deadly infants will be ranked on a great new airfield, stretching out from the assembly end of the plant, with enough white concrete runways to make a highway 22 miles long. From those runways the new born bombers will make their test flights, then take off for service.

* * *

Detroit has other enormous rooms, and out of them armies

Time - - -

(Continued on Page 5)

Labor Peace

PITTSBURGH, PENN. (UP)—"We will stay on the job until the war is won."

This is the pledge given by the Congress of Industrial Organizations and the American Federation of Labor. Philip Murray, president of the C.I.O., and William Green, president of the A.F. of L., appeared together for the first time here recently to give the joint pledge.

Magazine Cost Up

NEW YORK, N.Y. (AP)—The "Saturday Evening Post" and "Colliers" have raised their prices from 5 to 10 cents.

General Marshall Sets a Goal for Stars and Stripes

Gen. George C. Marshall, Chief of Staff of the Army who is in the British Isles inspecting United States Forces, Friday issued the following statement upon the publication of the first issue of The Stars and Stripes of 1942:

"Like any other veteran of the A.E.F. in France, I am delighted to welcome the new version of The Stars and Stripes. By a fortunate coincidence I happen to be in the British Isles as it comes off the press.

"'I do not believe that any one factor could have done more to sustain the morale of the A.E.F. than The Stars and Stripes,' wrote General Pershing of this soldier newspaper. We have his authority for the statement that no official control was ever exercised over the matter which went into The Stars and Stripes. 'It always was entirely for and by the soldier,' he said. This policy is to govern the conduct of the new publication.

A Symbol

"From the start The Stars and Stripes existed primarily to furnish our officers and men with news about themselves, their comrades and the homes they had left behind across the sea. A soldier's newspaper, in these grave times, is more than a morale venture. It is a symbol of the things we are fighting to preserve and spread in this threatened world. It represents the free thought and free expression of a free people.

"I wish the staff every success in this important venture. Their responsibility includes much more than the publication of a successful paper. The morale, in fact the military efficiency of the American soldiers in these Islands, will be directly affected by the character of The Stars and Stripes of 1942."

* * *

General Marshall, in addition to inspecting United States troops in the British Isles, has been meeting with high British officials on various aspects of the war. He was accompanied from the United States by Harry Hopkins, who is representing the president in talks on supply matters.

Both men held a press conference shortly after their arrival April 8 and both expressed themselves as confident that the

Marshall - - -

(Continued on Page 3)

Gen. Marshall . . "We will expand."

A.E.F. Paper Reborn for U.S. Forces

This issue of your newspaper, the first of a soldier weekly planned for distribution to United States service personnel in the British Isles, re-establishes The Stars and Stripes, famous publication of the American Expeditionary Force of the last war.

Permission to use the name was granted by the War Department upon request of Maj. Gen. James E. Chaney, commanding general of United States Army Forces in the British Isles.

The first issue of the original Stars and Stripes was published in Paris Feb. 8, 1918, and the seventy-first on June 13, 1919. At the height of that paper's circulation career, 400,000 copies weekly were distributed to troops in the trenches of France and Belgium.

The original Stars and Stripes became world-famous because of the excellence of its editing and reporting. The paper at that time also was noted for the humor which its reporters and editors injected, the excellence of its sketches by Baldridge; the beauty of its poems, selected and edited by Hudson Hawley, from contributions of service men.

Staff

Among the writers of that paper who later went on to fame in the same type of work after the war are Guy T. Vishniskki, newspaper and publication expert; Grantland Rice, the sports writer; Alexander Woollcott, the "Town Crier;" Franklin P. Adams of "Information please;" Hilmar R. Baukhage, radio and news commentor; Stephen T. Early, press secretary to President Roosevelt; Hawley, radio executive and writer; Adolph S. Ochs, II, member of the famous publishing family; John T. Winterich, author of "Squads Write;" Abian A. Wallgren, cartoonist.

The new publication will contain many of the features popular in the original weekly.

News Services

The Associated Press, United Press, International News Service, Chicago Daily News, Chicago Tribune, New York Herald-Tribune, New York Times, and Des Moines Register are among the news organizations that have volunteered to supply materal for the paper. King Features, McNaught Syndicate, Inc., McClure Newspaper Syndicate, Time and Life Magazines, National, Columbia, and Mutual Broadcasting systems, and Wide World and Acme also are offering their services and feature material.

Numerous other agencies, including many which ordinarily serve only the British Isles, are assisting, while Capt. Bruce Bairnsfather, creator of "The Better 'Ole," has accepted the position of cartoonist and will contribute weekly.

Each Sunday, The Stars and Stripes will be distributed to personnel of the United States Armed Forces throughout the British Isles. This task will be accomplished with the co-operation of the distribution agencies and facilities of the "News of the World," voluntarily placed at the disposal of The Stars and Stripes.

The staff will operate under the Special Services section, directed by Col. E. M. Barnum.

3d. THE STARS AND STRIPES 3d.
Weekly Newspaper of the U.S. Armed Forces in the British Isles

Vol. 2 No. 2 London, England April 25, 1942

General Marshall Inspects Troops in Northern Ireland

Gen. George C. Marshall, Chief of Staff of the Army, watches an Infantry unit march in review during his visit last weekend to Northern Ireland and the American troops stationed there. With General Marshall as he visited the troops were a number of high ranking Army officers and other officials of the British, Northern Ireland and United States governments. The officers included . . .

. . . Maj. Gen. R. P. Hartle, commander of U.S. troops in Northern Ireland, Lt. Gen. H. E. Franklyn, commander of British troops in Northern Ireland, and Maj. Gen. James E. Chaney, commander of American troops in the British Isles. General Hartle stands next to General Marshall, while General Chaney is at right. Story Page 3. (*Associated Press Photos.*)

Tell Pass Plan, Trips to London

Leaves and furloughs for a limited number of American troops in Northern Ireland will be granted after May 1, Maj. Gen. James E. Chaney, commander of United States Army Forces in the British Isles, announced Friday.

Nine days will be the maximum time for which either leaves or furloughs may be granted, but those having passes will be permitted to visit England, Scotland or Wales.

Of the total number allowed to be absent from their duties, no more than 50 men and 10 officers will be given permission to visit London, the remainder of those excused from duty being obliged to spend their holiday in other parts of the country.

Individuals may not have more than one leave or furlough in any three-month period and not more than 7 per cent. of a command may be absent at one time.

* * *

Men going on leave or furlough must:

1. Have sufficient funds to cover all traveling expenses during their trip and must purchase return-trip tickets before departure.
2. Have a furlough certificate or leave order.
3. Have their identity card.
4. Have British embarkation forms.
5. Have British leave ration book.
6. Have identification tags.
7. Have gas mask and helmet.

Other equipment will not be carried and hand luggage should be limited to what the individual can carry and maintain supervision over.

The route selected for travel of troops to and from Northern Ireland is such that meals may be obtained en route and personnel, therefore, need not carry luncheons when leaving their home stations.

* * *

Arrangements have been completed whereby men on leave or furlough who may become ill will be treated at the nearest British Army, Naval or R.A.F. station and at the Railway Transportation Offices in various railroad stations. Personnel becoming ill in London may visit a special Army dispensary which has been set up.

The American Red Cross field director will make arrangements for men wishing to avail themselves of invitations to visit private homes.

Dear Mom: I've Met 2 Heroes

SOMEWHERE IN NORTHERN IRELAND—Dear Mom: Let's forget about the sights I'm seeing and the things I'm doing this time, Mom. I want to tell you about some of the things I've been thinking since I first landed in Northern Ireland.

I guess maybe it's because I've been a little ashamed of myself and telling you about it will make me feel better.

You see, Mom, Americans, and especially American soldiers, are a queer breed. We like to think we're rough and tough, and we like to "take over."

I remember reading somewhere that America is a nation with a thousand mothers and a thousand fathers. Maybe that's the reason we want every one to think we're the original "Dead End Kids."

But too often, Mom, we get the idea that we've got a monopoly on the world's supply of courage. I suppose we have our share. You can tell a Yankee soldier anywhere. If he came into a store dressed in only a sheet you could spot him for a Yankee by the air of confidence he wears like a coat, by the look in his eye. You seldom see a Yankee not perfectly at ease, no matter what the surroundings.

T-Bone Steak

But here's what I mean. At first we got a big kick out of going into a restaurant and asking for a big T-bone steak, with fresh green beans, celery, mashed potatoes, apple pie and all the trimmings.

We knew darn well the chances were pretty good we wouldn't get it, but we wanted every one to know that's what we were used to before.

Well, Mom, we don't do things like that now. And we don't go into dime stores and ask for three bars of soap. And we don't ask anyone where we can get "some good American cigarets." Nobody told us to stop doing those nasty little things. We just came around to it gradually.

And it's because, whatever and

Heroes - - -

(*Continued on Page* 5)

Kansas City Police Sniff Breaths for Traces of Liquor

KANSAS CITY, MO. (Special Cable from Associated Press)—Kansas City police are halting city-bound cars Friday and Saturday nights and sniffing drivers' breaths to determine whether they have been drinking.

Police assigned to sniff must prove they haven't head colds, which would impair their smelling.

3 Weeks Holds Burma's Fate

CHUNGKING, CHINA — The next three weeks may seal Burma's fate.

They will decide whether the Japanese can reach the high and dry ground of the upper valleys in the race against the monsoons due by May 14.

They will reveal Japan's capacity to maintain her already overtaxed supply lines during the rainy season and to keep up the pressure necessary to expel the Allies.

Radio Program

The first of a series of radio programs for American troops will be broadcast Monday from 6.30 to 7.30 p.m. by the British Broadcasting Corporation. The program, arranged by the War Department, will feature guest stars.

News from American shortwave stations may be picked up at 6 p.m., while a number of commercial programs now are being sent via shortwave from the United States.

U.S. Rations Gasoline in 17 East States

WASHINGTON, D.C. (UP)—A temporary gasoline rationing plan is to be put into operation in 17 East Coast states May 15. The ration is expected to allow each motorist between two and a half and five gallons per week.

Boys Will Be Boys

WASHINGTON, D.C. (UP)—Japanese diplomats interned at Hot Springs, Va., have discarded western dress for the kimono—and a fan.

Tokyo Raid Upsets Japs

* * * * * *

See U.S. Blows at Nazis

— Tokyo —

By Drew Middleton

(Associated Press Staff Correspondent)

American bombers, flying high, wide and handsome over the supposedly sacred islands of Japan, hammered Tokyo, Kobe, Yokohama and four other cities last Saturday as the United States began sure repayment for Pearl Harbor.

By Japanese accounts only schools, hospitals and "cultural establishments" were hit. But the Japs have admitted damage by fire and there is no doubt that the bombers battered the heavy industries centered around Kobe and Yokohama.

This bold raid, which hit the body of the Japanese octopus as its tentacles felt southwards toward Australia and westward toward India, was the climax of a week of stirring Allied air successes.

It followed closely Brigadier General Royce's dashing attack on the Japanese in the Philippines from Australia and occurred almost simultaneously with the Royal Air Force's gallant and damaging blow at the great German factory at Augsburg.

Damage

The United Nations still await details of the raid on Japan. Thus far there has been no official word from Washington. The Associated Press has heard unvarying praise of the raid here in London. Most British officers believe considerable damage was done.

* * *

There are good reasons for an official silence in Washington.

If the raid was made by planes from an aircraft carrier, the ship must maintain radio silence until she is out of the cruising radius of Japanese submarines and patrol bombers.

Moreover, it is obvious the Japanese have no idea where the raiders came from or what was their destination. The Japanese high command, therefore, cannot make tactical dispositions to meet

Tokyo - - -

(*Continued on Page* 3)

— Nazis —

By Edward W. Beattie

(United Press Staff Correspondent)

As spring wears on toward the halfway mark and the usual spring hatch of rumors reaches a late April peak, Britain and Germany are dug in on two sides of their narrow sea—each prepared to defend itself against invasion.

As is usual during periods when the chief problem is "What that man is going to do next," the chief focus is on Adolf Hitler, although Nazi Field Marshal Karl Rudolf Gerd von Rundstedt and Sir Alan Brooke, British commander, may be pardoned for their considerable interest in each others specific plans for the months before the weather breaks sometime in late September.

Rundstedt, who is Hitler's commander in western Europe, probably would like to know, too, what Sir Alan and Gen. George C. Marshall, United States Chief of Staff, talked about because, according to all indications, German defenses along the great occupied coastline are going to have a very busy summer.

* * *

The coastline on both sides of the Channel can be penetrated by Commando raids and pounded with bombers during the next several months—but invading either with heavy forces and making the invasion stick is a problem which must be measured in scores of divisions, and thousands of guns and tanks, not to mention ships to transport the troops and then keep supplies rolling to them.

There has been unmistakable evidence recently, however, that the Germans are worried seriously by the growing aggressive spirit on this side of the Channel.

They know it will not be long before United States bombers begin to join the Royal Air Force in battering Germany and they know, too, that many thousands of United States troops soon will be perched in the British Isles, ready to jump upon any weak point in the Nazi defenses.

In Norway, where the normal

War - - -

(*Continued on Page* 3)

Pay Boosts Near Vote

WASHINGTON, D.C. (Special Cable from Associated Press)—Bills to raise the pay of soldiers, sailors and marines, Friday were approaching final action in Congress.

The Johnson bill, providing for an increase from $21 a month to $42 a month for privates and for corresponding increases through all grades and ranks to include second lieutenants, already has been passed by the Senate and now is being studied by a special military affairs subcommittee of the House.

At the same time, the War Department is sponsoring another measure which would provide subsistence allowances for all men in the services. This bill also would grant additional funds to dependents of service men whose allowances are insufficient to meet living expenses.

Several other measures of interest to the Armed Forces also are pending, including one which would defer income tax obligations until six months after termination of service.

3d. THE STARS AND STRIPES 3d.
Weekly Newspaper of the U.S. Armed Forces in the British Isles

Vol. 2 No. 4 | London, England | May 9, 1942

Madagascar Gives Up to Allies; Corregidor Surrenders to Japan

— France —

(Compiled from Late Cable Dispatches)

Fighting on Madagascar appeared to be drawing to an end early this weekend as Diego Suarez, important naval base, and Antsirana fell to British arms.

It was apparent, however, that some minor engagements were yet to be fought with Vichy France forces in scattered parts of the island, which combined British forces assaulted early in the week in an effort to prevent Japanese occupation.

Casualties among the British forces were not believed to have been light, and 1,000 men may have been lost in one engagement alone.

British naval units now are resting in Diego Suarez harbor.

— Philippines —

Corregidor and the other fortified islands in Manila Bay surrendered to the Japanese last week, giving over as prisoners what survivors there were of the 11,574 persons known to have been in the garrisons.

Lt. Gen. Jonathan Wainwright, commander, presumably was among those captured, the War Department announced in Washington.

The final attack on the island fortress began Tuesday about 8.30 p.m. and continued for about 33 hours before the Americans finally were forced to ask for terms.

The garrisons, including about 1,250 casuals and civilians, had been under constant bombardment from the air and from Japanese artillery for almost five months.

What It Means

By J. Wes. Gallagher
(Associated Press Staff Correspondent)

American soldiers soon may be taking a hand in Vichy France's affairs following Britain's land, sea and air occupation of strategic Madagascar, huge island outpost across the United Nation's shipping lanes to India and Australia.

President Roosevelt's blunt warning to Hitler's handpicked French premier, Pierre Laval, that any "warlike act" against Britain would be regarded as an attack against all the allies was followed closely by strong indications from the State Department that America is ready to send troops to occupy Martinique and other French possessions in the Western hemisphere.

Whether resistance to the British occupation of Madagascar, ordered by Vichy, will be considered a "warlike act" and therefore send American troops into action was not clear early this weekend.

It was more likely that the State Department would await the next move by Laval and his pro-Nazi cabinet.

Mr. Roosevelt also made it clear that American naval forces and presumably marines would be sent to help the British in Madagascar if they were needed.

Fence Yanked Out

Thus, fence-straddling Laval, who has been trying to keep on good terms with the United States and at the same time give Hitler every aid possible, suddenly found his fence yanked out from under him.

United States Ambassador Admiral Leahy already is in Lisbon on his way to Washington, ending months of effort by America to France - - -

(Continued on Page 5)

Red Cross Hotel Open

By Staff Sgt. Russell Jones

SOMEWHERE IN NORTHERN IRELAND—The first Red Cross hostel and recreation center for men in service was opened in Londonderry last week by Maj. Gen. R. P. Hartle, commander of American Army Forces in Northern Ireland.

In praising the Red Cross for its work, General Hartle said, "A man's body might be whole and well and still useless without the proper mental attitude—he needs mental rest and relaxation. In this clean and comfortable building, we have just that, through an organization that everybody knows—the Red Cross."

The Lord Mayor of Londonderry, F. J. Simmons, also welcomed the troops.

Bernard S. Carter, representative of the American Red Cross in the British Isles, was toastmaster.

More than 500 American and British soldiers and sailors and civilians were present for the ceremony.

Accommodation for the troops will include more than 80 bedrooms, a dining room, canteen, writing room, library, showers, recreation rooms, and a complete barber shop—including a shoe shine boy.

* * *

After the ceremonies tea was served, followed in the evening by a dance at which 75 Wrens were guests of honor. The music was typical American swing, furnished by the "Rhythm Majors" dance band from an Infantry regiment.

* * *

Alfred Cappio is director of the center and is assisted by Mrs. L. Kohler as program director. Arrangements are being made for dances, concerts, choral clubs and dramatics. Movies will be shown regularly in the dining room.

A second Red Cross center, with similar facilities, will be opened in the latter part of July in Belfast.

U.S. Navy Victory! 8 Jap Ships Sunk

WASHINGTON, D.C. (Special)—Eight Japanese ships, seven of them warships, have been sunk and four others seriously damaged in an action with United States forces off the Solomon Islands, 500 miles from the Australian coast.

In announcing the victory late Thursday, the Navy Department said it had "very excellent news," going on to explain that one light cruiser, two destroyers, four gunboats and one supply ship were the Japanese ships sunk.

Only three American airplanes were lost during the action.

Peep Passes New Tests, It Will Plow Gardens

SOMEWHERE IN NORTHERN IRELAND—The "Peep" has passed another test. Men of an Infantry battalion are using it in place of a tractor to plow their garden.

His Forces Fall

Lt. Gen. Jonathan Wainwright . . . Stays with Troops.

Message on Mother's Day

Maj. Gen. James E. Chaney, commander of United States Army forces in the British Isles, Friday issued the following statement on behalf of the troops:

"The members of the United States Army forces in the British Isles have only one message for Mother's Day.

"They want their mothers and relatives at home to know that they are well and that they are ready to play whatever part is allotted to them in this great joint fight we are waging to see that the American mothers of the future have a free and happy world in which to bring up their children.

"It might cheer our mothers and relatives at home to know that British men and women of all ranks and conditions are treating us with the utmost kindness and consideration.

"We are inspired to better work by the example of their patient fortitude and their determination to see this present task through to a victorious conclusion, cost what it may. They agree with us that a world under any other conditions would not be fit for us to live in."

Whew!

Presented herewith is a scientific treatise on Irish soldiers, their origin and background, care and equipment, and standard nomenclature list. Names and incidents mentioned are strictly coincidence and the views expressed do not necessarily represent the opinions of the War Department, Library of Congress, The Stars and Stripes, or the guy at the next bunk.

SOMEWHERE IN NORTHERN IRELAND—Whew!

What to See During Your London Visit

By Tech. Sgt. G. K. Hodenfield
(Chief Staff Correspondent)

Daniel Boone had a snap. He didn't have anyone to confuse him. All he had to do was cut a mark on a tree and then come back and find it.

But there aren't many trees in London. And a Bobby would glance your way with no little suspicion should you meander down the Mall with a two-bitted ax in hand.

And anyway, I'm no Daniel Boone.

* * *

The trip from Northern Ireland is a holiday. A boat ride, a train ride, and here you are. Like falling off a tram.

The first thing to learn when you visit London is not to ask directions. Just take a taxi, or start walking until you find yourself where you want to be.

The town is only 18 miles square, so you're bound to hit it right sometime. But if you start asking directions, you're lost. There just aren't any.

The longest street in London is about three blocks long, and it's a dead-ender.

If your legs and shoes hold out, you'll probably find yourself eventually in Trafalgar Square.

Eagle Club

From Trafalgar Square it doesn't cost too many bobs by taxi to the American Eagle Club, at 28 Charing Cross Road, W.C.2 (which, incidentally, means Westminster City, Second Postal District, or something). That's a good place to start.

They'll tell you where the best and cheapest hotels can be found and, if you're hungry, they'll fix up with the nearest possible facsimile to an American meal you can find in England.

And you'll be hungry by the time you find the place.

* * *

Another place that makes a good headquarters is the English Speaking Union, Dartmouth House, 37 Charles Street, Berkeley Square, W.1.

After that you start back for Trafalgar Square. If it's still daylight by the time you get there you can set out for the Houses of Parliament at Westminster, and Westminster Abbey. Big Ben is down that direction somewhere, too.

St. James's Park

A few questions, well-asked, will get you to St. James's Park, where Buckingham Palace is located.

Whitehall, a street which winds itself around the Houses of Parliament is also the location of London - - -

(Continued on Page 5)

U.S. to Pay Men Every Two Weeks

Effective about May 16, officers and enlisted men of the Army in Northern Ireland and the rest of the British Isles will be paid on a semi-monthly basis, Maj. Gen. James E. Chaney, commander of United States Army forces in the British Isles, announced Friday.

The new plan, which is to be tested during the next several months, is being adopted in an effort to reduce excessive spending and to curb what has become known as "the middle of the month blues."

Partial payments made in mid-month will be in even dollars and in amounts not exceeding the amount of pay due, less deductions for allotments, insurance and other expenses of the current month.

In case the total amount of deductions exceeds the amount of pay due, no partial payment will be made.

An example of how the plan will work would be that of a soldier earning $54.00 per month. His pay tabulations might look like this:

Pay for 15 days	$27.00
Soldiers' bond deduction	0.13
Allotments	5.00
Post exchange	5.00
Company fund	2.00
Laundry	1.75
Total deductions	13.88
Net amount due	13.12
Maximum amount of partial payment	13.00

The plan has been tried in other branches of the service and found to be satisfactory.

Payrolls for the partial payment must be submitted to the Finance Office by the twelfth of each month, necessitating some extra clerical work, the only known drawback of the plan.

* * *

Meantime, in Washington, D.C., legislation increasing pay of the armed forces continued to be bogged down by a series of amendments and proposed changes in the plan.

Speedy passage first was prevented by the clause providing extra allowances for dependents and, as this plan was studied, an amendment providing for creation of the women's reserve component was added, bringing on further discussion.

Then, last week, some congressmen attacked the Army's practice of granting so-called "quickie" commissions, necessitating further hearings and debate, and bringing from the bill's sponsors smiling complaints that counterproposals "must be the work of saboteurs."

Saves 2 Friends As Third Drowns

SOMEWHERE IN NORTHERN IRELAND—Private Ralph Hebling, 22, of Pittsburgh, Penn., drowned Tuesday when a makeshift raft on which he and four companions were paddling about a Northern Ireland lake started to capsize. His four companions were saved, two of them through the efforts of Private Elmer Clewicky.

The boats began to capsize 300 yards from shore. Private Hebling started to swim for the shore, then turned around and started for the raft.

Private William Nau, Pittsburgh, stayed with the raft and was rescued by a boat. Cpl. George Chmelicek of Cedar Rapids, Iowa, and Private Edward Fullerton swam to shore assisted much of the way by Private Clewicky.

Sharpening Up Firing Eyes

From a sandbag trench on a firing point Sgt. Herbert Brown (left), Private First Class Adolph Kessler, and Private M. E. Cooney, practice with machine guns during special drill.

3d. **THE STARS AND STRIPES** 3d.

Weekly Newspaper of the U.S. Armed Forces in the British Isles

Vol. 2 No. 8 — London, England — June 6, 1942

New 'V' Mail Will Speed Up Service

By Cpl. Bud Hutton
(Staff Writer)

"V Mail"—letters photographed on special film, flown to America and reproduced for delivery there—today became available to all personnel of the United States Armed Forces in the British Isles, Army officials announced.

The new method of mail delivery is designed to supplement, rather than replace, existing forms of postal service.

The "V Mail" will be free to all members of the armed forces here and at certain other points throughout the world. Army postal officials explained it would provide a means of delivery quicker than boat mail, somewhat slower than air mail.

Maj. Gen. James E. Chaney, commander of Army forces, officially opened the "V Mail" service Thursday with a letter to President Roosevelt.

Weight-Saver

Salient feature of "V Mail," as far as the Army Post Office and the air lines are concerned, is that by photographing the letters in the British Isles, then flying the film to the States for reproduction and delivery, tremendous savings will be made in bulk and weight of air mail.

A ton of letters is recorded on negatives weighing only 25 pounds, it was explained.

The system, which is officially designated V ...— Mail, with the three dots and a dash signifying "V" in Morse code, was named after the "V for Victory" slogan. W. J. Means, a post office inspector in the United States, who did the ground work for the new system here, first suggested the name for the service.

Explain System

In announcing the new form of mail deliveries today, Army postal officials explained the procedure for writing and posting "V Mail" letters.

Letters for "V Mail" will be written on special forms, available at company offices. The forms, as well as the delivery service, are free.

In a ruled box at the top of the sheet, the sender prints in large letters the name and address to which the letter is destined. The message is written below. Very small writing is not suitable, authorities pointed out, inasmuch as the letters are photographed and then reproduced on paper about five by four inches.

For letters of more than one page, separate forms must be filled out for each page.

After the letter has been written, it is handed in to the company office, as in the case of ordinary mail. Unit censors, after checking it, will indorse their name and rank at the top, and forward it within 24 hours to the officer designated to affix the censor's stamp.

Once censored, the letters are placed flat in a large envelope or packaged if quantity warrants, and mailed to the "V Mail" station.

Special Camera

Army postal authorities here then send the individual letters through a special camera which records each letter on a 16 mm. motion picture negative, 1,500 letters going on a single roll of the film.

The film is flown by air mail to the U.S., where it is reproduced on special "V Mail" paper, folded into an envelope so that the address on the top of the form is visible through a small "window" in the envelope, and finally is delivered as ordinary mail.

A positive check on delivery of all "V Mail" letters is made possible under the system whereby the originals of all letters are kept Mail - - -

(Continued on Page 3)

'Victory' Mail to Home

Capt. L. S. Fogarty, of Guthrie, Okla, writes a "V Mail" letter.

Big Raids On Nazis by the RAF

By Bill Downs
(United Press Staff Correspondent)

Intensive discussions were underway in Washington and London today settling final details for hurling hard-hitting units of the U.S. Air Corps into the United Nations aerial second front over Europe.

A British mission of service chiefs headed by Lord Louis Mountbatten arrived in Washington Wednesday with Lt. Gen. H. H. Arnold, chief of the U.S. Army Air Corps, to consult with President Roosevelt regarding extended co-operation between the two nations.

Bases Planned

In addition to plans for basing United States fighters and bombers in the United Kingdom, these meetings are believed to include plans for use of U.S. forces in the expanded land activities against the continent.

Meanwhile U.S. naval, military, and air officials in London are maintaining close liaison with Prime Minister Winston Churchill and British service headquarters. Lt. Gen. Brehon Somervell, U.S. chief of supply, Admiral John H. Tower, head of the U.S. Navy Air Corps, and other American officials for the last two weeks have been doing twenty-four hour duty with the United Nations military chiefs.

No Details Released

Only details released regarding the U.S. Air Corps units to operate from Britain were contained in General Arnold's statement that a "balanced force" of fighters and bombers would go into action under American command, from designated American airfields staffed by American ground crews.

Mr. Churchill in a statement in the House of Commons Wednesday said U.S. planes would join the R.A.F. offensive "very soon."

R.A.F. Raids

While something very definitely is "in the air" for the coming weeks, during the last seven days biggest aerial news was supplied by the R.A.F.

More than 6,000 fighters and bombers have attacked from British fields since the R.A.F.'s 1,000-plane "saturation raid" on Cologne Saturday night, all of them carrying bad news for Germany and German-occupied territory.

The 1,000-plane raid on Essen and the Ruhr Monday night proved that the R.A.F. had made history, and would continue to do so.

Tuesday night a "strong force" of R.A.F. bombers again struck at the Essen district with an estimated 350 planes. Wednesday night the R.A.F. continued its export to Deutschland program, when another 350 planes dropped their bombs on Bremen.

These raids were accompanied by diversionary activity by night fighters, bombers from Coastal Command and planes from the British Army's Cooperation Command.

Daylight Attacks

In addition, Spitfires, Hurricanes, Bostons, and Beaufighters carried out extensive daylight raids on northern France, the continent's invasion coast, climaxed by a series of sweeps throughout Monday wherein an estimated 1,000 fighters took control of the Luftwaffe's own private flying atmosphere.

Since the 1,000-plane raids on Germany last week, British air officials are allowing speculation that aerial striking power against the continent might be doubled—even tripled—in the near future. Informed sources, however, agree that night raids against Germany by 2,000 or more bombers probably must await inclusion of United States bombing units.

American flyers operating in the R.A.F. and the Canadian Air Force already have participated in the biggest-ever attacks on Germany.

Belfast Hostel Is Now Open

SOMEWHERE IN NORTHERN IRELAND—The American Red Cross Center in Belfast was opened unofficially this week. The official opening will be held next month.

Now open to all service men is the hostel with sixty beds, the canteen, the games room and the lounge.

June 10th, the Red Cross is sponsoring a dance in Belfast.

Red Cross Assures A Worried Soldier He Still Has Car

SOMEWHERE IN NORTHERN IRELAND—Alfred Cappio of the Red Cross tells this one.

It seems there was a soldier who was worried because he hadn't heard whether his wife was receiving monthly allotments. He appealed to the Red Cross for help and they checked up.

When they reported that everything was as it should be, the soldier heaved a sigh of relief and said, "I'm sure glad to hear that she is getting the money. I was afraid that she had let the payments on the car lapse."

Jap Planes Bomb Alaska

WASHINGTON, D.C. (UP)—In a futile attempt to stage another Pearl Harbor attack, Japan struck twice at Dutch Harbor, Alaska, last week. The raids were six hours apart.

Further reports of the Jap attack stated there were few casualties and warehouses were set on fire, but there was no serious damage.

Shipbuilding Record

WASHINGTON, D.C. (UP)—United States shipbuilding set up this world record in May: Delivered, 58 ships; launched, 65; keels laid, 75.

Suggest New Plan to End Pay Dispute

WASHINGTON, D.C. (Special Cable from the Associated Press)—Hopes for settling the Congressional controversy over the Military Pay Adjustment bill, and thus avoiding a political showdown on the issue of a base pay for the armed forces, this week-end seemed to rest on a suggested compromise offer.

The War Department was reported to be seeking to break the deadlock between the Senate and the House by urging a middle-of-the-road plan whereby the lowest ranking personnel in the Army, Navy and Marines would receive forty dollars cash per month and ten dollars in non-negotiable government bonds.

House-Senate Dispute

The House of Representatives has demanded a minimum basic monthly pay of fifty dollars. The Senate has voted for forty-two dollars. A joint House-Senate conference has been unable to settle the dispute.

Senator LaFollette of Wisconsin is said to be ready to press for a Senate vote on the motion to discharge the Senate committee who have refused to agree to the representatives' demand for a fifty dollar minimum.

Bill Compromise

An unidentified senator was quoted as saying there was little doubt President Roosevelt would veto the fifty dollar bill if it should pass.

The compromise suggestion of paying a basic monthly minimum of forty dollars in cash, plus ten dollars in non-negotiable bonds, would provide a savings fund for men in the forces, it was pointed out. Non-negotiable, the bonds could be held by the payees until they were redeemed by the government after the war.

20 Countries

SOMEWHERE IN NORTHERN IRELAND—A quartermaster unit claims to be a truly all-nations organization. Parents of the men hail from more than 20 different countries.

Seeks Dough, Dad Says No

SOMEWHERE IN NORTHERN IRELAND—We can't vouch for this, it's just something we heard somewhere:

One of the Yankee soldiers stationed in Northern Ireland is purported to have written the following letter:

"Dear Dad: Gue$$ what I need mo$t of all. That'$ right. $end it along. Be$t wihe. Your $on, Tom."

And the answer:

Dear Tom: NOthing ever happens here. Write us aNOther letter aNOn. Jimmie was asking about you Monday. NOw we have to say goodbye."

'No Tea Party!' Colonel Tells Women

DENVER, COLO. (Special Cable from the Associated Press)—Col. Thomas N. Gimperling, speaking to applicants for the Women's Army Officers Training School, laid down the law.

"This Corps will not tolerate petulance or capricious feminine temperament," he said. "You won't be able to get your commission and then quit. This is no tea party. Return qualifications within nine days, and I don't mean 10."

The applicants bit their lips, clenched their fists—but relinquished the last word.

Washington Gets Air Raid Test

WASHINGTON, D.C. (UP)—The staff of the White House grabbed their gas masks and ran to the air raid shelters when Washington had its first full-dress air raid test June 2.

When the sirens sounded all traffic came to a stop, while pedestrians ran to shelter. The test lasted 15 minutes.

Dislikes Lollypops

NEW YORK, N.Y. (AP)—Baby Jean Maura Fitzgerald, suffering from a rare metabolic malady, can't drink milk, dislikes lollypops—but thrives on soy beans.

3D. THE STARS AND STRIPES 3D.

Weekly Newspaper of the U.S. Armed Forces in the British Isles

Vol. 2 No. 9 London, England June 13, 1942

U.S. Planes Stop Japs At Midway

By J. Wes Gallagher
(Associated Press War Correspondent)

United States Army airmen, Marines, and the Navy gave Japan its first major setback of the war this week by sinking or damaging half of a 30-ship invasion fleet aimed at Midway Island.

In words of Admiral Nimitz, "Pearl Harbor was partially avenged" as thousands of Japs died in Pacific waters under a three-day rain of bombs and torpedos from American war-planes.

* * *

Looking for a "soft touch" the Jap fleet steamed toward Midway, and in the manner of Guam and Wake Islands unleashed waves of carrier planes. An estimated 180 fighters and bombers blasted the island in two short attacks, but in words of the defenders the Japs were "too busy after that protecting themselves to attack again."

Fortresses first sighted invasion fleet and with Marine and Navy planes pressed home attack after attack until the Nipponese Navy broke off the engagement and fled in disorder, leaving flaming and sinking ships scattered over a wide area.

Latest reports from Admiral Nimitz placed the Jap losses as follows: two or three aircraft carriers sunk with all planes destroyed; one or two additional carriers damaged and most of their planes lost; three battleships damaged, at least one seriously, four cruisers damaged, two of them badly crippled; one destroyer sunk and three transports damaged.

American losses included a destroyer sunk and an aircraft carrier damaged.

One American pilot of a torpedo plane which was shot down witnessed the destruction of two carriers from a "grandstand seat" in a rubber dinghy.

"Flames from both carriers roared high into sky," he reported in describing bomb hits, and explosions rumbled through the ships as a Jap destroyer tried to save the carrier crews."

He was later picked up by a Navy plane.

Colonel Walter Sweeney, leading a Fortress squadron, told of sighting more than 20 warships and transports.

"We laid bombs in pattern, scoring direct hits on one cruiser and one transport and possibly a second cruiser. One of our planes reported hitting a battleship."

"The Japanese started frantic escape maneuvers, but our pattern blanketed a carrier," he said.

Commanding officers reported the American flyers flew almost continuously during the battle "until they were dizzy with fatigue, but they kept it up."

* * *

Naval observers in London agreed if the Japanese could not take Midway, which is more than 1,000 miles from Hawaii, with their strong battle force, they stood little chance of success in ever trying to take Hawaii itself or attacking any place along the American coast or Panama.

Admiral King reported that the Japanese also had attacked Dutch Harbor in Alaska. A Tokyo spokesman claimed the Japs made landings in the Aleutian Islands and wiped out some American Army posts.

Washington reported the situation in the North was "obscure," but denied any Army posts had been wiped out or that any landings had been made on "occupied islands."

Only slight damage was reported

Midway - - -
(Continued on Page 3)

President's Son in London

Associated Press Photo

Lieutenant (Junior Grade) Franklin D. Roosevelt, Jr., U.S.N.R., son of the President of the United States, arrived in London this week. On the evening of his arrival he was the guest of Rear Admiral Alan G. Kirk, Naval Attache and Chief of Staff to Admiral Stark, and has paid courtesy calls on Major Gen. James E. Chaney, commanding U.S. Forces in the British Isles, and Winston Churchill, Prime Minister of Great Britain, at 10, Downing Street. All four of President Roosevelt's sons are in the armed forces. Franklin and John are in the Navy, Elliott is in the Army Air Corps, and James is in the Marine Corps. Lieut. Roosevelt is shown inspecting a hat of a Wren officer attached to the British Admiralty's Liaison Office at the United States Naval Headquarters.

Pay Boost Is Passed InCongress

WASHINGTON, D.C. (Special Cable from the Associated Press) —Within a few days President Roosevelt will sign his name on the dotted line—and American privates will become the highest paid fighting men of their rank in the world.

After weeks of wrangling the Senate and House finally got together on a bill which increases the base pay of every man in the armed forces, army, navy, marine, coastguard, public health service, and coast geodetic survey.

* * *

Under terms of the new legislation, privates and apprentice seamen will be paid $50 per month; first class privates and apprentice seamen, $54; corporals and first class seamen, $66; sergeants and third class petty officers, $78; staff sergeants and second class petty officers, $96; first or technical sergeants and first class petty officers, $114; master sergeants and chief petty officers, $138.

* * *

Second lieutenants and ensigns will be raised to $150 per month, nurses with less than three years service $90, and nurses with more than nine years service $135. Increases have also been voted in the rental and food allowances for officers.

The pay increase will be retroactive from June 1, 1942.

Those eligible under the 20 per cent increase for overseas service or sea duty will receive that amount in addition to the new base pay. Longevity pay for active service will be continued. (It is not known whether the $10 bonus for one year of service will be affected.)

* * *

Congress has already approved a measure, introduced by Senator Johnson of Colorado, which calls for payment by the government of stipulated amounts to dependents of men in the service.

The bill provdes that $22 shall be deducted from the soldier's pay each month, and $28 more shall be allotted by the government, in case of a wife, but no children. Twelve dollars shall be paid for the first child, and $10 for each child thereafter.

Under this bill an enlisted man with a wife and two children and on foreign service would be paid $110 per month, the private retaining $38.

Other allowances may be made for men whose dependents include grandchildren, brothers, sisters, and parents. All dependents' allowances will include men below the grade of staff sergeant or second class petty officer.

Potato Crop Needs Labor

BOISE, IDAHO (Special Cable from the Associated Press)—The depleted labor supply in Idaho is bringing sunburn, aching muscles, and blistered hands to Idaho's white collar workers.

To harvest Idaho's 74,000 acres of potatoes and sugar beets Boise stores were closed and State employees were released from the regular jobs to work in the harvest fields.

"Darned hard work," exclaimed Gov. Charles Clark, leaning on a hoe.

Loses Good-Luck Comb, So Sergeant Cuts Off His Hair

SOMEWHERE IN NORTHERN IRELAND — Staff Sgt. Dick Carney, Infantryman from Stillwater, Minn., very neatly solved the problem of a lost comb.

Sergeant Carney had carried the comb since his first days in the service, using it for his locks and as a good-luck piece. When he lost the comb, he had his hair cut short.

Jack Oakie is Ill

HOLLYWOOD, CAL. (UP)—Jack Oakie, the film actor, has been taken to hospital in Hollywood with a high fever. His condition is not revealed, although it was stated at the hospital that he was as well as could be expected. Oakie is 49 years old.

Hitler Wants Brain Dissected

NEW YORK, N.Y. (UP)—Hitler thinks so much of his head that he has ordered his brain to be dissected after he dies, according to Frederick Oechsner, for eight years head of the United Press Bureau in Berlin.

U.S. Navy Is With British Home Fleet

A task force of the United States Navy, under the command of Rear Admiral Robert C. Giffen, has been in British waters for weeks, and is co-operating with the British Home Fleet.

The announcement that the task force was in British waters was made after the King of England had made an inspection tour of American naval units.

The task force serving with Admiral Tovey's Home Fleet is another indication of the close co-operation between the British and United States governments in fighting the war.

The King's impressions may best be shown by the message sent to Admiral Giffen:

"It has given me great pleasure to have had this opportunity of visiting the United States ships and thus being enabled to meet some of the officers and men of the United States Navy Task Force of the Home Fleet.

"I have been deeply impressed by the smart and efficient appearance of the ships and the ships' companies, and I congratulate you and all those under your command upon the alert and cheerful spirit with which you are undertaking your duties in the common cause.

"The enjoyment of my visit was greatly enhanced by the presence of Admiral Stark. I send to you, your officers and men, my best wishes for your safe return to your homes when victory is won."

Admiral Giffen's reply: "The kind message relative to your Majesty's visit to vessels of this Task Force is deeply appreciated by Admiral Stark and me.

"It is with the greatest of pleasure that I pass your inspiring message on to the officers and men of my command.

"It is a great privilege to us of this Task Force to have been visited by your Majesty and to serve with the warriors of the Home Fleet."

More Troops Arrive Here

SOMEWHERE IN NORTHERN IRELAND — Another convoy of American troops, including a contingent of Negro soldiers, arrived in a Northern Ireland port this week.

This convoy is another link in the "ever-increasing flow of men and materials" which the United States is sending to the European battle front.

Included in the masses of cargo on the ships were a great number of tanks and guns and other supplies.

With a smoothness stemming from experience, officials at the points of debarkation had the troops loaded into trucks and trains and sent to their camps in a minimum of time.

'Yank' Newspaper For Enlisted Men

NEW YORK, N.Y. (Special Cable from the Associated Press)—When staff correspondents of "Yank," official army newspaper making its debut June 13, start scouring foxholes and trenches for stories they'll carry pencils, papers—and guns.

"Yank" will be patterned after "Stars and Stripes" (Ed. note—We're duly flattered), and will be by and for enlisted men. Says the editor of the "Yank": "Military rank has been forgotten. We're not interested in officers, not even generals."

Private in Ireland Wins $1300 Bank Night Prize at Home

SOMEWHERE IN NORTHERN IRELAND—Private Archie Hopkins, Infantryman from Council Bluffs, Ia., is very unhappy.

His girl friend wrote that his name was drawn as the winner of a $1,300 bank night prize. The winner had to be present to collect.

'Swing' Club Is Opened

SOMEWHERE IN NORTHERN IRELAND—American swing officially arrived in Northern Ireland with the opening of the "United States Swing Club" in a Northern Ireland town in which American troops are stationed.

Sergeants George Frode and Charles Beekman rented the local Orange hall, and with the aid of soldier volunteers, completely remodeled it. A stage, big enough for any theatrical productions, was made in Belfast and hauled forty miles by army truck for the installation.

The Rhythm Majors dance band from an Infantry regiment played for the dance Friday night which officially opened the club. Weekly dances are planned.

A burlesque show from Dublin will be shown Wednesday, June 17.

3d. THE STARS AND STRIPES 3d.
Weekly Newspaper of the U.S. Armed Forces in the British Isles

Vol. 2 No. 11 London, England 67209 June 27, 1942

Major General Eisenhower Is European Commander

Associated Press Photo

Maj. Gen. Dwight D. Eisenhower . . . assumes "the task of working out details of the Allied invasion of the Continent with the British."

By Tech. Sgt. G. K. Hodenfield.
(Chief Staff Correspondent)

Maj. Gen. Dwight D. Eisenhower, former chief of staff to General Douglas MacArthur in the Philippines, this week assumed command of the European Theater of Operations for United States Forces.

General Eisenhower, 51, came to London direct from Washington, where he sat in on one of the conferences being held this week between Prime Minister Winston Churchill of Great Britain and President Roosevelt.

* * *

In a formal statement issued to the press this week, General Eisenhower said:

"I have been assigned to command the European Theater for United States Forces. The formal establishment of a European Theater is a logical step in coordinating the efforts of Great Britain and the United States.

"Six months ago the Prime Minister of Great Britain and the President of the United States heartened the people of the United Nations by moving swiftly to merge the military and economic strength of Britain and the United States for a common effort.

"At that Washington conference they set a more effective pattern for unqualified partnership than has ever before been envisaged by allied nations in pursuit of a common purpose.

"Only recently they have met again to bring combined action into even closer coordination.

"The presence here in the British Isles of American soldiers and pilots in rapidly increasing numbers is evidence that we are hewing to the line of that pattern."

In an off-the-record conference with the press, General Eisenhower discussed public relations policies and renewed friendships made in the United States with correspondents and army officers.

* * *

General Eisenhower, until recently Assistant Chief of Staff, Operations Division, War Department General Staff, was born in Texas on October 14, 1890.

He attended schools in Kansas, from which State he entered the United States Military Academy at West Point, New York, in 1911.

He was an outstanding athlete, and a star halfback in the game of American football. Until a severe injury to his knee forced him to stop playing, he distinguished himself through his brilliant play on the Academy's team. Later, he acted as assistant coach of the team.

General Eisenhower was graduated from the Academy in 1915, and distinguished himself in the World War by his services in the Tank Corps, which was then in its earliest beginnings. As a result of his excellent organizational work in this field he became one of the youngest American Army lieutenant-colonels the World War produced, and was decorated with the Distinguished Service Medal.

* * *

After the Armistice, General Eisenhower served with line troops until 1926. In that year he attended the Command and General Staff School, from which he was graduated first in his class. He was graduated from the Army War College in 1928, and from the Army Industrial College in 1933.

General Eisenhower is known throughout the service as the MacArthur type of soldier; so it surprised no one that, when in 1935 General MacArthur went to the Philippines to take charge of the organization of the Philippine Commonwealth Army, Gen. Eisen-

General - - -

(Continued on Page 3)

Royal Pair Pay Visit To Ireland

By Sgt. Bud Hutton
(Staff Writer)

SOMEWHERE IN NORTHERN IRELAND — England's King and Queen have met the men and seen the battle might of United States Armed Forces in Northern Ireland.

In a day and a half visit with U.S. soldiers of the European Theater of Operations, Great Britain's rulers and a staff of ranking British officers toured American military establishments. They rode in "peeps," chatted informally with scores of soldiers, and lunched in an enlisted men's mess.

Atop a gorse-covered hill, England's royal pair watched American riflemen and machine-gunners, artillery men, signal men and tank men in a mock combat operation across rugged Irish terrain.

The visit of their Majesties lasted three days. Half of that time was spent with British forces—Navy and Army. The other half was spent with Americans.

Major General R. P. Hartle, commander of U.S. Forces in Northern Ireland, accompanied the King and Queen, introducing them to the various units.

Officers and men found the suntanned King a quiet, friendly man, who understood Army talk and asked pertinent questions about much of the modern mechanised equipment with which the U.S.A. Forces have been training.

In her turn, the constantly smiling and gracious Queen literally swept soldiers into a personal train of admirers by her friendly inquiries and sincere interest in their work and life.

By the same token, the King and Queen were obviously impressed with what they saw—and it was plenty!

It was no hurried, "official" inspection of whisking past ranks of men and guns. Rather, their Majesties moved patiently and with quite an apparent interest through encampment and across firing ranges, pausing to chat with soldiers at their jobs.

They asked questions of men and officers, and certainly did more honest-to-gosh good for Anglo-American relations than a thousand propaganda campaigns might hope to achieve.

Private Leo Bennett, Brooklyn, N.Y., signalman, summed up the

King - - -

(Continued on Page 3)

England's King George VI meets Maj. Gen. R. P. Hartle, commander of U.S. forces in Northern Ireland.

Pay Bill Gives Your Family An Allotment

WASHINGTON, D.C. (AP)—President Roosevelt signed the service men's pay allotment and allowance bill Wednesday, paving the way for financial aid to dependents of U.S. fighting men and the re-classification of married men for conscription.

It has also been learned that under the pay bill the $10 for more than a year's service has been discontinued as of June 1.

Further information has been received concerning allotments and allowances under the new pay bill.

Privates, corporals, and "buck" sergeants (Grade IV) who are married and have a Class A allotment will receive $28 monthly from the government to be sent with the Class A allotment to the dependent.

Enlisted men with parents, brothers, sisters, and grandchildren who are dependent will receive $15 for one parent and $25 for two. Five dollars monthly will be given for each additional grandchild, brother or sister. This is a Class B allowance.

Married couples with children will receive $40 a month if they have one child and $10 extra for each additional child. An enlisted man who has only a child to support will receive $20 monthly for that child and $10 for each additional child.

Sergeants of the first three grades (staff, technical and first, and master) are not affected by the new allowances. They will continue to draw the same amount as always.

To take advantage of these allowances an enlisted man must make an allotment of $22 monthly. This is mandatory, and will be taken from his pay. If he desires

Pay - - -

(Continued on Page 5)

Marriage Ban on U.S. Troops

WASHINGTON, D.C. (UP)—United States' Army personnel serving in foreign countries or possessions may not marry without the approval of the commanding officers of U.S. Army forces stationed in the area, according to an announcement by the War Department.

There had been increasing appeals by both U.S. Army officials and Irish authorities for American soldiers stationed in Northern Ireland not to marry.

Marriage did not guarantee the girls U.S. citizenship, they warned.

Churchill - Roosevelt Talks Encourage United Nations

(Compiled from late Cable Reports)

WASHINGTON, D.C.—One of the most important meetings between two national leaders since the war began, a meeting that will probably have far-reaching effect on the strategy of the United Nations, neared an end here this week.

Prime Minister Winston Churchill of Great Britain and President Roosevelt of the United States have been conferring behind closed doors with military leaders of the Pacific War Council, and have discussed the existing situation with Congressional leaders of both houses and both parties.

New Optimism

Although the conference took place while the Allied Nations were rocking under the blow of the fall of Tobruk, members of the Pacific War Council left the conference full of a new optimism.

Churchill and Roosevelt, they declared, had formulated a victory plan, and there is good reason to believe that major objective will be to stop Hitler this year.

The hardest task the two leaders faced was assuring China that the United Nations' first job is to whip Hitler. Australia and New Zealand approved the plan.

All China's representative would say was that he had no doubt his request for increased aid would be granted.

Mention Second Front

Congressional leaders, too, were optimistic. Representative Sol Bloom, chairman of the House Foreign Affairs Committee, said everyone had been "enlightened and encouraged," and added that although the establishment of a second front was not mentioned specifically, the "subject always comes up."

Speaker of the House Thomas Rayburn told the press they had been given a great deal of information of "military nature."

Joseph Martin, Republican leader in the House, said Churchill had given those who attended the

Roosevelt - - -

(Continued on Page 3)

Fix European War Theater

Formation of a European Theater of Operations for the United States Army, under command of Maj. Gen. Dwight D. Eisenhower, was announced Friday.

No territorial definitions, other than the general term "European Theater" have yet been applied to the command.

All U.S. Army forces, excepting representatives on the London Munitions Assignment Board, military attaches, and personnel attached to embassies, and including such part of the U.S. Marine Corps as may be detached for service with the Army, is included in the command.

Yank Swipes Man's Hand From Arm, Anyone Seen It?

The civilian wasn't foolin' when he walked in the barracks and asked the charge of quarters, "Where did that fellow go with my hand?"

The C.Q. knew that some Yankee soldiers had lost their hearts since coming to the British Isles, and that others had lost their heads. But he had heard no rumors about anyone picking up a spare hand.

"It was all in fun, see?" quoth the civilian. "We were having a couple and this bloke grabs my hand and runs away with it." To prove his point he held up his artificial arm, from which a hand was most certainly missing.

Anyone seen a spare hand?

Out of Gas

NEW YORK, N.Y.—It is estimated that 90 per cent of the gasoline filling stations in the New York metropolitan and many places in the Atlantic seaboard are without gasoline.

3D. THE STARS AND STRIPES 3D.

Weekly Newspaper of U.S. Armed Forces in the European Theater of Operations

Vol. 2 No. 13 London, England 67301 July 11, 1942

Forces End War Show In Ireland

By Staff Sgt. Russell Jones
(U.S.A.N.I.F. Editor)

SOMEWHERE IN NORTHERN IRELAND—Under the watchful eyes of General Sir Alan Brooke, Chief of the British Imperial General Staff, Major General Majendie, commander of the British Forces in Northern Ireland, and General Ladislaw Sikorski, Premier of Poland and commander-in-chief of the Polish Forces, American and British troops last week completed the biggest maneuvers ever held in Northern Ireland.

Maneuvers started on July 2, when the country of "Down" declared, in true totalitarian fashion, that "the continued refusal of 'Antrim' to grant plebiscite among the 'Menian' people or to allow them to determine their sovereignty has made it necessary for our Forces to cross the 'Menian border' early today to free that country from the yoke of 'Antrim' oppression."

The "Down" forces, composed of both British and American troops and commanded by Maj. Gen. Russell P. Hartle, drove north into "Antrim" territory, pushing back the outnumbered defenders.

As our pressed "Antrim" Forces fell back, barely maintaining order in their ranks, General Majendie, commander-in-chief, called on their ally, the country of "Tyrone," to fulfil their pledge to come to their aid.

The "Tyrone" Army answered by declaring war on "Down," and, by a series of forced marches, engaged the enemy on the second day of the war. The invading forces were now confronted by armies that were more than a match for their own, and they, in turn, called on their ally, the country of "Lancashire." Being across the Irish Sea from "Down," they immediately despatched a huge convoy bearing armored forces.

This convoy sailed the same day that "Tyrone" joined "Antrim," and was heavily attacked by submarines, "Antrim" claiming the destruction of most of it.

The "Down" and "Lancashire" Forces stated that actually their losses were very light. On the fifth day of the conflict, armored forces attacked in such strength that the Northern Allies fell back in considerable confusion.

It was a "free" maneuver, meaning that when troops got the starting signal both sides went at it, no holds barred, and may the best Army win.

American soldiers covered an average of more than 25 miles a day during maneuvers.

The long marches were designed as a test of the men's stamina and physical fitness. While most of the troops were slogging along on foot, specially trained men made daring commando raids deep into territory occupied by the opposing forces.

On one such raid by the "Antrim" Forces, General Hartle was surprised in his office and forced to escape through the window. Commandos under cover of darkness attacked enemy lines of communication. Both sides used freely "paratroops," represented by an R.A.F. regiment.

An interesting sidelight on the war were the daily newspapers printed by the opposing forces for the edification (or perhaps the confusion) of the press and spectators.

The newspapers were identical in make-up, both playing up to the extreme their victories and minimizing their losses.

General Franklin declared the maneuvers a complete success, especially commending the work of the staff and the warm cooperation between American and British troops.

Wack School Teachers Will Get No Dates

DES MOINES, IA. (Special Cable from the Associated Press)—With the nation's feminine eyes beamed towards Des Moines the approaching opening date of the W.A.A.C. officers' training school is bringing difficult tactical problems to veteran Colonel Duncan Faith, commandant of the Wack's training center.

Although mainly concerned with routine preparation problems, Colonel Faith is stumped on how to regulate women according to stiff Army standards.

Seven hundred female students and an all-male faculty forced Faith to rule bachelor officers are barred from dating unwed candidates. The faculty has also been warned to watch any picturesque language.

Fearing soprano sergeants will be unable to shout commands to the rear-rankers, the commandant has employed voice teachers to show the officers how to bring their voices from stomachs instead of daintily from throats.

Colonel Faith right now is watching the marching bottleneck. He is endeavoring to solve the problem that arises when a five-foot girl tries to take a regulation 30-inch step.

"Imagine Wacks and soldiers marching together with the same music, with the soldiers stepping 30 inches and the Wacks 20 inches," he moaned.

He is also worried about the possibility of woman bandsters carrying Sousa horns and bass drums.

New Helmets Are Tougher

PITTSBURGH, PENN. (AP)—Tough, light-weight plastic helmets that have the strength of steel, weight for weight, are now in mass production for Uncle Sam's fighting men, the Westinghouse Electric and Manufacturing Company has announced.

The plastic hats, inside half of the Army's new two-part double-purpose helmets, are designed to protect the soldier during behind-the-lines activities. The outer half, hung from the soldier's belt until slipped on over the plastic for front-line combat, is a two-pound steel shell. The combined helmet must withstand a crash resistant test of 50 foot pounds.

Weighing less than 12 ounces and made of cloth and resin, the plastic hats, or liners, must meet an army-specified crash resistant test of 15 foot pounds.

A small air space between the liner and the shell, together with the insulation properties of the plastic, provides heat insulation, making the two-part helmet more comfortable than the "tin hats."

Newlyweds Say, 'I do'—Phone Girl Says 'You're Thru'

SUMTER, S.C. (AP)—After an hour of nervous waiting, Private Weldon Tidwell got through a telephone connection to Miss Opal Carter in Mexia, Tex., and they were married by the Rev. W. D. Glateon in a streamlined three-minute telephone ceremony.

"Well, honey," Tidwell said as the vows were completed, "how does it feel to be married?"

"I'm sorry," interrupted the operator, "Your time is up!"

Conscription In Canada

MONTREAL, CANADA (UP)—Canada now has conscription. The Government bill amending the National Resources Mobilization Act passed its second reading in the House of Commons in Ottawa last week.

U.S. Pilots Bomb Targets In Nazi-Occupied Holland

Major General Spaatz . . . holds the D.S.C. Planet Photo

By Tech. Sgt. G. K. Hodenfield
(Chief Staff Correspondent)

It was the first communique to be issued from the European Theater of Operations, and its wording was terse:

"In a joint operation with R.A.F. light bombers, six American air crews attacked targets in German-occupied territory today.

"Two American planes are missing.

"The American crews flew A-20 type aircraft (Bostons) in a daylight minimum altitude attack."

Behind the officially-worded communique lies the story of America's first real blow at Germany, a blow that came appropriately enough on July 4. Behind it, too, lies the story of the heroism of Pilot Captain Charles C. Kegelman of El Reno, Okla., and his crew of three men, 2nd Lt. Randall M. Dorton of Long Beach, Cal.; Sgt. Robert Golay of Fredonia, Kan.; and Sgt. Bennie Cunningham of Tupelo, Miss.

* * *

It has been revealed that the six American crews were flying British planes, American-made, with R.A.F. markings. Their targets were airdromes in Holland, with the heaviest attacks being dealt those in Hamstede, Alkmaar, and Valkenburg.

The attacks were made in the face of heavy flak fire, and they swept back and forth over their targets bombing hangars, administration buildings and dispersal points. When they ran out of bombs they turned on their machine guns, leaving at least one enemy plane burning on the ground.

At Hamstede nearly 150 Germans were caught flat-footed in full flying kit as if they were lined up for mess or pay call.

After unloading their bombs the planes headed back for Britain, slowing down long enough enroute to bomb German patrol boats off the Netherlands coast.

* * *

The raid took place 150 miles inland in one of the heaviest Luftwaffe-guarded areas on the invasion coast. The distance made it impossible for the bombers to be accompanied by a protective umbrella of fighter planes. The bombers were over the target area of more than an hour.

The daring hedge-hopping cross-channel flight in broad daylight brought a message of admiration from British air force officials, who applauded the raid as a "daring event which, occurring on July 4, symbolized American ability once more to strike hard for freedom."

Participation in the raid brought the Distinguished Service Cross to Captain Kegelman. The award was made by Maj. Gen. D. D. Eisenhower, theater commander. In addition, Maj. Gen. Carl Spaatz, commanding the United States Air Force in the European Theater, directed, under the authority of General Eisenhower, that the Distinguished Flying Cross be given to the three members of Captain Kegelman's crew, Lieutenant Dorton and Sergeants Golay and Cunningham.

* * *

Captain Kegelman's plane was hit by flak over the target area. With the propeller and nose of the starboard section of one of his engines shot off and afire, and bullet holes in the tail section, the Boston bomber, already at near zero altitude, hit the ground, damaging the starboard wing and knocking a large hole in the plane's fuselage.

Captain Kegelman recovered control, and after leaving the target area on one engine, confronted intense fire from a flak

Bombs - - -

(Continued on page 5)

Major General Spaatz Is Air Corps Chief In Europe

A real "flying general" is Major Gen. Carl Spaatz, 51, Commander in Chief of the United States Army Air Force in the European Theater of Operations.

General Spaatz, whose work will be increasingly important as the United Nations begin intensive hammering of Germany from the air, holds active ratings as command pilot and combat observer. In the last war he shot down three enemy planes in the closing days of 1918.

* * *

General Spaatz spent many months on this side of the Atlantic during the Battle of Britain as an observer studying German tactics, especially at Dover. He later returned to the United States.

He returned to Great Britain last month to set up the ground forces necessary for America's constant expansion on the European front. His command includes all wings of the air force. His chief task will be to coordinate American air effort and to direct its policy in cooperation with the R.A.F.

Major General Carl Spaatz, Commanding General of the Air Force, European Theater of Operations, was born in Earlville, Penn., on June 28, 1891.

* * *

He was appointed to the United States Military Academy from Pennsylvania and entered there in June, 1910. He was graduated from the Academy four years later and was commissioned a second lieutenant. While at the Academy the General was nicknamed

Spaatz - - -

(Continued on page 3)

Quiz Machine for Navy Pilots

WASHINGTON, D.C. (AP)—The Navy has turned out a quiz machine to test aviation cadets on aircraft and ship identification.

When a control button is pressed, a question card pops out of a small window. The cadet studies the question and then presses one of a row of buttons corresponding to a variety of possible answers. A light panel flashes "correct" or "incorrect."

The cadet is scored both on the accuracy and speed of his answer.

Eisenhower Is Now Lt. General

WASHINGTON, D.C.—Dwight D. Eisenhower's promotion to the rank of lieutenant general has been confirmed by the United States Senate, it was announced by the War Department Friday.

Must Prove It

SOMEWHERE IN NORTHERN IRELAND—Over the door of the hut occupied by the squad of Sgt Jim Evans, Glenwood, Iowa, hung this sign: "Through these portals pass the best damn soldiers in the world." The sign isn't there any more. The regimental c.o. wants them to prove it first.

3d. THE STARS AND STRIPES 3d.
Weekly Newspaper of U.S. Armed Forces in the European Theater of Operations
Vol. 2 No. 16 London, England August 1, 1942

Reds Fight 'Till Death,' Halt Nazis

By John A. Parris, Jr.
(United Press Staff Correspondent)

Facing the gravest situation since the Germans launched their climactic campaign toward the Caucasus, Marshall Timoshenko's hard-pressed armies on the Lower Don appear to be stiffening their resistance as thousands of fresh reserves move into the battle lines.

In a dramatic appeal to the Red Armies, Stalin ordered them to halt their retreat and told every officer and every soldier to stand and fight until death.

"Not one step back," he ordered. "Such is the nation's will . . . victory or death. Execution of this task means the preservation of our country and the destruction of the hated enemy—a guaranty of victory."

The Russian position is extremely serious, but military observers saw one encouraging aspect in the general gloom of the great Red Army retreat—Timoshenko's armies have withdrawn with a deliberation which still suggests conformity to a preconceived plan.

Russian Reserves

It is noteworthy that for the first time Moscow dispatches are mentioning reserves being hurled into the battle. Some reports claim that the first of 2,000,000 Red Army reserves are now fighting on the Lower Don.

The Germans' main objective still appears to be the great industrial city of Stalingrad, lying just on the bend of the Volga. The immediate aim of Von Bock's forces apparently is to cut the most important Stalingrad-Tikhoretsk railway, which already is virtually within artillery range, if not cut.

New Stalingrad Menace

Latest Moscow reports revealed that Stalingrad is menaced from a new point in the Kletskaya area, slightly below the northern arms of the Don bend, sixty miles northwest of Kalach, where the Don nearest approaches the Volga.

Pressure toward Stalingrad likewise has been continued on the southern arm of the Don bend, where Soviet resistance appears to have stiffened, with no German progress reported during the past twenty-four hours.

In the battle for Kletskaya, 75 miles northwest of Stalingrad, the Germans appear to be trying their utmost to secure the right bank and establish a foothold for a further advance toward Stalingrad.

The Germans actually reached the Don at one point, but were compelled to retreat to their original position following a strong Russian blow from the flanks.

Rostov Occupation

Simultaneously with the occupation of Rostov, the Germans crossed the Don east of the city and developed an offensive beyond the river, where they are trying desperately to push southward.

Reports that the Russians have already retired into the Caucasus mountains are obviously to be dismissed, since the front is yet nowhere near even the foothills.

Fierce fighting, however, appears to be raging between Bataisk and the important junction of Tikhoretsk, where the Russians are waging a rearguard action. At no other point have the Germans advanced so far across the Don.

In spite of the impressive German advance of the past few weeks, Timoshenko's armies do not appear to be shattered or even highly disorganised. The Germans admit that the Russians have managed to get the majority of their tanks back across the Don in the Stalingrad area. This was the most difficult sector, as the Russian forces were somewhat

Russia - - -

(Continued on Page 3)

Bundles for Berlin

Associated Press Photo

The Flying Fortresses are arriving in Brit**a**in. The one pictured here is taking off from an airport "... newhere in Britain" on a test flight to get acquainted with the terrain, while the ground crew, mounted on bicycles, waves a "hurry back" greeting. According to late cable dispatches from the eastern front, "the Russian Air Force is now using Boeing Flying Fortresses in its battle against the Germans."

Facts and figures: The B-17 has four engines, and can fly on any two of them. The crew varies from seven to nine men. The wing span is 105 feet, the overall length of the plane is 70 feet, and the gross weight is more than 22 tons. In 1939 the B-17 set an altitude record of 23,800 feet, carrying a load of 11,000 pounds. Since that time alterations have been made to increase its power and altitude.

Congress Will Close Shortly

WASHINGTON, D.C.—Congress is expected to adjourn shortly for the summer until September 1, to enable members of the House of Representatives, all of whom face re-election, as do one-third of the Senate, to return to their constituencies to prepare their campaigns.

Meanwhile an agreement has been reached in the two houses that controversial legislation will be suspended until after the recess, by which time the Senate Finance Committee is expected to have ready proposals for meeting the U.S. $6,270,000,000 Tax Bill.

Iowa Infantryman and Air Girl Beat Wedding Deadline

SOMEWHERE IN NORTHERN IRELAND—Private First Class Robert Oliver, Infantryman, Mason City, Iowa, beat Uncle Sam by one day when he was married to Miss Mabel Adocock of the W.A.A.F. the day before orders were issued stating that American soldiers are forbidden to marry while overseas.

The young couple hope to coordinate their furloughs so that they may spend their honeymoon together in England.

Captain David O. Jones, Waterloo, Iowa, Infantry chaplain, officiated at the services.

Propose United Nations Chief

WASHINGTON, D.C. — It was disclosed that the elevation of General George C. Marshall to commander-in-chief of all the United Nations forces is under serious consideration if the Allies succeed in finding a satisfactory way to create a unified command.

Army Fighter Planes Now Based in Britain

By Sgt. Bud Hutton
(Staff Writer)

Three new factors—each part of a vast pattern of bad news for Berlin—last week made air news in England. They were:

Revelation of the presence of the first United States Army Air Force fighter group in England

The disclosure that American Air Force pilots, flying Spitfires, have been on operations against the enemy.

The announcement by Maj. Gen. Carl Spaatz, commanding the Air Force here, that ranking generals heading branches of the force have taken up their posts in these islands.

With these announcements, it became apparent that the groundwork was just about completed for the eventual aerial assault against Germany and the Nazi-occupied countries.

Establishment of the first all-American fighter group and the steadily swelling stream of men and material that is pouring across the Atlantic were described as "complements to the already established Flying Fortress and Boston bomber groups."

To coordinate the components of American aerial power in England, these officers have taken up command posts here:

Major General W. H. Frank, Commanding General United States Air Service Corps; Brig. General Frank O'D. Hunter, United States Fighter Command; Brig. General Robert C. Oandee, United States Ground Air Support Command; Brig. General Asa N. Duncan, Chief of Staff, Army Air Force.

But last week it was the revelation of the fighter group, flying

Fighters - - -

(Continued on Page 3)

Heavy Raids By the RAF

The R.A.F. continued its heavy raids on Nazi key cities last week by dumping tons of heavy bombs and incendiaries on Hamburg, Duisberg, and Saarbruecken.

Hamburg, biggest submarine building base in Germany, was hit with more than 700 tons of bombs in one night. Never, during the London blitz, were that many bombs dropped.

Meanwhile fighters and light bombers were scouring the occupied countries, shooting up railroad trains and transport facilities in general.

Locomotives have been their special targets, with the result that many German engines were punctured into uselessness by cannonfire.

Nazi Agents Lose Appeals

WASHINGTON, D.C. (UP)—The eight German agents arrested in the United States and now being tried by a military court have lost the first round in their fight to gain access to the civil courts.

When seven of them were represented before the Supreme Court, it was revealed that they unsuccessfully sought writs in a lower court yesterday.

They pleaded under Habeas Corpus writs that they should be allowed civil trials, and denied that they came to the United States to commit sabotage.

New Hostel Opens In Edinburgh

EDINBURGH, SCOTLAND—The first American Red Cross hostel in Scotland and the largest in the British Isles was opened here August 1.

In the building which formerly housed the Royal Hotel at 53 Princes Street, the Red Cross will be able to provide nightly lodgings for more than 450 men.

The new hostel is patterned after those already opened in London, Belfast and Londonderry.

Servicemen Only

Up to the time the Red Cross took over the building on July 6 the Royal Hotel was still accommodating guests. Now its only guests will be servicemen and their friends.

Men on furlough will be able to secure, at the new hostel, a room for a night and breakfast the following morning for the equivalent of 50 cents—one half-crown.

They may stay at the hostel for the length of their furlough and use it as their home while away from their station.

Other Services

The hostel will also provide other services for men in and near Edinburgh, such as providing them with tickets to various theatres and special events occurring in Edinburgh. Sightseeing tours are being arranged to such places as Edinburgh Castle and Holyrood Castle.

The Red Cross will also provide opportunities for U.S. Servicemen to accept the hospitality of the Scotch people by obtaining

Hostel - - -

(Continued on Page 3)

3D. THE STARS AND STRIPES 3D.
Weekly Newspaper of U.S. Armed Forces in the European Theater of Operations
Vol. 2 No. 19 London, England 67307 August 22, 1942

Commandos, Fliers Join in Smash at Dieppe

By Drew Middleton
(Associated Press War Correspondent)

I have just watched the R.A.F. and Royal Navy smash the Luftwaffe in the fiercest and most dramatic air-sea battle of the war in the west.

* * *

Our motor launch, which was about a hundred feet long, left a southern port Tuesday night escorting tank-landing craft. The moon was sinking toward the horizon as England dropped astern and the ghostly line of ships headed for France—and the enemy.

* * *

As light brightened we saw six Spitfires flying high overhead. We were still admiring them when there was a roar of planes to the port side, and two Focke-Wulfs began the attack on our convoy. They swept over us with every gun answering theirs. One climbed out of barrage, the second wavered, and slid into a smooth sea.

* * *

"Let's go and see some fun," said the captain after tank transports had run in to landings. We steamed through smoke and in early sunlight saw burning houses in Dieppe and heard the rattle of rifle fire and the chatter of machine guns.

Shells from four-inch guns of British destroyers began to whistle overhead.

* * *

Periodically we were strafed by Nazi fighters. Squadrons of Bostons flying very low were sweeping inland to bomb second line German defenses.

* * *

Four Dornier 17-Zs flying at about 6,000 feet in echelon came toward the long lines of British ships. Ship by ship anti-aircraft guns opened fire, and tracer bullets cut sharp patterns into the blue French sky. Dorniers looked big and very black as they roared closer. Our little ship jumped under the recoil of her anti-aircraft and machine guns.

* * *

The leading bomber swerved slightly and out of her belly tumbled four bombs. They landed with explosions that nearly lifted us out of the water. Second and third bombers dropped their loads, but anti-aircraft drove off the fourth. The bombs missed the targets.

* * *

By now everyone was watching the Dorniers. The first one was blazing from hits by anti-aircraft shells and the other two were being pursued by three Spitfires.

* * *

The first fell flaming into the sea near the shore. The other two tried desperately to evade the fighters, which hung like black crosses above them. There were furious bursts of machine-gun fire, then one after another two Dorniers turned lazily over, burst into flame and fell into the sea.

Cheers of sailors on other ships came faintly across the water.

After that there was a steady rain of bombs. Our ship shook and shivered. But R.A.F. fighters pressed attacks on German bombers. Few got a chance to make a run and take careful aim on targets. I saw only one small boat sunk by bombs, and I saw 17 German planes shot down as payment.

* * *

The sky was literally covered with fighters and bombers. Many more were flying so high that we couldn't see them. I counted 49 aircraft engaged in one pitched battle to the southwest. Twisting and gyrating madly, they filled the air with the sound of motors and machine-guns.

B-17's Start Day Raids On France

Bomb-laden Flying Fortresses struck at German-occupied France in high-level daylight raids last week, demolishing a railway terminus at Rouen on Monday, attacked a German fighter base at Abbeville during the Commando operations, Wednesday, and bombed railway yard and other targets at Amiens, Thursday.

All planes returned safely to their bases and a radio operator with an injured kneecap was the sole casualty. The raids proved, too, that the vaunted efficiency of the secret bomb sight is no myth.

Twenty-four Fortresses took part in the raid on Abbeville, but one of them had mechanical difficulty with the bomb doors and jettisoned its bombs in the English Channel on the return trip.

A report issued after the raid said:

"Direct hits were observed on the north-west dispersal area, as well as on the runways. Clouds of black smoke rose after bombs had been placed on fuel storage sites."

Accompanying the Fortresses during the Amiens raid were nearly 500 Spitfires, the greatest number ever to carry out a sweep. No enemy fighters were encountered by the huge B-17s.

* * *

As in the raid over Rouen, the Fortresses were accompanied by fighter squadrons of the Royal Air Force and the Royal Canadian Air Force. Little opposition was encountered in the air, but three bombers were struck by flak splinters.

Wing-Commander Kingcombe, who led one of the escorting fighter formations, said after the Abbeville raid:

"The American bomber boys were marvellous. They did not waste a single bomb on the middle of the airfield, but buildings around the edge went up in clouds of smoke and debris. Wherever the buildings were, the bombs landed on or around them."

* * *

Twelve bombers made the trip to Rouen, the first all-American raid on the continent. Again the protective umbrella of R.A.F. and R.C.A.F. fighter planes kept enemy aircraft interference at a minimum.

The last plane over the target, the "Birmingham Blitzkrieg," captained by 1st Lt. Tom Borders, was struck 11 times by flak and the one Messerschmidt 109 which broke. The Messerschmidt was shot down in flames by Sgt. Kent West, East Blocton, Ala., ball turret gunner in Lieutenant Borders' plane.

Brig. Gen. Ira Eaker, U.S. bomber command chief, made the trip over Rouen as an observer. He flew in a Fortress nicknamed

Bombers - - -

(Continued on page 3)

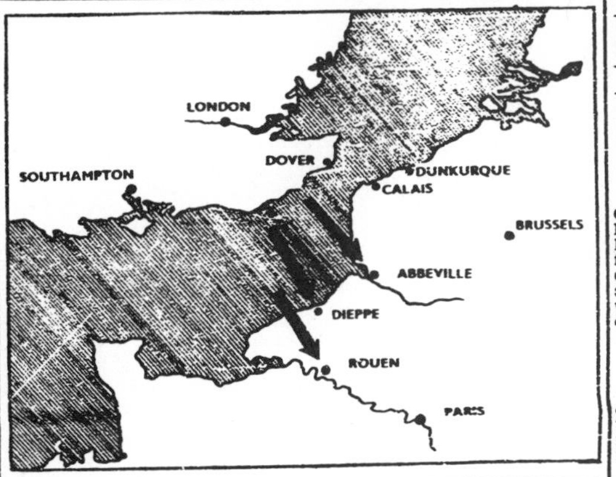

Task Force Voting Rights Are Sought

WASHINGTON, D.C. (UP)—Strong support is developing in the Senate for the passage of a bill approved by the House of Representatives to permit United States soldiers and sailors in Europe to send home their votes for district elections, it is learned in Washington.

The measure would provide that in time of war, notwithstanding any provision of state law relating to elections, including registration requirements, those in the armed services otherwise qualified should be entitled to vote for election of President, Vice-President, and Senators and House members.

Chase U-Boats Near Brazil

NEW YORK, N.Y. (UP)—More reports of German U-boat and surface raider activity in the South Atlantic have been received, while demonstrations in Brazil against the Axis continued to rage.

Following reports in Rio de Janeiro that R.A.F. planes based on British Guiana had attacked two U-boats off French Guiana, near Cape Orange and Brazilian waters, all Brazilian ships off the Brazilian coast were ordered into the nearest port.

The Rio newspaper O Globo reported that, in addition to one U-boat sunk and two others possibly sunk, two more had been located and were being chased.

Jack Benny Signs for 12 Million

HOLLYWOOD, CAL. — Jack Benny has been persuaded to become a movie producer for United Artists, the persuasion price being $12,000,000.

Plane Losses

Allied
Shot Down : 98
(30 Pilots Saved)

German
Shot Down : 91
Damaged : 180

Begin Call-Up Of 1-B Class

WASHINGTON, D.C. (AP)—The first of an estimated one million men holding a deferred 1-B classification in the draft because of minor physical defects are now being accepted for limited military service.

Undisclosed quotas to be filled by men with faulty eyesight, teeth and other defects which disqualified them for many combat duties, went out July 3 to local boards, to become effective August 1.

By calling each month a number of men who are physically capable of performing limited military service, it will be possible to release almost an equal number of qualified soldiers for duty with task forces, the War Department said in announcing the new policy.

Caucus Rejects F.D.R. Candidate

NEW YORK, N.Y. — State Attorney-General John J. Bennett will be the Democratic candidate for governor in the New York elections this fall.

He was picked at the Democratic state convention held in Brooklyn, and his selection is considered a rebuff to President Roosevelt. The President's candidate was Senator James Mead.

Rangers in Raid; U.S. Airmen Help

Snarling across the English Channel as their comrades in the Ranger Battalion were assaulting Dieppe, U.S. fighter pilots in Spitfires flew in to the thick of the dogfights that were going on "upstairs." Also flying with them were British, Belgian and Canadian units.

R.A.F. airmen, veterans of the Dunkerque fighting and the Battle of Britain, were full of praise for the Americans.

With six months' experience crowded into one day, the U.S. fliers came back with "sore necks" after hours of hard fighting in the skies of France.

"I never twisted and turned and looked behind me so much in my life. They were coming in all directions," exclaimed Lt. Harry Robb, New Philadelphia, Ohio.

Capt. Frank Hill, Hillsdale, N.J., probably accounted for a Focke-Wulf 190 for the first U.S. fighter victory of the war. "He came by in a dive and I turned in and caught him with a four second burst," Captain Hill explained.

"He spun down 2,000 feet, then seemed to regain control for a moment, then started spinning again. I think I got the pilot, but I couldn't wait around to see."

Brig. Gen. Frank O'D. Hunter, head of the U.S. Fighter Command, was full of praise for his pilots. "It was a hell of a hot show," he remarked.

Most of the American planes flew in the bottom layer of fighters, and some of the pilots had occasional glimpses of the fighting on the ground.

U.S. Fighters - - -

(Continued on page 3)

A strong force of Canadians, British, Americans and Fighting French Wednesday battered their way onto the beaches and quaysides of the French coastal resort town of Dieppe in the greatest Commando raid of the war.

The small detachment of United States troops—who thus became the first American soldiers to land on the Continent in World War II—was drawn from the Rangers, U.S. version of the Commandos.

For nine hours the battle on the ground raged, while the skies were filled with snarling fighter planes which spread a protective netting of steel and lead over the forces below.

Largest Raid Yet

The raid was the largest one yet attempted, and it marked the first time that tanks were landed in such an operation. The tanks were used as mobile fortresses, adding greatly to the fire power of the attacking forces.

German claims to the contrary, a number of the tanks were brought back when the Commandos returned. Others were destroyed in Dieppe, some by the Germans, some by the attackers.

Air Battle Rages

It would have been impossible to stage such a raid, especially in daylight hours, without the "magnificent" support of the fighter squadrons.

The Luftwaffe threw hundreds of planes at the attackers in an attempt to smash them into submission, but even greater numbers of Spitfires, flown by Canadians,

Commandos - - -

(Continued on page 3)

U.S. Rangers (Commandos) land somewhere in the British Isles, during a mock raid on the enemy.

3D. THE STARS AND STRIPES 3D.

Weekly Newspaper of U.S. Armed Forces in the European Theater of Operations

Vol. 2 No. 20 London, England 67808 August 29 1942

Reds Hurl Foes Back At Rzhev

By William King
(Associated Press War Correspondent)

Soviet Russia's indomitable warriors injected a ray of hope in the bleak picture of the war in Eastern Europe when they launched an offensive on the central sector of the front around Rzhev.

When a worried Allied world had just about decided there was no hope of holding Stalingrad—important industrial city on the Volga River—the Russians proved again their ability to attack at a moment when odds seem against them.

The threat to Stalingrad, which is menaced by three of Von Bock's armies approaching from three directions, was still grave despite the brave Red Army counter measures. The invaders first succeeded in crossing the Don River in force last Monday, and since that time they have succeeded in greatly extending their bridgehead in the elbow formed by the Don at the approaches to Stalingrad.

Must Make Stand

The Russians have reached the point where they can no longer fight in their classic pattern of slow withdrawal while inflicting the greatest possible loss on the enemy. Further withdrawals in the restricted area in which fighting is now going on before Stalingrad would mean that the city would almost surely fall.

Besides its industrial value, Stalingrad is vastly important to the Russians as the most important link in the only remaining communications route connecting the embattled Soviet armies fighting in the Caucasus with their sources of supply from the rest of Russia.

In the Caucasus, fighting has reached a fairly static state in the foothills of the range of mountains which cuts across the isthmus. The Nazis are still far from the main oilfields of the Baku. It is likely, however, that heavy fighting will be resumed in this sector, since the Germans must be anxious to smash through to manganese mines, seaports and main oilfields before impending snows.

Nazis' Weakened Lines

It is likely that the Germans weakened their lines on the Kalinin and central sectors to throw every available man, tank and gun into the fierce fighting around Stalingrad. This made it possible for the Russians to make substantial advances, which, according to them, are continuing.

The offensive, which was first announced in a special statement from the Russian high command Wednesday night, actually began two weeks earlier. Enemy defenses along a seventy-five mile line were penetrated, the announcement said. Advances

Russia - - -

(Continued on page 3)

Aircraft Workers Form Legion Post

SOMEWHERE IN NORTHERN IRELAND—American civilian aircraft workers attached to a service area depot who served in the last war have made application for a charter to organize an American Legion post.

This probably will be the first Legion post in Ireland.

Commander pro tem is the civilian depot chaplain, Dr. Norman Nygaard, former pastor of the First Presbyterian Church of Los Angeles, Cal. Acting as adjutant is Roy Adair, who served with both the Canadian and American forces during the war.

Celebrities to Entertain Troops

U.S. Signal Corps Photo

Al Jolson, Merle Oberon and other Hollywood film stars are dishing out G.I. entertainment for the United States troops in the British Isles now, and occasionally Al has to fill out one of those Army forms, but most of his writing (and his colleagues') is done in soldiers' autographs books. And are those boys happy about the whole thing!

Hollywood Stars Here

By Pvt. Mark Senigo
(Staff Writer)

Film stars Merle Oberon, Al Jolson, Patricia Morrison, Allan Jenkins and Frank McHugh have arrived in London on the first stop of a four-week tour through the British Isles to entertain the American Forces.

On the tour they will attempt to "hit" as many camps as possible in England and Northern Ireland. They will spend ten days in Ulster and the remainder in England.

Asked where they were going to put on their shows, Jolson remarked, "We don't care where we work. We'll work from the back of trucks, in mess halls, in huts, in theaters. Wherever we can get a bunch of the fellows together, we'll put on a show."

* * *

It will be a seven-day week for the stars while they are here. And they won't play matinees just on Wednesdays and Saturdays. If the facilities of the camp are not large enough for one show, there will be two or three.

At a preview performance in London, the celebrities brought down the house. With Merle Oberon as M.C. ("mistress of ceremonies" this time), Jolson sang the old songs for which he is famous — "Mammy," "Sonny Boy," "Brother Can You Spare a Dime"—with some ad libbing on the side.

Miss Morrison did some singing in a sentimental mood—and had the boys eating out of her hand—and then the daffiness twins, McHugh and Jenkins, did a comedy routine that was strictly not from hunger.

* * *

Beside entertaining U.S. forces, the group also will play in several British war industry factories for the workers during their free time.

This Hollywood quintet is the first of what is hoped will be a series of sorties from America by big-name stars.

Sponsors are the motion picture section of the U.S.O., in collaboration with Brig. Gen. Osborne, chief of the Special Service Section of the War Department.

Ranger Fights on French Soil for His 23rd Birthday

Aye!

NORTHERN IRELAND — Conversation overheard between two Yanks in Ireland:

"Did you eat with Company 'K'?"

"Aye."

"I?"

"No, K."

"But you just said 'I.'"

"Aye."

U.S. Launches Largest Ship

NEW YORK, N.Y.—What is almost certainly the world's largest and most powerful battleship slipped down the ways in a New York navy yard late last week.

The ship is the U.S.S. Iowa, a 45,000-ton sea monster completed seven months ahead of schedule at a cost of about $100,000,000. She is the fourth ship to carry that name. —her immediate predecessor was scrapped under the Washington treaty limiting naval armaments.

The Iowa is 860 feet long, only 200 feet shorter than such liners as the Queen Mary. Her main battery will consist of nine 16-inch guns. She also carries 20 five-inch guns.

Assistant Secretary of the Navy Ralph Bard declared at the launching that "the Iowa could fire faster and farther than any ship afloat," and is "a weapon far advanced over the battleships sunk at Pearl Harbor."

Mrs. Henry Wallace, wife of the vice-president and herself a native Iowan, broke a bottle of champagne on the bow to send the ship down the runways.

Censors Call Down First Lady

WASHINGTON, D.C. (UP)—Mrs. Franklin D. Roosevelt has revealed that she has received a stern letter from the censorship authorities rebuking her for mentioning the weather in her weekly gossip column.

By Tech. Sgt. G. K. Hodenfield
(Staff Writer)

It was the most exciting birthday party Cpl. Bill Brady had ever had. He ruined his best pair of tailor-made trousers and he only had 16 cents (American) to start with, and there wasn't any birthday cake with candles.

Big day, though.

Corporal Brady, you see, spent part of his 23rd birthday in France, around the beach of Dieppe.

Not too many years ago that might have been all the thing, a birthday party at the famous coast resort town. Bill's visit was strictly in the line of business.

* * *

Bill was one of the small detachment of American Rangers who made up part of the landing force which carried out the biggest Commando raid of the war. Come along with him, one of the first Americans to set foot on French soil in this war.

Bill has been in training with the British Commandos for some time. Several times, while telling his story, he said, without giving it a thought . . . "In the British Army we . . ." And don't kid him about it. Bill, and the other Americans who made the raid, won't have any of this loose talk about the British Tommy not being able to fight.

* * *

A volunteer for the American Rangers, Bill was one of the lucky ones to pass the rigorous exams. He used to play a lot of professional basketball around his home town of Grand Forks, N.D., and he's got the physique of a light-heavyweight.

Brady and the rest of the Rangers who made the trip didn't know it was anything special. They thought it was just another "maneuver." Not until they were on the boats and ready to take off for France were they sure that this was to be the real thing.

It was too late, then, to change pants, so Bill went to France with his very best pair of tailor-made trousers. They were something

Ranger - - -

(Continued on page 3)

Japs Lose Heavily In Sea Battle

Blasted by the savage blows of Flying Fortresses and carrier-based aircraft of the U.S. Navy, a Japanese expeditionary force seeking to regain the Solomon Islands has been smashed and driven from the area.

Communiques from the Navy Department and from the G.H.Q. of General MacArthur in Australia told of the repulse of the enemy armada which had come to counter-attack the American Marines now engaged in mopping up after their sudden descent on the Japanese positions in the Solomons.

Jap Carriers Hit

Extent of damage to either side in the combined sea and air battle off the Tulagi area was not revealed in the Navy communique which stated that the Japanese had withdrawn. But earlier announcements had told of successful blows against Japanese carriers and cruisers, as well as lighter craft which composed the Nippon striking force.

Meanwhile, a second Japanese force has effected a landing at Milne Bay, New Guinea, west of the Solomons and only 420 air miles from the Australian coast. But here, apparently, the United Nations had been waiting for such a stroke and immediately launched a battering ram of air power at the landing forces, sinking troopships and hitting warships to an extent that made the landing highly costly. American and Australian ground forces, as well, have moved up to check the Milne Bay landing and close fighting is in progress.

Marines Still Hold

There was no indication of the progress of the land fighting in New Guinea.

Tactically, the position in the Solomons is that the Japanese, despite their all-out attack, have thus far been unable to dislodge the U.S. Marines from their hard-won positions on Guadalcanal, Florida and Tulagi Islands.

Thirteen ships flying the Rising Sun have been damaged and a minimum of 33 of their aircraft shot down. One Japanese battleship and two carriers—one light and one heavy—have been severely damaged in the heavy fleet.

The lighter Japanese fleet escorting transports suffered extreme losses, some of which were treme losses, some of which even were acknowledged in an Imperial communique, including the loss of one destroyer. They claimed "heavy American losses."

Yanks Will Get 'Free Smoke' Kits

NEW YORK (Special Cable to Stars and Stripes)—United States soldiers overseas soon will be receiving free smokes from Uncle Sam.

Already more than 15,000 smoking kits have been packed by the Army in assembly line-like production for distribution in canteens at foreign posts.

Each of these kits contains enough cigarets and pipe tobacco to supply 200 men.

Soldiers Will Speak To European People

SOMEWHERE IN NORTHERN IRELAND—American soldiers of foreign parentage will be the stars of a series of broadcasts to be made by the B.B.C. directed toward the countries of occupied Europe. The broadcasts will be interviews in foreign languages, and are designed to reassure the oppressed people of the American intention to help them.

3d. THE STARS AND STRIPES 3d.
Weekly Newspaper of U.S. Armed Forces in the European Theater of Operations

Vol. 2 No. 22 London, England September 12, 1942

Fort Crew Tells About Air Battles

By Tech. Sgt. G. K. Hodenfield.
(Staff Writer)

ENGLAND—Sgt. John Edwards used to blow a mean trombone in a dance band at Platteville, Wis. But he probably never gave forth with a sweeter tune than he did with his machine gun over France during a Flying Fortress raid.

The tune he played was a rat-a-tat that saved the life of Pfc. Joseph Walsh, Scranton, Pa., who used to drive a truck to earn his daily bread.

Private Walsh has been recommended for the D.F.C.—he brought down a Focke Wulff 190 during the raid—but he wants it known that he wouldn't have been alive today if Sergeant Edwards hadn't beaten off a German pursuit plane that was diving at him. Private Walsh didn't have a chance to defend himself from the enemy plane, which was coming at an odd angle. He just sat in his rear gunner's turret and hoped to gosh someone would chase the Nazi away. Someone did.

Praise Spitfire Pilots

That's the way with the guys on these Fortress raids. They're always telling you about someone else. They tell you about the other guys in their crews, about the guys in the other crews, and about the British pilots who throw a protective umbrella of Spitfires over them.

Take Walsh, for example. He's only been in the Air Corps since last February. He insisted he wanted to fight, so they made him a tail gunner. He's been fighting. He was credited with one of the three enemy planes the Americans know they brought down on this particular raid, and he probably destroyed several others. But he likes to talk about Sergeant Edwards.

Sergeant Edwards likes to talk about the British pilots and their Spitfires. Sgt. David Fanning, Los Angeles, likes to talk about two things—his native California, and the way Corp. Raymond Ericksen, Chicago, chased Messerschmidts and Focke Wulffs away from the plane on their left. Corporal Ericksen talks about the other guys.

Biggest Raid Yet

The raid the men were talking about was one of the biggest yet. And the Germans didn't like the idea of the Flying Fortresses coming over, bombing the daylights out of them, and going back without a casualty. So the Nazis waited for them over the channel, fought them all the way to the target and back, and didn't leave until they were back over the

Forts - - -
(Continued on page 3)

Liner Manhattan Is Burned at Sea

(Special Cable to Stars and Stripes)

NEW YORK—In a dramatic rescue at sea, 1,600 passengers and crew members were safely removed from the 24,000-ton naval transport Wakefield (formerly the liner Manhattan) when it caught fire en route to the United States.

The transport was returning to the east coast after a successful ocean crossing with the largest number of troops ever ferried in a single operation.

The rescue was carried out by warships in the convoy, who were at the Wakefield's side 10 minutes after the alarm was given. Most of the passengers were women and children returning to America from England and Eire. Many of the passengers and crew members suffered burns, none fatal. The burned-out hulk was towed to port.

Hands Across the Sea

Keystone Photo

Admiral Stark, U.S. naval chief, congratulates the bride after the first wedding between members of the naval forces of the United States and Britain. The bride formerly was Second Officer Joan Mary Ferguson Casement of the W.R.N.S. The groom is Chief Yeoman Richard A. Templeton, Augusta, Ga., who has been in London since July, 1941.

Gen. Smith Heads Staff

Brig. Gen. Walter Bedell Smith this week became chief of staff to Lt. Gen Dwight D. Eisenhower, Commanding General, European Theater of Operations, United States Army.

General Smith replaces Brig. Gen. Charles Bolte, who also was chief of staff to Gen. Chaney, first commander of the American Forces in the British Isles.

Gen. Smith was assistant secretary and secretary of the War Department General Staff from Oct. 5, 1939, to Feb. 1, 1942, and United States secretary of the Combined Chiefs of Staff in Washington from Feb. 1, 1942, to Sept. 3, 1942.

Appointed 2nd lieut. in the infantry section, Officers Reserve Corps, on Nov. 27, 1917, Gen. Smith was made a first lieutenant of infantry in the Regular Army on July 1, 1920. He was promoted to captain Sept. 24, 1929, to major on Jan. 1, 1939, to lt. col. on May 4, 1941, to col. on Aug. 30, 1941, and to brig. gen. on Feb. 1, 1942.

A member of the General Staff Corps since April 23, 1942, General Smith was graduated from the Infantry School, advanced course, in 1932; from the Command and General Staff School in 1935 and from the Army War College in 1937. In 1933 and 1936 he served as assistant secretary and secretary of the Infantry School, Fort Benning, Georgia, and in 1938 he was there as an instructor in weapons.

General Smith was born on Oct. 5, 1895, at Indianapolis, Ind.

New Tank Vessel Is Launched in U.S.

PITTSBURGH (UP) — A new type landing ship for tanks was launched this week in the Ohio River.

Although the U.S. Navy refuses to give out details about the vessel, it claimed that it is the largest warship ever launched on inland waterways in the U.S.

Admirals Attend Wedding of U.S. Yeoman and WREN

Veteran Undergoes Operation to Enlist

SHEPPARD FIELD, TEX. (AP)—A 63-year-old private, whose military service in times of emergency dates back to the Spanish-American War, has joined the Army Air Forces technical training command at Sheppard Field.

He is Private Harry Rudolph of Brooklyn, who gave up a veteran's pension and underwent an operation on both legs to qualify for enlistment and a chance at specialized training for a ground crew post.

By Tom Bernard
(Yeoman Second Class, U.S.N.R.)

The first wedding between members of the British and American Naval forces in England took place Thursday, when Second Officer Joan Mary Casement, WRNS, and Chief Yeoman Richard A. Templeton, USN, were married in the chapel of the American Red Cross Milestone Club in London.

Three admirals, representing both the American and Royal Navies, attended the ceremony. Admiral Harold R. Stark, Commander, U.S. Naval Forces in Europe; Rear Admiral Alan G. Kirk, his Chief of Staff and Naval Attache, and Vice Admiral Sir Geoffrey Blake, R.N., Admiralty liaison officer to the U.S. Naval forces, were present.

Lieut. Col. David G. Cowie, R.A., retired, uncle of the bride, gave her away, and Chief Yeoman David Martin, of the flag office staff, was best man. Lieut. Silas L. Weems, U.S. Army Chaplain, performed the rites.

A reception for Navy men attached to the American Embassy was held Thursday night at the groom's home, Nell Gwynn House, Chelsea.

The couple left Friday morning for a week's honeymoon at the bride's home town, Bally Castle, County Antrim, Northern Ireland.

Templeton's home is in Augusta, Georgia.

Officers Must Fly On Raids

ENGLAND — Brig. Gen. Ira Eaker, commanding general, Bomber Command, Eighth Air Force, has issued orders that all staff officers, as soon and as often as practical, shall accompany Flying Fortresses on raids over Germany and German-Occupied Europe.

Every staff officer, if not already a qualified aerial gunner, shall take a course to qualify himself as such. No staff officer shall usurp the functions of a member of a combat crew, but neither shall he be carried as "dead cargo."

That the plan has merit was proven by Col. Newton Longfellow, Minneapolis, Minn. Colonel Longfellow was awarded the Purple Heart after a recent raid, which he made as an observer.

After a dog-fight with enemy planes he administered first aid where needed, saving the life of the co-pilot by prompt action, then took the place of the injured co-pilot, and helped to land the B-17 safely.

President to Order 35-mile Speed Top

(Special Cable to Stars and Stripes)

WASHINGTON, D.C.—Speed-crazy America is going to slow down—by order.

President Roosevelt has announced that as soon as possible he will impose a speed limit of 35 miles per hour on all motor vehicles and will restrict all cars to 5,000 miles per year "for necessary driving."

Nazi Drive Rolls On At Stalingrad

By William King
(Associated Press War Correspondent)

Nazi Germany's slashing offensive against Russia's key tank manufacturing city of Stalingrad, on the Volga river, entered its eighth week with invaders progressing inch by inch through fiercely defended outer fortifications which form a semicircle about the beleaguered city.

At week's end, as the hard-pressed defenders of the vital city were forced to yield three more strong points, crack Siberian regiments were called in to try and stall the Nazi drive.

Battle for Time

For Timoshenko and his Soviet battalions it was a battle against time and weather. Once again, as in every campaign the Germans have fought since their panzers first mowed down the Polish cavalry in September of 1939, the United Nations are counting on General Weather to halt the enemy.

As they did in their successful defense of Leningrad last year and in their unsuccessful but tenacious battle to hold Sevastopol three months ago, the Russians have again proven their willingness to exact the greatest possible price for every enemy advance into their territory.

In the advance on Stalingrad the Axis is probably paying a new high price for each foot of the undulating steppes over which the battle rolls. Von Bock, the Nazi commander, has thrown reinforcements and reserves of tanks into the attack on the city's western approaches and is making steady progress on this front.

Hold At Any Cost

The Red Army has been ordered to hold ground at any cost, however, and is using extensive minefields and heavy concentrations of artillery to slow the drive. Companies of machine-gunners and special anti-tank rifle detachments plant themselves in the path of the advancing enemy, levying heavy casualties on the invaders before being blasted from their positions.

Von Bock can only maintain the tempo of his attack by constantly drawing on reserves, which are mostly Italian and Rumanian troops of inferior quality. Russians also are calling upon reserves of men and materials as they constantly seek to offset the prepon-

Russia - - -
(Continued on page 3)

New Fighter Plane Ready

PHILADELPHIA (UP)—A 400-mile-an-hour U.S. fighter plane, which operates best above 25,000 feet, will soon make its appearance on the fighting fronts of the world, according to Lt. Gen. George Brett.

Gen. Brett, commander of the United Nations Air Forces in the Southwest Pacific, stated here that the new plane weighs 5,000 pounds more than the average pursuit craft and has a firing force equal to the impact of a five-ton truck smashing into a stone wall at 60 miles an hour.

Willkie Sees de Gaulle About U.S. Attitude

(Special Cable to Stars and Stripes)

BEIRUT—Wendell Willkie conferred with Gen. de Gaulle in Beirut on the attitude of the United States to the Fighting French. Willkie also called on President Naccache of the Lebanon Republic.

3d. THE STARS AND STRIPES 3d.

Weekly Newspaper of U.S. Armed Forces in the European Theater of Operations

Vol. 2 No. 23 London, England September 19, 1942

U.S. Army Parachute Troops Are in Britain

Story and pictures
by Sgt. Bud Hutton.
(Staff Writer.)

WITH U.S. PARATROOPERS IN BRITAIN—You hear them first . . . the basso thundering of a dozen big planes hammering along at tree-top height. Then, so low and so fast that they are above the cleared patch in the woodlands where you stand before you have accurately figured their direction, the white-starred monoplanes appear. A figure stands in the yawning open doorway of one of the planes. It jumps out.

So fast you scarcely can count them, dozens more follow that first one. And from each succeeding plane of the group they pour out. White umbrellas of parachute silk billow against the sky.

For a few seconds the figures beneath those parachutes pendulum from side to side. They have jumped from such a low altitude that the pendulum swing barely is corrected before they touch ground.

The 'chutes are "spilled" and collapse. For a moment, in which you wonder if the jumper has been injured, there is no movement from the men on the ground.

Abruptly, the figures leap up.

Stars and Stripes Photo

The sky of Britain is filled with white bits of silk, blossoming out as the paratroops leap from the carrier planes. (This picture was taken from a plane traveling with the paratroop formation.)

sprint to 'chutes which have dropped guns and munitions in canisters. Now another crouched sprint to the shelter of nearby woods.

Scant minutes—how many is a military secret—from the time the planes appear, a unit of United States Army parachute troops has jumped, set up headquarters and signals and is ready for action with a firepower that would have delighted an entire brigade and then some, of the last war's troops.

* * *

That cleared patch of ground amid woodland is "somewhere in Britain." The paratroops who jumped are here, ready for action.

Presence of American paratroops in Britain was announced this week by Lt. Gen. Dwight D. Eisenhower, commanding general, European theater of operations.

* * *

The airborne fighting men, necessarily spearhead and first to fight of any continental invasion, are completing the "polishing up" stages of training, cooperating with British paratroops in both tactics and general strategy.

Over an assault course that would leave the best-trained of athletes grunting for breath these men

Para - - -

(Continued on page 3)

New Solomon Attacks Held Off By Marines

By Bill Downs
(United Press War Correspondent.)

United States Leathernecks are stubbornly fighting against reinforced Japanese land, sea and air forces as the LYB's launch attack after attack in vain attempts to knock the Marines out of the Solomon Islands.

Both military experts and armchair strategists agreed that Jap determination to retake the islands was preparatory to another major thrust in the Southwest Pacific. Not even the Son of Heaven and all his cherry blossoms could make another thrust towards Australia with the United States and Australian navies itching to put a few broadsides into his left flank from their bases in Tulagi.

While the Japs are finding out just how tough a Marine can be, the American and Australian effort in this theater seemed mainly to concern itself with the destruction of Japanese air power.

It was reported from Pearl Harbor Wednesday that the 7,500-ton aircraft carrier Ryuzyo probably was sunk off the Solomons on August 24.

This makes a total of six carriers with which we've populated the bottom of the Pacific since December 7.

And since the Jap attack began August 7 they have lost some 300 planes.

NEW GUINEA

On the Southwest Pacific's other main fighting front in New Guinea, Australian soldiers are holding their own against strong, tricky Japanese jungle fighters who have used everything from firecrackers to human bait to advance their lines down the Owen-Stanley range towards Port Moresby.

Main forces of both the Australians and Japanese are now in contact as patrols probe around flanks looking for passage through the thick jungles which form the battlefield. The main fighting is believed proceeding somewhere south of Kokoda.

ALEUTIANS

U.S. Army and Navy bombers heavily attacked Japanese harbor forces and ground installations at Kiska in the Aleutians this week.

Yorktown Is Sunk by Japs

WASHINGTON, D.C.—The Navy Department announced this week that the 19,900 ton aircraft carrier Yorktown was sunk in the Pacific battle of Midway in June. Also sunk with the Yorktown was the destroyer Hammann.

The casualties of the sinking were light and were included in the still Midway casualty list, which totaled 92 officers and 215 men.

The carrier was first hit by aerial bombs on June 4. Immediately after the bombing she was hit by torpedoes. The crew abandoned the ship, but she stayed afloat and a salvage crew was put aboard in an attempt to bring her to port. The Hammann was put alongside for protection.

The Japanese renewed the attack on June 7, and, hit by torpedoes, both the Hammann and the Yorktown went down. With the sinking, the U.S. has lost two carriers and a converted carrier. The others lost were the Lexington and Langley.

U.S. Power

WASHINGTON, D.C.—Rear Admiral W. H. P. Blandy, chief of the Naval Bureau of Ordnance, declared that the United States forces in the Pacific now hold the balance of striking power.

His statement was based on observations made during a recently completed 35,000-mile inspection tour of Pacific bases.

The bombers were accompanied by pursuit planes which strafed Jap forces on the ground. Large fires and explosions were started, five ships were sunk, as well as others damaged. Estimated Jap casualties were 500 with two U.S. pilots killed when their planes crashed into each other.

Three Eagle Squadrons Go to U.S. Army

Three squadrons of American Eagles, the men who came from America to fight the battle of democracy long before their country entered the war, have transferred into the United States Army Air Force.

The squadrons will remain together and continue to fight as units, passing on their wealth of knowledge to their countrymen who are arriving here in ever-increasing numbers.

The Eagle Squadrons have accounted for at least 73 enemy planes, probably many more.

It has also been announced that arrangements are being made for the transfer to the U.S. Air Forces of all Americans in the R.A.F. and R.C.A.F. who wish to make the move.

Mickey's Wife Seeks Settlement

HOLLYWOOD, CAL.—Allegations of extreme cruelty were made by Miss Ava Gardner, actress wife of Mickey Rooney, when she sued for divorce in Hollywood.

She also alleged grievous mental suffering.

She asked for alimony in proportion with his salary of $5,000 a week.

Miss Gardner was 19 and Mickey Rooney 20 when they were married last year.

Japs Mysteriously Killed in Siberia

NEW YORK, N.Y. (UP)—Thousands of urns containing the ashes of Japanese soldiers are arriving every month at Harbin, Manchuria, where the general opinion is that they were killed in fighting on the Siberian border about which both the Japanese and Russians are keeping quiet.

It is pointed out, however, that the Japanese dead might be the result of Chinese guerilla activity.

Von Bock Fights Way to Stalingrad Outskirts

By Noland Norgaard
(Associated Press War Correspondent.)

Paced by the heaviest dive-bombing barrage ever concentrated in support of land forces, Field Marshal von Bock's German army fought its way into the outskirts of Stalingrad this week, and the greatest battle of World War II swirled with rising fury in and around the great Russian tank and tractor manufacturing city on the Volga.

Dispatches from Moscow told of German losses mounting sharply as the Nazis, forging slowly into the edges of the city, exposed themselves to concentrated fire from Red Army infantry and artillery screened by the ruins of shattered buildings.

But the Russians themselves made no effort to conceal the precarious position of their defense forces, aggravated by the German air superiority which enabled von Bock's dive-bombers to pulverize selected strong points and open the way for his tanks and infantry in narrow key sectors.

The battle for Stalingrad was more than a fight for a city. Upon its outcome hinged control of vital supply lines over which great quantities of war materials from the United States are routed to the Russian armies after transhipment across Persia and then through the Caspian Sea.

The Russian command already had given notice there would be no retreat from the city.

Through the Moscow press, the Red Army was reminded that in 1918 Stalin saved the same city by withdrawing the fleet of Volga river boats which afforded the only means of retreat and then promising to shoot any man who attempted to flee.

Aside from Stalingrad, the most significant fighting along more than 1,400 miles of the Russia front occurred at Mozdok and near Leningrad.

The swift dash of German Panzer forces toward one of Caucasus Russia's richest prizes, the Grozny oilfields, second [illegible] in the U.S.S.R., has been brought to a standstill in the Mozdok area.

R.A.F. Blasts At Ruhr Area

Carrying out the ninth big attack in 16 days, a very strong force of R.A.F. bombers, probably numbering many hundreds, attacked the Ruhr this week.

Thirty-nine R.A.F. bombers failed to return.

The concentrated attack lasted about an hour, and the bombs dropped brought to nearly 5,000 tons the weight of bombs dropped on Germany in the great September offensive.

No attempt is made officially to pretend that the losses are not heavy. Six or seven trained airmen constitute the crew of each of those big night bombers.

The size of the R.A.F. force engaged cannot be revealed, but it can be said that they unloaded more bombs on the Ruhr than was ever dropped on London on any one night during the blitz.

'Double-Time' Ends in States

WASHINGTON, D.C.—President Roosevelt this week signed an executive order prohibiting the payment of double time for work done on Saturdays, Sundays and holidays. Many unions have already modified their contracts in order to comply with the order.

Good Ideu!

FORT DEVENS, MASS. (AP)—Pvt. John J. Murphy dropped out of line as his outfit returned from a 14-mile hike with full field equipment.

To his captain he explained:

"I broke my arm last night, and I think I'd better have it put in a sling."

3d.

THE STARS AND STRIPES

3d.

Weekly Newspaper of U.S. Armed Forces in the European Theater of Operations

Vol. 2 No. 26 London, England October 10, 1942

Stalingrad Defenders Stand Fast

By Wes Gallagher
(Associated Press War Correspondent)

Russia's military miracle defense of Stalingrad continues unabated this week, with the Red Army and the city's "Minute Men" from the factories and docks repulsing every attempt by Hitler to take the burning and battered Volga port.

Berlin radio Friday night indicated that for the first time the Stalingrad battle had reached a stalemate and that mass infantry assaults would be called off. However, the Friday night Moscow communique reported that the attacks had not been called off and that fierce fighting continued with both infantry and mechanized forces.

Some military sources estimate German losses must be about the same as British losses in the Third and Fourth battles of Ypres, when 2,606 men were killed each day, and 379,000 men were killed between the third of July and the end of the year, along with 19,000 officers.

Marshal Timoshenko's terrific defense already ranks with General MacArthur's defense of Bataan in the military books. It is evident that Timoshenko, like MacArthur, believes the best form of defense is to attack. His counterthrusts northwest of Stalingrad and to the south both have made small but steady progress during the week, which is more than Hitler has been able to do, although at one time he is reported to have turned loose 1,000 bombers a day on the already shattered metropolis.

Italian reports said Timoshenko's forces had crossed the Don northwest of the city, but had been "thrown back." If the Italians did throw them back it is the first time they have been able to budge a Russian soldier since the war started.

Meanwhile winter is closing down on the northern fronts and moving rapidly down the Volga. As battered as Stalingrad is, it offers a hundred times better shelter for troops than the icy steppes west of the city, which are swept with blizzards and sub-zero temperatures. It was in November last year that Russian resistance and winter broke the back of the German offensive on Moscow and put the Wehrmacht on the defensive until this summer.

In the south, the German drive for the oilfields at Grozny has made as little progress as the attack on Stalingrad, with the Red Army beating off every attack.

Welles' Reply to Stalin Talk

WASHINGTON, D.C. (UP)—Commenting on Stalin's second front statement, Sumner Welles, U.S. Under-Secretary of State, said that he had read the statement carefully, and that every possible assistance, whether material or physical, would be given the Russians to the greatest extent possible, and with the greatest speed.

U.S. Strikes Cause Small Labor Loss

DETROIT, MICH. (UP)—Since Pearl Harbor, strikes have caused the loss of less than one-tenth of one per cent of the total time worked, U.S. Secretary of Labor Perkins told an American Federation of Labor convention.

They Fought Off Forty Focke-Wulfes

Associated Press Photo

With more than 200 holes in the fuselage of their Flying Fortress, two engines out of commission and half their controls shot away, this crew came back to tell the story. Studying a map of the territory they successfully bombed are: Lt. John Thomson, St. Louis, Mo.; Lt. Charles Paine, Waycross, Ga.; Lt. Stanley A. Komarek, Muskegon, Mich., and Lt. Robert H. Long, Sweetwater, Texas.

Yanks 'Lay It on the Line' for War-Orphaned Children

By Sgt. Bud Hutton
(Staff Writer)

The Yanks in the British Isles laid it on the line this week for the war-orphaned children of their Allies.

Into The Stars and Stripes War Orphan Fund came the first checks and money orders which will go toward the care of United Nations youngsters who have lost one or both parents during three years of war against the Axis.

No one, least of all the men "out on the line," tied any strings to their offers. They just reached down in their pockets and said, "How much does it take?"

* * *

The Non-Commissioned Officers Club of headquarters battery of an anti-aircraft coast artillery unit called a meeting as soon as The Stars and Stripes announced it would sponsor a fund to help care for war orphans.

The non-coms voted, unanimously, to send £20 monthly to the Fund until £100 has been raised, a sum sufficient to provide care and necessities for one child for five years, over and above what the British Government already provides.

"We'd like a girl orphan, three to six years old," wrote Master Sgt. Joe Bethea, president of the club. "And we would prefer a blonde."

What's more, the club promised that as soon as the first £100 is raised, they're going after a second £100 to sponsor another orphan.

* * *

Moved by the appeal for help in caring for youngsters who have been hit by war and aren't able to hit back, an American Air Force fighter squadron somewhere in England sent a check for £50 from the commissioned and enlisted personnel alike to "show appreciation of your truly American spirit of helping those less fortunate," as Capt. James G. Moore put it.

The unit didn't have enough cash right at hand to provide the full £100 and thus choose, if they wished, the type of orphan child they would help care for; they just dug down and laid it on the line.

An infantry unit in Northern Ireland telegraphed: "Sure we want one-twelfth dozen or more Orphans - - -

(Continued on page 3)

Kaiser Builds 64-Day Miracle

U.S. PACIFIC PORT—Henry J. Kaiser has done it again. The man who built a Liberty ship in ten days has just completed the construction of a shipyard in 64 days when experts told him it would take at least two years.

"Experts told us that we could not get the necessary cranes, so we pieced together cranes of our own from scrap metal, from ships and from girders left over from the building of the Coulee dam and from old oil derricks," he said.

Kaiser's representatives are now in New York canvassing for more labor for his shipyards.

Tommy Manville Takes 6th Wife

NEW YORK, N.Y. (UP)—Tommy Manville, the asbestos millionaire, has obtained a wedding licence to marry his sixth wife in New York.

"It's the real thing this time," vowed Manville. The sixth-to-be is Wilhelmina Boze, a 20-year-old showgirl.

New Tax Bill Will Raise Eight Billion

WASHINGTON, D.C. — The largest tax bill in the nation's history, which is designed to raise between $7,000,000,000 and $8,000,000,000 by adding millions of new taxpayers, has been completed by the Senate Finance Committee and sent to Senate floor for consideration. The bill would swell the annual Treasury receipts to $26,000,000,000.

Italy Claims U.S. Battleship Sunk

ROME, ITALY—A special Italian communique states that the Italian submarine Barbarigo, commanded by Lieutenant Enzo Grossi, sank with four torpedo hits off Freetown, Sierra Leone, the U.S. battleship Mississippi.

Cards Snap Yank Streak, Take Series

The St. Louis Cardinals, whom the experts said coudn't even win the National League pennant, stunned the sporting World this week by completing a four out of five sweep of the World Series and taking the championship back across the Muddy Mississippi.

To make their victory emphatic, the Cards completed the job in the Yankee Stadium, winning the only three games played in New York. More than 210,000 people saw the last three games—and they still don't understand it.

The Yanks, cocky and confident as only World Champions can be, took the first game in St. Louis, 7 to 4. Then Johnny Beazeley, the 23-year-old former boxer from the hills of Tennessee, evened the account in games with a 4 to 3 victory, then series moved to N.Y.

Then, right in its own den, the Cards bearded the mighty Yankee Lion. The third game was 2 to 0, the fourth, 9 to 6, and the fifth, 4 to 2.

And now the critics have their perfect answer to their mournful chant of "Break Up The Yankees." The Yankees were making their last appearance as a "wonder team," for the entire infield will be gone next year.

The Yanks lost the series, but World's Series - - -

(Continued on page 6)

Saturday's Bore

Ain't you glad you ain't home on Saturday afternoons?

Just sitting around the house bored to death, nothing on the radio but football games.

You spin the dial, and all you can get is GEORGIA TECH beating NOTRE DAME, TENNESSEE walloping FORDHAM, IOWA SEAHAWKS breaking MINNESOTA'S long winning streak, OREGON STATE scoring in the last 10 seconds to beat the UNIVERSITY OF CALIFORNIA, PENN beating HARVARD.

Ah, it's great to be over here.

(If you want to read football, it's all on page 6.)

Lone Fort Battles 40 NaziPlanes

This is a story of heroism—the heroism of men and their machine. The machine was a Flying Fortress, the men were the crew.

* * *

They were five miles above France, two engines were out of commission. In the plane were three shell holes in the rudder and three more in the stabilizer and another in the wing, half the controls were shot away, the landing gear was smashed, and there were more than 200 holes in the fuselage.

* * *

That was the result of direct anti-aircraft fire.

Then they were attacked by 40 FW 109's.

The crew members weren't professional soldiers with lots of experience. All were fresh from civilian life. The pilot and co-pilot were attorneys, the bombardier was a law student. The navigator was a questioner with a famous public opinion polling organization. A coal miner, an artist, and a printer manned the guns.

The crew members were:

Pilot—Lt. Charles Paine, 27, Waycross, Ga.; Co-pilot—Lt. Robert Long, 25, Sweetwater, Tex.; Navigator—Lt. John Thomson, 23, St. Louis; Bombardier—Lt. John Komarek, 27, Muskegon, Mich; Waist gunner—Sgt. Herbert Peterson, 21, Des Moines, Ia.; Upper turret gunner — Sgt. Thomas Coburn, 22, Forty Fort, Pa.; Ball turret gunner—Sgt. Ralph Sheeder, 23, Six Mile Run, Pa.; Radio-gunner—Sgt. Arthur Bouthillier, 22, Westcott, R.I.; Tail gunner—Sgt. Bert Taucher, 20, Rock Springs, Wyo.; Radio-gunner—Sgt. Walter Purcell, 20, Kingston, Wash.

* * *

And this crew, which hadn't even flown together as a complete unit before, brought their plane safely back to an English airdrome in one of the greatest flights of the war.

The Fortress "Phyllis" was the last bomber to approach the target. They just had crossed the target when Lieutenant Paine heard shouts from every quarter of the plane:

"Here they come!" "They" were 40 Focke-Wulfe 190's, including a Yellow Nose (Goering) squadron.

From every side they came, spitting machine gun bullets and cannon shells from every angle. Every gun in the Fortress burst into a staccato reply.

Bouthillier's oxygen mask broke away from his face and he slipped to the floor unconscious.

Purcell leaped to take his place at the gun which had jammed. By the time he was able to clear the gun a 20 mm. cannon shell from an FW cut his oxygen tube, and he also fell unconscious.

* * *

At the same time two cannon shells knocked one engine out of commission and "Phyllis" started losing place in the formation. The F.W.s swooped in for the kill.

Lieutenant Paine started a long glide down, to save the lives of the two radio men, as the plane was then too high for those without oxygen masks.

At this point anti-aircraft shells smashed into the right stabilizer, ripped a big hole in the wing, and three more shells tore a big chunk out of the rudder over Taucher's head.

* * *

"I was so busy shooting at German fighters coming up on us I didn't notice anything," said Taucher. When they landed Fortress - - -

Continued on page 3.

3D. **THE STARS AND STRIPES** 3D.

Weekly Newspaper of U.S. Armed Forces in the European Theater of Operations

Vol. 2 No. 28 London, England 61316 October 24, 1942

Rain, Mud Slow Down Nazi Drive

By Alfred Wall
Associated Press War Correspondent

Hitler's long campaign to take Stalingrad showed more definite signs of bogging down in Russia's prewinter weather at end of another week of bitter fighting for the battered Volga city.

The Russians announced the recapture of more positions.

The German radio hedged more and more about the campaign.

Some commentators thought Von Hoth's desperate "final" assault had been turned.

Even the most conservative of military observers permitted themselves to see evidence that Hitler had lost one of the greatest gambles in military history.

It was a fact that:

1. The Russian armies had not been split and still presented an unbroken front to the invaders.

2. The Nazis had failed to attain their land objectives—the oil of the Caspian shore and control of Stalingrad and the mouth of the Volga.

On the other hand, the German summer campaign had:

1. Added 800 miles of front which the Germans would have to defend during the terrific Russian winter.

2. Continued so far into the bad weather period that the Germans again faced a winter in the field.

3. Left the German left flank still menaced by the Russian salient at Voronezh.

It begins to look like the beginning of another winter of hardship and suffering for the Nazis in Russia—despite Hitler's promise that they would be better equipped this year.

Already the weather had taken a turn whch favored the Russians and made Stalingrad's position, which seemed somewhat grim early in the week, "decidedly more satisfactory," according to British military sources who received late dispatches from the front.

German dive-bombers were mired on soggy airfields and Stalingrad's defenders, relieved of harassment from the air, rallied and took a series of important heights outside the city.

On Wednesday the Russians got a direct message of encouragement from the American people, with President Roosevelt heading the list of signatories. It was a tribute to the valor of the Soviet peoples whose "courageous resistance has given us time to produce our arms, so that at the appointed time we may join in your triumphant offensive."

Forts Attack U-Boat Base

U.S. Flying Fortresses attacked the Nazi U-boat base at Lorient, in Occupied France, this week as well as an airfield at Maupertis.

Three Fortresses failed to return to their bases after the raid. The Vichy government stated that more than 100 people were killed in the attack upon Lorient and that 450 were injured.

At the same time fighter planes of the British Army Cooperation Command penetrated 750 miles into Germany to shoot up military camps and factories as well as targets in Holland.

Los Angeles Has 'Quake Shock

LOS ANGELES, CAL. (UP)—Buildings in Los Angeles swayed gently sideways when an earthquake shock was felt in the city Wednesday. The shock lasted one minute.

First Lady Will Visit Britain

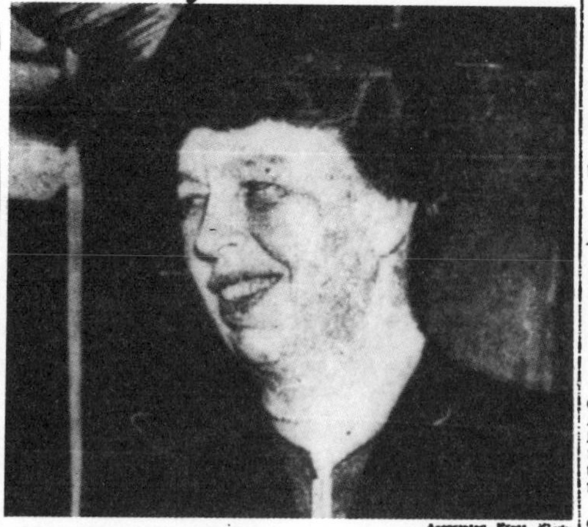

Associated Press Photo

Mrs. Franklin D. Roosevelt . . . First Lady of the U.S. . . . will visit U.S. troops in Britain.

* * * * * * * * * * * * * * *

Mrs. Franklin D. Roosevelt will arrive in England soon for a two-week visit of the British Isles. While here she will be the guest of the Queen, renewing a friendship first made when the Royal pair visited the U.S. in 1939.

The First Lady will also visit many of the bases at which U.S. troops are stationed in Great Britain. And, for the first time, she will see the three foster children she has adopted. They are a 17-year-old Polish girl, Janina Dybowska, and a Spanish boy, 14-year-old Kerman Garaie.

These two children are refugees from Europe. The third is Thomas Moloney, a 44-year-old son of Britain.

Stimson Asks NoLiquor Ban

WASHINGTON, D.C. (UP)—An appeal to Congress to reject a proposal by Senator Josh Lee to ban sales of liquor in areas in which service camps were situated was made in Congress this week by Henry L. Stimson, U.S. War Secretary.

He pointed out that if this ban were imposed the Government would also have to enforce prohibition in New York, Chicago, Los Angeles, or any other part of the country adjacent to military camps.

Denmark's King Suffers Head Injury

STOCKHOLM, SWEDEN (UP)—"I am no longer 18," were the first words of King Christian of Denmark after he had been thrown from his horse.

The latest bulletin says that the condition of the 72-year-old king is satisfactory and that he has sustained no concussion, while his skull is not fractured, but he will be confined to bed.

Ohio Factorymen Use 'Slanguage'

CLEVELAND, OHIO (UP)—"Slanguage" is making its appearance in factories around Cleveland.

If the foreman (the "pennydog") says: "Tell the gyppos to twiddle the gates a little faster. This is war and we've got to give her the gun."

"He really means to say, in plain English, that production will have to be speeded up and that pieceworkers will have to grind the valves faster.

Hotel Sailed to Washington

FORT LAUDERDALE, FLA. (UP)—A floating 75-room hotel sailed for 900 miles from Fort Lauderdale, Florida, to Washington to help relieve the housing shortage in the capital.

E.T.O. Chief Denies Claim

German claims made on Sept. 28 that several large liners "heavily laden with American soldiers" had been torpedoed were denied this week by Lt. Gen. Dwight D. Eisenhower, European theater commander.

General Eisenhower said that the "claims were completely unfounded." He added that the official announcement had been withheld "until every U.S. soldier that was on the Atlantic at the time of the German announcement had landed safely in the United Kingdom."

Edw. G. Robinson Arrives in Britain

Tough guy of the films, Edward G. Robinson, has arrived in London, preparatory to touring U.S. camps in the British Isles to entertain the troops.

From New York comes word that he is but the vanguard of another group of stars, including Carmen Miranda and Alice Faye, who are expected to arrive soon to give shows for Americans stationed here.

House Approves Teen-Age Drafting

WASHINGTON, D.C. (UP)—The Bill authorizing the lowering of the conscription age to 18 was passed by the House of Representatives in Washington this week.

Allied Heads Plan Campaign in India

NEW DELHI, INDIA (UP)—Three generals—Wavell, Auchinleck and Stilwell—are today planning new Allied campaigns from their headquarters in New Delhi.

New Stars and Stripes Will Be Daily Paper

The Stars and Stripes, official publication for the United States Armed Forces in the European Theater of Operations, will become a daily newspaper on Monday, Nov. 2.

As a daily, The Stars and Stripes, which first was published in the last World War and resumed publication as a weekly on April 18, 1942, will be distributed every day but Sunday to all American forces in the British Isles. It will not be for sale to the civilian public here.

With its entrance into the daily field, The Stars and Stripes becomes the first American newspaper other than the Paris Herald and the Paris edition of the Chicago Tribune (both now suspended) to be printed daily in Europe.

Written and edited by soldier-newspapermen in the Army, Navy, and Marines, the new Stars and Stripes will be published in four pages on Tuesday, Wednesday, Thursday, Friday and Saturday. On Mondays it will appear as an eight-page paper, carrying two full pages of sports results at home and with the forces.

* * *

Cost of the daily will be one penny per copy.

* * *

All six editions of The Stars and Stripes and the Sunday issue of Yank may be obtained at a total cost of sixpence a week. Subscriptions will be sold on a five-week basis at two shillings and sixpence. Single copies of Yank will be sold for threepence.

* * *

The European Theater edition of Yank will be distributed as the Sunday edition of the paper.

* * *

The daily Stars and Stripes will carry full wire reports of news from America, up-to-the-minute dispatches from the world's battlefronts, complete news from units in the field in the European Theater and feature stories about American forces in other theaters of operations.

* * *

A full page of sports news and pictures will be carried daily, with two pages on Monday.

* * *

The entire wire reports of the Associated Press, United Press, International News Service will be available to the paper, while the office of War Information in Washington and abroad will cable news and features daily especially for The Stars and Stripes.

A staff of enlisted men—reporters and photographers—will be in the field constantly, covering the European Theater's Army, Navy and Marine forces. Staff correspondents of the newspaper will accompany American forces in action.

Wirephoto pictures from America and the rest of the world will be available to the new daily, while other photographs will be flown from the U.S. regularly. Staff photographers and the U.S. Army Signal Corps will cover the forces afield, while the O.W.I. will provide pictures as well as stories of forces in other theaters.

The new Stars and Stripes will be printed as a morning paper by

Daily - - -

(Continued on page 3)

Correspondents Needed

Volunteer correspondents are urgently needed to fill the news requirements of the new, daily, Stars and Stripes. It is hoped to have at least one correspondent in every unit.

If there is now no regular correspondent in any unit, volunteers for the position may apply, with the approval of their commanding officer, to The Stars and Stripes, Printing House Square, London. It is necessary that qualifications for the job be given in writing.

Aid Pledged To Ten More War Orphans

In one pell-mell outpouring of good will and pound notes, American doughboys in the British Isles this week guaranteed the future happiness of ten war-orphaned children of the United Nations.

A disbanding non-commissioned officers' club of a bomber group turned over its entire treasury of £152 10s. to help care for one child for five years and provide £52 10s. toward the care of another.

The —st Service Squadron of an Air Service group laid it on the line with a check for £100 11s., the eleven shillings presumably being for administrative purposes!

The base military censors promised to take care of a child.

The first battalion of a regiment which a couple of weeks ago wired "Sure we want one-twelfth or more dozen orphans . . ." kicked in with another £100 for its own "sweetheart of the regiment."

* * *

But the prize of the lot was the second battalion of that regiment: They've asked for half-a-dozen!

* * *

That Northern Ireland Infantry regiment's full wire read:

"Sure we want one-twelfth dozen or more war orphans. Pick us one to be sweetheart of regiment. Funds guaranteed will follow." The wire was signed by Lt.-Col. H. Wulf.

It was just about that time that Major Bruno Marchi, Fort Dodge, Iowa, had a letter from Colonel Wulf. Major Marchi is commanding the second battalion of the regiment, and is stationed in England. He didn't know what the regiment had decided to do.

The letter from Colonel Wulf explained, and asked the Major if the "sterling second battalion" could raise £25 as its share.

Friday, Major Marchi walked into The Stars and Stripes office and laid down a bag filled with one-pound notes, 600 of them. The second battalion wanted to sponsor six orphans, one for each of the five companies, and one for the officers.

And a letter soon will be sent by Major Marchi to Colonel Wulf, explaining what the second battallion has done, and asking if it's all right if the battalion holds a bazaar now to raise the other £25 for the "regiment's sweetheart."

Here are the specifications set forth by the second battalion for the children they wish to help:

Headquarters Company, Girl, 5 years old, blonde, blue eyes; Company E—Girl, 5 years old, blonde, blue eyes; Company F—Boy, 4 to 6 years old; Company G—Girl, brunette, 5 to 7 years old; Company H—Boy, 5 to 6 years old, red hair, and Officers—Boy, 4 to 6 years old.

The N.C.O.s' club, representing the non-coms of two squadrons of a bomber group in England, voted unanimously to put their entire treasury into the war orphans' fund, they reported in their letter signed by Sgt. Samuel L. More

Orphans - - -

(Continued on page 3)

1D. THE STARS AND STRIPES 1D.
Daily Newspaper of U.S. Armed Forces in the European Theater of Operations
Vol. 3 No. 7 — London, England — November 9, 1942

U.S. Troops Invade North Africa

The French North African Coast

Map shows practically the entire North Africa field of activity for U.S. forces landing there. On the Atlantic Coast. Yanks attacked Casablanca. There were reports of a British radio offensive from Rabat. Gibraltar, famous British fortress at the gateway to the Mediterranean, is a key base. Americans also attacked at Oran and Algiers, using amphibious equipment and paratroops. The airport at Algiers was reported in Allied hands. Liaison already is possible, by air, with the Eighth Army, which faces Rommel 800 miles to the west.

Boats Land Forces In French Colonies From Huge Armada

Attack Before Dawn at Scattered Points On Atlantic, Mediterranean Coasts; President Hails Second Front

American soldiers, sailors and marines from the greatest naval armada ever engaged in a single military operation swarmed onto the Mediterranean and Atlantic coasts of Vichy-controlled North Africa before dawn yesterday in a bold stroke to break Axis control of the Mediterranean and provide what President Roosevelt termed "an effective second front for the assistance of our heroic allies in Russia."

Under an umbrella of British and American planes operating from aircraft carriers, American troops landed from assault boats at points hundreds of miles apart, and dispatches last night indicated that in most areas they were meeting with success.

Allied Headquarters, quickly established in North Africa, was silent concerning the exact points of invasion, but the Vichy Government admitted last night that the Americans had successfully effected landings at six points.

On the Mediterranean coast Americans have established a beachhead near Algiers, to the east of Oran, and on the Atlantic coast they have landed at Safi and Fedala in French Morocco, according to a Vichy communique. Further landings on the Atlantic coast—at Bouznika, 25 miles from Casablanca, and at Mehita, also in French Morocco—are admitted in a message from Gen. Nogues, Resident-General of Morocco, to Vichy.

Gen. Doolittle There

Landings at Oran and Algiers were announced in a communique issued last night in Washington, in which it also was disclosed that Brig. Gen. J. H. (Jimmy) Doolittle, who led the sensational bombing attack on Tokyo, was in command of the American air forces in the expedition.

In none of the Allied communiques was there any mention of the size of the invasion force, but Vichy radio said: "According to first estimates, 140,000 men are taking part in these operations."

Reports emanating from Vichy last night gave this picture of the position on the Mediterranean coast:

Allied units took up their positions offshore before the assault, with British warships forming a protective screen, shelling the French defenses at Algiers, while transports unloaded American commandos into motor launches, lighters and landing craft

Simultaneous uprisings by dissidents within the main French ports have failed to rally in sufficient strength to overcome loyal forces, thus leaving major operations in the hands of the Americans, Vichy said.

Fighting at Many Points

Vichy reported fighting at many points in Morocco and Algiers.

Big forces of U.S. troops were said to have come ashore and to be fighting in the streets of Safi, on the Atlantic coast of Morocco, while Vichy circles quoted by Berlin radio stated that the situation was serious.

First news of Vichy resistance was given in a communique early in the morning, describing landing attempts near Algiers and Oran, on the Mediterranean coast.

"In the region of Oran," said a later communique, "the port itself was attacked, and two British or American corvettes were sunk. Prisoners were taken to the east and west of Oran. Arzeu, 25 miles to the east of Oran, is practically occupied and the situation is confused."

In Berlin, Adolf Hitler's reaction to the news was as expected. Mocking the Allies' intention of bringing about an ultimate capitulation of Germany, he asserted in a radio address:

"In me, Germany has a man who does not know the meaning of the word capitulation."

Gen. Eisenhower Commands

Lt. Gen. Dwight D. Eisenhower, who "disappeared" from London a few days ago, ostensibly on his way to Washington for consultations with the President, was in command of the invasion force. Throughout the night the tall, greying, decisive commanding general of the European Theater of Operations worked ceaselessly directing the first great American blow at the Axis involving crack combat infantry, Rangers, airborne troops and the cream of America's airmen.

Primarily an American show at the start, the expedition soon will be augmented by divisions of British troops, it was announced.

At dawn low-flying American and RAF planes roared over the cities of French North Africa pouring white showers of leaflets which glittered in the low morning sun. The leaflets contained two messages—one from President Roosevelt, asking the aid of the French in lifting the yoke of Hitler rule from their country, and one from Gen. Eisenhower, asking the inhabitants to consider the invading troops as friendly and to obey their orders.

President Makes Appeal

Simultaneously, radio transmitters in the United States, Britain and Africa began to broadcast the messages over and over again to the people of France and French Africa.

"We are coming among you solely to crush and destroy your enemies," said the voice of President Roosevelt, speaking in French with a strong American accent.

"Believe us, we do not wish to do you any harm. We assure you that once the threat of Germany and Italy has been removed from you, we shall immediately leave your territory."

As he spoke troops already were setting foot on African soil and British and American naval vessels were laying down heavy barrages at each point.

Allied leaders obviously were hoping for a minimum of resistance from French colonial forces—or, even better, assistance from them. Soon after the start of the invasion Gen. Henri Giraud, anti-Vichy military leader who disappeared mysteriously from France a few months ago, made a dramatic appeal to his countrymen to aid the Allies. He said the landings of United States forces in North Africa constituted

(Continued on page 2)

Routed Enemy Fleeing Across Libyan Border

8th Army Smashes Onward In Pursuit; Captives Mounting

CAIRO, Nov. 8 (UP)—The bulk of the retreating German Army of the desert is now over the frontier in Libya.

Chased by the relentless Eighth Army, Rommel's Afrika Korps continues to retreat, constantly strafed from the air, its armor either surrounded or shattered.

Complete headquarters of three Italian divisions have been captured, the Germans making no effort to extricate the Italian divisions left in the pocket to the south of the general line of Axis retreat.

Not all of Rommel's armor has been surrounded, but some of his troops, fighting a delaying action in the Mersa Matruh area, have been encircled, according to Sunday's Cairo communique.

Allied Air Mastery

The communique referred to air activity over the desert: "Halfaya Pass and other frontier targets were bombed by our heavy and medium bombers during the night of Nov. 6-7. Large concentrations were attacked with great success. In addition our heavy bombers attacked aerodromes in Crete."

The picture is one of complete and continued Allied air and land mastery.

The Allies have taken prisoner between 30,000 and 40,000 men in the desert. They have destroyed at least 500 tanks and between 900 and 1,000 guns.

Allied planes have been bombing concentrations of Axis forces at Buq Buq, only 30 miles from the Libyan-Egyptian frontier, the Cairo communique states.

Fighting in the Mersa Matruh area was referred to by both the German and Italian communiques.

"Yesterday," said the Italian communique, "considerable enemy armored forces exercised strong pressure in the Mersa Matruh area, where prolonged and hard fighting took place.

"Axis air forces ceaselessly attacked enemy motorised columns and supply lines."

Italian Communique

The Italian communique admitted damage to town and harbor in Genoa, described damage as "huge," and said number of victims is not yet known.

It said British planes also dropped bombs on the outskirts of Milan, Savona and Cagliari "without causing damage."

(Continued on page 2)

It Took Desert Land Mine To Separate Lt. and Jeep

CAIRO, Nov. 8 (AP)—Lt. B. H. Charles, New York City, has parted company with his jeep.

It happened this way: He was driving the jeep through a minefield, looking over a U.S. plane forced down.

"I thought if airplane could land in minefield and not set things popping," he said, "I could do as well.

"I don't know exactly what happened. I didn't even hear an explosion. But suddenly I must have been 50 feet in the air with parts of the jeep sailing all around me, and without my shirt. I am pretty stiff, but outside that I feel okay."

Sunday Calm Shattered by African News

American intervention in Africa broke a cool Sunday's calm in England as Tube straphangers, waitresses, soldiers of all the United Nations and ordinary folks-in-the-street pored over headlines for more and more.

Some expressed their reaction in satisfied grunts. A bowler-hatted pedestrian in Fleet Street bit fiercely into his cigar and commented, "Bloody good job!"

Two church-bound stenographers in a city bus smilingly handed their paper to eager doughboys for just one look.

"The Best News"

Most exact paraphrase of public reaction possibly came from two Yanks sergeants—"The best news in a helluva time!"

There was realization of the seriousness and far-reaching effect of the Allied action.

"This is a great day for the free people of France," were the words of a battered French veteran of two World Wars, Raoul Jean Dormion, holder of the Belgian and French Croix de Guerre as well as the Military Medal of France.

"The French have great faith in America. This is good news," he added.

(Continued on page 3)

Hero of Tokyo Raid Heads U.S. Air Forces

WASHINGTON, D.C., Nov. 8 (UP)—The War Department has announced that the American air forces in the North African expedition are commanded by Brig. Gen. James H. Doolittle.

Maj. Gen. Lloyd is commanding the American landing forces at Oran.

Maj. Gen. Charles Ryder is commanding the forces at Algiers.

Maj. Gen. George Patton is commanding the American landing on the west coast of Africa.

Rear Admiral H. K. Hewitt is commanding the U.S. naval forces engaged in the occupation.

The communique also announces that Lt. Gen. Frank Andrews had assumed command of the U.S. forces in the Middle East, in succession to Maj. Gen. Russel Maxwell.

Germany Must Never Give In, Fuehrer Warns

Axis Can't Compromise, Hitler Says; Ignores U.S. Landings

"We know the fate that awaits us if we lost and for this reason we have not the remotest idea of a compromise," Hitler declared last night in a broadcast from Munich on the anniversary of his abortive "beer cellar putsch" of 1923, the Associated Press reports.

Hitler strove to put a bold front on the rout of his Afrika Korps by the British Eighth Army, declaring: "As far as I am concerned the British can advance in the desert as much as they like. They have already advanced several times and retreated again."

A hint that all was not well in National-Socialist Germany was seen in the Fuehrer's remarks thanking the S.A. and S.S. men who, he said, fought formerly against internal enemies, and are now fighting against "both internal and external enemies."

Ignores U.S. Landings

He devoted a large part of his speech to the customary gibes against the Allied leaders and "international Jewry."

He made only the briefest reference to today's landings in French Africa, saying: "We have always prepared our blows well and they have always succeeded."

Hitler spoke for one hour and 25 minutes.

"We have always had the Jews as internal enemies and now we have them as external ones," he said.

"It is no coincidence that today we have the same enemies as in 1915. Then his name was Wilson, today it is Roosevelt.

Referring to the Kaiser's capitulation in 1918, Hitler said the Kaiser was a man who had not the strength to see things through.

"In me, however, Germany has a man who simply does not know the word 'capitulation,'" Hitler boasted.

Have Raw Resources

"We have taken possession of raw materials which will enable us to win the war under all circumstances," he continued.

He called on every man and woman to think that this war was a fight for the existence of the German people so that every thought and action of theirs should be a prayer for Germany.

'Fate of France Rests On Campaign'—Giraud

WASHINGTON, Nov. 8 (AP)—The Foreign Broadcast Intelligence Service of the U.S. Federal Communications Commission heard General Giraud, who recently escaped from Germany, broadcast from Algiers to non-commissioned officers of the French African Army today.

The fact that he called on Frenchmen to side with the Allies was confirmed, and he added, "We have one passion—France; and one aim—victory. Be aware that the African campaign holds in its hands the fate of France."

1D. THE STARS AND STRIPES 1D.

Daily Newspaper of U.S. Armed Forces in the European Theater of Operations

Vol. 3 No. 9 London, England Wednesday, Nov. 11, 1942

Oran Falls, Allies Control North Coast

The North African War Front, From Egypt to Atlantic

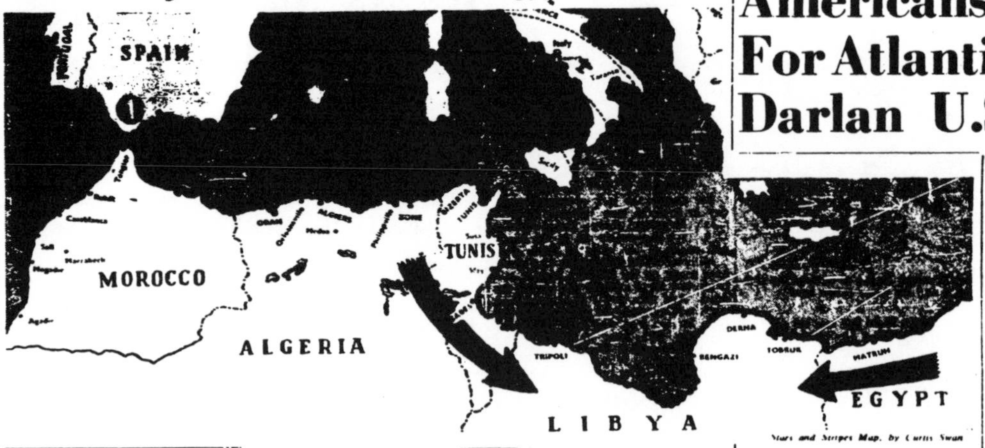

Stars and Stripes Map, by Curtis Swan

Success of the North African campaign will bring Vichy France and all Italy within easy range of Allied heavy bombers, as shown by map, besides establishing control of Mediterranean sealanes.

Fighting continued along the whole front yesterday, but Oran (3) and Algiers (4) were in the hands of American troops last night, virtually assuring success of the campaign.

Attention was focused on (1) Gibraltar, where Vichy reported presence of a huge Allied convoy, protected by the British warships Nelson and Furious. Axis radio has made frequent references to naval activity here.

U.S. forces, according to Vichy and Berlin, landed north and south of (2) Casablanca, and are executing a pincer movement. A naval engagement was reported, and sharp land fighting continues.

Gen. Eisenhower, Allied C.-in-C., last night announced capture of (3) Oran, which has four strategic airfields. Algiers (4) was already under Allied control. Adm. Jean Darlan, British-hating commander of the French fleet, is a " guest " of the American Government here.

The landing of American troops as far east as (5) Philippeville, near the Tunisian border, took on significance with President Roosevelt's request to the Bey of Tunis for passage through Tunisia. Beyond Tunisia lies Libya, into which remnants of Rommel's army are still fleeing from Egypt and the Eighth Army.

Americans in Battle For Atlantic Seaport; Darlan U.S. 'Guest'

AEF Now in Position To Hit Rommel And Italy

Lt. Gen. Dwight Eisenhower, commander of the Allied expedition to occupy Vichy-controlled North Africa, announced last night that the vital Mediterranean port of Oran, in Algeria, had fallen during the afternoon to the attack of American troops, only a few hours after the assault began.

The fall of the naval base virtually ended all French resistance in the Mediterranean after an unprecedented three-day campaign.

Allies Control Coast

With Algiers already firmly in American hands, the Allies were virtually in control of the coast, and in a position to strike eastward by land to contact the retreating North Afrika Corps, or northward by air to strike at Italy.

Bitter fighting still continued on the Atlantic coast, in French Morocco, where U.S. troops have been landing since early Sunday morning. American forces apparently were attempting a pincer movement on the port of Casablanca, but were meeting stiff resistance, judging from Vichy radio reports.

Meanwhile, Allied reinforcements kept pouring into French North Africa.

At Gibraltar, where a huge convoy assembled before the Allies moved into Africa, another big force was reported by Vichy radio to be gathering. The battleship Nelson and an aircraft-carrier, both British, were said to be among the ships. There were conflicting reports on whether the French fleet, idle almost since the fall of France, had left Toulon on the French Mediterranean coast

Darlan U.S. " Guest "

Adm. Jean Darlan, former supreme commander of all the Vichy fighting forces and an ardent advocate of French colaboration with Germany, was a " guest " of the United States Government, in Algiers, it was officially announced in London last night. Maj. Gen. Mark W. Clark, deputy commander of the expedition, has talked with Darlan, it was said.

The French leader apparently had been captured during the American occupation of the Algerian port, but he was not a prisoner, and was being treated with the respect due him, the London sources said.

In Vichy, 85-year-old Marshal Henri Pétain assumed supreme command of the Vichy forces and immediately ordered all Vichy commanders in Africa to keep up the fight against the Allied forces.

There was still no word last night of a reply from the Bey of Tunis to President Roosevelt's application for passage of the American Expeditionary Force through French Tunisia from Algeria to Libya, a move which would carry American troops into the path of Field-Marshal Erwin Rommel's retreating German Army.

Still Fighting

Likewise, there was no word as to whether the American forces had started such a journey. This was considered unlikely at this time, however, for although Lt. Gen. Dwight Eisenhower, commander of the African expedition, said yesterday morning that the campaign was ahead of schedule, there still appeared to be fighting to do before the force could head eastward across the border.

The fighting for Oran was brief, but fierce. American troops landed to the east and west on Sunday morning and reached the city proper yesterday. At 7.30 AM, according to Allied headquarters, an all-out attack began.

The original phases of the actual siege began at midnight, when a task force of tank and infantry forces started moving west to east. By 7.38 it had reached a point three miles from the heart of the city from a point west of Fort Mers el Kebir.

Another force began to push at the same time to the west from the east of the city and by 7.30 AM was seven miles from the centre of the town and pushing on rapidly. One column from this force east of Oran swung further to the east and pushed along the coast road towards

(Continued on page 4)

America Splits With Laval, Not French People

Nations' Interests Kindred, Roosevelt Says, Calling Laval Hitlerite

President Roosevelt, asserting that Pierre Laval evidently was still speaking the language prescribed by Adolf Hitler, expressed regret in Washington yesterday that Laval had severed diplomatic relations with the United States. The President added that nothing ever could " sever relations between the American people and the people of France."

Canada, Cuba and Mexico broke diplomatic relations with Vichy yesterday, less than 24 hours after the colaborationist Government of France had severed its ties with the United States as a result of the invasion by the Allies of French colonies in North Africa.

Berlin radio said unofficial reports were circulating in Paris to the effect that Peru also had broken with Vichy.

President's Statement

In his statement on the situation, President Roosevelt said:

" The representative of this Government at Vichy has reported that last evening Laval, chief of the Government at Vichy, notified him that diplomatic relations between Vichy and this Government had been severed.

" I regret this action on the part of Laval.

" He is evidently still speaking the language prescribed by Hitler.

" The Government of the United States can do nothing about this severance of relations on the part of the Vichy Government."

In Ottawa, Mackenzie King summoned the French Minister to Canada, M. Rene Ristelhueber, to his office and told him that Canada no longer recognized his Government. The Prime Minister later denounced the Vichy Government as a " German Puppet Government " without legal or constitutional rights.

" Protest " Resignations

In Mexico City President Avila Camacho announced his Government's decision in a radio speech and attributed the break to French resistance to the Allied occupation of French North Africa.

In Bogota, Colombia, M. Paul-Boncour, son of the French statesman, resigned his post as commercial attaché to the French legation yesterday. The newspaper El Liberal said he resigned because of Petain's order to French troops to fire on the Allied forces in North Africa.

Eisenhower Tells Russia U.S. Move Victory Step

MOSCOW, Nov. 10 (AP)—Lt.-Gen Dwight Eisenhower, Allied commander in North Africa, asserted in a greeting to the Red Army today that the current operations pointed the way to a decisive victory.

A telegram from Gen. Eisenhower in connexion with the 25th anniversary of the Soviet Revolution was published prominently in Soviet papers.

On the Shores of Tripoli Marines Celebrate Birthday

" From the halls of Montezuma to the shores of Tripoli — —."

Wherever U.S. Marines are found they sing that good old song, and yesterday, 167th birthday of Uncle Sam's proudest fighting corps, they actually were doing it —fighting all the way to Tripoli.

The marines have fought everywhere and fought successfully since their founding in 1775, but Nov. 10, 1942, they were ripping up more places of the earth than ever before at any one time.

" Marines Have Landed . . ."

At Casablanca, at Oran, at Algiers, " the Marines have landed and the situation is well in hand." They were better than holding their own in the southwest Pacific, where at Guadalcanal they were making their favorite enemies, the Japs, unhappy in lightning land-and-sea fighting that is just why the corps were born. To say nothing of Iceland, Newfoundland, Alaska, the Aleutians. Wherever Americans are fighting in this man's war, U.S. Marines are in it.

Lovers of parades and big brass bands, they nonetheless weren't in the Lord Mayor's Day festivities in London this week.

Too busy.

Embassy Guard Gone

Most of the lads who came to London to guard the American Embassy and military establishments as far back as last summer left recently. Their new assignment has not been made public.

However, at camps in the British Isles, Marines commemorated the time when Capt. Robert Mullan swore in the first U.S. Marine—in Philadelphia, 167 years ago—with a day of rigorous training maneuvers, or of guard duty at great American naval bases.

For luckier ones, it was a day crowned with hearty dinners and dances and heartier toasts.

There was no official Marine celebration in London.

U.S. Marine " Firsts "

Here are some " firsts " that Marines could point to on their birthday: First to fire a U.S. shot in World War I—Cpl. Michael Chockie. First to land in Japan, in 1853, with Perry. First to fly the U.S. flag over Alaska, at Sitka, Oct. 18, 1867. First to catapult a plane from a moving warship, Lt. Alfred Cunningham, 1916. First to loop the loop in a seaplane, Lt. Col. F. T. Evans, 1917.

Four days after Pearl Harbor Marines were first to sink a Jap ship. The feat was performed by Maj. H. T. Elrod and Capt. Frank Tharin, Dec. 11, 1941. Nothing in U.S. history compares to their defense of Wake Island in this war, when Lt. Col. J. P. S. Devereaux, asked if there was anything he needed, replied: " More Japs ! "

On African Coast

Today Marines are in the thick of assaults and mopping-up operations along the whole North African coastline. Their landing barges and crack machine-gunners led the way.

It is too early for stories of individual heroism, for any detail of this typical Marine smash. There have been casualties, as always there must be where soldiers—real soldiers—go in first. But Marines think of that afterwards.

This anniversary they rejoiced that once again U.S. Marines are in there. . . . " ——to the shores of Tripoli ! "

More Advances At Guadalcanal

WASHINGTON, D.C., Nov. 10 (AP) —Gen. Holcomb, commandant of the U.S. Marine Corps, reported today that " things are shaping up " so that it would be increasingly more difficult for the Japanese to put reinforcements on Guadalcanal Island in the Solomons.

Gen. Holcomb, just returned from a visit to Marine posts in the South Pacific, disclosed that the original Marine division which was sent into the Solomons to begin the first American offensive of the war was still on front line—probably a record for unbroken service under fire for Marine outfits.

The Navy Department announced that American troops on Guadalcanal made further advances on their eastern flank, while fighting to the west had apparently halted entirely.

British Capture More Prisoners In Egypt Desert

Spearhead of 8th Army Pushes Past Border After Rommel

CAIRO, Nov. 10 (AP)—The armored spearhead of the Eighth Army has driven across the Egyptian border, on into Libya, pursuing the disastrously routed Axis forces, while the main Allied units still are mopping up resistance on the Egyptian battlefields.

East of the border, British forces continued to mop up pockets of the enemy over a scattered area. Prisoners continued to arrive at the coast road in Egypt to give themselves up.

Most of the prisoners were Italian soldiers who walked out of the Alamein line and headed for British camps and safety from the desert. Many Italian troops died in the desert from lack of water and food and through walking under the hot desert sun.

Lost in Desert

Exhausted prisoners reported that hundreds and possibly thousands more Italian soldiers, left stranded by the retreating Germans, were lost in the desert and only immediate help would save them.

The British Army organized search parties, which headed into the desert, taking transport lorries and first-aid vehicles with them.

All the Italian prisoners were bitter about being abandoned by the Germans.

The exact position of the extreme forward British armor nearest to the main body of the fleeing Axis forces was not known, as the chase has been so fast that communications have been disrupted.

Some of the Eighth Army forces were known, however, to be operating inside Libya. The air force from new advance fields has been giving the enemy no peace as they race along the coast road.

One huge enemy convoy on the road from Sollum to Capuzzo was bombed and the road was blocked as huge fires burned for hours.

In Egypt special Eighth Army forces continued to gather up all types of heavy and light abandoned guns.

Lorries by the hundred were arriving at recovery camps, where they were being

(*Continued on page* 4)

Senate and House Agree On 'Under 20' Draft Bill

WASHINGTON, D.C., Nov. 10 (AP) —The Joint Senate-House committee agreed today on the draft bill eliminating the Senate provision requiring a year of military training before men under 20 could be sent into foreign combat.

Elimination of the provision cleared the way for speedy final approval of legislation lowering the draft age.

In approving a compromise which must be acted on by both Houses the committee agreed to accept the Senate amendment directing local selective boards to defer the calling of essential farm workers into the armed forces.

1D. THE STARS AND STRIPES 1D.
Daily Newspaper of U.S. Armed Forces in the European Theater of Operations
Vol. 3 No. 13 London, England Monday, Nov. 16, 1942

Allies Enter Tunisia, French Fight Nazis

Naval Clash Reported In SW Pacific

Decisive Engagement Now Being Fought by Big Fleets

The naval battle raging off the Solomon Islands may be the opening phase of the long-expected showdown between the main American and Japanese fleets in the Pacific, the United Press reports from Washington.

The battle started, according to information available there, when the Japanese appeared to be preparing for a heavy land attack on Guadalcanal.

This, it seemed likely, would be a prelude to a move south from the Jap bases at Rabaul and Truk.

A Japanese convoy so large that the whole of it is never in view at any one time is reported by Allied bomber pilots to be moving down on the southeastern Solomon Islands under repeated bombing attacks by U.S. aircraft.

No Losses Reported

A Navy Department communique said only that a battle is in progress. Losses were not disclosed. "No details will be reported while the battle continues," the communique added.

German radio quoted the usual fantastic "fishing expedition" of the Japanese Navy Department to the effect that American forces have lost one battleship, four aircraft carriers, five cruisers and one destroyer, and that many other U.S. ships have been damaged. In Washington no comment was made on the losses thus far for either side.

Further Jap claims report the appearance of American naval forces, including an aircraft carrier, off Santa Cruz, in the Philippines last Wednesday.

(In Melbourne, J. O. Makin, Australian Navy Minister, sounded a warning yesterday that on the outcome of the current Solomons battle depended the invasion of Australia, the Associated Press reported. Makin said that he had asked the Navy for the latest reports on the Solomons action and his warning was based on the latest information. He said there should not be undue optimism and complacency as the result of the Allied successes in New Guinea and North Africa.)

30 Japs Shot Down

Gen. MacArthur's headquarters in the South-West Pacific announced that 30 Japanese aircraft were shot down during an air attack which interrupted bombardments of Japanese ships massing in the Solomons naval base in the Buin-Fasi area for new attacks on U.S. positions.

While two enemy light cruisers received direct hits in the third day of the American onslaught, the U.S. heavy cruiser San Francisco was damaged when a burning, disabled Japanese plane crashed into her killing 30 of her crew. A five-inch shell from an enemy shore battery damaged the destroyer Buchanan and killed five of the crew.

"Bombs were dropped on the airdrome at Kahili, hitting runways and dispersal areas. All our planes returned.

"New Guinea: Wairopi, our ground troops reached the vicinity of Ilimow, where the enemy defending force has been surrounded," the communique said.

"Of the enemy detachment which was encircled and destroyed at Gorari, the bodies of five officers and more than 500 men have already been counted in the jungle.

"Allied fighters cooperating with ground units strafed and silenced enemy positions in the rear areas."

'Flit-Gun Squadron' Kills Another Kind of Germs

ALEXANDRIA, Nov. 15 (UP)—The "Flying Flit-Gun Squadron," consisting of one American pilot and a British Lysander aircraft, is dealing out death today to germs, not Germans—and has played a big part in the defeat of Rommel in the Middle East.

Part of the RAF's anti-malaria organization, its work is the gigantic task of wiping out the larvae of mosquitos in all potential danger zones from Libya to Persia and Irak.

Pilot Officer Buster Leach, 29-year-old Texan, one of the first Americans to join the Royal Canadian Air Force, has flown over Palestine, Syria, Transjordan, Persia and Iran, spreading larvae-killing powder from a special tube under the fuselage.

Old Glory Flies in Algeria

Supplies for American troops landed on the beach at a point west of Oran are stacked by soldiers beneath the Stars and Stripes.

Officers Calmly Gave First Aid As Shells Raked Crippled Ship

WITH AMERICAN EXPEDITIONARY FORCE, Oran, Nov. 13 (delayed) (UP)—The story of how a young U.S. Navy lieutenant and several U.S. Army officers saved the lives of many Americans and Britons when a cutter became disabled under the guns of Oran harbor before dawn Sunday was revealed here today.

With 320 American and British sailors and American soldiers aboard, the cutter lay helpless for an hour, her guns and engines useless, while shells from a four-inch coastal battery burst in the compartment where the soldiers huddled and machine-gun fire swept the survivors when fire forced them on deck.

With only slight protection on deck, the officers administered first aid and hypodermics to the wounded, blew up their life jackets and threw the men overboard. Most were rescued.

The cutter hit a reef outside the harbor boom as she came in about 3 AM. Backing away, she drew the fire of the coastal guns. As she passed the boom a direct hit blew up her boiler and another smashed her after guns. The forward guns fired on, but it was impossible to man her machine-guns because of the close-range fire from shore. Once inside the boom, the cutter drifted within 40 yards of a heavy French destroyer and also came under cross-fire from machine-guns in lorries along the port side.

One shell hit the forward messing com-

(*Continued on page 2*)

Rommel Departed Tobruk Clad in Shirt and Shorts

STOCKHOLM, Nov. 15 (UP)—British tanks, which surprised the headquarters of Gen. Rommel near Tobruk last Friday, nearly caught the general himself.

So close did they come to capturing him, that the head of the Afrika Korps was forced to run for it in his shirt and shorts, leaving behind his coat and his famous scarf, it was admitted here tonight by the Berlin correspondent of the German-controlled S.T.B. news agency.

This agency adds, however, that when Rommel arrived at his new base, he stated:

"Like Napoleon, I lost my equipment, but there won't be any Waterloo."

Snyder-to-Snyder-to-Nazis Is Air Force Double Play

ENGLAND, Nov. 15—The Eighth Air Force doubleplay combination of Snyder-to-Snyder is one of the best in the business. And we don't want to hear any squawks from the Sportsman's Park of Ebbet's Field clientele, either.

It's like this. Pa Snyder builds the engines for big bombers in Detroit's Studebaker plant and his 24-year-old son, Lt. Howard Snyder, helps fly 'em over here.

Young Snyder is co-pilot of the "Kissy-Me-Kowboy," a four-motored job that the old man helped build not many months ago. The Fortress was christened by its pilot, Lt. Clarence L. Thacker, Kissimee, Fla., a charter member of the Florida Chamber of Commerce.

The double play combination clicked like a dollar watch on a sortie over Holland. The Luftwaffe couldn't get to second base, the flak thrown up by the ground crews couldn't even get to first.

The "Kissy-Me-Kowboy" had dropped its load of high explosives on the target area and started for home. Flak popped around the plane like a July 4 celebration at the city park. Messerschmitts and FWs buzzed around, popping away whenever it looked safe, which wasn't often.

A high-explosive shell knocked out one of the engines. But Pa Snyder, back in Detroit, had done a good job. The other purred a sweet song of power.

One of two accompanying planes ran into trouble. The boys at the controls knew that Pa Snyder had helped build those engines, so, even with only three working, the "Kissy-Me-Kowboy" went back to lend a hand. It looked like the damaged plane might land in the channel and the "Kissy" was going to be there to drop a raft or send a position-report to the British Air-Sea Rescue Service.

Neither step was necessary. The badly hit plane struggled back to the home airdrome, escorted all the way by the "Kissy-Me-Kowboy" on three engines, which flew around like a fretful mother hen and its proverbial one chick.

The score: The target area bombed, with hits observed; two enemy fighters probably destroyed and three others damaged seriously, and one badly damaged ship convoyed safely home.

Tinkers and Evers and Chance couldn't do any better than that.

Scouts Map Routes For Main Advance Through Mountains

French Troops Heed Darlan's Call for Aid, Fire on Transports Bringing Men and Tanks to Tunisian Airfields

American and British reconnaissance parties have penetrated into French Tunisia to seek the best routes through the mountain passes for the main Allied Army driving from Algeria, Lt. Gen. Dwight D. Eisenhower, Commander-in-Chief of the North African operations, revealed last night.

French garrisons inside Tunisia were reported resisting the influx of Axis troops and firing on their transport planes, the general said in a summary of the operations. Further Axis landings were reported, mostly of Italians, bringing the total Axis forces in the country to an estimated 3,000.

Somewhere in Tunisia, unless the Axis evacuates first, American troops will encounter Italian and German forces in ground combat for the first time in this war.

French resistance to the Axis in Tunisia was reported by Allied pilots who flew over Tunisia to bomb and strafe Axis-occupied airfields. The pilots said they saw shooting by French soldiers on the ground and were certain the troops were not firing at the planes.

Advancing on Bizerta

Havas News Agency quoted a report attributed to Washington that American troops were advancing towards the naval base of Bizerta and the capital, Tunis, but Gen. Eisenhower's brief summary of the military situation contained only the information that small, scattered reconnaissance parties were crossing the Tunisian border at several points.

"We seem to be in that part of the operation that is not too filled with startling news," he said.

American and British parachutists who seized Bona, 50 miles from the Tunisian border, on Wednesday night, already have been reinforced in spite of feverish Axis efforts to disrupt the operation by bombing attacks, say reports from headquarters.

Meanwhile, thousands of British troops comprising the First Army are preparing for the principal drive with the Americans into Tunisia, headquarters added.

Violent Air Combats

Vichy radio said there were violent air combats over Tunisia between Allied and Axis planes yesterday. The radio added that there were similar combats over the Italian islands of Sicily and Sardinia, where American and English planes apparently were endeavouring to smash at fields from which troops were being flown to Tunisia.

Axis arrivals in Tunisia are reported by Allied headquarters to have come both by air and by sea, despite heavy blows by Allied air forces at communications.

RAF fighters downed six Italian transport planes loaded with German soldiers Thursday, and the fact they were flying north from Tunisia led to the supposition the Germans might be evacuating their air-borne troops in the face of the joint drive by the Allies.

Axis Flying Tanks

Reports from Allied headquarters that Germans had landed light tanks by air in Tunisia, however, indicated that the Axis was reinforcing its spearhead, rather than withdrawing manpower.

While visiting advanced headquarters, Gen. Eisenhower revealed last night, he pinned the third star on the shoulders of Gen. Clark, making him the youngest lieutenant-general in the U.S. Army. Gen. Clark is 46 years old. He was recommended for promotion by President Roosevelt after a daring mission with several other officers into North Africa to gather information while the Allied

(*Continued on page 2*)

Red Bayonets Halt Germans At Stalingrad

Hand-to-Hand Fighting As Soviets Hold New Push

MOSCOW, Nov. 15 (AP)—Employing bayonets in bitterly cold wind which whipped over the steppes, the Red Army defenders of Stalingrad have halted the latest German push before it made significant headway.

Dispatches said that the greatest hand-to-hand fighting of the current Nazi offensive occurred when the Fascists, with big forces of infantry and tanks, pushed ahead in one factory district.

Red Star said that the current German attacks were incessant. Infantry now being used was probably new or at best rested.

The battle area is now only a few hundred yards wide. Into this area the Nazi commanders hurled hundreds of infantry. Many fell but always some managed to crawl forward.

'Mountains of Dead'

The Germans made progress only over "literally mountains of bodies of their dead."

Stalingrad, situated high on the west bank of the Volga, is exposed fully to biting winds that come off the steppes both from the east and from the west, making present fighting conditions severe.

The horror of the situation was emphasized in an Izvestia report, which said that the locale was covered with the bodies of 100,000 German officers and soldiers, 800 wrecked tanks, and hulks of more than 1,000 planes.

In a big battle northwest of Stalingrad, in a sector which included a large hill and valley without natural obstacles, Soviet forces routed the Germans from strong fortifications.

A Pravda dispatch said that heavy volleys of big calibre trench mortars found the Nazis and drove them from their firing points. Some positions were abandoned intact and the Red Army men turned some of the weapons against the running Nazis.

The Germans hurried up reinforcements and halted what was turning into a rout.

The Russians improved their positions south-east of Nalchik in a two-sector battle.

Pravda Hails New Front With 30 Million Copies

MOSCOW, Nov. 15 (AP)—More than 30,000,000 copies of Pravda went out to the peoples of Russia on all fronts today proclaiming in bold headlines the Anglo-Soviet-American alliance.

The headlines—happiest which have yet appeared over the alliance—indicated the pleasure of the Soviet Government in the Anglo-American African successes.

Pravda said: "We are leading a great liberative war. We do not carry it on alone but together with our Allies. It brings victory over the mean enemies of humanity, over German Fascist imperialists."

Roosevelt Felicitates Eisenhower on Africa

WASHINGTON, Nov. 15 (AP)—President Roosevelt sent congratulations to Lt.-Gen. Dwight D. Eisenhower in a message published by the U.S. War Department last night for "the highly successful accomplishment of a most difficult task."

The President said that the North African occupation "caused a wave of reassurance throughout the nation" because of the skill and dash of the operation and also the perfection of the co-operation with the British.

1d. THE STARS AND STRIPES 1d.

in the European Theater of Operations

Vol. 3 No. 15 London, England Wednesday, Nov. 18, 1942

Jap Fleet Loses 23 Ships, Flees North

Big Clash Is Looming In Tunisia

French, U.S. Mobile Units Join British March Toward Cities

By the United Press

A major clash between Allied and Axis Forces in Tunisia at any time now was foreshadowed last night by reports of operations in North Africa.

British troops under Gen. Anderson pressing towards Tunisia were reported last night to have been joined by French and American mobile forces, and Berlin radio admitted yesterday that American and British forces were on the coastal road east of Bone, in Algeria, near the Tunisian border. This would mean they were driving towards the naval base of Bizerta.

British parachute troops have landed deep into Tunisia from American transport planes clearing the way for General Anderson's advancing armies, while a forward French patrol reported sighting a German reconnaissance unit, Allied Force headquarters reported last night.

Morocco radio, quoting what it called an announcement from Allied H.Q. to the effect that the First British Army was continuing its drive to the east, added "No details are yet available, although it is known that no large-scale battle has yet been joined."

Pincers Tighten

A summary of the position carried on the American short-wave radio, however, said:

"French garrisons are fighting the garrisons in Tunis and Bizerta. The Allied forces are now advancing from Algeria into Tunisia and, to the eastward, the British Eighth Army is daily narrowing the fighting in the area in North Africa which the German and Italian armies control."

The Vichy-controlled Saigon radio quoted what it called a broadcast by Paris radio for stating that the French fleet at Toulon was awaiting battle orders, although there is no record of any such broadcast from Paris. Saigon radio also said that an estimated 40,000 Axis troops were in Tunisia.

The German high command, tight-lipped as ever over events in any theater where they have been outmaneuvered, claimed only that Allied columns on the march had been attacked from the air, and that another Allied transport vessel had been sunk.

Axis Seeks French Aid

Gen. Nehring, commander of the Axis forces in Tunisia, quoted by Berlin radio from Tunis, has again appealed for French help.

A German military commentator, in a long review of the military situation in North Africa, last night declared that the "biggest mistake" made by the Anglo-American authorities in planning the operations in North Africa was that it had given the Axis an opportunity to occupy Tunisia which the Axis had not done before in order not to "extend the conflict to neutral countries."

The puzzle of Adm. Jean Darlan's status and future standing in North Africa remained as big today as ever.

Although most of his proclamations have been made in the name of Marshal Pétain, the German-controlled Press in Paris launched another attack against him yesterday, Marcel Déat, himself a quisling, referring to him as a traitor and to "the fateful and pernicious role played by Darlan, who is despised and hated by all true sailors."

Spain Mobilizes to Guard Neutrality, Berlin Reports

Berlin wireless, heard in New York, quoted a Madrid message yesterday to the effect that the Spanish Ministerial Council had ordered mobilization for the protection of Spain's neutrality, the Associated Press reported.

German radio reported from Madrid last night that Gen. Franco received yesterday morning for a farewell audience General Yague, the newly appointed commander of the tenth Spanish Army Corps in Melilla. Gen. Yague was leaving Madrid tonight for Morocco, it was stated, the Associated Press reported.

Commissioned Nov. 11 In 1918, Again in 1942

NEW YORK, Nov. 17—Waldow Thrasher has much by which to remember the date Nov. 11.

On that day, back in 1918 as warring powers signed an Armistice, Gen. Pershing signed papers commissioning him a second lieutenant in the Army. On Nov. 11, 1942, Gen. Eisenhower signed similar papers granting him the same commission, according to word received here from Allied Headquarters in North Africa.

Thrashero, a cameraman in the Signal Corps, is right hand man to Col. Daryll Zanuck who, with 90 cameramen and continuity writers, is filming the American offensive in North Africa.

Cold Weather Closes Down On Red Front

Nazis Reported Wearing Clothes Looted From Peasants

MOSCOW, Nov. 17 (UP)—The first severe frost in the Voronezh area and the Don Valley has caught the Germans unprepared.

As last winter, some Nazis are wearing looted peasant shawls, felt, rags and towing blankets. German prisoners explained that the High Command has not issued warm clothes because a mild winter was expected.

Snows also are reported on the entire Karelian front, where the first ski troops are already in operation.

(Latest dispatches from the Russian front southeast of Nalchik reveal the growing strength of a Soviet offensive in this area, according to the Associated Press. New attacks by the Red Army from the flanks drove the Germans from occupied lines and threw them into disorder on two sectors. The Germans suffered heavy losses from a rear attack on another sector.)

The main fighting at Stalingrad is centered in the northern factory district, where the Germans have been held for the past few days, unable to develop an offensive, according to Red Star. Small-scale fighting for individual houses is continuing.

The position on other Russian fronts today is: Central Caucasus: Russians have continued steady progress of reclaiming territory in the area southeast of Nalchik.

Mrs. Roosevelt Returns To U.S. from British Isles

WASHINGTON, Nov. 17 (UP)—Mrs. Roosevelt returned to Washington today from the British Isles. She was warmly welcomed at the airport by President Roosevelt. Chatting animatedly, she was driven off to the White House, where the President said he was going to get a complete story of his wife's trip.

Yanks Get Abbey For GI Chapel

Thanksgiving Services for U.S. Forces in Hallowed Westminster

For one November morning the most hallowed ground of all England will be America's.

Thanksgiving, at 10.30 AM, a U.S. Army chaplain will begin ceremonies of worship and gratitude in Westminster Abbey, where English kings since William the Conqueror have been crowned; where for 900 years the Empire has laid to rest royalty, nobleman, captain, and poet.

An American soldiers' choir will sing hymns; an American soldier will play the organ; many American servicemen will take part in non-sectarian services to give thanks not only for their own safety, but, at last, for victories in the field and at sea.

It will be the first time in history that services in Westminster Abbey have been conducted by other than the regular clergy there. Tender of this privilege was made by the Right Rev. Paul Fulcrand Delacour de Labilliere, Dean of Westminster, who has relinquished all control of the Abbey for the time necessary.

Exceptional Circumstances

"This is not an abandonment of our age-old position," the Dean said, according to U.S. Headquarters. "It is merely a deviation under exceptional circumstances."

Chaplain James L. Blakeney, United States Army, will be assisted by chaplains of both Catholic and Jewish faith.

The non-sectarian ceremonies will be opened by Chaplain Blakeney at 10.30AM, with upwards of 3,000 officers and enlisted men in attendance. It will be a representative gathering since invitations have been extended to all units in the British Isles, accommodations to be handled "first come, first served."

During the services President Roosevelt's Thanksgiving Day proclamation will be read by John G. Winant, American Ambassador.

Anthony J. Drexel Biddle, American Envoy to Allied Governments in Exile

(Continued on page 4)

Tiny Mountain Nation Too Small for Hitler

ANDORRA, Nov. 17 (AP)—The German Army occupying all France has halted at the frontier of this little republic of 5,231 people and 191 square miles, which lies high in the Pyrenees between France and Spain.

A German sergeant and soldier arrived at the Andorra border and told one of its seven guards: "We've orders to respect your frontier."

That is all Andorra knows about its international situation at present.

Biggest Sea Victory In American History Ends 3-Day Battle

Smashed Japs

Planet Photo

Vice-Admiral W. F. Halsey

Pilots Watched Fleet Massing

All-Out Attempt to Take Guadalcanal Suspected Early in October

WASHINGTON, Nov. 17 (UP)—The story of how the battle in the Solomons was fought, from the beginning until the Japanese naval units disengaged and fled northwards, is graphically described in the Navy Department communique.

Early in the month, air reconnaissance reports showed that heavy concentrations of Japanese naval units and transports were massing in the north-western Solomons at New Britain. Another attempt by the Japanese to recapture Guadalcanal Island was indicated.

On Nov. 10 Japanese naval forces approached the island from the north and south, and it became evident that the expedition was being launched in force.

Repeated attacks were made on part of the assembling Jap forces at Rabaul by Army bombers, both by General MacArthur's command and by other U.S. forces.

The spearhead of the attacking force, which was composed of two battleships of the Kongo class and a number of other vessels, reached the island shortly after

(Continued on page 4)

20 to 40 Thousand Enemy Troops Drowned

WASHINGTON, Nov. 17 (AP)—Remnants of the once mighty Japanese armada were withdrawing from the Solomons today after losing 23 ships, including one battleship, in what was hailed in Washington as the greatest naval victory in American history.

Besides the battleship, five enemy cruisers, five destroyers and 12 transports were sent to the bottom in the epic three-day struggle, which left U.S. forces in virtually full control of land, sea and air fronts and broke, temporarily at least, the threat of an invasion of Australia.

A second Japanese battleship and six destroyers also were damaged, the Navy Department announced, and between 20,000 and 40,000 crack combat troops were lost in the swirl of sunken transports. Eight of the transports were sent to the bottom by American bombers, some of which operated from Guadalcanal, the apparent objective of the enemy fleet.

8 U.S. Ships Lost

American losses were two light cruisers and six destroyers, and casualties were comparatively light, the Navy Department said.

Adm. Chester W. Nimitz, commander-in-chief of naval operations in the South-west Pacific, said in Pearl Harbor that the enemy forces involved comprised a large portion of the total Japanese fleet. The U.S. forces were under the immediate command of Vice-Adm. William F. Halsey. It was the biggest naval engagement since the Battle of Jutland in the World War.

Japanese losses were listed by the Navy Department as follows:

One battleship sunk.
Three heavy cruisers sunk.
Two light cruisers sunk.
Five destroyers sunk.
Eight transports sunk.
One battleship damaged.
Six destroyers damaged.
Four cargo transports destroyed.

Col. Frank Knox, Secretary of the Navy, said the United States had clearly won round two of the battle for the Solomons, but that it "must not be forgotten" that there might be a round three.

Calling the battle a major one, but not a decisive one, Col. Knox said that the effect of the losses obviously would be hurtful to the Japanese Navy, but he declined to say that the Jap fleet had been crippled.

MacArthur in Field

In Australia, meanwhile, it was announced that Gen. MacArthur had taken the field himself to direct the Allied campaign to drive the Japanese from their invasion base at Buna, New Guinea. Allied forces are closing in rapidly on Buna from the west and south, and the enemy is steadily retreating.

American B25s and Australian Beaufighters thrice bombed and strafed canoes in which remnants of the Japanese forces in the Wairopi area were attempting to escape in disordered flight.

Adm. Nimitz said in a communique: "By far the strongest Japanese attempt to date to recapture Guadalcanal has been completely frustrated by aggressive action by Vice-Adm. W. F. Halsey and his forces in the south Pacific area.

"The enemy transport force was almost annihilated so that little if any assistance reached the Japanese land

(Continued on page 4)

Mass Arrests Reported Of Anti-Fascists in Italy

Mass arrests have been made in Milan, Turin, Genoa and other Italian towns during the last few days, according to a Geneva message quoted by Moscow radio.

It is estimated that up to 3,000 people have been arrested. Among these there are many of the military and industrialists opposed to Mussolini, as well as several hundred civil servants opposed to the Fascist regime.

Battleship of This Type Lost By Japs

Battleship of the Kongo class (29,250 tons, about 30 years old) was one of the 11 warships lost by Japanese in Battle of the Solomons. Before it went down, however, shells from its 14-inch guns wrecked bridge of U.S. flagship, killing Rear-Adm. Daniel J. Callaghan.

1D. THE STARS AND STRIPES 1D.

Daily Newspaper of U.S. Armed Forces in the European Theater of Operations

Vol. 3 No. 16 London, England Thursday, Nov. 19, 1942

American Soldiers Land on Shores of Morocco

With Old Glory flying before them, U.S. troops move inland near Surcouf, Morocco, after being unloaded from assault boats.

Allies May By-pass Bizerta and Tunis In Drive Eastward

Move Reported to Occupy Old French Line Of Defenses Between Tunisia, Libya; Struggle On for Control of Air

By the United Press

Allied forces today are believed to be making a dash through southern Tunisia, by-passing the naval base of Bizerta, the capital of Tunis, and the other ports of the protectorate, to Gabes, in the southeast, commanding the narrow gap between the salt lakes and the sea.

Lt. Gen. Anderson's advance into Tunisia, according to a dispatch from the Allied expeditionary force, is expected to be made in three prongs. The first two would be aimed along the coast at Bizerta and Tunis.

The third, or southern column, is believed to have started from Tebessa, the road and railway junction on the Algerian-Tunisian frontier 100 miles south of the port of Bone, heading in the direction of Gabes.

Such a move, if successful, would enable the First Army to occupy the Mareth line, long prepared by the French to halt any Italian aggression from Libya, and block any attempt by Rommel or any other Axis force to force Tunisia from the east.

Contest for Air Control

(American and British air forces struggled yesterday for the mastery of the air, which is the key to the drive into Tunisia, while Allied ground forces thrust their way towards Bizerta and Tunisia from the border, according to Associated Press.

(The RAF advanced with Gen. Anderson's army as a protecting cover and even from Bone, captured several days ago, could strike at Bizerta, less than 200 miles away.

(Indications that the Germans were depending on the Luftwaffe to gain time to get their ground forces to meet Gen. Eisenhower's "blitz" was to be seen in reports that the Germans were rushing a large force of fighters into Tunisia from Sicily and Sardinia. Some field reports said that the Germans had already put 12 squadrons of fighters into Tunisian airdromes.)

Axis Claims Bizerta

The German-controlled Paris radio claimed today that the Germans and Italians had occupied Bizerta and had thus taken the initiative in the Tunisian fighting.

The Axis communiques today made no mention of this claim, merely asserting that five Allied planes had been shot down for the loss of three German ones off the North African coast, and that further raids had been made on the port of Bone and on Maison Blanche airdrome, near Algiers.

The Vichy radio said that a convoy of 16 ships had lost half its numbers and three others had gone aground while trying to take refuge in Algerian harbors in a great storm which had been raging in the Mediterranean in the last 40 hours. Another Vichy report was that Gibraltar harbor was full of damaged ships, and that hospital ships were arriving daily.

Wops Talk Big

The Italians, in reports quoted by the Paris radio, claimed that they had sunk two cruisers and two destroyers and damaged a number of other ships, including aircraft-carriers, between Nov. 8 and Nov. 16.

Allied losses in the North African operation were remarkably few, it was stated in London yesterday. Of the ships that were damaged, all but one had landed their troops and stores before the damage occurred.

This result was achieved in the face

(Continued on page 4)

Bomber Crew Got Four FWs In 25 Minutes

Fortress Crew Fought on Despite Wounds and Nazi Attacks

By Charles W. White
Stars and Stripes Staff Writer

A half hour of hell in a B-17 whose tail gunner kept on shooting with his whole side mangled; a cannon hole through the fuselage—waist gunner still firing; a motor and wing smashed, but all safe home. Four German fighters down for sure, four more probable, and they fought off 30.

That's the story of a bomber crew's heroism in a noonday's work over Lille which was released by Bomber Command, Eighth Air Force, yesterday, following announcement of more than 130 USAAF decorations.

The men: 1st Lt. Robert L. Riordan, Houston, Tex., pilot; 1st Lt. Edward P. Malisewski, Grosse Point, Mich., co-pilot; S/Sgt. John T. DeJohn, Ensley, Ala., tail gunner; Bombardier Gerald D. Rotter, Commerce, Okla.; S/Sgt. Anthony L. Santore, Houston, Tex., waist gunner; S/Sgt. John E. Owens, Roanoke, Va., gunner; 2nd Lt. George J. Spellman, Holyoke, Mass., navigator.

Six Decorations

The decorations: S/Sgt. DeJohn, Purple Heart and Air Medal, and Air Medals to Lt. Riordan, Lt. Spellman, S/Sgt. Santore, S/Sgt. Holloway, and S/Sgt. Owens.

The fight:

"They put a 20mm. cannon shell practically in our tail gunner's lap, but that gunner . . ." The gunner was S/Sgt. DeJohn. When the shell exploded beside him he reported over the intercom that his left gun was out of action. His whole left side was sprayed with steel fragments. But for the next ten minutes he fired his remaining gun with one hand and, when a Focke-Wulf 190 tried to close in on the Flying Fortress tail, DeJohn calmly shot it down in flames.

"When they put a bullet through our No. 1 propeller dome and knocked us out of formation," said Lt. Riordan, who told the story of the fight to the squadron "I" officer, "I knew we were in trouble. And when they slammed two cannon shells into our rudder controls I told the boys to get ready to bail out. We were lucky, I guess."

Lucky? There were four certain kills, four probables, and the ship was brought home after raiding Lille with one motor out, one wing-tip rolled up, rudder con-

(Continued on page 4)

U.S. Forts and Libs Bomb Nazi U-Boat Base Again

U.S. bombers struck St. Nazaire Tuesday in the third daylight bombing within a week, according to the Air Ministry and U.S. Air Force Headquarters.

Flying Fortresses and Liberators of U.S. Bomber Command, supported by RAF fighters, attacked the German submarine base during the afternoon, and observed many hits.

Severe opposition was encountered. Six enemy aircraft were destroyed. None of our planes is missing.

Paratroops Jumped to Attack African Airfield from Planes

By Frank Kluckhohn
New York Times Correspondent

A U.S. PARACHUTIST BASE, Somewhere in North Africa, Nov. 17—From a paratroop transport I watched United States parachutists leap to take an airfield somewhere along the Algeria-Tunis frontier.

American boys in their well-known paratroop blouses and baggy trousers, "jump boots" and steel helmets, rocketed groundward and successfully occupied a field which will be of the greatest use as a base.

They also blocked Germans occupying it, after flying through a war zone where Nazi planes were active.

Over mountains, across a torrid desert marked by an occasional green oasis, from an American plane I saw the commander lead his men in a jump to the ground, expecting possible opposition, because it was uncertain whether the French were informed of their coming.

I saw the parachutes open, despite the fact it was a low-level jump. Circling back with the plane bouncing on air currents, it was possible to watch occupation of the field. It was done, as far as we could see, without a shot being fired, although the "grim reapers" went down prepared for anything.

Roaring in over the field, supply planes dropped extra ammunition and food by parachute into the red sand, where men were waiting for it. We veered away for the perilous dash back to base, knowing Uncle Sam had scored another successful surprise move which will affect the campaign for Tunisia.

Three of us, who watched, were filled with admiration both for the courage and smooth functioning of these sky soldiers from New York, California, Rhode Island—the U.S.A.—who have been called "nerveless men," but were on this job because they are highly strung, well-trained soldiers.

We took off for an unknown destination, expecting enemy action. But this undercurrent of tenseness was relieved by the men themselves. They seemed to forget they were in North Africa on a critical assignment. Mess kits went into the air; they pushed, shoved and laughed at inexplicable soldier jokes.

They laughed and shouted—perhaps the reason was that now the fight was on and everything seemed funny, or something for weeping, or however you would want to take it.

We saw this from the air: an armored formation in movement; at another spot,

(Continued on page 4)

18-Year-Olds Must Register

WASHINGTON, Nov. 18 (UP)—President Roosevelt has ordered the registration for selective service of all youths who have reached the age of 18 since July 1, 1942, it is learned in Washington.

The registration will be spread over the last three weeks of December, and it is estimated that the order will make available 500,000 more youths for the armed forces.

The "Teenage Draft Bill" originally provided for the calling up of all youths of 18 and 19 for military service, and the Senate was urged by President Roosevelt last month to pass the bill in its original form without imposing any restrictions on the Government's freedom of action.

The Senate, however, overriding the President, amended the bill, and inserted a provision that no youth under the age of 20 should be sent overseas.

In this form the bill was passed by both the House of Representatives and the Senate, and was passed to President Roosevelt for signature last week.

A Red Cross club has been opened at Southport in a large hotel, with facilities for indoor and outdoor sports and recreation and sleeping accommodations.

Kaiser Sets Another Mark; Builds Auxiliary in 3 Days

NEW YORK, Nov. 18—Henry J. Kaiser, America's shipbuilding wizard, has set another record with the launching of a naval auxiliary craft in two days, 23 hours and 40 minutes after the keel was laid.

Previous world record for a ship launching was three days, eight hours.

Japan Has Lost Initiative to U.S. In SW Pacific

Has Sacrificed at Least 45,000 Lives in Fight For Control of Area

PEARL HARBOR, Nov. 18 (AP)—Japan, despite the might of her concentration of air and sea power in the south Pacific, has failed to shake the plans for an American offensive.

The Japanese appear to have lost the initiative in that sector, paying heavily in planes, ships and men.

Japanese loss of life has been heavy: 5,000 lost in the battle of the Coral Sea, 10,000 at Midway and perhaps 20,000 to 40,000 in the last battle, plus more than 5,000 on Guadalcanal.

But this is far less crippling than losses of flying personnel and carrier-based planes, of which it is believed an important part has been destroyed. This may be an explanation why no aircraft-carriers were used by the Japanese in their show-down effort last week.

All Forces Share Credit

All forces—land, sea and air, American and Australian—share the credit for the victorious thrust against the Japanese in New Guinea, the Australian Premier, John Curtin, declared last night in Melbourne.

Mr. Curtin revealed that Gen. Sir Thomas Blamey had been conducting operations personally in the field since Sept. 23 after the transfer of his headquarters had been decided upon in consultation with Gen. Douglas MacArthur, Allied commander, the southwest Pacific.

Mr. Curtin said that before and during these operations Gen. Blamey and American and Australian officers serving under him had personally reconnoitered the terrain selected for operations.

Gradual Ascendancy

Mr. Curtin recalled that Tokyo radio, in successive announcements after sea battles had "reduced" the United States to the status of, first, a third-class power, and second, a second-class power. Then he remarked: "This ascending scale led us to assume that the latest Japanese announcement would have reduced us to a first-rate power.

"This time, however, the American fleet has been 'completely annihilated,' according to Tokyo."

GI Zoot Suit Prompts Query: 'Whar At's My Shootin' Irons?'

BROOKLYN, N.Y., Nov. 18—Zack and Nick Zacharias, 20-year-old twins from Somewhere in the Hills of West Virginia, are in the army now. It took a long trek to the city, a lot of durn-foolin' with the law, and some work for an army barber—but the boys are happy about the whole thing.

Soon the twins may be strolling down Oxford Street looking for a shootin' gallery, maybe, in Piccadilly. They'll be better informed on the score than when Brooklyn police picked them up recently for questioning. Somewhat rustic hairdos attracted an officer's attention, and he asked to see draft cards.

The twins didn't have any draft cards. They had never heard of the draft law. It was news to them that the U.S. is engaged in a war.

Not their fault, really, because tests showed neither could read nor write.

"Don't you listen to the radio?" the detective demanded. Nope, they didn't. In the woods most of the time, they rarely got the chance. However, seeing the mess things were in, the twins at once sought the right to volunteer.

They were taken to a recruiting officer.

"Can you shoot?" he inquired tentatively. The lanky youths looked like good material.

Both laughed. "Cut our eyeteeth on a squirrel rifle!" From Whiteville, W. Va., they can pick off a squirrel at 500 yards.

One twin couldn't refrain from asking a question of the recruiting sergeant. He pointed to the non-com's uniform.

"Sir—do we git a fancy suit like that when we get in the army?" The sergeant said, "Yes."

"What at," inquired Zack, "is our shootin' irons?"

Halsey Fooled Enemy By Doing Unexpected

WASHINGTON, Nov. 18—Vice-Adm. William F. (Pudge) Halsey tossed the rule book out the porthole in his recent smashing victory over the Jap fleet in the Solomon Islands.

Explaining earlier successes, Adm. Halsey said in a message:

"We got away with it because we violated all traditional rules of naval warfare. We do the exact opposite of what they expect us to do. We deliberately put ourselves under fire from enemy batteries. We expose ourselves to shore based planes. We don't stay behind with carriers. Whatever we do, we do fast."

Mrs. Roosevelt Reports on Trip

WASHINGTON, Nov. 18 (AP)—Mrs. Roosevelt told reporters today that her trip to England convinced her that if American citizens could only realize that the length of the war would depend largely on what they did, "we might put a great deal more into our war effort."

The President's wife talked to reporters for an hour and a half. Asked for examples of what Americans could do, she said giving up non-essentials for one thing, also, if women were willing to do a great deal more work, more man-power could be relieved for war industry and the armed services.

Asked if she could sum up what she got out of her trip, Mrs. Roosevelt said: "I am glad I went because I learned a tremendous amount. I came back with enormous pride in the ability of human nature to rise above things that bother us most—the little inconveniences."

1d. **THE STARS AND STRIPES** 1d.

Daily Newspaper of U.S. Armed Forces in the European Theater of Operations

Vol. 3 No. 18 | London, England | Saturday, Nov. 21, 1942

U.S. Troops Repulse Nazis in First Clash

Soviets Rout Nazi Forces In Caucasus

Reds Turn Defensive Into Attack, Beat Back Force of 45,000

MOSCOW, Nov. 20 (AP)—The Red Army, having smashed the Nazi offensive at Ordzhonokidze, in the deep Caucasus, today pursued the beaten and disorganized Germans and their Fascist allies, piling up trophies and counting ever more dead.

As dispatches rolled in from the Caucasian front it appeared that at least four divisions, possibly 45,000 soldiers, had been defeated by the Red Army.

The Nazis' death roll exceeded 5,000 and wounded were probably more than 10,000. About 150 tanks were taken and many more smashed.

The newest victory eased pressure upon Grozny, one of Russia's finest oilfields and one on which the Hitlerites had fixed their eyes for months.

Ends Threat to South

The turn in events also removed somewhat the threat to the south Caucasian lands which are connected with Ordzhonokidze by the Georgian military highway.

Piling in large forces of men and machines southeast of Nalchik, the Nazis started an offensive which reached the approaches to Ordzhonokidze on Nov. 3, the Luftwaffe bombing Russian positions fiercely.

Then the Russians took the offensive, while on a nearby sector a large German group was cut off and driven to the slopes of the mountains, where they were blasted for five days by Soviet artillery and trench mortars and forced to retreat.

Began as Defensive

"Pravda" said today the Russian counter-blow did not occur after a long respite in positional warfare, but in the course of violent defensive combats while the Russians were retreating.

"Pravda" said the Germans employed a special shock group of forces, whose objective was to break through the Soviet defences, create panic and demoralize the ranks of the defenders of the Caucasus.

On Nov. 3 the Russians dropped 1,500 shells on these shock troopers, comprising one tank division and three infantry regiments, forcing the Germans to retreat in disorder, abandoning machines and munitions.

A dispatch to "Izvestia" from the Caucasus today reported that Nazi troops defeated at Ordzhonokidze were fleeing into the mountains and forests. The Germans left tommy-gunners scattered over the valleys while abandoning one line after another. Empty German cartridges, dated 1942, were made of iron, not copper, and unexploded German mines and shells were of poor quality.

Yank Will Fly Messerschmitt

WITH THE U.S. BLACK SCORPIANS, Cyrenaica, Nov. 18 (delayed) (AP)—One of Goering's late model Messerschmitt 109s will take to the air in a few days marked with the American star and with an American pilot at the controls.

The Germans could not get all their planes away when the army moved in a couple of days ago in a swift advance towards Benghazi. The plane was seized by an advance unit of the Black Scorpians which took over the landing ground to set up operations for fighters.

Pearl Harbor Anniversary To Go Unobserved in U.S.

WASHINGTON, Nov. 20 (AP)—Deciding against taking any official notice of the anniversary of Pearl Harbor on Dec. 7, President Roosevelt disclosed today that he thought it should be observed as a "day of silence in remembrance of a great infamy."

A White House statement said: "The President will not deliver an address on Dec. 7 nor take official notice of that anniversary."

Yes, Adolf, There is a Santa Claus

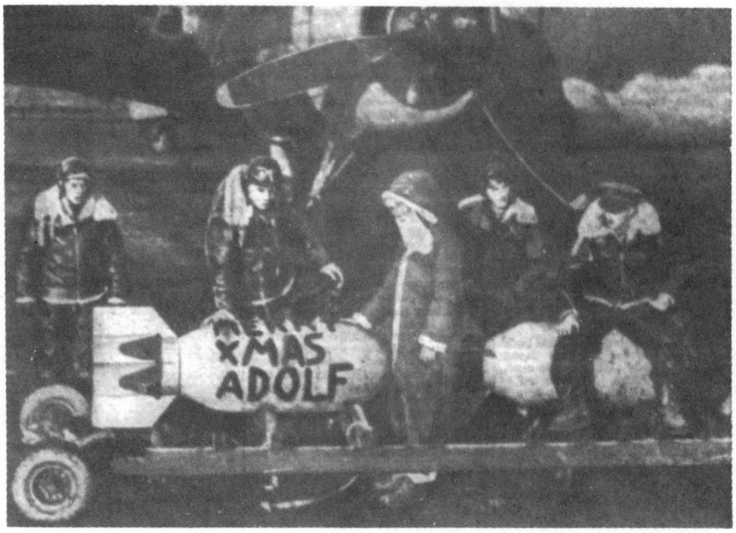

Heeding pleas for early Christmas mailing, the crew of a Flying Fortress plans to get this 500lb. present for Hitler in the mail right away. Lt. A. J. Davis, New York, plays Santa Claus and personally guarantees it'll be opened in time for Christmas. With him are members of the crew: Capt. William Anderson, Long Beach, Cal., pilot; S/Sgt. John Scott, radio operator, Lancing, Tenn.; Lt. Davis; T/Sgt. John Collier, Beaverton, Ala., gunner; and Sgt. Arthur Daugherty, Sharron, Pa., gunner.

Pilot and Co-pilot Wounded, Bombardier Flies Plane Home

He had been up in ships, but never flown them. He was a bombardier, not a pilot. Yet, with his pilot and co-pilot wounded and virtually out, 2nd Lt. Anthony Yenalavage, Kingstown, Pa., took the controls and, getting verbal directions from the others, flew a B-24 Liberator through flak and rotten weather home.

He sat the big bomber down, all safe—and probably doesn't know yet how it all happened, because it happened pretty fast.

The story of how this bombardier who had never before been at the controls of a four-motored bomber safely flew the Liberator back over the channel, after the pilot and co-pilot were wounded, was revealed last night by Eighth Air Force Headquarters.

The Liberator had been over Lorient with a formation of B-24s, planting bombs on German submarine pens and docks. They had scored hits. Everything okay so far. Now home.

2nd Lt. Yenalavage was riding in the nose of a plane flying in the "hot spot" at the tail of the formations. They were 60 miles on the homeward flight when three JU88s made for the rear ship. Seemingly out of nowhere, they made eight savage attacks.

The B-24 was riddled. They sent one Hun into the sea, another trailing smoke home. Though they were now getting the worst of it, they had to stay in and fight in order to support a sister ship which had lost a motor.

At this point the JU's got Lt. Yenalavage's pilot in the arm. Then the co-pilot was struck, possibly by the same slug. The pilot couldn't handle the controls, but the co-pilot carried on for 20

(*Continued on page 4*)

Japanese Fleet Lost 28 Ships

WASHINGTON, Nov. 20 (AP)—The United States Navy has dealt the Japanese fleet its most disastrous defeat in modern naval warfare. It became apparent today with the disclosure that enemy losses in last week's three-day battle probably reached the staggering proportion of 28 ships destroyed and 10 more damaged.

This setback, believed to have cost the Japanese two battleships, six heavy cruisers, two light cruisers, six destroyers and 12 transports and cargo ships, became even more crushing with the news that Allied bombers had sunk another cruiser and a destroyer in the New Guinea area.

The U.S. Navy cautioned that the latest claims might include some damage previously reported.

If Allied troops succeed in ousting the Japanese from their base at Buna, these naval victories would open the way for an Allied invasion of Lae, Salamaua and Rabaul.

In New Guinea Allied ground forces have pinned the Japanese down to a

(*Continued on page 4*)

This Is Getting To Be Habit—Another GI Needs New Shoes

The Stars and Stripes campaign for "a pair of shoes for every soldier" continued yesterday, with Pfc Dewey Livingston, size 13 EE, almost equipped and a new footman in the field—this time Cpl. Donald Mann, Buena Park, Cal., size 13½ D.

A quartermaster company read about Dewey and sent a wire declaring they have the shoes. The Stars and Stripes sent out a call for Dewey, who may be flatfooting it for Printing House Square from Somewhere in England, although Dewey isn't here yet, nor are his shoes, but there are lively hopes of a meeting soon.

Meantime, the case of Cpl. Mann came to notice. He is six feet two and wears the rare size 13½ D.

Cpl. Mann, who is in a chemical company, came to England with a single pair of GI shoes, which had been repaired again and again.

One day, while the corporal was marching in the shoes, the shoes marched off from the corporal. Or so to speak. Anyway, Donald has gone through the only known pair of 13½ D buskins in the British Isles, and now, naturally, is looking around for more leather.

Moral: Anybody who knows where to beg, borrow, or steal a pair of 13½ Ds, kindly report the fact to The Stars and Stripes, Printing House Square, London, E.C.4.

Allied Losses Were Cut By Agents' Work

Nazis' Own Fifth Column Technique Aided Drive Way into Africa

By Drew Middleton
New York Times Correspondent

ALGIERS, Nov. 12 (delayed)—Swift and cheap occupation of Algiers is due as much to the work of scores of British intelligence agents and hundreds of patriotic French men and women as it is to the skilful attacks on eastern and western sections of the city by United States and British forces.

It was largely a result of their efforts that American troops were able to land unopposed and find reliable guides ready. Political agents working for many months prepared the bulk of French officers and men to accept Allied occupation, not as a military move against Algeria but as a step toward ultimate liberation of France.

Today hundreds of French troops and officers, shocked by the invasion of unoccupied France, are believed to be willing to serve with Allied armies in any theater of the war.

Intelligence reports on Algiers, furnished by the British, were complete to the last detail.

Guided by these reports and hundreds of aerial photographs, American troops had no difficulty in finding their way through strange country. The principal building in each town was identified in the reports, and homes of the leading military and civilian figures were marked.

Familiarity with conditions in the country had much to do with the relatively low American casualties. It is literally true that landing forces knew the location of every French battery, strength and ammunition supply of every troop

(*Continued on page 4*)

U.S. Hopes to Double Plane Output in 1943

WASHINGTON, Nov. 20 (UP)—The United States aircraft production goal for 1943 was fixed at more than double this year's production. Donald Nelson, head of the War Production Board, announced today.

Nelson gave no precise figures. The original target was set at 60,000 planes for 1942, but this figure was later reduced.

Allies Strike Hard Blows At Panzers

Americans Repel Four Attacks in Tunisia; First of War

ALLIED FORCE H.Q., North Africa, Nov. 20 (AP)—Allied combat teams, driving on Tunis and Bizerta from several directions in the first heavy fighting in Tunisia, destroyed one-third of a German panzer column between 30 and 40 miles from Bizerta, forcing it to retreat, and drove back two other German columns to the south.

Although the Germans used their best medium tanks and dive-bombers, Allied losses were described as "minor" in the opening battle for the control of Tunisia.

(The first ground clash between American and German troops since the beginning of the war occurred in the battle United Press reported, quoting an announcement at Allied Headquarters. This was not counting the fighting which a handful of Americans performed in the raid on Dieppe Aug. 19.

(American troops advancing in Tunisia won a short, sharp battle in which four German attacks were thrown back, UP reported. The Allies suffered some losses, and the enemy's losses are reported to have been considerable.

Nazis Digging In

"It appears that the Germans are digging in about 30 miles southwest of Bizerta and Tunis, making a stand," a headquarter's spokesman said today. "Although the French situation is extremely confused, it appears that almost all the rest of Tunisia is either controlled by pro-French garrisons or occupied by the Allies.

"German losses in yesterday's clashes were quite heavy but they are pouring in reserves and it looks like we are in for considerable fighting," the spokesman continued.

Crack new American mobile artillery units helped the British and French forces to shatter an advance German motorized column about 20 miles south from the area near the coast where the main tank clash took place.

French Capture Germans

Small German units trying to push south along the Gulf des Gabes have been captured by pro-Allied French units, which have also driven off German attempts to land troops by air transport in this area.

"The French are doing exceedingly well despite great confusion as a result of local commanders issuing contradictory orders to surrender to the Germans in one case and to fight in the next," the spokesman said.

"It is a hell of a mess, but most of the French appear resolved to carry on the fight against the Axis."

The Germans have been pushing out columns from their newly formed lines around Tunis and Bizerta, but in every clash have been driven back.

Flying Fortresses striking in daylight without loss pounded German air strength and harbor installations in the raid on Bizerta yesterday with good results.

Allied forces are converging on the German bridgehead around the two great ports from all sides.

The Luftwaffe in a futile attempt to

(*Continued on page 4*)

Fortresses Rule Air Over North Africa

ALLIED FORCES H.Q., North Africa, Nov. 20 (UP)—There are so many Flying Fortresses now in North Africa that the Axis air strength has been completely overwhelmed.

And there are more on the way.

When these Fortresses arrived, or where they came from, cannot be disclosed, but they are here in such numbers that the Axis will be unable to furnish anything to meet the display.

In the first operation of its kind in this area, Fortresses raided Bizerta yesterday. They passed over the target at a low altitude and hits were registered on oil storage dumps. Only light anti-aircraft fire was encountered. One Fortress shot down a Me.109 on the return journey.

1D. THE STARS AND STRIPES 1D.
Daily Newspaper of U.S. Armed Forces in the European Theater of Operations
Vol. 3 No. 20 London, England Tuesday, Nov. 24, 1942

Nazis Face Encirclement at Stalingrad

Dakar Joins Adm. Darlan With Allies

West African Naval Base Was Long Doubtful; Tunisia Clashes

By United Press

French West Africa has placed itself under Admiral Jean Darlan's orders, according to a broadcast by Dakar radio last night.

The radio quoted an announcement to this effect by M. Boisson, Vichy Governor-General of French West Africa.

The accession of French West Africa means that the Allies now have the big port and base of Dakar, on the Atlantic coast, falling into their hands without any trouble.

(Broadcasting over Radio Algiers last night, Admiral Darlan said that French West Africa had placed itself freely at his disposal, the Associated Press reported.)

French West Africa comprises a vast stretch of country bordering on Nigeria in the south and running up the western part of the African continent to Algeria, Morocco and Tunisia. Dakar, bulging out into the Atlantic on its western sea coast, is its great base.

French Ships at Dakar?

Some French naval forces are reported to be in Dakar, among them the battleship Richelieu, three heavy cruisers and an unknown number of destroyers. The Richelieu was crippled in the British attack in 1940, and her heavy guns were later reported to have been taken away to reinforce the coastal defences.

The evacuation of women and children from Dakar was announced early this month by M. Boisson, when he declared that Dakar was determined to fight it out against anyone who tried to take it away from Vichy.

Three Tunisia Clashes

Meanwhile three separate Allied forces were reported to have engaged Axis forces in Tunisia.

One attack, according to the unofficial Morocco radio, was launched against enemy forces entrenched in the region of Tunis and Bizerta.

This was followed by the announcement that enemy forces, which had infiltrated into the region of Gafsa, about 70 miles inland from the Gulf of Gabes, had been thrown out of the oasis of Gafsa by a counter-attack by French troops, supported by Allied forces.

Quoting what it called communique No. 4 from French headquarters, Tunisia, the station also said that the enemy infiltrations had been enlarged on all fronts between Gafsa and Kairouan, some 75 miles southeast of Tunis. At Gafsa, where there is an airdrome, prisoners were taken, it was added.

'Battle for Harbor'

Meanwhile Axis radio stations had little to say concerning the Algerian-Tunisian situation.

Berlin radio, quoting what it called Anglo-American sources, declared that a violent battle was taking place for a harbor 30 miles from Tunis.

Repeated successful attacks on Allied airdromes, during which 17 planes were destroyed on the ground, were claimed by the Italian communique.

Commenting on Adm. Darlan's position, Radio Morocco denied reports that the American military authorities have presented the French with demands which have nothing to do with military necessity.

"We are authorized to state that the High Commissioner, in full agreement with the representatives of the American Government in Algeria, formally denies these rumors. Adm. Darlan would never

(*Continued on page 4*)

Axis Planes Raid Algiers, Meet Heavy A-A Barrage

ALGIERS, Nov. 22 (delayed) (AP)—Axis raiders bombed Algiers intermittently during an hour-long raid tonight and were met by a thunderous anti-aircraft barrage.

It was the third successive night attack on the city and vicinity. Earlier, in daylight, the guns opened fire twice on high-flying intruders, believed to have been Axis reconnaissance planes.

P38s Are Flying From British Fields

Stars and Stripes Photos

Flying against the Luftwaffe over Europe from bases in the British Isles are American P38s, or Lightnings, manufactured by Lockheed and serviced and flown by the Eighth Air Force.

American P38s In Action Here

400-Mile-an-Hour Plane Used as Escort for Fortresses

U.S. P38s, the fastest, highest-flying fighter planes known, have been in action from British bases since Sept. 1, it was revealed yesterday.

The P38s, called Lightnings when they first were manufactured and test-flown by Lockheed, have been escorting American Flying Fortresses and Liberators on bombing raids over Nazi-occupied Europe, Eighth Air Force headquarters disclosed.

Thus far, the 38s have been unchallenged, cruising even above the high-flying Fortresses as a ceiling cover for the bombing operations.

The P38, designed years ago by far-seeing technicians, is putting into actual operation one of the most amazing set of performance statistics in any air force.

What these sensational flying bullets can do is almost unbelievable.

Speed: 400 miles per hour, plus.

Range: 1,500 miles (maximum), more than enough to get to Berlin and back.

Flying altitude: 40,000 feet.

Armament: One 20mm. cannon, four machine-guns.

Weight: Only 15,000lbs.

These twin-engined streaks are operated

(*Continued on page 4*)

Yanks Will Be Guests In British Homes Xmas

American soldiers will fill the chairs left empty by British fighting men this Christmas, the Special Service section of Headquarters, Service of Supply, has announced.

Invitations from British families who have sons who are either fighting on one of the overseas fronts or who have lost their lives in the war will be filled first. List of men who wish to spend the day in a British home will be given by unit commanders to the British Army welfare office and forwarded to the Ministry of Information for assignment.

As many men as possible will be given the day off, but for those who must remain on duty Army cooks will prepare a traditional Christmas dinner.

U.S. Pilot Crashes To Death In Flames To Save Civilians

A 23-year-old American pilot, who only a month ago transferred to the U.S. forces from the Canadian Air Force, crashed to death in flames Sunday to avoid striking a row of civilian homes in a London suburb.

He was 2nd Lt. Harvey Dalton Johnson, Westville, N.J.

Johnson's disabled plane was in flames above suburban homes near an empty football field at Walthamstow. Although he might have saved his life by baling out, he cleared rows of houses in the closely populated district before jamming his disabled ship into a nosedive.

Thousands in the suburb heard the ship, its motors missing fire. They saw flames spurt from the engine as the low-flying craft headed for a row of closely packed houses.

(An accident there recently took lives of more than a dozen civilians when a military plane crashed into a row of houses.)

Thomas Curd, civilian worker, dragged the charred body from the ship and reported to authorities.

"All of us," Curd said, "want to do something to show our gratitude. This pilot saved dozens of our lives."

Curd and neighbors made persistent inquiries from military headquarters, trying to get the name and address of the pilot, then unidentified.

"If we can get his name and address, we want to write to his parents and——"

U.S. Airforce Headquarters Tuesday were able to release particulars as to the pilot. Unmarried, he was the son of Mr. and Mrs. R. B. Johnson, Philadelphia. A former member of the Royal Canadian Air Force, he transferred to the U.S. service Oct. 13.

1,910 Casualties In Africa for U.S.

360 Dead, 1,050 Wounded, 500 Missing, Reports Washington

WASHINGTON, Nov. 23 (AP)—The U.S. Army announced today that American casualties during the initial landings in North Africa were estimated at 1,910 killed, wounded and missing.

The communique said that Gen. Eisenhower reported that he was not yet able to obtain careful confirmation of the casualties, most of which occurred in the capture of Oran and Casablanca.

Very few men were lost in the operations around Algiers. The total was 350 killed, 900 wounded, 350 missing in the Army and 10 killed, 150 wounded and 150 missing in the Navy.

"It is probable that most of those reported missing were drowned," a communique said. "The next-of-kin will be notified as soon as the casualty lists have been received. Afterwards the lists will be released for local publication."

Gen. Eisenhower was quoted as saying that "but for the cooperation of the French with our movement in Tunisia, we would have suffered heavy casualties."

Petain About to Jo in U.S When Captured—Pearson

WASHINGTON, Nov. 23 (UP)—Drew Pearson, Washington "Merry-Go-Round" columnist, asserted in a broadcast today that the Nazis captured Marshal Pétain as he was preparing to leave France and join the U.S. forces in French North Africa.

They did not dare intern him, however, as they did Weygand, Pearson added. He said that Admiral Darlan probably saved 30,000 lives by ordering cease fire, otherwise fighting would still be in progress.

Red Drive Unchecked In 3 Days

Thousands Killed, Huns Strive to Avert Major Disaster in East

MOSCOW, Nov. 23 (AP)—The Germans, who failed to take Stalingrad in three months pitched battle, have suddenly been put in peril of disastrous encirclement by a Red Army counter-offensive which was reported today to be progressing northwest and southwest of the Volga city.

Nazi losses, which were estimated at more than 14,000 dead and 13,000 prisoners in the first three days of the Soviet drive, mounted as the German command threw in fresh forces but failed to check the Red Army rush across the steppes, which has already reached the Don at one point at least.

(Enemy losses are reaching colossal proportions considering that the offensive has apparently not yet reached its climax, the United Press reported from Moscow. The number of dead alone is reported to be nearing the figure of 25,000.)

Rumanian troops, whom the Germans had been using behind the front lines at Stalingrad, were being taken prisoners.

Sharp Turn in War

The Soviet drive from Stalingrad, following the defeat of the German Army in the Caucasus above Ordzhonikidze, brought a sharp turn in the fighting on the eastern front.

After pushing east to the Volga and south to the Caucasus during the summer and autumn, the Germans are now placed in a perilous position as winter sets in with their units at Stalingrad menaced by a giant pincers movement and the Caucasus force still at a standstill.

While the shattered Nazi divisions reeled back, leaving behind them thousands of dead, thousands of prisoners, and war material of all kinds in such quantities that only tentative estimates had been given by the Soviet authorities, today's Soviet communique reported progress on every section of the Stalingrad-Don front.

'Heat Turned On'

The Columbia Broadcasting System reported said on Moscow radio: "In the battle for Stalingrad, when the time came to turn on the heat, it was the Russians who turned it on. It looks as if the 'squeeze play' of United Nations has begun."

Troops, tanks and guns pursued the broken German divisions through minefields and fortifications northwest and southwest of Stalingrad in the biggest Russian offensive of this year's campaign.

(Berlin is still reluctant to admit the scope of the Russian offensive. Berlin radio sought to claim that Russian attacks near Stalingrad had been repulsed, although admitting heavy fighting on the defensive in the great bend of the Don, United Press reported.)

The Stalingrad offensives stretched two arms 125 miles apart round the German advance guard still holding their positions in the city of Stalingrad.

One-Hour Barrage

Dispatches disclosed that the offensive was begun with an hour's artillery preparation so intense that, when firing ceased, only isolated enemy guns replied, the others having been silenced by the Russian shells.

Red Army scouts exploring enemy terrain had marked down enemy emplacements as targets for the gunners.

Following the artillery preparation, Red Army infantry and tanks smashed through the German front line, routing the enemy out of some advance points with hand-to-hand fighting and driving them from their trenches into the open steppes.

Deep in German ground, dispatches said, the Red Army blasted the enemy fortifications, threaded their way through minefields, cut down barbed wire barriers and suppressed anti-tank guns.

Front Lines Overwhelmed

During the first day of the drive the Russians captured several successive enemy lines, heights and settlements.

The German front line was overwhelmed by the fierceness of the start of the Russian offensive, but on the second day the Nazis brought up new guns and launched counter-attacks at some points. Red Army infantry, tanks

(*Continued on page 4*)

1D. THE STARS AND STRIPES 1D.
Daily Newspaper of U.S. Armed Forces in the European Theater of Operations
Vol. 3 No. 24 London, England Saturday, Nov. 28, 1942

French Navy Scuttles Ships at Toulon

Reds Draw Closer On ThreeSides

Nazis Fight to Retain Corridor of Escape From Stalingrad

MOSCOW, Nov. 27 (AP)—The huge German army before Stalingrad was experiencing increased pressure from three sides today—eastward from Stalingrad itself, northwestward from the Soviet army pounding upon the communications' corridor, and from the south by still another Red army.

The biggest threat to German forces was that the corridor behind them would be closed before they could withdraw.

South of Chernyshevskaya, which is almost 90 miles behind the Germans at Stalingrad, Red Star said, the Russians advanced several miles and captured several settlements.

1,320 Tanks Taken

(Earlier the Russians announced the occupation of 14 more towns or villages and the capture of an additional 12,000 prisoners, bringing the total in eight days to 63,000. Booty taken in the same time, Moscow said, amounted to 1,320 tanks, 1,863 artillery pieces, 3,851 machine-guns, 50,000 rifles, 9,000 horses, and 108 food and ammunition dumps.)

There were still no indications that the Nazi forces were ready to withdraw and give up the battle for Stalingrad. They were still strong before the city, and while they were being slowly edged from their positions, they were clinging to every fortification.

As the total of prisoners taken mounted toward the 75,000 mark, the Russians threw their army into the Don elbow positions with fresh fury.

Fighting for Corridor

Dispatches said that the Germans were trying hard to keep on fixed lines, which means that they are seeking to keep open the vital corridor which extends from the deep rear to the streets of Stalingrad.

On the northwest edge of this corridor stubborn battles developed. The main German force took up positions on a hill in this region. The Russians advanced upon the German lines, but heavy artillery and trench-mortar fire turned them back. Then Soviet mobile artillery hurried into position and turned blazing muzzles upon the hill positions.

After a fierce barrage two Russian tank groups rushed the hill. Several advanced firing points were suppressed, and two infantry groups then piled into the fray, putting the Germans to flight.

Caught Unawares

At another place, Red Star said, the Soviet forces surrounded numerous German detachments. The swiftness of the blow caught the Nazis unawares and nearly all perished or were captured. A huge number of trophies was taken.

Within the Don elbow, the Russians drove the Germans and Rumanians from three settlements, but there were reports that the Nazi commanders were moving new troops into the corridor from other fronts. Despite this, the Red Army continued to forge ahead into new areas, liberating more places and gradually closing the corridor which leads to Stalingrad.

Southwest of Stalingrad, where the Russians were driving north and northwest against corridor positions, the Red Army occupied seven new settlements, all strategically important.

R.A.F. Bombers Attack Marble Arch Air Base

CAIRO, Nov. 27 (AP)—Striking at concentrations of Rommel's depleted supporting air forces, RAF medium bombers carried out a raid against the important air base at Marble Arch in Tripolitania during the night of Nov 25-26.

Marble Arch is so called because of the triumphal arch built in 1937 to commemorate Mussolini's visit to Libya. It is 40 miles west of El Agheila. Several fires were started in the target area among aircraft and transport.

RAF medium bombers attacked Tunis in two waves the previous night. Fuel dumps were hit by the first party and the second arrived to see fires spreading rapidly. The only enemy opposition was inaccurate ackack.

Violent Battles in Don River Area

Red Army guardsmen with tommy guns advance on German snipers in the Don River area, where violent engagements are taking place as Soviet armies slowly close in on Nazi forces before Stalingrad.

U.S. Railroad Engines Here

Yank-Built Locomotives For Use in Isles and Europe Arrive

Locomotives built in the United States and designed especially for service on British railroads, have arrived in Britain it has been disclosed. The first shipment was unloaded with ceremony at its port of arrival in the presence of Allied officials, and more are coming, according to Headquarters, European Theater of Operations.

Built to conform to British and Continental loading gauges, the engines are equipped with a dual braking system which enables them to work trains using either Westinghouse or vacuum brakes. The dual arrangement is essential, as much rolling stock in the United Kingdom uses vacuum brakes, while in Continental Europe the air brake system is widely employed.

The design of the American-built locomotive is simple, yet robust, incorporating features of both British and American design. They are small in comparison with most U.S. locomotives.

Among officials present to inspect the new locomotives were: Maj. Gen. D. J.

(*Continued on page* 4)

Mustang Best Fighter In 1943, Hitchcock says

WASHINGTON, Nov. 27 (AP)—Maj. Thomas Hitchcock, air expert, said in an interview last night that, in the opinion of both American and British fliers, the United States P51 fighter, known as "the Mustang," would be the best fighter for 1943.

Maj. Hitchcock was in England for seven months as Assistant Military Attaché for Air, and made a study of fighter planes now in service or in the blueprint stage.

"We are drawing freely on engineering skill and productive power both in England and the United States to beat the Germans in the race for air superiority," he said.

17,252 Navy Casualties Since Pearl Harbor

WASHINGTON, Nov. 27 (AP)—A naval spokesman reported today that the American Navy's losses in killed, wounded, and missing since Pearl Harbor totalled 17,252 officers and men.

Up to Nov. 15 the Navy, Marine Corps, and Coast Guard casualties totalled 4,929 dead, 2,157 wounded, and 10,166 missing as a result of world-wide operations.

Controls Blasted, Fort Crew Still Licks Nazis, Gets Home

A 21-year-old red-headed Flying Fortress pilot who forced his bullet-riddled ship to carry him and his wounded crew home after a successful attack on a European target limped into dinner on a wounded foot after a hazardous landing. The rest of the mess wanted to know how he flew the big bomber home with a slug in his foot.

"It was nothing much," he said. "I didn't have any control rudders left to use the foot on, anyway."

It was the second time in three weeks that the same Fort with the same crew had successfully fought off a Nazi fighter plane attack and returned safely home.

This perfect team is headed by 1st Lt. Charles "Red" Cliburn, Hazelhurst, Miss., who brought his riddled Fort and wounded crew back the last time with a Jerry slug in his foot.

Focke-Wulf 190s caused the trouble this week after Cliburn's four-motored bomber had dropped its load of destruction on St. Nazaire, German submarine base. The Fortress formation was attacked by two three-plane flights of FWs. Several picked on Cliburn's ship.

First the rudder control lever was shot away and Cliburn was unable to keep the plane in formation. Then 2nd Lt. Clyde De Baum, Bicknell, Ind., the co-pilot, was hit. Tech. Sgt. Louis Vingo, Spokane, Wash., the tail gunner, had his

U.S. Army Signal Corps Photo

1st Lt. Charles "Red" Cliburn

oxygen mask shot away but kept on firing. The plane's radio receiver and compass were blasted out of commission

(*Continued on page* 4)

BBC Changing Forces Shows

British Broadcasters Plan More 'Zip and Zing' For Yanks

BBC is going to make changes in its variety programs to meet the needs of the American forces in this country, it was disclosed last night.

Starting today, the broadcasters plan to inject more "zip and zing" in their shows for the Yanks, Pat Hillyard, BBC assistant director of variety, said.

Hillyard, who has just returned from a four-week inspection tour of broadcasting in the United States, also announced that there will be at least three all-American shows broadcast over BBC every week—the Bob Hope and Jack Benny shows, as well as "Command Performance"—and more soon will be added.

In addition, Hillyard said he soon intends to put visiting Hollywood stars on the air as a unit show, written by American script writers.

"In that way we'll be able to reach those isolated troops who at least will be able to hear the show they couldn't see," he explained.

OWI Helps

These programs also will inaugurate a big "get-together" movement between American and British stage, screen and radio stars. The plan is a result of conversations between the American Office of War Information in London and the BBC.

Tonight at 6.30, Tommy Handley (the British Fred Allen) and Geraldo will have Edward G. Robinson on their program. Robinson made a recording especially for them just before he returned to the U.S. At 7 PM, the American Sports Bulletin goes on and immediately after that, the four Hollywood stars—Mitzi Mayfair, Kay Francis, Carole Landis and Martha Raye—are scheduled to be guests of Jack Buchanan, popular British musical comedy star. Kay and Mitzi, both recuperating from bad cough and sprained shoulder, still hope to be able to take part on the program.

Venezuela, Colombia Cut DiplomaticTiesWithVichy

CARACAS, Venezuela, Nov. 27 (AP)—The Government tonight recalled diplomatic representatives from France. The Foreign Ministry declined to call the move a rupture of relations, but indicated it was rather because the Vichy Government had ceased to exist.

BOGOTA, Colombia, Nov. 27 (AP)—The Foreign Ministry announced that it no longer recognized M. George Helouis, France's Minister to Colombia, because "the French Government had ceased to exist as a sovereign independent entity."

Vichy Men Fight Nazis Taking Port

Fire on Force Arriving To Seize Fleet in Mediterranean.

Adolf Hitler yesterday ordered the demobilization of the French army and sent his troops into the great French naval base of Toulon, but the French Mediterranean fleet at anchor there was scuttled—at least in part—by its officers and men before the Nazis could take it over, according to Marseilles reports quoted by the Havas (French) News Agency.

French naval forces resisted the occupation, fired at Nazi planes, and attempted to slip some of the ships out of the port, but failed, Havas reported.

Scuttling of the fleet, if true, gave final answer to the question of whether its vessels ever would fight again, either on the Axis side or the Allied. It was a question that had been asked since the fall of France, but more frequently and with more import since the Anglo-American expedition in North Africa, when Allied leaders called upon the French naval officers to bring their ships into the war to liberate their own country.

German radio denied last night that all of the ships were scuttled, and said it had guards on those still afloat to prevent them from being blown up.

"To Prevent Treachery"

In a letter to Marshal Pétain, Hitler said the occupation of Toulon was prompted by evidence of "treachery" among the officers of the fleet. Two statements in the German High Command communique which announced the occupation indicated that the officers had decided at last to join the Allies.

The base was occupied, the radio said, "to prevent treacherous acts by certain elements in league with De Gaulle which, in spite of the promises given, were prepared—and about to carry out their plan."

It also said that "the systematic instigation of the French Army, which was ready to collaborate, by Anglo-Saxon influences, continued to spread and in the last few days reached the fleet at Toulon."

According to the Havas reports, the Strasbourg—one of three battleships in the port—was scuttled first, and other units followed in quick succession.

Latest information on the French fleet at Toulon was that it included the modern battleships Strasbourg and Dunkerque, the old 22,000-ton battleship Provence, the 10,000-ton seaplane carrier Commandante Teste, four 10,000-ton heavy cruisers, the Algerie, Colbert, Foch and Dupleix, four light chuisers, 25 destroyers and 26 submarines.

"Some Ships Saved"—Berlin

Berlin radio said last night that not all of the ships had been sunk. Broadcasting an eye-witness account, which mentioned "columns of smoke and sheets of flame over the whole area" and repeated explosions, the speaker said:

"Our engineers and sappers are on all the ships which have not yet been blown up, searching for charges in order to prevent further explosions and in an effort to save whatever ships can be saved.

"Now, at 8 AM, we are in the center of the harbor area. Standing on the Longue Quai, I have a good view of the ships. Some have sunk, some are still sinking, but some appeared to be undamaged so far."

At 3 o'clock yesterday morning, Havas reports, a great wave of German bombers passed over the port, dropping flares to find out where the ships were lying. Other planes flew over the outer harbor, dropping magnetic mines, while bombers flew in over the defense forts.

Toulon's anti-aircraft defenses immediately went into action, while many of the ships began to steam towards the port exits, Havas continued. Meanwhile, German columns streamed into the town, occupying the harbor itself.

Storm Naval Headquarters

Naval headquarters was stormed by German troops who entered the upper windows by scaling ladders. Other German units entered the arsenal, while soldiers were posted with machine-guns in the Vauban Basin, one of the great

(*Continued on page* 4)

THE STARS AND STRIPES

U. S. Army Newspaper
Published Weekly in Africa

Through Facilities of
Stars and Stripes and Yank

Vol. 1 - No 1 - Wednesday, 9 December, 1942 — ALGIERS — TWO FRANCS

First Army Strikes At Two Cities In Tunisia

Light Forces Held Up For Reinforcement But Air War Still Rages

Four weeks after Allied forces under the command of Lieut. Gen. Dwight D. Eisenhower moved into French North Africa, a campaign in the protectorate of Tunisia, about 100 miles across the Mediterranean from Italian - owned Sicily was shaping up.

This campaign centered around Tunisia's two largest cities—Bizerta, the big French naval base, and Tunis, the capital. Shortly after the Allies set foot in North Africa, the British 1st Army, having landed at Bone and Philippeville, moved across the Algerian border into Tunisia. This was admittedly a not-too-heavily equipped nor very large force, but at that time it was hoped that it might get to Bizerta and Tunis before the Germans arrived in strength.

The Nazis, however, quickly, landed air-borne troops, took over important airdromes at eboth these cities and began shifting a considerable part of the Luftwaffe to this new theatre of war. They were able to operate on the coastal plains of Tunisia, whereas Allied forces had to cross difficult mountains in which roads were poor and forward air bases few. The result is that the British - American forces have been held up, pending reinforcements, at points in the hills from 15 to 30 miles outside the two cities.. The British in this area now outnumber the Americans by about three and a half to one, with most of the Americans being in armored or air force units.

Another Allied force, composed mainly of Col. Edson Raff's famed paratroopers, have been operating in southern Tunisia in the general neighborhood of Sfax. This part of Tunisia was supposeldy defended by Italians, but the other day Col. Raff's men caught a few Nazis "wandering" about their territory and captured 100 of them.

In the north, several small-scale indecisive battles have been waged, with rarely more than 25 or 30 tanks of either side taking part in them. Air battles have, however, been growing in intensity as Allied fighters and bombers make daily sweeps over the Tunis and Bizerta airports and the Nazis reciprocate by bombing, almost nightly, our forward bases in Algeria.

Allied bombers used in these battles have been DB7s, B26s, B25s and the B17s. The British have also used a new bomber in the twin-engined Bisley, which is akin to the Blenheim. The C-47 transport has been used to haul men and materiel to foward positions. Th P-38 has been used as a fighter as well as the British Spitfire.

Perhaps the week's most important and encouraging event was a sweep made by the Royal Navy in waters between Italy and Tunisia. Four Axis merchantmen, including two troop transports, and three enemy destroyers, were sunk.

Japs Lose Double U. S. Sunk Warships

Washington — An official recapitulation of the naval losses sustained by the United States and Japan in the year since Pearl Harbor follows:

United States — One battleship, four aircraft carriers, seven cruisers, 24 destroyers.

Japan — Two battleships, six aircraft carriers, 11 cruisers, 59 destroyers. These figures do not include damaged warships, in which category Jap losses were twice as great as American losses

A Message From The C-in-C

Lt. Gen. Dwight D. Eisenhower

I welcome the publication of *Stars and Stripes* in Africa, as will every man of the Allied Forces. We are a long way from home. Only people who have experienced the isolation inherent in extended military operations can fully appreciate the value to the soldier of news from home and friends. We have come to depend on *Stars and Stripes* for such news.

It is especially gratifying to know that the Army weekly, *Yank*, has joined its facilities and personnel to those of the *Stars and Stripes* in North Africa to give us widespread coverage of news from our home countries. The two staffs will render a service of immediate and inestimable value to our Armed Forces in North Africa and to the cause for which we fight.

Dwight D. Eisenhower,
Lt. Gen., U. S. Army
Allied Comander-in-Chief, North Africa

Yank Solve Language Troubles, French Now Speaking English

By LINCOLN BARNETT
(Correspondent for Life)

Algiers—Just three weeks ago this city blazed with the light of sullen neutrality. Germans and Italians lounged in its hotels. Its forts and garrisons were mere dormitories for idle and discontented soldiers.

Now Algiers is dark, but alive. Allied transports, freighters and warcraft move ceaselessly in and about its magnificent hill-cradled harbor. Its streets are jammed with wide-eyed Yanks staring at befezzed moslems and veiled Arab women. Lorries and jeeps roar down boulevards that last month heard only the clatter of donkey carts and trams and the occasional burp of an Italian Fiat. American movies, baned by Vichy, have returned to every theatre in town. They are old, but they are American.

For the first time since World War I an American Army of occupation stands guard in a modern European city. For though it lies in Africa, Algiers is no colonial outpost but is politically and culturally part of metropolitan France. Handsome store fronts on the Rue Michelet are more reminiscent of Fifth Avenue than anything Americans saw in Belfast, Glasgow or Liverpool. After the misty British Isles, U. S. troops are gaping with pleasure at the glistening white buildings of Algiers which, many say, remind them of Mexico or California or Arizona.

(Continued on Page 3)

By ROBERT NEVILLE

Oran — American soldiers stationed here and French civilians living here are having a wonderful time getting acquainted. So far everything's been rosy as a honeymoon in Utopia, with the French trying hard to explain how glad they are to have us here and the Americans reciprocating by spending beaucoup francs and by passing out unheard of quantities of such previously unobtainable tidbits as chewing gum, candy bars and cigarettes.

Although Oran was perhaps the toughest city in North Africa to take, all that seems now to be forgotten. The other day two units, one a Zouave detachment and the other an American company, which fought against each other in an engagement near Oran, paraded side by side, in columns of three each, down the Boulevard Clemenceau after a joint flag-raising ceremony in the local Place de la Bastille.

The M. P.'s and the Oran police cooperate nicely in keeping order, and while some of the boys are momentarily inclined to overestimate their wine capacity, the town shuts up tight after 10 p. m., when no dogface is allowed to be about except on very special business. Another new regulation in force now here is that all men in town must wear blouses (not field jackets), must not wear leggings, must sport a tie and, in general, be spic and span in appearance.

(Continued on Page 3)

FDR Bans Volunteers Between 18 and 40

Washington — Men between 18 and 40 can no longer volunteer for the Army or Navy, according to an executive order issued by President Roosevelt. Hereafter, both civilian and military manpower needs will be met through a special commission headed by Paul V. McNutt. Selective service will be transferred to the commission.

Secretary of War Stimson announced that hereafter no men over 38 years old would be drafted. The War and Navy secretaries have been ordered to determine and present their estimates to this new commission. Certain enlisted men particulaly those over age who are unable to perform military service satisfactorily may now be honorably discharged from the Army.

Clark Gets D.S.M. For His Part In Secret Trip

Huddles In Cellar With Bribe Money And Gun Unused

An award of the Distinguished Service Medal to Lieut. Gen. Mark W. Clark, Deputy Commander-in-Chief of the Allied North African Force, was made last week at AFHQ by Lieut. Gen. Dwight D. Eisenhower, the Commander-in-Chief.

Gen. Clark received this high American decoration for his part in carrying out a "vitally important and hazardous mission" to Algiers weeks before the first Allied troops landed in North Africa. Flying first to Gibraltar, Gen. Clark and a party of seven other American and British officers then transferred to a submarine and set out for a prearranged rendezvous in a lonely house on the North African coast. Signals somehow got switched, however, for that first meeting, and the party left to return at a new and also pre-arranged time.

The eight men huddled behind bushes and trees, scarcely moving and not daring to whisper, until a light flickered in the windows. Then they moved into the house, and carried out important negotiations almost under the noses of Axis agents. As Gen. Clark himself told this part of the story:

"The house was filled with French military officers in uniform, although they had come in civilian clothes. We conferred all day and night, stopping only to cook our own meals, until we had gathered all the information we wanted.

"Meanwhile, the Arab servants who had been dismissed for safety's sake by the head of the household had decided something suspicious was going on and had gone to the Axis-controlled Vichy police. Our conference received word that the police were on the way. A French general in a military uniform changed into civilian clothes in a minute. I last saw him going out of the window. Other French officers were going in all directions. Our staff gathered papers and guns and hid in an empty wine cellar, listening intently as our host talked to the owner of the house over our heads.

"I had 15,000 francs in my pockets and a revolver in my hand. I was undecided, if the police came down, whether to shoot them or bribe them. But after we had spent an hour in hiding the police departed."

Leaving the scene, the party had to cross a nearby body of water in a rowboat. The weather was rough and each of the officers took off his uniform and

(Continued on Page 3)

U. S. War Output Shatters Record One Year After

O. W. I. Warns 1943 Means More Sacrifice And More Goods

Washington, Dec. 7—This first anniversary of the Japanese attack on Pearl Harbor has been a time here at home for checking up on our accomplishments during the last twelve months.

The Office of War Information released impressive figures of American war production, but added the sober warning that the year 1943 would entail still further sacrifices. Donald Nelson, chief of the Office of War production, estimated that the United States alone was now producing twice as much war materiel as all our enemies combined.

Here were the OWI figures for 1942:

49,000 airplanes, with emphasis on heavy bombers.

32,000 tanks and self-propelled artillery.

17,000 anti-aircraft guns of more than 20-mm. calibre.

8,200,000 tons of merchant shipping.

The miracle of American rearmament was demonstrated in the fact that a year ago 7,000,000 Americans were working on war orders as against 17,500,000 One ... About 47,000,000 dollars was badly on war production, which mean that 40 cents of every dollar of the national income went into munitions. Of this amount, some 13,000,000 dollars were collected in taxes. Americans bought 33,000,000 dollars worth of war bonds during the last year.

The volume of railroad and truck traffic exceeded in 1942 anything known before and 1942 also set an all-time high record for food production, being 12 per cent greater than 1941 and 40 per cent greater than 1918. It was estimated that fully 25 per cent of our food goes either to the Army or abroad on lease-lend arrangements. Living costs this October were estimated at 16.1 per cent higher than the year before.

The OWI's report ended with a warning against too great optimism. "The production tasks of 1942 will seem easy compared with those which loom ahead," it said. "For next year our program calls for so great an increase in munitions production that we will have to produce two-thirds again as much as we did in 1942. Next year calls for greater tasks and presents us with equal if not greater obstacles. The record of the past year gives us no cause for feeling the job cannot or won't be done."

As an added fillip to the anniversary, 15 warships, including an aircraft carrier and the new 45,000-ton battleship New Jersey, were launched in a single day.

Heartening news came from the Pacific theatre of war, too, on this anniversary. The Japs now hold only a tinu beach head near Gona, New Guinea, against advancing Australians and Americans. In the Solomons, U. S. forces took five Jap bases on Guadalcanal and again routed Jap naval units bent on reinforcing their units there.

The full story of what happened at Pearl Harbor a year ago was also released in detail. On the morning after the Jap attack there was scarcely a warship and not very many combat planes in the Hawaiian area able to repel further attacks. The warplanes were replaced in a few days and now, a year later, of nineteen warships damaged on that historic occasion, eighteen have been repaired.

The report disclosed that the Japs made four attacks with 21 torpedo planes and that 30 dive bombers came in eight waves during a half-hour period.

THE STARS AND STRIPES

U. S. Army Newspaper
Published Weekly in Africa

Through Facilities of
Stars and Stripes and Yank

Vol. 1 - No. 4 - Wednesday, 30 December, 1942 ALGIERS TWO FRANCS

Giraud Named High Commissioner Following Murder of Admiral Darlan

French troops paraded past the bier of Admiral Darlan, in front of the summer palace of the Governor General. Parade took place soon after final services were held in the Cathedral.

Lt. Gen. Dwight D. Eisenhower, C-in-C of Allied forces in North Africa, pays his respects to Mme. Francois Darlan, wife of the assassinated French leader. Photos by Sgt. Pete Paris

Assassin Ambushes Admiral in Own Office, Dies by Firing Squad 36 Hours Later; Council Names Giraud Successor

General Giraud, 63-year-old hero of two wars, was appointed High Commissioner of French Africa this week in succession to Admiral Francois Darlan, who was assassinated on Christmas Eve as he entered his office in the Summer Palace at Algiers. Already C-in-C of French forces in North Africa, General Giraud thus became, by the unanimous vote of the Imperial Council, the political and civil leader, as well as the military chief of French North Africa.

The assassin of Admiral Darlan, a young man about 20 years of age, was executed by a firing squad on Dec. 26 a few hours after the death sentence had been imposed upon him by a military tribunal.

GEN. HENRI GIRAUD

His identity has not been divulged.

It was shortly after 3 p.m. when Admiral Darlan's limousine rolled through the gates of the Summer Palace on Rue Michelet. At that moment his assassin was sitting in the waiting room outside the admiral's office. He had called during the morning, but had failed to see Darlan. As the admiral passed through the waiting room and opened his office door that afternoon, the young man jumped to his feet, whipped a .25 calibre pistol from his pocket and fired.

The first bullet grazed Admiral Darlan's mouth. The second, more deadly, entered his chest. As the admiral collapsed unconscious in the doorway, the assassin leaped over his body into the inner office. Commander Hourcade, Darlan's naval ordnance officer, dashed into the waiting room, stooped momentarily over the admiral's motionless form, then bounded into the office after the fleeing murderer.

GENERAL AT FRONT

Turning, the youth clipped Hourcade's ear with a third bullet and hit his leg with a fourth. Other staff officers and attaches then poured through both doors of the office and the assassin was disarmed and overpowered. A priest was summoned and administered last rites to the unconscious admiral. He died en route to the Hospital Maillot. One of those who rode with him in the ambulance declared that in a brief moment of lucidity, the admiral struggled, despite his mouth wound, to utter some final words. But they were unintelligible.

All afternoon on Christmas Day, thousands of Algierians filed up to the big Government General Building, where Darlan lay in state in a catafalque, covered by a huge Tricolor and topped by the admiral's uniform hat. An honor guard of four French officers stood with drawn sabres at its corners. At one moment during the afternoon gendarmes cleared a path for General Giraud, who approched the catafalque, saluted, knelt a moment in prayer and left.

On the day of the assassination, General Eisenhower was at the front, but at 11 p. m. Christmas Eve he started back for Algiers by car. He ate Christmas dinner by

(Continued on Page 3)

Stars and Stripes Writer Hits Front – Front Hits Back

Dedges Nazi Bombs But Gets Blitzed By G. I. Coffee

By Sgt. JAMES A. BURCHARD

ALGIERS, Dec. 29—The urge to slap out one of those "I-have-just-returned-from-the-front" things is overwhelming to this correspondent, who is otherwise winning eternal fame by becoming the only reporter in World War II not to write a book on his experiences.

My impressions, bared to a hungry populace, no doubt will fail to change military history in North Africa, but I don't care. I may never get another chance like this.

The newcomer frequently finds it difficult to believe he is at the front at all. There are the same soldiers, the same guns and the same chow he's been seeing all along. I know my first day in the battle area was most tame. Except for a topkick giving me hell when I tracked mud into headquarters, I might have been back at Camp Upton enjoying an afternoon of goldbricking.

TWO-SIDED WAR

But do not trust that first impression. If you do, you'll probably get your GI block knocked off by shrapnel. It had just become dark that first night when I was convinced there actually were Germans in the war as well as Americans.

A siren went off about a mile away. I stood there wondering what it was all about when a colonel sprinted past me and nose-dived into a fox hole. I told him he would dirty his nice, shiny uniform. He replied:—"Don't worry about this uniform, you jackass. Have you got anything I can use for a shovel?"

All at once there was a queer whistling noise, followed by a terrific explosion. It sounded as though one thousand hungry lions had seen a fat missionary at the same time. I don't know exactly how I got there, but I found myself beside the colonel digging straight down with both hands. I got at least one foot lower before the second egg arrived.

ONE NIGHT ENOUGH

Jerry let go eight bombs on that occasion. They seemed to be coming on a straight line toward our fox hole. The colonel said:—"I just hope he runs out of ammunition soon, or we won't need an airplane to fly after him."

Right here I would like to state that all schools for airplane identification should be held at the front. When a guy's longevity depends on split-second recognition of JU 88's, ME 109's or FW 190's he displays amazing mental agility no matter how many times he flunked out of kindergarten back home.

One night at headquarters was enough for me. There was too much brass that seemed to attract those bombs like magnets. We had to leap out of bed (two blankets

(Continued on Page 3)

Santa Claus in Khaki Brings Christmas Cheer

Mud and rain slowed down Santa Claus as well as battle operations during the holiday week. The assassination of Admiral Darlan on Christmas Eve put a damper on such programs of gayety as were planned, while a Christmas night bombing of Algiers was not conducive to sleep.

In the actual battle area it took a lot of gumption to have fun. One week of heavy rain was enough to bring curses instead of cheers. But somehow the boys managed to observe the festive occasion. Enough turkeys, ice cream, cigarettes, chewing gum and such like were flown to the front to gladden many a dogface's stomach.

Some of the British guards preferred to express their holiday hurrahs through action. At 5 p.m. Christmas Eve they launched an attack northeast of Bedjez-el-Bab. Scrapping continued Christmas Day, with the guards holding, against persistent counter-attacks, most of their newly-won positions.

Lt. Gen. Dwight D. Eisenhower made a hurried trip to the front, returning quickly when he got word of Admiral Darlan's death. The C-in-C reported the morale of the men at the front as high.

The 12th Air Force did itself proud by holding a swell party for orphan kids at Algiers. The GI's dished out 150,000 francs, plus candy, soap and gum rations to 200 orphans of four faiths—Protestant, Catholic, Jewish and Moslem. A fat Frenchman played Santa Claus, aided by a 16-foot Christmas tree. In addition to magicians and acrobats, there was a choir of 20 soldiers under the direction of Chaplain Horace N. Cooper, of Denver, Colo.

All through North Africa the boys in khaki did their darndest to be real Santa Clauses for the kids.

One party was held in the big room of an ancient monastery where an eight-year-old French boy got up and spoke in slow, hesitant English to air force headquarters units. He said:—"We heartily thank you gentlemen for all the gifts you have given us. Our fervent prayers will always be with you. Merry Christmas, Happy New Year and Long Live America."

At another party 275 quarts of ice cream made a tremendous hit. As related by Lt. John E. Kieffer, of Buffalo, N. Y., "anybody up to

(Continued on Page 3)

War Ace Tells Story of Rescue

Rickenbacker Prays For Food and Gets Results

WASHINGTON — Capt. Eddie Rickenbacker told reporters this week the story of his experiences on a life raft for 22 days after his plane was forced down in the Pacific last October. He said that he and his six fellow-survivors couldn't have lasted another 48 hours.

"We were all out of water and our food consisted of four oranges," he said. "Pvt. John Bartek had a Bible, which we used to conduct

(Continued on Page 3)

ON THE FIGHTING FRONTS

ALGIERS—Ground activity on the Tunisian front was held to a minimum by continuing rain. Weather made plane operations difficult and air activity over the front was the lightest in weeks. Flying Fortresses of the 12th Air Force, however, punched deep into Tunisia over the week-end, scoring direct hits on troop concentrations, harbors, installations and shipping at Sousse. On a strafing sweep over Libya U. S. fighters attacked an Axis convoy only 30 miles this side of Tripoli. It was the first time our fighters had roamed so deep into Axis territory from this side of Africa.

CAIRO—The 8th Army occupied Syrte, about two-fifths of the way from El Agheila to Tripoli. Rommel's Afrika Korps was still retreating.

MOSCOW—The Red Army this week continued its drive to the west, freeing cities that the Germans have held for more than a year. In 11 days, according to a Soviet communique, Marshal Timoshenko's forces in the south have captured 812 Nazi-fortified places, including eight cities and eight important railroad stations. The Russians reported they took 56.000 prisoners during the period.

TOKYO—Admiral Shimada, Japanese naval minister, speaking before the Japanese Diet, warned of an allied counter-offensive in the Pacific. "The war," he said, "is now entering into a decisive phase and the enemy, counting on his productive capacity, is now capable of launching a counter-offensive."

NEW DELHI—The allied advance into Burma continued this week but without conclusive results.

ON THE HOME FRONT

WASHINGTON, D. C.—Leon Henderson, Chief of the Office of Price Administration, has announced his resignation because of illness. Most likely successor is Senator Prentice Brown, who has recently been defeated for re-election in Michigan. The Henderson program of keeping prices down will probably remain intact.

NEW YORK — "White Christmas" has sold 600,000 more copies over a 10-week period than any other Irving Berlin song. Evidently song-lovers prefer the sleet and hail of New England to the palms of Hollywood, and this has catapulted the Berlin ditty into the first sentimental hit of World War II.

WASHINGTON, D. C.—Henry Morgenthau, Secretary of the Treasury, announced this week that Americans have subscribed a record-breaking 10 billion dollars in government securities since the launching of the "Victory Fund Drive" on December 1. The largest previous total was the seven billion dollars collected in three weeks for the Fourth Liberty Loan in 1918.

PHILADELPHIA — Judge Harry McDevitt has ruled that all women air raid wardens must be accompanied by a man while performing duties during blackout.

TOPEKA, KAN.—They're eating horsemeat back home and liking it. Hill Company Packers, who have been dealing in horsemeat since 1929, formerly shipping all of it to Europe, are now doing a boom-

(Continued on Page 3)

1D. THE STARS AND STRIPES 1D.
Daily Newspaper of U.S. Armed Forces in the European Theater of Operations
Vol. 3 No. 51 London, England Friday, Jan. 1, 1943

Reds Say Nazis at Stalingrad Wiped Out

Forts, Libs Upset Air War Theory

Heavy Bombers Altered Concept of Daylight Raids in '42

German planes shot down: 200-plus.

U.S. planes shot down: 42.

That was 1942's score in the aerial warfare over Europe between the Eighth Air Force and the Luftwaffe.

Listing a total of 26 bombing raids against Nazi targets in Europe, approximately 1,350 offensive fighter patrols and nearly 900 defensive operations, Eighth Air Force yesterday reviewed its operations in the year in which American heavy bombers started a revolution in the theory and practice of aerial bombardment.

How great was the revolution was told in the "box score" for the 25 heavy bomber operations. (There was one light bomber attack, by Bostons, in July.)

FW190s Badly Beaten

The Flying Fortresses and Liberators, armed with potent, far-reaching .50-caliber machine-guns, shot down more than 200 of Germany's best fighter planes, most of them FW190s, while losing 33 bombers of all classifications. Nine fighters were lost in the year, according to the recapitulation.

In announcing its year-end score, Headquarters, Eighth Air Force explained that results of the Dec. 30 raid by American heavy bombers on German sub pens at Lorient were not yet available, pending complete survey of operational reports. Up to that time a total of 195 enemy aircraft had been chalked up and the official pronouncement on the Lorient raid was that, "a number of enemy aircraft were destroyed."

Credit for some of the plusage on the 200-figure must go to American fighter pilots who participated with RAF, RCAF, Dominion and Allied fighter escorts in providing umbrellas for the heavy bombers within their useful range. Making day raids in mass formation, American bombers concentrated on such targets as submarine pens, vital manufacturing and railway centers, harbor installations and enemy dromes.

First Raid on July 4

American bombardment aircraft made their first raid on occupied Europe on July 4, when six US crews took Boston attack bombers on a low level raid against Nazi targets in Holland. Two of our aircraft were lost on the first operation.

American pilots took the B17—Flying Fortress—over Europe for the first time on Aug. 18, when 12 of the heavy bombers struck at railway yards at Rouen and returned safetly, shooting down one FW190.

Twenty-four Forts, with Allied fighter escort, raided the enemy fighter base at Abbeville on Aug. 19 in conjunction with the Dieppe landing. All returned.

B17s destroyed an FW190 during a raid against the Amiens railway yards on Aug. 20. Other bombing raids during August took place on the 21st, 27th, 28th, and 29th, when B17s dropped high explosive on the shipyards at Letraid and Rotterdam, the aircraft factory at Meaulte, and a German drome at Wevelghem, near Courtrai, Belgium. From these raids all our Fortresses returned. Six enemy aircraft were destroyed, with bombers and Allied fighter escorts sharing the victories evenly.

Railway Yards Hit

On Sept. 5, 6, and 7 American bombers were over the railway yards at Rouen and Utrecht, the Schieden shipyards at Rotterdam and the Le Havre docks, the Meaulte aircraft plant and airfields at Abbeville and St. Omer. In

(Continued on page 4)

U.S. Army, Navy Report 56,075 Casualties So Far

WASHINGTON, Dec. 31 (AP)—The cost of America's growing offensive in Naval dead, wounded and missing amounted to 20,397 casualties since Pearl Harbor.

The preponderance of new casualties, the U.S. Navy Department said, resulted from direct action with the enemy, but the total included those lost in accidents at sea and in the air on duty directly connected with wartime operations.

Casualties reported so far by the U.S. army up to Dec. 7 brought the total for the American armed services to 56,075.

Flew Plane Home the Hard Way

U.S. Army Signal Corps Photo

The pilot and co-pilot of their Flying Fortress wounded, Capt. Alexander Bright, Cambridge, Mass., left, and T/Sgt. Clarence V. King, Island Falls, Maine, brought their Fort safely home. Lt. John R. Bell Jr., Prescott, Ariz., right, rubbed King's arms to keep him from freezing.

Pilots Wounded, Fort Is Flown Home by Sergeant, Ex-Broker

A sergeant engineer and a former Boston stockbroker who was along just for the experience brought a crippled Flying Fortress safely back from Wednesday's U.S. raid on Lorient after the pilot and co-pilot of their ship had been knocked out by German shells.

The two men, who came back from the raid as heroes, are Capt. Alexander Bright, Cambridge, Mass., and T/Sgt. Clarence V. King, Island Falls, Maine.

Capt. Bright, not required to fly by his ordinary duties, was on the raid to get experience valuable in briefing pilots.

A shell exploded in the cockpit of their Fort. They saw the pilot collapse over the wheel and the co-pilot, also wounded, lose control. Sgt. King jumped forward, carried the pilot aft, and Capt. Bright administered first aid.

Sergeant Took Controls

Then King took the pilot's vacant seat. He got the plane out of a dive and levelled off for its base in Britain. To prevent the arms and hands of Sgt. King and the injured co-pilot from freezing, Lt. John R. Bell Jr., Prescott, Ariz., bombardier, rubbed them vigorously.

The destruction of two Focke-Wulfs and a probable Me109 was claimed by the crew. One of the enemy fighters claimed destroyed was shot down by the tail gunner after he had been hit by a Nazi shell.

Three Fortresses failed to return from the raid against German submarine pens at Lorient.

Flyers who were still being interviewed yesterday indicated the score of FW190s downed is high enough to make it another major U.S. air victory.

Figures on German fighters shot down were withheld, pending completion of official interrogations.

T/Sgt. B. C. Farmer, Bailey, N.C., left waist gunner aboard the bomber piloted by Capt. Sidney Smith, Santa Barbara, Cal., was credited with one FW destroyed. It was seen to dive into the sea after being hit.

Early reports showed that, among others, Sgt. E. L. Bates, Tule Lake, Cal., gunner on the Fort piloted by 1st Lt. D. M. Daniel, Eagle Butte, S.D., was credited with one enemy fighter destroyed.

Capt. E. E. Tribbett, Thorntown, Ind., made an emergency landing near his home base. His telephone report was

(Continued on page 4)

Curtiss Wright Output Soaring

Producing in Week More Than Yearly Rate of Short Time Ago

NEW YORK, Dec. 31 (AP)—The Curtiss Wright Corporation, America's largest airplane, engine, and propeller producers, announced today that current production for a single week exceeded the annual rate for a short time ago.

G. W. Vaughan, president of the company and head of the Aircraft War Production Council for the East Coast, said that the industry would expand its output in 1943 to what formerly was considered impossible proportions.

Vaughan added that "aerial box scores in the current war communiques hint only vaguely at miracles of design and production performed by the aviation industry in the production of war planes for all fronts over which we are engaged.

"During succeeding months this superiority will be more pronounced as we reach an output rate that even we thought impossible until Pearl Harbor. Workers in our drawing offices, machine shops, and assembly lines are seeing to that."

And We'll Deliver 'Em

WASHINGTON, Dec. 31 (AP)—The War Department, in a year-end review, said among other things that the United States was producing enough rifle and machine-gun ammunition each month to fire 833 rounds at every Axis soldier.

Flood Spreads to Six States, Plants Shut, 17,600 Homeless

PITTSBURGH, Dec. 31 (AP)—The worst December flood in the history of the upper Ohio river watershed was reaching its crest after forcing numerous war plants to close and disrupting railway and bus traffic. Many steel plants and other factories along the banks of the flooding rivers were virtually paralysed.

The American Red Cross was caring for 7,500 persons in the Pittsburgh area, driven destitute from their homes in low-lying sections, and it was estimated that 10,000 others were homeless in Pennsylvania, West Virginia, Ohio, Kentucky, Tennessee and Alabama.

A weather forecaster announced at midnight that the Ohio river had reached its crest with a level of 36.5 feet, which is 11.5 feet above flood level but still 11 feet below the disastrous St. Patrick's Day flood of 1936, of which there is no danger of a repetition. The forecaster predicted that a gradual fall in the level would begin at dawn.

The muddy waters covered many downtown streets. Four theaters and four large bridges were closed and there was water several feet deep on the lines of one railway near a station.

There was five feet of water in the courtyards of the Western Penitentiary, but it was not expected that it would endanger the hundreds of prisoners.

The inhabitants of Wellsburg, W. Va., which was devastated in the 1936 flood, left for the hills as the Ohio reached a level of 42 feet. Residents of Wheeling Island, in the middle of the Ohio river, as well as at South Wheeling were leaving by thousands. The river there was 40 feet

(Continued on page 4)

Claim 95,000 Slain, 72,000 Imprisoned, When Trap Closed

Italians Are Delighted: They Defeated Germans

CAIRO, Dec. 31 (AP)—Details of a pitched battle between Italians and Germans near Alamein were revealed today in enemy documents captured in Libya. The Germans surrendered to the Italians before the mistake was discovered.

The tone of the documents, pertaining to the subsequent court of inquiry, indicated the Italians were delighted.

An Italian battalion, ordered to advance on foot in a general attack, was fired on and gave battle. After hours of fighting the Italians' opponents surrendered. They were found to be part of a German battalion, which had advanced by motor faster than the Italians and on seeing them approach believed them to be British. Twenty Germans and five Italians were killed or wounded.

French Moving Up from South To Hit Rommel

Lake Chad Force Is Seen As Threat to Axis Flank in Desert

By the United Press

While the advance patrols of Gen. Montgomery's Eighth Army are still skirmishing with Rommel's rearguard in the rocky terrain between Sirte and Misurata, a Fighting French force is streaming northward from the direction of Sebha Oasis, south of Wadi-el-Chebir.

This new development, which constitutes a serious threat to the left flank of Rommel's retreating forces, was made known in a communique yesterday afternoon from Gen. Le Clerc's forces, who began their advance from the Chad territory, in the heart of the desert.

The Bretagne Squadron, a Fighting French bomber reconnaissance unit, attacked the airdrome at Sebha Oasis, which is on the Trans-African highway, and the destruction of a number of enemy aircraft on the ground is reported.

Rommel Avoids Stand

Rommel's forces have abandoned Wadi Bei-el-Chebir, which was regarded as a likely defense point, and are now apparently in the neighbourhood of the Wadi Zemzem, 70 miles from Sirte. The only remaining defense line between this point and Misurata is the Wadi Sofezzin, 50 miles further to the west.

Increased air activity on both sides over the battle area is reported today.

The capture of a group of British parachutists, commanded by a senior officer, in the Sirte area was claimed in the Italian communique, which also said that a number of motor vehicles, including some armored ones, were destroyed in the Libyan desert.

The German communique said there was assault troop activity at some points in Libya. It claimed hits on our motorized columns.

Air Action in Tunisia

ALLIED HQ, North Africa, Dec. 31 (AP)—Flying Fortresses made six attacks on Axis supphy bases between Tunis and Tripoli yesterday.

Two-to-Four-Year War In Pacific Is Predicted

WASHINGTON, Dec. 31 (UP)—A forecast that the war in the Pacific would last between two and four years, depending on how long it took to defeat Hitler and what material was concentrated against Japan, was made by the Dutch Vice-Admiral, C.E.L. Helfrich, when he visited Sumner Welles, Under-secretary of State, today. Ships and planes, he said, were the greatest need in the Pacific.

Middle Don Victories Doomed Axis Units, Moscow Says

Moscow radio, in a special communique last night, said the German army in Stalingrad was completely liquidated.

Ninety-five thousand Germans were exterminated and 72,000 captured. In the course of the battle the second, fifth, sixth, ninth, 13th, 14th and 15th Rumanian infantry divisions were completely destroyed, the communique said.

The communique made the following claims:

The Red Army advanced between 45 and 90 miles in Stalingrad offensive between Dec. 16 and 30. Thirteen inhabited places were captured.

Seventeen German divisions and one Rumanian division were surrounded in the Stalingrad offensive, as well as 11 German regiments.

Don Offensive Did It

Russian troops in the middle Don area fulfilled the task set by the Soviet High Command to break the defense front Novaia Kalitva to Monastir.

The Germans made a desperate attempt to free the encircled divisions at Stalingrad but were successfully frustrated by the Red Army. The Germans concentrated their forces at Kotelnikovo for the purpose of freeing encircled divisions. This was frustrated in the third phase of the Soviet offensive.

Since Nov. 19, 175,000 Germans were killed and 137,650 taken prisoner, the communique said.

"On Nov. 19 the Red Army launched an offensive with the forces on the southwest front, the Don front and the Stalingrad front and inflicted a powerful blow on the enemy," the communique said.

Lists Units Routed

"The task given by the Supreme Command to Russian troops operating northwest and southwest of Stalingrad was to rout the flank forces of the German and Fascist troops at approaches to Stalingrad and by means of an enveloping movement to surround the bulk of enemy forces at Stalingrad. This aim was achieved by Russian troops. In the course of the offensive our troops routed the following enemy forces:

"The 2nd, 5th, 6th, 9th, 13th, 14th and 15th Rumanian infantry divisions, the 7th and 8th cavalry divisions of Rumanians and the 1st Rumanian tank division, the 44th, 376th, 384th German infantry divisions and the 22nd German tank division.

"In addition heavy losses were inflicted on three other German infantry divisions. During these battles our troops destroyed 95,000 of the enemy and captured 72,000."

Drive Gains Speed—

By Maurice Handler
United Press War Correspondent

MOSCOW, Dec. 31—The German front south and southeast of Stalingrad is in imminent danger of collapse.

Within the last 48 hours the Red Armies have carried out a series of well-coordinated unbroken advances and freed thousands of square miles of Russian territory south and southeast of Kotel-

(Continued on page 4)

Goebbels Tells Reich of Peril

Josef Paul Goebbels, Nazi Minister of Propaganda, broadcasting a New Year's speech on the German radio last night, said that last year the Germans only succeeded in countering the gigantic Russian war machine by the greatest efforts.

It was clear that Germany could and must be saved, but this was possible only with a tremendous effort of will power, Goebbels declared.

The situation had to be examined carefully, he said, adding that events had proved that "what does not kill us makes us stronger."

1d. THE STARS AND STRIPES 1d.
Daily Newspaper of U.S. Armed Forces in the European Theater of Operations
Vol. 3 No. 68 London, England Thursday, Jan. 21, 1943

London Rescue Crews Search for Raid Victims

Associated Press Photo

Shortly after a bomb dropped on this bank in a London area yesterday, ARP workers swarmed over the debris in search of victims buried beneath the ruins. At several points where German fighter-bombers attacked, American soldiers helped to clear away the ruins and give aid to the injured.

Eighth Army Nears Tripoli; Axis Tanks Advance in Tunisia

Nazis Push French Back Seven Miles In South

By the Associated Press

Strong enemy tank attacks on the Allied southern flank have strengthened the supposition that the Axis plans to make its final African stand in Tunisia.

While parts of Rommel's fleeing force were reported to be retiring even beyond Tripoli, towards the other Axis forces in Tunisia, enemy tanks struck about seven miles through French positions southwest of Pont du Fahs, in Tunisia, apparently in an effort to create a diversion which would allow Rommel to retreat into southern Tunisia.

The Axis attack was part of what an Allied spokesman called "a good deal of armored movement by the enemy with heavy air support."

Seven-Mile Advance

The Allied communique issued here yesterday said:

"Minor engagements continue in the Bou Arada-Goubellat area.

"Enemy forces moving southwest from Pont du Fahs have penetrated about seven miles. One advancing column was attacked effectively by Hurricane bombers and Spitfires.

"Bisley bombers attacked roads and railways in the area Tunis-Sousse on the night of Jan. 18-19. A train was destroyed and hits were made on motor transport.

"Yesterday, objectives in the Tunis area were bombed by Flying Fortresses.

"In the south, B25s bombed targets at Medenine.

"Lockheed Lightnings attacked a column of enemy vehicles near the Tunisian frontier, destroying about 20 of them.

"From all these operations two of our aircraft are missing."

New Tank Commander

The German tank forces, which slashed through the French positions in a drive along the road from Pont du Fahs southwest towards Robaa, now are known to be commanded by Gen. von Arnim, who has replaced Gen. Nehring.

Von Nehring apparently considers the hills northeast and northwest of Bou Arada vital to the defense of Axis holdings in coastal and Southern Tunisia.

The heights command the whole of the Goubellat plain, in addition to the valley extending from Bou Arada to Pont du Fahs.

The tank thrust by the Germans was stopped by combined Allied air and artillery action, a spokesman said, declaring there had been considerable enemy tank losses.

A theory was advanced by observers that the push was von Arnim's initial step to protect Rommel's retreat from Tripolitania to Tunisia by drawing off Allied forces from the Southern Tunisia sector which might launch an attack on Rommel's exposed and retiring flank.

New Algeria Governor

ALLIED HQ, North Africa, Jan. 20 (AP)—The appointment of Marcel Peyrouton, described as a deadly political enemy of Laval, as Governor-General of Algeria is taken to be a sign that there will be a thorough cleaning out of pro-Vichyites in minor positions in Algeria.

British Are Reported Past Homs On Coast Road

By The United Press

The Eighth Army raced into the home stretch to Tripoli yesterday, with one flank hugging the coast and snapping at the fleeing heels of Field-Marshal Rommel, while a western force drove northward through the interior toward the same goal.

Although it seemed certain that the Axis would make some sort of a stand—possibly a decisive one—at Tripoli, there were grounds for reports that Rommel would not attempt much more than a strong rearguard action at the much-battered port.

A Morocco radio report said last night that part of Rommel's army already was fleeing west of Tripoli towards the Tunisian border.

It seemed likely that the commander of the broken Afrika Korps would make his stand in the hills along the border of Tripolitania and Tunisia, where the Mareth line of fortifications is said to have been rearmed.

Allied Air Attacks

Meanwhile, Allied air power from the East, from Malta and from North Africa was doing its best to make certain that there was little in Tripoli worth fighting for. Bombers kept up their day and night attacks on the harbor.

The Eighth Army, continuing its advance with still less opposition from the Axis during the past 24 hours, has now reached the so-called "Jebel Line," which consists of broken, hilly country running from Homs through and beyond Tarhuna to the southwest.

Despite the nature of the country, however, and the plentiful sprinkling of mines by the enemy, there has been no lessening of British pressure on the Germans and Italians, either on the ground or in the air.

Morocco radio late yesterday said the Eighth Army was at Homs, the last big port on the road to Tripoli, 50 miles away.

Another Morocco radio broadcast said that advance forces were within 30 miles of Tripoli, but there was no confirmation of this.

Report Axis Embarkation

Another—and unconfirmed—radio report from Morocco said Rommel was embarking some of his troops from Tripoli in the face of the heavy Allied bombings.

Another big air attack has been carried out on Castel Benito airdrome, which Rommel must use to defend Tunis from the air. Large fires were seen among aircraft dispersed round the field. At the same time, fighters and fighter-bombers harassed the Axis columns retreating from the Tarhuna area, south of Tripoli. The harbors at Tripoli and Sousse were bombed again by Liberators, and during the raids they shot down three enemy fighters.

Bombers, torpedo-carrying aircraft and "intruders" have been operating from Malta, attacking shipping in the Sicilian narrows and striking at enemy communications with Sicily. Two ships were torpedoed in the Sicilian narrows, one a large supply ship and the other a medium-sized supply ship.

Parachutists Near Algiers

ALLIED HQ, N. Africa, Jan. 20 (AP)—French military authorities in North Africa have published a newspaper notice offering a reward for German parachutists who have been dropped in Algeria.

The order was signed by the commander of the city of Algiers, indicating that the parachutists were dropped near Algiers, itself, and were presumably making their way citywards.

London School, Suburbs Blasted By Nazi Raiders

11 Enemy Planes Destroyed In First Daylight Attack Since July

German fighter-bombers, sweeping in from the southeast coast at roof-top height, bombed and machine-gunned several suburban sections of London yesterday noon. Eleven of the attackers were shot down in the biggest daylight dogfight over the city since the Battle of Britain.

The raiders dealt their most devastating blow in the heart of a suburban London residential district, where they bombed a school and trapped nearly 100 children and teachers at their lunch tables.

Rescue workers discovered the bodies of 30 children, six to 14 years old, and continued to remove baskets of debris in search for the 30 to 60 more children and three teachers who were trapped under the rubble.

All were seated at luncheon on the first floor of a four-story brick building. The room in which they were lunching was almost leveled by the attack.

More than 200 men, including the grey-haired vicar of the district, and several women continued to work to clear the ruins last night. Only 11 children and one teacher emerged alive, and some of them were seriously injured.

Some American soldiers on leave in London assisted ARP workers in searching the debris for victims.

Observers estimated that only six of the thirty German raiders, FW 190s and ME 109s, which sped over the Channel under cover of clouds and with an escort of 100 fighter planes, reached London.

Heavy London Barrage

Heavy and light anti-aircraft guns opened up in the heart of London a half hour after the first warning was sounded. A heavy barrage lasted ten minutes.

The attackers blasted several houses, shops and a train in at least four other

(Continued on page 4)

U.S. Shipments To Russia Rise

WASHINGTON, Jan. 20—America has sent more than 3,200 tanks, 2,600 planes, 81,000 motor vehicles and other large quantities of war materials to Russia during the 15 month period ending Jan. 1, Edward R. Stettinius Jr., lend-lease administrator, said today.

The total of airplanes shipped to Russia under lend-lease agreements was larger than that sent to the United Kingdom or any other military theater under lend-lease, he reported.

In addition to the U.S. shipments, Stettinius declared, the United Kingdom has sent Russia over 2,600 tanks and over 2,000 planes on a similar basis.

November, 1942, was a record month for Russian shipments. Exports were 13 times the total sent in January, 1942. Two-thirds of the value of items sent were of a military nature and the balance was composed of industrial materials and food.

Yanks Keep One Eye On Sky, One On Vets

American soldiers have kept one eye on the sky and the other on London's veterans of the blitz during the air raids of the last four days.

Nazi bombs and English ack-ack are new to them, but they realize that the often-blitzed Londoner knows what to do better than anyone else in a raid.

So the Yank goes to the shelter when the Londoner does, and stands in doorways and windows watching the sky when the Londoner does.

His army training has taught him to be a bit more cautious about the flak which killed several civilians Sunday night. He stays clear of open sky but still peeks cautiously out at the aerial show.

No injuries to army personnel have been reported.

Tax Returns Due After War

Soldiers Given 3½ Months After Return to U.S. To File

Military personnel in the European Theater of Operations need not file Federal income tax returns until the 15th day of the third month after their return to the U.S., according to a Headquarters, ETO, announcement.

A circular issued in the ETO, quoting an opinion of the Judge Advocate General of the Army, set the date when returns are due from men serving outside the U.S. It applies to all individuals overseas, prisoners of war, beleaguered, etc.

Finance Department authorities yesterday held that "Victory Tax" payments, likewise, would not be deducted from soldiers' pay, although they would be taken from that of U.S. citizen civilians. All U.S. personnel, however, are subject to the tax as from Jan. 1, 1943, and eventually may be expected to pay it.

According to the Judge Advocate General's opinion quoted in the circular, an individual serving outside the continental United States is deemed to receive his entire pay at his station, regardless of allotments made by him. Military personnel need not include as items of gross income allowances for quarters, subsistence, uniforms, or equipment in connection with federal income tax.

Income tax returns will be available, the circular states, in all finance offices as soon as received.

Allied Victory in 1943 Predicted by Jim Farley

MEXICO CITY, Jan. 20 (AP)—James A. Farley, former Postmaster General, who is noted for the accuracy of his political predictions, said today that the Allies would defeat Germany before the end of this year.

"It is my honest opinion that Germany cannot last another winter, and after Germany collapses it should not take long to finish Japan," he said.

Reds Still Drive Nazis Westward On All Fronts

Stiff German Resistance On Leningrad-Volkhov Battle Area

MOSCOW, Jan. 20 (AP)—From the frozen Neva in Russia's far north to the Kuban in the northern Caucasus, the Red Army drove the defeated German armies ever westward.

The Germans put up their most stubborn resistance on the broken Leningrad-Volkhov front, where they still possess numerous fine fortifications, and an abundance of munitions, weapons and troops.

Red Star described a German stronghold on the Volkhov front as "the main stronghold in this sector." The heights governing the settlement were the key to the situation and there was a series of enemy defenses to be overcome.

Despite intensive shelling the Russians reached the German trenches in the north-eastern part while they were already carrying out an encircling movement to the west. The Germans rushed up reinforcements from the rear, and heavy fighting was still in progress.

At the same time Russian units on the Leningrad front were fighting stubbornly for another large center of resistance in two adjoining villages. Every foot of

(Continued on page 4)

News of Soviet Advance Brings Panic to Budapest

ISTANBUL, Jan. 20 (UP)—A wave of panic swept through Budapest yesterday afternoon after the issue of the Hungarian communique admitting the Russian break-through on the Voronezh sector held by the Hungarians, state the latest reports reaching Istanbul.

The panic was increased by a later announcement cancelling all army leave and asking men to rejoin their units a week earlier.

Many men will not be able to find their mauled units, which are retreating in disorder.

Exchange Stores Cut Prices; Cigarettes 2-4d, Juices 3-7d

A reduction in the price of cigarettes was announced today by the U.S. Army Quartermaster Exchange Stores in the ETO in conjunction with the circulation of a new price list.

Popular brands of cigarettes that previously sold for 6d. now cost 4d. Other brands have been cut to 2d. and 3d.

The new price list is already in effect in some Exchange Stores, and after today all stores throughout the European Theater of Operations will sell on the new scale.

Some of the reduced items on the new price list include toilet articles, lighter fluid, shaving cream, fruit juices and cookies.

New prices on some of the standard purchases are cigars 2d. and 4d., candy 2d. and 3d., chewing gum 2d., peanuts 1s., fig newtons 5d., vanilla wafers 2d., cheese niblets 2d., Colgate tooth paste and Lyons tooth powder 9d., cough drops 2d., Lifebuoy shaving cream 1s., Barbasol shaving cream 4d., shoe polish 4d., grapefruit juice 3d., orange juice 3d. and 7d., Edgeworth and Prince Albert smoking tobacco 5d., chewing tobacco 3d., and popular brands of soap 4d.

The reduction in prices is due to the non-profit operations of the QM Exchange Stores which recently took over the operation of these stores from the Army Post Exchange Service, it was pointed out.

Old prices prevailed until the QM could clear the shelves of PX stock and organize the handling of its own.

Atlantic U-Boat Sinkings Climbing, OWI Chief Says

WASHINGTON, Jan. 20 (UP)—U-boats have sunk more Allied shipping in the Atlantic so far this month than in the first 20 days of last month, it was revealed today by Elmer Davis, head of the Office of War Information.

The U-boat menace, he said, would remain serious for a long time to come, but other aspects of the war were much brighter.

1D. **THE STARS AND STRIPES** 1D.

Daily Newspaper of U.S. Armed Forces in the European Theater of Operations

Vol. 3 No. 69 | London, England | Friday, Jan. 22, 1943

Army Takes Over Posts In Solomons

Marines at Guadalcanal, In Combat Five Months, Are Given Rest

WASHINGTON, Jan. 21 (AP)—The United States Marines who knocked the Japs out of Henderson Airfield and then waged a campaign of elimination against enemy forces in the Guadalcanal jungle are headed for a rest today after spending more time in battle than any other unit of American troops in recent history.

Under-Secretary of War Robert Patterson disclosed today that Army ground troops have replaced the Marines in the Solomons under command of Maj. Gen. Alexander Patch, who moved his headquarters from New Caledonia to Guadalcanal.

"The Marines who fought so long and well in the Solomons are now getting a chance to rest," Mr. Patterson said.

Gen Patch, who commanded the Army troops which landed at New Caledonia last year, relieved Maj. Gen. Alexander Vandergrift, of the Marines, not quite a month ago, Mr. Patterson said.

Army There For Months

The Navy Department, announcing the change simultaneously, gave no indication of what assignment would be given to Gen. Vandergrift, who has been in command since the initial occupation of the position on the island.

"The Marines have been operating jointly with Army troops in this area for several months, during which period most of the Marines who made the original landing on Guadalcanal were replaced by Army personnel," a Navy communique said.

The Marines leaped from their landing barges onto the narrow beaches of Guadalcanal in August, 1942, and wrested the partially completed and strategically important airfield from its Japanese builders and pushed the enemy back into the jungle.

In Constant Warfare

Just when they were relieved cannot be stated, but they have been moving out of the Solomons in small groups for nearly a month prior to the announcement today. They had spent at least 150 days on the island in almost constant combat.

Available records show that the first division in France in the last war had the longest period in battle—223 days in the front line, including short training periods. The Marines on Guadalcanal lived a life of constant warfare, with patrol engagements under way at all hours and aerial attacks a nightly event. Sleep was snatched by day or night.

Gen. Patch, who is 53 years old, is a veteran of a quarter of a century of Army service. Born at Fort Huachuca, Ariz., son of an Army officer assigned there, he was graduated from West Point and went to France in the World War with the 18th Infantry.

At various times Gen. Patch has been stationed at Washington, Fort Benning, Ga.; Staunton Military Academy, Staunton, Va.; Ft. Eustis, Va; Ft. Bragg, N.C., and Camp Croft, S.C.

Gen. Vandergrift, who is 55, was born in Charlotteville, N.C. He was appointed a second lieutenant in the Marines in 1909 and attained his present rank in

(Continued on page 4)

New Guadalcanal Chief

Associated Press Photo

Maj. Gen. Alexander M. Patch

Camp Bound on Guadalcanal

Associated Press Photo

Wearing two-toed shoes for jungle tree climbing, a captured Jap fighter pilot walks with a U.S. Marine Corps interpreter through the hot damp jungle of Guadalcanal island in the Solomons, where American Army units took over this month, giving the Marines their first rest since occupation last August.

Britain's Reciprocal Aid to U.S. Grows as More Troops Arrive

WASHINGTON, Jan. 21 (AP)—An administration spokesman told newspapermen today that an increase in reciprocal aid from Great Britain was foreseen as the number of American troops abroad grew.

The spokesman, who declined to permit use of his name, stated that Britain had already spent $500,000,000 on construction for the American air forces in the United Kingdom alone. A vast amount of guns, ammunition, bombs, military engineers' equipment, shipping and other services were also given to the Americans not only in the British Isles, but throughout the Empire and North Africa. A large amount also had been sent to the United States, particularly in the months immediately following Pearl Harbor.

These and additional facts about the benefits of lease-lend will be presented to the ways and means committee of the House of Representatives when the appropriation for non-military lease-lend supplies is discussed next week.

The appropriation for military lease-lend includes War and Navy Department bills.

The spokesman also said that a considerable increase in lease-lend food exports was expected this year, with more supplies going to Russia than to Britain.

The statement was intended as preparatory to offset Republican criticism in Congress on lease-lend, which may be debated in the House of Representatives next week.

Cabled Money Orders Banned

Army Postal Order Only Method to Send Funds Home

Soldiers in the European Theater of Operations now may send money back to the States only by Army postal money order, it was announced yesterday by Army postal authorities.

Under new regulations funds no longer may be cabled home through the agency of a bank.

At the same time Army postal officials yesterday said they were unable to list a single item that a soldier in the ETO can request from home and still stay within new regulations.

The new regulations, designed to save shipping space, state that servicemen may ask the folks back home to send them only items which cannot be purchased or issued in this theater.

However, servicemen are still within their rights to seek permission from their battalion commanders to make a request. If written permission is granted, the soldier's family must show such approval to the home town post office before a package is accepted for shipment.

New Entertainment Unit Arrives to Give Shows

A new unit of stage, screen and radio entertainers has arrived in the British Isles to provide shows for the forces.

Julia Cummings, Peggy Alexander, "Stubby" Kaye, Paul Le Paul and Olya Klem comprise the unit, which has appeared before more than 200,000 soldiers in training camps in the States.

Maj. Theodore R. Phalen, Milwaukee, head of the Theatrical and Cinema Division, Special Service Section, SOS, who is handling their schedules, said the unit will take the road early next week.

Allies Nearing Hills Surrounding Tripoli; City Pounded by Air

Fleeing Axis Columns Are 'Strafers' Paradise'

CAIRO, Jan. 21 (UP)—"Strafers paradise"—That is how airmen returning from raids on Rommel's fleeing columns describe the road west from Tripoli, reporting that a solid line of traffic is leaving the city.

"We started fires among five or six miles of traffic moving in dispersed groups," said one pilot.

"Our pilots are shooting up these vehicles, blowing many of them up and starting many fires." The enemy's withdrawal is so hurried that the vehicles are traveling with all their lights on at night until they are attacked.

Red Offensives Gain in Fury On Vast Fronts

Soviets Capture Caucasus Prize, Important Rail Junction

MOSCOW, Jan. 21 (AP)—The Red Army's six major-scale offensives have not slackened anywhere along the vast front, and although there was no specific news today from the Leningrad-Volkhov sector, gains of from 10 to 20 miles and a considerable penetration of the Ukraine supported the theory that the tempo of the Soviet rushes was increasing rather than slowing down, despite the fact that the Russians at some places were battling in deep defenses with reinforced troops.

The latest and most impressive Caucasian prize was Nevinnomyskaya on the Kuban river. Situated on the Rostov-Baku railway, Nevinnomyskaya is also the junction for the line running into the mountains.

Down this branch line the Russians captured Ikonkhalk, Erkanshakhar, Erkankhalk and Klychevsky: all small towns, but the fact that they lay about 100 miles southeast of the Maikop oil-fields was the thing that counted.

The Red Army now has bases from which the direction of another blow could be aimed at the German-held oil lands. The forces advancing towards Stavropol are a threat from the north-east.

Feverish Nazi Efforts

Feverish efforts by the Germans to fix themselves on a stable line south of the unfrozen Manych river were failing.

A Red Star dispatch said that the Russians were pouring over the quiet, lake-like river, capturing populated points as the Germans were rapidly retreating, blowing up bridges and trying to lay more mines.

The Germans already were driven from a number of positions on Salsk side of

(Continued on page 4)

Quick Juncture With Axis in Tunisia, Rommel's Plan

By the Associated Press

Sweeping westward from Homs and northwest from Tarhuna, the Eighth Army yesterday neared the hills surrounding Tripoli without a pause in keeping its steady pressure on Rommel.

Under mounting air blows the Axis withdrawal was showing further signs of disorganization, but there was yet no authoritative indication that Tripoli it self was being evacuated, British military sources said.

While Gen. Montgomery's progress was eminently satisfactory, the sources warned against "crystal gazing." Reports from other parts of Africa credited the British with greater progress than they actually had made, it was pointed out. It was emphasized that after Tripoli at least another 100 miles of fighting must be done before the army could cross the border into Tunisia.

French Whereabouts Secret

The actual whereabouts of Gen. LeClerc's Fighting French forces was a secret, but British sources lauded their "masterly operation" of advancing 1,200 to 1,500 miles over difficult country and their capture of 700 prisoners, 40 guns and 18 tanks.

The British occupation of Tripoli was regarded as a matter of time—possibly a few days—but the Eighth Army's main objective and stiffer task was preventing the bulk of the remaining Axis forces from moving into Tunisia.

British observers, looking ahead of the Libyan offensive now in its final phases, declared the Tunisian campaign should be concluded by April if the Allies hope this summer to take full advantage of the North African springboard for a real European second front.

Tripoli Hit By Air

Allied aircraft smashed at targets in a close arc around the town of Tripoli yesterday. To the east, between Homs and Tripoli on the coastal road, enemy troops which were entrenched in defensive positions were attacked, while to the south and west streams of motor transport were strafed by continuous intruder patrols.

While fighters and fighter-bombers maintained a steady ring of pressure, American heavy bombers pounded at the harbor of the Tripolitanian capital. The daylight air offensive was followed on by relentless night attacks by aircraft of all types, including night fighters.

On land the Eighth Army continued to mop up pockets of resistance occupying Homs—onetime summer residence for Italian colonial officials—and Tarhuna, on top of the Jebel Nefuza range, which forms part of Tripoli's last natural defense line.

British Throw Foe Back

ON THE TUNISIAN FRONT, Jan. 20 (delayed) (AP)—British infantry and tanks which defeated the German effort to break through the Goubellat road defenses and to capture the Bou Arada area, followed up their success by pushing the Nazis back along the road from Bou Arada to Pont du Fahs.

The Germans, who had worked feverishly throughout the night to recover the knocked-out tanks they had sent along this road in a two-pronged attack on the British fell back slowly in the face of quick jabs and short enveloping movements.

Fortress Plunges 7,000 Feet As Pilot Fights for Control

A U.S. BOMBER STATION, England, Jan. 21—Controls gyrating so wildly that the pilot and co-pilot were hurled from their seats, a Flying Fortress plunged toward the English Channel.

Struck simultaneously on both wings by cannon fire from Nazi FW190s, the ship, which had just completed its bombing run over Lorient in a recent raid, twisted out of control and went into a dive.

While crew and everything movable within the Fortress were hurled about the interior, the big B17 screamed down from 10,000 feet. FWs followed its crazy course, firing. Ammunition spilled out of the racks and rattled around the metal skin of the ship until the crew thought the plane was breaking up.

At 3,000 feet Capt. E. E. Tribbett, Thornton, Ind., finally struggled back to the controls and wrenched the bomber out of its dive.

That was the story revealed yesterday by Eighth Air Force intelligence officers who interrogated the crew and pieced together the facts of the yarn over a period of several days.

One of a formation of heavy American bombers attacking the U-boat harbor that day, the ship was navigated by 2nd Lt. E. H. Vanhala of Duluth, Minnesota.

Arriving over the target, the Fortress made its bombing run. The bombardier, 2nd Lt. Julius Dorfman, of Philadelphia, Pa., got the sub pens squarely in his sights. They saw their bombs burst and Capt. Tribbett, a former Indiana carpenter, turned back to sea.

Almost immediately they were intercepted by six enemy fighters which circled overhead, diving in pairs. The tail gunner, S/Sgt. C. S. Johns, San Jose, Cal., shot down two of them in flames. At the same time a cannon shell ripped into his own turret, causing such heat that his oxygen mask melted away and his ammunition box caught fire. As he was forced back into the waist of the ship, the

(Continued on page 4)

Nazi 'Peace Plan' Trap Is Described by Davies

LOS ANGELES, Jan. 21 (AP)—Joseph Davies, former U.S. Ambassador to Russia, revealed that in 1940 he was approached by a Nazi spokesman at a New York conference suggested by "certain well-meaning citizens of our own country" with a proposed peace treaty to be signed by the German military or other government officials, under which Hitler would be "retired."

Mr. Davies said on the face of it their proposal seemed very fair, but careful study showed the condition for this peace was that Germany should "keep the dominant place it had achieved by conquest in Europe and be permitted to project its new order in Europe without interference."

"I made it clear to these gentlemen that in my opinion it was an impossible peace," Mr. Davies said.

THE STARS AND STRIPES

U. S. Army Newspaper
Published Weekly in Africa

Through Facilities of
Stars and Stripes and Yank

Vol. 1 - No. 8 - Wednesday, January 27, 1943 | ALGIERS | TWO FRANCS

FDR, Churchill Meet in Casablanca; Demand "Unconditional Surrender"

Tripoli Falls; 8th Army Pursuing Axis Remnants

Voronezh Taken As Russian Attack Gains Ground

With forces of Generals Montgomery and Anderson executing the pincer movements on a scale unheard of by the Nazis, in their squeeze play on Tunisia; with the Russians advancing along two-thirds of the 2,000 mile front, occupying Voronezh and threatening the Axis anchor point of Rostov; and the Japs being pushed back steadily in the 'ferocious fighting in the South Seas, forces of the United Nations are on the offensive on every front in the world.

NORTH AFRICA

As the British 8th Army swept by Tripoli and neared a junction with the Allied forces under General Dwight Eisenhower in the West, the Axis armies in Africa are crowded into the narrow corridor of Tunisia. The fall of Tripoli marked the end of Mussolini's dreams of a Roman Empire. Now Il Duce has only his dissafisfied country, tiny Albania and the Dodecanese Islands under his ever-weakening rule.

And as units of the British 7th Armored division, the famous "desert rats," entered Tripoli, Allied submarines sank the one millionth ton of Axis shipping in the Italian "Mare Nostrum" and Montgomery was closer to Algiers than he was to Benghazi, his last big port to the East. Soldiers set to work immediately repairing the port so that it may be used for ships that come the more than 1,000 miles from Alexandria that Montgomery has chased Rommel. Italians said that the evacuation was part of a plan, offered as proof the fact that the British encountered no resistance. The German radio announced that Rommel was "continuing his advance to the West," shortening his lines of communications and consolidating his forces with those of General Von Armin, commander of the Axis army in Tunisia.

Rommel, who, only a few months ago was looking down on Alexandria and preparing for a victory march into it, is now entering Tunisia, with the battered fragments of the once-proud Afrika Korps dependent on the success of the drive to the West by Von Armin to hold off Anderson while they reach safety. The best that the Axis can hope for is either a drawn-out siege or an evacuation from the bomb battered ports of the East coast and Bizerta.

Von Armin's drive down the East side of the Ousseltia valley was held after the Germans captured the hill of Djebel Bou Dabous. From advanced airports on both sides of the Axis, Allied bombers were dumping tons of high explosives on the ports of Bizerta, Sfax, Sousse and LaGoulette. Elsewhere, the front has been comparatively quiet.

RUSSIA

On the Russian front, although the Germans seemed to be fighting desperately, the Red Army contin-

(Continued on Page 3)

THE PRIME MINISTER

THE PRESIDENT

HOME FRONT: Airplane Crash Takes 35 Lives

Author Eric Knight, Wm. Hodson Die

WASHINGTON—The most disastrous accident in American airplane history took place recently off the coast of Surinam, in the northeastern part of South America, where 26 passengers and nine crew members lost their lives.

Among those killed when the big four-motored American transport plane crashed, were Army's Major Eric Knight, author of the best seller, "This Above All," William Hodson, New York City Commissioner of Welfare, P. L. Foxworth, assistant director of the F. B. I., in charge of the New York City office and a specialist on sabotage cases, Morris Lewis, volunteer writer for the soldier's pocket-book guide, and Capt. Basil Gallagher, who was on a mission for Yank, the Army weekly.

Frances Isn't Crazy

LOS ANGELES — Mrs. Lillian Farmer, mother of film actress Frances Farmer, said: "My daughter is no more insane than you or I. She just needs a rest." Frances is now under observation in the psychopathic ward of a hospital. She recently was sentenced to six months in jail for failing to pay all of the previous 250 dollar fine for drunken driving and also a

(Continued on Page 3)

Tour Thru Camp Startles Troops

By RALPH MARTIN
(Stars and Stripes Staff Writer)

RABAT, Jan. 26—Surprise is too mild a word to describe how the troops felt when their Commander-in-Chief unexpectedly dropped in to look them over one day last week. Since nobody had dreamed that the President was any nearer to North Africa than Washington, they were simply overwhelmed.

The GI's first recognized the familiar, unmistakable Roosevelt countenance as the President, riding in the back seat of a jeep, drove past a line of tanks, trucks, ambulances and men. Riding with him were Harry Hopkins, the President's personal adviser, and Lt. Gen. Mark W. Clark, commander of the new 5th Army.

Driving the President's jeep was S-Sgt. Oran E. Lass, of Kansas City, Mo., who was altogether the proudest soldier of the day. Sgt.

(Continued on Page 3)

Official Communique

CASABLANCA, Jan. 26—Here is the text of the official communique released at the end of the President's and Prime Minister's ten-day conference:

January 24, 1943

The President of the United States and the Prime Minister of Great Britain have been in conference near Casablanca since January 14. They were accompanied by the combined Chiefs of Staff of the two countries, namely, for the United States: General George C. Marshall, Chief of Staff, U. S. Army; Admiral E. J. King, Commander-in-Chief, U. S. Navy; Lieut. General H. H. Arnold, Commanding U. S. Army Air Forces, and for Great Britain: Admiral of the Fleet Sir Dudley Pound, First Sea Lord; General Sir Alan Brooks, Chief of the Imperial General Staff; Air Chief Marshal Sir Charles Portal, Chief of the Air Staff.

These were assisted by: Lieut. General B. B. Somervel, Commanding General, Services of Supply, U. S. Army; Field Marshal Sir John Dill, Head of the British Joint Staff Mission in Washington; Vice Admiral Lord Louis Mountbatten, Chief of Combined Operations; Lieut. General Sir Hastings Ismay, Chief Staff Officer to the Minister of Defense, together with a number of staff officers from both countries.

They have received visits from Mr. Murphy and Mr. Macmillan; from General Eisenhower, the Commander-in-Chief Allied Expeditionary Force in North Africa; from Adrimal of the Fleet Sir Andrew Cunningham, Naval Commander Allied Expeditionary Force in North Africa; from General Spaatz, Air Commander Allied Expeditionary Force in North Africa; from General Clark, U. S. Army; and from Middle East Headquarters, from General Sir Harold Alexander, Air Chief Marshal Sir Arthur Tedder and Lieut. General F. M. Andrews, U. S. Army.

The President was accompanied by Mr. Harry Hopkins and was

(Continued on Page 3)

CASABLANCA, Jan. 26—After the historic Roosevelt-Churchill press conference President Roosevelt, at Mr. Churchill's suggestion, asked the correspondents to come by, shake hands and give their names and papers.

When meeting *The Stars and Stripes* representative, the President stopped him and began to ask questions. He asked whether it was possible to print the paper daily, what kind of presses we used and whether we had enough newsprint on hand to supply the American soldiers with reading matter. The President was interested in the fact that *The Stars and Stripes* had been using French presses and borrowed French newsprint.

President Calls For Destruction Of "Philosophy Of Hate" And End Of Axis War Power

By ROBERT NEVILLE
(Stars and Stripes Staff Writer)

CASABLANCA, Jan. 26—The President of the United States and the Prime Minister of Great Britain have just ended here an unprecedented ten-day conference at which Allied military plans for the year 1943 were formulated.

Arriving at Casablanca by air and in all secrecy, Mr. Roosevelt and Mr. Churchill brought with them the chiefs of the American and British Army, Navy and Air Forces, who immediately settled down to a routine of working 18 hours a day. The war was reviewed theater by theater and decisions were made which, although now military secrets of the highest order, will doubtless become apparent as the events of the year unfold.

But more came out of the conference than purely military plans. In an informal press interview held at the end of the meeting on the lawn of a handsome modernistic villa, the President and Prime Minister also served notice on Germany, Italy and Japan that those nations need not ever ask for peace terms. Nothing less than the "unconditional surrender" of the Axis could be accepted, the President said and he asked the press to call this meeting at Casablanca the "unconditional surrender" conference.

"Unconditional surrender," the President explained, did not mean the destruction of Axis populations, but rather the destruction of their philosophy of hate and fear which causes the subjugation of other peoples. Only by the total elimination of the Axis war power, the President said, can the world again have a reasonable assurance of peace.

Premier Joseph Stalin, of Russia, was invited to become a third party to the conference, but because of the winter Russian offensive, which Premier Stalin as Commander-in-Chief of the Red Army is personally directing, he was unable to come. The decisions of the conference, one of which was to relieve the Nazi pressure on Russia in every possible way, have already been communicated to the Kremlin.

It was the first time since Woodrow Wilson attended the Versailles peace conference that an American President had crossed the Atantic while in office and the visit gave President Roosevelt his first opportunity to see American troops in a theater of war. The Commander-in-Chief of all U. S. armed forces spent a day in the field, rode in a jeep, ate a GI lunch served in a mess kit from a portable field kitchen and reviewed both infantry and armored units. After that he visited a war cemetery near Port Lyautey, where he placed wreaths on both American and French graves.

The President, at the press conference, said he had found the troops in "excellent health and high spirits" and the Army in a "state of great efficiency." "I'm sure they are eager to fight again," he added.

During his stay in French North Africa the President also gave a dinner party for the Sultan of Morrocco, Sidi Mohammed, and his son, the heir to the throne. Mr. Roosevelt also paid tribute to the French who were killed during the Allied landing last November, adding that after the armistice was signed the French civil and military authorities gave the Allied Forces complete cooperation. The President added that the time was past when the population of North Africa would be robbed of the food they produce.

But the conference was practically all work and very little play. For this period a large part of the general staffs of London and Washington were brought to Casablanca. For these days this shining white city on the Atlantic, with its white stucco buildings, its Moorish architecture, its spirited Arabian horses and its bicycle taxis, became the capital of the Allied war effort. The mixed Arab, Spanish and French population living here was unaware that a conference of such proportions was taking place practically on its doorstep.

A large section of a rich and modern suburb, situated on a rolling hilltop overlooking the city, was commandeered for the occasion. Several strands of barbed wire were strung around the area, while sentries patrolled every inch of the territory night and day. A constant and impressive air patrol was always to be heard and seen overhead.

Allied military chiefs came from far and wide to this secluded and protected spot to confer with the President and Prime Minister. Accompanying the President were Gen. George C. Marshall, Chief of Staff of the U. S. Army; Admiral E. J. King, Commander-in-Chief of the U. S. Navy, and Lt. Gen. H. H. Arnold, commanding

(Continued on Page 3)

THE STARS AND STRIPES

U. S. Army Newspaper
Published Weekly in Africa

Through Facilities of
Stars and Stripes and Yank

Vol. 1 - No. 11 - Wednesday, February 17, 1943 ALGIERS TWO FRANCS

Germans Launch Two Big Central Tunisian Drives

Gafsa Evacuated As U. S. Troops Face Nazi Veterans

American troops are now engaged in their first major battle with the Germans in the African campaign as two Nazi columns of tanks and infantry drive toward Sbeitla in an all-out attempt to gain unhampered control of the central coastal corridor in Tunisia.

Field Marshal Erwin Rommel's forces in central Tunisia, only recently arrived from Tripoli, struck to the west at 0700 hours last Sunday. Heavily supported by Stukas and tanks, one column drove almost directly west from the Faid district, and at last reports was within 15 miles of Sbeitla. The second, launching its attacks from further south, at first drove toward Gafsa and suddenly swung northwest, thus attempting to execute a pincer movement.

TANKS IN BATTLE

Held by only a small American force, Gafsa was evacuated and our position was established some 40 miles to the north. Armored units of the German army entered Gafsa at 1630 hours Monday to complete an advance of 20 miles.

Bitter fighting is taking place southwest of Faid, with American armored units counter-attacking. We continue to hold high ground over an extended area in this district, but the battle is still joined and the result at this writing inconclusive. Losses have been severe on both sides. At least 20 German tanks have been knocked out and our artillery has been hard hit. The Germans in this drive are veteran soldiers from a division of Rommel's famed Afrika Korps.

While it is too early to guess Rommel's intentions, it appears he is attempting to widen his territory through the sheer necessity of obtaining more room for his operations in Tunisia.

"He won the first round," admitted a U. S. Army spokesman, "but his movement could not be termed a complete surprise."

AIR FORCES ACTIVE

Air forces on each side have been unusually active in supporting troops and bombing objectives. Stukas were responsible for many of the American casualties, while our planes maintained a dawn-to-dusk offensive on enemy positions.

Eleven enemy aircraft were destroyed Monday alone, with three of our planes missing. Spitfires and P-38's destroyed nine trucks, one half-track and other cars. Eight gun posts were silenced. Two waves of bombers — B-26's and B-25's — blasted the airdrome at Kairouan. Many fires and huge columns of smoke resulted.

As an added measure, Fortresses struck at the harbor of Palermo, Sicily in their first daylight attack on this objective. Hits were observed on the dock area, oil tanks and a large vessel.

Jap Forces Abandon Guadalcanal Island

WASHINGTON — After six long months of desperate fighting, the Japanese have quit Guadalcanal in the Solomon Islands, Secretary of Navy Frank Knox announced last week. Tokyo confirmed the operation on the same day.

The move is characterized here as a "major rout and catastrophe" for the Jap forces. The Jap losses during the various battles amounted to 50,000 men, more than 1,100 planes, 71 warships and transports sunk and 11 more probably damaged. The Jap evacuation cost the enemy seven destroyers and 8,000 casualties.

U. S. Marines first landed on the shores of Guadalcanal on Aug. 8. The Japs staged three terrific attempts to recapture the island and airport, but failed with costly results.

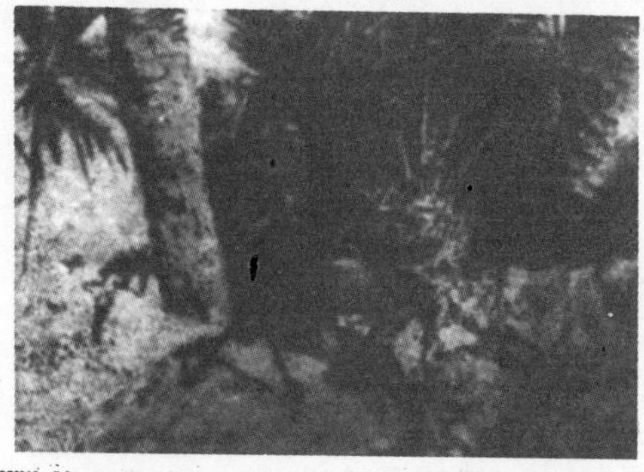

With his weather eye peeled for the enemy, Pvt. SAM de CRISTO, of Rome, N. Y., is on the alert at an advanced infantry position on the Tunisian front. His automatic rifle is ready at a moment's notice.

Roosevelt And Churchill Promise Action In 1943

LONDON—The position of the United Nations in the fourth year of the war was reviewed by Prime Minister Winston Churchill last week before an enthusiastic House of Commons which had waited impatiently for the British leader's return from the Casablanca conference and from a swing around the Near East to Turkey.

Speaking in a sober but generally optimistic tone, the Prime Minister told his audience which interrupted him frequently with sustained applause, that the Allies had formulated plans of action for the next nine months.

TURKEY OUR ALLY

Commenting on the state of Anglo-Turkish relations, the Prime Minister stated emphatically: "Turkey is our ally and our friend and we hope that her territory, her rights and her interests will be preserved at all costs."

Comforting words were expressed on the U-boat menace which the Prime Minister did not attempt to minimize. Here he spoke confidently and frankly. Mr. Churchill declared that during the last three months the Allies have been destroying enemy submarines at double the rate of last year.

Mr. Churchill also stated that "the merchant fleet of the United Nations has more than 1,000,000 more tons than it had six months ago."

How the striking power of enemy submarines has been diminishing was described by the Prime Minister. He said according to figures from the Admiralty, one German submarine during the first year was considered to have accounted for 19 ships; 12 during the second year of the war, and seven during the third year of the war.

WASHINGTON, D. C.—Determination of the Allies to end the war as quickly as possible on the uncompromising terms of "unconditional surrender" applies to Japan as well as to Nazi Germany, President Roosevelt declared in a Lincoln's Day address before the White House Correspondents Association.

In his first public address since his return from the Casablanca conference, the President stressed the complete accord between the United States and Great Britain on pooling all their resources with China in the out-and-out final attack on Japan should Germany be conquered first.

Mr. Roosevelt told how Prime Minister Winston Churchill desired to make a formal agreement along these lines and that he told the Prime Minister no formal statement or agreement was the least bit necessary. "The American people accept the word of a great English gentleman," was the President's tribute to Mr. Churchill.

BATTLE OF TUNISIA

Discussing the massing of the British, French and American Armies in North Africa for one of the major battles of the war, the President said the enemy's purpose in the battle of Tunisia is to hold at all costs their last bridgehead in Africa, and to prevent the Allies from gaining control of the straits that led to Nazi-dominated Europe.

"Our prime purpose," Mr. Roosevelt asserted, "in this battle of Tunisia is to drive our enemies into the sea."

The President emphasized the high costs in maintaining supply

(Continued on Page 2)

Reds Capture Rostov, Open Three - Pronged Assault On Kharkov

German Retreat Threatened By Disaster As Russians Continue Steady Sweep From Don Area Toward Dneiper

Rostov, gateway to the Caucasus, resounded early this week to the triumphant echoes of the boots of the marching Red Army soldiers who recaptured this key city at the mouth of the Don, and thus climaxed a Russian winter offensive that has smashed the power of the mighty Wehrmacht in the Caucasus and the Donetz Basin.

The loss of Rostov, an important port and railway junction, with a population of 500,000, was as severe a blow as the Nazis have sustained in a winter of rude shocks. Only a few days before Russian troops entered the city, Nazi officials had distributed posters advising: "Don't listen to rumors. We are not leaving Rostov."

Further to the northwest, the Soviet troops were wheeling their big guns up within range of Kharkov. They were advancing upon the city from three sides and were reported within five miles of the capital of the Ukraine and chief Nazi supply base. Already there were indications that the Nazis were evacuating Kharkov, which has been in German hands since September, 1940.

Gathering momentum like a rolling snowball, the successful Russian offensive, now in its third month, has presented the German high command with the strategical problem of averting a full disaster by maintaining a semblance of a controlled retreat westward to the Dneiper River.

SOVIET SWEEPS ON

The amazing sweep of the Soviet Armies through the Donetz Basin has more than nullified the German gains of the last summer's campaign. An idea of the scope of the Russian drive is given by one report which points out that the Russians have regained territory, more than half the size of Germany.

Following the epic victory at Stalingrad and the liquidation of the Nazi forces in that area, the Red Armies have cut a wide swathe through the southern Caucasus and the Don region. When the week was over, the winter forces of the Russian Armies extended from a point west of Orel, approximately 150 miles north of Kharkov, down through Rostov and south to another key railway junction, Krasnodar, in the Kuban region.

SUPPLIES TRAPPED

In the wake of the speedy Soviet advance were large stores of German supplies and thousands of Nazi prisoners trapped by the skillfully executed enveloping movements of the Red Armies. At Voronezh alone, the last German spearhead on the Don, the Russians have captured more than 75,000 officers and men.

In their defensive strategy the Nazis reckoned without the brilliant and unconventional tactics of Marshal Semyon Timoshenko and his aides. The Red Armies accomplished the seemingly impossible. They left the expected routes of attack and struck over areas heavily covered by snow. How they managed to transport their men and equipment to execute devastating double envelopments on Nazi strongholds is still not explained by cautious Russian communiques.

Tribute to the Red Armies was

(Continued on Page 2)

Four Stars, Full Command Here For Eisenhower

Dwight D. Eisenhower has been promoted from lieutenant general to full general and simultaneously with his promotion, Gen. Eisenhower has been placed in supreme command of Allied North African operations.

Under the new four-star American general will come Gen. Sir

New Four-Star General

Harold Alexander, who has been the British chief of the Middle East Command; Air Marshal Sir Arthur Tedder, who will be in command of air operations in the

(Continued on Page 2)

Guardhouse Artist Draws Repentant Cartoons

TUNISIAN FRONT — Sgt. Kenneth Farmer was a section leader of machine guns until that night when the court martial met in the dining room of a hotel in this place. They sat Kenneth down in a chair facing the court assembled and threw the book at him. He thereupon became a private and went to the jug.

Kenneth admits he deserved the jug. He had been a special MP, assigned to defend the law, and somehow he got hold of a big bottle of vin rouge. But the details don't matter.

What does matter is that he's an artist. The night he faced the court martial, the major who was performing the duties of chief justice had trouble controlling his features when the captain, sitting next to him, passed him a small scrap of paper signed by Kenneth Farmer, drawn in the guardhouse while Kenneth was awaiting trial.

It was a cartoon of the court sitting on his case. The major, who is ordinarily a happy man, was drawn with a face as stern as an Anti-Saloon Leaguer. The other members of the court didn't look any more affable. The balloons drawn above most of the court members said: "Guilty as hell!" Variations on this theme included: "Give him three months." "I raise you six." "Make it a year."

The guardhouse for this infantry outfit is small, square and has white calcimined walls. For the average jailbird, there's nothing to do in a guardhouse but sit. For the special type of convict, a jail is a fine place to be if you want to get away from things and do a little creative work. Adolf Hitler wrote "Mein Kampf" in prison; Jawaharlal Nehru, the Indian nationalist, wrote his fine autobiography; Leon Trotsky penned most of his abstruse political theory in jail and ex-Sgt. Kenneth Farmer became a muralist on the whitewashed walls of his guardhouse cell.

In one month, Kenneth has worn out several lead pencils he borrowed from his fellow-inmates, who are great admirers of his work. They like the back view of a voluptuous blonde, who stands on one side of a home-made calendar, in which the dates are ticked off day by day.

Then there's a drawing of Pluto, running in circles, evidently trying to get out of the room. Below a sign that says: "There's No Place Like Home" is a drawing of Broad St. and Market in Farmer's home town on a busy day. There's one elaborately printed sign that says: "Buy U. S. War Bonds—Help Win the War."

The masterpiece of the whitewashed walls is a drawing of a chaplain holding the Bible facing the prisoner, pointing a finger and saying: "You are a bad boy!" The prisoner, dressed in a striped suit, has horns coming out behind his ears, carries a pitchfork and looks extremely repentant.

Kenneth Farmer, the artist, will continue to draw until the pencils run out, the walls cave in or his sentence expires. When that happens, he'll go back to his machine guns. His friends say he can draw a pretty sharp line with .30 caliber lead, too and Farmer's anxious to get back to work.

Allies Land 780 Ships Lose Under 2 Percent

Seven hundred and eighty ships have landed six and one-half million tons of supplies at North African ports since the Allied landing it was revealed this week by Admiral Sir Andrew Cunningham, Allied Naval Commander in the Western Mediterranean.

Less than two per cent of the number of ships coming to North Africa have been sunk, the Admiral added.

"Axis attacks on Mediterranean convoys have become better organized and planned than before," he said, "but so has our defense."

1D. **THE STARS AND STRIPES** 1D.

Daily Newspaper of U.S. Armed Forces in the European Theater of Operations

Vol. 3 No. 100 London, England Saturday, Feb. 27, 1943

Panzers in Full Retreat Beyond Pass

How It Feels to Bomb Germany . . .

By Andrew A. Rooney

Stars and Stripes Staff Writer

A U.S. BOMBER STATION, Feb. 26—From the nose of Lt. Bill Casey's Banshee, I saw American Fortresses and Liberators drop a load of destruction on Wilhelmshaven today.

We flew to Germany in the last group of a Fortress formation and Banshee was in the trailing squadron.

Soon after dawn the bombers thundered down the runway. Lt. Casey's windshield was splattered with mud on the way. It really was a blind take-off.

Like a pickup football team on a Saturday morning, we grew in strength as we flew, until all England seemed to be covered with bombers.

Everything was quiet—almost monotonous—for an hour after we left the English coast.

Sees First Enemy Plane

Then the trouble began.

Peeling out of the sun came shining silver German fighter planes, diving at one bomber in the formation and disappearing below the cloudbanks as quickly as they had come. They seemed tiny, hardly a machine of destruction, and an impossible target.

Andy Rooney . . . went to Germany

My first glimpse of a German fighter came when the navigator, 2nd Lt. William H. Owens, of Tullahoma, Tenn., nearly knocked me into the lap of 2nd Lt. Malcolm A. Phillips Jr., the bombardier, whose home is in Coffeyville, Kan. Owens swung around at what appeared to be an Me109 as it whipped down through the clouds on our left.

From that time until three and one-half hours later, when we were half way home, no one had to look far to see a German fighter. They were all over and they were all kinds of planes—Me109s, Ju88s and Me110s. There were no FW190s, by far the best plane Jerry has to fight the Forts. Their absence strengthened Allied contentions that Germany is desperately short of fighter planes.

From a vantage point in the pilot's cabin Lt. Casey and his co-pilot, 1st Lt. Kelly G. Ross, were calmly giving information over the inter-com.

"Here comes one at 2 o'clock, Elliott. Get the son-of-a-bitch."

T/Sgt. Wilson C. Elliott, of Detroit, Lt. Casey's top turret man, is the only man from the original Banshee crew left.

Before we were very deep into Germany deadly black puffs began to appear around us. It seemed as though they were "air mines" that were touched off as we came to them. A puff would appear to our right and then in quick succession a row of five more black splotches flowered out, each one closer as they caught up to us.

Lt. Casey zigged, and the puffs appeared in the tracks of our zag. He was one jump ahead of the flak. All but once he was one jump ahead.

Thought Plane's Nose Torn Off

Lt. Phillips was leaning far forward in the nose, between his guns and bomb-sight, when suddenly the whole nose seemed to break out of the ship. My first impression was that they had given up the flak and had thrown the gun at us.

Lt. Phillips sat back on his heels and covered his eyes with his hands. Splinters of flexiglass formed coating over his helmet. It was a minute before he recovered from the shock to open his eyes and find that he could see and was unhurt.

What appeared to be the nose being ripped off actually was only a small hole the size of a man's fist.

The formation was perfect, and the German sky dotted with Forts in front of us and Liberators behind us was comforting. Below, the land seemed to be farmland for the most part. Even that was divided into aggravatingly square plots. It looked German and unfriendly. You had the feeling you would have known it was Germany even if you hadn't attended the briefing.

German flak didn't seem to bother German fighter planes. They poured in even when their own flak was thickest.

Approaching the bombing run, the doors of the ships in front of us could

(Continued on page 4)

Allied Tanks, Planes Blast Fleeing Foe

8th Army Pilots Also Hit Columns Withdrawing Toward Gafsa

ALLIED HQ, North Africa, Feb. 26 (AP)—Pursued by Allied ground and air forces, Rommel's panzers appeared in full retreat in southern Tunisia today. American and British infantry and armored formations snatched the initiative by recapturing the vital Kasserine Pass.

Tommies and doughboys drove up the mountains on each side of the pass yesterday afternoon, driving the Germans into the foothills beyond and allowing the British and American tanks through the gap on the heels of Rommel's withdrawing forces.

By day and night American and British bombers and fighters poured destruction on panzer columns moving southward towards Gafsa.

Bisleys raided Gafsa and Sbeitla, giving the Germans no rest. Pilots reported large fires in both places. The Middle East air forces were working in close cooperation all the time, giving a hand in chasing Rommel.

Engineers Remove Mines

United States forces on the Tunisian front regained Kasserine Pass—the vital gateway to the Hatab Valley—without a fight after the enemy's columns had retreated through the gap and continued to move southward through Feriana, presumably towards Gafsa. The wide valley through which the battle raged for three days was strangely serene as American engineers moved gingerly forward through the pass, lifting elaborate minefields which the Germans and Italians had left to protect their retreat.

The quiet was broken only by the occasional detonation of a mine. British units also edged down the Thala road removing mines left behind when the German tanks retreated along that route after their thrust northward had been doomed by Allied blows at their flank.

Approximately a dozen light Italian tanks, some of whose armor was pierced by American .50-caliber guns, were left on the field, but the Germans had removed their own disabled tanks.

Eisenhower Back from Front

(Gen. Eisenhower returned to Allied Headquarters in North Africa Thursday from the Tunisian front, United Press said. He watched the turning of the German tide at Kasserine and had long conferences with Gen. Alexander and with Gen. Fredenhall, who commands in the southern sector.)

Over the battle area, American fighters maintained constant patrol making harassing attacks on German tank forces.

There were no reports of land activity from the Eighth Army, but Middle East bombers carried on a softening-up process against Axis positions with a raid on the Mareth Line.

American and British infantry wrested the last remnant of the initiative from the German panzers by attacking the mountains on either side of the Kasserine Pass yesterday, allowing Allied tanks to proceed five miles through the pass itself to the eastern mouth.

Further north in the Sbiba area the Germans were in flight, pursued by Allied forces which reached within nine miles of Sbeitla.

Allied forces progressed 15 miles from Sbiba, while it was not known how far beyond the Kasserine Pass the American and British armored units have gone.

Reports from the front gave no indication how far the Germans plan to retreat before making a stand, but it was clear that Rommel has lost the initiative he has

(Continued on page 4)

Wilhelmshaven Blasted Second Time by Yanks

Fortresses and Liberators Smash at Naval Base; Seven Planes Lost

Flying Fortresses and Liberators bombed Wilhelmshaven again yesterday. It was the second daylight attack on the Nazi naval base by U.S. planes and the war's third American raid on Germany proper.

The Eighth Air Force bomber crews fought off heavy enemy fighter opposition to press home their attack on the port, at which a considerable portion of Nazi U-boats are constructed. Crews reported direct hits.

Seven bombers were reported missing from the mission.

Enemy fighters went up to meet the Americans before the formation reached its target, pressed home attacks during the bombing run and followed the American planes for some distance back over the North Sea.

There was no estimate of the number of enemy fighters shot down.

RAF fighter squadrons met the bombers on the way home and escorted them through the latter part of the journey.

Enemy fighters, which followed the bomber formations some 30 miles back over the North Sea after a running fight up to and over the target, consisted largely of Me109s, Ju88s, and Me110s. While some formations were attacked by FW190s, crews of other groups reported that not a single FW190 had been seen, possible indication of severe strain on the Nazi fighting strength, since the Focke Wulf is the Luftwaffe's best weapon against the heavy U.S. bombers.

While some squadrons reported lighter

(Continued on page 4)

German Home Affairs Now In Goebbels' Hands

STOCKHOLM, Feb. 26 (UP)—Hitler is devoting his whole time to military matters in Germany, the newspaper Aftonbladet said today, leaving the whole "home front" administration to four men, headed by Dr. Joseph Paul Goebbels.

Soldiers going to the front, the paper's former Berlin correspondent wrote, get only six weeks training. Much of it consists of lectures on the outlook of a good Nazi. This indoctrination is considered necessary since most of the reservists are lukewarm in their support of the Nazi Party.

U.S. Air Force to Match Axis, Giving Allies 2-to-1 Odds by '44

WASHINGTON, Feb. 26—An American air force equal to the entire Axis air strength by the end of 1943, giving the combined Allied forces a two-to-one advantage over their enemies, was revealed today to be the goal of U.S. military officials. It also was disclosed that the Army intends to have a total overseas force of 4,750,000 by the end of 1944.

The figures were made public by the Senate Appropriations Subcommittee, which is inquiring into U.S. manpower problems, particularly whether the nation can support an armed force of 11,100,000 by the end of 1943 as the War and Navy Departments plan.

Donald Nelson, chairman of the War Production Board, told the committee yesterday the United States could equip and maintain such an armed force without cutting civilian economy down to bedrock.

Lt. Gen. Joseph T. McNarney, deputy chief of staff, said an Army Air Force of 900 squadrons projected for this year to match the Axis would include a personnel of 2,450,000 men. His testimony along with that of witnesses during the month of closed hearings, was made public today.

This force, added to the 900 squadrons of the other United Nations, would give the Allies a two-to-one superiority, Gen. McNarney said. The Axis, including Japan, has 900 squadrons consisting of 25 fighters and eight bombers.

The testimony showed that the Axis probably would retain its superiority in ground forces next year despite the increase in the American armed forces.

(Continued on page 4)

Fourth of Food Going to Forces

But Ample Supply Left To Feed America, Wickard Says

WASHINGTON, Feb. 26—Secretary of Agriculture Claude R. Wickard said here yesterday that approximately one quarter of the food produced in the United States this year will go to fill military and lease-lend requirements.

In order that supplies be available for American soldiers and those of other nations joined with the United States in the war, American civilians will have to hold their total consumption to pre-war levels, he declared.

Secretary Wickard said that 20 to 25 per cent of the nation's beef output, practically all of it for the American Army, would be required; 30 to 35 per cent of the pork output, 25 to 30 per cent of the nation's eggs, 15 to 20 per cent of the butter and 40 to 45 per cent of the cheese would all be unavailable to civilians. But the situation, he said warranted "neither complacence nor hysteria."

'Enough Food'

"I have told the American people numerous times in recent months," he said, "that there is going to be enough food for essential diets in this country, provided we manage our foods wisely."

Secretary Wickard said the most notable change in the supply of staple foodstuffs for civilians was in dried peas and beans.

"We started 1943 with a record supply of those" he said, "but during the first six weeks of the year it became apparent that the needs for shipment to the fighting fronts and for accumulating reserves of these easily-stored foods against future contingencies, would take more than we had calculated early in January."

As a result, Wickard said, civilians will receive about two pounds less of these foods during 1943 than they did last year.

Wickard explained that the "Russian Allies need 5,000,000 bags of beans out of our total of 23,000,000 bags for their troops who are breaking the back of the Axis power in Europe."

Stiff Resistance Slows Russians In Donetz Basin

Weather Hinders Drives As Well, But More Villages Are Taken

MOSCOW, Feb. 26 (UP)—With heavy air and land reinforcements, the Germans have forced slower Russian progress on the fronts west of Kharkov and near Orel, and are making a determined bid to send their tanks and motorized forces behind the Red Army's lines in the Donetz Basin.

Here furious battles are raging, particularly between Kramatorskaya and Krasnoarmeisk, where the Germans are attacking in great force to try and restore the strategic communications of the area.

In spite of this greatly increased resistance, however, the Russians are continuing to push on even though progress is slower.

The weather is no longer on the side of the Russians. The Donetz fighting areas are a morass, roads are quagmires, without any snow.

The heaviest fighting in the Donetz Basin is centered between Krasnoarmeisk and Kramatorskaya and southwest of Voroshilovgrad.

On the latter front the Russians have managed to push ahead and capture a

(Continued on page 4)

Yanks Took Pass Without a Shot After 155s Finished Their Job

By Philip Ault

United Press War Correspondent

WITH UNITED STATES FORCES, Kasserine Pass, Feb. 25 (delayed)—United States troops occupied the Kasserine Pass this morning without firing a shot, after shelling it all night. The German artillery withdrew during the night, leaving heavy minefields to delay the pursuit.

The Germans are also believed to have left the town of Kasserine and withdrawn their main forces from the Gafsa area.

American 155-mm. guns—called into action on this front for the first time—fired into the pass for hours during the night. Then, at 6.30 A.M. the infantry attacked over the right shoulder of the pass, but met with no opposition. Next a tank destroyer unit and some medium tanks crept up the shell-torn road into the pass.

British forces, which had advanced from Thala without meeting with any opposition, were moving along the left shoulder of the pass at noon, through minefields.

I stood on a rocky knob at the northern end of the pass with an advanced platoon of tanks, and watched the engineers below lifting mines. These were laid in a criss-cross pattern at ten-foot intervals.

Behind, the tanks maneuvered into position, waiting to go on through the pass as soon as the way was cleared.

Burned Italian and German tanks, vehicles and guns were scattered around the crater-pocked pass, victims of the intense bombing and the artillery barrage.

On a plain north of the pass were the charred remains of more than a score of lorries and at least eight Axis tanks, as well as a number of freshly dug German and Italian graves.

American troops were now advancing in strength over this plain.

Libs Bomb Italian Ports, Hit Naples and Crotone

CAIRO, Feb. 26 (AP)—Liberator bombers of the Ninth U.S. Air Force bombed the harbors of Naples and Crotone in Italy last night, a U.S. communique said today.

"In Naples direct hits were observed on the docks and in the harbor area generally," it said. "In Crotone bomb hits were seen in the area of the quay and railroad lines leading to it. Enemy aircraft were present over Naples, but offered no resistance. All our aircraft returned safely to their bases."

1d THE STARS AND STRIPES 1d

Daily Newspaper of U.S. Armed Forces in the European Theater of Operations

Vol. 3 No. 102 | London, England | Tuesday, March 2, 1943

Nazis Rush Supplies for Vital Donetz

Germans Try to Avert Disaster in Heaviest Fighting of War

MOSCOW, March 1 (UP)—The heaviest fighting of the winter campaign is now going on in the northern part of the Donetz salient, where the Germans are pouring in all available tanks, armored vehicles, aircraft and infantry to keep open the vital 70 miles between their lines and the Sea of Azov and thus avert a repetition of the Stalingrad encirclement.

The battle has now been swaying to and fro for the past three weeks. Few details of its latest developments are available in Moscow today. Fighting has shifted from the south-west of Kramatorskaya to what the overnight communiqué called the "Kramatorskaya area."

Here the Germans threw in scores of tanks in a continuous succession of attacks in an endeavor to drive through the Russian lines, but the attacks were beaten back.

The area in which the Donetz Battle has been waged between Kramatorskaya and Krasonoarmeisk is one which gives its possessor control of vital railways which connect the Donetz with the Crimea and southern Ukraine.

Artillery Duels Near Rostov

In the eastern area of the Basin fighting seems to have subsided to some extent. West of Rostov the Russians are consolidating their positions, and engaging in artillery duels with the Germans who are holding the fortified line which defends the approaches to Taganrog in this area.

It was in this area that the Russian advance from Rostov last winter was ended.

The Germans are holding a line of hills which offer ideal defensive positions for the Germans and which also provide opportunities for the German counter-attacks which are now going on with growing force.

Spring Weather

Spring weather now prevails in this area. While it hampers ground fighting it has caused an increase in air operations from the Sea of Azov to the Kuban. Exceptionally fierce air fighting is reported from the latter area where the Germans are grimly hanging on to their bridgehead on to the mainland.

In the Kursk-Kharkov area the Russians are maintaining their offensive and have gained more ground west of Kharkov and Kursk. Several villages and small towns have been liberated, but no major advance has been reported.

Berlin claims that fierce fighting has been going on on the central front. Moscow says nothing about this area, which follows its usual custom of keeping quiet about operations until some positive development in the fighting.

Fierce fighting has been going on both north and south of Orel. It was admitted that the Russians had made what were described as "temporary break-throughs," which, it was claimed, were cleaned up by the Germans.

Berlin tonight claimed that, in the Orel fighting, the Russians had lost 19,000 men killed and 1,700 taken prisoner since Feb. 4.

TankDestroyer MatchesNazi88

DETROIT, March 1 (AP)—The production of a powerful new tank destroyer, a land cruiser which can cope with anything yet thrown into battle by Germany, was announced today by the General Motors Corporation.

The destroyer, one of three newly designed models, is known as the M10 and is being built on a volume basis at the tank arsenal of General Motors Fisher Body division.

The destroyer has already been tested in battle and its performance was described as "excellent."

With the permission of the War Department, E. F. Fisher, general manager, gave this brief description of the destroyer:

It is of welded construction and is faster than the ordinary tank. It is heavily armored, has great maneuverability and carries terrific fire power.

Although the caliber and range of the big gun mounted in the turret are secret, Army officials said that it could trade blows on an even basis with the much discussed 88mm weapons found on the most recent German tanks in North Africa.

This Is The Cavalry's Newest Mount

U.S. Army Signal Corps Photo

This is the new light tank of the cavalry, an armored reconnaissance vehicle designed to carry 37mm. firepower to the enemy at a speed which keeps it alongside the half-tracks and motorcycles. Weighing 15 tons, the new M5 light tank has speed to spare over its prototype, M2A4, and more maneuverability. It carries machine-guns to supplement the 37mm., and is now in use by cavalry training in the ETO for the invasion of Europe.

Rationing Begins in America, 125,000,000 Register in Week

WASHINGTON, March 1—Mrs. America went shopping today with ration book No. 2—along with cash—in her handbag, necessary now under regulations controlling the retail sale of practically every foodstuff except meat, fresh vegetables, fresh fruits and bread.

Rationing authorities said approximately 125 million copies of ration book No. 2 had been distributed.

Canned and processed foods of all types come under the regulations which went into effect today. As they were set up, the new rules made it pretty dangerous—as well as unpatriotic—to try to chisel. Applications for the books, without which no housewife could buy a can of beans or a carton of frozen brussels sprouts, had a space for a declaration of how many cans were on the pantry shelf. False returns carried the penalty of a $1,000 fine upon conviction

No Dangerous Shortage

Government officials, announcing the ration system the 21st of last month, said no dangerous food shortage existed in the United States and that the rationing was being put into effect to see that no one consumed more than his fair share and, at the same time, to provide for military and lend-lease needs.

Nevertheless it appeared that the average American family was going to be forced to tighten its collective belt a notch or two.

Introduction of the new rationing for civilians came on the same day that soldiers in the European Theater of Operations went on a new diet which adjusted mess-hall meals to include more English-produced vegetables in place of other foods formerly shipped from the United States.

Allied Post-War Conference

WASHINGTON, March 1 (UP)—All the Allied countries will be asked to send representatives to a meeting at which post-war problems will be discussed, Sumner Welles, Under-Secretary of State, said today. Mr. Welles said the meeting is planned for the near future.

Air War Rolls IntoFourthDay

RAF Dumps 1,000 Tons Onto St. Nazaire in Half-hour

A trail of ruin and rubbles across Hitler's Europe, from Nuremberg north to Wilhelmshaven and west to St. Nazaire and Brest today forms a bomb-battered monument to the biggest air offensive of the war.

Dumping more than 1,000 tons of high explosives and incendiaries onto the U-boat base of St. Nazaire in little more than half-on-hour, RAF heavy bombers polished off more than three days of unrelenting battering of Nazi objectives which began Thursday night.

Yesterday, American bombers were not over, but the RAF, in its coup de grace on St. Nazaire, cascaded enough blast-force on the docks and freight yards to quiet German defenses.

Bomber crews reported great fires that spread all over the base, and one huge explosion which dwarfed all the fires.

With the St. Nazaire raid the Allied air offensive from bases in Britain entered its second month of paralytic bombing. The pattern of smashing the bases and factories behind the Nazi U-boat warfare continued in the St. Nazaire mission, which cost the RAF five planes. Other scattered bombing sorties were staged against western Germany.

Unofficial compilations placed the tonnage dropped by the RAF on Germany during February higher than the total dropped by the Luftwaffe on Britain during three months of the heaviest blitz, when London was raided for 57 consecutive nights.

During February, unofficial tabulation disclosed, Allied bombers made 31 raids

(Continued on page 4)

Jap Air Force Reserves Sinking, Chennault Says

CHUNGKING, March 1 (AP)—Brig. Gen. Chennault, in an interview today, expressed his belief the Japanese air force had "hit its peak and is now on the downgrade."

The commander of the China Air Task Force said, "From the evidence of various sources, the enemy has run into two bottlenecks—aircraft production and the training of airmen." His reserve stock of planes was being used up and he was getting short of trained personnel because of heavy losses, Gen. Chennault said.

Feriana Reoccupied By American Forces; Nazis Press Attacks

Ex-Bookie Calls Odds As He Goes Into Battle

NEW YORK, March 1 (UP)—"Fifty to one . . . 20 to one . . . eight to one . . . seven to two. . . ."

An American private who used to be a bookmaker shouted these words as he took part in a charge on Japanese positions in Guadalcanal, according to a story repeated here by Eddie Cantor.

He was calculating the odds on his reaching the objective without being killed, Cantor related.

Foe Pays Heavily for Three-Mile Gain In the North

The town of Feriana, evacuated last week by American troops before the overwhelming weight of Field Marshal Erwin Rommel's Panzer assault, was in Allied hands again last night.

American engineers were the first to enter the town, 40 miles west of Gafsa, as American and Allied forces continued to pursue the retreating Axis forces east of Kasserine Pass.

The engineers were kept busy clearing mines and booby traps left by Axis forces.

Nazis Pay For Gain

Further north, Nazi Gen. Von Arnim, beaten back in five of his six local attacks, threw his armor and infantry toward Beja for a three-mile gain, despite heavy losses in tanks and men from Allied ground and air attacks.

Spitfires and Hurribombers caused great havoc among German transport columns in dawn-to-dusk attacks, while American Flying Fortresses struck a heavy blow at the Axis port of Cagliari, Sardinia, hitting at least four ships used to supply the Axis forces in Tunisia.

Although the German Panzers made a local advance in the Beja sector, Allied positions were not seriously endangered.

Algiers radio said Feriana fell into Allied hands after Anglo-American aviation had made a record number of sorties in the last 24 hours. Retreating German troops were being subjected to a violent bombing from the air. Great confusion had been observed in their rear lines.

Mareth Line Pounded

Eighth Army aviation was pounding the Mareth line, the radio said.

The Eighth Army offensive was only a question of days if not hours, Paris radio said. Earlier, Ankara (Turkish) radio, quoting an Algiers message, said the Eighth Army had begun an offensive against the line, and German radio asserted the 44th and 51st British infantry divisions, as well as three tank brigades with special service troops, were drawn up facing the German and Italian front in North Africa.

Von Arnim's attacks on Beja in northern Tunisia have progressed three miles beyond Sidi Nsir, despite great losses, while on the rest of the front the German attacks were flattened.

The Germans threw their full weight into Beja, after being held back by attacks from the northern front, although fighting is still continuing on most sectors.

The Allies fought to the last man before giving ground in the vital Beja area, taking heavy toll in their attacks. The air support given by RAF Spitfires and Hurricane bombers was described as "magnificent." Pilots reported scores of hits on 50-odd armored cars, tanks and trucks on the vehicle-crowded roads in the Medjez, Bou Arada and Pont du Fahs area.

Fierce resistance at Medjez El Bab and along the Mediterranean was described as particularly stubborn.

Line's Position Vague

The exact position of the Allied line remains in doubt, but it is apparent in the three days of steady attack that the Germans have not been able to make a definite break in the Allied positions.

Even in the three miles of the Beja thrust, Von Arnim's troops are in danger of being cut off if the Allies continue to hold positions behind and on each side of them, as it now appears they are doing.

Charles Collingwood, CBS commentator, speaking over Algiers radio, said that during the last two days 500 prisoners were taken in the northern sector.

(Continued on page 4)

JapsStrengthen Island Positions, Allies Warned

MacArthur Says Troops Massed 'in Readiness' North of Australia

ALLIED HQ, Southwest Pacific, March 1 (UP)—Japanese strength in the islands north of Australia has been increasing through the past week, Gen. Douglas MacArthur's headquarters revealed today.

Based on reports brought back by reconnaissance pilots after flights from Timor to the Northern Solomons, the communique said the Jap concentrations indicate they are taking up "a position in readiness."

"The military expression 'position in readiness' means either offensive or defensive military operations," a spokesman at Gen. MacArthur's headquarters explained.

(An authoritative analysis of Japanese strength—and weakness—is carried on page two of today's Stars and Stripes.)

Raids on Japs

Fighting in the Southwest Pacific area was limited to raids by United Nations' aircraft today which pounded Japanese installations at nearly a score of points. A Bombay communique claimed the sinking of a 7,000-ton Jap cargo ship.

(In a broadcast message to the American Red Cross from "Somewhere in the Pacific," Rear Adm. Chester W. Nimitz said today that we are "now at the crossroads of the Pacific campaign. Through the unmatched devotion of the men who held the lines in the trying months of the past year," he declared. "We have turned back the enemy in the South Pacific. The loss of Guadalcanal marks the first defeat of that kind suffered by the Japanese in modern times." Admiral Nimitz is Commander in Chief of the U.S. Pacific Fleet.)

14 Enemy Planes Downed

Yesterday's Allied HQ communique claimed the destruction of fourteen Japanese planes in operations over the Jap airbase at Koepang and said Jap ground troops had been pushed back 30 miles from the scene of their defeat at Wau, Allied advanced airdrome in Northern New Guinea.

Other successful raids were carried out at Kai Island, Lae and Finschafen, New Guinea.

Maj.Gen.H.C.Ingles Named Deputy Commander of ETO

The appointment of Maj. Gen. Harry C. Ingles to be deputy commander of the European Theater of Operations was announced yesterday by Lt. Gen. Frank M. Andrews, ETO commander.

Gen. Ingles succeeds Maj. Gen. Russell P. Hartle, who will command troops in the field, according to the announcement.

A graduate of West Point, Gen. Ingles served on border patrol in Arizona in 1916 and the early part of 1917. Later in 1917, he was senior instructor at the Signal Officers' Training Camp at Leon Springs, Tex.

After the first World War he served at a number of stations including the Philippines, and for a time was assigned to duty with the organized reserves at the University of Minnesota. He has been an instructor in the Command and General Staff School at Ft. Leavenworth, Kan., and was graduated from the Army War College. After graduation from the Army War College he was director of the Army Signal School, Ft. Monmouth, N.J.

A high point in his more recent military career was his assignment in May, 1941, to duty as Chief of Operations Division in the Carribean Defense Command.

In March, 1941, he was assigned as chief of staff of that command and in January, 1942, to command the Panama Mobile Forces.

Gen. Ingles is a native of Pleasant Hill, Neb., but he considers San Antonio, Tex., his home. He has one daughter and two sons. One son, John S. Ingles, is an enlisted man attending an officers' candidate school in the States.

Finland Will Fight On, Re-elected President Says

"The war will be continued and it demands the whole attention of the people," declared re-elected President Ryti of Finland.

Again and again, he said, Finland was confronted with new and difficult decisions. We wanted nothing but friendly relations with all countries. After Finland had fought by herself against immensely superior forces when she was attacked by Soviet Russia she had withdrawn from the war because her strength was diminished.

1d. THE STARS AND STRIPES 1d.

Daily Newspaper of U.S. Armed Forces in the European Theater of Operations

Vol. 3 No. 110 London, England Thursday, March 11, 1943

Munich Digs Out of Ruins As Nazis Cry

Second RAF Night Raid Brings Howls From German Radio

German radio said yesterday: "The enemy has no pity . . . we hate this kind of warfare."

The statement came while Munich and Nuremberg were still digging their way out of the wreckage left by two consecutive RAF night raids to southern Germany.

The Allied air offensive, which has pounded around the clock for 14 days with only one night's interruption, continued Tuesday night with what the Air Ministry said was a "heavy" attack on Munich, birthplace of Nazism and manufacturing and rail center. The night before, the RAF hit Nuremberg, leaving great fires and causing what the Germans admitted was heavy damage.

The Munich raid, along with smaller bombing missions to western Germany, where the sirens have wailed almost every night for a month, and the laying of mines in German coastal waters, cost a total of 11 aircraft, the Air Ministry said.

St. Nazaire Still Burns

Even as the RAF bombers were soaring over Munich with their incendiaries and high explosives, Vichy radio reported that fires were still burning in St. Nazaire, western France U-boat base, from the bombing attacks on it eight days ago. Vichy also announced that the entire port was to be evacuated as soon as possible, and that plans were being made to evacuate all other towns on the coast.

Munich, the Germans' fourth largest city, had been bombed four times before by the RAF, the last time on Dec. 12, 1942. It has locomotive and car repair works, as well as Diesel engine and airplane engine factories.

Berlin radio declared that three art galleries were destroyed by the night's raids.

From Stockholm, meanwhile, came reports that Nuremberg, plastered the night before by four-engined RAF bombers, had been damaged more extensively than Lubeck and Rostock, which were razed by huge raids last year. According to stories reaching Sweden from Berlin, much of Nuremberg "is in ruins."

'Revenge a Thousand Times'

Berlin radio, commenting on the raids on Berlin, Essen, Nuremberg and Munich, declared that all Germany must be prepared to "withstand blows which are unavoidable at the moment in order later to retaliate on the enemy in the knowledge that revenge is a thousand times justified." (The Krupps munitions plant at Essen was hit squarely by RAF bombs last Friday night, according to word reaching London yesterday.)

German retaliation yesterday and the night before consisted of hit-and-run raids on the coast and attacks at points in the southwest and south.

The Germans claimed to have hit Hull Tuesday night and Worthing in a daylight attack. The British Air Ministry said two raiders were shot down after an attack on a south coast town. One raider was brought down Tuesday night. Damage was caused and there were casualties, it was announced, in the raid Tuesday afternoon and night.

Germans Rushing French Defenses, Madrid Hears

MADRID, Mar. 10 (UP)—German precautions against a Second Front have greatly increased during the past ten days, according to reports from France reaching Madrid.

Special teams of engineers from the Todt organization are hurriedly building defenses along the southern European coasts, chiefly in France, Italy and Greece. The defense works are practically the same as those established on the Channel and Atlantic coasts of France.

41 Years' Canned Goods On Shelf—No Coupons

WASHINGTON, Mar. 10 (UP)—A family in Pennsylvania is 41 years ahead of its rations.

When they applied for their three new ration books recently, they confessed they had 4,502 excess cans of fruit and vegetables, it was learned here.

So the government ordered all coupons for canned goods be removed from future ration books.

At the present rate, it will take the family 41 years to pay back the coupons.

Sabotage, Resistance Spread in France

Guerrilla Outbreaks In Channel Ports; Deat Attacked

French guerrillas carried their attacks on German occupation troops to the frequently bombed Channel ports of Brest and Lorient yesterday. Other outbreaks occurred in Lyons and Marseilles and in the industrial centers of Normandy, Brittany and Alsace Lorraine.

Advices to Fighting French headquarters in London estimated that close to 300 Germans, mostly officers, had been killed in the last three days.

Paris radio said last night an attempt had been made to shoot the French Fascist leader, Marcel Deat. The shots missed, the radio said.

So widespread were the outbreaks that two more regiments of SS troops have been sent to Paris, and several motorized groups and armored units have reinforced the German garrison there, Morocco radio said last night.

Terror Reprisal

From Alsace it was reported the Germans had introduced terror measures, and that many persons were jailed, several deported and two young men executed for refusing to obey German labor orders, the radio said.

In addition to the bombings, shootings and stabbings in Paris and Lille on Monday and elsewhere in France yesterday, there has been a wave of sabotage which left freight trains piles of smoking, twisted steel and crippled vital links in the Nazi-controlled French rail network.

Regarded as sporadic and disconnected when they were first reported early this week, the outbreaks are now taking on the character of a nation-wide revolt.

What touched them off, apparently, was the agreement of Pierre Laval and his Vichy government to Nazi demands for the conscription of French labor.

The call for 400,000 French workers, to which Laval agreed, was described by the Germans as necessary for war production. Underground French leaders, however, have become convinced that the plan is really intended to strip France of every man who might be able to aid the Allies in their expected invasion of France.

Fragmentary reports, sifting out of France through underground channels, made it difficult to estimate accurately the effectiveness of the fighting. Many outbreaks occurred which have not been reported in detail, it was known here.

Theater Attacked

In Brest the fighting started when guerrillas, armed with hand grenades, attacked a theater filled with German troops at the moment that a newsreel shot of Hitler was being shown. Two German soldiers were killed and many others injured.

German patrols appeared in the streets and were fired on. Fighting became general, including a grenade attack on the Hotel de la Poste, where two more Germans were slain. Hand-to-hand fighting in the streets ended when the guerrillas withdrew after suffering only small losses, secretly transmitted dispatches said.

In Lorient, still smoking from American bombs, the fighting followed a similar pattern. Guerrillas bombed a German naval canteen, hang-out for U-boat crews,

(Continued on page 4)

Scenes like this were being repeated throughout France yesterday as the French resisted Hitler's labor conscription. Here a man, shot by SS troops during a Paris demonstration of resistance, is carried into a Nazi army car.

Patrols Harassing Rommel, Foe Shows No Sign of Fight

ALLIED HQ, North Africa, Mar. 10 (AP)—Eighth Army patrols harassed Rommel's crippled Panzers in southern Tunisia today, knocking out more tanks, while the other fronts were relatively quiet and bad weather restricted operations by the Allied air forces.

Commenting on the German withdrawal after the abortive drive on the Mareth line, a military spokesman said:

"We knew we won the first round and the enemy is showing no willingness to come up for round two. We know he lost more armor than he can afford."

It was announced that the total German tanks knocked out had been raised to 52 by yesterday's losses.

Taking up the burden dropped by their armored forces, German fighter bombers attempted evening attacks on the Eighth Army area. One group of fighters was driven off before they could drop any bombs.

Allied planes flew offensive patrols in the northern and central sectors without encountering Axis air opposition.

There was little activity in northern Tunisia but the Anglo-American First Army patrols were "extremely active."

In the far south the French completed the occupation of Tozeur, south west of Gafsa, and their reconnaissance patrols were active.

Not Just Probing Thrust

WITH THE EIGHTH ARMY, Mar. 8 (delayed) (AP)—The battle of Medenine was no thrust to probe British defenses. It was an attack in force to drive the British back. It failed because the Eighth Army was ready with guns which laid down a fire equal in intensity to the bombardment which preceded the British attack at El Alamein.

Today the morale of this army is higher than at any time during the campaign across Africa.

Rommel changed his tank tactics in the battle of Medenine. Instead of sending a full force of tanks against one sector of the front he spread them in groups along

(Continued on page 4)

26 Bombers Hit Allied Air Base

Light Damage, Casualties; Libs Blast Targets in Shortland Islands

ALLIED HQ, Southwest Pacific, Mar. 10—Twenty-six Japanese twin-engined bombers attacked the Allied airdrome at Wau, New Guinea, yesterday, causing little damage and light casualties, according to the official communique issued here today.

Escorted by 21 fighter planes, the enemy bombers came in from the northwest flying at 15,000 feet and dropped their bombs on the base all at once.

No mention was made in the communique of any planes shot down. Wau is about 35 miles southwest of Salamaua and 425 miles south of Rabaul, main operating base of the Japs in New Britain.

A heavy Allied bomber on reconnaissance duty near New Britain ran into nine Jap fighters and shot down four of them, probably a fifth, and returned to its base safely.

Japanese planes dropped bombs on

(Continued on page 4)

Chennault, Flying Tiger Chief, Heads New Air Force in China

CHUNGKING, Mar. 10—Brig. Gen. Claire Chennault, former Louisiana high school principal, who led the American Volunteer Group ("Flying Tigers") into combat against the Japanese long before the United States and Japan were at war, was given command today of a newly created China Air Command, comprising the 14th Air Force.

His appointment was announced by Lt. Gen. Joseph Stilwell, commander of U.S. forces in India and China and chief of staff of Generalissimo Chiang Kai-shek. Chinese quarters rejoiced at the appointment. It was considered that in his new post Gen. Chennault would be one of the key men in the air offensive against the Japanese.

Creation of the separate air command was believed to be one of the concrete results of Mme. Chiang Kai-shek's visit to Washington. It was taken for granted in Chungking that Gen. Chennault's air force would be considerably strengthened.

Gen. Stilwell's announcement said: "Upon the decision of the War Department, the 14th Air Force was activated today under the commanding general of the U.S. Army Forces in China, Burma and India. The 14th Air Force, com-

(Continued on page 4)

Brig. Gen. Claire Chennault

66 Torpedo Survivors Rescued in Icy Seas

Sixty-six survivors from a torpedoed American freighter are safe at a U.S. Seamen's Service club in Britain, the War Shipping Administration revealed yesterday. They were rescued by a British corvette.

Nine of the crew are unaccounted for.

'Priest,' With its 105, Again Rips Up Nazis

ALLIED HQ, North Africa, Mar. 10 (UP)—Reports of Saturday's battle show that the 105mm. gun mounted on the chassis of a General Grant tank—known as the "Priest"—created havoc among Rommel's panzer formations.

The "Priest" played an important part in the El Alamein battle, where it outshot the German 88mm. gun, as revealed by Mr. Churchill in the House of Commons. Another of its assets is its speed of 30 miles per hour, which enables it to keep up with an advancing army.

Nazis Block Red Drive in Donetz Basin

Outreaching Supply Line, Russians Retreat from Important Towns

MOSCOW, Mar. 10 (UP)—Fierce counter-attacks in the Donetz Basin area forced Russian units to retreat today—the first setback the Soviet fighters have received in more than three months of offensive warfare.

Elsewhere along the far-flung front the Russians hold the advantage, pushing ahead against wavering German defenses or, at least, holding the positions they had already won.

Russian communiques admitted that Krasnograd, Lozovaya, Pavlograd, Krasno-Armeisk, Kramatorskaya, Barvenkovo, Slaviansk and Lisichansk—several of them important points—had been abandoned, and that Russian troops were meeting heavy German attacks on a new line east of those points.

Red Star, Russian Army newspaper, summed up the new situation by assigning a defensive role to Russian units in the southern area. Their duty, said the paper, would be to "wage defensive warfare and stubbornly and firmly hold their positions and repulse all attacks."

Outreached Supply Lines

The Russian setbacks came when spearheads, striking to the southwest, outreached their supply lines. Short of ammunition and food, their situation complicated by a sudden thaw which turned frozen roads into quagmires, the advance Red units found themselves in danger of encirclement. A retreat was ordered.

News from the Vyasma area was especially good from the Russian point of view. There the German retreat is gaining speed and the Russians have scored very important successes in the last 36 hours. From the east, southeast and north, Red Army columns are closing in on the great German "hedgehog" position.

Two Rail Points Fall

They have taken Tumanovo, a railway station on the Vyasma-Moscow railroad, 19 miles east of Vyasma; and they have taken Temkino, on the Kaluga-Vyasma line, 40 miles north of the town.

Further north, Gen. Timoshenko's armies are within 16 miles of Staraya Russa and are closing in for the final assault on that German stronghold.

On the Kursk-Orel front slow but steady progress goes on without any notable successes.

The battle for Smolensk continued yesterday with Russian columns striking to the west and southwest of Sychevka despite deep snow, bitter winds and blinding snow. Red troops occupied a former German concentration camp in the area and liberated many Russian civilians who had been left there by fleeing German guards.

Soviet Mines Take Toll

Russian dispatches from the fighting fronts yesterday used the sharp-focus technique of telling the story of single units in action with the enemy.

"Southwest of Voroshilovgrad," one such dispatch read, "a group of our sappers planted 650 mines at night and under enemy fire. On these mines, eight German tanks and many trucks loaded with infantrymen and supplies were blown up."

The dispatch described how the Russian engineer troops crawled to their positions, planted the deadly little tins of explosive, and withdrew despite the spattering fire of Nazi machine-guns and snipers.

When the German mechanized units attempted a dawn advance, first one, then another vehicle ran over the hidden mines, exploded them and were wrecked.

Swedish Mental Specialist On Rush Trip to Germany

STOCKHOLM, Mar. 10 (AP)—Dr. Oliver Crona, famous Swedish mental specialist, is reported to have left suddenly for Koenigsberg, East Prussia. No explanation was given here as to why he might have been summoned to Germany.

It was regarded as possible, however, that if he was on his way to attend some German leader it might well be Luftwaffe chief Hermann Goering, who often goes to East Prussia on hunting trips. After the last war he was in a Swedish mental hospital for treatment as a drug addict.

J. P. Morgan [illegible]

BOCA GRANDE, [illegible] —J. [illegible] [illegible]

1D. THE STARS AND STRIPES 1D.
Daily Newspaper of U.S. Armed Forces in the European Theater of Operations
Vol. 3 No. 126 London, England Tuesday, March 30, 1943

Mareth Line Falls, Trap Closing on Axis

Rocket Gun Is One-Man Tank Buster

U.S. 'Bazooka' Furnished To Allied Forces Here And in Tunisia

A new anti-tank gun, described as so powerful it can stop any armored vehicle known, yet so light it can be fired from the shoulder by a single man, is now in the hands of American soldiers in combat in North Africa and those awaiting action in Great Britain.

Dubbed the "bazooka gun" by men using them in Africa, the weapon was a closely guarded secret until yesterday, when Army officials in Washington described its successes against Rommel's tanks in Tunisia, and authorities in London disclosed that some men in the European Theater of Operations were armed with it. Enough have been manufactured to supply Allied forces as well, Washington sources said.

Maj. Gen. L. H. Campbell Jr., Army Chief of Ordnance, describing the gun to the Associated Press, said it would make every lone foot soldier "the master of any tank which may attack him."

Penetrates Armor Plate

He said the new guns, now being produced in quantity, are rocket-guns "built on a Fourth of July principle." The gunner loads and fires the weapon in a normal fashion, he said, but from there on the projectile behaves in an abnormal, and still secret, manner.

"Bazooka" rocket-shells, Gen. Campbell declared, will penetrate armor plate, drive through brick or stone walls, shatter bridge girders and "perform other seeming miracles."

On one occasion in Africa, recently, the ordnance chief said, an American bazooka-gunner was attacked by six enemy tanks. He fired one shot, which missed the lead tank but shattered a tree beside it. The tank crew, seeing the tree blown into splinters, thought they were under point-blank fire from a 155 and surrendered.

One Shot Does Trick

In Africa the Bazooka is being used to smash field fortifications as well as to stop tanks. One shot wrecks a machine-gun post, several will destroy a bridge or a building.

Gen. Campbell said that bazookas have been in mass production long enough so that they are being supplied not only to American troops but to the troops of Allied armies as well.

Explaining that the gun is not a substitute for any existing weapon but is intended to supplement them all, the general emphasized that it is a short-range weapon for shattering tanks, pill-boxes or fortifications.

Tables of Basic Allowances are being revised and it is expected that the guns will be used in defensive operations by chauffeurs, truck drivers, ammunition carriers, orderlies, mess personnel and other available men.

Regular line companies will continue to use their standard weapons, backed up by the bazooka men in emergencies.

Need 'Good Healthy Hate' Says Air Marshal Bishop

NEW YORK, Mar. 29 (AP)—Air Marshal Billy Bishop, the Canadian ace, said here that "a good healthy hate" for the Axis was necessary in war, and, referring to recent Allied bombings, that he did not care "if there is no one house left standing in Germany."

Air Marshal Bishop described Sir Arthur Harris as "a tiger with no mercy in his heart" towards the enemy. Sir Arthur, he added, told him at a time when England's back was nearly broken that "he was going to give it all back a thousandfold and he will do it."

Famous Pianist Dead

BEVERLY HILLS, Cal., Mar. 29—Sergei Rachmaninoff, 69, world renowned pianist and composer, has died here. His preludes in C sharp minor and G minor, written in his teens, are among the most popular of classical pieces although, in the light of his more mature compositions, Rachmaninoff considered them his worst efforts.

Report Brazil Force to Africa

RIO DE JANEIRO, Mar. 29 (UP)—Brazil, deciding to take a still more active part in the war, is going to send an expeditionary force abroad, probably to Africa, within the next few months, according to a usually reliable source in Rio de Janeiro.

Allied Thrusts Close in on Rommel

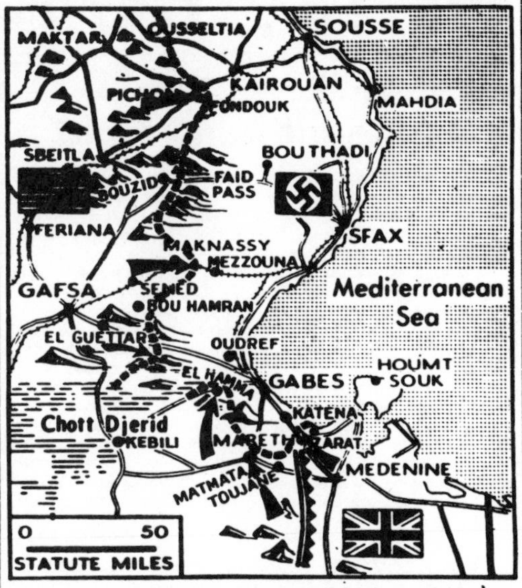

Rommel lost the Mareth Line yesterday as the Eighth Army took Matmata, Toujane, Mareth and El Hamma. Further north the Americans are closing in to cut off the Axis retreat by three thrusts to the coast from Maknassy, Fondouk and El Guettar.

Nazaire Aflame After RAF Raid

46th Blow of War on Sub Pens Follows U.S. Trip to Rouen

The RAF, which followed up the bombing of Berlin and the U.S. attack on Rouen with a night blow at the Nazi submarine base at St. Nazaire Sunday night, devastated much of the town and started huge fires which were still burning yesterday, reconnaissance photos showed.

Reconnaissance planes which were over St. Nazaire yesterday at 9.15 AM reported great columns of smoke rising 15,000 feet. Eleven hours earlier, crews of RAF bombers in mid-channel said they could see huge fires raging in the city as they winged homeward.

Weather during the raid was excellent, with good visibility, an Air Ministry communique said.

The St. Nazaire operation, the 46th attack on that town since the war began and the fifth rair this year, came on the anniversary of the Commando raid on the base there.

American heavy bombers have hit St. Nazaire six times since they began their heavy attacks on Germany and German-held territory last Aug. 17.

Enemy air activity over Great Britain was limited to one hit-and-run raid on a south coast town yesterday. Fighter Command Spitfires intercepted four FW190s as they streaked for home, shot down one and damaged another.

U.S. 90mm. Guns Down One Plane per 50 Shots

CINCINNATI, Mar. 29 (AP)—The average "bag" for U.S. 90mm. guns in operation against Jap planes over Guadalcanal was one plane brought down for every 50 rounds of ammunition fired, according to statistics given by Maj. Gen. Levin Campbell, Ordnance chief of the Army at a press conference.

During the first world war 17,000 rounds of anti-aircraft fire were needed to hit, but not to bring down, a plane.

U.S. Gained In 'Lend' Swap

WASHINGTON, Mar. 29 (AP)—Lend-Lease Administrator Edward Stettinius, summarizing lend-lease food shipments today, said that during the last year Australia and New Zealand gave more beef to U.S. forces in the South Pacific than the U.S. had shipped to other countries.

In terms of the U.S. population, he explained, food shipments to the Allies during each week of January and February, were equivalent to a weekly personal allowance of a quarter of an ounce of beef, three ounces of pork, three-fifths of an ounce of lamb and mutton, a quarter of an ounce of butter and even smaller amounts of cheese, edible fats, oils.

573 Air Awards Announced In ETO's Largest List Yet

Eighth Air Force Headquarters announced 573 decorations yesterday, conferred on men in the European Theater of Operations. It was the largest single honors list announced here since the war began.

Among the awards were a second and third Oak Leaf Cluster to the Air Medal, 12 posthumous Air Medals, and a Purple Heart.

Sgt Frank W. Bartlett, of Whitesville, W. Va., bomber gunner, received the second and third Oak Leaf Clusters to a previously earned Air Medal for the destruction of two enemy aircraft.

The Purple Heart was awarded to Sgt. James E. MacCammond, of Darien, Conn., and presented by Col. John H. Hayden, of Tampa, Fla., during presentation ceremonies. Col. Hayden also presented an Oak Leaf Cluster to S Sgt. Walter L. Hazleton, of Heuvelton, N.Y., and Air Medals to 39 bomber crewmen, all of whom won the awards for taking part in five missions over enemy territory in Europe.

The posthumous awards, read out during the presentation ceremonies, were made to 1 Lts. Walter R. Erness, Rochester, N.Y.; Estell Q. Martin, Miami, Fla., and Robert A. Johnson, Denison, Ia.; 2 Lt. Keal W. Alford, Jeffersonville, Ind.; M Sgt. Oscar L. Olsen, Chicago, Ill.; T Sgt. James E. Davis, Louisville, Tenn.; S Sgts. William J. Nagle, Roselle, N.J.; Samuel S. McNeeley, Oak Hill, W. Va.; Samuel F. Powell, Salt Lake City, Utah; Jack E. Pinion, Chattanooga, Tenn., and William L. Stammer, Argos, Ind., and Sgt. Kenneth L. Pastrof, Union, N.J.

Air Medals, awarded "for exceptionally meritorious achievement, for ten fighter missions over enemy territory, for five bomber missions over enemy territory or for destruction of an enemy air-

(Continued on page 4)

Naval Vessels Shell Axis Port of Gabes As Rommel Retreats

Eighth Army Takes All Mareth Positions, Americans Advance Further North, Threatening Foe's Escape

By the Associated Press

The Eighth Army cracked the Mareth Line yesterday after nine days of battering from the air and land, and reports from the battlefront said Rommel was withdrawing his forces in an apparent last-minute attempt to avoid the trap set by British and United States troops in his rear.

The British and Americans were reported closing in still more on the Axis escape corridor to the north with three thrusts toward the coast—from El Guettar, Maknassy and Fondouk.

The area around Gabes, major Nazi supply port, where Rommel was expected to make his strongest stand, was being subjected to a heavy naval bombardment by the Allies, according to dispatches last night. Reports from Cairo that Luftwaffe personnel were plowing up the airfields at Gabes, as they have done elsewhere when retreat was imminent, indicated Rommel might give up the vital port without much resistance.

The communique announcing the breakthrough and the capture of Mareth, Toujane and Matmata reported the "whole of the strong organized defenses of the Mareth positions now are in our hands." Six thousand prisoners had been taken, it was said.

The Mareth Line took nine days to break—the same time as the Eighth Army's massed artillery, bombers and infantry needed to eat through Rommel's first line at El Alamein 1,500 miles farther back.

The Axis withdrawal, the communique said, was forced on Rommel by an attack south of El Hamma made by an Eighth Army force that swept 150 miles around the Mareth positions.

Algiers radio quoted an announcement that El Hamma itself was in Allied hands, leaving only a 16-mile corridor between the little town and the coast through which Rommel could attempt to withdraw his estimated 85,000 men to the north.

If Rommel is able to run that gauntlet under artillery fire and attacks from aircraft operating from newly captured airdromes, including one at El Hamma, he will meet American forces driving towards the sea from Maknassy and El Guettar in twin thrusts. The communique announced the El Guettar column made progress yesterday.

Fondouk Force Advances

Eighty miles further north another American force was knifing into the narrow Axis-held coastal strip. After the capture of Fondouk, announced Sunday, this column was reported by Algiers radio to have advanced to within 18 miles of Kairouan.

Broadcasts by Axis-controlled radio stations yesterday were anything but optimistic. The Berlin military spokesman spoke significantly of a "last stand" by Rommel in positions which, he said, would be "determined by tactical and strategic considerations," while German-controlled Paris radio said last night that the battle for Tunisia was "unequal" and the Allies were bound to win.

"Generals Patton and Montgomery only started their offensive when they were in a position to be certain of victory," said a military analyst on Paris radio.

The suggestion that Rommel was planning a swift withdrawal even from the Gabes area was given in a Cairo report that the two main Axis landing grounds at Gabes were being ploughed up deliberately by Luftwaffe personnel.

Observers expressed the belief that if Rommel left Gabes he probably would attempt to withdraw along the entire Tunisian eastern coast to link up with Von Arnim's forces for a last-ditch

(Continued on page 4)

Yanks Driving Toward Coast

Three American Columns Narrowing Rommel's Escape Corridor

Three American columns drove forward from Maknassy, Fondouk and El Guettar yesterday in an ever-growing offensive designed to reach the Tunisian coast and cut Rommel's corridor of escape.

American infantry stormed 1,500-foot Jebel Mcheltat, chief German position in the Guettar area, early yesterday and drove the German defenders from the horseshoe-shaped hill with bayonet and bomb.

It was one of several objectives captured as American and French troops, based on newly-taken Fondouk, continued their drive toward the coast.

The enemy fell back to the Jebel Chemsi further east on the road to Gabes, and dug in for another stand. One American column, on the right of the Gabes Road, is still attacking the eastern slope of the Jebel Berda, where Nazi artillery covers the advance zones. American and German guns opened a fierce duel there yesterday.

Stiffening German resistance indicated Rommel was determined to hold the road to Gabes and the coast at all costs.

Further north, other American troops were reported by Algiers radio to have advanced to within 18 miles of Kairouan, "Holy City" of Tunisia. To the south, along what is called the Grand Dorsal, American guns hacked at German positions on high ground East of Maknassy. German radio said attacks there had been repulsed with heavy losses.

The main attack, in the El Guettar area, lasted all day. Soldiers crept forward over hills and up ravines under constant shell and mortar fire.

The Germans were well entrenched behind barbed wire, provided with machine-guns, mortars and field pieces.

Despite the opposition, American patrols inched forward taking more than three-quarters of a mile at one point.

Gen. Doolittle Awarded Air Medal for Five Raids

WASHINGTON, Mar. 29—The War Department announced today that an Air Medal has been awarded to Maj. Gen. James H. Doolittle, commander of the Twelfth Air Force in North Africa, in recognition of five sorties he led against the enemy.

Gen. Doolittle had previously been given the Congressional Medal of Honor for his bombing raid on Tokyo and other Japanese cities last April. He also holds the Flying Cross, with Oakleaf Cluster, for other feats.

Soldier Travel Cut for Easter

Restrictions on passes, furloughs and travel over the Easter holidays were announced by ETO Headquarters yesterday.

Soldiers who are on pass or furlough must arrange their trips so that they will not travel by train on either Easter Sunday, April 25, or Monday, April 26, it was announced.

Furloughs will not be granted between April 22 and April 26, and furloughs granted prior to this period will not terminate on either April 25 or April 26. Short passes of 48 or 72 hours will not be granted between April 20 and April 26, inclusive.

There is no restriction on travel by any means other than rail during the holidays, and, if necessary, soldiers may use trains to attend religious services, it was announced.

THE STARS AND STRIPES
AFRICA
Vol. 1 - No. 18 - Friday, April 9, 1943 U. S. Army Newspaper Two Francs

Yanks, British 8th Army Meet; Allies Swing North After Rommel

British And American Recon Patrols Merge Amid Desert Wastes

Sgt. Joe Randall Of State Center, Iowa Greets Sgt. A. W. Acland Of London, "Hello, You Bloody Limey!"

By MILTON LEHMAN
(Stars and Stripes Staff Writer)

WITH THE AMERICAN FORCES IN SOUTHERN TUNISIA, April 7—"Hello, you bloody Limey!"

That was the affectionate hello given by Sgt. Joseph A. Randall, State Center, Iowa, to Sgt. A. W. Acland, of Maida-Vale, London, as the reconnaissance patrols of the British 8th Army and American armored forces headed eastward, met in the historic juncture of the two armies, on the macadam road, 42 miles from Gabes amid desert wastes

"Very glad to see you," answered Acland, with typical British restraint.

And these two enlisted men—the helmeted, grinning American and the freckled-faced, red-haired Britisher with a blue beret and a turtle-necked sweater — stepped forward and shook hands for the first formal contact uniting British forces which pursued Rommel for 1,500 miles and the Americans who slapped back the Germans 140 miles from Kasserine Pass in six weeks. This is Acland's story of the meeting for which soldiers on both sides have been eagerly looking forward to for weeks:

"At first we thought you were Jerries because of your helmets. We had been having trouble with Jerry all the night before and all this morning we had been picking up Italian prisoners.

"We were seriously considering opening fire on you, especially when we saw the big gun sticking out of your armored lorries. Then we got the idea that it was you. We remembered that everybody was saying yesterday that we would meet the Yanks today and when you fellows started running out of your vehicles we recognised you.

"Then everything happened at once. We were in a big stretch of wasteland with bare mountains in the middle of nothing. There were five armored cars on your side—your halftracks with 75 mm. guns—and we had three armored dingos, or scout cars, each holding two persons.

"One Yank hollered, 'Christ, what's this' when he saw everybody ahead of him start throwing their arms around each other. All of us were chuckling and laughing. I'm a British Army photographer so I was already busy taking pictures of the scene.

We met at exactly 1525. I looked at my watch to note the time.

(Continued on Page 8)

EISENHOWER TO ALEXANDER:

'A Magnificent Fight'

Following the juncture of the American and British 8th Army in southern Tunisia, Gen. Dwight D. Eisenhower, Commander-in-Chief of the Allied Forces, sent the following message to his Deputy Commander-in-Chief, Gen. Sir Harold R. L. G. Alexander, who is in charge of the Tunisian campaign:

"I hope that you and all ranks serving under you will accept my personal congratulations and those of the entire Allied Headquarters on your recent successful operations which have joined up the victorious Eighth Army with the British, French and American forces that have been carrying on through four months a magnificent fight in Central Tunisia under most unfavorable conditions. While everyone of us fully appreciates that great difficulties and bitter fighting still lie ahead of you, and that beyond this campaign lie still greater hardships and sacrifices, still you and your 18th Army Group, and the Navy and the Air Force are now in position to exact the full price from the enemy confronting us in Africa. You may be sure that the whole democratic world is applauding your successes against forces that have outraged our concepts of freedom and human rights. Good luck!

(Signed) DWIGHT D. EISENHOWER

Historic Union Crowns Drives By Both Forces

French Contact Main U. S. Positions East Of El Guettar

(By a Staff Writer)

WITH AMERICAN FORCES IN SOUTHERN TUNISIA, April 7—An American armored column, after rolling 20 miles on the heels of the retreating enemy east of El Guettar met forward units of the British 8th Army on the Gafsa-Gabes road in an historic union today and immediately swung north together to finish the job of chasing the Axis from Africa.

While the advance patrols of the two armies met at 1525 about halfway between Gafsa and Gabes, the formal juncture of the two armies in force came 30 miles northwest of Gabes at 1610. Extended patrol tentacles of both armies also met at other points and it appeared a matter for future historical debate just when two forces met and merged.

With Rommel pulling out his legions overnight, the road to Gabes was clear sailing today for American tanks. While the Germans rushed to the north for shelter and to prepare new positions, the only enemy the American force met along the macadam Gabes-Gafsa road were large groups of Italians left behind as rear guards. With nothing left to guard and no heart in the fight, many of the Italian groups came down from the hills to the road to surrender to the Americans. Most of them seemed relieved that their fight was over

PRISONERS POCKETED

The juncture of the two armies left a vast pocket of enemy troops east of Gafsa and another pocket of prisoners developed when the French army under General Bosseau contacted main American infantry positions east of El Guettar near Djebel Berda.

The French troops brought 70 Italian prisoners along with them whom they had captured on the way.

With the Germans retreating to the north, the road to Gabes was open to Allied traffic and the road from Gabes to Sfax seemed next in line.

The historic juncture of the two armies was no surprise to the men here. We had been expecting it for days but what held up the meeting was the large number of mines left behind and the fact that the Nazis had concentrated a strong striking force of troops and tanks in the sector separating the two forces.

The British break-through to the north involved the taking of high ground in front of a well fortified Wadi. Once that barrier was broken, there was little but a long flat plain behind. In its move

(Continued on Page 2)

Prisoner Hans Insists Nazis Will Win—Soon!

By RICHARD BRUNER
(Stars and Stripes Staff Writer)

NEAR THE TUNISIAN FRONT—There's a German youngster named Hans with an American bullet in his belly in a prisoner of war camp up here. He's only 20 years old, and about the nearest thing he has to a God is his former leader, Field Marshal Erwin Rommel. He thinks Hitler is all right, too

The same icy stare which seems a part of all Nazi troops was frozen on Hans's face as Pfc. Ralph Safdieh, an MP from Brooklyn, and I approached his hospital cot. Safdieh was to act as interpreter, but that turned out to be unnecessary. Hans had studied English in his home town, Berlin, and spoke it well.

Hans was bitter towards the war in Russia. "The Russians," he muttered, "don't fight fair. They fight just like animals. The soldiers of the Reich fighting in Russia," he said, "are anxious to come to Tunisia and fight the British and Americans because," he insisted, "we put up a fair fight.

Hans assured us that the Allied prisoners of war received excellent treatment in German camps and he was enthusiastic about the work of the American doctors. "They are very good," he admitted.

He grappled for the pack of American cigarettes as we handed them to him and his eyes sparkled as we promised to let him have some American magazines. "I'd like to go to a prison camp in America," he exclaimed. "I'm tired of North Africa." Hans has been with Rommel a year.

We brought the only smile of the day to his stern face when we asked him if he had a girl-friend back home. He nodded and said his girl understood what the war meant to both of them and would wait for him to return victorious.

We didn't have the heart to tell him she would have quite a wait

(Continued on Page 2)

"Doughnuteers" Popular Visitors At Front Airbase

Airmen Slick Up In Sunday Best For Red Cross Girls

By RED MUELLER
(Correspondent for Newsweek)

AN AMERICAN AIRBASE IN TUNISIA—You could tell right away something was up.

A month ago, you hobnobbed with a bunch of dirty, bearded, mud-stained fighter pilots and bomber crews, full of frontline battle talk seasoned with plenty of four-letter words, and looking forward to chow time as their chief diversion from the strain of constant war duty.

Now, from brass hats to the lowest dogface, these guys were clean-shaven or industriously trimming beards and mustaches; wearing shirts and ties under spotless uniforms, and flashing brilliantly shined shoes. Even their language was toned down to a kind of sedate parlor talk.

Were Generals Eisenhower or Doolittle expected to visit the field? The answer was a surprised "Oh no"

DOUGHNUTEERS

Neither was Archbishop Spellman due nor had American nurses moved into the neighborhood, the fellows were quick to assure you. As they continued to refuse the desert and tea with sheepish and guilty grins, and you'd just about decided they were all goldbricking their way into the nearest rest home, the object of their attendance hove into sight. It looked like a cross between a station wagon and a nightmare by Rube Goldberg. But what stepped out on both sides and began unloading more Goldberg contraptions were strictly refugees from Hollywood.

Both wore smartly tailored, grey uniforms, pert hats, silk stockings and black shoes, and on each shoulder was a little, white badge marked "Red Cross." One of them, a sedate beauty, could have doubled for Greer Garson, and the other was a statuesque blonde in the best Ziegfield tradition. We began to understand.

If you could get near the former and ask why she left films she'd say you're very nice to say such sweet things but she is only Peggy

(Continued on Page 2)

It's An Order

Propaganda Chief Dr. Paul Joseph Goebbels told German women this week that they would be expected to do their all for the total Nazi war effort. At the same time he told the girls that it was their duty to make themselves as attractive as possible for husbands, fiances or friends at home on furlough

"The more that young girls fulfill their duties willingly, joyfully and without compulsion the better it will be for the nation," he said. was broken, there was little but a long flat plain behind. In its move

NEWS FROM HOME

Chicago's Subway Roars In Dry Run; White House Cancels Its Egg Rolling, And Marriage Booms, Among Other Things

Subway Born

CHICAGO — The long-awaited, much-disputed Chicago subway has finally come to life, although it will be some time before it will be ready for the cash customers. All that happened this week was that a newly-painted, specially decorated, eight-car train, carrying mostly officials, sped through the new underground in a special dry run

Coincident with the birth of the new subway was the death of "Burma Road," the name Chicagoans called the torn-up streets through which the underground runs. For years now the citizens here have become accustomed to traffic jams, trip-ups and extended detours caused by the ripped-up streets.

The subway, a modest affair as far as big cities go, was built to relieve the traffic problem in the famous "Loop" area which, up until now, has had to accommodate buses, trolleys and an elevated railroad. The subway runs north and south on State Street.

Cupid In Khaki

NEW YORK — Marriages last year reached an estimated record-breaking total of 1,800,000, of which two-thirds had servicemen as bridegrooms. This is 11 percent more than in 1941 and 83 percent more than in 1932.

The greatest increases took place in the Far West where San Diego, Cal., scored a 159 percent jump to lead the United States. San Antonio led the Southwest with a 62 percent rise.

One magazine attributed the marital boom to the lower draft age, the increase in the armed forces and the war production rise bringing greater employment.

Easter Casualty

WASHINGTON—The traditional Easter egg-rolling ceremonies on the White House lawn have been cancelled again this year. The Department of Agriculture asked that Easter eggs this year be used only for eating and hatching. The Department is also trying to discourage Easter purchases of baby chicks and ducks as pets.

Women MD's In Army

WASHINGTON — Women doctors will soon have direct commission in the Army and Navy, if

(Continued on Page 3)

1D. THE STARS AND STRIPES 1D.
Daily Newspaper of U.S. Armed Forces in the European Theater of Operations
Vol. 3 No. 136 New York, N.Y.—London, England Saturday, April 10, 1943

Allies Advance, 10,000 Prisoners Taken

U.S. Freezes All Salaries, Prices, Jobs

Drastic Orders from FDR Issued to Halt U.S. Inflation Swirl

WASHINGTON, Apr. 9—All wages, salaries and prices in the United States have been frozen at their present levels in a sweeping series of Executive Orders which are the most drastic steps the United States has taken to halt the inflationary spiral. Under the measures, workers may not change to higher priced jobs unless the move benefits war production.

The basic order was signed by President Roosevelt yesterday and today the chiefs of the prices, food and manpower commissions were busy getting out amplifications and drafting specific rules to adapt the order to their particular fields.

Under the order there will be no further increases of wages or salaries, beyond those provided in existing agreements. The order will have the effect of damping demands for wage increases which have been growing apparent recently—particularly on the part of John L. Lewis' United Mine Workers. An exception is made to permit the functioning of the so-called "Little Steel Formula"—wage increases to meet rises in the cost of living index.

It was not clear, from the original order, whether it would have the effect of establishing the $25,000 salary roof which Congress rejected recently.

Price Levels to be Set

Levels will be established for all commodities which may be altered later by the Office of Price Administration. They may be reduced to stop profiteering, or increased when production is threatened by retail prices which make production uneconomic.

As it affects the manpower commission, the order provides that workers may not change to higher-paid jobs unless the change is in the interests of war production. This gives authorities an unparalleled control over labor in the United States, bringing the country almost into line with regulations in force in Great Britain.

The last major price control step was taken last October when "ceilings" were established on food and innumerable household goods. The orders being written today carry out the same plan but go into much greater detail, stopping up leaks which developed in the original order.

Despite the earlier regulations, prices have been working their way up and there have been demands for wage increases to meet them. The present orders seek to halt both price and wage increases.

U.S. Navy to be Increased By Two-Thirds in 1943

INDIANAPOLIS, Apr. 9—The tonnage of the U.S. battle fleets will be increased by two-thirds this year, without allowing for probable losses, Secretary of the Navy Frank Knox said here today.

The efforts of the Navy Department this year, he said, would be marked by two special accomplishments on which the department has put all energy and will aircraft carriers and destroyer escorts.

The number of carriers completed this year, he said, would multiply many times the carrier strength at the end of 1942.

The number of destroyer escorts, for anti-submarine work, will be greater than the total number of all destroyers in service at the end of 1942.

Lehman Here to Study Post-War Relief Problem

Herbert H. Lehman, Director of the U.S. Office of Foreign Relief and Rehabilitation Operations, who is in London to study the problem of feeding, clothing and housing the population of Axis-dominated countries after they have been freed by Allied forces, visited British Foreign Secretary Anthony Eden with U.S. Ambassador John G. Winant yesterday.

Lehman resigned as Governor of New York Dec. 3, 1942, to accept the job which he called "the greatest opportunity for service ever offered." The organization already is providing relief in North Africa in the sections around Algiers and Morocco.

Loading for The Kill

At a base in Algiers, U.S. crews load General Sherman tanks to be sent to the Tunisian battlefields. Yesterday American armored forces were credited with aiding the Eighth Army advance toward Sfax by battering the bulk of Rommel's armor protecting the coastal plains surrounding Sfax.

Easter Cards, V-Mail Style, Flying Home by Thousands

Easter greetings from American soldiers in the ETO are flying back home by the thousands on illustrated V-Mail blanks. Thousands of forms already have been distributed and mailed, while increased demands for more have kept GI artists and mimeograph operators working overtime to get them out in time to reach the States by Apr. 25.

Postal officials report the flood of V-Mail Easter greetings is almost as great as it was at Christmas, when soldier cartoonists first turned out specially designed greetings in mass production.

Special Service Section, London Base Command, said yesterday 10,000 blanks were distributed from its office in the last two weeks, including 1,000 Passover greetings for Apr. 20 to soldiers of Jewish faith. An additional 6,000 Easter forms were available today for late comers.

With only a limited number of conventional Easter cards on sale at stationery shops near an infantry division base in Britain, the popularity of mimeographed V-Mail greetings swept camp like rumors at an induction center.

Among the half-dozen designs of Easter bunnies, baby chicks and eggs circulated throughout the division was a creation by S Sgt. Edward F. Fieseler, of Annapolis, Md., mess sergeant, who drew sketches between meals.

Sgt. Elmer J. Holdsworth, of Elsmere, Del., cut the stencil and Pvt. Marty Willen, of Baltimore, ran off mimeographed copies.

The blanks circulated by the LBC Special Service Section resulted from the work of Pfc Joseph Cunningham, of Brooklyn, staff artist and former Associated Press cartoonist. Cunningham also illustrated the Passover forms.

RAF in 'Heavy' Attack on Ruhr

21 Planes Fail to Return, Weather Described as 'Bad' by Crews

Heavy bombers of the RAF attacked Germany's industrial heart Thursday night in the second blow against the Ruhr in less than a week. An Air Ministry communique yesterday said 21 planes failed to return.

The weather over Germany was "bad," returning crews reported, and the effects of the bombing were difficult to observe. Beyond describing the attack as "heavy" the communique gave no indication of how many planes were involved or the amount of explosives dropped on Hitler's arms-producing center.

In the earlier blow at the Ruhr on Saturday, a great fleet of four-engined air freighters raided the Krupp works at Essen and unloaded a 900-ton cargo of bombs. Essen was the target for two big raids last month.

In addition to bombing the heavily-defended Ruhr, British planes laid mines in enemy waters Thursday night, the Air Ministry said.

The Ruhr is the best defended area in all Germany. More than 1,000 heavy guns are believed to be concentrated there with at least 300 at Essen alone. For every heavy gun there are at least two

(Continued on page 4)

10,000 Warplane Reserve In the States, Report Shows

ALLIED HQ, Southwest Pacific, Apr. 9 (UP)—America already has built up a reserve of 10,000 warplanes in the U.S., according to an authoritative estimate made here today.

This reserve does not include any part of American plane production either shipped overseas or assigned to other theaters of war, the estimate showed.

Alexander Lauds U.S. Second Corps For Part in Drive

Desert Air Force Pounds Fleeing Enemy, Yanks Mop Up El Guettar Sector, British Reach Mahares Line

ALLIED HQ, North Africa, Apr. 9 (AP)—The blitz forces of the British Eighth Army pursued Rommel's beaten Afrika Korps up the Tunisian coast today as the Desert Air Force pounded the enemy troops fleeing northeast from Mazzouna and north from Mahares. The Eighth Army had taken 9,500 prisoners since the initial attacks on Tuesday morning.

The American Second Corps mopped up the El Guettar area, taking 1,300 prisoners. Its achievement in engaging the bulk of the enemy's armor earlier this week on the Eighth Army's flank was highly praised by General Alexander at a press conference.

Raids by British and American aircraft were maintained against the retreating foe during the last two days. A total of 130 enemy vehicles have been destroyed and 200 damaged.

U.S. troops today captured the Djebel Mazaila height in the mountain range north of Maknassy.

Rommel, pressed hard by Gen. Montgomery's forces, was growing short of transports to extricate his rearguard.

In the Medjez El Bab sector of northern Tunisia, the British offensive operations continued and long-range guns knocked out two enemy tanks.

One enemy tank concentration in this area was observed being violently attacked yesterday by German Stukas, which had obviously mistaken their target.

It was not known how many Panzers were knocked out by the Stukas' error, but the British troops were jubilant at the sight and trusted that the German results were effective.

The Eighth Army now has reached a line running roughly from Maknassy to Mahares, on the coast of Tunisia a little more than 20 miles from Sfax. The railday from Sfax to Gafsa, which branches off from the coast near Mahares, is assumed to be partly in their hands.

As they advance the Eighth Army men are carrying out outflanking maneuvers similar to that which trapped large Axis forces at different stages of the long retreat across the desert.

Windy, rainy weather hampered ground operations in the north, however. Roads and fields were turned into the same "gooey" mud which the Allies had endured all winter.

More than 400 prisoners had been taken in the Medjez El Bab fighting since Wednesday.

Gen. Eisenhower, in a message to Gen. Alexander, declared the Allied forces in North Africa were "in a position to exact a full price from the enemy now confronting us in Tunisia."

Winston Burdett, CBS radio commentator, broadcasting from Algiers, said the Eighth Army, going as strong as ever after two major battles, was about 45 miles from Sfax.

The North African air forces hit 66 Axis ships during March, he said, sinking 17, severely damaging 23 and damaging 16. Nineteen small craft, hit in the Sardinia area, were not included in these figures.

"If Rommel intends to go home in ships, he will not have a picnic," he said.

In the central sector enemy transports moving north to Zaghouan, 15 miles east of Pont Du Fahs, were attacked by RAF Spitfires and four vehicles were damaged. American Spitfires damaged one Messerschmitt during battle patrols.

In a blistering attack which lasted from

(Continued on page 4)

Jap Withdrawal At Lae for New Base Reported

Enemy Hastily Developing Airports Near Wewak, 300 Miles North

A Japanese withdrawal from Lae and Salamaua in British New Guinea is believed to lie behind considerable enemy activity along the northeast coast of the island, according to reliable reports from the Southwest Pacific.

The Japs are hastily developing Wewak, 300 miles north of Lae, as their main base, and Mandang, 150 miles north of Lae, as their main forward base.

A huge airfield is under construction with fighter fields nearby in Wewak.

A single Hudson bomber on reconnaissance yesterday bombed and strafed 12 Japanese supply barges for one hour off Kaukenau, on the coast of Dutch New Guinea, today's Allied communique says.

Fires were started on a patrol boat and three power-driven barges. The remainder were hit and damaged.

The communique also revealed that 34 instead of 37 Jap planes were shot down near Guadalcanal yesterday.

The Japanese, in a communique today, stated that in a battle off the Florida Island coast, a U.S. cruiser and a U.S. destroyer had been sunk, as well as ten transports.

Off Aru Islands another Hudson strafed seven small native praaus. Hudsons also raided Timika airfield and Saumlaki jetty. In the northeast sector heavy bombers bombed the new Panapai airfield at Kavieng, then bombed and strafed various targets at Finschafen.

Tokyo Radio Warns U.S. Planning Raids on Japan

NEW YORK, N.Y., Apr. 9—Two Tokyo radio commentators have warned the Japanese people within the past 48 hours that the U.S. might be planning to bomb Japan.

One announcer said that it would soon be the anniversary of the first bombing, and that a new attack might come at any time from China, the Aleutians, or from aircraft-carriers. He added that American naval construction was making "frantic headway."

P40 Finally Gets Smart Aleck Jap

NEW DELHI, Apr. 9 (AP)—An American kid in a streamlined P40 wrote finish—in blood—to the taunting of a Jap smart Aleck who used to irritate the boys up in Assam when he came over in a high-flying twin-engined reconnaissance plane.

The Jap, nicknamed "Photo Joe," used to come in at 26,000 and 28,000 feet to take pictures of American bases. His radio was on the same frequency as American sets, and insults were freely exchanged.

"Never mind trying to come after me, boys. Stay down on the ground where you belong," the Jap would say in good English. "I getting out now."

The Jap was serenely smug and self-confident. He knew the Yanks hadn't anything that could climb fast enough to catch him. So he always got away, leaving Yanks swearing impotently on the ground below.

Impotently—well, maybe for a while. But Yank ingenuity wouldn't let this insult continue indefinitely. The boys went to work on a P40 and stripped it until it was capable of getting upstairs in time to make the yellow son of a turtle eat his own words. Then they "layed for him."

Thursday he came over again.

Young Lt. Charley T. Streit, Newburgh, N.Y., jumped into the streamlined P40 and took off for "Photo Joe" who was circling around, broadcasting his usual taunts between clicks of his camera shutter.

"Think fast, Mister Photo Joe," Charley said in effect. "Here I come."

A few seconds later he was on Joe's tail and was pressing the firing button. But Joe didn't fall—not this time, for Charley's guns jammed.

Joe by this time was hightailing for home, but Charley kept right on his tail.

Charley got his guns unjammed and fired again. Still no luck. One burst and the guns jammed again. The guns, in fact, jammed a total of three times, until Charley finally got in an effective burst that sent Joe, and his crew of two accompanying him, to a reunion with their Hon. Ancestors On Other Side of River.

This was the second Jap plane officially credited to Charley, who, incidentally, was a New York State neighbor to President Roosevelt.

Lt. Streit previously destroyed a bomber, for official credit.

It was at least the third Jap "recce" plane destroyed over Assam within a few months.

'Snooze And You Lose,' Nazi Prisoner Knows

WITH U.S. ARMY, Southern Tunisia, Apr. 9 (AP)—One drowsy German soldier has slept himself right into an American prison camp.

"We saw this fellow as we were mopping up hills," said Capt. Henry V. Meddlewerth, 23, of Rockville Center, L.I. "I got out my jeep and sent my driver one way toward the German while I got behind him.

"When he saw we had him from two directions he threw up his hands and surrendered. It turned out he had lain down for sleep and his unit had moved out in the night overlooking him in the darkness. He sure was one lonesome lost soldier."

THE STARS AND STRIPES

ALGIERS DAILY

Vol. 1 - No. 1 - Thursday, April 15, 1943 U. S. Army Daily Newspaper for troops in Algiers area 1 Franc

Yanks, Cards Are Choice To Repeat

Draft-Riddled Clubs Open Season On Wednesday

The baseball season opens Wednesday and the 16 clubs are going ahead despite the fact that many of the key players are in the service and others are slated to go.

The future is uncertain but in Washington, President Roosevelt, an ardent baseball fan, received his annual gold-engraved American League pass from Owner Clark Griffith and said he'd try his darndest to be on hand to toss out the first ball in the game between the Senators and the Athletics. This game will be played a day earlier in the nation's capital.

One thing the experts agree on this year and that is, that the American and National Leagues will stage the hottest race in its history. The following article cabled especially to The Stars and Stripes, will give you an idea of what to expect from the major leagues in 1943.

By ARTHUR PATTERSON

(New York Herald Tribune Writer)

NEW YORK, April 14—Colonel William Harold (Bill) Terry retired generalissimo of the New York Giants, took time out from his Memphis farm the other day to predict there will be another nickel World Series this year—but all five cent carfares, Bill said, would be paid to St. Louis conductors.

Yes sir, Colonel Bill, looking at baseball as a disinterested party thinks not only will the St. Louis Cards win the National League pennant, but Luke Sewell's St. Louis Browns will cop the American League pennant and be the October classic competitors. And the Browns never won a pennant yet.

CLOSE RACE

There are many—this correspondent included—who disagree with the Colonel but his startling statement gives a fair idea of what kind of flipflop baseball has taken. Only one thing seems certain as teams move toward the opening day April 21—both leagues will present the keenest competition from gong to gong and at least four clubs in each circuit should be in the running as late as Sept 1.

From this corner it looks like the Yankees and Cardinals again with the St. Louis Browns, Boston Red Sox and Detroit Tigers giving Marse Joe McCarthy's athletes considerable annoyance and with the Dodgers, Cincinnati Reds, Chicago Cubs heckling Billy Southworth's Redbirds right down the finish. We regret to state that the New York Giants look definitely second division calibre despite their surprising third place finish last year under Mel Ott's leadership.

Pitching will tell the story in both leagues. Strangely few hurlers have been inducted into the service. They must be the marrying kind. The Yankees lost Red Ruffing to the Army and traded El Goofo Gomez to the Boston Braves but they have a stalwart

(Continued on Page 2)

Sights, Downs JU-52 In Three Minutes

Reminiscent of the American pilot's now famous words, "sighted sub, sank same," is the following cryptic entry made in the log of an RAF Beaufighter observer, Sgt. Fred Baker:

"11.13, sighted JU-52.

"11.14, JU shot down into sea.

"11.15, resumed course."

The Beaufighter was piloted by Flight Officer Gordon Link, 23, of the Royal Canadian Air Force. The JU-52 was sighted off the Sicilian coast.

Stars And Stripes Begins Algiers Daily

With this issue, *The Stars and Stripes* of Africa begins publishing a daily newspaper for troops stationed in the Department of Algiers. The Algiers Daily is not to be confused with the weekly *Stars and Stripes*, which will continue to be circulated throughout North Africa.

The Stars and Stripes Algiers Daily will be published five times weekly, Monday through Friday. Beginning next week, April 24, *The Stars and Stripes* weekly paper for North Africa will be published on Saturday instead of on Fridays, as heretofore.

The Algiers Daily is the first of a series of daily *Stars and Stripes* contemplated for the North Africa theater of war. As rapidly as possible, dailies will be initiated in other key centers. Plans also are under way for organizing a mobile publishing unit to print a daily bulletin for troops in the combat areas.

The Algiers Daily will be ready for early morning distribution, but mechanical difficulties force us to close the daily forms at 1900 hours —five hours earlier than the local French morning newspapers close. For this reason, we will be unable to print news breaking in the five hours from 1900 to midnight, and therefore will be printing such news one day late.

The Algiers Daily will be distributed through military channels to major camps and units in the area. It will also be on sale by civilian newsdealers.

Here are the three ways you may secure your copy of the Algiers Daily:

1. Call at the *Stars and Stripes* office, 10 Blvd. Baudin, 5th floor of the Red Cross Service Club, or phone 336.60 Extension 66 and place an order for your unit.

2. Place your order with the nearest civilian newsdealer, arranging with the dealer for him to deliver it or for you to pick it up.

3. Buy it individually from a local newsdealer or boy.

In order to prevent a burden on army transportation facilities, it is urged, wherever possible, you make arrangements to secure your Dailies through civilian newsdealers or boys in the street, or that you arrange to pick up your papers for your unit at the *Stars and Stripes* office.

Free distribution will be made to patients in British and American hospitals.

The price to all other soldiers is one franc. No subscriptions can be accepted for the Algiers Daily either for individual delivery in Algiers or to the States. You are permitted to mail your copy home, if you wish.

You may subscribe for the WEEKLY edition to be sent home at any time. The cost is 100 francs for one year's subscription.

Big Ovation For Wallace

Peruvians Cover Him With Flowers

CUZCO, Peru, April 14 — Vice-President Henry A. Wallace's trip through the Latin American republics continues to be a succession of triumphs. When he arrived here four days ago, he drove to the town hall and was literally covered with flowers thrown by people standing along the road who shouted: "Long live the democracies." After that he became an honorary member of the faculty of the University of Cuzco.

The academic ceremony was followed by a tremendous reception held in the honor of the Vice-President. Dr. David Chapparro, president of the university, assured Mr. Wallace of his conviction that President Roosevelt's plan for post-war reconstruction was the basis of a lasting peace with security for all nations and peoples.

Mr. Wallace, who pleased his audience when he spoke in Spanish, devoted much of his speech to the contributions to modern agriculture made by the peasants who settled near Cuzco centuries ago. He said they were a symbol of the free America and he expressed the hope that they would contribute largely to the much-needed supply of foods to war-devastated Europe.

Summer Vacations For War Workers

WASHINGTON, April 14—Workers will be permitted to have summer vacations this year after all. The government wants them to relax for a time, according to Donald P. Nelson, who holds that short vacations for industrial workers will pay dividends later on.

"Experience has proven," he said, "that volume production is increased if workers can restore their energies through periods of physical and mental rest. Vacations must be planned so that substitutes may step into the jobs in order to keep up the production goals for this year, which are twice as large as last year."

New War Bond Drive Opens

NEW YORK, April 14—The second war loan drive, which has a three week goal of 13 billion dollars, opened officially at Carnegie Hall when Treasury Secretary Henry Morgenthau appealed to Americans to tighten their belts and send more of their dollars into the war effort.

Cheers resounded through the meeting-place when Morgenthau said that the United Nations were piling up "thunderclouds of the greatest attack in history."

A tremendous response from the nation was reported. Banks, insurance companies and investors from every walk of life were pitching in their dollars to make the drive a success.

Anti-Fascist Says Eyeties May Mutiny

NEW YORK, April 14—Luigi Antonini, president of the Italian American Labor Council, said last night that underground reports from Rome say an anti-fascist revolt is brewing and that a military mutiny this month is likely.

His statement was made at a dinner honoring Attorney General Anthony Biddle who was presented with the Council's Four Freedoms Award.

In his acceptance speech, Mr. Biddle said it was time for the Italians to quit dying for the Germans.

Four Convicts Fail In Alcatraz Break

SAN FRANCISCO, April 14—Floyd Hamilton, one-time Public Enemy No. One, and three other convicts made a sensational attempt yesterday to escape the Federal Prison at Alcatraz in a vain dash for liberty.

After slugging two guards, the four notorious criminals jumped into the bay but their efforts ended in disaster. Only Harold Brennan, Pittsburgh kidnapper and bank robber, was caught trying to swim ashore. James Boarman, serving 20 years for robbery, was drowned.

Hamilton and Fred Hunter, gangmen pals of the notorious Alvin Karpis, are still missing but authorities said they had probably drowned in the strong rip tide.

Alcatraz, known as "The Rock" to the underworld, is considered escape-proof.

To this foreboding prison built on a small rocky island in the San Francisco harbor are sent the nation's most desperate criminals. Al Capone served his sentence here. The last attempt to escape was made five years ago by two Oklahoma bandits, Theodore Cole and Ralph Roe, who leaped into the bay and were never seen again.

Dorothy Thompson To Wed Refugee

NEW YORK, April 14—Dorothy Thompson, the columnist and commentator on international events, is going to become a June bride.

Not long ago Miss Thompson, who almost always is to be found entertaining refugees from Hitler's Germany in her Central Park West apartment, agreed to sit for a portrait to be painted by Maxim Kopf, a Czechoslovakian painter. The result was the forthcoming marriage.

Miss Thompson is the former wife of Sinclair Lewis, the novelist and Nobel Prize winner. They have one son. Miss Thompson was a former correspondent for the New York Post in Vienna and Berlin, having left Germany only when Hitler came to power there and she was forced to leave. She had one famous interview with Hitler, after which she was quoted as saying that Hitler would never come to power in the Reich.

Knox Dispels Aussies' Fear Over Japs

But Tells Press About Threat To Alaska

WASHINGTON, April 14 — Secretary of Navy Frank Knox today went far in dispelling fears of a Japanese invasion of Australia raised by Gen. Thomas Blamey, commander of the Australian Army and deputy to Gen. Douglas McArthur.

Gen. Blamey said the Japs had massed 200,000 men on the islands north of Australia, but Knox countered by saying that a concentration of an enemy fleet would be a necessary prelude to an invasion and there were no signs of such a fleet in that area.

Discounting the South Pacific somewhat, Knox focused attention on the Aleutian Islands again. He said that despite frequent bombings and naval assaults, the Japanese are building a string of air bases from Tokio toward Alaska which even fighter planes can span. He said that the enemy has constructed a half mile runway at Kiska and a long bomber field at Attu, the island furthest west in the Aleutians.

Meanwhile, there has been a considerable renewal of air activity in New Guinea. The Allied air offensive against Japanese land bases continued unabated with American airmen accounting for 52 enemy planes over Port Moresby and Oro Bay.

Further attempts of the Japs to mass planes in the Islands north of Australia for an air attack suffered a stinging setback when Gen MacArthur's bombers downed 76 aircraft in two days.

Eighth Army Drives For Enfidaville

RAF, Fortresses Smash Axis Lines Of Supply

ALLIED FORCE HEADQUARTERS, April 14—While the 1st Army continued to punch eastward in the Medjez-el-Bab—Munchar area against the Germans' hard-pressed flank, today, the 8th Army pushed north toward Enfidaville and threatened the weakened base of Rommel's army

Enfidaville, which has been mentioned in communiques during the last few days, is located north of Sousse at the southern end of the last tier of German defenses of the Tunis-Bizerte area. It protects the German position in the north. Enfidaville is also a strong Axis airbase and has been used as a forward field for Luftwaffe missions this week.

Ground activity today consisted mostly of powerful combat patrols of both 1st and 8th Armies. French patrols of Gen. Biosson's army moved out from strongly-held ridges in the range of mountains northwest of Kairouan to probe the enemy's position.

It was a much bigger day in the air than on land.

SICILY HIT

During yesterday and today, the Allies air forces pounded Jerry at his rear airbases in Sicily and his forward fields near Tunis. A total of 73 enemy aircraft were destroyed yesterday on the ground at Castelvetrano and Milo, Sicily, by American Flying Fortresses of the Northwest African Air Forces. Most of these planes, according to photo reconnaissance which provided the day's totals, were giant transports designed to supply Rommel's retreating forces.

At the Castelvetrano airport which the Fortresses dropped their bombs were 112 large transports. Of these, 51 were blasted to bits and others were seriously damaged. At Milo, 105 planes were on the ground when the airport was attacked and 22 of these were wrecked. In addition, U. S. flyers set fire to a gasoline dump. Four Axis planes in the air were also destroyed at Milo.

In today's operations, Beaufighters of the Coastal Airforce, commanded by Air Vice-Marshal Hugh Lloyd, intercepted a formation of more than 12 Axis torpedo-carrying planes. They shot down two of these, damaged others and forced the remainder to jettison their torpedos and run for it. A JU-88 and a DO-217 were destroyed.

TUNIS FIELDS BOMBED

Other heavy attacks were launched against the Megrine airdrome at Pochville, on the outskirts of Tunis. Bisleys and Wellingtons of the strategic Air Force bombed Megrine, operating as teams for the night attack. One team dumped the incendiaries and the other scored with fragmentation bombs.

The Oudna landing ground south of Tunis was also hit today by B-25 Mitchells with an escort of Spitfires and Hurricanes. In the Medjez-el-Bab sector, RAF fighters intercepted three ME-109's. Many hits were observed and plumes of white smoke poured out. Pieces fell off the ME-109 and it crash-landed.

Credit for one of yesterday's air victories, according to an announcement here, goes to Americans aboard Fortresses over Milo, they brought down four enemy planes. They include S-Sgt. B. M. MacGill, of Lakeland, Fla., Sgt. Joseph Ribec, of Worchester, Mass., T-Sgt. William Sibeski, L. I., N. Y.

In the attack on the 12 Axis torpedo-carrying planes by Coastal Air Force Beaufighters, F-O M. J. Gloster, of Solihull, Warwickshire, got one of the planes, thereby bringing his total victories in North Africa to five. F-O H. K. Humphreys, of Hampton Arden, Warwickshire, scored the other victory. Humphreys joined the squadron only two days ago. This was his first operational patrol with them.

1d THE STARS AND STRIPES 1d
Daily Newspaper of U.S. Armed Forces in the European Theater of Operations
Vol. 3 No. 147 New York, N.Y.—London, England Saturday, April 24, 1943

Allies Advance in North and Along Coast

Tokyo Raid Fliers Slain, U.S. Reveals

Executions Enrage Nation; New Attacks Demanded; Airmen Volunteer

WASHINGTON, Apr. 23—Thousands of American airmen, enraged by a White House disclosure that the Japanese had executed some of the American fliers captured after the Tokyo raid, were volunteering today for further raids on Japanese cities, and a wave of angry demands for such raids was sweeping the nation.

President Roosevelt revealed the executions "with a feeling of deepest horror, which I know will be shared by all civilized peoples." The Japanese government, in an official communication to the U.S. government, had admitted executing some of the fliers after trying them on charges of intentionally bombing non-military objectives.

Immediately after the announcement, Gen. Henry H. Arnold, commander of the United States Army Air Forces, in a message to air forces throughout the world, urged them to redouble their efforts until "the inhuman war lords" of Japan have been "utterly destroyed." In Africa, Maj. Gen. James H. Doolittle, who led the historic raid, expressed his anger and vowed that "soon our bombers will be there again."

Berlin Condones Executions

Berlin radio condoned the executions in a broadcast which said: "Murder has been committed exclusively by those who with their air terror against women and children, spurn all the laws of humanity. The execution of the American assassins will be considered a just punishment by every right-thinking person."

News of the executions, in violation of the Geneva convention on treatment of prisoners, infuriated the nation as nothing has since Pearl Harbor, and everywhere there were demands that immediate heavy raids be made on Japan in retaliation.

Americans were particularly horrified by the President's statement that only by torture could the Japanese have obtained the confessions they claimed were made by members of the raiding party that non-military objects were picked out.

No Reprisals on Prisoners

The U.S. government quickly announced that there would be no reprisals against Japanese prisoners in U.S. hands -but that reprisals would be made after the war against the officials responsible.

The President called attention to the fact that the press had just published the full details of the Tokyo raid, in which eight of the 80 participants were known to have been captured after crash-landing in Japanese territory and two others were still unaccounted for.

On Oct. 19, he said, the United States learned from Tokyo broadcasts "of the capture, trial and severe punishment of those Americans." Communicating through the Swiss government, the United States finally received an admission from Tokyo on March 12, 1943, that the captured crew men had been tried and sentenced to death.

"It was further stated," the President said, "that the death penalty was commuted for some, but that the sentence of death had been applied to others."

In a formal communication sent to the

(Continued on page 4)

First American Freed by Italy

ANKARA, Apr. 23 (AP)—Alan Stuyvesant, of New York, believed to be the first American prisoner of the Axis to be exchanged, arrived here yesterday in a group of British prisoners who are being repatriated in exchange for sick and wounded Italians.

Stuyvesant brought news of a number of other American prisoners captured in Tunisia and now held at a camp near Rome. He said Red Cross packages, important to the men, have begun arriving at the camp.

The other Americans who Stuyvesant saw, all of whom he said were well and fairly happy, were:

Glenn Wilson, Ann Arbor, Mich.; Lt. Conrad Kreps and Capt. Harry Frazee, both of Akron, Ohio; Bob Weigand, Cincinnati; Richard Yeats, Monroe, Mich.; Frank Hawkins, Toledo, Ohio; Henry Wyssen, Youngstown, Ohio; Al Barnes, North Martinsdale, W. Va.; Ray Bulek and Ed Mullen, both of Chicago; Flying Officer Dan Newman, San Diego, Cal.; Pilot Officer Claude Weaher, Oklahoma City, and J. Williams, Carlsbad, N.M.

Historic Take-off to Tokyo, 800 Miles Away

Keystone Photo

With Jimmy Doolittle at the controls, a B25 Mitchell bomber leaves the deck of the aircraft carrier Hornet on the historic bombing mission to Tokyo—800 miles away. Maj. Gen. Doolittle, now leader of the Strategic Air Force in Africa, baled out over China after the daylight raid. (Photo just released by the War Department and radioed to London.)

AEF Observes Second Easter In British Isles Tomorrow

By Bryce W. Burke
Stars and Stripes Staff Writer

Members of the U.S. forces throughout the British Isles will celebrate Easter tomorrow at religious services in city parks, old English cathedrals, neighborhood churches and in their own camps and installations.

Beginning at sunrise, ceremonies will be held throughout the day at which Americans will join with civilians and members of the Allied forces in commemorating the Resurrection of Christ.

In Hyde Park, London, the British public will be guests of the American Army at a sunrise service which will be followed in the afternoon by a Vesper service in St. Paul's Cathedral.

In addition to religious observance of the day members of the U.S. Forces will be hosts to evacuated and orphaned children at camps all over the Isles. During the 15 months of the second AEF these parties have become features of holidays.

At the open-air ceremony in Hyde Park, which will begin at 6.45 AM, more than 4,000 persons are expected to be present when Chaplain Chester R. McClelland, of Dallas, Tex., gives the call to worship and invocation, after which Brig. Gen. Pleas B. Rogers, of Austin, Tex., Commanding General, London Base Command, will read the Scripture lesson.

LBC Chorus to Sing

Following the singing of "The Holy City" by the LBC chorus, Chaplain James L. Blakeney, theater chaplain from Little Rock, Ark., will read his Easter message to the troops.

After the hymn "Low in the Grave He Lay," and the Benediction, the service will close with the playing of the Star Spangled Banner by the LBC band under the direction of W/O Frank Rosato, of New Orleans.

The Vesper service at St. Paul's will begin at 4.45 with a procession, during which Cpl. Heinz Arnold will be at the organ. Chaplain McClelland again will give the call to worship with the invocation by Lt. Col. E. J. Blakely Jr., of Lexington, Va. Gen. Rogers will read the scripture lesson and Chaplain Blakeney will give the sermon. Following the hymn "Onward Christian Soldiers" will be the Benediction and the recessional.

Soldiers who wish to bring friends to this service may obtain reserved seats from their company commanders or at the

(Continued on page 4)

Bomber Men To Stage An Egg-Rolling Contest

A U.S. BOMBER STATION, England, Apr. 23—Although no eggs will be rolled on the White House lawn this Easter, an egg-rolling contest is going to be put on here.

The contest will take place in front of Chaplain Eugene L. Lamb's office.

All the eggs will be powdered and rolled in the can.

ETOUSA Rules On Commissions

Direct Appointments Only In Special Cases; 1942 Quota Exceeded

Officer candidates in this theater are to be commissioned only on completion of training at the American School Center, and direct appointments for commissions will be given only in special cases and at the discretion of the Theater Commander, according to a bulletin issued by Headquarters, ETOUSA.

The bulletin followed an announcement by the War Department that the training program for officer candidates in 1942 was so successful as to reduce materially the number of candidates needed for 1943.

The next course of OCS in ETO will start on or about May 15 and will last for a period of 12 weeks. New courses will start at intervals of six weeks.

Applicants for these courses, except those in the basic arms, must have sufficient training in their branch or service to insure their ability to become officers in that branch or service.

Men who don't have the military background required for the theater school, but have civilian experience or education which would qualify them for training, will be sent to schools in the United States.

Men whose civilian background has specially qualified them as officer material for either the Signal Corps or the Corps of Engineers will be sent to the United States by the first available transportation.

Also sent to schools in the United States will be men who have qualified for officers' training in the postal, machine records and censorship sections of the Adjutant General's Department, Armored Forces, Cavalry, Coast Artillery, Field Artillery, or as Aviation cadets.

On completion of the courses, each candidate will be commissioned a second lieutenant in the Army of the U.S.

63 Nazi Planes Shot Down by U.S. at Bremen

Final Total on Raids Week Ago Set New Mark For USAAF

Sixty-three German fighter planes were destroyed by American bombers over Bremen last Saturday, it was officially announced by Eighth Air Force Bomber Command yesterday.

This figure tops by 11 the previous record of 52 enemy aircraft destroyed in one raid—on Vegesack Mar. 18, which was carried out by both Fortresses and Liberators.

The official total of 63 destroyed does not include the number of German planes crews claimed as "probably destroyed" or "damaged."

Information gathered by intelligence officers from Fortress crews indicated that there were 150 German fighters sent up to engage the USAAF bombers over the Focke-Wulf plant in Bremen. Ninety-five of the 150 were shot out of action, either destroyed or damaged.

Most Bombers Lost

Sixteen bombers were lost on the Bremen raid, more than twice the number lost on any previous raid. Seven planes were lost Jan. 3, over St. Nazaire, and seven failed to return from the Wilhelmshaven raid, Feb. 26. Only two bombers were lost in the raid on Vegesack, less than 20 miles from the Focke-Wulf factory target in Bremen.

The number of Fortresses taking part in the raid was not announced. On a previous occasion Maj. Gen. Ira C. Eaker stated that the combined Fortress and Liberator strength on March raids had ranged from 85 to 120.

Light U.S. and British bombers were reported by Vichy radio to have dropped "about 20 bombs" on the suburbs of Boulogne-Sur-Mer yesterday. There was no confirmation from the Eighth Air Force.

Yesterday the Air Ministry reported that RAF bombers mined enemy waters the night before at a loss of two planes.

Germany Warned of Gas Raids If Axis Uses It Against Reds

A stern warning by Prime Minister Winston Churchill that the Allies will use gas against Germany should the Nazi forces use gas against the Russians was being broadcast to Germany yesterday by BBC.

"Reports have been issued from several sources that Hitler is making preparations for using poison gas against the Russian front," Mr. Churchill said. He warned that any use of poison gas against the Russians "will immediately be followed by the fullest possible use of this process of war upon the German munitions centers, sea ports, and other military objectives throughout the whole extent of Germany."

He added that "British resources and scale of delivery have greatly increased since last year. The necessary precautions against German reprisals have already been enjoined by the competent authorities throughout the United Kingdom."

Following the Prime Minister's first warning to Germany June 10, 1942, Home Secretary Herbert Morrison told the British that "for all we know gas attack may never come." On Tuesday, however, he warned the public not to assume that the possibility of enemy gas attack had ended.

The strongest deterrent against a German chemical warfare offensive is the fact the Allied aircraft now rule the European air, and should the RAF decide to carry gas into Germany the results would be considerably more effective than anything the enemy could offer, London observers declared.

Every Yard Is Contested By Rommel

First Army Gains 3 Miles, Eighth Goes 6; Another Big Air Victory

ALLIED HQ, Apr. 23 (AP)—Gen. Alexander hurled the Anglo-American First Army into the attack against Rommel's mountain positions today, driving three miles forward on a nine-mile front near Bou Arada, while the Eighth Army smashed six miles north of Enfidaville.

In the air Allied fighters wiped out an air fleet of 20 giant German six-engined transport planes—six-engined Messerschmitt 323s, each capable of carrying 140 men—over the Sicilian Straits. In the day's activity they accounted for 38 Axis planes. An official spokesman estimated that the 20 enemy transports were equal to the carrying capacity of 100 Ju25s.

Joining the Eighth Army in the assault on Rommel in the Bou Arada area, the First Army "achieved all initial objectives," headquarters said. Its advance between Goubellat and Bou Arada was made against "stubborn resistance."

Advanced elements of the Eighth Army, moving north along the coast towards Bou Ficha, reached a point six miles north of Enfidaville.

Pincer Movement

The First and Eighth Armies are now executing a pincer movement on Rommel's second mountain position.

The First Army's advance has taken it about 24 miles from Tunis on the western slope of the steep and difficult hills.

Bloody fighting was in progress on the Medjez El Bab sector, and it appeared that Alexander's tactics were becoming increasingly effective against Rommel's defenses along the whole line of the western front.

The Eighth Army advance along the coastal strip pushed forward through marshy ground against "extremely difficult and most stubborn resistance," a spokesman said. "Each inch of the ground is being vigorously contested."

Strike Long Stop Hill

In the First Army offensive in north-eastern Tunisia, Thunderbolt-like attacks swept the enemy perimeter defenses on half a dozen or more points before the dawn of Good Friday.

During a night in which rain, hail and stars alternated in the sky, heavy concentrations of British guns opened fire on a mile-wide objective and poured their deadly fury on Long Stop Hill, the strongest known enemy fortified point between Medjez El Bab and Tunis, 30 miles away.

Hard-fighting British infantry followed the creeping barrage to the face of Long Stop Hill, six miles northeast of Medjez El Bab, and since midnight their signal flares indicated that they were winning back this concrete ridge, where the Coldstream guards fought and died during Christmas week.

Hill Well Fortified

Long Stop Hill, between Djebel Ang and Djebel Ahmour, stands directly beside the road from Medjez el Bab to Terbourba and Tunis and its slopes are clustered with trenches, weapon pits, concrete gun emplacements and mines.

At midnight, as we watched, Long Stop Hill seemed to twinkle with the winking lights of British shell bursts. Near our vantage points a long convoy of ambulance drove forward, for victory has its price.

The biggest hole on the western front was punched by the British yesterday afternoon in the Sidi Ahmour area, 12 miles southeast of Medjez el Bab and five miles southeast of Goubellat.

German's Flying Tank In Action in Tunisia

ALLIED FORCE HQ, North Africa, Apr. 23 (AP)—The Luftwaffe's flying tank, which first appeared in Russia, has been used in the Western Desert fighting and has also been seeing duty in Tunisia.

The aircraft—Nenschel 129—was designed as an anti-tank plane. It is equipped with 30mm. cannon, the largest caliber gun yet found on German aircraft, and has a cockpit so heavily armored that it resembles part of a tank.

THE STARS AND STRIPES

Oran Daily

Vol. 1. - No. 1 - Monday, May 3, 1943 | U. S. Army Newspaper | One Franc

GOVERNMENT SEIZES STRUCK COAL MINES

Red Cross To Celebrate Four Gala Openings

All Oran Clubs To Take Part In Day's Events

The American Red Cross will hold formal openings for four Oran service clubs today which will combine ceremonies with celebrations marking five months of remarkable achievement here.

The base commander will head an official party which will conduct formal opening ceremonies at each of the four service clubs. In the party wil be Hon. William H. Shott, United States Consul; Col. George B. Pence, Chief of Staff; Lt. Col. P.C.R. St. Aubyn, British liaison officer; Lt. Col. Enos W. Curtin, Special Services Section; Lt. P. L. A. Des Landers, French liaison officer; Capt. P. H. Spellman, U. S. Navy; and [illegible] B. Brandreth aide to [illegible]

Th[illegible] established [illegible] time and now offer officers, and enlisted men many forms of entertainment, amusements, athletics, conveniences and special services.

A skeleton staff of workers organized and established the Allied Club here in December, and since then the growing organization has established the Officers club, for officers and nurses; the Empire Club for enlisted men, and the Alcazar Club, for Negro servicemen.

Although new facilities constantly are being added to the big Empire Club, enlisted men now enjoy the privileges of an air raid shelter, game room, 36 shower baths, badminton and volleyball, table games, telephone service, Office of Military Welfare, snack bar, souvenir card room, sketch room for artists, athletic equipment, loan library, state registration room, dance room, powder room for women, lounge and library.

The Empire Club also operates a theater for officers and enlisted men, where movies are shown both in the afternoon and night, and dining rooms, all at minimum cost to servicemen.

The Empire Club celebration will start at 2 PM this afternoon with a swing concert by the Engineers Band in the recreation room. The orchestra will play for an enlisted men's dance at the Club, starting at 6:30 PM. Three hundred tickets will be issued for the dance, 150 to be given to the first GI's who ask for them during the afternoon, and 150 to enlisted men who present

(Continued on Page 2)

How To Get Oran Daily

STARS AND STRIPES, Oran Daily, will be published Monday, Tuesday, Wednesday, Thursday and Friday of each week. On Saturdays, the weekly will be issued as heretofore. There will be no paper on Sundays.

Both Oran Daily and the weekly may be procured for any unit by arranging direct w[illegible] the STARS AND STRIPES office, 6 rue Hotel de Ville Oran Phone 25957 or, preferably, by placing your unit order w[illegible]h the nearest civilian newsdealer. Single copies may be bought from civilian newsdealers--daily one franc, weekly two francs.

The War Department does not permit individuals to mail Oran Daily to the U. S. (Unit censors please note) but subscriptions will be accepted for the daily at 250 francs per year.

You may subscribe for the weekly to be sent home, as heretofore, at 100 francs per year.

Shipyards Boost 1943 Launchings

NEW YORK, April 29--Speaking at the 31st annual meeting of the U. S. Chamber of Commerce here, WPB Vice-Chairman William Batt and Rear Admiral Emory Land, Maritime Commission chairman, gave an insight into the nation's production figures on planes, cargo vessels and tankers for 1943.

Admiral Land said that U. S. shipyards will build 19,000,000 deadweight tons of cargo vessels and tankers this year, as compared with 8,000,000 tons in 1942. He revealed that the nation's output of planes in '43 will be nearly 100,000 planes, thus doubling last year's production.

Reds Make Plans For New Drives

MOSCOW, May 2—Behind the bloody, hardfighting front lines the Russian people celebrated May Day yesterday with displays of bunting, messages of encouragement and with renewed preparation for an onslaught which they hope may soon free the Ukraine and the Crimea from the Nazi yoke.

Moscow was decked out in flags and finery for the traditional celebration. Broad strips of bunting decorated the balconies of the principal buildings. One of them carried a greeting to the "Anglo-American forces i n Tunesia." Through the color and the air of holiday was stamped the awareness of the grim struggle that continues from Leningar dto the Black Sea.

Observance of the revolutionary holiday started with an order of the day issued by Premier Stalin the night before, and broadcast over the Moscow radio. Said Stalin: "I congratulate you. The peoples of our country are celebrating May Day in stern days of patriatic war. They have entrusted their fate to the Red army and have not been mistaken in their trust. "The Soviet armies are defending their country with their breath. During the winter campaign of 1942-43, the Red Army has inflicted serious setbacks on the German Army, has wiped out large numbers of the enemy's men and great quantities of his war material: has encircled and liquidated two enemy armies before Stalingrad, and has taken prisoners more than 300,000 enemy officers and enlisted men.

Meanwhile, Soviet soldiers had resumed their offensive in the Kuban region, where they recaptured several key positions.

Berlin admitted strong Russian attacks, saying that the Red Army had rolled out tanks, 10 divisions of infantry, and a concentraton

(Continued on Page 2)

Epic Storm Batters Ohio

AKRON, Ohio, May 2 — This state's worst storm since the Lorain tornado 19 years ago, caused the death of three and injury to 200 or more, with this city and Cleveland and their suburbs bearing the brunt of the damage.

In this city alone, at least, 2,000 homes were damaged at losses estimated at 3,000,000 dollars while at Cleveland damage to property and personal goods will run into at least 1,000,000 dollars.

The dead were listed as Arthur Cawrea, of Cleveland, killed on his farm at Oberlin, and Richard Paternoster and Anthony Pernibeck, Akron orphans, who were trapped in a collapsed barn at Medina.

Yanks Take Hill Blocking Mateur Road

By DAVID GOLDING
(Stars and Stripes Staff Writer)

ON THE TUNISIAN FRONT, May 2—After a bitter 72-hour battle, bayonet-charging American troops have captured Hill 609, the German stronghold which blocked the road to Mateur on the western flank of the Tunisian Front, and the drive toward Tunis and Bizerta to the north continues. Rangy 2nd Corps riflemen, composed mainly of lads from Minnesota, took the heights of the hill with artillery support at 0845 hours Friday.

Desperately defending the mountain position were some of Hitler's crack air-borne infantry, whose machine guns had swept the broad valley approaches with malten, almost impenetrable cross fire for three days. The attack opened at dawn after a surprise all-night march, asd in three hours and 45 minutes we had cleaned out Jerry's machinegun nests at the base of the rise.

On clear days, from the topside, good eyes can see the buildings of Tunis and Bizerta.

Probing their way through the grey dawn, riflemen guided the fire of artillery by shooting tracers into German gun emplacements, and as the attack proceeded our artillery supported the advance.

Casualties were surprisingly low among our forces.

Capt. Harold Edward Doyle told a Stars and Stripes reporter who followed the advance that a platoon led by S-Sgt. Rot Mangenio had wiped out German machine gun crews with the bayonet.

Capt. Doyle said his men wanted to push right on into Tunis, but said he, I had to call them back, or they'd have run into our advanced artillery fire smashing at Jerry's heels.

The Germans had held on to hill 609 with desperate tenacity. It remained as the most formidable barrier to our advance on Mateur and some of the best of Hitler's troops were assigned to holding it.

Laval Hurt In Explosion

LONDON, May 1—Vichy Dictator Pierre Laval has been wounded by a bomb explosion in a sleeping car in which he was returning to France from Berlin.

Several times before, Anti-Nazi elements have made similar attempts to assassinate the Axis collaborationist who forced himself into power over Marshall Petain.

Laval's wound is described as slight. More seriously wounded in the same explosion was Laval's finance minister, Pierre Cathala, who had accompanied his boss to a conference with Der Fuehrer.

German Prisoners Say Tunisia Lost

ALLIED FORCE HEADQUARTERS, May 2—Captured German troops on the Tunisian front are comparing their plight in North Africa with the entrapment of German Armies at Stalingrad. They speak of Tunisia as "Tunisgrad," expecting to meet the same fate as Nazi divisions destroyed and captured in the disasterous effort to take the Russian steel city.

Second Corps officers at the front describe German air strength in the area as "pitiful." On the comptain bitterly that Allied aircraft are strafing and boming unceasingly. They are convinced for the most part that the campaign in Africa is lost.

Hull Recalls Consul From Martinique

WASHINGTON, May 2—Secretary of State Cordell Hull has recalled the United States consul general from Martinique and has sent to Admiral Georges Robert recalcitrant French high-commissioner on that French island, a blistering piece of his mind.

In recalling the U. S. diplomatic representative on Martinique, Hull declared that the island is now an "integral part of the Nazi system" and notified Admiral Robert that his continued show of allegiance to Nazi-controlled Vichy government of Pierre Laval makes it impossible for the United States to do business with him.

More to the point, the secretary of state also abruptly cancelled the agreement of May, 1942, under which Martinique had a sort of favored refugee status among colonial lands of the Western Hemisphere. Martineque lies well within the reach of our gulf ports and has long been uder constant surveillance as a possible base of operations for German submarines.

In Martinoque's harbor lie unused French war and merchant shipping, among them the aircraft carrier Bearn, the minelayer cruiser Emile Bertin, several smaller craft, six tankers and four merchant ships.

Early last fall, Washington believed that negotiations were nearly complete for the transfer of the merchant ships to Allied service and eventually the warcraft were expected to follow. But then came the invasion of North Africa. With that, Robert refused to listen to any new proposals and his attitude has been conspicuously uncooperative ever since.

Sentiment of the French rank and file on Martinique has been decidedly pro-Allied, especially since the United States began to ship food in under the May, 1942, agreement. Those shipments ceased in November in the belief that the people deprived of such aid, would force Robert into line.

A GI Newspaper For Oran

With this issue The Stars and Stripes, Oran Daily, makes its bow.

It is a modest beginning, but the paper will endeavor to bring to its readers each day an account of the progress of the war in Tunisia and throughout the world, a certain amount of current home news, and such local news as is available for publication. Emphasis will be placed on the news that is of most interest to the soldier. Sports news will be covered as thoroughly as is possible.

Because of mechanical limitations, it will be necessary to close the forms at 1800 hours on the day preceding the issue. This will result occasionally in this paper's being "scooped" by the local French newspapers.

The Stars and Stripes will publish each day a special feature, "The Oran Datebook," which will list social functions, entertainment, and other activities and places of interest to the soldier, and the permanent facilities of the Red Cross.

All units are invited to contribute news items about their dances, athletic activities, and other events of general interest. Remember that censorship regulations will not permit the publication of your outfit's official name. Give your teams names such as the Signal Singers, the Aviators, the Tigers, etc.

The Stars and Stripes will be edited by enlisted men who are experienced newspapermen in civil life. The friendly co-operation of the management of L'Echo d'Oran is acknowledged with thanks.

FDR Says War Effort Protected

Workers Expected Back In Mines By This Morning

WASHINGTON, May 2— CIO coal miners throughout the bituminous fuel belt of the eastern states are expecting to get back on the job tomorrow morning (Monday) in mines now controlled by the United States government. Federal control of the mines was ordered by President Roosevelt after more than 400,000 members of John L. Lewis's United Mine Workers union walked out in a wage dispute at Friday midnight.

Their action in calling for a strike paralysed almost the entire soft coal industry upon which the steel mills of the Birmingham and Pittsburgh areas depend for fuel. The President declared that the action of the CIO threatened the entire war production industry.

In a second order to Secretary of War Stimson, the President, warning that "the national interest is in grave peril and the production of coal must and shall continue," directed that armed troops be dispatched, where necessary, to protect miners who wanted to return to work Monday, and to guard against violence or sabotage.

Appealing directly to the miners, ordered to stop work by UMW President Lewis when efforts to obtain a two-dollar-a-day wage said, "I ask that you return immediately to the mines and work for the government; your country needs your services as much as those of the armed forces.

"I am confident you do not wish to retard the war effort and that you will promptly answer this call to perform this essentiol war service."

White House Secretary Stephen T. Early announced that the President's directive to Secretary of the Interior Harold L. Ickes for taking possession of the mines also included orders to take over any and all real or personal property, franchise rights, facilities, funds and other assets and operate them on the government's behalf.

Early also announced the President would speak to the nation and the miners by radio Sunday night at 10 PM (3 AM Oran time) in which the chief executive would put "bluntly" the vital necessity of coal to win the war.

The President's action came in swift reply to Lewis' defiance of a White House ultimatum that miners return to work by 10 AM Saturday morning following the mass walkout midnight Friday, when the old contract of the UMW with mine operators expired.

Hurling his challenge to the presidential ultimatum, Lewis renewed his demand for continued negotiations through collective bargaining and repeated his contention that War Labor Board of William H. Davis had "pre-judged" the miners' case and was "packed against labor."

In stating the miners' position, Lewis charged that living cost has increased more than 15 per cent, and that because spiraling living costs were not being met by higher wages, the UMW was forced to withdraw its "no strike" pledge.

The miners' yearly contract with the operators expired March 31 and at that time both participants in the wage dispute agreed to a presidential request that the mines be kept open and negotiations continued for a settlement beyond April 1 deadline, with any agreement to be made retroactive.

Both parties also agreed to extend the old contract to April 30.

THE STARS AND STRIPES

Oran Daily

Vol. 1 - No. 6 - Monday, May 10, 1943 U. S. Army Newspaper One Franc

50,000 PRISONERS CAPTURED

Press Hails Victory As Turning Point Of War

Axis propagandists were kept busy over the weekend giving alibis to the peoples of Germany, Italy and the other occupied countries for the defeat in Tunisia.

Radio Berlin explained that the Axis defeat at Tunis and Bizerta was, "the physical overwhelming of a brave outpost by ten to one odds in men, planes, tanks and equipment."

From the Italian radio came the excuse that "four continents" had poured out men and equipment against the defenders of Europe.

Radio Rome said the Allies had assembled "a most military machine" the fruit of the mobilization of thousands of officers, millions of men and billions of dollars and pounds Sterling to crush the Axis forces.

The Axis propaganda machine generally tried to minimize the Allied victory and repeatedly used to describe what had happened such expressions as "delaying action," heavy losses on both sides," "siege conditions" and "tenacious defense."

The German High Command report on the Battle of Tunis admitted that the British 1st Army had smashed a wide gap through the Axis lines and exploited this success in true Blitzkrieg fashion. Hundreds of enemy tanks poured through this break to threaten major Axis forces at Tunis and Bizerta.

It said, "The order for withdrawal was therefore given and a special force was posted in Tunis to delay the Allied advance. Every crossroad was tenaciously defended, tying up the Allied spearhead."

There was no mention in any German broadcast of the reembarkation of troops. Instead, the home public was told that the men would continue to hold their positions to the last moment as part o their vital delaying role, and warned that none of the men in Tunisia should be expected to return.

On the consequences of the fall of the last two major Axis bases in Africa, DNB, the official German news agency, claimed that Tunis and Bizerta weren't important ports anyway.

"Even the loss of this bridgehead will no longer be of any decisive significance," DNB declared.

Italians today are celebrating the seventh anniversary of the Italian occupation of Ethiopia, known as Empire Day. Nevertheless, the Italians are continuing their explanations of the loss of Tunis and Bizerta, asserting that Axis units are fiercely continuing the fight east of Bizerta and in the central and southern sectors.

Postpone Third Loan Drive

WASHINGTON, May 9—Because the American people oversubscribed th. second War Loan drive by more than 5 billion dollars a third War Loan drive, slated for July, will be postponed until early October President Roosevelt announced. The President said that of 6,000,000 people working for the war effort or in the armed services 50,000,000 own bonds worth 10 billion dollars. Bond sales were widely scattered throughout the nation and individuals as well as large commercial firms went over their quota.

Invertors other than commercial banks bought over 13 billion dollars worth of bonds, although their goal was only eight billion. Direct purchases by individuals totalled three billion while insurance companies and savings banks contributed three and one half billion.

Quintuplets Get Two Big Thrills

SUPERIOR, Wisc. — The Dionne quintuplets got two new thrills on their way to this place to christen five liberty ships launched simultaneously Sunday.

The initial one came with their sleeping in separate rooms for the first time in their already eventful lives. Each was assigned to her own Pullman compartment of the southbound train and enjoyed the novelty.

Their second thriller came with the unscheduled derailing of their Pullman in the Superior yards. All five of them and their special party esc[illegible] injury.

Jimmie Durante Ill

NEW YORK—Jimmie "Schnozzola" Durante, veteran stage and screen comedian, is under treatment in a local hospital for a respiratory infection. His conditon s termed serious but not dangerous.

General Pays Tribute To War Mothers

WASHINGTON, May 9—The Nation's military leaders joined today in celebration of Mother's Day.

Gen. George C. Marshall, Chief of Staff said, "The courage of our men on the fighting front is less great than that of mothers who can only stand and wait."

Hundred of letters to me from mothers who have lost their beloved sons are my great inspiration in these terrible days of trial and suffering.

"The patriotic resolution that shines through their heartbreaks is a wonderful thing-a perfect example of pure pariotism and self sacrifice to the great cause for which we are fighting.

"I wish people througout the country could have the same inspiration that fortities me and strenghens me today."

Gen. Dwight D. Eisenhower sent this message. "The observation of Mother's Day this year came at a time when patriotic Americans are devoting all their talents in the effective prosecution of the war. Now our nation is engaged in world wide struggles on behalf of freedom everywhere. We are fighting to destroy oppression and to create conditions under which people everywhere may enjoy the four freedoms.

"On behalf of the Allied forces in North Africa I proudly salute the brave and sacrificing mothers of our fighting men who have given or are risking their lives for their country in this worldwide war to eliminate aggression and dictatorship.

Mrs. Thomas F. Sullivan, mother of five sons who were lost in the Solomons last year, said: "Today we mothers are helping their sons at the front by working in war plants that produce fighting equipment.

"I even heard of one case where a mother helped to make the very lifejacket that saved her son. What wonderful satisfaction that must have been. It must be great inspiration to all those working mothers to know every day that they're backing up their sons."

In a Mother's Day broadcast, Secretary of the Navy Frank Knox spoke of the peace after the war.

Only Shreds Of Once Great Army Survive

ALLIED FORCE HEADQUARTERS, May 9—The following special communique was issued here tonight at 7:30 o'clock:

The second U. S. Corps continued mopping up in the areas around Bizerta, where organised resistance has ceased.

Three German divisions, their commanding officers and staffs, have been captured.

The commanding officer and remnants of the 15th Panzer Division surrendered to their old enemies of the 7th British Armored Division.

Heavy fighting continued in the area of Hammantif and in the area north of Zaghouan. Since May 7, 50,000 prisoners have been taken.

No enemy aircraft has been seen over Tunis, and the German air force appears to have been withdrawn from the battle.

ALLIED FORCE HEADQUARTERS, May 9—The Air Force made the heaviest bombardment of the North African war tonight on Palerme, Sicily.

The weight of bombs dropped was five times as great as that of any former attack on Italian bases.

All of the pilots were Americans. They flew in B 25 Mitchells, B 26 Marauders, and T 28 Lightnings, accompanied by their escorts.

Great damage was done, and the smoke was so thick that it was impossible to take pictures.

ALLIED FORCES HEADQUARTERS, May 9—What is left of the Axis forces in North Africa was crumbling to pieces today.

The American 9th Infantry Division had mopped up the last sinuer resistance in Bizerta and the British 78th Division had all opposition cleaned up in Tunis by yesterday morning.

The forces that had blasted their way into the capital and harbor cities last Friday were now hammering without pause at the only two ground pockets left to the forces of Col. Jurgin Von Arnim.

One of these pockets lies along the coast on the western edge of the Gulf of Tunis, pinned in by Bizerta on the north and Tunis on the south.

The other last possible stamping ground of the Axis in Africa was on the 40-mile-long, 25-mile-wide Cape Bon peninsula.

Since the climactic blow was struck last Friday, there has been no letup in the hammering punches of the Allies. Today there is no talk of a Dunkirk from Cape Bon. Instead, for the collapsing German forces only final surrender or annihilation was possible and nothing that Von Arnim could say or do could altar things much.

In Germany Dr. Josef Goebbels had already written off the remnants of the African forces. Berlin radio announcers last night tolled off the list of the German divisions pocketed in Tunisia, naming the division and the town in Germany from which its men came. For Germans it was a death roll.

The African outpost to Axis Europe was being overrun. All the Germans claim was that the war in Tunesia had fulfilled its mission by helping to delay the events to come.

In Allied Force Headquarters, reports that came in today were all good. At least 20,000 prisoners were reported to have been taken since the drive to Tunis and Bizerta began and a vast amount of war material remained to be collected.

Turis and Bizerta and on Cape Bon were the rest of the forces, badly disorganized and virtually prisoners now because all routes of escape were quickly being cut off.

The Tunis-Bizerta stretch was meeting a drive from the north and south. Two American infantry and one Armored division were pushing down from Bizerta and Mateur and units of the 1st Army were coming up from Tunis.

In Cape Bon, with its three servicable airports, rocky hills and very poor harbors, the Germans, who were better organised than in the north, were met by another drive that threatened to cut them in two.

Carthage and La Goulette airport, outside of Tunis, were in Allied hands and the British 6th and 7th armored divisions were pressing on to the small key town of Solinan and a road that, when taken, will cut off any further retreats to Cape Bon.

Further south, French forces, with new American armor had made a considerable advance over difficult hill country and now occupied the town of Zaghouan.

The 8th Army, halted by thickly planted mine fields, was beginning to move north again.

While ground forces continued to press their advantage to the limit, the Northwest African Air Force was providing what may be the severest air pounding the Germans have ever seen. They had complete mastery of the air in Tunisia.

The Tactical Air Force, with its close ground coordination, and immediate objectives, was blasting enemy troops, vehicles and air fields on Cape Bon.

Around the coasts of the peninsula, shipping was also heavily attacked and direct hits were scored on several vessels. With the bombers and fighter bombers of the Straights of Sicily under constant watch, the Axis line of supply was broken and the line of evacuation broken with it.

The news of the German defeat came to the world with dramatic suddenness. In Washington, wires of congratulation were pouring in from all Allied capitals and were also going out to commanders and their troops in the field.

In Russia's capital, all official spokesmen expressed the highest praise for the rapid culmination of the campaign. In neutral countries, observers noted the great show of strength in the Tunision forces.

Throughout occupied Europe, unrest was bound to grow as the full story of mounting Allied strength could no longer be kept from the oppressed peoples.

In Tunisia, the Allies' victory was received with rejoicing and also with a quick taking-over of civil government by General Juin, commander of the French troops in the field.

He was named temporary resident general by Gen. Henri Giraud, until the arrival of Gen. Maste, who is now recovering from serious injury in Beyrouth. Gen. Maste will be Resident General of France at Tunis as soon as he is fully recovered.

Of all the towns the Allies entered, only one failed to give them a reception fit for a conquering hero. That town was Bierta, which was empty. Its great docks had been ripped to pieces under the intense Allied air attacks and the Germans, before they had evacuated, had wrecked nearly everything in sight. Bridges were blown up. The town was full of booby traps.

The people of Bizerta, almost to the last one had moved south to Ferryville before the Yanks entered. At Ferryville, however, the streets were lined with men, women and children, who, according to Seymour Korman correspondent for the Mutual Broadcasting System, tossed bright bouquets of spring flowers on the soldiers, rushed up to kiss them and generally went mad with joy.

In Tunis, the capital of Tunisia, it was the same story, said Korman.

On one of the street corners an old Frenchman, in his best Sunday Black suit, stood erect as the Brit[illegible]

(Continued on Page 2)

Propagandists Try Hard To Explain Defeat In Africa

By JOHN WILLIG
(Stars and Stripes Staff Writer)

Reaction to the swift sudden fall of Tunis and Bizerta brought enthusiastic and optimstic comments from Allied capitals throughout the world yesterday. Most press and radio announcements of the news hailed this latest Allied victory as the turning point of the war and echoed the sentiments of some United Nations leaders that the African downfall was the beginning of the end for the aggressor nations.

In Moscow, block long ques lined up before news stands to read of this final collapse of the Nazis in Africa the news drawing the greatest flood of praise given to foreign powers in the history of the Soviet Union.

Press radio declared it was being treated as the biggest victory since Stalingrad—as if it had been won by Red Army soldiers.

Premier Joseph Stalin in identical messages to President Roosevelt and Prime Minister Winston Churchill declared: "I congratulate you and the gallant British and American troops on the brilliant victory which led to the liberation of Bizerta and Tunis from Hitlerite tyranny I wish you further successes."

[illegible] of our aggressive effort and the end of Hitler's mad dreams."

President Roosevelt's own comment to the all-but-closed chapter brilliantly planned American campaign was significant in that it was contained in a cable to Gen. Dwight D. Esenhower and Gen. Henri Giraud Commander-in-Chief of the French forces in North Africa on the occasion of ceremonies commemorating the transfer of American equipment to the new French Army. The President referred to things to come and the "final victory."

Comment of Washington officials was short and brisk. Chairman Andrew J. May of Kentucky of the House Military Affairs committee said, "A whale of a good job." Texas Tom Connally Chairman of the Senate Foreign Affairs Committee said, "Glorious news. The begin-

"Herbert Lehman said that plans already were made for extending immediate American aid to the freed people in Tunis and Bizerta would begin at once.

"We have asembled stocks of basic foods, medical supplies and clothing for the relief of the Tunisian population in Algiers and even in Tunisia, within close reach of the devestated areas." Lehman said, We've already made some distribution of supplies under military control and direction at Sfax, Gabes and Sous[illegible].

The Yugoslav Constantin Fotitch said the Yugoslav people now "are much nearer the day when they'll reveal their re-accumulated strength."

While a spokesman from the Norweigian Legation expressed pride in the part played by Norweigian warships and merchantmen in the victory. "When this news reaches Norway the people of our occupied land will take new courage. The news will make them feel that liberation is certain," the spokesman said.

THE STARS AND STRIPES

ALGIERS DAILY

Vol. 1 - No. 21 - Thursday, May 13, 1943 | U. S. Army Daily Newspaper for troops in Algiers area | ONE FRANC

Africa Campaign Ends; General Arnim Captured

Churchill In U.S. For Talks With FDR

Army, Navy Chiefs With Prime Minister On Fifth Meeting

WASHINGTON — Official announcement was made yesterday of the arrival of Prime Minister Winston Churchill at the White House to confer with President Roosevelt. Accompanied by both military and naval staff experts, Churchill was met by the President and will be his guest for the duration of the visit.

The Prime Minister's departure from London was most secret He met his special train outside the city. The most travelled Prime Minister in England's history, Churchill has now had five meetings with the President since August, 1941, when the two drafted the Atlantic Charter on the high seas.

The whereabouts of the Prime Minister was unknown until Maj. Clement Attlee, the Laborite leader, deputizied for him in the House of Commons Tuesday morning. It then became apparent that the Prime Minister was again out of the country on an important mission. Attlee made the government statement of the virtual end of the Tunisian campaign— an occasion which Churchill would not have foregone if he had been able to make the statement himself.

When the Prime Minister's absence was known, there were some hints from American sources that he had gone to Washington The German radio, however, broadcast their own version of the meeting saying that "Churchill is in Cairo to attend a big military conference of the Allies." The Scandinavian Telegram Bureau, a German-controlled station, claimed that "Stalin, Churchill and Roosevelt are meeting in Moscow."

It is believed in London that at

(Continued on Page 2)

Fletcher's Castoria Nauseates Buyers

WASHINGTON, May 12—The Cantaur Co., manufacturers of Fletcher's Castoria, a laxative, has spent thousands of dollars in newspaper and radio advertising to warn the public not to use their product.

This unusual practice was started when the U. S. Food and Drug Administration learned that the laxative was making its customers ill and nauseated. All wholesale-retail stocks are being withdrawn to insure that no more Fletcher's is sold until the nauseating element is discovered.

Hull Scores Critics Of Trade Plans

WASHINGTON — Secretary of State Cordell Hull, who has been under Congressional fire several times lately for his part in the reciprocal trade agreements as they affect agriculture, Monday struck back at his critics in a letter to Robert L. Doughton, chairman of the House Ways and Means Committee.

In his letter Secretary Hull refuted charges that American agriculture has been "sold down the river" under the trade agreements program, and also denied that the program runs counter to the farm program. He asserted that the trade agreements program is not in conflict with, but to the advantage of, the domestic farm program.

The Secretary wrote that his reciprocal agreements have assisted the farm program efforts to secure and maintain parity prices for agricultural products.

"It ought to be clear to anyone," he said, "that a program which helps to re-open and expand export outlets for our great farm surpluses, as the trade agreements have done, must enable the growers of the great export crops to obtain a closer approach to parity prices for a larger amount of output than would otherwise be possible."

House Acts To End All War Strikes

No Lock-Outs For Textile Workers

WASHINGTON, May 13—Congress today speeded up action on the Connally anti-strike bill to get in under the line of the expiration of the John L. Lewis 15-day strike truce which ends May 18

The House Military Affairs Committee voted 21 to nothing to write into the bill provisions to end all threats of labor stoppages for the duration of the war. The bill also decrees that a union must hold a secret ballot before calling a strike and must give employers 30 days' notice of the intended strike. The union must withhold a walk-out for 60 days after the WLB takes jurisdiction and must register with the NLRB full financial statements of receipts and expenditures by each union. The bill also gives the WLB the power to subpoena witnesses and data.

Rep. Landis, of Ind., author of the bill requiring the unions to furnish the labor department with periodical financial statements, said that the bill would "get at those racketeers who charge big iniation fees" on war construction jobs, then fire the workers.

At the New York City convention of the Textile Workers Union, (CIO) Emil Rieve, union president, said:

"Nothing has happened which should cause labor to deviate one iota from its pledge of unbroken production throughout the war."

In regards to the recent coal strike, Rieve told the union members that no matter how great were the coal miners' grievances and no matter how much the coal operators sought to take advantage of the situation, there couldn't be any justification of a halt in production. "No matter what the provocation, we'll keep production going," Rieve promised.

Allies Encircle Germans On Cape, Find No Resistance

150,000 Prisoners Taken Including Twelve Generals, As Last Pocket Falls

Special Communique

The following communique was released by the 18th Army Group tonight at 2015 hours:

Organized resistance except by isolated pockets of the enemy has ceased. General Arnim, commander of the Axis forces in Tunisia has been captured. It is estimated that the total number of prisoners captured since May 5 is about 150,000. Vast quantities of guns and war materials of all kinds have been captured, including many guns and aircraft in a serviceable condition.

In addition to the above communique, which virtually announced the end of the North African campaign, it was also stated here that the number of general officers captured since May 5 now totals 12. The capture of Maj. Gen. Graf von Sponeck, commanding the 90th Light Division, and Maj. Gen. Proice, commanding the 10th Panzer Division, was announced. Nearly 400,000 prisoners have been taken since the North African campaign commenced two years, eleven months, ten days ago. During this time 11 German and 26 Italian divisions have been wiped out.

Early today Gen. Freyburg, commanding the 90th Light Division, was presented terms of unconditional surrender and refused, saying that he would fight until he ran out of ammunition. But then he and his staff officers changed their minds.

Col. Gen. Jurgin von Arnim, whose capture was announced earlier this evening, was believed to have been taken on the Cape Bon peninsula.

ALLIED FORCE HEADQUARTERS, May 12—Col. Gen. Jurgin von Arnim, commander of all the Axis forces in North Africa, has been captured, it was officially announced here tonight. Arnim, a close friend of Field Marshal Erwin Rommel, who commanded the famed Afrika Korps, came from a distinguished German Junker family in which have been admirals, generals, statesmen and even poets. The general was a tank expert. Rommel left Africa about two months ago. The German radio during the last several days has announced that he was convalescing.

ALLIED FORCE HEADQUARTERS, May 12—The Axis territory in Tunisia has now been reduced to a pocket 18 miles wide by 15 miles long, in which the last German resistance of the North African campaign is being staged British and French troops are now tearing that pocket apart.

Yesterday the British 1st Army after slicing through to Hammamet at the entrance to Cape Bon in the morning, completely encircled the peninsula. Whatever idea the Nazis had of staging a "Corregidor" on Cape Bon is now dissipated.

Inside the Cape Bon noose that these Empire troops threw around the peninsula, there were little more than German service units. And these troops, who no longer had any service to render, were burning the few supplies and equipment which they would never be able to send down the line. There was no serious resistance expected from them.

In the pocket to the south, there was slight resistance and this resistance was doomed to disaster as fighting French forces and British troops crush it with a cordon of steel. The only gateway to the sea a gateway with the watchdogs of

(Continued on Page 2)

Air Force Pounds Germans; RAF Cites Accurate Bombing

ALLIED FORCE HEADQUARTERS, May 12—Unrelenting bombing and strafing of Axis troops still resisting British and French forces in the Allied trap south of the Cape Bon peninsula continued yesterday without let-up. Light bombers carried out more than 100 sorties in the area, attacking gun positions.

Concentrating on the pocket around St. Marie du Zit, Grombalia and the area north of Enfidaville and Zaghouan, American and British bombers dumped load after load on the encircled Axis remnants and inflicted heavy punishment. On the Cape Bon peninsula itself, the advance of the 1st Army up the parallel sides of the coast was so swift bombing had to cease. Nowhere was any enemy aircraft spotted during the day's operations.

Early in the morning, however, RAF Wellingtons and Bisleys bombed scattered enemy remnants at Hammamet and Menzel Temime. Attacks also were made over enemy transport and troops on the peninsula, with direct hits on supply dumps, motor traffic and guns, some of them concealed in olive groves.

Night flying Hurricanes intercepted a few JU-52 troop carrying aircraft apparently attempting to rescue some of the trapped Germans and one was shot down.

Tuesday's devastating raid over Marsala, Sicily, which leveled docks, warehouses, hangars and repair installations at the great seaplane base, also netted 15 enemy aircraft destroyed over the city.

Among the targets was a huge winery whose building contained tons upon tons of war materials. Crew members said flak formed a blinding sheet of fire over the target. Marsala has been serving as a supply depot for the Afrika Korps and as a port for dispatching supplies.

1st Lt. Daniel C. Emrich, of Britton, Okla., was among those assigned to the winery target. "We took care of that. Right over the target, we were attacked by about 15 enemy fighters. One came so close I could see the pilot's face He was frowning. One of our waist gunners brought him down." the lieutenant said.

Sgt. James A. Brehm, Enon Valley, Pa., a tail gunner, remarked, "After that bombing, there won't be any use in going back—to where Marsala was."

Gunners from the heavy and medium bombers accounted for 12 of the enemy interceptors and the escorting P-40 Warhawks brought down three more.

In the Bizerta and Ferryville areas the RAF reported results of an investigation to determine the amount of damage done by the Allied Air Forces. Almost without exception, the bombing was described as "remarkably accurate and entirely restricted to military targets."

Ferryville residents remarked about the "miracle"—the fact that although the whole dock area was blasted to bits, not a single house in the town, which is less than a mile from the waterfront, was hit. Civilian authorities said that during the entire dawn-to-dawn bombing campaign, there were only 20 casualties among the civilian population and these re-

(Continued on Page 2)

THE STARS AND STRIPES
CASABLANCA DAILY

Vol. 1 - No. 1 - Wednesday, 19 May, 1943 . U. S. Army Newspaper for troops in Casablanca area — One Franc

Lewis Extends Coal Truce at Ickes' Request

Last Minute Action Averts Threatened Bitter Union Fight

NEW YORK, May 18—The 15 day coal strike truce, which was to have expired at midnight, was extended today until May 32 by John L. Lewis, United Mine Worker's president, at the request of Fuel Administrator Harold L. Ickes. The labor chieftain's last minute decision changed a situation which threatened to percipitate a bitter union struggle.

Lewis on Monday flouted a War Labor Board an order directing the resumption of collective bargaining between coal miners and operators.

He refused to send representatives to the WLB hearing in Washington, stating that jurisdiction in the dispute no longer lay with the WLB, but with Coordinator Ickes, who is operating the mines for the government.

In return, the WLB stamped the defiance of Mr. Lewis as a challenge to the United States sovereignty. The War Labor Board meanwhile, proceeded toward a decision on the controversy without any participation by the United Mine Workers. The board closed the hearing with the statement that Lewis is giving aid and comfort to our enemies, and that any new strike in the mines would violate the contracts which the government, acting under its war powers, had directed to be extended until the settlement of the wage dispute.

Lewis later said he would continue to negotiate with the mine operators in New York, but reiterated that he would not participate in any hearing before the WLB.

He called the WLB "malignant." Lewis' decision to ignore the War Labor Board in the controversy was prompted by the WLB order which indicated stricter enforcement of price ceilings. The board intimated it was willing to approve an agreement, including a guarantee of a six-day work week, but not an in-

(Continued on Page Four)

GI's Get Bath-House Blues, Sweat Out Rationed Water

Shower baths aren't necessary! You'll find it so in black and white if you'll refer to Administration Memo No. 61, Par. 3 b HQ, dated 16 May, 1943.

Just shake it off and pray for a strong wind, or grab yourself a nice clean "C" ration can and hop in: It's the fashionable thing to do in Casablanca these arid days. (Ref. par. 3 c): "Adequate personal hygiene may be obtained from use of water in small containers such as tin cans, basins, or small buckets."

But, before you get the idea that bathing is passé, hark to Par. 3 d: "Organizational commanders will establish and maintain bath rosters to insure that no individual receives more than three (3—count 'em) showers per week." And be absolutely sure, my knight in shining perspiration, that a commissioned officer is present at this triweekly ablution to see that you get just so wet, and not more. (Par. 3 h).

If this sort of supervision seems a bit hard at times, just remember General Sherman's famous words. If, however, it's a little more than you can bear, have a confederate, preferably a M-Sgt. who has recently been "busted," slip the officer a "hot-foot." The confusion which must ensue will allow the bather time to get a once-over-lightly in the shower and be dressed before the officer can say "Hello Gabriel."

But before you get the idea that we are trying to pan this "Keep Clean on Less" drive, bear in mind that there is always a reason behind rules and regulations.

Engineers Section says the present supply of water for Casablanca, Rabat, Fedala, and Port Lyautey is insufficient for present demands. It is imperative that available water be strictly conserved. And it is true that many fellows do take more showers than

(Continued from Page One)

FDR Hits Tax Plan as Partial to Rich

WASHINGTON, May 18—Because it would favor the rich and work undue hardship on the masses, President Roosevelt implied today that he would veto the Senate-approved "one hundred percent forgiveness" Ruml tax plan.

In letters to Chairmen George and Doughton of the Senate and House committees, the President raised no objection to the House-approved bill forgiving 75 percent of a year's taxes. The President added that he favored "pay as you go" legislation, but insisted on a "bill that I can sign."

Allies Pound Axis Islands

ALLIED FORCE HEADQUARTERS, May 18—The Allied air offensive against Axis-held Mediterranean islands continues with unabated fury, with the port and airfield at Alghero on the northwest coast of Sardinia as the principal target in Monday night's attack.

The raid was carried out by RAF Wellington Bombers. Bombs were seen to burst in both target areas and large fires were left burning. A direct hit was scored on a train. The raiders, guided by bright moonlight, made a second run over the town and strafed the area from as low as 200 feet. One pilot was forced to lift his wing sharply to avoid a church steeple.

A lone Beaufighter of the RAF coastal air force on night patrol took on a formation of German aircraft near the North African coast shooting down two of them. The others became so panicky that they started shooting at each other, according to the Beaufighter pilot, Flying Officer K. G. Rayment

(Continued on Page Four)

RAF Bombers Crack Open Two Great German Dams, Panic Reigns on Rhine

4,000 Killed, Floods Break on Vital Nazi War Centers

LONDON, May 18—At least four thousand persons were killed and 120 thousand made homeless as a result of the RAF raids which pierced the industrial heart of Germany by the bombing of dams in the Ruhr and Eder Valleys. Although the damage reports came from private channels within the Reich, even the German High Command found it necessary to admit that civilian casualties were "heavy."

Lancasters of the British Bomber Command burst two of the largest dams in the country during the mammoth attacks, which took place over an area embracing Berlin, the Ruhr and the Rhineland. Two-thirds of the entire water capacity of the Ruhr basin are controlled by these two dams—the Mohne on the Mohne River, which flows into the Ruhr, and the Eder on the Eder River.

The A.: Ministry painted a scene of panic and desolation caused by the water pouring in torrents through the ruined dams. Bridges in the Ruhr Valley were torn apart by the floods, hydro-electric stations destroyed or damaged, and freight yards inundated. Railways were reported at a standstill.

At Duisburg and Muntheim, there was said to be wild tumult and disorder. The public has reason to be jittery about further air raids because the shelters are flooded.

It is understood that martial law has been declared in an attempt to bring the alarming situation under some sort of control.

Reconnaissance later established that Mohne Dam had been breached over a length of one hundred yards, and the power station below swept away by the floods. Eder Dam, which controls the headwaters of the Weser and Fulda Valleys, and operates several power stations,

(Continued on Page Four)

Yanks Advance in Attu Fight

WASHINGTON, May 18—Seven more Jap vessels ,including a destroyer and a patrol craft have been sunk off Attu Island, the Navy announced today. At the same time it appeared that conclusion to the land fighting in the seven-day-old battle for the fog-shrouded bit of land, 750 miles west of Dutch Harbor, would be possible as soon as the constant heavy weather cleared.

Navy Secretary Knox announced today the American capture of a high ridge on Attu which had been held by the Japanese since the American invasion of the westermost Aleutian Island a week ago. The successful maneuver left the main Jap force at Holtz Bay wide open for an all-out American assault.

Knox said that, despite difficulties of water and stubborn

(Continued on Page Four)

Late News

LONDON, May 18—U. S. Air Headquarters announced tonight a shattering new blow to Germany's fighter planes strength when it was disclosed that our bombers and fighters in three days destroyed 121 German fighter planes. The communique covered operations carried out by American Air Forces over Europe on May 14, 15 and 16.

WASHINGTON, May 18—The Canadian Government announced that Prime Minister Mackenzie King is expected to reach Washington today to take part in talks being conducted by Prime Minister Churchill and President Roosevelt. Mackenzie King and his party are scheduled to meet the Prime Minister and the President tomorrow.

LONDON, May 18—Roaring flood waters loosed by the RAF attacks on the Mohne and Eder dams have swept far into eastern Germany. This was announced tonight by the Air Ministry after photographs were taken earlier today by RAF reconnaissance planes. Unusually high waters were also observed at Duisberg.

ALLIED HEADQUARTERS IN NORTH AFRICA, May 18—General Eisenhower announced tonight the bag of Axis prisoners taken in North Africa now exceeds 200,000 German and Italian troops. The previous highest estimate had been 175,000 prisoners.

WASHINGTON, May 18—The House sounded the death knell of the Ruml hundred percent forgiveness of 1942 income tax levies today by a vote of 202-184. The measure goes to a joint House Senate Committee where a compromise will be sought that is acceptable to President Roosevelt.

Stars and Stripes Daily Opens Up in Casablanca

With this issue, *The Stars and Stripes of Africa* begins publishing a daily newspaper for troops stationed in the Casablanca area. The Casablanca Daily is not to be confused with the weekly *Stars and Stripes*, which will continue to be circulated throughout North Africa.

The Stars and Stripes Casablanca Daily will be published six times weekly, Monday through Saturday. Beginning Sunday, May 21, *The Stars and Stripes* weekly paper for North Africa will also be published in Casablanca.

The Daily, as well as the Weekly, will be on sale at civilian newstands and by newsboys on the streets of Casablanca and other important cities in Morocco. The wholesale distribution will be handled by the Messageries Hachette who correspond to the American News Co. in the U. S.

Units which draw a quantity of papers for their outfit may place an order with one of the Hachette Agencies or with any civilian newsdealer. A list of the principal Agencies is given herewith.

A coupon is also printed on page four for your convenience in ordering just in case your French isn't up to a conversation of that magnitude. Just clip the coupon, fill it in and hand it to a newsdealer or to a Hachette Agency. When the light of comprehension dawns in those friendly French eyes you will know they compree and your papers will arrive the next day. Then you can change your order up or down each day as you wish.

HACHETTE AGENCIES

Rabat—Place de la Gare.

Port Lyautey—Rue Albert 1st.

Meknes—Rue de la Poste.

(Continued on Page Four)

Soviet Front Rests Static

MOSCOW, May 18 Soviet forces today hurled back German troops aiming to break the Russian arc that is constantly drawing tighter around the Nazi-held Black Sea port of Novorossisk.

The Russian mid-day communique told how the Red Army in repulsing the German counterattacks during night engagements, killed 100 of the enemy in one sector and wiped out a whole company of German troops in another.

Although the Soviets continued yesterday to inflict heavy losses on the Germans, the communique stated that no important changes took place along the battle lines.

Another German attempt to break the Russian Novorossisk encirclement met with the loss of several tanks. At the same time Red artillery put out of action several Nazi gun emplacements.

Soviet planes enjoying their newly-gained air superiority, hedge-hopped in to help maul and repulse German tank support in the Kuban area. There, Red airmen, in carrying out the day's operations, downed 14 Nazi planes.

Two other planes were shot down at Leningrad and three more at Sevsk. London heard a Russian radio report that the Luftwaffe lost 27 planes last night during a raid 50 miles east of Kursk.

1d. **THE STARS AND STRIPES** 1d.

Daily Newspaper of U.S. Armed Forces in the European Theater of Operations

Vol. 3 No. 174 New York, N.Y.—London, England Wednesday, May 26, 1943

U.S. and British War Chiefs Meet With FDR, Churchill

President Roosevelt and Prime Minister Churchill, with their war chiefs, attending White House conferences. British leaders (left to right): Field Marshal Sir John Dill, chief military representative to the U.S., Lt. Gen. Hastings Ismay, Chief of Staff to Churchill; Air Chief Marshal Sir Charles Portal, RAF; Gen. Sir Alan Brooke, head of Imperial General Staff, and Adm. Sir Dudley Pound, First Sea Lord. U.S. leaders (left to right): Adm. William Leahy, President's Chief of Staff; Gen. George C. Marshall, Army Chief of Staff; Adm. Ernest J. King, Naval Chief of Staff, and Lt. Gen. Joseph McNarney, deputy Army Chief of Staff. Photo radioed here yesterday.

Sardinia Hammered By 300 U.S. Planes; Air Defense Fading

Italians Warned Allies Can Pick Landing Spots

Italians were warned last night that the Allies would land wherever they chose.

Algiers radio said:

"The last battle is approaching. It will be felt from the toe to the top of Italy. What has happened in one day in Pantellaria will happen all over Italy. Ask the population of Sicily, Sardinia and Naples. Your industries will be completely razed if they continue to work for Germany. Only you people can stop the ruin.

"The Italian soldiers who have died on the battlefield have not died for Italy—they have died for Germany."

Ferry Ports in Sicily Also Hard Hit in Growing Assault

The steadily growing might of Allied air power in the Mediterranean was turned against Sardinia yesterday, when more than 300 American planes attacked nine important enemy defense targets on the large Italian island.

Bomb-ravaged Pantellaria also was raided twice by American fighter-bombers in a continuous air offensive against the Axis southern front. Many planes were destroyed on the ground, the number of which has not officially been ascertained. The total number of Axis aircraft destroyed in the last two days is now 317.

Waves of Flying Fortresses, Marauders, Mitchells, Lightnings and Warhawks rolled over Sardinia, where German troops were recently announced to have landed, and unleashed a merciless storm of bombs.

The Fortresses dealt the heaviest blows at Sardinia, the Axis base west of the Italian mainland. Docks, shipping and airfields suffered heavily. One supply ship blew up, four small vessels were sunk and seven others were damaged by bomb hits. The Americans lost three planes.

Sicilian Ferry Ports Hit

Although Sardinia was the principal target of the growing offensive, the Sicilian ferry ports of Reggio di Calabria and San Giovanni—the only real links [illegible] also were plastered by heavy bombers.

Liberators of the Ninth U.S. Air Force, based in the Middle East, attacked the ports in daylight Monday. Two large ammunition supply depots were demolished and ferry installations and shipping heavily damaged by 150 tons of American bombs.

At Reggio di Calabria, aerial photographs taken during the raid showed sheets of flame shooting thousands of feet into the air and billowing black clouds of smoke. An observer said the ground in the vicinity seemed to be swallowed up in the explosions.

From Cagliari, the capital of Sardinia, and many other towns in Italy's toe and islands, refugees were streaming north to escape the Allied bombardment, said a report from Zurich, Switzerland. Rome already has received thousands.

Duce Desperate?

The appointment of Prince Umberto to commander-in-chief of Italian infantry is regarded as Mussolini's desperate step to prevent further demoralization of the Italian army, which has recently assumed threatening proportions, said a Tass (Russian) report from Geneva.

Although DNB (German news agency) reported yesterday that German troops were sent to reinforce the defenders of Sardinia, Allied pilots reported that Axis air squadrons had vanished from the Italian outpost islands on Sunday, and only three planes were reported lost yesterday out of "large formations" swarming over Sardinian ports and airfields.

Meanwhile the Italians were told by radio from Algiers that the bombing raids on Italian towns so far are child's play compared with what is being prepared for them.

"The Allies will deliver much harder blows at Italian airdromes, ports and in-

(*Continued on page 4*)

Germans Admit Havoc Is Great In Bombed Area

Not One Resident Escaped Some Loss in Four Industrial Cities

The official German press admitted yesterday that there is not a single German in Essen, Duisberg, Dusseldorf, Dortmund and the surrounding territory who has not suffered personally, or sustained the loss of property, as a result of RAF bombings of the Nazi industrial area.

Printed by the Voelkischer Beobachter, the statement was one of the very few Nazi admissions of the extent of the havoc created by the Allied bombings of western Germany.

Reports from Switzerland said the Dortmund attack Sunday caught the Nazi ARP services with one-quarter of their force working miles away from the city on the scene of floods caused by the destruction of the Mohne dam, and that the sirens in Dortmund were not sounded until several minutes after the attack had started. There is no official estimate yet on the raid dead in Dortmund but 37,000 people are reported homeless.

Swedish dispatches, quoting the German paper, also told of growing disaffection among Nazi troops in Norway. The recent sinkings of two ships and an oil barge in Oslo harbor, Norwegian reports to Stockholm said, may have resulted from acts of sabotage on the part of German marines stationed there.

It is known, Stockholm said, that a number of marines had been arrested and that police duties have been taken over by the Army.

Nazis Shoot Officer

German troops stationed at Kristiansund, Norway, are reported to be particularly demoralized. Recently, it was reported through Norwegian underground channels, an officer was shot and killed in a cafe by four marines whom he had rebuked for drinking brandy.

Norwegians reported that at least 1,600 German deserters have been imprisoned in Norway.

The Germans were said to be hurrying defense preparations in Norway, including the placing of torpedo-nets in the Moesvatn and Skarsfoss dams.

Inside Germany itself, the Gestapo chief for Central Europe has been ordered to the bombed and flooded Ruhr district, Algiers radio reported yesterday. The broadcaster said the move followed disorders at Kassel, described as a "movement of rebellion."

Four Nazis Destroyed In Day Raid on Coast

A dozen German fighter-bombers attacked an English southeast coast town in daylight yesterday, causing deaths and casualties with bombs and cannon fire.

Anti-aircraft fire destroyed three FW190s and a Typhoon interceptor shot down one more of the same type.

RAF intruders were over the Continent the preceding night, but there was no heavy bombing.

War Conferences Reach Crux, Word Expected From President

WASHINGTON, May 25—The world waited anxiously tonight for an expected statement from President Roosevelt and Prime Minister Churchill on the result of their conferences on the future conduct of the war.

For two weeks, the two chiefs of state have been holding almost daily talks. At the same time conferences of the utmost importance have been going on between their aides.

The highest naval and military chiefs of the two nations, as well as specialists in various types of warfare, have been checking, conferring and planning.

Today the President and Mr. Churchill lunched with 60 chiefs of the various staffs, and their subordinates, and it was expected that a statement—which may be every bit as important as was the Atlantic Charter declaration—would be made within a matter of hours.

Sunday night the two British and American leaders were closeted in a White House study from 11 PM to 2.30 AM. Presumably they reviewed the whole progress of their two-weeks' conferences, probably with special consideration of the part Russia will play.

There had been no official reaction from Moscow, where former Ambassador Joseph Davies has just presented a letter from the President to Prime Minister Josef Stalin.

It is known here, however, that among the subjects the President and Mr. Churchill would like to take up with Premier Stalin are the following:

1—An understanding on the treatment to be accorded Germany after her defeat.

2—The extent to which Russia will participate in a post-war United Nations' security system to maintain peace.

3—Russia's attitude toward the Pacific after the defeat of Germany.

There seemed good reason to believe that both the President and the Prime Minister are firmly agreed that Germany must be knocked out of the war before the all-out attack is launched on Japan.

FDR May Visit Canada

OTTAWA, May 25 (UP)—Premier Mackenzie King, on his return here yesterday from the Washington conferences, said President Roosevelt was anxious to visit Canada and would do so as soon as he could leave U.S. domestic problems.

Snow, Sleet Slow U.S. Attu Drive

Knox Denies Jap Claim Of U.S. Battleship, Cruiser Sunk

WASHINGTON, May 25 — With drizzly sleet and snow handicapping operations, American forces on Attu Island slowly advanced on the corralled Jap forces on the peninsula of Chicagof Harbor, the Navy Department announced today.

Secretary of the Navy Frank Knox said today there was no fresh information beyond the communique, but he called a Jap claim that a U.S. battleship and cruiser had been sunk off the Aleutians "just another fishing expedition."

Asked whether any reports had come in to show that the Attu airfield being built by the Japs was serviceable, Knox said, "I assume that what the Japanese have started, the Yanks can finish."

The Navy chief disclosed that the Jap bombers which attempted to raid Attu on Saturday and Sunday probably came from the Kurile Island, 800 miles west. The enemy raiders headed westward after they were chased from the island by P38s, earlier communiques show.

Russell Annabel, United Press war correspondent with the U.S. forces on Attu, reported that "Japanese snipers wait for the chance to pick off stretcher bearers evacuating American wounded as they hide in their cock niches on Attu.

Japanese machine-gunners pinned down 20 stretcher bearers with 12 wounded for

(*Continued on page 5*)

Every Man Expected to Have $10,000 in Insurance by Aug. 9

Every American soldier in the European Theater of Operations is expected to have a $10,000 policy in National Service Life Insurance by Aug. 9, it was made clear yesterday by Headquarters, SOS, ETOUSA.

Soldiers who, for some reason, prefer not to take out the maximum amount allowed will be required to sign a statement which will be filed with their permanent Army records.

Headquarters pointed out that soldiers still have 76 days in which to take out or increase insurance without having to undergo medical examinations and without medical history statements. On Apr. 12 the War Department announced that regulations for taking out insurance would be relaxed for 120 days, during which time no examinations or medical statements would be required. The deadline is Aug. 9.

Up to that time insurance may be taken out even by men now hospitalized or men who have previously been rejected for any reason whatever, headquarters said. Even men hospitalized for mental disorders will have applications submitted for them.

The War Department urgently desires all men—both officers and EMs—to take advantage of the offer, SOS officers said. They added that the opportunity to acquire protection, without regard to the customary rules of insurability, is probably without parallel in insurance history.

The $10,000 policy costs from $6.40 a month for 18-year-olds to $12.70 for men of 50. Rates above 50 are proportionately higher. Premiums are deducted from pay, and the policy cannot lapse no matter where its holder is sent.

After one year the policy can be converted to one of three permanent forms—ordinary life, 20-pay life, or 30-pay life.

(*Continued on page 4*)

Eden Watches Opening Fights For ETO Titles

18 Servicemen Advance Through First Round At Rainbow Club

Eighteen U.S. servicemen yesterday advanced through the first round of The Stars and Stripes ETO boxing championships.

Anthony Eden, British Foreign Minister, was a ringside spectator in the evening bouts.

As expected, the favorites came through without too much difficulty. All the Division entries made the grade.

There were three knockouts on the afternoon card and four in the evening.

Yesterday's bouts were the first in the four-day tourney to determine the fistic championship of the ETO in eight weight divisions. Winners will form an 11-man team to meet the British Army champions, June 10, at Royal Albert Hall.

More Fights Today

Two more sets of bouts will be held at the Rainbow Corner this afternoon and tonight.

Pvt. John Robinson, of Kansas City, Kan., and Pfc Harold Alle, of North St. Paul, Minn., welterweights, opened the tournament, with Robinson beating out a hard-earned decision over Alle. It was a contest of left hands most of the way, with Robinson's jab making Alle miss his powerful hooks. Robinson also showed a little more stamina and finished fresh. It was his fifth victory at the Rainbow Corner.

Pfc John Shikolak, lightweight, from Whitehouse, N.J., scored the first knockout of the afternoon, when S/Sgt. Harold Cross, of Chicago, was counted out on one knee in 1:52 of the second round. Shikolak's aggressiveness gave him a slight edge in the first round, but in the second he began to connect with his two-fisted attack, putting Cross down for nine and again for no count before the final knockdown.

Spontak Batters Silverman

Pvt. Mike Silverman, East Chicago, Ill., lightweight, never had a chance in his fight with Cpl. George Spontak, of Pittsburgh, Pa., but he was the crowd's favorite as he took everything Spontak could throw and came back for more.

Hopelessly outclassed and so short that his feet didn't touch the floor as he sat on his stool, he kept wading into his tough opponent while the audience shouted to have the fight stopped. The referee sent

(*Continued on page 4*)

German Admits U-Boats Having A Tougher Time

STOCKHOLM, May 25 (UP)—Allied counter-measures are successfully thwarting the German U-boat campaign against merchant ships, a spokesman for the German Government admitted, according to Swedish newspaper correspondents.

The spokesman said "the present low level of our sinking figures" can be explained by the fact that, "just as in every other form of warfare, experience leads to the adoption of new methods and to counter-measures. We know very well that the enemy merchant navy is protected by an ever-increasing fleet of naval units and aircraft."

DSC Pilots Died To Save Crew

Two USAAF pilots who sacrificed their own chance of escaping from a bomber forced down in the North Sea in order to help save fellow-crew members have been posthumously awarded the Distinguished Service Cross, Headquarters, ETOUSA, announced yesterday.

The pilots were 1/Lt. Allen Brill, of Sedalia, Mo., and his co-pilot 1/Lt. Allen W. Lowry, of Richmond, Cal.

The citation says that while on a bombing mission over enemy-occupied continental Europe their bomber was attacked by enemy fighters, and after a "long and gallant fight" went into the sea.

"In utter disregard for their [illegible] safety, Lts. Brill and [illegible] their posts and aided [illegible] to leave the plane [illegible]

1D. THE STARS AND STRIPES 1D.

Daily Newspaper of U.S. Armed Forces in the European Theater of Operations

Vol. 3 No. 180 — New York, N.Y.—London, England — Wednesday, June 2, 1943

Coal Strike Imperils U.S. War Output

Forts Strike Air Gateway To Balkans

Foggia Airdrome Blasted; Allied Planes Attack At Will in Italy

By Chris Cunningham
United Press Correspondent

ALLIED HQ, North Africa, June 1—Foggia, the great airdrome which is the "air gateway" from Italy to the Balkans, again was pulverised in another big attack by Flying Fortresses of the strategic air force yesterday.

When the Fortresses swept across the field they found large numbers of planes, chiefly Junkers 88's, on the ground and dropped scores of tons of bombs among them. They also scored direct hits on barracks, hangars, administrative buildings and the railway yards that serve the airdrome as well as the city.

This was the third big raid by Fortresses in four days, the first being against Leghorn on Friday and the second against Naples Sunday.

Striking at Will

Their ability to strike at will anywhere well inside the theoretical area of Italian fighter protection without meeting with any very strong opposition is one of the most amazing features of the "softening-up" process that Air Chief Marshal Tedder is now conducting.

Foggia is not only a big air center but a vital communications center at a point where Italian communications down into the heel of Italy start to run a little thin. The continued plastering it is now getting from Allied planes is a tribute to its strategic importance in any developments of the campaign.

Elsewhere air activity was on a smaller scale than for some days. Lightnings attacked Sardinia damaging a small cargo-boat at Porte Ponto Romano and dropping bombs among a collection of small boats in the harbor at Cagliari, at the southern end of the island.

Eight Axis fighters followed the formation for more than 80 miles as they

(Continued on page 4)

Big Ship Movements Reported at Gibraltar

A record number of merchant ships—104—are concentrated at Gibraltar, according to a United Press report from La Linea, the Spanish town which adjoins Gibraltar.

Most of them are transports and tankers, which arrived Monday night, said the report, one of several suggesting an Allied invasion fleet is being massed.

Berlin radio, quoting reports from Algeciras, across the bay from Gibraltar, said three British aircraft-carriers, three battleships and a number of destroyers left Gibraltar Monday, some headed for the Atlantic but most steaming east. Later a cruiser and four destroyers arrived. The Axis reported great numbers of invasion barges concentrated at all Allied ports in the Mediterranean.

RAF Gets Five Of 12 Raiders

Five of an attacking force of 12 German FW190s which raided a southeast English town yesterday were shot down by RAF Typhoons—a dogfight percentage of 41 2/3.

By usual standards for air fighting, a sustained ten per cent loss is all any attacking formation can stand.

Later in the day RAF fighters, in sweeps over northern France, shot down another five Nazi planes, losing one in the process. The two encounters made it ten to one for the day's exchange.

The coast raid was the second of the day in which enemy planes were over English territory. Early yesterday two raiders crossed the south coast and dropped bombs in the London area. Slight damage and a small number of casualties, some fatal, resulted.

Yank Who Got Malta's 1,000th Plane

The 1,000th Axis plane destroyed by the RAF on Malta is chalked up on the Spitfire of Squadron/Ldr. J. J. Lynch, of Alhambra, Cal., who knocked out a Ju52 for the new mark. Lynch was awarded the DFC for the 1,000th plane destroyed.

Most VD Infections Spread By 'Piccadilly Commandos'

One third of all venereal disease cases in the ETO are contracted in the London area, according to Lt. Col. Paul Padget, chief of the section for the control of venereal disease of the division of preventive medicine, Office of the Chief Surgeon, ETO.

Most of the infections acquired in this area are picked up from the "Piccadilly Commandos" or their sister prostitutes in other sections of London, he added.

Almost all cases are contracted through wilful or ignorant negligence on the part of the soldier, Col. Padget emphasized.

"Education is the only way to combat venereal diseases," he said. "The soldier must not forget what he has been taught and should remember that it isn't smart to get hurt."

Quick Cure Assured

If, however, a man does get caught off base, he should report to the dispensary at once. Eighty-five per cent of the time gonorrhea can be cured in from five to ten days if treated immediately and no complications arise. The other 15 per cent, Col. Padget said, fail to respond to the sulfathiazole treatment and "are in for a bad time."

The treatment of syphilis, he continued, has made rapid advancement recently although no new drugs are being used. The "sulfa" drugs have no effect on the disease.

The cure for the majority of the gonorrhea infections has been made so simple by the use of sulfathiazole that the patient loses no time from duty and therefore suffers no loss of pay. A few pills a day for five days, complete abstinence from all types of liquor, spices and sexual activity for approximately a month and the cure is effective.

Col. Padget and his staff keep close tabs on the diseases. One officer is assigned to each base section and spends his full time fighting the disease. Maj. Peter Pullman is located in the Central Base Section, Capt. Goran at Southern Base, Capt. Barron Knox at Western Base and 1/Lt. Albert Leroy at Eastern Base.

Capt. Raymond Heitz, of Louisville, Ky., is Col. Padget's assistant while 1/Lt. Charles Anderson directs the "contact investigation" work of the four nurses;

(Continued on page 4)

Germans Admit They Need Lull

Can't Hide Allied Blows, But Pin Faith On U-Boats

STOCKHOLM, June 1 (AP)—Reeling under constant Allied blows and awaiting further attacks—perhaps this month—Germany no longer can hide the crippling effects of the Russian and North African defeats, informed Berlin quarters told neutral correspondents yesterday.

The Axis needs a "calm year" to recover from the damage caused by bombing raids, to repair battered transport facilities, reallocate the shrinking supply of raw materials and train millions of laborers for war factories, the Berlin correspondent of the Stockholm Tidningen reported.

"Germany is suffering from a bleeding wound," he said.

Calm was not only needed to replenish supplies of weapons but to give the army time to drill and train 3,000,000 more men.

The mobilization of 3,000,000 men gave an indication of Nazi losses and explained the disruption of the factory labor situation. The cream of Germany's manpower has been fighting for three years. New conscripts are coming from the factories, where their places were taken by women and foreign workers.

The Berlin correspondent of both the Stockholm Tidningen and the Svenska Dagbladet said that the Nazis continued to pin their hopes on "tiring out" the Allies in submarine warfare, although acknowledging that it would take a long time.

Talks by Giraud, De Gaulle Are Stopped Temporarily

ALGIERS, June 1 (UP)—Negotiations between Gen. Charles De Gaulle and Gen. Henri Giraud, which are expected to result in the formation of the first Democratic government of France since her capitulation in 1940, were temporarily suspended today until certain points of disagreement can be ironed out.

Disagreement is understood to center around whether the Gov.-Gen. of Algeria and Resident-General of Morocco and French West Africa should be allowed to remain at their posts in view of Gen. De Gaulle's insistence that all former collaborationists should be ousted from high positions.

Lewis Calls 500,000 From Mines to Force $2-a-Day Pay Raise

Government Already in Control of Mines; Negotiations Continue as Troops Stand Ready to Move In

The United States coal industry, vital to the war effort, was virtually paralyzed yesterday as nearly half a million miners went on strike to enforce a demand for a new contract, calling for $2 more a day to meet increased living costs.

The strike was called by John L. Lewis, chief of the independent United Mine Workers of America, at the close of a 28-day truce in which negotiators for the union and the operators had failed to reach an agreement.

The U.S. government already was in control of the mines. On instructions from President Roosevelt, Secretary of the Interior Harold L. Ickes had taken possession May 2 when 500,000 workers quit, staying out for one day before the truce was arranged. Troops were held ready to enter the mine fields, but up to a late hour last night no such action had been ordered.

Both the White House and the union headquarters in New York were silent on the situation.

Reserve Supplies Short

No information was available last night on how much reserve coal supplies American war industries had on hand, but when the original walkout occurred May 2 most war plants reported they had enough coal for only a few weeks' operations, and it was assumed the same was true now. The vital steel works had only enough for two weeks, and many plants manufacturing plane, tank and gun parts had only half that.

As the nation waited tensely for governmental action—possibly occupation of the mines by the Army—it appeared inevitable that drastic steps would be taken to conserve the fuel supply so vital to America's war industries. All non-essential railway travel may be banned, and a nationwide dim-out may be imposed.

In Washington Lewis and the mine operators resumed negotiations without comment yesterday morning.

The strike appeared to be nearly 100 per cent effective in all coalfields operated by United Mine Workers personnel, although a number of mines worked by non-union or independent union workers continued production.

Anthracite Miners Join

Pennsylvania's 1,600 soft coal mines were idle as 100,000 workers obeyed Lewis' injunction not to trespass on the mine properties without contracts. There was scattered picketing.

Pennsylvania's 83,000 anthracite miners also refused to work.

Eastern Ohio's rich coalfields, which employ 16,000 of the state's 21,000 coal miners, also were idle.

In West Virginia more than 130,000 men refused to report for work.

The importance of the strike to the American war effort was clearly stated by President Roosevelt in his radio appeal to the miners just before the truce was announced May 3.

"These are not mere strikes against employers to enforce collective bargaining demands," he asserted. "They are strikes against the United States government itself and a direct interference in the prosecution of the war."

At that time it was made clear that the government would not force the miners back to work, but would, if necessary, send American soldiers into the mines.

The strikers' reply was: "You can't dig coal with bayonets."

The background of and reasons for the strike are described in the following dispatch, cabled from Washington by The Associated Press last night at the request of The Stars and Stripes:

The soft coal miners' contract expired but the United Mine Workers and the

(Continued on page 4)

Chinese Encircle Five Divisions In Big Offensive

U.S. Planes Help Smash Jap Air Protection; Enemy 'Doomed'

By the United Press

From four to five Japanese divisions have been surrounded and doomed to destruction in an all-out Chinese offensive against the Japanese forces on the Yangtse front, the Chinese High Command announced yesterday in Chungking.

It was one of the biggest victories for Gen. Chiang Kai-Shek's armies in the whole Sino-Japanese war, and the most shattering joint Chinese-American air victory over the Japanese ever achieved in China.

First news of the new offensive, given by a Chinese communique, indicated that the mopping up of the beleaguered Japanese troops was progressing satisfactorily.

Changyang, which was captured by the Japanese little more than a week ago, is now threatened by Chinese forces which have reached the city's outskirts as part of a general drive on a 50-mile front southwards from Ichang on the Yangtse River.

U.S. Planes Help

American heavy bombers and fighters, supporting the Chinese counter-offensive, smashed at three of the main Japanese bases in central China—Ichang, Shasi and Yuchow—all in the Yangtze area.

The attacks were admitted by Tokyo radio today, which said that the raids were carried out by 14 bombers, escorted by 30 fighters.

The Chinese report that signs of cracking are evident in the Japanese rear as the result of the new attack and the additional strain of bombardment of their vital bases and centers.

The defeated Japanese divisions had been intended to form the spearhead of a vast southwesterly push to Chungking down the Yangtse.

Fighting also is reported to be in progress south of the Yangtse River, where Chinese forces have been making co-ordinated attacks on enemy positions along the Hunan-Hupeh border area.

Wounded Gunner Fixes Radio, Keeps Log As Nazis Pop Away

A U.S. BOMBER STATION, June 1 (UP)—S/Sgt. Isaac A. Flesher, of Towanda, Ill., was the toast of both officers and men at this Liberator station after a raid in which the wounded gunner not only kept a log all through the action, but used his own body to test a damaged radio set.

As the plane neared the target, Flesher left the radio room to help open the bomb bay doors which were jammed by a loose shell case. The men were unable to open the doors at first, and while they were working on them Flesher was struck in the face and legs with flak. At the same time a 20-mm. shell crashed through the dynamo, knocking out the radio and intercom system, as well as the radio compass.

The interphone is vital over the target, so Flesher hustled to establish an emergency system and then began to repair the radio set. He said "there must have been 20 or 25 jerries popping away at us." With all temporary connections made, Flesher used his own body to test the equipment to see if the radio was getting the proper current. He took one lead in one hand and the other lead in the other hand to test the juice. After the current was established, he returned to aid the other gunner who had been wounded, and although his face was bleeding profusely, he finally got the bomb bay doors open.

During the time the action took place Sgt. Flesher kept a neatly itemized log—marred here and there with a drop of blood—and coolly turned in the log when he landed.

British Empire Casualties 514,993 in Three Years

Casualties in the British Commonwealth and Empire forces during the first three years of the war were 514,993 killed, wounded, missing and prisoners of war.

Figures revealed yesterday in the House of Commons showed 92,089 killed, 88,294 wounded, 226,719 missing and 107,891 prisoners of war. The total included casualties in the armies, navies and air forces of the United Kingdom, Canada, Australia, New Zealand, South Africa and the colonies.

Civilian casualties during the first three years throughout the Empire amounted to 47,291 killed and 35,643 injured.

1d

THE STARS AND STRIPES

1d

Daily Newspaper of U.S. Armed Forces in the European Theater of Operations

Vol. 3 No. 189 | New York, N.Y.—London, England | Saturday, June 12, 1943

Pantellaria Surrenders Under Air Blitz

VictorySets Pattern for Next Steps

Italy Felt More Bombs In 12 Days Than Rest Of Axis in Month

Pantellaria's defeat by terrific bombing alone, without risking large numbers of men in landing operations, was seen last night as a possible pattern for future operations against Axis territory—particularly Italy.

Officers at Allied headquarters in North Africa, aware of Brig. Gen. Lauris Norstad's comment that the final raid knocking out Mussolini's "little Malta" was "a scientific job prepared with a slide rule," hailed the success of the operation and said it augured well for future operations not only in North Africa but elsewhere.

More bombs were dropped on Pantellaria during the last few days than were dropped on Tunisia, Sicily, Sardinia and Italy together during the whole of April, Algiers radio said. Between May 29 and June 10, Algiers added, the weight of bombs dropped on the island equalled that dropped in May in all other theaters of warfare.

From the East, Too

Simultaneously Gen. Lewis H. Brereton, commanding U.S. forces in the Middle East, disclosed at Cairo that the Ninth Air Force stepped up its blitz by 25 per cent in May compared with the preceding month. Three and a half million pounds of explosives were dropped on the enemy in 200 missions during the month, he said.

Five hundred tons of bombs were dropped by Liberators on the ports on either side of the Messina straits at Regiio di Calabria and Messina, the Cairo statement added. Fighters made 162 missions, shot down 23 enemy aircraft, sank seven Axis ships, and left 12 others probably sunk and 30 damaged.

The U.S. Navy, as well as the U.S. Air Force, has begun to worry the Italian high command, it was evident from a Rome broadcast by Adm. Auturo Riccardi, under-secretary of state for the navy.

He said the war in the Mediterranean, waged by the Italians for three years "with comparatively small means," had become "still more difficult by the added weight of the U.S. Navy in that theater of war."

Nevertheless, said Adm. Riccardi, in a statement interpreted as indicating an Italian intention to challenge Allied naval forces, "our navy is ready for further defense and even to strike at the enemy."

Fighters Sweep France, Holland

RAF fighter squadrons swept over France and Holland yesterday, destroying three enemy fighters in dogfights with interceptors.

British fighters also escorted Ventura bombers in raids on coke ovens and benzole plants at Zeebrugge. Heavy smoke which boiled up from the target area after the bombs landed convinced pilots that they had scored.

Later, Spitfires flown by Polish, Norwegian and Dominion pilots challenged the enemy over Abbeville, France.

Washington Recognizes Argentine Government

WASHINGTON, June 11 (AP)—The United States recognized the new Argentine government of Gen. Pedro Ramirez today, Secretary of State Cordell Hull announced this afternoon. He said most of the other American republics had done the same thing, and that the rest would do so within a few days.

A reporter asked the Secretary if Great Britain had been consulted in the matter, and Hull replied that the United States had acted "on its own initiative," although other American republics had been consulted, "as usual."

Fathers in the Draft

WASHINGTON, June 11 (AP)—A married man of military age with children has about 17 chances in 100 of being drafted before next year, statisticians figured today. Those who are farmers will, however, be deferred for the most part for occupational reasons. The drafting of fathers is expected to begin in August.

Allied Stepping Stone to Europe

Occupation of Pantellaria extends by nearly 100 miles the fighter protection for bombing raids on Sicily and Italy's toe. Lampedusa is expected to fall at any time, providing still another stepping-stone to Europe.

15-Star Unit Arrives by Boat To Entertain Yanks in ETO

The first unit of USO-Camp Shows Inc. to travel to Britain by troop transport has arrived here and will begin a tour of ETO installations next week.

Aboard ship they gave four performances, improvising a stage out of six mess hall tables and planks.

All 15 members of the party, one of the largest groups to come to the ETO, said they were happy to be here. They explained they had volunteered for "overseas duty" a long time ago.

The new "entertainment task force," according to William Dover, executive administrator, of USO-Camp Shows, reflects the organization's determination to "follow the men wherever they go, subject only to policy restrictions of the army."

Nine Camp Shows already are on tour in the British Isles, and soon there will be 15, Dover said, promising a talent pool that will remain active for the duration.

"American entertainers are eager to come over here," he declared. "The only problem has been transportation."

Hal Le Roy, Broadway and Hollywood dancing star, summed up the attitude of the group. "It's swell to get over here at last. It's where we want to be. We're anxious to get to work—and fast."

Francetta Malloy, blues singer, said she was afraid that appearing before American troops would affect her specialty. "I won't feel blue," she explained, "playing for the boys."

Dorothy and Helen Blossom, comedy dancing team, who intend to get soldiers from their audiences to jitterbug with them, said that all their dancing was "on the bias" while afloat. "It was OK with us when the boat rocked," Dorothy said. "That only made for better jitterbugging."

Other entertainers in the group, which will cover every installation in the ETO during the next six months, "and longer if necessary," are Hank Ladd, radio star; Elsie Hartley, singing accordionist; Brucetta, acrobatic dancer; Patricia Melville, accordionist; Dorothy Deering, acrobatic dancer; Eddie Cochran, magician, and company; Don Rice, comedian; Mildred Anderson, accordionist; Wally West, mimic; and "Limberlegs" Edwards, dancer.

Pay-As-You-Go Tax Bill Signed

First Deduction in July; Most 1942 Taxes Are Cancelled

WASHINGTON, June 11—America's income taxpayers were put on the "pay-as-you-go" basis yesterday as President Roosevelt signed a bill cancelling from 75 to 100 per cent of last year's taxes. Beginning July 1 all salary and wage earners will have at least 20 per cent of each pay check deducted and paid to the government.

Before enactment of the law, taxes were paid a year in arrears.

Persons owing less than $40 on their 1942 income, under the old system, will pay no taxes for last year. They must, however, pay this year's taxes this year.

Those paying more than a $40 tax for 1942 will have fractional amounts remitted, depending on the size of their incomes. All uncancelled taxes must be paid this year in addition to the "pay-as-you-go" sums. Such payments will be spread over the coming months.

The President's action formally ended a bitter legislative battle in which House Democrats defeated the Republican-sponsored Ruml Plan three times. The Ruml bill would have cancelled an entire tax year.

Adrift 132 Days on Raft

MIAMI, Fla., June 11 (UP)—Poon Lim, 25-year-old Chinese steward of a torpedoed British merchant ship, is recovering in a hospital here from his ordeal of 132 days on a raft. Previously, the longest time a man had been known to live under those conditions was 87 days. Lim lived on fish he caught with a bent nail. Rain provided him with drinking water.

'In a Month or Two'

WASHINGTON, June 11 (AP)—"In a month or two" we should see what the invasion talk flooding Europe's capitals is about, Harold Butler, representative of the British Ministry of Information, said today in a brief interview.

Allied Troops Land To Prepare Island For Blows at Italy

Air Power Alone Achieved Victory Over Land Force First Time in History; FDR Asks Revolt on Duce

The tiny Italian island of Pantellaria surrendered yesterday, giving the Allies possession of the first stepping-stone to Europe.

Its white flag was hoisted after 13 days of continuous air assault, swelling in the final 24 hours to the greatest air blitz of the war, in which more than 1,000 planes were employed. The pounding was such as no other target of similar size ever has received.

It was the first time that air power alone had knocked out an important fortress without ground troops having been landed. The air forces were given some assistance by several naval bombardments.

Capitulation of Lampedusa and Limosa, two other small Italian islands, was forecast almost immediately. Tokio radio said a surrender demand already had been sent to Lampedusa. From Pantellaria's airfields and underground hangars Allied fighters now can command Sicily.

In the violent crescendo of the final 24 hours of air assault, more Fortresses than ever before were used in the Mediterranean theater led the assault.

The rain of explosives smothered gun emplacements, airfields and other targets. The island's single town and fort became an inferno. Allied planes, mostly American, made a hundred-odd sorties. Thirty-seven enemy fighters fell in dog fights all over the island.

Capitulation, after two Allied demands for surrender, came in the midst of the raid. A white flag fluttered from Semaphore Hill, a mile inland from the harbor. Twenty minutes later Allied troops began landing.

At first there was slight resistance, because all of the garrison had not been informed of the decision to surrender. But within 22 minutes of the first landing all the primary objectives had been taken.

Forts Held Their Bombs

The surrender signal was first seen by Flying Fortresses, which circled over the island shortly before noon and then returned to their bases without dropping their loads. Previously, more than 100 Fortresses had begun a pattern bombing of the island, starting on the coastline and gradually moving their bomb-patterns inland.

About the same time the senior Italian officer on Pantellaria sent a message to the Allies, apparently by radio, saying: "I beg to surrender because of lack of water."

Allied headquarters in North Africa disclosed last night that Gen. Dwight D. Eisenhower, Allied commander-in-chief in North Africa, and British Adm. Sir Andrew Cunningham, commanding Allied sea forces in the Mediterranean, were on board British cruisers which led Tuesday's naval bombardment of the island.

In Washington, President Roosevelt said the victory was very good news, and appealed indirectly to Italy to withdraw from the war. He told a press conference that the Italian people could be assured that after Fascism had been suppressed and the Germans driven from Italy they would have an opportunity to choose the kind of non-Nazi, non-Fascist government they want.

Every type of plane was thrown into the final assault—from Fortresses to bomb-carrying Lightnings. Traffic over the target was so heavy that some formations had to circle offshore for several minutes until there was room to make their runs.

'Class-room Classic'

"This operation will go down in history as a class-room classic," said Brig. Gen. Lauris Norstad, chief of operations of the strategical air force. "It was prepared with particular care by a large competent staff—a scientific job prepared with a slide rule."

He said that by dusk Thursday Pantellaria was through. "We knocked out all gun positions, which included many coastal pieces of four-inch to nine-inch bore."

Fall of the Italian "Malta"—whose

(*Continued on page 4*)

Allied Triumph Heartens Reds

Aerial Attacks Increase As Radio Tells News Ahead of Time

MOSCOW, June 11—Heartened by news of the latest Allied triumph in the Mediterranean theater, the Russians intensified their air blows against vital German targets on the central front today in preparation for an all-out offensive, apparently timed to coincide with the Allied blow at Europe.

Russia heard the news of the fall of Pantellaria six hours earlier than usual. There is usually a time lag of 12 hours in Moscow radio's broadcast of foreign news, but the victory was broadcast soon after 6 PM.

Russian planes struck twice more at German offensive power in Russia. The first blow came when strong Soviet forces battered five key enemy airdromes at night.

For the second time within a week, they destroyed large numbers of grounded German planes—possibly those which the Nazis have used to strike at targets of Gorki and Yaroslavl. Ammunition and fuel dumps round the airdromes were seen to explode.

All the raiding aircraft returned safely to their bases.

The second blow was struck not by bombers but by fighters which intercepted 100 German aircraft over the approaches to Leningrad.

They attempted a daylight raid on the city and were badly carved up by the Russians who intercepted them. A total of 22 German aircraft were destroyed, most of them Heinkel 111's, Focke Wulf 190's and ME 190's.

The raid failed although there were roughly two fighters for every bomber.

Hell's Angels Completes 28 Raids

EIGHTH AIR FORCE STATION, June 11 (AP)—Hell's Angels, a Flying Fortress which has dumped more than 150,000 pounds of bombs over Germany in the last seven months, is still going strong with only a few patched-up flak tears and a lone bullet hole to show for her 28 raids on Europe.

The unequalled record of the big B17 is matched by the record of her crew: of the original group of men who flew and fought her, only two have been lost, and both were flying in other planes at the time.

Plowing through German flak and swarms of Luftwaffe fighters, Hell's Angels has bombed Wilhelmshaven, Kiel, Bremen, Hamm, Vegesack, St. Nazaire, Lorient, Romilly and Paris. Other Forts sometimes faltered and turned back before reaching their target, but the Angel, carrying as her insignia a haloed, wing-sprouting cherub, bearing a bomb over one shoulder, completed every mission.

Other stations have dubbed Hell's Angels the "luckiest Fortress in the ETO." That burns the men of this station. "Her flying crew and groundmen just know their onions," they say.

The plane's first navigator, Capt. Harold Fulghum, of Lubbock, Tex., was taken prisoner after he was forced to bail out while flying in another plane during a raid on St. Nazaire last November. He was replaced by 1/Lt. Paryley W. Madsen Jr., of Provo, Utah, who was lost while flying in another Fortress which failed to return from St. Nazaire.

These are the men who completed the missions with the plane: Capt. Irl Baldwin, Yakima, Wash., pilot; 1 Lt. Donald R. Bone, Temple, Okla., bombardier and Sgts. James E. Rodrigues, South Ozone Park, N.Y., top turret gunner; Russell M. Warren, Sante Fe, N.M., radioman-gunner; Allerton F. Medbaugh Jr., New Milford, Conn., waist gunner; Harry J. Brody, Glendive, Mont., ball turret gunner; Dennis Weiskopf, Miami, Fla., waist gunner, and Harold E. Godwin, Los Angeles, tail gunner. They have been transferred to another station, presumably preparatory to going to the United States. 1 Lt. Ripley W. Joy, of San Francisco, co-pilot, is staying here on operations.

Members of the ground force are: Sgts. Fabian F. Folmer, Mansfield, Ohio, crew chief; Robert C. Whitson, Achille, Okla.; Ernest Touhey, Mountain Home, Ark.; John J. O'Brien, Boston, Mass.; Edward A. West Jr., Newport News, Va.; George A. Roberts, Statesbury, W. Va.; Wilson F. Fairfield, Sturbridge, Mass., and Kasmer Wegrzyn, Chicopee, Mass.; Cpl. John R. Kasilla, North Tarrytown, N.Y., and Pvts. William C. Holman, Northport, Ala.; George C. Kelly, North Hollywood, Cal., and Ival E. Salisbury, Howard, Kan.

Maneuvers in U.S. Seen As Rehearsal for Invasion

SPARTANBURG, S.C., June 11—Maneuvers described as a dress rehearsal for invasion have just been completed in South Carolina by the largest force of paratroopers, airborne infantry and ground-air cooperation units ever assembled in the United States.

Huge troop transports, gliders and even parachute artillery outfits took part in the test.

In a single day of operations, thousands of paratroopers were dropped in "enemy territory" under conditions approximating those of an actual invasion.

THE STARS AND STRIPES

Oran Daily

Vol. 1 - No. 35 - Friday, June 18, 1943 | U. S. Army Newspaper | One Franc

Japs Drop Poison Gas On Chinese

King Sees His Forces In Africa

A NORTH AFRICA PORT, June 16, (Delayed)—The King of England continued his visit here in North Africa with a review of British and other Allied warships.

Later in the day he greeted another part of the forces, the war correspondents. The British ruler, a navy man himself who saw action at the Battle of Jutland in the last war, spent the better part of the morning inspecting detachments of sailors and marines, chatting with WRENS, the British equivalent of WAVES, and touring several warships.

His Majesty arrived at the docks accompanied by Admiral Sir Andrew Cunningham, Commander of Allied Naval Operations in the Mediterranean, Sir Clinton Danby, Britain's sea transport chief, and Gibson Graham, of the Ministry of War Transport.

The waterfront was a mass of white uniforms gleaming brightly in the warm sun with the sparkling blue water for a backdrop.

A comparatively small group of men stood out for they were not in white. They were merchant seamen. They were praised highly by the King for their work in manning the "bridge of ships" from home fronts to war fronts.

For more than an hour King George walked slowly up and down the vast docks, chatting with some of the British tars just back from the bombardment of Pantelleria and Lampedusa, inquiring about the experiences of some of the WRENS who were torpedoed while enroute to North Africa, and displaying much interest in the American gobs, with many a salt mile of convoy duty to their credit.

The men of the sea were drawn up in long lines that stretched all the way from the warehouses nearest the street to the waterfront.

Two of the American officers who accompanied him on the review were Vice Admiral H. K. Hewitt and Rear Admiral J. L. Hall.

The King then went aboard one of Britain's heavy warships, being piped over the side by a guard of honor composed of Royal Marines.

He next visited an American warship, her gun turrets turned skyward in salute. As he departed the sailors threw their white caps in the air and gave three rousing cheers.

The French people had watched the colorful procession from harbor villas and apartment balconies and as he drove away from the docks and through the city they, too, joined in the wild cheers.

Clapping Arab children ran after the royal car but, of course, were not allowed to approach too near.

(Continued on Page 2)

Crippled Bomber Fights Off Two Attacking Planes, Lands Safely

ALLIED FORCE HEADQUARTERS, June 17 — Unfavorable weather yesterday restricted the Northwest African Air Force to routine patrolling. Heavy and medium bombers were grounded.

However, five more planes can be added to the 11 Axis craft shot down in raids over Sicily on Tuesday, the Allied Force communique revealed.

These victories had not previously been reported.

To fill in the quiet day there was the story of a Martin Marauder bomber which fell out of a recent Pantelleria-bound formation because of motor trouble, was jumped by two German fighters. He shot down one of them and then returned 60 miles to a base on one motor, safely making a "hot" landing.

Let Lt. Kenneth G. Ross of Huntington, Ind., the pilot of the unlucky B-26, tell his own story.

"Just as we opened our bomb bay doors on the bomb run I had trouble with the right engine and it started smoking. I put on the rich fuel mixture and put the blower on full power but the engine kept falling off and we were dropping behind the formation. About then at least two ME 109's hit us.

"I looked out my window and saw a big bullet hole in the cowling above my left engine. Tracers were flying by the cockpit. Right then I forgot about the target and cut across our course to catch up with the formation.

"The oil pressure of the shot-up engine started fluctuating and then dropped like a shot I feathered the propeller immediately. Fortunately, the other engine picked up."

Meanwhile the bombardier navigator S-Sgt. Edward L. Baker, of Murphysboro, Ill., had closed the bomb bay doors. He was the first man to sight the enemy fighters.

"We were so far behind that I couldn't even see the target. A little later, when we were over the water, the co-pilot gave me the order to salvo the bombs."

The tail gunner, Sgt. James R. Williams of Milwaukee, Wis., took over the story.

"We saw those old black crosses as plain as day," he said. "That's the one I shot at. I got in three good bursts, and saw the tracers go into him. I think I hit the pilot because he headed right down. I was too busy with another baby to keep my eyes on him all the time."

S-Sgt. John K. Moberley, of Frederick, Md., the turret gunner, who also got a crack at the Messerschmitt, said his shots failed to strike home.

After its encounter, the crippled Marauder received a protecting cover from elements of it's formation and from P-40's. The problem now was to get back to the African coast on the one remaining lung, and it was coughing.

The B-26 lost altitude all the way but Lt. Ross managed to keep it at 2,500 feet along the coast of Cape Bon until he sighted a fighter field.

"I had to make a hot landing," the pilot said. "My air speed indicator, which is essential in landing a B-26, went out when the wing tip was shot up. When I tried to put the flaps down I could get them only a quarter open.

"With no way to cut the speed, the ship touched ground at 170 miles an hour. These ships have a high landing speed but, hell, I was going too fast. Regardless, it was a nice landing.

"There's nothing wrong with my ship that a new engine and a little sheet metal work won't fix up," chuckled Lt. Ross.

Report Ship Loaded With Gas Shells

WASHINGTON, June 17 — Following closely on the heels of President Roosevelt's stern warning to the Axis on the threatened use of gas, a Chinese military spokesman revealed that Japanese planes dropped poison gas bombs over China yesterday on the Province of Suicynan.

It was also reported that Japanese artillery fired gas shells at Matousshan in Southern Shansi and that last month a Jap ship anchored at Woosung, off Shanghai, was loaded with 120 poison gas containers and 50 tons of poison gas shells.

Only recently did the President reaffirm the Allied position regarding gas. At the time he said: "We promise to any perpetrators of such crimes full and swift retaliation in kind, and I feel obliged now to warn the Axis Armies and Axis people in Europe and Asia that the terrible consequences of any use of such inhumane methods on their part will be brought down swiftly and surely upon their own heads."

On that occasion the President revealed that there was increasing evidence that "the Axis powers are making significant preparations indicative of such intentions."

He revealed that he had received numerous reports from a variety of sources that the Axis powers were preparing to use gas.

Premier Hideki Tojo, Japanese War Minister, neither affirmed nor denied the Chinese accusation but warned his people to expect new blows by the United Nations, including raids on the Japanese mainland.

"The enemy is not only trying to raid our bases," said Tojo, "but they are attempting to raid our mainland and shut off our supply routes."

He also told the Japanese people that the Chinese Air Force had begun to receive the help of American personnel and equipment.

"In New Guinea," continued the Premier, "battles are growing fiercer and fiercer." Tojo blamed the recent Japanese defeat on the island of Attu to bad weather and the fact that the enemy was fully prepared.

Decision In Wage Fuss Is Expected

WASHINGON, June 17—The final decision of the War Labor Board in the wage controversy between the coal miners and the operators is expected to be handed down Friday.

No one knows, though, whether the board's verdict will stave off the third strike of the coal miners, slated to begin at the expiration of the truce deadline, Sunday midnight.

John L. Lewis, president of the United Mine Workers, has defied continually during the negotiations the power of the board to adjust the grievances and settle the dispute.

The final decision of whether the miners will strike, no doubt, will be up to him. On the basis of past performances, it is doubtful whether Lewis' antagonism to the board will abate unless the board proposes what he considers a satisfactory solution.

Lewis has studiously ignored the board to carry on his negotiations with the operators.

It appeared today that the UMW and Illinois coal owners were putting on the finishing touches preparatory to signing a contract before the deadline.

The UMW's negotiations with the Central Pennsylvania operators has broken down.

The latter group broke away from the joint Appalachian conference last week and Charles O'Neill, spokesman for the Pennsylvania operators, said he notified the board of the failure of negotiations with the miners and that his group will abide by the board's decision.

As this issue went to press, the president had not taken any action on the anti-strike bill, which labor leaders have denounced.

If the President signs the bill and the miners go out on strike, Lewis faces the possibility of a conviction and a jail sentence under such a law.

To Review Food Setup

WASHINGTON, June 17 — Food distribution and price problems of the nation will be reviewed by the Office of War Mobilization at the behest of President Roosevelt.

Meat shortages, OPA subsidy payments and price checks will be considered.

James F. Byrnes, War Mobilization Director, who is often called "assistant President in charge of the home front," is expected to get the job of handling the complex situation.

OPA head Prentiss Brown and CIO president Philip Murray support the OPA plan to pay subsidies to producers as a way of rolling back the cost of eating Murray has declared that if such a program is not instituted all control over wages must be broken.

Plan Another Food Parley

LONDON—Another International Food Conference is tentatively scheduled for Washington next month, Hugh Dalton, president of the Board of Trade, said in an address at the Labor Party Conference this week.

Plans call for the gratifying of the draft agreement on the program for a United Nations Relief and Rehabilitation administration and the setting up of the machinery immediately.

He said negotiations between Britain, Russia, the United States and China on postwar relief had

(Continued on Page 2)

Exonerate FDR's Grandson In Shooting

MORRISTOWN, Pa.—A coroner's jury exonerated William Donner Roosevelt, aged 10, in the accidental fatal shooting of a playmate.

The boy is President's Roosevelt's grandson and the son of Col. Elliot Roosevelt.

Sunday's Boxing Card Is Billed As Africa's Biggest

The biggest boxing event ever held in Northern Africa will be staged Sunday, June 20 at 1700 hours when the Allied Boxing Tournament takes place. Place d'Armes, scene of this outstanding event, is the open square between the Continental Hotel and the M. P. Headquarters.

Heretofore unmatched Ed Tipton will go eight rounds with Hernandez, a heavyweight from Oran

Tomitch, former heavyweight champion of Yugoslavia, will battle it out with Brown of the U. S. Army

Also on the card in the lightweight division is LaGrange who will meet Battling Hal

Hal hails from French Morocco and is present contender for the light-heavyweight title of France

LaGrange is a former National Gloves winner and also won the Diamond Belt in England All pro fights will be eight rounders, three minutes each.

In addition to these professional bouts there will be five amateur matches featuring a rematch between Sgt Broussard of the infantry and Johnny McCoy Hale, of the U. S. Navy

Other amateur bouts are:

Charles Boland, Royal Navy vs LeRoy Foreman, Infantry in a three rounder Dave Stemmuller, Signal Corps vs Garcia, a local boy from the Gallieni Club Two local Frenchmen in the flyweight class who hail from the Gallieni Club will conclude the program

Tickets will be on sale in the offices of Stars and Stripes and at Serva's Tobacco Shop, in front of the Barclay Bank Ringside seats will range from 25 francs to 125 francs.

Bayard Veiller, Playwright, Dies

NEW YORK, June 17—One of America's best known playwrights Bayard Veiller 74, author of the "Trial of Mary Dugan," died here in a hospital after being ill for several months.

His famous court room play was one of Broadway's all-time smash hits and was acclaimed by Presidents Wilson and Theodore Roosevelt.

Mr Veiller, who also wrote "Within the Law" was born in Brooklyn and worked for New York San Francisco and Chicago newspapers before seriously turning to the drama.

Charlie Chaplin Marries Daughter Of Gene O'Neill

SANTA BARBARA, Cal., June 17—Comedian Charlie Chaplin today married June O'Neill, 18, daughter of playwright Eugene O'Neill, in the small town of Carpinteria, near Santa Barbara.

The surprise wedding catapulted the 54-year-old actor's name back into the headlines less than a week after he had occupied the front pages in defending himself against the accusation of Joan Barry, his protege, that he is the father of her unborn child.

Miss Barry reportedly went into a state of collapse earlier in the day after hearing that Chaplin and Miss O'Neill had been issued a marriage license.

"I can't believe it," she said over and over again.

Onna O'Neill is one of the playwright's two daughters by his second wife, Agnes Boulton, whom he married in 1918 and divorced 11 years later. He also has a son, Eugene, by his first wife.

O'Neill, Pulitzer Prize winner for drama in 1920-22-28, and recipient of the Nobel Prize for Literature in 1936, now lives a retired life in a hillside cottage near Oakland, Cal.

Chaplin and Miss O'Neill left Hollywood secretly last night and turned up accompanied by friends at the Santa Barbara City Clerk's office half an hour before the office opened.

Deputy Clerk Ira Altshul, who issued the license, said, "the comedian was so nervous he could hardly hold the pen."

The Justice of Peace of Carpinteria performed the marriage ceremony.

Chaplin and his bride met at a party eight months ago. She is his fourth wife, Chaplin having formerly been wedded to Mildred Harris, Lita Gray and Paulette Goddard.

Chaplin recently made a settlement for the temporary care of Miss Barry pending the birth of her child, and the legal determination of its paternity.

THE STARS AND STRIPES
CASABLANCA DAILY

One Franc

Vol. 1 - No. 41 - Tuesday, 6 July, 1943

U. S. Army Newspaper for troops in Casablanca area

Allies Edge Closer to Jap Base

Salamaua Is Threatened

WASHINGTON, July 5—(S-S)—Increased aerial attacks marked action in the South Pacific over the weekend, while land forces concentrated on consolidating bridgeheads within striking distance of the two Japanese anchor bases in the New Guinea-Solomons line, Salamaua and Munda.

Allied Air Forces dealt heavy new blows on New Georgia island and have taken a heavy toll of enemy planes attempting to interfere with Allied troop movements, a communique from Allied Pacific Headquarters revealed.

Japanese positions in the Munda area of New Georgia island are being consistently hammered from the air and by coastal batteries on nearby Rendova island.

150 PLANES BLASTED

Twice Jap aircraft attempted attacks in force on the new U. S. positions on Rendova, and twice they were beaten off.

The Japs lost 21 planes over the island yesterday, bringing Nipponese aircraft losses to more than 150 since the battle began last Wednesday.

In New Guinea, the Americans who landed at Nassau Bay are still consolidating their positions as fierce patrol clashes are continuing on the Jap supply lines from Salamaua to Mubo.

STORM VILLAGE

Gen. Douglas MacArthur is in personal command of the New Guinea front, where U. S. and Australian troops are drawing in on the Japs' Salamaua base.

Just south of New Georgia, Allied forces have followed up their recent sea and air bombardment of Vanguno Island by storming the Jap-held village of Vura.

When Allied troops went ashore, they immediately overpowered the garrison and left 200 enemy dead in the village area. Remnants of the garrison fled inland, the communique said.

Finn Unit Seeks U. S. Good Will

WASHINGTON, July 5—An open Finnish bid for better relations with the United States in disregard of German pressure on Finland aroused interest in diplomatic quarters here today.

Organization of a Finnish-American society at Helsinki composed only of Finns was announced during the past week to "cultivate good relations between Finland and the United States."

Its chairman is Eljas Erkko, newspaper editor and former foreign minister. Its organizers have long been considered pro-American. What interested Washington observers was the fact that they should announce such an organization while subject to German pressure.

Medina is Quarter of Mystery and Intrigue; 'Off Limits' to GI's Only for Sanitary Reasons

Scribe Visits Scene, Arabs Friendly

By RALPH H. MAJOR, JR.

Medina, the "off limits" quarter of mystery and intrigue, probably would be voted "the place we'd most like to go" by servicemen in the Casablanca area if Army officials should attempt such a poll.

Out-of-bounds to all American personnel, the Medina now is patrolled by MP's who have orders to halt any American—whether colonels or corporals—who wish to inspect the twisted streets, the colorful residents and the aromas which are distinctive of Casablanca's Medina.

Officially, there are two Medinas— the Old Medina and the New Medina, both off limits to servicemen—but the one which arouses most interest and speculation is the Old Medina, near the Place de France, a square mile of crooked streets, hole-in-the-wall shops and intriguing villas. The name "Medina," which characteristically is applied to Arab sections of North African cities, is taken from the ancient Moslem city of "Medina."

"L'AFFAIR MEDINA"

"Why is the Medina off limits?" is a question which has been expounded.

To discover the reason behind the Medina ban and to tear the curtain of mystery from Casablanca's "Casbah," The Stars and Stripes went to the proverbial headquarters with the questions, and seeks now to publish a story of the behind-the-scenes history of "l'affair Medina."

"The Medina is off-limits because of sanitary reasons alone, and not because the Military Police wish to guide the morals of American soldiers," according to Capt. Raymond E. Klein, of the Military Police office. Recognized in MP

(Continued on Page 4)

—U.S. Signal Corps Photo—T-4 Paul Sherman

An "off limits" placard and an efficient MP bars the way to Casablanca's mysterious forbidden city, the Old Medina, Pfc. Ignatius Colluva, of New Orleans, La., shown above at one of the main entrances to the Medina, must explain to GI's the reasons behind the official ban on servicemen-visitors.

Greeks Strike Against Nazis

LONDON, July 5—(S-S)—The Axis has been faced with new difficulties in its fight to hold the conquered Greek people in servitude, BBC reported.

A general strike, the fourth in 15 months, broke out in Athens June 25, resulting in street fighting with German soldiers in the Greek capital and demonstrations in other sections.

Previous strikes in 1942 and the spring of this year forced occupation authorities to gr^nt some concessions to the people.

Sicilian Industries Feel Allied Mastery

WASHINGTON, July 5—(S-S)—Allied mastery of the air and seas around Sicily is seriously hampering communications to the mainland, reports from Berne said.

Sicilian industrialists last month advised clients in Italy that they could not guarantee a definite date for delivery of merchandise because of air raids on their factories, the report stated.

Commerce at Naples also has been paralyzed by air attacks that have damaged the city's harbor and railroad stations.

First Airfreight Train Crosses Atlantic with 2½ Tons of Cargo

LONDON, July 5—(S-S)—The first transatlantic airfreight train composed of a glider towed by a two-engined Douglas transport landed in England today after a 28-hour trip from Canada.

The glider, carrying two and a half tons of freight, including vaccines for Russia, and raido and aircraft motor parts, was piloted by RAF Squadron Leader R. G. Seys.

The ship had no automatic pilot, and Seys said the job demanded almost hypnotic concentration by glider pilots.

The Waco-designed sailplane had an 87-foot wing spread.

Further experiments with gliders in airfreight transportation will be made, the Air Ministry announced.

Polish Leader Killed in Crash

ALGIERS, July 5—(S-S)—Gen. Wladyslaw Sikorski, prime minister of the Polish government in exile, was killed today in an airplane crash at Gibraltar, according to news dispatches received here. He was 61 years old.

Gen. Sikorski was prime minister of Poland in 1922-23, after which he retired. In 1939 he returned to active service as prime minister of the Polish government in exile in London. He visited Washington last January.

AN APPEAL

Once again The Stars and Stripes is reaching the bottom in its supply of zinc. To be in a position to present local personages and scenes, such as the Medina series opening today, a newspaper must have zinc. If any unit or GI in the area can supply this precious metal, suitable for cuts, this sheet will drop an editorial orchid in your lap every day for a year.—Ed.

WAC Marries Britisher

ALGIERS, July 5—(S-S)—The first overseas WAC marriage took place yesterday afternoon on America's Independence Day when T-5 Josephine McCase, of Pittsburgh, became the bride of Lance Corporal Hubert Heckman, of the British army and Devonshire, England.

The ceremony was held in the Algiers villa of Robert Shuchan, former U. S. consul at Martinique.

The marriage ceremony was conducted by Chaplain Paul E. Winslow, of Chicago.

Cpl. Jane Strauss of St. Paul was bridesmaid and Earl Pittman of Chicago acted as best man.

As Chaplain Winslow pronounced the newlyweds husband and wife, a shower of rice descended upon their heads thrown by the large group of WAC's that were present to see the first of their number to marry overseas.

A short reception was held after the ceremony.

Shortly after the reception, the couple left for a three-day honeymoon.

NEW NAZI UNIT

STOCKHOLM, July 5—A Berlin dispatch to the Newspaper Aftonbladet reported today that a new German "general service" military branch headed by Grand Admiral Raeder had been created apparently to combat an Allied invasion.

'MALE' GI'S

WACO, Texas, July 5—(S-S)—At the first GI dance attended by WAC's at Blackland Army Air Field, a sign was posted, "Beginning immediately, dancing classes will be held for male soldiers."

Axis Air Shield Is Bolstered

New Opposition Met by Allies

ALLIED FORCE HEADQUARTERS, July 5—(S-S)—Attempting to shield its Eastern Sicilian airports from the July Fourth attack of heavy and medium bombers of the NAAF, the Axis threw up the heaviest fighter opposition since the end of the Tunisian campaign.

During the terrific air battles over Catania and Gerbini, 38 enemy planes were shot down to an Allied loss of three aircraft. Catania, which is one of the keys to Sicily's single line railway system and a port town in the center of the eastern coast within the shadow of Mt. Etna, answered the B-17's with swarms of intercepting Italian and German fighters.

In spite of the air bombing tactic and aggressiveness of the Axis planes, the Forts sprayed runways and dispersal areas with fragmentation bombs that sent up white smoke which soon turned black with shooting flames.

At Gerbini, also in Eastern Sicily, the raid over Axis airdromes was conducted by Mitchells and Marauders, medium bombers of the Strategic Air Force. The Mitchells dropped bombs among enemy aircraft on the ground and their P-38 escort shot down six enemy planes in the air.

14 DOWN

The Marauders attacking Gerbini shot down 14 enemy planes in what they reported as the most hotly contested dogfights they had ever been in.

Sicily, which has been under constant attack by the long range bombers of the Strategic arm within the past few days, has begun to feel the weight of the light and medium bombers of the Tactical Air Force.

In daylight raids on July 4, A-20 Bostons, B-25 Mitchells and RAF Baltimores attacked Sciacca, Comiso and Milo air fields.

Over Sciacca, the A-20's, covered by P-40 Warhawks, met about 30 enemy fighters. In a series of dogfights, while the bombers blasted the air field, the P-40's destroyed five ME-109's and damaged others.

TWO FIRES

At Comiso, the Mitchell bombers attacked the air field and landed several bombs among enemy aircraft, oil storage and workshop areas.

In the raid over Milo, the Baltimores encountered heavy ack-ack and bad visibility, but their bombing resulted in two large fires in the southeast corner of the airfield.

The night before, the western port town of Trapani in Sicily was bombed by strong formations of RAF Wellingtons, which also bombed Lido di Roma Airport 15 miles from Rome.

A Baltimore on reconnaissance in the Tyrrhenian Sea north of Sicily sighted a float aircraft bearing Italian markings. After three attacks during which the enemy aircraft returned fire without causing any damage, the Baltimores sent it crashing into the sea where the float machine burst into flames.

THE STARS AND STRIPES
AFRICA

Vol. 1, No. 31, Saturday, July 10, 1943 — U. S. Army Newspaper — Two Francs

SICILY INVADED

Allied Forces Begin Landing Operations On Axis Island

Sicily—New Allied Battlefield

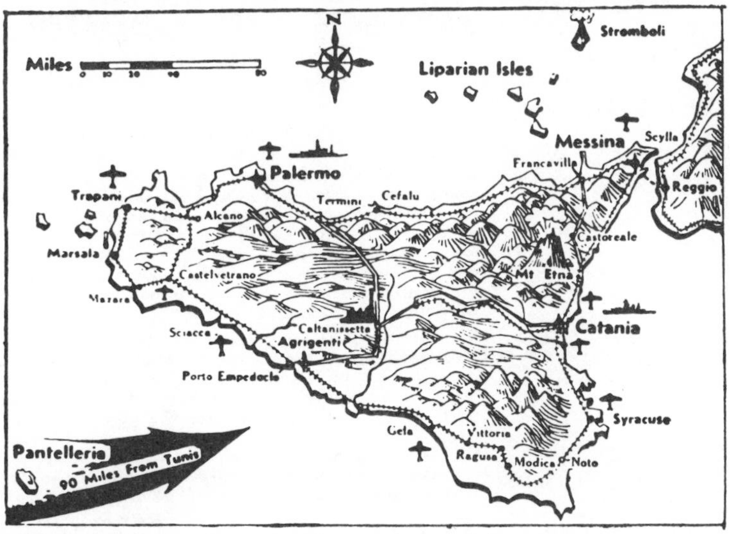

Radios Warn French People To Wait For Right Moment

SPECIAL COMMUNIQUE

ALLIED FORCE HEADQUARTERS, July 10—This special communique was issued here at 6 AM today:

ALLIED FORCES UNDER COMMAND OF GENERAL EISENHOWER, BEGAN LANDING OPERATIONS ON SICILY EARLY THIS MORNING. THE LANDINGS WERE PRECEDED BY ALLIED AIR ATTACK. ALLIED NAVAL FORCES ESCORTED THE ASSAULT FORCES AND BOMBARDED THE COAST DEFENSES DURING THE ASSAULT.

Simultaneously with announcement of the invasion of Sicily, Allied radio stations throughout the world broadcast a warning to the people of metropolitan France and underground workers instructing them to remain calm lest they give themselves away by premature action. The warning came from Gen. Dwight D. Eisenhower, Allied Force commander, and read:

"The United Nations Armed Forces have today launched an offensive against Sicily. It is the first stage in the liberation of the European continent. There will be others. I call on the French people to remain calm, *not* to allow themselves to be deceived by the false rumors which the enemy might circulate. The Allied radio will keep you informed on military development. I count on your sang-froid and on your sense of discipline. Do *not* be rash for the enemy is watching. Keep on listening to the Allied radio and never heed rumors. Verify carefully the news you receive. By remaining calm and by *not* exposing yourselves to reprisals through premature action you will be helping us effectively.

"When the hour of action strikes we will let you know. Till then help us by following our instructions. That is to say: keep calm, conserve your strength. We repeat: when the hour of action strikes we will let you know."

No details of the size of the attacking Allied Forces were given, and it was too early to say what kind of opposition the Allied Forces met on the initial operations. There could be little doubt, however, that the enemy would put up the stiffest opposition for such a strategic island.

As the zero hour for Sicily approached, the bombers and strafing planes of the Northwest African Air Force had the island staggering with day and night attacks that went on for a week.

Sicily's air defense had taken a terrific pounding. The relentless aerial offensive had smashed at airports and transportation centers. All the ports around the triangular island were singled out and shellacked by light, medium and heavy bombers. Varying the all-out onslaught were the fighters

(Continued on Page 8)

Il Duce's On The Spot; Pleads For Support

Tells People Invasion Must Be Resisted To Last Man

Axis sentries from Greece to Norway walked the rim of the European Fortress with one eye to sea and the other turned nervously inland last week as invasion tension and internal dissension, especially in weak-sister Italy, mounted to fever pitch.

At Rome, Mussolini frantically tried to jack up Italian resistance to an invasion threat and break down a growing mass indifference to Fascism; in Greece, the Germans met an outbreak of strikes, demonstrations and guerrilla activity that forced them to declare a "state of revolution" in the country; in Holland, the Swiss reported huge numbers of German troops arriving at the Dutch coast, and in France, key coastal cities of the Mediterranean and along the southern Atlantic were ordered evacuated.

Il Duce and his faltering Fascists took the spotlight, when Radio Rome Wednesday broadcast 13 days late an amazing speech delivered by Mussolini June 24 before the Fascist Party Directorate.

A strange mixture of rebuke and flattery, Mussolini's address was the most revealing to come from any totalitarian leader in the present war. He admitted that growing labor unrest, with strikes at Milan and Turin, necessitated more stringent labor compulsion. He acknowledged black markets and the failure of Party economic measures. But mostly he pleaded for a return by the Italian people to a faith in the party itself.

"The Fascist Party is still the party of the masses," he declared. "A nation of 46 millions needs to be led by several thousand political leaders, helped by hundreds of thousands of collaborators inspired by the same faith. The figures concerning the numerical forces of the Party are really imposing.

"Of course there are negative and opposing elements to the Party," he admitted, "but we control all that and they will never be in a position to extirpate the regime. Where the laws in effect

(Continued on Page 8)

Air Arm Batters Island All Week

ALLIED FORCE HEADQUARTERS, July 9—Hundreds of bombing, strafing planes of the Northwest African Air Forces have kept Sicily reeling all week with unending blows at the island's air, transport and communication installations.

Stinging day and night raids have been made on the triangular island by first-line American bombers—Flying Fortresses, Mitchells, Marauders, Bostons and Baltimores—working with British night-bombing Wellington s and fighters — Lightnings, Warhawks and Spitfires.

While heavy and medium bombers were setting down tons of explosives on Sicilian targets, fight-

(Continued on Page 8)

Think It's Hot Now? Wait Till Next Month

By Cpl. JOHN M. WILLIG
(Stars and Stripes Staff Writer)

The weatherman at AFHQ, wiping his face determinedly with a sweaty old handkerchief, remarked with frayed humor that being hot in Africa was all a matter of humidity, just like in New York or Wabash, Ind.

"If you think you were hot this week with the temperature mostly hitting the 100-degree mark or around there, what are you going to do in late July and August, when the temperature shoots up to 112 along the coast and as much as 120 degrees inland?" he asked coolly.

He had to agree, though, that even the natives complained about the heat wave during the week and admitted it was a bit out of order. At Algiers, soldiers sweated as the mercury climbed to 96 degrees. Souk Ahras reported a high of 100 degrees in the shade and Constantine sweltered under a record-breaking 108 degrees on Tuesday. Farther west, the mercury dallied around the 100-degree mark, with Oran getting a 97 and Oujda a 98.

Some small comfort was forthcoming when the weatherman took that old saw about heat and humidity apart.

Actually, you won't be as hot in

(Continued on Page 8)

THE STARS AND STRIPES
ALGIERS DAILY

Vol. 1, No. 69 · Tuesday, July 20, 1943 U. S. Army Daily Newspaper for troops in Algiers area ONE FRANC

AIR ARMADA BOMBS ROME

* * * * * * * * *

Yanks Capture Caltanissetta

Unity Italy's Sole Hope, Scorza Says

Fascist Secretary Makes Final Call For All To Fight

By Pvt. AL KOHN
(Stars and Stripes Staff Writer)

A final "call to arms" Monday night by Italy's man of the hour, Carlo Scorza, was a last-ditch summons for Italian unity in the moment of her greatest peril.

Speaking to the nation over Radio Rome, the secretary of the Fascist Party said "Italy is now in the greatest danger she has faced in all her history."

"Resist, resist, resist," he exhorted them time after time. "It is not enough for the enemy to hurry. It is indispensable for him to go like wildfire if he wants to retain any hope of victory. Today the enemy has the strategic initiative; if we resist, the initiative will go to pieces in his hand."

There was a lack of boasting and an impression of frank speaking in the speech by the Fascist official who during the last month has replaced Mussolini in shouting the rallying cry for the Italians.

Italian cities have been destroyed before but from the wreckage arose the unity of the Italian people, Scorza declared to a people whose unity has been noticeably wavering recently.

The Italian people were told openly that they were responsible for their entry into war. "We hold that the war, rather than an inevitable strategic, political and economic necessity, was an unavoidable demand on our race," the secretary shouted.

Scorza pointed to Britain's heroism as an example for the Italian people. Admitting that the Italian Navy which ruled the Mediterranean for two years is now dominated by the Allies, he asked, "Shall we despair because of this? Especially when the enemy did not

(Continued on Page 4)

B-26 Flies 350 Miles On One Good Engine

ALLIED FORCE HEADQUARTERS, July 19 — Setting a new distance record for flying a B-26 Marauder on one engine, Capt. Curtis A. Miller, of Tampa, Fla., back from a Naples raid, covering 350 miles in the two and a half hours. The action occurred July 17, it was announced today.

Besides the non-functioning engine, Capt. Miller's plane had a shot-up electrical system and a broken hydraulic system, and he could not transfer gasoline from the useless right tanks to the left engine.

They had to jettison everything on the plane except the one good engine. The men organized a bucket brigade. The radio operator and co-pilot passed stuff to the navigator, who gave it to the gunner, who threw it out the camera hatch. They took an axe and hacked away what they could not pry loose.

Agrigento Is Rich Prize

By JAMES A. BURCHARD
(Stars and Stripes Staff Writer)

AGRIGENTO, Sicily, July 18 (Delayed)—The fall of Agrigento and adjoining Porto Empedocle, finest seaport on the South Sicilian coast, proved a rich harvest for the Americans.

The Americans counted an Italian brigadier general among the 5,000 prisoners taken when the town of 28,000 population fell. Four battalions of big guns also fell into American hands.

The drive on Agrigento started at 0300 hours on July 16th when American artillery moved to positions commanding the city. They cut loose at daybreak, displaying beautiful marksmanship.

For a time, Italian artillery replied, but it was a hit-and-run performance. Once our shells started to land in their midst, however, they tossed in the sponge.

I watched the entire show from

(Continued on Page 4)

U.S. Troops Sweep Into Inland City

British Only Three Miles Outside Key Port Of Catania

ALLIED FORCE HEADQUARTERS, July 19 — Bowling over weakening enemy resistance in a large advance into the heart of Sicily, the American 7th Army has captured Caltanissetta, a town of nearly 40,000 population which commands the island's central rail lines and highways, it was announced here today.

As all Allied forces moved northward, the British were within three miles of important Catania on the east coast and Americans, British and Canadians in the center of the front made long advances. At some points the Allies had penetrated 50 miles into the island.

The taking of Caltanissetta in the heart of Sicily's sulphur mining industry undoubtedly presages a combined move of the 15th Army Group to converge on the key central town of Enna, only 12 miles away.

With Enna in their hands the Allies will control the whole inland transportation system.

Catania's approaches have seen

(Continued on Page 4)

3rd Division Sees Action

Group Completes Smashing Drive

By RED MUELLER
(NBC Correspondent

A cryptic radio message came in from the beach just after dawn, when the American 3rd Division and its supporting elements were sweeping ashore in overwhelming strength on Sicily.

"To Cruiser Dodger, from number three beach. Battery behind hill shelling our barges."

The cruiser's reply was brief: "You mean the one three thousand yards inland. We've got it spotted. One minute please."

The air rocked with the concussion of three rapid-fire broadsides, and then the third and final message crackled "All quiet number three beach. Nice shooting. Thank you."

Thus ended the last beach resistance that met the smashing drive of the 3rd Division, which in a few hours put ashore more than a division and a half of combat troops and all their vehicles, including armor. The speed and organization of that disembarkation was magnificent, and just the physical process of carrying it out, despite seven dive-bombing attacks in ten hours, was a stupendous task.

On the extreme left flank of the American front, 3rd Div's orders were to get ashore with all possible speed, establish a bridgehead eight miles deep and twelve miles long and organize a base

(Continued on Page 3)

Military Objectives Shattered In Heavy Attack On Capital

By T-SGT. MILTON LEHMAN
(Stars and Stripes Staff Writer)

ALLIED FORCE HEADQUARTERS, July 19—Rome burned today. The communique which will soon arrive from here will tell you about the railroads, marshalling yards and air installations that were bombed at points known as Littorio, San Lorenzo and Ciampini in the capital city of Mussolini's long-suffering empire, give the overall picture of one of the greatest air attacks ever launched from the continent of Africa and the heaviest air bombardment Italy has ever suffered.

At this time I don't know how many bombers and fighters went over the targets nor how much damage was done—these figures have not yet been released by Allied Force Headquarters. But from what I could see leaning over the pilot's compartment in Miss Maisie, a B-25, and from what I heard the returning crews say about the raid, it appears tonight to have been a gigantic success. If the Axis was not surprised by the arrival of one of the greatest, if not the greatest, air armadas to leave the shores of North Africa, then it was totally unprepared to receive it.

Yesterday, together with a group of selected correspondents, I listened to a 36-year-old one-star general, who is assistant chief of staff and operations chief for Lt. Gen. Carl A. Spaatz, commanding general of the Northwest African Air Force, describe the mission set for today, it's significance and projected effect.

"The attack on Rome," he said, "has been considered for some time. It was avoided as long as possible. But the line of Axis communications through Italy runs through Rome, making it a vital military objective once the military operation reaches the stage where an attack on Rome cannot be avoided.

"We have now reached a point," said the general, "where it is necessary to attack Rome."

Rome is obviously a target providing the Axis with food for its propaganda, at a time when Axis propaganda is having a hard time making reasonable copy. But Rome today was attacked with the utmost scientific precision ever required of a bombing mission and bombing is always a precision device.

To get back to what the operations general had to say:

"We have selected the best, most expert groups in this theater for this job," he said. "Rome will be attacked only by those units who have demonstrated without doubt their accuracy."

Not only were the units selected with care, but every military target in Rome that was bombed today was selected after a careful consideration of the safety factor. The target closest to any significant religious institution is over one mile and a half away—and our bomber crews have demonstrated that they can bomb as close as 1,000 yards to our troops as they did during the landing on Pantelleria—without having a single bomb go astray."

The mission for today's bombing

(Continued on Page 4)

Sicily Likes Allied Rule

ALLIED FORCE HEADQUARTERS, July 19 Crowds of Sicilians at the southeastern town of Noto broke into frantic cheering when an AMGOT civil affairs officer read to them the proclamation of Gen. Dwight D. Eisenhower expressing the Allies' determination to destroy Fascism, it was declared here today.

A British officer who witnessed the demonstration has returned from a tour of occupied territory on the island with reports of many instances of Sicilian friendliness.

After the AMGOT officer had finished reading the proclamation the delirious populace swept him up and carried him on their shoulders in a triumphal procession through the town.

Later the Bishop of Noto conducted a high Mass at which the AMGOT officer occupied the seat of honor, for 20 years reserved for the town's Fascist chief.

Everywhere the Briton went the people exhibited a fervent desire to cooperate with AMGOT — the Allied Military Government of Occupied Territory.

In Syracuse the visiting officer was deeply impressed with the orderliness of the town and the lack of effective damage to the port installations. It was here that he heard the most bitter recriminations heaped on the heads of the Germans who had been quartered on the island. The Allies here were greeted as liberators and the impoverished people broke out gifts

(Continued on Page 4)

The following is a translation of the text of leaflets dropped in yesterday's raid over Rome:

"TO THE CITIZENS OF ROME"

You have already been warned that military objectives in the vicinity of Rome are liable to be bombed by the Allied Air Force.

When this occurs the Fascist government, who have consistently concealed from you the facts about the war, will pretend that we are trying to destroy those culural monuments which are the glory not only of Rome but of the civilized world.

It is possible, moreover, in order to lend plausibility to their lying statements, that the Fascist government or their German associates will themselves arrange for bombs to be dropped on the center of Rome and even on the Vatican City.

We leave it to your intelligence to decide whether it is likely we should waste our efforts on targets whose destruction is useless for our purpose.

We have declared and we repeat that we shall be aiming at military objectives—communications, war industries, military installations, air ports, all of which are being used for the sole interest of the Germans.

These objectives have been carefully chosen and our pilots have been specially trained in accurate bombing. It is, however, impossible, while aiming at military objectives, to avoid some destruction to civilian buildings. It is our intention to reduce this destruction to a minimum.

Since our attack will be in daylight you will be able to see for yourselves that these statements are true.

You can therefore conclude that any bomb which drops far outside the target area will be the work of the Fascist government in a deliberate attempt to deceive you.

THE STARS AND STRIPES

AFRICA

Vol. 1, No. 33, Saturday, July 24, 1943 — U. S. Army Newspaper — Two Francs

Palermo Taken As Americans Cut Across Island To North Coast

Nazi Offensive On Eastern Front Becomes Retreat

Red Army Pounding At Orel, Key Enemy Defense Base

The great German offensive on the Russian front went into reverse gear this week. Not only had the drive launched early this month by the vaunted Wehrmacht been stopped dead, but the Red Army was sweeping forward in a powerful counter attack that threw the Germans back beyond their starting positions.

By the week's end, Soviet forces were pounding at the gates of Orel, key Nazi bastion on the central front. The fury of the Russian drive marked a critical point in the Battle of Eastern Europe. A break-through at Orel would threaten the German-held cities of Smolensk and Kharkov, on which the entire Nazi defense line in the East rests.

But much more significant than mere territorial gains or losses was this testimony that the power of the Wehrmacht was definitely on the wane. Always in the past a carefully prepared and seriously launched German offensive had netted at least big early gains. This time the drive was held almost from the beginning.

For two years the Germans had fortified and strengthened Orel against this very battle. They were sure they could hold it against the best opposition the Red Army could offer. Now Orel is tottering and the Germans don't have an equally strong fortress or natural defense for at least 200 miles. Kharkov is about 200 miles due south and already threatened by a Russian salient extending west from Belgorod. Smolensk is the same distance to the northwest and likewise imperiled by the Russian line at Velikie Luki to the

(Continued on Page 2)

Sicilians Dislike Il Duce's Fascism

WITH THE AMERICAN TROOPS IN SICILY—You can't tell us that these Sicilians want to fight. Not us, not now.

Not when their kids scrounge our garbage cans for food scraps; not when their women line up along the streets laughing and cheering as our troops march through their rubbled town; not when their soldiers parade up in hundreds, hunting for somebody to surrender to.

In any one of the many towns we've captured, you can see these Sicilians walking around with civilian clothes and army boots, and you know that maybe a few days ago, these guys had guns in their hands waiting to shoot you. But maybe they saw too many of our planes dropping too many bombs, so they just dropped their guns, went home, changed clothes, and went back to work.

If it were not for the few German divisions, threatening them from the rear and for the Fascist officers who see nothing but death in an Allied victory, this show would have been over in a week. As it is, it may take a little longer.

These people have nothing to fight and die for. They hate Mus-

(Continued on Page 2)

Hitler's Youth At Play

THESE TWO GERMAN YOUNGSTERS, playing at the grim game of war in the front of their home at Stuttgart, Germany, already are being molded to become model members of Hitler's Youth. This revealing photograph was found by Stars and Stripes photographer S-Sgt. Phil Stern in a portfolio belonging to Oberlieutenant Rudolph Brenner, of Stuttgart. The portfolio containing the snapshot of his children had been left behind by the Nazi officer who pulled out in a hurry when the Allies invaded Sicily.

Allies Shift Aerial Offensive To Italy

By S-Sgt. GEORGE M. HAKIM
(Stars and Stripes Staff Writer)

ALLIED FORCE HEADQUARTERS, July 23—Allied air power cast an ominous shadow over the Italian mainland this past week as American and British bombers highlighted the week's aerial activity with mass raids on the Imperial City of Rome and the important port of Naples.

Photo reconnaissance revealed that the attack on the Italian capital, which was carried out by one of the largest armadas of planes ever to leave North Africa, was highly successful. The Northwest African Air Forces, coordinated with the 9th U.S. Air Force, confined all their bombs to the target area and inflicted severe damage to railroad yards, factories and an airdrome outside the city.

Heavy damage was done to the San Lorenzo marshalling yards where traffic was completely blocked. Direct hits were scored on both round houses, rolling stock and other railroad installations. The yard is an important servicing and repair center for rail facilities. Highly electrified, it is on the belt line joining with the two main lines from Florence and Naples, and on the coastal line from Genoa.

The Littorio marshalling yard, four miles to the north of Rome, was hit at least 50 times, and was 50 percent blocked to traffic. Through this important rail center passes the bulk of all freight traffic from the industrial areas of northern Italy to Rome, Naples and the southwest coast.

Both marshalling yards are of vital military importance to the Axis war strategy. They bottleneck all rail, passenger and freight traffic in the southern Italian peninsula.

Allied bombers also carried their attacks to the important Tavonelli steel plant and a large chemical works nearby. They ranged over the Ciampino airport outside the city and left several hangars and a large number of parked aircraft burning. The Littorio airport, which is near the railroad yards, was also hard hit.

The air fighting of the past week was marked by a scarcity of

(Continued on Page 16)

Airborne Troops Held Enemy For Two Days

LONDON, July 23—The work done by U.S. airborne troops in the initial invasion of Sicily advanced Allied progress by a week, reporters were told today by Maj. Gen. Joseph M Swing, coordinator of plans for airborne troops, who left the island a few days ago.

The airborne troops took the brunt of the attack and held off the enemy for two days until they were reinforced, Gen. Swing explained. He described their operations as the greatest airborne invasion ever attempted, larger in scope than the German attack on Crete.

Move Isolates Axis Forces In Western Part Of Sicily

By Sgt. GEORGE DORSEY
(Stars and Stripes Staff Writer)

ALLIED FORCE HEADQUARTERS, July 23—Advance elements of the American 7th Army occupied Palermo, Sicily's largest city, yesterday at 1000 hours, according to a special announcement made here today.

In view of the rapidity of its fall, Palermo could not have been seriously defended, but there were no details of the northern coastal city's capitulation in the first reports. A general statement was made here, however, which revealed that the rapidly advancing American troops met little resistance as they swept north toward their objective.

"Poorly equipped Italians showed little desire to impede the American advance," the special announcement read.

The quick break-through to the northern coast of Sicily was the climax of a campaign barely two weeks old. In those 14 days the Allies established long beachheads, brought in formidable modern equipment, set up air bases and moved forward in a continuous surge to take at least two-thirds of the strategic island.

The capture of Palermo, a world famous port, gave the Allies extensive docks and shipping accommodations that should be of great value to future operations. With its population of more than 300,000, the city is also an important highway and rail terminus, being linked to the eastern, western and central portions of the island.

In occupying Palermo, the troops under Lt. Gen. George S. Patton, Jr., have cut Sicily in two in a move which spells the doom of any enemy forces which may still attempt any resistance in the western part of the island.

PERHAPS TO EAST

What is probably more important, the 7th Army can be expected to turn toward the east where the formidable Axis forces have been hotly contesting the determined advance of the British 8th Army on Catania; east coast stronghold. Troops now in Palermo are over 120 miles from the east coast, but other Allied elements are doubtless making their way to the east along the northern coast.

There the Allies have a new approach to Messina, the northeast ferry terminus city which has from the beginning of the Sicilian campaign been acknowledged as holding the key to the island's fate. The position of the Axis troops defending the Catania area would rapidly become untenable if Allied forces in strength began attacking Messina from the west or charged down on the enemy flank along the inland road which skirts the slopes of Mt. Etna and ends in Catania.

The occupation of Palermo followed by 58 hours the fall of Enna, the central city from which roads stem to Catania and to north coast points about half way between Palermo and Messina.

It was two weeks tomorrow that a mighty armada landed on Sicily's southern shores the men and material that constituted the Allies' first great blow to the Fortress Europa that the Axis insisted could not be stormed. Now, just 14 days later, American and British troops occupy at least two-thirds of an Italian outpost island of 9,860 square miles and nearly 4,000,000 people.

Most of this territory has fallen into Allied hands during the past

(Continued on Page 2)

Palermo: A City Of Lore, Lemons And Good Docks

With the fall of Palermo, the Axis has lost the largest city in Sicily and the Allies have captured their most important prize to date. Palermo has a normal population of 301,166, but during the last several months, especially since the heavy bombings began, there has been quite an exodus from Sicily and especially from such important targets as Palermo. Heading these migrations were the Fascist leaders who began to grow uneasy as time passed and sought refuge in the comparative safety of the mainland.

The port of Palermo has an important shipbuilding yard and drydock and ranks next to Genoa, Naples and Trieste as one of Italy's best ports. One of the island's finest airdromes is just outside the city. It had a reputation for throwing up more flak than any other airfield on the island.

The original city was built on a tongue of land between two inlets of the sea. The present main street, the Cassaro, Via Marmoria or Via Toledo represents the line of the ancient town with water on either side of it. The two ancient harbors

(Continued on Page 2)

Frenchmen Decorate Gen. Eisenhower

ALGIERS—Gen. Dwight D. Eisenhower, Allied Commander-in-Chief, has received France's highest decoration, the Grand Cross of the Legion of Honor, it was revealed here.

Among other American and British officers who received lesser awards for their part in the Tunisian campaign was Lt. Gen. Mark W. Clark who, as Gen. Eisenhower's Deputy Commander-in-Chief helped to carry out the Allied landings in North Africa last November.

Forts Hammer Norway, Hamburg and Kiel

1D. THE STARS AND STRIPES 1D.

Daily Newspaper of U.S. Armed Forces in the European Theater of Operations

Vol. 3 No. 226 New York, N.Y.—London, England Monday, July 26, 1943

King Dismisses Mussolini

U.S. Heavies Follow RAF To Nazi Port

1,800-Mile Trip to Arctic B17s' Longest; Mediums Attack Belgium

American heavy bombers pounded the German ports of Kiel and Hamburg in daylight yesterday, only a few hours after the RAF had unleashed its heaviest blow of the war and within 24 hours of the USAAF's first raid on Nazi targets in Norway. The RAF's "heaviest yet" attack also was on Hamburg.

The mission to Hamburg marked the first time Eighth Air Force heavies had followed up an RAF night attack.

American medium bombers also were out yesterday, attacking industrial sites near Ghent, in Belgium.

The unprecedented 24 hours of attack was opened in daylight Saturday when Flying Fortresses hammered the Nazi U-boat bases in Trondheim, near the Arctic Circle on the far northwestern coast of Norway, and an aluminum plant 65 miles from Oslo.

Sicilians Cheer 7th Army

The Trondheim raid, covering 1,800 miles round-trip, was the longest U.S. mission yet in this theater and possibly the longest raid ever carried out by Fortresses anywhere.

That night, RAF heavy bombers in "very great strength" dumped more than 2,500 tons of high explosives on Hamburg, Germany's largest port and submarine building center.

The RAF force set three records of its own: The bomb load was greater than any announced before, it was dropped in the record time of 50 minutes, and only 12 planes were lost during the night's operations, the lowest yet percentage for a major assault.

Another force of RAF bombers—Lancasters—struck without loss at the port of Leghorn on Italy's northwest coast on their way back from North Africa.

Aluminum Plant Blasted

The Fortresses were making the fifth USAAF bombing operation of the month Saturday when they struck Trondheim, Nazi submarine base and repair center far up the northwestern coast of occupied Norway, and an aluminium plant at Heroya, near Oslo, and much closer to bases in Britain.

It was the first American raid on Norway and brought to five the number of Nazi-held countries to which the Forts and Liberators have flown from England. The first four were France, Holland, Belgium and Germany.

Some of the crew members, who came back with stories of dead-accurate bombing which left fires and explosions

(Continued on page 2)

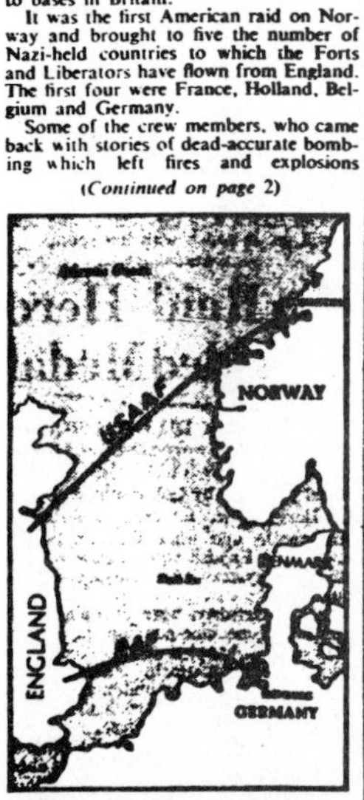

Eighth Air Force bombers travel approximately 1,800 miles round trip from England to blast U-boat bases in Trondheim, Norway. RAF heavies dump 2,500 tons of bombs on Hamburg, in northwest Germany.

The Battle in Sicily As Il Duce Resigns

Axis forces now are squeezed in Sicily's northeast tip as U.S. Seventh Army captures Marsala and traps more than 25,000 Axis prisoners between Trapani and Palermo, Sicily's capital city. Other U.S. columns press against Axis rearguard units on the north coast. British and Canadians meet stubborn resistance at Catania.

ETO's Greeting to WAAC Over; Members Stand Reveille Today

By Philip Bucknell
Stars and Stripes Staff Writer

WAAC REPLACEMENT DEPOT, England, July 25—The WAACs are ready for work after a week of parades, reviews and dances. The ETO's greeting to the First Separate Battalion of the WAAC to land has ended.

The festive atmosphere here will be replaced this week by the routine the WAACs have been trained to perform. They have been oriented, given physicals, classified, assigned and entertained by a program that was topped off with Bob Hope. They like it, but they came over here to work, they point out, and are anxious to begin their jobs with the Air Force.

At a final review by Maj. Gen. Ira C. Eaker, Eighth Air Force commander, and Maj. Gen. Jean Knox, ATS controller, the GI Janes ended their first week in Britain. Gen. Eaker told them they were the ambassadors of their country.

Precision Formation

Gen. Eaker took the review in company with Gen. Knox and Capt. Mary A. Halleren, five-foot commander of the battalion. Capt. Anna Wilson, the WAAC ETO commander, remained modestly at the rear of the stand, and made up the back file when the line was trooped.

With the precision that is now expected of the WAACs, the battalion marched on to the reviewing field, led by Capt. Mary Dixon, executive officer, of Ithaca, N.Y. On their shoulders were the insignia of the AAF, and on their chests the ETO ribbon, which had been pinned on previously by Capt. Thomas Shallcross, Philadelphia; 1/Lts. Arthur Berman, San Antonio, Tex.; Wern G. Isenburg, Haddon Heights, N.J.; A. Abrams, of Philadelphia, and 2/Lt. R. L. Zogg, of Syracuse, N.Y.

There was no hesitation or fumbling as the girls entered in column formation, faced and formed up in front of the reviewing stand. The flag was carried in by the color guard, Pfc Mary C. Waterman, of Appleton, Wis., Pvts. Ethel D. Rudolph, of Milwaukee, Wis., and the bearer, Dorothy E. Whinnery, of Anoka, Minn.

While the CBS band softly played "Over the Waves," the diminutive Capt. Halleren led tall Gen. Eaker along the line of WAACs. He told her after that

(Continued on page 2)

Jap Seaplane Carrier Sunk

ALLIED HQ., Southwest Pacific, July 25—U.S. torpedo and dive-bombers with a strong fighter escort sank a 9,000-ton Japanese seaplane carrier and its 20 aircraft Saturday morning out of a convoy attempting to run supplies into Buin, main Jap base in the northern Solomons.

Land-based enemy fighters attempting to intercept were driven off with the loss of five Zeros. Three U.S. fighters were lost.

As American troops were tightening the ring around Munda on New Georgia, U.S. dive-bombers blasted the Jap base with 60 tons of bombs.

In New Guinea a strong force of Mitchells with P40s escorting made long bombing and strafing sweeps along the coasts of Huon Gulf, about 40 miles east of Lae, and destroyed 12 barges and either destroyed or seriously damaged 13 more barges. Other attacks were made on barges in Cape Busching area. One, apparently loaded with oil, exploded and two others were set afire.

Both in the Solomons and in the northwestern islands, Allied bombers have attacked Japanese seaplane bases. Rekata Bay on Santa Ysabel Island received a visit from Mitchells and Dauntlesses. Installations were attacked and fires started. Taberfane in the Aru Islands was attacked yesterday afternoon by formations of RAAF Beaufighters. They damaged three floatplanes caught on the beach and strafed shore installations along the coast.

Big China Air Victory

CHUNGKING, July 25—Maj. Gen. Claire Chennault's 14th Air Force de-

(Continued on page 2)

Casualties Far Below Last War

WASHINGTON, July 25—American Army casualties are about one-quarter what they were in the first world war, although the United States has been in the present war longer.

Acting Secretary of War Robert P. Patterson revealed that Army casualties up to July 1 totalled 65,130. The total in World War I was 248,589. Of the casualties in the present conflict, 7,471 soldiers have been killed as compared with 37,568 in the last war.

In this war only 677 men have died of wounds which are not immediately fatal, while 13,942 died of such wounds in the world war

Badoglio Appointed As Premier of Italy, Rome Radio Reveals

Badoglio Declares: 'The War Continues'; All West Sicily in Allied Hands As U.S. Takes New Towns

With dramatic suddenness last night Rome radio broadcast the news that Dictator Benito Mussolini had been dismissed from office and that the King had assumed the post of commander-in-chief, with Badoglio as Prime Minister.

The radio said: "The King has accepted the resignation of the prime minister and secretary of the Fascist party Benito Mussolini and has appointed in his place Marshal Pietro Badoglio."

The radio then broadcast the text of two proclamations signed by King Victor Emmanuel and Marshal Badoglio.

Marshal Badoglio, in his proclamation taking command of the military government, said: "The war continues."

The text of the Rome announcement is: "H.M. the King has accepted the resignation from the post of chief of government, prime minister and secretary of state, by his excellency Cavaliere Benito Mussolini.

"The King has appointed as chief of the government, prime minister and secretary of state, his excellency Cavaliere Marshal of Italy Pietro Badoglio.

"H.M. the King Emperor has issued the following proclamation to the Italian people: 'Italians, from today I assume the command of all the armed forces. In the solemn hour which has occurred in the destinies of our country, each one must again take up his post of duty. No deviation can be tolerated.

'Every Italian must stand firm in face of the grave danger which has beset the sacred soil of the fatherland.

'Italy by the valor of her armed forces, by the determined will of all Italians will find again the road of her destiny.

'Italians, I feel myself today indissolubly united more than ever with you in unshakeable belief in the immortality of the fatherland.

Signed:
Vittorio Emmanuele.
Countersigned:
Badoglio.'"

The dramatic news came as virtually all of Sicily except the northeastern corner was in Allied hands.

The U.S. Seventh Army had occupied the major ports of Marsala and Trapani, then swept east and captured Termini, 20 miles southeast of Palermo.

With the Axis in flight from the west and the Americans in possession of more than 50,000 prisoners and much booty, including 200 artillery pieces, everything was ready for the battle of the Etna triangle—the final operation to drive the Axis out of Sicily.

It was a race against time, and Lt. Gen. George S. Patton's armored columns were rolling swiftly along the north coastal road toward Messina in an effort to get behind and encircle the enemy before he becomes solidly entrenched behind the Etna defense line running northwest from Catania to the coast.

Somewhere near the center of this line Canada's First Army was pushing forward against desperate resistance from the German 15th Panzer Division. And at the sea end, outside Catania, Britain's Eighth Army remained stymied by fierce resistance from German panzers. The

(Continued on page 2)

Orel Fight Near Decisive Stage

The battle for Orel was rapidly approaching its decisive stage last night as Russian forces, having turned the German offensive into slow but steady retreat, pushed doggedly north along the Kursk-Orel line, gradually reducing the chances of escape for the German troops in the Orel sector.

South of the city, where the Germans were putting up the stiffest resistance reported anywhere on the front, Soviet forces fought their way into the railway town of Zmiyevka, representing an advance of 12 miles in six days. Eighteen less important towns and villages also were captured.

North of the city the Nazis hurled in the bulk of their air forces in an attempt to stem the Russian advance. A decision is imminent in this area, the United Press reported from Moscow last night.

Russian forces were heartened in their struggle by a special order of the day from Premier Stalin, which revealed that Hitler's abortive summer offensive had cost Germany more than 70,000 men killed, 2,900 tanks and 1,392 planes, as well as a huge amount of other material.

The order, congratulating three generals and the troops under them, pointed out that the Germans not only had been pushed back to their starting point after achieving an advance of only 17 miles, but at points they had been pushed back at least 15 miles beyond their original line.

"Thus the plan for a summer offensive must be considered completely frustrated," Stalin said.

21-Year Rule Comes to End For Italy's 'Sawdust Caesar'

Benito Mussolini, the man who reconstructed Italy, gave it an empire and lost it again, has ended 21 years of supreme power by his resignation.

Son of a blacksmith, Mussolini increased the world importance of his country in exchange for total obedience to his new political system and his word.

Formerly a Socialist editor, Mussolini came to power in 1922 together with his Fascist party.

This total change in his political beliefs was brought about by open disagreement with the Socialist party's last war policy. His own Fascist party was created by him to counteract Socialism, although he continued to apply some of its principles in the field of social legislation.

He founded the first elements of the Fascist party in Milan in March, 1919. This included the first storm troops. His first followers pledged themselves to fight socialism, and communism together with any enemies of the country who tried to throw away Italy's fruits of the war.

Italy at that time was ripe for a revolution.

At the Fascist congress at Florence in 1919 he was called "Il Duce" for the first time—in recognition of his leadership.

In 1922, confident of the country's support, he decided to strike. On October 24, at the Naples congress, he issued a statement challenging the government.

"The government shall either be given to us or we shall take it, closing in on Rome and seizing the miserable dominant class by the throat," it declared.

Three days later a mobilisation of the blackshirts took place and on October 28 the "march on Rome" was begun.

'Peace' Shouts in Rome, Other Cities, Reported

MADRID, July 25 (UP)—Shouts of "Peace" and "Make Rome an open city," were heard at a huge demonstration in one of the central squares in Rome, according to reports reaching Madrid by way of France.

Many peace meetings took place in Venice, Milan, Turin, Florence, Bologna and Trieste on Tuesday, according to these reports. The police and blackshirts are said to have ignored them.

Strikes were reported spreading in factories throughout northern Italy, especially among workers on the night shift. Sabotage of electric supplies, both for power and lighting, is said to be frequent.

THE STARS AND STRIPES
ALGIERS DAILY

Vol. 1, No. 50, Wednesday, August 18, 1943 — U. S. Army Daily Newspaper for troops in Algiers area — ONE FRANC

ALL SICILY FALLS TO ALLIES
Americans Capture Messina
Marseilles Airfields Bombed

Flying Forts Raid French South Coast

Unescorted Planes Strike Nazi-Held Fields Near City

ALLIED FORCE HEADQUARTERS, Aug. 17—In the first NAAF raid on German-occupied France, a large force of American Flying Fortresses this afternoon heavily bombed the airdromes at Istres le Tube and Salon, both about 25 miles northwest of the big Mediterranean port of Marseilles. The historic raid involved a round-trip of approximately 1,000 miles.

Returning observers said that many bombs burst among parked aircraft. Several explosions and fires were seen as the heavy four-motored sky queens left the two airfields, which are near the shores of an inland marsh lake, Etang de Berre.

Recent reconnaissance had shown that a large number of Heinkel-111 torpedo-carrying aircraft have their headquarters at Salon. ME-323 six-motored transports are known to use the Istres le Tube field.

Only a few enemy aircraft came up to oppose the unescorted bombers, but considerable flak was encountered.

As the Sicilian campaign reached a climax disastrous for the enemy, Tactical Air Force bombers were out every minute of the day and night. Messina's beaches were bombed, escape vessels in the narrow straits between the island and the mainland were hunted out and subjected to furious attacks. All along the Italian toe and up the west coast of the peninsula to Pizzo traffic was disrupted as relentless Allied airmen brought new ruin to overtaxed transportation routes.

For the second night in a row.

(Continued on Page 4)

Victorious Generals

THE COMMANDING GENERALS of the victorious 15th Army Group are shown above viewing operations in Sicily. Gen. Sir Bernard Law Montgomery, commanding the British 8th Army, left, watches with Lt. Gen. George S. Patton, Jr., commanding the U.S. 7th Army. —Photo by Army Pictorial Service

Island Defense Cost Nazis Two Divisions

By SGT. JACK FOISIE
(Stars and Stripes Staff Writer)

WITH AMERICAN FORCES APPROACHING MESSINA, Aug. 15 (Delayed)—The defense of Sicily has cost the German High Command about two divisions, it was revealed in a checkup taken here as the fall of Messina and the end of the island campaign seemed imminent. No accurate count of Italian losses can be made yet.

Occupation of Sicily has given the Allies three definite tactical advantages:

(1) Insured protection of the Mediterranean sea route.

(2) Bottled up a good part of the Italian navy in its home bases on the coast to the northeast of Sicily.

(3) Has given the Allied Air Forces bases from which its fighters can reach most of southern Italy and its fighter-bombers, a large sector of Italy.

The operations which routed the Germans from their mountain defense lines and the five-day battle for Troina were termed here "the stiffest fighting for American troops since the last war." The enemy launched 24 separate counterattacks in a desperate effort to keep the high ground which commanded the terrain east of Mt. Etna and controlled all inland communications. American commanders committed five regiments of infantry and 15 battalions of artillery to the taking of the Troina ridgeline.

German prisoners taken during the battle described the artillery as "worse than Stalingrad"; they called it "zauberfeuer," meaning "magic fire."

One of the tactical lessons of the campaign was the German demonstration of masterful retreat through the maximum use of demolitions and mine fields.

On the other hand the Yanks showed the enemy the value of well-executed amphibious warfare. Twice in five days they landed behind the Axis lines. More than 1,000 prisoners were taken in the second thrust at Cape Orlando, all but 100 being Italians. The Germans burst out of this trap, but not without large losses. The Americans lost a considerable amount of materiel in this action.

Tribute was paid the American

(Continued on Page 4)

Gen. Eisenhower Urges WACs To Continue Their Good Job

ALLIED FORCE HEADQUARTERS, Aug. 17—In plain and simple words, Gen. Dwight D. Eisenhower, Allied Commander-in-Chief, addressed his command of WAACs on Sunday afternoon and told them how necessary they were to the fighting ahead. Today these women soldiers were no longer WAACs. They are now WACs, with their auxiliary status gone forever, and today they faced the 64 dollar question of whether to go home or enlist for the duration.

"If a single one of you goes home, it's too many," Gen. Eisenhower told the ladies in his brief speech, urging them to continue the good work they have done thus far. The General had just returned by plane from a conference with his senior commanders in the forward area.

"A WAAC often does the job—in her particular sphere—of two men," Gen. Eisenhower declared. Going directly to the question of whether a woman auxiliary should enlist in the Women's Army Corps—should become a WAC instead of a WAAC—the General said:

"As far as I'm concerned, that's just a technicality. I'm too simple a soldier to see the difference."

The possibility of losing some of these skilled workers in high army offices became a source of concern when it was revealed that in some WAAC companies in the States, 20 percent of the members had chosen to return to civilian life, even before they had completed the training for which they had volunteered.

Incidental to his address, Gen. Eisenhower gave the WAACs a scoop. He told them flatly: Messina will fall tonight or tomorrow."

Amphibious Raids Feature Closing Phase Of Battle

By Pvt. PAUL S. GREEN
(Stars and Stripes Staff Writer)

ALLIED FORCE HEADQUARTERS, Aug. 17—The Allies today closed the books on another successful campaign with the complete collapse of enemy resistance in Sicily.

The Axis was shoved off its last island toe-hold when Messina fell to triumphant troops of the American 7th Army who swept through the city early this morning. Yanks of the 3rd Division had reached the outskirts at 2000 hours yesterday under cover of a heavy artillery barrage.

As British 8th Army troops pushed up the east coast and joined the Americans within Messina, artillery from the Italian mainland began to shell the city.

The eagerly-awaited announcement came at 2053 hours today with the issuing of this special communique:

"American troops captured Messina early this morning. Some artillery fire is being directed on the city from the Italian mainland."

Although it was officially announced that no organized resistance remains anywhere on the island, there was no immediate estimate of the number of prisoners captured or the amount of equipment taken. There was no comment on Axis reports that all enemy troops were successfully evacuated early this morning.

The drama of the last hours was heightened by two new amphibious landings—one by the 7th Army in the north and the other by British Commandos eight miles south of Messina. The whole campaign has featured four sea raids, all in the past ten days.

The end came almost exactly 38 days after Allied invasion forces landed on the beaches of southern Sicily, and 24 days after Il Duce bowed out of the Italian scene.

The doom of Messina was foreshadowed when the Americans effectively split the Axis forces in half by taking Palermo on the north coast on July 22. The actual capture of the city was the culmination of a concerted Allied push that began after the British seizure of Catania on the east coast Aug. 5.

The drive was slowed down until combined British and American troops broke through at Randazzo, north of Mt. Etna, four days ago. After that, there was no holding the Allies as they swept up the north and east coast roads and smashed their way to the beaches of Messina.

The Allies are now closer than ever before to the mainland of Europe, Messina harbor being two miles away from Italy at the closest point. This indicates a continuing artillery duel between Axis and Allied gunners, who may blast away at each other at will over the Straits.

The Germans remaining behind hung on by the hooks of their swastikas in the final moments be-

(Continued on Page 4)

Battle Rages In Kharkov

Difficult Terrain Slows Soviet Push

LONDON, Aug. 17—The battle of Kharkov has reached its climax and Russian troops are overwhelming German resistance in the northern suburbs only a mile from the city, front-line dispatches said last night. On the south, too, the Soviet tide surged forward, and the army which captured Chuguev last week was reported less than four miles from Kharkov.

In a move to protect their escape corridor west of Kharkov, the Germans are bringing fresh reserves to the sector south of the steel center as well as along the Kharkov-Poltava railway where fierce resistance is slowing the Russian advance westward.

Continuing their progress toward Bryansk, the Red army occupied the city of Zhisdra, 40 miles to the north, and advanced on the entire sector east of the central front stronghold. It was revealed in Moscow that large guerilla forces have been aiding the regular Russian army in the heavy forests which lie around Bryansk.

In some spots the terrain which forms a natural barrier to the Soviet offensive is said to be almost jungle-like in denseness, and thousands of swamps make the

(Continued on Page 4)

Army Approves V-Mail Balloting

WASHINGTON—The Army and Navy have approved plans for V-mail voting by soldiers and sailors in next year's presidential election, the Senate elections committe reported. Special voting days would be held in overseas Army camps and on ships in advance of the regular election day, it was proposed in one bill which permits ballots to be counted if received within two weeks after the election.

1D. THE STARS AND STRIPES 1D.

Daily Newspaper of U.S. Armed Forces in the European Theater of Operations

Vol. 3 No. 252 | New York, N.Y.—London, England | Wednesday, Aug. 25, 1943

Berlin Gets 1,900 Tons in Heaviest Raid

Gestapo Controls All Germany

Hitler Gives Home Rule To Himmler

Move Seen as Desperate Attempt to Avert Internal Collapse

Adolf Hitler placed all of Germany under the iron control of the Gestapo yesterday, naming Gestapo chief Heinrich Himmler as the new Minister of the Interior and general plenipotentiary for Reich administration.

The drastic action came as a wave of revolt swept occupied Europe, particularly Denmark, and only a few hours after the biggest RAF raid on Berlin, for which the German capital had been preparing frantically ever since the blitz of Hamburg.

Allied and neutral observers expressed the belief that Hitler, under direct impact of Allied air attacks and military defeats in Russia and Sicily, had taken a desperate step to prevent internal collapse.

Revolt had reached such proportions in Denmark that between 40,000 and 50,000 German troops and a number of tank divisions were rushed across the border to occupy Copenhagen and other centers of disorder, the United Press reported from Stockholm. A state of emergency was proclaimed in the Danish capital and five other cities as rioting and sabotage, particularly of war plants and transport lines, spread.

French Keep Gestapo Busy

Travelers reaching Switzerland from France said disorders also were spreading in that nation and the Gestapo was increasingly busy trying to control the people. All of France, they said, was waiting tensely for the Allied invasion.

Hitler's appointment of Himmler as virtual dictator of the home front was part of a sweeping shakeup of Nazi chiefs.

Into the hands of the cold, remorseless fanatic, it places unparalleled power over the civil population, with full control of the Gestapo, uniformed stormtroopers and police to carry out his orders.

The Gestapo chief replaced Dr. Wilhelm Frick, who had been Minister of the Interior since Hitler's rise to power. It was Frick who made the Austrian paperhanger a German citizen. As police chief in Munich before the beer-cellar putsch of 1923, Frick appointed Hitler a policeman, which under the law gave him citizenship automatically.

Frick, in turn, was named yesterday to succeed Konstantin von Neurath as "Protector of Bohemia and Moravia," a post which Hitler was believed to have created only to keep von Neurath satisfied. The latter, it was announced, was relieved of his post "at his own wish."

Moscow radio also reported a sweeping shakeup of the German Army and quoted Stockholm rumors that Field Marshal Brauchitsch, one of Hitler's foremost generals, had died suddenly.

Siege Law in Denmark—

STOCKHOLM, Aug. 24 (AP)—A state of emergency was proclaimed in six Danish cities as police and German soldiers met increasing difficulty in subduing "the people's revolt" against German occupation.

The Stockholm press heard that during the weekend the Germans rushed tanks, armored vehicles and about 40,000 soldiers into Copenhagen. Clashes between Danish soldiers and Germans in Odense resulted in at least 50 deaths, and 20 Germans were killed at Svendborg, reports said.

Welles Resigns, Capital Hears

WASHINGTON, Aug. 24 (AP)—The Washington Star said today that Sumner Welles, Undersecretary of State, had submitted his resignation at President Roosevelt's request after ten years in the State Department.

The paper said the resignation was on the President's desk to be acted upon after his return from Canada.

Mr. Welles, at Bar Harbor, Me., for a short holiday, refused to comment.

The Star said there had been increasing difficulties between Secretary Hull and Mr. Welles, and that Mr. Hull finally told the President to choose between them.

SS Repel Food Riot in Denmark

Evidence of the mounting disorder in Denmark is shown in this picture from Copenhagen, radioed to London via Stockholm, Sweden. The scene is outside a Danish restaurant where black uniformed Nazi Storm Troopers and brown-shirted Danish Fricorps charge crowds during riots one of the city's meatless days.

Axis Saving Planes in Italy; Allies Bomb Twice Unopposed

Two Allied bombing attacks on southern Italy without opposition from a single enemy fighter indicated yesterday a sudden Axis decision to conserve fighter strength after the loss of 114 interceptors in four days.

Air crews from North Africa smashed bombs onto key rail centers at Battipaglia and Bagnoli without meeting a single enemy fighter, but Middle East Liberators attacking Bari encountered 30 or 40 Axis interceptors and destroyed 14. None of the B24s was lost.

American Mitchells covered the yards at Battipaglia, 45 miles southeast of Naples, and British Wellingtons followed up with a night attack on yards at Bagnoli in the suburbs of Naples itself. The Middle East Liberators, bombing not only the railway yards at Bari but also the airdrome, dropped 55 tons of bombs in spite of the heaviest opposition they had met in some time.

Badoglio Fights Fascists

Meanwhile Switzerland heard that Marshal Badoglio, to avert a possible Fascist attempt to seize power again, had ordered a series of arrests to prevent formation of an "iron guard" under the leadership of Roberto Farinacci, former Fascist secretary and editor.

Madrid said the Italian fleet, increasingly endangered by the growing Allied sea and air strength in the Mediterranean, had been ordered, nevertheless, to remain inactive so long as there is any chance for peace.

Correspondents at Allied headquarters said the fleet either would have to stay at Taranto, menaced by bombers, or run the gauntlet of strong British naval forces in a dash for the Adriatic. Even if some units reached the refuge of the Adriatic they would only be trapped there for the duration.

Russians Flank Key to Dnieper

Poltava Push Threatens Nazis' Front in Ukraine; Kharkov Only Ruins

A Russian thrust at the strategic rail junction of Poltava, behind German forces in full retreat from burned and blackened Kharkov, jeopardized the entire German front in the Ukraine yesterday.

Poltava, 80 miles beyond Kharkov, defending the approaches to the Dnieper, was outflanked from the north by the Red Army's drive west from Kharkov to Oposhnya, 21 miles from the new Soviet goal. A second thrust south of Kharkov stretched the Russian lines toward the vital Donbas mining region.

Kharkov itself was a shambles. Red Army troops who wrested the great industrial and rail center from the Germans Monday said Nazi demolition squads had methodically dynamited the city's streets and buildings and left great incendiary-built fires raging everywhere. Where the streets were not great bomb craters they were piled high with the rubble of adjacent buildings, now only hollow walls.

Robert Magidoff, U.S. broadcaster in Moscow, said the Russians already had driven the German artillery beyond range of the city and were extending their advances.

Some of the Kharkov defenders were retreating west toward Poltava, forced on to secondary country roads by the Russian advance along the Kharkov-Poltava railroad to Vodyanya, 42 miles from Poltava. Others were moving southwestward along the railway leading to Krasnograd. Still others were retiring towards the Dnieper along railways leading to Dnepropetrovsk.

German Confidence Shaken?

MADRID, Aug. 24 (AP)—The loss of Kharkov, which even the German in the street considers the gateway to the Ukraine, prompted Spanish correspondents in Berlin to write of "German confidence in their army which up to now has not been shaken."

Joe Louis to Visit Australia

MELBOURNE, Aug. 24 (AP)—Sgt. Joe Louis will visit Australia soon according to the Melbourne Sporting Globe which claims that with other world-famous performers he will be a member of a special service department of the U.S. Army.

RAF Over Capital 50 Minutes; USAAF Hits Foe in West

Huge Fires Burning in Berlin After Assault Twice as Large as City Felt Before; Big Fort Formations Over Europe

Fires raged across Berlin yesterday in the wake of the German capital's heaviest raid, and even as the Nazis tightened the ring of their defenses, American daylight bombers split it open again with a smashing attack in the west.

U.S. bombers poured explosives down on German installations in occupied France in a day marked by possibly the heaviest air traffic across the Channel since the Battle of Britain, and fighters and Allied planes swept constantly to the attack across the coastline.

Eight enemy fighters were destroyed without U.S. loss during operations over enemy territory yesterday, Eighth Fighter Command reported. Maj. Eugene P. Roberts, of Spokane, Wash., was credited with destroying two Me109s, and thereby officially becomes an ace. He downed three enemy fighters on July 30. 2 Lt. William E. Julian, of Dallas, Tex., was credited with destroying two enemy fighters.

As the attack rolled on through the day and into the evening, reconnaissance pilots brought back from Berlin reports describing the destruction left by the enormous RAF night armada which late Monday unloosed nearly 2,000 tons of destruction over Germany's first city.

The scale of what in 50 minutes became the heaviest raid yet on Hitler's capital was measured in the RAF loss—58 planes, the highest number ever reported missing by British Bomber Command.

1,900 Tons on City

With the bomb tonnage dropped officially reported at 1,700 long tons—approximately 1,900 U.S. tons—it was likely that the attacking force numbered about 700 planes, since the RAF has been reported averaging about 2.8 tons of bombs per aircraft on heavy raids.

Reconnaissance reports told of four-mile columns of smoke towering above fires which still burned in Berlin in daylight yesterday, and one reconnaissance pilot said Berlin appeared to be in worse shape than Dusseldorf, which was smashed last June 13 in a saturation attack.

Berlin had not undergone a heavy raid since March 29, when the fifth heavy blow in two and a half months was handed out to the capital, but on a scale scarcely half Monday night's.

Mosquito bombers, however, have kept the sirens wailing in Berlin for three weeks, following the ten-day blitz which reduced Hamburg to rubble and ruin and which prompted the Nazis to order evacuation of the Reich capital by non-essential civilians.

Some index of the extent of the damage was found in the immediate clamping down of censorship regulations on all neutral correspondents in Germany. From usually voluble Stockholm and Berne came only thin reports telephoned out from Berlin to the effect that damage had been widespread but there had been no panic.

Paris Reported Hit

(The industrial western suburbs of Paris were named as targets for daylight raids yesterday in a broadcast late last night by Rome radio.)

That the Nazis—and particularly the Luftwaffe, which controls not only the air defenses but the ack-ack—had been expecting Berlin would "get it" on the scale of Hamburg was apparent in the swarms of night fighters sent up to meet the RAF bombers. Pilots reported they had never seen anywhere near as many enemy planes at night. The Air Ministry said a "number of enemy planes were destroyed."

In addition to its strategic and tactical value as the seat of government and as a communications center from which the

(Continued on page 4)

FDR, Churchill Say Stage Is Set For Next Moves

Strategy Drawn for Blows In Europe and Pacific, But Details Secret

QUEBEC, Aug. 24—Prime Minister Churchill and President Roosevelt, concluding their sixth war conference, announced tonight that "the necessary decisions have been taken" to "spread and deepen" the war effort against the Axis.

"It would not be helpful to the fighting troops to make any announcements of decisions which have been reached," said a joint statement. "These can only emerge in action.

"It may, however, be stated that the military discussions of the chiefs of staff turned very largely on the war against Japan and the bringing of effective aid to China. . . . In this field, as in the European, the President and the Prime Minister were able to receive and approve the unanimous recommendations of the combined chiefs of staffs."

Later, talking to 150 reporters assembled on the terrace outside the Citadel, President Roosevelt hinted at big things to come. He pointed out that the June, 1942, conference laid the ground for North Africa and the Casablanca meeting produced the Tunisian and Sicilian campaigns. The implication was that similar operations were planned here.

Mr. Churchill said the world could expect another Allied achievement to be forthcoming now that Sicily was prostrate. Great steps were being taken, he added, to batter down the antagonists of the Allies one after the other.

The joint statement said that another British-American conference would be held before the end of the year "in addition to any tripartite meetings which it may be possible to arrange with Soviet Russia." It added that full reports of the Quebec decisions, "so far as they affect the war against Germany and Italy, will be furnished to the Soviet government."

Fighter Pilot Tells the Story Of His First Victory—a Triple

A USAAF FIGHTER STATION, Aug. 24—2 Lt. Glen D. Schiltz, of North Canton, Ohio, drew 36 blanks before he hit the jackpot and became the second Thunderbolt pilot in the ETO to score a triple victory over Nazi fighters. Today he told the story of the Aug. 17 dogfight which brought him his triple.

His first mission was a flat failure, with German fighters chasing him home. Smarting from the defeat, he planned just what he would do the next time he met a Nazi pilot, but during the next 35 trips he didn't have a chance to fire a round from his guns. "I just made 35 milk runs," he said. "Finally I gave up. I made up my mind that I just wasn't going to get a chance and then it came just as I had visualized it and the whole plan unfolded without my even thinking about it.

"We entered Holland and proceeded southeast to look for the bombers. We spotted them over Liege, flying in perfect formation. We made our turn and were circling over them. At first they looked like flies on a window pane. But when we closed I spotted about 30 FWs making head-on attacks against them.

"I broke away from my flight and headed down, but two of the FWs turned up to meet me, head on. Believe me, it doesn't take long to close in under that set-up. I opened fire on the leader at 400 yards and let him fly through my fire. That was the last I saw of him. I pulled up to the right and started to circle, when I spotted four FWs flying in a string at my level. I was sure they didn't see me, so I eased in closer. The two end men broke away, leaving me the number two straight ahead. I closed to 300 yards and opened fire and then stopped. At 200 yards I could see my bullets lighting up a half-box pattern on his left wing, cockpit and engine. The pilot slumped over his controls and the plane headed down in a tight spin, with pieces flying off and smoke trailing.

"I looked about and saw the FW leader slightly above me. I slid over and opened fire at 300 yards with a burst of four seconds. I watched his right wing

(Continued on page 4)

FBI Makes First Arrests Of War for Espionage

WASHINGTON, Aug. 24 (UP)—A man and three women have been arrested in Detroit on charges of espionage, the FBI announced today. This is the first case of actual spying in the U.S. during the war, although several have been arrested for sabotage and aiding Nazi fugitives.

The names of the two women are given as Mrs. Theresa Behrens, a German-Hungarian and secretary of the YWCA in Detroit, and Grace Buchanan Dineen, a Canadian-born woman who entered the U.S. from Lisbon.

1d THE STARS AND STRIPES 1d
Daily Newspaper of U.S. Armed Forces in the European Theater of Operations
Vol. 3 No. 256 New York, N.Y.—London, England Monday, Aug. 30, 1943

Biggest Air Battle Cost Nazis 307 Planes

Danish Navy Scuttles 45 Of Its Vessels

Nine Others Escape As Germans Put Country Under Martial Law

Denmark's Navy scuttled 45 ships at dawn yesterday and sailed nine others—two small destroyers, six torpedo-boats and a minesweeper—into Swedish ports to prevent their seizure by the Germans.

The scuttling, climaxing a clash between Danes and Nazi military forces in the Copenhagen naval yard, occurred almost simultaneously with the German military commander's publication at 4 AM of a proclamation placing all Denmark under martial law.

Stockholm heard last night that several persons were killed, a number wounded and scores arrested as a result of riots in Copenhagen. These reports said German air squadrons circled over the city in great numbers all day.

Nazis Tried to Halt It

The navy yard battle apparently was one of the first clashes. It started before daybreak, a Dane who escaped to Sweden said, when the Germans tried to force their way into the yard to prevent the scuttling. Stockholm heard from another traveler that another battle occurred in Copenhagen barracks yesterday afternoon between the Danish Royal Guard and German troops.

The ships that fled to Sweden brought with them a large number of civilians as well as naval officers and enlisted men.

Telegraphic communication between Denmark and Sweden, cut at 5 PM Saturday, remained broken yesterday, but the Danish radio announced that strikes would be punished by death, that German military courts would be set up to try offenders under the new regulations, that meetings of more than five persons were forbidden and that a curfew at dusk would be instituted.

Little was known in Stockholm of the reported scuttling beyond the assertions of the officers reaching Sweden that vessels which could not escape were blown up to prevent their falling into the enemy's hands.

'Ruthless' Action Threatened

Denmark's entire navy numbers little more than 60 vessels, many of them tiny coastal patrol ships. The fleet includes 17 torpedo-boats, most of them less than 300 tons, and 12 submarines, the largest of which is only 380 tons. The navy's largest ships are two coastal defense craft of 3,800 and 3,500 tons respectively.

The German military commander's proclamation of martial law warned the Danes that "in the event of assaults or gatherings, armed force will be used ruthlessly."

An announcement in Berlin said martial law was proclaimed "in order to secure the European coast and to form a counter-measure against the increased activity of enemy agents in Denmark. The necessary measures have been carried out without a hitch. No incidents worth mentioning took place."

U.S. to Punish Nazi Atrocities

WASHINGTON, Aug. 29 (AP)—The U.S. government reaffirmed today that "it is resolved to punish the instigators and the actual perpetrators" of German atrocities against the people of Poland.

The State Department in "a declaration on German crimes in Poland" said trustworthy information had reached the U.S. government regarding "crimes committed by the German invaders" against the Polish population. The State Department said these were carried out with "the utmost brutality."

"Since the autumn of 1942 a belt of territory . . . has been systematically emptied of its inhabitants," the statement said. "In July, 1943, these measures were extended to practically the whole of the province of Lublin, where hundreds of thousands of people have been deported from their homes or exterminated.

"These measures are carried out with the utmost brutality. Many victims are killed on the spot. The rest are segregated. Men from 14 to 50 are taken away to work for Germany. Some children are killed on the spot, others separated from their parents and either sent to Germany to be brought up as Germans or sold to German settlers or dispatched with the women and old men to concentration camps."

The Miracle Tribe's Lady Moe

Planet Photo

Lady Moe, donkey mascot of the Fortress The Miracle Tribe, peers from a waist gun position with S Sgt. Lou Klimchak, of Josephine, Pa., and Sgt. E. O. Matthews, of Porter, Tex., after a flight from Africa in the B17 which bombed Bordeaux, France, before landing at its home base in the ETO. Lady Moe, bought for 400 francs from an Arab desert dweller, wore a special oxygen mask on the mission—the home leg of the USAAF's first shuttle raid from the ETO to Africa.

Nazis Map Dnieper Retreat; Ploesti Raid Helped Defeats

The Russian drive to smash the German supply lines in the Donetz Basin gained speed yesterday, as the German war machine, handicapped by the destruction of their Ploesti oil supply in the American Liberator long-range bombing attack, was reported mapping a retreat to the Dnieper River.

The Russians advanced yesterday on two of the most vital railroads in southern Russia—the line from Bryask through Konotop to Kiev and the Poltava-Kiev line.

On all three fronts the Reds launched new offensives at widely separated points. South of Bryansk, the Soviet troops advanced from four to eight miles and occupied more than 50 inhabited places. South and west of Kharkov, the Russians beat off fierce German counter-attacks and advanced three and one-half to seven miles. On the Mius front the Russians reported new advances.

Meanwhile, the Rumanian military experts were quoted as expressing the belief that the dislocation of Rumanian oil exports were largely responsible for the German defeats in the last three weeks.

Since the start of the Russian invasion the Germans have been transporting oil directly to their armies from Rumania. Before the Ploesti raid it was estimated that any interruption in the flow of oil

(Continued on page 2)

Fighters Attack Anti-SubPatrol

Biscay Bay Battle Reveals New Tactics Against Coastal Command

Packs of German fighters have been thrown against American and British anti-sub aircraft over the Bay of Biscay, it was revealed yesterday.

The Air Ministry announcement, which was the first reference in two months to U.S.-manned Liberators with Coastal Command, provided confirmation that two types of U.S. aircraft, flown by U.S. personnel, are operating from British bases against the Nazi subs. It was revealed two weeks ago that Catalinas, Navy flying patrol boats, are operating with Coastal Command.

Disclosure that the Germans are sending out their fighters in packs came with the announcement that a Liberator, piloted by Lt. K. H. Dustin, of Ausable Forks, N.Y., was attacked by a swarm of ten Ju88s over the Bay of Biscay. During a 40-minute battle, the Lib destroyed one enemy plane and damaged three others.

The JUs ganged up on the B24 and attacked in pairs, groups coming from both sides simultaneously, the Ministry reported. On the first attack a cannon shell crashed into the right side of the cockpit, wounding the co-pilot, just as another hit the left side and injured the pilot. The top turret and radio gunners received minor wounds, one engine was hit and the landing gear knocked out in five attacks.

Lt. Dustin managed to nose his ship, V for Victory, into cloud cover and

(Continued on page 2)

Germans Use Mark V Tanks In Frantic Effort to Halt Reds

The Germans are scraping the bottom of their military arsenal to halt the Russians' summer offensive, according to a roundup yesterday of dispatches from Moscow.

In a frantic effort to halt the Soviet drives, the Nazi armored force has unveiled the Mark V Panther tank, hitherto missing from the consecutively numbered series of panzerwaggonen. Red anti-tank gunners say it is highly vulnerable.

Going to the opposite extreme, the Germans also have come up in the last three weeks with almost primitive means of defense against the Soviet attacks, using armor-plated shields and ready-made concrete pillboxes in multiple storeys similar to stockade towers of 18th-century warfare.

The Russians don't think much of the Mark V Panther.

"Any man can destroy these novelties," the Soviet newspaper Red Star said yesterday, after revealing that the Mark V is being used on a mass scale along with Tigers and Ferdinands in an effort to halt the Russian drive to regain possession of the Ukraine.

The Panther weighs 45 tons—15 less than the Tiger—carries a crew of five, is armed with a 75mm. long-barrelled gun and a 7.92mm machine-gun, roughly equivalent to a .30 cal.

The new tank is approximately the same

(Continued on page 2)

Shuttle Raid Forts Got 140, Schweinfurt Force 147, P47s 20

Gunner Hangs by Toes From Fort Ball Turret

A USAAF BOMBER STATION, England, Aug. 29—Hanging by his feet from the ball turret of a Fortress, thousands of feet in the air, gave S Sgt. Aubrey R. Bartholomew an upside down view of Nazi fighters pressing home an attack during the USAAF's England-North Africa shuttle raid.

Bartholomew tumbled from his turret when the door came off on the outward flight near Regensburg. Luckily, his toes hooked the range pedal of one of his guns. He hung there, without a parachute and with enemy fighters attacking his formation, until he lifted himself "up by the toes."

When Bartholomew, Canadian-born gunner on the Raunchy Wolf, arrived back in Britain he received word his four-year quest for U.S. citizenship had been approved.

Weekend Offensive Hits Nuremberg, Enemy Fields

American airmen scored the biggest aerial victory of the entire war in their battle with Luftwaffe fighters during the Regensburg-Schweinfurt raids of Aug. 17, it was revealed yesterday.

Three hundred and seven enemy aircraft were destroyed in aerial combats by the gunners of Flying Fortresses and the P47 Thunderbolt pilots who flew to Germany to escort some of the formations back to Britain.

One hundred and forty planes were shot down by the Fort formations which battled their way across the Reich, shattered the Messerschmitt fatcory at Regensburg and then shuttled on to Africa, Eighth Air Force headquarters announced last night after a check of intelligence reports.

One hundred and forty seven Nazi planes were destroyed by the Fortresses which struck the key roller bearing plant at Schweinfurt at the same time, and the Thunderbolt guns accounted for 20 more, making a total of at least 307 confirmed victims.

RAF's Best Score

The battles over Germany provided far and away the biggest air victory on any single day of the war—Allied or Axis. At the height of the Battle of Britain, the best day's score for the RAF—on Sept. 15, 1940—was 185 German planes shot down. The previous high for the Eighth Air Force was the tally of 87 chalked up on June 11 when the targets were Wilhelmshaven and Cuxhaven, in Germany. Eight Forts were lost that day.

The record score, however, was only a small portion of the day's achievements, since the bombs which burst across the Messerschmitt factory cut 30 per cent off the German production of day fighters for the next six months, according to official reports. The Regensburg factory was geared to turn out between 1,000 and 2,000 day fighters—depending on supplies—during the next six months.

In addition, uncounted scores of completed and nearly completed fighter planes were destroyed on the factory's vast dispersal area.

59 Bombers Lost

For the record score, the Eighth Air Force paid a known total of 59 bombers, the highest Allied loss of bombers on a single day's or night's mission yet in the war. Twenty-three Forts were reported missing from the Regensburg attack, it was announced, but the crews of four are known to be safe. It previously was announced that 36 bombers were lost on the Schwienfurt attack.

Commenting on the Regensburg operation, Brig. Gen. Frederick L. Anderson, Eighth Bomber Command chief, said: "Our bomber crews destroyed one of Germany's most important aircraft factories, one which had a potential production of more than 1,000 fighters over the

(Continued on page 2)

Allied Bombers Again Blanket Italy's Railways

Yards and Depots at Dozen Points Are Battered By Day and Night

ALLIED HQ, Aug. 29 (UP)—One of the most extensive bomb-blankets ever dropped on any country's transport system has battered Italian railways during the last 24 hours.

Nearly a dozen targets were attacked by Allied bombers. Railway yards and depots at Taranto, Crotone, Cancello, Aversa, Terni, Lamezia, Catanzaro, Castrovellari and Cadenza all were hit heavily.

The Tactical Air Force alone dropped a heavier bomb-load on Italy than at any other time since the end of the Tunisian campaign.

In addition, U.S. Liberators from the Middle East raided shipping at Taranto, damaging an enemy cruiser, while fighter-bombers from the North African Air Forces attacked targets in Sardinia.

One of the biggest attacks was made on the railway yards at Terni, 45 miles north of Rome and on the line from Rome to Ancona.

The attack, concentrated into five minutes, was made by more than 100 planes, including Fortresses escorted by Lightnings.

Besides the repair shops and the railway yards, targets hit included the royal arsenal, an electrical works and the gas works. At least one large explosion and a number of fires were seen. About 40 enemy fighters came up, and at least six Me109s were shot down.

The important junction at Aversa, 15 miles north of Naples, was attacked by

(Continued on page 2)

School Hours Rearranged For War-Working Pupils

PHILADELPHIA, Aug. 29—Dr. Alexander Stoddard, superintendent of schools, announced today that if school interfered with the war plant jobs of some 15,000 Philadelphia pupils school hours would be changed for them.

He urged as many pupils as possible to attend during regular hours after the summer vacation ended, but said that classes would be arranged "at odd hours and on Saturdays for those who feel they must work." Pupils will receive laboratory credit toward diplomas for their work in war factories.

Nearly 15,000 Wounded Flown Out in Five Weeks

In the five weeks between July 6 and Aug. 14, 14,898 wounded and sick were flown from Sicily to hospitals in Algeria and Egypt by RAF-USAAF medical services, the Air Ministry reported yesterday.

The two air forces collaborated completely, pooling their planes. In some cases, the RAF provided orderlies to fly on American ambulance transport planes.

THE STARS AND STRIPES

MIDDLE EAST

VOL. I No. 21 — CAIRO — FOUR CENTS — SEPTEMBER 3 1943

Island Raid Gives Japs The Jitters About Mainland

Marcus Island, Japanese-held base 1200 miles south-east of Tokyo, was raided by a United States Naval Task Force on Wednesday. To Washington observers, this attack appears to be the first blow in a possible offensive opening a direct invasion route to Japan.

This naval bombardment is the first action to be brought against the outpost since March 4, 1942. Marcus Island stands guard over vital Japanese positions in the central Pacific. Military opinion is that United Nations sea and air power throughout the Pacific has now reached a point were hit-and-run raids are unlikely. Hence the Marcus Island action looks like a step toward an offensive.

Could Have Gone Further

Radio Tokyo announced to its Japanese listeners : "Marcus Island is halfway between Japan proper and Wewak, New Guinea. The enemy could have raided the mainland if he wanted to. The people of Japan must solidify their defense against the enemy."

Declared Under Secretary of War Robert Patterson in Melbourne, "You won't have to wait long for the bombing of Japan."

Mr. Patterson praised the spirit of the Allied forces in the South Pacific which he said were receiving war materials in sufficient quantities.

Prisoner Exchange

As a transport of Japanese POWs slipped out of New York en route to an exchange for American POWs, Red Cross Chairman Norman Davis in London remarked : "We have had no trouble getting supplies to prisoners of war in Germany and Italy, but we have never been able to work out a satisfactory arrangement with Japan."

Meanwhile, Japanese authorities issued the new requirement that messages to Americans in Japanese prison camps be limited to 25 words.

The Allied triumph over Wewak in New Guinea has forced the Japanese air force to shift its bases 200 miles west to Dutch New Guinea, leaving behind nearly 400 wrecked planes and unsupported ground garrisons. Fighting for Salamaua is still in the seesaw stage.

Transatlantic Bombers On The Way, Arnold Says

WASHINGTON—Mighty bombers of the future, capable of carrying half a carload of bombs across the Atlantic and flying home without stopping, were foreseen this week by Gen. Henry "Hap" Arnold.

The AAF chief pictured the bomber of the future as having numerous "blisters"; multiple-gun power turrets controllable from sighting stations; sights that compensate for every possible error encountered in firing fast moving targets and gun-sights as revolutionary as our present bomb-sights.

"They will carry bombs of completely different design and may mount heavy caliber cannon of an entirely new principle. And fighter planes will have advanced almost beyond recognition in form and combat equipment."

Earlier in the week, it was announced that U.S. plane production for July had hit 7333.

Cheops' Big Tee

Here's Slamin' Sarge Ted E. Bodle Jr. atop the Great Pyramid addressing the historic golf ball that relegated the golf myth of the Pyramid to the dead letter office. A few seconds later the ball was bouncing around the base of the Second Pyramid in the background.... a drive of 382.3 yards. Just to the left of the ball is an inscription in the rock which reads "Prince Edward of Wales—1915", the point where the Prince phizzled his shots.
(Signal Corps Photo)

GI Golfer Smashes Legend, Drives Ball From Pyramid

By S/Sgt. Gene Lynch

For the next couple of thousand years or so tourists who scale the sun-baked sides of the Pyramid of Cheops will gaze on a trophy of World War II. It's a can of GI Spam cemented into the top of this rock of ages, bearing the following inscription, "From this spot, on August 28, 1943, S/Sgt. Ted E. Bodle, Jr., of the U.S. Army drove four golf balls clear into the realm of the Second Pyramid." Within the can, preserved by the indestructible and ageless ersatz boloney, nestle the four historic balls.

It all came about when Sgt. Bodle heard of the legend that no one had ever been able to drive a golf ball off the top of the Pyramid and clear the base... a distance of but 127.3 yards. Many failures to accomplish the feat lent support to the popular legend. The most notable failures were reportedly made by the Duke of Windsor, then the Prince of Wales, and Bob Ripley of "Believe It or Not" fame, whose futile drives dribbled down the sides of the rock pile into the limestone gulch.

Among the theories which were supposed to make the feat impossible were : the attraction of a large body for a small traveling object, updrafts, down currents, the eclipse of 1666 and the curse of Apis the Bull. Since Saturday, the legend has taken on a strong bull odor.

Four Long Drives

Last Saturday Sgt. Bodle, oddly enough from Granville, Ohio, rather than Missouri, decided to take a hand in the matter of the myth...and a golf club. Armed with a battered and borrowed driver which someone must have been using to hammer rivets and four ancient golf balls as lively as a mummy, young Bodle ascended the 450-foot high Pyramid, accompanied by several witnesses. After catching his breath and teeing a ball up on sand, the Slammin' Sarge wound up and wham !... he scattered the old golf myth of the Pyramid all over the place like so many pieces of shattered alabaster. His first drive not only cleared the base but also a smaller pyramid, several tombs, and over the fence surrounding the Second Pyramid. Just to make it stick he hit three more balls in the same neighborhood. Bodle's longest drive landed 240 yards from the base of the Great Pyramid and rolled and additional 15 yards...an actual horizontal distance of 382.3 yards.

Old Hand At Game

Sgt. Bodle, the pyramid pulver-

(continued on page 2)

5th YEAR DAWNS BLACK FOR AXIS

The fifth year of "the most formidable, destructive and devastating war of all time," opened this week with the Axis warlords staring at a long series of sombre facts :

They had not won a single military or political victory in more than a year;

The Nazis were taking one costly beating after another from the battle-wise Red Army;

German home morale was tottering under Allied bombs;

Italy was being flattened for use as an Allied bombing base;

The neutral nations, led by Sweden, were stoutly resisting Nazi threats;

The satellite governments were looking for the way out;

The captive people of the entire continent were ready to rise — 12,000,000 of them with arms — the moment the United Nations landed their impatient armies in Europe proper.

Denmark Seething

"We see the Germans hated as no race has ever been hated in human history, or with such reason," said Winston Churchill, pointing to seething Denmark. There, despite rumbling tanks and goose-stepping Nazis, strikes and sabotage continued. Part of the Danish navy, bearing several hundred prominent Danes, escaped to Sweden and was welcomed there. Most of the rest was scuttled.

Sweden called the Germans down for sinking Swedish fishing boats in the Skaggerak, firmly held to her decision denying transit of Nazi war materials to captive Norway. The Germans fulminated.

In Bulgaria, where King Boris lay mysteriously dead, trouble brewed for the Nazis. It brewed in war-weary Finland, in tortured Poland, in Greece, Yugoslavia, France. Trains were wrecked, power lines damaged, grain fields set afire. It was plain that the big Allied second front would open a thousand small ones from one end of Europe to the other.

In Belgium, near Malines, patriots armed with revolvers and Tommy guns held up a train deporting 1,500 Jews to Poland, liberated several hundred of them.

Berlin Blasted

For the second time in eight days, Berlin was blasted by the RAF. Night-flying bombers fought their way through swarms of "cat-seye" fighters for nearly 400 miles to dump their bombs on the target. Searchlights and guns were massed along the route.

Over Berlin itself the enemy tried a new trick. Aircraft at great height dropped flares which burned slowly and brilliantly as they fell, but they showed up Nazi planes as well as British.

The raid left great fires raging in the German capital. Nearly 50 bombers were lost.

Russians Drive On

U.S. bombers concentrated as usual on precision daylight bombbing. The Eighth Air Force based in England plastered 16 enemy airfields during August. The Ninth and Twelfth continued their pin-point attacks on strategic Italian rail junctions.

The 700-mile Eastern front continued to move Westward over bare fields and in dense forests in a series of co-ordinated Russian offensives.

The new Russian advances posed a great threat to Smolesk, one of Hitler's headquarters ; out-flanked the companion fortress of Bryansk; brought the key Bryansk-Konotop railway within artillery range ; drove closer to the Dnieper Bend west of Kharkov; and chewed up the remnants of the trapped German garrison of Tangarog where 35,000 Germans were reported slain near the ruined Chekov-Museum on the sea of Azov.

In some areas, including the Northern Ukraine, the German retreat showed signs of becoming a rout with tanks and guns being abandoned intact.

The fall of ruined Yelnia, chief German bastion on the central front, gave particular satisfaction to the grim Russians. Two years ago, in the first Russian success against the Nazi invaders, young General Sokolovsky routed eight German divisions to capture the town. Now the same young General had done it again, and this time for good. Stalin ordered 12 artillery salvoes from 124 guns in Moscow to celebrate the victory.

U.S. Forces Are Invited To British Boxing Shows

American forces are invited to attend the two British boxing shows to be held this week-end at Almaza. Friday night at 6 o'clock the preliminaries of the Cairo area amateur boxing championships will be run off. On Saturday night at 8.30 the semi-finals will be held. Admission is free to both shows. To reach Almaza, ride the Heliopolis "Toonerville" to the end of the line.

BANGTAIL SETS RECORD

NEW YORK. — "Prince Quillo" set a new track record for the mile, winning the 63rd running of the $25,000 Saratoga cup at Belmont Park. The time was 2.56 4/5, clipping 4/5 sec. off track record.

At Chicago, "Askmenow" won the American Derby nosing out "Bold Captain". "Slide Rule," the current hoof sensation, ran next to last.

HOLIDAY WORK ASKED

WASHINGTON. — Charles Wilson, executive vice chairman of WPB, has asked war plant workers to give up the Labor Day holiday. "To get out the munitions our men need in battle," he said, "it is imperative that all producers of war material operate full work schedules on Labor Day."

SPOTTERS' CONTEST

A "Plane Spotting" Contest is one of the highlights this weekend at the Red Cross Club, Cairo. Four o'clock's the time, the first floor recreation lounge the place.

Small models of various plane types will be numbered and contestants will try to supply their names. Yes, there are prizes for top scores.

WASHINGTON. — Read Admiral Chares E. Rosendahl, dirigible expert and Chief of the Naval Airship Training program, has been awarded the Navy Cross for heroism while serving as commanding officer of the cruiser USS Minneapolis during the Battle of Lunga Point, 1943.

THE STARS AND STRIPES

SICILY

Vol. 1 - No. 7 - Friday, Sept. 3, 1943 | U. S. Army Newspaper | 2 Lire

ITALY INVADED

Soviet Attacks Threaten Every Nazi Position

Greatest Offensive Of War Brings Reds Close To Smolensk

BULLETIN

In a special order of the day Premier Stalin has announced the capture of Sumy on the central front and Voroshilovsk in the heart of the Donets Basin. The fall of Voroshilovsk indicates that German forces in the Donets Basin not only are surrounded but are practically cut in two.

LONDON, Sept. 3—The greatest of Russian offensives is hurling the Nazis back along an 800-mile front stretching from Smolensk to the Kuban Peninsula. In what may be one of the decisive battles of the war six great Soviet spearheads have pierced weak spots in the German armor. As yet none of these Red thrusts has been stopped.

Smolensk is under attack by one wing of the Russian armies encircling Bryansk, while the other wing is driving deep into the joint between two Nazi commands. Kiev is threatened by one arm of the Soviet pincers hinging on Kharkov while the other Red arm is cutting off the Donets Basin. In the far south two Russian armies are marching along the Sea of Azov towards the Crimea.

SMOLENSK THREATENED

The Russians are striking between the fortified keystones of the German line—Smolensk, Bryansk, Kiev, Poltava, Stalino and Novorossisk. It is too early to tell in which direction any one of the Soviet spearheads will move, yet it seems clear that Red strategy is aiming at the encirclement and annihilation of troops rather than the capture of cities. The problem of the Wehrmacht now is less to defend its lines than to extricate its trapped armies.

Smolensk, whose capture would open the way to Poland, is under direct attack by the Red divisions which crossed the River Desna to take Yelnya. In German hands since 1941, Yelnya is 35 miles by rail from Smolensk. Its capture endangers the railroad from Smolensk to Bryansk.

Bryansk is not only under fire of Red guns nine miles away, but its rail connections southwards to Kiev are menaced by a hard-driving Soviet column moving from Sevsk towards the juncture of the northern and central Nazi armies. The railroad from Kiev to Poltava is on the point of being cut, while the tracks from Poltava to Stalino are in Russian hands at several points.

Along the shores of the Sea of Azov Soviet troops claim to have liquidated 40,000 Nazis at Tagan-

(Continued on Page 4)

Bette Davis' Husband Dies In Hollywood

HOLLYWOOD — Actress Bette Davis, on the verge of hysteria after the death of her husband, Arthur Farnsworth, an aircraft technician, has been placed in the care of physicians. She was at her husband's bedside when he died after a fall on Hollywood Boulevard

WHERE BRITISH HIT

Sicilian Engines Run Fine For U. S. Crews

By JAMES A BURCHARD
(Stars and Stripes Staff Writer)

Wherever an American soldier goes, you'll almost always find some more American soldiers bringing up a railroad train right behind him.

This was true in Tunisia. It also was true in the Sicilian campaign where the 727th Railway Operating Battalion turned in an amazingly efficient and speedy job under pressure. In one respect, these men who rushed tons of supplies to the front lines deserve an equal share of credit with the infantry, guns, tanks and planes that handled the actual combat assignments. They get that credit, too, as evidenced by many messages of commendation.

Twenty-four hours after they landed at Licata on July 15, the battalion had trains in operation.

Today their lines of freight cars cover the island over some 600 miles of track. Approximately 50 trains chug forth each day. They run from Trapani to San Stefano on the north, across the island to

The 727th Railway Operating Battalion put Sicily's railroads in order for Allied uses with a minimum of mishaps. There was one wreck in the Licata area, where several men won Soldier's Medals for saving equipment under hazardous conditions. One train was strafed near Cefalu and several times the cars were bombed. But losses throughout the campaign remained surprisingly small.

Castelvetrano and go all the way east to Gerbini. British handle the rest. When an American train comes to British territory, the train is turned over to a British crew and vice versa.

In addition to the freight trains, many of the passenger variety are operated for the benefit of civilians. These, in a sense, also serve the U. S. Army as they bring workers from the small towns to the city.

There are plenty of headaches, however, before the present smooth state of operations was achieved. You can find this out by conversing with 1st Lt. Ralph G. Hickey, of Cleveland, Tenn., formerly yard master for the Southern Railway.

He's now yard master and RTO officer in Palermo, where he is assisted by S-Sgt. William D. Farrell, of Fort Wayne, Ind., and T-Sgt. Norwood L. Stone, of St. Louis.

"Our main problem was repairing bridges and tracks," said Lt. Hickey. "Many bridges and even tunnels were wrecked. All told we had to repair at least 15.

"Curiously, we found much equipment, especially locomotives, in good shape. A lot of stuff was destroyed, but there was plenty left that wasn't. We put in a great deal of new roadbed and rails. Part of the repair equipment we brought with us, and some we found in Sicily. The locomotives, Italian or German, provide few problems to our engineers. After one hour they have them completely solved."

BRAKES, ANYWAY

The engineers agree. Three of them were located in their billet, a former Italian schoolhouse. They introduced themselves as Sgt. Willard Quillan, of Steubenville, Ohio; Sgt. Frank Hayden, of North Platte, Neb., and Sgt. Vincent Stiles, of Kansas City. Quillan used to be a Pennsy engineer; Stiles and Hayden are ex-firemen from the Union Pacific.

"Anyway," said Quillan, "the rails are standard guage and these Sicilian engines have brakes. In Tunis we had to go into reverse when we wanted to stop."

"Yeah," supplemented Hayden, "these engines are OK, but they aren't up to the American brand."

(Continued on Page 4)

Bricker Will Seek '44 GOP Nomination

CHICAGO—Sen. Robert A. Taft, Republican of Ohio, has announced that Ohio's Gov. John W. Bricker will definitely seek the G. O. P. nomination for President in 1944. Mr. Taft and Gov. Bricker was talking over his campaign with Republican leaders, including Alf M. Landon, G. O. P. nominee in 1936. The first Republican to announce his candidacy for the 1944 nomination was Wendell Willkie.

British Troops Attack Across Messina Straits After Mighty Barrage

By T-Sgt. HILARY LYONS
(Stars and Stripes Staff Writer)

Italy is being invaded today! Canadian and British 8th Army forces are swarming into the toe of Italy, fanning out over the province of Calabria.

The invasion, according to an official communique, was preceded by a spectacularly heavy barrage across the straits by Sicilian shore-based batteries and ships. The landings were covered by very strong sea and air forces. For several days at least the Allies have controlled the straits. Their planes have operated over the narrow passage at will and British battleships only two days ago entered the straits to silence Italian batteries on the mainland.

The news of the invasion was given in a special communique from Allied Force Headquarters at 0745 hours today. The special communique stated that amphibious landings across the Straits of Messina were still in progress at that time, but no further details of the invasion, which fell on the fourth anniversary of Britain's entrance into World War II, were given.

General Dwight D. Eisenhower, Allied Commander-in-Chief, was named as commander of the expedition, serving in the same capacity as for the Sicilian and North African campaigns. The appointment of Gen. Eisenhower as commander led to the belief that American forces would almost certainly be used at a later stage of the Italian campaign and that Italy, like Sicily and North Africa, would be a joint Allied undertaking.

QUICK ACTION

The invasion of Italy followed by less than three weeks the collapse of Italo-German resistance on Sicily. The island, which is only three miles from the Italian mainland across the Messina Straits, fell to the 15th Army Group, composed of the U. S. 7th and British 8th Armies plus Canadians, on Aug. 17.

For the invasion of Italy the British used their outstanding veterans. Tested in the African deserts and the Sicilian mountains, the Eighth Army, led by Gen. Sir Bernard Montgomery, is generally regarded as Britain's most rugged and seasoned battle force.

The accelerating pace of Allied warfare is shown by the fact that while there was a gap of more than two months between the conquest of North Africa and the invasion of Sicily, less than a month elapsed between the fall of Sicily and the drive into Italy.

Italy's ability to resist an all-out attack is open to question. If reports from all neutral countries are correct, the Italian masses long for peace, and the Italian army, judged by its performance in Sicily shares the sentiments of civilians.

ITALIAN MORALE

On the other hand, the government of Marshal Badoglio, set up after the fall of Benito Mussolini last July, has consistently tried to persuade the Italians that they must stay in the war. To some observers it has seemed that fear of German reprisals was partly responsible for the aged Marshal's stand.

The number of German troops in Italy is a matter for guesswork. Some reports told of an influx of Nazi forces into Italy after Mussolini's exit. More recent reports have told of German withdrawals, though the Nazi troops which fled into Italy after they were soundly beaten in Sicily may not have had the opportunity to leave the peninsula.

The invasion of Italy has been looked for as the next logical Allied step after Sicily's fall. Even before the island fell Allied planes were ceaselessly bombarding airfields and lines of communications

(Continued on Page 4)

All New Georgia In Allied Hands

ALLIED PACIFIC HEADQUARTERS, Sept. — Allied forces have moved a step nearer the complete re-conquest of the Solomons by overcoming all Jap resistance on New Georgia island, whose chief base, Munda, fell to our troops last month. The quickening tempo of Allied action in the Southwest Pacific is indicated by the fact that the New Georgia campaign took less than two months, while nearly half a year was required to win Guadalcanal.

The tone of communiques from General Douglas MacArthur's headquarters grows increasingly optimistic. A recent communique declares that the Japs last month lost as many planes as their factories produced. In the Solomons thus far this week the Japs have lost 36 out of 60 fighters in a series of Allied attacks on Nip airfields.

Raids on New Ireland and New Britain, lying between New Guinea and the Solomons, are mounting and General MacArthur promises that a heavier air offensive lies just ahead. The Tokyo radio has expressed alarm over a recent Allied raid on the Marshall Islands, 1,300 miles from Tokyo. The Jap capital may soon be under bombs again, the Jap commentator stressed.

New Air Attack Staggers Berlin

LONDON, Sept. 2 — Berlin has received another terrific air blow. For 45 minutes last Tuesday night, an undisclosed number of Allied bombers, fighter-bombers and fighters swept over the Nazi capital, dropping tons of incendiaries in a raid as heavy as any yet staged on the city. Shortly after midnight, the air armada nosed homeward and observers could see many fires burning.

The Luftwaffe was ready for the raid. Aided by searchlights, a fleet of fighters was raised which harassed the attackers and made the bombers fight both coming and going from the target. Allied aircraft accounted for 16 German fighters; 45 of our bombers and one fighter are missing.

RAF and USAAF bombers based in Britain continue to carry out relentless day attacks on Axis air fields in Northern France and the Low Countries. Beaufighters and Flying Fortresses have made repeated calls on already well-bombed military installations near Am-

(Continued on Page 4)

THE STARS AND STRIPES

Fifth Army Edition

Volume 1, Number 4 — Thursday, September 9, 1943 — FREE

ITALIANS SURRENDER

People Called On

The Italian people were being informed of the armistice and the surrender of their army and government through the spreading of leaflets in all the populous cities of the state.

The leaflets called upon the Italians to enter actively in the cause of the United Nations. It was pointed out that Italy now has behind it all the might of the Allies.

"Italy now has the opportunity of taking vengeance upon her oppressors," read the leaflets.

In all areas occupied by Allied soldiers the Italian people were urged to give every assistance they can.

In all German-occupied areas, they were told to do nothing to assist the Germans.

It was pointed out that the war in Italy will become a war of transportation. Railways, roads, shipping facilities will become all-importaint. The people were urged to see that no single train bearing German soldiers and supplies is permitted to pass. They were told to see that no shop carried Germans, and no roads were used by the Germans.

During the crucial week to follow the announcement of the armistice, it was said, one supreme heroic effort must be made by the Italian people to paralyze their German enemy.

What will become of the Italian fleet was an ever pressing question in the minds of military and naval men. The Germans were expected to seize the Italian ships in all harbors wherever possible.

Italians were warned not to scuttle their ships. Those ships now in Mediterranean ports were told to make for Allied ports, and those in the Black Sea to make for Russian.

At Number Ten Downing Street last night, an official statement was issued saying that the United Nations will recognize in the Italian surrender the further signal weakness of the Axis forces. The prime minister, it was stated, will make a full discussion of the subject when parlament next assembles.

Italy entered the war on June 11, 1940 when France was on the verge of collapse

(Continued on Page 2)

Russians Capture Stalino To Dominate Donbas

Stalino, great industrial city in the heart of the rich Donets River Basin, fell into Russian hands Wednesday. Berlin announced its evacuation by the German Army.

The capture of this city of half a million people, mining and steel center and the hub of the Basin railway system, is regarded by many experts as of greater military importance than the taking of Rostov.

Russia now controls the communication lines of the Basin besides well over two-thirds of the land. The push westward is expected to be accelerated with the fall of this strongpoint. Berlin said the evacuation was according to plan. Russians called the German withdrawal a rout.

On the central front the Soviet troops pushed on from Konotop, where they have scored one of the greatest tactical successes of their offensive. There they are driving a wedge beyween Hitler's armies of the center and the south.

Aiming at Bakhmach the Red Army was intent upon cutting the main railway link between the two German armies. The fall of this vital section is regarded as certain. Already the line has been cut north of Bakhmach, and the railway-junction city itself was under Russian gunfire on Wednesday, with Red troops only three miles away.

At the southern tip of the 600-mile front of Mariupol on the Sea of Azov was a near prospect, the Red Army by-passing this in their sweep through the Donbas.

Victory Certain

WASHINGTON — General George C. Marshall, Chief of Staff of the United States Army, has issued a detailed report on the progress of the war.

The Marshall report points out that "the end is not yet clearly in sight but victory is certain." After reviewing the struggles of the earlier months of American participation, the report sums up the present situation as one in which the strength of the enemy is steadily declining and that of the United Nations steadily increasing.

Armistice Signed

Italy has surrendered unconditionally.

That news, announced at 1730 hours Wednesday at Allied Force Headquarters in North Africa, sent a stir throughout the world. The end of one of the great Axis powers had come. A moment of great triumph had come for the United Nations.

General Eisenhower, commander in chief, made the announcement of the render.

A military armistice has been granted to the Italian government. The terms that armistice have been approved by governments of the United States, Great Britain and Soviet Russia.

"The Italian Government has surrendered its armed forces unconditionally," read the statement of Gen. Eisenhower. "As Allied Commander in Chief I approved a military armistice which met with the formal approval of governments of the United States, Great Britain and Russia."

The armistice was signed by representatives of Gen. Eisenhower and of Marshal Badoglio, the Italian prime minister, who succeeded Mussolini to power in Italy.

The statement of Gen. Eisenhower pointed to the cessation of hostilities and further stated that all Italians who now act to eject the German armed aggressor from Italy will have the assistance of Allied force.

It was revealed that Italian peace feelers were sent some weeks ago. A meeting was arranged between Italian representatives and Gen. Eisenhower's representatives, taking place in a neutral country. At once it was explained by the United Nations that only unconditional surrender was acceptable.

On Sicily on September 3 at Allied headquarters the terms of the armistice were agreed upon and signed.

At that time it was made a condition that the armistice was to come into force at a moment most favorable to the Allies. That moment, it was decided, had arrived yesterday.

One clause of the terms imposed binds the Italian government to comply with political, economic and military con-

(Continued on Page 2)

THE STARS AND STRIPES

Fifth Army Edition

Volume 1, Number 6 — Saturday, September 11, 1943 — FREE

Kiev, Dneiper Russian Goals

More than 300 towns, including some important rail junctions, were liberated on the 600-mile front of the Russian offensive Friday as the triumphant Red Army went on with its ruthless smashing of the Nazi armies.

Main objectives of the Russian drive are now Kiev in the upper Ukraine and Dnepropetrovsk, at the great bend of the Dneiper river in the lower Ukraine.

From Bakhmach, the most important communication center and strongpoint on the way to Kiev, which the Russians occupied Thursday after 48 hours of fierce street fighting, the Red Army was thrusting southwards towards Priluki. This thrust was a further penetration of the great wedge which is being driven between the German armies of the central front and of the south.

Just north of this fighting the Bryansk area also saw heavy action Friday. North of Bryansk, advance Russian units recaptured Lyndinovo and were within 50 miles of much-bombed Roslavl, key town on the railway line between Smolensk and Bryansk.

Just south of the drive towards Kiev is the Kharkov front, and there the Russian troops on Friday were threatening Barvenakova on the only railway line to the south from Kharkov. They reached Gusarouka, only six miles east of Barvenkova.

Mariupol Taken

The capture of the city of Mariupol on the Sea of Azov was reported Friday in Marshal Stalin's order of the day. This important seaport is about 65 miles west of Taganrog. Its taking was accomplished largely as a result of Russian troops bypassing it when they swung northwards towards Stalino after taking Taganrog.

Another great victory for the Russians on Friday was the capture of Chaplino, some 75 miles due west from Stalino. This rail city is only 45 miles from the Dneiper bend. Its quick seizure, only two days after the winning of Stalino, is indicative of the complete rout of the Germans in this region, and the great speed of the Russian offensive.

Allied submarines sank eight large ships in the Adriatic and nine small vessels during the first days of the Italian mainland campaign, it was reported.

Mighty Good

"From where we were sitting the invasion looked mighty good," said an air force colonel Friday after coming back from flying over the Naples area. "Thousands of our troops could be seen ashore. The boys on the ground were going right to work."

British Move Ahead

Connection was made Friday between the main advancing force of the British Eighth Army moving up the west coast and the troops who cut behind the German rear the day before by landing on the Gulf of Eufemia some 30 miles ahead. As a consequence the coastline of the Italian toe is now held from Pizzo in the Eufemia gulf to Monasterace on the eastern coast, considerably above Locri.

In closing the 30-mile gap between the main army and the seaborne troops, the invaders forced the Germans to take hasty retreat, and captured many prisoners.

Up both the eastern and western coasts, following the coastal road they now control for such a stretch, the British Eighth Army went on progressing Friday despite some German resistance.

Most German opposition, however, still took the form of demolitions. What contact there was, took place with light rearguards left by the Nazis to engage the British-Canadians and detain them as long as possible.

Army air force flyers on Friday were giving excellent support to the Eighth Army. They were concentrating here, as well as in the Naples area, upon smashing German motor transports on which the Germans must rely for reenforcements and for retreat, since the railways are so badly disorganized.

Over the Eighth Army front, 96 enemy trucks were destroyed, and 133 others damaged by fighter bombers.

Taranto Falls

The taking of Taranto, the great Italian naval base on the Gulf of Taranto in the Ionian Sea, was announced Friday. Occupation of this important city, where often the Italian fleet took shelter or from which it steamed to do battle, was made by British forces.

Landings began Thursday, and the British troops slowly made their way into the city, encountering no strong opposition. Ships of the Royal Navy supported the landings. Taranto is a city of 150,000 population, largest in the southern tip of Italy.

Fifth Army Hits Nazis At Naples

The Fifth Army, spearheading the great Allied offensive in the Naples area, was fighting its way inland on Friday from various landing points, overcoming strong German resistance.

An Allied Force Headquarters communique said that the first groups of the Fifth Army have established themselves successfully in the Naples area.

The Germans were reported to be putting up as stiff resistance as was anticipated. Five German counterattacks were made with savage force, and the Fifth repulsed them and moved forward.

Fighting was heavy Friday in the Salerno sector where another Allied landing had been made. In the battle there, the German 16th Panzer division was identified. This division was reported wiped out before Stalingrad, but evidently has been reformed.

A headquarters communique said that Salerno represents one of the extremities of the Fifth Army's line. It is about 30 miles south of Naples.

A diversional force on Friday captured Ventolene Island, some 20 miles off the Italian mainland and 40 miles west of Naples. The garrison surrendered to the attacking force.

Landings continued in the Naples area. About 30 German fighters interfered with them at one time during the day, but were driven off.

Mines laid off the beaches had to be cleared by minesweepers. Naval forces still remained offshore helping in the landings, and protecting the work of unloading ships which went on without intermission.

Naval Forces immediately engaged in the landing operations are under the command of Vice Admiral Henry K. Hewitt, United States Navy. The Army landing operations are commanded by Lieut. Gen. Mark Clark, as announced yesterday.

There were no reports and no confirmations, on Friday regarding other landings on the coast of Italy above and below Rome.

Rome Bombed

Several unidentified planes were over Rome on Friday and dropped bombs on the city. Some casualties were caused and some houses hit. The bomb fragments are being studied to determine the identity of the planes.

THE STARS AND STRIPES

Fifth Army Edition

Volume 1, Number 7 — Monday, September 13, 1943 — FREE

Soviet Advance Rings Bryansk

As the Red Army advance went rolling westwards Sunday, the city of Bryansk appeared to be the next large base certain to fall again into Russian hands. This German-held strongpoint in the north-central part of the vast front was nearly isolated by the oncoming Russian troops, and the Nazi defenders were in danger of encirclement

Soviet soldiers were 25 miles southwest of the city. Striking north from that point, they had only 15 miles to go in order to cut the Bryansk-Minsk railway in back of the German garrison. On the southeast they reached a belt of marshyland which encloses the city in that direction.

The Russian drive made progress over the weekend towards the two main objectives of Kiev in the center and the great bend in the Dneiper at Dnepropetrovsk in the south.

On the road to Kiev, the Russians were striking within 15 miles of the railway junction at Nezhin, the only lateral railway east of Kiev still in German hands. The Nazis were reported to be backtracking from this region in front of Kiev so rapidly they aren't carrying out heavy demolitions.

In the drive towards the Dneiper, the Red Army was nearing Pavolograd In this region beyond Stalino, the Germans are threatened with having their escape route from the Crimea cut off.

The taking of Mariupol on the Sea of Azov was speeded by the landing of seaborne troops west of the city, it was revealed Sunday. On the Black Sea, at the German-held port of Novorossisk there appeared to have been activity over the week-end, the Germans claiming that Russians landed in the harbor and were annihilated in a bitter battle.

Dancing In Kharkov

MOSCOW— Russian trains are already moving into recaptured Kharkov. Some shops are open and a number of theaters even are in operation.

The leading Russian ballet star Lepeshinskaya is now dancing in that city which was in German hands so short a time ago, and which is still in ruins from the battles that have swept back and forth across it.

Seventy percent of the buildings were found to be damaged.

Spectacle

Naval history's greatest event since Germany surrendered her fleet at Scapa Flow in 1918 took place late Saturday afternoon when the surrendered Italian fleet sailed colorfully into the harbor of Valletta at Malta.

Stretching out a distance of more than four miles over the blue Mediterranean, the warships of the Italian Navy came steaming into port, their great force no longer a threat to Allied supremacy of the sea. They had successfully evaded German efforts to secure them and to sink them. They were surrendered in accordance with the terms of the armistice.

Standing on the deck of the Royal Navy Warship, Hamilton, the commander in chief of Allied operations, Gen. Eisenhower, and the commander of naval operations, Admiral Cunningham, watched the impressive sight of the incoming warships

Malta made it a gala day. Flags were flying from all public buildings of the gallant island city in this moment of its greatest glory. When, later, the Italian admiral formally surrendered his ships to Admiral Cunningham there were great crowds in the square attending the ceremony.

In the surrendering fleet that came into Malta harbor at 1630 Saturday were two battleships, five cruisers and four destroyers. Earlier in the day other ships had been coming in, bringing the total surrendered to four battleships, seven cruisers and 10 destroyers. Three more destroyers steamed in on Sunday to surrender. Two of the battleships were Italy's most modern and largest.

Six other ships of the Italian navy were reported to have reached Allied

(Continued on Page 2)

Allied Unity

LONDON — Means of developing a closer military and political unity between the United States, the British Empire and Russia are being prepared. Under discussion is a plan for a permanent three-power commission with authority to make recommendations and take action regarding problems arising from current military operations.

A conference of the foreign ministers of the three Allied nations is expected to be held next month with a view to promoting such closer collaboration. It is expected that problems requiring joint handling may arise before long from the collapse of Italy and the disintegration of the new German order in the Balkans also from any military operations in western Europe.

British Troops Take Brindisi

The Fifth Army, leading the battle in the Naples area, at Salerno, and elsewhere in that vicinity, was reported Sunday to be continuing its progress. The communique from Allied Force Headquarters stated also that German resistance continued strong.

Meanwhile on the beaches there is vast activity. Reinforcements are constantly being brought up, as Gen. Clark's spearheading Army gathers strength and takes shape for the fiercer drives to come. Germans have launched heavy air attacks on these preparations but the Allies have countered sharply.

The most marked successes of the Italian campaign reported on Sunday had to do with the progress of the Eighth Army and of the British and Canadian troops generally in the southernmost section of Italy. Practically the whole of the foot of Italy, toe and heel and all, was in Allied hands Sunday.

The troops who captured Taranto pushed east to the Adriatic coast and took Brindisi, port and factory city of 40,000 population. They reported the bombed factories were soon in operation, the Italians cooperating, this time turning out materials for the Allies.

Other troops who fanned out from Taranto after the taking of that great Italian naval base headed northwards and came into contact with German soldiers, some of them the 1st German Parachute Division. This German force was said to have been bottled up by the advancing British.

The Eighth Army men moving up the east coast from Reggio reached as far north as Catanzaro, which they occupied on Sunday. This, too, is a city of 40,000 and an important capture. The line around the coast from west to east now stretches from San Eufemia La Maza to Catanzaro, and is some 80 miles above Reggio.

Golfer Here

LONDON—Robert Sweeney, American golfer who won the British amateur golf championship in 1937, was the captain and pilot of a Libertaor bomber that accounted for two of the German submarines sunk in the recent blasting of seven subs in the Bay of Biscay. He received the DSC for his services.

1D. THE STARS AND STRIPES 1D.

Daily Newspaper of U.S. Armed Forces in the European Theater of Operations

Vol. 3 No. 294 New York, N.Y.—London, England Wednesday, Oct. 13, 1943

1373 Treaty Gives Britain Azores Bases

That USED to Be One of Biggest FW Assembly Plants

U.S. Army Air Force Photo

[illegible] of smoke rising in the wake of the B17 Virgin's Delight is the plant which is believed to have [illegible] nearly half of Germany's FW190s. The photograph leaves no doubt of the thoroughness with which the Forts wiped it off the map. The plant is at Marienburg, East Prussia—200 miles beyond Berlin.

Vital Outpost in War On U-Boats Acquired In Deal With Portugal

Churchill Dusts Off Old Pact, Takes Axis By Surprise; British Troops Are Reported Already in Isles

Bantam Portugal, which has ruffled its feathers in Tokyo's nose the last week, threw total neutrality out the window yesterday by granting Britain bases in the Azores which will complete the great circle of island outposts guarding the all-vital Atlantic sea lanes.

Swiss reports last night said that Allied warships already had been patrolling off the Azores a day before the surprise agreement, under a Britain-Portugal treaty of 1373, was announced yesterday in the House of Commons by Prime Minister Churchill, and Lisbon reports received in Madrid last night said that Portugal's Premier Salazar announced that British troops had disembarked in the islands.

This combined military and political bombshell must have caused an explosion of consternation in the mind of an evidently greatly surprised Adolf Hitler, that old and growing older one-time master of the war of nerves.

Talks a Complete Secret

For Churchill's announcement was the first word the world had had of negotiations leading to the agreement. The discussions had been kept a complete secret.

The Prime Minister drew a laugh in Commons when he solemnly began his revelation:

"I have an announcement to make to the House arising out of the treaty signed between this country and Portugal in the year 1373 between King Edward III and King Ferdinand and Queen Eleanor of Portugal."

The immediate effect of Portugal's action was the subject of hot speculation in London. First and foremost important result for the Allies will be to give them one more valuable base from which to combat the U-boat which, while beaten into submission this summer, is expected to return to the fray in full power this winter.

The Azores, a group of nine islands about 800 miles west of Portugal, constitute a vital crossroads of Atlantic shipping. They are about 1,000 miles from Newfoundland to the west and 1,400 miles from Britain to the east. From the isles, which contain a number of fine harbors and an excellent seaplane base, the Allies can complete an aerial umbrella over Atlantic convoys.

U.S. Ships May be Affected

So far as could be learned last night in London, United States ships will not be based in the Azores, but it was felt that normal refuelling restrictions in the islands would be relaxed for the benefit of Allied war and merchant craft. In this connection, it was recalled that in World War I the United States Navy set up a base in the Azores when the submarine problem became acute.

Washington was kept fully informed of negotiations for bases in the islands, which President Roosevelt said in his famous May 27, 1941, broadcast that he would not permit the Axis to occupy. It was said that the President expressed accord with the agreement prior to its announcement. The State Department approved the alliance officially after it was made public. Russia was informed of the agreement, but not of preliminary negotiations.

It was understood that Spain, a big question mark in the current international situation, was informed by her tiny neighbor of the agreement and presumably raised no objection.

Emphasis was placed in British Foreign Office circles on the assertion that Portugal still remained a neutral, although her relations with Japan have been strained of late owing to Japanese occupation of Portuguese Timor in the South Pacific.

The 570-year-old treaty, which has been renewed and broadened ten times, called directly for "mutual assistance."

Announcing that arrangements for the

(Continued on page 4)

Dnieper Battle Reaches Climax; Nazis Repulsed

German Resistance at Its Peak, but Reds Drive Forward Steadily

MOSCOW, Oct. 12 (UP)—The Battle of the Dnieper appeared to have reached a climax today as Russian spearheads drove forward around Kiev and before Gomel in spite of stiffening German resistance, now at its height.

Russian reinforcements poured across the Dnieper at scores of points without interruption, although the Germans threw in more and more tanks against the bridgeheads. Their tank losses were continuing to mount and today had become almost double what they were four days ago, a sharp indication that the peak of the German defensive movement has now been reached.

With the failure of each counter-attack against the bridgeheads the Russians seized the initiative and smashed forward again, backed up by a wealth of men, tanks and guns, rolling up behind them.

The plan of the Russian general staff was to try to overwhelm German resistance on the river itself by hitting strongly at as many points as possible, in the hope that in the end German resistance would be completely disorganized and the way opened for the next great advance towards the west.

One Russian thrust was directed against the Dnieper bend—from the rear. From the Kremenchug bridgehead Russian forces threatened the whole German position inside the bend along the Dnepropetrovsk-Zaparozhe line. If they were to break through the German defenses and sweep south here the Germans in the bend would be faced with headlong retreat—or another Stalingrad. This is why the Germans have tossed large reserves of tanks, planes and men into the battle of the Kremenchug bridgehead.

Farther north, the Russians struck a vital blow at Gomel by capturing Novo Belitza, a suburb three miles east of the German stronghold from which the vital Gomel-Pinsk communication line runs.

U.S. Could Have Captured Wake

Planes Flew 830 Sorties From Carrier Flotilla; Little Opposition

PEARL HARBOR, Oct. 12—Wake Island could have been "invaded and captured," but apparently the "high command didn't want the island this time," Mark Johnson, United Press war correspondent aboard the flagship aircraft-carrier during the attack, said today.

A concentration of aircraft-carriers, described as the biggest in the history of naval warfare, took part in the mission. fighters, torpedo-planes and dive-bombers flew more than 830 sorties against the island, the reporter said.

All air opposition was apparently eliminated on the first day. On the second day, the Japs sent air reinforcements but they did not send a single surface vessel to interfere.

Nearly every military target on the island was completely destroyed.

Long Attack to Celebes

ALLIED HQ, Southwest Pacific, Oct. 12—Liberators made a round trip flight of 2,400 miles from Australia to attack the Japanese-held Macassar island, in Dutch Celebes, for the fourth time in the war. Twenty-five tons of bombs were dropped, today's official communique said.

Chennault's Men Active

CHUNGKING, Oct. 13—Maj. Gen. Claire Chennault's 14th Air Force has carried out widespread missions in the past two days against targets in Yunnan, Indo-China and off the China coast. A small tanker was sunk and widespread damage was inflicted on airfields and military installations.

Casualties Total 114,359

WASHINGTON, Oct. 12—The announced casualties of the armed forces from the outbreak of the war to date total 114,359, the Office of War Information announced yesterday. This figure, arrived at by combining War and Navy department reports include 22,892 dead, 32,912 missing, 33,072 wounded and 25,483 prisoners of war.

Mrs. FDR 59 Years Old

HYDE PARK, N.Y., Oct. 12 (AP)—Dinner with a few friends and a new "hair do" were Mrs. Eleanor Roosevelt's only concessions to her 59th birthday.

Bombless Forts Blast Path for Rest—Berlin

On an obvious "fishing expedition" for information, German radio newscasters said that "super Flying Fortresses," armed as aerial dreadnoughts but carrying no bombs, were leading USAAF raids against the Reich.

Describing the planes as "four-engined fighters," the German broadcasters said they mounted .50 cal. guns at several more places in the plane than standard B17s. The "fighter Forts" were flying ahead of bomb-carrying formations to clear the sky of Luftwaffe fighters, according to the radio.

From USAAF sources in the ETO there was, naturally, no comment.

U.S. to Eat Less Meat; Army, Allies Need More

WASHINGTON, Oct. 12 (AP)—Americans will eat less meat in 1944, because of a 25 per cent increase in military and lend-lease requirements, the Bureau of Agricultural Economics announced yesterday. Total food production in 1943 will be five per cent. higher than in 1942, the bureau said.

Bombs Batter Corfu Airfield

Crete, Rhodes Also Blasted As Battle in Italy Slows To a Virtual Halt

ALLIED HQ, Italy, Oct. 12—With land fighting bogged down in rain and mud across the entire Italian front, Mitchell bombers flew from bases in Italy yesterday to deliver a smashing blow at a Nazi airfield on Corfu, the strategic Greek island dominating the entrance to the Adriatic.

In addition to the Mitchells' attack, escorting Lightnings scored two direct hits on an enemy merchant vessel in Corfu harbor.

New raids also were made by Liberators on airfields at Rhodes and Crete, in which bombs were dropped on buildings and parked aircraft.

Torrential rains virtually brought land activity in the Italian battle to a halt. While the left wing of the Fifth Army continued to bring up strength for an eventual crossing of the Volturno River, some slight gains were made in the central sector by other units of the Fifth, and farther to the east by one Eighth Army column driving northwest from Foggia.

Allied planes continued to sweep behind the enemy lines, attacking communication points.

B17 Gunners Claim 12 Nazi Planes

AN EIGHTH BOMBER STATION, Oct. 12—Gunners of the B17 Ohio Air Force claimed 12 enemy aircraft destroyed for a new ETO record Sunday in a 400-mile running battle to get home from Munster, the day's target in Germany. The claims have been confirmed by Bomber Command.

The total, which included a Dornier 217 bomber, was one higher than the previous mark of 11, and may be a world record for enemy airplanes destroyed by one aircraft.

High scorer of the crew was 2/Lt. Robert H. Winnerman, of Newark, N.J., who was credited with three planes. Winnerman, the bombardier, manned the center and right nose guns, and destroyed the Do217 as well as an FW190 and an Me210.

The Ohio Air Force, piloted by 2/Lt. John Richey, of Steubenville, Ohio, had just completed its bombing run over Munster and was making the turn for home when the B17 on its left was knocked out of formation. A moment later a plane in front of and above the Ohio Air Force was hit and Richey was forced to swerve out of formation, and before he could rejoin the rest of his squadron Nazi interceptors swooped in and the plane was left to fight its way home alone.

"Just like all B17 pilots, I've always wanted to see what a Fort could do: well, I found out Sunday," said Richey. "That plane did a slow roll, just as if it had been a fighter. And every man on the crew has bruises to prove it. That's about as evasive as evasive action can get."

(A slow roll, basic fighter maneuver, is virtually unheard of in a four-engined bomber. It involves rolling a plane completely over around its line of flight.)

With the Ohio Air Force separated from its formation, the Luftwaffe threw everything it could spare at the ship, and crewmen reported that several times twin-engined planes fired rockets at the Fort from a distance, while faster fighters harried them from close range.

Gunners said that from the time they left Munster probably 200 fighters attacked them, with one relay picking up when another had run out of gas. Not a single man on the Ohio Air Force crew was wounded.

Everyone on the plane was credited with at least one enemy aircraft except the pilot and co-pilot, who fired no guns but spent the entire time in heaving the big Fort around the air in evasive action. Co-pilot was 2 Lt. Thomas A. Helman, of Medford, Ore.

Radio operators seldom get credit for an enemy plane, since their one gun has a limited traverse immediately above the ship, but T/Sgt. Milton V. Lane, of Collingswood, N.J., shot down a Ju88 during a heavy attack.

Two gunners got two planes each: S/Sgt. Jack T. Gesser, of Bellevue, Ky., tail gunner, knocked down an Me109F

(Continued on page 4)

Fort From Canada Gets Lost, Lands in Spain

SEVILLE, Spain, Oct. 12 (AP)—A U.S. Flying Fortress, one of a group of ten which became separated by storms while flying to Africa, made a forced landing three miles south of Seville Sunday night. The crew said that after flying 18 hours from Canada they lost their way and circled Tablada airport, Seville.

Their gasoline exhausted, the weary crew landed safely Sunday night and surrendered their ship to the Spanish authorities.

THE STARS AND STRIPES

Oran Daily

Vol. 1 - No. 119 - Thursday, October 14, 1943 | One Franc | Daily Newspaper For U. S. Armed Forces

Italy Declares War On Nazis; Gets Status Of Co-Belligerent

About-Face Comes After 3 Years Of Axis Partnership

ALLIED FORCE HEADQUARTERS, Oct. 13—The Italian government of Marshal Pietro Badoglio today declared war on Nazi Germany and received the status of co-belligerent from the Allies.

The declaration of war constituted one of the most amazing about-faces in all history. It was on June 11, 1940, that Il Duce took Italy into the war against Great Brittain, and as recently as two months ago Marshal Badoglio, having succeeded Benito Mussolini as Premier, was still calling for the continuation of hostilities against the Allies.

Telling the Italian people that "There will not be peace in Italy as long as a single German remains upon our soil," the Marshal informed his nation that "His Majesty, the King, has given me the task of announcing today, the 13th day of October, the declaration of war against Germany." The Italian ambassador in Madrid was instructed to inform the German ambassador there of the declaration.

There was no immediate statement concerning the number of Italian soldiers ready for action against the Germans, but almost the entire Italian fleet is already available to the Allies. Only yesterday Prime Minister Winston Churchill told the House of Commons that more than 100 Italian warships and more than 150,000 tons of Italian merchant shipping are now in Allied hands. He announced that the position of the ships and their crews is still under active consideration. So far there have been no indications that Italian soldiers are fighting alongside the Americans and British in Italy.

The war declaration recalled the fact that Marshal Badoglio had conducted peace negotiations with the Allies under the very noses of the Germans, and then announced the armistice on September 8, the evening before the invasion. The armistice was signed secretly in a command tent in Sicily, with Gen. G. Castellano representing Italy.

In the official proclamation on the state of war, the Marshal reviewed the record of German ill-treatment of Italians since the armistice. From that time on, he said the Germans not only disarmed Italian units, but "in most cases, they proceeded to a decisive attack on our troops."

"But German arrogance and ferocity did not stop here," he continued. Even while the Germans were allied to them, he pointed out, they committed "abuses of power, robbery and violence of all kinds" in Catania. More savage incidents against the unarmed population took place in Calabria, in the Puglie, and in the Salerno area, "but where the ferocity of the enemy surpassed every limit of the human imagination was at Naples."

Marshal Badoglio called on the Italians to march forward, shoulder to shoulder, "with our friends of the United States, Great Britain, of Russia, and of all the United Nations." Italian troops in Yugoslavia, Greece and Albania were ordered to resist "to the last man."

The Allied acceptance of Italy as a co-belligerent was announced in a declaration issued simultaneously in Washington, London, and Moscow. In the statement, President Roosevelt, Prime Minister Churchill and Marshal Stalin made it clear that the relationship of co-belligerency cannot affect the terms of the armistice between Italy and the Allies, and that the armistice can be modified only by

(Continued on Page 2)

Battles Rage In Kiev Outskirts, Gomel Streets

Russians Pour Reinforcements Into Ukraine

LONDON, Oct. 13—Fighting raged in the outskirts of Kiev today at the same time as Soviet troops were hammering their bloody path into the streets of Gomel in White Russia, correspondents reported from Moscow tonight. The Russian offensive against Kiev continues to gain strength, it was said, since powerful German counterattacks have been unable to halt the stream of Red Army troops crossing the Dnieper river on pontoon bridges north of the city. An ever-present Red Air Force protective umbrella has played an important part in breaking up enemy resistance along the river, Moscow sources indicated.

At Kremenchug, 170 miles further down the Dnieper, the Russians are steadily widening their wedge on the western bank and are pouring large bodies of troops into the fight for the last important German bases in the Ukraine. The Russian advance in White Russia continued in spite of the heavy autumn rains which have begun "in earnest", one reporter said.

The battle for Gomel was in its final stages today, and a Soviet victory was expected within a short time. German resistance has been as stiff here as in any city the Nazis have given up this year, but the overwhelming power of Soviet armor and infantry was slowly battering down the last fortifications of the city.

In the Vitebsk sector, however, mud has taken over the direction of the current campaign, and the Soviets have shown signs of floundering in highways that now resemble quagmires, reports said. The wooded and marshy terrain has added to the Russian difficulties, and the Germans apparently will receive a slight respite from Red Army pressure. No rain appeared in the south, though, and the Russians began their first softening up bombardment of the Crimea since the Nazis were driven from the Kuban. Heavy Soviet guns have started hurling shells across the narrow Kerch straits separating the Taman peninsula from the Crimea.

Pointing up a full-scale onslaught against the Crimea in the near future, a Soviet landing party of the Azov fleet Monday night landed in the rear of the enemy lines near the settlement of Yalta, an official communique reported. Final results of the amphibious raid were not announced, but the party held two German attacking waves with great valor, the announcement added.

Repeal Of Chinese Exclusion Act Asked

WASHINGTON, Oct. 13—President Roosevelt asked Congress yesterday to strike the Chinese exclusion act of 1882 from the statute books and extend the privileges of citizenship to Chinese residents of the United States. "Such action," he said, "not only will strengthen China's faith in her fighting Allies but will correct a historic mistake and silence the distorted Japanese propaganda."

Legislation pending in the House would permit 105 Chinese to enter this country annually and grant citizenship privileges to Chinese already here. Mr. Roosevelt emphasized that this small quota would put Chinese immigrants on a par with those of other nations and could not reasonably result in unemployment or provide competition in the search for jobs. It would be additional proof, the President added, that we regard China not only as a partner in waging war but that we shall regard her as a partner in days of peace.

British Midget Subs Hit Tirpitz

LONDON, Oct. 13 — Midget British submarines, passing through mine fields and negotiating the intricate Norwegian fiords, have carried out a successful attack on the German battle fleet lying in Alton fiord, the admiralty announced yesterday.

The 35,000 ton battleship Tirpitz, sister ship of the Bismarck, was badly damaged during the daring raid. Air photographs taken after the battle show the Tirpitz surrounded by thick oil which covered the fiord where she lay and extended more than two miles from her berth. The photographs also show a number of small unidentified craft alongside the battleship, presumedly repair crafts or ships which supply power and lift.

The attack took place on September 22 but lack of enough evidence of the result delayed the communique. Three of the small subs are missing from this attack.

NAAF Bombers Concentrate On Italy

ALLIED FORCE HEADQUARTERS, Oct. 13—NAAF planes blasted trains, trucks, roads and bridges in Italy yesterday as unfavorable weather conditions over the target areas prevented continued bombing of other Axis positions. It was the first time in eight days that airfields in the Adriatic area were not visited by Allied bombers.

On the 8th Army front in Italy, USAAF Warhawks smashed an entire train and destroyed eight additional railway cars filled with trucks. The bomb-carrying P-40's caught the train on the coastal railway northwest of Termoli and Pescara, and crews observed numerous fires and explosions after making direct hits. Two locomotives were included in the bag. Other Warhawks, paving the way for Allied troops in the central sector, attacked gun positions at Ceremaggiore and surrounding areas. RAF Baltimores smashed road junctions and other enemy communications near Landiano and at Vasto, 20 miles north of Termoli.

Before dawn this morning RAF Wellingtons of the Strategic Air Force hammered railway bridges and yards at Civitavecchia on the west coast of Italy northwest of Rome. The crews reported explosion after explosion among the choked points at this repeatedly visited target. A large fire was seen burning in a nearby barracks. Not a plane was lost in the day's operations.

Photographs taken of the October 10 raid on Latoi near Athens by B-17's reveal that one-third of the planes on the field were destroyed, it is now announced.

Naples' Railway Service Resumed

NAPLES, Oct. 13—The first railway service in and out of Naples since June was inaugurated yesterday with a run of the "General Greunther" special, named after Lt. Gen. Mark W. Clark's chief of staff, Maj. Gen. Alfred M. Greunther. The run was experimental, aimed at testing the ground against time bombs and hidden mines left behind by the Germans along the track at intervals of only a few feet at many places. The trip was successful and the line pronounced fit for regular runs henceforth. U.S. engineers repaired the railway line and put locomotives in working conditions by assembling spare parts from more than a score of engines. The "General Clark" is the name given to another Italian locomotive.

Allies Gain In Central Sector; Take San Croce

ALLIED FORCE HEADQUARTERS, Oct. 13—Allied troops in Italy made extensive advances in the central sector yesterday, but along the Volturno river 5th Army troops were still jockeying for position before making the difficult crossing. Activity of the 5th Army was again restricted to patrols which reported the enemy is continuing to build up his forces to considerable strength. German artillery kept up a heavy shelling of positions on the south side of the river.

The Allied line in the central sector was further straightened out when our troops pushed ahead nine miles to capture San Croce, north of the Calore river and northeast of Pontelandolfo, which was taken two days ago. Eighth Army units took Riccia, southwest of Gambalesa, and then met the heaviest fighting of the day before they occupied Bonefro, four miles northwest of Colletorto.

Meanwhile, advance British patrols reached San Elia, six miles southwest of Colletorto. The progress in the central sector placed Allied forces within striking distance of the important town of Campobasso, which is astride the main road leading from Termoli in the east clear down through Italy and ending up in the Volturno river area. Capture of Campobasso would give the Allies the use of this important north-south artery, and would enable our forces to threaten the enemy's Volturno positions.

The 8th Army advanced about four miles up the east coast road in the Termoli area. In most of this fighting Allied troops met only spasmodic enemy resistance, and moved ahead despite demolitions and the difficulties of the mountainous country.

Fighting Heavy Near Finschafen

ALLIED SOUTH PACIFIC HEADQUARTERS, Oct. 13—While Australian troops, forcing their way down the Ramu valley toward Madang in New Guinea, met some resistance from Japanese defending hilltop positions, the most bitter fighting on the island today was in the Finschafen area, where mopping-up operations continued. Although trapped and surrounded, the Japanese lost more than 400 dead.

In the air, Japanese fighters and bombers attacked Lae and Wewak on New Guinea. The three night raids over Lae were described as "light and ineffective." Over Wewak fighter patrols reported intercepting an enemy formation of 32 fighters and 12 bombers, shooting down eight Jap fighters and probably destroying two others. On the western end of the island, in Dutch New Guinea, Allied Liberators bombed the ports of Manokwari, Bira and Fakfak, where they sank a Japanese tanker. Medium bombers also attacked the Japanese-held island of Amboina, which lies off the west coast of Dutch New Guinea.

In the Solomons, Japanese torpedo planes attacked Allied shipping near Guadalcanal, while Al-

(Continued on Page 2)

AA Guns Credited With 646 Planes

Allied antiaircraftsmen have accounted for a confirmed total of 646 enemy planes in North Africa and Sicily, the antiaircraft and coastal defense section, AFHQ, officially announced yesterday.

Of these, 526 were shot out of North African skies, 118 out of Sicilian. The majority of planes accounted for by AA, it was said, were JU-88's.

Figures for Italy have not yet been released, but the AA and CD Section, AFHQ, reports that one Bofors gun crew, at the time of the 5th Army's initial landings, turned its attention to ground targets and knocked out two enemy tanks with only five rounds.

U. S. Shares Use Of Azore Islands

WASHINGTON — The United States has the right to share wartime bases in the Azores under the agreement between Great Britain and Portugal, President Roosevelt disclosed yesterday after telling correspondents that the agreement was planned when Prime Minister Winston Churchill visited the White House last May.

It was recalled here that U. S. Naval forces were based on the Atlantic islands during World War I and Mr. Roosevelt said that there would be no question but that joint operations would be conducted from the strategic Azores whenever necessary.

In addition to shortening the air route for warplanes of all types, use of the bases in the Azores will give the Allies new advantages in the war against German submarines. Observers pointed out that transportation of American troops will be made safer because of the strategic position of the islands in the Atlantic approaches to Gibraltar.

Allied troops have already landed in the Azores it was announced, but President Roosevelt, in answer to a question, said Portugal's Cape Verde islands, 300 miles west of Dakar, did not enter the picture at the present time.

Although the German propaganda line emphasized that Berlin realized Lisbon submitted to the agreement under pressure, and that Germany would maintain friendly relations with Portugal, Lisbon and other large cities last night were blacked out. The war regulation was said to be part of the Portuguese government's offer to prepare the people in the event the nation decided to abandon neutrality.

America, Japan To Exchange Nationals

MARMOGOA, PORTUGUESE INDIA, Oct. 13—Fifteen hundred Americans interned by Japan will be exchanged for a similar number of Japanese during the coming week end at this neutral port. The Swedish repatriation liner Gripsholm coming from America and the liner Teia Maru from Japan are expected to arrive here Friday carrying in addition to their passengers 2,000 tons of Red Cross parcels.

The Gripsholm has 1,500 tons comprising 51,000 parcels for the U.S. nationals in China, while the Jap liner has 500 tons for the Japanese nationals in the U.S. The exchange operations will last for six days.

Front Line Paper of the 5th Army

THE STARS AND STRIPES

COMBAT EDITION

VOL. I, NO. 1 Italy, 20 October, 1943 FREE

Russians Expand River Bridgehead

MOSCOW, Oct. 19 — Russian troops at various points along the vast Dniepr River battle line were fighting fiercely today to expand their bridgeheads. The most important gains of the day were made southeast of Kremenchug in the center of the Kiev-Dnepropetrvosk section. There, on the lower Dnieper, the Russians broke through to establish a flanking threat to Dnepropetrovsk.

At the far south of the line, near the Sea of Azov, street fighting in Melitopol grew into a full-scale battle of tanks and heavy artillery. The Russians progressed in the city to strengthen their hold within it.

German resistance along the Dnieper is desperate. Under penalty of death Hitler has ordered his troops to hold the right bank of the river, after they had failed to hold the left. Fresh Nazi divisions are being brought up and thrown into battle in incessant counter-attacks in which they are suffering enormous losses.

The advance of the Russians southeast of Kremenchug took them five miles beyond the right bank of the river. Several villages were taken.

In the middle reaches of the Dnieper, south of Kiev, Russian troops improved their positions on the right bank. They also advanced slightly north of Kiev.

The Germans resistance north and south of Kiev is especially strong. Russian strategy aims at outflanking this fortress city. Its vast network of fortifications and minefields make it virtually impregnable against frontal assault.

Japs Blasted

ALLIED Hq., China, Oct. 19 — Lieut. Gen. Joseph Stilwell announced that American bombers inflicted heavy casualties on Japanese troop concentrations and supply dumps along the Salween River.

Numero Uno

Presented herewith is the first issue of the Combat Edition of *The Stars and Stripes*, country cousin of the military newspapers printed and published by U. S. Army personnel a Algiers Oran Casablanca and Palermo.

This newspaper is printed and published primarily for the fighting men of the Fifth Army in the front lines. It is our hope to build up our circulation rapidly to allow every Fifth Army soldier in the front lines to read the news of the day, what is happening at home, what is happening across the next hill from him, what is going on in the sports world, how the war is going in the South Pacific and on the Russian front.

The unit is equipped for mobility (even though some one made away with our presses before they reached us) and we hope to move forward as the battle line moves toward Berlin.

Moscow Confab Opens

MOSCOW, Oct. 19 — The Three Power Conference of delegates from the State Department and Foreign Offices of the United States, Great Britain and Russia opened here today. Preliminaries were under way within two hours of the arrival of U. S. Secretary Cordell Hull and British Foreign Secretary Anthony Eden.

Giant four-motored planes brought the American and British representatives. Soviet fighters escorted them for part of the trip and were diving and zooming over the airfield as they came in to land at the Moscow military airport.

A large number of State Department and Foreign Office officials accompanied Hull and Eden.

The Russian Commissar for Foreign Affairs Viacheslav M. Molotov was at the airport to meet them. There were bands and crowds of pressmen and photographers. A military cadet guard of honor marched past the delegates as they left their plane.

"Diplomats must learn from soldiers who keep step harmoniously, and we must also keep step," Molotov remarked to Eden.

Allies Advance Beyond Volturno

ALLIED Hq., Oct. 19—The Allied line in Italy moved forward today. The Fifth Army took six towns as it strengthened its position beyond the Volturno River. The Eighth Army captured Montcilfone.

Along the Volturno, Gen. Mark Clark's troops seized Gioia, Liberi, Alvignano, Pontelatone and Brezza. On the right flank of the Army San Stefano as taken by the advancing Americans.

Gen. Kesslring's forces moving back from the river were faced with an increasing threat from Gen. Clark's swing north of Capua which penetrated four miles deeper in the last 24 hours. This is in a rugged region with many ridges which afford the Germans excellent defensive points.

The Fifth Army is now firmly established across the Volturno from the sea to Capua. Fresh bridges are being constructed. More tanks and heavy equipment are being moved north of the river.

The Americans now face an uphill fight for Mt. Messico ridge along the west coast. They are also confronted with a rugged sector near the Garigliano river. The present front is slightly in advance of the line; mouth

(*Continued on Page 4*)

Prisoners Exchanged

GOTHENBURG, Sweden, Oct. 19—Trains arrived here today bringing British wounded prisoners and other prisoners from Germany for repatriation to Great Britain. They were transferred to the Swedish liner Bromtningham.

There were 1,250 men among the British prisoners. Within the next few days the Swedish liner, with the British hospital ship, Atlantis, and the Empress of Russia, which brought Germans who are being repatriated to their homes, will be leaving for Britain.

FIFTH ARMY
THE STARS AND STRIPES
COMBAT EDITION

VOL. 1, NO. VII | BE ALERT AND LIVE | Italy, 27 October, 1943

Nazis Flee Russ Trap

Fifth Gains Heights

FIFTH ARMY HEADQUARTERS, Oct. 27—General Mark Clark's Fifth Army has pushed forward another several miles on both sides of the Volturno River and had, yesterday at noontime, gained strategic heights northeast of Pietravairano.

This advance on the right flank of the Fifth was coupled with an advance of central front Fifth Army forces as far as Ailano, southeast of Pratella. Meanwhile, the left flank has been pushing strongly against well entrenched German forces on the west coast along the Gulf of Gaeta.

Allied air forces coordinating their attacks with the Fifth have put down a heavy bomb load on Vairano, continuing the far-ranging fighter and bomber activity which has been directed effectively against Nazi installations over a large area of Italy. German air activity over the front has been meager.

ALLIED HQ., Oct. 26 (Delayed),—Before a determined Allied push that captured strategic towns, the Germans were withdrawing today towards rugged country which will give them their best natural defenses short of Rome.

The troops of Gen. Kesselring were retiring upon a high Apennine mountain line from Mt. Massico on the

(*Continued on Page* 4)

Nazis Need Machinery

ALGIERS, Oct. 26—Italian workers were warned to prevent machinery from falling into German hands, in a United Nations broadcast tonight. It was pointed out that the Germans need Italian machinery to replace losses they have suffered in Allied air raids.

The Italians were urged to frustrate the German plans. It is much better, the broadcast said, to have broken down machinery in a factory than to let the Germans dismantle it and take it to Germany.

You're In Italy

FIFTH ARMY HEADQUARTERS, Oct. 27—You fellows on the Fifth Army front are now officially in Italy. The Censor says so. He says it's OK to announce your change of station in the datelines of your letters.

But that's just about all you may reveal. Mention of cities and identifiable geographical characteristics of the country is forbidden. However, if you've got any combat experiences you wish to write about, go ahead—but keep out information useful to the enemy.

Steamrolling Reds

MOSCOW, Oct. 26—Striking accounts of the immensity of the battle now taking place in the Dnieper bend are coming from correspondents at the front. Every story emphasizes the near-panic among the Germans and the might of the Russian onslaught.

The Russian drives from the north and the south into the bend are developing into the largest penetration battles ever fought by the Red Army, reports a Swiss correspondent.

He says that Berlin is amazed at the vast number of troops and heavy weapons the Russians are throwing incessantly into the battle.

For nearly three months now, he points out, the Russians have been pouring in men, tanks, and planes from a seemingly inexhaustable reservoir.

The German armies inside and below the Dnieper bend are in about as complete a tangle as Soviet strategy could devise, writes another correspondent.

Going Up Front

Starting with this issue *The Stars and Stripes Combat Edition* will be distributed up at the front line. APO circulation in rear areas will be curtailed.

Disaster Looms

MOSCOW, Oct. 26—Disaster was growing ever more imminent today for the German army battered by the Russians within the great bend of the Dnieper River.

Moving in three irresistable prongs, the Soviet troops were swiftly closing the last avenue of withdrawal for the Nazi divisions inside the bend. Miles in the rear of these Germans, the Russians had only to shut a narrow opening and cut the last railway line westwards to complete their trap.

The Germans, their communications in chaos, were racing against time to get out of the bend, moving away from Dnepropetrovsk and the Dnieper River as fast as they could. The roads were littered with German dead, smashed tanks and broken lorries. Rarely in this war have the Nazis been so exposed to unrelenting attack from all sides.

One Russian prong was moving upon KrivoiRog, city of iron and steel industries, in the heart of the bend. Another was stabbing south and southwest from captured Dnepropetrovsk. The third, much farther to the south, was sweeping west from Melitopol across the open steppes of Nogaisk.

The sector of greatest menace to the Germans was the railway line from KrivoiRog northwestwards to Znamenka. The cutting of this line will nearly seal the fate of the Germans, closing their last rail exit. The Russians were within five miles of the line today.

Named For Cities

WASHINGTON, Oct. 26—Eighty United States cities and one Alaskan city, as well as 21 British colonies and protectorates, will be honored by having new U. S. or British frigates bearing their names, it was announced today by U. S. Secretary of the Navy Frank Knox.

The first of several U. S. frigates and twin-screw corvettes of new design were built in Canada.

1D. THE STARS AND STRIPES 1D.
Daily Newspaper of U.S. Armed Forces in the European Theater of Operations
Vol. 4 No. 1 New York, N.Y.—London, England Tuesday, Nov. 2, 1943

Moscow Accord Bared; Unity Cemented

U.S. May Seize Struck Mines

530,000 Out; War Plants Shy of Coal

FDR Ready to Act; UMW Is Reported Frigid to Peace Offer

WASHINGTON, Nov. 1—An executive order under which the Government would again take over strike-bound coal mines was awaiting President Roosevelt's signature today, the United Press reported, as the United Mine Workers Policy Committee deliberated here whether to order its 530,000 striking members back to work or officially sanction their pay-increase demands.

It was understood that the President would proclaim Federal operation of the mines—the "decisive action" he had promised—if the union leaders failed to heed his warning and end America's fourth great work stoppage in six months in the vital coal industry.

As the nation tensely waited for either executive or union action to end the walkout, which became general at midnight last night, its impact was felt almost immediately in the war plants which depend on an uninterrupted coal supply.

Steel Output Slashed

The great steel-producing mills in the Birmingham area of Alabama announced that their output had been curtailed drastically. In Pittsburgh, the site of many of America's largest steel plants, it was reported that there was only enough coal to last for 12 days.

Fuel Administrator Harold L. Ickes stopped all domestic anthracite deliveries of more than half a ton. At the same time, he prohibited all shipments to domestic consumers who had more than a ten-day supply on hand.

This diverted coal, it was apparent, would be used for war plants.

It seemed unlikely tonight that the strike would be ended by John L. Lewis' UMW. Although the union as yet has issued no call for a strike, it made no appeal to halt the walkout or postpone the end of the no-strike truce set by Lewis June 23 at the end of the third work stoppage.

Little Hope of Settlement

There was little hope in Government circles that the 200 conferring union leaders would accept the War Labor Board's offer of a daily wage increase of 32.2 cents and other concessions amounting to an additional 20 to 25 cents a day instead of the $2-a-day raise the miners had demanded. Lewis, who called the meeting of the Policy Committee, already has indicated opposition to the Government's plan.

President Roosevelt himself already has established a precedent for federal seizure and operation of the pits if the union does not accept the government's terms.

When confronted by a similar situation early last May the President instructed Fuel Administrator Ickes to take immediate possession of all struck mines and authorized use of the U.S. Army, if necessary, to do so.

If the President again takes this action he will have at his command the drastic powers given him by Congress after the June strike to threaten the union leaders with heavy fines or imprisonment.

The Connally-Smith-Harness anti-strike law, passed by Congress over the Presi-

(*Continued on page 4*)

Moscow Pact in Brief

Representatives of the United States, the United Kingdom and Soviet Russia at the Moscow conference agreed upon:

1—Establishment of a European Advisory Commission in London to study and make recommendations on common problems.

2—Establishment of an "advisory council for matters relating to Italy," to be composed of representatives of the three governments and also of the French Committee of National Liberation. Provision also is made for the addition of representatives of Greece and Yugoslavia.

3—Restoration of Austria's independence after the cessation of hostilities.

4—Establishment of democratic government in Italy.

5—Provisions to return Germans who have committed atrocities in occupied territories to them for trial and punishments according to the local laws.

6—Collaboration and cooperation in the post-war era.

7—Principles for a general international organization to be established at the earliest practicable date.

8—A cooperative plan to regulate armament of nations in post-war era.

Great Invasion Army Shaped In Rehearsals on British Coast

By Charles F. Kiley
Stars and Stripes Staff Writer

U.S. ASSAULT TRAINING CENTER, England, Nov. 1—American assault divisions, already designed to attack Nazi-held shores of Europe, are staging their rehearsal for the invasion here along the English coast, where thousands of troops are taking part in the most intensive amphibious exercises undertaken by U.S. forces in this theater.

The large-scale invasion maneuvers, coordinating operations between the Army, Navy and Air Force, have been in progress for several weeks, but not until now has censorship allowed such a disclosure.

"Never in all history has there been an attack like the one we propose," Col. Paul W. Thompson, 37-year-old commander of the Assault Training Center and one of America's leading experts on German warfare, told reporters. "The men who will undertake this tremendously important task must be thoroughly acquainted with the job, and we are giving them the training here."

The technique employed in these amphibious exercises leading up to the "unparalleled attack," according to Col. Thompson, was decided during a 30-day conference between Army, Navy, Marine and Air Force experts who were associated with the planning of, or had taken active parts in, the invasions of North Africa, Sicily, Italy and islands in the southwest Pacific.

A great many improvements in tactics previously used by invasion forces are incorporated in those developed for the training of troops here, Col. Thompson said.

The forces undergoing this specialized assault training are not hand-picked, but are hard-bitten infantry soldiers, most of whom are getting their first taste of amphibious exercises.

In planning a training area, Col. Thompson and his staff reproduced fortifications corresponding with those the enemy has stretched along the continental European coastline, details of which were gathered by aerial reconnaissance, secret service and from reports of Dieppe. On the beaches and beyond the sand dunes of this sector of England are concrete pillboxes, machine-gun nests, coastal gun locations, thousands of feet

(*Continued on page 2*)

Elections Today In Four States

Democratic Win in N.Y. Would Spoil Dewey's Plan to Run in '44

WASHINGTON, Nov. 1—New York, New Jersey, Pennsylvania and Kentucky voters will give the nation tomorrow its first test of Democratic and Republican strength prior to the opening of next year's Presidential campaign.

Nation-wide interest centered on New York's contest for lieutenant governor, because of its bearing on the national elections. If the Republican candidate, Joe Hanley, defeats the Democratic and American Labor Party choice, Lt. Gen. William N. Haskell, Gov. Thomas E. Dewey will be free to declare his bid for the GOP's Presidential nomination.

Dewey, the leading Republican aspirant, according to a straw poll conducted by Fortune magazine, would be honor-bound to remain in Albany if Haskell should win, as his resignation to run for President would give the state a Democratic executive.

Election in New Jersey

In New Jersey, former Senator Walter Edge, Herbert Hoover's ambassador to France, was running for governor against the Democratic mayor of Newark, Vincent Murphy.

Some political circles looked for the Jersey election to supply a gauge of Wendell L. Willkie's popularity and his chances to gain a second Republican nomination for President. The 1940 GOP candidate last week endorsed Edge in a speech at Paterson in which he made a bitter attack on President Roosevelt's foreign policy.

Kentucky's governor, Lyter Donaldson, was opposed in his bid for re-election by Republican Judge Simeon Willis.

In Philadelphia's mayoralty race, Democrats banked on William Bullitt, former ambassador to Russia and France, to end 60 years of Republican municipal rule. His opponent was Bernard Samuel.

Most political observers predicted Kentucky would go Democratic, New York and New Jersey Republican and Bullitt would be defeated.

Bananas Sought To Save a Life

An appeal for bananas to help save the life of an English child suffering from a rare disease was made to members of the U.S. forces yesterday through The Stars and Stripes.

In the belief that American ferry pilots, Air Force men or merchant marine personnel may have access to a supply, a social worker called the U.S. Army's attention to the case of three-year-old Peter James Brockwell, who is suffering from coeliac disease.

Bananas are essential for his diet, since the boy's system can derive no nourishment from ordinary fats, it was explained. Without them his health is deteriorating rapidly, a doctor said.

If any branch of the U.S. forces can supply bananas, communicate either with The Stars and Stripes or directly with Mayday Hospital, Croydon, Surrey.

British First Sea Lord Lauds USN Enterprise

ALLIED HQ, North Africa, Nov. 1—Adm. Sir Andrew Cunningham, new British first sea lord, in a letter to Vice Adm. Henry K. Hewitt, USN, today lauded the "high standard of courage and enterprise shown by the U.S. Naval forces" in the Mediterranean.

Adm. Cunningham said, "great things have been achieved" through the close cooperation of the U.S. and British navies.

Solid Front Erected To Hasten Nazi End, Chart Peace Course

Joint Commission to Be Set Up in London; Austria Promised Independence; China In on Agreement

The decisions reached at the Moscow conference were announced simultaneously in Washington, London and Moscow last night in one of World War II's most important declarations.

It assured the people of the increasingly victorious United Nations—and warned the waning Axis powers—that there was unquestionable unity among the crusaders against totalitarianism; that the military plans for quick victory had been studied in great detail; that there would be as close collaboration after the war as there is now, and that many of the steps to be taken in re-establishing Europe under a democratic setup already were in the process of being planned.

The announcement, vague though it was as to the imminence of the great Allied blow at Europe, was of such a nature as to offer Germany—already beset with invasion fears and striving to brake a downhill plunge toward defeat—no hope of escaping the demanded "unconditional surrender."

Indeed, the announced decisions singled out Germany as the arch foe in the Western world and indicated an attitude of lenience for other peoples—the Italians and the Austrians, for example—who had fallen under her influence years before.

Plan Independence for Austria

Six declarations set forth the main results of the conference:

Austria, as the first nation to be overrun by the Nazis, should be given her independence under a democratic regime after the war.

Italy is to be helped in establishing a government of and for the people.

War criminals, sponsors of atrocities in occupied countries, will be handed over to the governments of those countries for trial and punishment.

A practicable method of regulating armaments in the post-war period is to be established.

A European Advisory Commission is to be established in London to make joint recommendations to the American, British and Russian Governments.

An advisory council on Italy is to be formed, with French, Greek and Jugoslav representation, as well as American, British and Russian.

Bid for Austrian Move

The agreement to give Austria an independent government of the people's choosing was regarded in some quarters as not only a promise to the nation which was first to feel Nazi aggression but also as a direct bid to the Austrian people to join other conquered countries in resistance to the Germans.

It was looked upon also as a possible factor in prompting revolt among Austrian troops now serving with the Wehrmacht.

The three-power conference was joined by still a fourth nation—China—in at least one stage, the declarations revealed. A Chinese signatory added his country's pledge to a "declaration of general security," which provided for closer collaboration than ever in the prosecution of the war and "in all matters pertaining to the surrender and disarmament of the enemies with which the four countries are respectively at war."

In this clause the one word "respectively" apparently alone kept Russia from becoming signatory to a joint pledge by her three partners to smash Japan. The stipulation was clear, however, through use of that word, that Russia, not being at war with Japan, would leave that task to the other three already seeking that end.

Observers throughout the United Nations hailed the sweeping declarations as a death-blow to Germany's most effec-

(*Continued on page 4*)

German Flight In South Turns Into Slaughter

Red Bombers Pound Nazi Columns; Thousands Taken Prisoner

The great Russian offensive south of the lower Dnieper last night had turned into a slaughter of routed and disorganized German forces being pounded to pieces by hundreds of Russian bombers.

Dispatches from Moscow said that the campaign which ensued in the drive west and south from Melitopol would go down in history as one of the most disastrous defeats the Germans ever have sustained.

With the Crimea already sealed off by Soviet forces which had by-passed the Perekop Isthmus, German columns retreating to the lower Dnieper were in chaotic condition. Their tanks, trucks, guns and men jamming roads leading to the river were mass targets for the Red Air Force.

A fast mobile column had penetrated to within 12 miles of Kahkova, the river crossing of the Dnieper opposite Beryslavl, while to the south, another Russian force was 40 miles from Kherson, where the Perekop-Nikolaiev railway crosses the lower Dnieper.

Behind these units were tens of thousands of Germans who had not managed to escape, and these were being mopped up. Thousands of prisoners were streaming to the rear, said Moscow in its first reference in some time to large numbers of captives being taken in the current great southern offensive.

Between Nikopol and Kahkova the Russians were within striking distance of the Dnieper, and German positions were being overrun at will.

Meanwhile, inside the Dnieper Bend, to the north and east of the great Russian victories, heavy fighting continued, particularly at Krivoi Rog as the Germans battled fiercely to keep open the neck of the "Dnieper sack" long enough for their troops to escape to the west.

Formulated the Eight-Point Pact

Cordell Hull — Anthony Eden — Vyacheslav Molotov

Their countries will cooperate in the Post-war era.

America's 4.2-Inch Mortar Has Power of 155Mm. Gun

OSHKOSH, Wis., Nov. 1 (AP)—America's secret weapon—a 4.2-inch mortar with the power of a 155mm. gun—is holding its own, workers at the factory producing it were told by Col. Harry Lebkicher, head of the Sixth Service Command's Chemical Warfare Service.

He said the weapon, which has seen action in all major theaters of war—the southwest Pacific, Attu, North Africa and Italy—could be carried by its crew to any advanced position and assembled in three minutes. Every two seconds, Col. Lebkicher disclosed, it poured out shells comparable to a 155mm. gun.

THE STARS AND STRIPES
ITALY

Vol. 1, No. 1, Wednesday, Nov. 10, 1943 — For U. S. Armed Forces — TWO LIRE

Vatican Raid Damages St. Peter's; Nazis Stiffen North of Isernia

Reds Threaten Break-Through In White Russia

Push 45 Miles From Kiev in Two Days

LONDON, Nov. 9—A large force of Russian tanks in rapid pursuit of the defeated Germans retreating from Kiev threatens to overwhelm the enemy in a greater break-through than at Melitopol, Reuter's correspondent in Moscow reported today. It was at Melitopol that the Soviets won the first great victory of the campaign that ended in the capture of Kiev and the fall of the Crimea.

Reuter's reported that in two days the Red Army has pushed 45 miles southwest beyond Kiev along the Fastov railway while to the northwest Soviet troops were already 31 miles from the Ukrainian capital.

On other active fronts the Russians were also gaining. At the eastern gateway to the Crimea, Red Army soldiers and marines were steadily closing in on Kerch from north and south in the face of stiff resistance. Troops which made new landings on the peninsula have been reinforced by tanks, Moscow radio reported.

To the north, the Russian drive toward the Baltic is proceeding through half frozen lakes and swamps. Although Moscow gave few details of fighting in this area, the German - controlled Scandinavian news agency reported that battles raging west of Nevel were even fiercer than those at Kiev. A fierce tank engagement is now in progress at Nevel, the agency added, with new and more powerful weapons being used by the Russians. "The Soviet Command has launched what appears to be a general offensive toward the Baltic," it stated.

Summing up the battle for Kiev, the Soviet Information Bureau disclosed that in three day's fighting 15,000 Germans were killed, 6,200 taken prisoner and 12 divisions routed.

Reinforced Germans Slow 5th Army Drive

WITH ALLIED TROOPS IN ITALY, Nov. 9—Heavy fighting was in progress northwest of Isernia and Venafro today as reinforced German troops attempted to stop dead the steady plodding advance of the 5th Army, while in the 8th Army sector the British consolidated their positions around the port of Vasto on the Adriatic.

The advance of Gen. Bernard Montgomery's men up the east coast of Italy was beginning to shape into a definite threat to the seven German divisions known to be committed to the defense of Rome according to authoritative military observers. But the stout resistance on the 5th Army front continued, and there was no indication of a withdrawal except possibly from the port and peninsula of Gaeta, 50 miles north of Naples.

Lt. Gen. Mark W. Clark's men are now on the edge of the town of Calabritto, five miles from the important communications center of Mignano amid the broken Apennine ridges. The fighting is being done in rugged country with movement being hampered by rain and mud, mines and demolition.

Before the 8th Army is a formidable German defense line—the Sangro river. Latest on-the-record information from Allied Force headquarters put their advance elements at about five miles from the river.

By air the Allies struck deep in northern Italy as heavy daylight bombers from the Mediterranean area made their first raid on the important ball-bearing works at Turin according to an Algiers broadcast. Close support air operations were limited by poor weather yesterday

THE ALLIED LINE in Italy runs from the mouth of the Garigliano River, on the west, to Venafro, taken by American troops of the 5th Army, thence across to the south side of the Trigno River. At a point 10 miles from the mouth of the Trigno the line crosses the river, then curves upward in a semi-circle to Vasto. 8th Army troops carved the semi-circle north of the Trigno in some of the bitterest fighting they have yet had in Italy.

Bombs Shatter Priceless Glass In Famed Church

Numerous priceless stained glass windows of world-famous St. Peter's in Vatican City were shattered in Friday night's bomb blast, the Vatican radio revealed yesterday. Among the more celebrated windows destroyed was the "Altar" in the Apse of St. Peter's. On Sunday morning, it was announced, worshippers were permitted inside St. Peter's after it was shut one full day for "urgent repairs."

It was also stated that the Vatican radio station, although near the bombed zone, had suffered only slightly.

Vatican authorities, meanwhile, kept silent on the nationality of the bombing planes. From Catholic churchmen throughout the world messages of sympathy poured into the Vatican. Among the typical ones was a note from the Primate of Ireland, expressing on behalf of Catholic Ireland profound sympathy on "the cowardly outrage," but placing no specific blame.

Although the German radio continued to claim that Allied planes had dropped the bombs, the Allied and neutral world had no doubt whatsoever that this was another "Reichstag fire" perpetrated by the Nazis to turn Roman Catholics against the Allies. Just as in 1933 the Germans did not hesitate to set fire to the Reichstag to throw the blame on their internal political enemies, so it is now believed certain that they would destroy the Vatican to benefit themselves.

A Nazi attempt of exactly this character was predicted on July 1 when, during an Allied raid on the San Lorenzo

(Continued on page 3)

Hitler Speaks His Yearly Piece But Not So Loud

Time was when the world eagerly waited Adolf Hitler's annual speech in the Lowenbrau beer cellar at Munich. It was his habit to let his old Nazi cronies catch the scent of what was ahead for the powerful Reich.

Hitler spoke again there Monday night on the 20th anniversary of the founding of the German Workers' Party, which became the Nazi Party.

What was ahead for the once powerful Reich was not the fate which Germany suffered at the end of the first World War, said Hitler. "Whatever happens we will overcome all obstacles and in the end victory will smile on us," he promised his old party veterans — of whom he is but charter member number 7.

"Our day of vengeance will come and if we cannot reach America there is a state very near us which will pay dearly," glowered the Fuehrer, presumably a threat directed at England.

He admitted the battle against Russia was the "hardest the German people have ever known" and that the Italian collapse could not be without consequences on the war situation as a whole.

Summing up the state of German morale, he embarked on the state of his own: "Everything is possible but that I should lose my nerve is impossible."

Churchill Discounts Nazi Collapse Hopes

In his annual address at the Lord Mayor's banquet in London last night Prime Minister Winston Churchill warned the people of Britain that there is no indication of an early collapse in Germany despite the continuing tide of Allied victories. Mr. Churchill contrasted the dark days of November, 1940, when England stood alone, with the successful campaigns of 1943. England's war leader asked that the people continue to give their full attention "to the vast task" ahead.

Gotham Shimmers In "Brownout" Splendor

By T-Sgt. JOHN WILLIG
(Stars and Stripes Staff Writer)

NEW YORK—The lights are winking all over Manhattan now that the dimout has been shucked and the place almost seems the way it used to be.

For the first time in 18 months, jam-packed Broadway is giving intr customers some of the old brilliance and sparkle and once more you can stand in Times Square, look down 44th and see what's playing at the Shubert theater. A bit of the old nostalgic shimmer has come back to 42nd Street, and over on Fifth Avenue, frustrated window shoppers are happier than they've been for a long time gazing against the world's most costly come-ons.

It is almost like good old pre-Pearl Harbor days, but not

There are still plenty of black splotches mixed in with the blazing brightness. Huge spectacular animated signs in Times Square are still dark and the New York Times has turned off its moving news sign at the corner of Broadway and 42nd Street to save fuel and electricity. There is still something called "brownout" and it's figured that the lights are only 40 percent brighter than they were under the gloomy dimout.

Besides there is a 10 PM curfew for all the bright lights so that the town's new glory has a sort of Cinderella-at-the-ball ending. From twilight the place goes full blaze. When the dark hour comes, though, it changes

(Continued on page 3)

The Stars And Stripes Starts A New Edition

Depending upon the highly temperamental Neapolitan power system, Vol. 1, No. 1 of the Italian edition of *The Stars and Stripes* comes off the presses today. It is being published at the plant of Il Mattino at 266 Via Roma, in Naples, and it will be sold on the streets of Naples and environs. The price is two lire. For distribution in outlying areas, units are requested to speak up and name their wants. Special Services officers are particularly asked to get in touch with us to initiate distribution to their units. We hope to make *The Stars and Stripes* available to every American soldier in Italy.

Today's edition joins *The Stars and Stripes* family of newspapers under circumstances reminiscent of the first publication of *The Stars and Stripes* almost a year ago. When that first issue was undertaken in December, 1942, in the French composing room of L'Echo d'Alger in Algiers the mechanical staff faced the problems of the French language, a linotype keyboard different from the conventional American keyboard, unfamiliar type faces which included neither the American dollar sign nor quotation marks, and the circulation staff faced a shortage of transportation.

Much the same situation exists at the newspaper plant of Il Mattino, where the present edition is being published. As in Africa, the type faces familiar to American

(Continued on page 3)

FIFTH ARMY
THE STARS AND STRIPES
COMBAT EDITION

VOL. I, NO. XXXIII — "BE ALERT AND LIVE" — Italy, 24 November, 1943

Berlin Burns After Flattening Raid; Reds Close Escape Gap from Gomel

Bombload Exceeds Any Dumped on Hamburg

BULLETIN

ZURICH, Nov. 23—The Kroll opera house where Hitler used to address meetings was demolished in last night's raid on Berlin. Evidence of the concentrated weight of the raid lie in reports that the former British and Italian legations were destroyed; that the Swiss legation was badly damage; and that other embassies and official buildings south of the Tiergarten were also severely hit.

STOCKHOLM, Nov. 23—A British-based Allied raid on Berlin last night is said to have left no part of the city unscarred by bombs. Neutral source reports reaching Stockholm assert that the raid was heavier than any raid ever made on Hamburg—and that city is described as being all but flattened to the ground.

From Zurich comes information that even Berlin's suburbs suffered in the widespread devastation; and that damage was particularly heavy in the center of the city, especially near Unter Den Linden and the Alexanderplatz. Friedrichstrasse is said to have been shattered.

When first reports of the attack reached Stockholm there were huge fires still burning throughout the city. In some places as many as eight and 10 buildings adjoining each other were roaring masses of flame.

Fifth Army

COMMUNIQUE, 23 November

Though slightly less rain fell in the last 24 hours, the recent heavy storms have turned the battle area into a sea of mud. Rivers and streams are in flood. Little activity has been possible on any part of the fronts.

Contact became a little more brisk along our army fronts as weather cleared somewhat. Northwest of Agone in the Eighth Army sector light Canadian forces were attacked by German troops in strength. After a two hour action, the Germans were forced to withdraw. Our troops in the area around San Pietro found many villages which had been destroyed by the

(*Continued on Page 4*)

Roosevelt Proposes

WASHINGTON, Nov. 23 — President Roosevelt in a message to Congress has asked for immediate consideration of a three point program financed by the Federal government to aid ex-service men during the post war period. The plan calls for:

Uniform payment and reasonable mustering out of all members of the armed forces upon their honorable discharge or inactive duty status.

A uniform system of handling unemployment after the demobilization, which will be fixed regardless of the variance of state laws.

Full benefit to members of the armed forces including the merchant marine, for old age and servicemen's insurance covering their period of military service.

Senator Dies

WASHINGTON, Nov. 23—Senator Warren W. Barbour, 55, of New Jersey, is dead of a heart attack. Barbour was appointed to the Senate in 1931 to fill the vacancy caused by the death of Dwight Morrow.

Icy Waters of Dnieper Take Toll of Nazis

MOSCOW, Nov. 23—The fighting for Gomel, the fortress stronghold at the end of the German White Russian line, is entering its final stages. Soviet troops are fast closing the last retreat exit for the German garrison. Russians have only six miles to go to cut the westward railway.

Berlin announces that southwest of Gomel their troops are being withdrawn.

German troops are practically cleared from the right bank of the Dnieper below Rechitsa. All organized resistance ceased some hours ago, and the only resistance left is at the crossings.

The Germans are defending these crossings with strong artillery fire in an effort to withdraw from the Gomel trap. They have suffered large losses at these crossings and hundred of them have drowned in the ice-cold water of the Dnieper.

The new Russian push in the Dnieper bend goes ahead fiercely. Many German troops from the Zhitomir fighting are being drawn south by this determined Red Army drive. This

(*Continued on Page 4*)

The Combat Edition Passes

With this issue *The Stars and Stripes Combat Edition* ceases publication for troops of the Fifth Army. The fighting front which this paper served, more or less well, has been taken over by *The Stars and Stripes* city edition printed in Naples.

The Combat Edition is a rolling printing plant. It was designed to operate in front line combat areas, within easy reach of fighting troops. From the start, its intention has been to serve only troops in the line.

The supposition was (when first we came to Italy) that no commercial plants would be within easy reach of the front. The Combat Edition could be. The fighting man could have his news daily.

However, the Italian peninsula has turned out to be as narrow as we always knew it was. And its cities are not really so far apart. The Naples edition can take care of the front just as easily as we could—and supply the front with far more copies of *Stars and Stripes* than the Combat Edition could possibly produce.

The time has come for us to move on into other fields. Another front, perhaps. The war is not yet done.

There should be no parting without apologies for bad behavior; without many thanks for favors received

The instances of willing cooperation and generous help received from the Fifth Army are numerous beyond memory. Recognition of the freedom of our small press was absolute.

We recall our meeting with General Mark Clark. If you need anything, said he, ask for it. We did. We got it. Our presses and other printing equipment were lost or stolen somewhere along the line of shipment. A thousand and one "bugs" were discovered as we started operation for the first time. Only now is the end of our experimental stage in sight. Next time our job will be simpler and better done. —ED.

NORTHERN IRELAND EDITION

1D. **THE STARS AND STRIPES** 1D.

Daily Newspaper of U.S. Armed Forces in the European Theater of Operations

Vol. 1. No. 2. New York, N.Y.—Belfast, Northern Ireland. Tuesday, Dec. 7, 1943

Big Three Plan Triple Smash on Reich

Nazis Prepare For Blow In South Russia

White Russia's Weather Favorable to Nazis, Reports Say

MOSCOW, Dec. 7 (UP)—The Germans in Southern Russia are preparing a desperate effort to recapture the initiative and restore their Dnieper winter line.

Taking advantage of the late winter which has prevented the maximum use of the Russian cold-weather equipment, the Nazis have regrouped their forces and poured in reinforcements for the blows.

The weather is showing little signs of improvement, and continuous rain and slush in White Russia and the Southern Ukraine has bogged down armour and helps to keep the planes on the ground—both points which favour the enemy

The sector of the Russian front where results can be expected soonest is the White Russian area where the Reds yesterday steadily worked their way towards the important junctions of Moghilev, Rogchev and Zhlobin in spite of appalling weather. Even on this front, however, the Russians are unable to exert their maximum striking power until the marshes and rivers freeze and their excellent winter equipment can be brought into use.

At present there are three main drives going on in White Russia. One is being made by the column of Gen. Rokossovsky's force, which is less than 20 miles from Mogilev. A second column is moving west towards Orsha, the big German air base north of Mogilev, while the third drive is being made towards Zhlobin and Rogachev, key points in the intricate railway network south of Mogilev.

Curtin Asks For More Aid

CANBERRA, Dec. 7—John Curtin, Australia's Premier, said today that if Allied Forces were given a "heightened scale of striking power" they could break into Japan's conquered Empire before it can be fully exploited."

"Then," he continued, "we can strike at the inner Empire and finally at Japan herself."

In a review of the past two years since Australia entered the war against Japan, Curtin said:—

"Authoritative conclusions demonstrate that to regard Japan as a sideshow to be disposed of easily after the war has been won over Hitler is not only idle but dangerous talk. It would suit Japan's strategy to hold her from further conquests for an unfixed period.

"Allied forces with limited resources have taken every Japanese military position they have attacked."

Japan, added the Australian Premier, was prepared to sacrifice five million men in a war of attrition.

British Reveal Secret Cable Cutting Device

LONDON, Dec. 7—The British Air Ministry has disclosed that every RAF bomber now is equipped with 16 cable-cutting devices capable of slicing through cables — especially those on enemy barrage balloons—in one-thousandth of a second. The bombers, equipped with these instruments, can sweep a field of operations clear of enemy balloons before beginning low-level attacks

Zoo Director Claims Snakes Doing Part Too

TULSA, Okla. Dec. 7.—The director of the city reptile garden here says that rattlesnakes are playing an integral part in the war effort. Rattlesnake venom, he explained, is being used in the treatment of shock and nervous disorders among troops, and that the venom is necessary in the manufacture of a serum to control hemorrhage

Ulster Presses Roll

—U.S. Army Signal Corps Photo by Ogawa.

After pressing the button which started the presses rolling, Brig. Gen. Leroy P. Collins, Northern Ireland base section commander, looks over the initial issue of the Stars and Stripes' Ulster edition at its debut Monday.

U.S. Navy Planes Assist in Sinking Six Nazi U-Boats

U.S. Navy Raids Marshall Isles

WASHINGTON, Dec. 7.—The Navy department announced late today that a "heavy carrier task force" had carried out a raid on the Japanese occupied Marshall Islands in the Central Pacific, Saturday.

Because of the necessity for radio silence, details of the raid had not been reported from the task force.

Allied long-range planes based in Northern Ireland played a major part recently in sinking six Nazi submarines and attacking nine others when United States Navy, RAF and Canadian aircraft battled two big packs of U-boats for eight days.

The British Admiralty, in a communique issued yesterday, stated that "aircraft of Coastal Command and aircraft of the U.S. Navy, operating with Coastal Command, inflicted severe losses on U-boat packs which recently attempted to attack three trans-Atlantic convoys."

It was reported that one U.S. Navy squadron flying Venturas, took part in the "kills." Four-engined Liberators and Sunderlands and two-motor Venturas and Hudsons were thrown into the attack. The Libs sent three U-boats to the bottom, and the other three types bagged one each.

The Admiralty communique said:

"On the first day two of the convoys were escorted by aircraft from Iceland. No U-boats were sighted near the convoys, but three were attacked by aircraft sweeping the approaches.

"Next day Liberators provided close cover for the convoys, while Hudsons and Venturas of the U.S. Navy flew offensive sweeps in the neighbourhood.

"Soon after dawn a U-boat was attacked by a Hudson, but bad weather made it impossible to observe results. Later a Ventura of the U.S. Navy sighted a U-boat on the surface and straddled it with depth charges.

"Later the third convoy was threatened by a concentration of U-boats and on the sixth day a Liberator attacked a surface U-boat near the convoy.

"An hour afterwards the Liberator renewed the attack on the U-boat, which had resurfaced. The submarine went down stern first, leaving wreckage and bodies in the water.

"The Liberators then sighted another U-boat. A second Liberator of the same squadron was brought to the scene and attacked, but the U-boat crash-dived and results were not observed.

"An hour and a half afterwards the second Liberator returned to the same position and saw a third Liberator attacking a surfaced U-boat, probably the same one. Both attacked with depth charges and the U-boat's crew came out on deck and inflated their dinghies."

The U.S. Navy squadron was commanded by Cmdr. C. L. Westhofen.

Army Downs 13,500 Planes

WASHINGTON, Dec. 7 — Gen. Henry H. Arnold, U.S. Army Air Force commander, revealed to-day that 13,500 enemy planes had been destroyed or damaged since the Pearl Harbour incident by army combat planes.

Arnold said the army air force now totalled 2,300,000 men, and had flown more than 225,000 individual plane flights, fired 41,000,000 rounds of ammunition, and consumed some 2,000,000,000 gallons of gasoline.

"In every theatre," Arnold said in The Army and Navy Journal, "the enemy is reeling from unceasing pressure. Target after target is being demolished. The offensive will continue to mount until the Axis has neither the will nor the ability to resist."

Report Ciano Executed For Betraying Il Duce

MADRID, Dec. 7—Milan reports reaching Madrid today said that Count Ciano, Mussolini's son-in-lay, had been executed in Northern Italy following a trial on charges of betraying Il Duce.

The reports said Ciano stressed his loyalty to King Victor and Italy, but the court ruled he was the ringleader in what was termed "the betrayal of Mussolini."

There's Still Hope for Stripes Aplenty in N.I.

ETO headquarters announced yesterday that restrictions on promotions of enlisted personnel, reported in Monday's Stars and Stripes, applied only to soldiers working at theater headquarters

The ETO headquarters order said that no promotion would exceed more than one grade at a time, and at least 30 days must elapse from the date of last promotion before the soldier is eligible for further promotion.

Berliner on the Blitz.

STOCKHOLM, Dec. 7.—The Stockholm Tidningen yesterday reported a Berlin resident had told a neutral:

"The reason for Berlin's miseries is that a man once said 'I will erase your cities.' But the others happened to have better erasers."

F.D.R. Tips Off Yanks In Iran Of Conference

CAIRO, Dec. 7—American troops at the Amirabad hospital camp, near Teheran, were among the first outsiders to learn details of the historic meeting between Roosevelt-Churchill and Stalin, it was disclosed today.

President Roosevelt visited the camp last Thursday and told the troops: "I've had a conference with Marshal Stalin and Mr. Churchill during the past four days—very successful, too—laying plans, as far as we can, to make it unnecessary for us again to have Americans in Iran—just as long as we and our children live."

The President then visited the American army camp at Amirabad, where he said to an audience of surprised soldiers:

"If you had said to me or I had said to you three years ago that we would meet in Iran to-day, we would have probably said we were completely crazy.

"I got here four days ago to meet the Marshal of Soviet Russia and the Prime Minister of England to try to do two things. The first was to lay military plans for cooperation between the three nations and looking forward towards winning the war just as fast as we possibly can, and I think we have made progress towards that end.

"The other purpose was to talk over world conditions after the war—to try to plan for the world, for us, and for our children when war ceases to be a necessity. We have made great progress in that also."

Nazis Routed By Fifth Army

Clark's Men Ready for Final Assault On Rome Barriers

The Fifth Army yesterday routed German troops defending three of the most important heights in the Mount Camino and Mount Maggiore areas of Western Italy, then made ready for a last assault on the well-fortified positions blocking the route to Rome.

On the Adriatic front the Eighth Army advanced to the Moro River, less than 12 miles from Pescara, the main lateral road to Rome. Bitter fighting, reminiscent of Verdun, took place in the slippery peaks commanding the great plain on the main route to the Italian capital as the Germans battled furiously to retain their last mountain footholds.

In spite of the resistance, however, General Mark W. Clark's forces continued to advance, the Allied communique said, new heights were gained and the positions previously won were consolidated.

In the face of murderous mortar and machine-gun fire dispatches from the front said the Fifth Army opened breaches in the main bastions of the German western defense line.

As General Montgomery's troops pushed the Germans back in the Moro River sector the Germans rushed fresh troops to the front. Bridges across the river, a stream between two lateral roads running inland from the Adriatic, were blown up by the retreating Germans.

In five days the Fifth Army has captured 11 peaks from the Germans.

(Continued on Page 4)

Nine Nazi Divisions Face Allies In Italy

ALGIERS, Dec 7—Reports reaching here today stated the Germans have four divisions facing the Eighth Army and five more against the Fifth Army in Italy.

The Nazi divisions on the Eighth Army front were reported to be the 26th Panzers, 90th Panzer Grenadiers, 1st Parachute, and 65th Infantry

On the Fifth Army front the 15th and 29th Panzer Grenadiers and 44th, 94th, and 305th Infantry divisions are fighting for the Nazis

The Hermann Goering and Third Panzer divisions are being held in reserve

Landing In Norway?

NEW YORK, Dec. 7—Swiss radio today quoted Scandinavian sources as reporting that an Allied party landed and blew up the foundry at Arendal in Southern Norway on the night of November 20.

Agreement For Lasting Peace Bared

Teheran Pact Provides Blows from East, West and South

Declaring "complete agreement" had been reached on the scope and timing of Allied operations against Germany from the east, west and south, a joint statement on the history-making Roosevelt-Stalin-Churchill conference at Teheran was released to the world last night.

The statement by the leaders of the United States, Russia and Great Britain said "we are sure that our concord will make it an enduring peace."

The communique announcing the historic military and diplomatic agreement was announced at Cairo. The urgency of the military plan was underscored when the combined Anglo-American general staff returned from Teheran to Cairo and started concentrated planning sessions which lasted from Friday until yesterday.

Berlin Reaction.

The "big three" pledge of Teheran of an ever-swelling three-way assault on Germany was hailed in Britain as a terrible warning that Nazi military might may be wiped off the face of Europe.

Anticipated in Berlin, it set German leaders to talking desperately of defenses against any eventuality. Nazi chiefs told a special press conference that an Allied invasion of western Europe was expected soon; that a Russian winter offensive also was anticipated; and that German bombing reprisals against the Allied countries were to be launched shortly.

One full scale meeting of President Roosevelt, Premier Stalin and Prime Minister Churchill lasted more than nine hours and produced perhaps the most significant agreement. From it came this statement:

"Big Three" Statement.

We, the President of the United States of America, the Prime Minister of Great Britain, and the Premier of the Soviet Union, have met these four days past in this, the capital of our Ally, Iran, and have shaped and confirmed our common policy.

We expressed our determination that our nations shall work together in war and in the peace that will follow.

As to war, our military staffs have joined in our round-table discussions, and we have concerted our plans for the destruction of the German forces. We have reached complete agreement as to the scope and timing of the operations which will be undertaken from the east, west, and south.

The common understanding which we have reached guarantees that victory will be ours, and as to peace we are sure that our concord will make it an enduring peace.

We recognise fully the supreme responsibility resting upon us and all the United Nations to make a peace which will command the goodwill of the overwhelming masses of the peoples and of the world and banish the scourge and terror of war for many generations.

With our diplomatic advisers we have surveyed the problems of the future. We shall seek the co-operation and the active participation of all nations, large and small, whose peoples in heart and mind are dedicated, as are our own peoples, to the elimination of tyranny and slavery, oppression, and intolerance. We will welcome them as they may choose to come into a world family of democratic nations.

No power on earth can prevent our destroying the German armies by land, their U-boats by sea, and their war plants from the air. Our attacks will be relentless and increasing

From these friendly conferences

(Continued on Page 4)

Nazis Claim Turkish Chief Meeting F.D.R.

German news sources reported yesterday that the President of Turkey, Ismet Ineunu, was meeting with President Roosevelt and Prime Minister Churchill at Cairo.

THE STARS AND STRIPES

MIDDLE EAST

VOL. I No. 35 — CAIRO — FOUR CENTS — DECEMBER 10 1943

Mighty Triumvirate At First Meeting

"We came here with hope and determination. We leave here friends in fact, in spirit and in purpose" — Marshal Stalin, President Roosevelt and Prime Minister Churchill at the Teheran Conference. (U.N. Photo Pool)

Roosevelt, Churchill and Inonu Meet While Turkey Ponders War Issues

STOCKHOLM, (UP) — Both Germans and Turks continue to concentrate troops on both sides of the Turko-Greek and Turko-Bulgar frontiers, according to Swedish press reports from Sofia.

The Germans have ordered two divisions from Svilengrad in Southern Bulgaria to move to the south in the direction of Tokatosi Valley, near the Turkish frontier.

Turkish troop concentrations are reported to have been observed near Edirne and Ipsala, both close to the Greek frontier. All traffic across the Turko-Bulgarian frontier has been suspended..

President Roosevelt and Prime Minister Churchill returned to Cairo from the Teheran Conference for another portentous meeting — this with President Inonu of Turkey. A statement by the leaders announced "identity of interest and of views" of the three powers with the Soviet Union, which was represented at the talks by the Soviet Ambassador to Turkey.

While no military advisers came to Cairo with the Turkish president, the Teheran talks and the long-standing Anglo-Turkish treaty combined with the meeting to give rise to war talk in the Turkish capital.

In a delayed dispatch from Ankara, written while the meetings were in progress, UP correspondent, Eleanor Packard cabled that Turkey feels "the hour of acceptance or rejection by Turkey of the invitation for the war is at hand." The reporter cabled reasons underlying both war and peace arguments from the viewpoint of the Turks. Those for war are :

1.) If Britain chooses to invoke the treaty, Turkey must either aid Britain or refuse to honor her signature,which would be repugnant to the general public and government circles.

2.) Turkey's desire to participate in the post-war set-up would not be fulfilled should she choose the isolationist role in the critical period of the war.

(Continued on page 8)

Six Nip Ships Sunk As Offensive Opens On Marshall Islands

Six Jap vessels, including two cruisers, have been sunk and four others damaged and more than 72 planes destroyed by strong U. S. task carrier forces which attacked the Jap held Marshall Islands. The action is interpreted as a warning to Japan that the recent conquering of the Gilbert Islands, to the south, was only a prelude to a great offensive in the Central Pacific.

The U.S. forces under the command of Rear Admiral Charles Pownall successfully fought off vigorous and prolonged aerial torpedo and bombing attacks. Of one group of seven attacking torpedo planes, six were destroyed by AA fire. Only one U.S. ship suffered minor damage.

The Marshall Islands had been attacked only once before, on February 2nd of this year, though American land-based planes had struck there 14 times previously.

In commenting on the new offensive, Admiral William Halsey said: "This I can promise — we shall have offensives. Taking back what was ours originally is just a start. Each one of us has an appointment in Tokio."

Jap Raid Repulsed

Nine Jap planes raided the new U.S. air base on Tarawa in the Gilberts but the damage was slight.

The battle for Bougainville has passed its critical stage and it is only a question of time until the Americans complete the conquest of the last remaining Jap positions in the Solomons. The intensiveness of the attack is revealed in the report that more than 2,000 bombs were dropped in nearly 200 sorties against Jap airfields on the island on one single day. The air attacks were reinforced by sea bombardments from U. S. destroyers.

In the Wares sector of New Guinea the Allied forces continue to move northward along the coast of H[illegible] north of Mongora in the [illegible] Jap resistance

Becomes Human Decoy To Save Wounded Pals

SYDNEY, AUSTRALIA, (OWI).— Sgt. Gail E. Frederick, a radio operator aboard a U.S. troop carrying plane, was cited for heroically allowing himself to become a decoy for Japanese strafing planes to save the lives of two wounded companions.

According to "Yank Down Under," Frederick's transport plane was attacked by two Japanese fighter planes while over New Guinea and a crash landing was made. After helping two wounded buddies to cover, Frederick dashed into the open to draw the fire of the Jap planes trying to strafe the survivors.

Miraculously, Frederick escaped injury, and he and his two companions were back on operational flights three days later.

Leipzig Becomes Berlin's Gomorrah

LONDON—A new "feinting" tactic in the aerial strategy of the Allied Air Forces has resulted in one of the greatest air raids of the war when Allied heavy bombers deluged Leipzig with 1,500 tons of explosives.

A force of Mosquitos and heavy bombers flew on a direct line almost to Berlin to draw German fighter planes out of position. A short distance from the German capital the bombers veered off to drop their loads on Leipzig while the Mosquitos continued on over Berlin.

Reports from neutral sources indicate that half of the city of Leipzig was left in ruins and it is believed that 100,000 persons are homeless.

Architects of Future Draft War and Peace Blueprint in Iran

The history making declaration signed by President Franklin D. Roosevelt, Prime Minister Winston Churchill and Premier Josef Stalin at the close of the four-day conference in Teheran offers Germany the alternatives of unconditional surrender or massive new assaults by the combined Allied Powers.

The joint declaration by the three Allied leaders discloses that the Three-Power consultation has blueprinted a plan for German destruction if the Reich does not capitulate.

"As to the War, our military staffs have joined our round table discussions and we have concentrated our plans for destruction of the German forces," said the Allied statement. It continued, "We have reached complete agreement as to the scope and timing of operations which will be undertaken from the East, the West and the South. No power on earth can prevent our destroying the German armies by land, their U-Boats by sea and their war plants from the air. Our attacks will be relentless and increasing."

Also emerging from the historic meeting is the promise binding America, Great Britain and the Soviet Union in joint responsibility for peace which would "banish the scourge and terror of war for many generations."

New hope for minority nations of Europe in the post-war world was promised as Allied leaders declared, "We shall seek the active participation of all nations, large and small, whose peoples in heart and mind are dedicated as are our own people', to the elimination of slavery, oppression and intolerance. We will welcome them as they may choose to come into the world family of Democratic nations."

The Teheran Conference also pledged economic aid and continued freedom to Iran in recognition of that nation's aid as a lifeline of supply to the Soviet Union.

Military observers have interpreted the Teheran victory pledge to as an early invasion of Western Europe. These observers suggest that General Marshall may not return to Washington from the Cairo and Teheran Conferences though no great significance should be attached to his return if he does re-appear with President Roosevelt.

The declaration by the Big Three it is said, seems to remove all doubts whether the Allies would venture to attack from the west for which they have been steadily assembling powerful forces.

(Full text on Page 2)

Artillery Blasts At Hill Defenses On Road To Rome

Both the Fifth and Eighth Armies advanced steadily this week on the road to Rome despite counter-attacks by the Germans and torrential rains which frequently kept Allied planes from aiding their advancing forces.

Southwest of the tottering capital, Yanks of the Fifth won emplacements for their artillery in the Camino-Maggiore mountains, while Eighth Army tanks and infantry forced the Moro River on the Adriatic Coast. All along the mountainous front heavy Allied guns blasted away at Jerry, hidden in caves where machine-gun nests kept up the fight although their lines of supply had been cut off for four days.

A Yank medical carrier, Pvt. John Gurley, reported that many of the Germans killed by the Allied artillery barrage showed no signs of external injury but were victims of concussion and one correspondent gave this impression of the start of the big Fifth Army offensive near Mignano :

Artillery Dazes Enemy

"The ground trembled and a storm of sound filled the valleys. Gun flashes lighted the sky so you could have read a newspaper. The artillery of one group alone hurled 2,000 tons of explosives and steel into a narrow sector from where the Germans had observed Allied moves in the valley below. German prisoners, trapped in their foxholes by the steady pounding, were dazed by the concussion of the exploding shells."

Another correspondent wrote : "Far down below the mass of peaks, our bombers come over in

(Continued on page 8)

Pendulum Battles Rage Around Kiev

Bitter local fighting is waging in the snow and slush of areas west and south of Kiev with neither side able to swing the tide of battle. Russian successes which included the cutting of the railway line between Znamenka-Nikolayev and Krivoirog have been tempered by the Nazi forcing of other localities in the area of Chernyakhov.

In the Dneiper Bend, Soviet troops have occupied several strongly fortified centers after fierce fighting. In this area, 96 German tanks were destroyed or disabled.

The Germans made unsuccessful attempts to win back the penninsula of Kinduskava Koss, west of the Crimea on the east side of the Dneiper mouth. German landing parties had swarmed ashore and captured two towns in this area but were wiped out after several days fighting.

EX-BANKER DIES PENNILESS

NEW YORK. — Julius Lehrenkrauss, 76, former wealthy head of Brooklyn banking firm of the same name, dies in comparative poverty. He had served three years in prison for grand larceny in connection with financial manipulations when firm went bankrupt in 1933. Recently he had worked in a shipyard.

ACCUSED W.O. FILES APPEAL

GEORGETOWN, DEL. — Notice of appeal has been filed by U. S. Army Warrant Officer Carl Mouline of Fort Miles, after conviction of involuntary manslaughter in slaying of Warrant Officer John H. Worthington. He faces from one to 30 years in prison as outgrowth of shooting in Worthington beach home where Worthington accused Mouline of intimacies with his wife Elaine, 25.

THE STARS AND STRIPES

TUNIS

One Franc

Vol. 1—No. 1—Tuesday, 21 December 1943 Newspaper for U. S. Armed Forces in Tunisia

Nazi Defenses Crumble In White Russia Drive

Yanks Advance Past San Pietro Along Liri Plain

Germans Hard Hit On British Front

ALLIED FORCE HEADQUARTERS, Dec. 20—American infantrymen in the 5th Army central front struck forward yesterday from San Pietro to attack San Vittore two miles westward on the road to Rome There was no mention of tank action at San Vittore and it was assumed the town was under attack by the infantrymen which Saturday captured San Pietre, last Nazi barrier to the Liri plain.

At the northern end of the 5th Army front Allied troops, fighting in the mountains, gained two miles against strong enemy resistance.

Allied troops reported that the bodies of many Germans were found in the northern sector, indicating a rapid withdrawal. Only under severe pressure will the Germans retreat without burying their dead, a military commentator pointed out.

On the 8th Army front British troops, supported by tanks, made a short advance near the coast. The tanks caused heavy losses to the enemy by overruning their positions at one point in the center of the 15-mile front between the Adriatic Sea and the Maiella mountains. The town of Consalvi, just above the road from Ortona to Orsagna was occupied.

Fifty Germans were captured from the 1st Parachute Division recently brought into the line as reinforcements, and five tanks were knocked out.

The 9th Panzer Grenadiers division has lost 2,500 of its estimated 5,000 infantrymen in the last 14 days. Of the three original battalions in the division, one has been wiped out and the other two have lost so heavily that they were consolidated into one unit

No Scotch and Soda For FDR, Hopkins

LONDON, Dec. 20—When American security men bottle up the possible approaches to a travelling President they really bottle them up. Sitting in the study of U. S. Minister Dreyfus in Teheran, Harry Hopkins, Reuters reports, asked for a whisky and soda. The butler reappeared a few minutes later and reported: "Sorry Mr. President and Mr. Hopkins, but the American security men who were here earlier have bricked up various doors of the legation, unfortunately including the wine cellar door.

Texans Advance To Edge of Jap Base at Arawe

ALLIED SOUTH PACIFIC HEADQUARTERS, Dec. 20 — Advance spearheads of Gen. Walter Krueger's 6th Army yesterday lunged six miles north of their Arawe bridgehead on the southwest coast of New Britain to reach the approaches of the Jap-held Arawe airfield.

The Texas jungle fighters pressed forward behind an intense barrage of artillery weapons brought ashore a few hours after the first landings east of Arawe Peninsula.

American patrols probed the enemy positions east and northeast of captured Unlingolu village, a mile east of the neck of the peninsula. Gains up to four miles east of the original landing point were reported in an Allied communique.

Squadrons of Jap bombers continued to swoop in low over the harbor attempting to harass reinforcements coming ashore but Jap air resistance decreased yesterday as increasing numbers of Yankee fighters rose to meet them. Two Jap fighters and one dive-bomber were bagged in the

(Continued on Page 3)

Vol. 1, No. 1

With this issue, another edition of The Stars and Stripes is born in Tunisia. This latest addition to the large chain of soldier newspapers in the Mediterranean area will be published semi weekly and will be available to troops in and around Tunis, Bizerte, Mateur and Ferryville. The two issues will come out in addition to the Sunday paper which troops in this area are already receiving.

THE STARS AND STRIPES is your newspaper. It will be put out by soldiers for soldiers and the staff welcomes all advice and criticism so that it may be possible for us to give you the kind of a newspaper you want. Our Mail Call columns are open to all your opinions and gripes and our Puptent Poets section to your poetical efforts, anytime the spirit moves you.

We will make available to you as many copies of The Stars and Stripes as you feel your unit can use. It is requested that you come in for your papers between the hours of 8 AM and 12 noon on Tuesdays, Fridays and Sundays. We cannot accept home sub scriptions to the new dailies since postal regulations specifically prohibit it.

Papers for troops in the Tunis area will be available at The Stars and Stripes office at 20 (bis) Avenue de Paris (Lycee Carnot) instead of at the Depeche Tunisian building at No. 2, Avenue de Paris. In the Mateur area, papers may be picked up at Depot, Special Service, Mateur; in Bizerte at Special Service, EBS; and in Ferryville at M. Bele, Journal Ferryville.

Industrial Germany Is Pummeled In Hardest Aerial Blow of Month

ALLIED FORCE HEADQUARTERS, Dec. 20—Mediterranean-based heavy bombers made their deepest penetration of prewar Germany Sunday in blasting the industrial city of Augsburg and the railway yards at Innsbruck to score the greatest aerial victory of the month.

Allied Headquarters announced it was the first raid from the south on Augsburg 100 miles north of Brenner Pass.

The two attacks were part of widespread activity over the Reich, Italy and the Adriatic, which resulted in destruction of 43 enemy planes. Sixteen of our planes failed to return, but some are believed to have landed in friendly territory.

The fortresses weaved a systematic pattern of destruction in the Innsbruck railway yards besides ripping through track and rolling stock in the yards, an important junction in western Austria and eastern Germany for supplies to Italy. Bombs fell on oil installations in the vicinity, causing large explosions and fires.

The B-17's of the 15th AAF, escorted by P-38 Lightnings had to battle with 70 to 90 enemy fighters. At least 24 were shot down by Fortress gunners.

Returning crew members said the fighters made no attempt to prevent the bombers from carrying out their mission, but swarmed in for the attack immediately after the bombing.

"Fighters came in so close you could practically reach out and touch the pilots," said Capt. Phil.

(Continued on Page 4)

Reds Surround Vitebsk Salient

LONDON, Dec. 20— A sudden Soviet blow has crumbled the German defenses on a [illegible]-mile front in the Nevol area of White Russia and the Red Army has penetrated more than 18 miles in the first five days of the new offensive, biting into the German defenses south of Nevol.

The Russians, an official communique announced last night, have killed at least 20,000 enemy soldiers and taken huge quantities of materiel. The frigid northern sector, of Vitebsk two months ago, has become the scene of a vast new conflict, observers reported, with battles raging from the Vitebsk area north almost to the Leningrad region.

Vitebsk has been outflanked on the north and it appeared the position of the German garrison there was rapidly becoming untenable. The new drive has carried the Russian army of General Bagranyan to within 60 miles of the old Latvian border and offers a distinct threat to the railway junction of Polotsk, an important point on the supply route serving the Nazi beseigers of Leningrad.

Powerful tank forces, well supported by cavalry and ski troops, are now in a position to roll back the Leningrad line. Further advances by the Red Army would start an encircling movement at the rear of the Germans in the north, forcing them to evacuate or be trapped between two Soviet armies.

The current offensive was announced for the first time last night by the Soviets, but German

(Continued on Page 4)

Senate Passes Bonus Proposal

WASHINGTON, Dec. 20 — The Senate passed yesterday and sent to the House a bill providing servicemen with mustering-out pay raging from $200 to $500 depending upon length of service.

The bill, sponsored by Sen. Alben W. Barkley (D. Ky.) would allow $500 for those serving outside of the U. S. for 18 months or more; $400 for those serving overseas for from 12 to 18 months; $300 for less than 12 months service abroad or $300 for more than 12 months service within the continental U. S.; and $200 for those who have served less than 12 months within the U. S. The measure would be retroactive to Pearl Harbor.

Under Sen. Barkley's bill, one-third of the amount would be paid upon honorable discharge and the balance in equal installments. Within two months all enlisted men and officers, up to and in-

(Continued on Page 3)

Five GI Rangers Take on 100 Germans in Italy

By Sgt. RALPH G. MARTIN
(Stars and Stripes Staff Writer)

WITH THE 5TH ARMY — The five Rangers with their heads low were moving quickly up the slope. They were heading for the tiny pimple on top of the nob of the hill. It was the highest observation point overlook ing that entire valley. From there an OP could direct artillery fire on German-held bivouac areas and gun positions.

The Rangers sent five men—all they could spare—with simple orders:

"Take the pimple. Stay there until we send you reinforcements."

There were about 100 Germans coming from the other side of the hill with the same orders.

It was a sharp-raising, rocky slope and the five Rangers raced up, stumbling, falling. The looey in charge of the four-man patrol was Iowa-born Lester Kness. Kness covered his men from the rear.

"The slope was lousy with snipers," Kness said, "They forced us to fall flat four different times when they opened up on us.

"I got three of them," he said. He also helped to get ten more a few minutes later.

They had reached the top of the hill when they spotted the ten Germans clambering on to the pimple from the steepside. Kness and T 4 Leroy Robinson, Memphis, rushed up with a Browning automatic and a tommy gun and opened up simultaneously. They got all ten. Three of the ten, standing near the brink of the ledge, fell straight down over the side landing on top of some of their buddies beneath them.

Kness laughed grimly: "You ought to hear those Heinies yell down there . . . they just didn't know what was happening.

"They sent up a few more men to look around . . We let them get up all right . . .

" . . . but they never got back to report," he said, laughing again.

By this time the five Rangers were carefully scattered around the pimple, all facing the ledge, their guns pointed, waiting for the next German targets to show themselves. They showed themselves about two minutes later—swarms of them. They were coming up from every part of the

(Continued on Page 4)

London Bombed

LONDON, Dec. 19 — A formation of German bombers roared over the English Channel last night and dropped bombs in the London area and in the Thames estuary district. Little damage was reported.

NORTHERN IRELAND EDITION

1D. THE STARS AND STRIPES 1D.

Daily Newspaper of U.S. Armed Forces in the European Theater of Operations

Vol. 1. No. 18. New York, N.Y.—Belfast, Northern Ireland. Tuesday, Dec. 28, 1943.

Army Takes Over U.S. Railroads

Allied Invasion Staff Is Named

Eisenhower In Command; Tedder 2nd

Senator Says Yanks To Make Up 73% Of Assault Force

One of the most historic weekends of the war—four drama-packed days that saw Gen. Dwight D. Eisenhower named Supreme Allied Commander for the invasion of Europe, the 26,000-ton German battleship Schornhorst sunk by the British Home Fleet, and an American air assault which proved Allied control of the invasion coast—came to a surging climax yesterday with a flat, unqualified prediction by the new Generalissimo that victory would be won in 1944.

Declining to hedge his statement in nay way, the new supreme Allied chieftain confidently told a farewell press conference in North Africa before leaving for England to take command of the invasion forces; "We'll win the European war in 1944."

The new Allied supreme commander, after his "farewell press conference" in North Africa, was expected in London at any time, possibly within a matter of hours.

At Press Conference

General Eisenhower told correspondents he doubted that bombing alone could defeat Germany, but he looks on the air offensive as a "valuable adjunct" to the assault on Germany from the west.

Disclosure last night in a joint communique from President Roosevelt and Prime Minister Churchill that Air Chief Marshal Sir Arthur Tedder will be deputy to Eisenhower capped these weekend developments.

(1) Roosevelt and Churchill revealed the Allied lineup for invasion would run this way;

Eisenhower, Supreme Commander of British and U.S. Expeditionary Forces organizing in the United Kingdom for the liberation of Europe; Tedder, Deputy Supreme Commander under Eisenhower; General Sir Bernard Montgomery, Commander-in-Chief of British group of Armies under Eisenhower; General Sir Henry Maitland Wilson, Supreme Allied Commander Mediterranean theater; General Sir Harold Alexander, Commander-in-Chief all Allied Armies in Italy; General Sir Bernard Paget, Commander-in-Chief in Middle East under Sir Maitland Wilson; Lieut.-General Carl Spaatz, Commanding American Strategic Bombing Force operating against Germany.

Senator's Statement

(2) Senator Edwin C. Johnson (Dem., Colo.), of the Senate Military Affairs Committee, asserted in Washington that invasion plans called for the U.S. to furnish 73% of the assault force, Britain and the Dominions 27%.

(3) More than 2,000 Allied planes—with more than 1,500 of them USAAF bombers and fighters, including well over 500 heavy Fortresses and Liberators—delivered a series of devastating attacks against the Northern France "rocket coast" the day before Christmas without loss of a plane.

(4) One of the Nazis' three capital warships, the battleship Scharnhorst, was sunk off the northern tip of Norway Sunday evening by Home Fleet units guarding a convoy, a terse British Admiralty communique announced.

(5) A German communique told of a British-French Commando raid on

(Continued on Page 2.)

Latrine Lawyer Gets His TS Slip Bit Early

FORT LEAVENWORTH, Kan., Dec. 28 (AP) One American gave the following reason for asking for draft deferment:—"I'm recuperating from traumatic perrosynovitis of the flexor digitorum sublimus in the profundus muscle at the metacarpophalangeal joint."

The Army, however, said no. A sore finger was not a good enough reason for deferment.

Nazi Warship Sunk In Fight

The 26,000-ton German battleship Scharnhorst, sunk off Norway's northern tip Sunday evening by units of the British Home Fleet after a battle which began in the afternoon and ended in darkness, was one of the Nazis' three capital warships.

'This Is The Army' Opens In Belfast January 13

Irving Berlin's all-soldier musical "This Is the Army" will open a 10-day run at the Opera House in Belfast, Thursday, January 13, it was announced today.

Sgt. Ben Washer, in charge of public relations for the show, said that no details had been worked out for the number of complimentary tickets to be distributed among Allied servicemen for each show.

However, it was expected the same set up which has prevailed at other stops in the ETO—that of setting aside one-third of the house for men and women in uniform—would prevail at the Northern Ireland performances.

"This Is the Army," which boasts a cast of 150 soldier performers, currently is playing at Bristol, England.

Toured United States

The GI's who make up "This Is the Army" have done their stuff from New York to Hollywood in the States, and since arriving in the ETO have played London, Glasgow, Manchester, Liverpool and Birmingham, in addition to Bristol. While in Hollywood, they made the screen version of "This Is the Army," which, incidentally, has its British debut in London Friday.

In the States, the show raised $200,000 for Army Emergency Relief. It is expected that the picture will earn at least ten millions more for the army service in the States.

"This Is the Army" is a series of scenes emanating for the most part from the lives of GI's. There are a couple of scenes which see men appearing as women one of them in particular based on the goings-on at New York's famed Stage Door Canteen.

Irving Berlin introduced a new song when the show opened in London. Known as "My Buddy," the tune has proved popular with the audiences—which have been capacity at every show.

U.S. Gets Raid Scare On Xmas

NEW YORK, Dec. 28—The Eastern Defense Command revealed today that it had alerted all military and civilian defense agencies along the Atlantic seaboard, because of "receipt of a report that a sneak air attack might be attempted by the enemy on Christmas day."

The Command said the alert was cancelled at 9.05 PM Christmas night after army protection units had been standing by for the preceding 24 hours.

Residents of New York state flooded newspapers and radio stations with telephone calls after a warning message was broadcast.

In Washington, a War Department spokesman said he was unable to give the source of the report that America might undergo a Christmas air raid, but added that the Eastern Defense Command apparently considered the source authentic enough to broadcast warning rumors spread up and down the Atlantic coast that an aircraft carrier had been sighted about 700 miles off the coast. But this and scores of other rumors as to why the alert was ordered all lacked official comment.

FDR Orders Stimson To Operate Lines; Gen. Cross In Charge

War Labor Board In Special Session After 122,000 Steel Workers Walk Out In Six States

WASHINGTON, Dec. 28—The U.S. Army today operated the nation's vast system of railways after taking possession of them late last night on orders issued by President Roosevelt.

The seizure order was carried out by Lt. Gen. Brehen Somervel, chief of the Army Service Forces, acting on behalf of Secretary of War Henry L. Stimson.

Maj.-Gen. C. P. Cross, head of the Army Transportation Corps, was placed in charge of the operating lines.

The seizure was ordered to insure the "movement of troops, war necessities, passenger traffic, supplies and food for the armed forces and the civilian population, and everything essential to the successful prosecution of the war," the President stated.

"I am obliged to take over at once the temporary possession and control of the railways to insure their continued operation," the President explained in the executive order under which the seizure was made.

'Strike Against Govrenment'

"Major military offensives now planned must not be delayed by interruptions of vital transportation facilities," Mr. Roosevelt added. "If any employes of the railroads now strike they will be striking against the government of the United States."

He also pointed out that the "government still expects every railroad man to continue at his post of duty."

The seizure order also applied to railroad express companies and car companies owned or controlled by the railroads.

The order directed the Secretary of War to operate or arrange for operation of all the railroads, but stipulated that the present administrative officials should remain at their positions as far as possible.

President Roosevelt issued the order after three of the Operating Brotherhoods had failed to call off the strike scheduled to begin Thursday. Two of the Operating Brotherhoods and the 15 Non-operating Brotherhoods had agreed to the President's offer to arbitrate and had called off the impending strike.

Mr. Roosevelt explained that he could not wait "until the last minute to see that supplies to our fighting men are not interrupted."

Steel Workers Strike

Meanwhile, the War Labor Board was called into special session to deal with the threatened strike of the nation's steel workers, amid growing indications that the government also might take over operation of the steel mills.

There has been no strike call among the steel workers, but more than 122,000 already have stopped work in a move to force the WLB to approve a wage increase of 17 cents an hour. More than half of the strikers who started the walkout at midnight Saturday when the union's contract expired, are in Ohio, but the stoppage has spread into Pennsylvania, West Virginia, Indiana, Michigan, and New York.

If the wage controversy is not settled by next week, when other contracts expire, more than 500,000 men are expected to be on strike.

The War Labor Board has refused to grant the union its wage demands, insisting that any increase would violate the little steel wage formula which limits war time pay boosts.

British Sink Scharnhorst

Nazi Warship Meets End In Battle Off Norway's Northern Tip

The German battleship Scharnhorst, one of the Nazi's three capital warships, was sunk off the northern tip of Norway on Sunday evening by units of the British Home fleet guarding a North Russia convoy.

Sinking of the 26,000-ton battleship, which for four years has staged sporadic forays against Allied shipping in the Atlantic, was announced in a terse communique late Sunday by the British Admiralty, and confirmed shortly afterwards by German radio.

No Details Issued

The Scharnhorst was sunk after a battle which began in the afternoon and ended in darkness, the Admiralty announced. The German announcement said the warship went down only after a long fight with "superior British heavy naval forces." The Nazis claimed "damage was inflicted by the Scharnhorst, which fired to its last shell."

Twentyfour hours after the battle, the Admiralty still had not announced how the Scharnhorst was sunk. It was presumed that at least one British ship of the King George V class, with 30 knot speed and long range 14 inch guns, must have engaged the 29 knot Nazi craft.

The Scharnhorst, with nine 11 inch and 12 5.9 inch guns, together with its sister ship Gneisenau had been holed up in Baltic Sea ports, usually Gdynia, since their escape from Brest and passage up through the English channel last February in one of the most daring naval exploits of the war.

Occasionally either the Scharnhorst or Gneisenau slipped out of the Baltic, ran through the narrows off Sweden and headed north through the maze of fjords along the western and

(Continued on Page 2.)

Threat Rouses Fliers' Wrath

American bomber crews yesterday answered German threats of reprisals against captured Allied airmen with a vow to "drop twice as many bombs" on Nazi military targets for every captive flier molested by the Germans.

The latest Nazi threats against captives said that civilian residents of the city of Hamburg would be called as witnesses at special trials at which the airmen will be charged with "deliberately dropping their bombs on residential quarters of German cities."

First German threats to try the airmen came immediately after the Russian trials of Germans who mass-murdered civilians in the Kharkov area.

Yesterday a survey of American airmen at bomber bases in Britain brought a reaction only of renewed determination to press home the bombing attacks on Nazi military targets until the war is won.

Pope Calls For Peace In Yule Eve Address

The havoc and horror of war is a challenge to independent and enlightened minds, Pope Pius XI said in his Christmas Eve broadcast to the world.

"We look forward to a new order of peace, of right, and of work. In this new order there must be no people left to whom justice and equity are not applied. If any gaps are left in the organization the whole structure would be in danger," the Pope said.

THE STARS AND STRIPES DAILY

Vol. 1 - No. 175 - Friday, December 31, 1943 | One Franc | Daily Newspaper For U. S. Armed Forces

ARAB BOWL TOPS NEW YEAR

Oran, Casa Teams Fight For Crown

Termites Face Rabchasers In Feature Game

By Sgt. JIM HARRIGAN
(Stars and Stripes Sports Editor)

Hailed far and wide by sports enthusiasts as the biggest sports extravaganza projected thus far in the current war by members of America's Armed Forces overseas, the No. 1 gridiron classic outside of the continental United States will be unveiled in Oran tomorrow as a fitting celebration by and for the service men in this area commemorating New Year's Day in North Africa.

Topping the day's events is the clash between the Termites of Oran, local league champs, and the Rabchasers, winners of the Casablanca Football League, for the football championship of North Africa.

Inaugurating the day's events will be a military parade in town at 11 AM followed by spectacular camel and donkey races. Jockeys for the camels will be WACs representing MBS, Special Services, The Stars and Stripes, SOS, Chez Oran of the American Expeditionary Station and the American Red Cross. Other WACs will pilot the donkeys, with the course for both races scheduled from Gallieni Garage on Gallieni Blvd. over to Blvd. Clemencau and up to the Barclay Bank Bldg., where the finish will be broadcast over a public address system by staff members of Special Services.

Lt. Col. Egbert White, Publications Officer, Natousa, in charge of the Stars and Stripes, arrived by plane yesterday afternoon. Col. Leon T. David, Special Services, Natousa, is expected sometime today with other officers from Algiers.

Brig. Gen. Arthur R. Wilson, commanding general of MBS, is

(Continued on Page 3)

CARRY CASA'S COLORS INTO BOWL

WATCH THESE RABCHASERS tomorrow afternoon as they endeavor to whip Oran's Termites for the football championship of North Africa. Pictured above are Shoemake, McCall, McKibben, Willis, Pepper and McDonald, part of the Casablanca squad.

—Photo by Connell (USAAF)

2,000 Ton RAF Raid Stuns Berlin

LONDON, Dec. 30—More than 2,000 tons of bombs were dropped by the RAF on Berlin last night in the second air raid on the German capital within six days, and the eighth since mass attacks on Berlin began November 18. Fires were visible around the whole horizon and a heavy pall of smoke rose 14,000 feet, according to the Berlin correspondent of a Stockholm paper, who was permitted to telephone a brief dispatch.

The raid was officially announced here three quarters of an hour after midnight, the earliest hour a night assault on the Reich has ever been disclosed. British bombers now have been over Berlin 30 times and dropped more than

(Continued on Page 4)

Bombs Answer GI's Plea For Smokes

NAPLES, Dec. 30—"And if you wish long enough . . . wish strong enough . . ."

First Sgt. Marvin J. Heine, Kim Mott, Texas, wanted a cigarette. He wanted it so bad that he was willing to walk a mile for it, whether the tobacco was toasted or not.

Somehow the boys of his 36th Infantry Division unit failed to respond. One of the boys said, "Hell, you can't smoke now, there's an air raid on."

And just then, all of them heard the loud screaming of a bomb coming almost straight at them.

Seconds later, when Sgt. Heine opened his eyes he saw five beautiful cellophane-wrapped packages of cigarettes lying at his feet.

The bomb fragments had hit a barracks bag, scattering its contents.

Red Offensive Crushing Nazis In Dnieper Bend

Gen. Marshall Voted 'Man Of The Year'

NEW YORK, Dec. 30—Gen. George C. Marshall, American chief of staff, has been selected by Time Magazine as the "man of the year" for 1943.

General Marshall was selected by the editors of the news magazine on the basis of nominations by readers, as one who had effected the most dramatic change in the course of history during the preceding 12 months.

General Marshall, according to the citation, has transformed the "worse than disarmed United States into the world's most effective military power."

New Drive Perils German Railway Communications

LONDON, Dec. 30 — German troops in the Dnieper bend were being drawn today in the claws of a giant pincers after the Russians last night announced a new offensive in the sector opposite Zaporoshe.

The rapid advance of Gen. Nikolai Vatutin's army on the Kiev salient is pressing the rear of the Nazi armies in the bend by threatening railway communications at Berdichev and Kazatin and the latest drive, with the offensive around Kirovograd, is slowly crushing the Nazi divisions in a grip showing no signs of weakening.

The capture of Korosten yesterday highlighted Soviet gains in the Kiev salient, but the Russians also recovered 25 other towns in their drive toward the Polish border. The Korosten victory, freeing the northern flank of the bulge, was accomplished, observers reported, by simultaneous blows from the front and flanks. Machine gunners mounted on tanks and armored cars by passed the city and are now behind the German lines, attacking escape routes. Stormovik dive bombers ranged over the area west of Korosten, pounding the retreating Germans. South of Korosten, the Russians are now within a few miles of all three of the Wehrmacht's communication keypoints—Zhitomir, Berdichev and Kazatin—and the Nazi Panzers, correspondents reported, are finding their freedom of motion increasingly restricted. The

(Continued on Page 4)

Marines One Mile From Jap Airfield

ALLIED SOUTH PACIFIC HEADQUARTERS, Dec. 30—As the Japs continued to dash in for bayonet fighting, U. S. Marines at Cape Gloucester, New Britain, met them with flame throwers. The Japs were literally singed back for half a mile toward the big Gloucester airdrome.

While the Marines drove to within a mile of the airfield, overhead relays of attack and dive bombers swept in low over the field and big Yankee "Long Toms" added to the devastation by pouring hundreds of shells onto the hangars and ground installations.

More than 200 Japanese were killed in hand-to-hand bayonet fighting, an Allied spokesman said as it became evident that the Japanese intend to fight a desperate, bitter battle for the strategic airfield, which is within 270 miles of Japan's big sea and air bastion at Rabaul, on the northern tip of the island.

Down the south coast of New Britain at Arawe, bitter fighting tapered off to light patrol clashes north of Pelho. Supporting bombers strafed enemy supply trails along the Pulie River.

After smashing stubborn resistance Australian tank forces stormed Blucher Point on New Guinea's Huon Peninsula coast.

Heavy Allied bombers damaged two Jap transports near Celebes in the Dutch East Indies.

DAY OF PRAYER

A PROCLAMATION BY THE PRESIDENT OF THE UNITED STATES OF AMERICA

At the end of the year 1943, which has not only made manifest the devotion and courage of our nation's sons but has also crowned their efforts with brilliant success on every battle front, it is fitting that we set aside a day of prayer to give thanks to Almighty God for His constant providence over us in every hour of national peace and national peril.

At the beginning of the new year 1944, which now lies before us, it is fitting that we pray to be preserved from false pride of accomplishment and from willful neglect of the last measure of public and private sacrifice necessary to attain final victory and peace. May we humbly seek strength and guidance for the problems of widening warfare and for the responsibilities of increasing victory. May we find in the infinite mercy of the God of our Fathers some measure of comfort for the personal anxieties of separation and anguish of bereavement.

NOW, THEREFORE, I, FRANKLIN D. ROOSEVELT, President of the United States of America, do hereby appoint Saturday, the first day of January 1944, as a day of prayer for all of us, in our churches, in our homes, and in our hearts, those of us who walk in the familiar paths of home, those who fight on the wide battlefields of the world, those who go down to the sea in ships, and those who rise in the air on wings.

IN WITNESS WHEREOF, I have hereunto set my hand and caused the seal of the United States of America to be affixed.

DONE at the city of Washington this 3rd day of December, in the year of our Lord nineteen hundred and forty-three and of the Independence of the United States of America the one hundred and sixty-eighth.

(SEAL)

FRANKLIN D. ROOSEVELT

By the President:
CORDELL HULL,
Secretary of State.

Churchill On Job Tho' Sick

LONDON, Dec. 30—Despite his recent illness, Prime Minister Churchill was at no time forced to relinquish his part "in the direction of affairs," he said in a personal statement released at No. 10 Downing Street today.

His departure from where he was hospitalized to an "unknown destination" to spend a few weeks convalescing in the sunshine was also revealed. He will continue to maintain full daily correspondence with London. He said he felt better now than at any time since leaving England.

Mr. Churchill, who praised the physicians who treated him, disclosed that he had planned to visit Italy "but on the 11th of December I was so tired out that I had to ask General Eisenhower for a few days rest before proceeding. This was accorded me in a generous manner."

"The next day," continued the Prime Minister "came the fever and the day after when the photographs showed that there was a shadow on my lungs, I found that everything had been foreseen by Lord Moran. The most excellent medical authorities in the Mediterranean arrived from all quarters as if by magic."

"After one week's fever," said the Prime Minister, "I was on the way to recovery. I hope that all our battles will be as easily won and as well conducted."

Complete 65 Flights Refuse Rest in U. S.

SLATON, Texas—Capts. R. F. Spikes and James M. Bugbee, pilots of AAF B-25 Mitchells, recently declined to return to the U. S. for a rest upon completion of 60 missions, it was announced yesterday. Capts. Spikes and Bugbee, who are in the same squadron, both completed 65 missions last week end.

Each has received commendations from Gen. Henry H. Arnold, commanding general of the AAF. They participated in the Tunisian, Pantellerian, Sicilian and Italian air campaigns and led two of the first flights of medium bombers in raids on the Balkans.

8th Moves On Pescara

ALLIED FORCE HEADQUARTERS, Dec. 30—Tough Canadian troops of the 8th Army who knocked the Germans out of Ortona Tuesday found the wrecked town heavily mined and filled with booby traps. Houses and public buildings contained the same type of vicious time bombs the Germans left in retreating from Naples. Sappers began work immediately to clear the city.

Meanwhile, other troops advanced about a mile up the coastal area toward Pescara, another important Adriatic port. Here the road also was heavily mined and progress was slow as cold and cloudy weather settled over the 8th Army area, patrols continued sniffing at enemy defenses west of Ortona. Infantrymen occupied an important height a half-mile northwest of Villa Grande.

On the 5th Army front, the fighting subsided at Pontafiume, where the Germans had attempted a large-scale attack, which was repulsed. The town is at the point where the Garigliano River enters the Tyrrhenian Sea.

Localized, but extremely stiff, fighting continued in the heights a half-mile above the Colli-Atina road. Allied infantry, struggling against snow and rugged terrain as well as determined German defenders, stormed a 1030-foot peak, the highest point on the southerly tip of the Catanella-Della Mainarde ridge.

THE STARS AND STRIPES

SICILY

Vol. 1 - No. 41 - Friday, Dec. 31, 1943 | For U. S. Armed Forces | 2 Lire

8th Drives On Pescara After Taking Ortona

ALLIED FORCE HEADQUARTERS, Dec. 30—Field Marshal Albert Kesselring today is concentrating six-barreled mortars and 88 mm. self-propelled guns in an all-out attempt to check the 8th Army's twin thrusts towards the Rome-Pescara road in Italy.

Canadian troops are continuing their advance toward the vital Adriatic port of Pescara, leaving behind them the charred and mined ruins of the German fortress of Ortona.

The Canadians seized Ortona after eight days of fierce house-to-house fighting, the toughest of the entire Mediterranean campaign. They strong-armed their way to the northwest rim only after the Germans yielded ground yard by yard. While being punched out of one important stronghold, however, the Germans amassed a large force to attack the British on the left flank of the 5th Army's line at [illegible].

ORTONA DEVASTATED

The Canadians, described as "the best street fighters in the world," found Ortona nearly devastated. Doorways, basements, streets were littered with battered tanks which the Germans had used as pillboxes. The town's dock area had been burned as the Germans scorched the ground before they gave up.

Rubble, debris and wreckage made many streets impassable. Burial details found much work to do.

Knocking the little Adriatic seaport town apart wasn't the Germans' only satisfaction. They had fought desperately to win time, and they won eight precious days. Feverishly, they strengthened other positions to the north of Ortona.

Continued on Page 4

Marines Capture Gloucester Field

ALLIED SOUTH PACIFIC HEADQUARTERS—United States Marines today are in full control of grimly-contested Cape Gloucester in New Britain. The Leathernecks seized the Cape Gloucester airfield after Jap pillboxes were knocked out by flame throwers.

Earlier, in a bloody series of savage, hand-to-hand bayonet clashes, the Americans repulsed four Japanese counter-attacks and stabbed inland in a torrential rain to within a mile and a half of the chief enemy airdrome.

The Yanks threw in everything they had as the Japs, for the first time, emerged from shell-shattered bunkers to dispute the American advance. While the shock forces of both sides fought at close range, heavy American guns were lobbing hundreds of shells at the big Jap airdrome, ripping hangars and ground installations.

Marine tank spearheads moved in near the field as the Nips were hurled back, leaving large quantities of supplies, field guns and ammunition.

Seventy miles down the south coast of New Britain at the Arawe bridgehead, the Jap hurled a large force of dive bombers against the American defenders. Allied fast fighters shot down 30 out of 60 bombers and fighters, and ship guns got four more.

Muss 'Dies' Again

MADRID — Mussolini is dead again. At least, such is the report being widely circulated in this city. The ex-Duce originally was said to be a suicide several weeks ago. The latest story has him a victim of internal ailments and a mental crackup. At the rate he is dying, Mussolini will take more killing than the proverbial cat.

HAPPY NEW YEAR

For a couple of weeks we've been trying to figure out how to give all you soldiers and sailors in Sicily a real New Year's treat. We can't hand out individual drinks, because our colonel might object to the bar bill. Luckily, one of our guys who looks and acts like "The Wolf" spotted a picture in a magazine. It was a photo of a gal with a low-slung chassis whose mere smile should start 1944 off right for everyone. So here she is. We don't know her name, age or telephone number, but who cares? In addition to those beautiful eyes, we wish all of you hearty cheer, success and a furlough to the States for the Nuovo Anno. Here's looking at all you guys. Bottoms up!

Allies Sink Three Nazi Destroyers

The German navy ain't what she used to be.

Over a four-day period the Allies have dealt crippling blows to Adolf Hitler's hopes for maritime glory. They started by sinking the pocket battleship Scharnhorst near the northern tip of Norway. They followed up by sending three Nazi destroyers to Davy Jones locker in a bristling engagement in the Bay of Biscay.

Two important cargo ships also were included in the German casualties. One plunged to the bottom in the Biscay fracas. The other, a 6,000-ton job, ran afoul of Allied planes off the Dalmatian coast in the Adriatic.

As though the fate of the Scharnhorst weren't sufficiently convincing, German destroyers and other fighting craft attempted to provide protection for a blockade off the coast of France.

Naval observers commented that the blockade runner must have carried highly essential supplies for the Germans to risk so many destroyers, since the Nazi fleet is especially weak in that category. Since the outbreak of the war, the Germans have lost at least 48 destroyers and torpedo boats.

The blockade runner first was sighted by a Sunderland flying boat. Other Allied aircraft were diverted to the area, and the cruisers Glasgow and Enterprise dispatched to intercept. For several hours, pending the arrival of the cruisers, aircraft shadowed the ship. A Liberator of the Czech squadron scored a direct hit on the stern, causing an explosion of such intensity that the plane, 600 feet above the stricken vessel, was rocked and severely shaken.

Flames spread throughout the blockade runner, and the crew abandoned ship. About 70 survivors were sighted in lifeboats or rafts. Destroyers, attempting to protect the ship and valuable cargo, soon were engaged by cruisers. Three of the destroyers were sunk and the remainder took off for sanctuary.

Press commentators pointed out that a series of losses such as the two just sustained by the Germans had led directly to a mutiny at Kiel in 1918. The loss of the Scharnhorst and three destroyers, observers added, would not help to strengthen morale of the German naval personnel if it was at all shaky.

Latest details on the Scharnhorst sinking reveal that only seven of the 1,400-odd crew escaped with their lives. A survivor told of wild scenes during the battleship's final minutes. Many men were trapped below decks, and others leaped overboard when one of the gun turrets received a direct hit. Hundreds were dragged down by the ship's suction when she finally plunged.

Both President Roosevelt and Premier Stalin sent congratulatory messages to Prime Minister Churchill following the sinking of the Scharnhorst.

Said President Roosevelt: "Sinking of the Scharnhorst has been great news to all of us. Congratulations to the home fleet."

Said Stalin: "I send you personally and also to Admiral Sir Bruce Fraser and valiant sailors of the Duke of York my congratulations on this splendid blow."

There were no additional comments from Germany.

Eisenhower Predicts Allied Victory In '44

ALLIED FORCE HEADQUARTERS—General Dwight D. Eisenhower, at a "farewell" conference for the war correspondents in this theater, declared:

"It is my conviction that the Allies will win the European war in 1944."

Just back from a tour of the front, General Eisenhower is expected to leave shortly to take up his new duties as supreme commander of Allied operations against Germany from the United Kingdom.

Korosten Falls As Red Assault Batters Ahead

LONDON, Dec. 30—The guns of Moscow once again are saluting the conquests of Russia's armies in the Kiev bulge.

Striking with tremendous force over a wide area, General Vatutin's troops have advanced from 30 to 60 miles in the past six days. They have liberated over 1,000 towns and villages, completely shattering the German lines as 14 infantry and six panzer divisions reeled backward under the sledge-hammer blows of the attackers.

Climaxing the great Russian advance was the capture of Korosten, key rail junction 86 miles northwest of Kiev. As the old year comes to an end, the Soviets have swept ten miles past Korosten and momentarily are expected to retake Zhitomir.

FAST COMEBACK

Thus in one week the Russians have reconquered more than half of all the territory gained by the Germans in their all-out five-week offensive for Kiev. And those three titanic attacks by the Nazis cost them heavily in tanks, guns and men—a fact which now is playing into the hands of the Reds.

Korosten's loss was a severe blow to the Germans. This city is a juncture of five railway lines, and it commands many roads. Korosten first was captured by the Russians on Nov. 17, and then reoccupied by the Nazis Nov. 30. It is only 55 miles from the old Polish frontier.

Germans are defending the approaches to Zhitomir to the last man. They made their first "suicide" defense at Korostishev, a small town of 7,000, and one of the bloodiest battles of the Soviet offensive resulted. They dug in on an 800-foot hill, and not a single Nazi remained alive when the Rus-

(Continued on Page 4)

Eighth Major Air Raid Rocks Berlin

LONDON, Dec. 30—Berlin took it squarely in the neck again last night by one of the most powerful concentrations of RAF bombers yet to visit the German capital.

More than 2,000 tons of bombs were dropped on the already gutted city, and returning pilots reported seeing vast columns of flames and smoke rising two miles above the target.

While the powerful formation of heavy bombers was smashing at Berlin, Mosquitoes attacked targets in western and northern Germany and in northern France.

Of the hundreds of British aircraft employed in these important raids, only 22 failed to return. At least 28 German fighters were bagged.

The raid on Berlin was the eighth of a large scale carried out by the RAF since November 18. The raid was conducted during the early hours of the evening.

Wallace Sees Finish Of Nazi Might Soon

WASHINGTON—Vice President Henry A. Wallace predicted in a radio interview the destruction of Germany's war might within a "few months" after the expected invasion across the English channel. He said such a drive coordinated with a full-scale Russian offensive, would quickly place the Nazis "in an impossible position."

"We must not only completely defeat and disarm the enemy," Mr. Wallace said, "but through the agencies of the United Nations make it possible for all people of the world to help themselves as fast as possible in their last fight against hunger, disease and unemployment."

Germany, France Hit as USAAF Opens '44 Offensive

1D. THE STARS AND STRIPES 1D.
Daily Newspaper of U.S. Armed Forces in the European Theater of Operations
Vol. 4 No. 54 New York, N.Y.—London, England Wednesday, Jan. 5, 1944

Nazi Front Caves In, Reds Enter Poland

Northwest Reich Blasted Through Clouds by New 'Magic Eye' Technique

Marauders Pound Targets Along the Invasion Coast

American bombers and fighters opened their 1944 air offensive in daylight yesterday with dawn-to-dusk attacks on Nazi targets from France to northwestern Germany.

Vast formations of Flying Fortresses and Liberators, protected by shuttle relays of USAAF fighter planes, swept over northwest Germany and bombed through solid clouds with the secret technique called by Swedish scientists the "magic eye." Eighteen heavy bombers and two fighters were reported missing.

Marauder medium bombers, together with RAF medium, light and fighter-bombers, stormed the invasion coast of northern France in a literally unending series of attacks on military installations—probably more secret rocket-gun emplacements. The first Marauders climbed up from their fields in the pre-dawn darkness, and the last of them were coming home after dusk. Four bombers and one fighter were reported missing from the joint medium operations.

Some bomber crews reported temperatures of 55 degrees below zero and winds of almost gale-like velocity.

Wait Reconnaissance Photos

In line with policy, no immediate official announcement was made of the heavy bombers' objectives in yesterday's attacks pending later reconnaissance, inasmuch they bombed through clouds.

The day's operations were the first in the new year for all U.S. forces, which last were out on Dec. 31 when the 1943 offensive wound up with the USAAF's largest assault of the war.

For the Marauders, whose formations were in the air almost all through the day, yesterday's attack marked the completion of 1,500 consecutive sorties—on seven operational days—without loss, it was announced, leaving the inference that the four bombers reported missing were RAF or Allied aircraft. The U.S. mediums last lost a plane on Dec. 13.

The day-long attack came after a night in which the RAF interrupted its Battle of Berlin and only stirred the German sirens with intruder and nuisance forays into the western zones of the Reich. Meanwhile, however, reports continued to come from neutral sources substantiating Sunday's rumors that much of the civilian population of the Nazi capital was being evacuated to safer areas.

Forced Down in Sweden

Although there was no official announcement on yesterday's target for the heavy bombers, dispatches from Sweden told of at least one flak-scarred U.S. bomber being forced down there, which may have been an indication that the object of the day's attack was well in the north of the Reich, from which it would be easier for a crippled aircraft to reach Sweden than attempt the trip back to England.

Some crews reported they saw fires in the target area through a break in the clouds.

"We were lucky enough to pass over a break in the overcast and see part of the place burning," said Capt. Wayne L. Horr, Auburn (N.Y.), pilot of the Fortress Mission Belle. The day's mission was Horr's 25th.

Combat crews praised their fighter escort.

"It was good and there was certainly a lot of it," said S/Sgt. Oren C. Becke, of Swea City, Ia., tail gunner on Shackeroo II. "The only trouble was it was damn cold up there today."

No Board, No Draft

JACKSON, Miss., Jan. 4—Nobody has been drafted for military service in Alcorn County since Oct. 2, because there's no draft board to call them up. Three board members resigned Oct. 2 after a dispute over Selective Service regulations, and everyone asked to serve since has declined appointment.

Hitler Won't Live to End

WASHINGTON, Jan. 4 (AP)—M. Masaryk, Czechoslovak Foreign Minister, predicted that Hitler would not live long enough to be brought up for trial as a war criminal. "He will either be taken care of by the military or will commit suicide," he said.

Blitz Firemen's Methods Save U.S. Motor Pool

A U.S. ARMY POST, England, Jan. 4—Employing British fire-fighting methods developed in the 1940-41 blitz and taught to them in a four-week instruction course by Sgt. L. G. Martin of the Royal Engineers, Negro soldiers stationed here saved their unit's motor pool from destruction by fire, it was disclosed today.

During the course, 14 soldiers working in teams of four became proficient enough to lay 300 feet of discharge canvas hose and extend two lengths of suction hose from a booster pump in 75 seconds. They won honors in tournaments with both British and American units.

A month after the course, the motor pool, filled with vehicles and large quantities of gas and oil, was discovered ablaze. The 14 firefighters went into action and quickly extinguished the fire.

15th Forts Hit Bearing Plant

Italy Factory First Target By Twining's Command; Land Battle Quiet

ALLIED HQ, North Africa, Jan. 4 (AP)—German communications at Turin and the vital Villa Perosa ball-bearing factory yesterday felt the crushing weight of 15th Air Force Fortresses, while soggy ground and snow "stymied" large-scale land activity today in Italy.

The U.S. heavy bombers, flying for the first time under the command of Lt. Gen. Nathan Twining, almost completely wrecked the ball-bearing plant.

Photographs showed that main buildings, 600 feet wide and 1,200-feet long, received direct hits, with further damage from near misses. Other direct hits were scored on adjacent buildings which apparently housed workers.

The raid was another blow in the intensive campaign against plants producing ball bearings—one of the most vital necessities of the war since they are used in planes, tanks, submarines and most other military machines.

Algiers radio today said that while the weather on the Italian front had improved, it was not hard enough underfoot to permit of any major action. One report said that the whole of the Eighth Army front apart from the small coastal belt was under snow.

On the Fifth Army front Allied patrols probed the enemy defenses yesterday.

The Tidal Wave Rolls West

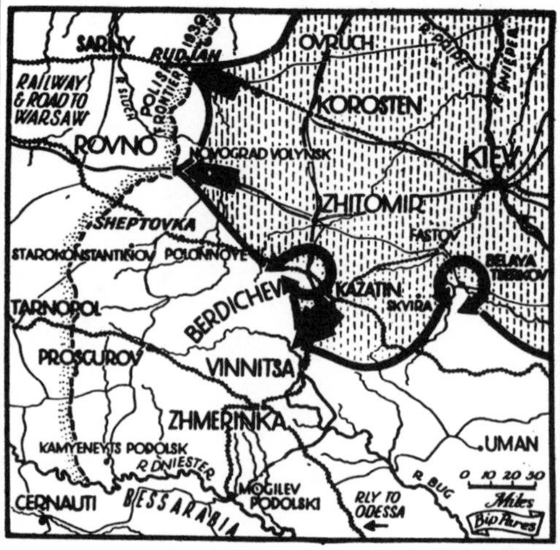

Daily Express Map

Russian Cossacks crossed the Polish border northwest of Korosten yesterday as the entire German front crumbled along a 50-mile stretch south to Novograd Volynski. South of the growing Kiev bulge the Russians captured the railway stronghold of Belaya Tserkov (shown here as encircled).

30 Indicted as Having Plotted With Reich to Seize U.S. Reins

WASHINGTON, Jan. 4—Indictment of 28 prominent pro-Fascist men and two women—including William Dudley Pelley, George Sylvester Viereck, Gerhard Kunze and Mrs. Elizabeth Dilling—on formal charges of conspiring with the German Reich to overthrow the American government stirred a sensation today in the U.S.

Attorney Gen. Francis Biddle announced the indictments late yesterday. He said they resulted from investigations begun as long ago as June, 1940.

The 30 were charged with having knowingly conspired with officials of the German Reich with intent to interfere with and impair the loyalty, morale and discipline of military and naval forces in the U.S.

They were accused of distributing printed matter urging disloyalty and mutiny and also were charged with having joined a movement launched by the German Nazi Party intended to undermine loyalty and morale in the U.S.

Pelley, head of the semi-Fascist American Silver Shirts, once was said to have planned a march on Washington to seize power. He was accused in 1940 of plotting overthrow of the government with a number of U.S. Army officers.

Viereck, newspaper writer and author of pro-Fascist booklets, was sentenced last year to serve two to six years in prison for failing to disclose his activities as a German propagandist.

Kunze, leader of the German-American Bund in the United States, was sentenced at Hartford, Conn., in August, 1942, to serve 15 years in prison for conspiring to send military and defense information to Germany and Japan.

Mrs. Dilling, a supporter of Spain's Gen. Franco, gained fame as author of "The Red Network," a book which labelled many prominent Americans as Communists.

Other defendants included Lawrence Dennis, known as "the brains of American Fascism," and Joseph McWilliams, Bronx (N.Y.), accused jew-baiter.

Pelley, Viereck and Mrs. Dilling were among 33 persons indicted a year ago on charges of sedition.

Single Liberty Ship Gets 6 Nazi Planes on Voyage

U.S. EAST COAST PORT, Jan. 4 (AP)—A Liberty ship has docked here after a hazardous voyage to the Mediterranean in which its naval gun crew accounted for six German planes.

The vessel drew first blood while lying off Gela, when it brought down an FW190. Half an hour later it accounted for another.

Several weeks later, while proceeding towards Gibraltar, the ship was attacked by a large German formation and the crewmen shot down two Ju88s and two Heinkels.

Jap Siberian Islands Hit by U.S. Bombers

WASHINGTON, Jan. 4 (UP)—Paramushir, Japanese base in the Kurile islands, which run north from the Jap mainland to the Siberian peninsula of Kamchatka, was bombed New Year's Eve by Army planes, the War Department revealed today. All planes returned safely.

Blackened Skies Over Reich—FDR Pledge Becoming a Fact

By Earl Mazo
Stars and Stripes Staff Writer

AN EIGHTH BOMBER STATION, Jan. 4—The boys of Eighth Bomber Command got on with the job of working over the German war machine today, and in their opening Fort-Liberator mission of the new year brought closer to complete reality one of President Roosevelt's first war-time promises to the Nazis: To cover completely the daylight skies over Germany with American bombers.

As observer-gunner on Mr. Smith, one of the hundreds of heavies doing today's job on a vital northwest Germany target, I was with a formation in the middle of the whole show and saw swarms of Forts and Libs going in and coming out—like so many huge dump trucks buzzing around a road project.

That dumping wasn't going on unchallenged, however. There was plenty of flak bursting like exploding kegs of nails all over the place, and an occasional Ju88 or FW190 poked its nose up through the overcast, only to be driven off or engaged by the American fighter support, which seemed to be circling the target area at will when our particular Fortress formation came over.

Mr. Smith, the Fort christened for the average American Smith, and piloted by 1 Lt. Chester (Doc) Doron, of Rochester, N.Y., took off this morning as it always does to the tune of "Nas-Zdrowie," shouted by the whole crew in unison.

According to the crew's only Pole, S/Sgt. Edward Berowski, of Buffalo, N.Y., top turret gunner, "Nas-Zdrowie" brings good luck and its repetition before each trip is greatly responsible for Mr. Smith's 20-odd successful missions against the Nazis to date.

Berowski explained this belief as the Fort took its place in the combat wing's formation and headed out over the icy North Sea. When Berowski finished, the interphone conversation became heated. T/Sgt. Donald Hughes, radio-gunner

(Continued on page 4)

Gen. Sultan Is Appointed To Southeast Asia Post

ALLIED HQ., New Delhi, Jan. 4—Maj. Gen. Daniel Isom Sultan, 58, has been appointed Deputy Commander-in-Chief of U.S. Army troops in China, Burma and India, it was announced today.

Sultan, a veteran of 36 years in the regular Army, served as an instructor at West Point before World War I, in which he served as a member of the general staff. At West Point he played on the same football team as Gen. Dwight D. Eisenhower.

FDR Is Recovering

WASHINGTON, Jan. 4 (AP)—President Roosevelt is continuing to recover from his attack of influenza but he remained in his bedroom today on doctor's orders and his press conference was canceled.

Line Yields To Cossacks West of Kiev

Soviets Over Border First Time Since June of 1941; Enemy in Utter Rout

Swift Cossack patrols, racing ahead of the main Russian columns west of Korosten, were reported yesterday to have crossed the Polish border at several points as the Soviet Ukrainian Army gathered in hundreds of square miles of new territory and overwhelmed the Nazi railway stronghold of Belaya Tserkov, 50 miles south of Kiev.

The Cossacks' advance carried the Russians back to Polish soil for the first time since June 28, 1941, a week after Hitler began the attack on Russia.

Dispatches from the front indicated the Russian drive was continuing unabated, with the Germans nowhere able to make a stand. On a 50-mile front between Olevsk, northwest of Korosten, and Novograd-Volynski, key rail junction west of Zhitomir, Marshal Von Manstein's troops fell back in utter rout.

Rich Booty for Russians

The advancing Russians gathered in a rich haul of booty as they drove the Germans back. Moscow said the trackless forests and swamps of the battle area—some of the most desolate country in the world—yielded large numbers of guns, trucks and other materials.

So fast were the Russians moving that correspondents in Moscow were unable last night to fix their front lines exactly. Main forces on Gen. Nicolai Vatutin's right flank were well west of Olevsk, five miles from the Polish border, and south of the bulge were approximately 15 miles from the railway town of Vinnitsa, one of the two keys to the communications of the Dnieper Bend.

Fall of the town and large railway station of Belaya Tserkov, announced in a special order of the day by Marshal Stalin last night, opened the way for strong Russian forces to swing southwest toward Vinnitsa, on the Bug River, and Zhmerinka, 25 miles beyond, on the vital Odessa-Lwow railroad.

The threat to the large German forces fighting in the Dnieper Bend against the Russian offensive aimed at Nikopol thus grew measurably greater as the Russian steamroller crushed its way toward the Rumanian border and the railways that feed the Dnieper Bend.

Big Attack on Berdichev

Only the almost encircled railway junction of Berdichev, south of Zhitomir, and the communications center of Sheptovia, 60 miles west of Zhitomir, still stand as Nazi bastions in the northern Ukraine, and Berlin radio said last night that the Red Army was now attacking the northern part of Berdichev with unabated fury.

The Cossack sweep across the Polish border was reported by Reuters in a Moscow dispatch, but though the Russians passed it through censorship they made no announcement of their own in the capital, apparently waiting for Gen. Vatutin's main forces to clear the last of the Germans from Russian soil west of Korosten. A Stockholm report said the Cossacks occupied the small Polish town of Rudjah-Gorodnitsa a mile or two west of the frontier.

Sarny, 45 miles west of Olevsk, on the road west from Korosten, and Rovno, 55 miles west of Novograd Volynski, were the Russians' next objectives in this sector. Both can be reached only over a veritable no-man's-land, sparsely populated, almost roadless country.

Moscow dispatches told of new gains on the White Russian front but gave no details.

Nazis Entered Russia Just 2½ Years Ago

It was on June 28-29, 1941, that German troops first crossed the original Polish-Russian frontier. The crossing came in the Minsk area, less than a week after the Germans made their first attack on Russia.

The main Nazi thrust in the general direction of Moscow was made through the "Baranowicze gap" and resulted in a battle between 4,000 tanks.

NORTHERN IRELAND EDITION

1D. THE STARS AND STRIPES 1D.

Daily Newspaper of U.S. Armed Forces in the European Theater of Operations

Vol. 1. No. 26. New York, N.Y.—Belfast, Northern Ireland. Thursday, Jan. 6, 1944.

Reds Drive To Spring Dnieper Bend Threat

USAAF Bombers Hammer Two Airfields In France

Kiel Hit 2 Straight Days; 3,000 Allied Planes Out Tuesday

Eighth Air Force heavy bombers, ranging far over occupied Europe from the Baltic to the Bay of Biscay, struck heavily at German airfields at Bordeaux and Tours in France yesterday and for the second time in two days droned the long 850-mile round trip to Kiel to hammer vital Nazi shipping.

The multi - pronged raids — unidentified targets in western Germany were also attacked—were the second days operations in a row for the American four-motored bombers and their long-range fighter escort. Kiel and Munster were attacked in Germany Tuesday in a day of aerial assault, which saw some 3.000 Allied warplanes take part.

American fighters escorted the bombers on all of yesterday's missions except the long looping run over the Bay of Biscay to Bordeaux. Fortress crews who had to go in there without their usual P38 and P47 protection returned telling of fierce enemy interceptor attacks

Tougher Than Schweinfurt

The Bordeaux raid was described by one pilot, Maj. Thomas Kenny, of Youngstown, Ohio, skipper of the Fortress Fertile Myrtle, as more difficult than the costly attack on the Schweinfurt ball-bearing works in Germany last October.

"I've been on 19 missions, including Schweinfurt," Kenny said, "and this was the most difficult yet. We were attacked by 50 fighters all the way from the target to the coast."

Other crewmen reported heavy flak, but said that in spite of it the airfield was heavily bombed.

Besides the heavy-bomber operations RAF and Allied medium bombers and RAF fighter-bombers, escorted by RAF and Allied fighters, attacked military objectives in Northern France yesterday again without loss.

One of the raiding Fortresses came down in a forced landing in Sweden, northwest of Trelleborg, in the southern part of the country. Dispatches from Stockholm said the ten members of her crew were uninjured.

It was the second American plane to land in Sweden in two days, and brought the total of interned American airmen to 86.

Eighth Air Force, announcing the targets of yesterday's attacks, said that losses and claims would be announced "as soon as they are evaluated, probably Thursday morning."

Mosquitos Hit Berlin

The American heavies went out in daylight yesterday after RAF night forces had kept up the ceaseless hammering of military targets in Northern France—presumably rocket-gun emplacements along the French invasion coast.

The RAF's operations Monday night also included Mosquito attacks on Berlin, which started the sirens screaming in the German capital after a 24 hours let-up following the assault early Sunday. Not a single plane was ...ted missing from those and other ... operations, which included **New Dodge.** western Germany and ...YN, N.Y. enemy waters.

The do... ...onged attack on Kiel and Munster, which was ...ried o... while the mediums of both Air Forces were pounding the French rocket-gun coast, was supported by long-range American fighters in one of their

(Continued on Page 2)

Raid on Schweinfurt Aided Them, Reds Say

The American heavy bomber raid on Schweinfurt two and a half months ago has had a direct and disastrous effect on Germany's Eastern Front, a radio broadcast from Moscow declared yesterday.

The Oct. 14 assault, which cost the USAAF 60 heavy bombers, its biggest single loss of the war, crippled the plant at Schweinfurt which was turning out possibly 50 per cent of the ball bearings used by the mechanized Wehrmacht.

"This was a hard blow to Hitler's war machine," the Soviet commentator said. "It reacted disastrously for Hitler on the Eastern Front."

Nazis Bombed by New 'Magic Feet' Technique

AN EIGHTH BOMBING STATION, Jan. 6—Henry Brirton, of Jamaica, L.I., N.Y., a Fortress bombardier, danced a gig five miles up over Naziland in order to drop his bombs in yesterday's attack on Northwest Germany.

The bomb-bay doors jammed and several explosives failed to drop, authough released from the shackles.

Brirton crawled down into the bomb bay. Holding on to the sides of the bomb rack, he jumped up and down until the door jarred open, allowing the bombs to fall while the plane was still over the target.

Sofia's Rail Line Bombed

2 Other Balkan Bases Blasted As 8th Gains On Adriatic

ALLIED HQ., Jan. 6 (AP)—U.S. bombers struck at German communications in the Balkans hitting at three points in Bulgaria and Jugoslavia as the armies in Italy gained two commanding positions against fierce opposition.

With heavy clouds hiding most of the Italian targets, Fortresses of the 15th Air Force smashed the railway yard and bridge at Dupnitsa, 50 miles south of Sofia on the main line.

Mitchells of the 12th Air Force scored five hits on a railway station at Doboj, 55 miles north of Serajevo, as well as on barracks and troop concentrations at Travnik, 30 miles northeast of Serajevo. Two German planes were destroyed. All the U.S. planes returned.

Tough Fight for Heights

Tough local fighting for heights at the Adriatic end of the Eighth Army's line continued, while Indian troops advanced a few hundred yards in the mountain ridge under German machine-gun fire southwest of San Tommaso.

Troops of the Fifth Army advancing a little more than a mile west of Venafro stormed a 2,300-ft. height in Sammucro Ridge about two miles northeast of San Vittore to gain some dominance of that bastion on the German winter line.

Lightning fighters escorting small formations of Forts on the Dupnitsa raid shot down a Heinkel 111 and a Gotha 242 glider which was encountered when they were strafing locomotives on their way home. Two locomotives were destroyed and a train of 40 cars damaged.

Lt. Gen. Leese Will Command 8th Army

ALGIERS, Jan. 6 (AP)—Lt. Gen. Sir Oliver Leese will be the new commander of the Eighth Army in succession to Gen. Montgomery, it was announced here to-day.

Gen. Leese commanded the Eighth Corps during the march from El Alamein to Tunis.

74,000 Tons Dropped By USAAF In 'Med' Area

ALLIED HQ North Africa, Jan. 6 (AP)—The North African air forces announced today that the Strategic Air Force alone had dropped 74,000 tons of bombs on Axis targets in the Mediterranean during the past year.

Planes of the Strategic Air Force shot down 3,146 Axis planes during 1943 for the loss of 819 aircraft, while 2,426 more enemy planes were destroyed on the ground.

During the year 70,000 sorties were flown by Maj. Gen. James Doolittle's command, during which 101 ships were sunk, ranging in size from cruisers to German torpedo boats. In addition, 216 ships were seriously damaged.

Targets included Germany, Austria, the Balkans, Italy, North Africa, France, and most of the islands of the western Mediterranean.

The Scotch Famine

WASHINGTON, Jan. 6—Even the British Embassy here cannot get any Scotch!

The Russian Front Today

Anybody Wearing the Bronx Ribbon?

The Story's Out—New York City Bombed Once—By U.S. Plane!

By Andrew A. Rooney
Stars and Stripes Writer

A MARAUDER-BASE, Jan. 6—Greater New York City has been bombed in this war and how it was done was told here today by the man who did it.

He is Sgt. Weldon K. Fulton, of Danville, Va.—unassigned at this station—who for the first year after America's entry into the war was an enlisted bombardier in medium bombers. The bombing of New York, he explained, was done with depth charges from a crippled U.S. plane—and the depth charges didn't explode.

On Dec. 21, 1942, Fulton said, the bomber in which he was bombardier was returning from the day's anti-submarine patrol over the Atlantic.

As the pilot whose name Fulton can't recall now, headed the ship toward land the starboard engine cut out.

The bomb load anti-submarine depth charges pulled the bomber down despite the pilot's efforts. "We were struggling to hold altitude," Fulton recalled today, "but it was no good. Just about that time we were coming over part of Long Island.

Dropped On Park

"The pilot had to make a quick choice whether to let us crash with the depth charges aboard and possibly kill a lot of people as well as the crew or to jettison the depth charges and hope they wouldn't go off. He thought fast and told me to drop them in an open park as we crossed it."

Fulton set his sights on the park and pressed the bomb release. The depth charges tumbled down to a small stream about 50 yards from a house. They did not explode. (Anti-submarine depth charges detonate as a result of under-water pressure after they are dropped into the sea and sink. They explode at a depth predetermined by the setting of the pressure fuse.)

The plane, rid of its cargo, limped safely to base, Fulton said, and turned in a report on the first bombing of Greater New York City.

Seek Will Rogers Post.

LOS ANGELES, Jan. 6—Leland M. Ford, who represented the 16th district in Congress from 1938-1942, announced that he would run again for Congress. Dr. Jesse R. Kellems, an Assemblyman, also has announced his intention to run for the same office. Both are Republicans. They said they would seek both the Republican and Democratic nominations. The 16th district is represented now by Will Rogers, Jr.

No Bulgarian Coup, Report

German motorized troops were reported moving up to strategic points in Bulgaria yesterday amid a flood of contradictory dispatches from neutral capitals purporting to describe the latest crisis inside that war-weary Balkans nation.

Travellers arriving in Turkey from Sofia, the Bulgarian capital, denied earlier reports that a pro-Allied coup d'etat had occurred in which the government of Premier Boshilov had been overthrown.

Boshilov's regime, though still in power, was described as so shaky, however, that the Germans were rapidly converting their "control" of the nation into occupation. Istanbul heard that they had practically taken over the administration to forestall rioting.

Berlin radio admitted for the first time yesterday that Jugoslavia Partisans attacking the railway town of Banjaluka in Bosnia were conducting an offensive against Nazi troops.

Tobacco Redrying Plants Placed On 4-Day Week

LEXINGTON Ky., Jan. 6 — The eight-state Burley tobacco belt went on a four-day week yesterday. The move was made necessary because redrying plants are experiencing difficulty keeping up with deliveries due to man-power shortage. Friday sales will be discontinued at least temporarily.

No Feature Section Today

Because of transportation delays, today's edition of The Stars and Stripes appears without the Thursday Feature Section, "Terry and the Pirates" and "Li'l Abner." It is hoped that the Feature Section and the comics will be included in Friday's edition.

Soviets Take Berdichev As Nazis Retreat

Germans Admit Lines On East Front Have Been Split

As the Soviet First Ukranian Army launched a great drive to clear at least a half-million Nazis from the Dnieper Bend, Marshal Stalin announced last night that Berdichev, key Nazi hedgehog stronghold in the Kiev bulge, had been captured by Russian Army units.

The Germans earlier had announced that the Russians had split their Eastern front west of Kiev and that under pressure of superior Soviet forces the Nazis had to abandon the eastern portion of Berdichev, the position from which the Germans had been centering their defensive campaign to hold up the Russian drive into the pre-1939 Polish territory.

Berdichev's fall was regarded by military observers as an important forward move in Gen. Vatutin's drive to trap the German armies in the Ukraine.

Powerful Russian mobile forces, striking from the plains south of liberated Belaya Tserkov, drove forward against Germans strung out all the way from that important railway center, 50 miles south of Kiev, to Nikopol deep in the bend.

First Counter-Attack in Poland

Marshal Von Manstein ran the risk of a major military disaster if the Russians achieved their encirclement. Red Army columns drove southwest toward the railway towns of Vinnitsa and Zhmerinka while, south of the Lower Dnieper, Gen. Holbukhin's steppe army, opposite Kherson, stood ready to surge across the river to shut the southern jaw of the trap.

Meanwhile, the First Ukraine Army beat off a German counter-attack on the Russian side of the 1939 Polish Border near Novograd Volynski. The Russians appeared to have decided to consolidate their positions here before driving farther across the boundary over which advance Cossack patrols penetrated Tuesday.

Abandonment of the eastern part of Berdichev was revealed in the German communique a few hours after a Wilhelmstrasse spokesman speaking to Swedish correspondents in Berlin admitted that the Red Army had split the Nazis into two fronts of 360 and 480 miles each.

The Press conference was held in the bomb-damaged foreign office, while fires still burned in the capital from Sunday's and Monday's heavy raids

Two-Prong Drive

With Berdichev's fall expected within 24 hours, the way seemed clear for a rapid advance toward Vinnitsa and Zhmerink. Moscow reports said yesterday that Gen. Vatutin had apparently decided to consolidate his positions around Novograd Volynski, the key junction 60 miles north-west of Zhitomir, and concentrate his main thrust to the south-west toward the Bug and Dniester rivers.

Vatutin appeared to be cutting a wide encircling sweep round the Germans in the Dnieper bend, his right wing driving for Vinnitsa and his left wing pushing on from Belaya Tserkov, south-east to the Nazi's Cherkassy bridgehead on the Dnieper.

A new Russian offensive on the front joining the Zhitomir and Vitebsk sectors was reported by Berlin yesterday, as Gen. Ivan Bagramyan's White Russian Army around Nevel launched a major drive down the Veliki Luki-Riga railway.

'Help Soviets,' Poles Are Told

The Polish Government in London has instructed the leaders of its underground movement inside Poland to cooperate with the Soviet commanders when they enter Poland and when diplomatic relations between the two countries are resumed

This is disclosed in an official Polish Government statement issued last night which said:

"Poland naturally is entitled to expect full justice and redress as soon as she is liberated from enemy occupation.

"The first condition of such justice is the earliest re-establishment of a Polish sovereign administration of liberated territories in the Republic of Poland and the protection of life and property of Polish citizens."

THE STARS AND STRIPES
MIDDLE EAST
VOL. II No. 2 CAIRO FOUR CENTS JANUARY 14 1944

President Calls for Nation Service Law

President Roosevelt's annual State of the Union message to Congress recommended "A National Service Act" which, "with certain appropriate exceptions, will make available for war production or for any other essential services every able-bodied adult in this nation."

Besides outlining a five-point program for Congressional action, the President also asked the legislators to make it possible for soldiers, sailors and marines to vote in the coming elections. Under existing state laws the voting machinery is left entirely to the States; both the Army and Navy have reported that it will be impossible effectively to administer 48 different soldier voting laws. "It is the duty of Congress to remove these unjustifiable discriminations against the men and women in our armed forces — and to do it as quickv as possible," the President urged.

He condemned the attitude of "half-an-eye on the battlefronts abroad and the other half-an-eye on personal, selfish or political interest here at home" and asked the Congress adopt:

1. "A realistic tax law — which will tax all unreasonable profits both individual and corporative and reduce the ultimate cost of the war to our sons and daughters. The tax bill now under consideration by the Congress does not begin to meet this test."

2.) "A continuing of the law for the renegotiation of war contracts which will prevent exorbitant profits and assure fair prices to the government. For two years I have pleaded with the Congress to take undue profits out of war."

3.) "A cost of food law — which will enable the government (a.) to place a reasonable floor under the prices the farmer may expect for his produce and (b.) to place a ceiling on the prices a consumer will have to pay for the food he buys. This should apply to necessities only and will require public funds to carry out. It will cost in appropriations about one percent of the present annual cost of the war."

4.) "Early re-enactment of the stabilization statute of October 1942. This expires June 30, 1944 and if not enacted well in advance, the country might just as well expect price chaos by summer."

"A National Service Act" was the fifth of these proposals, which the President said he would not recommend "unless other laws were passed to keep down the cost of living, to share equitably the burdens of taxation, to hold the stabilization line and to prevent undue profits."

He pointed out that "I have for three years hesitated to recommend a National Service Act. Today, however, I am convinced of the necessity. Although I believe we and our Allies can win the war without such a measure, I am certain that nothing less than total mobilization of all our resources of manpower and capital will guarantee an earlier victory and reduce the toll of suffering and sorrow and blood.

"National Service is the most democratic way to wage a war. Like Selective Service for the armed forces, it rests on the obligation of each citizen to serve his nation to his utmost where he is best qualified. It does not mean reduction in wages. It does not mean loss of retirement and seniority rights and

(continued on page 2)

Old Glory Flies Over Tarawa

Victorious U.S. Marines raise the American Flag over the captured Jap base on Tarawa in the South Pacific after three days of bitter fighting in which 1,092 Marines lost their lives. The entire enemy garrison of 5,700 Japs were annihilated to the last man. A war-torn palm was drafted to do the honors of a flagpole.

Fifth Army Faces Gates of Cassino

After weeks of bitterly-contested struggle, the Fifth Army on the Italian front this week was within four miles of Cassino, toughest German bulwark on the road to Rome.

The Yanks began clearing Mount Trocchio, last of the mountain barriers before the city. Every yard of the slippery, rock-strewn surface was savagely defended by the Germans, who had orders to hold to their positions to the point of virtual suicide.

Further inland, the British troops of the Fifth crossed a fording of the Peccia river, giving the army a foothold at the lower end of the broad Liri plain, immediate goal of the advance.

Rising temperature in the central mountains had turned the front into a huge swamp, but from behind the lines USAAF and RAF planes took off to paste the four-mile gap between Cassino and Cervaro. In these hills advancing Yank troops have been for-

(Continued on page 5)

WAR NEARS BALKANS

LONDON. — Radio Berlin said Thursday that "War has practically come to the front door of the Balkans."

The Turkish Minister of Education told Turkish students in Berlin to continue their studies in Switzerland.

In Sofia, the Bulgarian Radio ordered all military and railway personnel to rejoin their units.

USAAF-Luftwaffe In Gigantic Battle

Matching might and wits against the Luftwaffe, an armada of 700 Liberators and Flying Fortresses of the U.S. Army Air Forces battled Tuesday in German skies with unprecedented fury.

Luftwaffe opposition tactics resembled those of a naval battle, employing "destroyer" planes with smokescreens and broadside rocket shelling in an attempt to prevent the raiders from reaching their target.

It was evident that the Germans assumed this was to be the first daylight American attack on Berlin whereas it actually was a series of three targets the USAAF bombardiers were prepped for — fighter plane plants at Brunswick, Oschersiben and Halberstadt. These factories, which supply ME 110s, Fock-Wulfe 190s and JU 86 and 188s, are reported to have been successfully bombed.

Of the estimated 700 heavy bombers the USAAF sent over, 59 have not returned to their bases, while of the fighters which escorted them part way over and partially back, five are missing. In the three hour air battles, Yank pilots estimate the Germans lost from 100 to 300 fighter craft.

These attacked the bomber formations in swarms of between 20 and 30 each, including twin-engined night fighters in their all-out opposition. While our losses are not regarded as overly high, it is estimated that the German fighters destroyed or downed may set a record.

Russian Troops Pour Through New Gap In German Lines

The battle of Russia continued in all its fury as Soviet armies in North White Russia pierced German lines northwest of Vitebsk. Fighting was reported behind the German lines. At the same time, General Vatutin's First Ukraine Army launched a powerful new drive towards Poland north of the Pripet marshes and a break-through of eight miles was reported.

After a battle representative of the war's bloodiest, Sarny was captured despite strong German counterattacks in a desperate attempt to stem the advance of Soviet Armies which closed in on three sides. Sarny, a large railway junction lying 30 miles west of the 1939 Polish border, is the furthest town reached in the first thrust into Poland.

Soviet offensive operations along the two vast fronts of the First and Second Ukraine Armies developed steadily. Battles are reported to be raging night and day with German suicidal attempts to chop into the Soviet flanks and cut off the Russian troops from the masses of reserves streaming up from the rear.

Railway Menaced

The Russians are within a few miles of the Bug River and form an immediate menace to the important Oedssa-Lvov railway. German pantzer troops, fighting fiercely to prevent the Russians from crossing the river and cutting off their main escape line from the Dnieper Bend, have brought up reinforcements to the northern banks of the Bug.

Another prong of the Soviet offensive in pushing towards Shep-

(Continued on page 5)

Pocket Closing on Japs in New Guinea

Allied forces are closing the trap on the Japs in New Guinea. Australian forces, following a heavy artillery barrage have driven past Sharnhorst Point and have the Japs in full retreat. Meanwhile American Sixth Army units are making steady advances in the direction of Madang. Allied fliers hit Madang with 243 tons of bombs.

A light U.S. naval force intercepted an apparent Jap attempt to reinforce their isolated forces on New Guinea and sank seven barges jammed with troops and supplies.

On New Britain, U.S. Marines are making slow progress in the hills south of Gloucester. Heavy fighting is being waged for the possession of Hill 660, important observation post still in enemy hands.

Allied headquarters have announced that Marine casualties at Cape Gloucester have been less than 15 per cent of the losses inflicted on the Japs.

Solomons-based American bombers hit Rabaul, New Britain, as other U.S. planes struck at Cape St. George on the southern tip of New Ireland in the face of stiff ene-

(Continued on page 5)

Reversal of Senate Vote Action Sought

WASHINGTON. — Sen. Scott Lucas, Illinois Democrat, has introduced a new soldier vote bill intended to reverse the Senate action that approved the measure placing responsibility for service ballots on the individual States.

The new bill provides a federal ballot for president, senators and representatives but sets up local election boards as sole judges of the remainder of the ballot. Blank spaces would allow serviie personnel to write in choices for federal offices in the field ballot. Ballots would be returned to local election boards under auspices of U.S. Ballot Commission.

President Summons Labor Chieftains

WASHINGTON (UP)— President Roosevelt summoned the antagonistic labor leaders William Green, President of the A.F. of L.; and Philip Murray, President of the C.I.O., to the White House to discuss the labor draft legislation.

At the same time, the Senate Committee started hearings on the Republican sponsored legislation to achieve the same end.

A first check of labor sentiment showed disappointment that the President had proposed National Service Legislation.

It is expected that William Green will, not less than his C.I.O. colleague Richard Murray, oppose the legislation on the grounds that the closed or union shop controversy cuts across the labor draft problem, although the leaders concerned are so far avoiding the issue.

Strikes Continue

Meanwhile, in Philadelphia 17,556 striking employees of the Cramp Shipbuilding Co. failed to return to work despite orders to do so from the Navy WLB and the Industrial Union of Marine and Shipbuilding Workers. Strikers stated that they have eight grievances which they will discuss when they meet on Sunday to decide whether or not to return to work. Simultaneously, 3,500 city employees spurned appeals to return to work, leaving piles of uncollected garbage and trash and other public utilities tied-up.

"We will continue to strike until we get our ten cents an hour increase," said the strikers. Convicts from two prisons operated the water pumping stations so that Philadelphians might have water.

Irked workers of Pittsburgh utilities went into their third day of a sit-down strike to demand the return of a fired supervisor. The people of Pittsburgh, however, took the strike without complaint. The strikers' jobs were to prepare and mail gas and electric bills, and the mailing of 500,000 bills was held up by the strike.

NORTHERN IRELAND EDITION

1D. THE STARS AND STRIPES 1D.

Daily Newspaper of U.S. Armed Forces in the European Theater of Operations

Vol. 1. No. 36. New York, N.Y.—Belfast, Northern Ireland. Tuesday, Jan. 18, 1944.

Gen. Bradley Heads U.S. Invasion Troops

Reds Across Bug River, Nazis Admit

Bitter Fighting In South; Leningrad Rail Line Cut By New Soviet Drive

Russian mobile units cut one of the Nazi rail lines to Leningrad and rolled back the enemy in a rapid advance toward the Baltic yesterday as the Red Army on the central front pushed within 40 miles of Pinsk, and the Germans admitted that at one point Soviet tanks had crossed the Bug River near Vinnitsa, in the south.

Powerful Red Army armored forces, rolling forward in what may become a major thrust to the Baltic, surged westward through a widening gap in the enemy lines at Novo-Sokolniki, 25 miles north of Nevel and a little more than 70 miles from the Latvian border.

Capture of the railroad station at Nasva, 17 miles north of Novo-Sokolniki, cut the rail line running north to Leningrad, isolated the German garrison at Novo-Sokolniki, and left the Russians free to strike west toward the Leningrad-Polotsk railway, one of the last two lateral supply lines the Germans hold south of Leningrad.

Bitter Fighting In The South

On the southern end of the front, bitter and bloody fighting continued along the 80-mile front from Vinnitsa to Uman, where the Germans were making as many as 20 counter-attacks a day to hold back the Russians from the Bug River and the vital Odessa-Lwow railway.

Crossing of the Bug was admitted by a Wilhelmstrasse military spokesman, quoted by the Berlin correspondent of the Stockholm Dagens Nyheter. He said the vanguard of a strong Russian force succeeded in spanning the river, but German reserves counter-attacked and encircled one unit "now apparently facing defeat unless the Russians are able to bring up reinforcements."

In some places on the southern front, notably north of Uman, the Nazis hurled as many as 120 tanks against the Russian positions. Nearly half were destroyed, the Russians reported. Meanwhile, the Russians said they took terrific toll of the German armor and kept their own lines intact.

A gauge of the cost to the Germans was the Soviet Information Bureau's assertion yesterday that more than 100,000 Germans were killed in the first three weeks of Gen. Nicolai Vatutin's offensive west of Kiev—between Dec. 27 and Jan. 13. More than 7,000 were taken prisoner.

2,204 Tanks Destroyed

The Russians claimed they destroyed in the same period 2,204 tanks, 1,174 guns of various caliber, 3,173 machine-guns, 4,686 trucks, and 27 ammunition dumps.

German resistance appeared to be stiffening in the Pripet area, where Gen. Constantine Rokossovsky's forces which took Mozyr and Kalinkovichi drove westward 18 miles within shelling distance of the railway connecting Minsk and Pinsk.

At the same time Gen. Vatutin's right flank continued its pressure toward Pinsk from the south in an effort to cut the Mozyr-Pinsk railway and join up with Rokossovsky's columns moving west along this line.

Other columns of the First Ukrainian Army swung south-west of Sarny, the rail junction 35 miles beyond the 1939 Polish border, and pushed within 16 miles of Rovno, through which rail lines run to Berdichev, Lwow, Brest-Litovsk, and Minsk.

Bazooka Gun Rushed To Reds Aided '43 Stand

WASHINGTON, Jan. 18—The Bazooka gun was credited today with playing a large part in the successful Russian defense of Kursk and Orel in 1943.

Col. James Miller, of the Army's Ordnance Department, disclosed here that the weapon was rushed to the Russians, and aided in stopping the mass German tank attacks on the central front last summer.

Four New Points In Russia

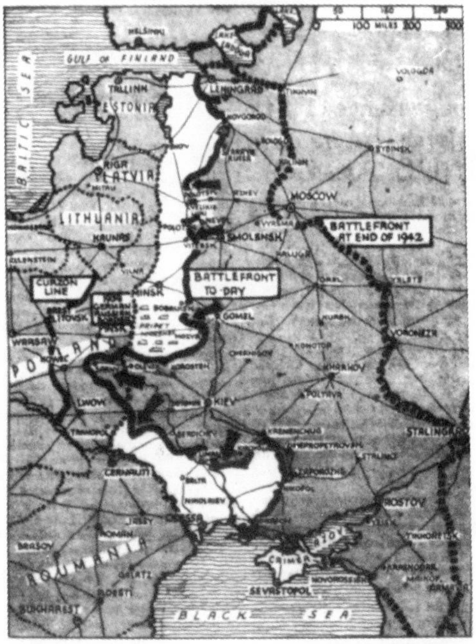

Belfast Telegraph Map.

The giant Russian offensive continued yesterday as the Germans admitted that Soviet forces had crossed the River Bug. This map of the entire Eastern front shows the battle line a year ago, the present line, the dwindling territory in German hands and the Curzon Line, recently mentioned in the Polish-Soviet boundary discussions.

British Deny Pravda's Report Of 'Separate Peace' Meeting

The British Foreign Office last night completely denied a report from Cairo published by Pravda, Moscow newspaper of the Communist Party, that "two leading British personalities" had conferred recently with Hitler's foreign minister, Joachim Von Ribbentrop, to discuss a separate peace with Germany.

The Pravda report, quoting "reliable Greek and Jugoslav sources," created a sensation in United Nations capitals.

Headed "Rumors from Cairo," the dispatch was attributed to Pravda's Cairo correspondent, who said he understood that the meeting in one of the sea coast cities of the Pyrenees peninsula "did not remain without results."

London and Washington quickly expressed amazement at Pravda's implication that Britain was sounding out Germany on the possibility of a separate peace.

The British Foreign Office, branding the report "absurd," quickly issued a "complete denial" and asserted flatly "There is no truth whatever in this story."

Secretary of State Cordell Hull told a Washington press conference he had no information whatsoever about the dispatch.

Both capitals pointed out that Britain had committed herself many times against a separate peace, and

(Continued on Page 4.)

U.S. Offers Aid In Polish Talks

WASHINGTON, Jan. 18—Secretary Cordell Hull said today the State Department, at the request of the Polish Government-in-Exile, had telegraphed the Soviet Government it was willing to attempt mediation of the Russo-Polish boundary dispute if the Russians were agreeable.

The Secretary said the Department's offer was made Saturday night, but no reply had as yet been received from Moscow.

Mr. Hull's press conference came a few hours after the Soviet Government had announced in Moscow that since the Poles apparently had rejected the Curzon boundary agreed upon by most of the Allies in 1919, the Soviet Government could not enter into negotiations.

4th War Loan Drive Starts In U.S. Today

WASHINGTON, Jan. 18 — The nation's fourth war loan drive gets under way today. Many cities will signal the start of the drive by ringing church bells and blowing sirens for five minutes at noon.

Motion picture houses throughout the country will hold 2,500 war bond premieres in an effort to sell 12,000,000 individual bonds—one for every theater seat.

Overscribes Fourth Time

COLUMBIA, Mo., Jan. 18 — Taney county, first in the nation to oversubscribe in the third war loan drive, has done it again. Although the fourth drive opens today, the county's $82,000 quota is oversubscribed already.

Known As 'Doughboy's General;' Eisenhower Hails Softening Blows

Leads U.S. Troops

Lt. Gen. Omar N. Bradley has been named commander of American ground forces in the European Theater preparing for the coming invasion of Europe. This photo was taken when Bradley, as a major general, was commanding the American Second Corps in the Tunisian campaign.

Gen. Wilson Hints Attack From South

Lt. Gen. Omar N. Bradley, who commanded the American Second Corps in the campaigns in Tunisia and Sicily and was one of Gen. Eisenhower's chief assistants in the Mediterranean theater, has been named commander of American ground forces in the European theater preparing for the coming invasion of Europe, it was announced yesterday.

Gen. Bradley, who is recognized as one of the foremost Infantry experts in the U.S. Army, was given a large share of the credit for the American successes in the North African fighting, and was credited with holding casualties in the final battle for Tunisia to a minimum.

Gen. Bradley has been an Infantry officer so long that he is known today as "The Doughboy's General." Fifty years old, with graying hair and a square-hewed chin, he was graduated from West Point as an Infantry lieutenant in 1915, served through the last war as a foot soldier, and was in command of Fort Benning when the U.S. entered this war.

Spadework Already Done

"It is the Infantry," Gen. Bradley has said, "which must bear the brunt of battle. The Infantry must have the will and the ability to close with the enemy and destroy him. It must expect to suffer a high percentage of casualties."

Meanwhile, the picture of Allied might menacing Hitler from the West nad South, as well as the East, grew clearer as Gen. Eisenhower disclosed that the pre-invasion task already was far advanced in Britain, and Gen. Sir Henry Maitland Wilson, Allied commander in the Mediterranean, hinted of blows in fresh quarters in that theater, possibly in southern France.

Gen. Eisenhower, in his first press conference as commander-in-chief in the West, gave warm praise to the Air Forces for the blows they are inflicting now on the enemy, and paid particular tribute to the infantrymen in the United Kingdom, who, he said, "are getting themselves ready and toughened for any job that lies ahead."

At a similar conference at Allied Headquarters in the Mediterranean, meanwhile, Gen. Sir Maitland Wilson said that "with luck" the European war would be won this year. He spoke of blows from any direction, indicating that the Axis could not expect to hold the southern flanks merely by a stout defense in Italy alone.

Generous Praise from Chief

Gen. Maitland Wilson said that southern France, like any other area along the Mediterranean front, might be turned into a battlefield if the opportunity for successful operations there developed. He disclosed that he was to confer with Gen. Charles De Gaulle to-morrow.

Gen. Eisenhower, whose arrival in England after conferences with Prime

(Continued on Page 4.)

Nazi Plant Is Hit In Austrian Alps

Two Fort Raids Top Day Of Varied Attacks; Allies Reach Rapido In Italy

ALLIED HQ, North Africa, Jan. 18—The Flying Forts hit the important German aircraft factory at Klagenfurt in the Austrian Alps twice Sunday within 90 minutes in a day of widespread assaults on German targets in which Liberators, Marauders, Mitchells, fighter-bombers and fighters took part, it was announced yesterday.

In Italy, American troops swept forward two miles from captured Mount Trocchio to reach the east bank of the Rapido River and the so-called Nazi Gustav Line as French units of the Fifth Army advanced to within 1,000 yards of San Elia, an anchor of the German Cassino fortifications.

While Forts yesterday pounded the Messerschmitt components plant at Klagenfurt, 14 miles from the Jugoslav border, Liberators raided the German-held port of Zara in Jugoslavia through which Germans supply their Balkan and Adriatic troops.

Another Fortress force bombed Villaorba airfield, five miles north of Venice. Liberators swept the northern Italian airfield of Osappo. Mitchells hit Terni, 30 miles north-east of Rome, and Marauders blasted Orte, 30 miles north of Rome.

Air Power Alone Cannot Win War In Europe, Tedder Admits

ALLIED HQ., North Africa, Jan. 18 (AP)—Air power alone could not decide the conflict with Germany, Air Marshal Sir Arthur Tedder, deputy supreme commander for the invasion of Western Europe, said yesterday in an interview.

"Perhaps if we'd started building air fleets five years ago with that idea in mind it might have come about, but bombing cannot do it alone," he declared. "It will take all arms, and particularly the splendid effort by the Russians."

Air superiority will be the key to the opening of a successful second front, the Air Marshal said. He expressed doubt that the Germans would be able to spring anything of a secret-weapon nature which would be a deciding military factor.

"I don't think we'll be able to knock the Germans completely out in the air over any second front. We'll gain superiority and keep them from unduly interfering with ground and sea operations, but they'll keep coming on and we'll have to beat them back again and again," he said.

Emphasizing the importance of air power in years to come, Air Marshal Tedder declared that the "people of America and Britain don't realize that air power has built itself a place in history—in fact, the future of the history of the world will depend largely on air power.

600,000 Over 65 Work Instead Of 'Cashing In'

WASHINGTON, Jan. 18—More than 600,000 men and women over 65 have chosen to postpone their social security benefit claims to continue work, Federal Security Administrator Paul v. McNutt revealed today in the eighth annual report of the U.S. Social Security Board.

The report urged that old age and survivors insurance be extended to include farm and household workers, employes of public organizations and the self-employed and stressed the need of protecting the social security rights of servicemen.

NORTHERN IRELAND EDITION

1d. **THE STARS AND STRIPES** 1d.

Daily Newspaper of U.S. Armed Forces in the European Theater of Operations

Vol. 1. No. 41. New York, N.Y.—Belfast, Northern Ireland. Monday, Jan. 24, 1944.

Allies Driving Inland Near Rome

Your Chance Of Voting . . .

13 States So Far Have Laws To Give Soldier Vote

What is your chance of voting in this year's Presidential election? President Roosevelt last week warned Congress that if it failed to establish a centralized federal set-up to handle the vote and left it to the individual states, many soldiers would be deprived of their ballot. Discussions still are going on in Washington, but indications in Congress are that the task will be left to the states. The Stars and Stripes asked The Associated Press for a survey of what the states have done and are doing to provide the soldier with an absentee ballot. Here is the round-up.

Special Cable to The Stars and Stripes

WASHINGTON, Jan. 24—Rep. Eugene Worley (D., Tex.), chairman of the House Elections Committee, said he was making "every effort to have Congress enact a simple election law that would insure American soldiers abroad a vote in the coming presidential election."

At the moment the voting situation by states shapes up as follows: Sixteen state legislatures are meeting now or are about to meet in regular or special session with an opportunity to enact liberalized election laws. Others are waiting on Congress to see whether their final draft of the vote facilitation measure requires any supplemental action on their parts. Still others, like **Pennsylvania**, may be able to solve the puzzle through the application of state war emergency powers.

The **Georgia** legislature was the first to pass a liberalized election law, completing on Jan. 7 a bill permitting absentee voters to register and vote by mail instead of in person as at present and setting up a state commission with final authority over the ballot. The bill has been signed by the governor. **Illinois**, **Wisconsin** and **West Virginia** were quick to follow, enacting bills to allow soldiers to vote.

Other state legislatures now meeting or to meet this month are those of **Kentucky**, **Mississippi**, **New Jersey**, **New York**, **Rhode Island**, **South Carolina**, **Virginia**, **Connecticut**, **Iowa**, **Colorado** and **Michigan**. The meeting of the **Louisiana** legislature is scheduled for May. **California** and **Maryland** are other possibilities for early meetings.

Governor Edward Martin (R.) of **Pennsylvania** said that his state's law needed changing to speed the delivery of ballots to absentees; an effort will be made

(Continued on page 3)

New Landing 32 Miles South Of Eternal City Virtually Unopposed

Invaders Advance Along Vital Railways And Roads In Attempt To Trap 100,000 Germans

After bold amphibious landings south of Rome, American and British troops of Lt. Gen. Mark Clark's Fifth Army today were driving toward vital railroad and highways running south of the Italian capital in an attempt to trap German armies in western Italy, estimated at 100,000 men.

From secure bridgeheads—reported by the Germans as about 32 miles south of Rome—Allied troops, led by U.S. Rangers and British Commandos, Sunday had captured heights dominating the coast and last night were reported sweeping inland to within striking distance of Kesselring's main communication lines.

The Germans apparently were thrown completely off balance by the unexpected blows early Saturday along the beach, which they were unable to defend.

Only scattered and weak German resistance was met by the Allies for 24 hours after the initial landings, but late Sunday night an NBC commentator, quoted by Reuter, said German artillery fire had increased and "U.S. doughboys inland were beginning to meet enemy patrols."

A 47-Mile Jump North

Although Allied communiques have not revealed the exact location of the new offensive, German and neutral reports said that the Fifth Army had stormed the coast between the "mouth of the Tiber and Nettuno," 32 miles south of Rome and 67 miles from the 5th Army front.

The surprise landings confronted the Germans with two alternatives. Kesselring's nine divisions now holding back other units of the Fifth Army along the Garigliano and Rapido rivers—the so-called Gustav Line—may attempt a withdrawal by the roundabout Avezzano road to Rome, or attempt to hold the Allies while troops are rushed to Rome from the north to establish an improvized defense.

So unexpected was the new Allied maneuver that Rome at present probably is not guarded in strength. Only last week three German armored divisions were sent south to bolster the Gustav Line, it was reported.

Admitting that the Allies had captured the town of Nettuno with the aid of "gigantic air support," a German military spokesman predicted that if the Fifth Army could hold its bridgeheads the German front in Italy would fold and Rome would fall in a short time.

"Decisive Battle"

Other German sources declared that the decisive battle of the Italian campaign had begun.

German Radio, in spite of the Allied announcement that the landings were unopposed, claimed that the Nazi Air Force attacked the landing fleet, sinking four large landing vessels and heavily damaging eight major units and several landing boats.

In an effort to isolate Rome and cut off the German divisions to the south, the British and Americans pushed inland toward the Rome-Capua railroad, the Appian Way

(Continued on Page 2.)

Reds Closing On Rail Line To Estonia

Begin New Pripet, Kerch Drives; Enemy Attacks Near Vinnitsa Cease

Advancing Red Army troops, now in control of all railroads and highways within a 20-mile radius of Leningrad, closed in on the lateral railway running westward to Estonia yesterday as the Russians opened a new offensive north of the Pripet Marshes and began a strong attack against the Nazi stronghold of Kerch, in the Crimea.

German defenses around Leningrad crumbled rapidly as the Soviet offensive in its ninth day took on the proportions of a major operation along a 50-mile front.

While one advance column moved into the outskirts of Tosno, 30 miles southeast of Leningrad, where the lateral rail line to Narva, in Estonia, joins the Leningrad-Moscow trunk, another brought up strong artillery forces four miles north of Krasnovardeysk, the most important railway and highway junction in the area 22 miles southwest of Leningrad.

New Attack Near Kirovograd

East of Vinnitsa, in the Dnieper Bend, where Gen. Nicolai Vatutin's Army was reported building up new troop concentrations, only local fighting was reported, but the German military commentator, Col. Ernst Von Hammer, described new Soviet attacks and a flare-up of fighting around Kirovograd.

A new offensive by Gen. Constantine Rossovsky's troops north of the Pripet aimed at the railway junction of Bobruisk, on the railway to Pinsk, was described by the Germans. They said the Russians brought up several fresh infantry divisions and a number of tank units in an effort to force a break-through "at all costs."

In the Crimea, Von Hammer said, the Russians landed southeast of Kerch and after a fierce barrage advanced against the town coincident with strong attacks from the Red bridgehead to the northeast. His broadcast said fierce fighting had been going on since yesterday morning, but did not add the usual claim that the Russians had been repulsed.

The Red drive in the North to cut the vital supply line to Narva threatened to trap some 15 to 20 German Divisions. An even larger trap

(Continued on Page 2.)

Wisconsin Passes Bill For Soldiers To Vote

MADISON, Wis., Jan. 24—A soldiers' vote bill enabling overseas servicemen to vote in this year's primary and Presidential election was passed unanimously by the Assembly and Senate.

Local election officials will make up registration lists and will mail the ballots, making it unnecessary for each serviceman and woman to apply for an absentee ballot.

Eisenhower ETO Chief; Lee His 2nd In Command

Gen. Dwight D. Eisenhower, in addition to his duties as Supreme Allied commander, has assumed the post of commanding general of the European Theater of Operations, it was announced yesterday. He immediately consolidated ETO headquarters with SOS, ETO, headquarters and named Maj. Gen. John C. H. Lee as deputy commander.

Maj. Gen. John C. H. Lee
New ETO Deputy Commander

General Lee, who will retain his post as commanding general, Services of Supply, served on Gen. Eisenhower's staff in 1942 in the preparations for the North African landings. His appointment as deputy theater commander will leave Gen. Eisenhower free to devote the major portion of his time to his duties as Supreme Allied commander.

Other steps in the consolidation included the appointment of Lt. Gen. Walter Bedell Smith as chief of staff, ETO, in addition to his duties as chief of staff, Supreme Headheadquarters Allied Experitionary Force, and the appointment of Col. Royal B. Lord as deputy chief of staff, ETO, in addition to his duties as chief of staff, SOS, ETO.

Elements Under Eisenhower

Under General Eisenhower, in his role as theater commander, are the three elements of the U.S. army—Air Forces commanded by Lt. Gen. Carl A. Spaatz, Field Forces commanded by Lt. Gen. Omar N. Bradley, and Services of Supply commanded by Maj. Gen. Lee.

As Supreme Commander, Allied Expeditionary Forces, Gen. Eisenhower commands all Allied forces in the United Kingdom.

Among the responsibilities assigned Gen. Lee by Gen. Eisenhower was the operation of all administration and supply for American troops in the United Kingdom, and for continental operations. Other duties assigned Gen. Lee remain secret.

Gen. Lee was graduated from West Point in the Corps of Engineers in 1909. After service in the Panama Canal Zone and the Philippines, in

(Continued on Page 2.)

Lowell Bennett, Of INS, Safe—A Captive Of Nazis

Lowell Bennett, International News Service correspondent who was reported missing in the Nov. 2 RAF raid on Berlin, is a prisoner of war in Germany.

The INS bureau chief in London, Leo Dolan, received a letter from Bennett yesterday written "Somewhere in Germany, Dec. 11——." In his letter the correspondent noted, "That's a helluva dateline, but it could be worse."

"I'll try and give the INS some invasion scoops," he said and finished with the warning, "watch out for the secret weapon."

Secret Letter From Knox To An Admiral Is Stolen

SEATTLE, Wash., Jan. 24 (Reuter)—Rep. Warren G. Magnuson (D., Wash.), a member of the Alaskan International Highway Commission, said today that a confidential letter given him by Secretary of Navy Frank Knox for delivery to Vice Adm. Frank J. Fletcher, commander of the northwest sea frontier, was stolen this week in Vancouver, "possibly by an enemy agent."

Nazi HQ In Italy KOd By Bombs

Surprise Blow By A36s Comes Just Before New Landing By The Army

ALLIED HQ., Italy, Jan. 24—In a surprise raid, U.S. A36 Invader dive-bombers wiped out the German military headquarters in Italy a few hours before Fifth Army units made their new landing south of Rome, it was announced yesterday.

A36 pilots, under the command of Lt. Col. Harold E. Kofahl, of Fellows, Cal., scored 26 direct hits on the headquarters, a villa near Franscati, 15 miles south of Rome, and about five miles from the Pope's summer residence at Castel Gandolfo.

Big explosions left the place wrecked, and not a single German aircraft was encountered.

(Before the Allied landings on Sicily last summer, U.S. dive-bombers destroyed the Axis headquarters on the island, seriously disrupting enemy communications for many days.)

Two-Billion Tax Bill Wins Senate's Unanimous OK

WASHINGTON, Jan. 24—A \$2,000,000,000 tax-increase bill—criticized by President Roosevelt as "unrealistic"—went to conference with the House today after unanimous passage by the Senate.

The measure would yield less than a fifth of the \$10,500,000,000 revenue suggested by the President as the "least" Congress should raise.

USAAF Marauders Again Bomb France's 'Rocket Gun' Coast Area

The "rocket-gun area" of France's Pas de Calais, pounded on Friday by the largest force of American and Allied planes ever sent out in a day's operations was attacked again yesterday by formations of U.S. Marauder medium bombers and Allied fighter-bombers.

As the attack—details of which still were lacking early today—was in progress German fire-fighting crews still were engaged in battling blazes in the city of Magdeburg in central Germany, where the RAF dropped more than 2,000 tons of high explosive and incendiary bombs Friday night.

Reports reaching Stockholm yesterday said that the 34-minute RAF raid has resulted in direct hits on factories manufacturing tanks, Diesel engines and synthetic fuel, and damage in the IG Farbenindustrie chemical factory, the customs building and a sugar refinery where 4,000 tons of sugar were reported destroyed. The Magdeburg raid cost the R.A.F. 52 bombers.

The Friday USAAF and RAF assault on the "rocket-gun" coast, an official communique announced, cost the American Air force six heavy bombers, two light bombers and three fighters.

U.S. Airmen destroyed 14 enemy fighters in the attack, headquarters said, heavy bombers getting seven and fighters seven.

Meanwhile, goaded by the war's biggest blow on Berlin by the RAF on Thursday night, the Luftwaffe slashed back at Britain with two sharp raids Friday night, giving many American soldiers their first taste of what the blitz of 1940-41 was like.

The raids actually were only miniature replicas of the blitz battles when hundreds of enemy bombers ranged over England, but the heaviest ack-ack in many months was thrown up at attacking German planes and flares dropped by enemy planes added to the spectacle.

Of 90 bombers sent over England by the Luftwaffe about 30 reached the London area, the Air Ministry said. Twelve of the entire force were shot down, it added.

Biddle Joins Eisenhower As A Lt. Col. On His Staff

WASHINGTON, Jan. 24—Anthony Biddle has resigned as Ambassador to the governments-in-exile in London to accept a lieutenant-colonel's commission on the staff of Gen. Dwight D. Eisenhower, it was announced yesterday. Col. Biddle will serve as liaison officer to the exiled governments.

In accepting the resignation, President Roosevelt told Biddle that he considered it wise "to take the military side of the restoration problems." Biddle was envoy to the governments of Poland, Norway, Belgium, Czechoslovakia and Luxembourg.

THE STARS AND STRIPES
TUNIS

One Franc

Vol. 1—No. 11—Tuesday 25 January 1944 Newspaper for U. S. Armed Forces in Tunisia

Nazis Reply To Allied Landings With Fierce Drive Near Cassino

5th Army Within Artillery Range of Key Road to Rome

ALLIED FORCE HEADQUARTERS, Jan. 24—Furious German counterattacks along the entire 5th Army Front, which developed into the bitterest hand-to-hand fighting of the Italian campaign, today was Marshal Albert Kesselring's answer to the surprise Allied amphibious landing south of Rome and far to his rear.

While the Allied advance inland from the beachhead north and south of Allied-held Nettuno continued to progress with little enemy opposition, the Germans hurled themselves recklessly against the strongly-held positions of General Clark's forces 80 miles to the south.

Mostly the Germans spilled blood in vain, but at one point they did force an American withdrawal to the east bank of the Rapido River in the San Angelo area. The withdrawal came only after the Americans had inflicted extremely heavy casualities, and, having exhausted their ammunition, retired across the 120-foot stream.

Heaviest fighting in the south developed around the French-held Mt. Croce area, but the French beat off all enemy efforts and continued their pressure toward the west, seriously menacing the Wehrmacht's Gustav Line. Simultaneously, south of the Garigliano, in the vicinity of Minturno and Castelforte, the British hammered back the strong enemy efforts, inflicting heavy casualities. Principal target of the Nazis was the Damiano ridges a mile west of Castelforte.

It was apparent that Marshal Kesselring had decided on a bold attempt to upset the Allied lines before his own Gustav defenses, and if successful, to retire on his own conditions to meet the Allied threat to his rear. In doing so, in the opinion of mili-

(Continued on Page 4)

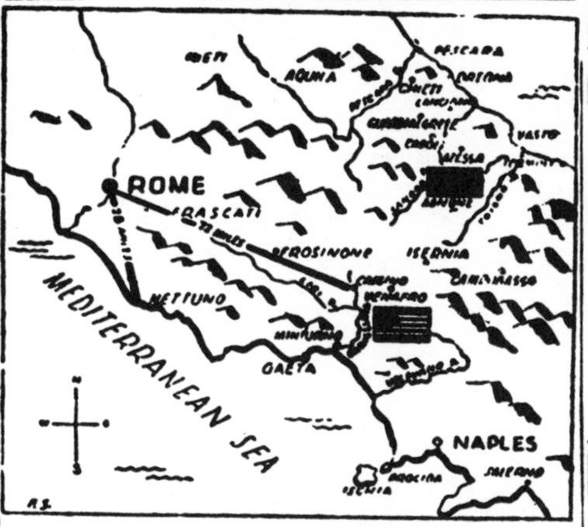

IN A DARING, DRAMATIC STROKE, Allied forces of Lt. Gen. Mark Clark's 5th Army struck at the heart of the Nazi bastion in central Italy in a series of amphibious landings south of Rome. Under cover of a powerful air umbrella Allied troops swarmed ashore and captured Nettuno, 28 miles south of Rome, while fighters and fighter-bombers paved the way by knocking out the Axis headquarters at Frascati.

Soviets Threaten Encirclement of 400,000 Nazis

Three Red Units Form Giant Pincer

LONDON, Jan. 24 — A vast German army of 400,000 men is fighting today for its very life in a huge salient southwest of Leningrad, as Red Army units converged on the Nazis from three sides in bitter north front battles.

The point of the salient is formed by the fortress of Tosno, railway junction 15 miles southeast of liberated Leningrad. The right side of the frozen arena extends southwest from the city in front of the chief Leningrad-Moscow railroad as far as the Volkhov River, and the left, west along a fortified line protecting the rail line from Tosno to Estonia, now the enemy's most important supply route.

Red Army units were pushing toward the Estonian railway south and southwest of Krasnoye Selo, and in the center of the battle line, Soviet forces freed by the reduction of the Nazi bastion of Mga, captured a number of populated places north and northeast of Tosno. On the right, the Russian surge carried units close to the Leningrad-Moscow railway and wiped out a strong German bridgehead on the east bank of the Volkhov.

In the western Ukraine, the Soviets drove deeper across the ice-encrustd marshes west of Novgorod. Action west of Mozir resulted in the capture of Lelkdchy, and the progress of the offensive through the deepest fortifications ever built by the Germans in Russia was seen by military observers as an indication of the difficulties being imposed upon the Nazis, trying to hold a line extending from the Gulf of Finland to the Black Sea.

There was little doubt that the Red Army campaign in the north was tying down thousands of German reserves, hindering every enemy effort to rescue their armies in the south.

Meanwhile, there were no fresh reports of the fighting below the Kiev bulge, where for more than two weeks the Russians have been slashing German divisions in the Dnieper Bend.

Stars and Stripes Reporter Sees Landing from Bomber

By Sgt. JACK FOISIE
(Stars and Stripes Staff Writer)

AN ADVANCED AIR BASE, (Delayed) — I flew over the vicinity of the newly-won Allied beachhead today, and then deep into German territory to bomb Frosinone, key junction town on the road to Rome.

This is what I saw from the plexi-glass nose of the American A-20 Boston bomber:

The Allied invasion fleet, extending in a long line, three or four ships abreast, from the beach out many miles into the mist.

To us at 10,000 feet, they were but dark slivers on a calm sea, but the reports were that landings were progressing rapidly, due to an untroubled sea and feeble attempts of the Luftwaffe to molest the operation.

Time and time again Allied pilots returning to their advanced fighter strips spoke almost identical words:

"Certainly nothing like Salerno," or "A soft touch compared to Sicily."

While over the beachhead, I did not observe any naval firing whatsoever. This was at 1500 hours. Early-morning patrols had reported some naval firing, but few returns from the enemy.

Farther inland, I could see vehicular movement on the road. They must have been ours, for P-40s, A-36s and P-38s were over the territory constantly, going down to the deck to investigate any suspicious activity. And around the beachhead they found none, although inland, on the main roads, enemy traffic was moving at a hurried pace, though without panic.

It was our first mission to bomb the town of Frosinone, to tumble the buildings into the street and block the main artery. Each plane carried 250-pound demolition bombs for the job — and there were a lot of planes.

This was all part of the overall coordination of air and ground in their efforts to protect the convoy and landings, while the fighter-bombers and bombers cut the main routes of communications to forestall enemy reinforcements converging on the assault force until it had had time to establish itself and gain position.

How well the air force has been able to do the job will be told in the fighting of the next few days.

The full strength of the 47th Bombing Group, commanded by Col. Malcolm Green, San Francisco, took off at 1410. It took them a full hour to assemble, gain altitude and pick up fighter escort.

During that hour, I saw at least 200 planes, the sky was drenched with them. Far below us we could see fighters, seemingly drift along at cross angles to the curious patchwork appear-

(Continued on Page 4)

Bombs Protect Invasion Troops

ALLIED FORCE HEADQUARTERS, Jan. 24—Bombs and bullets poured from great numbers of Allied aircraft yesterday to protect new landing operations on Italy's west coast south of Rome and to make impossible the avenues of supply—or retreat—for German forces on the Gustav Line.

What appeared to be the enemy's only attempt to impede landing operations was ended even before it was started with eight Nazi planes being shot down. For the day Allied victories totaled 11 at a cost of three Allied aircraft. Fighters in great strength continued to patrol over the beachheads and the Rome-Florence area.

Key roads and bridges between the new beachhead and the 5th Army front around Cassino continued to be the targets of Allied heavy, medium and fighter bombers.

B-17 Flying Fortresses of the 15th AAF destroyed one bridge at Pontecorvo and hit another at Caprano, both towns being northwest of Cassino. Marauders and Mitchells of the 12th Air Force took care of various objectives around Avezzano, an important Liri valley junction leading to the east coast from Rome.

The east coast of Italy in the vicinity of Ancona, particularly the town of Portocivitanova,

(Continued on Page 4)

General Eisenhower To Command ETO

LONDON, Jan. 24 — Gen. Dwight D. Eisenhower, Supreme Commander of Allied Expeditionary Forces in the United Kingdom, has also been named commander of the European Theater of Operations, U.S. Army, it was announced here yesterday.

Gen. John C. S. Lee, commander of U.S. Army Service Forces in the European Theater, has been named deputy commander to General Eisenhower.

Maj. Gen. Walter D. Smith, chief of staff to General Eisenhower in the Allied Expeditionary Force Command, will serve in the same capacity in the European Theater of Operations, U.S. Army, it was announced. Col. Royal B. Lord will be the deputy chief of staff.

In Washington it was announced that Anthony J. Drexel Biddle, Jr., American ambassador-minister to the Allied governments in London, has resigned to accept a commission as a Lieutenant Colonel in the U.S. Army.

Col. Biddle will serve on General Eisenhower's staff as a liaison officer in the governments of occupied countries abroad.

FDR Creates Organization For Persecuted Minorities

WASHINGTON, Jan. 24 — A war refugee board charged with effecting the immediate rescue from the Germans of the oppressed European minorities—racial, religious or political, has been established by President Roosevelt.

In an executive order Saturday creating the board, the President named as its members Secretary of State Hull, Secretary of the Treasury Morgenthau, and Secretary of War Stimson. He directed them to enlist the cooperation and participation of foreign governments in plans for the rescue, transportation, relief and establishment of havens of temporary refuge for the victims of enemy oppression.

The President stressed in an accompanying statement the necessity of urgent action "to forestall the plan of the Nazis to exterminate all the Jews and other persecuted minorities in Europe." He expressed confidence in the cooperation of the United Nations.

Expressing its "profound appreciation," the American-Jewish conference said, "the action promises life to people who were otherwise doomed to destruction and will be welcomed by millions of Americans who have been deeply concerned with this pressing problem."

Dr. Israel Goldstein, president of the Zionist Organization of America, described the action as "a gratifying culmination of the efforts on the part of recognized American - Jewish bodies, functioning through the American-Jewish conferences, to arouse the democratic world to the scope and gravity of the refugee problem and the need of

(Continued on Page 4)

Marauders Hammer French Coast Again

LONDON, Jan. 24—Following up Friday's crushing 1000-plane assault on northern France, more than 200 Marauders dropped 300 tons of high explosives yesterday in the Calais area along the English Channel.

The Marauders, escorted by British, New Zealand and American fighters, swarmed across the Channel in mid-afternoon. Returning pilots reported good bombing results.

Earlier in the day Thunderbolts, serving as fighter-bombers, plastered the Gilb-Ripen airfield, 30 miles southeast of Rotterdam, for the first time. Strong formations of medium bombers and fighter-bombers attacked another airfield at Maupertuis, on the Cherbourg peninsula.

NORTHERN IRELAND EDITION

1D. **THE STARS AND STRIPES** 1D.

Daily Newspaper of U.S. Armed Forces in the European Theater of Operations

Vol. 1. No. 46. New York, N.Y.—Belfast, Northern Ireland. Saturday, Jan. 29, 1944.

Japanese Atrocities Stun U.S.

U.S. Heavies Hit North France

Berlin Gets 1,750 Tons In 12th Assault

Capital 'Half Wiped Out;' Northern France Struck By Lib Force

American heavy bombers, striking at the enemy in their eighth major operation of the month, attacked military objectives in Northern France yesterday a few hours after a large force of RAF Lancasters dumped 1,730 American tons (1,500 British tons) of bombs on Berlin in a concentrated 20-minute assault.

The night attack on the German capital, the 12th heavy bombing since the Battle of Berlin" began last Nov. 18, started numbers of fires which quickly spread to a great conflagration marked by violent explosions.

Some air observers, calculating that about 23,000 tons of bombs now have been dropped on the capital, suggested that the job of wiping out the city was about half done after Thursday night's attack.

34 British Planes Lost

Other RAF planes, carrying out what German Radio described as a feint, attacked Heligoland and Northern France about the same time the main bomber formations headed for Berlin. A small force of Mosquitoes roared over the German capital about an hour later. In all these operations the British lost 34 aircraft.

Yesterday's USAAF raid carried out by a striking force of Libs with Thunderbolt escort was aimed at Northern France targets, where Allied bombers have struck again and again in recent weeks—possibly the site of German rocket gun emplacements.

The bombers met no enemy opposition and little flak and all returned safely.

Crews said the daylight sweep to France was "the milk run of all milk runs." S/Sgt. Edward G. Hutchinson, a ball turret gunner from Surveyor, Pa., declared upon his return, "The hardest job we had today was getting out of bed for the briefing."

2/Lt. John Gaffney, of Philadelphia, a co-pilot, described it as easier than even a practice mission.

Glow Seen 200 Miles

The Air Ministry said the attack on Berlin was carried out through very thick clouds. Pathfinder planes laid a dense concentration of sky markers promptly at zero hour, 8:25 P.M., and soon afterward the clouds were lit from below by the glow of fierce fires.

Rear gunners of the main force could see the red glow from a hundred miles away, but by the time the Mosquitoes were coming away the fires had spread so that they could be seen 200 miles. Crews told of seeing the flashes of several violent explosions

American General Sees Reds Using U.S. Aid

MOSCOW, Jan. 29 (Reuter)—Maj. Gen. Donald H. Connolly, chief U.S. Persian Gulf Command, completing a five-week tour of Soviet battle fronts, said to-day he had seen great numbers of American trucks carrying supplies to support the advance, American equipment in use and American food being eaten at the front.

"The Russians asked me what I wanted to see, let me go every place I asked to go and let me see everything I wanted to see," Connolly said. "At every place I went they held nothing back."

Accompanied by a group of U.S. Army supply, signal and communications experts, Connolly visited Stalingrad, Leningrad, Kiev, the country west of Moscow, Orel, Kursk, Zhitomir and an area 25 miles southwest of Zhitomir.

The Bridgehead Broadens

Americans and British reinforce Anzio-Nettuno bridgehead, hurl back the second major counter attack by the Nazis and drive on toward the Rome-Gaeta railroad after capturing Litteria and Aprilia.

Invaders Gain In Italy; 50 Nazi Planes Downed

After hurling back the second major counter attack since the amphibious landings south of Rome, Allied troops drove on yesterday toward the Rome-Gaeta railroad.

Coupled with this victory over German infantry and tanks was a crushing defeat of the Luftwaffe in the greatest Mediterranean air battle since the Tunisian campaign.

At Carrocetto only 3½ miles from the Rome-Gaeta line—one of the main supply routes along which the Nazis are rushing reinforcements toward the Allied bridgehead—the 29th panzer Grenadiers, withdrawn from the main Fifth Army front to the south, launched a heavy counter attack on advancing British troops. The Germans quickly were forced to retreat.

Meanwhile, the greatest Allied air victory of the Italian campaign was achieved, when 50 German planes were destroyed over the bridgehead and the French Riviera within 24 hours

21 Down Over France

Twentyone of the 50 were shot down in a series of heavy air battles over southern France by fighters escorting heavy bombers in attacks on three bases in the Montpellier and Marseilles area, from which the Germans are raiding Allied shipping south of Rome.

Although Allied planes flew more than 1,400 sorties while hitting German targets and blasting Nazi supply lines, only seven Allied planes were lost in all operations.

The enlarged bridgehead yesterday was said at Gen. Alexander's headquarters to be at least six miles deep at all points. Previous announcements had placed Allied troops 12 miles inland at some points.

Cairo Radio, with an unconfirmed

(Continued on Page 4)

Nazis Retreat Toward Baltic

Disordered Flight Harried By Reds; Rearguard Is Being Cut To Pieces

Beaten German forces rolled westward to Estonia in full retreat yesterday on the front southwest of Leningrad.

While they fled to the Baltic, nipped by fast Russian tanks and cavalry, and harried by bridges-blasting Red bombers, other Nazi units to their rear were being cut to bits near Tosno—a regular massacre in the words of a Reuter correspondent in Moscow.

In this sector, the last German-held section of hte Moscow - Leningrad trunk railroad, 30 miles southeast of Leningrad, the enemy fled in disorder across marshland between Tosno and the German Baltic base at Luga.

"Many units completely broken up, isolated and wandering lost in the northern forests are being rounded up by Russian cavalrymen," the Reuter report said

"They have completely lost touch with their neighbouring units in some sectors and are being herded back on the Novgorod railway line like sheep."

The Russians, after smashing their way through Volosovo, last fortress town short of Estonia, were less than

(Continued on Page 4)

2,300,000 Officers, Men In U.S. Army Air Forces

FORT WORTH, Tex., Jan 29 (Reuter)—The American Air Force now numbers more than 2,300,000 officers and enlisted men, the Air Force Training Command said today. The figure includes 100,799 pilots, 20,086 bombardiers, 18,805 navigators, 107,218 aerial gunners and 555,891 ground and air combat technicians.

Overcoats Stay In, Strawberries Come Out

Midwest Winter Does A Fadeout In Warmest January In Years

CHICAGO, Jan. 29—A record-breaking winter "heat wave" has made overcoats unnecessary throughout the Middle West, sent the temperature in Chicago soaring to its highest January mark since 1882 and caused some concern that drought conditions might imperil food production.

Discovery of a blossoming strawberry plant in a Chicago garden gave visible proof of the unseasonable weather.

This week saw the thermometer climb to 62 in Chicago, 56 in Des Moines, 63 in Minneapolis, 62 in Detroit, 69 in Omaha and 62 in Indianapolis.

Although many farm experts claimed the unusual weather would not harm the corn and wheat crops, delegates to the American Dairy Association convention here predicted that the drought might "mean trouble for the future civilian food supply."

Dr. Robert Prior, of Seattle, Wash., vice-president of the dairymen's organization, said that some reservoirs in Washington and western Montana were 50 feet below usual levels.

The Chicago Weather Bureau predicted that winter soon would be back.

Official Report Tells Of Barbaric Cruelty To The Men Of Bataan

Torture, Thirst, Starvation, Slave Labor Described By Escaped Eyewitnesses

A wave of anger such as the United States has not felt since the war began swept the nation today as the War and Navy Departments issued a report telling a ghastly story of Jap atrocities on American and Filipino soldiers taken prisoner on Bataan and Corregidor

The report, containing sworn statements by three American officers who escaped after a year of imprisonment, said that thousands of prisoners had met death through starvation, slave labor, torture and wanton murder.

It was released by the government, according to Stephen Early, President Roosevelt's private secretary, only when it became evident that further relief supplies from the U.S. could not be expected to reach prisoners.

Simultaneously Anthony Eden, British foreign secretary, delivered to a shocked House of Commons in London, a similar report on Jap atrocities committed upon British prisoners. He added that Japan had withheld permission for neutral inspection of any prison camps.

Enraged U.S. Cries Revenge

Presented under screaming headlines, the two atrocity reports whipped Americans to fever pitch far beyond that which greeted news of the execution of the American airmen who bombed Toyko.

Heavy police guard were thrown around Japanese internment camps for fear of mob retaliatory action.

Voices from Washington's Capitol Hill clamored for immediate revenge, demanding that the entire Navy be mobilized for attack and that Japan be "bombed out of existence" and vowed that the war would never end until the Nipponese had paid in full for their heart-sickening deeds.

Secretary of State Cordell Hull, characterising the Japs as fiends, answered a reporter's question as to whether the U.S. planned to protest to Japan through the Swiss Government by saying that he had sent one protest after another but had never received a satisfactory response.

He said the U.S. was gathering all possible information so that the Japs responsible could be punished after the war.

The American report was based solely on the eyewitness testimony of Cmdr. Melvyn H. McCoy, U.S. Navy; Lt. Col. S. M. Melinik, Coast Artillery, and Lt. Col. William E. Dyess, Air Forces, following their escape from the Philippines.

Dyess later died in an air crash at Burbank, Cal., while training to return to combat against the Japs. Melinik is now with Gen. MacArthur, and McCoy is on duty in the U.S.

Several times more prisoners have died than the Japs have admitted, mostly from starvation, forced hard labor and brutality, the report said.

550 Die Each Day

At one prison, Camp O'Donnel, about 2,200 Americans died in April and May, 1942; in another, at Cabentuan, 3,000 had died up to the end of October, 1942, and still heavier mortality occurred among the Filipinos, it was said.

The report said that the "calculated Japanese campaign of brutality" began soon after Bataan's fall with what the survivors called a "march of death." Thousands of prisoners were marched 85 miles in six to 12 days through sun without food and water, beaten with sticks and dragged out to almost certain death if they became sick or delirious.

"Our thirst was intense," Col. Dyess testified. "Many of us went crazy and several died." He added

(Continued on Page 2)

Soviets Charge Germans Shot 11,000 Poles

Red Group Claims Nazis Conducted Mass Killings Of Prisoners

SMOLENSK, Jan. 29 (AP) — The ghastly graves on the goat hills in a nearby forest have given up evidence which the Soviet Special Commission calls "indisputable proof that the Germans conducted a mass execution of Polish prisoners in August and September, 1941."

The commission after reconstructing the crime, offered its solution of one of the major mysteries of the war and a major political issue.

It found that the Germans killed 11,000 Poles by shooting them in the back of the head, cast them in mass graves, had them dug up again by 500 Red Army men who were prisoners in their hands, who were in turn shot, and then prepared the "provocation" charge that the Russians killed the Poles.

British and American newspaper correspondents who saw the exposed and documentary evidence, and heard the commission, experts and witnesses, are convinced that this is the best possible explanation of the crime.

It was because the Polish government in London took up the German story that the Poles were shot by the Russians in March and April, 1940, and asked the International Red Cross to investigate it, that the Soviet Government severed relations with the Poles

The party of British and American newspapermen taken to the scene of the crime by special train were shown the bodies in mass graves, medical experts at work making post-mortems, and the special commission hearing the testimony of witnesses.

Among the party was Kathleen

(Continued on Page 4)

Jap Attache In Bucharest Is Reported Under Arrest

ANKARA, Jan 27 (delayed)—Rumanian police have arrested the Japanese military attache in Bucharest on a charge of communicating illegally with Moscow by radio, reliable reports from the Rumanian capital said today. They added that the man attempted suicide when seized. The Bucharest correspondent of Domei (Japanese official news agency) has been expelled for sending untruthful reports about Turkey.

THE STARS AND STRIPES

TUNIS

One Franc

Vol. I—No. 14—Friday, 4 February 1944

Newspaper for U. S. Armed Forces in Tunisia

Russians Chase Germans Across Estonian Border

Nazi Troops Flee Toward Narva

LONDON, Feb. 3—Red Army units rolled over wreckage-strewn roads today right up to the Estonian Border as the Germans raced across the frontier toward Narva, their important base four miles inside Estonia.

In the absence of official word from Moscow, there were indications that in places along a wide front the Russians already had crossed the border in pursuit of the Nazis, and were driving hard toward Narva, which the Germans must hold if they are to keep the Red Army from over-running Estonia.

Gen. Leonid Govorov's spearheads were aimed at the 25-mile gap between the Gulf of Finland and the northern end of Lake Peipus. The offensive had liberated Fedorovka, less than a mile from the Estonian border and seven miles northeast of Marva; Vanskila, 11 miles north of Narva, and Krivayaluka, a little more than a mile south of Narva, according to an official Soviet communique.

To the southeast, the Germans were streaming toward their fortress at Luga, slogging through an oblong-shaped stretch of swampy territory with Soviet forces closing in from the north and northwest, and from the east and southeast.

Commenting on Gen. Meretskov's advance, the Soviet Army newspaper, Red Star, reported that in the first six days of the offensive below Leningrad approximately one-third of 3000 Spanish Legion troops had been decimated by the Russians. Red Star claimed the Spaniards, remnants of the Spanish Blue Division, had reached the front during the closing days of December.

The Moscow radio, replying to an assertion by the Hungarian news agency that Hungarian troops in the east are not in the front lines, declared that 11 Hungarian infantry divisions and one cavalry division were in action on the Soviet-German front.

No Extra Cost For Supplement

We have been advised that some vendors of The Stars and Stripes have attempted to charge two francs for the Tuesday and Friday editions of the paper. Despite the addition of the Readers Digest supplement, the price of the paper remains the same: Two francs for the weekly (Sunday) edition and one franc for all others. American troops are requested to have the nearest MP arrest any vendor asking more than the price printed on the top right-hand corner of page one.

U.S. Heavies Hit Northern France

LONDON, Feb. 3—American heavy bombers attacked military targets in the Pas de Calais area of northern France, their fifth daylight offensive in six days. Covering an area that has been repeatedly bombed in recent weeks by Allied forces, the Liberators were escorted

LONDON, Feb. 3 — A fleet of 1100 American bombers and fighters attacked the great German naval and submarine base at Wilhemshaven in a daylight raid today.

by Thunderbolts but encountered no enemy fighters.

Other Thunderbolts and Lightnings accompanied medium American bombers in raids on airfields in Normandy. Two bombers failed to return from the day's operations.

Further reports from Stockholm told of indescribable destruction in Berlin following the RAF's attack Sunday night. Fire brigades were rushed from as far distant as Jutland to extinguish the flames that covered the city under a pall of heavy black smoke.

The 16,500 tons of bombs unloaded on Germany by the RAF Bomber Command during January is 500 tons greater than the previous record month of August, 1943. Of the nine major assaults made by the RAF in January, six were directed against Berlin compared with four in the previous month.

Roi, Vital Jap Airbase, Is Taken by U.S. Marines

Since Pearl Harbor

Vast Fleet In Support

BULLETIN

WASHINGTON, Feb. 3 — Troops have completely occupied Namur Island in the Marshalls Group, it was announced tonight.

PEARL HARBOR, Feb. 3 — Veteran Marine forces last night captured the strategic Roi air base, major Japanese airfield in the heart of the Marshall Group in the central Pacific, and today completely occupied all of Roi Island, after mopping up a few fanatical snipers, it has been officially disclosed.

New landings were made on Namur Island, south of Kwajalein Atoll, as the Nipponese defenders were hurled back to only a small area of the northeastern beach.

Bayonet fighters of the 7th U.S. Infantry Division today had occupied a third of Kwajalein Island, driving the defenders to the narrow eastern end.

Meanwhile, the mightiest Allied invasion armada ever assembled continued to cover the landing operation with a staggering concentration of explosives.

Carrier bombers, taking off from the greatest collection of aircraft carriers ever gathered in one place for a single operation, were giving close support to the assault forces by continually slugging away at enemy ground defenses. An official Naval communique issued here today asserted that the American forces had suffered no naval losses and casualties were termed "very moderate."

Press dispatches disclosed for the first time that the amphibious forces changed the tactics they had used in the successful, but costly, operations against Tarawa in the Gilberts last Nov-

(Continued on Page 4)

Fifth Army Batters Way To Outskirts of Cassino

ALLIED FORCE HEADQUARTERS, Feb. 3 — The long, bloody battle for Cassino was about to end in an Allied victory, but the fury of the three-month fighting on the main 5th Army front might yet be eclipsed by the struggle brewing on the Anzio-Nettuno beachhead south of Rome. Today American troops were on the fringe of Cassino itself and only about two and a half miles from Highway 6 at a point about an equal distance west of Cassino. The main assaults on the city were coming from the north and east of it, from American tanks and infantry, which with support from the French, had widened the breach in the Gustav Line to more than four miles.

At one point the Americans had slugged their way to within 500 yards of the city, but, according to front line dispatches, their progress was slowed down later in the day by very heavy fire from six-barrelled mortars, machine guns and self propelled weapons which the Germans had planted around and in the city.

American artillery cleared the path for the advance from the north by slamming shells all day long into Highway 6 which splits the town, even as advanced American units were infiltrating into the outskirts.

U. S. INFANTRY

Simultaneously, according to reports, other American infantrymen swept down from the mountains from the northwest to within a mile and a half of the city, threatening to cut the road behind Cassino and trap such German defenders who might still be within it. This force, probably was not large, for the Germans were depending not so much on manpower as on the skillfully placed self-propelled weapons and their Neberwerfer "screaming meemies."

The Nazis, under Marshal Albert Kesselring, were throwing in considerable manpower in frantic efforts to turn the Allied advancing right flank which yesterday firmly established itself on heights in the Calle Abate region, a mile and a half northeast of the village of Terelle, three miles northwest of Cassino. Here the French troops, holding the northern slopes of the feature, beat off two furious counterattacks. The Germans called off their assaults on the

(Continued on Page 4)

Jittery Nazis Rule Rome With Iron Hand

By Sgt. MILTON LEHMAN

(Stars and Stripes Staff Writer)

WITH THE 5TH ARMY AMPHIBIOUS FORCES — (Delayed) — A bad case of jitters is affecting the German troops stationed in Rome, according to Italian civilians who slipped out of the city yesterday and are now safely behind the new Allied frontline. News of the sudden landings on the beaches 35 miles south of Rome swept through the Eternal City like a whirlwind, they reported.

To counter the elation of the civilians the Germans have drawn a cordon of guards around the city to prevent anyone from entering or leaving and have also stiffened their curfew and blackout restrictions. In the words of Riccardo Gatti, a wine merchant of Nettuno, who came home yesterday:

"Now if an Italian even looks a German in the face, he gets slapped."

Gatti went on to say that resistance forces in Rome composed of civilians and former soldiers continued to snipe at Germans at every opportunity.

Although the Germans have tirelessly hunted out civilian firearms, placing heavy sentences on anyone found with them, the resistance groups still have managed to hide away many weapons and are keeping them ready for the right moment.

Amerigo Procaccini, a 16-year-old engineering student at the Leonardo da Vinci school in Rome, narrowly escaped German guards on his way out of town yesterday. When he heard that the Allies had landed, he decided to get away from Rome in the excitement and return to his parents who live in a small town in the beachhead area.

He hitched a ride to the southern suburbs of Rome, Amerigo told me today. "Then," he said, "I saw the Germans coming toward me and I made a run for the bushes and walked in the rest of the way, not staying near the main roads."

Food stocks in Rome have been steadily depleted in recent months, Riccardo Gatti reported. Grain is extremely scarce, he

(Continued on Page 4)

FDR Explains U.S. Objectives in India

WASHINGTON, Feb. 3 — "American objectives in India or elsewhere in continental Asia are to expel and defeat the Japanese, in the closest collaboration with our British, Chinese and other Allies in that theater." President Roosevelt declared in a recent address.

Mr. Roosevelt noted that the task of expelling the Japanese is military, and that the British and Dutch are as determined "to throw the Japanese out of Malaya and the Dutch East Indies as we are determined to free the Philippines." He declared that each is prepared to help the other "on roads and waters and above them, eastward to these places, westward from where the Allied forces also are fighting and beyond Tokio."

The President explained that there will be plenty of problems and that their solution will be easier if the utmost forces of "good will and good faith," of all are employed. "Nobody in India or anywhere else in Asia," Mr. Roosevelt continued, "will misunderstand the presence there of American Armed Forces if they believe, as we do at home,

(Continued on Page 4)

THE STARS AND STRIPES
MEDITERRANEAN

Vol. 1, No. 75, Friday, February 11, 1944 — ITALY EDITION — TWO LIRE

Large Areas Restored To Italian Government

19 Nazi Divisions Lost In Ukraine, Russians Claim

Oredezh, In North, Falls; Threat To Luga Increasing

LONDON, Feb. 10 — Nineteen German divisions have been either destroyed or defeated with heavy losses in the Russian capture of Nikopol and the smashing of the Nazi Dnieper River bridgehead below the city, according to frontline Soviet observers.

Seven divisions—three of them armored—were routed in the initial breakthrough toward Nikopol, another five were cut off and wiped out in the next phase of fighting and seven more were smashed up in the Nikopol bridgehead. All these defeats were sustained by Germany's Ukraine armies in a space of ten days and the Wehrmacht in the whole of southern Russia gives the impression of a series of disconnected forces, all of them in mortal danger. There seems to be a complete absence of any overall strategic plan.

An important new development in the Nikopol region is a drive by one of General Rodion Malinovsky's columns to the west of Apostolovo, flanking the big iron oré producing center of Krivoi Rog. The Russians yesterday captured the town of Aleksandrovka, 15 miles southeast of Krivoi Rog.

Russian forces in the northern part of the Dnieper bend were methodically hacking to pieces the ten German divisions isolated in the Kanev-Smela pocket. Red Army troops have captured the town of Gorodishche, which was the largest town held by the doomed force. Intercepted radio messages have asked Field Marshal Fritz von Mannstein to relieve them "before it is too late."

While part of his forces were consolidating their victories of the past few days in the north, one of General Leonid Govorov's columns continued to drive down the Leningrad-Batetskaya railroad, capturing Oredesh, 18 miles northeast of Luga. Then Russian spearheads pushed on across the Oredesh River at a point only ten miles north of the German base at Luga. General Kyril Meretskov's army, pushing west from Novgorod, was also getting closer to Luga.

Finland Weighing Position In War

LONDON, Feb. 10—Neutral reports from Europe today told of Finland's increasing anxiety over its war position.

A Swiss newspaper disclosed that the Finnish government met in secret session Tuesday night to examine the warning of Secretary of State Cordell Hull to get out of the war. Earlier, a Stockholm paper said that Hull's warning was published prominently in Helsinki newspapers and caused dismay throughout the country.

In a leading editorial the Russian Communist Party newspaper, "Pravda," noted that Finland had grown fearful of the consequences of being a Nazi ally only after the defeat of the German army south of Leningrad.

Kids Make It Rough For Movie Snipers

KANSAS CITY, Mo., Feb. 10—Youngsters in the audience of a movie here could not contain themselves during a showing of the picture "Guadalcanal Diary", which portrays action in the Southwest Pacific.

When the showing was over, the manager counted 55 holes in the screen, all blasted by juvenile members of the audience who were picking off Jap snipers with their air rifles.

Great Air Battle Rages Over Reich

LONDON, Feb. 10—Flying Fortresses roaring forth on a bombing mission against the German aircraft center of Brunswick today became involved in a long and furious battle with hundreds of Luftwaffe fighters in the air five miles above the Reich.

The Fortresses and their escort of Thunderbolts and Lightnings were attacked continuously by German fighters from the time they crossed the enemy coast line until they reached the target. The Germans then followed the American bombers all the way back to the English channel, weaving in and out with their fighters unleashing rocket shells and hot streams of machine gun bullets. As many as 100 to 200 enemy planes attacked the U.S. armada at a time.

Despite the heavy German onslaught, the B-17s carried out their assault on the central German industrial city in full force. American bombardiers plastered their targets with unerring accuracy. Brunswick is a big aircraft production center for the Germans, manufacturing Messerschmitt fighters and much other essential material for the Luftwaffe.

Powerful formations of Allied bombers, fighter bomber and fighters streaked across the English Channel yesterday to continue their hard-hitting attacks on targets along the French invasion coast and further inland.

In one of the busiest days since the opening of the campaign to soften up German installations on the west coast of France, Allied aircraft flew at least 1,000 sorties. German fighter opposition was unusually weak. Few Allied airmen were called upon to fire a shot in their own defense and only one plane was missing from the day's operations.

Starting the onslaught off at dawn, Typhoons and Hurricanes dropped bombs in the often-hit Pas de Calais area. Then 200 fast, deadly American B-26 Marauders launched a surprise attack on the key rail center at Tergnier, in northwestern France midway be-

(Continued on page 4)

Men Discharged Face Second Draft

WASHINGTON, Feb. 10—Some service men who were wounded in action and received medical discharges are being drafted again after their complete recovery, the Associated Press said today.

Veterans who are taken back into the services get their old rank back, according to an unnamed Army spokesman, who said that it was unlikely that men in this category would be sent overseas again.

Germans Press Beachhead Drive

WITH 5TH ARMY AMPHIBIOUS FORCES, Feb. 9 (delayed)—The Allies today continued fiercely to resist the Boche effort to push a spearhead into the 100 square mile beachhead. Wave after wave of tank-supported infantry stormed beachhead lines in a drive launched late Monday evening.

To resist the first German thrust under Monday night's bright moon the Allies rushed up strong forces of American tank destroyers and, with a determined counterthrust by British infantry, succeeded in driving back the enemy in that sector.

A beachhead strongpoint was the scene of the most bitter fighting since the Anzio operation began. Attempting to infiltrate the Allied lines against one of the heaviest artillery barrages mustered by the Allies, the Boche struck in a spearhead with heavy losses in the torrential assault.

A British officer who had been in the forward lines the last two days of the heavy German assault declared the Boche drive as "the most furious I have ever seen." He related:

"They came into us like a pack of wolves. When we mowed down the first ones, others followed. They assailed our outposts, leaving their wounded and dead where they lay."

The first German troops to attack the beachhead positions, according to this officer and other witnesses, were battle-worn but determined. The waves that followed them were fresher and troops who met them were impressed with their strength. While the Allies threw in their most concentrated artillery hammering

(Continued on page 4)

5th Tanks Fight In Town Streets

ALLIED FORCE HEADQUARTERS, Feb. 10 — American and German tanks were slugging it out in the streets of Cassino yesterday. The Yanks made some progress, but the desperately resisting enemy continued to hold the bulk of the town.

The German hold on Abbey Hill, towering upward southwest of Cassino, was still firm, but American troops on the other side of the town were fighting up steep hillsides, smashing pillboxes and heavily fortified gun emplacements as they went. One German counterattack on Allied hill positions was driven off.

British troops in the lower Garigliano River region made a slight advance and improved their positions in the mountainous area three miles north of Suio. But resistance was stiff here, too, and the Tommies had to repulse two local counterattacks.

On the 8th Army front there were patrol clashes and exchanges of mortar and artillery fire.

Patterson Predicts Stiffer Nazi Push

WASHINGTON, Feb. 10—Under Secretary of War Robert Patterson today told reporters that although the greatest weight of German pressure on the beachhead at Anzio is still to be felt "our men are firmly established."

Mr. Patterson pointed out, however, that German threats should in no way be minimized, adding that the enemy had massed tanks, artillery and men for the counterblow. He added that unfavorable flying weather had prevented full use of Allied air power in the beachhead area.

Bombers Active South Of Rome

MAAF HEADQUARTERS, Feb. 10—American four-motored heavy bombers were called in for the first time today in the battle of the Anzio beachhead to blast German forces at five points just ahead of Allied ground troops.

Points attacked were Albano, Cisterna, Cecchina—hit by B-17 Flying Fortresses — and Velletri and Campoleone, which were targets of B-24 Liberators. Crew members reported heavy bomb concentrations on enemy troops and strong points.

The 15th Air Force heavy bomber attack was made despite bad weather, which may have accounted for the complete absence of enemy fighters, and marked the first time since the Battle of Salerno that the big planes had been switched over to tactical work.

In a further effort to crack the Nazi ring around the beachhead, P-38 Lightnings, also of the 15th Air Force, returned to bombing and strafing tactics for the first time since October to attack rail and highway targets just east of Rome, on the main routes to the 8th Army front. P-47 Thunderbolts also took part in these attacks.

Other Lightnings ripped into targets of opportunity on the

(Continued on page 4)

U.S. Legation In Iran Raised To Embassy

WASHINGTON, Feb. 10 — The United States has decided to elevate the status of its diplomatic mission at Teheran, Iran, from that of a legation to an embassy, the State Department announced yesterday.

The Iranian government has notified the U.S. that it intends to take corresponding action with regard to the status of its diplomatic mission in Washington.

This action was agreed upon, the U.S. State Department said, in recognition of the greatly increased relationships which have recently developed between the two countries and in accordance with the status of Iran as a full member of the United Nations.

Allies Transfer Territory To King, Badoglio

ALLIED FORCE HEADQUARTERS, Feb. 10—All of Italy south of the northern boundaries of the provinces of Salerno, Potenza and Bari, together with the islands of Sicily and Sardinia, will be restored to the jurisdiction of the Italian government at midnight tonight, it was announced today by Lt. Gen. Sir Henry Maitland Wilson, Allied Supreme Commander. The islands of Pantelleria, Lampedusa and Lampione were not included in the order.

King Vittorio Emmanuele III and the government of Marshal Pietro Badoglio will take control of approximately 30,000 square miles of Italian territory with a population of about 5,000,000. This partial restoration of Italian suzerainty was in accord with principles set forth at the Moscow conference. One of those principles was that the Italian people should be given opportunity to establish a democratic government.

The Allied Advisory Council for Italy, representing the United States, Great Britain, the Soviet Union and the French Committee of National Liberation, last December set the boundaries of the territory to be returned to Italian jurisdiction under provisions of the Moscow parley.

"The transfer," said General Wilson, "was recommended with the understanding that it should be subject to two conditions: That the administration, central and local, should be carried on by officials of substantial good faith and Allied sympathies, and that the transfer should involve no commitment to the present administration after the capture of Rome."

It was stated that the change would not affect rights of the United Nations under the terms of the armistice with Italy. Although the Allied Military Government which has been operating in this region is thus terminated, it will be replaced by regional controllers in Sardinia and Sicily and south of the Salerno-Potenza-Bari line who will advise the Badoglio administration.

These three regional Allied executives are members of the Allied Control Commission. They will insure, General Wilson said, the use of Italian resources in the war against Germany, and provide the people of Italy with opportunity to develop their political activities.

General Wilson added that AMG would continue to operate in the combat zones immediately behind the 5th and 8th Armies. As the Allied armies advance and normal conditions are restored, future transfers of jurisdiction to the Italian government will be made.

Enlarging upon General Wilson's statement, Lt. Gen. Sir Noel Mason MacFarlane, chief civil affairs officer for the ACC, declared:

"This is the first major step we are taking to hand back to the Italians the government of their own territory. On this depends

(Continued on page 4)

THE STARS AND STRIPES
MEDITERRANEAN

Vol. 1, No. 81, Friday, February 18, 1944 ITALY EDITION TWO LIRE

1,000 Yanks Lost When Ship Is Sunk

Atlantic Sinking Believed Worst In U.S. History

WASHINGTON, Feb. 17—One of the worst disasters involving American forces at sea since the start of the war—the sinking of an Allied troop ship with American soldiers on board, somewhere in European waters, was officially announced late tonight by the War Department.

Approximately 1,000 men are reported missing and about 1,000 others have been rescued, according to the brief official statement. The War Department release said:

"Military authority now permits the disclosure that an Allied troop ship was sunk on an undisclosed date in European waters. The sinking was caused by enemy action at night time. Emergency addressees of the missing troops have now been informed. It is believed that the enemy does not know the results of this action and therefore the date has been withheld."

No further information was released.

Although the name and registry of the ship were not disclosed, it is believed here that the vessel was British. It is not known whether there were any other than American troops on board.

The tremendous loss would indicate that the transport must have suffered at least one direct hit below the water line. American emphasis on boat drills and abandon ship training on transports would otherwise have prevented such a large-scale loss.

Naval circles here said that the disaster must have been caused by submarine or surface attack since aircraft would have had to have scored a lucky bomb hit directly down a funnel to gain the speedy sinking indicated by the large loss.

German news agencies had made no mention of the disaster prior to the War Department announcement.

NEW TRAP FORMING

CRUSHING SOVIET STEAMROLLERS were pursuing the disordered German forces fleeing south to Pskov and west into Estonia yesterday. The forward-sweeping Russians appeared on the way to new triumphs over the faltering Wehrmacht as they threatened to trap another German army at Staraya Russa.

Reds Wipe Out 52,000 In Dnieper Bend Pocket

MOSCOW, Feb. 17—In a special Order of the Day, Marshal Joseph Stalin late tonight announced the "liquidation" of the Kanev pocket of ten trapped German divisions in the central Ukraine.

Fifty-two thousand Germans were killed and 11,000 were taken prisoners.

The order said that the battle lasted 15 days, ending in the annihilation of ten German divisions and one brigade, forming part of the German 8th Army. All German equipment and arms were captured.

The order of the day, directed to General Koniev who directed the encirclement operation, added:

"Troops of the 2nd Ukrainian front, who completed the annihilation of the trapped Germans, will be saluted by 20 salvos from 224 of Moscow's guns. Soviet units which participated will receive the name of 'Korsun.'"

Moscow also reported that the Red Army was hammering at the gates of Narva and Pskov yesterday and outflanking the bristling Nazi system of fortifications at Staraya Russa.

Red soldiers had crushed forward to a point less than 25 miles north of Pskov and other Red Army men were in the suburbs of Narva, while the Germans fought futilely to stem the tide from the north.

Indications that the battle for Staraya Russa at the southern end of Lake Ilmen was about to open were reported by the German-controlled Vichy radio which said that the Russians have started local attacks south of this powerful fortress.

Tass, the Soviet news agency, reported yesterday that the Red Army had forced the Wehrmacht to change the whole character of its defense system. For two years the Germans relied on a network of strong points and hedgehogs, but Soviet mastery of methods to overcome this type of system has caused the enemy to resort to the solid lines of trenches of the last war, Tass said.

A supplement to the Soviet communique said that a Hungarian light infantry division had surrendered to the Russians and thousands of Poles were reported drifting through the Soviet lines near Luck and Rovno, offering themselves as recruits for the Polish brigade operating on that front.

RAF Bombings Leave Berlin A City Of Fire And Death

LONDON, Feb. 17—A horror picture of the Berlin of today has been brought back to neutral countries by eye-witnesses of Tuesday night's RAF "cascade" raid in which 2,500 tons of block-busters and incendiaries were dropped on the German capital at the rate of over 60 tons a minute in a little more than half an hour.

Witnesses said that flames flared from unshapely snarls of masonry and twisted steel. Miles of firehose serpentined around great holes in boulevards and over heaped remains of houses in the streets. Block-long lines of people formed in bitter cold behind Wehrmacht soup kitchens.

Largest city in continental Europe, Berlin has now rocked and shuddered from a total weight of 23,500 tons of bombs which have made almost total wreckage of partial destruction and have converted rubble to dust since the "Battle of Berlin" started last November. The Reich capital is now said to be from 70 to 80 percent destroyed.

The northeastern section of the city suffered the most damage in this latest raid. Large fires were started throughout the entire area and the Heinkel and Osram factories and the gas and electric plants were wrecked. Swiss dispatches said.

Civilian losses, it was reported were enormous and emergency graves had to be dug to dispose of the dead. The great number of casualties was attributed to the fact that many of the buildings damaged in previous raids could not stand the blast this last time.

Swedish survivors arriving in Stockholm today from Berlin said that bombs fell all over Berlin at the same time. The fire brigade organization broke down, they reported, and huge fires blazed all over the city with no engines available to fight the flames.

Army Discharges Total Of 776,000

WASHINGTON, Feb 17 — The War Department announced recently that 776,000 men had been honorably discharged from the Army between Dec. 1, 1941, and Nov. 30, 1943. About 200,000 of these were discharged as overaged.

Of the remaining 576,000 discharged, the majority were for physical disability. Others discharged were minors, key men in industry, volunteer officer candidates and men who joined other branches of the service.

Allies At Anzio Beat Off Nazis

Von Kesselring Unleashes Four New Armored Counterattacks

By Sgt. MILTON LEHMAN
(*Stars and Stripes Staff Writer*)

ON THE ANZIO BEACHHEAD FRONT, Feb. 16 (Delayed) — The largest-scale German attack since the landing was resumed today at 0630 hours. For the forces of Field Marshal Albert von Kesselring and for the tightly-packed Allied troops defending this 100-square mile beachhead south of Rome, today, by all signs, was der Tag.

Plunging their armored probes into at least four sectors of the beachhead, the fierce German assaults had been blocked initially at all points.

In the besieged "factory" area near Carroceto, the Germans have massed a strong force of infantry and tanks. Early this morning, German artillery hammered out the heaviest barrage they have launched in this beachhead's history.

German tanks, tightly coordinated with infantry, stormed up to the Allied lines under the cover of smoke. As of noon today, incomplete reports state that the Allies have already knocked out ten of these tanks. Beside these flaming and crippled tanks, hundreds of German assault troops lay dead before they had succeeded in penetrating the Allied first line of defense.

One spearhead of the German's attack around the beachhead perimeter was launched in two prongs against the eastern sector, where the Mussolini Canal swings south to the Tyrrhenian Sea. Bridges crossing the canal, which were the most-contested objectives during the first week of the beachhead battle, were apparently once more under fire.

Of the two prongs of the German assault in this sector, one was cut short soon after it was launched. The second was repulsed later.

German fighter planes were supporting the drive in this sector, and elsewhere on the beachhead perimeter. Frontline ack-ack crews were attempting to beat back the German air threat. Along the Mussolini Canal the Germans conducted at least one strafing mission.

But the battle now raging on the Carroceto area appeared hourly to be the most severe of all the German thrusts. The embattled "factory" and surrounding terrain dominates the approaches to the road joining the Appian Way and Anzio. And it is in this area that the Germans staged their heaviest assault. Last week the Germans recaptured the community center known as "the factory," have held it against repeated bombings and artillery "timed crashes."

This morning's assault followed a three-day lull in the beachhead fighting. Last night, however, the Germans stepped up their air as-

(*Continued on page 4*)

Air Support At New High

MAAF HEADQUARTERS, Feb. 17—The full power of the Allied air arm in Italy today was thrown against German forces attacking on the Anzio beachhead front in what was believed to be the greatest ground support of the Mediterranean campaign.

The attack was headed by B-17 Fortresses and B-25 Liberators which smashed at a concentrated area containing massed enemy troops, gun emplacements and vehicles on the main highway from Anzio to Frascati.

Dropping fragmentation bombs—used with best effect against men and their machines — the four-motored bombers reported blanketing completely a crossroads area between Anzio and Rome.

The heavy bombers reported extremely heavy flak over their target area. The only enemy fighters encountered by the heavies was a formation of 25 German aircraft which attacked one B-24 flight. Preliminary reports gave no details of the combat results.

A special announcement tonight from Lt. Gen. Ira Eaker's MAAF headquarters said the four-motored planes roared over the beachhead in wave after wave for three hours beginning at 10 a.m.

Twelfth Air Force B-25 Mit-

(*Continued on page 4*)

Press Deplores Italy Censorship

LONDON, Feb. 17—The London press today was virtually unanimous in deploring editorially censorship regulations applying to war correspondents writing from the Anzio-Nettuno beachhead.

The Daily Mail, the Daily Herald and the Daily Telegraph all spoke their minds on the subject. The Daily Mail charged that "dispatches from the beachhead are being deliberately delayed," while the Daily Telegraph said that the remedy for faulty reporting was to "insure that correspondents receive a correct picture of events." All three protested against the denial of radio facilities to the correspondents.

Meanwhile, in Parliament, pointed questions were asked of Sir James Grigg, the War Minister, who promised to look into the matter. Elmer Davis, head of the U.S. Office of War Information, also announced that he was looking into the matter.

Simon Says Cassino Treasures Removed

LONDON, Feb. 17—Viscount Simon, speaking for the British Government, told the House of Lords yesterday that all monks of the Montecassino Abbey retired to Rome before the Allied bombardment Tuesday.

The former British Foreign Secretary emphasized the fact that many of the monastery's art treasures had been removed before German military use of the holy buildings had precipitated Allied attacks on the abbey.

THE STARS AND STRIPES

SICILY

Vol. 1 - No. 60 - Tuesday, March 7, 1944 For U. S. Armed Forces 2 Lire

Soviets Spring New Offensive Near Tarnopol

Red Army Shatters Vital Nazi Railway From Dnieper Bend

LONDON, March 6—A Stalin Order of the Day tonight revealed a dramatic breakthrough of Russian troops on the South Polish front, spearhead of the entire Soviet-German battle line, which carried the Red Army to within ten miles of the great railway junction of Tarnopol less than 50 miles southeast of Lvov.

Led by Marshal Gregory Zhukov, the red-starred legions of the First Ukrainian Army advanced along a 120-mile front, smashing four German tank and eight infantry divisions and at last reports had cut the trunk railway between Odessa and Warsaw, main supply route of hapless Nazi Field Marshal Fritz von Mannstein's armies in the Dnieper Bend.

Marshal Zhukov, victor at Stalingrad and hero of the repulsion of the Nazi Army from Moscow, took the command from General Nicolai Vatutin who is ill. According to the Paris radio, Marshal Zhukov has 14 battle-tried divisions engaged in action.

The new offensive threatened the Nazis with still another major disaster and Marshal von Mannstein, victim of a ten-division loss at Cherkassy, his second inside of a month. Group by group his estimated 50 or 60 divisions force, not far short of 750,000 men, are being forced into a new big retreat.

With Soviet artillery and air support, Marshal Zhukov is aiming a three-pronged thrust toward the Carpathians. His central advance is crashing forward south of the

(Continued on Page 4)

Finn Peace Move Seen In Few Days

BULLETIN

STOCKHOLM, March 6 — The Swedish newspaper Margentidningen is quoted by a UP correspondent as saying that former premier Justo K. Parsinkivi, who negotiated the Russo-Finnish peace in 1940, will leave for Russia within a few days to begin formal negotiations for a separate peace.

MOSCOW—There is no official indication from Helsinki concerning what the government will do following Soviet publication of peace terms, Reuters reported. The Finnish radio is said to have broadcast an editorial from an Helsinki newspaper saying "one must constantly remember it is our sincere endeavor to extricate ourselves from this war . . . It is now the government's task to examine the situation."

The Swedish Minister of Foreign Affairs has denied the report that the Germans sounded out the Swedish government relative to evacuating Nazi troops from Finland by way of Sweden, according to Reuters. The Swedish Minister said he had received no request of this kind

Chief of 'Murder, Inc.' Executed With Aides

NEW YORK — Louis "Lepke" Buchalter, the chief of "Murder, Inc.," went to the electric chair Saturday night after last minute attempts to save him had failed. His henchmen, Louis Capone and Emanuel Weiss, were executed at the same time.

"Murder, Inc.," organized killing on a business basis and is believed to have been responsible for at least 80 murders.

Screen Newcomer Wins Coveted Acting Award

HOLLYWOOD—A comparative newcomer to the screen, Jennifer Jones, was voted best actress of the year and received the coveted "Oscar" when the movie industry handed out its annual awards to the best performers, films and technicians of the year. Miss Jones played bits in hoss operas before she was given the title role in "The Song of Bernadette."

"Casablanca" was adjudged the best picture of the year and its director, Michael Curtiz, the outstanding director. Paul Lucas won the award for his performance in "Watch on the Rhine." Best documentary was the British Army Film Unit's "Desert Victory," record of the Eighth Army's North African campaign.

U.S. Breaks Off With Argentina

WASHINGTON, March 6—The United States has suspended recognition of the new government of Argentina, it was officially announced by Acting Secretary of State Edward Stettinius. U.S. Ambassador Norman Armour has been instructed not to carry on official diplomatic relations with General Edelmiro Farrell's regime.

It is understood that the British Ambassador to Argentina has also been instructed not to take any formal steps which could be interpreted as recognition of the Farrell Government.

The Bolivian regime, which likewise has not received U.S. and British recognition, announced that it had entered into diplomatic relations with the new Argentine Government.

In Buenos Aires, General Farrell told Reuters that his regime was "determined to eradicate from the country anything which may signify the remotest danger to continental security."

Since taking over the government, the Farrell regime has cut down at least one revolt by army and navy groups, but because of strict censorship on press and radio, the outside world has only a dim picture of conditions inside Argentina. Farrell declared recently that he and his group were preparing the country for elections.

Enemy Halted After All-Out Beachhead Bid

Weather Whittles All Peninsula Activity To Minor Skirmishes

ALLIED FORCE HEADQUARTERS, March 6—Rains and squalls yesterday closed in on all Italian fronts, greatly reducing both ground and aerial operations. In the Anzio beachhead activity was whittled to a brief enemy flareup in the Cisterna region which Allied mortar and artillery screens held for no gain.

This lull came as a breathing spell for the still groggy German forces which late last week were stopped cold in their third major attempt to catapult the Allies back into the Tyrrhenian Sea.

Field Marshal Albert Kesselring had nothing to show for his three-divisional assault but another mountain of casualties after hitting an Allied stone wall which an official announcement revealed to be composed principally of the American Third Division.

Long-range shelling of Anzio harbor by the enemy lessened yesterday, and in spite of enemy air attacks and heavy swells, the orderly task of unloading reinforcements and supplies in the area continued.

Six weeks after their landing in the beachhead, Allied troops have gained three major victories over the Germans attempting to dislodge them. Beachhead forces are now well dug in and fortified despite every enemy effort in long-range shelling.

Now, as on the first day of their landing, they constitute an irritating potential threat to German communications south of Rome. They are containing ten German divisions and inflicting heavy casualties—already well over 15,000.

Laval Threatens French

LONDON—"The German army will tolerate no disorder." Pierre Laval, French quisling Prime Minister, told the people of France, according to PWB, threatening them with German ruthlessness if they assist the Allies in the event of an invasion of the continent.

Yank Planes Score First Berlin Raids

Stimson Values Lives Over Cultural Sites

WASHINGTON—Religious and cultural targets in and around the Rome area will be bombed if the Germans use them for military purposes, Secretary of War declared in a review of last week's operations on all fronts.

Every attempt is being made to respect the neutral status of Vatican City, Mr. Stimson said, but he emphasized that religious and historical targets could not be spared if their use by the enemy endangered American lives.

The Secretary of War pointed out that Rome's rail lines and yards make it an important communications center through which most of the enemy forces pass on their way to the Anzio beachhead and the main front in southern Italy.

Americans Strike West Of Saidor

BULLETIN

LONDON, March 7—American forces have made a seaborne landing behind the Japanese lines 30 miles west of Saidor in New Guinea, BBC reported this morning. Patrols driving in the direction of Madang, Japanese port southeast of the great base at Wewak, have reached a point twenty miles west of Saidor.

ALLIED SOUTH PACIFIC HEADQUARTERS, March 6—U.S. cavalry troops are striking northward from captured Momote airfield on Los Negros in the Admiralty group after inflicting one of the bloodiest defeats of the Pacific struggle upon the Japanese garrison.

All night long the Japanese commanders sent their men against the machine guns and bayonets of the First Dismounted Cavalry Division in an attempt to recapture the strategic Momote aerodrome, only to be cut to pieces by the strongly reinforced Americans. In the battle for the air base, the Jap-

(Continued on Page 4)

Monday Total: 83 Nazi Planes

LONDON, March 6—Bombing of Berlin by United States planes was inaugurated over the week-end when Flying Fortresses Saturday followed the trails blazed for them by a formation of American Lightning fighters who flew over the Nazi capital on Friday to become the first American aircraft to hit the city.

Today the American air forces were at it again, as it was announced that very strong forces of United States heavy bombers escorted by large formations of fighters attacked the Berlin district. Factories, air fields and other military installations of the city were pounded with "good results."

In today's attack Allied fighters destroyed 83 German fighters for a loss of 11, while American heavy bombers also destroyed a large number of German aircraft whose total is not yet ascertained. One bomber division is known to have destroyed at least forty. Sixty-eight U.S. bombers failed to return. Seven Flying Fortresses are reported to have made forced landings in Sweden.

It was the third raid within four days and the fifth time within six days that heavy bombers attacked Nazi targets in daylight. And late today it was announced that the RAF had sent heavy aircraft over the channel.

Returning pilots said that anti-aircraft fire and fighter opposition was much lighter than anticipated, except directly over the target.

After Saturday's historic American daylight attack on Berlin, Air Chief Marshal Sir Arthur Harris sent the following telegram to Major General James Doolittle: "Hearty congratulations on the first U.S. bombing of Berlin. It is more than a year since they were last attacked in daylight but now they know they have no safety by day or night. All Germany learns the same lesson."

509 Italians Die In Train Tragedy

NAPLES, March 6—Five hundred and nine Italian civilians lost their lives when a train broke down in a railway tunnel in central-southern Italy last Friday evening, according to official preliminary reports.

Most of the victims died of asphixiation within a few seconds. It was learned that at the train's last stop hundreds of Italians had swarmed onto the already crowded train.

Rome Radio stated that the train was compelled to stop in the tunnel "for reasons that are not yet known," and that the smoke of the engine made the air so "unbreathable" that more than 500 persons lost their lives.

An additional 49 persons were taken to the hospital in serious condition, according to a Rome Radio version.

Marine Kills 19 Japs In Single-Handed Feat

NAMURA, Kwajalein Atoll—Pfc. Joseph P. Mammott, Buffalo, N. Y., killed 19 Japanese single-handed during a short-lived Japanese attempt to attack an American Marine dugout in the Marshalls campaign.

Mammott laid the barrel of his machine gun across his arm and blasted away when he discovered that the tripod on the gun prevented the barrel from lowering far enough. He was wounded in the arm by a Japanese bullet.

BEACHHEAD'S FOXHOLE HOSPITAL

INDISCRIMINATE BOMBING and strafing of all ground objects in the Anzio beachhead has forced the hospitals to place beds below ground level as protection against this enemy action. In this British hospital, the wounded are placed in slit trenches. *Photo Through PWB*

NORTHERN IRELAND EDITION

1d. THE STARS AND STRIPES 1d.

Daily Newspaper of U.S. Armed Forces in the European Theater of Operations

Vol. 1. No. 83. New York, N.Y.—Belfast, Northern Ireland. Monday, March 13, 1944.

Travel Between Ireland, Britain Restricted

Reds Destroy 500 German TanksinDrive

Dnieper Spanned From South In New Threat Against Nazis

Destruction of 500 German tanks and armored cars, the equivalent of four divisions' equipment, in a big four-day battle on the front opposite the Rumanian border, was reported by the Soviet News Agency last night as Gen. Feodor Tolbukhin's Fourth Ukrainian Army swung into action across the swollen Lower Dnieper.

Tolbukhin's seasoned troops, veterans of the campaign which wrested Melitopol from the enemy last fall, forced the river, apparently near Kakhova, and captured the town of Berislov, 40 miles from the Black Sea port of Kherson, in the rear of the Germans retreating from Krivoi Rog.

Only a few of Tolbukhin's great force appeared to have been engaged, but the mere fact that the steppe's army was on the move again for the first time since it smashed the Nazis' left bank bridgehead opposite Nikopol a month ago indicated the Red Army's southern offensive still had not yet reached its climax more than a week after it began on March 4

Big Trap Taking Shape

The river crossing appeared likely to trap possibly large forces of Germans retreating under the pressure of Gen Rodion Malinovsky's Third Ukrainian Army, advancing from the Krivoi Rog area.

Soviet News Agency gave no details of the tank battle on the First Ukrainian Army's front, but it seemed likely it may have been in the Tarnopol sector, where Russian reconnaissance planes earlier spotted 400 Nazi tanks coming up to the front lines.

The Germans brought up powerful forces, including heavy artillery and armored trains, but in spite of the strength pouring into the western section of the city, Pravda said Red infantrymen were fighting their way into the city house by house.

Counter-Attack At Proskurov

Red Star said the Germans, regardless of losses, were fighting fiercely for every hilltop, stream and road in that sector and making their main stand west of the city, where they mounted a large number of big guns on hills commanding the junction.

A sharp German counter-attack was reported in the Proskurov sector, 60 miles east of Tarnopol, where Marshal Gregory Zhukov's men were steadily

(Continued on Page 2.)

Foe Calls Raids, Red Push Preliminaries To Invasion

U.S. raids on Germany and new Soviet offensives on the southern sectors of the Eastern Front are the preliminaries to the invasion of Europe, according to German sources quoted by Budapest radio

The War Today

USAAF—Unescorted Libs blast Pas de Calais for second time in two days without loss.

Eire—Allied "economic squeeze" on Eire predicted after DeValera's rejection of U.S. request to ban Axis consuls

Russia—Reds destroy 500 German tanks, armored cars in four-day battle opposite Rumanian border

Italy—Scattered patrol clashes feature land action on Italian front; better weather conditions promise large scale operations.

Burma—U.S., Chinese troops advance 150 miles through Jap-held jungles, kill 800 Japs in week's fighting.

Pacific—Marines seize Talasea and airfield, cutting off thousands of Japs on Williamauz Peninsula, north of Talasea

Yanks Advance In Far East

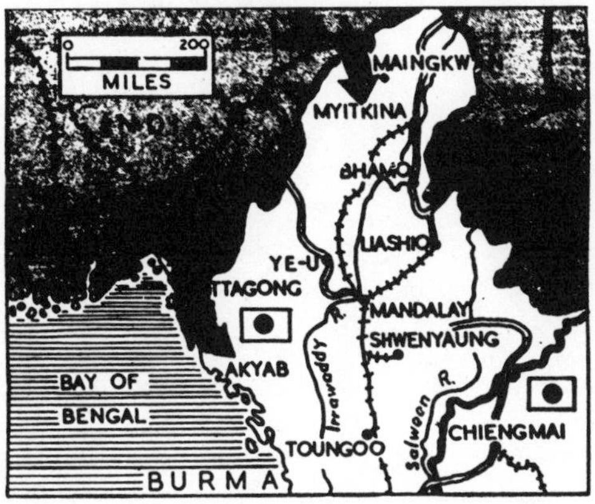

Stars and Stripes Map by Marsh

Yanks, Chinese Push 150 Miles Into Burma; Only 2 Men Killed

WITH U.S. FORCES, NORTHERN BURMA, March 13—American and Chinese troops, commanded by Brig. Gen. Frank Merrill, at a cost of only 39 casualties—two killed and 37 wounded—have advanced 150 miles through solid Jap-held jungle and killed at least 800 Japs in one week's fighting.

The week's whirlwind drive has been so successful tha. Lt. Gen. Joseph Stilwell has flatly predicted that "the Hukawng Valley will soon be ours."

Gen. Stilwell's troops are still mopping up Jap remnants in two sectors. While one Allied force is relentlessly pushing the enemy back, another force has crossed the Nampyek River and has cut the only motor road to Kamaing.

In Southern Burma Allied troops have ambushed Jap patrols west of the Mayu Range and are advancing steadily. East of the hills only a few scattered parties of enemy troops are left.

RAF heavy bombers have attacked the Mongaung-Kamaing road and dumps in the Mongaung area. Large fires were started and three direct hits were scored on a railroad bridge.

Speedy Burma Advance May Open Ledo Road

NEW DELHI, India, March 13 (AP)—So fast is Lt. Gen. Joseph Stilwell forcing the pace in North Burma that a crisis is approaching which will make or break this year's Burma campaign.

He has forced his way 150 miles into Burma, and the Japs must now either withdraw troops from other fronts or see Gen. Stilwell accomplish his objective of smashing a corridor across north Burma from China and open the Ledo road from India.

His strategy in diverting an American infantry column into direct cooperation with his American-trained Chinese troops was a drastic revision of an earlier plan to make only a long range harassing penetration into Burma

Instead, the Americans have spread confusion in the Jap defenses by cutting in ten miles behind their lines.

Libs Hit Calais; Not One Is Lost

Luftwaffe Fails To Oppose Unescorted Bombers In Sunday Raid

Unescorted Liberators of the U.S. Strategical Air Forces in Europe blasted the Pas de Calais "secret weapon" coast of France yesterday for the second time in two days, and returned without the loss of a single bomber to report the same astonishing lack of German fighter opposition encountered in Saturday's Fortress raid on Munster.

Not one enemy aircraft was sighted, and not one bomber was lost when the Forts, escorted by P47s and P51s slashed 300 miles into Germany to Munster to hit the vital rail and waterways junction through clouds

30 Forts Lost

Thirty Forts and two Thunderbolts were lost at Munster in October in furious air battles in which 102 Nazi planes were shotdown

P38s which escorted Libs to Pas de Calais on Saturday "played with each other for lack of something to shoot at, according to B24 crewmen.

P47s, in addition to escorting the Forts to Munster, carried out an offensive sweep over Occupied Europe. Pilots reported heavy flak, but no German planes as they shot up high-tension towers, gunposts, machine-gun emplacements, and gun crews.

Not one U.S. bomber was lost in the day's operations, but four fighters failed to return.

U.S. Marauders Saturday afternoon joined with small forces of RAF and Allied Mosquitos and Typhoons to hit targets in Northern France as other RAF Typhoons carried out offensive patrols. Only one Typhoon was lost. The B26s were escorted by Allied Spitfires.

Knudsen Sights Demands For 12 Million New Cars

NEW YORK, March 13 (AP)—Lt Gen William Knudsen, the Army's war-production chief, said today that Americans would want 12,000,000 new cars after the war and would begin to get them within six months of the war's end

He said the first available cars would be 1942 models, that so-called super-cars wouldn't be much like those depicted by artists today and that the main development in aviation would be in the direction of bigger planes rather than private planes.

Who's Who In Jap, German Eire Legations

By Jules B. Grad

Stars and Stripes Staff Writer

The international spotlight today was focused on the personnel of the German and Japanese embassies in Dublin, which U.S. Secretary of State Cordell Hull requested Eire's government to remove from the Irish Free State.

Mr. Hull, in his note to Eire's President Eamon De Valera, pointed out that Axis "diplomatic and consular representatives still continue to reside in Dublin and enjoy the special privileges and immunities customarily accorded such officials."

Doubtlessly referring to the South American activities of the German and Japanese representatives there, Mr. Hull added:

"That Axis representatives in neutral countries use those special privileges and immunities as a cloak for espionage activities against the United Nations has been demonstrated over and over again."

"It would be naive to assume," Mr. Hull's note continued, "that Axis agencies did not exploit the conditions in full in Ireland as they have in other countries"

Meet Herr Hempel!

Heading the German legation staff is Dublin is Eduard Hempel, who gained the ability to evaluate military information as a Saxon liaison officer to the Kaiser's general headquarters at Charleville during World War 1. After the armistice he became Saxony's representative to the central government in Berlin.

In 1927, six years before Hitler's rise to power, Hempel entered the Wilhelmstrasse Foreign Office. At one time, he was charge d'affaires in Norway, since fallen to the Wehrmacht as the result of a Berlin inspired fifth column movement

Although information about the personnel of the German legation in Dublin has been scarce, recent reports stated that the staff includes:

Henning Thomsen, secretary of the legation, and Robert Wenzel and Herr Mueller, consular secretaries.

The London Daily Express reported Saturday that Thomsen's rank was "Chief of Intelligence, Western Europe"

Thomsen Has £1,000,000 In Eire

"Thomsen is the man who runs the German spy system in Eire, the Express said "He nominally serves under Hempel, but actually he is Hempel's boss."

"He is also boss of the third member of the German legation triumvirate, Dr. Carl Petersen who went to Eire before the war as a German newspaperman, then assumed the title of press attache at the German legation.

The Express also reported that Thomsen has a million pounds sterling

(Continued on Page 2.)

Flying Boat Mars Sets Record For Mail Load

WASHINGTON, March 13 — The Navy announced yesterday that its giant flying boat Mars had broken another record

The transport landed at San Francisco this morning carrying 800,000 letters weighing 23,846 pounds—largest mail load ever shipped by air from the Pacific

In addition, the plane carried more than half a ton of war materials

15 More Days Of Aerial Combat And Luftwaffe's Done—Mahurin

A FIGHTER BASE, March 13 (AP)—"Give us 15 more good days when we can get the Jerries up and I think it will mean the war is won as far as the Luftwaffe is concerned," Captain Walker Mahurin, America's leading fighter ace in the ETO, said yesterday

While his prediction is definitely on the sunny side, his statement showed how fighter pilots feel about the week's savage battles in which Thunderbolts, Lightnings, Mustangs and Spitfires shot down 197 enemy aircraft

Mahurin's score of 20 victories now is only six under the American record established by Eddie Rickenbacker in World War 1. Before the war, Mahurin was a clerk in Fort Wayne Ind

Thus far in the battle of Berlin begun with the fighter sweep over the German capital ten days ago American fighters and bombers have gotten a combined bag of 351 Nazi planes. Fighters alone got 84 March for a new day record and then matched it on March 8, both times on Berlin jobs

Mahurin likes to see Berlin as the target. "It shows the trend more than anything else when we can go all the way there and shoot them up. We definitely have superiority now." Then he made his optimistic victory prediction

Mahurin frankly admits that he is "scared to death" on every flight

"I think a lot of us are," he added. A fellow pilot, however, asserted that Mahurin never showed fear in the way he dived into swarms of German fighters.

Mahurin, a good-looking 25-year-old flier who is all wrapped up in airplanes, declared that he "gets lots of fun out of combat, especially after you've got a Jerry."

Order Follows Eire's Reply To Hull Note

Economic Sanctions Seen Unlikely, Though U.S. Refuses Ship Sale

Britain today clamped down tight restrictions on cross-channel travel—including movement from Great Britain into either Northern Ireland or Eire—in a swift aftermath to De Valera's refusal to accede to the United States' request that she oust Axis diplomatic representatives to prevent seepage of invasion information.

The action, likely to prove a blow to pocketbooks in Eire—haven for the war-weary—came just two days after disclosure of Eire's position, and will affect not only civilians, but men and women in the services.

The order, which affected all travel

The texts of the U.S. and Eire notes appear on Page 6

except those on missions of vital military necessity, stated:

"The government has decided that, subject to certain exceptions, all travel between Great Britain, on the one hand, and Northern Ireland and Eire, on the other hand, must be suspended forthwith for military reasons.

Service Personnel Included

The order also stated that no "further leave certification for Irish workers to return from Great Britain would be granted, except for business or work of urgent national importance or on compassionate grounds of the utmost urgent and compelling character."

"Similar restrictions on leave of service personnel are being imposed," the order said

While the border restrictions were anticipated generally as a result of the President Eamon De Valera decision to keep his country aloof from the war, it was not expected in informed diplomatic quarters that it would be followed by imposition of economic sanctions

Earlier, both the American and British press had predicted an Allied "economic squeeze" on the Irish Free State following De Valera's flat rejection of the U.S State Department's demand that Eire close its German and Japanese legations and consulates

U.S. Refuses to Sell Ships

A refusal by the U.S. to permit Eire to buy two badly-needed American merchant ships—Ireland has only about ten, which are insufficient for her needs—indicated that such a policy might already be in force, although it was possible the refusal had been made prior to transmission of the U.S demand

There was no expectation of military action

The State Department re-published

(Continued on Page 2.)

Their Billet Doux To Nazi Captives Trap Three WACs

DENVER, Colo., March 13 (UP)—Three WACs have been sentenced to four to six months' imprisonment for writing love letters to German prisoners of war, and two other WACs are accused of the same offence, it was revealed today

Also, eight U.S. soldiers have been charged with aiding German prisoners to escape. Three of the soldiers confessed their guilt; all will be court-martialed.

The discoveries followed the escape of two German prisoners from a camp near Denver

Six Die In Richmond, Va., Hotel Fire; 12 Others Hurt

RICHMOND, Va., March 13—Six persons, including a state senator, were burned to death over the week-end when they were trapped in a fire which damaged the Jefferson Hotel here. Twelve others were seriously injured.

THE STARS AND STRIPES

MEDITERRANEAN

Vol. 1, No. 104, Thursday, March 16, 1944 | ITALY EDITION | TWO LIRE

Cassino Pulverized By MAAF; Fortresses Hammer Brunswick

Soldier Vote Bill Passed By Senate

Democratic Leader Forsees Possible Presidential Veto

WASHINGTON, March 15 — After bitter debate, the Senate yesterday passed by 47 votes to 31 the "States' Rights" soldiers vote bill, in spite of a hint by Democratic leader Alben W. Barkley (D., Ky.) that President Roosevelt may veto it.

The bill was scheduled to be taken up in the House, where Speaker Sam Rayburn (D., Texas) had previously announced he would support it. An unfavorable vote by the House would send the bill back to conference, but the House was expected to pass it.

As the bill stands now, the servicemen and women could receive, under certain conditions, a Federal ballot which would carry no names and would cover only the elections for President, Vice-President, Senators and Congressmen.

These are the conditions: first, the governor of the serviceman's state must declare the Federal ballot legal under state laws, and secondly, if the governor does so certify, the serviceman must swear that he applied for the ballot by Sept. 1 and failed to receive a regular state ballot by Oct. 1. Otherwise the soldier must vote under the regular state laws.

There is also a provision which sponsors claim would permit the Federal ballot to be used in New Mexico and Kentucky, the two states which do not provide for absentee voting—if approved by the two governors concerned.

This week also saw Gov. Thomas E. Dewey submit his own plan to the New York Legislature for a simple soldier-voting bill. At the same time Dewey strongly attacked the Roosevelt Administration for "attempting to force on people of this country a soldier ballot limited to the election of Federal officials."

The Dewey plan, which is certain of passage, will allow New Yorkers to vote for Federal, state and local candidates by requesting ballots from the War Ballot Commission in Albany. Any New Yorker can start making his request by giving his home and present APO address. As soon as the primaries are over on July 19, a state ballot will be prepared and sent out to serv-

(Continued on page 4)

Eight American Planes Downed To Nazis' 36

LONDON, March 15—The Allies slugged back in the European battle of the air today as the Americans loosed great fleets of heavy and medium bombers and fighters for daylight assaults on central Germany and northern France.

Waves of Flying Fortresses and Liberators, strongly supported and escorted by Lightnings and Thunderbolts, pierced deep into the heart of the Reich to strike Brunswick, important Nazi aircraft manufacturing center. The bombing was done by instrument as the city was obscured by a heavy overcast. The Luftwaffe offered only spotty opposition — some bomber crews reported seeing no German planes at all—and lost 36 planes to an American loss of three bombers and five fighters. This was the first time in a week that the Luftwaffe challenged an American raid over the continent.

While the heavies were pushing through the German skies, U.S. Marauders, escorted and covered by RAF and Allied fighters, winged over the English Channel to continue the day-by-day hammering of military targets in northern France and Belgium. Later in the day, American Thunderbolts roared unchallenged over northern France in a low-level offensive sweep. Divided into two formations, the P-47 squadrons strafed coastal targets, dipping almost to roof top height. The initial operation of this type for these versatile fighters, which once were used exclusively for high altitude encounters, was made last Saturday over the same area.

Meanwhile, the Luftwaffe came over London last night in an attempt to fire-blitz the British capital. British night fighters and ground defenses knocked down 13 German planes in one of the fiercest sky engagements of the year.

At least two waves of German bombers employed the Luftwaffe's new tactics of approaching London in a spread-eagled formation. An intense ack-ack barrage over the British capital compelled them to bomb haphazardly.

(Continued on page 4)

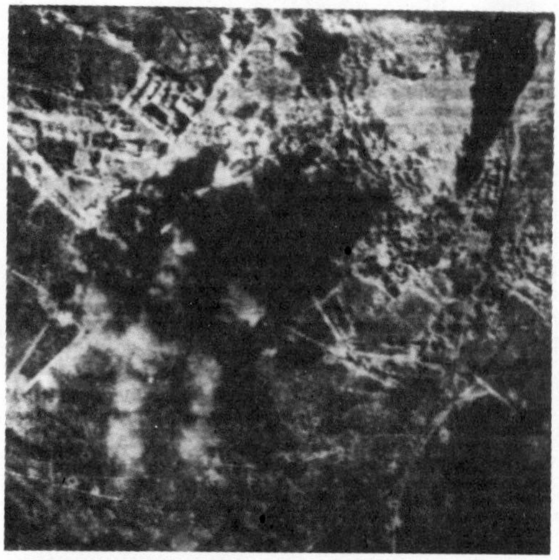

BOMBS FALL ON CASSINO in an all-out effort to end the stalemate on the southern 5th Army front. Stars and Stripes staff photographer Max Montgomery, who took the picture, said: "As we approached the town, we could see the Allied artillery firing below. The whole area was pocked with shell craters. Over the target, we watched the bombs fall until suddenly billowy clouds of black smoke mushroomed up from the town. Even while we were completing the run, we could see other bombers coming in."

Russians Cross Bug River In 60-Mile Break-Through

BULLETIN

LONDON, March 15—Soviet troops under the command of Marshal Ivan Konev have smashed across the Bug River along a 60-mile front and are now less than 30 miles from the old Rumanian border and the River Dniester, according to tonight's Soviet communique. Moscow listed the capture of several towns, including Olgopol, which is 30 miles beyond the Bug.

LONDON, March 15—Moscow reports indicated today that several divisions of battered Germans were locked in the jaws of the Soviet trap sprung in the Kherson-Nikolaev region yesterday.

The Germans have already suffered more than 14,000 casualties in dead and captured inside this new circle of Soviet steel, which is centered around Snigirevka on the west bank of the Ingulets River, 30 miles north of Kherson and 36 miles east of Nikolaev. Soviet reports claimed that only 20 miles separated the jaws of the Red Army trap grinding together relentlessly deep in the Ukraine. This latest success of Soviet arms was implemented by the army of General Rodion Malinovsky, captor of Kherson earlier this week.

Early Russian capture of Nikolaev, the big railroad center and port near the mouth of the Bug River, seemed a certainty today, as Soviet tank spearheads pounded to within 19 miles of the city from the north. The main body of the offensive against the Black Sea city moved in a continuous flow across the estuary of the Dnieper, through Kherson and along the railroad from the east.

Three other German fortresses appeared likely to crash before Russian onslaughts in the Ukraine:

Vinnitsa—Two Soviet forces converged on the town with great mo-

(Continued on page 4)

Theater Record Made As Allies Drop 2500 Tons

By JOHN O. KEARNEY
(Stars and Stripes Staff Writer)

ON THE FIFTH ARMY FRONT BEFORE CASSINO, March 15 — Cassino is flattened. Waves of Allied bombers, totalling almost 400 Liberators, Fortresses, Marauders, Bostons and Mitchells, unloaded 2,500 tons of bombs on the battered town for three and one-half hours this morning, in the largest single air attack any town in the Mediterranean theater has ever suffered.

M A A F HEADQUARTERS, March 15—Lt. Gen. Ira C. Eaker, MAAF commander, in a short-wave broadcast to America, said today that his airmen flew more than 3,000 sorties against Cassino this morning, dropping more than 2,500 tons of bombs.

"Generals Alexander, Devers, Clark and I watched Cassino melted down today," General Eaker reported. "It was by long odds our greatest effort."

"Today we fumigated Cassino," he declared, "and I am most hopeful that when the smoke of today's battle clears we shall find more worthy occupants installed with little loss to our men."

And when the smoke and the stone dust cleared away in the light wind a few minutes after noontime, Cassino had been smashed into a mass of rubble indistinguishable from the jagged, rocky base of Mount Cassino itself.

With all sizes of bombs and finally with an intensely heavy artillery barrage that picked up where the planes laid off, Allied forces attempted to crack the resistance of a pivotal German stronghold which has held out against us since early last month.

Troops of the New Zealand Corps, who have been fighting room to room through the streets of Cassino since the American 36th Division was pulled from that part of the line, were withdrawn from their positions in and around the town before dawn. Civilians also had been evacuated from the bombing area.

At 0830 hours the first wave of 18 B-25s came over in three groups of six. Visibility was excellent. Most of the bombs of this first wave hit the town squarely. They struck with quick stabs of red flame from which knife-like geysers of black and white smoke and stone dust spurted, and then spread and billowed into the air to a height higher than the monastery.

From that time forward, on a 15 minute schedule throughout the morning, waves of planes kept up the bombardment. An extremely small percentage of bombs failed to land either within the streets of the town or on Kraut positions on its perimeter, or immediately south along Cassino's highway 6 exit. Several bombs landed on the monastery itself, from which in the darkness of last night observers had seen German tracer fire directed against Allied troops.

By 1030 hours the whole of

(Continued on page 4)

GI Heaven: Anzio Rest Camp

By Cpl. WADE JONES
(Stars and Stripes Staff Writer)

ON THE 5TH ARMY ANZIO BEACHHEAD FRONT, March 15—A beachhead 12-piece band was playing "Honeysuckle Rose" so close to the frontlines today that they had to tell the drummer not to beat so hard.

The scene was a secluded glade where one of the advanced rest camps has been set up. Some of the men there had come out of the line only last night and none had been out for more than three days, except a few who were being treated for trench foot.

Men are driven to the camp directly from the front and they stay two days and nights and then other groups come in. They get hot showers from a 16-nozzle portable Italian shower machine captured back in Sicily, and then they are given a complete change of clothing.

For entertainment, there is a dance band composed of men from the same unit which runs the camp. Movies are also shown four times a day; but a good deal of the men just like to sit around and talk.

Many of the men reaching the camp shave for the first time in weeks and when the beards were removed, their jaws and cheeks were left white and razor-nicked. The rest of their faces were dark from the sun and the wind and the dirt that wouldn't wash off.

Their shirts, trousers and wool caps were brand new and most of the boys had forgotten to pull the tags off. Some of them had such bad cases of trench feet from standing in water for days, that they were hobbling about on improvised crutches and canes.

They laughed very little and they didn't smile much, but they were getting the most out of their precious two days. The band was very good and they gathered around it appreciatively. The musicians were standing and playing with helmets on. Sgt. Edward L. Martin, Maysville, Ky., the bass viol player, solemnly took off his helmet, mopped his forehead and hung the helmet over the neck of the big fiddle. For some reason that seemed amusing and the act drew a few smiles.

When one shell landed with a particularly loud explosion, every one looked with mock accusation at the drummer, Cpl. Gordon L.

(Continued on page 3)

Giant Air Base Planned

LONDON, March 14—The world's greatest air base with seven concrete runways at least 1,500 yards long for land planes and a two-mile "runway" for flying boats is being planned for London, Brig. Gen. A. C. Critchley, director general of the British Overseas Airways Corporation, said yesterday. The proposed airport will be 14 miles from the heart of London and will cover 2,800 acres

1d THE STARS AND STRIPES 1d
Daily Newspaper of U.S. Armed Forces in the European Theater of Operations
Vol. 4 No. 121 New York, N.Y.—London, England Thursday, March 23, 1944

Berlin Hit Again; Luftwaffe Shuns Fight

Puppet Tells Of New Rule In Hungary

Cites Aid to Nazis Against Common Foe; Report Rumanian Thrust

In high-sounding phrases full of "traditional friendship" and "comradeship in arms," a new Hungarian government headed by an apparent Hitler puppet last night confirmed that the German Army had occupied the country "to assist Hungary against the common enemy."

In the first Axis admission that Hungary had been invaded, the communique announced that Premier Nicholas Kallay had resigned and that Adm. Nicholas Horthy, the regent, "has entrusted M. Doeme Sztojay, up till now Hungarian minister in Berlin, to form a new government."

The announcement, delayed until German troops had achieved complete domination of the country, came at a time when Hitler appeared to be holding a threat of similar occupation over Bulgaria and Rumania unless they intensified their war efforts.

Budapest Radio Off

Possible Russian countermeasures to check Hitler appeared under way, with Soviet bombers reported flying over Hungary's eastern frontier yesterday and Budapest radio off the air at 7.48 PM last night—possibly because of new Red air sorties.

The new Hungarian premier, well known for extreme pro-Nazi sympathies, has been minister to Berlin since 1935. Sixty years old, he was attached to the Austro-Hungarian general staff in the last war and from 1925 to 1933 he was military attache at Berlin.

The official communique said the German Army had arrived in Hungary "on the strength of a mutual understanding" to aid prosecution of the war "and in particular to intensify the effective struggle against Bolshevism."

Shortly after a transmitter identifying itself as Free Hungarian Radio broadcast that Adm. Nicholas Horthy, regent of Hungary, and his aides had been imprisoned in Germany, the Swedish press printed Swiss dispatches saying that more than 600 persons had been arrested in Budapest alone in the first two days of the Nazi occupation.

Hungary's Parliament appeared to have abdicated for the duration, having adjourned "for an unspecified period."

In Bulgaria, telephone, telegraph and radio services were reported by Ankara to be firmly under German control. Another Turkish report, quoted by Hitler's own German radio, said two Nazi security divisions had arrived in Rumania. Their purpose ostensibly was to round up German deserters from the Eastern Front.

The German activity in the Balkans undoubtedly stemmed from the unexpectedly speedy advance of the Red Army toward the border of Rumania proper. Hitler, preferring not to rely on the none too certain loyalty of his satellites, appeared to have decided to control the lines of communication through Hungary himself and to establish German troops in the Carpathian passes now being approached by the Russians.

N.Y., Arizona OK Vote Bills

WASHINGTON, Mar. 22—Two more states—New York and Arizona—enacted legislation yesterday which will allow servicemen to vote under a state-regulated system.

Gov. Thomas E. Dewey, meanwhile, informed President Roosevelt by telegram that his state's new voting law complied in every respect with provisions of the federal bill relating to state ballots. Under terms of the bill, the State War Ballot Commission will receive applications and mail ballots through noon Oct. 15. Marked ballots will be accepted through Nov. 3. A postcard application will be sent to every member of the armed forces eligible to vote.

At a special session of the Arizona Legislature, Gov. Sidney P. Osborn signed a bill which advances the state primary from Sept. 12 to July 18, and calls for the airmailing of small, lightweight ballots to members of the armed forces 60 days before an election. Arizona's bill also provides that registration of a soldier, sailor or marine may be made by parents, spouse, next of kin, or a friend.

Caught With Their Panzers Down

Planet Photo

Tanks and armored vehicles of Germany's elite panzer corps stand wrecked and deserted in the mud near Uman, city on the southern Ukraine front captured ten days ago by the Reds. Yesterday Russians were reported 120 miles southwest of Uman.

Strongpoint Guarding Odessa Falls; Reds Open Vitebsk Push

Pervomaisk, one of the two principal Nazi strongpoints guarding the great Black Sea port of Odessa, was captured by the Russians yesterday even as Berlin revealed the launching of a new Soviet offensive southeast of Vitebsk in White Russia, far to the north.

Seizing of Pervomaisk, about 125 miles up the Bug from Odessa, wrested from the enemy an important railway junction where the line from Kirovograd to Balti crosses the river.

Thus it narrowed the Nazi bulge east of the Bug, laid open Nikolaev to the southeast to an outflanking attack and increased the danger to an estimated 12 Nazi divisions threatened with encirclement.

Moscow said nothing about an offensive in the north, but Col. Ernst von Hammer, military commentator of German News Agency, reported seven Red infantry divisions and several tank brigades attacked and achieved breakthroughs at some points.

Might Unhinge Front

Vitebsk, at the northern end of the central front, has been regarded as the key to the Baltic states and its fall might unhinge the Nazi line all the way to Riga.

In the south, with advance units of Marshal Ivan Koniev's army only 20 miles from the Pruth River and the Rumanian border, fierce air battles raged over the Dniester crossings as the Russians poured more and more troops into Bessarabia.

Their bridgehead here was 40 to 50 miles wide and ten to 20 miles deep. Heavy fighting was reported northeast and north of Balti, the rail junction from which a line runs south to Jassy and the Danube port of Galatz.

Von Hammer said the main weight of the Soviet attacks along the Dniester had been shifted to the Tarnopol-Proskurov sector southeast of Lwow, where what he described as "extraordinarily strong forces" attacked with 250 to 300 tanks and "an array of rifle divisions."

Midget PX Kit Set for Invasion

Tiny Unit to Supply Free Tobacco, Candy, Gum, Toilet Articles

PX kits designed to supply U.S. soldiers with a ration of tobacco, candy and toilet articles will accompany the Army in the invasion of Europe.

Already in use in Pacific combat areas, the kits, which contain enough goods for 200 men, will be distributed to front-line troops who are unable to visit mobile sales stores.

Weighing only 65 pounds, the "midget PXs" can be operated by only one man, are easily stored in landing craft and are quickly handled under combat conditions.

Plans call for soldiers, if circumstances permit, to receive a free daily ration of a pack of cigarettes, or pipe or chewing tobacco, a box of matches, a stick of gum and some hard candy or tropical chocolate. "Invasion" chocolate has been specially prepared to remain fresh in hot weather.

Toilet articles, including razors, blades, tooth powder, tooth brushes, shaving cream and soap also will be stocked.

The kits will be issued free by the Quartermaster Corps at invasion embarkation points.

29 U.S. Soldiers Killed By Accidental ETO Blast

Twenty-nine American soldiers were killed and eight injured, at least one seriously, when explosives were set off accidentally in training activities somewhere in England, ETOUSA headquarters announced yesterday.

Arnold Asks Girl Army Pilots; Men All Going Across

WASHINGTON, Mar. 22 (UP)—Legislation to give women pilots commissions in the regular Army was urged today by Gen. Henry H. Arnold, Army Air Force chief, who explained: "I expect to have every man flier out of the U.S. and overseas fighting."

Women pilots now are used for ferrying planes: their status is that of civilians.

The need for fighting men is so severe, Gen. Arnold said, that the air forces have returned to the ground forces about 36,000 men rather than hold them until there is room for them in flying schools.

20 Nazi Planes Blasted By Two Mosquito Pilots

Luftwaffe ground crews yesterday were sorting out the wreckage of 20 aircraft destroyed by two pilots, an American and a Canadian, in one of the biggest bags ever claimed by two planes on a single patrol. Two RCAF Mosquitoes on a 1,000-mile round trip destroyed three Nazi aircraft in combat, left four others blazing on the ground and damaged 13 more parked on airfields.

Piloting one Mosquito was 1/Lt. James Luma, 21, of Helena, Mont. Originally with the RCAF, he was transferred to the USAAF and is now assigned to his old outfit. F/Lt. D. MacFayden, of Toronto, piloted the other Mosquito.

Reluctance Mystifies Yanks; Cloud Was No Deterrent, They Say

Estimated 1,400 Tons Hurled Onto Reich Capital, Possibly Including Some Of New Giant Incendiaries

Virtually unchallenged by the Luftwaffe, Flying Fortresses and Liberators of the U.S. Strategic Air Forces bombed Berlin for the fifth time yesterday, loosing an estimated 1,400 tons of bombs on the battered German capital.

The size of the force was not officially disclosed, but it was estimated to be around 600 heavy bombers, escorted by approximately 800 fighters. Preliminary reports indicated that losses were comparatively light.

Skies above Berlin were cloudy enough to force the American bombardiers to use the scientific cloud bombing method, but both fighter pilots and bomber crews said upon their return that cloud conditions were not sufficient to have kept Luftwaffe fighter planes on the ground.

Flak, however, was the heaviest yet experienced over Berlin, they said.

Thirteen bombers and nine fighters failed to return, headquarters announced.

Huge fires in the capital were reported by the returning airmen, who said they could see great stretches of the city through breaks in the clouds.

Some of the smoke pillars, they said, rose as high as 5,000 feet.

The lack of fighter opposition was the chief subject of discussion among returning crews. They said the clouds appeared to start about 1,000 feet off the ground, thus giving German fighters ample opportunity to take off, and extended to 10,000 feet, with clear sky above.

The Luftwaffe, far from beaten, possibly had decided that conditions were not ideal for visual bombing and therefore it was not worthwhile to risk its dwindling fighter strength in attacks on the heavies.

Thunderbolts, Lightnings and Mustangs shuttled back and forth over Germany for more than six hours without opposition, including two hours spent over Berlin itself. A few of the fighters then swept down to shoot up a dozen locomotives, three coastal vessels and other targets. Only one aircraft was claimed and that was an He177 four-engine bomber that was shot down as it took off from a German airdrome.

A few bomber crewmen and fighter pilots said they had spotted German fighters, which kept their distance.

"I thought I saw some Messerschmitt 109s on top of the cloud," said 1/Lt. Gerald Leinsweber, of Houston, Tex., a Lightning pilot. "We dived down there, but before we reached them they stuck their noses into the clouds and disappeared."

Another P38 pilot, Capt. Joseph Meyers, said: "I kept wondering all day what had happened to the Luftwaffe, since I didn't even have a single report of 'bandits' on the radio. Nobody seemed to be even discussing them any more."

In addition to high explosives and other incendiaries, the American bombers possibly hurled on the German capital 500-pound "block-burner" incendiaries, known as the M-76, use of which in the European theater was revealed in Washington yesterday.

The War Department said that the huge incendiary, whose destructive power was "tremendous," could not be extinguished once it had started to burn. It contains a mixture of jellied oil and powdered magnesium.

Incendiaries now form about 60 per cent of the bomb loads dumped on

(Continued on page 4)

Marines Seize 2 Islands North Of New Ireland

Complete Big Encirclement And Take Bomber Line 580 Mi. From Truk

Marines have seized two Japanese-held islands 85 miles north of Kavieng, New Ireland, completing the Allied encirclement of enemy bases in the Solomons, New Britain and New Ireland—75,000 Japs are believed garrisoned in the three island groups—and advancing the Allied bomber line to within 580 miles of Truk, Japan's great Carolines stronghold to the north.

Going ashore against slight opposition, the U.S. troops were supported by a great naval fleet which for several hours bombarded the two islands—known as Emirau and Elomusao in the St. Matthais group.

A few hours before, battleships had poured more than 1,000 tons of shells onto Kavieng itself in the greatest bombardment executed in the Southwest Pacific since the invasion of Guadalcanal.

Emirau, larger of the two islands, is an irregularly shaped coral isle eight miles long, part of it thickly wooded, but suitable for the building of extensive airfields.

Meanwhile, eight different types of planes struck at Rabaul, on New Britain, dumping more than 300 tons of bombs on the base without loss.

Pilot Training Programs Are Lengthened in U.S.

FORT WORTH, Tex., Mar. 22—The Army has added nine weeks to the training period for fighter pilots and five weeks for bomber pilots. The revised program is now in effect at all AAF flying schools. It was announced that the reason for the longer course was that requirements of combat air forces were being filled adequately and that it was possible to slow down the tempo of pilot training.

No Guns, No Hits, No Errors

Yank Yells in His Best German To Capture a Shot-Down Nazi

A U.S. BOMBER BASE, England, Mar. 22 (AP)—A former Buffalo (N.Y.) fireman armed with nothing but nerve and an ability to speak German captured a Nazi airman singlehanded less than five minutes after the latter parachuted from a Ju88 that crashed in the middle of the landing field here early today.

The plane, one of a German force trying to reach London, was shot down by a RAF night-fighter in a spectacular dogfight.

Roaring down over this base's barracks, the Ju88 ploughed into a parked bomber, killing two men in the Nazi crew. One other crewman also bailed out but was captured near another airfield.

S/Sgt. Stephen J. Gehl, chief of the aviation fire-fighting platoon, was racing to the crash on a bicycle when he sighted a floating parachute less than 100 yards away.

"I was probably just as scared as he was, but I jumped off the bicycle and shouted to him to halt," Gehl said. All his conversation with the prisoner was in German.

"He got up on one knee as I approached and then threw his hands over his head. I could see him only as a shadow in the glow of the burning plane."

"Are you German?" Gehl demanded.

"Yes," came the quick reply.

"Then advance."

A husky German flying officer obeyed the command without offering a sign of resistance.

"He appeared pretty badly wounded and seemed damned glad to be captured," Gehl said.

"When I asked him if he was hurt he held out both hands as if his wrists were broken and asked if I had any bandages. His face was bleeding badly."

The German had a pistol holster, but it was explained that he must have lost his gun on the way down.

P47s Dive 25,000 Feet, Blast Huge Nazi He177

A THUNDERBOLT BASE, Mar. 22—Four Thunderbolt pilots, on the way to rendezvous with American heavy bombers, today destroyed a Heinkel 177, Germany's biggest bomber—bigger than the B17—as it was taking off from a field just inside Nazi territory.

Capt. Earl L. Abbott, of Erie, Pa., leading the flight, which included 1/Lts. Richard C. Brookins, of Los Angeles; John F. Thornell Jr., of East Walpole, Mass., and Edmond Zellner, of Hazleton, Pa., spotted the plane, when they were flying at 25,000 feet. They dived so fast they were close enough to fire before the Nazi had climbed above 150 feet.

THE STARS AND STRIPES
MEDITERRANEAN

Vol. 1, No. 116, Thursday, March 30, 1944 ITALY EDITION TWO LIRE

Soviet Forces Cross Border Of Rumania

Zhukov's Armies Enter Cernauti; Take Kolomyja

MOSCOW, March 29—The Red Army invaded Rumania today.

Marshal Gregory Zhukov's troops have forced the River Pruth, border of the province of Bessarabia and Rumania, in a dual drive west and south of the recently-captured city of Kamenets Podolsk, the Soviet communique announced.

Street-fighting has been reported between advance Russian elements and German rear guards in Cernauti, on the west bank of the Pruth. Second largest city in Rumania, Cernauti lies on the strategically important Lwow-Bucharest railway, the last lateral trunk route connecting German forces in Poland with those in Rumania.

The invasion of Rumania overshadowed today's earlier capture of Kolomyja, southwestern Polish city which also straddles the Lwow-Bucharest rail line. The advance into Kolomyja, less than 30 miles from the Hungarian border, marks the westernmost thrust the Red Army has yet made.

While German dead were still heaped high in the streets of newly captured Nikolaev, the Red Army began the final clearing of the Ukraine with a piledriver blow at German positions guarding the northeastern routes to Odessa. Boiling over the River Bug on a 30-mile front above Voznesensk, the Russians hit the wobbly Wehrmacht with a punch that followed closely the collapse of the eastern end of the German line.

The fall of the Black Sea port of Nikolaev, which was given great importance in the German scheme of resistance, was described by the Soviet Information Bureau in these terms:

"Soviet troops broke through the

(Continued on page 4)

Lost Nurses Return Safe

ADVANCED ALLIED HEADQUARTERS, March 29 — Three American nurses who have wandered about German-held Albania for months since the plane they were in was forced down there last November have been rescued and are safe and unharmed in Allied territory, it was disclosed here today.

The repatriated nurses are 2nd Lts. Helen Porter, Hanksville, Utah; Ava Ann Maness, Paris, Texas, and Wilma Dale, Butler, Ky. All other occupants of the plane escaped from Albania in January.

The nurses' story began when a plane full of medical personnel used on air evacuation missions took off from Sicily and headed for Italy. The weather was bad and when the plane broke through the clouds the pilot didn't know where he was. He spotted an airfield and started to land. But when he found he was being fired upon, he pulled away. Two Messerschmitts chased him and he shook them by diving into some clouds. Later he made a forced landing on an ordinary field.

The nurses were never in German hands. They were befriended by Albanian patriots who hid them from the Nazis and passed them through the underground.

BLAMED

PIERRE LAVAL
... at the bottom of it

French Court Rules Death

ALGIERS, March 29—A French Military Tribunal today sentenced former Vichy Officer Lt. Col. Pierre Cristofini to death after finding him guilty of treason in a brief session here.

Christofini, a Corsican, was convicted of recruiting forces to fight the Allies in North Africa. Documents presented by the prosecution revealed that the 40-year-old officer had been sent by Vichy to North Africa to organize the "African Phalanx" to fight against the Allies in Tunisia. The documents identified Vichy French Premier Pierre Laval as the man behind Christofini's recruiting mission.

Cristofini was arrested by Corsican patriots on Sept. 7, 1943, three days before the landing of French forces on the island. At that time, it was said, he readily discussed details of his recruiting mission with his captors.

The trial was held in the same courtroom where Pierre Pucheu, former Vichy minister, was sentenced to death on a similar count. Cristofini's opening defense move to adjourn the hearing until after the liberation of France was turned down by the president of the court, Louis Ohlman.

First Defeat Made Issue By Churchill

British Minister Says Action Shows Little Confidence

LONDON, March 29 — Prime Minister Winston Churchill today made an issue of a minor government defeat on a strictly domestic matter and took the dramatic and uncompromising stand that a further approval of an education bill amendment would be considered a "no confidence" vote and would result in the resignation of his government.

The amendment which provoked the storm is an equal pay provision for women teachers, which was attached as a rider to the routine government education bill. Over government protest, the House of Commons yesterday approved the rider by the narrow margin of only one vote and thus gave the Churchill administration its first parliamentary defeat of the war.

Churchill has demanded that the amendment be deleted and the bill presented to the House again in its original form at the next sitting. If the government does not secure a majority on this second test, resignation of the administration will be mandatory by normal British constitutional procedure. Churchill's statement on the question reads:

"Events of yesterday require alteration in government business. It would not be possible for the government to leave matters where they stood when the motion to report progress was accepted last night. At this very serious time in the progress of the war, there should be no doubt of the question of support which the government enjoys from the House of Commons."

Miss Cazalet Keir, mover of the amendment which brought about the defeat of the government and the subsequent furor, said: "This vote is not a vote against the government or against the government's conduct of the war. Neither is it a vote against the education bill. Equal pay for men and women teachers has nothing to do with war."

Nazi Troops Regain Two Vital Positions On Monastery Hill

Invasion Imminent, Henderson Warns

LONDON, March 29—The Allied invasion of Europe is imminent, Arthur Henderson, British War Office financial secretary, told a Trafalgar Square meeting today.

"The hands of the clock are turning," said Henderson. "They have reached five minutes to twelve. When twelve o'clock strikes, Allied armies of liberation will move forward."

MAAF Raps Nazis Hard

MAAF HEADQUARTERS, March 29 — All three divisions of the MAAF, tactical, strategic and coastal, combined yesterday to give the enemy in Italy one of his heaviest pummelings in recent weeks.

Flying a total of 1,500 sorties, MAAF pilots hit the Germans along both 5th Army fronts and also blasted his lines of supply far into the north of occupied Italy. Ten Allied aircraft are listed as missing while strong enemy formations encountered during the day limped home minus at least 12 planes.

Hardly a railroad junction in north or central Italy escaped yesterday's blasting. While Flying Fortresses were returning from a blistering attack on the main yards at Verona, B-24 Liberators escorted by Lightnings plastered the east railroad yards of the same city. The Verona yards are at the junction of the Brenner Pass route from Germany and the North Italian network. The Liberators knocked down two German fighters, while the Forts and the P-38s bagged seven.

Other Lightning-escorted Liberators attacked the Mestre yards just west of Venice with good results and still smaller formations of the big B-24s bombed bridges at

(Continued on page 4)

Action At Anzio Paced By Heavy Artillery Fire

ADVANCED ALLIED HEADQUARTERS, March 29 — German soldiers today hold the positions on Hangman's Hill and Hill 202 which Indian and New Zealand troops captured in conjunction with the assault on Cassino March 15.

Today's communique announced the news in 13 words:

"Our advance detachments on the eastern slopes of Monastery Hill have been withdrawn."

In view of the inability of the Allied forces which attacked Cassino to throw the Germans out of the town immediately, the two hard-won heights had become more of a burden than an asset. It was necessary to supply the Gurkhas on Hangman's Hill by air and his method of bringing in food, water and ammunition could not be considered sound over a period of time. In addition, there were the extreme difficulties involved in the evacuation of wounded from this rugged height.

Castle Hill on Montecassino's slopes was still held by Allied troops, who were under fire from German mortars at the Continental Hotel in Cassino and from tanks near the hotel. Allied artillery took up the challenge and pounded the hotel area anew. A German patrol which advanced east of the Continental's ruins was driven back.

Under a creeping artillery and mortar barrage, the Germans launched a raid on Hill 915, scene of frequent fighting just east of Terelle in the region north of Cassino. French troops holding this sector hurled the attackers back.

American troops defending the Cisterna sector of the 5th Army beachhead made it hot for their German opponents. One enemy company forming for an attack three miles west of Cisterna was dispersed in a drowning concentration of artillery fire at dusk Monday. Yank gunners also knocked out of action two German tanks dug in five miles northwest

(Continued on page 4)

Clean-Up Begins Around Vesuvius

By Sgt. VICTOR DALLAIRE
(Stars and Stripes Staff Writer)

SAN GIUSEPPE VESUVIANO, March 29—As the sensational phase of the eruption of Mt. Vesuvius came slowly to an end, this and neighboring communes today turned to the back-breaking job of removing thousands of tons of volcanic sand from streets and roadways.

Allied Military Government officials headed by Lt. Col. James L. Kincaid, Naples Provincial commissioner, have already established one-way traffic on main highways and streets, but the bulk of the clean-up job will have to be carried out by the communes themselves. Colonel Kincaid said quick clearance of the high-priority routes was possible only through the cooperation of British and American Army units who cheerfully turned over equipment and men.

San Giuseppe itself, under three feet of the slate-gray volcanic discharge, was not so hard hit as Terzigno and Poggiomarino, where the covering reached a depth of three to four feet. In places, the wind drifted the heavy sandy material as high as rooftops and AMG officials believed that until the deposit was removed or ploughed under it would keep drifting across highways, making the progress of traffic difficult and hazardous.

A survey of the nine square miles affected on the east side of the volcano showed that residents lost all of their spring gardens, thus adding civilian relief to the problems of AMG authorities. An emergency food and candle distribution was made here yesterday by Capt. C. A. P. Bertelli, in charge of local relief. Capt. Bertelli said that the first shipment of forage for horses had also been distributed.

Some of the patient Italian gardeners have already begun the task of turning the volcanic layer under in preparation for new gardens. Vineyards which produce the famous Lacrima Christi wine will probably benefit from the eruption because previous years in which the highly-mineralized sand was blown over the countryside proved to be great vintage years.

The experience of digging out is not a new one to the 17,000 residents of San Giuseppe, although the job is made more difficult this time because of lack of equipment. In 1906, San Giuseppe and Ottaiano to the west were buried in an avalanche of the dry, volcanic substance. The new deposit on the mountainside above San Giuseppe will probably slip down one of these days but old-timers said it was not so deep as after the 1906 eruption.

WACs' Smoking In Public OK'd

LONDON, March 29—Although smoking on streets and other public places is outlawed for British girls in the Auxiliary Territorial Service, ETOUSA officials today announced they planned no similar rule against smoking by Wacs.

Under a new order, ATS girls, counterpart of American Wacs, are not allowed to smoke in many public places. Male members of the British Army may light up when they please.

ETOUSA officials said they expected the Wacs to observe the tenets of good judgment but as "members of the U.S. Army we desire to treat them as we treat men. As our soldiers are permitted to smoke in streets, Wacs are naturally given the same privileges."

THE STARS AND STRIPES
ALGIERS DAILY

Vol. 1, No. 251, Thursday, March 30, 1944 | For U.S. Armed Forces | ONE FRANC

Air War Switches To Reich Targets In Daylight Raids

Doolittle Discloses 2,100 Nazi Planes Downed In 8 Weeks

LONDON, March 29 — Allied planes which for the past three days have been plastering Nazi air bases and first-line defenses along the invasion coastline returned to targets in Germany today. BBC reported bombers were over the Reich but gave no details of the attack.

American bomber crews expressed amazement at the lack of fighter opposition in the assault on German-held airfields in France yesterday. An official announcement said that not a single German interceptor came up to challenge the hundreds of bombers or their Thunderbolt, Lightning and Mustang fighter escorts which struck at Chartres, Chateaudun, Rheims and Dijon.

At least 30 German planes, including many bombers, were destroyed on the ground, and more than 20 others were damaged. Two Fortresses and three fighters failed to return.

Lt. Gen. James H. Doolittle, commander of the 8th AAF, in a radio address from Britain to the National Press Club in Washington last night, said "that an estimated 2,100 German planes had been destroyed in the past eight weeks by the 8th and 9th AAF.

He disclosed that more than 26,000 tons of bombs had been dropped on Germany and an additional 11,000 tons on occupied countries since Feb. 1. He said "that since Feb 20 16 major factories producing aircraft or integral parts for the Luftwaffe had been destroyed or so severely damaged that production had ceased entirely or been greatly curtailed."

Churchill Seeks Confidence Vote

LONDON, March 29—As the result of passage by the House of Commons of a government-opposed amendment to a new education bill, Prime Minister Winston Churchill today announced that he would call for a vote of confidence at the next sitting of Parliament.

The Commons by a one-vote majority passed an amendment providing equal pay for men and women teachers. The government had endorsed the education bill as a whole but opposed the amendment and it therefore suffered a technical defeat when the amendment passed.

Mr Churchill said that at the next sitting the government would move for the deletion of the amendment and that the vote on the motion would be considered a vote of confidence in the government, with the usual consequences if the government did not get an adequate majority. This would mean that the members of the Churchill cabinet would resign.

Explaining his reasons for calling for a vote of confidence Mr. Churchill said "At this very critical time in the progress of the war, there must be no doubt of the support which the government enjoys from the House of Commons."

UNRRA Funds Bill Signed By Roosevelt

WASHINGTON, March 29—President Roosevelt yesterday signed the bill authorizing American participation in activities of the United Nations Relief and Rehabilitation Administration to the extent of 1,300,000,000 dollars. Specific appropriation of the funds remains to be made by Congress.

Burma Battle

DEEP IN THE jungles and mountains of Burma, bitter fighting is under way on three fronts. Allied forces are stabbing toward Myitkyina; Japanese columns are driving toward Imphal, India, in Central Burma, and in the southwest a British offensive, aimed at Akyab, is in progress.

Allied Units Withdrawn From Precarious Perches

ALLIED FORCE HEADQUARTERS, March 29 — Some of the Allied troops stranded on the eastern slopes of Monastery Hill when the all-out attempt to capture that German stronghold bogged down in heavy rain on the night of March 15 have been successfully evacuated, it was officially announced today.

Those withdrawn came from Hangman's Hill and Hill 202, and they left behind them equally gallant bands still holding out on Hill 193 under German fire from at least four directions.

All other reports from the Italian war fronts followed a familiar pattern—reports of artillery exchanges and patrol actions; disruption of a small-scale enemy attack on the Anzio beachhead sector before it got started; a futile air raid on Anzio harbor.

Official reports did not tell the full saga of Hangman's Hill and Hill 202; of the suffering endured for nine days by men who were dependent on parachuted food, water and ammunition, but fought on nevertheless. Their's apparently was a lost cause from the moment it was evident that the 5th Army would be unable to capitalize speedily on the record air bombardment of Cassino and vicinity the morning before the attempted charge to the German fortress atop the 1,700-foot mountain overlooking Cassino.

Attempts to resupply these men by porter packs were extremely perilous for the men who tried to climb the crags and skirt the ravines which were being raked day and night by withering enemy fire. For five straight days daring Invader pilots dropped bundle after bundle of necessaries by parachute, and at the time it was announced that up to 95 percent of all these bundles were delivered successfully.

New Zealand, French and British—were previously announced as fighting it out on the slopes of Monastery Hill. Their full story is

(Continued on Page 4)

Billion For Navy Bases Approved By House

WASHINGTON, March 29—A Navy appropriations bill authorizing 1,664,373,024 dollars for construction of shore installations was passed by the House yesterday and sent to the Senate.

Of the total, 1,900,000,000 dollars was earmarked for advanced bases overseas. Another 228,375,000 dollars will be spent for naval air-base facilities, 120,000,000 dollars is intended for ordnance work and 46,579,670 dollars will go for housing and training facilities.

The Appropriations Committee estimated that approximately 41,716,500 dollars would be needed for development of fleet operating facilities within continental limits of the United States during the 1945 fiscal year.

Fighting Rages Inside Cernauti

Plane Taxi Service Aids Burmese Drive

NEW DELHI, March 29—U.S. Army aircraft have established an air taxi service to carry reinforcements, materiel and orders to British troops operating inside Burma, front-line dispatches disclosed today.

Pilot-sergeants operating single-engined, two-seater liaison planes fly from India to the British troops and then carry wounded to safety on their return journey. Nearly every one of the pilots was said to have brought out at least 50 wounded soldiers since the service was established.

Allies Hamper Jap Imphal Push

NEW DELHI, March 29—Allied forces have handed Japanese forces driving toward Imphal, capital of India's Manipur State, a major setback and shot down 30 Japanese planes over Burma in a series of brilliant air victories, Lord Louis Mountbatten, Allied Supreme Commander in South East Asia, reported in today's communique.

British troops struck at a Japanese column advancing along the road which loops 100 miles northwestward from Tiddim, Burma, to Imphal, and inflicted severe casualties in bitter fighting, the communique said.

Despite the loss of a considerable amount of equipment, the Japanese were said to be continuing to exert pressure along the India-Burma border. The British victory was reported to have precluded any immediate advances of importance, however.

AAF P-40s and P-51s intercepted Japanese bombers headed for communication lines in India's northern Assam province and shot down 11 bombers and 13 escorting fighters, the communique disclosed.

Six other Japanese planes were "probables" and several others were damaged as against the loss of two U.S. pilots. Six other Japanese planes have been destroyed and an equal number damaged in other actions this week.

On the northern Burmese front, U.S.-trained Chinese forces driving southward in the Mogaung Valley today were reported only five miles north of Shaduzup.

New Russian Drive Routs Reich Units

LONDON, March 29 — Soviet troops tonight are fighting in the streets of Cernauti, northern Rumania's most important railhead, after smashing across the Pruth River for the first time earlier today.

Other forces of the First Ukrainian Front meanwhile had dashed to within 30 miles of pre-war Czechoslovakia—the westernmost point yet reached by the Red Army—by capturing the important railway junction of Kilomyja, 42 miles northwest of Cernauti on the line to Lwow. Marshal Gregory Zhukov, the official communique reported, had taken the city by a clever maneuver of tanks and infantry. So rapid was the Red Army advance that it captured, an incomplete account showed, at least 13 Tiger tanks, 15 trains filled with war material and 45 locomotives.

The Pruth River crossing marked the first time Soviet soldiers had entered pre-World War I Rumania (Bessarabia had been part of the Russian empire). Capture of Cernauti would virtually eliminate any slim escape chances held by the thousands of Germans fleeing across the southern Ukraine before the blows of the Soviets who captured Nikolaev yesterday.

The southernmost Russian drive to expel the last Nazi from the Ukraine maintained its pressure today in the form of a pincers with one arm reaching out for Odessa and the other punching west from Pervomaisk, 90 miles north of the Black Sea port.

Waves of Red Army troops which swarmed across the Bug River yesterday captured Balta today, advancing across the muddy

(Continued on Page 4)

Milan Battered By MAAF Bombs

ALLIED FORCE HEADQUARTERS, March 29—B-24 Liberators struck the rail yards at the great Po Valley city of Milan today just 12 hours after Wellington bombers last night gave the communications and industrial center its first night raid from bases in this theater, it was officially announced tonight.

In a day of varied activity against northern Italy communications points MAAF bombers struck at Bolzano, Turin, Leghorn and other cities. Shipping in the harbor of Porto Ferraio on the historic island of Elba was among MAAF's less familiar targets.

ALLIED FORCE HEADQUARTERS, March 29—Milan's big railroad yards felt the lash of MAAF's extending whip when RAF Liberators and Wellingtons gave the northern Italian city its first night pounding from this theater as part of the non-stop assault on enemy lines of communications.

Milan, anchor of rail lines to France, Germany and the Balkans, was not the only target. Brescia, just east of Milan, and Rimini, on the Italian east coast, also suffered from RAF night raiders. Yesterday American heavy bombers pocked Verona, in northeastern Italy; Mestre, a few miles west of Venice, and bridges between Pescara and Ancona on the Italian east coast. Italy's east coast has been receiving increasing attention from Allied bombsights the past two weeks.

In addition, there was plenty of work for the Tactical Air Force's medium and light bombers, which

(Continued on Page 4)

Three Nurses Return From War Odyssey

Three Army nurses—"Sure glad we are Americans"—arrived in Italy a few days ago after spending nearly four months as the uninvited but welcome guests of patriots behind the German lines in Albania, it has been reported by the United Press from 12th Air Force Headquarters.

The nurses' safe arrival recalled the dramatic story, announced about six weeks ago of the nine-week trek of 27 nurses and Air Forces men through the wilds of Albania to the coastline and their rescue by Allied boats.

The three nurses—2nd Lts. Helen Porter, Hanksville, Utah; Ava Ann Maness, Paris, Texas, and Wilma Dale Lytle, Butler, Ky.—had become separated from the rest of the party about one week after the forced landing of their off-course transport plane bound from Sicily to Italy to evacuate wounded soldiers.

The nurses were extremely reticent about their adventure when interviewed at 12th AAF Headquarters. They declined to say anything which might conceivably endanger the natives who helped them or the Allied officers who brought them out. The intelligence officer who presided over their press interview described them the UP said as the "most security-minded people I've ever met."

The nurses were communicative, though, when it came to more personal matters. They said they had been well fed, well taken care of and even, according to Lt Porter, "gained a little weight." The people with whom they stayed "refused to let us pay anything."

The "toughest part of the trip was worrying about our folks and our dislike at our confinement," according to Lt. Maness.

"Our hosts wouldn't let us do anything except wash dishes a couple of times," Lt. Porter said "We played three-handed bridge

(Continued on Page 3)

1d.

THE STARS AND STRIPES

1d.

Daily Newspaper of U.S. Armed Forces in the European Theater of Operations

Vol. 4 No. 129 | New York, N.Y.—London, England | Saturday, April 1, 1944

Navy Strikes 500 Mi. From Philippines

Twin Peril To Odessa Developing

Reds Seize Port to East; Zhukov in Carpathians 15 Mi. From Hungary

While Russia's First Ukrainian Army surged forward at record speed within 15 miles of the Hungarian border northwest of Cernauti, Soviet artillery and Marines yesterday captured a port only 40 miles east of Odessa, thus confronting that Black Sea base with the threat of attack from the sea, as well as from the land.

Fall of the port Ochakov to troops under Gen. Rodion Malinovsky was announced in an order of the day by Marshal Stalin last night even as another wing of Malinovsky's Third Ukrainian group threatened Odessa from 34 miles to the northeast.

Stalin's order described the port as a "fortress" and "an important strongpoint in the German defenses blocking the entrance into the Dnieper-Bug estuary." The town faces Odessa across a 40-mile bay.

Northwest of Cernauti in the Carpathians, Marshal Gregory Zhukov's First Army troops pressed forward high up in the Pruth valley to a point 2,000 feet above sea level, within ten miles of the Tartar pass leading through the mountains into the Tisa valley. The valley has belonged to Hungary since the partition of Czechoslovakia in 1938.

Another force, thrusting south from Cernauti, was reported within ten miles of the frontier station of Dornesti on the Rumanian border.

A hundred miles to the south, along the Pruth in the Jassy area, Marshal Ivan Koniev's armies marked time, growing in strength for an early push across the river there into Rumania. Koniev's left wing, gaining 12 miles in a day, pushed within 45 miles of the Moldavian capital of Kishinev, where the Red Army apparently hoped to cut the lateral railway running west from Odessa to Jassy.

Less than ten miles separated Zhukov and Koniev along the upper Pruth, and the latter's right wing was reported racing west to link up with the First Army troops which captured Cernauti.

Stanislavov, the oil and rail town about midway between Cernauti and Lwow, on the line linking those two cities, was reported encircled, and Col. Ernst von Hammer, military commentator of German News Agency, described a new Soviet attempt to storm the town with tanks. He said tank-busters repulsed it.

Von Hammer, telling of new attacks on Brody and Kovel in Poland, also revealed that the Red Army was continuing to hurl strong forces at the Nazi lines on the central front east of Mogilev in an effort to achieve a major breakthrough.

British Mistake U.S. Plane For a Nazi, Shoot It Down

WASHINGTON, Mar. 31 (AP)—British fighter planes from a carrier shot down a U.S.-Army transport plane and its crew of six by error in the Atlantic this week, the War Department and the British Admiralty announced jointly today.

The fighters were protecting a convoy and apparently mistook the four-engined C54 transport for a German Focke Wulf 200 bomber.

Clocks in U.K. Go Ahead An Hour Starting Sunday

Double summer time goes into effect at 1 AM Sunday, if you're up that late. If not, set your watches ahead one hour when you roll in for taps Saturday.

The "double" part is due to the fact that under the war schedule clocks are already one hour in advance of Greenwich mean time.

Cannon Sponsors Bill To Turn Back Clocks

WASHINGTON, Mar. 31—A bill introduced by Rep. Clarence Cannon (D.-Mo.) asks Congress, which set the nation's clocks ahead one hour in 1942, to set the time back again. Cannon said he had received hundreds of protests against daylight saving time.

Soviet Forces Japan to Accept Cut in Vital Oil, Coal Supply

Soviet Russia, frankly admitting that she was giving "due consideration" to the Allies' war in the Pacific, announced yesterday a new pact with Japan—reclaiming from Tokyo's control an important source of Japan's oil and coal and sharply restricting Japanese fishing concessions in Arctic waters.

Under the new pacts, Japanese coal and oil interests in northern Sakhalin, a Russian-owned island, ended 26 years ahead of schedule.

Diplomats in Moscow said flatly that the change was a staggering blow to the Japanese war machine, a great contribution to the Allies' war on Japan and one of the greatest diplomatic victories in the war.

The newspaper Izvestia, mouthpiece of Soviet policy, made it clear that Russia had forced Japan into the new agreements and declared that Red Army successes against Germany and "developing military operations of our Allies" had played a part in "sobering up" Japanese politicians stalling since 1941 with a hopeful eye on Hitler's blitzkrieg.

Up-to-date statistics are not available on the island's production of coal and oil. It probably does not represent a large percentage of the total Japanese supply, but its loss to the Japanese war machine is appreciable, since Japan's resources cumulatively fall short of requirements. Output in 1939 was about 1,000,000 tons a year.

Observers in London and Washington declared it was a definite sign of weakening in Tokyo.

In brief, Japan agreed to cancel 26 years before they expire the oil and coal concessions granted by the Soviet in 1925 and to transfer to the Soviet for 5,000,000 rubles all Jap oil and coal properties in northern Sakhalin. Russia agreed to supply Japan with 50,000 tons of oil annually—but not

(*Continued on page 4*)

President Won't Sign It, But Lets Vote Bill Get By

WASHINGTON, Mar. 31—President Roosevelt notified Congress today he would allow the soldier-vote bill to become law at midnight without his signature, although he considered it "wholly inadequate" in providing servicemen and women an opportunity to cast their ballots.

In a message sent to Capitol Hill, he appealed to the states to cooperate in making the measure "as fully effective as its defective provisions will allow" and at the same time asked Congress "to take more adequate action to protect the political rights of our men and women in service."

He proposed an amendment to permit all persons in uniform who had not received state ballots by an appropriate date, regardless of whether formal application had been made, to use the federal ballot without previous express authorization by the states.

"If the states do not accept the federal ballot that will be their responsibility, and that responsibility will be shared by Congress," the message said.

"Our boys on the battlefronts must not be denied the opportunity to vote simply because they are away from home.

"They are at the front fighting with their lives to defend our rights and our freedoms. We must assure them their rights and freedoms at home so that they will have a fair share in determining the kind of life to which they will return."

The compromise measure adopted by House and Senate after four months' legislative discussion provided that servicemen and women overseas might use federal ballots only if they had applied for state ballots before Sept. 1 and had not received them by Oct. 1. In addition, governors of their states would have to certify that federal ballots would be acceptable under state law.

In a telegraph poll of all governors, the President learned that at least 20 states planned to do nothing about authorizing the use of supplementary federal ballots: that 19 would permit their use, or probably would, and that nine were noncommittal.

Nazis Quitting South Greece?

Turks Hear of Evacuation; Possibly Made in Fear Of Balkans Debacle

ISTANBUL, Mar. 31 (AP)—Evidence has reached Istanbul of German military movements which indicate a complete or partial evacuation of southern Greece.

Incomplete reports show that the Nazis are moving north and perhaps west. These reports indicate that no replacements are arriving, although it was previously reported that the Germans had ordered, or shortly would order, the Bulgarians to widen their Balkan police duties in order to free German troops for duty in actively menaced areas.

Analysts suggested two possibilities: (1) That the Germans, fearful of a coup in the eastern Balkans which would isolate them in Greece, are on their way to the Dinaric Alps and the Danube-Carpathian line through upper Jugoslavia, Hungary and Rumania; (2) that they may be preparing for a quick getaway in the event that Soviet forces smash through Rumania and the Bulgarians go over to the Russians, while preserving positions to guard against an Anglo-American attack from the Adriatic.

This WAC Group Shed Stripes to Get to ETO

More than 200 WACs will be processed for jobs at ETO headquarters today, all of whom have voluntarily agreed to be "broken" to private from grades as high as first sergeant in order to get to the ETO.

They were told that only the stripeless would be sent to Spamland, and girls who had worked for their chevrons for up to 18 months said, "Take 'em away."

With the group are six WACs who do rate as high as corporal, but they are intended as replacements in special jobs.

Fear of Reds Spreading In Germany, Swiss Hear

ZURICH, Mar. 31 (Reuter)—Stark fear of the Russians is spreading through Germany, despite the fact that the German public is about a fortnight behind in its news from the Eastern Front, according to travelers arriving here.

Official anxiety also is becoming more apparent, and Berlin is at a loss to know how the Wehrmacht can cope with the Soviet advance, according to the Berlin correspondent of the Tribune de Geneve.

House Group OKs Putting 4Fs in Plants or Labor Units

WASHINGTON, Mar. 31 (Reuter)—The House Military Sub-committee recommended that the War Department take positive action to force men classified as unfit for military service into essential industries or induct them into the Army as labor battalions.

Daring Fleet Foray Coincides With New Air Assault on Truk

Big Bill's Hidden Hoard Of Over Million Found

CHICAGO, Mar. 31 (UP)—Lawyers searching for the will of William Hale (Big Bill) Thompson, former Chicago mayor who died recently, opened two safe deposit boxes and found a hoard of old-style large dollar bills and gold certificates worth $1,200,000. Three more boxes have yet to be opened, and another two boxes are known to be in existence.

Previously it had been reported that Thompson left an estate estimated at $150,000.

The will has not been found yet.

Nuremberg Hit Hard by RAF; 94 Planes Lost

Luftwaffe Is Up in Record Numbers; Pitched Battles Bring Highest Toll

Ninety-four aircraft—the heaviest loss ever sustained by an Allied force—failed to return early yesterday from the RAF's great raid on Nuremberg and other German targets.

The losses, exceeding by 15 the previous high of 79 RAF planes downed in the raid on Leipzig Mar. 19, were poignant evidence that the Luftwaffe still can launch, if it wishes, enough aircraft to give stiff opposition to an assaulting force.

However, the theory that the Germans have brought into use a reserve "secret air force" was discounted by commentators. A story from Switzerland had suggested the existence of such a force.

Probably more than 1,000 planes flew into the Reich to hit the transport and industrial center of Nuremberg, in the south, and other targets in western Germany. An estimated 2,000 tons were dropped on Nuremberg.

Three-Hour Pitched Battle

For three hours, the Air Ministry said, a pitched battle was fought between a "very strong" force of Lancasters and Halifaxes and the largest numbers of fighters the Germans have ever hurled against the RAF.

Apparently anxious to protect the city from the great destruction wrought in Frankfurt by the RAF Mar. 22, the Germans appeared to have sent up the greater part of their entire force of night fighters.

One experienced pilot, now on his second tour of operations, said that he had never seen so many hundreds of fighters as in yesterday's unsuccessful but determined Nazi attempt to keep the bombers from their targets.

The Germans opened their attack, described by returning crewmen as one of the bitterest since the beginning of the Battle of Germany, shortly after 1 AM—before the moon had set. Fighter packs engaged the bombers soon after the

(*Continued on page 4*)

Jap Warships Flee Before Stab Into Enemy Waters

A powerful U.S. naval armada, including a fleet of aircraft-carriers, has struck at the Palau Islands, westernmost of the Caroline Islands and located 500 miles due east of the Philippines, in an attack described in Washington naval circles last night as the "first deliberate challenge to the Japanese fleet to leave its hiding places and come out and fight."

A few hours before the attack began late Wednesday—it has been continuing ever since—U.S. reconnaissance planes observed a fleet of "Japanese ships fleeing from the area," an official Navy Department announcement said. Late dispatches last night claimed that a tremendous naval bombardment was continuing against the Palau Islands, which guard the eastern gateway from the Pacific into the rich Jap-dominated East Indies.

Almost simultaneously with the Palau attack, Liberator bombers from Gen. Douglas MacArthur's Southwest Pacific bases gave two islands in the Truk group

Map on Page Four

their first attack, scoring 200 direct hits on vital installations while shooting down 20 aircraft and destroying or severely damaging another 94 Jap planes caught on the ground.

Following up Gen. MacArthur's air blow, bombers of the Seventh Air Force operating from bases in the Gilberts smashed three times in 24 hours at Truk, leaving great fires burning on two islets of the group.

In the brief communique announcing the Palau Islands action, the Navy Department said that enemy scouting planes either from Dutch New Guinea or from Palau itself apparently had spotted the American task force as it approached the islands and given warning to Japanese ships in the area.

The attack, still apparently continuing last night, is one of the most audacious thus far in the Pacific war and indicates

(*Continued on page 4*)

Wingate Killed In Plane Crash

Maj. Gen. Orde Charles Wingate, DSO, who planned the recent Burma operation in which British airborne troops were landed far behind Japanese lines by American gliders under command of Col. Philip ("Flip Corkin") Cochran, was killed Mar. 24 in an airplane crash in Burma, the British War Office announced last night. He was 41.

Wingate, an anti-aircraft officer in Kent at the outbreak of the war, organized Wingate's brigade of jungle commandos who waged guerrilla warfare hundreds of miles behind the enemy lines in Burma for months, supplied only from the air.

The recent airborne operation 200 miles in the Japanese rear, largest Allied air landing of the war, was planned by Wingate in conference with Lord Louis Mountbatten after Wingate accompanied Prime Minister Churchill to the Quebec conference last summer.

Wooden Bullets Used By Germans in Italy

BATTLE CREEK, Mich., Mar. 31 (Reuter)—German use of wooden bullets in Italy was disclosed with the approval of Army authorities by returned wounded at an Army hospital here.

Soldiers said the bullets had a maximum range of 100 yards and were used only in attacks from the rear to eliminate overshooting into other Nazi troops. Several cases of the ammunition had been captured, they said.

Father of 14 Enlists

WATERTOWN, N.Y., Mar. 31—A 46-year-old father of 14 children has applied, together with his 17-year-old son, for enlistment in the Navy here. Leo Thesier, of Lowville, and his son Paul will be given final examinations next month.

Some Milk Run

Panting Stork Flies In 7 Babies To 2 Mamas in Adjoining Beds

Special to The Stars and Stripes

NEW YORK, Mar. 31—The wife of Cpl. Herbert Bachant—the latter is somewhere in the British Isles—gave birth to triplets yesterday in Sloane Hospital only 24 hours after the birth of quadruplets in the same hospital to Mrs. Harry Zarieff.

All seven babies and their mothers, who occupied adjoining beds while expecting, were reported to be in excellent condition.

Mrs. Isidore Miller, maternal grandmother of the quads, said that although her son-in-law had been in 1A, proof the quads were coming got him one of the most unique deferments of the war.

Arrival of the triplets made Sloane Hospital in the eyes of the nation a monument to maternity and multiple births.

The hospital superintendent's latest communique said that the mothers and babies slept well during the night. The infants were sleeping in air-conditioned cribs, wearing just diapers and shirts and feeding well.

THE STARS AND STRIPES

ALGIERS DAILY

Vol. 1, No. 259, Tuesday, April 11, 1944 | For U.S. Armed Forces | ONE FRANC

Soviets Capture Odessa, Greatest Black Sea Port

Pacific Air Force Continues Hitting Great Truk Base

Liberators Of 7th Press 'Softening Up' Raids On Stronghold

PEARL HARBOR, April 10—Truk Atoll, the massive Japanese naval fortress which guards the Caroline Islands in the southwest Pacific on the northwest approach to the Japanese mainland, was slashed Friday night for the 16th time in nine days by Liberators of the 7th AAF. A tip-off on the significance of the latest attack came yesterday in a communique from Pacific Fleet headquarters, which reported that "operations to soften up Truk continue."

The raid followed by a day what the Associated Press and the United Press described as "the greatest yet launched from southwest Pacific bases" against Truk. The four-engined Liberators scored clean hits on wharves and fuel dumps on both Moen and Dublon, inside the atoll.

Southwest of Truk, in the same group of islands, Mitchells of the 7th AAF, escorted by gull-winged Corsair fighters of the 4th Marine Aircraft Wing, gave Ponape a going-over Friday, busting up a bauxite works—starting step in the production of aluminum—and bombing and strafing an airfield.

Adding insult to injury, a single Liberator bombed Japanese installations at Ponape later in the day as it impudently toured the Carolines and the westernmost Marshalls. Army, Navy and Marine elements teamed up to attack four other enemy-held atolls in the Marshalls.

Farther southwest, Allied bombers swept down Saturday along the northern coast of New Guinea, the dinosaur-shaped island above Australia, dumping 281 tons of bombs on Hollandia, Wewak and Hansa Bay. General Douglas MacArthur's communique today said it was the third time in a week that

(Continued on Page 4)

France, Belgium Heavily Attacked

LONDON, April 10—Heavy bombers of the 8th AAF, which brought the Allied aerial assault from Britain to within 300 miles of the German-Russian battlefront yesterday, switched their attack to France and Belgium today. Their targets, however, were the same as those which have occupied them throughout the Greater Reich for the last three days—aircraft factories, assembly plants and parts manufacturing centers.

Up to 750 Liberators and Flying Fortresses of the 8th AAF, escorted by equally strong forces of Thunderbolts Mustangs and Lightnings, lashed at aircraft repair works and an airdrome in the Brussels area and an aircraft factory at Bourgesin, France.

Last night, bombers of the RAF made a heavy attack on Lille and Villeneuve-St. George near Paris. Mosquitoes bombed Mannheim and objectives in western Germany and an extensive mine laying operation was conducted. Eleven planes failed to return.

Approximately 800 heavy bombers and a thousand fighters took part in the several attacks on Poland and Germany yesterday. They smashed at plane factories at Posen and in the Gydnia area of Poland. They struck at Marienburg in east Prussia and at Tutow and Warnemunde in northeast Germany near the Baltic coast.

The five Nazi factories, which had been assembling Focke-Wulfs or producing parts for these Luftwaffe fighters, were bombed in

(Continued on Page 4)

Anthony Eden Stays As Foreign Minister

LONDON, April 10 — Anthony Eden will remain as British Foreign Minister and no changes will be made in the government at present, according to an official announcement here. Reports had been current that Mr. Eden would leave the Foreign Office to give more time to his duties as leader of the House of Commons.

New Zealanders Inflict Casualties

ALLIED FORCE HEADQUARTERS, April 10—The lateral road connecting the Appian Way and Highway Six, and in front of the 16-mile Allied line from Cassino to Minturno took on increasing significance in official reports today.

It was along this stretch in the lower Garigliano Valley that New Zealand troops stormed two enemy strongpoints which had been partly destroyed by artillery and "inflicted casualties on the enemy." It was also near the road that winds through the Ausente Valley that Allied artillery shelled 21 enemy tanks and selfpropelled guns on Saturday and succeeded in knocking out about five of them. Throughout this region numerous "small groups" of enemy troops were under observation.

Much of the day's official reports was given over to activities in this sector. Reports from all other battlefronts followed the usual pattern of "patrol actions and exchanges of fire" both of which were reportedly lessened on the Allied beachhead.

The enemy reportedly threw plenty of mortar shells into Allied positions in Cassino and into the Allied-held portions of the upper Rapido Valley, which was shelled again by leaflets, contents undisclosed.

The strongpoints assaulted by the New Zealanders were around San Angelo in Teodice, about three miles south of Cassino and two miles east of the lateral road.

It was at dusk on Saturday that the big enemy tank movement was spotted along this road about two and a half miles northeast of Minturno and brought under fire. Shortly after the Allied guns opened up, the enemy covered their movements with a smoke screen and further results were not observed.

Bad weather reduced MAAF activities yesterday to about 400 sorties against communications north of Rome, German-held towns between the Garigliano River front and the Allied beachhead, shipping along the Dalmatian coast and a

(Continued on Page 4)

Dock Demolished

SMOKE RISES FROM bursting bombs after planes of the Mediterranean Allied Air Force attacked harbor installations at Leghorn, important enemy supply base. (Photo by PWB)

Another Drive Now 40 Miles Into Rumania

LONDON, April 10 — Odessa, greatest port and industrial center on the Black Sea and the last important German stronghold in the rich south Ukraine, has fallen to the Red Army.

While Soviet units poured a hail of explosives on the city in a mighty frontal assault, Kuban cavalry, motorized units and infantry executed what was cryptically described as a "clever and unexpected maneuver" to break through German defenses and capture the fortress city, which defended the approaches to the central regions of Rumania.

Marshal Joseph Stalin announced the great victory in a special order of the day tonight. In Moscow a 24-salvo salute thundered from 324 guns while the shores of the Black Sea echoed a 12-salvo barrage from 120 guns as the Black Sea fleet celebrated the liberation of its greatest base.

Disclosure that Odessa had finally succumbed to the mighty Soviet sweep across the Ukraine came at a moment when long columns of Red Army tanks, guns and infantrymen pushed steadily southward over rain-soaked hills more than 40 miles within Rumania.

Northward another Soviet army had battled its way over snow-mantled crags and was poised on the summit of the Carpathians along the Czechoslovakian frontier.

On the Rumanian invasion front, Marshal Ivan Konev's forces captured more than 200 Rumanian towns yesterday as they moved ahead over mud-mired soil laced by hundreds of gullies. The advancing Russians by-passed the heavily fortified rail center of Jassy as they captured Zahorna, seven miles to the north, and then pivoted south toward the Ploesti oil fields and Bucharest, still some 200 miles to the southwest.

The battering assault which has

(Continues on Page 4)

World Body To Maintain Peace Begun, Hull Says

WASHINGTON, April 10—Secretary of State Cordell Hull last night told the nation that work had begun on "an international organization to maintain peace and prevent aggression."

Mr. Hull asserted in a broadcast that neither he nor President Roosevelt "has made or will make any secret agreements." The Secretary of State, who has asked Congress to designate a group to consult with him on postwar policy, expressed the hope of constant bi-partisan help and advice from members of Congress.

Mr. Hull, in the most detailed exposition of U.S. foreign policy in his more than 11 years in office, declared that the American people have learned that "free governments and Nazi and Fascist governments cannot exist together in this world."

The Secretary of State dealt quite specifically with the questions of France, Italy and neutral countries.

He said that the French Committee of National Liberation should exercise leadership to establish law and order in France under the supervision of the Allied commander in chief. He noted that the Committee "is, of course, not the government of France and we cannot recognize it as such." But he went on to recall that the Committee has "given assurance that it wishes at the earliest possible date to have the French people exercise their own sovereign will in accordance with French constitutional processes."

Mr. Hull described the Committee as "the symbol of the spirit of France and of French resistance," and said that the "central and abiding purpose" of the U.S. government "is to aid the French people, our oldest friends, in providing a democratic, competent and French administration of liberated French territory."

In Italy, Mr. Hull said, as in any other country, there can be no compromise with Fascism and the U.S. is interested in the establishment at the earliest possible moment of a free Italian government. He expressed regret that military events have not progressed according to hopes so that enough of Italy would have been freed before this time to permit the expression of the Italian will.

The Secretary of State, recalling the Moscow decisions of the American, British and Soviet governments concerning Italy, said that the policy had been carried out with the exception of that part calling for the introduction of more democratic elements in the central government. This exception, Mr. Hull said, does not represent any change in policy but is the result of the opinion that the military situation would be preju-

(Continued on Page 4)

Yanks, Nazis Pause For Easter Services

WITH THE 5TH ARMY IN ITALY, April 10 — Thousands of American doughboys knelt in foxholes less than 400 yards from German outposts in a dramatic sunrise Easter service conducted by three chaplains Sunday.

German and American soldiers alike paused on the battlefield to hear the Prince of Peace honored in services which were broadcast over a public address system so that all could participate in the Easter ceremony.

High on a rocky ledge overlooking the wide, haze-obscured valley, a makeshift altar had been created. A six-foot board was stretched between two 25-gallon gasoline cans and covered with a canvas tarpaulin. On it rested a tiny cross, two candles and a Bible.

From that altar Lutheran Chaplain Oscar Reinbeth opened the service with an address to the Germans within hearing.

"Happy Easter," the chaplain said. "As an American chaplain, I greet Protestants and Catholics of the German army. Should not all Christendom be jubilant on this day? Should not all people rejoice now that Christ died and rose again for all men — for Germans and Americans alike? Therefore, I wish you also today, in the name of my soldiers, Happy Easter."

Protestant Chaplain Early Hayes and Catholic Chaplain Leo J. Crowley then continued the service in English.

Amidst less warlike settings throughout the United States, the multi-colored uniforms of United Nations service men also marked Easter services.

In Washington, where the finest Easter weather in years enticed throngs to stroll beneath the blooming cherry blossoms, General George C. Marshall, Army Chief of Staff, addressed a sunrise service at Arlington Memorial Cemetery.

Mrs. Franklin D. Roosevelt was

(Continued on Page 4)

President Takes Holiday To Recover From Illness

WASHINGTON, April 10—President Roosevelt has left for a two-week vacation in the South, the White House announced today.

Mr. Roosevelt will cut short his trip "in the event of an unexpected emergency," the statement said. His destination was not revealed. The President is recuperating from a recent attack of bronchitis.

Hull's Policy Talk Lauded By British

WASHINGTON, April 10 — The discussion of United States foreign policy by Secretary of State Cordell Hull last night "will be warmly welcomed everywhere except in the enemy countries," the British Embassy in Washington commented today.

"Mr. Hull has not only made it clear how necessary the maintenance of unity is among the Allies, he has also shown how, in fact, they are working out agreed policies on all the difficult problems of the present and, what is more, how they are already underway to working out agreed policies on the great problems of the future," the Embassy said.

Rep. Sol Bloom (D., N. Y.), chairman of the House Foreign Affairs Committee, declared that "Secretary Hull's convincing speech on foreign affairs should satisfy the people of the entire nation that a definite foreign policy already exists to establish postwar peace throughout the world."

Sen. Styles Bridges (R., N. H.), expressed disappointment "because my search for concrete evidence of current steps being taken with the other United Nations to work out the basic terms of the peace was unrewarded. In general, I agree with Secretary Hull and his laudable aims and principles."

In New York, the Times and the Herald Tribune editorially praised Mr. Hull's speech.

"On the verge of great events, when the Allied world awaits the

(Continued on Page 4)

THE STARS AND STRIPES
SICILY

Vol. 1 - 73 - Friday, April 21, 1944 | For U. S. Armed Forces | 2 Lire

Allied Bombers Batter Railroad Yards In France

LONDON, April 20—The round-the-clock Allied air offensive against enemy targets in northern France and Germany continued with unabated fury as large forces of American Fortresses and Liberators, supported by swarms of Mustangs and Thunderbolts, attacked targets in northern France today.

The American daylight attack was followed by heavy RAF attacks on military objectives in western Germany and northern France. No official announcement of the raid has yet been made by the Air Ministry.

On Wednesday morning a force of at least 750 American bombers, with long-range fighter escort, ranged deep into Germany to deliver another whack at the Luftwaffe reserve. Aircraft factories and the airfield at Kassel as well as the airfield at Hamm were all soundly plastered. Enemy fighter opposition was light, although one flight of 100 fighters swept through the bomber formation over Kassel but quickly dispersed when American fighters appeared on the scene.

Five enemy craft were shot down by the bombers, 16 by the fighters. Two fighters and five bombers are missing from the American attacking fleet.

The daylight assaults followed the mightiest raids yet to be struck in this war by any air force. RAF Bomber Command on the preceding night sent close to 1,000 bombers, mostly Lancasters and Halifaxes, to drop a record weight of 4,000 tons of bombs on French rail centers. Among the targets hit were Ternier, in the north; Rouen, on the coast at the mouth of the Seine River near Le Havre, and centers in the Paris area.

Reconnaissance photos showed that the bombs fell well within the target areas. Enemy opposition in

Continued on Page 8

Nazi Anti-Semetic Board In Hungary

WASHINGTON — The Germans have set up a special administration in Hungary for the sole purpose of "liquidating thousands of Jews," Senator Alben A. Barkley, Democratic Majority Leader and member of the Senate Foreign Relations Committee, declared.

"If the Germans choose to follow in Hungary the pattern of liquidation of Jews and other persecuted minorities in Poland, then the prospective victims will be deported to isolated places to be dealt with by ruthless guards."

Recalling the President's warning to the Fascist war criminals, Mr. Barkley said "None who participate in these acts of savagery shall go unpunished and all who share in the guilt shall share the punishment."

He appealed to the Hungarian people to continue their "Christian charity" and to show their disapproval of the Nazi philosophy of brutality by counteracting the "sinister" and inhuman measures of the German tyrant and his minions.

U. S. Bread Rationing Called 'Inevitable'

BALTIMORE—A prediction that bread would be rationed in the United States before Christmas was made by B. B. Derrick, secretary-treasurer of the Maryland and Virginia Milk Producers Association. Derrick declared in an interview that bread rationing this year was "inevitable" because reserve stocks of wheat had been largely exhausted and because this year's planting had been curtailed.

Turks Reply To Allies On Trade With Germany

LONDON, April 20—The Turkish reply to the Allied note on the supply of chrome to Germany, delivered on Monday, was couched in general but accomodating terms. Turkish newspapers say that the delivery of chrome to Germany has been considerably cut down during the last few days owing to transport difficulties.

A spokesman of the British Ministry of Economics Warfare told the House of Commons that Turkey had exported 14,800 tons of chrome to Germany during the first two months of 1944, as against 1,870 tons to the United Nations.

Partisans Attack In Western Serbia

LONDON, April 20—A communique broadcast from Marshal Tito's Headquarters announced today that Partisan troops of the Yugoslav Army of Liberation had routed the Pozega Chetnik Corps of about 4,000 men in western Serbia.

In the Sanjak sector between Montenegro and Serbia, Partisan units were said to have succeeded in halting any further advance by the Germans. An earlier communique from Yugoslav headquarters reported the routing of Bulgarian quisling forces in a prolonged battle in the Studenica Valley in Serbia, south of the capital, Belgrade, where Germans, Bulgarians and traitor General Neditch's troops are bringing up reinforcements to prevent the Partisans from widening their offensive operations.

The Free Yugoslav Radio reported today that relations have now been established and missions will be exchanged between the Greek Committee for National Liberation, headed by Colonel Bakirtzis, and Marshal Tito's Yugoslav National Liberation movement.

From Budapest, the German-controlled Hungarian Radio announced that the Chief of the Hungarian Military Staff, General Szombathely, has been relieved of his post "at his own request." At the same time the German News Agency said that four more opposition parties have been dissolved in Hungary and seven more Hungarian publications have been banned.

Meanwhile reports from neutral Switzerland said that 15,000 Hungarian students who participated in anti-German demonstrations have been confined in the recently organized concentration camp near Budapest.

ACC Restores Art Treasures In Palermo

NAPLES—Recent reports emphasize the vigilance with which the Allied Control Commission is working behind the Italian front to preserve art treasures. At Palermo, Sicily, bomb blasts blew out two bays of the wall of a famous church. All the stones were found and numbered and the wall has now been rebuilt in its original state. In the Sicilian capital alone "first aid" has been given to six damaged churches and two oratories.

House Committee Rejects New 4-F Legislation

WASHINGTON — Congress has tossed the 4-F problem back into the laps of the executive agencies. At a closed meeting climaxing weeks of study of how best to utilize the services of draft-age men rejected for military duty because of physical disabilities, the House Military Committee decided against 4-F legislation on the grounds that already existing agencies had the power to deal with the question.

ANZIO SHELL GAME

AMERICAN SOLDIERS OF AN ARMORED regiment piling up used shells after an enemy attack was repulsed on the Anzio beachhead. All of these were used to stop one thrust.
—Photo Through PWB

MAAF Mines Danube; Adriatic Area Active

ALLIED FORCE HEADQUARTERS, April 20—While activities on all sectors of the Italian fronts were in the main limited to patrolling and artillery exchanges, increased Allied raiding parties are reported in the 8th Army Adriatic sector, as well as on the 5th Army bridgehead, with the enemy suffering casualties at Arielli.

An 8th Army raiding party captured 16 prisoners after some brisk skirmishes, a communique stated. A sharp patrol clash occurred about a mile northeast of Guardiagrele, and another southeast of Tollo, supported by our artillery.

At Tollo, the enemy fired propaganda leaflets—with no visible damage—while south of here, they shelled Fallascoso. In the vicinity of Appollinare, an enemy petrol dump was discovered by Allied tanks, and large fires were started.

ALLIED FORCE HEADQUARTERS, April 20—The greatest waterway through the Balkans, the Danube river, was mined by RAF heavy and medium bombers, it was dislosed for the first time by an air communique. Liberators and Wellingtons belonging to a famous group which has a distinguished record of service in the Mediterranean carried out the operations.

For several nights Allied airmen performed their unique mission well behind enemy lines. It was a part of the coordinated day and night bombing of German communications to the southern Russian front.

It was announced by Bucharest and Budapest radio that Hungarian and Rumanian shipping companies have stopped all traffic on the Danube due to the danger of mines. Already one large ship and two smaller vessels have been sunk.

At least 91 planes, most of them rocket-firing Messerschmitts used for intercepting bomber formations, were destroyed on the ground in twin raids by the United States 15th Air Force on the Tokol and Veses airfields near Budapest on April 13, it was officially disclosed.

On Thursday, RAF Halifax heavy bombers attacked targets in Plovdiv, second largest city in Bulgaria. Through an early morning haze, pilots saw bomb flashes on the targets, and the glow of the fires was visible to crews after they had bombed their objectives.

In direct support of movements on the ground fronts, medium bombers of the 1st Tactical Air Force yesterday bombed railway yards at Piombino and Ancona. Fighter bombers attacked railroads, bridges and other communications in the Florence area.

Italy Reminded Of Fascist Past

NAPLES, April 20—Palmiro Togliatti, leader of the Italian Communist Party, told a Reuter's correspondent that "Italy must not forget that she is obliged to make good the injuries and losses inflicted by Fascism on people against whom the Fascists have committed acts of aggression.

"We will do everything in our power to ensure that the Italian working class gives steadily a larger contribution to the war for the liberation of their own country from the invader," he said.

Meanwhile Marshal Pietro Badoglio, Italian Prime Minister who earlier this week handed the King the resignation of his entire cabinet, continued his discussions with former opposition party elements while the Italian National Committee of Liberation studied plans for the possible makeup of the new democratic coalition government to be composed of all anti-Fascist Italian parties.

Party leaders were scheduled to meet individually with Marshal Badoglio today in Naples.

FDR's Son Divorced

FORT WORTH, Tex.—Mrs. Ruth Goggins Roosevelt was granted a divorce from Col. Elliot Roosevelt, second son of the President.

French Court Sentences Five Fascists To Death

ALGIERS, April 20—The French military tribunal here returned verdicts on Wednesday night in the cases of the 27 former members of the Vichy-recruited Fascist Phalange Africaine, organized to fight with the German army against the Allies in Tunisia.

The tribunal, headed by President Paul Cordier, condemned five of the men to death, 13 to forced labor for terms ranging from ten years to life, and nine men to five years in prison. Five of the defendants received suspended sentences.

Soviets Fight In Sevastopol; Balaclava Falls

LONDON, April 20—The Russian noose is rapidly closing in the Crimea as harried German troops are falling back toward the sea in the shell-shattered city of Sevastopol. From all sides Red Army troops are surging into the city and have overrun the village of Balaclava, roughly ten miles from the Black Sea port.

The Soviet Maritime Army, under General Yeremenko, smashed its way through a formidable line of pill boxes, tank barriers and mine fields to take Balaclava, famous as the scene of "The Charge of the Light Brigade." The capture of the town has broken the outer ring of Nazi defenses from the southwest and Red Army troops are swarming through the gap toward Sevastopol.

Inside of Sevastopol, German commanders desperately gambling that the bloody losses they are suffering in prolonging the defense of the city will gain the precious time needed to bring up shipping for an evacuation of the Crimea, are throwing every available man into the battle.

Barricades have been thrown up across every street, with German and Rumanian troops fighting fanatically for time in a desperate, last ditch stand with their backs to the sea. Hundreds have already been forced into the sea from the high cliffs above Balaclava. Others trying to get away in powered barges from the beaches further west have been drowned in their attempt to escape.

Sevastopol, in flames and in ruins, is now a grim death trap sealed off by land, sea and air. Land batteries, a powerful screen of warships, Stormoviks and bombers have almost completely shut the door on the port's sea exit. The Nazis have been herded into a poc-

(Continued on Page 4)

Naval Forces Hit Sumatra Shipping

CEYLON, April 20—The British Admiralty today announced a successful attack by an Allied naval force against Sabang, at the northern end of Sumatra. The force suffered no damage.

Sabang lies on a small island 10 miles off Sumatra and is an important shipping center. The attack was preceded by a daylight attack by heavy bombers of the 10th USAAF on the shipping at Port Blair in the Andeman Islands, 400 miles northwest of Sabang in the Bay of Bengal.

In northern Burma, the Chinese 22nd Division is now fighting desperate Japanese resistance in the north Burma town of Warazup, one of the enemy strongpoints in the Mogaung Valley sector. The Japanese are surrendering each yard of ground only after bitter hand to hand fighting with the steadily advancing Chinese troops.

ALLIED SOUTH PACIFIC HEADQARTERS, April 20—The Allied air offensive against Japanese positions in the central and south Pacific continued this week with new and heavy blows against objectives in the Carolines, New Britain and New Guinea.

Allied Solomons-based Liberators made a daylight attack on the enemy airfield on Satawan Island southeast of the powerful Japanese base of Truk in the Carolines. Medium and light bombers from Southwest Pacific bases struck at Rabaul, while Mitchells of the 7th USAAF, based in the central Pacific, smashed at airfields and ground installations in the eastern Carolines and Marshalls.

THE STARS AND STRIPES

VOL. II No. 17 — CAIRO — MIDDLE EAST — FOUR CENTS — APRIL 28, 1944

Government Seizes Ward Mail Stores

CHICAGO — President Roosevelt is reported to have issued an executive order for seizure of the Montgomery Ward mail order company and Department of Commerce officials were expected to take over operations immediately.

This action came after President Roosevelt issued a "back-to-work" ultimatum to striking employees. At the same time, he ordered the management to comply with WLB's order and sign a new contract with CIO. Workers voted to return to their jobs but the managers ignored the executive warning and refused to extend the contract which expired December 31.

The strike began on April 12 as result of the management's refusal to sign a new contract with CIO, labor union with which retail wholesale and department store employees are affiliated. Managers claimed that the union no longer represented the majority of their workers and challenged CIO's right to represent M-W employees.

When the walk-out occurred, President Roosevelt intervened immediately. To the company's president, Sewell Avery, went a telegram which said in part : "The strike is taking place in the heart of one of the most vital war production centers in the country. It is causing delay in the delivery of farm equipment and machinery repair parts, electrical appliances, automobile tires and other goods essential for the economy in wartime. I shall take such action as the interest of the nation requires."

Lack of War Spirit Ires U.S. Under-Secy.

NEW YORK — Under-Secy. Robert P. Patterson warned that the spirit of unity which gripped the nation immediately after Pearl Harbor has dwindled away under the complacent feeling that the war is as good as won.

Patterson called upon Americans to attain a unity of purpose through trust in our Allies, faith in our military leadership and linking ourselves in thought and action with the nation's fighting

Chowhounds Up Front

(Above) U.S. Army nurses dangle mess kits as they line up for chow somewhere behind the Allied Fifth Army front in Italy. Judging by the size of those lovely smiles the chow must be pretty good. All nurses in the front-line areas wear the buxom GI regulation overalls. (Below) An MP and a jeep jockey grab a couple of handsful of sinkers served by a Red Cross clubmobile man. The coffee will be out in a few minutes. (OWI Photos.)

Nazis Wait Invasion As Air Blitz Mounts 5th Pushes at Anzio

The war of nerves, which brought the Germans their earliest World War II successes, this week brought butterflies to millions of German stomachs as their once-confident government warned of Allied invasion by the end of the month.

The Allied high command said nothing, but tufts of its long-planted plans sprouted from Scandinavia to Spain, from the Straits of Gibraltar to the Bosphorus. The Allies moved with their priceless advantage of timing, gave their own people little hint of whether the inevitable "Now" would occur in a matter of hours or months. But if they didn't speak, these actions did :

Not a day went by without thousand-plane raids over Germany, Belgium and France. Monday night's RAF Berlin raid was described by the Germans as "the heaviest ever," allowing no time for recovery after USAAF's bomb load of the previous day.

German posts along the channel were on the alert for landings as Nazi spokesmen pointed out high tides the last ten days of the month would be most favorable to landings.

Britain "Sealing Up"

On the Italian front, gains were made at Anzio, through Carano, center of the Allied line, and at Cisterna at the right flank; artillery duels continued at Cassino, but the general atmosphere was one of waiting. Again the Germans displayed their defensive attitude by pointing out that "the new Allied concentrations are not consistent with present activity and a new offensive in Italy is expected to be timed with the landing attempts in the west."

In Italy, too, court-martialed pilots and non-coms, physically fit released prisoners and political dissenters appeared on the Nazi fronts. Prisoners reported drinking water on the German side was foul and that their food is now poorer than several weeks ago. The Nazis ordered their troops to loot for clothes in Italy to be sent

(See INVASION on Page 8)

Soviet Troops Mass For Spring Thrusts

A strange lull descended across the Russian front this week after nearly ten months of fierce, continuous offensives but the lull was described as a calm before the storm. Moscow correspondents reported that the Red Army is completing its regrouping in several sectors on the vast front and is now ready to launch more powerful new offensives, perhaps coinciding with the Anglo-American invasion of western Europe. Unending streams of reinforcements and supplies are flowing up to the entire Eastern front in preparation. And while Russian troops paused after their winter of success, Spring was drying out the Ukraine and melting the deep snows on the central and northern front.

Berlin, however, reported that violent fighting is flaming again on the lower Dniester after fierce artillery barrages and air attack in the area of Kishinev, capital of Bessarabia. Other battles were reported progressing south of Ti-

(See RUSSIA on Page 8)

Gen. Giles Praises USAFIME After 18,000-Mile Inspection

Returning early this week from an 18-day and approximately 18,000-miles air tour of USAFIME, Brig. Gen. Benjamin F. Giles had high praise for the spirit being shown and the work being done by the officers and men of his Command.

"What impressed me most on the whole trip", said Gen. Giles, "was the fact that all the troops, regardess of where stationed, seemed conscious of the real importance of their jobs and were working with spirit and enthusiasm to do their jobs well. To me this is the test of a real soldier, and it makes me proud and happy to have such soldiers in my Command.

"The men of USAFIME obviously realize", the General continued, "that the troops at the front can continue to carry on only when the troops in the rear keep their organizations running smoothly and the flow of supplies moves forward without interruptions.

"Dakar Still Vital"

The General praised the construction work done at Benghazi by Major Burg and his men, and added that the post was of real importance both from the tactical and supply point of view.

At Tindauf, locale of the famed book, "Beau Geste", he saw American troops that reminded him, he said, of an American Foreign Legion, and they were doing splendid work in a mighty hot spot.

Winging over to Dakar, Gen. Giles was mightily impressed with that busy station and the work being done by Col. Keen and Major Peters and their men. "Dakar may be out of the news these days", said the General, "but the quiet job being done there, in keeping planes and supplies moving, is vital to our war plans".

At Roberts Field, Liberia, Gen. Giles found "a fine body of our Negro troops doing some outstanding engineering and supply work, with a snap and polish that was good to see".

Praises South Africa

Bustling Accra, headquarters of the Central African Wing of ATC and hub of USAFIME activities in that area, was, the General said, a model post. "The troops under Col. McMullen and Col. McClendon are exceptionally neat in appear-

(See GEN. GILES on Page 8)

Japs Flee Into Jungles As Yanks Expand N. Guinea Beachheads

Two of Hollandia's three airdromes have been captured by American invasion forces in Dutch New Guinea.

Madang, Jap naval and air base in British New Guinea, has fallen to Australian forces.

In what appears to mark the beginning of the end of the New Guinea campaign and the setting of the stage for the battle of the Phillipines, huge American forces are expanding their bridgeheads which they carved out on both sides of Hollandia, Dutch New Guinea, and another 150 miles southwestward at Aitape.

Using the greatest number of troops ever used in the Southwest Pacific and supported by a large fleet of warships and carriers, the U.S. forces swarmed the Hollandia beaches to recover the first Netherlands territory of the war.

Gen. MacArthur, who witnessed the operation, described it as "Bataan in reverse," and asserted that the isolation of another 60,000 Japs between Hollandia and Madang leaves 150,000 enemy troops neutralized and "strategically impotent" from New Guinea to the Solomon Islands. American casualties were extremely light.

The fall of the three aerodromes at Hollandia, which will bring Mindanao in the Philippines within the range of heavy bombers, is

(See PACIFIC on Page 8)

PLANE CRASH IN STREET

MONTREAL — An RAF bomber exploded in mid-air this week and plunged into downtown Montreal, razing three buildings and damaging others. Authorities revealed that the plane was operated by the RAF transport command and carried a crew of five. Nine bodies have been found in the burning debris of buildings.

THE STARS AND STRIPES
MEDITERRANEAN

Vol. 2, No. 23, Saturday, May 13, 1944 — For U. S. Armed Forces — TWO FRANCS

Allied Armies Ram Gustav Line

Force Of 1,000 Bombers Blasts Leipzig Works

Synthetic Oil Factories Target As Air War Ends 27th Day

LONDON—A force of 1,000 Flying Forts and Liberators of the 8th AAF bombed four major synthetic oil plants in the Leipzig area of Germany today and one at Rux, inside the Czechoslovakia border, carrying the unabated air assault against Europe into its 27th straight day. The heavies were escorted by equally strong forces of Thunderbolts, Lightnings and Mustangs of the 9th AAF.

Targets listed included the big Leuna oil plants at Merseburg, 18 miles west of Leipzig, and other plants at Lutzkendorf, 14 miles south of Halle, and one at Bohlen, just outside of Leipzig and Zeitz.

Since daylight and through dusk on Friday all types of aircraft were reported crossing the Channel coast of England. One observer reported the noise of Europe-bound bombers "is so continuous that the silent periods are most impressive."

There was no Allied confirmation of German radio reports that the American bombers in several waves attacked Moselle and other targets in the Rhineland.

In the House of Commons, Air Minister Sir Archibald Sinclair disclosed that about 26,000 German and Italian aircraft had been destroyed in the air by American, British and other Allied forces since the beginning of the war. This figure, he said, excluded the aircraft destroyed by Soviet forces and aircraft destroyed on the ground.

German-occupied Europe was rocked by tons of explosives for the sixth consecutive night Thursday as aircraft of the RAF Bomber Command were out "in great strength" over France and Belgium.

The assault was made practically continuous with another daylight pounding by what was termed in press reports as "the greatest aerial

(Continued on Page 16)

Germans Stalled In Dniester Bid

LONDON — As Russian burial squads continued to carry German and Rumanian bodies out of the ruined buildings in captured Sevastopol, Nazi forces opened a large scale offensive at week's end on the Soviet bridgehead on the right bank of the Dniester River opposite Tiraspol.

Large numbers of German shock troops, supported by tanks, were thrown at the bridgehead, formed by units of General Rodion Malinovsky's 3rd Ukrainian Front about five weeks ago and which threatens Nazi positions in southern Bessarabia.

German dispatches asserted that Nazi divisions mopped up the entire bridgehead, but the Moscow midnight communique on Thursday said that the German attacks had been repulsed and heavy casualties inflicted.

In the far north, Soviet torpedo planes sank a 7,000-ton German transport off the coast of Norway. And in a raid on an unidentified enemy port, Russian naval planes sank 25 small ships, damaged a transport and set a transport afire.

Duncan Hooper, special Reuter's correspondent, wrote that it was possible to count the few buildings

(Continued on Page 15)

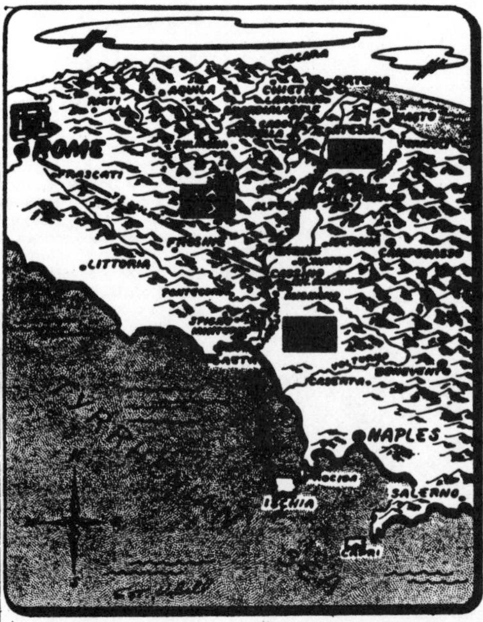

ALLIED GROUND FORCES, covered by the Mediterranean Allied Tactical Air Force, struck in a mass assault Thursday night against the Gustav Line—outer ring of defenses shielding Hitler's Europe.

Invasion Fever Mounts As U. S. Awaits D Day

By Sgt. DAVID GOLDING
(Stars and Stripes Staff Writer)

NEW YORK, May 12—The invasion fever kept mounting this week in America.

There is growing tension evident everywhere as day after day newspapers emphasize "pre-invasion" bombing of Hitler's fortress.

"When will D Day be?" is the question everyone is asking today. But the date of the western invasion of Europe looks like the best-kept secret of the war.

All eyes were turned toward the White House this week, where the nation's Commander in Chief returned after a month's vacation. Rumors were particularly rife during the President's absence. Whisperers had the President, among other places, in London to be on hand for the invasion.

But President Roosevelt is back in Washington giving the impression he is ready for anything. People know now where the President rested, which spiked a lot of invasion guessing. However, speculation over when it will happen has been stimulated anew by the President's presence in the nation's capital.

People also were informed that announcement of the invasion, when it comes, would come from the Allied Command in London. Elmer Davis, OWI chief, told the nation to disregard all phony reports of second-front operations emanating from Joe Goebbels' rumor mill.

Coverage of the invasion will be unprecedented, and newspapers and radio are sweating out the first invasion flash. Some afternoon newspapers already have informed advertisers that they will

(Continued on Page 16)

Heavy Artillery Barrage Precedes Mass Drive

By Pvt. STAN SWINTON
(Stars and Stripes Staff Writer)

ALLIED FORCE HEADQUARTERS, May 12—The 5th and 8th Armies, striking the first blow in the all-out assault on Germany's European fortress, have funneled their might between Cassino and the Tyrrhenian Sea in a great new offensive aimed at smashing the Gustav Line.

Thousands of artillery pieces unloosed one of the heaviest barrages of the war at 11 o'clock last night and continued for hours to blast the powerful belt of defensive positions ranging across the Italian peninsula. Then ground troops struck, concentrating against German positions in the Liri Valley, which is approximately six miles southwest of Cassino.

The 8th Army, which had been secretly moved across the Apennines from its former positions, sent British, Dominion, Indian and Polish troops into the Liri Valley assault.

The 5th Army, after successfully completing extensive regrouping activity, launched a parallel drive northwards on the Tyrrhenian coastal flank to clear the mountains ahead which form a part of the Gustav Line and separate the Anzio beachhead forces from the main body.

Reuter's late today quoted the New York radio as reporting the Allied advance has gained more than a mile in the central sector and an unnamed town has been occupied.

The MAAF went all out in support of the new offensive, sending Flying Fortresses and Liberators aloft on 700 sorties against west coast harbors and railroad centers in close co-ordination with the ground operations. Escorting fighters flew another 200 sorties.

The German Headquarters towns of Civita Castellana, 15 miles north of Rome, and Massa D'Albe, three miles north of Avezzano, were bombed by the heavies with good results. While only eight of the 18 primary targets set for the heavies could be assaulted because of bad weather, the formations struck at secondary targets when their prime objectives were inaccessible.

The Fortresses and Liberators

(Continued on Page 16)

Satellite Nations Get Joint Allied Note To Quit War

WASHINGTON—Four Axis satellites—Hungary, Rumania, Bulgaria and Finland—were warned Friday to quit the war or "go down in utter defeat with Germany" in a joint declaration issued by the United States, Great Britain and Russia.

"There is yet time for the people of these four satellites to contribute to the coming Allied victory," the declaration read, urging the quartet to withdraw from hostilities, to cease collaboration with Germany, and to resist the Nazis by every possible means.

"Through the fateful policy of their leaders," the declaration continued, "the people of Hungary are suffering the humiliation of German occupation. Rumania is still bound to the Nazis in a war now bringing devastation to its own people. The governments of Bulgaria and Finland have placed their countries in the service of Germany and remain in the war at Germany's side.

"The governments of Great Britain, the Soviet Union and the United States think it right that these peoples should realize the following facts:

"One—The Axis satellites, Hungary, Rumania, Bulgaria and Finland, despite their realization of the inevitability of a crushing Nazi defeat and their desire to get out of the war, are by their present policies and attitudes contributing materially to the strength of the German war machine.

"Two—These nations still have it in their power, by withdrawing from the war, ceasing their collaboration with Germany and by resisting the forces of Nazism by every possible means, to shorten the European struggle, diminish

(Continued on Page 15)

Nazis Lose Five Aircraft In Raid

ALLIED FORCE HEADQUARTERS, May 12—The Coastal Air Force, which had pinned the Luftwaffe's ears back six times before in the past four months, shot down another five German aircraft last night, when between 25 and 30 swastika-marked planes launched an unsuccessful twilight torpedo attack against an Allied convoy in the Algiers area.

British Beaufighters and Mosquitoes joined with French Airacobras to bring the Coastal's total to 25 victories against convoy raiders since Feb. 1. The German planes swept out of the twilight in two waves, one ten miles behind the other, and descended to deck levels before firing their torpedoes.

Intercepting Allied aircraft followed the intruders down toward the sea and the ensuing dogfights took place at levels of 100 feet and under within ten miles of the convoy. Two Beaufighters got a Heinie shot down and another damaged apiece; two Mosquitoes scored one victory each, and a French pilot got the fifth plane.

Coastal planes were equally busy yesterday over the Adriatic. Spits chased one ME-109 around the heel of Italy for an hour before sending it spiraling down from 29,000 feet in flames. A few min-

(Continued on Page 16)

'G-5' Created To Administer Countries Freed In Invasion

LONDON — Plans for the temporary administration of Germany and territories liberated by the invasion forces were disclosed Thursday to Allied correspondents at a press conference at G-5 headquarters—the Civil Affairs Section of the Supreme Allied Command—somewhere in England.

Nations whose territories will be affected by the plan are Norway, Denmark, Holland, Belgium, Luxembourg, Germany and, perhaps, Austria. Reuter's said that Yugoslavia, Greece and Albania would fall within the sphere of the Mediterranean command and that the Balkans would be in the Russian sphere.

Allied spokesmen said that in friendly countries, Civil Affairs teams of from ten to 44 specially-trained officers and enlisted men would enter a village, city or province in the wake of the Allied Armies accompanied by a representative of the country's government abroad.

In Germany, the Civil Affairs group will function along the same lines as AMG does in Italy, although no agreement has yet been signed with the Russians with respect to the civil administration of the Reich. Reuter's reported that many questions remained to be settled as to collaboration in the occupation of Germany.

The Associated Press said that in the case of France, the representative accompanying the Civil Affairs team would be from the French Committee of National Liberation.

(Secretary of State Cordell Hull, in his foreign policy address of April 9, and Anthony Eden, British Foreign Secretary, speaking in Commons last week, said that the FCNL would be the recognized civil authority in France.)

The Associated Press said that agreements for the administration of liberated Norway, Belgium and the Netherlands were almost ready for signature. Reuter's said Denmark would be treated as an ally—on the same basis as other liberated countries—in view of her assistance record.

Reuter's also reported that discussions toward an agreement concerning France had been started with the military mission of the FCNL now in London, but that the ban on diplomatic travel

(Continued on Page 15)

THE STARS AND STRIPES
TUNIS

One Franc

Vol. 1—No. 44—Friday, 19 May 1944

Newspaper for U. S. Armed Forces in Tunisia

Cassino, Rome Gateway, Captured

Allied Soldiers Seize Important Burma Airport

Myitkyina Taken In Surprise Move

KANDY, Ceylon, May 18 — Chinese and American troops have captured the southern airport of Myitkyina and are pouring mortar fire into the town, according to the Chinese high command communique reported by Reuter's today.

Siege of the airport was reported in today's communique from southeast Asia Command headquarters. The attack on the main Jap base in upper Burma held by the enemy for the past two years began yesterday after a 20-day march by three columns of both Chinese and American troops.

The Allied forces under command of Brig. Gen. Frank Merrill secretly made their way over a rough and tortuous ground from the Kumon hills on the eastern rim of the Mogaung Valley to take the Japs by surprise. Shortly after establishing positions around Myitkyina, American glider-born engineers were flown to aid the action.

Latest reports of the Chinese advance from Yunan Province tell of continued successes in the face of repeated Jap counterattacks. After crossing the Salween River in a number of places, several Chinese columns are well on their way to crossing the 17,000-foot range of mountains—known as the hump—still separating them from Lt. Gen. Joseph W. Stillwell's forces around Myitkyina.

AP Says President Can Get First Ballot

WASHINGTON, May 18 — President Roosevelt is assured of the Democratic Presidential nomination on the first ballot if he wants it, according to an Associated Press compilation which indicates that by next Tuesday night, the President will have 677 delegates pledged or claimed as against 589 needed for the nomination.

The United Press reported that Gov. Thomas E. Dewey, N. Y., may be the first ballot nominee of the GOP convention "as delegate sentiment for first place is recorded so far."

The AP's political writer, Jack Bell, said that Gov. Earl Warren, Calif., "can have the GOP Vice Presidential nomination if he wants it but Republicans wish they knew whether the governor means it when he says he is not a candidate."

The AP writer adds, however, that Gov John W. Bricker, Ohio, would "be a strong Vice Presidential nominee from an important state with 25 electoral votes. Former governor Harold E. Stassen, Minnesota, would have considerable support. Not to be overlooked are Rep. Everett Dirksen, (R., Ill.), who is campaigning for a place on the ticket and Eric Johnston, West Coast industrialist, who just has been re-elected president of the U. S. Chamber of Commerce."

Ask Fast Action In Neglect Trial

WASHINGTON, May 18 —A resolution that would require the War and Navy Departments to start court martial proceedings within the next three months against Rear Admiral Husband E. Kimmel and Maj. Gen. Walter C. Short, who were in charge at Pearl Harbor when the Japanese struck was introduced into the House yesterday by Rep. Dewey Short (R., Mo.).

Soviet Air Force Hammers Nazis

LONDON, May 18—While the rumble of artillery and the persistent jabbing of patrols marked the continuing lull in ground operations along the eastern front, The Red Air Force continued its offensive against German communication centers by sending large fleets of long-range bombers against the railroad junctions of Minsk, Baranovich and Kholm.

At Minsk, on the north-central front, the Red-starred strategic heavies set seven large fires which burned together and became one huge blaze. Eighty miles southwest along the same rail line, trains loaded with enemy troops and equipment were smashed at Baranovich.

In other aerial activity, the Red banner Baltic Fleet air arm intercepted a German convoy in the Gulf of Finland and sank three trawlers and two coast-guard launches while knocking down 16 enemy planes.

Ground activity continued to be on a small scale. Southeast of Stanislavov, in eastern Galicia, 500 Germans were killed and 150 captured when the Red Army seized a line of enemy trenches and then held them against two counterattacks.

Niedzielski To Play

The world-famous Polish pianist, Niedzielski, will present an all Chopin program on Sunday, May 21, at 6:00 PM at the Municipal Theater in Tunis. Tickets may be obtained at the theater which is located on the Rue Jules Ferry.

Refineries, Rail Yard Bombed In Balkan Raid

Ploesti's Oil Stores Get Sixth Pounding

ALLIED FORCE HEADQUARTERS, May 18 — Forces of American Liberators and Flying Fortresses, numbering between 500 and 750, today bombed Ploesti, Rumania and Belgrade and Nis, in Yugoslavia, against strong enemy opposition and in very bad weather, MAAF said in a special announcement late this afternoon.

It was the sixth raid of the war against refineries and rail yards at Ploesti, last visited by Mediterranean-based planes on May 5th. It was Belgrade's 4th raid, the last being on April 24th. Crewmen returning from Nis, last attacked April 16th, reported the bombing results as "good" with the railroad on the Belgrade-Sofia line well plastered by bomb hits.

Frosinone, the most important rail and road junction between the Italian battle front and Rome, was pounded day and night yesterday in a mighty air force effort to place a crippling bloc in the path of Nazi supplies. But it was only one of numerous targets of the busiest day of this week for Allied airmen.

Frosinone got most of the punishment from 4,000-pound block busters dropped last night by RAF Wellingtons, from American Mitchells and Marauders and from lighter Allied craft. The Wellingtons gave special attention to the junction of Highway 6 and another road that swings northward from Frosinone. The Marauders aimed at and probably hit a bridge at Frosinone and others in the same general area. Meanwhile Warhawks, Spitfires, Thunderbolts and Invaders ranged up and down the highway in the same vicinity destroying motor vehicles.

Medium forces of American Liberators out for the first time since Sunday took over the

(Continued on Page 8)

Officers Maintain Order As Sedition Trials Open

WASHINGTON, May 18 — Federal marshals were called to keep order yesterday as the sedition trial defendants shouted interjections and the defense attorneys objected to prosecutor John Rogge's statement that the government would prove the 29 persons had a Fuehrer in mind to establish a Nazi regime in the United States

Attorney Rogge also declared that the defendants accused of seditious conspiracy had joined a "world wide Nazi movement"

The defense counsel clamored for a mistrial on the ground that Mr. Rogge's presentation was inflammatory and had prejudiced the mind of the jury. Mistrial motions were denied.

Defendant James Edward Smythe, New York, who loudly demanded a mental examination for himself had his request granted for the guidance of the court.

Lois De Lafayette Ashburn, another defendant, arose and yelled, Your Honor, I resume my challenge. But the marshals put her back in her seat before it was known just what challenge she wanted to make.

Attorney Rogge asserted the defendants claimed the whole democratic system was rotten, corrupt and about to fall, and that they called all Jews Communists. He said defendant Gerald Winrow was the first to call President Roosevelt a Jew.

Some of the defendants went to the German embassy and others to the German consul, Mr. Rogge claimed, while others went to Germany to learn how Nazis came into power.

Hitler Line Contacted; 5th Army Drive Rapid

ALLIED FORCE HEADQUARTERS, May 18—Cassino, for seven bloody months a stubborn barrier in the battle for Rome, today lay behind Allied forces rushing into contact with the Adolf Hitler Line, but the fall of the most popular prize of the Italian campaign was almost overshadowed by the brilliant dash across the Liri River by American and French units of the Fifth Army.

The capture of Cassino and towering Monastery Hill at the western end of the German bastion, was announced in a special Allied communique late this afternoon. The victory was achieved in a brilliant, fiercely-prosecuted pincer movement, executed by Polish and British troops of the Eighth Army with comparatively few casualties.

The town itself fell to the British troops who had first cut Highway 6, the only escape route from Cassino, three miles west of the town. The hill on which St. Benedict's Abbey once stood, fell to Polish soldiers who completely out-manoeuvered the vaunted fanatical Nazi parachutists who had been the bulwark of Cassino's long defense.

Hours before the official Allied announcement, which fixed the victory hour as noon today, the Germans were insisting that the citadel, long known as "the Gateway to Rome," had been successfully evacuated. But the Allied report of 1,500 prisoners from among the Fourth Parachute Regiment, a regiment of the 15th Panzer Grenadier Division and the 376 Regiment of the 305th German Infantry, and tremendous casualties from among the units, belied the Nazi claim.

In fact they indicated strongly that Marshal Albert Kesselring, reported by German news agencies to be on the Cassino front, waited too long before trying to extricate his men from an untenable position.

Quite possibly, Kesselring expected just another of the many Allied frontal attacks on Cassino which failed to neutralize the bastion despite thousands of tons of bombs, multi-thousands of rounds of artillery shells, and high casualty lists among the American 34th and 36th Divisions, the French, British, New Zealanders, Indians and Poles since the first big attack on Cassino in mid-January.

The Allies did not play according to Kesselring's plan. The Poles who had been pinned down by the parachutists since the start of the Gustav Line offensive last Thursday night, pushed off again from north of Cassino on the heels of a terrific artillery barrage that was

(Continued on Page 8)

British Task Force Raids Enemy Waters

LONDON, May 18—Carrier-based Hellcat fighter-bombers protected by Wildcat and Hellcat fighters have roared over the coastal waters of occupied Norway Tuesday to set fire to two medium-sized supply ships, damage three other vessels and knock down nine German fighters, the Admiralty announced last night.

Striking once again at the sea-lanes over which the enemy transports iron ore from northern Norway, the British task force steamed so close to the shore that the mountains could be seen in the distance. The British force lost five aircraft but suffered no damage to its warships despite futile efforts by Luftwaffe planes to break through the ack-ack and fighter protective ring.

The first carrier-based attack Tuesday was against German shipping anchored near the shore. Witnesses said that in a few minutes the fleet air arm planes turned the peaceful anchorage into a cauldron of smoke, steam and flying metal. Two ships were hit, three possibly damaged and Heinkel float planes buffetted.

Wednesday, the task force made another surprise attack 200 miles to the south near Stadlandet, most westerly point of Norway. Oil tanks and a fish oil factory were hit and two armed trawlers shot up.

Forrestal's Nomination Due Senate Approval

WASHINGTON, May 18 — The Senate was expected today to confirm the nomination of James V. Forrestal as Secretary of the Navy, International News Service reported.

The Senate Naval Affairs Committee unanimously approved the nomination a few minutes after Mr. Forrestal appeared before it yesterday. The entire committee arose and greeted the nominee with applause in a special tribute. The usual questions were waived. Mr. Forrestal would succeed the late Frank Knox.

Prisoners Exchanged

BARCELONA, May 18—The Gripsholm and Gradesca arrived here today within an hour of each other, to effect an exchange of war prisoners.

Allies Catch Fleeing Enemy Near Aitape

ALLIED SOUTHWEST PACIFIC HEADQUARTERS, May 18—Allied troops who have patiently been chasing fleet-footed Japs into the interior of northern New Guinea between Aitape and Hollandia have at last caught up with them, General Douglas MacArthur indicated in today's communique

The Aussies and Yanks who have had to be content with meeting occasional and small pockets of resistance here and there, made contact with some substantial forces 34 miles southeast of Aitape. Attack planes and fighter-bombers also attacked enemy-occupied villages and troop concentrations all along the coast.

NORTHERN IRELAND EDITION

1D. **THE STARS AND STRIPES** 1D.

Daily Newspaper of U.S. Armed Forces in the European Theater of Operations

Vol. 1. No. 144. New York, N.Y.—Belfast, Northern Ireland. Wednesday, May 24, 1944.

Allies Open Big Drive at Anzio

Luftwaffe's Nests Hit By U.S. Bombers

Heavies, Fighters Sweep Europe Looking For A Scrap; Nazis Refuse

Three thousand American and Allied warplanes stretched an aerial dragnet across the skies of western Europe yesterday, hunting down the German air strength Hitler is saving for invasion day.

From the edges of the Biscay provinces eastward to the Reich itself more than 1,000 American fighters escorted some 800 Fortresses and Liberators to six of the Nazis' key air bases, to two rail yards around which central European transport hinges, and 10 other unspecified targets within western Germany.

It was the greatest fighter cover ever sent out on a single mission from Britain.

The big air fleet which pounded out from British bases at dawn's first light split into task forces across western Europe as it carried into its fourth day the newest phase of the pre-invasion offensive aimed at destroying the Luftwaffe and neutralizing the German capacity to shift men and material to meet the Allied D-Day.

1,000 Bomber RAF Raids

Nazi sirens had barely quieted after a night in which the RAF, working on the same plan of widespread attack, had dispatched more than 1,000 heavy bombers to six targets in Germany and the occupied countries.

But where the RAF had flown into occasional bitter combats with night fighters, the big fleet of United States daylight heavies and their escorts found almost no resistance, and bomber crews and fighter pilots, alike, came home with stories of Luftwaffe interceptors which refused to give battle and left their bases to be destroyed without interference.

While the heavies were bombing and some of the fighters were dropping to hedge tops to strafe transports and communications targets, the RAF sent out light daylight forces in sweeps over the Low Countries and France.

As the daylight forces sought in vain to lure the Luftwaffe to combats, the Forts and Libs made virtually unopposed runs over the railway junctions of Epinal and Chaumont, in southeastern France near the Swiss border, and over six of the main German airfields, just behind the first line coastal defences—Caen, Avord, Orleans-Bricy, Bourges, Chateau Dun and Etampes, all within a 120-mile arc south and southwest of Paris.

Planes Out Last Night

And early yesterday evening German Radio announced that "several enemy planes are over western Germany."

A small force of Ninth Air Force Marauders, escorted by Thunderbolts, joined in the day's assault by attacking military objectives in northern France without loss.

More than 1,000 Eighth and Ninth Air Force Thunderbolts, Lightnings, and long-range Mustangs flew with the bombers, and when it became obvious the Luftwaffe would not fight, went down to earth and strafed locomotives, military trains, airfields, hangars, and gun emplacements.

Only one bomber group reported

(Continued on Page 4)

The War Today

Italy— Anzio beachhead troops open big offensive; 8th Army launches all-out drive against last of Hitler line.

Pacific— Navy Department still silent on enemy-reported carrier raid on Marcus Islands, 550 miles from Jap mainland.

Air War— U.S. heavies, fighters blast key airfields and rail yards in France; Luftwaffe refuses combat.

Asia— Chinese seize Chefang to cut old Burma road, 24 miles from Burma border, as savage for Myitkyina.

Russia— Eastern front lull enters second month, with Moscow silent on operations.

Nazis Face Encirclement

Sunday Observer Map

Encirclement of Nazi units in Italy was threatened today after Allied forces in the Anzio beachhead sector (upper left) opened a two-way offensive for Rome and the main Fifth Army front while Eighth Army troops began a drive between Pontecorvo and Aquino to capture the few remaining elements of the tottering Hitler line.

Rails in France a Mess—Nazis; Blame Bombings and Saboteurs

A Nazi radio commentator said yesterday that "the French railroad system is in complete chaos" as a result of Allied bombings and attacks by saboteurs.

And another Nazi broadcaster asserted that Gen. Eisenhower had "3,250,000 troops in Southern England" ready for the invasion jump. This was the largest Axis estimate to date of the strength of Allied forces in Britain.

"The Allies have successfully pulverized into rubble whole marshalling yards, they have destroyed countless locomotives and have made scores of railway stations unusable," said Robert de Beauplan on the Paris radio.

"The rest of the destructive work, which could not be done by the Allied pilots, has been accomplished by saboteurs."

Electric System Hampered

Beauplan said saboteurs also had put out of action the entire hydro electric system in France, forcing cuts in electricity consumption. Rivers and canals no longer can be used for transport, because saboteurs have blown up locks and other facilities, he said.

"The temper of the population," Beauplan said, "is rising because no food is available and nobody can travel. Frenchmen are blaming the Germans for all this misery." What prompted Beauplan to broadcast these dour assertions was a puzzle, but he may have been attempting to stir up resentment against the Allied bombings, incite Frenchmen against the patriots and whitewash the Germans, some sources declared.

Casualty Rate Shrinks

A U.S. EVACUATION HOSPITAL, Fifth Army Front, Italy.—A survey disclosed today that less than one-half of one per cent of battle casualties reaching evacuation hospitals die—an extraordinarily low mortality rate contrasting with the 15 per cent mortality of the last war.

U.S. Blacklists Swedish Firms

38 Named; SKF Bearing Omitted Leading To Rumors of Deal

WASHINGTON (Reuter). — The State Department yesterday issued a list of 38 Swedish firms which are to be placed on the blacklist in keeping with the new U.S. foreign policy of applying pressure on firms in neutral countries which have helped the enemy through trade.

SKF, the giant Swedish ballbearing firm was not on the list, which led to the belief that current negotiations to stop bearings shipments to Germany from Sweden might have succeeded.

"It was announced last week here that Stanton Griffis, a special representative of the Foreign Economic Administration, had arrived in Stockholm to seek an agreement with SKF on control of bearing shipments.

Reliable reports later said that Griffis was authorized to spend up to $30,000,000 to buy all the SKF output to keep it from Germany.

Air Attacks Precede Smash to Break Out Of Bridgehead Area

Rome, Main Front Key Objectives Of Two-Way Thrust in Italy

NAPLES—The Allied troops massed in the Anzio area exploded a big offensive yesterday in both directions from the beachhead, in which they have been cooped up for four months.

Their long awaited push was preceded by a devastating aerial attack, in which more than 500 Flying Fortresses and Liberators joined smaller bombers in tactical raids against German troops concentrations and other targets in the area, and by an intense dawn artillery barrage.

At the same time, the Eighth Army opened an all-out assault on what remained of the Hitler line, in the Liri Valley.

Allied heaquarters, announcing the twin attacks, said that "the battle in Italy has started upon a new phase."

Lt. Gen. Mark W. Clark, commander of the Fifth Army, went to Anzio in person yesterday and set up an advanced command post in the beachhead. No official details of the day's fighting there were issued immediately.

(A Reuter dispatch direct from Anzio said that a British attack on the left sector of the beachhead, launched at 8:30 last night, led the all out drive).

Report Two Pronged Drive

The German High Command, which gave the first word of the offensive, indicate that the push was from both sides of the beachhead—northwestward toward Rome, and eastward toward other Fifth Army forces battling through the central Italy defenses some 20 miles away.

After reporting the intense Allied artillery barrage, the Nazi communique said: "With the support of battleplanes, and with strong Infantry and tank forces, the enemy then went over to the attack, southwest and west of Aprilia, on the northern flank, and in the Cisterna, Littoria (eastern) sector. Fighting is in full swing."

A correspondent at the front, quoted by German Radio, called it a "decisive offensive, and said that the battle rages like hell, under a scorching sun."

He reported that the Allies used parachutists, and had the support of warships off shore, but claimed that the German lines remained intact. Before the drive opened, Gen. Von Mackensen had reshuffled his German Tenth Army troops around the beachhead under a dense smoke screen.

Fierce Battle at Piedimonte

The Eighth Army attack, with several hundred guns firing heavy preliminary barrage, was hurled at dawn against a sector of the Hitler line between Pontecorvo and Aquino. Later in the day, Pontecorvo, southern strongpoint of what is left of the line, was wreathed in smoke.

At the northern end of the line, the Germans pushed out of Cassino sought to make a "Little Cassino" out of Piedimonte, six miles back.

Polish and British troops almost

(Continued on Page 4)

Anzio Eyewitness' Story

U.S. Doughboys Charge Out In Wake of Tanks

By Daniel DeLuce,
Associated Press Correspondent.

ANZIO BEACHHEAD — American tanks and doughboys smashed at the smoke-shrouded German line guarding the Appian Way yesterday in the beachhead's greatest attack since the Allies landed Jan. 22.

Under the eyes of Lt. Gen Mark W. Clark, thousands of veteran U.S. Infantrymen began their attack an hour after dawn, when massed artillery loosed a 30-minute barrage and light bombers rained destruction on enemy forward targets.

Supported by the fire of American warships offshore, British Tommies stormed German positions along Moletta creek in a simultaneous action on the northwestern extremity of the beachhead.

Trained specially with tanks for the last month, the Infantry swarmed across the flat, green No Man's Land in the wake of scores of Shermans, their guns blasting in German foxholes at point-blank range.

With heavy advantages in armor and artillery, the troops went into battle vowing they would fight through to Rome.

Thick in dust, a mile-long column of tanks appeared over a ridge and clanked ahead to a dispersal field close to our old outpost.

At H-hour, with tanks lumbering ahead along the white-taped tracks marked by sappers, doughboys charged. Many had their belts hung with grenades, and riflemen ran with bayonets fixed. Heavy weapon squads kept close at their heels.

This was the day of destiny for the beachhead.

Anzio Yanks Are Big, Plenty Tough—Berlin

STOCKHOLM (Reuter)—A Berlin military spokesman quoted by Svenska Dagbladet yesterday paid this compliment to American troops at Nettuno and Anzio:—

"They are mostly farmers from Texas and Alabama, broad shouldered and strong. They have good weapons and know how to use them. They can fight well, particularly in hand to hand battles.

Sacrifice of a Life for a Pal Wins Congressional Medal

NECHE, N.D.—The Congressional Medal of Honor has been awarded posthumously to Pfc Henry Gurke, a 22-year-old Marine who gave his life to save a pal on Bouganville, in the Solomon Islands.

The official citation reads: "When a Jap grenade dropped squarely into the foxhole, Gurke, mindful that his companion manned an automatic weapon of superior fire power and, therefore, could provide more effective resistance, thrust him aside and flung his own body over the missile to smother the explosion."

4 Who Fought in the Blitz Join WAC

By Arthur W. White
Stars and Stripes Staff Writer

Four American girls who fought the Luftwaffe from gunsites in London and Coventry in the days and nights of the blitz have joined the WAC in London. One-time members of the British ATS, they were among 47 American citizens in that service and the WAAF who transferred at the Army's recruiting office.

The girls, who were sworn in by W/O C. W. Williams, of San Antonio, Tex., came from practically every branch of the two services. They were either living in Britain when war was declared, or came over to join up before Pearl Harbor. Many applied for transfers more than a year ago.

The four "combat veterans" are Pvts. Beatrice Chadwick, of Massapequa, N.Y.; Ruth Winters, of Dillon, Mont.; Dorothy M. Motroni, of Bolton, England, and Clarissa M. Goldie, of Flint, Mich.

When they don their new uniforms today with the rest it will probably mark the first time that the U.S. Army has had battle-trained WACs serving in the ranks.

Miss Motroni has never seen the States. She was born here of American parents, and was registered at a U.S. consulate. Her father, Pvt. Harry Montroni, born in Chicago, joined the U.S. Army at the same office two years ago and now is in Ireland. Miss Chadwick's brother Henry followed suit seven months later and is serving with the Air Force.

Dorothy served for 16 months on a London barrage battery, working on a predictor and other instruments. She said none of the girls actually handled shells or fired the guns, they were near enough to make little difference.

Miss Goldie, a trained searchlight operator, came to England with her parents when she was 14. She joined the ATS two years ago.

Miss Winters was an aircraft spotter—a job which called for recognition in ten seconds of any one of more than 100 types of aircraft. She had to be prepared to "call" instantly any plane which the searchlights coned — say whether it was German or Allied—before the guns began firing. Her old battery was credited with six kills.

Miss Chadwick was at Coventry in that city's first big blitz, and her site was one of those which recently joined in the "lend-lease personnel exchange" with the U.S. Army.

Yesterday the new WAC company —quietly termed "The International Brigade" by recruiting sergeant Al Young, of Philadelphia—was preparing to leave for the replacement center where they will get basic training along lines followed in the U.S. Their instructor will be 1/Sgt. Virginia Rosekrans, of Chicago, first WAC top-kick in the U.S., who arrived with the ETO's first WAC contingent.

Most of the girls were looking forward to two important items — the four pairs of rayon stockings that are WAC issue, and American chow. One called "thrilling" the hot dogs they were served at the Army mess in London.

THE STARS AND STRIPES

SICILY

Vol. 1 - No. 83 - Friday, May 26, 1944 | For U. S. Armed Forces | 2 Lire

Fifth Army Meets At Anzio

Austria, France, Yugoslavia, Reich Hit Round-Clock

LONDON, May 26 — From both ends of the continent, German and satellite targets were bombed in a giant "squeeze play" by day and night.

Five hundred American Liberators and Flying Fortresses of the Mediterranean Allied Air Force pounded German-held air installations in Austria and Yugoslavia. An airplane factory was hit southwest of Vienna, and two other airfields were raided in the Fina and Neustadt vicinities.

Other German targets were blasted near Gratz, in Austria, and at Zagreb, in Yugoslavia.

In the latest attack by MAAF bombers based in Italy, rail yards in the Toulon and Lyons area were air-attacked.

From airdromes in Great Britain, American planes escorted by Spitfires attacked an airfield at Chievres in Belgium, and others smashed up railway centers at Gisors and Buchy in France.

Three railway bridges crossing the Meuse River near Liege were blown up by American raiders, together with barges northeast of the city. In the same offensive swoop, airfields at Debain and Monty-Breton were bombed.

In their third major operation in 24 hours, Marauder crews who attacked bridges reported bomb bursts on all targets. More than 100 tons of bombs were released on bridges and airfields in the morning's operations.

Night forays by the Royal Air Force accounted for good scores on railway targets in Aachen in western Germany, a motor assembly plant at Antwerp, and on military objectives in France, the RAF Bomber Command announced.

At the same time, Mosquitoes attacked Berlin. Swarms of German fighters attempted to intercept the bombers attacking Aachen, and there were running combats from the coast to the target area and back again.

Patterson Lauds Records Of ASF

WASHINGTON The U. S. Army Service Forces "have mastered the greatest supply problem that has ever faced an army in the history of the world," Under Secretary of War Robert P. Patterson asserted this week.

Reviewing the accomplishments of the ASF under the leadership of Lt Gen Brehon B. Somervell, Mr Patterson noted that 1,800,000 troops and 28,000,000 tons of supplies were carried overseas in 1943. Operating over 56,000 miles of sea and land routes, he said, the ASF is the "Army's link to the productive power of our nation."

"The invasion of Europe will call for service troops to perform hundreds of specialized missions," Mr Patterson continued. "Service troops will be needed for reconstruction work, building airfields, clearing and rebuilding the ports.

"I can assure you myself that we are producing more in 1944 than we did in 1943. Last year ASF produced 150 new weapons for our troops. More are on their way."

Lt Gen John C. Lee, Commanding General of the Services of Supply in the European Theater of Operations, on behalf of General Dwight D. Eisenhower, Supreme Allied Commander, thanked the ASF and the American people for the support given the Allied fighting forces.

YANKS SURGE FORWARD

AMERICAN TANKMEN MOW DOWN a barbed wire entanglement put up by the retreating Germans in an attempt to slow down the advance of the Yanks into Scauri.

Army, Navy Depts. Tell Demobilization Plans

WASHINGTON, May 25—The Army can be partially demobilised after the defeat of Germany but the Navy must be maintained at present strength until Japan is defeated, according to estimates submitted by the War and Navy Departments to the Senate Postwar Committee.

Under Secretary of War Robert Patterson showed the committee an estimate that 200,000 to 300,000 men can be released monthly for a year after Germany falls, although the rate depends on the shipping situation.

Red Fleet Sinks Two Nazi Vessels

MOSCOW, May 25—The Soviet communique once again reported "no material changes at the front."

Nevertheless, there was fierce local action in some sectors of the land front, and the Red Air Force was active both over the battle lines, where 17 German planes were shot out of the sky yesterday, and in the Gulf of Finland, where aircraft of the Red Banner Baltic Fleet sank two enemy transports, one of 4,000 and the other of 3,000 tons.

Northwest of Tiraspol, German tanks and infantry attacked Soviet Guards all day Wednesday, with heavy losses in men and materiel and not a single inch of territory regained. Four hundred dead Germans were counted on the field of battle as the Nazis finally withdrew at the end of the day, and 20 enemy tanks were destroyed.

The Germans have been persistently attacking in this sector for two weeks, trying to reduce or neutralize the Soviet bridgehead over the lower Dniester before it can become an important springboard in future Soviet offensive operations.

Only minor skirmishes were reported from the Galician front southeast of Stanislavow and west of Mozr.

On Tuesday, units of the Soviet Black Sea Fleet sank a German U-boat. On the same day, the enemy lost 27 tanks and nine planes on all fronts.

Aid To Turkey Halted

WASHINGTON, May 25—U. S. Secretary of State Edward R. Stettinius yesterday confirmed reports that the United States and Great Britain have halted all lead-lease shipments to Turkey. Shipments were discontinued some time ago, Mr. Stettinius declared.

Partisans Wreck Ten Troop Trains

LONDON, May 25—German communications in northwestern and western Yugoslavia received a severe jolt today when ten Nazi troop trains were wrecked by Marshal Tito's Yugoslav Partisans.

Two of the trains were destroyed on the Belgrade-Zagreb railway line; two between Trieste and Ljubljana; three on the Zagreb-Karlovac line; two near Sisak, southeast of Zagreb; and one between Sarajevo and the German-held ports of Dubrovnik and Cattaro.

In his mountain cave headquarters, meanwhile, the Yugoslav Marshall celebrated his 52nd birthday today. In Moscow, the all-Slav committee sent a message in honor of the occasion, stating that "the struggle against the Fascist invaders waged by the peoples of Yugoslavia, who are united by your efforts and under your leadership, is highly praised by all freedom-loving peoples."

In London, BBC broadcast the second and third messages of operational instructions to the people of Europe this week, asking them to gather information which might be of value to the Allied forces when the invasion starts. Like the operational broadcast last Sunday, the message was introduced by a member of the staff of the Supreme Commander of the Allied Expeditionary Force, General Dwight D. Eisenhower.

10,000 German Troops Captured In 14 Days

ALLIED FORCE HEADQUARTERS, May 25—Achieving the goal they set out to attain only 14 days ago, troops of Lt. Gen. Mark W. Clark's 5th Army have climaxed a spectacular, 60-mile lightning advance to join hands with the bridgehead forces south of Rome.

The dramatic junction of bridgehead patrols with patrols from the main 5th Army front occurred early Thursday morning a mile south of the bridgehead perimeter on the coastal highway between Terracina and Anzio.

At the same time, the new Allied bridgehead thrust, spurred by large numbers of tanks, continued to force the enemy back around the entire perimeter, cutting the road north of Cisterna and taking more than 1,000 prisoners.

BBC announced early today that the bridgehead forces had fought their way into Cisterna.

Pouring through the breech they forced in the Hitler Line on Tuesday, Canadians of the 8th Army followed a tremendous artillery barrage to overrun enemy defenses and sweep up the Liri Valley to reach the Melfa River, 13 miles beyond Cassino.

The swift Canadian advance forced the Germans to yield Pontecorvo, key defense point of the Hitler Line, along with 500 prisoners.

THREE-PRONGED DRIVE

Prisoners taken since the Allied assault was launched the night of May 11, now total in excess of 10,000 and are equal in number to a full German streamlined division.

The drive from the main 5th Army front, meanwhile, continued to surge ahead in three main directions. To the northwest, 5th Army troops advanced to capture the mountain village of Roccasecca de Volsci, which overlooks the Amaseno Valley, across the river from Priverno.

American troops, fighting side by side with the French of General Alphonse Juin, have occupied Monte Portino and proceeded on

(Continued on Page 8)

Tor River Forded In Guinea Drive

ALLIED SOUTH PACIFIC HEADQUARTERS, May 25—American forces who recently landed on the coast of Dutch New Guinea opposite Wadke Island, have pushed forward five miles and have reached an important Japanese airfield.

The landing was effected while other U. S. amphibious forces overran Wadke Island, now completely in Allied hands and already an important base for present and future operations in the New Guinea area.

The Tor river, which had to be crossed in several places before a major push inland could begin, is several hundred meters wide, with swampy banks, and the crossings had to be made with strong artillery support in the face of determined enemy resistance and even counter-attacks.

Farther down the coast, in the Wewak area, American forces advancing from Aitape have been engaged in sharp patrol clashes with Japanese units, while various points along the coast were bombed from the air and shelled from the sea.

Heavy bombers of the central Pacific command under Admiral Chester Nimitz have again raided Ponape, east of Truk, and targets in the Kurile Archipelago.

American submarines in the Pacific have sunk 15 more Japanese ships, including one destroyer and four transports, according to a special Navy communique issued in Washington.

Bombers of the Southwest Pacific command kept up their determined offensive against widely scattered targets in enemy-held territory. Manokwari, in the western corner of Dutch New Guinea, and the nearby Schouten Islands bore the brunt of the attacks.

Plane Contract Ended

WASHINGTON—On the grounds that fighter plane losses in combat have been far less than anticipated, the Navy has announced the termination of a contract with the Brewster Aircraft Corp. for the production of Corsair fighter planes.

Vaunted Hun Superiority Belied By Italy Action

ALLIED FORCE HEADQUARTERS, May 25—Ruthless training camp commandos fleeing in terror at the first sound of actual gunfire; hundreds of Teller mines being rushed to the front, useless because their igniters were forgotten; hasty rechristenings of defense lines to avoid serious losses of prestige—as the lines fall before oncharging Allied troops.

These are some of the stories that belie Nazi military superiority as gleaned from the more than 10,000 prisoners taken since the Allied 5th and 8th Armies started their offensive which, in 14 days, smashed all of the Gustav Line and half of the once-called Adolf Hitler Line.

What had been known for months as the Hitler Line became, with the first signs of rupture, the Doro Line, named for a mountain now more than ten miles behind the present front. The Adolf Hitler Line, it seems, has now been assigned to some other defense positions still to be discovered farther north, which the official AFHQ commentator said, is a device "which can be used again and again until the Hitler Line coincides with the 'Unter Den Linden'."

The snafu of the Teller mines was attributed to an Austrian engineering outfit which had been rushed to the front to try to stop the Allied thrust on the Pignataro-Pontecorvo Road. Many of the mines were laid hurriedly, and quickly spotted by Allied sappers.

(Continued on Page 8)

Two U-Boats Sunk In Convoy Attack

LONDON, May 25—One of the two largest Russian-bound convoys ever dispatched from Britain has delivered 250,000 tons of vital war material to the Soviet Union without losing a single merchant ship despite a dramatic running battle which continued for 12 days in mountainous seas, blinding rainstorms and 11 below zero temperatures.

Royal Navy destroyers and carrier-borne Swordfish and Wildcats sank two Nazi U-boats, probably destroyed two more and damaged several others during the engagement. In addition, two of 13 German aircraft were damaged and the others driven off, the Admiralty announcement this weekend said.

The 1,920-ton British destroyer Mahratta, whose loss had been announced earlier, was the lone Allied casualty and because of the pitch darkness and raging seas only "a handful" of survivors were rescued. No officers survived.

British Prisoners Flee During RAF Bombing

LAUSANNE—A dispatch to the Lausanne Gazette over the weekend reported the escape from a Nazi prison camp near Epinal in western France of several thousand British prisoners during the confusion of an RAF raid. Groups of these prisoners, most of them Indian troops, have been crossing the Swiss frontier for several days.

THE STARS AND STRIPES
TUNIS

One Franc

Vol. 1—No. 48 — Friday, 2 June 1944

Newspaper for U. S. Armed Forces in Tunisia

Au Revoir

It had to come sometime, and this is it.

With this issue, the staff which has prepared and brought you your Tunisian edition of The Stars and Stripes for the past six months strikes its tents, packs its equipment and leaves Tunisia for other ports. Beginning Monday the Algiers edition of the paper will be distributed daily throughout the area in place of the current Tunisian edition.

It's not because it's the thing to do that we say we're sorry to leave. We regret going because of the splendid hospitality shown us by the many families whom we are happy to number among our friends. Despite the thrill of preparing for other missions, it is with real reluctance that we say goodbye to tree-lined Jules Ferry, to La Marsa's stretch of white beach, to Sunday afternoons' promenades on Avenue de Paris.

Sure we've had our troubles: Linotype machines and presses regarded as hopeless derelicts after six months of German abuse; news wires that went temperamental at press time; muddy winter roads that almost dared us to d liver the papers to the widely scattered American units

Yet, whatever our handicaps, we could never forget that our problems were picayune compared with those confronting our fellows risking everything at Anzio, Cassino and in the South Pacific Cajoling a prima donna linotype machine for a 16-hour stretch is no fun, but it still isn't in the same class with lying in a front-line foxhole not knowing which screaming-meemie has your number. Most of us have gone through that and know.

And we also know that whatever our problems, they might have been insurmountable had it not been for the unstinting assistance of those in a position to lend a helping hand. To the personnel of the "Depeche Tunisienne," printers of The Stars and Stripes, we extend our hearty thanks for their full cooperation in helping us solve our manifold technical problems. To EBS Special Service we toss a verbal bouquet for its invaluable assistance in distributing The Stars and Stripes.

Above all, now that we are pulling out and cannot be suspected of "bucking," we thank the EBS commanding officer for his complete understanding, cooperation and assistance. Never have we encountered such a profound interest in the welfare of enlisted men, extended to the full limits permitted by military considerations. Never, to our knowledge, has any idea designed to improve the status of enlisted men in this base section failed to receive a sympathetic hearing by the commanding officer. That is the kind of military leadership we like and we take this opportunity to pay it our respects. We trust it will always be our good fortune to be associated with commanders motivated by the same principle.

And so, despite our knowledge that closing this chapter of The Stars and Stripes represents another step toward the homeland to which we all yearn to return, we leave Tunisia with a heavy heart. To our military friends, we express the hope that we meet again — in Rome, Berlin or Tokyo. And to the civilians who have shown us a brand of hospitality we didn't suspect even existed in North Africa, we say, "Thanks," "Au revoir," and, as the Arabs put it, "Filamen."

THE STAFF

Rare Historical Treasure Turned up Here by Nazis

By W. I. BERMAN
(Stars and Stripes Staff Writer)

Rarely have the Germans, in their sacking of the art treasures of two continents, been credited with contributing to civilization's store of culture. And yet, ironically, the last Nazis to hold out against the conquering Allies in Tunisia last year disclosed to the world a wealth of historical relics the full extent of which is only just now being explored by La Direction des Antiquities et Arts de Tunisie.

all happened when the final K a:i hold-outs, driven to the furthest extremity of Cape Bon after the liberation of Tunis, were seeking desperately some refuge from the relentless Allied aerial strafing. The plains of Dameus Gattous were covered with the massed Axis troops. The rocky terrain offered little protection from the pursuit ships that droned overhead, then swooped over the pride of the Afrika Corps, tatooing a staccato of riccocheting bullets against the rocks and the beaten, desperate troops.

Then some smart Nazi, it has been learned, noticed an ostensibly man-made cut-back under an overhanging rock. He called his "Kameraden" and together they dug under the rock until they came to a thick rectangular slab standing upright, very much in the position of a door. They pried behind it, toppled it forward and walked over it into the chamber it had concealed.

The room was obviously a tomb. Yellowish skeletons lay along both sidewalls and between them lay dusty pieces of pottery, covered with the sands

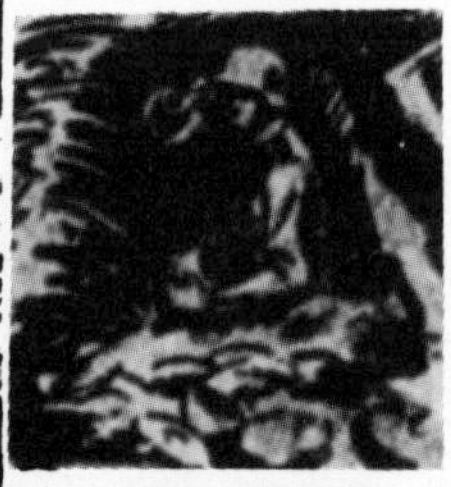

. . . *Tombs were foxholes*

of countless centuries It is doubtful that the Nazis, in the stress of their plight, pondered the historical significance of their discovery; they knew only that they had found a safe refuge from the strafing and that was sufficient. They tossed the skeletons and relics out of the mouth of the tomb and installed themselves in their shelter.

But the chamber could hold

(Continued on Page 4)

Bombers Smash At Anti-Invasion Transport Lines

Marauders Pound Targets on Coast

LONDON, June 1—About 1,000 RAF bombers last night maintained the systematic destruction of Nazi anti-invasion transportation and communications by plastering three important rail lines in northwestern France.

Targets for the British bombers, announced today by the Air Ministry, were Tergnier, Trappes and Saumur. First reports indicated the bombing was well concentrated, and raiders of Trappes said a violent explosion midway in the attack literally wiped out the target markers dropped by pathfinders.

The night attack followed an unopposed raid by Fortresses and Liberators of the 8th AAF on railway targets at Haam, Osnabruck, Schwerte and Sceat, in Germany. Nazi fighters stayed well away from the heavies with their 1,200 escorting Lightnings, Thunderbolts and Mustangs, and the day's loss was one bomber and four fighters.

One force of P-47s, returning from the target, encountered a flight of 30 FW-190s and reported five shot down. Other fighters hitting at airfields and rail targets shot up 35 locomotives and a number of planes on the ground. An additional target for heavy bombers during the day was the Luxu l airdrome, near the French city of Mulhouse.

Kimmel Trial to Be Extended to Dec. 7

WASHINGTON, June 1 — A Senate judiciary sub-committee voted yesterday to extend the time from court martial proceeding against Rear Admiral Husband E. Kimmel and Maj. Gen. Walter C. Short to Dec. 7, 1944—exactly three years after the debacle at Pearl Harbor for which they were criticized.

On Monday, Admiral Kimmel publicly demanded a free, open and publ c trial at the earliest possible date on charges he was derelict in his duty.

The sub-committee's action came shortly after Secretary of the Navy James V Forrestal expressed opposition to court martial now for Admiral Kimmel "It seems quite clear," he said, "that during this war and certainly its immediate phase, I personally would not be in favor of conducting such a trial"

Attorney Goes Free In Doctor's Slaying

WASHINGTON, June 1 — Robert I Miller, 67 year-old attorney, without a show of emotion gravely thanked the jury yesterday as they declared him not guilty in the "love triangle" slaying of Dr John K Lind, noted psychiatrist.

The jury of 11 men and one woman deliberated little more than an hour before adjudging the lawyer blameless for shooting Dr. Lind as he sat in a parked car with Miller's wife in downtown Washington last February.

Rome in Sight Of Allied Lines

'Marryin' Lady' Nabs 15 Hubbies

DETROIT, June 1—Titian-haired Mrs. Marion Stankowich, 35-year-old dress designer who admits marrying 15 men since 1926, today faced charges of fraudulently receiving dependency allotments following her arrest by the Federal Bureau of Investigation.

While G-Men seized her only because she has received $1,500 in allotments from three soldier husbands, Mrs. Stankowich admitted marrying at least 12 other men in Michigan, Indiana, Texas, Colorado, New York, Ohio, Arizona and Florida.

"I guess it was 15 but I think three of them divorced me," Mrs. Stankowich was quoted as saying. She added she wasn't quite sure how many husbands she had married.

German Ultimatum To Bulgaria Scores

NEW YORK, June 1—The Bulgarian Regency Council has prepared an affirmative answer to the German ultimatum that the nation either break off diplomatic relations with the USSR or face occupation, the New York Times reported from Berne, Switzerland, today.

The Times said its information was the first direct word received from Sofia since communications with the outside world were severed last Friday. From Stockholm, it was reported that the five point ultimatum to which Bulgaria has decided to bow called for:

(1) Formation of a "pro-Bulgarian"—that is, pro-Nazi—cabinet; (2) Rupture diplomatic relations with the USSR, Bulgaria's Slavic neighbor and long-time "big brother nation; (3) Increase industrial co-operation with Germany; (4) The Bulgarian High Command and the Bulgarian Army must be placed under the German High Command to fight against the Allies, and (5) Bulgarian workmen will be mob lized to work for the German Todt organization in Bulgaria The number will be set later

Stars & Stripes Sales Continue

Units will communicate with The Stars and Stripes offices in Bizerte or Tunis for information on points of distribution commencing tomorrow, Saturday, 3 June 1944. Telephones: Bizerte, 178, Tunis, 0305.

De Valera Re-Elected

DUBLIN, June 1 — Prime Minister Eamon De Valera and at least six of his cabinet members retained their seats in the Dail (Eire parliament) as a result of the general election Tuesday, it was indicated yesterday as the ballot counting got under way.

Wedges Cut In Defenses

ALLIED FORCE HEADQUARTERS, June 1—Allied troops today were within sight of Rome from positions on the slopes of the Coli Laziali mountain mass and the vicinity of Lake Di Nemi where they had driven deep wedges into the enemy's defenses.

Today's official reports credited the 5th Army's infantry with consolidated advances of up to 3,000 yards both northeast and northwest of Velletri, the center of the Valmontone-to-the-sea defense perimeter where the Krauts are making their final stand in a losing fight. Despite the fact that their comrades were in full retreat from all positions east of Valmontone, the Germans were holding tenaciously to their final line against steady pressure from the ground, sea and air.

Yesterday's Allied achievements were more important than spectacular. Two American naval vessels made successful bombardments of Nazi coastal positions against which British troops were driving relentlessly north of Ardea and far across the Moletta River. As in the greater part in the Italian campaign, the right flank terrain favored the Germans who were doing their utmost to keep Highway 6 open between their front lines and Rome.

Allied pressure on the flank, the sea bombardment, and swarms of Allied planes smacking at every German-held spot between the frontlines and Rome

(Continued on Page 4)

Soviets Crush Nazi Attacks Near Jassy

LONDON, June 1 — While massed Luftwaffe squadrons roared overhead to blast the way, German tank spearheads supported by infantry tommy gunners pounded relentlessly against Soviet lines north of Jassy, Rumania, yesterday only to be thrown back without gain after suffering heavy losses.

The German southern offensive, credited Tuesday with driving "an insignificant wedge" into the Red Army positions, failed to score any additional gains. Furious battles were continuing today. Moscow commentators predicted the next 24 hours would show the full scope and objective of the German onslaught

Marshal Ivan Konev's Second Ukrainian Army disabled or destroyed 23 German tanks and shot down 50 enemy planes in stemming the assault yesterday. Tuesday the Germans lost another 95 tanks and 106 planes around Jassy out of 97 tanks and 142 planes destroyed on the entire eastern front.

The midnight supplement to last night's Soviet communique said that "Soviet infantrymen, artillerymen and tank troops, by powerful fire and counter-blows, successfully repelled all Hitlerite attacks. Thousands of enemy dead and a great number of disabled or burned-out German tanks, self-propelled guns and armored carriers were left on the battlefield."

NORTHERN IRELAND EDITION

1d. THE STARS AND STRIPES 1d.

Daily Newspaper of U.S. Armed Forces in the European Theater of Operations

Vol. 1. No. 153. New York, N.Y.—Belfast, Northern Ireland. Saturday, June 3, 1944.

Yanks Fly to U.S. Bases in Russia

U.S. Troops Take 2 Key Positions

Tank Thrust Block Nazis' Escape Line

Ferentino Falls to Eighth Army; Foe Fights Hard For Mountain Route

NAPLES—Twin German fortress towns constituting the strongest of the last barriers remaining on the two main roads to Rome— Valmontone on Highway 6 and Velletri on Highway 7—fell to American fighting men yesterday.

And while the Yank infantry and Sherman tanks finally severed at Valmontone the main escape route of the German Tenth Army below there the Allied Eighth Army drew its trap tighter around those Nazi forces by taking Ferentino, just 18 miles from Valmontone, on Highway 6 (the Via Casilina).

The fall of the Valmontone and Velletri bastions after days of bitter fighting—the most significant stride toward Rome since the ex-beachhead forces went into action—was announced in a special communique, which also identified the American tank troops with the Fifth Army as the U.S. First Armored Division, commanded by Maj. Gen. Ernest N. Harmon.

Goering Division Beaten

Even before the investment of Valmontone, Allied artillery had rendered the highway there virtually impassable for the German forces retreating from the south, but Field Marshal Albert Kesselring rushed the crack Hermann Goering Division into the line there in a futile attempt to hold it at all costs.

The Valmontone-Velletri keypoints became virtually untenable for the German defenders, however, when Artena, two and a half miles south of Valmontone, and Lariano, roughly mid-way on the road linking the two "V" towns, were taken.

While the Eighth Army pounded up both sides of Highway 6 to capture Ferentino, the last important town before Valmontone, the French colonials of the Fifth Army advanced westward in that direction through the Lepini mountains.

These forces took Morolo, about five miles south of the Highway. Thus the Germans were left in a box only five miles deep south of the road.

Yanks Enter Velletri

On the "beachhead" front, Yank infantrymen entered Velletri, a bastion of the Rome defense line, late Thursday and fought at close quarters to clean out mobile mortar batteries, stone pillboxes and snipers holding out from back yards, wine cellars and attics.

The Americans previously had the town encircled on either side. An American armored thrust on the coastal side beyond the Anzio-Rome road advanced yesterday seven miles beyond Velletri.

Light and fighter bombers blitzed Nazi troops' bivouac areas, motor pools and gun positions in the battle zone along with rail lines and bridges in central Italy, while mediums attacked troop concentrations, roads, and bridges in the battle zone and to the north of Rome.

The War Today

Italy—Americans capture Valmontone and Velletri, principal remaining German strongpoints on Highways 6 and 7 to Rome, and bastions of whole defense belt, after bitter fighting.

Air War—Nearly 1,000 British-based Fortresses and Liberators pound Pas de Calais; while Italian-based U.S. heavies raid five rail yards in eastern Hungary and Transylvania.

Russia—Soviet tanks and infantry open counter-attack north of Jassy after three days' fighting; drive enemy out of positions with "terrific" losses; Germans report other Red attacks in Carpathian foothills and Pripet Marshes.

Asia—Chinese report 250,000 Jap troops massed in Hankow area of southeastern China.

Worst Mississippi Flood at St. Louis

Keystone Photo

View of the highway from the east approach of Rocks Bridge, in the St. Louis flood belt, after the levee at Chouteau Island broke early in May, loosing Mississippi waters upon thousands of acres. It was called the worst Mississippi flood in 100 years, destroying millions of dollars worth of crops and washing out many homes.

Keep Vatican Clear of Battle 'At Any Cost,' Pope Pleads

With the Italian front a dozen miles from Rome, Pope Pius XII, broadcast an urgent appeal yesterday that the Holy City might "in any case and at any cost be spared from becoming a field of battle."

Calling anew for a "reasonable peace," he spoke out against war aims of "total victory or complete destruction," which, he said "compel the peoples to resist at all costs, prolonging the war and threatening economics and social afflictions in the post-war period."

"Whoever should dare to lift his hand against Rome would be guilty of matricide, and would bear a grave responsibility," he said.

Expressing his hope for a peace with justice and clemency, the Pope declared:

"It is certainly significant that while the tools of military destruction have reached a stage of power never known before, and the world is on the eve of still more dramatic and, as some believe, decisive events, discussions about fundamental laws and the particular terms of the future peace attract more and more people, who show an ever-increasing interest in the matter.

"However, against these voices of wisdom and moderation there are also others with open demands for vengeance.

"In this way, the fear has arisen among many that there was no alternative other than complete victory, or complete annihilation. Once this dreadful dilemma penetrates the minds of the people it acts as a stimulant for the prolongation of the war, even with those who by an inner impulse toward realistic considerations would be inclined to a reasonable peace."

June 15 'Infantry Day'

WASHINGTON (Reuter)—June 15 has been officially set aside as "Infantry Day" in tribute to the American footslogger. Special ceremonies will mark the day in Army installations throughout the U.S.

U.S. Toll Light In S.W. Pacific

Deaths Less Than at Anzio Envoy Reports; New Action in Solomons

ALLIED HQ., NEW GUINEA — Fewer U.S. troops have been killed in action in the entire Southwest Pacific operations than on the Anzio bridgehead in Italy, Nelson T. Johnson, U.S. Minister to Australia, reported today.

Discussing light combat losses in New Guinea, Johnson said that wherever possible Gen. Douglas MacArthur had by-passed rather than attacked enemy strength.

Meanwhile, Gen. MacArthur's communique announced that reinforcements were being poured into Biak Island, off northwest Dutch New Guinea, to support the drive for three vital airfields within bomber range of the Philippines.

In the northern Solomons, Americans went into action for the first time in several months, amphibious forces moving seven miles to the southeast of the Torokina River in Bougainville's Empress Augusta bay area. It was the first advance beyond the bay's bridgehead since it was established last November.

RAAF Catalinas from Australia completely smashed a Jap air strip on the Dutch East Indies island of Amboina. Liberators of the Seventh Air Force hit Guam, Truk, Wake and Ponape, while other bombers struck Saipan, in the Marianas, and Woleai and Alet, 300 miles west of Truk.

Nazis Reported Building Invasion Wall in the South

The Germans are rushing to completion a line of anti-invasion blockhouses stretching around the Gulf of Genoa from Spezia to Toulon, a correspondent of the Zurich newspaper Neue Zurcher Zeitung, quoted by Reuter, reported yesterday.

"Apart from the blockhouses built into the ground and the concrete walls," he said "the Todt organisation is also building 'nests' in the coastal rocks, tank traps and—between the ruins of bombed coastal villages — barbed-wire defences and tank obstacles."

24 Hours Near Enemy Coast, Fort Crew Rescued From Sea

A FORTRESS BASE — What it's like to float around in the North Sea for more than 24 hours within a few miles of occupied Europe was told yesterday by members of the crew of the Flying Fort piloted by Lt. J. P. Rogers, of Wilson, N.C.

Coming back from a recent raid on Berlin, Rogers was forced to ditch his ship after two of its motors were knocked out by enemy fighter action. Although one gunner was injured during the landing, the entire crew managed to scramble into dinghies.

"We could hear a plane (from the British Air/Sea Rescue service) coming after us, but it got dark, and we couldn't raise contact," S/Sgt. Russell E. Gately, Jr., of Needham, Mass., a gunner, said. "So we sat waiting all night, hoping we wouldn't drift on to enemy shore."

The next afternoon one of Coastal Commands's lifeboat carriers appeared overhead and dropped a craft complete with motors. T/Sgt. Dick Kendall, of Virginia, knew something about operating such boats, and with Gately's help got it started.

"We set course for home," Pilot Rogers said. "However, we ran into heavy seas, and had to keep baling out water. We took turns during the night steering for home."

Three days later a high-speed British launch, 100 miles from its home base, picked up the Fort members. Three Thunderbolts, circling overhead, escorted the launch to a British dock.

Bombers, Apparently From So. Italy, Land After Shuttle Attack

USAAF, Soviet Fighters Escort Planes To New Fields

U.S. Army Air Force long-range bombers, apparently flying from Italy, landed at American bases "somewhere in Russia" yesterday to complete the first leg of a history-making Allied shuttle bombing operation over eastern Europe, the War Department announced in Washington last night.

USAAF P51 Mustangs and Russian Yak fighters escorted the "heavies" to their bases after they had dropped their bombs.

The announcement, made simultaneously in Washington and Moscow, came a few hours after Allied Headquarters in Italy had reported that between 500 and 750 escorted heavy bombers had attacked Balkan targets, including Cluj, the Transylvanian capital, which lies 150 miles from the Soviet-German battlefield north of Jassy.

From Allied bases in southern Italy to the area behind the Soviet front line in the south is roughly 900 miles.

American and Soviet personnel, who had worked day and night for several months to prepare bases—under an agreement reached at Moscow last October—serviced the aircraft with fuel and ammunition for another call on the Axis when they return to their home bases.

Number of Bases Ready

It was revealed that a number of American air bases had been established in the Soviet Union, and that all were ready for the servicing, refuelling, re-ammunitioning and turning around of the U.S. bombers for a return visit to Axis targets across many hundreds of miles of enemy territory.

Photographic reconnaissance, it was reported, had been made over the various possible shuttle-bombing routes for some time, and that the first mission of this type was carried out by Col. Paul Cullen. Col. Elliott Roosevelt, second son of the President, who is assigned to an aerial reconnaissance unit, recently was seen in Moscow.

Bases Cut Flying Distance, U.S. General Says

MOSCOW—A statement issued today under the authority of Maj. Gen. John R. Deane, chief of the U.S. military mission in Moscow, stressed that the operations carried out yesterday marked the first large-scale physical collaboration of air forces from Britain and Russia.

"Henceforth," the statement said, "a new menace hangs over Germany and her vassals—shuttle bombing by which American aircraft, after bombing their targets, can fly east or west to prepared bases. This cuts down enormously the total flying distances involved when certain targets in eastern Germany or eastern Europe are attacked."

Staffs In 'Direct Contact'

MOSCOW—Moscow radio said last night that "direct contact between the respective staffs" of the Allied Air Forces had been established "to insure that the efforts of the combined air forces shall be concentrated on the most important objectives."

Calais Sector Gets Its Biggest Attack of War

1,000 Heavies From U.K. Rip Coast; Force From Italy Hits Hungary

Huge fleets of American heavy bombers yesterday thundered over France's channel coast to give the Pas de Calais its heaviest single pounding of the war while at the same time Italy-based U.S. heavies raided railyards in eastern Hungary and Transylvania.

After a night in which the RAF struck at targets from Denmark to the Balkans, a force approaching 1,750 USSTAF bombers launched another north-south offensive to hit the so-called invasion coast of France and five Balkan rail junctions.

Possible 3,000 tons of explosives were heaped on Germany's west wall defenses by nearly 1,000 Britain-based Forts and Libs. Not one enemy fighter was encountered as the heavies, shepherded by about 500 Eighth Air Force P47s, P38s and P51s, dropped their bombs through cloud. Not one aircraft was lost.

The Return To Calais

The raid marked the return of U.S. heavies in strength to the battered Pas de Calais after nearly two weeks in which major blows from Britain had been directed at strategic targets deep behind the coast and in the Reich itself.

Almost simultaneously in another sharp attack on German rail lines in the Balkans MAAF U.S. heavy bombers plastered railroad yards at Miskolcz, 100 miles northeast of Budapest; Szolnok, 55 miles southwest of Budapest; Szeged, five miles from the junction of the Jugoslav, Rumanian and Hungarian borders, and Telaj and Simerio in Transylvania.

For the Szolnok area through which the Germans funnel supplies to their eastern front, it was the second attack in hours by Mediterranean-based aircraft.

Shortly after midnight yesterday a small force of RAF bombers swept over Saumur in the second attack in as many nights on the French rail center, 150 miles southwest of Paris.

Meanwhile, USSTAF headquarters announced that American heavy bombers had rained more than 63,000 tons of bombs on German occupied Europe in May.

In May, the USSTAF spread its 63,000 tons of bombs from battered Pas de Calais to the Balkans. Operating from bases in Britain and Italy, the American bombers made a total of 30,106 sorties.

FDR Offers a New Name For It: The Tyrants' War

WASHINGTON — The "Tyrants' War" is what President Roosevelt proposes to call this World War II.

The President, who asked some time ago for suggestions as to a name for the war, said the "Tyrants' War" was one title that had been sent in and that he liked it very much.

THE STARS AND STRIPES

Vol. 1 - No. 1 PUBLISHED IN ROME Rome, June 5 1944

WE'RE IN ROME

Old Order Changeth

ROMANS CHEERED and laughed today at the words of a new balcony speaker in the Piazza Venezia. He is Sgt. John A. Vita (with arm upraised) and he promised caramelli instead of castor oil.
(Photo by Pfc. Martin Harris)

NO LETUP AS ALLIED FORCES CHASE FLEEING GERMANS NORTHWARD

By Sgt. PAUL GREEN (Stars and Stripes Staff Writer)

ROME, June 5 — The kraut was fleeing today along the roads that lead north from Rome as 5th Army troops poured through the Italian capital in relentless pursuit of the decimated enemy forces. Exactly 24 days after the first guns boomed from Minturno to Cassino, the Eternal City was completely in Allied hands

There was no letup in the crushing offensive as American, British and French soldiers — taking in stride their magnificent victory in liberating Rome — kept on going with a good chance of cutting off and annihilating many thousands of Jerries before they could reach some stable line of defense.

The world rang with praises of the campaign that has been climaxed with the capture of the city. Rome has fallen many times to military conquerors, but this is the first time that it has been taken from the south. That was something for the GI to talk about at his next bull session.

But GI Joe was a little too tired today to realize the full importance of what he had done. It's been a tough fight all along the line, and the dogfaces are plenty weary. You

walked through the streets of Rome. You could feel it from the tired nods as they answered the cheering of the people.

The GIs who passed through the cito today could relax their trigger fingers for a while. The city was theirs — completely. It was especially the pretty signorinas who caught the eye of appreciative Yanks. Far-seeing ones scrawled down a few addresses for reference later on when they come back to Rome on leave. Others took a little time out to get a quick look at the famous ruins.

But to most of them, Rome is just another stop — although, a main one — on the road that leads home. The GI who saw Africa last year or Sicily has marched on a long trail since then. Others have joined him. The trek that led through the toughest, most gruelling days o fthe Mediterranean campaign opened up for its last chapter at Salerno

(Continued on page 4)

VITA! VITA! REPLACES OLD CHEER FOR DUCE

By Sgt. GEORGE DORSEY
(Stars and Stripes Staff Writer)

PIAZZA VENEZIA, Rome, June 5 — The crowds gathered in the Piazza Venezia again and stood cheering wildly under Mussolini's historic balcony, but the speech they heard today was verry little like the old days.

Sgt. John A. Vita, a 27-year-old Italian-American from Port Chester, N. Y., leaned over the marble railing of the balcony and to a sea of friendly ci vilian faces promised death to Mussolini, to the tedeschi and to the Fascisti.

Sgt. Vita, who landed with the American infantry at Anzio and came all the way with them, through Cisterna, through Velletri and Valmontone to Rome, knew his speachmaking and paused after each significant phrase while the people applauded enthhusiastically. He parodied a Mussolini speech, starting out with «Vincere, Vincere, Vincere» (conquer, conquer, conquer) then added, «Not for Mussolini, the Fascists or the Germans, but for the Allies».

«Instead of castor oil», he told his eager listeners, «we bring you caramelli and food».

The bearded American sergeant made his historic speech at 0730 hours of this first morning that the Allies have spent in the Italian capital. Despite the earliness of the hour, the Itafians had risen in strength to greet the Americans and the audience ran into thousands.

Sgt. Vita's speech was the result of a promise made to his mother in Port Chester eight months ago. «We're going to Rome», he said, «and the first thing I'm going to do when I get there, Mom, is make a speech from Mussolini's balcony». His mother was born in Reggio Calabria.

over there maps and conferred while scores of photographers and reporters milled about, recording the historic moment.

General Clark then paid a brief tribute to "the men and women of the 5th Army who made the supreme sacrifice so that we could keep going to Rome and begone".

He said that "this great day for the 5th Army" was made possible by the combined efforts of "French, British and American troops". "I also want to mention the support given the advance by General Eeaker's Air Force".

General Clark said that the French were fighting the Germans in the north, but, added that the German forces which had been defeated in the battle for Rome and retreated so fast that contact was lost. Five minutes later, General Juin, French Corps commander, who had been delayed, arrived to take part in the dramatic meeting.

General Clark said that the 5th Army had smashed two German Armies in the drive from the south and the attack launched from the beachhead. "I would estimate conservatively that at least 20,000 prisoners have been captured", he stated.

Neither he nor his two American corps commanders could name the number of Germans kil-

(Continued on page 4)

Generals Plan Further Drives

(By a Staff Correspondent)

ROME, June 5. — Lt. Gen. Mark W. Clark arrived at the Campidoglio, Rome's city hall, at 1000 hours today to confer with his corps commanders, Major Generals Geoffrey Keyes, Lucien K. Truscott and General Alphonse Juin, to coordinate the further advance against the enemy.

At the foot of the steps of the ornate bulding, beneath Allied flags fluttering lazily in the spring breeze, the generals pored

IL MESSAGGERO PRESS TURNS OUT ROME EXTRA

This first number of *The Stars and Stripes* to be published in Rome has been made possible through the pressmen of *Il Messaggero*, who have turned to on their linotypes and pressed with as much enthusiasm in getting this first edition of the press as the people of Rome have in welcoming the 5th Army volumos. Besides few of them understand a word fox of English. They are proud and so are we. Other numbers will follow. Welcome to Rome.

Rome Untouched By Battle Marks

ROME, June 5 — For the people of the first Axis capital to be liberated by the Allies, the coming of the Yanks opened a new era of freedom. Wildly enthusiastic men women, kids gavethe Roman welcome in the Broadway ticker-tape tradition.

The city it self ws almost untouched by marks of battle. Only in the suburbs did the rubbled homes and pock-marked roads tell of the rear-guard action fought by the Germans y[illegible]rday. The rest of the city seemed almost like Naples except for the ancient ruins that give Rome its oPmpeii-like atmosphere.

It was hard to find out exactly how many Romans were there to greet the Americans Estimates of the capital's war-swollen population ranged from two and a half to three million Rome usually has only somewhat more than one million and the rest were all refugees from other parts of Italy.

Naturally, rooms were at a premium. Civilians told of sleeping

(Continued on Page 4)

Tanks Push On Beyond Tiber

WITH THE 5th ARMY, June 5 — Key positions facing the 5th Army south of Rome along the Appian way have fallen. And at dawn this morning the armored units had succeeded in sweeping across the Tiber River bridge network to secure a bridghead of several miles to the west and and northwest of the city.

In the wake of this part of the Fifth Army advance lie the former German strongpoints of Lanuvio, Genzano and the town cluster around Albano. Infantry soldiers who had for three days been unable to get into Lanuvio finally did so, two days ago, making a mighty assault in the nick of time. For Jerry had started to run.

This smash presaged the southern drive on Rome itself. With infantry sweeping the hills, all day yesterday, armored forces pierced along the road west of Lanuvio to the Appian way at Albano. Signs of German retreat were everywhere, although it was not as a mad a scramble as the big German defeat at Cori shortly after the bachhead offensive began.

At shell pocked Albano a man and a little boy claimed the Germans had left there only two hours earlier. The forward elements of the tank caravan met some of the retreating German tanks just outside the city and were held up for a while.

Jerry planted mines, machine gun nests and small clusters of tanks everywhere along the roads and in the hills before the advancing tanks and foot soldiers. But these were chiefly harrassing actions with no thought of real defensive intentions.

(Continued on page 4)

EVERYONE'S MIXED UP BUT HAPPY HERE TODAY

By Sgt WADE JONES
(Stars and Stripes Corraspondent)

ROME, June 5 — Ro[illegible] at noon today is a city of confusion; of parades, of bright sunshine; of reunions and victory.

[illegible] 4 Salvatore Curiale, Newburgh, N. Y., who swears by all that's holy that he [illegible] into Ro[illegible] proper 3:30 p. m. yesterday in the first American party to enter the city has already lost his outfit

«I was radio operator for the colonel commanding my regiment and since we were in touch with everybody else coming into the city, I know we were first. But then something happened and nou where the hell am I? I got separated and now I'm lost. Ain't these Roman gals lovely?». They sure as [illegible] are, Curiale they sure as hell are.

Rome is a big city and there are a lot of other fellows in Curiale's shape. They've lost their outfits and they stand on street corners and hail you and ask if you know where such and such an outfit is.

Rome today is a city of parades. Every time a civilian here sees a group of American vehicles moving along a [illegible]et he begins to wave and cheer and try to climb on vehicles.

The Italians make signs of cutting the throat with their finger and the Americans say, «That's right, cut his old throat. Cut old Musso's throat».

Rome today is a city of reunions. Reynolds Packard, who was head of the Rome bureau of the United Press before the war was once jailed here for writing what he thought, arrives before the 5th Army Public Relations building in a jeep with his wife, Eleanor

Italian civilians who remember the Packards, jump up in the back seat of the jeep and kiss the Packards and yell «Viva Packard», with the accent on the last syllable

Packard, an old sentimentalist, grabs them around the neck and hugs them while his wife tries to maintain a little dignity. It's quite a scene and a lot of people fall out of the jeep.

At the Prison of Via Tasso, where the Germans kept many other political prisoners, two Yugoslavs met today. One of them had bee nearly starved to death by the Germans in the last seven months. Both have served terms in the Via Tasso prison. The two men had never met until they bumped into each other at the prison and then they had to much o say they could hardly say it.

(Continued on page 4)

Vatican Awes Battleworn GI

THE VATICAN, Rome, June 5 — A bearded, dust-grimed American infantryman, holding his helmet in his hand, stepped inside the vast, vaulted coolness of St. Peter's Cathedral at 3:15 this morning, only a few hours after Allied troops had entered Rome.

He stood loocking straight ahead and then up and he gulped and blinked his eyes and said in a quiet, shaky voice: «I never thought there was a place in the world as wonderful as this. I didn't know there was anything so beautiful».

He wold not give his name, his organization or anything else. «I'm just here», he said, «and I know what I'm seeing is too big to talk about». And he walked out, down under the great high ceiling toward the tomb of St. Peter I., at the far end of the great entrance way

Outside the Vatican, British soldiers, American and French strode beside the great fountains while Piper Cubs swooped down low overhead and guns roared in the distance.

Then bells began tolling from somewhere in the Vatican City And the soldiers, nearly everyone of them, stopped in their tracks. You had the feeling they were all walking on tip toe.

A British jeep driver from the

(Continued on page 4)

THE STARS AND STRIPES

Vol. 1 - No. 2 PUBLISHED IN ROME Rome, June 6 1944

INVASION

Second Front In France

LONDON, June 6 — Allied forces landed this morning on the northern coast of France, it was announced at 0945 hours from General Dwight Eisenhower's Supreme Headquarters of the Allied Expeditionary Force in England. The German official news agency said that Allied airborne and seaborne troops which landed on the coast of the Seine Bay early this morning had been reinforced. The agency added that Allied airborne landings in Normandy were made in great depth. Allied naval forces, supported by strong air forces, began landing armies early this morning and reinforcements followed the initial sea and airborne assault waves. It was announced that General Sir Bernard Law Montgomery, former chief of the Eighth Army, is in command of the combined American, British and Canadian army group carrying out the assault.

Ground Forces Pursue Krauts

By Sgt GEORGE DORSEY
(Stars and Stripes Staff Writer)

WITH THE 5TH ARMY NORTH OF ROME, June 6 — With Rome taken and the second front begun, infantry and tanks of the 5th Army continued their hot pursuit of the battered German forces. Today they were pounding ahead in two powerful drives, one north to Lake Bracciano along the roads that lead to Florence and the other veering to the northwest up the coast road toward Civitavecchia, important port city in central Italy.

The Germans especially in the coastal area, are hindering the advance with bridge demolitions and mines, but Allied troops are pushing forward with all speed to keep the Germans from organizing a stable line. The inland drive, along and between Highways 2 and 3, is being opposed by a few self-propelled guns and tanks, and some thus-far inaccurate artillery fire.

(Continued on Page 4)

MAAF Bombers Land In Russia

MAAF HEADQUARTERS, June 6 — Strategic bombers and fighters of the Mediterranean Allied Air Force have shuttle-bombed targets in southeastern Europe, taking off from Italy and landing in Russia, it was announced today.

The news was first revealed in Moscow that Allied bombers and fighters which bombed Rumanian targets Friday had flown straight on to land at Allied bases in the U. S. S. R. A special communique from Allied headquarters said:

« As announced by Moscow yesterday, a force of Allied strategic bombers and fighters attacked enemy targets in Rumania yesterday and proceeded to Russian bases. As is customary, no further details can be given on this operation except by the Air Commander in Russia. Complete details will be made available when publication will in no way jeopardize the success of combat operations ».

MAAF aircraft based in Italy have bombed targets in Rumania, Hungary and Bulgaria for several months but had previously been forced to return to their home bases, a long and costly round trip. With bases in Russia, the attacking formations will be able to hit their targets both on the

(Continued on page 4)

THE SEINE BAY, where the Germans have announced Allied landings, is the entrance to Normandy, one of the richest and most densely populated sections of France. At the mouth of the Seine is Le Havre, second largest of France, with a population of about 140.000. Le Havre is connected by a dense network of roads and railroads to Paris, all of northern France and Belgium. North of the mouth of the Seine lie a number of little fishing and bathing villages, among them Dieppe. The beaches near Dieppe are broad and only the bluffs behind them interrupt the flat land stretching to Paris.

Caen, where the Germans say the invasion spearhead has hit, lies just south of the Seine where the beaches are fair but high hills form a barrier across the interior. At the end of this stretch of coast is a peninsula at whose tip lies Cherbourg, the closest to England of the large French ports.

GIs Hardly Believe Big News

By Sgt JAMES P. O'NEILL
(Yank Correspondent)

The dogface in Rome today is a very befuddled gent. He didn't have a chance to get over the 5th Army's historic and raucous entry into Rome before the biggest news of World War II, the opening of the Second Front, dropped like a bomb on the local scene. We went out in the noisy streets of Rome and asked four startled GIs the question, « What do you think of the opening of the Second Front? ». Here is what they said:

Pvt. Robert Kinchen, is an artilleryman from Verro Beach, Flo., where, long, long ago he grew oranges for a living. Kinchen had been guarding one of the main streets of Rome since 5 A. M. He was tired but very anxious to contribute his two cents about the big news. He had heard the news an hour before.

Said Kinchen: « I didn't believe it. In fact I'm taking your word for it. Damned glad it finally came. For a long while, especially when we were at the beachhead, I thought they had given up the idea of a Second Front. Hope the boys didn't meet to much stuff when they hit shore. If the beachhead sticks in France, I guess we'll have the Germans whipped before the year is out ».

Pvt. Jerome Kern, Detroit, Mich., was riding down a side street on a borrowed Eyetie bicycle. He rammed the bike to a stop. « You aren't kidding? » he said. « I heard it from an Eyetie over on the square. I didn't believe it, because the state this town's in today, they are liable to tell you anything. If it is true, it sure is wonderful news. I don't mean to be selfish, but I hope it means we can relax a little. We had our stomach's full at Anzio and the push up here hasn't been a cinch. I got two good pals with an infantry outfit over there. I sure hope they get through it okay ».

Pfc. Bill Ellis, Mobile, Ala., was walking down the street searching for his pals who had whipped off in a weapon's carrier and left him stranded.

Like most GIs in Rome, Ellis' had heard the news second — hand and didn't quite believe it.

«Sure is a hunk of news» he declared. « I've been waiting for it since North Africa. It won't be long now till Jerry gives in, I hope. Rome and the Second Front will be too much for him. We oughta be home in six months, I hope ».

S Sgt. Carl Johnson, an artilleryman from Hartland, Minn., was parked in a jeep outside an office building waiting for his CO. Johnson heard the news by radio. He heard both German and BBC announcements. He also heard Eisenhower speak to the people of France.

« Boy, the guys at our CP went crazy when BBC went on. Personally, I got a tickling sensation in the pit of my stomach when I heard it. I'm happy it came at such a swell time.

Giving the latest news of the landings, Prime Minister Winston Churchill disclosed this afternoon that 4,000 ships crossed the Channel and that up to 11,000 Allied aircraft are taking part in the operation.

« Masses or airborne landings have been successfully effected behind the enemy's lines and the landings on the beaches are proceeding at various points », Mr. Churchill said. « Already there is hope that an actual technical surprise has been attained. The battle has begun well and will grow in scale and intensity for many weeks to come ».

The German news agency reported this afternoon that at two points the Allies have penetrated several miles to the south. « We must be patient », warned the announcement. « Fighting », it added, « is at present going on in the Isigny-Carentin area at the Vire estuary where German Atlantic Wall troops are battling against four Allied airborne divisions. » The agency said also that Allied troops have landed on Guernsey and Jersey islands, 15 to 20 miles off Cherbourg peninsula.

Allied authorities declared that more than 640 naval guns from four to 16 inches are bombarding the beaches and enemy strongpoints.

The troop landing was preceded by the heaviest assault ever executed by the RAF bomber command. Monday night 1,300 aircraft bombed German naval guns and howitzers along the invasion coast.

This afternoon Supreme Headquarters announced that planes carrying airborne troops accomplished their mission earlier in the day and returned « without heavy casualties ».

The weather, so important in an amphibious operation, changed for the better. After a shower soon after daybreak this morning, there was sunshine in the Straits of Dover. But the outlook was less settled and the wind had blown fairly hard during the night.

Each soldier was handed an order of he Day, from General Eisenhower as H-hour approached. The dramatic document stated.

« Soldiers and airmen of the Allied Expeditionary Force. You are about to embark upon a great crusage towards which we have striven these many months. The eyes of the world are upon you. The hopes and prayers of liberty-loving people everywhere march with you.

« In company with our brave Allies and brothers in arms on other fronts, you will bring about the destruction of the German war machine, the elimination of Nazi tyranny over the oppressed peoples of Europe and security for ourselves in a free world.

« Your task will not be an easy one. Your enemy is well-trained, well-equipped and battle-hardened. He will fight sa-

(Continued on Page 4)

1D. THE STARS AND STRIPES 1D.
Daily Newspaper of U.S. Armed Forces in the European Theater of Operations
Vol. 4 No. 185 New York, N.Y.—London, England Wednesday, June 7, 1944

Allies Driving Into France

Opposition Less Than Expected; Troops 10 Mi. In

Allied armies, supported by more than 4,000 ships and 11,000 warplanes, stormed the northern coast of France in the dark hours of yesterday morning to open the decisive battle for the liberation of Europe, and by nightfall had smashed their way ten miles inland to Caen, between the vital ports of Cherbourg and Le Havre. Enemy radio stations said heavy street fighting was in progress.

By reaching Caen, the invasion forces may have cut the railway running from Paris to Cherbourg, main route for the supply of Hitler's troops on the peninsula.

German opposition in all quarters—sea, air and land—was less than expected, according to information reaching supreme headquarters and losses appeared to be astonishingly light.

American naval losses were only two destroyers and one LST (landing ship, tank) craft, while American air losses were kept to one per cent, President Roosevelt revealed in Washington on the basis of a noon dispatch from General Eisenhower. The President said operations were "up to schedule."

Losses of troop-carrying aircraft were extremely small, although more than 1,000 of such planes were used, headquarters disclosed. The airborne troops themselves were "well established," Prime Minister Churchill had announced earlier.

And as for the forces which landed on the beaches, Adm. Sir Bertram Ramsay, Allied naval commander-in-chief, reported that "naval ships landed all their cargoes 100 per cent." He added that there was "slight loss in ships, but so slight that it did not affect putting armies ashore. We have got all the first wave of men through the defended beach zone and set for the land battle."

Along a front described by the Germans as 80 miles long—from the mouth of the Seine River at Le Havre to the tip of the Cherbourg peninsula—American, British and Canadian troops landed on French soil from the choppy waters of the English Channel and from the storm-studded skies.

From 600 naval guns, ranging from four to 16 inches, and from massive fleets of supporting planes, ton upon ton of high explosives thundered into the concrete and steel of the West Wall which Hitler erected to guard his conquered countries.

The actual landings took place in daylight after an aerial assault on the coastal defenses which lasted from before midnight to dawn, a communique disclosed late last night. The airborne troops, however, had landed behind enemy positions during darkness.

Between 6.30 and 7.30 two naval task forces—one commanded by Rear Adm. Sir Philip Vian, aboard HMS Scylla, and the other by Rear Adm. Alan Goodrich Kirk, aboard the U.S.S. Augusta—launched their assault forces at enemy beaches.

It was on the cruiser Augusta that President Roosevelt and Prime Minister Churchill signed the Atlantic Charter in August, 1941.

The mightiest air and sea armadas ever assembled paved the way for the successful landings. American warships participating included battleships, cruisers and destroyers, as well as hundreds of smaller craft and troopships.

Thirty-one thousand Allied airmen, not counting airborne troops, made a continuous road through the night in the skies over France. Between midnight and 8 AM more than 10,000 tons of high explosives were hurled upon the Normandy invasion area by Allied aircraft, which flew 7,500 sorties.

Against this aerial might the Luftwaffe was able to mount only 50 sorties, despite an order of the day from Goering that "invasion must be beaten off even if the Luftwaffe perishes." Allied fighters swept 75 miles inland without opposition.

After an initial communique made the momentous announcement of the landings, Prime Minister Churchill gave the first word that the assault had been successful. To a cheering House of Commons he announced shortly after noon that landings were proceeding according to plan, that sea obstacles planted by the Nazis had been less serious than had been feared, that the fire of shore batteries had been largely quelled, and that airborne landings had been effected successfully behind the enemy lines.

Later, after visiting Gen. Eisenhower's headquarters with King George VI, Churchill said that "many dangers and difficulties which appeared at this time last night to be extremely formidable are behind us. The passage of the sea has been made with far less loss than we apprehended."

A spokesman at Supreme Headquarters Allied Expeditionary Forces (SHAEF) declared last night that the "first four or five hurdles" in establishing Allied forces on the Continent had been overcome, and that the positions of the Allied troops definitely gave "no cause for pessimism." No specific information was given on the landing points or the progress made.

It was left to the Germans to give most of the details, and all day long came a steady stream of reports from German agencies of new airborne and sea landings, most of them between Le Havre and Cherbourg and some airborne landings southwest of Boulogne.

Enemy radio stations late last night painted a picture of growing Allied successes, with new beachheads established and a general spreading-out from positions on coastal stretches already occupied.

German Overseas News Agency said fierce fighting was in progress along the whole 19-mile stretch of road between Carantan and Valognes on the Cherbourg peninsula. Paratroops established themselves on both sides of the road and later were reinforced by glider troops, the agency added.

Vichy radio said Allied reinforcements were pouring into the beachheads and "it must be admitted the Allied landing area has been considerably extended."

The French radio station at Brazza-

(Continued on page 4)

Greatest Umbrella for Landing

Armadas of Allied Planes Hammer Nazi Targets

Unleashing the full fury of Anglo-American air power, Allied aircraft yesterday bombed and strafed mile after mile of French beaches, seizing undisputed mastery of the air and heaping record-breaking tons of explosives on Nazi coastal installations in providing the greatest umbrella in history for the invasion forces.

Between midnight and 8 AM yesterday alone, 10,000 tons of steel went cascading down on German targets on the coast of Normandy. In the same period more than 31,000 Allied airmen, not including airborne troops, dominated the sky over France.

It was estimated that in a final recapitulation the number of sorties flown yesterday would soar to more than 20,000.

In spite of the staggering number of sorties flown by the Americans only 1 per cent of the aircraft operating were lost, President Roosevelt announced in Washington at noon.

Luftwaffe Stays Down

So sparse was Luftwaffe opposition that most airmen did not encounter a single German fighter. Few of the 1,750 fighter planes which it is estimated the Nazis can muster to oppose the invasion put in an appearance.

High-ranking officers of Supreme Headquarters emphasized, however, that there was no reason to believe the Luftwaffe had been defeated.

"Fighting of the greatest severity is in store before the Luftwaffe is wiped out," according to one air officer.

American heavies, flying three missions for the second time in four days, roared out at 6 AM, at noon and again in the mid-afternoon at a cost of only four bombers.

In the first assault a record force of more than 1,300 Fortresses and Liberators struck more than 100 German targets on the French coast. Later in the day a medium force of B24s and B17s flew behind the West Wall to pound a defended German position. Most of the bombers in the second raid returned with their loads because the presence of Allied troops made it inadvisable to bomb through overcast. Another Nazi strongpoint was battered on the third mission.

Not one enemy fighter was encountered

Bombing, strafing and patroling fighter aircraft of the Ninth Air Force were in the air continuously yesterday from 4.30 AM, covering the movement of the Allied Expeditionary Force over sea and on to the beaches, and probing ahead of the landing parties for tactical objectives beyond the operations zone.

Starting yesterday morning with air-

(Continued on page 3)

'This Was the Invasion'

Flying S & S Writer Files First Eyewitness Story

By Bud Hutton
Stars and Stripes Staff Writer

Six thousand feet below, troops surged over the beaches of France and against Hitler's Atlantic Wall, and as the first black dots moved over the white sand a gunner said over the interphone: "Jesus Christ! At last."

On the dirty dark green of the Channel waters, battleships, cruisers, destroyers and more man-carrying craft than you could count rolled steadily toward the green fields and the white towns the Nazis had taken from France. Through a smoke screen the wraith-like shapes of warships loomed a moment, chameleoned into blobs of flame as another broadside roared off to find some Wehrmacht strongpoint beyond the coast.

This was the invasion.

North and south, all across the Channel and deep into the reaches beyond the concrete-bound coasts of the Continent, some 7,000 American and Allied warplanes flew in the greatest aerial armada in history. They drove the Luftwaffe from the skies with guns, and with bombs the German gunners and infantry from their camouflaged strongpoints beneath. Marauders and Havocs, Fortresses and Liberators, Mustangs, Thunderbolts, Lightnings and all the myriad craft of the RAF filled the sky until there was no room for more.

From a Marauder medium bomber of

(Continued on page 4)

Teheran Set Landing Time With Stalin's OK, Says FDR

WASHINGTON, June 6—President Roosevelt disclosed today that the approximate invasion time was set at the Teheran conference last December and that Marshal Stalin was completely satisfied with it. The precise date, however, was determined only within the last few days.

Citing losses far lower than expected, Mr. Roosevelt told his press conference that politicians who had been demanding a second front for months would see now why the Allies had waited—the extra time had enabled Gen. Eisenhower to have many more divisions and landing craft.

Eisenhower's Order of Day

The following order of the day was issued yesterday by Gen. Eisenhower to each individual of the Allied Expeditionary Force:—

"Soldiers, sailors and airmen of the Allied Expeditionary Force!

"You are about to embark upon the great crusade, toward which we have striven these many months. The eyes of the world are upon you. The hopes and prayers of liberty-loving people everywhere march with you.

"In company with our brave allies and brothers in arms on other fronts, you will bring about the destruction of the German war machine, the elimination of Nazi tyranny over the oppressed peoples of Europe, and security for ourselves in a free world.

"Your task will not be an easy one. Your enemy is well trained, well equipped and battle hardened. He will fight savagely.

"But this is the year 1944! Much has happened since the Nazi triumphs of 1940-41. The United Nations have inflicted upon the Germans great defeats in open battle, man to man. Our air offensive has seriously reduced their strength in the air and their capacity to wage war on the ground.

"Our home fronts have given us an overwhelming superiority in weapons and munitions of war, and placed at our disposal great reserves of trained fighting men. The tide has turned! The free men of the world are marching together to victory!

"I have full confidence in your courage, devotion to duty and skill in battle. We will accept nothing less than full victory!

"Good luck! And let us beseech the blessing of Almighty God upon this great and noble undertaking."

The order was distributed to assault elements after their embarkation. It was read by commanders to all other troops in the Allied Expeditionary Force.

Late Bulletins

FIRST U.S. RAID FROM USSR BASES

U.S. BOMBER BASE, Soviet Union, June 6 (Reuter)—In the first American raid of the war from new shuttle bases on Soviet soil, scores of U.S. heavy bombers showered tons of high explosives and incendiaries on airdrome installations at Galatz, Rumania, today and then returned here.

STALIN LAUDS ALLIES ON ROME

A congratulatory message from Marshal Stalin on "the great victory of the Allied Anglo-American forces" at Rome was made public last night by Prime Minister Churchill. Stalin wrote that the news of Rome capture was "greeted in the Soviet Union with great satisfaction."

INVASION JAMS U.S. PAPERS

WASHINGTON, June 6 (Reuter)—Many newspapers announced tomorrow's editions would not contain advertising because of pressure of space.

THE STARS AND STRIPES

MEDITERRANEAN

Vol. 2, No. 27, Saturday, June 10, 1944 — For U. S. Armed Forces — TWO FRANCS

Bitter Tank Battle In Normandy

West Wall Going West

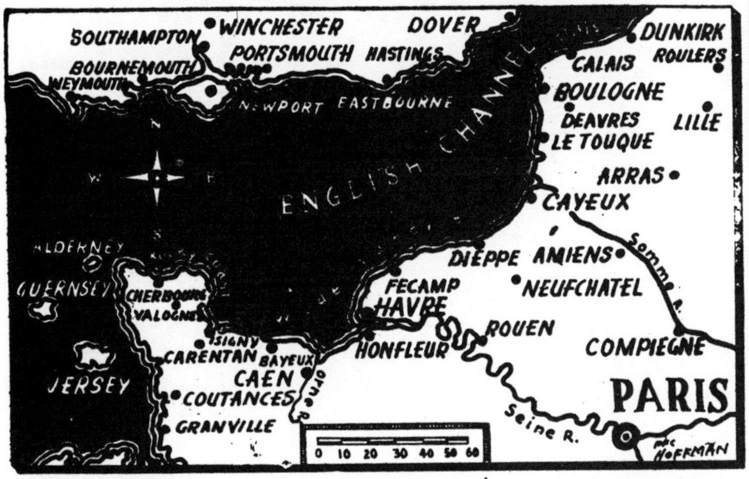

ALLIED LIBERATION TROOPS who landed on the Normandy coast of France Tuesday were engaged in grim fighting along a 70 mile front extending east and north from within 12 miles of Cherbourg on Friday. Hand-to-hand fighting was reported within the city of Caen and tank battles were in progress in the rolling country west and southwest of Bayeux, first important town to fall to the Allied airborne and ground troops.

Allied Troops Pushing Forward Past Bayeux

By Sgt. DON WILLIAMS
(Stars and Stripes Staff Writer)

Fierce fighting raged on a 70-mile front on the Normandy coast of France Friday as Allied liberation forces, under the personal command of General Sir Bernard L. Montgomery, met with increasingly heavy opposition in efforts to push across the Contentin peninsula and isolate the great port of Cherbourg.

Heavy tank engagements were reported in progress in the rolling Normandy fields several miles to the south and southwest of captured Bayeux, five miles from the coast and first important town to fall to the American, British and Canadian forces.

The Associated Press reported that Allied troops had advanced five miles south and west of Bayeux. And the Transocean German News Agency announced this afternoon that the Allies had driven a wedge southwest from the Bayeux railroad junction toward St. Lo for a distance of six miles.

Allied and German troops were reported locked in savage street fighting in the battered strategic city of Caen, 15 miles to the east of Bayeux. And the United Press said in a dispatch from Supreme Headquarters, Allied Expeditionary Force, that at least one junction had been effected between amphibious and airborne Allied troops on the north side of the peninsula about 12 miles east of Cherbourg. Allied planes were said to be giving strong tactical support to the ground troops as they streamed toward the port.

Supreme Headquarters of the Allied Expeditionary Force announced Friday night that operations were making satisfactory progress and that beachheads continued to be enlarged against stiffening resistance.

Main German counterattacks were reported to be in the Caen area with German armor well forward. Ground has been gained in this sector, it was announced. French parachutists were reported to be taking part in the Caen action.

Earlier Friday afternoon a com-

(Continued on Page 16)

MAAF Plasters Munich In First Blow From Italy

ALLIED FORCE HEADQUARTERS, June 9 — Strong forces of American heavy bombers today pressed home the first attack on the Nazi shrine of Munich from Italian bases and used, for the first time on record in this theater, equipment for accurate bombing despite overcast conditions.

Although the special MAAF announcement tonight revealed no details, the force of more than 750 four-motored bombers and their escort of Lightnings, Thunderbolts and Mustangs was reported to have encountered considerable enemy opposition.

The Mustangs, in particular, were said to have had their hands full.

The German submarine drydocks at Pola, 85 miles south of Trieste, were attacked yesterday with fair results by American heavy bombers, while last night RAF heavy and medium bombers resumed their offensive against enemy communications in the Balkans.

Details of the American bombers' operations were sparse. It was stated that no enemy aircraft were encountered and that the flak ranged from moderate to intense.

The night operations were against big railway repair shops at Nis, in eastern Yugoslavia, on the direct express route from northern Europe to Istanbul. It was the first night attack on the Nis yards, and crews reported direct hits in the target area. All bombers returned safely to their bases, it was reported.

Coastal Air Force planes also were over Yugoslavia as well as the Marseilles sector of southern France yesterday on bombing and strafing missions against transport vehicles and communications lines.

MAAF announced the loss of six Allied planes and claimed the destruction of four enemy aircraft.

Fifth Captures Viterbo 45 Miles From Rome

By Sgt. LEN SMITH
(Stars and Stripes Staff Writer)

ALLIED FORCE HEADQUARTERS, June 9—Viterbo, important airport and road junction on Highway 2, 45 miles north of Rome, was captured today by Allied troops who were skillfully overcoming demolitions, scattered rear guards and more Italian mountains in their drive to wipe out the surviving one-fourth of General Field Marshal Albert von Kesselring's once-mighty armies.

Also occupied today by the 5th Army's advance on the western side of the Tiber were Tarquinia, 12 miles north of Civitavecchia on Highway 1, and Vetralla, due east of Tarquinia at the junction point of Highway 2 and 1B.

All Allied reports today told of advances everywhere in Italy—still quite rapid in the 5th Army sector, and not so fast, but just as decisive along the far-flung 8th Army front from the east bank of the Tiber to the Adriatic. The Adriatic area, largely static for more than five months appeared to be coming to life, with enemy withdrawals reported between the coast and Crecchio, about five miles inland.

The announcements tonight of the occupation of Viterbo, Tarquinia and Vetralla represent advances in 24 hours of up to 20 miles. The tone of official announcements indicated almost negligible resistance in this area.

It would appear that the Allied Air Force's "Operation Strangle" which once made Viterbo an almost daily target, not only neutralized this important base as a supply depot, but made it well nigh indefensible by the retreating Krauts. On the other hand the 5th Army appeared equal to the task of circumventing the Nazi and Allied-made demolitions.

This morning forward elements were reported in the vicinity of Lake di Vico, about eight miles

(Continued on Page 16)

Russians State No Drive Yet

MOSCOW—While the Germans claimed the Russians had begun a major offensive in Rumania, Thursday's Soviet communique declared "there is no material change on any front," and the newspaper Red Star predicted an imminent Russian drive westwards.

The only action reported by the official communique was an attack north of Jassy which put Red Army troops in possession of "a height of considerable importance, and killed 200 German officers and men."

Meanwhile, Red Star, the Soviet Army organ, said a great Russian drive would open soon. The newspaper declared, "our tanks are starting a race for the pavement of Berlin. Our infantry will soon march over German land."

Hume Claims Rome Near Normal Again

By Sgt. PAUL GREEN
(Stars and Stripes Staff Writer)

ROME—Brig. Gen. Edgar E. Hume, senior civil affairs officer for the AMG Rome region, revealed in his first report to press correspondents this week that the Italian capital is rapidly returning to normal.

General Hume indicated that all the problems associated with a huge metropolis turned over from one army to another—food, police, public utilities, health, education, art, refugees—are all under control and present no serious difficulties.

For the time being the Allies will be able to give out as much food as the Germans did. Later the food ration will be increased. Food trucks have arrived from Anzio and food will be distributed immediately.

Soup kitchens will be set up at once to accommodate 400,000 people. Much more food will have to be sent in, since there are more than two million people in this city, which normally holds only somewhat more than a million. In the emergency, the Vatican has placed its food stocks at the disposal of the Allied authorities.

There will be no water famine in Rome, AMG officials promised. Machinery has been brought in for distilling the water of the Tiber and plenty of chlorine is available for purification.

The electric current is off in some parts of the city but coal has been obtained to increase the supply. Telephone service has been started for a limited number of phones, and shortly many others will be put into operation. Gas has been provided for hospitals, and will slowly be extended elsewhere on the basis of need. Bakeries are next on the priority list. The Germans had cut off the gas entirely on the pretext that there was no coal.

Health in the city is good, General Hume said, and there is no fear of malaria or intestinal diseases getting out of hand. The

(Continued on Page 15)

Educational Benefit Set In 'GI Bill Of Rights'

WASHINGTON — Conferees on the "GI Bill of Rights," the veterans' aid bill, agreed Thursday on a maximum educational benefit of 500 dollars a year for not more than four years.

Sen. Scott W. Lucas (D., Ill.) said agreement had been reached on the language of the bill making it certain no new Federal controls over state educational systems would be effected.

The education provision is designed to assist veterans to complete education interrupted by induction for Army or Navy service. Other disputed sections of the legislation remain to be worked out.

Jim Farley Resigns As Committee Head

NEW YORK—Former Postmaster General James A. Farley Thursday announced his resignation as Chairman of the New York Democratic Committee, a post he held for 14 years.

Mr. Farley said he resigned because business duties and obligations would not permit him to give necessary time to committee affairs in the forthcoming national election. He told a press conference that he would go to the national convention as a delegate.

As National Committee Chairman, Mr. Farley directed the campaigns that led to President Roosevelt's first two terms. He was opposed to a third term. In recent years, observers have noted a definite break between Mr. Farley and the President.

Consider Partial Pay In France

LONDON—Negotiations are now in progress between General Charles de Gaulle and Prime Minister Winston Churchill and other Allied officials in an attempt to prevent inflation in liberated France because American and British troops are bringing in large sums of Allied military currency.

It appears that the principal measure under consideration is to "hold back" a portion of soldiers' pay in order not to dislocate French economic life.

So far as the Americans are concerned, the exact proportion to be withheld has not been disclosed. It is understood that the British War Office has made arrangements whereby British soldiers will not be paid in full, and the balance held in Great Britain as credit.

American and British soldiers entered France with large quantities of French bank notes of special design.

The backing for this Allied military currency will normally be that of the Bank of France, but it is practically certain that the French national bank will be paid for and credited in dollars and sterling, which the future French government will be able to spend in due course.

THE STARS AND STRIPES
ORAN DAILY

Vol. 2, No. 32, Thursday, June 15, 1944 — One Franc — Daily Newspaper For U. S. Armed Forces

NAZI RESISTANCE STIFFENS

Germans Still Back Toward Florence Line

5th, 8th Armies Smash Obstacles In Italy Advance

ALLIED FORCE HEADQUARTERS, June 14—All along a front extending 150 airline miles from the Tyrrhenian to the Adriatic, at one place nearly 70 miles above Rome, Allied troops today were closing in on enemy "delaying points" below the Pisa-Florence-Rimini defense zone.

Although official reports this morning continued to stress strong enemy resistance at some places, both the 5th and 8th Armies were moving forward in a co-ordinated advance.

The area of resistance, as in the last three days, has been between the Tyrrhenian coast and the west bank of the Tiber River, south of Highway 74, one of three main lateral roads below Florence.

This morning Allied reconnaissance elements were north of this important artery at one point and threatening it at two other spots—at Latera, west of Lake Bolsena, and on the east side of the lake near the junction of Highway 74 and Highway 2 about six miles south of Orvieto.

From the Tiber's east bank to the Adriatic, there was resistance of varying degrees. In the Tiber valley, British armored forces were closing on Narni, on the Nera River and Highway 3, about six miles from Terni. Here the enemy was directing heavy shellfire against the Allied troops from dominating observation posts high in the hills.

From all appearances the admittedly retreating enemy was

(Continued on Page 8)

YANKS IN FRANCE

AN AMERICAN INFANTRYMAN stops to talk to French people and admire the baby during a march through a French town.

Yank Marianas Raid Cost Japs 13 Ships, 141 Planes

PEARL HARBOR, June 14—The American task force which over the weekend banged the Marianas Islands in the Central Pacific sank 13 Japanese ships, damaged 16 others and destroyed 141 enemy planes, Admiral Chester W. Nimitz, Commander in Chief of the Pacific Fleet announced today in a communique.

The gigantic attack on the islands, 1,000 miles east of the Japanese mainland, had been previously announced, but it was not until today that the thumping box score was made public.

The Jap ships which hit the bottom included a destroyer and three corvettes. Altogether, the announced loss totalled 15 American planes, mostly fighters.

The vast operation has four objectives: Guam, Saipan, Tinian and Rota, all of them thoroughly combed over by carrier-based planes.

Beginning the attack last Saturday, American fighter planes swept the objectives in force and destroyed 124 enemy aircraft, a large majority of them in aerial combat. Our losses were 11 Hellcat fighters and eight pilots. The attacks were continued Sunday, when 16 enemy aircraft were toppled.

At the same time the attackers sank two small cargo ships at Saipan and a small oiler northwest of the island. A formation of enemy ships, apparently attempting to escape from Saipan was brought under attack Sunday.

The communique continued, "one large oiler, one destroyer, three corvettes, one large cargo ship, one medium cargo ship and three small cargo ships were sunk. Five medium cargo ships and five escort vessels were damaged.

"A second formation of enemy ships several hundred miles away was attacked and heavily damaged by our aircraft Monday. These were three destroyers, one destroyer escort and two large cargo ships.

"In the Monday operations, our losses were four aircraft and seven flight personnel. On Saturday night, several enemy planes approached our force but failed to drive home an attack, and one of them was shot down by anti aircraft fire."

Bombings significant in their

(Continued on Page 8)

Americans Gain in Center; Huns Attack Before Caen

SUPREME HEADQUARTERS, ALLIED EXPEDITIONARY FORCE, June 14—Grim battles of increasing intensity were reported at both ends of the 90 mile battle line in Normandy Wednesday night as American troops punched out gains in the central sector on the fourth anniversary of the Nazis' triumphal entry into Paris.

Four German panzer divisions were reported to be throwing repeated and furious counterattacks in the Tilly Sur Suelles-Caen sector where British and Canadian armor was trying to push the right claw of the pincer around the Nazi bastion of Caen.

Fluctuating fighting was reported in progress at the tip of the left claw of the pincer in and around the city of Troarn, seven miles east of Caen.

Big guns of the British battleships Nelson and Ramilles were throwing innumerable ponderous shells in support of the liberation forces who took the city in a five mile leap on Tuesday. Frontline reports from this sector indicated uncertainly as to whether the city itself still was in Allied hands.

German claims that the key city of Montebourg, near the western end of the line, 15 miles southeast of the great port of Cherbourg, had been retaken by their forces were neither confirmed nor denied at SHEAF.

Capture of the city after days of bitter fighting by the 4th Division, in which battleships were called upon to demolish the tower of a medieval church being used by the Nazis as an observation post had been reported on Tuesday.

The midnight communique of SHAEF Tuesday night told of strong Nazi counterattacks in the area by Nazi armored forces. A headquarters spokesman said the push was backed by mortar support as well, and that American troops had been forced to give some ground. It was not clear, the

(Continued on Page 8)

Jerrys Offer Slight Aerial Opposition

SUPREME HEADQUARTERS, ALLIED EXPEDITIONARY FORCE, June 14—The Luftwaffe, after the beating it had taken on Monday when at least 80 of its planes were destroyed in combat and on the ground, failed to rise to meet the continued Allied air assault Tuesday. Officially, enemy fighter opposition was described as sporadic, although Allied aircraft encountered strong ack-ack.

Despite a worsening of weather conditions as compared with the perfect weather prevailing the day before, Allied planes were out in one of their most concentrated efforts since the opening of the campaign.

At least 4,000 planes were reported to have taken part in the all-day offensive directed primarily against airfields in the battle zone and between battered Caen and Paris. Marshalling yards, bridges and fuel dumps also were the targets for strong attacks.

Heavy bombers of the 8th AAF were dispatched against Nazi airfields after reconnaissance disclosed that the Germans had moved more than 500 single engine fighters within tactical range of Normandy battlefields and had concentrated an additional 500 bombers between Caen and Germeny.

Flying Forts struck at air bases at Evreux, Pauville, Dreux and Illiers—Levequex, boosting to 19 the number of enemy airfields which had been bombed within a 24-hour period. Late in the afternoon the Forts carried out a second air base mission and blasted two key fields north of Paris. Medium bombers attacked the field at Rennes.

A United Press dispatch reported that the Luftwaffe had abandoned

(Continued on Page 8)

Soviets Test Finns' Front

MOSCOW, June 14 — Swift thrusts of the Soviet armored columns on the Karelian isthmus have been replaced by a more cautious probing advance as the Red Army moves deeper into the maze of lakes, streams, woods and marshes dotted with fortifications shielding the strength of the old Mannerheim Line, front line dispatches said today.

While assault parties are picking new openings in the complex Finnish defenses, the main Russian forces are apparently regrouping and reinforcing for a drive on the port city of Viipuri, 30 miles to the north.

Yesterday's Soviet communique stated simply that "our troops continued their advance on the Karelian front and captured several enemy strongpoints."

Reports indicated today that during the last 24 hours Finnish reserves, including artillery, have been brought up and sent into ac-

(Continued on Page 8)

King Leopold Held As Captive in Reich

LONDON, June 14—King Leopold III of Belgium is now a captive in Germany. The Belgian government-in-exile in London officially announced that they had received confirmation of the news that the king was sent to Germany on June 7.

The Associated Press reported that ever since the Allied landings the Germans had removed the King as a security measure—an understandable move since Leopold is technically commander in chief of the Belgian army and a potential rallying point for resistance.

Night Raiders Bomb Munich

ALLIED FORCE HEADQUARTERS, June 14—RAF heavy and medium bombers crossed the Alps from Italian bases for the first time last night to attack Munich's main railway station a few hours after American heavies from Italy had attacked the same area in strong force.

The raid also marked the first time both Italy-based and Britain-based bombers flew against inner Germany on the same night.

Halifaxes, Liberators and Wellingtons, the latter specialising in two-ton block busters, participated in the raid. The crews saw some night fighters over the birthplace of Nazidom, which in the last week has had more visits from Allied bombers than from Reichsfuehrer Adolph Hitler himself.

The Luftwaffe lost 35 planes, two over the Central Italy battle area.

In the Munich dogfights the winners included Maj. Herschel H. Greene, Mayfield, Ky., whose 14 victories top all other American fighter pilots' scores in this theater.

Two planes were shot down over Munich by S-Sgt Herbert L. Townsend, Detroit, Mich., who manned a Liberator waist gun when the regular gunner was killed. Townsend is an aerial photographer.

Today American heavies raided seven oil refineries and airfields in Hungary and Yugoslavia, it was announced this afternoon, but no details of the missions were released.

GI 'Bill of Rights' Goes to President

WASHINGTON, June 14—The House of Representatives unanimously passed the GI "bill of rights" today and sent it to President Roosevelt for his approval or rejection. Yesterday the Senate likewise unanimously passed the bill after agreeing that any benefits a veteran receives be deducted from any bonus he may be voted after the war.

The bill contains three major provisions: 1) Unemployment compensation of 20 dollars weekly for a maximum of 52 weeks for veterans without jobs in the first two years after their discharge.

2) Government-financed education with the United States paying a maximum of 500 dollars tuition and 50 dollars monthly for a veteran's subsistence and another 25 dollars for dependents.

3) Guarantee by the government of 50 percent of private loans up to 4,000 dollars to help veterans establish themselves in business or for purchase of homes and farms.

Joseph Stalin Cheers Allied Invasion Feat

MOSCOW, June 14 — Marshal Joseph Stalin, who knows a few tricks about killing Germans, yesterday characterized the Allied landing in France as a brilliant success and the channel crossing as a feat which neither the "invincible Napoleon nor the hysterical Hitler had been able to pull off."

"One must admit," he said in reply to a correspondent's question "that the history of wars does not know any undertaking so broad in conception, so grandiose in its scale and so masterly in its execution.

"In summing up the result of the seven days of liberation by the Allied troops who invaded northern France, I may say without hesitation that the large-scale forcing of the channel and the mass landing of Allied troops have fully succeeded.

"As is known, 'invincible Napoleon shamefully failed in his time with his plan of forcing the channel and of capturing the British Isles. Hitler, the hysteric, who for two years boasted that he would carry out the forcing of the channel did not even attempt to carry out his threat.

"Only British, American and Canadian troops succeeded with honor in carrying out this immense plan of forcing the channel and landing troops on a vast scale. History will take note of this achievement of the highest order."

In W[illegible]ton, President Roosevelt [illegible] Marshal Stalin, in [illegible] Ambassador W. [illegible] had elaborately [illegible].

Southern California Feels Earthquakes

LOS ANGELES, June 14 — Two earthquakes jarred Southern California yesterday, rattling dishes and waking light sleepers in some areas. No damage was caused.

The first shock was felt distinctly in nearby Pasadena and Laguna Beach, police said. The second rocked Los Angeles briefly and was reported also in Pasadena, Long Beach and other Los Angeles communities.

NORTHERN IRELAND EDITION

1D. THE STARS AND STRIPES 1D.

Daily Newspaper of U.S. Armed Forces in the European Theater of Operations

Vol. 1. No. 164. New York, N.Y.—Belfast, Northern Ireland. Friday, June 16, 1944.

Super-Forts Bomb Tokyo

Yanks Menace Lines to Cherbourg

Two Towns Recaptured By Germans

Americans Already Have Part of Eastern Lines; Small Port Taken

Yank infantry and armor, pushing westward across the Cherbourg peninsula on a nine-mile front, threatened yesterday to sever the enemy's last communications lines to the deep-water port of Cherbourg itself.

The Americans, in the only important Allied gain of the day in Normandy, advanced from between Carentan and Le Ham to within six miles of the high ground around La Haye du Puits controlling the western highway and railroad up to the important harbor at the tip of the peninsula.

The eastern road and rail lines were already in U.S control from Carentan up to Montebourg which the Germans claimed to have recaptured from the U.S. Fourth Division in heavy fighting.

The American capture of Quineville, five miles northeast of Montebourg, on the peninsula coast, was announced at headquarters of the 21 Army Group. Capture of this small port represented the northernmost advance along the side of the peninsula.

As the Allied threat to isolate Cherbourg mounted, the Nazi-controlled Swedish Telegraph Bureau reported in Stockholm that the Germans had blown up the harbor facilities at Cherbourg, where vessels up to 30,000 tons may be docked.

Germans Retake Troarn

At the far eastern flank of the front in France, Allied headquarters acknowledged that the Germans retook Troarn, and some of the fiercest fighting since D-Day raged from Troarn westward through the Caen sector to the St. Lo area.

The main fighting took place before Villers Bocage, southwest of Caen. After the Nazis recaptured Villers Bocage, Allied troops occupied high ground facing the town a quarter of a mile away, with the Seulles river dividing them and the German forces across a 500-yard valley. As the Germans threw in their panzers, the Allies countered with planes. Marauders in answer to an urgent call from the ground forces, dumped 50 tons of bombs on the highway junction and bridge at Villers.

North of Villers the village of Tilly-sur-Seulles changed hands several times, but to the west the Germans admitted that the British held Caumont.

The Allied troops knocked out 17

(Continued on Page 4)

The War Today

Pacific—B29 super Forts bomb Tokyo. . . American troops land on Saipan, in Mariana Islands, 100 miles north of Guam and 1,300 miles from Yokohama, supported by "largest Allied task force in Pacific war."

France—Americans gain in westward push on Cherbourg Peninsula, threatening Germans' last communications line to port. . . . Germans recapture Troarn. . . . Allies knock out 17 enemy tanks in heavy fighting on central front.

Air War—More than 1,300 U.S. heavies raid airfields, rail targets and other objectives in France and Germany. . . . Marauders bomb front-line town of Villers Bocage. . . . New blows fall in daylight assault on Le Havre's E-boat pens by RAF.

Russia—Finns report Soviet breakthrough northwest of Terijoki in drive for Vipuri. Moscow communique reveals capture of several strongpoints and claims 3,000 Finns wiped out.

Italy—Fast-moving armor smashes German attempt to curb Allied advance. . . . Eighth Army takes Orvieto. . . . Fifth Army circles port of Orbetello, traps Germans there.

First Full American Squadron Sets Down on French Airstrip

By Bud Hutton
Stars and Stripes Staff Writer.

AN AIRFIELD IN FRANCE, June 14 (Delayed)—The first squadron of American fighter planes set down on this newly-built airstrip at 8.15 last night after a combat mission, refueled and flew back to home base in England. Use of the strip, which had been carved out of the Norman fields by Air Force engineers under fire, made possible the tactical doubling of the fighter's range—which almost automatically shoves the line of Allied aerial mastery even deeper into the continent.

First man down in his P47 Thunderbolt was Capt. Richard E. Leary, of Annapolis, Md., operations officer for the group commanded by Col Gilbert Meyers, and as his wheels kicked up the dust of the strip, it marked the first planned use of airstrips onto which Allied warplanes have been landing for emergency refueling and rearming the last four days.

From now on it will be a question of moving fighter units onto newly-built strips as fast as the engineers can skin turf and trees

(Continued on Page 4)

1,300 Forts, Libs Paste Foe in France, Germany

Another huge force of American heavy bombers dumped lethal explosives on enemy targets in France and Germany yesterday, and Ninth Air Force warplanes joined in the fierce struggle raging for the Normandy town of Villers Bocage. In an early morning operation British Lancasters smashed at Le Havre's E-boat pens with 12,000-pound blockbusters in the RAF's first high altitude precision bombing.

More than 1,300 Eighth Air Force Fortresses and Liberators, mounting their third huge attack in four days at a cost of only three bombers, flew 300 miles south of the battle zone in the deepest penetration of France since the European landings to hit airfields including one at Bordeaux, French rail junctions, rail bridges, and aircraft assembly plants. Unspecified objectives in the Reich also were struck.

German radio reported that the great industrial city of Hanover was bombed.

No Luftwaffe opposition was encountered by most of the heavies, but one Liberator combat wing drove off two sharp assaults near Tours by 50 German fighters—the largest number seen by the bombers since the start of the continental campaign.

Twelve enemy planes were shot down in all, seven by the B17s and B26s and five by escorting P51s, P38s and P47s.

In addition, the Eighth pursuits carried out low-level strafing attacks on transport, shooting up two locomotives, four freight cars, six flak towers, five trucks and other ground targets. Three fighters were lost.

Carrying tactical support to within a very short distance of the American lines, Marauders rained steel on a road junction and bridge in Villers Bocage, scene of a stiff tank battle. Rocket-firing Typhoons also struck in support of Allied ground units.

As a smashing follow-up to Wed-

(Continued on Page 4)

Army May Keep Two Million In

500,000 to Be Released Monthly After Peace, Group Estimates

WASHINGTON—A Senate postwar planning committee estimated yesterday the armed forces would discharge five to six hundred thousand men a month after peace comes, but two to three million men would be retained in service.

The report warned that "large pools of unemployed in war boom areas" would be "inevitable . . . regardless of the overall national situation."

If the nation is to enjoy "real prosperity" after the war, it added, American industry will have to employ eight to ten million more persons than held jobs in peacetime. Full employment, it said, must be available for 54,000,000 to 56,000,000, as compared with a pre-war peak of 46,000,000.

British NCOs in Reich Moved to Luxury Camp

One thousand British non-commissioned officers who are prisoners of war in Germany have been moved from various prison camps throughout the Reich to a new "luxury camp" near Berlin, where they are housed in comfortable huts, guarded by English-speaking sentries and given a small wardrobe each, the International Red Cross at Geneva reported to British authorities yesterday.

Red Cross officials expressed the belief that the move indicated a German feeling that the end of the war was near and a desire to have British NCOs report good treatment by their captors. Similar action was taken by the Germans towards the end of the last war.

Prisoners moved to the new camp were taken on sight-seeing tours in Germany and given "ample freedom" at various stops, the Red Cross report said.

Leopold Sent to Germany

King Leopold of the Belgians was sent to Germany the day after the Allies landed in Normandy, the Belgian government-in-exile said yesterday, according to a Reuter dispatch.

Believe Giant B29s Struck From China; Called 'the Beginning'

'We'll Strike Again and Again,' Patterson Asserts; Damage Great, Losses Light, House Told; New Bombers Carry 8 Tons

WASHINGTON—America's monster new monarchs of the skies—the B29 Super-Fortresses—were hurled at the heart of Japan yesterday in a sensational assault which not only blasted the Japanese home islands, but signalized the start of a bold new strategy in aerial warfare. The principal target was Tokyo itself, the House of Representatives heard from "a reliable source."

The War Department disclosed that the Super-Forts, with a range and striking power far beyond that of the heaviest bombers previously in action, have been organized into an independent arm known as the 20th Air Force, headed by Gen. Henry H. Arnold himself, which will be controlled by the joint chiefs of staff and used against the Axis on a global scale.

Their initial blow at Japan yesterday was made from distant land bases somewhere in the China-Burma-India theater. Just where was not revealed, but it was generally believed the big planes operated from China bases.

Rep. Joseph Starnes, of Alabama, told the House that he had received official confirmation that Tokyo had been bombed with "great destruction" by a large number of planes, which probably suffered "negligible" losses. The number of planes, the targets, and the results were not announced by the War Department, which issued only this brief but electrifying announcement: "B29 Super-Fortresses of the USAAF 20th Bomber Command bombed Japan today."

'Just a Beginning'

Robert Patterson, Undersecretary of War, said. "We shall strike at the heart of Japan again and again. The bombing of the islands of Japan by our new super-Fortresses is just a beginning."

Secretary of War Henry L. Stimson added that no corner of the Japanese homeland was now safe from attack. "The new long-range bombers have overcome the tremendous barriers of distance to bring the heart of Japan under the guns and bombs of the U.S. Army Air Forces," he said. "The pioneers who planned this action and manned the aircraft have shortened our road to Tokyo."

Tokyo radio, which gave the first news of the bombing raid led by Lt. Gen. (then Lt. Col.) Jimmy Doolittle on Tokyo and other cities on Apr. 18, 1942, had nothing to say immediately about the new assault. But the bare news that Japan had been bombed flashed instantly by press and radio across the U.S., caused a sensation throughout this country and dwarfed for the time being even the war news from France. Crowds in New York's Times Square cheered exultantly.

The long-awaited news that the super-Forts at last were in action and that their initial target was Japan boldly underscored the words of President Roosevelt when he told the country in a radio address opening the Fifth War Loan only two days ago that the Japanese now could be forced "to unconditional surrender or national suicide much more rapidly than had been thought possible."

Along with its brief announcement, the War Department released statements from Gen. George G. Marshall, U.S. Army chief of staff, and Gen.

(Continued on Page 4)

Yanks on Island 1,300 Mi. From Japan Mainland

New Invasion Supported By Pacific's Greatest Naval Task Force

American assault troops have landed on Saipan, in the Mariana group, 100 miles north of Guam and 1,300 miles from Yokohama, Adm. Chester W. Nimitz, Pacific Fleet commander, announced last night.

"Assault troops have effected landings on Saipan Island after an intensive preparatory bombardment of Saipan, Tinian, Pagan, Guam and Rota islands by carrier-based aircraft, and by a portion of the battleships, cruisers and destroyers of the Pacific fleet," Nimitz's communique said.

Preliminary reports, the official statement said, indicated American casualties were moderate, although "the landings are being continued against strong opposition under cover of a supporting bombardment by air and surface forces."

Earlier fleet headquarters at Pearl Harbor announced that battleships, cruisers, destroyers, and carrier-based planes attacked enemy bases in the Marianas, which are about 1,500 miles from the Philippines.

This task force officially described as "the largest in the Pacific war," directed its assault against Saipan and Pinian, Japan's two main bases in the Marianas. Twenty enemy ships, including four destroyers, were sunk and 17 more damaged.

The armada's initial attack on the Marianas was made last Saturday, when carrier-based planes bombed enemy installations and continued the attack Sunday. Warships' big guns shelled Saipan and Pinian Monday and planes attacked again Tuesday.

The Mariana group consists of 14 islands, covering an area of 246

(Continued on Page 4)

Path of Glory Leads to Clink For Glider-Borne Stowaway

By Bruce Munn
United Press Staff Writer

AN ALLIED TROOP-CARRIER BASE—This is the story of a man who is in the guardhouse because he invaded France.

It began in a U.S. barracks in England. The airborne boys trooped in shouting gleefully—"The invasion is on." One private was quiet. He was not an airborne trooper, but he had made up his mind that he was going.

The second part of his story began in a Horsa glider being towed across the Channel. The private, Charles Schmelz 20, of Pittsburgh, Pa., was crouched in the tail, a stowaway. He took with him a machine-gun, helmet, trench shovel and two bars of chocolate.

After 20 minutes he rapped on the door and the airborne troops let him out, gave him some rations and fed him anti-airsick pills.

"We landed about 100 yards from the enemy lines," Schmelz related, "and it was a good thing I got out of the tail, because it was torn off when we came down. The airborne troops advanced four miles. We slept that night in trenches listening to the gunfire ahead."

Next morning the unit pushed on and spent a nerve-shattering time under direct fire from German guns.

"We lay in a shallow trench for five and a half hours listening to the shrapnel," Schmelz said. "I prayed—I am not ashamed to admit it—I prayed almost all night.

"We moved on, going very carefully in order to escape German bullets."

At this point—three days after he landed—Schmelz was sent back to England.

Now he is in the guardhouse, and he may be court martialled for being AWOL.

New Jet Propelled Plane, P59 Airacomet, in Use

WASHINGTON—The new jet propulsion planes, designated P59s and called Airacomets, are now in use, the War Department announced yesterday.

It disclosed also that production had begun of two new planes, the A26 Invader, a light bombardment plane described as an improvement on the A20 Havoc, and the P66 King Cobra fighter said to be a larger and improved version of the P39 Airacobra.

The Department said that the recently disclosed night fighter the P61 Blackwidow, has 2,000 H.P. engines and four-bladed standard propellers. It weighs more than 25,000 lbs. and is armed with 20 mm. cannon and .50 caliber machine-guns.

THE STARS AND STRIPES
MEDITERRANEAN

Vol. 2, No. 29, Saturday, June 24, 1944 — For U. S. Armed Forces — TWO FRANCS

Soviets Launch New Offensive

Germans Make Last Man Stand For Cherbourg

Von Rundstedt Orders Assaulted Port Held Despite Cost

By Sgt. DON WILLIAMS
(Stars and Stripes Staff Writer)

American troops were locked in an all-out struggle with bitterly resisting Nazi forces for control of the great Channel port of Cherbourg on Friday.

The full-scale Allied assault of the naval fortress, begun after the Nazis had failed to reply to a surrender ultimatum broadcast from an American field headquarters in Normandy, was in its second day.

Supreme Headquarters, Allied Expeditionary Force spokesmen expressed the belief that the city would be captured fairly rapidly and that a siege was unlikely to develop. The capture of the eastern of the three hill positions holding up the fall of the city was reported.

In Washington, President Roosevelt declared that the operations at Cherbourg were proceeding according to schedule.

Yank doughboys, making a frontal assault from the south and southwest upon the strongly-fortified port, were fighting their war forward yard by yard under heavy air and artillery support. Enemy pillboxes guarding the smoke-wreathed city were being reduced one by one.

Into the bomb-shattered inner defense zones, the Nazis had crammed all of the troops they were able to withdraw from the east

(Continued on Page 16)

Nazi Resistance Grows In Italy

ALLIED FORCE HEADQUARTERS, June 23 — German troops, strongly placed along a broad front about 20 miles south of Arezzo, a Foggia-like air, rail and highway center below Florence, today were reported holding on desperately in spite of Allied advances everywhere around them.

On both the Tyrrhenian and Adriatic flanks the Allies maintained their steady advance against slackening enemy resistance on the east coast and against increasing pressure on the west.

In its coastal sector American armor and infantry units pushed ahead against increased artillery fire along Highway 1 to within seven miles of the seashore town of Follonica, less than ten miles from Piombino. Lt. Gen. Mark W. Clark's forces held high ground on both sides of the highway in this area. Further inland, other American units were fighting their way forward on Highway 73 and along a road northeast from Paganico to within two and a half miles of Roccastrada. The Americans fought through heavily mined areas covered by artillery and self-propelled guns.

French troops of the 5th Army also were encountering mounting opposition in their push northward in the vicinity of Cinigiano, Montenero and Castiglione D'Orcia, near where the 5th Army line merges with that of the 8th Army of General Sir Oliver Leese. The 8th Army, according to today's reports, was meeting determined resistance from forces which gave no indication of withdrawing from strong positions between Lakes Trasimeno and Chiusi, and others east of Lake Trasimeno and around

(Continued on Page 16)

Big Brother

AMERICA'S NEW B-29 SUPER-FORTRESS is shown for the first time in this photo released by the War Department following news of its first mission against Japan. Some idea of the giant bomber's size is given in the photo, in which a Culver target plane is dwarfed by the nose of the huge ship. (Official U. S. Army Photo)

Most Powerful Force Ever Afloat Hits Japs

WASHINGTON—Task Force 58, the hard-hitting American armada which battered a concentration of the Japanese Imperial Fleet on Monday between the Marianas and the Philippines, is "the most powerful and destructive in the history of sea warfare," a U. S. Navy spokesman revealed Thursday in making public for the first time a partial report on the 5th Fleet's spearhead.

While definite figures on the size of the task force were not given, a Navy statement issued later Thursday evening said that nearly 100 American aircraft carriers were now operating in the Pacific.

This statement apparently was in conflict with one made Monday by Rear Admiral Dewitt C. Ramsey, Chief of the Bureau of Aeronautics, who had stated that the Navy would have 100 carriers in commission by the end of this year.

One indication of Task Force 58's tremendous wallop came in the disclosure that the unit can launch more than 1,000 planes from its carriers. The spokesman said the force "probably had 20 carriers."

"Just where this floating strategic air force will strike next," the spokesman said, "is a constant source of conjecture and worry for the Japanese."

The task force includes the latest and swiftest aircraft carriers, battleships, cruisers and destroyers and it has been given "the entire Pacific Ocean all the way to the gates of Japan as its stamping ground."

Task Force 58 first operated as a unit immediately after the occupation of the Marshalls last winter. It covered the landings in the Gilberts, supported the attack on Hollandia, in New Guinea, and has twice raided Truk. Its very identity had been kept secret until this week, following the running engagement in which at least four Jap warships, including a carrier, were sunk; 10 heavily damaged; three tankers sunk; one destroyer possibly sunk, and another carrier possibly sunk, in addition to 353 aircraft destroyed.

At the same time, an official an-

(Continued on Page 15)

Bolivia's Government Receives Recognition

WASHINGTON — The United States, Great Britain, and 17 other American Republics Friday recognized the government of Bolivia.

An announcement by the U. S. Embassy in La Paz declared that "the provisional government of Bolivia has carried out a number of decisive and affirmative acts in support of hemisphere solidarity and the cause of the United Nations." The consensus was, the note said, that there was no longer any reason for withholding recognition.

Shipyard Completes LCI In Seven Hours

BOSTON—Workers of the Lawley yards at Neponset, urged on by loudspeakers and pinup girls, established a new all-time shipbuilding record Wednesday when they launched a 158-foot prefabricated landing craft just seven hours and one minute after construction began.

Only the yard's regular 300-man crew were engaged in the performance that smashed the previous record for LCI production of between four and five days. The record astonished the most optimistic officials who had set a goal of 18 hours for the launching.

President Signs GI Bill Of Rights

WASHINGTON — President Roosevelt has signed the Soldier Benefit Bill—"GI Bill of Rights"—providing for federally-financed education, government-guaranteed loans and unemployment compensation and services for veterans.

In a statement issued after the bill became law, the President said: "The well-rounded program for veterans is nearly completed. It gives emphatic notice to the men and women in the armed forces that the American people do not intend to let them down."

The President pointed out that by prior legislation the government had already provided service men and women with many benefits. Among those he listed adequate dependency allowances; mustering-out pay; generous hospitalization, medical care and vocational rehabilitation and training; liberal pensions in case of death or disability in military service; substantial war risk life insurance and guarantee of premiums on commercial policies during service; protection of civil rights and suspension of enforcement of certain civil liberties and liabilities during service; emergency maternal care for wives of enlisted men, and reemployment rights for returning veterans.

In addition to all of these benefits, most of which accrue to soldiers while they are in the service, the new GI Bill of Rights mainly provides:

1. An opportunity for service men and women to begin or resume their education with the government paying tuition up to 500 dollars a year for four years. During this period, 50 dollars a

(Continued on Page 15)

Russians Crack Nazis' Positions Around Vitebsk

Berlin Claims Minsk Objective Of New Red Army Push

MOSCOW—Russia launched the long awaited full scale offensive against the Germans on the Eastern front early Friday, an official Soviet communique announced.

Behind a massed artillery barrage, and with close support of the Red Air Force, Soviet troops in White Russia crashed through powerful German positions both northwest and south of Vitebsk, a keypoint of the Nazi line.

Friday's Soviet communique declared: "On June 23 northwest and southeast of Vitebsk our troops, with support of artillery and air force, passed to the offensive.

"Northwest of Vitebsk our troops broke through strongly fortified enemy defenses on a front 20 miles wide, and advanced from eight to ten miles.

"They have occupied over 100 inhabited localities, including Shumilin, the district center of the Vitebsk region, and the railway stations of Sirotkino and Shatviza, both on the Polotsk-Vitebsk line."

The communique added that Soviet forces had also cut the vital Vitebsk-Orsha railway.

First news of the powerful Russian drive came from a Berlin broadcast, which declared that the main assault force of Soviet troops were massed along the Smolensk-Orsha highway. The Germans admitted that the Nazi lines had been overwhelmed at several points, but claimed that the breaches had been

(Continued on Page 16)

New Drive Begun On Saipan Island

PEARL HARBOR—U. S. Marines and Army troops, shielded by a great American battle fleet standing off the Marianas, launched Thursday morning a major attack to expand their positions on Saipan Island, pushing ahead on a four-mile front.

In the bitter fighting since their landing on the island a week ago, the Yanks have captured about one-third of the island's southern sector, including two airfields. One of these was the Aslatic airdrome, most valuable in the Marianas, which was ready for operation Friday after Seabees repaired and extended its 3,600-foot main runway.

The Japanese defenders fought ferociously and had the advantage of entrenched positions along the steep ridges. They used considerable land mines and booby traps, as well as artillery.

In one hard-fought engagement on the hill overlooking Magicienne Bay, Jap artillerymen ran their field pieces out of caves, fired, and then ducked back in again. The Americans finally captured these and similar positions elsewhere, using flame throwers in several instances.

One of the big advantages the invading Americans had was artillery superiority, achieved in the first few days. During the landing, scores of heavy guns were lugged ashore across the reefs. In addition to these big guns, U. S. warships were busy all day long pumping shells into Jap positions. Most enemy shore batteries already have been knocked out.

Latest reports indicated American troops had advanced more

(Continued on Page 15)

Landon Sees Dewey First Ballot Choice

CHICAGO, Ill.—A prediction by Alfred M. Landon Thursday that New York's Governor Dewey would be nominated for President by the Republican Convention on the first ballot found immediate support from a prominent Pennsylvania delegate who said that his state's 70 votes would go to Dewey when balloting begins this Wednesday, two days after the Convention opens.

From Sen. Robert Taft (R., Ohio), however, came the statement that Ohio's Governor Bricker "has a good chance" for the nomination despite mounting predictions of an early Dewey victory.

Roy Moore, Governor Bricker's campaign manager, branded as "fantastic" the claims of strength made by Dewey's managers. "Numerous states which haven't been caucused have been claimed in entirety for Dewey, in some instances where delegates have publicly announced for other aspirants," Mr. Moore said.

The Associated Press reported that Lt. Cmdr. Harold E. Stassen's managers stated that "Stassen could put on a campaign such as this nation has never seen," urging that the former Minnesota governor be named as the presidential choice. Lt. Cmdr. Stassen has made known that he would reject the nomination for Vice President.

The Resolutions Committee, with Sen. Taft as chairman, heard the plea from National Chairman Harrison E. Spangler to keep the GOP platform down to some "reasonable length."

"If we don't keep it short, instead of being published in the press it will go into the waste paper basket," Mr. Spangler said. He urged that the platform deal only with fundamentals, a proposal which Taft seconded.

Sen. Warren Austin (R., Vt.), brought to Chicago a one-page typewritten declaration of foreign policy which, he said, was patterned after the Mackinac pledge advocat-

(Continued on Page 16)

NORTHERN IRELAND EDITION

1d. THE STARS AND STRIPES 1d.

Daily Newspaper of U.S. Armed Forces in the European Theater of Operations

Vol. 1. No. 172. New York, N.Y.—Belfast, Northern Ireland. Monday, June 26, 1944.

Cherbourg Lost, Germans Concede

Reds Encircle 'Key to Balkans'

Trap Closes On Garrisons Inside Vitebsk

Road Now Open to Minsk, White Russia Capital; 5 Divisions Cut Off

Mighty concentrations of Soviet artillery and tanks have battered wide breaches in the Germans' vaunted "Fatherland Line" in White Russia, and last night, 72 hours after launching of the Red Army's summer offensive, only 20 to 30 miles of the original 160 miles of fortifications remained intact.

Vitebsk, long regarded as the key to the Baltic states, was completely encircled, Moscow announced at midnight. Five infantry divisions were said to be cut off in the city, where street fighting already was in progress. Encirclement of the fortress city opened the road to Minsk, capital of White Russia, 140 miles to the southwest.

Evacuation of Vitebsk already has been decided upon, according to the Berlin correspondent of the Stockholm Aftonbladet, who reported that the situation was viewed in the German capital as critical.

From Berlin, meanwhile, came a report that the offensive has been extended south to the Bobruisk area above the Pripet Marshes. Col. Ernst von Hammer, military correspondent of German News Agency, coupled this report with one that the Russians have thrown in 80 rifle divisions and one tank force.

Drive Ahead In Finland

In Finland the Russians pressed back the Finns at top speed along the Aunus Isthmus, between Lakes Ladoga and Onega, pushing on towards Petrozavodsk, capital of the Karelian Republic. North of Onega, the Russians were reported freeing additional miles of the Leningrad-Murmansk railway.

The White Russian offensive was launched with four main thrusts—northwest of Vitebsk, south of Vitebsk, north of Orsha and at Mogilev. Of these, the attack above Vitebsk by the First Baltic Army of Gen. Ivan Bagramyan made the greatest initial gain—an advance up to 28 miles through a breach widened to 50 miles in 48 hours.

It was this force which reached the Dvina, leading across Latvia into the Baltic at Riga.

Gains on the other fronts ranged from nine to 15 miles through gaps 50 miles wide south of Vitebsk, 30 miles wide at Mogilev and 112 miles wide north of Orsha.

As the advance progresses, the Russians will move into difficult country infested with swamps, but ahead lies the core of the German defenses in White Russia, airdromes at Orsha and Bobruisk, the vital railway link of Minsk, and the Baranovici pass, gateway into Poland.

The War Today

France—Germans concede loss of Cherbourg and tell of U.S. tanks entering city as defenders run out of ammunition. . . Latest Allied reports tell of fierce fighting for fourth day. . . British advance in Tilly sector. . . Allied planes pound targets in France from Spanish border to Pas de Calais, hitting oil dumps, airfields and robot coast.

Pacific—Japs viewing Saipan as direct threat to Japan proper and Philippines promise all-out battle to throw out the Yanks now holding half of Marianas Island, 1,200 miles southeast of Tokyo. . . Carrier planes bomb Bonins, 550 miles from Yokohama.

Russia—German line in White Russia shattered . . . Vitebsk encircled and way clear for Red advance on Minsk, White Russian capital . . Finns being pushed back toward Karelian capital.

Italy—Enemy reported abandoning port of Leghorn . . . Nazi counter-attack forces Allied line back along Adriatic.

This Is What Vets Will Get Under the 'GI Bill of Rights'

WASHINGTON—When President Roosevelt, using ten pens so that interested legislators and veterans' officials might have souvenirs, put his signature last week on the so-called "GI Bill of Rights" he wrote into law probably the most comprehensive measure yet enacted for soldiers of the current war.

Education benefits up to $500-a-year tuition, plus subsistence pay, unemployment compensation of $20 a week for 52 weeks, and $2,000 loans for the purchase of homes, farms, or businesses—these are the bill's principal points.

To answer the questions that will inevitably arise concerning the law's provision and veterans' eligibility to participate under them, the following detailed roundup of the legislation's benefits has been prepared by Army News Service.

Exceptions to and restrictions on these benefits are many, and some provisions which are not clearly defined in the text will have to be covered in regulations. But here, as they stand now, are high points:

Education—Up to $500 a year tuition and expenses for laboratory fees and books at any recognized private or public secondary business school college, including religious school. A subsistence allowance of $50 a month, plus $25 a month for dependents.

Education benefits are available only to veterans who were under

(Continued on Page 7)

Republicans on Convention Eve Talk of Dewey-Warren Slate

CHICAGO—Republicans gathering here last night for their first war-time national convention since Lincoln was renominated in 1864 talked of a "Hands-Across-the-Nation" ticket, headed by Gov. Thomas E. Dewey of New York for President and Gov. Earl Warren of California for Vice-President.

The convention opens today, but tomorrow, when the resolutions committee headed by Sen. Robert A. Taft of Ohio presents the 1944 platform for adoption, it is generally expected to put the party and its nominee on record as favorite full American participation in a post-war international organization to maintain peace

If predictions of the Dewey supporters that their candidate will be nominated on the first or second ballot materialize, the Presidential balloting should be completed Wednesday. The convention then could complete its work Thursday with selection of the Vice-Presidential nominee and acceptance speeches of the standard-bearers.

Warren, who will deliver the convention keynote speech today, released the California delegation of 50 which had been pledged to him and said he did not seek either first or second place on the ticket. His name, however, was that most frequently mentioned for the Vice-Presidential choice, and Rep. Joseph W. Martin of Massachusetts, House minority leader and permanent convention chairman, predicted that Warren would accept.

Dewey himself, for that matter, has not publicly announced his candidacy. There were some who thought earlier this year, before his boom attained its present proportions, that the former "racket-bust-

(Continued on Page 2)

Nazis Giving Up Port of Leghorn

Demolishing All Docks Not Already Bomb-Levelled; 5th 50 Miles Away

Reconnaissance disclosed yesterday that the Germans in Italy were abandoning the bomb-shattered west coast port of Leghorn with the rapid approach of Fifth Army spearheads, now only 50 miles to the southeast.

As Fifth Army armor and infantry gained all along the Tyrrhenian coast, occupying Fallonica, Monte Rotondo, and Montcalio, all astride Highways 1 and 3, it was revealed at 15th Air Force headquarters that the Germans were blowing up all Leghorn docks not damaged by Allied raids in the last 15 months.

In the mountainous sector of central Italy, where the Germans marshalled their forces for a stand, Eighth Army units attacking east and west of Lane Trasimeno occupied the towns of Sarteano, Pescia, and Caselvieto.

Several Allied tanks yesterday penetrated into Chiusi, mainstay of the Nazi line in central Italy, and 23 miles to the northeast British troops made some gains around Perugia.

Strong enemy counter-attacks along the Adriatic coast meanwhile forced the Allies back along the general line of the Chienti River, some 25 miles southeast of the naval base of Ancona.

Bonds in Hitler's Name Outlawed by Treasury

SIOUX FALLS, S.D. — The Treasury department has clamped down on the War Bond buying of Dr. O. Charles Ericksen, who has been listing such people as Tojo and Hitler as co-owners, with the money payable to him at their deaths.

According to regulations, bond purchases are restricted to residents of the U.S. and its possessions or citizens abroad temporarily.

For Ex-Presidents Only

WASHINGTON—Rep. Gordon Canfield (R., N.J.) has introduced a bill to create the office of senator-at-large for all former Presidents of the U.S. The ex-Presidents would have all senatorial rights and privileges except one—voting.

Fierce Bombardment Caps 4-Day Assault To Capture Vital Port

Allies Claim Only That Troops Are Inside City; Berlin Says Nazis Ran Out of Munitions; Pall of Smoke Nearly Hides City

The loss of Cherbourg and its great port was conceded by the Germans at 7.30 last night after four days of a fierce American assault capped by a pulverizing naval bombardment.

"In view of the enemy's crushing superiority, particularly in heavy arms and air power, it is to be assumed that the Americans have succeeded in taking possession of the town of Cherbourg in the course of today, Sunday," said the official German News Agency. "German grenadiers, fighting in self-sacrificial close-range combat, destroyed numerous American tanks with high explosives, but were, however, unable to prevent them penetrating into the city as they ran out of ammunition."

Latest Allied reports from the front had told of American patrols penetrating into the main street of the smoke-shrouded city to feel out the German defenses, while fierce fighting continued against the pillboxes and other fortifications.

By indicating the fall of the city in advance of any Allied announcements to that effect, the Nazis may have hoped to cushion the blow from a propaganda standpoint and put across their excuse that ammunition ran out in their laudatory accounts of their troops' last-ditch stand.

The German Version

Their story was that the Americans mustered heavy armament against Cherbourg Saturday night and early yesterday morning "began an extremely heavy bombardment on all quarters of the town, singling out the southeastern city limits. About noon the fortifications of Cherbourg harbor were subjected to an extremely heavy naval bombardment directed from the air by artillery reconnaissance planes.

"A few hours later, the American infantry and tank formations, held in readiness in the area of Octeville went over to the attack. Heavy bitter and bloody fighting developed the already depleted ranks of the German defenders fighting with determination to the last."

The Nazi commander, Gen. Vondohlieben, had issued a new order: "Anyone failing to defend the city to the last will be shot."

Nevertheless, more than 1,800 prisoners were taken by the Yanks in the 24 hours up to 9 AM, and the Germans were observed to be firing their motor pools and even ammunition dumps. Dense clouds of black smoke from these demolitions and from fuel dumps rolled across the city and almost blotted it from the view of the U.S. attackers. The Germans mined the roads into the city and prepared the buildings for a house-to-house defense.

10 U.S. Divisions, Paris Says

The Germans, acknowledging that the Americans had penetrated some of their defenses gave this picture of the fierce resistance in a high command report: "German grenadiers and artillery units bypassed by the enemy have formed islands of resistance in the enemy's rear in hamlets, parks, thickets and valleys. Frequently local German headquarters and artillery positions are meeting the enemy with cold steel at points where he has broken in."

Paris radio put the strength of the American attackers at ten divisions.

The heights overlooking Cherbourg were reported from the front to be firmly in American hands. While heavy American artillery and mortar fire continued, the troops hacked their way through the pillboxes with grenades and bayonets, and used flame-throwers on the toughest points.

(Continued on Page 2)

Tokyo Worried, Terms Saipan Battle 'Decisive'

Assures Japan Big Forces Will Be Sent Against Advancing Yanks

While American troops increased their grip on Saipan in the Marianas, 1,200 miles southeast of Tokyo, to encompass half the island, German News Agency yesterday quoted a member of the Japanese High Command as saying the Japs were ready to throw in everything to keep the island.

The Japanese spokesman said that fighting for Saipan "has developed from just another invasion into the greatest decisive battle of the war. We are set to commit major army, air and naval power into the struggle."

He assured the homeland that the high command was doing its utmost to repel the enemy.

"We realize that the allied landing is a direct threat to Japan proper and the Philippines," he said.

The American forces pushing northward made new gains along the shore of Magicienne Bay, the allied communique reported. A Reuter dispatch said the Japs were consolidating and increasing their defenses along an extended line and were fighting a delaying action while preparing for a last stand.

Meanwhile, U.S. carrier-based planes struck Friday at Iwojina, in the Bonin Islands, only 550 miles from Yokohama.

In further attacks the carrier planes sank five Japanese ships and destroyed 72 planes in a series of blows at four airfields in the Marianas.

U.S. Liberators smashed at Yap, in the southwestern Marianas, and knocked down 12 enemy aircraft and

(Continued on Page 2)

'We're in Cherbourg!' They Shriek

Prisoners Stream Out of City As Yanks Patrol for Snipers

By Richard McMillan
United Press Correspondent

WITH U.S. TROOPS, Before Cherbourg.—With German guns putting up a heavy cross barrage, American troops swept into Cherbourg yesterday afternoon.

They pressed down the sunken road to the coast and then smashed their way eastwards into the port against heavy machine-gun and long-range artillery fire.

The first troops entered the city at noon. The Americans started to patrol the streets and round up snipers. I saw many hundreds of German prisoners pouring out of the city along the roads. One American officer, badly wounded and his arm bleeding profusely, held his revolver in his left hand and brought a German officer out of a house.

The streets of Cherbourg were heavily defended, but there was not nearly as much resistance as was expected in the outlying houses.

The final attack started after artillery had blasted the strongpoints. I went and stood on high ground to watch the battle.

Tanks rumbled along the country track past dead Germans lying in rows under hedges, their bodies covered with dust thrown up by tanks [illegible] accompanied the tanks downhill into the field to get the latest news from battalion headquarters, and then the German barrage opened up at full blast.

A shell fell ahead of us to the left. Another came down nearer to the right. A third one fell in the field 15 or 20 yards away. The sergeant beside me was killed, and several officers nearby were severely

(Continued on Page 2)

Nomination of Colonel, 28, To Be General Approved

WASHINGTON—Two Air Force "youngsters" were among 63 Army officers whose Presidential nominations to the rank of brigadier general were approved by the Senate Military Affairs Committee.

The two are Col. Richard C. Sanders, 28, commander of a bombardment wing in the ETO, and Col Clinton D. Vincent, the 14th Air Force in the China-Burma-India Theater.

The committee at the same time approved promotions of 30 officers to temporary grade of major general.

1D.

THE STARS AND STRIPES

1Fr.

Daily Newspaper of U.S. Armed Forces in the European Theater of Operations

Vol. 4 No. 211 — New York, N.Y.—London, England—France — Friday, July 7, 1944

Robot Toll 2,752; London Worst Hit; Yanks Quit La Haye; Rundstedt Ousted

Reds Smash Near 3 Key Rail Towns

Vilna, Dvinsk Threatened; Russians Only 10 Miles From Baranovichi

The Russians' swift drive west on the central front increased the threat to the Germans' Warsaw-Leningrad supply line yesterday as the Red Army pressed closer to the rail junctions of Dvinsk, Vilna and Baranovichi.

The latter town, guarding the approaches to Brest-Litovsk 120 miles beyond, felt the pressure of the Soviet advance, with Marshal Rokossovsky's troops less than ten miles away.

The Russians were less than 40 miles from Vilna, from where a branch line runs west to feed Kaunas, in Lithuania, and Konigsberg, in East Prussia. At Dvinsk, commanding the Dvina valley leading to Riga and the Baltic, they were reported already in contact with Nazi defensive positions southeast of the town.

Moscow dispatches were not clear just how close the Red Army had moved to Dvinsk, northern end of the Nazi defense line, but a German Overseas News Agency report that the Russians "attempted to outflank the strong German positions" suggested a considerable advance beyond their last reported position some 45 miles from the city.

Sweeping Nazis Away

Izvestia said the Germans were launching repeated counter-attacks "with considerable forces" in front of Baranovichi, but the paper added that the Russians were "sweeping the Germans away."

Berlin dispatches forecast both an attempt to break through to Vilna from the fortified town of Molodechno, which fell to the Russians Wednesday after a three-day battle, and a thrust down the Dvina valley toward the Baltic. They said the strongest Soviet concentrations now were in the Dvinsk area.

Capture of the railway junction of Kovel, 100 miles north of the Polish base of Lwow, was announced by Marshal Stalin last night, 24 hours after the Germans announced its evacuation. The town was taken by southern units of Marshal Rokossovsky's First White Russian Army group.

Moscow reported the Germans were losing heavily in their retreat beyond Minsk. A supplement to the nightly Soviet communique said 2,700 were killed west of Minsk in two days and 2,000 others were taken prisoner.

On the Finnish front, the Red Army advanced another ten miles on the Karelian Isthmus.

Yanked From Japs

Stars and Stripes Map

American troops yesterday were reported in possession of seven-eighths of Saipan Island, in the Marianas, 1,200 miles from Yokohama.

Saipan Victory Near—Nimitz

While Adm. Chester W. Nimitz announced that the American battle for Saipan in the Marianas was nearing a successful conclusion, U.S. troops seized the second of two important airfields on Noemfoor Island, 100 miles west of Biak, off northern Dutch New Guinea.

Nimitz said "we have the situation well in hand" in pointing out that Saipan casualties compared with those in Normandy, "indicating the toughness of the opposition we are meeting." A New York broadcast, quoted by Reuter, said American forces now controlled seven-eighths of the island.

Capture of Koransoren airfield on Noemfoor was accomplished with only minor opposition, Gen. Douglas MacArthur's communique said. The Americans were reported converging on Namber, Noemfoor's only air base still held by the Japs.

Meanwhile, Tokyo Radio reported a U.S. task force off the Bonins, only 550 miles from the Jap mainland, and speculated on possible landings there shortly.

Fire in Ringling Big Tent Traps Circus Spectators

HARTFORD, Conn., July 6 (Reuter)—Fire broke out in a big tent of the Ringling Brothers and Barnum & Bailey circus today at the afternoon performance. First reports said the tent collapsed, trapping an undetermined number of persons beneath it.

Von Kluge Takes Over In France

Americans Seek to Bypass La Haye; Fierce Battle For Carpiquet Airfield

As U.S. troops were forced out of La Haye du Puits but made gains elsewhere against stiffening German resistance yesterday, Hitler disclosed that Field Marshal Gerd von Rundstedt had been replaced as Nazi supreme commander in the west.

A communique from Hitler's headquarters explained that Von Rundstedt was "unable to carry out his duties for health reasons." Replacing him was Field Marshal Gunther von Kluge, the Prussian Junker who led the German armies to the gates of Moscow and who is, at 69, the oldest Nazi field commander.

Although the Yanks were forced to withdraw from La Haye, six miles inland from the west coast of the Cherbourg peninsula, they began to bypass the town on both sides, and captured three villages. East of La Haye, they drove six miles to capture La Butte. Southwest of La Haye, they took Glatiny and Soorman, both about four miles from the town.

Battle for Airfield

Canadian forces, who retained a firm hold of Carpiquet, three miles west of Caen, struggled to capture the fiercely-defended airfield.

Along the 25-mile arc of the American drive between the west coast of the Cherbourg peninsula and Carentan, First Army men met stiff German opposition at many points as they came to defense positions which the Germans had thrown up in the last few days, but the Yanks

(Continued on page 4)

The War Today

France—Americans gain on both sides of La Haye du Puits but are forced to withdraw from town as German resistance stiffens . . . Von Rundstedt replaced by Von Kluge as Nazi supreme commander in west . . . Canadians continue grim battle to capture Carpiquet airfield.

Russia—Red Army advance menaces Germans' Warsaw-Leningrad rail line feeding Baltic states, with advance spearheads reported already in contact with defenses outside Dvinsk, gateway to Latvia and Baltic . . . Rokossovsky's troops reported ten miles from Baranovichi, fortified town guarding approaches to Brest-Litovsk, 120 miles beyond on Minsk-Brest railway.

Italy—Eighth Army closes to within three miles of Arezzo, communications center 37 miles from Florence . . . Allied troops now eight miles from Ancona on Adriatic and 10½ miles from Leghorn on the west coast.

Pacific—Adm. Chester W. Nimitz reports battle for Saipan in Marianas nearing successful conclusion. . . Americans reported in control of seven-eighths of island. . . . U.S. forces seize second airfield on Noemfoor Island, 100 miles west of Biak, off northern Dutch New Guinea. . . . Tokyo Radio speculates on possible American landings in Bonin Islands, 550 miles from Japanese mainland.

Asia—U.S. Chemical Warfare Service officer confirms Japanese use of mustard and Lewisite gas against Chinese in Hunan Province campaign . . . Chiang Kai-Shek in message on war's seventh anniversary sees victory in Europe before "too long" and pledges China to keep on fighting.

Rocket-Bomb Attacks On N.Y. Held Possible

HOLLYWOOD, July 6 (AP)—Louis P. Lochner, former chief of the Associated Press Berlin bureau, in an NBC news commentary last night, said there was a possibility of a Nazi attack on the Atlantic Coast with rocket bombs or airplanes catapulted from U-boat trailers.

"As a measure of desperation and in order to bolster up home morale," he said, "the Nazis may actually one unexpected day release rocket bombs at the Atlantic Coast, aiming them, I suppose, at New York."

He said information about such a plan was given him by a German refugee—now an American citizen—who was in a position to study Nazi robot planes in their early stages.

Japs Using Gas, Yank Confirms

CHUNGKING, July 6 (UP)—Definite confirmation of Chinese reports that the Japanese were using poison gas was given today by Capt. Ralph Thompson, an intelligence officer of the U.S. Chemical Warfare Service.

Returning from Hengyang, the "bomb-Tokyo" town and air base taken by the enemy a few days ago, he said the Japs in this operation used a mixture of mustard gas and Lewisite

The Chinese for the last two years have declared that the Japanese were using gas in their land campaign in China.

(President Roosevelt warned the Axis some time ago, following Soviet reports that the Germans had used gas in Russia, that the U.S. and its Allies were prepared to reply in kind. There was no immediate comment from Washington officials on Capt. Thompson's report.)

'Situation is Tense'

Meanwhile, Generalissimo Chiang Kai-Shek, in a message to the nation on the seventh anniversary of the war against Japan, declared that "the situation is grave" in southeastern Hunan Province, where the Japanese have made "rapid advances," but that their drive there was "five years too late."

Chiang expressed the belief that "it will not be too long before the war in Europe is brought to a successful conclusion," and pledged that the Chinese would continue fighting "until victory has been attained and our lost territory recovered."

By the drive in Hunan along the Canton-Hankow railroad, Chiang said, "the enemy aims at reducing the Chinese field forces before the Allied counter-offensive; secondly, to destroy Chinese air bases and minimize the danger of an air offensive; and thirdly, to control Chinese trunk lines as avenues of retreat for the troops now in Burma, Indo-China, Siam and Malaya.

"To date, he has not accomplished any of these three objectives."

Buzz-Bomb Facts Issued By Churchill

Premier Lifts Censorship On New Blitz; Reveals Yanks Among Killed

Breaking the rigid veil of censorship surrounding round-the-clock assaults by flying bombs, Prime Minister Winston Churchill, in a frank address before the House of Commons yesterday, revealed for the first time that London was bearing the brunt of Germany's "indiscriminate" new weapon.

Churchill, making no effort to "underrate the serious character of this form of attack," disclosed that since the Nazis began to hurl the lethal missiles at England, 2,752 persons had been killed and 8,000 injured.

A number of service men and women, including Americans, were among those killed and injured. U.S. soldiers were killed and wounded when a club was hit; another bomb barely missed quarters occupied by WACs. Several British WAAFs were killed when a bomb landed on a building in which they were housed.

The figures released by Churchill showed that more Britons were killed by the winged bombs than met death in the first 15 days of the Normandy fighting. In that period, 1,842 Britons died in France.

100-150 Bombs Daily

In the last two weeks or so, he said, 2,754 of the buzz bombs had been launched from the Continent and between 100 and 150 of them were being catapulted daily.

The Prime Minister promised that casualty lists would be published monthly, "as this battle may be a somewhat lengthy affair."

Indicating the seriousness with which the government viewed the new blitz, Churchill disclosed that children already were being sent away from the capital and that the evacuation of other persons was not being discouraged, since "we do not want more people in London than are required for business purposes of peace and war." The situation does not justify government compulsion on evacuation, he said.

About 5,000 children left from four main London railroad stations before noon yesterday bound for the north and west, with a teacher in charge of every ten children. It was expected that eventually 15,000 children would be leaving daily.

The Prime Minister stressed that despite measures taken to meet the new threat "we shall not allow the battle operations in Normandy or the attacks

(Continued on page 4)

Something New Has Been Added

For Every 6 Months Overseas, You'll Now Sport a Sleeve Bar

WASHINGTON, July 6—The War Department has authorized a cloth bar to indicate overseas service for officers and enlisted men, and officials said today that steps were being taken to make it available to troops as soon as possible. The bar will be worn on the left sleeve, as is the insignia denoting overseas service in the last war, and will be in addition to the chest ribbons denoting service in the various theaters.

The bar is to be worn four inches from and parallel with the end of the left sleeve. It is one-quarter inch wide and three-eights of an inch long on a cloth background with a border one-eighth of an inch wide. For wear on blouses, field jackets and battle-dress, the background will be olive drab and the border gold lace or bullion. For wear on shirts, it will be khaki background with a yellow cloth border.

Men who wear service hashmarks or World War I chevrons will wear the new bar above them.

One bar will be worn for each six months of overseas service, computed from the date of departure from the U.S. to date of return, during the period between Dec. 7, 1941, and six months after the end of the war.

The Quartermaster Corps has ordered a quantity of the bars for shipment to men now overseas. Officials said that until the issue arrives, overseas commanders are authorized to obtain a supply from other available sources. Authority to wear the bar will be entered on men's service records and officers' qualification cards. Periods of desertion and AWOL will not be counted toward service.

At the same time, the department announced regulations covering the new glider badge for officers and enlisted men. To qualify for it, an individual must be attached to a glider or airborne unit or to the airborne center; must participate in at least two glider flights under tactical or simulated tactical conditions; and must complete a course in lashing and loading equipment.

Men authorized to wear both the glider and parachute badges may wear only one at a time—the choice is optional with the individual.

Stories From WACs Buzzed by Bombs

Ceiling, Floor, Panes Mashed, 'But Nothing Happened to Me'

By the Associated Press

A number of American soldiers were killed recently by the flying bomb, and a group of WACs who escaped said the tragedy struck so quickly they had time to be frightened only when they saw bodies lying in the street.

Sgt. Rhoda Laird, of Houston, Tex., and Cpl. Mary Lou Bernick, of Sarasota, Fla., were eating breakfast about 7.30 in the basement when the blast occurred.

"It all happened so suddenly," said the sergeant. "The door was blown off right behind me. Windows were broken. We ran upstairs to see if anybody was hurt. No one was. Then we got the nerve up to go out and see what happened."

The corporal said: "I don't feel like talking about that part of it."

Some of the soldiers killed were in a truck waiting to go on rescue work to help victims of other bomb hits, Sgt. Laird said.

In the room where the two girls had been sleeping for safety, the beds were covered with glass. In their regular room, nothing was broken but a small mirror.

Sgt. Laird said 1/Sgt. Mary D. Thatcher, of Indianapolis, Ind., was "the most wonderful one of us all. She came running downstairs, got into a jeep and made trip after trip with the wounded to a hospital."

Pfc Dorothy Lacey, of Cincinnati, was knocked down by the blast with a tray and cup in her hand, but received only a nick on her hand.

"Those boys visited us all the time," said Pfc Lacey. "It was a horrible shock."

Pvt. Mary Jane Nevel, of Williamsport, Pa., was in her room when the bomb hit. She said: "The ceiling came down, the floor came up, the windows blew in—but nothing happened to me. I expected when such a thing happened we would all have hysterics, but none of us did."

Pfc Janet Lippincott, of New York, got a mule kick from the blast and, though unhurt, she wound up sitting in the sink.

CONTINENTAL EDITION

1 fr.

THE STARS AND STRIPES

1 fr.

Daily Newspaper of U.S. Armed Forces in the European Theater of Operations

Vol. 1 No 7 — Printed "Somewhere in France" — Tuesday, July 11, 1944

Yanks 3 Miles From St. Lo; British Attack S.W. of Caen

Reds Mop Up In Vilna, Push On for Baltic

East Prussia Looms As Battleground

MOSCOW, July 10 — The Red Army, fighting less than 100 miles from East Prussia on both sides of Vilna, has cut the rail line between Daugavapas and Kaunas, the prewar capital of Lithuania.

The Russians, mopping up in the battered streets of Vilna, reported captured yesterday, had that city surrounded on three sides. Radio Berlin said Nazi defenders barricaded themselves in the center of town and that house-to-house fighting was in progress for every foot of ground.

The broadcast said the Russians were sweeping northeast past Vilna toward Kaunas, 50 miles to the west. Tilsit, in East Prussia, and Riga, the Latvian port on the Baltic, appeared to be the main objectives of the offensive.

London heard the Germans already had declared East Prussia "an area of operations" and were planning swift withdrawals from Psyovnarvo, a sector of Estonia in the Northern Baltics. The Nazi plan called for evacuation of all Estonia and most of Latvia in order to conserve forces for the defense of East Prussia, cradle of Junkerism.

With Vilna virtually encircled, the Russians also swept south, taking 150 towns on a front of more than 100 miles, including Lida on the Vilna-Baranowicze railway.

German news commentators admitted the Reds, attacking with ten infantry divisions and three tank brigades, had broken through the German lines on the east bank of the Bug River, west of Kowel, but added the customary claim that penetrating units had been destroyed.

Tank 'Darlings' Make a Hit With Their Pet Boom

A TANK UNIT, Normandy, July 10—They gave John Derden a tank fitted with a retrieving boom instead of a gun, but that didn't keep him out of combat. He and his repair crew figured if they couldn't fight, they could fix tanks that would—and that's how "Derden's Darlings" have been operating since early in the invasion.

During one battle near Carentan, the Ellijay, Ga., warrant officer and his men went into the middle of the fight to pull out five crippled mediums and one banged-up light tank. Then their tank retriever was knocked out.

Within hours "Derden's Darlings" had three of the tanks and their vehicle back in the fight.

Another time they went behind the German lines to bring in a white-starred armored car, light tank and assault gun lost out of their outfit some time before.

The "Darlings" are Sgt. Frank Hans, of Baltimore; Cpls. Loren Golo, and Walter Kirbauer, of Chicago; T/4 Dan Juhl, of Burbank, Cal., and T/5 Kenneth Beckham, of St. James, Mo.

BOLIVIAN LEADER SHOT

LA PAZ, BOLIVIA, July 10 (Reuter)—Joe Antonio, leader of the left - wing revolutionary party, was wounded by a bullet fired by two unidentified men. His condition is serious.

Majority of GIs in France Are Eating B Rations — And Some Get Oranges!

The majority of Yank soldiers in France are now eating B rations—such as chicken, sweet potatoes white bread and cherry cobbler—the First Army Quartermaster officer disclosed yesterday.

Fresh fruit has been on the menu for men in the front lines, he said. American troops at the front have received two issues of oranges.

Fresh frozen meat will be added to rations as quickly as possible, the officer promised.

He said besides the 50 per cent of troops on B rations, 25 per cent are being fed the "10-in-1" food, 15 per cent are issued C rations and the remaining 10 per cent are still eating K rations.

The "10-in-1 rations are issued in large cans so that one issue will feed 10 men. Containing canned vegetables and a variety of meats, they are distributed to men who are not at the front, where the troops eat on C and K rations.

Here's a typical breakfast of B rations: stewed prunes, rolled oats, milk which is canned or dehydrated, pork sausage, plain omelet, toast, apple butter, coffee.

The dinner menu consists of corned beef, baked macaroni and cheese, buttered peas, peach shortcake, bread and jam, lemonade.

Chicken with cranberry sauce tops the supper menu, with steamed rice, spinach, bread and butter, coffee and sliced pineapple for dessert.

The First Army QM said bread is being issued in Normandy on the basis of 25 pounds per 100 men. This will be increased as additional equipment arrives.

The CO of the Quartermaster office presented the first loaf of bread baked here to a wounded soldier in a Normandy hospital on July 4.

Besides getting fresh bread, the front-line soldier will get first crack at cigarettes, smoking and chewing tobacco, shaving cream, razors and razor blades, tooth powder, brushes and hard candy, the QM said.

Chocolate candy and other soft confectionaries are not authorized for free issue but will be sold as soon as the first PX supplies arrive in France. However, GI Joe can munch on a some vitamin-packed bars of chocolate in his K ration.

Jerries in Normandy Are Learning Our 'Big-Gun Serenade' the Hard Way

By Earl Mazo
Stars and Stripes Staff Writer

A FIELD ARTILLERY BATTALION, July 10—Like their cohorts in Africa and Italy, the Germans facing American artillery in France have learned the hard way that a Yank "big-gun serenade" is anything but sweet music.

Here are some reasons:

Sgt. James W. Byrd, a Tampa, Fla., infantryman, noticed something moving in a tree several thousand yards in front of his line. He pointed it out to Lt. Dick Moses, of Brooklyn, who was forward artillery observer that day. Moses decided it was a German observer, and ordered the spot shelled. The first battery burst ringed the target.

Capt. Ralph Slaine, of Columbus, Ohio, a battery commander, was up front looking over the situation when he noticed some enemy movement in and out of a farm house. The first five shells he ordered obliterated that house. That day Capt. Slaine's battery also accounted for an enemy ammunition dump.

The little incidents of artillery accuracy add up; German prisoners attest to that. One captured officer asked if the Americans had sniper sights on their big guns.

He might have known about a Tiger tank which Capt. Slaine's battery knocked out. After the tank was hit, some Germans went forward to bed the remains down as a pillbox. A battery burst killed them all. Some more went forward; they, too, were blown to bits. That went on for half a day until the Germans abandoned the idea.

46,819 Captives Taken by Yanks

General Bradley's headquarters disclosed last night that American troops have captured a total of 46,819 German prisoners since D-Day. A staff officer announced that the American Army since the invasion started has buried 5,030 dead Nazis, but cautioned against attempting to calculate losses from that figure.

"I presume the Germans buried a lot more than that themselves," the spokesman said.

6 Robot Planes Are Shot Down; Some Fall Short

LONDON, July 10 — German robot planes were directed at southern England again last night and in daylight yesterday. A British anti-aircraft battery was reported to have shot down three of four flying bombs engaged while an RAF Coastal Command plane and two Polish fighter planes brought down one apiece. Several of the missiles were said to have dropped into the English Channel before reaching the coast.

Gen. Eisenhower, in a statement on the use of robot planes, termed them "the makings of a cheap air force," and added that every one was aware of the trial undergone by people in London and southern England during the flying bomb raids.

Early yesterday morning a strong force of RAF Lancasters raided what was announced only as military targets in France after Mosquitoes had struck at enemy oil installations at Gelsenkirchen for the eighth time in ten days.

Allies Advance Slowly in Italy

ROME, July 10—Overcoming bitter German resistance, U. S. troops who yesterday captured the German stronghold of Volterra have knifed forward another four miles and driven a wedge in enemy defenses fronting the so-called Gothic Line.

The American advance was described officially as "a setback" to the enemy's intention of imposing maximum delay on the Fifth Army's drive along the Arno River toward Florence and Pisa.

Progress was slow along the entire Italian front as German troops continued to mass guns and troops to fight desperately from every vantage point.

On the west coast, American doughboys made an advance of three miles to within ten miles of Leghorn despite heavy enemy fire of all kinds. Another Yank force moved up to Pomaja, eight miles inland and 14 miles southeast of Leghorn.

45,000 Germans On U. S. Front

Spearheaded by tanks, American troops bursting the German bulge south of the Vire River drove to a point a little more than three miles northwest of St Lo yesterday while German forces began to withdraw south of La Haye du Puits, Reuter reported.

In the British-Canadian sector around Caen, Gen. Montgomery yesterday launched a fresh attack southwest of the city. The assault was preceded by a heavy artillery barrage and air support by rocket-firing Typhoons of the RAF. The drive threatened to outflank German forces still defending the city's southwest fringe.

An official spokesman at Gen. Bradley's headquarters disclosed last night that some 11 or 12 German divisions—a total of probably 45,000 fighting men—are now facing the entire American front.

Two counter-attacks around Caen yesterday afternoon were beaten off, one by British Churchill tanks. The first counter-blow came at noon, the second at 1600 hours.

Tanks Support Doughboys

Grinding through a misery of mud, tanks helping doughboys deepen an eight-mile-wide bridgehead swept through a number of villages and hamlets to reach the northern edge of Pont-Hebert, about five miles due south of St. Jean de Daye. Pont-Herbert is on the main lateral road leading from St. Lo to Carentan.

Other American forces were already poised at a point about three miles northeast of St. Lo. Simultaneous with the expanding of the Vire bridgehead, the Germans, having lost dominant high ground in the La Haye area, began withdrawing as the Americans raced forward to a point about two miles south of La Haye.

The German withdrawal was being made through a seven or eight-mile bottleneck, flanked on either side by swamps, and was believed to be a move to avoid being trapped and also to establish shorter defense lines.

Nazi Thrust Repulsed

The fight between the Vire and Taute rivers was the heaviest of the entire front. The Germans threw in some tanks—principally Mark IVs—in an effort to check the American sweep southwestward, but in the words of a staff officer, the counterattack "slowed but didn't halt the advance."

Principal gains made in the day's drive were an advance to the north of Le Desert, about two miles southwest of St. Jean, engulfing Meauffe, some four miles southeast of St. Jean, and a thrust to the northern edge of Pont-Herbert.

The Vire bridgehead now extends more than three miles west of the Vire where the original crossing was made and nearly five miles south from the Vire et Taute Canal where that stream was first bridged.

Meanwhile, German artillery fire increased all along the Americans' offensive front, probably because better artillery is attached to crack units such as Das Reich Division now in the line.

Just Rows of Hedges, Eh? — Like Hell They Are!

By William Stringer
Reuter Correspondent

"So that's a hedgerow," said the GI as he poked through the bushes and saplings lining the road.

Pfc John Lepore, of Jersey City, N. J., was having his first close-up look at hedgerows — those tangled mattings of brush, trees and dirt which delayed the American push through Normandy.

"Beats Hell"

"It beats the hell out of me." Lepore said. "I had heard about this fighting from hedgerow to hedgerow and I wondered what was so tough about it.

"I thought they were just rows of hedges and I couldn't figure out why we didn't just spray them with lead and blast out the Jerries."

But now, after walking through the heavily-fortified underground maze which constitutes a hedgerow, he knows what makes it virtually impregnable to everything but the infantry's bayonet and hand grenade.

Lepore, like hundreds of other Yanks with behind-the-line jobs, had no idea what hedgerow battles were like. In weeks of living in the front lines and watching scores of hedgerow fights, I've seen some of the toughest the Germans have built —some that mortars or even tanks with 75s couldn't crack.

The hedgerow is more than a mere line of hedges—usually it is a dirt embankment three to four feet high covered with a tangle of bushes and trees which often make it a total height of six feet or more.

Boundaries

Most hedgerows are two to four feet thick. In Normandy they bound each field and road and alongside each is a shallow drainage ditch two or three feet deep and about three feet wide. Almost every ditch has been dug out by the Germans into protected trenches five or six feet deep.

In some places the Germans covered the trenches with layers of eight-inch logs and padded the top with thick chunks of sod.

Every hedgerow has a maze of interconnecting tunnels—through the hedgerows themselves, between hedgerows, sometimes across entire fields.

"Like Rats"

The Jerries must've lived like rats in these holes," Lepore said. And he wasn't far from wrong.

One group of hedgerows I saw near La Haye du Puits was worked on unsuccessfully for two hours by virtually every type of U. S. firearm. After being blasted by artillery, mortars, and tanks we figured surely the Jerries had been blown to hell, but they popped up and began firing as soon as we exposed ourselves.

The hedgerows, like many another German defense in Normandy, are strictly a job for the infantry—nothing else.

Stalin Cites Son, Ace Soviet Flier

MOSCOW, July 10 (AP)—Col. Vassily Stalin, 24-year-old son of the Marshal, led a fighter force which operated in mass raids on Lida before that city fell, Pravda disclosed today. A few hours later the Soviet supreme commander cited his son in an order announcing the city's capture.

CONTINENTAL EDITION

1 fr. THE STARS AND STRIPES 1 fr.

Daily Newspaper of U.S. Armed Forces in the European Theater of Operations

Vol. 1 No. 15 Printed "Somewhere in France" Thursday, July 20, 1944

BRITISH DRIVE IS BIGGEST SINCE D-DAY; AMERICANS CLEAN UP POCKETS IN ST. LO

Soviets Have 100 Mi. to Go To Warsaw

In the Russians' farthest advance west, Soviet tanks yesterday blasted their way to the railway between Brest-Litovsk and Bialystok, 100 miles from Warsaw.

Thus in 26 days since their summer offensive began behind the Vitebsk-Orsha-Mogilev line on June 22, the Russians have advanced three-fourths of the way to the Polish capital.

Advance units were reported already in the suburbs of Brest-Litovsk, even as Marshal Ivan Konev hurled a tremendous weight of armor at Lwow and by German admission, penetrated deeply into the enemy lines north of that well fortified base.

> As the fronts stood yesterday, the Russians were roughly 450 airline miles from Berlin and the western Allies about 530 miles.

Outflank Two Cities

The Soviet thrust to the lateral line between Brest-Litovsk and Bialystok, automatically outflanking both junction fortresses, was reported by German News Agency's Col. Ernest von Hammer. He said bitter fighting was in progress.

Several Soviet infantry divisions led by two tank brigades and cavalry, attempted a "surprise" assault" on Brest-Litovsk from the southeast yesterday, Col. Alfred von Olberg of German Overseas News Agency said last night. He claimed the breakthrough attempt was foiled.

To the south, Konev hurled masses of armor into the battle for Lwow where the Germans admitted the Russians were gaining because of superiority in men and equipment.

winter drive from Kiev had swung

Marshal Stalin's Order of the Day said the Russians had punched a hole 128 miles wide in the Kari line an advanced 32 miles through "strictly fortified, deeply echeloned defenses."

436 Believed Dead In Navy Explosion

MARTINEZ, Cal., July 19—Up to late last night only four bodies of a mounting death toll unofficially placed at 436 had been recovered in the wreckage of an explosion Monday night of two 6,500-ton ammunition ships which shattered the Port Chicago naval ammunition depot.

Early estimates on the number of dead ranged as high as 650, but 12th Naval District headquarters subsequently announced that casualties would not run that high. Official figures listed the known dead as 256 sailors, nine officers, seven merchant seamen and four civilians. A party of 40 armed guards aboard the ships and a combined civilian crew list of about 130 were also presumed lost.

Between 600 and 800 persons, the majority of whom are Navy personnel, were reported injured.

Material damage reports exceeded $5,000,000.

U. S.-ITALY MAIL

WASHINGTON, July 19, (Reuter)—Resumption of civilian mail service for personal correspondence between the U. S. and Rome and the Vatican City has been announced.

But Captured City Is Under Heavy Shell Fire

U. S. FIRST ARMY HQ., July 19 (Reuter)—Battling fierce mortar and artillery fire, American troops mopped up important St. Lo today and severed another highway leading from the city, while the Luftwaffe made its first sizeable appearance.

Except for one stubborn pocket still holding out in the northern suburbs and occasional snipers, St. Lo had been cleared of Germans.

The St. Lo saucer, nestling in the center of a near-circle of high ground, was mopped up under savage pasting from German artillery and mortars from hills southwest and southeast of the city.

Simultaneous with the clearing of the town, doughboys pressing forward northwest of St. Lo slashed the important St. Lo-Periers highway at a point about six miles from the medieval cathedral city.

Meanwhile, the Luftwaffe, in a desperate attempt to halt the spreading American flood, sent over between 15 and 19 ME109s on strafing missions.

The daylight mission, which cost the Nazis two planes, was the first sizeable appearance of the Luftwaffe over the American sector since D-Day. One German plane was shot down by anti-aircraft fire and another by a U. S. fighter.

Resistance along the entire front was, in the words of an Army spokesman, "stiff." Southeast of Carentan, veteran U. S. troops were meeting some of the fiercest resistance they have ever met—principally from crack paratrooper units. All fronts remained fairly static, the principal gains being made northwest of St. Lo, and southeast of Carentan.

'FOLDING BAZOOKA' IN USE

WASHINGTON, July 19—American jungle and parachute troops are being equipped with "folding bazookas" while Army planes in the China-Burma-India theater are using new large 4½-inch bazookas, the War Department disclosed today.

The new 2.36-cal rocket launcher doesn't actually fold, as its name implies, but can be assembled in a few seconds to form a bazooka 61 inches long.

One of First Men to Enter St. Lo Is Borne Into City in Hero's Funeral

St. Lo, July 19—There was a strange funeral procession which entered this town when it fell last night. Riding in state, in an ambulance sandwiched between tanks and armored cars, was the flag-draped body of the major who a few hours before had led his men to take the last hill in front of St. Lo.

The commanding general of the division ordered that the body of the Virginia battalion commander who had died so that others might reach the town would enter St. Lo with the first troops.

The major, whose name is not releasable, was laid in state on top of yellow block stones which crumbled down from the arched Norman walls of a church in the center of St. Lo.

The pile of yellow rubble running down from the undamaged windows of the church was the highest and most prominent in the city and the sun seemed to shine more brightly on the yellow blocks of stone and the American flag over the bier.

The ambulance used as a hearse was driven by Pfc Emerson Ensor, of Texas, Md. when the armored vehicles formed on the road to go into St. Lo.

"We thought we were just going to treat casualties along the way," said Capt. Herman Tannebaum, the doctor in the ambulance. "Just before we went in they told us to take the major's body into the shrine inside the city and place it there. We thought we would pick some flowers on the way in."

Today, as German mortars fall through the American-occupied town, the major's body still lies on the high spot overlooking the town he died to free.

Byrnes Withdraws As Candidate For Vice-Presidency

CHICAGO, July 19—War Mobilization Director James F. Byrnes withdrew from the race for the Vice-Presidential nomination as the 1944 Democratic National Convention opened today, saying he was acting "in deference to the wishes of President Roosevelt."

At the same time, Vice-President Henry A. Wallace continued to take personal charge of his campaign for renomination, following a virtual SOS from leaders of his home-state delegation.

Many delegates believed the announcement by Byrnes foreshadowed a more positive move by Mr. Roosevelt to point out his preference for a running mate, as he did in 1940. Byrnes' withdrawal apparently left Sen. Harry S. Truman of Missouri as Wallace's leading contender, although Sen. Alben W. Barkley, of Kentucky, also had supporters.

The selection of a Vice-Presidential candidate and the delicate question of Negro rights were two of the principal matters before the convention.

144 Nazi Planes Bagged as Reich Is Pounded Again

LONDON, July 19—Unloosing the sixth paralyzing American blow against the Reich in nine days, about 3,700 warplanes yesterday raided more than 12 key targets in Southern Germany and boosted the toll taken of the decimated Luftwaffe in 48 hours to at least 144.

From Britain more than 1,100 Fortresses and Liberators convoyed by nearly 750 pursuits smashed at more than four plants feeding the enemy war machine as well as oil pools and Luftwaffe stations, while from Italy up to 500 15th AF B17s and B24s escorted by fighters struck aircraft factories, airdromes and ordnance plants near Munich.

As a smashing sequel to the previous day's assault in which the Eighth AF shot down 21 interceptors, fighter pilots and bomber gunners yesterday destroyed 30 Nazi aircraft, of which the P51s, P47s and P38s bagged 17—17 in the air and 26 on the ground. U. S. losses were 16 heavies and seven fighters.

Preliminary reports did not indicate how many had been destroyed-

Continued on Back Page

Monty Says Nazis In Normandy Lost 156,000

British and Canadian tank columns, spearheading the new Allied breakthrough toward the heart of France, smashed forward several miles through the breach in the German's Orne River defenses yesterday, while an estimate by Gen. Montgomery placed German losses in the 43 days of fighting in Normandy at 156,000.

The new offensive, heaviest in weight of troops and armor that the Allies have unleashed in Normandy, penetrated six miles to Cagny, in the wide plain southeast of Caen and on the road to Paris—Highway 13 from Caen—German radio admitted.

A powerful German counter attack with armor has been launched, supreme headquarters announced, but it was stated that the battle was going "extraordinarily well" for the Allies.

British forces captured Hubert-Folie, a stumbling block, two and a half miles southeast of Tilly-sur-Seulles.

Montgomery, declaring that the Allied offensive "is" to "bleed" the German military machine to death," announced that the Allies had taken 60,000 prisoners and buried 7,400 German dead since D-day and estimated total German casualties at 156,000. He said that British and Canadian casualties in the first day of the new offensive were extremely light—"almost negligible."

Before the breakthrough southeast of Caen the allies slammed down 14,000 tons of explosives on various targets, one dispatch said yesterday, and near Colombelles, northeast of Caen there was a gigantic pall of smoke 50 miles wide, 20 miles deep and five miles high. German defenders were left so shaken that many of those captured were not able to work the bolts of their rifles.

The fury of the greatest aerial bombardment ever dealt on such a concentrated battle area and the swift advance—after tanks surged across three Orne bridges which had been secretly built the night before—apparently left the German High Command confused as to the status of the battle and the depth of penetration.

2nd Nazi General In France Is Fired

Adolf Hitler has fired Gen. Von Falkenhausen, German commander-in-chief in Belgium and northern France, and also changed the administrative setup governing the two areas, a German News Agency announcement quoted by United Press said yesterday.

Von Falkenhausen is the second German military leader in the battle area dismissed in two weeks. The first was field marshal Gerd Von Rundstedt.

The German announcement said Von Falkenhausen handed over civil affairs to a new Reich commissar, Grohe, and military duties to Gen. Grase, who will take over in Brussels.

GERMAN 'WACS' SEIZED

CAEN FRONT, July 19 (AP)—German "WACs" were among the prisoners captured in the sudden onslaught yesterday east of the Orne River. They were the first women of the German Army captured on the British front in Normandy and were a disheveled lot, too dazed to bother to put on any makeup.

St. Lo 'Living Hell' Under German Fire

By Andy Rooney
Stars and Stripes Staff Writer

ST. LO, July 19—This town, from which the Germans raided the Cherbourg peninsula, is battered and broken tonight.

St. Lo was a town of 10,500 people, but there are no French here tonight but the dead. Down the main street the furniture hangs out of the broken buildings like the intestines of the cows in the field outside the town.

From the hills south of St. Lo the Germans are sending artillery and mortar fire into the town and U. S. troops walking through the streets are sticking close to the sides of buildings with an eye on the nearest door on constant watch for snipers.

The GIs who came in yesterday morning and who once pushed one-half mile south of town said St. Lo was "a living hell."

"I thought I'd never see hell but I guess I'm right in it now" said Pvt. Harry Elder, of Rifle, Col.

At the entrance to the town there is a large factory. Some of the boys guarding it say it's a distillery which makes Calvados (renamed Jersey Lightning). Some claim it's a power plant for the city and a few swear it is a cement factory. Bob Casey, Chicago Tribune correspondent, observed there wasn't a lot of difference.

Further on into the town there is a little cemetery which has been shelled. There are wrecked vehicles in the cemetery streets and people long dead have been shaken out of their graves by bursting shells. Out on the steps of the stone mausoleum of La Famille Blanchet soldiers are stopping to eat their K rations. The Blanchet family's mausoleum makes a handy shelter.

St. Lo was the German field headquarters for their governmental control over the French people in this section. The town is third in size and importance in Normandy behind Cherbourg and Caen.

"Rehabilitation will be much more difficult in St. Lo than it was in Cherbourg," said Maj. Asa B. Gardiner, of Baltimore, senior civil affairs officer with the division which took the town.

"It will take the engineers a good week to clear the streets and it will be at least two months before anything like normal life is restored in the town," Maj. Gardiner said after an early reconnaissance.

"The Germans are backing up French civilians with them as they are driven back and at some points we will have a flood of French refugees coming into our lines," he added.

THE STARS AND STRIPES

MEDITERRANEAN

Vol. 1, No. 39, Friday, July 21, 1944 | Published In Italy | TWO LIRE

BOMB INJURES HITLER

High Officers With Fuehrer Reported Severely Hurt

BERLIN, July 20—An attempt was made today to assassinate Adolf Hitler, it was officially announced from Berlin. High explosives burst near the Fuehrer and his entourage of high ranking generals and admirals, the German News Agency said, wounding several, but Hitler escaped with light burns and slight contusions.

Details of the effort at assassination were not revealed by the Nazi-controled press. It was not disclosed where it occurred or how, nor was the would-be assassin's identity made known, nor the state of the country which gave rise to the attempt at the Fuehrer's life.

ADOLF HITLER
Too Bad

The German official statement, admitting that it was "an attempt upon the life of the Fuehrer," listed the injured as: "Lt. Gen. Schmundt, Col. Brandt and Collaborator Berger, severely wounded; Lt. Col. Borgmann, Col. Gen. Jodl and Generals Korten, Buhl, Bodenschatz, Heusinger and Scherff and Admirals Voss and von Puttkamer and Naval Capt. Assaman, slightly wounded."

Hitler, it was claimed, received no injuries, other than the burns and contusions. It was pointed out that "he at once began to work again."

The Fuehrer, the news agency said, proceeded upon schedule to receive Benito Mussolini for a long meeting.

Shortly after the attempt, Reichsmarshal Hermann Goering went to see Hitler. The Nazi air marshal and Number 2 man, on learning what had happened, paid a hurried call to see how his leader was getting along.

Lt. Gen. Schmundt and Col. Gen. Jodl are the best-known among the injured high rankers. General Schmundt is chief of the personnel department of the German army and has been chief military aide to Hitler for several years. He is responsible for advising Hitler on promotions and appointments. Col. Gen. Jodl is chief of Hitler's personal military staff and is one of the professional military leaders who have surrounded him for the wartime years.

Lt. Gen. Buhl has for several

(Continued on page 4)

Entire Japanese Cabinet Resigns

WASHINGTON, July 20—The entire cabinet of Premier General Kideki Tojo has resigned, "apologizing for the Government's meager power to the men on the fighting front and the people of Japan," Domei, Japanese News Agency announced today. Emperor Hirohito is reported to be much concerned over "the stage existing today."

The dispatch, picked up by the Federal Communications Commission, was directed to Japanese occupied areas and quoted a statement by the Japanese Board of Information. The announcement came one day after Tojo was divested of his concurrent post as Army chief of staff in continuation of the High Command shake-up which began Monday.

General Kuniski Koiso, Governor-general of Korea, and Admiral Mitsumasa Yonai, former Premier, have been chosen to form a new cabinet, according to the Jap news agency.

Explaining the reasons for the resignation of the cabinet, Domei said in part: "In face of the grave situation, and realizing the necessity of strengthened personnel in time of urgency for the prosecution of the war, it was decided to strengthen the cabinet by a wider selection of personnel.

"By utilizing all means available, the present cabinet was not able to achieve its objective; so the government decided to renovate its personnel in order to continue to prosecute the war totally.

"Having recognized the fact that it was most appropriate to carry out the total resignation of the cabinet, Premier Tojo gathered together the resignations of each member of the cabinet and presented them to the Emperor July 18th.

"At this time of decisive war, to have reached the stage existing today is causing the Emperor much concern, because of which the cabinet is filled with trepidation and in

(Continued on page 4)

Still Another Drive Started By Soviets

MOSCOW, July 20—Soviet troops have launched another new offensive west of Kowel in central Poland, Marshal Stalin announced tonight in a special order.

The order, addressed to Marshal Rokossovsky, Commander on the 1st White Russian front, said that Russian armies had broken through German defenses along a 95-mile front, occupied 400 inhabited places and advanced 30 miles to the western bank of the Bug River.

Announcement of the new drive came as Soviet troops pressed their drives in Poland and toward East Prussia which led Ilya Ehrenberg, commentator for the Red Army publication, Red Star, to declare that the "German armies in White Russia have been completely destroyed beyond hope of reorganization."

This statement, first that such a definite assertion had been made by a responsible Moscow source, came as Soviet armies smashed to within nine miles of Lwow; fanned out inside the border of Latvia; pressed on toward East Prussia west of Grodno, and developed their threat to the German bastions of Brest-Litovsk and Bialystok.

[The German Overseas News Agency reported tonight that bitter fighting was raging at Augustovo, less than 12 miles from the East Prussia frontier.]

The German position at Lwow

(Continued on page 4)

All Ice Cream Stands Placed 'Off Limits'

Establishments in Rome selling ice cream, lemonade and other soft drinks have been placed "Off Limits" to all Allied troops in the city, the Rome Area Allied Command announced yesterday. Analysis of samples of soft drinks has shown that these liquids are contaminated and are a potential source of intestinal diseases. Raw milk produced in the Rome area and used in the manufacture of ice cream may often contain the organisms of undulant fever. Also, there is a high rate of tuberculosis present in many milk cows in this area, the announcement said.

5th Army Controls Vital Hill Masses

ADVANCED ALLIED HEADQUARTERS, July 20—Pushing relentlessly ahead after capturing Leghorn, American troops of the 5th Army established complete control today of the hill masses overlooking the Arno River from the south, seizing dominating terrain giving artillery observation over the river valley and forcing the Germans along a 25-mile front to withdraw to the north bank.

A torrential rain over the battlefront seriously interfered with the 5th Army's forward movement, said the morning's communique. The advance north of Leghorn, however, met with only scattered resistance. The Nazis left behind them mostly sniping parties armed with automatic weapons to cover demolitions and minefields.

Slightly west of this sector other troops of the 5th gained between two and three miles and cleared the towns of Varna, Certaldo and San Donato. Other elements took the town of Colle Salvatti, seven miles northeast of Leghorn.

Troops of the 34th Division and attached units were the first 5th Army men to enter Leghorn, it was reported. The 442nd Inf. Regt. which saw bitter front-line action

(Continued on page 4)

Heavy Bombers Assault South German Targets

MAAF HEADQUARTERS, July 20—For the third consecutive day, medium forces of fighter-escorted 15th AAF heavy bombers today raided targets in southern Germany. Liberators attacked three objects at Friedrichshafen, while Fortresses bombed two airfields southwest of Munich.

Escorted by Mustangs, the Liberators went for the Maybach components shop, the Zeppelin works and the Lowenthal airdrome, all in the immediate outskirts of Friedrichshafen, across Lake Constance from Switzerland.

Democrats In Battle Over Wallace's Job

CHICAGO, July 20—The Democratic party whooped up its first wartime convention in 80 years today while President Roosevelt mixed in the tumultuous scrap over the selection of his running mate by waving War Mobilizer James F. Byrnes out of the contest, according to the Associated Press.

Racing through the convention crowd went word apparently based on good authority that Roosevelt's second and third choice for Wallace's post were Sen. Harry S. Truman and Supreme Court Justice William O. Douglas. There were key developments as delegates swarmed about bunting bedecked Chicago Stadium for the first session which was to be devoted mostly to organization formalities.

Mr. Byrnes announced "in deference to wishes" of President

(Continued on page 4)

Battered Guam Gets 15th Daily Attack

PEARL HARBOR, July 20—Battered Guam received no r--nite when American planes and [illegible] vessels carried the softening-up operations against the island into its 15th consecutive day, Admiral Chester Nimitz' communique reported last night. In two days, Allied planes have flown 650 sorties over the target while battleships, cruisers and destroyers have laid down a continuous barrage into Guam's defensive positions.

Meanwhile the Navy department announced from Washington that U. S. submarines have sunk 14 more Japanese ships including a destroyer and a medium class naval auxiliary.

Nazis Fail To Halt Normandy Assault

SHAEF, July 20—Fierce German counterattacks failed to stop the mighty Allied drive in Normandy and powerful British and Canadian armored forces battled forward today in all directions to widen the breach in enemy defenses below Caen.

Late reports placed forward British patrols at a railway station half a mile from Troarn, an important road junction seven and a half miles due east of Caen. After smashing their way through the crossroads west of the station, the Tommies poured fire into strong German defenses inside the town.

Other British spearheads reached Cagny and Grentheville about five miles south of the jumping-off point. Both towns lie southeast of Caen.

The offensive was reported gathering weight at every yard as it surged on after cracking the crust of German opposition. Heavy tank battles were raging in country swarming with enemy anti-tank guns and crack panzer divisions.

Considerable mopping up operations and the annihilation of snipers continued. POW cages were filled to the tune of 1,250 Jerries, bringing the total captured since the invasion to well over 60,000.

Front-line reports described the unparalleled ferocity of the struggle. In haystacks and hedges,

(Continued on page 4)

8th AAF Pummels Reich, Smashing Big Factories

LONDON, July 20—American air power delivered punishing new blows to the Nazi Reich today when more than 1,200 8th USAAF heavies made simultaneous attacks on engine factories, fighter assembly plants, synthetic oil plants and other targets in the Leipzig area of central Germany.

Summing up recent raids against Germany, an Allied spokesman said that a great air offensive comparable to that carried out in February, which dealt the Luftwaffe a crushing blow, was delivered this week by English-based and Italy-based aircraft. On Wednesday planes from both sectors hit Munich at the same time.

Kerr Hails Democrats As 'Achievement' Party

CHICAGO STADIUM, July 20—Gov. Robert S. Kerr, of Oklahoma, hailed the party of Franklin Roosevelt last night as a party of achievement and assailed the Republicans and their youthful standard bearer, Thomas E. Dewey, as untried and untested, broken by disunity and having "no program except to oppose."

Keynoting the Democratic National Convention before cheering thousands, the 245-pound six-foot, three-inch oilman-governor drew back the curtains on a preview of the democratic campaign arguments for the presidential race ahead.

The world, Kerr said, has the right to ask "where we stand." He declared, "Our aims are complete and speedy victory. Our goals are a just and abiding peace. Our promise to a world at peace is responsibility and cooperation. Our pledge to America at peace is a government responsible to the needs and hopes of every citizen, even the humblest; a government which will not shirk or fail but will fulfill with gratitude and fidelity our sacred obligation to returning servicemen and women."

Kerr defended leaders of the Roosevelt administration against Gov. Dewey's charge that they are "tired, quarrelsome old men." He asserted that the Republicans are "incapable either of learning anything or forgetting anything." He accused GOP leaders "after World War I" of having "sabotaged every effective vehicle for keeping peace" and of major opposition to preparedness for World War II.

Cried Kerr as the Klieg lights shone on the bunting-festooned speakers' stand: "In this hall last month the Republicans nominated as their candidate for president a man selected for them four years ago by Herbert Hoover. As America looked on, she saw the mantle of Herbert Hoover not falling upon but being placed upon the shoulders of his cherished disciple, Thomas

(Continued on page 3)

Five More Provinces Returned To Italians

ROME, July 20—In line with the Allied policy of returning liberated areas to Italian administration, the Allied Control Commission announced today that five more provinces have been transferred to the jurisdiction of the Italian government.

These provinces include Foggia, Campobasso, Benevento, Avellino, and Naples, except the city of Naples. Municipal Naples remains under Allied control with the agreement of the Italian authorities because of its importance as a port for Allied supplies.

CONTINENTAL EDITION

1 fr. THE STARS AND STRIPES 1 fr.

Daily Newspaper of U.S. Armed Forces in the European Theater of Operations

Vol. 1 No. 17 Printed "Somewhere in France" Saturday, July 22, 1944

NAZIS ACT TO QUELL ANTI-HITLER REVOLT

Yanks Invade Guam, First U.S. Isle Lost

American infantrymen and Marines yesterday pushed inland from beachheads firmly established on the island of Guam after pouring ashore Wednesday under a thunderous supporting barrage from warships and aircraft.

Guam, first bit of U. S. territory seized by Japan in the Pacific shortly after the bombing of Pearl Harbor, had been under an unprecedented attack by U. S. battleships and war planes for 17 days prior to the landings. As thousands of Marines and doughboys swept in from their beachhead positions the terrific shelling continued to tear at remaining Jap defenses.

The rescue of Guam from Japan, presently struggling to replace the Tojo government, will extend Allied control of the Marianna Islands. This string of 14 islands extends from Uracas, about 900 miles below Tokyo, southward to Guam, 1565 miles from the Japanese capital.

Saipan, conquered after the most bitter but strategically most valuable of Pacific battles, already is providing a base from which Japan's Bonin and Kazan Islands have been bombed.

The Guam garrison apparently was as strong as that which defended Saipan where 20,000 troops confronted Americans. The Yanks had to kill nearly every Jap there to clinch the victory after 25 days of bloody fighting.

Japanese radios were silent on the Guam landings but cryptic Domei broadcast suggested that Emperor Hirohito's war lords had reconsidered the idea of having two premiers to succeed Tojo. The Imperial Rule Assistance Association at a special meeting unanimously pledged to give support to a new cabinet which will be formed under Gen. Kuniaki Koiso or Adm. Mitsumasa Yonai. This indicated that only one of them would get the No. 1 position.

Child's Remark May Be Nemesis Of Robot Bomb

NEW YORK, July 21 (AP)—A seven-and-one-half-year-old boy, Frederick Adrus Gauteson, of Plainfield, N. J., was credited by the president of a precision instrument company today with the discovery of a new physics principle which might lead to the defeat of the robot bomb.

Mrs. H. M. McNab, president of McNab, Inc., of Bridgeport, Conn., declined to elaborate on the new device or the principle from which it was developed, but said that the scientists believe it is sound and a step in the direction of repelling the robot bombs and any weapon that may come from Germany."

The device was developed after the child remarked to a mechanic on a similarity of the movement between a garter snake and an elastic watchband.

The principle of the device, a director of the firm said, questioned Newton's third law of motion that "every action has equal and opposite reactions."

Democrats Assail GOP 'Inexperience' After Nominating FDR on First Ballot

CHICAGO, July 21 — With President Roosevelt nominated overwhelmingly for a fourth term and the Democratic campaign launched on the issue of the Republican ticket's "inexperience and immaturity," Democratic National convention delegates came back to Chicago Stadium today to wind up their three-day session with the selection of a Vice-Presidential candidate.

Choice of the second man on the ticket was the only controversy left after the Rules Committee had rejected Southern demands for restoration of the two-thirds rule. The Platform Committee had turned a cold shoulder on a Dixie plea for a "white supremacy plank" and the Credentials Committee had seated two rival delegates from Texas, each with half the normal vote.

National Chairman Robert E. Hannegan's last-minute disclosure that Mr. Roosevelt had written him a second letter saying he would "be very glad" to have either Sen. Harry T. Truman of Missouri or Supreme Court Justice William O. Douglas as his running mate, suggested that party leaders were finding a way out of the controversy surrounding efforts to renominate Henry A. Wallace.

The President accepted his fourth nomination by radio from an unidentified Pacific coast naval base shortly after the convention gave him a rousing first ballot endorsement, 1,086 votes out of a total of 1,176—almost 500 more than the necessary majority of 589. Sen. Harry F. Byrd of Virginia polled 10 and former Postmaster General James A. Farley one.

Highlights of the Democratic platform as adopted by the convention were:

Foreign Policy—Pledges U. S. membership in an international organization open to "all peace-loving states, large and small," for the "prevention of aggression which the nations would maintain and make available "for joint

Continued on Back Page

Heavy Rain Slows Allies in France; British Consolidate Newest Gains

The heaviest downpour of rain since D-Day slowed the Allies all along the Normandy battlefront yesterday.

British and Canadian forces dug in and consolidated 30 square miles of territory occupied since the Orne breakthrough Tuesday, while American troops occupied two villages a few miles north and northeast of Periers, junction of the St. Lo-Periers-Lessay road and of Highway 171, which runs southwest from Carentan to Coutances on the west coast. Tanks in St. Lo were surrounded on three sides by heavy German resistance.

Canadian infantry and armor, forced to withdraw from Bourguebus, four miles due south of Caen, in the face of a heavy German counter-attack, fought their way back through a quagmire of mud and recaptured the town 24 hours later. Canadian and British infantry captured St. Andre-sur-Orne, about four and a quarter miles south of Caen.

British and Canadians also took Granville, about 16 miles west of Caen, which gave them control of the Caen-Caumont road.

On the American sector of the front doughboys captured Seves and Raids, which put them about two miles north and three miles northeast of Periers.

A German strongpoint also was wiped out south of Amigny. A region where the Yanks have already cut the St. Lo-Periers-

Continued on Back Page

1,100 Forts, Libs Raid Reich Again

LONDON, July 21—More than 1,100 American Fortresses and Liberators, escorted by fighters, today pounded war factories deep inside Germany for the third straight day, hitting the ball bearing plant at Schweinfurt and the aircraft assembly center at Regensburg.

The blow was coordinated with one from Italian-based heavies which raided targets in the Sudetenland, only 125 miles south of Berlin. It was one of the longest trips made by the 15th Air Force into Germany.

On the run to Schweinfurt and Regensburg, the Eighth Air Force bombers lost 35 while their escorting fighters lost 11. Sixteen enemy interceptors were shot down by the U. S. Thunderbolts, Mustangs and Lightnings.

BEEF STILL RATIONED

WASHINGTON, July 21—All beefsteak and beef roasts will remain on the list of rationed meats at least until Aug. 15, despite a War Food Administration order to the contrary, an Office of Price Administration spokesman indicated yesterday.

The OPA, it is understood, vigorously objects to the decision by Marvin Jones, head of WFA, to make most beef grades point-free next month and plans to postpone the effective date of the directive.

SPELLMAN OVERSEAS

NEW YORK, July 21—Archbishop Francis Spellman, head of Catholic chaplains in the armed services, has left on his second overseas trip to visit chaplains and confer with Pope Pius XII in Rome.

Plot by Generals to Form New Peace Government Thwarted, Berlin Asserts

Adolf Hitler's Third Reich was shaken yesterday by the first obvious tremors of internal eruption.

Twenty-four hours after an unsuccessful attempt had been made to assassinate the German Fuehrer, Nazi authorities were taking swift and drastic steps to quell what neutral sources described as a widespread revolt led by some of Germany's highest military leaders. Berlin said the conspirators aimed to set up a new government and sue for peace. There was every evidence that the crisis was not over, the conservative BBC reported.

Indications that the Reich, under growing pressure from east, west and south, had entered upon the last lap—long though it may be—to defeat were contained in these developments:

1—Nazi authorities moved swiftly to tighten the bonds between the Nazi party and the German military forces. Air Marshal Goering instructed the Luftwaffe to take orders from no one except himself; Adm. Doenitz gave similar instructures to the Navy; pledges of loyalty were demanded from all army commanders.

2—Berlin, acknowledging the fact that the attempt to kill Hitler with a time bomb had been made by a German military clique, announced that the leader of the conspirators—Col. Gen. von Stauffenberger, member of the general staff—had been executed and the others rounded up.

3—Hitler himself went on the radio with an address notably lacking in confidence, in which he told the German people he had "done his best" for Germany.

4—Nazi authorities appealed to the people for loyalty, declaring that the threat on Hitler's life should make all Germans rally to his support.

Hitler, in his radio speech, said the assassins planned to set up a government which would sue for peace and "carry out a stab in the back as in 1918."

Allied radios in Britain and Russia quickly seized the chance to fan the embers of rebellion. BBC told the Germans civil war had broken out in their country.

Berlin radio said the revolt was plotted by a small clique of generals and other high officers, among them Gen. Beck, chief of staff until 1938 and generally regarded as one of Germany's best military brains. An opponent of the occupation of Czecho-Slovakia in 1939, he was a victim later of one of Hitler's bloodless purges. Berlin radio said Beck was "no longer among the living."

Although Berlin tried to give the impression that the revolt was local and short-lived, neutral sources said there was ample evidence that it was widespread. Stockholm heard that measures had to be taken to quell disturbances and demonstrations in the heart of Berlin Thursday night, and also that two armored divisions on the East Prussia front had revolted.

Berlin also sought to prove the loyalty of German troops by telling how soldiers reported to the authorities a fake order by which the anti-Hitler conspirators attempted to seize the military quarters in Berlin. Reports reaching Stockholm, on the other hand, said members of Hitler's own guard were arrested and many had been shot.

Telephone communications between Germany and Stockholm, severed Thursday morning, were partially restored yesterday.

Sources in the Swedish capital which BBC considers reliable expressed the belief that around [illegible] Germany's highest generals [illegible]

Continued on Back Page

Russians Smash Bug River Line, Reach West Bank

The Red Army smashed the German's Bug River line on a 47 mile front yesterday and bridged the last natural obstacle before Warsaw, 100 miles away. Marshal Stalin announced in an order of the day late last night that his troops already had advanced five miles on the west bank of the river.

The Russians reached the Bug after a 31-mile advance in a new offensive which had smashed a 93-mile gap in the German line south of Brest-Litovsk. Farther south, the Rusians were only five miles outside the important supply base of Lwow.

The new outflanking wedge between Brest-Litovsk and Lwow coincided with fresh gains on the Baltic front, where Soviet forces to the southwest of Dvinsk cut the enemy rail line running 60 miles west to Panevezys.

Lwow seemed likely to be the next Nazi stronghold to topple before the Soviet juggernaut. Outflanking columns swung wide beyond the city to north and south—the one to the north forcing its way into Rava Ruska, 40 miles northwest of the Lwow base on the highway to Lublin. At this point the Russians were 83 miles to the west of the Bug.

CAPITAL 18 HOURS AWAY

WASHINGTON, July 21 (Reuter)—The first non-stop flight from London to Washington was made this week by a U. S. Army C54 transport plane, the War Department announced yesterday. The 3,800-mile trip took 18 hours.

U.S. Troops Make Gains Toward Pisa, Nazi Suicide Squads Defend Arno

Strong suicide detachments of Germans, with the advantage of terrain and extensive minefields, impeded Fifth Army patrols attempting to cross the Arno River in Italy yesterday, although troops north of Leghorn hammered out small gains in their advance toward Pisa.

The Eighth Army in central and eastern Italy shortened its approach to Gothic Line positions, seizing Monte Querciabella and Monte San Michele in a five mile thrust beyond Radda, which brought it to within 14 miles of Florence. The Eighth also was closing in on Citta Di Castello, east of Arezzo.

In the Ancona sector, Polish troops crossed the River Esino on a 15 mile front. They have 85 miles to go in difficult mountain country before they reach their end of the Gothic Line.

The Allied Control Commission announced the transfer to the Italian government of five additional provinces, Foggia, Campobasso, Benevento, Avellino and Naples. By agreement with the Italian government, Naples remains a military zone under Allied control, owing to its importance as a port and supply base.

1D.

THE STARS AND STRIPES

1Fr.

Daily Newspaper of U.S. Armed Forces in the European Theater of Operations

Vol. 4 No. 235 New York, N.Y.—London, England—France Friday, Aug. 4, 1944

Yanks Take Rennes, Brittany Capital; Russians Believed on German Soil

Reds Pierce Nazi Lines At Prussia

Stalin Is Expected to Issue Historic Order Marking Border Crossing

There were strong indications last night that Soviet armies were at last fighting on German soil in pre-war East Prussia.

With armored forces of Gen. Ivan Chernyakhovsky pressing their attack near towns only three miles from the eastern boundary of the Reich province, Moscow censors early in the day permitted correspondents to speculate that the frontier would be passed by nightfall.

Soon afterward German Overseas News Agency reported that the Red Army had broken through Wehrmacht defenses at Augustovo, at the southern end of the front below the Suwalki triangle, eight miles from the pre-war East Prussian boundary.

First Shells on Reich

It was obvious no news of a border crossing would come from Moscow until the Soviet High Command was ready to celebrate it with an historic order of the day and a booming salute of guns in the capital. The Nazis, too, were in no hurry to proclaim the Reich itself invaded.

Nevertheless, the Russians along a 20-mile front on either side of the Kaunas-Koenigsberg railway were within artillery range of East Prussian border towns and there was no reason to doubt that the first Allied shells to land in Germany in this war already were being hurled across the boundary.

Inside Warsaw, the long-suppressed Polish underground came into the open again to engage the German garrison in bitter street fighting and wrest parts of the center of the capital, as well as some of its southern, western and northern districts.

A radio message received by the Polish Telegraph Agency in London yesterday

(Continued on page 4)

The War Today

France—Americans drive southwest in Brittany to capture Rennes, original capital of Brittany, and reach Dinan in westward push threatening big port of Brest . . . British and American troops in Normandy advance against increased German resistance between Vire and Villers-Bocage . . . Allied total of German prisoners taken approaches 100,000.

Russia—Russians believed fighting on German soil along border of East Prussia . . . Red Army within artillery range of Reich along 20-mile sector astride Kaunas-Koenigsberg railway . . . Polish underground wrests center of Warsaw and outlying districts to north, west and south from enemy in bloody street fighting, as Rokossovsky masses for final assault.

Italy—Eighth Army tightens arc around Florence within five-mile radius . . . South Africans span river Greve and capture Strada . . . Vichy radio reports possible new Allied landings in northern Italy or southern France.

Pacific—Americans seize strategic airfield and three more towns on Guam . . . U.S. forces expand and consolidate positions on Sansapor in Dutch New Guinea . . . New Jap attempt to turn Allied flank near Aitape in New Guinea repulsed.

Asia—Chinese troops capture Tengchung, 20 miles west of Burma Road . . . Attempts by Japs retreating from India into Burma to make a stand are beaten off . . . Battle for Myitkyina, in north Burma, reported to have reached a crisis for Japanese.

Where Robots Were Ro-Botches

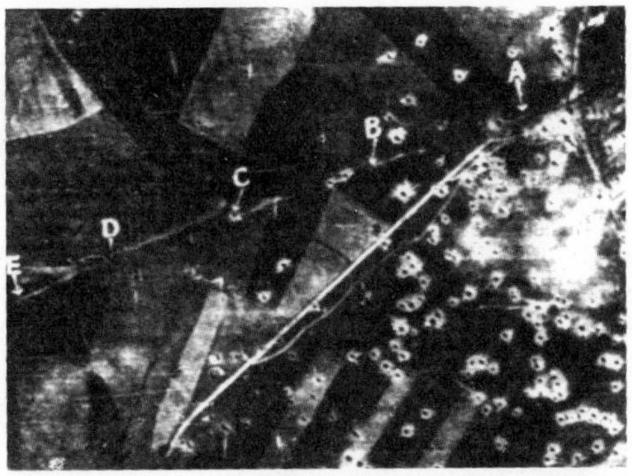

Bomb craters around this robot launching ramp (A) in Pas de Calais were made by attacking Allied planes. But craters B, C, D and E were made by flying bombs themselves which crashed upon launching; streaks behind holes were made by robots sliding along ground.

Robots Hit Seven Hospitals In One of Heaviest Attacks

In one of the heaviest attacks since the flying bomb was introduced seven weeks ago, wave upon wave of robots roared over London and southern England Wednesday night and early yesterday. Seven hospitals were hit or damaged.

At a hospital for the aged and chronic sick, ten patients were known to have been killed when a bomb crashed on a second-floor ward occupied by elderly women. Damage was estimated at $600,000. All of its more than 200 patients had to be evacuated.

At another, two patients, one a British soldier, were buried in a ward beneath the nurses' kitchen, where a bomb made a direct hit. Little hope was held for their survival.

Come in from East

Some sources said the Germans apparently took advantage of heavy cloud over the Straits of Dover to launch a saturation raid. Many robots were shot down by ack-ack and fighter planes.

Many came in on long shallow glides, their jet propulsion engines shut down and their only warning a high-pitched sustained whistle. Coastal observers said they appeared to be coming from a more easterly direction than usual.

The bombings produced numerous stories of remarkable escapes—and two children were born in the maternity ward of the most heavily bombed hospital within an hour or two of the raid.

A bomb fell on a covered corridor connecting a men's ward and a children's ward in a fever hospital but only two men were killed. Flying glass and falling plaster covered another children's ward but all escaped because nurses had

(Continued on page 4)

Allies Tighten Arc at Florence

Tightening the arc less than five miles around the southern half of Florence, Eighth Army troops yesterday threatened to encircle the historic city as an Indian unit crossed the Pesa River to the west on a wide front.

Strong German resistance from dominating hill positions continued. In the past six days, five Nazi counter-attacks have delayed the New Zealanders at Mont La Poggiana and on one occasion forced them to withdraw from their positions, which are the most advanced of the entire Allied offensive.

South African elements to the east of Highway Two spanned the Greve River to capture the town of Strada in their march on Impruneta, which the enemy holds in strength. Other British units approached Incisa, ten miles southeast of Florence.

Vichy radio reported that large Allied reinforcements pouring into Italy indicated that Gen. Sir Harold Alexander planned "a new landing in northern Italy or the south of France."

Tito's Son in Red Army

MOSCOW, Aug. 3 (UP) Marshal Tito's son is fighting with the Red Army on the Polish front and was recently decorated for bravery, Red Star revealed today.

Bombers Blast Nazi Transport

German freight yards at Saarbrucken, Mulhouse and Strasbourg and oil storage dumps at Merkwiller were pounded yesterday by Fortresses of the Eighth Air Force after fighter-bombers, slashing at enemy communications Wednesday evening in one of their most effective assaults since D-Day, left trains shattered and burning north of Paris from Rouen to St. Quentin.

The heavy toll in destroyed or damaged rail and motor equipment included 243 railroad cars, 62 locomotives, 47 motor trucks and a vehicle convoy. Bombs also were dropped on 20 railroad yards, ten factories and two airdromes, as well as railroad bridges, tank cars, flak and radio towers, pill boxes and canal locks.

Enemy fighter opposition was virtually non-existent. An Me109—the only German plane reported destroyed—was bagged by Lt. Col. Ben Rimmerman, of Omaha, Neb., a Thunderbolt group commander.

In a second mission, Eighth heavies attacked flying bomb sites in the Pas de Calais and four bridges southeast of Paris. From the day's total operations, seven bombers and nine fighters were missing.

Friedrichshafen, center of the German aeronautical industry, was attacked for the eighth time by Italian-based heavy bombers. Medium bombers hammered bridges north of the French Riviera and attacked a torpedo factory at Valence, on the Rhone.

The Mediterranean Allied Air Force

(Continued on page 4)

26-Mile U.S. Surge To West Threatens Brest, U-Boat Pens

American armored forces yesterday kept up the fastest movement of the war in France by a 34-mile drive southwest from Pontorson to capture Rennes, the original capital of Brittany, strategic center for the conquest of the entire Brittany peninsula, and a westward surge of 26 miles to Dinan, on the main road to the great port of Brest.

British and American troops near the center of the front, in the area of Vire and Villers-Bocage, advanced against stronger opposition as the Germans tried to delay an eastward onslaught and the possibility of a major retreat to the Seine.

Rush Paris Defenses

Germans at Paris were feverishly hurrying preparations for defense of the city and mining roads inside it, according to two French people who arrived near Vire from Paris two days ago, and who saw en route what they described as a near catastrophy in the German Army's retreat from the American breakthrough.

In Washington, Secretary of War Henry L. Stimson said that the advance in Normandy in the past nine days was "the most satisfying accomplishment" since D-Day, and added: "It even overshadows the swift envelopment and liberation of Cherbourg."

Gen. Montgomery, described as obviously in good spirits at his Normandy headquarters yesterday, declared:

"We have taken a lot of prisoners, and the Allied total is now approaching 100,000—quite apart from those we have written off. We are hitting the Hun a good crack."

Germans Admit Crisis

As U.S. tank spearheads raced deeper into Brittany, a German correspondent at Field Marshal von Kluge's headquarters admitted that "the situation is critical for German forces there."

The American thrust westward to Dinan threatened to isolate the second largest French port, Brest, 115 miles west of Dinan, while the drive southwestward to Rennes threatened to cut off the German U-boat pens at Lorient, 88 miles southwest of Rennes, and at St. Nazaire, 60 miles south of Rennes.

Brest, the great debarkation point for the AEF in the first World War, has a larger cargo capacity than Cherbourg. American control of both ports would allow a direct flow of war supplies from the U.S. to France. Capture of Lorient and St. Nazaire would virtually end the U-boat menace in the Bay of Biscay.

Patriots Kill 3,000

No reports of any strong German opposition in Brittany were available yesterday. German power was spread thinly in large areas, after four divisions

(Continued on page 4)

Double Summer Time Is Extended to September 17

Double summer time in Britain will be extended until Sept. 17, the latest since it was inaugurated four years ago, and the blackout will continue indefinitely, Home Secretary Herbert Morrison announced yesterday.

Morrison said the blackout would be relaxed as soon as possible. Last year double summer time ended Aug. 15.

16th and 116th Fought Bloody D-Day Battles

War Department Discloses Role of Two Regiments Which Stormed Beach

Stars and Stripes U.S. Bureau

WASHINGTON, Aug. 3—The War Department today described the bloody D-Day battle in which two U.S. infantry regiments defied withering enemy fire and at heavy cost drove through Hitler's Atlantic Wall to establish the beachhead which for two days remained the Allies' principal gateway to Normandy.

The two spearheading regiments were Virginia's 116th Infantry from the 29th Division and New York's 16th Infantry from the First Division. The landing cost the 116th more than 800 casualties, while the 16th lost at least one-third of its assault strength. The First and 29th Divisions were assigned to storm the beach just east of Carentan which bristled with concrete pillboxes, machine-guns and sniper nests. Moreover, an entire German division was in the same area on a maneuver.

Swamped by Sea

The 16th was heading for shore near Colleville-sur-Mer when it was swamped by violent seas and hurled from assault boats into mined waters. Struggling toward shore, the entire regiment became the target for point-blank fire from the enemy cliff positions. Slowly the regiment regrouped. They answered German artillery and machine-guns with rifles and rifle-propelled rockets.

A breach was blown in the barbed wire and the 16th poured through—but at terrible cost. Lt. Gen. Omar N. Bradley said "individually and collectively, members of the 16th Regiment turned threatened catastrophe into glorious victory for the American Army."

Infantrymen of the 116th went ashore near Ville-sur-Mer at a beach heavily fortified with barbed wire, concrete walls and land mines. The 116th neutralized cliff positions, forged through mines and routed the enemy.

Strategic Base Seized on Guam

American troops on Guam have occupied the strategic Tiyan airfield along with three more towns and are chasing the Japanese toward the heavily-wooded plateau sector in the north, while U.S. ground forces on Sansapor, in Dutch New Guinea, have expanded and consolidated their positions, Allied communiques announced yesterday.

Reporting the Guam successes, Adm. Chester W. Nimitz said that the Americans were making their headway despite stiffer enemy resistance.

Fresh details of the surprise landing at Sansapor contained in a New Guinea dispatch to Sydney said the village was taken without a shot being fired by either side. Americans hacking their way through the jungle there seized great quantities of supplies and medical stores.

In the Aitape sector of New Guinea the Americans repulsed another attempt by the trapped 18th Jap Army to turn the Allied flank to the south.

New Boots for Engineers

New high-type black boots are being issued to ETO engineer forestry companies, specially-organized units designed to convert local timber resources into finished lumber for construction use, it was announced yesterday.

Strike Renewed in Philly; Army Set to Take Charge

Stars and Stripes U.S. Bureau

PHILADELPHIA, Aug. 3 — Philadelphia's transportation system came to a complete standstill again last night after failure of a brief attempt by volunteer crews to operate several subway trains.

(An Associated Press dispatch reported that Maj. Gen. Philip Hayes, commander of the Third Service Command, arrived on the scene as the Army prepared to take over the transport lines.)

A walkout, unauthorized by the CIO Transit Workers' Union, started Tuesday when the company began training Negro employes for operational jobs. The resulting dispute caused police to confiscate knives, razors, clubs and guns and violence occurred throughout the city.

This was the outstanding strike of many recent walkouts which have made more than 25,000 workers idle and hampered war production. However, more than 4,000 returned to their jobs yesterday.

President Roosevelt was expected to take early action in the transportation dispute, possibly through a return-to-work appeal or government seizure. The facts of the strike were assembled by Mobilization Director James F. Byrnes and transmitted to the President, who is away from Washington, and the War Labor Board asked Mr. Roosevelt to "take appropriate action."

The Navy estimated that its output of war material in this area was cut by 70 per cent on account of the strike, and the Army said its production was curtailed 50 per cent.

!EXTRA!

THE STARS AND STRIPES
MEDITERRANEAN

Vol. 1, No. 234, Tuesday, August 15, 1944 ITALY EDITION • • TWO LIRE

ALLIES INVADING SOUTH FRANCE

Bombers Support Landings

14,000 Combat Men Used By MAAF In Attack

More than 14,000 air combat men of the Mediterranean Allied Air Forces, equivalent to the line strength of two divisions, were airborne this morning against German strongholds on the coast of France in the port of the invasion.

An hour before the first troops were landed, the beaches felt the devastating effect of cascading tons of bombs, designed to knock out or render ineffective invasion obstacles and coastal defenses.

MAAF threw into the gigantic aerial assault its full striking force to help blast a way inland for the invading troops.

The entire Strategic Air Force, composed of 15th USAAF and RAF night bombers, was switched into the tactical attack.

The heavy bombers joined forces with Tactical Air Force's fighter bombers, and light and medium bombers to drop thousands of tons of bombs on gun emplacements, strong points, coastal defenses, troop concentrations, supply dumps and beachhead obstacles.

Farther inland, airfields and lines of communications through the beachhead area were attacked.

Fighters normally used for escort work in the 15th AAF teamed up with tactical fighters and fighter

(Continued on Page 2)

"Try to say sumpin' funny, Joe."

Yanks, British, French In Push

Initial Objective Said Won During First Hour

ADVANCED ALLIED FORCE HEADQUARTERS, Aug. 15 – American, British and French troops, strongly supported by Allied air forces, are being landed by fleets of the three nations on the southern coast of France, it was announced this noontime in a special communique. A Navy announcement indicated that the landings were being made between Nice and Marseilles.

Specially trained troops, among them airborne forces, are among those participating in the latest Allied assault on the continent went ashore from the invasion fleet at several points along a wide front.

An American broadcast from Allied Headquarters in Italy reported by Reuter's said "the minimum of German resistance was met in landing. The first objectives were reached in less than an hour. In less than two hours, seven waves of infantry ha. been put ashore. Paratroopers were landed two miles in shore before dawn."

The seven waves, with 2,000 men or more, were in France before 1000 hours, it was said.

Following the reading of the first Special Communique from Allied Force Headquarters in the Mediterranean Theater, General Sir Henry Maitland Wilson, Allied Supreme Commander, broadcast a statement directed to French underground forces in the region of the landings.

Speaking in English, then in French, General Wilson said that every Frenchman, whether soldier or civilian,

(Continued on Page 2)

THE FULL WEIGHT OF ALLIED LAND, AIR AND SEA power was directed against areas along the southern coast of France between Nice and Marseilles. On the left of the landing points is the Rhone River

1D. THE STARS AND STRIPES 1Fr.
Daily Newspaper of U.S. Armed Forces in the European Theater of Operations
Vol. 4 No. 245 New York, N.Y.—London, England—France Wednesday, Aug. 16, 1944

Allies Invade South France; Half of Nazi Army Still in Trap

Another Front, Another Hitler Bellyache

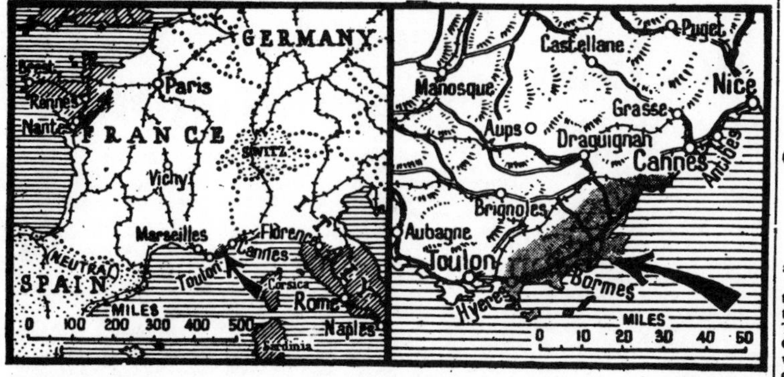

Stars and Stripes Maps

U.S.-British-French Assault Army Wins Beaches on Riviera

Opposition Light as Giant Sea-Airborne Forces Land; Falaise Gap Narrows; Foe Runs Gantlet of Shells, Bombs

Allied armies landed in southern France yesterday to open a fifth front against Hitler's hard-pressed forces.

To the north, 450 miles away, the Allies in northwestern France squeezed the Falaise sack and narrowed its neck, but front-line dispatches reported that half of the German Seventh Army there had escaped from the trap. The plight of the forces remaining was desperate under all-out attacks by Gen. Sir Bernard L. Montgomery's forces above and the Americans below, with Lt. Gen. Omar N. Bradley leading the Yanks as a full field commander of a new 12th Army Group and Lt. Gen. George S. Patton's Third Army heading the drive.

The sea and airborne forces which landed on a front of nearly 100 miles between Nice and Marseilles from North Africa, Italy and Mediterranean islands—U.S., British and French troops—aim "to effect a junction with the Allied armies advancing from Normandy," said Gen. Sir Henry Maitland Wilson, Supreme Commander in the Mediterranean Theater.

50,000 Reported Still in Bulge

Approximately half of Marshal Von Kluge's desperate German Seventh Army was reported last night to have escaped from the closing Allied trap at Falaise, but the sack itself and its bottleneck at the east were screwed relentlessly tighter on the forces that remained.

A Reuter dispatch from the British front which reported that "half of Kluge's army inside the Normandy pocket is now believed to have escaped" said that "the number of Germans still in the sack is estimated at 50,000."

Associated Press dispatches from the same front said that "the tempo of the German withdrawal is increasing hourly. Von Kluge is pulling back his armor and best infantry first. And again, as he did two days ago, he is withdrawing by day despite ideal bombing weather, a move which indicated his desperation."

Half of Armor Out?

All reports from the front agreed that some of the crack Nazi panzer divisions had withdrawn through the closing gap. Reuter's correspondent estimated that half of the vast armor concentration originally in the area was now east of Falaise.

The escape gap itself narrowed to about (Continued on page 4)

Several Miles In On South Coast

Shepherded by the greatest naval fleet ever employed in the Mediterranean and preceded by wave upon wave of paratroops and glidermen, strong American, British and French assault forces landed at a number of points along the southern French coast between Marseilles and Nice yesterday—and by last night appeared to have won control of the beaches.

Some elements already were several miles inland last night, an American correspondent broadcasting from field press headquarters said. "We landed almost without opposition," he added, "and only a few lives were lost."

The landings, climaxing five days' intense aerial hammering of the Mediterranean coast and the Rhone valley leading north into the heart of France, confronted Adolf Hitler—the man who wanted to fight on only one front at a time—with his fifth front: Russia, western France, southern France, Italy and the air over Festung Europa.

Opposition is Light

"By mid-morning," said a communique from Allied headquarters last night, "all landings were proceeding successfully according to schedule against only light ground opposition and no air opposition. Supporting airborne operations were also successfully executed."

The assault forces, numbering the first French forces participating in an invasion to recapture their homeland, were led, United Press said it understood, by Lt. Gen. Jacob L. Devers, former ETOUSA commander. Devers' chief, Gen. Sir Henry Maitland Wilson, announced soon afterward that their mission was to join up with the Allies in the north, in effect to create a giant nutcracker to break the Nazis in France.

Overnight, by their new operation 450 miles south of the fighting in the Seine-Loire wedge, the Allies doubled the scale of their assault in western Europe and set their feet on the traditional invasion route into France from the south—up the Rhone gap between the mountains that overspread southern France.

Best Allied opinion last night was that the Germans in southern France have at most only seven divisions, in an area where the underground has been reported strong. The enemy's biggest strategic re- (Continued on page 4)

Allied Planes Batter Airfields; Blitz on France Continues

In a closely co-ordinated joint operation—in which Eighth Air Force fighters for the first time escorted RAF bombers as well as their own Fortresses and Liberators—Allied planes struck at enemy airdromes in the Lowlands and Germany yesterday, while fighter-bombers maintained their campaign against enemy communications in France.

Halifaxes and Lancasters concentrated one of the heaviest attacks of the war upon nine airfields in Holland and Belgium, and Eighth bombers plastered Luftwaffe bases and airfields from the Rhine to northwest Germany.

More than 5,000 tons of bombs were dropped by the RAF, the average of 550 tons on each airfield amounting to more than dropped on the whole of London in any single night during the blitz. In its end of the operation, the Eighth hit targets at Cologne, Wiesbaden, Frankfort, Wittmund, Bad Zwischenahn, Vechta and Hansdorf, as well as airdromes in Holland and Belgium.

Enemy aircraft intercepted the Fortresses near Wiesbaden and Liberators near Vechta in the Reich. Sixteen bombers and five fighters were missing from the raid. The bombers shot down 13 enemy craft while the fighters accounted for 14 in the air and eight on the ground.

In addition to escort work, Eighth fighters battered German rail and other transport targets, shooting up 62 locomotives, 188 railroad cars, four military trucks and a number of canal barges, tugboats, gun batteries and radio stations.

Add to the Toll

Ninth Air Force Marauders and Havocs added to the toll of Nazi communications with attacks upon a railway center at Serqueux, 25 miles north of Rouen, and two bridges spanning the Oise, north of Paris. All the bombers returned and reported heavy damage both at Serqueux and at Auvers sur Oise, 15 miles north of Paris, and L'Isle Adam, two miles farther north on the Oise.

Marauders, carrying 2,000-pound bombs, blasted heavy gun batteries guarding the port of St. Malo, in Brittany, splattering huts and other installations with incendiaries in the attack. No enemy fighters or flak were encountered.

In more than 1,200 individual attacks by fighter-bombers Monday, the Ninth toll of Nazi equipment included more than 300 military transport vehicles destroyed and 108 damaged. Twenty-five tanks were knocked out and 19 damaged.

RAF pilots guarding the Nazi escape gap at Falaise reported the appearance (Continued on page 4)

The War Today

France—Allies invade southern France coast between Marseilles and Nice, secure beachheads against light ground opposition and none from air . . . New blow, with French invading homeland for first time, threatens Hitler with giant pincers squeeze against Seine-Loire armies . . . Lt. Gen. Devers reported leading combined sea-air operation . . . Half of Von Kluge's army believed to have escaped in Falaise gap . . . Canadians and Americans draw closer together as gap is narrowed, with an estimated 50,000 men of German Seventh Army still within bulge . . . Allied air forces continue to batter roads and enemy positions . . . Roads within gap under Allied shellfire.

Russia—Germans report Russians regrouping for new thrust toward East Prussian border after successful breaching of Biebrza River defenses northwest of Bialystok. . . . Offensive continues west of Pskov.

Pacific—Gen. MacArthur announces that Allied air attacks have "practically neutralized" Japanese airdromes and "immobilized" ground forces on Halmahera, Philippines stepping-stone . . . American heavies drop 60 tons of bombs on Manowari in Dutch New Guinea.

Asia—Takao, Formosa's chief port for Jap supplies in Chinese and Philippines area, blasted by American bombers. . . . Three freighters sunk in China Sea. . . . Chinese forces in Hunan Province recapture strategic points on the Canton-Hankow railway 35 miles south of Hengyang. . . . Japs fall back to within five miles of Burma frontier in Tiddim Road sector.

Italy—Allied positions in Florence improved as German shelling of city decreases . . . Eighth Army blasts Nazi toeholds on Arno River east and west of the city . . . Poles capture Frontone and seize Monte Fecchio in Adriatic sector . . . Rome reports indicate cabinet reshuffle to include Orlando as premier and Badoglio as foreign minister.

Ready Assault On E. Prussia

Red Army Pushing Ahead, Berlin Admits; Russians Gain on Other Fronts

Gen. George Zakharov's Second White Russian Army, successfully past the Biebrza River and fortifications guarding the southeastern corner of East Prussia at Osowiec, was reported by Berlin yesterday to be preparing for a new spring at the Reich border less than 16 miles beyond.

Though the bulk of Zakharov's armor was said to be "regrouping and absorbing fresh reinforcements" in the sector northwest of Bialystok, German News Agency's Col. Ernst von Hammer conceded that some Soviet elements were "pressing hard after the German disengaging movements in this area." He admitted that Red columns had pushed farther west.

On the Estonian front, the Russians apparently were throwing in strong forces to break through the remaining 17 miles to Valga, the junction where they can cut the Tallinn-Riga railway. Von Hammer said they made some gains.

Thirty-five miles south of Warsaw, where the Russians hold a bridgehead west of the Vistula near Warka, the enemy reported that a major Soviet attack punched "a number of wedges into the German lines," but claimed these were sealed off.

Britain, U.S. in Accord On World Security Unit

WASHINGTON, Aug. 15 (AP)—Secretary of State Cordell Hull said last night that Russia, China and Britain had been fully apprised of America's plans for a post-war world security organization.

Britain and the U.S. are in substantial accord on the main lines of the proposed agency, he reported.

Hull said the Russians within the last two days sent a memorandum on their own security ideas, but that he had not had time to study it thoroughly enough for comment.

Brittany Thrust Led by Patton

Bradley Heads Army Group; Status Equal to Montgomery's

By Wes Gallagher
Associated Press Military Correspondent

SHAEF, Aug. 15—Gen. Eisenhower has taken personal charge of operations in the Battle of France with establishment of an American Army Group under Lt. Gen. Omar N. Bradley, composed of at least the First and Third Armies, and with Bradley on an equal status with Gen. Sir Bernard L. Montgomery.

Both Montgomery and Bradley report directly to Eisenhower, who, from his command post in France, directs operations of both groups.

The change in command took place immediately upon Eisenhower's arrival in France more than a week ago, it became known tonight.

The new Army Group under Bradley will be known as the U.S. 12th.

Heading the American Third Army is Lt. Gen. George S. Patton Jr., "Old Blood and Guts."

Bradley's strategic genius and Patton's driving ability accomplished the unique feat of creating a new army while actually engaged in an offensive. When Bradley launched his great breakout offensive July 25, all the American forces were in the First Army. Then, as the campaign hit high gear on Aug. 1, a small segment

Associated Press Photo

Lt. Gen. George S. Patton Jr.

was broken off as the Third Army and placed under Patton to drive down the west coast of the Cherbourg peninsula.

Then, with new forces piled up on the beach behind, Patton drove that Third Army through Coutances, down the coast (Continued on page 4)

Parisian Patriots Burst Into Song at the News

MADRID, Aug. 15 (UP)—People rushed out into the streets in Paris and sang the Marseillaise when they heard the news that a French army had landed in France again, said reports reaching Madrid today. The Germans were powerless to stop them.

Sporadic fighting was reported between patriots and collaborationists, but the German military rule over Paris is still maintained rigorously.

1d.

THE STARS AND STRIPES

1 Fr.

Daily Newspaper of U.S. Armed Forces in the European Theater of Operations

Vol. 4 No. 247 | New York, N.Y.—London, England—France | Friday, Aug. 18, 1944

Americans 25 Miles From Paris; 50-Mile Solid Front on Riviera

French Without Tears

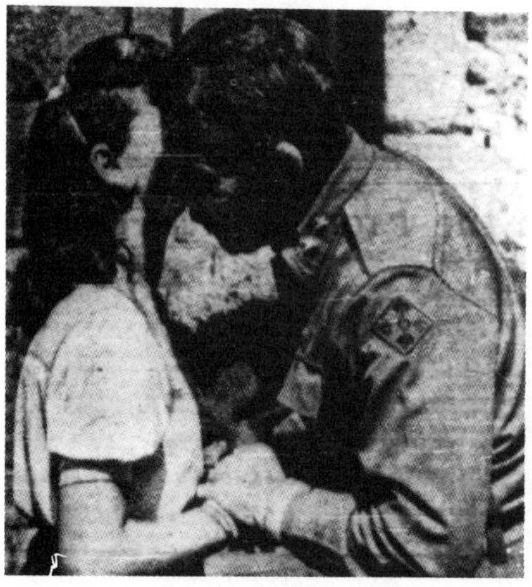

Maj. Gen. Raymond O. Barton of the Fourth Division gets a bouquet and a kiss from a French girl near his headquarters. Signal Corps photographer who took the picture said she was pretty.

Two Big Fleets Now Ready To 'Powerhouse' Japs–Nimitz

Even as Adm. Chester W. Nimitz declared at Guam yesterday that the American Third and Fifth Fleets were " ready to wage non-stop war against Japan " with the use of " powerhouse tactics." a Japanese spokesman warned his people of a two-pronged American offensive in which the Japs will face " an enemy superiority of three to one."

The Tokyo Radio statement sought to prepare the Japanese people for " a decisive battle between the Philippines and Japan proper," adding that the twin Allied pincers would consist of " 11 divisions of ground troops " under Nimitz and " 24 divisions, 17 of them American," under Gen. Douglas MacArthur.

The spokesman added that " the American air force in the Pacific area is superior to the Japanese. Ours is one third of the enemy's."

Tokyo Radio also reported three American air raids on widely scattered

(*Continued on page 4*)

The War Today

France—Gen. Patton's Third Army within 25 miles of Paris after crossing Aunay River. . . . Yanks capture Chartres, Orleans and Dreux, key cities on three main roads to capital. . . . German report says gunfire heard in Paris from three-pronged American drive. . . . All beachheads in southern France joined in continuous front 50 air miles wide. . . . Allies are more than ten miles inland and hold 500 square miles. . . . Seven towns firmly held. . . . Stockholm hears Nice and Cannes also taken.

Pacific—American fleets are ready for "non-stop war against Japan." Adm. Nimitz says. . . . Japs claim Allies have a 3—1 edge in superiority and forecast "decisive battle between the Philippines and Japan proper."

Russia—Germans admit Soviet breakthrough four miles from East Prussia. . . . Russians admit loss of town seven miles east of Warsaw to counter-attacking German panzers.

Italy—Germans using tanks in Florence streets to shoot down civilians and military police, according to patriots returning across Arno demarcation line. . . . Allies hold mountain strongholds from Empoli, 15 miles west of Florence, to Pontassieve to the east.

Asia—Allies drive remnants of Japs' "invade India" force across frontier and smash forward three miles into Burma. . . . Thaikwagon, 21 miles down Mandalay railway from Mogaung, cleared of Japs. . . . Chungking announces heavy air assaults on Tengchung garrison.

Unit Bombed With Plasma

A NINTH AIR FORCE BASE, France, Aug. 17 (AP)—Less than two hours after an American armored unit in the thick of the fighting had sent an SOS for blood plasma, a dive-bomber drove down through a wall of enemy ack-ack to within 50 feet of the ground to be sure of the mark—a big red cross marked on the ground—and dropped a carefully-packed belly-tank loaded with plasma and drugs.

"I tried to drop the tank containing plasma and dressings into some trees to prevent it from breaking," said the pilot, Lt. Willard R. Haines, of Atlanta, "but the ack-ack was so fierce I didn't wait to see where it landed."

The armored unit's radio man, however, reported a few minutes later that the package fell "in the field next to us—they're getting it now. Thanks a lot."

FDR Returns to Capital After Trip to the Pacific

WASHINGTON, Aug. 17 (Reuter)—President Roosevelt returned to the White House today after his 15,000-mile Pacific trip.

He told a press conference that Allied troops would drive in and occupy Germany and Japan even should resistance collapse short of the enemy borders.

Allies Hold 500 Sq. Mi. Of S. Coast

Drive Nearing Toulon, Cannes; Nice Seized, Stockholm Hears

All beachheads in southern France have been joined to form "a continuous front inland with anchor points more than 50 air miles apart" and some 500 square miles of coast are in Allied hands, a special communique announced last night.

"The swift advance of American and French troops inland continues," the communique said, "and numerous additional towns and villages have been taken."

The regular Allied communique revealed earlier that some troops were more than ten miles inland and still going forward.

" Unloadings have exceeded expectations," it said. Soon afterward, Acting Secretary of War John J. McCloy told a Washington press conference that the invasion was one day ahead of schedule. And from Advanced Allied Headquarters came a Reuter correspondent's report that Allied casualties were moderate, while enemy losses were believed heavy.

The latest official summary of the three-day-old Riviera operation placed the coastal towns of St. Tropez, St. Maxime, St. Raphael, Frejus and Le Levandou—as well as the inland towns of Le Muy, Le Luc and Moru—" firmly in our hands."

Allied forces, it said, " are now within ten miles of both Toulon and Cannes." Earlier the German communique had said the Allies, " after a heavy struggle, succeeded in penetrating into Cannes " and Berlin dispatches reaching Stockholm reported Cannes and Nice had been captured. German News Agency at the same time reported new Allied " landing attempts on both sides of the fortress of

(*Continued on page 4*)

Some Shortages, but None At the Front, Nelson Says

WASHINGTON, Aug. 17 (Reuter)—Donald M. Nelson, chairman of the War Production Board, told the Senate War Investigating Committee today that while "specialized shortages" existed in the war supply program "there is no shortage at the battlefronts," committee members said.

At a closed session, Nelson emphasized that the WPB order lifting the ban on the production of hundreds of civilian articles in areas where the labor situation is not critical and material is available "will in no way interfere with the war effort."

Orleans, Chartres, Dreux Fall; Police In Capital on Strike

Lt. Gen. George S. Patton's Third Army troops neared Paris last night after capturing Chartres, Orleans and Dreux—three key cities on three main roads into the French capital. The German High Command reported heavy fighting about 25 miles from Paris near St. Arnoult, on the main Chartres-Paris road.

The sensational American advance broke through on a 60-mile front between Orleans and Dreux in what Berlin termed "an all-out drive for Paris" by strong tank and motorized artillery formations.

Paris was already a front-line city, said a German report. The people heard U.S. gunfire. The police were on strike and the subway out of action.

As Berlin reported that three American columns were advancing on the capital, a United Press dispatch from the U.S. front said that one column jumped the Aunay River and had a bridgehead across it only 32 miles from Paris, 13 miles beyond Chartres. Another spearhead crossed the Eure River, the UP said, and a third captured Chateaudun, southwest of Chartres.

Light Resistance Indicated

Berlin spoke significantly of the American drive being met by German "covering forces"—a phrase that usually means screening forces, not in very great strength.

It was officially announced that the Third Army had accounted for about 100,000 German casualties, including 11,000 killed, 41,300 captured and 47,000 wounded.

On the Falaise front, dispatches indicated that confusion was spreading in the German ranks. Prisoners captured over a 12-hour period represented 12 different divisions, the AP reported: many of the captured Germans had had no food, while some had no shoes. "The German Army is completely disorganized," British staff officer told a Reuter correspondent.

Other than that, the situation in the Falaise gap—Falaise itself was captured but there were no reports of the gap actually being closed— remained obscure. Dispatches on the number of Germans still inside the pocket were widely at variance, as were estimates of what percentage of Von Kluge's armor had managed to escape. One report said flatly that the bulk of Kluge's panzer force had gotten out.

However, a Canadian Army spokesman told a Reuter correspondent that the Germans had not been able to get any great amount of men or material out. The spokesman said that " a number of panzer and infantry divisions " were still

(*Continued on page 4*)

112,673 U.S. Casualties

WASHINGTON, Aug. 17 (AP)—American losses on the Normandy sector from June 6 to Aug. 6 were 16,434 killed, 76,535 wounded and 19,704 missing for a total of 112,673, the War Department announced today.

Mediums Bomb West of Falaise

Risle River Bridges Hit; 8th AF Sums Up Two Years of Operations

Eighth Air Force fighter-bombers hammered enemy communication lines in Germany, France and Belgium and railway lines south of the Rhine yesterday as Marauders and Havocs of the Ninth Air Force poured over 400 tons of explosives on roads and highway bridges across the Risle River west of the Falaise battle area.

Figures released by the Eighth Air Force on the occasion of its second anniversary of flights across the Channel into occupied Europe disclosed that its individual airmen had made 1,750,000 crossings into enemy territory in two years.

From the date of the first venture, Aug. 17, 1942—when 12 Forts dropped 18 tons of bombs on railway yards at Rouen, in France—the Eighth has flown 301,000 sorties, 162,000 by Forts and Liberators and 139,000 by Mustangs, Lightnings and Thunderbolts.

Over 8,500 enemy planes were shot out of the air, 5,688 by bomber gunners and 2,913 by fighter pilots, apart from 1,150 parked enemy planes strafed and those destroyed in frequent bombing attacks upon enemy airdromes. The Eighth losses in the two-year campaign were 31,000 men listed as killed or missing in action—a large number are known to be prisoners of war—and 2,900 bombers and 2,000 fighters due to enemy action.

Yesterday's raid was the eighth time since the Allies began closing the Argentan-Falaise gap that Ninth medium and light bombers struck at rail and road targets ahead of the actual battle area.

Targets along the Risle, which extend in a line more than 20 miles south from

(*Continued on page 4*)

Crack Nazi Line Near E. Prussia

A Soviet breakthrough at the northeastern edge of East Prussia, less than four miles from the pre-war border, was admitted by Berlin last night while German panzers 200 miles to the south launched a series of frenzied counter-attacks east of Warsaw after wresting the suburban town of Ossow from the Russians.

The loss of Ossow was the first town the Red Army admitted evacuating in two months, but Moscow's communique described it as " insignificant " and dispatches from the Soviet capital said the Germans had driven only a narrow wedge into the Red lines seven miles east of the capital.

The Soviet breakthrough apparently was achieved west of Virbalis in Lithuania. Meanwhile, Moscow reported the German garrison of Sandomierz, 120 miles south of Warsaw, almost completely surrounded and likely to fall soon.

Maquis Using Airborne Artillery

GENEVA, Aug. 17 (UP)—Artillery parachuted to the Maquis was in action tonight for the first time following risings in the Haute Savoie near the Franco-Swiss frontier.

A Foot Wedged in Hitler's Door

Fuller Brush Man in GI Clothes Spins a Glib Fib, 406 Nazis Quit

By Bud Kane

Stars and Stripes Staff Writer

BOURG BLANC, Aug. 17—Sgt. Alexander Balter, of Pittsburg member of an armored unit sweeping up through the Brittany peninsula, personally captured 406 Germans within 24 hours—and never fired a shot. In fact, the entire day's haul for his reconnaissance unit was more than twice the total number of men in his company.

At the request of his commander, Capt. Allen A. Scullen, of Boston, Balter took a jeep with a white flag attached, rode into an enemy stronghold and gave the commander a word picture of his situation which was far from true—although the German didn't know that.

"You are surrounded on three sides," said Balter, "and our air forces are awaiting the time, one hour from now, when they will bomb your entire area. In addition, our artillery will deliver a barrage guaranteed to destroy your forces. You can surrender now and avoid all this."

The Nazi commander asked how Balter could prove it. Balter turned over his field radio receiver, which had been tuned all the time to Scullen.

"The captain will corroborate my statements," said Balter.

Scullen attested to all that Balter had said and added:

" Tell him that 20 minutes already have passed and that he has little time left to make up his mind."

Balter relayed the message, and reminded the commander of a bombardment and barrage which had taken place several miles down the coast.

The barrage evidently was fresh in the German's mind, because he considered only a minute and then said, " I will surrender."

In less than 20 minutes 246 men comprising the garrison marched out.

Inside three hours, two other garrisons, with a total of 160 men, had surrendered to the same line of talk all because Balter could speak German convincingly.

1 Fr.

THE STARS AND STRIPES

1 Fr.

Daily Newspaper of U.S. Armed Forces in the European Theater of Operations

Vol. 1 No. 45 — New York—London—Rennes — Thursday, Aug. 24, 1944

PARIS IS LIBERATED

Rumania Is Out of the War

Soviet Peace Bid Accepted By Satellite

Balkan Nation Wants To Join In Fight Against Nazis

In an eleventh-hour bid to climb on the Allied band wagon, Rumania last night became the first of Hitler's Balkan satellites to get out of the war. Radio Bucharest broadcast a royal proclamation stating that Rumania has accepted Russia's peace terms and wants to become an ally of the United Nations.

The proclamation said a new national government will be formed with Gen. Konstantin Sanatescu as premier. Two cabinet members thus far announced are Bratianu and Maniu.

Bucharest radio said that the Vienna Pact—under which Germany's satellites were pitted against each other and under which Rumania ceded the larger part of Transylvania to Hungary—has been rejected.

"Rumania is taking her fate into her own hands and will fight against the enemy. All citizens are to rally around the throne," the royal proclamation said.

Reds Capture Four Strongholds

Capture of four enemy strongholds by Russian Armies on the first, second and third Ukranian fronts was announced by Marshal Stalin last night in three Orders of the Day.

The first Order of the Day reported that troops on the second Ukranian front had captured Vaslui, enemy strong point and communications center in Rumania, 36 miles south of newly liberated Jassy between the Sereth and Pruth Rivers.

The second Order of the Day said troops on the third Ukranian front had captured by assault the towns of Akkerman and Bendery 21 miles southwest of Odessa, important strongholds of the German defense system on the lower Dniester.

The order announced that troops on the first Ukranian front captured Debica, center of the aircraft industry 60 miles east of Cracow. The [illegible] big German base guarding the approaches to Silesia, Debica stands on the eastern bank of the Vistula River and [illegible] the Lwow-Cracow railway line.

U.S. Planes Blast Wall for Chinese

Fighting their way into Tengchung through breaches blasted in the city walls by U.S. 14th Air Force, Chinese troops now hold a third of the city, a Chungking report announced last night.

Meanwhile, Jap counter-attacks were reported repulsed by Chinese on the highest peak of Sungshan near the Salween River.

First 'Duckmobile' Brings Java, Sinkers

A BEACHHEAD IN NORMANDY, Aug. 22—Sailors can [illegible] "Duck" for doughnuts they [illegible] from [illegible] A. Becker of Lynchburg, Va., American Red Cross "duckmobile girl."

Using a converted duck to [illegible] small craft and [illegible] [illegible] Miss Becker makes [illegible] "doughnuts and coffee [illegible]" in three hours. She is assisted by Sgt. [illegible] Kennedy of Brooklyn, who serves as a "[illegible]."

Paris, 'City of Conquest,' Free Again

Seven times captured, twice threatened with seizure during its long history, Paris is free again today after four years of German control. Picture above show the capital's 107-year-old Arc de Triomphe.

Paris Watched in Silence As Boche Entered in 1940

On June 14, 1940, German tanks rumbled into Paris. They passed through otherwise silent streets. Many thousands—some reports said two-thirds of the population—had evacuated Paris and the remainder stayed indoors.

Paris had been declared an open city a few days before. A valiant effort had been made to save the city, but the fight was a desperate and losing one against an army with vast superiority in armor. Marshal Petain, who assumed office shortly after the occupation, signed an armistice with the Germans on July 24, and formal hostilities in France ceased the next day.

Paris cafes, shops and stores, the cinemas and most of the hotels were shut. Women made pilgrimages to the Arc de Triomphe and, bowing their heads, cried bitterly. The Germans ordered a 9 PM curfew and the city of light lost its brilliance in a blackout as complete as that of London.

Thus began life under the German

Continued on Page 4

FDR Lists Aid To Free French

Says Lend-Lease Put De Gaulle's Army Back in War

WASHINGTON, Aug. 23—President Roosevelt informed Congress today that the U.S. commanding general in the field in France had been sent $428,399,989 worth of lend-lease equipment for delivery to the French in addition to the vast quantities already received by the French forces now fighting on their homeland.

"With the fall of France, the French Army was virtually destroyed," he said. "Now there is an army in France again. It is equipped with lend-lease arms."

The French are back in the fight, the President said, because "we have sent them Sherman tanks, American half-tracks and artillery and other equipment to replace what they had [illegible]."

The President added that "the French are providing many supplies and services to U.S. forces in the Mediterranean theater as reverse lend-lease, the estimated value being [illegible] by the first of this year."

FLY OUT 300 WOUNDED

ROME, Aug. 23 (UP)—United States Dakotas in the greatest air evacuation of wounded since the [illegible] began, carried 300 wounded patients out of Yugoslavia Tuesday. The [illegible] also carried food into Yugoslavia and flew hundreds of miles [illegible] enemy held territory.

Patriots Clear City In Four-Day Battle As U.S. Army Nears

French Armored Unit Reported Inside; Marseilles and Grenoble Also In Hands of the Allies

Paris is free.

Its liberation, after four years and two months of German occupation, was announced yesterday at the headquarters of Gen. Charles de Gaulle's National Committe of Liberation.

French Forces of the Interior, with the aid of unarmed citizens encouraged by the approach of American armies to the gates of the city, effected the liberation, according to the announcement, and French armored troops already were reported to have entered the city as the vanguard of the liberation armies which landed in France two months and 13 days before.

Almost simultaneously with the disclosure of the freeing of the city, which is the symbol of liberty to France and to much of the world, Allied headquarters in the Mediterranean announced that Marseilles, France's largest southern port, had fallen to French and U. S forces advancing from their south coast beachhead. Only small pockets of resistance remained to be cleared up, it was said.

Mediterranean headquarters also announced the fall of the rail center of Grenoble and revealed that Allied troops had advanced as much as 150 miles inland from their landing points. Heavy fighting was reported in Toulon, great French naval base.

The battle for control of Paris began inside the city Friday night, when street fighting broke out, according to reports from French sources. On Saturday the prefecture was occupied. SS troops placed machine-guns in key posts to combat the increasing menace of the FFI troops.

It was estimated that 50,000 armed FFI men, plus several hundred thousand unarmed patriots took part in the battle.

By Tuesday night all of the key public buildings had been seized as the Germans left the city.

Meanwhile, the U.S advance southeast of Paris was obscure because of Allied silence. There was no information whether Gen. Patton's forces had gone beyond the city of Sens, which they were reported to have reached Tuesday. This city lies 60 miles southeast of Paris.

Algiers radio, however, reported that American forces had reached the Marne River, northeast of Paris, which was the scene of the 1918 battle in which the Allies stopped the German advance toward the capital.

In western France the German Seventh Army continued to retreat with Allied forces in close pursuit. Their escape corridor toward the Seine was narrowed to about 20 miles as the Americans proceded west along the Seine toward the mouth of the river and the British and Canadians advanced eastward toward Paris.

3-Inch Heads Tell the News In U.S. Papers

Freeing of Paris Stirs America Out of Its Near Apathy

Stars and Stripes U. S. Bureau

NEW YORK, Aug. 23—America greeted the liberation of Paris today with something more than the almost apathetic calm which has marked—or failed to mark—most news from the front since D-Day.

Newspapers dragged out three-inch type. Some organized groups called for celebrations and prayer services. Mostly, however, it was business as usual.

Newspapers, using their biggest type since the invasion, headlined the news with "Paris Is Freed," and "Paris Is Liberated," while the radio networks aired special shortwave broadcasts from the French battle fronts.

The New York Times said editorially: "If Paris was freed solely by foreign troops one could be glad—but the French did all that man can do to free himself. With every passing day—indeed, with every passing hour—new areas are freed. Visibly France is rising from her ashes."

Gen. John J. Pershing, who commanded the American Expeditionary Force in World War I, described the liberation as "a great step forward along the road to Berlin."

The aged general said: "Today Paris is freed and the sons of America who fought to preserve the freedom of Paris in 1917 and 1918 have had a permanent role in the liberation of 1944 by their coopera-

Continued on Page 4

Pilot Returns With Prisoner After Landing In Enemy Area

NINTH AIR FORCE HQ, France, Aug. 23—Unarmed and hunted by a squad of German soldiers after he had parachuted behind enemy lines from his flak-crippled fighter-bomber, a Ninth Air Force Thunderbolt pilot captured a Storm Trooper noncom, disarmed him, and after a 3½-hour pilgrimage through no-man's land, was safely back at his base today.

Capt. Frederick Heitrecht, Beeville, Texas, the pilot, jumped from his Thunderbolt and landed in an open field. He ran to a hedgerow, but was spotted by a Storm Trooper corporal armed with a rifle.

Capt. Heitrecht said: "I yelled 'achtung'—the only German word I know—and pretended to cover him with a pistol, although I was unarmed. The Jerry dropped his rifle and yelled back 'Kamerad.'"

Motioning his captive to turn around, the Thunderbolt pilot snatched up the rifle, relieved the soldier of his ammunition belt, and led him back into the bushes. In a few minutes, six Germans came across the field, coming within 30 yards of the crouching pair. "I threatened my Jerry with his own bayonet, and then put my finger to my lips. He nodded and remained silent while that pick-up patrol went away."

The American flyer and the German foot soldier remained in their hedgerow for two hours while P47s, artillery, tanks and retreating German troops made the area hot with lead and steel. Capt. Heitrecht relieved the German of papers but let him keep a photograph of his fraulein and his watch. In handing

Continued on Page 4

8 German Ships Sunk Off Lorient by British

LONDON, Aug. 23—The British Admirality announced tonight that eight German vessels were sunk this morning off the French coast near Lorient by British warships, under the command of Capt. W.W. Davis in the cruiser Mauritius. The British ships suffered neither damage nor casualties.

A German supply ship was sunk early Wednesday morning. A Nazi minesweeper and escort vessel were driven ashore in the same engagement.

Later, the British ships encountered a small German convoy with one medium-sized ship and one small supply vessel accompanied by a minesweeper and two heavily-armed escort vessels. The convoy and escort vessels were all destroyed.

1D. THE STARS AND STRIPES 1Fr.
Daily Newspaper of U.S. Armed Forces in the European Theater of Operations
Vol. 4 No. 253 New York, N.Y.—London, England—France Friday, Aug. 25, 1944

Marseilles Falls; Capture of Bordeaux Reported

* * * * * * * * *

Germans Renew Fight in Paris

Rumania Gives Up; Balkan Crash Seen

Allied Armistice Terms Accepted By Bucharest

The entire Rumanian front before the Russians was reported crumbling yesterday following Rumania's capitulation to the Allies, while rumblings from other satellite nations indicated a possible swift crackup in the whole Nazi edifice in the Balkans.

Rumania's exit from the Axis camp, proclaimed by King Michael Wednesday night, came as a grim surprise to Berlin, where official spokesmen were speechless until late yesterday.

The move could be expected to expose to the advancing Red armies an estimated 250,000 German troops locked in Rumania, leave open all passes into Hungary, and deny the oil-thirsty Nazis further access to the Ploesti oilfields.

In announcing acceptance of Allied armistice terms, the King revealed that the United Nations had guaranteed the independence of Rumania, and that the Vienna award under which Transylvania was ceded to Hungary under Axis arbitration was thrown aside. No further terms were made public, although London diplomatic circles described them as "generous."

Antonescu Flight Reported

The King named Gen. Konstantin Senatescu as the new prime minister to succeed Marshal Antonescu, the pro-Axis leader who was reported to have fled to Germany. Other members of the new cabinet included M. Juliu Maniu, Peasant Party chief, Foreign Minister M. Niculescui-Buzesti and M. Bratianu.

Berlin's belated reaction was typically

(*Continued on page 4*)

The War Today

France—Allied troops battle toward Paris after Germans repudiate "armistice" with French Forces of Interior and patriots call for help. . . . U.S. armor in 25-mile drive along west bank of Seine captures Elbeuf, within artillery range of German supply base at Rouen and 25 miles from Canadian pincer of trap. . . . Two more Seine crossings made beyond Paris. . . . Marseilles taken, Swiss report U.S. tanks at Swiss border 220 miles north of Toulon. . . . Unconfirmed dispatches list Bordeaux and Lyons as in French hands.

Russia—Germans admit deep Soviet penetrations on Rumanian front as result of satellite troops' "confusion" over King's decision to quit war. . . . Moscow reports say Nazis are shooting Rumanians attempting to retreat. . . . Russians find hidden nest of evacuated German war plants 65 miles east of Cracow.

Italy—Allies approach Gothic line along whole Italian front. . . . British and Indians capture Mount Foresco, 10 miles from Nazi bastions. . . . Poles cross Metaura River in Adriatic sector, five miles south of Fano.

Pacific—Chinese Minister of Information says China is in favor of Allied military occupation of Japan. . . . Japanese provincial governors and cabinet reaffirm to Emperor their determination to insure victory. . . . Allied bombers continue softening-up attacks from Moluccas to Bonin Islands.

Asia—Allied 14th Army troops ten miles inside Burma along Tiddim Road again contact enemy successfully attacking Japanese position.

Naziland No More

Stars and Stripes Map

Russians Spur Rumania Drive

German troops on the Rumanian front continued to resist the advancing Russians yesterday, but "confusion among the Rumanian units" permitted the Red Army to penetrate deeply toward the lower Danube, German News Agency admitted last night. There were reports from Moscow that the Nazis were machine-gunning Rumanians who tried to retreat.

The Russians reported their five-day-old twin offensive in the south moving at increasing speed, with Nazi reserves unable to stem the Red tanks and artillery. One entire German division was wiped out by Stormoviks.

Capture of Kishinev, Bessarabian capital 60 miles east of Jassy, was announced last night by Marshal tSalin.

North of Warsaw the Soviets' newest assault—aimed at breaking the enemy's line above the Polish capital—increased in intensity as the Russians closed within five miles of Lomza, about 20 miles from southeastern East Prussia.

Sixty-five miles east of Cracow, according to the Associated Press, Marshal Ivan Koniev's army wrested "hundreds of German war factories" hidden in woods around the city of Debica, an apparent evacuation area for machine shops moved to thwart Allied bombers.

Fighting in the south, Berlin said, centered at Roman, 35 miles southwest of captured Jassy, from which a direct rail line runs to Ploesti, 180 miles beyond. Earlier Moscow reported capture of Akkerman, at the mouth of the Dniester; the rail town of Tighina, 60 miles upstream on the Dniester, and Vaslui, 85 miles north of the Danube mouth.

Wilson Quits WPB

WASHINGTON, Aug. 24 (Reuter)—The White House announced today that Charles E. Wilson had resigned as vice-chairman of the War Production Board.

U.S. Column Said to Be at Swiss Line

Broadcasts Cite Drives Far Past Grenoble; Toulon's Fall Held 'Imminent'

Liberation of southern France progressed by leaps and bounds yesterday, as hour by hour the Allies and Fighting French announced fresh successes over a weakened and confused enemy.

These were the highlights in 24 hours.

Marseilles, second city of France, was taken by French troops.

Bordeaux, France's fourth city and center of the last German resistance in southwest France, fell to Allied troops and French Forces of the Interior, Radio France at Algiers announced.

Swiss radio said a "hush hush" force of U.S. tanks which took Grenoble had pushed 55 miles farther north into Annecy, center of Maquis resistance in Upper Savoy, 190 miles north of Toulon.

An unconfirmed Reuter dispatch from Geneva, repeated later by a CBS correspondent at Berne, said it was reported there the Americans had reached the Swiss border at St. Julien, south of Lake Geneva, 27 miles north of Annecy and nearly 220 miles above Toulon.

Toulon's Fall 'Imminent'

In Toulon the German garrison continued to resist obstinately in house-to-house fighting and the commander of the attacking French reported his troops were "killing literally thousands." Berlin admitted the French had reached German naval headquarters, though the harbor was still in Nazi hands. Fall of the base "appears imminent," according to a Reuter dispatch from Allied headquarters.

France's third city, industrial Lyons, 175 miles up the Rhone valley, was liberated by the FFI at 5 AM, according to an unconfirmed Reuter report from the Swiss frontier last night. At the time, American forces striking from Grenoble

(*Continued on page 4*)

U.S. Special Service Will Keep 'Em Busy

At the risk of making Hans an even duller boy, German radio yesterday broadcast this all-work-and-no-play note:

"Work must be the order of the day, and social and welfare facilities must take a back seat

"Public assistance and entertainment for troops will cease, as German troops have no time for recreation anyway."

Tear Up Armistice; Allies Move on City

Cheese It, the Yanks

U.S. Army Signal Corps Photo

Concrete German pillbox looks like Swiss cheese after American tankers go to work on it.

1,300 Heavies Hit at Nazi Oil

Eighth Air Force heavies yesterday battered five targets in one of the war's heaviest assaults on German oil supplies.

After a day in which Italian-based American planes shot down 45 Nazi craft over central Europe to boost their two-day score to 99, more than 1,300 U.S. heavy bombers, escorted by up to 1,000 fighters, flew from Britain to paste aircraft and industrial objectives over a wide area of north and central Germany, as well as vital oil installations.

Among the targets pin-pointed visually by the raiders were synthetic-oil plants at Merseburg, in Prussia, and at Brux, in the Sudetenland—two of the three largest enemy oil production centers still in operation.

Also pounded were synthetic oil plants at Misburg and Ruhland; an oil refinery at Freital, near Dresden; aircraft plants at Brunswick; Luftwaffe stations at Kolleda, near Merseburg, and Langenhagen, near Hanover; a radio equipment factory at Weimar, and industrial targets at Kiel.

Ninth Bomber Command Headquarters revealed, meanwhile, that Havocs had

(*Continued on page 4*)

USAAF Plans to Station Units in Europe After War

WASHINGTON, Aug. 24 (ANS)—Maj. Gen. O. P. Echols, assistant chief of staff of the Army Air Forces, told a House committee today that the AAF had made plans for stationing Air Force units in Europe after the capitulation of Germany.

He declared that certain units would be kept in Europe for the time being, that others would be sent to the Asiatic theater and that some would be returned to the U.S.

Town Near Rouen Seized as Trap Threat Grows

Allied troops battled their way toward Paris yesterday after the Germans apparently repudiated an "armistice" under which the French Forces of the Interior had announced the capital liberated. The French then called for help.

But while popular interest centered on the struggle for Paris, an operation of far greater military significance down the Seine River found American armor driving 25 miles along the west bank to capture Elbeuf in a move to shut the trap on German forces between there and the sea. At Elbeuf the Yanks were 25 miles from a Canadian pincer at Trouville, near the river mouth, and within 10-12 miles of the German supply base at Rouen.

Meanwhile, Third Army troops forced two more crossings of the Seine southeast of Paris and headed toward Germany on a front which dispatches from the field estimated at 25 to 60 miles broad.

Evoked Roosevelt Statement

The premature announcement by Gen. Koenig, head of the FFI, on the liberation of Paris had evoked celebration and jubilation around the world, plus congratulatory messages which were climaxed by a special statement from President Roosevelt yesterday saying that "we rejoice with the gallant French people at the liberation of Paris."

Secretary of War Henry L. Stimson, too, referred to the "liberation" at a press conference in which he termed the battle of Normandy "a major victory" and said that German casualties exceeded 300,000.

But at SHAEF, where Gen. Koenig's communique had previously been neither confirmed nor denied, the following statement was issued last night:

"An agreement was made by the FFI in Paris with the Germans for some sort of armistice in the capital. It was intended to let the Germans clear out, but evidently they changed their minds and threatened to destroy everything.

"The French in Paris called for help, and we are furnishing that help for them now. Allied forces began moving on Paris this morning, but it is not yet

(*Continued on page 4*)

Remember Danielle Darrieux?

Fleur de Paris Blooms Despite Patched Petal

By James McClincy
United Press War Correspondent

NEAR PARIS, Aug. 24—Danielle Darrieux was in good form when we reached her home Tuesday, except that she had no cigarettes and no wine and she had a patch on her blue slacks.

Although there have been reports about Danielle being a collaborationist, they are not true. Rather than work for the Germans she had refused to make films in France, where the film industry was under German or Vichy control. She has been living quietly with her husband, Robert Rubirosa, son of a Dominican diplomat.

I was taken to her home by five members of the resistance movement—the kind who would not get any closer to a collaborator than necessary to shoot or spit at him.

Danielle said apologetically: "I only have water to offer you." So we sent the jeep driver for a bottle of wine, at the same time trying to keep our eyes on that neat little patch on Darrieux's "derriere."

She eagerly accepted American cigarettes and promised an interview some day when we were not in such a hurry to get to Paris. As we left, she stood smiling, her teeth glistening 50 yards away.

"The hell with Paris," our driver muttered.

U.S. Guns Purred It to This Tiger

U.S. Army Signal Corps Photo

GI gunnery blasts a German Tiger tank into a holocaust of flames and flying debris near Chartres.

1D. **THE STARS AND STRIPES** 1Fr.

Daily Newspaper of U.S. Armed Forces in the European Theater of Operations

Vol. 4 No. 254 | New York, N.Y.—London, England—France | Saturday, Aug. 26, 1944

French Tanks Smash Into Paris

Hustling Along

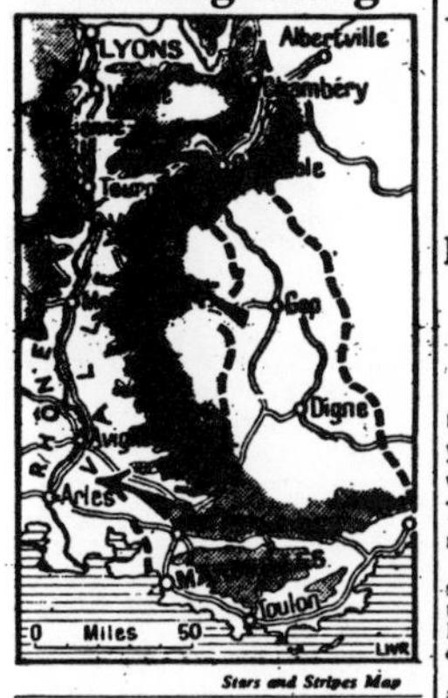

Stars and Stripes Map

Rumania Units Quit, Nazis Say

Berlin Concedes Russia A 'Cheap Victory' In the South

Berlin frankly admitted last night that the Rumanians had quit on them in the south and given the Russians "a cheap victory."

In the enemy's first confession that his erstwhile allies had deserted, Col. Ernst von Hammer of German News Agency told the Reich:

"The Rumanian divisions, which only a few days ago fought magnificently at the side of their German allies, have abandoned well-fortified front sectors together with their arms, regardless of their German brothers-in-arms."

The Russians, after sweeping most of the enemy's strongpoints in Moldavia and Bessarabia, were reported nearing Focsani last night, little more than 100 miles northeast of Bucharest and hardly 40 miles from the Danube port of Galatz. In 48 hours they had covered nearly half

(Continued on page 4)

The War Today

France—French armored troops battle Germans in center of Paris, as Berlin reports Americans in suburbs attacking German defenders from west, southwest and southeast. . . . One report says liberation of Paris is now a fact. . . . German forces west of Seine River are nearly encircled, as Canadians sweep around from mouth of the river. . . . British reach the Seine within sight of Le Havre. . . . Communique announces capture of Cannes but situation in Marseilles left obscure by correspondent's report that city has not been taken in spite of Allied claim.

Russia—Berlin admits Rumanian divisions at southern end of front have laid down arms and quit, giving Russians "cheap victory." . . . Red Army, with most of Moldavian and Bessarabian strongpoints in its grasp, advances swiftly within 100 miles of Bucharest and only 40 miles from lower Danube port of Galatz.

Italy—Eighth Army takes Acqalagna against weakened German resistance, arousing speculation Germans have determined on withdrawal to Gothic line ten miles beyond. . . . Only patrol activity in Florence sector.

Pacific—Adm. Nimitz says most of Pacific now is under Allied domination and that Jap supply lines are being severed. . . . Gen. Vandegrift emphasizes Jap's fanaticism. . . . Halmahera again bombed by American planes.

Allied HQ Claims Fall Of Cannes

But Earlier Announcement Of Marseilles' Capture Is Disputed

Allied Headquarters announced the capture of Cannes, on the Riviera, yesterday, but it was anybody's guess who held Marseilles, in spite of Thursday's flat official communique reporting the city's seizure.

"Marseilles has not yet been taken, in spite of previous statements to the contrary," a CBS correspondent with the French reported. He said the French held only a third of the city.

Yesterday's communique said that inside the city "moppi -up of enemy resistance near the port is in progress."

Although official silence hid the whereabouts of a U.S. column reported at the Swiss border Thursday, other Allied forces pushed west within eight miles of Arles, 26 miles up the Rhone from the sea, while French troops cleaning up Toulon met stiff German resistance around the base's naval arsenal.

French and American warships heavily shelled Toulon's coastal guns, which were also targets for Thunderbolt dive-bombers.

Capt. Ludwig Sertorius, German military spokesman, meanwhile reported "fast enemy detachments, with the support of Partisans, have now reached the Rhone between Montelimar and Valence," 85 to 110 miles from the

The count of prisoners taken in the 11-day operation officially passed the 25,000 mark, of whom 5,000, including two German generals, were reported seized at Marseilles.

Giving Lip Service to Joy of Liberation

U.S. Army Signal Corps Photo

Mademoiselles greet U.S. infantrymen with kisses as they march through Rennes.

Fall of City Is Believed To Be Near

Nazi Forces Are Battered In Seine Pocket; Claim Yanks Near Troyes

French armored troops of the U.S. Third Army fought the Germans in the heart of starving Paris side by side with French underground forces yesterday, as Berlin reported that American troops in the suburbs were attacking German defenders of the capital from the west, southwest and southeast.

Heavy air support aided strong Allied tank forces, Berlin said, and it appeared from field dispatches that Allied possession of the whole capital was a matter of hours.

Most reports agreed that the Allies controlled a majority of the city and suburban areas. An American broadcast from Gen. Eisenhower's Headquarters declared that the liberation of Paris was a fact.

Drawing Pocket Tight

Northwest of Paris, meanwhile, Allied troops strengthened their grip on the pocket gradually encircling German forces west of the Seine River. Although the Germans threw the bulk of their forces in the Elbeuf area against the Yanks, who were threatening to cut off their escape entirely by driving 25 miles farther to the mouth of the Seine, the Canadians were reported to be sweeping around the Germans from their position near the mouth.

British, Canadian and Polish troops ... smashing up to 12 miles toward the Seine on a 20-mile front. The British reached the Seine within sight of Le Havre, which was already within range of Allied guns only four or five miles from the great port.

Allied planes, out in force, hammered the Germans fleeing across the river and retreating from Le Havre toward the Pas de Calais. Reports from SHAEF said there was no evidence of any real defense line west of the Rhine. This was virtually admitted by a German military commentator, who said that German strategy now was to concentrate the German Army in the west along "the shortest possible line falling short of the German frontier."

Night reports from Allied pilots told of German trucks racing eastward along the rocket coast—their headlights full on

(Continued on page 4)

Unit Officers Are Named To Take GIs' Negatives

Army Exchange Service announced yesterday that unit exchange officers had been appointed who would accept film from GI amateur photographers for developing and printing in the event regular PXs were not accessible. Film should not be sent to the Photographic Division of AES by individuals.

Charges, collected in advance, will be on a flat roll basis in accordance with a price list. Negatives and prints will be returned directly to the soldier, or, at his request, to friends or relatives in the States.

Reich Gets New Double Blow; Oil Output Halved in 90 Days

In a furious co-ordinated assault more than 1,350 heavy bombers of the Eighth and 15th Air Forces yesterday pounded German aircraft plants, airdromes, air-force stations and other objectives.

Yesterday's attack followed Thursday's massive offensive by more than 1,900 British-based and Italian-based heavies—the largest number of USSTAF bombers ever dispatched. The record task force battered seven enemy oil-production centers in another of the Allied assaults which in a 90-day campaign slashed Nazi oil and gasoline production by more than 50 per cent, according to a joint statement released yesterday by the USSTAF and Air Ministry.

In a three-month drive which ended in July, the announcement said, the Eighth, 15th and Royal Air Forces, flying from Britain, Italy and Russia, cut the enemy's output of finished oil products by an estimated 49 per cent. Gasoline production alone was reduced 55 per cent and lubricants an estimated 62 per cent.

Although aircraft objectives, as well as the Peenemunde robot and rocket experimental station, bore the brunt of yesterday's blows, Eighth heavies kept the offensive against oil targets rolling

(Continued on page 4)

National Guard May Be Kept On

WASHINGTON, Aug. 25 (AP)—The War Department has begun a study looking toward revamping the National Guard in the post-war military organization.

No hint of the specific problems to be tackled by a special six-man committee was contained in an announcement yesterday, but the question of political control of appointments of high officers in the peace-time National Guard was known to be a matter of considerable concern to the Army.

The Army high command is believed to favor retention of the Guard as an agency of the states except in national emergencies, although with an extension of the War Department's authority over training and over qualifications of top Guard officers.

When the Guard was ordered into federal service before Pearl Harbor the efficiency of organizations varied sharply. Some are still fighting under the same officers they had in peace-time, but in many units a number of officers were weeded out when they failed to measure up to standard during training and maneuvers.

Security-Talk Censorship Stirs U.S. Press Angers

WASHINGTON, Aug. 25 (ANS)—The issue of secrecy surrounding the Dumbarton Oaks world security conference threatened to overshadow the three-power talks themselves as Undersecretary of State Edward R. Stettinius, chief American delegate, told correspondents today that he would consult with Russian and British delegates to see if "something can not be worked out."

Stettinius made his statement after receiving protests from correspondents over the skeleton communiques which have been issued thus far reporting only mechanical aspects of the meeting.

Rumania, Nazis Reported at War

A Rumanian declaration of war against Germany after Bucharest had been heavily bombed by the Luftwaffe was reported late yesterday by Cairo radio, relaying a Bucharest radio announcement. Rumanians were urged by their new government to rise and fight against the Nazis, the report stated.

The reported declaration of war clarified the Rumanian picture, which had been confused by the absence of official recognition in Moscow of Rumania's surrender, coupled with reports that Germany sought desperately to establish a new national government which would keep Rumania's armies in the Nazi fold.

In a special announcement on Moscow Radio, which strangely omitted any mention of King Michael's proclamation that Rumania had quit the war, the Soviet Foreign Commissariat stated that Russia considered it "imperative to restore the independence of Rumania."

The announcement added, "If Rumania ceases military operations and takes up

(Continued on page 4)

Fighting Irishman Doing a Foine Job Of Leading Maquis

ORLEANS, Aug. 25 (AP)—A Gallic Robin Hood, leader of 5,000 fighters of the French Maquis who have been giving the Germans hell for two years, goes by the name of Patrick O'Neill—and he doesn't care if the Germans know it.

He and his band operated for six months before the Allies landed, using deep forest shelters from which they emerged to raid German units.

It has been a long time since this wiry, six-foot colonel or his clan kissed the Blarney Stone, but he still has all the battling skill of his ancestors who forsook Erin for France.

Wonder Who Da Babe Is?

BROOKLYN, N.Y., Aug. 25 (ANS)—A police report on a 16-year-old girl victim of amnesia found wandering in Brooklyn described her as "slender and attractive" and added: "Speaks with an out-of-town accent."

We Might Even Go Extra

Plans to Cut Army at Defeat Of Reich Soon to Be Revealed

By Ben Price
Stars and Stripes U.S. Bureau

WASHINGTON, Aug. 25—Secretary of War Henry L. Stimson announced today that the order of priorities in which veterans will be discharged when the war with Germany ends would be made public shortly by the War Department.

(This appeared to indicate that the Army expected to discharge some men following Germany's defeat and before the war in the Pacific is won, although the dispatch was not specific on this point. Lt. Gen. Ben Lear, chief of the Army Ground Forces, said recently that some soldiers from Europe would be sent to the Far East.)

At the same time, Secretary of the Navy James V. Forrestal disclosed that the Navy had completed its plans for mustering out reservists but that they would not take effect as early as the Army discharges unless Japan's collapse accompanied Germany's. Generaly speaking, he told a press conference, the Navy will retain its men a good deal longer than the Army.

The War Department also announced that first had been taken to plan the makeup of the post-war Army which may have occupation and policing duties in both Germany and Japan.

Stimson declined to discuss any of the proposed Army discharge details. He also refused to comment on a speech by Maj. Gen. Lewis B. Hershey, chief of Selective Service, who forecast that victory in Germany would be followed by the release of between 1,000,000 and 2,000,000 men.

The New York Herald Tribune, quoting a Selective Service spokesman, said that Hershey was not acquainted with the War Department's plans. "The general was sizing up the situation as a layman when he ventured his estimate," the spokesman said.

1D. THE STARS AND STRIPES 1Fr.

Daily Newspaper of U.S. Armed Forces in the European Theater of Operations

Vol. 4 No. 255 New York, N.Y.—London, England—France Monday, Aug. 28, 1944

Paris Crowd Gunned; de Gaulle Safe

U.S. Signal Corps photographer, J. A. [illegible] this graphic panoramic sweep of the Place de la Concorde, tells better than a thousand words the story of a jubilant Parisian crowd turned suddenly into a horror-struck mob when hidden Nazis opened fire with machine-guns and rifles as Gen. deGaulle led processions through Place de la Concorde. Some abandoned their bicycles and plunged for cover in the barbed-wire street barricades and behind poles, while others, too paralyzed to move, looked in dumb terror upon their assailants.

The War Today

France—Last German resistance overcome in Paris except for snipers. . . . German air raid and reported attempt to kill De Gaulle mark weekend. . . . Yanks press on toward Germany. . . . Further bridgeheads established across Seine. . . . Allies in south take Avignon, Arles and Tarascon, as French complete occupation of Toulon.

Russia—RAF Lancasters from England, American heavies from Italy raid East Prussia and Rumania to aid Russians as Red Army cuts way to lower Danube, within shelling distance of Galatz river port. . . . Luftwaffe bombs Bucharest, but Rumanians report Nazi ground forces in city encircled and in danger of "imminent" liquidation.

Air—Eighth AF heavies blast Reich for fourth straight day. . . . Allied planes hammer Germans' escape routes in France. . . . RAF makes deep daylight raid.

Pacific—Allied bombers destroying what is left of Japanese air force. . . . Liberators bomb Ceram and Amboina: other bombers score direct hits on transport off Boeroe Island: Koror, in Palau group, left blazing. . . . Japanese air force reported moving out of East Indies. . . . Manila evacuation measures speeded up.

Italy—Eighth Army assault forces span Metauro River and establish bridgeheads from Brogo Lucrezia, 64 miles from the Adriatic, inland to Monte Felcino. . . . British and Indian troops progress east of Florence.

Asia—SEAC calls over-all picture in Burma encouraging, with Japs continuing to withdraw . . . British 36th Division advancing along important railway . . . Emmhaven, on west coast of Sumatra, attacked by task force of Eastern Fleet.

10 Reich Cities Pounded by Air

U.S. Heavies Hit Germany 4th Day in Row; Escape Routes Are Blasted

Eighth Air Force heavy bombers slashed into Germany yesterday for the fourth straight day to climax a weekend in which more than ten Nazi cities felt the weight of Allied explosives and Wehrmacht escape routes in France were blockaded continuously from the air.

Joining the force of nearly 500 Fortresses and Liberators in the revitalized Battle of Germany were RAF Halifaxes which struck Ruhr synthetic-oil plants in the deepest British daylight penetration of German territory in strength. It was the first long-range daylight attack by RAF heavies in more than two years.

In the savage campaign to close air, sea and ground channels of escape for the enemy's battered troops in France, Allied aircraft attacked naval and merchant shipping, transport planes, enemy troops, vehicles, tanks and supply lines.

Spearheading the assault, Thunderbolts of the Ninth Air Force's 19th Tactical Air Command bombed and strafed Brest

(Continued on page 2)

Maurice Chevalier Slain By Maquis, Patriots Say

PARIS, Aug. 27 (Reuter)—Maurice Chevalier, the former French film idol who became a collaborator in 1940, was killed by the Maquis last Friday, French patriots said today. He was 55.

Chevalier achieved world fame when he was signed by Paramount studios and co-starred with Jeannette MacDonald in the early talkies. In World War I Chevalier was captured at the front by the Germans.

Nazis Retreat Toward Reich As Allies Push On From Seine

All Toulon Seized; Tanks Driving Up The Rhone Valley

While twin tank columns pursued the enemy up both sides of the Rhone Valley after seizing Avignon, Arles and Tarscon, the French yesterday completed occupation of the city of Toulon and thus achieved the liberation of an area officially described as "all southern France east of the Rhone and south of Avignon."

The Seventh Army's bag of prisoners passed 23,000 as the French mopped up pockets of desperately-resisting Germans in Marseilles and American troops advanced eastward along the Riviera coast after taking Cannes and Antibes. Artillery and minefields slowed their push toward Nice.

Meanwhile, French authorities in the Franco-Spanish border town of Hendaye reported the surrender of 10,000 Germans who had been surrounded by American and French forces 30 miles south of Bordeaux, on the Bay of Biscay coast. The surrender, according to the French at Hendaye, ended all organized German resistance in southwest France.

A hundred miles north of Cannes, American troops extended their control almost to the Italian border by seizing, with Maquis help, the 4,500-foot heights of Briancon, five miles west of the line and 50 miles west of Turin, commanding the passage between Grenoble and Turin.

Avignon was passed by so quickly that the war did little damage to its medieval streets, a Reuter correspondent reported. He said the famed 12th-century Palace of the Popes was untouched, although Allied bombs had caused damage around the railway station.

Enemy Squeezed Tighter In River Pocket, Hit Hard by Planes

Allied troops swept eastward yesterday toward the German frontier from eight bridgeheads across the Seine River, both northwest and southeast of Paris.

German forces east of the Seine were retreating in a due easterly direction, leaving scattered rearguards behind, field dispatches indicated.

On the western bank of the Seine, Germans in an unorganized rabble were scrambling to cross the river under heavy Allied air attacks, as American, British and Canadian troops squeezed the Seine pocket around them between the river itself, the Risle River on the southwest, and a point south of Rouen across the Seine.

Rouen was also threatened, and there were indications that Le Havre, at the mouth of the Seine, might fall with little resistance. One dispatch said that garrison troops and demolition squads had been left behind in Le Havre.

The nearest point to the German bor-

(Continued on page 2)

Unconfirmed Reports Tell Of the Death of Von Kluge

Two Stockholm newspapers reported yesterday that Von Kluge, the German commander in Normandy, was dead.

Dagens Nyheter, quoting a source from inside Germany, said that he had been killed under unknown circumstances. Aftontidningen said that he had, according to unconfirmed rumors, committed suicide because of German defeats. It recalled that he was reported to have resigned a few days ago because of bad health.

Capital Bombed By the Luftwaffe

Eisenhower Enters City; Nazi Resistance Ends, 10,000 Captured

A heavy German air raid on Paris and a reported attempt to assassinate Gen. Charles de Gaulle rimmed Paris' heady cup of liberation with violence over the week-end.

But SHAEF announced yesterday that all formal German resistance within the French capital had ceased, except for some sniping, and that approximately 10,000 enemy troops, including the German commander and his staff, were taken prisoner.

Gen. Eisenhower followed his U.S. and French troops to Paris, said an American broadcaster quoted by Reuter, to tour the city and pay an official call on Gen. Koenig, its military governor.

Tribute to the Parisians

"I have come here to pay the tribute of the Allied forces to the indomitable spirit of Paris," Eisenhower was quoted as telling Koenig.

The attempt on de Gaulle's life was reported by another radio reporter quoted by the United Press.

The general was taking part in a triumphant procession through Paris when a shot was fired at him in the Place de la Concorde Saturday afternoon, the broadcaster said.

One shot followed another and the crowds paid little attention at first until machine-guns started to rattle, sending the masses of cheering Parisians into panic. It was apparently a well-laid plot, because in a matter of minutes there were rifle shots and machine-gun fire coming from all over the place.

The people scattered and ran as the bullets sprayed over them. Then Allied machine-guns opened up against the

(Continued on page 2)

THE STARS AND STRIPES

MEDITERRANEAN

Vol. 1, No. 253, Wednesday, Sept. 6, 1944 ITALY EDITION TWO LIRE

Yanks In Germany

LIBERATION EXPRESS ROLLS ON

SPEARHEADED BY the 2nd British Army, Allied troops are reported to have swept on 30 miles north of liberated Antwerp and taken the Dutch town of Breda. The U. S. 1st Army, its progress veiled in official secrecy, was last reported driving on from Tournai, below Lille on the French-Belgium border. German troops in the white corner above Lille are said to be hopelessly trapped. A few hours after the map was drawn, Aachen, about 80 miles east of Brussels, was reported taken along with Saarbrucken, about 25 miles from Metz.

AP Says Aachen, Saarbrucken Won

LONDON, Sept. 5—American troops are fighting on German soil.

An Associated Press dispatch from the French frontier reported this afternoon that the Allies have captured Aachen and Saarbrucken, on both ends of the Siegfried Line. The German News Agency reported that American troops had entered "southwest Germany's frontier region."

At the same time the AP reported that tanks of Lt. Gen. George S. Patton's 3rd Army had reached Strasbourg, capital of Alsace. Strasbourg is on the west bank of the Rhine and faces German territory.

The incredible onward sweep of the Allied forces deep into Nazi-held territory was so fast today that headquarters maps were changed hourly. Familiar place names of western Europe were captured by the score.

Louvain, Antwerp, Lille—all fell before the Allied steamroller. The Grand Duchy of Luxembourg was entered. A part of the Netherlands was taken, thus making another nation either liberated or on the point of being liberated.

Out of the thousands of reports came a picture of a German army beaten, disorganized, cut off from contact with the Reich and surrendering individually and collectively at every opportunity.

Frank Gillard, BBC reporter, said that despite "startlingly lengthened" Allied supply lines, the situation had been foreseen and that future supplies are assured. He said that so far the Allies in Belgium had encountered little flooded country.

Although there has been no official word for three days on American forces which broke into Belgium at Sedan, it was believed likely that they formed a line which cut off the German escape route east of Mons.

British troops driving in on the estimated 5,000 pocketed Germans at Le Havre were meeting considerable resistance and received no immediate reply to an ultimatum for surrender.

The Swedish radio said German administrative officers in Copenhagen were burning their official papers preparatory to pulling out of the Danish capital.

Ronald Clark, United Press correspondent who was one of the first to enter Brussels, described the entry as the most enthusiastically welcomed he had ever seen. Civilians waved flags and cheered as patriot forces took care of the Nazi rearguards left to cover the Germans' retreat. The British, he said, had no mopping up to do.

Rumors Begin

LONDON, Sept. 5—Reports were circulating today to the effect that Germany had capitulated. The exact origin of the rumor could not be traced, but it was repeated in Belgian broadcasts with strict reserve as to its accuracy.

Russians Declare War On Bulgaria

MOSCOW, Sept. 5—"A state of war" exists between the Soviet Union and Bulgaria, the Moscow radio announced tonight.

The Bulgarian minister, says the broadcast, has been informed that Russia regards this nation as an enemy not only of the United States and Great Britain, with whom Bulgaria has been at war for more than a year, but of the U. S. S. R., as well, with whom Bulgaria has hitherto been at peace.

The Russian government's declaration comes at a time when its troops are on—and possibly over—the Rumanian-Bulgarian frontier, and while a Bulgarian delegation waits in Cairo, Egypt, for the reply of Great Britain and the United States to its request of a week ago for an armistice.

Earlier today Tass, official Soviet news agency, had declared that the new Bulgarian cabinet, not yet a week old, must either cast its lot with the Allies by entering the war against Germany or stand responsible for the consequences.

With the statement came unconfirmed reports that the Red Army is establishing bridgeheads on the Bulgarian side of the Danube River.

Nazis In Italy Reeling

Allies Win Tank Battle

ADVANCED ALLIED FORCE HEADQUARTERS, Sept. 5—Bewildered German troops, kept off balance by vicious, well-screened Allied thrusts, reeled toward destruction in northern Italy today.

Their rear was exposed to increasing numbers of well-organized armed Italian Patriots, augmented by French Maquis pouring through the gaps in northwestern Italy.

The German flanks, particularly their vital eastern flank guarding the gateway to the Po Valley and to northeastern Italy, was duck soup for Allied naval guns. Their Gothic Line has proved as formidable as a Goebbels promise.

With the same ruthless fanaticism that has marked his tactics throughout the Italian campaign, Marshal Albert Kesselring has sent troops into suicide positions to screen withdrawals. He still was tardy in ordering withdrawals until such time as it was no longer possible to pull out in an orderly manner.

General Sir Harold L. Alexander used the same trick that worked in front of Cassino in preparation for the May offensive. With lightning speed and complete secrecy, General Sir Oliver Leese's 8th Army's 80,000 vehicles, 1,000 tanks and 1,000 guns, were moved across the Appenines from Florence to the Adriatic.

Kesselring, thinking he had only

(Continued on page 8)

7th Army Advances Far North Of Lyons

ADVANCED ALLIED FORCE HEADQUARTERS, Sept. 5—Nazi remnants, after looting Lyons and other French cities, today apparently had outdistanced American and French troops of Lt. Gen. Alexander M. Patch's 7th Army, forward elements of which were more than 75 miles north of Lyons.

The American troops, well beyond Mentrevel where they suffered some losses in a stiff fight Sunday, met no serious opposition yesterday, it was stated officially. French regulars, speeding up Highway 6 through the Saone valley, were at the outskirts of Macon, 68 miles north of Lyons, without making contact.

The French columns were less than 75 miles from Dijon, junction of all important rail and highway lines between the Saone-Rhone area and Paris. Dijon is less than 50 miles from the area in which the U. S. 3rd Army was reported moving before operational security shrouded its positions.

The greatest impediments to the advancing forces from the south were bridge demolitions and ever-growing parades of prisoners. The French took some 2,400 in mopping up Ville Franche, to bring the 7th Army's total to more than 65,000 for the 21 days of the campaign.

140,000 Tons Dropped On Europe In August

LONDON, Sept. 5 — The RAF and the U. S. Strategic Air Force dropped a record of 140,000 tons of bombs on all enemy targets in August, the United Press reported.

Air Marshal Sir Arthur Coningham's 2nd Tactical Air Force reported scoring a record toll in August against enemy war materiel, destroying 10,500 German transports and 850 tanks.

Typhoons and Spitfires of the 2nd Tactical Air Force pounded enemy communications during the heavy fighting in Normandy.

Fighting Seemed Miles From Liberated Lyons

By Sgt. STAN SWINTON

(Stars and Stripes Staff Writer)

WITH THE AMERICAN FORCES IN LYONS, Sept. 3 (Delayed)—The kissingest, happiest musical comedy chapter in the war of southern France was today's liberation of Lyons.

Human road blocks of deliriously happy French women and cheering men turned the streets leading westward to the Rhone into a four-mile canyon of kisses. Dazed American doughboys, matinee idols for the day, were surrounded by surging mobs of pretty mademoiselles, mothers and white-haired grandmothers.

The snarl of snipers' rifles was forgotten as the populace pelted autos with flowers and scrambled for the privilege of touching the liberators.

It was still war, but it was fantastic war. The German garrison fled day before yesterday, abandoning the renegade Vichy militiamen who served them. Today FFI patrols roamed the streets seeking the trapped traitors, who sniped from buildings throughout the city.

There was unreality about the little organized fighting remaining. At the Cours Gambetta, close by the Rhone, T-Sgt. Robert W. Korthals, North Collins, N. Y., and the 25-man American patrol which en-

(Continued on Page 8)

London—New York
Paris—Rennes
Thursday, Sept. 7, 1944
Vol. 4 No. 264, 1 Penny

THE STARS AND STRIPES

Daily Newspaper of U.S. Armed Forces in the European Theater of Operations

Daily French Lesson
Je Suis Americain
Juh Sweez ah-mayreekang
I am an American

Army Bares Discharge Plans

Yanks Enter Belgium—First Picture

U.S. Army Signal Corps Photo

These Yanks, first to cross Belgian border, enter Macon on their way eastward.

Parenthood And Service Will Govern

Childless Husbands Get No Preference; Age Also Immaterial

(Complete text of demobilization plan—Page 2)

WASHINGTON, Sept. 6—The War Department announced today that just four factors will determine the priority in which it will discharge such soldiers as are considered unessential after Germany's defeat:

1—Service credit, based on total length of service since Sept. 16, 1940, when the draft law was passed.

2—Overseas credit, based on time served overseas.

3—Combat credit, based on the number of a soldier's medals, bronze stars and battle participation stars.

4—Parenthood credit, given for each dependent child under 18 up to a limit of three children.

Which of these factors will count the most, and how much weight each will carry in relation to the others, was not disclosed. The Department said that the value of point credits for each category would not be announced until after hostilities end in Europe.

No Preference to Husbands

Thus married men were given no preference over single men unless they were the fathers of dependent children.

Age likewise will not be a factor; nor will it matter whether a soldier has a civilian job to return to or not.

At the same time there were ifs and buts, and plenty of warnings that it might take "many months" to discharge soldiers no longer needed after Germany's defeat—and even stronger warnings that the Pacific war must come first.

After months of study it was determined, the Department said, "that the fairest method to effect partial demobilization would be through the selection of men as individuals rather than by units" although it would have been simplest to return whole units to this country and discharge all their personnel at once.

The principles finally adopted were to a large extent dictated by soldiers themselves, it said, explaining that "thousands of soldiers both in this country and overseas were interviewed to learn their views." Ninety per cent of them, it added, favored priority for men overseas and men with dependent children.

With "thousands of ships required to supply the Pacific theater," only "very few" will be returning to the U.S. from Europe and "it may take many months" to return surplus ETO troops to the states, the department warned.

"Regardless of a man's priority standing," it added, "certain types of personnel can never become surplus as long as the war against Japan continues." At the

(Continued on page 4)

Nazis Admit Likely Drop In Robots for England

As Allied armies rolled up the rocket coast of France, Belgium and Holland, a German radio commentator acknowledged yesterday that "in future V1 may not be launched against England with the same regularity as hitherto."

The commentator, as quoted by Reuter, reassured the Germans, however, that flying bombs could be used by the Nazis against European targets and claimed that "the weapon will lose nothing of its importance."

Entry Into Germany Official

Nazis Say Reds Enter Bulgaria

Sofia Tells of Armistice Plea But Moscow Keeps Silent

While Moscow preserved an enigmatic silence over Sofia Radio reports that Bulgaria had asked the USSR for an armistice in their one-day war, Berlin Radio reported last night that the Red Army had begun to march into Bulgaria across the Rumanian border.

The Russians meanwhile pushed deep into western Rumania and closed within 55 miles of the homeland of Marshal Tito's Jugoslav Partisans after capturing the communications town of Craiova, 115 miles beyond Bucharest and only 60 from the Danube's "Iron Gate" gorge near Turnu Severin, on the Jugoslav border.

Gains in the south meant no slackening in the three-day-old offensive north-

(Continued on page 4)

The War Today

France—American patrols crossed German border and returned after quick reconnaissance, Third Army headquarters reveals. . . . Patton's troops across Moselle River, last water barrier before Germany. . . . U.S. First Army reported to have taken 20,000 prisoners in Belgium, and Nazi casualties estimated at more than 15,000 dead and wounded. . . . U.S. First links with British Second in double-edged drive through Belgium. . . . Canadians attack Calais from east and west. . . . German "ghost army" of 50,000, trapped along Channel coast, tries to escape across Scheldt River. . . . Allied Seventh Army chasing German 19th Army north from southern France is 30 miles from Belfort Gap, last escape route into the Reich.

Russia—Germans report Red Army has crossed border into Bulgaria. . . . No confirmation in Moscow of Sofia report that Bulgaria has asked armistice in one-day war. . . . Berlin describes new Soviet "offensive" from north bank of Bug River toward southern East Prussia.

Italy—Desert Air Force pounds German positions in front of Eighth Army troops attacking at Rimini, on Adriatic front. . . . On west coast Fifth Army thrusts toward Pistoia. . . . Patriots reported rising on Swiss frontier.

Pacific—Allied planes sink or damage 13 troopships off the Menado coast in the Celebes. . . . Catalina flying boats sink or damage eight Japanese merchant ships and 13 barges off Halmahera Island.

Asia—Heavy bombers attack Sangkhla area in Siam on the Burmasian railway. . . . Chinese casualties from the beginning of the war with Japan until June 31 total 2,802,220, Chinese National Military Council announces. . . . Japanese casualties placed at 2,144,000.

Third Army Patrols Cross Border as Forces Build Up

Official word that American patrols have crossed the border into Germany—they withdrew after quick reconnaissance—came yesterday from Third Army headquarters.

Field dispatches from the Third Army stressed that Gen. Patton's forces on the German frontier were still essentially in the building-up stage, and that his patrols were meeting increased resistance as they jabbed out toward the Reich itself.

Also confirmed were reports that Third Army troops had crossed the Moselle River, last water barrier before the German homeland. Heavy artillery was met by troops on the far side of the Moselle.

Pierce Maginot Line

U.S. patrols must have passed through the Maginot Line to enter Germany. They were known to be operating beyond Thionville, from which it is only 12 miles to Germany at Perl, which unconfirmed reports last week said had been entered by Americans.

Following an unconfirmed report that Strasbourg, on the French frontier, had been captured, the Swiss radio said yesterday that it was still in German hands and no Allied troops have yet been seen in the city or its surroundings.

The U.S. First Army in Belgium has taken 20,000 prisoners, and Nazi casualties are estimated at 15,000 to 30,000 dead and wounded, a Blue Network battlefront report declared. At British Second Army headquarters, a senior staff officer was quoted by Reuter as saying: "The speed of the American advance is dynamic. When the Americans reached Mons, the German High Command thought they were 50 miles away."

First Army troops, after capturing the communications center of Namur in a 45-mile advance across the Belgian frontier, linked up with British forces in a

(Continued on page 4)

Gas Flown In, Division Cheers And Takes Off

By Tom Hoge
Stars and Stripes Staff Writer

SOMEWHERE IN FRANCE, Sept. 6—The men of the 90th Division threw up their helmets and cheered yesterday when a number of C47s landed at an air strip here with thousands of gallons of gasoline.

"That's the prettiest sight I've seen in a long time," said a colonel with a sigh of relief. "Napoleon may have said that an army marches on its stomach, but, brother, it also takes plenty of fuel to move an outfit in this man's war. Now we can push on."

Led by Maj. Daniel F. Elam, of Duncan, Okla., of the Ninth Air Force, each plane in the flight brought in hundreds of gallons of gas.

"We got the order to shoot the fuel to the 90th at lunch time," said Elam, "and in 30 minutes we were ready to move out. Two hours later we were here."

A certain amount of fuel could be brought up from beachhead supply dumps, but not always enough to supply the urgent demands of the vehicles. It was then the C47s were called upon.

"What the hell they wanted green coffee beans for I'll never know," said Elam, "but we delivered them."

In addition to this the planes have carried back thousands of wounded and taken over vast quantities of medical supplies.

"For more than a month after D-Day we hardly brought anything over, their supply stock had been so well planned," said Elam, "but after the breakthrough at Avranches they began to move in high gear and the need for stuff began to mount."

Army Ordered to Run Struck Graphite Works

WASHINGTON, Sept. 6 (Reuter)—President Roosevelt today ordered the Army to take over the plants of the Cleveland (Ohio) Graphite Bronze Co., where the output of bearings has been hampered by a six-day strike of 7,000 employes.

The strike began on Thursday morning when the independent unionists walked out in protest against the discharge of an employe for allegedly breaking the lock on his company locker.

B26s Hit Brest In Twin Attack

Marauders From French Bases Carry Assault To Fourth Day

French-based Ninth Air Force Marauders, in an all-out aerial offensive against the besieged port of Brest, made two attacks yesterday, battering enemy strongpoints and installations in the city at mid-afternoon.

The second attack, which lasted more than an hour, marked the fifth time in the last four days that the B26s had hammered the key port, and the first time that U.S. medium bombers based in France have carried out two missions in one day.

A few hours earlier, 16 waves of Marauders and Havocs, led by the B26s flying from French bases, attacked the fortresses guarding the Atlantic port where Nazi defenders were still holding out.

The disclosure that Marauders now are operating from bases in France—the first Allied bombers to operate from the Continent—was made by Maj. Gen. Hoyt S. Vandenberg, Ninth Air Force commander. The first France-based mission was flown Aug. 28 by the White Tail B26 group commanded by Col. Wilson R.

(Continued on page 4)

Bishop Cannon Dead

CHICAGO, Sept. 6 (Reuter)—Bishop James Cannon, Jr., of the Methodist Episcopal Church, died today after a week's illness. He was 79. Cannon was a leader of the prohibition movement and took a prominent part in the presidential campaign of 1928 when former Gov. Alfred E. Smith, of New York, was defeated.

Action at the Marne

U.S. Army Signal Corps Photo

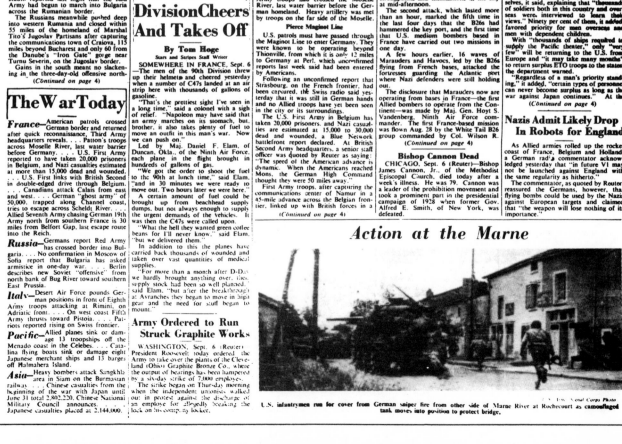

U.S. infantrymen run for cover from German sniper fire from other side of Marne River at Rochecourt as camouflaged tank moves into position to protect bridge.

THE STARS AND STRIPES
MEDITERRANEAN

Vol. 1, No. 13, Tuesday, September 12, 1944 | Printed In France | ONE FRANC

Yanks Liberate Luxembourg

FDR, Churchill Meet Again

Quebec Scene Of Ninth Conference Between Two Allied Chiefs

QUEBEC, Sept. 11 — President Roosevelt and Prime Minister Winston Churchill arrived in this picturesque French-Canadian city today for their ninth conference since 1941. The Allied leaders have not met since the momentous Teheran conference of Nov. 26-Dec. 2, 1943.

Mr. Churchill arrived at Halifax, Nova Scotia, yesterday, and was greeted by tumultuous crowds as he landed. Two trains were required to carry the full personnel and advisers who accompanied him. Mr. Roosevelt reached this city later on his special train.

Just as the first Quebec meeting of Aug. 24, 1943, planned the final assault on Hitler's Europe, so it was believed that this meeting will be mainly concerned with the climactic blows against Japan. The strategic policy against Japan is expected to be put into operation even before the collapse of Germany releases masses of men and materials for the Pacific operations.

The "Sunday Times" of London wrote that besides the war in the Far East, the future of Germany will doubtless play a large part in the discussions. The newspaper believed that on the question of the Reich there was general agreement on the establishment of a Supreme Commission of Control, with its seat in Berlin.

The "Sunday Times" said that the commission will be composed of the commanders-in-chief of the three main war theaters—General Dwight D. Eisenhower from western Europe, General Sir Harold R. L. G. Alexander from Italy and presumably Marshal Gregory Zhukov representing the eastern front—and three civilian members with ministerial status.

The commission was described as forming a sort of cabinet with such departments as finance, interior and health. There seemed a slight difference of opinion, according to the paper, as to how much authority should be invested in these departments.

The laws to be introduced in Germany, continued the article, are already in print and will decree the complete dissolution of the Nazi party. Political activities for certain persons will be prohibited as military security requires. In the industrial field, Russia is believed to be demanding much of the equipment of Germany's heavy in-

(Continued on page 4)

Conference In Canada

. . a few things to talk over

New Bulgar Government Pledges Soviet Alliance

LONDON, Sept. 11 — Bulgaria announced today the establishment of what it called "The People's Government of the Fatherland Front," an aftermath of the bloodless revolution that overthrew the pro-Axis regime and put into office an administration that is at war with Germany.

The new government pledged a permanent alliance with the Soviet Union as well as friendly relations with Marshal Tito's Yugoslavia. It asked the Bulgarian partisans to come out of the mountains to take part in the new regime, and promised a democratic press in which all popular elements will have a fair say.

As the new officials consolidated their control, more quislings were reported to have fled to Germany.

Meanwhile, from Ankara it was indicated that the Bulgarian peace delegation at Cairo, appointed by the ousted government, was being changed. The Turkish report said that the delegation had arrived at Ankara on its way back to Sofia.

With very strong Russian forces on their way to Sofia, other Soviet units in Rumania made more progress in their pincer movement on Transylvania. From the east they advanced through the Carpathians along a main railroad, taking a town en route over which the Germans had been entrenched for 24 hours before being tossed out.

From the south, Russian and Rumanian troops also moved along the railroads, and penetrated well into northern Transylvania. The Hungarian radio said they had captured Cluj, capital of the province. If that is confirmed, it means that they made a 40-mile gain in this sector. Cluj is on the communications route from Rumania to Budapest, and is 200 miles from the Hungarian capital.

First contact between General Rodion Malinowsky and Marshal Tito was believed made by Rus-

(Continued on page 4)

Germans Report Air Battles Over Leipzig

LONDON, Sept. 11—Heavy air battles were reported over Leipzig today by the German radio as Allied Air Forces continued their assault on western Germany.

Berlin was the target last night for Mosquitoes of the RAF and yesterday communications centers and airfields in western Germany and Holland were the targets of more than 1,100 heavy bombers of the 8th AAF.

Six German aircraft were shot down and 119 were destroyed on the ground in the day's operations. Allied loses were 12 bombers and 15 fighters.

Nazis Fighting Grim Rear-Guard Action

LONDON, Sept. 11—A new Allied threat to the Siegfried Line developed near its center today when the American 1st Army liberated Luxembourg, capital city of the Grand Duchy of Luxembourg, and drove to within ten miles of the German frontier.

Nazi rear-guard units were fighting desperately to impede the American push, blasting bridges and erecting road blocks along the path of the Nazi withdrawal. Allied heavy artillery covering the advance of the Yank armored columns, dropped their first shells on German soil as the drive continued.

At the same time, British 2nd Army units on the northern end of the Allied line in Belgium pushed beyond the Albert Canal, and established a bridgehead over the Escaut Canal. At last reports they were less than two miles from the Netherlands frontier. Some patrols were already across the border.

In eastern France on the Moselle River front, American 3rd Army troops broke into German defenses near the Nancy anchor and strengthened the several bridgeheads already established across the Moselle between Nancy and Metz.

American 1st Army troops also occupied Hasselt, 22 miles northwest of Liege in Belgium and Verviers, 13 miles east of Liege. It was announced that the 1st Army had taken 148,000 prisoners up to and including Sept. 9.

Meanwhile, a full scale attack was launched by Allied ground, air and naval forces upon the German garrison still holding out in the great port of Le Havre at the mouth of the Seine River in western France, and late yesterday it was reported British troops had entered the outskirts of the city.

Tank and ground forces inched their way toward the Nazi stronghold from the east as British battlewagons stood offshore and fired broadsides at the isolated fortifications in which the Germans are

(Continued on page 4)

General Pershing Cited 'Greatest U. S. Soldier'

PHILADELPHIA, Sept. 11 — General John J. Pershing, commander of the American Expeditionary Forces in the last war, was listed last week as recipient of the Medal of Honor awarded annually by the Army and Navy Union for outstanding service to the nation by an individual.

General Pershing, who celebrates his 84th birthday Sept. 13, was cited as "the greatest soldier in modern history."

Patch's Troops Swinging North

ADVANCED 7TH ARMY HEADQUARTERS, Sept. 11 — The distance between Allied armies in northern and southern France was lessened today as 7th Army forces last reported 25 miles from the Belfort corridor to Germany, switched their attack to the north and drove to the Ognon River.

No indication was given of any weakening resistance by Nazi rear-guard forces fighting below Belfort and engaged in a screening action for remnants of the German 19th Army pulling back to the German frontier below the Siegfried Line.

The Ognon River parallels the Doubs River Valley along which the 7th Army has been pursuing the 19th Army northeasterly from Besancon.

To the west, French troops pressed into the outskirts of the railway junction and industrial town of Dijon as the opposition decreased. Other advances were reported by French units 40 miles farther to the west.

The determination of the Nazi High Command to delay as long as

(Continued on page 4)

5th Army Clears Pistoia Of Krauts

ROME, Sept. 11—The 5th Army today spanned another hurdle in its steady drive toward the heart of the Gothic Line in western Italy as it cleared all Germans from Pistoia, 20 miles northwest of Florence and on the direct road to Bologna.

Other units of Lt. Gen. Mark W. Clark's forces took Prato, halfway between Florence and Pistoia. Preparing for a strong assault on the enemy fortifications, the Yanks were slowly pushing the Germans back to their main defenses.

Gains were also made in the central sector when United Kingdom troops of the 8th Army advanced to a point 15 miles northeast of Florence.

There was little change in the bitter fighting raging on the Adriatic front. Although enemy shelling decreased somewhat yesterday, correspondents still described the battles as some of the fiercest fighting ever seen in Europe. There were heavy casualties on both sides as 8th Army forces unsuccessfully tried to shove the Germans off the Coriano and San Savino ridges between the broken Gothic Line and the port of Rimini.

Field Marshal Albert Kesselring threw all his available tanks, men and guns into an all-out attempt to stem General Sir Harold Alexander's thrust toward the plains of Lombardy.

Starting yesterday morning, one German counterattack after another was launched under a lashing rain and through deep mud. All Nazi attacks have thus far been stopped.

Lost Airmen Return From Bucharest

By Sgt. LEN SMITH
Staff Writer

15TH AIR FORCE HEADQUARTERS, Italy—More than 1,000 of the 2,000-odd Allied airmen who were shot down in the great battle of Ploesti, Rumania, since Aug. 1, 1943, have come back from the dead in a dramatic mass air evacuation by the 15th AAF.

From the nose of a shiny Flying Fortress I watched the process of repatriation both at Bucharest, Rumania, and at the airfield here; saw the released men rush crazily into prop wash to get near once more to an American plane that wasn't bombing their concentration camp; saw them reach the journey's end in Italy, for many only a brief stopover point on the way to America.

They poured from 37 Flying Fortresses here, the wildest, most cheering, and, from their own observation, the loudest men imaginable. They kissed the dusty earth; they kissed the pilots and crew members who brought them back from the concentration camp in Bucharest where they were held prisoners; they kissed generals, colonels and buck privates; they whooped and hollered and brought tears to the eyes of strong men.

They cheered the fact that soon they would be getting good old GI rations instead of black bread and bean soup—their fare for three meals a day. They cheered the announcement that many of them would soon be on their way to their homes in the States and in England. They cheered the announcement that some soon would have a chance to get back into the air war against the Axis. They cheered the announcement that first all would be put through a delousing process, and for the latter promise they cheered loudest of all.

They looked like what you might expect to see at a Hobos convention. None had uniforms alike. They were a bedraggled bunch, dirty and tired and they had no words to express their emotion now that it was all over. Some said, "We're home, boy." Others shouted: "Ain't this some joint." They sang a song of their own composition entitled "The Bucharest Cannonball." And they nominated for king of the universe one Lt. Col. James A. Gunn, 3rd, of Keiseyville, Calif., the man who made a sensational flight from Bucharest to here, told their story to Maj. Gen. Nathan F. Twining, 15th AAF commander, and brought about the miracle of their release.

They were grateful men; overwhelmingly thankful for the packs of American cigarettes they were handed as they left their planes, and were only to glad to hand over to spectators the stinking, unsmokable "weeds" that some had been forced to smoke for 13 months or go without. They were disciplined men, only too eager to board the trucks that were to take them to baths and clean sheets and new clothes.

It's hard to tell where this saga of the American Air Force begins. Whether it's with Colonel Gunn, who was shot down on Aug. 17, and spent only a relatively few days in the flea-infested Bucharest schoolhouse that was the airmen's prison or with men like Lt. Worden Weaver, Theodore, Okla., or Lt. Worthy Long, Lubbock, Texas, or Lt. Elmer H. Reinhart, Oakland, Calif., who were shot down in the first Ploesti raid from Eastern Mediterranean bases on Aug. 1, 1943.

All of them had interesting stories to relate. Lt. Robert H. Minervini, N. Y., found three members of his crew in the prison, but failed to find eight others after he was shot down on May 31. Lt.

(Continued on page 3)

London—New York
Paris—Rennes
Wednesday, Sept. 13, 1944
Vol. 4 No. 269, 1D

London Edition

THE STARS AND STRIPES

Daily Newspaper of U.S. Armed Forces in the European Theater of Operations

Daily French Lesson
Tout droit
too DRWAH
Straight ahead

U.S. Tank Division Enters Reich; 3rd, 7th Armies Join; Havre Won

Philippines Attack Sinks 52 Jap Ships

First Big Sea-Air Raid On Islands Meets No Jap Naval Defense

American carrier planes destroyed 52 Japanese vessels and 68 planes when they swept over Mindanao Friday in the first big U.S. naval and air attack against the Philippines, Adm. Chester W. Nimitz announced yesterday.

A United Press dispatch said that the total number of ships destroyed, including a convoy of 32 fully-laden coastal vessels and 20 sampans caught in a bay northeast of the island, may have exceeded 89.

The attack followed more than two months' continuous bombing of the East Indies and the Philippines.

The U.S. carrier force, commanded by Adm. William F. Halsey, had a strong screen of cruisers and destroyers, but not a single Jap warship came out to intercept and every one of the eight planes encountered by the warships was shot down.

Other Allied aircraft from New Guinea made a separate attack on the island, second largest in the Philippines, scoring two direct hits on two 7,000-ton merchant ships. The communique said no U.S. ships were damaged and aircraft losses were very light.

In the East Indies Liberators escorted by long-range fighters carpeted Mapanget airfield with 159 tons of bombs. No enemy fighters came up, but when Jap bombers, in their first operation for several weeks, attacked airfields at Biak and Owi, off New Guinea, Black Widow night fighters destroyed two.

Meanwhile a Navy communique reported that U.S. submarines had sunk nine more Jap ships, three of them fighting craft, to bring the total since the beginning of the war to 732.

Big Three Reach Accord On Forming Security Body

WASHINGTON, Sept. 12 (ANS)—With agreement on all major issues of a world security organization assured American, Russian and British conferees at Dumbarton Oaks today drew near conclusion of their exploratory talks.

Meantime, Anglo-American delegations prepared to start similar negotiations with the Chinese. The Chinese phase of talks will last about a week.

17 Jap Ships Smashed By RAF in Andaman

KANDY, Ceylon, Sept. 12—In a bitter 33-hour battle described officially as "the greatest single air-sea victory in this theater," rocket-firing RAF Beaufighters smashed a large escorted convoy of Japanese merchant ships in the Andaman Sea Saturday and Sunday, scoring hits on 14 cargo-carriers, two sloops and one gunboat.

The Beaufighters, none of which was lost, made 21 attacks at extreme range, beginning at dawn Saturday. Many of the merchantmen, believed to be carrying supplies to Burma, were left burning.

FDR, Churchill Plan Jap Drive Without Russia

QUEBEC, Sept. 12—President Roosevelt and Prime Minister Churchill, after working far into the night, spent long hours together today, apparently discussing plans for an all-out Anglo-American offensive against Japan after Germany's defeat.

The two leaders have set out to plan victory in the Pacific without counting on Russian assistance, according to Henry C. Cassidy, former Associated Press bureau chief in Moscow, now covering the Quebec meeting.

Marshal Stalin's message declining to come to Quebec—because he could not abandon direction of the Red Army while it was developing its offensive—limited Mr. Roosevelt and Mr. Churchill, Cassidy said, "to a consideration of their own resources, confidently expected to be more than enough for Japan. They could not calculate on direct Red Army support or on bases in Siberia."

Readjustment of British and American land, sea and air power in the Pacific and Asiatic areas was reported to figure prominently in th conference. Another Associated Press dispatch said:

"It is understood that questions are being discussed as to whether a powerful thrust should be made across Japan's water lifeline to the East Indies, isolating them for a British reconquest and marking Japan proper for an American assault."

Hurricane Warnings off Miami

MIAMI, Fla., Sept. 12 (Reuter)—Hurricane warnings were ordered today from the Northern Bahamas and Miami to Cape Hatteras.

Yanks' First German Drive Gains 10 Miles Toward Ruhr

Stars and Stripes Map.

U.S. First Army troops invaded Germany in force by storming across the frontier northwest of Trier, and the Third Army breached Hitler's Moselle River defense line yesterday, while Third Army units linked up with the Seventh west of Dijon.

North-South Link Bolsters Block At Belfort

An American armored division roared into Germany yesterday—the 26th anniversary of the great American offensive at St. Mihiel in 1918—after forward elements of the U.S. First Army had crossed the frontier and driven eight to ten miles toward Coblenz in the industrial Ruhr.

Germany was invaded in strength by U.S. troops, making a large-scale assault against German soil for the first time in history. Elements of the Third Army previously had crossed the border into Hitler's Reich, but in patrol strength.

As First Army men plunged into the Battle of Germany the Third and Seventh Armies linked west of Dijon and strengthened the barrier before the Belfort Gap, escape route to the Reich for German forces trapped in eastern and southwestern France.

3,000 Captured at Havre

And the great Channel port of Le Havre surrendered to British troops of the Canadian First Army.

The German garrison at Le Havre capitulated just 36 hours after the British launched an all-out offensive on the city. At least 3,000 of the garrison, numbering more than 5,000, were captured, and many others were killed and wounded by the terrific Allied bombardment.

Smashing across the frontier northwest of Trier, strong First Army forces drove deep into the forest zones before the Siegfried Line toward a road network leading to Coblenz and the Ruhr. A UP dispatch from 12th Army Group said Gen. Hodges' men had not yet reached the Siegfried Line, which, in this sector, lies about 12 miles back from the German frontier.

From the German-Luxembourg border an AP dispatch said American troops

(*Continued on page 4*)

Who Said Blitzkrieg?

Americans captured the great Belgian fort of Eben Emael faster than German paratroops seized it in 1940 in the blitzkrieg which the Nazis filmed and circulated all over the world as propaganda.

B26s and A20s Blast Reich 1st Time, Hit Siegfried Line

While British and French-based Marauders and Havocs of the Ninth Air Force yesterday bombed targets in the Reich for the first time, up to 1,000 Fortresses and Liberators of the Eighth Air Force assaulted Hitler's synthetic and natural oil plants and other industrial targets in eastern and central Germany for the second straight day.

Early reports indicated that more than 500 P38s, P47s, and P51s, escorting the B17s and B24s, took a second successive day's heavy toll of the Luftwaffe, shooting down 50 and destroying 26 more on the ground. Forty-five heavy bombers and 17 fighters were lost.

Three strong waves of medium bombers swept over the Siegfried Line blasting a path for advancing units of U.S. armor and infantry. There was not a single burst of flak from the line, pilots reported.

All Bombers Return

The force of about 150 medium and light bombers returned safely from their initial blow at Germany.

Two forces of A20s attacked rail yards at St. Wendel, 17 miles north of Saarbrucken, while French-based B26s dropped 1,000-pound bombs on reinforced concrete pillboxes in a loop of the Our River on the Luxembourg-German frontier.

Anti-tank traps and enemy troop shelters at Scheid, just inside the German border, 32 miles south of Aachen,

(*Continued on page 4*)

On the Road to Berlin

U.S. Army Signal Corps Photo

First Army troops led by Lt. Gen. Courtney H. Hodges (circle) are now inside Germany in force. But they had to battle to get there, as witness these infantrymen pinned down by German small-arms fire in Libin, Belgium, as they try to move forward with machine-gun. Hodges' forces were first in strength to invade Germany.

Soviets Menace Key to Prussia

Red Army troops striving to smash through hard German defenses between Warsaw and East Prussia fought their way into the important road junction of Lomza 22 miles from the southeastern corner of East Prussia yesterday. Moscow dispatches last night said the town's fall was imminent.

Neutral reports meanwhile asserted the Germans had begun to evacuate the islands of the northern Aegean, including Chios, 200 miles north of Crete, and Mytilene, 45 miles farther north.

Although the Stockholm Tidningen included Crete among the islands being cleared, Cairo dispatches quoting "reliable sources" said there were no signs the Germans were quitting the bigger islands like Crete and Rhodes.

The Red Army stepped up its advance on both sides of Hungarian-occupied Transylvania, pushing beyond Sighisoara, 55 miles northwest of Brasov, on the main railway to Budapest.

Marshal Tito's Jugoslav Partisans, advancing to link up with the Russians in Rumania, seized the town of Surdulica, only 15 miles from the Bulgarian border and 72 miles west of Sofia.

FDR Nominates Bradley For Permanent Two Stars

WASHINGTON, Sept. 12 (Reuter)—President Roosevelt today nominated Lt. Gen. Omar N. Bradley for promotion to the permanent rank of major general in recognition of his accomplishments on the battlefields of northern France.

THE STARS AND STRIPES
MEDITERRANEAN

Vol. 1, No. 264, Tuesday, September 19, 1944 ITALY EDITION TWO LIRE

BRITISH 2nd IN HOLLAND

Massed Dutch Landing Scatters Enemy

Vital Nazi Defenses Straddled

SUPREME HEADQUARTERS, ALLIED EXPEDITIONARY FORCE, Sept. 18 — The brilliantly executed mass landing of Allied airborne troops in Holland yesterday has cleared the Germans from several Dutch towns, correspondents report, and the Allied communique, although still not revealing exact location of the troops, stated the operation was going well.

An Allied Press correspondent, who went in on the fourth glider radioed back that British and American troops of the 1st Allied Airborne Army were "established" in the liberated towns and that losses from flak were slight.

The airborne forces were reported in some dispatches to have "straddled" the great water belt dividing the upper two-thirds of Holland from the lower third. The barrier, described as Germany's most powerful line of defense in western Europe, extends from the northern end of the Siegfried Line to the North Sea.

Significance of the operation was indicated in a pre-takeoff statement to his men by Lt. Gen. Lewis Brereton, Commander of the 1st AAA, who flew with a spearhead formation.

"You are taking part in one of the greatest operations in military history," he said. "On navigation and flying skill, courage of the air crews and speed in landing rests the difference between a quick decision in the west and a long, drawn-out battle."

Colorful accounts of the operation—said to be the largest ever carried out in daylight—were given in on-the-spot recordings of radio broadcasters and the dispatches of correspondents.

Edward Murrow, Columbia Broadcasting System European chief, who recorded from a C-47 carrying paratroopers, said the spectacle was amazing if from the standpoint of color alone.

"Below us," Murrow said, "are clouds of vari-colored smoke marking the various landing zones. The parachutes of the men and their equipment are bright green,

(Continued on page 8)

NAZI DEFENSES ARE IN DUTCH

WHILE AMERICANS poured through the hole in the West Wall south of Aachen, in the first operation of its kind the 1st Allied Airborne Army yesterday leapfrogged German water barriers along the coast and landed inland on the Rhine delta, at several points in the Eindhoven area.

Russian Drive Into Greece Aimed At Cutting Off Enemy In Macedonia

Soviet Army Pushes Across Bulgarian Frontier

LONDON, Sept. 18—A part of the Red Army is today in Nazi-occupied Greece, according to the Istanbul, Turkey, correspondent of the Exchange Telegraph.

According to the report, Russian forces have crossed the Bulgarian-Greek frontier and are moving in the direction of Salonika, a maneuver which would cut off the escape of such German forces which remain in the Macedonian section of Greece to the east of Salonika.

Joint Yugoslav-Russian operations, reported today, include the occupation of the central Dalmatian islands, which control Adriatic Sea routes by which Germans in

(Continued on Page 8)

Enraged Romans Lynch Former Fascist Warden

(By A Staff Correspondent)

ROME, Sept. 18—Hundreds of enraged Romans—some of them widows and relatives of the 320 victims of the massacre of the Ardantine Caves — stormed the great gray Palace of Justice today and lynched Donato Carretta, Fascist ex-warden of the Regina Coeli Prison amid some of the wildest scenes Rome has ever witnessed.

The crowd, which started collecting long before dawn this morning for the trial of Pietro Caruso, Fascist ex-police chief of Rome, accused of collaboration with the Nazis, killed Carretta after beating him to a pulp and throwing him off a bridge into the Tiber.

Carretta was to have been one of the prosecution's principal witnesses in Caruso's trial. It was from Carretta's prison that most of the Ardantine slaughter victims were taken.

Carretta never reached the witness box. Women's hands clawed at his clothing, U. S. war correspondent Pat Frank reported. Men's hands reached for his throat while hundreds of other Italians

(Continued on page 8)

Nazis Show No Sign Of Cracking In Italy

ADVANCED ALLIED FORCE HEADQUARTERS, Sept. 18—There was no indication from official reports today that Field Marshal Albert Kesselring intends to withdraw before or surrender to the 8th Army, now two and a half miles from Rimini on the Adriatic Sea, or to the 5th Army, bucking the Gothic Line at its strongest point, the Futa Pass, some 25 miles north of Florence.

All along the snaking 150-mile front, small but significant gains were reported, principally by Canadian and Greek troops of the 8th Army who reached the northwest corner of the Rimini airfield, about three miles from the town itself.

The 8th Army bridgehead across the Marano River has been widened to eight miles, extending from the eastern borders of San Marino, tiny neutral republic inside Italy, to the Adriatic Sea, a

(Continued on Page 8)

15th AAF Heavies Aid Russian Drives

MAAF HEADQUARTERS, Sept. 18—Continuing to hamper movements of German troops trapped in the Balkans by the Russian offensives, medium forces of 15th AAF heavy bombers today attacked important targets in Hungary and Yugoslavia.

Today's missions followed similar attacks made yesterday.

Flak was heavy at some of the targets. Only one enemy aircraft was encountered.

Foreign Labor Delegates Study Conditions In Italy

By Sgt. HERBERT MITGANG
(Stars and Stripes Staff Writer)

ROME, Sept. 18 — Five visiting foreign labor delegates, representing the Congress of Industrial Organizations, the American Federation of Labor, British Trades and International Federation of Trades Unions, yesterday issued a joint report on general economic conditions and future trade union developments in Italy.

The joint report will be embodied in specific reports which the delegates will make to their own councils in the United States and Great Britain. Delegates emphasized that their visit did not imply any material promises to the Italian Labor movement, but rather that they would assist trade unionism only after the Italian people by their own actions had made an effort to establish a unified and democratic trade union movement.

Walter Schevenels, Secretary General of the International Federation of Trades Unions, declared that both Italian and foreign delegates had put aside political differences in an effort to improve employment and working conditions of the Italian people through trade unionism. He pointed out, however, that the existing trade union movement in Italy sprang from the Communist, Socialist and

(Continued on page 8)

New Drive, Air Action Dovetailed

SUPREME HEADQUARTERS, ALLIED EXPEDITIONARY FORCE, Sept. 18 —In coordination with the 1st Allied Airborne Army's invasion of Holland, the British 2nd Army has opened a major offensive from the south and has broken across the Dutch frontier at several points.

Field dispatches reported that the British already were two miles inside Holland, driving toward the cities of Tilburg and Eindhoven, where the German News Agency previously claimed that Allied airborne units had landed.

Both Dutch cities are within ten miles of the Belgian border, and Lt. Gen. Sir Miles Dempsey's troops were reported swinging towards them after breaking out of their eastern bridgehead over the Escaut Canal.

Meanwhile, the U. S. 1st Army continued to fight its way ahead east of encircled Aachen, after throwing back a furious German counterattack. Farther south, other Americans of the same army drove across the Luxembourg - German frontier at two new points.

After hurling back waves of frantic German infantry, Lt. Gen. Courtney H. Hodges' troops fighting on the eastern side of the Siegfried Line were last reported beyond the town of Stolberg and only 26 miles from the Rhineland city of Cologne.

Official sources said that new penetrations of Germany were made by the 1st Army at Echternach and Dullendorf, both about 17 miles northwest of the Reich city of Trier on the Luxembourg border.

Further advances of the left wing of the U. S. 1st Army, reported yesterday to have taken the Dutch town of Maastricht and to have neared the German frontier, were screened by official silence.

(Continued on Page 8)

Navy Planes Blast Crete Transports

ADVANCED ALLIED FORCE HEADQUARTERS, Sept. 18 — Naval aircraft accompanied a force of escort carriers in a low-flying attack on enemy motor transports on the Island of Crete, it was announced today. This was the first indication that aircraft carriers were operating in the Aegean Sea.

The carriers were under the command of Rear Adm. Thomas Trowbridge, RN, and the planes reported that 23 vehicles were destroyed on this island off the coast of Greece.

Eighty miles north, off the Island of Melos, three large and two small sailing craft were sunk and one merchant ship was damaged. All of the aircraft returned safely.

On the same day, Melos was bombarded by HMS Aurora.

New York—London
Paris—Rennes
Saturday, Sept. 23, 1944
Vol. 1. No. 70

THE STARS AND STRIPES

Daily Newspaper of U.S. Armed Forces in the European Theater of Operations

Ici On Parle Français
N'oubliez pas de m'écrire
Noobleeay pah duh mayKREER
Please be sure to write

Skyborne Army Rescued

Ike Praises Truckmen Of Red Ball

Twenty-five thousand American soldier-truckers and auxiliaries riding the Army's famed Red Ball Highway—400-mile supply lifeline from the ports to the combat areas—were told yesterday in a congratulatory message from Gen. Eisenhower that they were shaping the war's destiny as greatly as any combat troops.

Later, the Communications Zone chiefs who planned and who control the Highway revealed some of its secrets at a Paris press conference, and a 12th Army Group staff officer said that upon it depended how soon came a mass thrust into Germany.

Hughes Speaks for Gen. Ike

Eisenhower's tribute to the supply men was paid on his behalf early yesterday morning by Maj. Gen. E. S Hughes, who drove outside Paris to meet a line of trucks driven by Negro troops of a truck company.

In a field by the roadside, he decorated Cpl. Robert P. Bradley, of Lynchburg, Va., with the Bronze Star Medal for meritorious service. None of the men was aware of what was to occur when the convoy was waved to a halt and they were asked to assemble near by.

Hughes told the surprised truckers that he would have liked to give all of them a medal. "Bradley was chosen as a representative of the whole Red Ball Highway, including the men who repair the roads and bridges, put up the telephone wires and do all the service work in the rear," he said.

"Gen. Eisenhower realizes that you men seldom get the same recognition as soldiers in the front line and wants you to know that the part you're playing is vital. His message is for every man engaged on this vast project; the troops at the front couldn't do without you."

At the press conference, Maj. Gen. Frank E. Ross, chief of transportation, CZ, said Red Ball Highway—four times as long as the Burma

(Continued on Page 4)

No Tape in Red Ball, Congressmen Learn

The Red Ball Express waits for nobody, as 10 junketing congressmen discovered yesterday. Driving from an airfield near Paris to Gen. Eisenhower's headquarters, the congressmen were delayed when they had to stop while a Red Ball convoy roared by en route to the front.

Borrowed Flak Suits Shielded Engineers

Flak suits borrowed from the Air Forces were used on D-Day to protect engineer bulldozer operators on the beaches of Normandy, Maj. Gen. C. R. Moore, ETO chief engineer, has disclosed.

The suits afforded a measure of protection against shrapnel and small-arms fire as the engineers launched bulldozers through the su[illegible] to the invasion beaches. Shells from heavier German weapons, however, took a heavy toll of the giant engineer machines.

Come On Out, Bud, But Not to Play

Framed in a window of a shell-scarred house at Illy, France, a Nazi officer surrenders to a Yank armed with an automatic rifle. The smoke of battle still hangs over the town, liberated by American troops in their drive to the Belgian border.

Germans Shell Own Towns In Futile Effort to Halt Yanks

By G. K. Hodenfield
Stars and Stripes Staff Writer.

ON THE SIEGFRIED LINE, Sept. 22.—M/Sgt. Jack Harvey, of Ravenna, N.Y., was about four blocks away when the shell from a German artillery battalion landed at an intersection of a tiny village about halfway through the Siegfried Line defenses. Four German civilians were killed, two were injured and two homes were completely wrecked. The total damage to the Allied war effort was two slightly-wounded American soldiers.

This shell answered a big question for Harvey. He hadn't believed that the Germans really would shell their own cities and villages. He knows it now, and although now it's their own countrymen the Germans are killing, he hates the Jerry just a little bit more. That's saying quite a bit for a man who's seen action in Africa, Sicily and Italy and in France, Belgium and Germany.

After two years of it, Harvey is beginning to understand the German soldier. But he admits he can't make heads or tails of the German civilians he has met thus far. They don't fit into any pattern.

"Some of them," Harvey said, "smile and wave when we go by and others just scowl at us. I can understand either emotion, but what I can't understand is that entire villages will be divided. They'll be smiling from one house and scowling from the next.

"A lot of them are scared because they've been told we will shoot them when we capture a town, and they aren't quite certain just what they should do. Others will run up to give us information, which most of the time is accurate. They seem

(Continued on Page 4)

Japs on Edge In Philippines

The Japanese proclaimed martial law in the Philippines yesterday "in view of the danger of invasion being imminent," as Adm. Chester W. Nimitz announced carrier-based planes Wednesday launched their heaviest raid against the Manila Harbor area.

Eleven Jap ships were sunk and 26 damaged, and 205 enemy planes were destroyed in the air and on the ground, Nimitz revealed. Tokyo said 5[illegible] U.S. planes participated in the attack, which hit Clark Field, Mitchell Field and Cavite naval base, as well as Manila Harbor.

A Tokyo broadcast picked up in New York last night reported that 200 U.S. planes had made another attack on Manila yesterday.

2-Way Blow by Heavies Rips Targets in Reich

Strong forces of British-based Fortresses and Liberators, escorted by Mustangs, attacked industrial targets in the Kassel area of central Germany yesterday, while more than 500 heavies from Italy bombed Munich and rail yards at Larrissa, Greece.

U.S. medium bombers dropped about 2,000,000 war-news leaflets over German resistance pockets in the Calais and Dunkirk areas.

SPELLMAN IN GERMANY

KORNELIMUESTER, Germany, Sept. 22. — Archbishop Spellman celebrated his first mass in Germany since 1932 today with several hundred civilians in the audience.

Field Uniform Is Paris Style, New CO Rules

The prescribed uniform for soldiers in Paris was outlined last night by Brig. Gen. Allen R. Kimball, whose appointment as headquarters commandant of ETO and Communications Zone Headquarters was announced yesterday.

Until further notice the proper uniform for both officers and men will consist of helmet liner, OD trousers, OD shirt, field jacket and leggings or their equivalent.

A graduate of West Point, Kimball began his military career as an infantryman and later transferred to the Quartermaster Corps. Prior to his new appointment, he was ETO deputy chief quartermaster, with headquarters in the United Kingdom.

In his new post, the general is responsible for the billeting, messing and discipline of the several thousand officers and men assigned to the headquarters, which was transferred to Paris as soon as hostilities in the capital ceased.

Thus far, 169 hotels have been taken over as billets for personnel and more than 20 mess halls have been established, many of them with French staffs.

Greek Troops 200 Yds. From Po Valley Gateway

Greek troops of the Eighth Army fought to within 200 yards of the edge of Rimini, gateway to the Po Valley, yesterday while rain slowed the Fifth Army offensive after the Americans had captured heights dominating the Firenzula junction on the road to Bologna.

American troops were driving down the slopes of the last mountain barrier guarding the plains of northern Italy and toward Santa Lucia, part of the Futa Pass defenses of the Gothic Line.

Push Lifts Nazi Siege In Holland

British armor and American paratroops drove north in Holland from liberated Nijmegen yesterday to relieve a force of airborne units which had been cut off at Arnhem, while to the southeast, the greatest tank battle of the campaign in Western Europe raged in the Moselle Valley.

Before the junction of the two forces in Holland, the position of the beleaguered skyborne army at Arnhem had been described as critical, but not hopeless. To effect the junction, elements of the British Second Army and American paratroops thrust eight miles north of Nijmegen, where earlier the combined force had seized a great bridge over the Rhine (the biggest of two branches of the lower Rhine and called the Waal by the Dutch).

Nazis Battle Fanatically

The rescue was effected only after one of the stiffest battles of the war, according to front-line dispatches which emphasized the stern resistance being put up by the Germans, well aware that a continued Allied [illegible] in this [illegible] meant an outflanking of the Siegfried Line from the north and a development of the threat across the Rhine, already crossed at Nijmegen.

After the loss of 130 tanks in five days, the Germans yesterday flung against Lt. Gen. George S. Patton's Third Army forces virtually their last remaining armor in the Moselle Valley in a desperate bid to hold the approaches to the Siegfried Line.

In Germany itself, Lt. Gen. Courtney Hodge's First Army, moving to widen the gap blasted in the Reich's vaunted frontier defenses, encountered continued fierce resistance in the Hurtgen forest. Meanwhile, an American broadcast

(Continued on Page 4)

Germans Told To Revolt Now

An unidentified German radio station, believed to be near the French border, was heard Thursday night and early yesterday appealing to the German people for revolt against the government.

A "high officer" broadcast that the Nazi government had ordered the Wehrmacht to force back civilians evacuating regions threatened by the Allied advance. He said that such an order, if carried out, would cause civil war and that already he had shot and killed the officer who had issued such an order to troops in his area.

Hear Germans Waver

BRUSSELS, Sept. 22. — Reports reaching here from Germany today indicated that the German people were increasingly in favor of capitulation and that some quarters were urging unconditional surrender as an act of true patriotism.

Danish Strike Ends

STOCKHOLM, Sept. 22. — The general strike in Denmark, which was called as a protest to the dissolution of the Danish police force, ended yesterday under orders from the Danish Freedom Council. Reports reaching here indicated the Nazis were conducting widespread searches for policemen who had escaped an initial roundup.

London—New York
Paris—Rennes
Tuesday, Sept. 26, 1944
Vol. 4 No. 280 1D

London Edition
THE STARS AND STRIPES
Daily Newspaper of U.S. Armed Forces in the European Theater of Operations

Daily French Lesson
Vous allez beaucoup me manquer
Voo zaLAY boKOO muh monKAY
You are going to miss me very much

50 Miles of Big Guns Bombard Reich

Jap Fleet and Air Force Driven From Philippines

Japan's air force in the Philippines has been "destroyed" and her naval units stationed in the islands have been forced to withdraw to new refuges as a result of two "daring and highly successful" carrier-based attacks on the Manila Bay area last Wednesday and Thursday, Adm. Chester W. Nimitz announced yesterday.

The Pacific commander-in-chief said that in two days the Navy put out of action 405 enemy aircraft—169 destroyed in combat, 188 destroyed on the ground, 45 damaged on the ground and three damaged by gunfire from ships.

In addition, the raiders sank or damaged 103 ships and small craft, including 40 ships sunk, 11 probably sunk, 35 damaged, six small craft sunk and 11 damaged. Two floating drydocks were also damaged.

Peleliu Attack Thwarted

Nimitz' recapitulation of the Manila attacks was made public at the same time his headquarters announced U.S. warships on Saturday frustrated a Japanese attempt to reinforce Peleliu island in the Palau group by destroying a convoy of 13 barges and one motor sampan carrying troops and equipment. The convoy was attacked northeast of Peleliu, 600 miles east of the Philippines.

The Japanese "suffered heavily" in the two-day strike at Manila, Nimitz said, reporting "extensive destruction" at and near Clark and Nichols fields in the Manila harbor area and Cavite naval base.

Besides the toll of planes and ships, "extensive damage was done to buildings, warehouses, railroad equipment, oil storage tanks, harbor installations, hangars, shops and stored supplies.

"Our own losses were 11 planes in combat, ten pilots and five air-crew men. There was no loss or damage to any of our surface ships."

Withdrawal Forced

The admiral concluded that the Third Fleet's attacks, under Adm. William F. Halsey, "have forced the enemy to withdraw his naval forces from their former anchorages in the Philippines and to seek new refuges in the same general area, have disrupted inter-island communications and have destroyed his air force in the Philippines."

Liberators under Gen. Douglas MacArthur's command dropped 105 tons of bombs on Jap airdromes on Dutch Celebes, and patrol torpedo boats sank at least two enemy ships carrying troops and supplies in Morotai strait between Morotai and Halmahera islands.

Says LaGuardia Will Rule Italy as a Major-General

NEW YORK, Sept. 25 (Reuter)—Drew Pearson, American columnist, stated in a broadcast tonight that Fiorello LaGuardia, mayor of New York, will take over the entire Allied administration of liberated Italy as a result of decisions made at Quebec.

The mayor will be given the rank of major-general, he added.

Secretary of State Cordell Hull told his press conference today, however, that he knew of no decision to send LaGuardia to Italy.

Nazis See Next Stop Riga For Stalin Express

A massive Soviet assault to capture Riga was forecast last night by German News Agency's military commentator, Col. Ernst von Hammer, reporting that the Red Army has concentrated 1,000 tanks 25 miles southwest of the Latvian capital "with the apparent intention of breaking through to Riga bay."

"Strong air attacks are heralding the impending offensive and Soviet artillery has already begun to find the range," he added.

A hundred and fifty miles to the north, the Germans dragged out the battle for Estonia to the bitter end by concentrating strong forces on three islands at the entrance to the Gulf of Riga, in position to interfere with Soviet shipping in and out of the Gulf of Finland.

Retake Finnish Gulf Base

Not far away the Russians recaptured the Finnish Gulf base of Paldiski, on Estonia's northwest coast, after breaking out into the Baltic from Kronstadt for the first time since the siege of Leningrad. The sortie was marked by the sinking of five Nazi troopships, one of them a 10,000-ton transport, by torpedo bombers off the Latvian coast.

Inside Warsaw there was little change in the military situation, according to the Polish underground army's Gen. Bor. His communique hinted at German withdrawals in a cryptic sentence describing "increased movement of enemy units from the battle front on the southern outskirts of the capital." He also reported destruction of the last bridge over the Vistula.

Unofficial Moscow reports placed Russian columns 25 miles inside Slovakia and said Russo-Rumanian formations were within 25 miles of Szeged, Hungary's second largest city.

He a Section 8? We're Not So Sure

The Stars and Stripes yesterday received the first request of its kind—one asking for some "dope" on the Army of Occupation.

The writer said he wanted to know (1) about the application for service therein, (2) period of service, and (3) probable duties.

"I'm not a 'Section 8,' either," the writer added.

The Help Wanted Department suggested the man seek a transfer to the MPs, the logical branch to serve after the fall of Germany.

Nazis Fight to Cut Corridor

Stars and Stripes Map

Nearly 2,000 U.S. Planes Blast Reich Through Clouds

After a weekend lull because of bad weather, more than 1,200 Fortresses and Liberators of the Eighth Air Force yesterday swarmed over western Germany to blast railroad yards and other military and industrial objectives. Bombing was done with the aid of special instruments through solid cloud.

For the first time since D-Day, both Eighth and Ninth fighters, numbering nearly 750 Mustangs, Thunderbolts and Lightnings, escorted the heavies. Part of the escorting force also strafed enemy supplies and reinforcement facilities in the Ruhr—north of Marburg and in the vicinity of Pederborn.

Although no enemy pursuits were encountered and anti-aircraft fire was comparatively light, nine bombers and three Eighth fighters were lost.

The B17s and B24s pounded two railroad yards at Frankfurt, two at Coblenz and one at Ludwigshafen, as well as the Oopau chemical and synthetic oil plant. The railroad yards are important distribution points for German troops and supplies sent to the western front.

Ban Purchase of Dollars With Francs by Troops

PARIS, Sept. 25 (UP)—The sale of dollar money orders bought with francs at U.S Army post offices in the Paris area by U.S. troops has been stopped.

This development apparently was the result of a report, since denied, that the dollar value in francs was going to be increased above the present rate of 50 francs to the dollar.

First Army 240s Open Vast Attack

Airborne Men at Arnhem Get Some Relief But Still Wait Linkup

A devastating artillery attack on Germany launched along the whole U.S. First Army front from a 50-mile wall of powerful long-range guns, which plastered enemy traffic centers and military installations was reported in field dispatches yesterday.

Huge 240mm guns—the largest artillery pieces in the European theater—bombarded a ling line of towns serving German forward troops, and pounded targets only 18 miles from the Rhine.

Cross Rhine in Ducks

In Holland, relief for the trapped British airborne division at Arnhem dribbled across the lower Rhine River in ducks and assault boats under heavy fire from every sort of weapon the Germans could muster, but no solid link-up was reported in field dispatches last night.

There was no mention of the vital Rhine bridge at Arnhem either from SHAEF or field dispatches. Instead the emphasis was on a developing British thrust into Germany south of that area.

The two walls of the Holland corridor stretching up to Arnhem were strengthened in the face of German counterattacks. The Nazis broke through the Eindhoven-Arnhem supply line once, but the gap was sealed again.

Guns Hammer Duren

First Army artillery fire concentrated against Germany was reported to be equal in effect to air bombing, restricted by weather in the past few days. Guns blasted at Duren, 16 miles east of Aachen. Two villages were set on fire when shells exploded gasoline dumps.

Very heavy fighting was in prospect along the whole line as all signs indicated the Germans were determined to make a last-ditch stand for their homeland.

Immediate measures for full-scale defense of the Rhine line have been ordered by the German High Command, according to captured German officers, and Nazi construction crews were throwing up fortifications east of the river.

As the First Army pounded Germany with a terrific softening-up bombardment, Gen. Eisenhower issued a message to all foreign workers in Germany whose countries are at war with Germany. "The hour for action has come," the message said, listing instructions on sabotage.

Stands in Fear

"Remember that today the Gestapo stands in fear of the 12,000,000 foreign workers who, by acting now, can seal the fate of the Third Reich," the message ended.

British forces broke across the German frontier for the first time, crossing in two places. U.S. paratroops were with British tanks that pushed inside the Reich east of Nijmegen to capture Beek, while five miles to the southeast another British force crossed the frontier from the Reichwald Forest area.

Spearheads of Third Army armored attacks halted momentarily against strong enemy positions on and east of the Moselle River. German radio said Gen. Patton's armies were reaching back for a blow aimed straight at a sector of the West Wall.

On the Seventh Army front, U.S. infantrymen captured Epinal, about 40 miles southeast of Nancy, in a fast outflanking manoeuver after they stealthily crossed the river by night above and below the town.

Mess of Kraut Put in Storage

WITH U.S. FIRST ARMY ON THE SIEGFRIED LINE, Sept. 22 (delayed)—A Sherman tank and a dozer, temporarily too busy to take prisoners, joined forces here to pen up some Jerries in a pillbox for a day and then returned later for the capture.

When the men of an armored column fighting their way through this German line came to a pillbox half full of Germans, they didn't have time to bother with it. They called for one of their tank dozers and the Sherman with the blade on its bow pushed a mountain of dirt up against the only door of the pillbox.

The following day when they had more time the men came back and demanded that the trapped Germans inside surrender. The German commander refused, so the dozer shoved the dirt away and a Sherman, backing off a few yards, blasted away at the door with its 75. The Jerries came out.

A Combat Double Play

U.S. Army Signal Corps Photos

American infantrymen and armor demonstrate team play in these two combat photographs. As the infantrymen (left) made a dash for the bank of the Meurth River, which flows beyond Nancy and Lunelle about 14 miles from the German border.

Nazi snipers in the house (arrow) took their toll until the tank (right) was called into action to blow the structure to pieces and set it aflame. The house stored ammunition with which the Germans stocked up for action against the Allied Forces.

THE STARS AND STRIPES
MEDITERRANEAN

Vol. 1, No. 10, Tuesday, October 10, 1944 — Printed In France — ONE FRANC

Yanks Cut Aachen Roads

Cardinals Win World Series

Beat Browns, 3-1, As Wilks Saves Lanier

Relief Pitcher Fans Four, Holds Brownies Hitless

		R	H	E
Browns	010 000 000	1	3	2
Cardinals	000 300 00x	3	10	0

Batteries: Potter, Muncrief (4), Kramer (7) and Hayworth; Lanier, Wilks (6) and W. Cooper.

ST. LOUIS, Oct. 9—The St. Louis Cardinals, the Gas House Gang of the major leagues, came out on top of the baseball heap again today with a 3-1 victory over the St. Louis Browns in the sixth game of the World Series.

Lefty Max Lanier was the winning pitcher, but little Ted Wilks was the fireman who pulled the game out of the fire for him. Wilks, who was batted out of the box in the fourth inning of the third game, turned in a relief chore that was a masterpiece. In the three and two-thirds innings he worked, Ted allowed nary a bingle and struck out four Browns.

The only man to reach first base during Wilks' tenure was Mark Christman, Brownie third baseman, who made it on a fielder's choice as Whitey Kurowski was tossing out Chet Laabs at the plate in the sixth. Wilks wound up the ball game in a blaze by fanning pinch hitters Milt Byrnes and Mike Chartak.

Incidentally, the last seven pinch

(Continued on page 4)

Fireman

TED WILKS

Yank Column Just 10 Miles From Bologna

ROME, Oct. 9—American troops of the 5th Army in Italy were moving forward today on a broad front less than ten miles from Bologna while their big guns pounded enemy targets on the outskirts of the Po Valley city.

In less than two days, the mud-spattered Americans, beating the best the enemy and the worst the weather had to offer, pushed ahead four miles to reach the rolling country below the city on a front 15 miles wide. Enemy resistance was mounting as the Yanks drew nearer their goal.

The American breakthrough in the lower ridges of the Central Apennines climaxed more than a month of fighting in some of the most rugged country encountered during the long campaign. Capture of Bologna would paralyze German communications below the Po River and probably force Field Marshal Albert von Kesselring to withdraw to his reportedly powerful Po defenses.

British and Dominion troops of both the 5th and 8th Armies scored new gains in the face of chilling downpours and continuing enemy opposition. Ten miles inland from the Adriatic, 8th Army troops were across the flooded Fiumicino River in force after having been held up for several days.

Rain pinned down most Allied aircraft but fighter bombers were out over the Adriatic and Gulf of Genoa shipping routes.

150,000 Nazis Imperilled In Baltic Attack

Soviets Cut Gap 185 Miles Wide, Racing For Sea

MOSCOW, Oct. 9—Two powerful Russian armies, pouring through a 185-mile gap torn in the German lines following the resumption of the new offensive on the Baltic front four days ago, were racing yesterday across the plains of central Lithuania toward the Baltic Sea.

This twin Soviet drive, which threatens to cut off approximately 150,000 Germans in Latvia, has been progressing at a pace rarely equalled on the eastern front. Nazi troops, stunned and demoralized by the suddenness and intensity of the new Red Army push, are retreating frantically toward the Baltic in an effort to escape encirclement and annihilation.

The northern army, under General Bagramyan, is rapidly approaching Liepaja, on the Baltic coast, while the southern army, commanded by General Cherniakovsy, has pushed to within 30 miles of Memel, large Lithuanian port 30 miles from the East Prussian frontier.

The new offensive was opened last Friday when Soviet planes and guns pounded German positions and opened the way for Russian troops who poured through the exposed and shattered Nazi defenses.

With the Red Baltic Fleet operating in the Gulf of Riga, keeping close watch on the beleaguered German garrison trapped in Riga, Soviet troops are slowly closing in on the city from three sides.

Six hundred miles to the south, tanks and fast-moving Cossacks are spearheading Russian infantrymen advancing across the plains of eastern Hungary toward Budapest. Red Army troops were last reported to be a little more than 70 miles from the Hungarian capital, sweeping shattered and demoralized German and Hungarian troops before them.

The Germans and Hungarians are retreating in great disorder.

Advancing along a 40-mile front, Red Army troops captured three important towns beyond Karcag yesterday.

Churchill, Stalin Meet In Moscow

MOSCOW, Oct. 9—British Prime Minister Winston Churchill and Foreign Secretary Anthony Eden arrived here today for conferences with Marshal Joseph Stalin and Russian Foreign Minister Viashylev Molotov.

The Prime Minister and Mr. Eden were accompanied by British Chief of Staff Field Marshal Sir Allan Brooke and other high civil and military officials. It was believed that the leaders of the two nations would discuss postwar aims, since most of the broad military problems were ironed out last fall at the Teheran conference, which was also attended by President Roosevelt.

Four Powers Reveal Peace Body Plans

WASHINGTON, Oct. 9 — The governments of the United States, Great Britain and Russia announced today the results of the recently-concluded Dumbarton Oaks four-power conference and outlined the structure of the proposed organization to maintain world peace and security. The plan will be immediately submitted to all member nations for their approval, as well as to the governments of the four nations which participated in the conference.

It was decided at the conference that the organization would be called the United Nations, and that membership in the body would be open to all peace-loving countries on the basis of soverign equality.

The proposed organization would be comprised of four separate bodies: A General Agency, Security Council, Court of Justice and Secretariat.

The Security Council will be made up of 11 members, four of which, the U. S., Great Britain, Russia and China, and in "due course" France, would be permanent. The remaining places on the council would be rotated among the other member nations.

The purpose of the organization, as outlined in the conference plan, is to "remove the threat to peace and prevent acts of aggression through collective means."

Sea, land and air forces, to be provided by the member nations, would be used to preserve peace should any nation fail to abide by the decisions of the proposed organization.

The conference members also recommended complete international co-operation in the achievement of world economic and social security.

Landing Made Along Scheldt By Canadians

German Escape By Land Route Now Impossible

SHAEF, Oct. 9—The Germans holding out in the hotly-contested city of Aachen were virtually cut off today from the rest of Germany as troops of Lt. Gen. Courtney Hodges' 1st U. S. Army extended their spearheads north and south of the city to positions astride all the main roads leading east, northeast and south of Aachen.

Fighting their way through the maze of Siegfried defenses against bitter enemy opposition, the doughboys, spearheaded by strong tank formations, captured a dominating hill three miles east of the city.

A captured railroad car loaded with dynamite was sent careening into Aachen, and it exploded violently when it hit German installations within the city.

In western Holland, troops of the 1st Canadian Army made an amphibious landing yesterday to the rear of the German pocket south of the Scheldt Estuary. Their aim was to relieve the pressure on the powerful Canadian spearheads which crossed the Leopold Canal and which are engaging the Germans in a bitter struggle near the estuary.

While the new landings did not take the Germans completely by surprise, they were carried out successfully under cover of darkness early in the morning. The Canadians landed anti-tank guns and mortars on the east flank of the Nazi salient despite vigorous enemy attempts to prevent them from establishing a bridgehead.

Northeast of the new operation, other Canadian forces yesterday expanded their spearhead north of the Leopold Canal and drove

(Continued on page 4)

U. S. Batters Marcus Isles

PEARL HARBOR, Oct. 9—U. S. Navy headquarters here announced today that units of Admiral William F. Halsey's far-ranging 3rd Pacific Fleet had battered important Japanese installations in the Marcus Islands, 1,200 miles east of Tokio. The communique reported that the task force had wreaked considerable damage with "deliberate and destructive" gunfire.

One big coast battery was known to have been silenced.

General Douglas MacArthur's Allied Southwest Pacific Headquarters meanwhile reported that American bombers, for the third time in a week, had slugged Japanese refineries on Borneo, in the Netherlands East Indies.

Other U. S. bombers went again after Rabaul, the big Jap base at the northeastern tip of New Britain. The object here was to keep the base neutralized. Some 60,000 Jap troops are garrisoned there, but they have been virtually cut off from help from any other source, and to all intents and purposes are useless to the Japanese war effort.

Meanwhile the Allied war of attrition against Jap shipping continued over the weekend with excellent results. 25 vessels were sunk or damaged around Ceram and elsewhere in the southwest Pacific. Correspondents reported that the Japs were even beginning to use sailing craft to make up for their expensive losses.

General Tells Story Of Paratroop Battle

SHAEF, Oct. 9—A dramatic first person story of the paratroopers' stand at Arnhem was told here yesterday by Maj. Gen. Urquhart, commander of the British 1st Airborne Division, who was with his gallant men throughout their ten-day battle. Here is the general's account:

"There were several considerations which affected the issue. The main one was that because of flak the RAF could not land us nearer than eight miles from the town. It was intended to get the complete division down in one lift and that would have made a marked effect on the outcome.

"The fighting was absolutely first-class. Our parachutists moved off 100 percent strong. We never got more than 60 percent in practice. We bumped into opposition rather stronger and earlier than we had expected. Things did not go according to plan or anywhere near that in the early stages.

"At the end of the first day one battalion was on the bridge and the rest of the division on the outskirts of the town. The battalion removed charges and the bridge was secure and ready for anyone coming up from the south.

"The other brigade was to hold a [illegible] for the other forces coming up the next day. It was not long before we were separated. The second lift, because of bad weather, did not arrive until the evening of the second day. It became obvious that the chance of creating a perimeter around the town had gone.

"When we decided to form a perimeter on the river and hold the ferry crossing, the brigade recalled from north of the railway ran into a column of Germans with tanks, and it suffered a tre-

(Continued on page 4)

Allied Kindness Amazes Germans

CORNELIMUNSTER, Germany, Oct. 9—Civilians in this Catholic area of western Germany are taking the severe Allied restrictions in very good spirit and so far there have been no reports of civilian violence against American troops, Allied Military Government officials said today.

One of the burgomeisters, who have full responsibility for seeing that their people are fed and cared for, said of the Allied entry into Germany:

"We feared much worse. We expected we would be tortured and shot and that the day after you came our streets would be full of civilians with their throats cut."

Peloponnese Said Cleared

ROME, Oct. 9—No official news on the progress of British troops in Greece came today, but dispatches from correspondents indicated that the entire Peloponnese had been cleared of enemy occupation forces.

Land Forces Adriatic troops were last described as approaching the major city of Corinth, which commands the land connection between the upper and lower parts of the Greek mainland. Press dispatches today said that Greek Patriots had seized control of Corinth and were ready to turn it over to the Tommies when they arrived.

RAF pilots were out on patrol of the German land and sea escape routes again during the night, but little movement was spotted. So far, German security troops in Greece and the Aegean islands have been more agile at surrendering than in attempting escape.

The MAAF disclosed today that the 1,100 bombers which carried out the pre-landing bombing of Greece dropped more than 2,000 tons of bombs. Targets included the Eleusis, Tatoi and Kalamaki airdromes in the Athens area, the port of Salonika, a naval base north of Piraeus and a sub base on a small island near Piraeus.

THE STARS AND STRIPES
MEDITERRANEAN

Vol. 1, No. 285, Friday, October 13, 1944 — ITALY EDITION — TWO LIRE

Gigantic Bomber Attack Blasts Nazis In Bologna

Guns, Planes Lash Aachen; Foe Fights On

Fighters, Bombers Rip Nazi Stronghold In 5-Hour Attack

SUPREME HEADQUARTERS, ALLIED EXPEDITIONARY FORCES, Oct. 12—German stormtroopers, hopped up by extra whiskey rations to withstand the terrific bombardment they are now getting, still held out today in the battered German stronghold of Aachen. Following a continuous five-hour fighter-bomber and artillery pasting yesterday afternoon, some of the Nazi garrison rearguard took to the nearby fields and surrendered. Others, who pulled out earlier, sat expressionless in a field and watched their comrades inside Aachen.

(An Allied patrol was reported today in one dispatch to have sneaked into the south end of the blazing dust-billowing city. Several such previous reports have never been officially confirmed.)

Although there was nothing specific to indicate that the Germans in Aachen were ready to throw in the towel, the complete lack of enemy air opposition over the city and a familiar crack from the German radio were seen as a possible tip-off that the end might not be far off.

Not one of the hundreds of Allied fighter-bombers in the attack yesterday was lost and there was practically no flak. Some pilots reported seeing Germans in vehicles streaking eastward from Aachen towards their only escape gap.

The German radio said that Aachen was such a wreck that it had lost its military importance.

(Continued on Page 8)

Preliminary Terms Accepted By Bulgaria

MOSCOW, Oct. 12—Bulgaria has accepted preliminary terms of its armistice with the Allies, according to Moscow Radio tonight, and the preliminary terms include withdrawal of Bulgarian forces from Greece and Yugoslavia within the next two weeks.

No Fags, Coeds Try Corn Cob Smoking

LAWRENCE, Kans., Oct. 12 (ANS)—The cigaret shortage has caused feminine smokers to turn to pipes. A clerk in a downtown drug store reports she sold a whole card of "two-bit" corn cob pipes to women this week. Another said three University of Kansas coeds turned in desperation to pipes when butts were not forthcoming.

Rival Government Premiers Arrive For Moscow Talks

LONDON, Oct. 12 – Arrival in Moscow, where Marshal Stalin and Prime Minister Churchill are in the midst of discussions, of the heads of the two rival Polish governments was announced today.

Their arrival and the report that Marshal Tito of the Yugoslav National Army of Liberation is also enroute to Moscow reflect the importance of the conferences now under way.

The two rival Polish groups are the Polish Government-in-Exile, with headquarters in London, and the Polish National Committee of Liberation, with headquarters in Lublin, Poland.

The prime minister of the London group, Stanislaw Mikolajczyk, and the chairman of the Lublin committee, Edward Osubka-Morawski, are both in Moscow now, the latter accompanied by the Commander-in-Chief of the National Liberation committee's armed forces, Gen. Michael Rola-Zymierski. The commander of the London group's forces, who was captured by the Germans following his order to Warsaw's fighters to surrender to the Germans, is Gen. Tadeusz Komorowski, better known as General "Bor."

Marshal Stalin, Prime Minister Churchill and the U. S. Ambassador to Russia, W. Averell Harriman, were closeted at the British Embassy until well past three o'clock this morning, after a small dinner given by the British ambassador Sir Archibald Clark Kerr.

WHAT TALKS ARE ABOUT

WASHINGTON, Oct. 12 — The Associated Press lists questions of Anglo-Russian interests in the Balkans, the Polish question, the

(Continued on Page 8)

THE PUSH ON BUDAPEST

AIDED BY YUGOSLAV, Rumanian and Bulgarian troops, the Red Army is all set to make a little goulash in Hungary this week. The map shows the approximate location of the principle Russian salients aimed at Budapest, capital of the last of Hitler's Balkan satellite governments. Belgrade, capital of Yugoslavia, is now completely surrounded—either by Russians or by Marshal Tito's Yugoslav army.

Red Army Forcing Reich Doors Open

LONDON, Oct. 12—Although the taking of Szeged, Hungary's second city, and Cluj, capital of Transylvania, during the past 24 hours are spectacular gains for the Red Army and its partisan allies, still more significance attaches to the Baltic area where the Russians are forcing open new doors into the Reich itself.

Germany's defenses set up to protect East Prussia have suffered a severe blow by the loss of Taurage, one of the key-points in the defense system in this area.

The Daily Telegraph's Moscow correspondent points today to the way in which the tables have been turned on the Germans in the Baltic. Not only have the Germans' hopes of cutting off Russian forces south of Riga collapsed, but their own groupings are now without land escape routes.

Correspondents expect that losses of the Germans in manpower and in munitions will be astronomical, for the Red Army has made destruction of Germans and German arms its main objective, even at the expense of territorial gains. Yesterday's score alone included

(Continued on Page 8)

Raid Larger Than Those On Cassino

ADVANCED ALLIED FORCE HEADQUARTERS, Oct. 12—Black with bombers, the skies over Bologna rained fiery death on the Germans for many hours today as extraordinary forces of 15th AAF Liberators and Fortresses laid upon the key Italian city load after load of explosives in preparation for the 5th Army's expected assault on the area.

"A bigger job even than the bombing of Cassino," is the way veteran airmen described today's raid. It was the greatest attack, as to number of 15th AAF planes ever concentrated on one objective.

Barracks, bivouac areas, ammunition dumps and other vital military objectives were among the targets today.

The attacks from the air were a part of the Allies' answer to stiffened German resistance, reported recently by both Allied armies operating on this front.

In contrast to previous tactics, so the reports have run lately, the Germans have been fighting until killed or captured.

While the 5th Army was coiling itself to spring into action after the end of today's aerial show, the 8th Army continued in its forward drive from Savignano on Highway 9 to a point about two miles farther up the road.

The successful actions fought by British and Indian troops of the 8th Army in the foothills south of this Rimini-Bologna road during the last few days, despite bad weather conditions, have compelled the Tedeschi to withdraw to positions running northeast and southwest of Gambettola, about four and one-half miles from Cesena — first large Po Valley city ahead of the 8th Army.

The communique, as in the past five days, revealed scarcely any changes in the 5th Army's positions. The British troops, who have been advancing along the right flank up Highway 65, broke up another counterattack on Mount Battaglia (Battle Mountain) capturing 75 prisoners. Last week, Battle Mountain was captured, lost and recaptured. The enemy continued

(Continued on Page 8)

Bologna Raid Was 'Milk Run'

By Sgt. ED CLARK
(Stars and Stripes Staff Writer)

WITH THE 15TH AIR FORCE, Oct. 12—Bologna, target of the 5th and 8th Armies for many a week, really caught hell today from the air.

Great forces of Italy-based Flying Fortresses and Liberators—in fact, the greatest number of 15th AAF heavy bombers ever sent against a single objective—laid it on every military objective around the city, from mess lines to railroad yards, and from warehouses to latrines.

If there are any military installations left in Bologna tonight that are worth anything to the Germans, it's because the Nazis have forgotten the war and gone into the salvage business.

From the start, it looked as if it might be a good day to strike an all-out blow from the air in support of a final break-through by the ground forces into the Po valley.

The lead plane of the B-24 group, commanded by Col. Horace D. Aynesworth, Childress, Texas, flew through weather that might have been ordered by the High Command in the latter stages of its flight. There were a few puff clouds, a few mountain peaks already capped with early snows, but nothing to mar visibility over the target.

Then just short of those Appenine stretches known now as the Gothic Line that same array of clouds that have made things miserable for the doughfeet below spread their soggy blanket between the Liberators and the ground.

But somebody must have been working on the the day's work — for just north of the Appenines the cloud cover has been rolled back to the Alps, and the Po Valley was bright with sunlight.

Thousands of feet below the Liberator piloted by Maj. Darwin E. Swanson, Mineral Point, Wis., lay Bologna — ready for her bomb-load!

Things were already a bit hazy over the city, not because of the weather, but because another group of B-24s had just sent their bombs home. Through the dust and smoke, group after group of the heavy bombers let go at military targets in the stricken city.

Looking back at Bologna, little could be seen. A great pall of red and black hovered over the city and spread slowly across the Po Valley — here and there a ball of ack-ack blast puffed out in blacks and whites.

Veteran fliers call it a "milk run." A few planes did not come back, but not because of the Luftwaffe.

Homeward Bound? Here's The Schedule

AFHQ, Oct. 12—Clarification of the schedule to be followed by servicemen returning to the States on rotation was made today by the Office of Information and Education, SOS, NATOUSA.

According to the Adjutant General, the announcement stated, the procedure upon arrival in the States for rotation personnel is as follows:

(1) Short stay at the U. S. port of debarkation for a physical inspection required by law, distribution of necessary clothing and arrangement for transportation to the Reception Center nearest the returnee's home. (2) Short stay at the center to pick up additional clothing, if necessary, to collect maximum partial pay and to receive orders to a Redistribution Station or Reassignment Center with a 21-day delay (leave or furlough) at home or other place of choice enroute. (3) Several days at the Redistribution Station or Reassignment Center for a rest, complete physical exam to determine ability for future duties, recon-

(Continued on Page 8)

Government Of China Plans Relief Program

WASHINGTON, Oct. 12 — The Chinese government yesterday made public a program for relief and rehabilitation in China calling for the import of 10,000,000 tons of supplies valued at 2,500 million in United States dollars, in addition to internal expenditures estimated at more than 2,500 million in prewar Chinese currency.

Thirty-seven percent of the total import requirements is requested from UNRRA. Relief and rehabilitation operations will be conducted primarily in areas now under Japanese occupation and only to a "relatively small extent" in free China, the statement said.

THE STARS AND STRIPES

MEDITERRANEAN

Vol. 1, No. 290, Thursday, October 19, 1944

ITALY EDITION -:- TWO LIRE

HITLER MAKES PEACE BID

Jap Boats Told To Run For Shelter

Yank Bombers Roam Pacific; B-29s Hit Formosa Again

HONOLULU, Oct. 18 — Japanese freighters, whose normal job is to keep 'em sailing between Japan's stolen island empire and the home base, have scurried for cover under the impact of continuous air and sea attacks, and United States fliers and sea-fighters are keeping up the pressure today with additional assaults on Japanese strongpoints.

Radio Tokio is warning Japanese shipping to speed for shelter—but it won't do them a lot of good, for bombers of the 14th AAF are continuing their attacks on such Chinese harbors as Hongkong, striking at enemy ships seeking refuge there.

The latest Hongkong harbor score made public is that of Monday: two oil tankers sunk, three freighters and one other large cargo vessel, to a total of 48,000 tons of shipping. The docks were badly damaged, and one 5,000-ton Jap cruiser there to protect the freight ships was blown up.

Superfortresses from Chinese bases struck once more yesterday at the island of Formosa, choosing the Einansho airbase, a defensive field important to the heavily fortified naval port at Takao, as principal target.

Admiral Chester W. Nimitz announced today that troops of the U. S. Army's 81st Division nearly a month ago had occupied Ulithi Atoll in the West Caroline group of islands, and six other small islands in the same area. The fact has been kept a secret up to now so the Japs wouldn't find out.

The Office of War Information

(Continued on Page 8)

READY TO QUIT?

ADOLF HITLER

. . . not victory but peace.

Ten Large Red Armies In Motion

LONDON, Oct. 18 — Ten large Soviet army groups are in motion against the Germans today, all the way from the extreme northern front in Finland to southern Yugoslavia near the Greek border, and one of these Red Army salients—with Marshal Tito's Yugoslav soldiers giving substantial assistance—is driving the Germans out of Belgrade, capital of Yugoslavia, literally block by block.

Tito's headquarters say today that the Allied forces have now reached the main center of Belgrade, the downtown business section, and that all of the city except the Savamale and Darco sections has now been cleared of Germans.

As an example of the bitterness of the fighting, the Yugoslavian communique says: "The first floor of the State National bank is in

(Continued on Page 8)

Allies Take Venraij, Big Rail Center

British Column Now Eight Miles From German Border

SHAEF, Oct. 18 — British troops, supported by American armor, steamrollered into Venraij today and crushed all organized resistance in the important railroad and highway junction.

Venraij is on the long British 2nd Army spearhead thrust into Holland and is only eight miles from the German frontier. Its capture followed days of heavy fighting through minefields embedded in thick mud.

At the same time, the Allies smashed at shattered Cologne again with 600 Fortresses and Liberators escorted by nearly 500 American fighters, for the fourth major raid in five days.

Key junction of five major highways, Venraij marked the only big advance on the entire western front, along which a lull, spotted by bloody local engagements, has existed the past few days.

Military commentators pointed out that the lull might prove similar to the one that preceded the breakout from the Cherbourg Peninsula in Normandy, since the Allies are everywhere exerting tremendous pressure on the Siegfried Line.

Aachen was being mopped up steadily by American troops using

(Continued on Page 8)

Seaborne Forces Arrive In Greece

ADVANCE ALLIED FORCE HEADQUARTERS, Oct. 18 — The disembarkation at Athens of the initial sea contingent troops and stores has been completed and further drops by parachute troops have been carried out at fields already occupied, according to today's communique from Land Forces Greece and official naval statements.

In spite of the initial delay caused by the necessity of extensive mine sweeping, the further unloading of supplies and equipment is expected shortly "to catch up with the original timetable," the naval statement read.

Members of the Greek Cabinet were expected to make their official arrival in Greece today, coming ashore from the Greek cruiser Averof, the Allied Navy release further disclosed. They will be accompanied by military and naval force commanders.

The island of Scarpanto in the Dodecanese group has been liberated by unopposed landing parties from the British destroyers HMS Terpis, Terpischore and Cleveland.

An observer with an RAF regiment, which was among the first Allied troops to enter Athens last Saturday evening, describes how that night, from 40 miles away in the mountains, "a white glow could be seen in the sky, eastward.

Tells People Hope Is To Save Reich

ROME, Oct. 18—Hitler made a bid for peace today.

In a proclamation broadcast over the German radio today and quoted by Reuter's news agency, the Fuehrer made the startling admission that the uppermost thought in his mind at present is not a Nazi victory, but a peace that will safeguard Germany from destruction.

"We must and we shall succeed," he declared, "not only in breaking the enemy's determination to destroy us but in driving hostile forces back and keeping them clear of the Reich until a peace is guaranteed which safeguards the future of Germany, her allies and thereby Europe."

Only an incomplete part of the Broadcast reached here at a late hour tonight. In his opening, Hitler admitted that "after five years of struggle the enemy has by a defection of all our European Allies has at some points come near the German frontier and at others reached it."

His reference to "all European allies" was believed by observers here to indicate that all was not going so well in Hungary, despite the pro-Nazi coup d'etat following Count Nicholas Horthy's appeal for peace and subsequent removal from the regency.

This mobilization, Hitler declared, will be a "second large-scale mobilization," the first having been, according to him, in the autumn of 1939 immediately after the outbreak of the war.

He directed that "in all Gaus (administrative districts, headed by Nazi Gauleiters) of the Reich a German 'Volkssturm' comprising all able-bodied men from the ages of 16 to 60 be set up."

This "Volkssturm," Hitler continued, "will defend the home soil with all weapons and all means suitable."

"Secondly, the Gauleiters will be entrusted with the establishment and command of the German 'Volkssturm'; thirdly, I hereby appoint as the chief of staff, S. A. Scheppmann, inspector of rifle training, and corps leader of the

(Continued on Page 8)

5th Army Progress Measured In Yards

ADVANCED ALLIED FORCE HEADQUARTERS, Oct. 18—Progress along key Highway 65 to Bologna was being measured in yards—500 yards yesterday—as American troops spearheading the 5th Army advance went into their 38th day of relentless attack with their objective, the Po Valley, now just less than ten miles away.

Heavy fighting continued for hills and escarpments on either side of the highway; they must be taken before sizeable gains along the mountain road itself can be registered. West of 65 the battle was for the hill mass of Monte Ramici. East of 65 air support was used in advancing toward Mt. Belmonte, the most northernly point of Allied progress in the Apennines.

Farther east 5th Army troops captured the towns of Trebo and Santa Anna—one of three similarly-named towns in the fighting area.

On the 8th Army Adriatic coastal sector, patrols again crossed the Fiumicino River and yesterday they got as far as the Rigossa River, about a mile farther north. On Route 9, the other main highway leading to Bologna, 8th Army elements reached the Pisciatello River, putting them two miles south of Cesena and 15 miles from Forli. This advance of about a mile in the last 24 hours was made on a front of about four miles, extending west to Macerone.

On the other extreme flank of the Apennine front, units of the 5th Army, including Brazilian and Negro troops, maintained pressure on the enemy, the communique said.

U. S. Will Receive No More Refugees

WASHINGTON, Oct. 18 (ANS)—John W. Pehle, director of the War Refugee Board, announced yesterday that no more refugees would be brought to the United States. There are now enough temporary havens in the Mediterranean area for refugees, Pehle said.

Forgotten By Homefront, Italy Campaign Still Vital

(By A Staff Correspondent)

WITH THE 5TH ARMY, Oct. 18—The current hard-bitten relentless struggle now being waged by the 5th Army in fighting its way through to the Po valley has raised a series of questions:

1. How does the Allied effort in Italy fit into the "big picture" of the war to crush Hitler?

2. Why is the Wehrmacht making, at great cost, such, a determined stand on the back slopes of the Apeninnes when it could presumably contain the Allies so much more economically on the southern slopes of the Alps?

All and all, when the question can be fully answered and after you've seen the terrain over which the American divisions, spearhead of Lt. Gen. Mark W. Clark's 5th Army, have fought since Sept. 10, the Gothic Line campaign becomes a military epic.

Military security necessarily keeps hidden many of the facts, but this much can be said on the subject:

The 135-mile, two-army Allied front in Italy is currently being defended by elements of 27 German divisions, or just about half the number defending the thrice-as-long 400-mile Siegfried Line front, where some 55 divisions are known to be opposing four Allied armies.

Thus, from a pure mathematical standpoint it would appear that the 5th and 8th Armies are battling against forces superior to those defending what is admittedly a more serious threat against the German homeland. Actually, of course, in modern mobile war, overall mathematical strength is generally not the determinating factor. The disposition of troops and their ability and will to resist in a crucial spot, as indicated by the defense of Aachen, is the key to the toughness of German forces along the western front.

But then, the 5th Army itself has a potential Aachen in Bologna. Of those 27 divisions in Italy, the

(Continued on Page 8)

Rotation Of 30,000 Men Monthly Called Maximum

WASHINGTON, Oct. 18 (ANS)—The War Department, reporting it now is returning to this country approximately 30,000 men monthly, says it cannot increase the number substantially and continue to press the war "vigorously to an early conclusion."

The report to the House Military Committee was prepared as a result of increasing requests for furloughs for men serving abroad. To permit the return of even 30,000 men monthly, the Department said, "we must immobilize four to seven times this number, or the equivalent of eight to 14 divisions. For every man we add to this number being returned, the army would lose the effective use of from four to seven additional soldiers."

Selections of individuals to be returned under the quotas assigned to the overseas commanders, the report explained, is "the sole responsibility of the authorities in the theater."

Determination is based on local conditions with consideration given to the length of service of each individual, his value to his unit and the morale of individuals in the unit, including the extent of rebuilding of mind and body which is required.

"In no instance can a soldier be assured he will be returned as soon

(Continued on Page 8)

Daily German Lesson

Sprechen Sie langsam

Sprechen Zee lahngzahm

Speak slowly

New York — London Edition — Paris

THE STARS AND STRIPES

Daily Newspaper of U.S. Armed Forces in the European Theater of Operations

VOL. 4 No. [illegible]—1d. SATURDAY, Oct. 21, 1944

Daily French Lesson

Je vous remercie de m'avoir offert a boire

Juh voo remairSEE duh mav-war o-fair a bwar

Thanks for the drink

Nazis Lose First Big City as Aachen Falls

* * * * * * * * *

Smash Inland on Philippine Isle

A Testimonial To Hitler Cry: O, My Aachen Back

U.S. Army Signal Corps Photo

This pock-marked dwelling-house, like many others in fallen Aachen, seems smitten by a bad case of smallpox after the city's terrific bombing and shelling. U.S. engineers are shown clearing debris as the battle raged just ahead.

Reds Capture Belgrade; Push On in Hungary

Soviet armies yesterday captured Belgrade, capital of Jugoslavia, and the Hungarian communications center of Debrecen, 115 miles east of Budapest, while on the East Prussian front a relentless Russian offensive overran 15 miles of Reich border and seized an estimated 40 square miles of German territory.

Fall of Belgrade and Debrecen was announced by Marshal Stalin last night in separate orders of the day.

Shortly afterward the Moscow communique announced an enemy force southwest of Belgrade had been "liquidated" with a loss to the Germans of 9,000 killed and 8,000 captured.

Belgrade, mopped up with the aid of Marshal Tito's Jugoslav Partisans, was the seventh capital to be entered by the

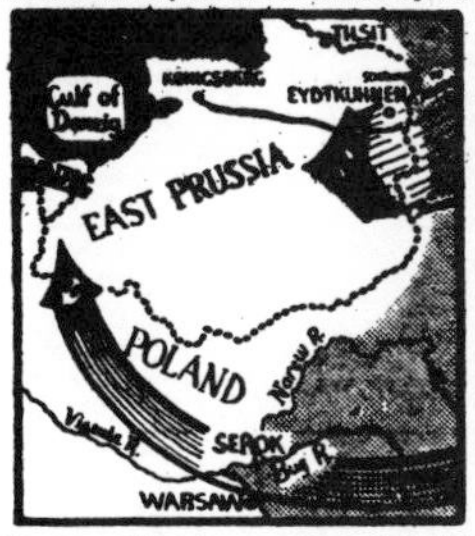

Russians—following upon Helsinki, Tallinn, Riga, Kaunas, Bucharest and Sofia.

Debrecen's seizure came on the 13th day of a gigantic tank battle still raging south of the city. Almost simultaneous with Moscow's announcement of its capture, German News Agency's Col. Ernst von Hammer reported a Soviet armored spearhead had reached a railway town 30 miles beyond Debrecen—suggesting the Russians were moving through Hungary much faster than their communiques indicated.

Moscow still cloaked the Red Army's two-way blow at East Prussia in operational silence, but German reports indicated the Russians to the north had pushed within 30 miles of the rail hub of Insterburg.

Churchill Quits Moscow And Stalin Sees Him Off

MOSCOW, Oct. 20 (UP)—Prime Minister Churchill and Foreign Secretary Anthony Eden left Moscow today after an 11-day visit.

They were seen off at the airport by Marshal Stalin, the first time Stalin personally has bade farewell to any foreign leaders.

Trap SS Remnants In Aachen's Outskirts

The week-long battle for Aachen ended at 3:30 PM yesterday when U.S. First Army doughboys cleared the last fanatical SS troops from the ruined frontier city—the first German city of importance to fall in this war.

A small pocket of Germans was still holding out beyond the city limits, but the city itself was completely in the hands of Lt. Gen. Courtney H. Hodges's army.

Dispatches said that for all practical purposes Aachen was destroyed. Its famed cathedral was almost undamaged, however, indicating how accurately American guns and Allied planes had struck against purely military objectives in the punishment administered the city after the Nazi commander had rejected surrender terms offered on Oct. 10.

Ordered by Hitler to hold the city at all costs, because its fall would have an ominous significance for every other city in the Third Reich, the SS troops held out to the last.

A 155-mm. gun literally blew apart the building which the Nazis had turned into a last strongpoint.

"Aachen is ours," said an American officer at the front. "When we knocked out that building we knocked out the guts of their defense. Now we hold all of the city proper and have only a clean-up job in the outskirts."

Casualties are Light

A correspondent broadcasting from the front said the casualties in the battle for the city were the lightest ever sustained in an action of this kind.

The fight for Aachen was a battle within a battle, for while the Americans inside the city had been beating down the SS garrison other First Army units had thrown back repeated German counter-attacks against the encircling forces.

Now the SS troops—estimated to number between 500 and 1,000—have been forced into a narrow trap in the outskirts of Aachen. About 2,000 of the garrison have been captured since the battle began.

Apparently realizing the city was lost to them, the Germans turned heavy artillery against Aachen Wednesday

(*Continued on page* 4)

Planes Sweep Rhine Valley

Communications in the Rhine Valley were attacked yesterday by 150 Ninth Air Force fighter-bombers, while Italy-based 15th Air Force heavies plastered German, Czechoslovak and Italian targets.

About 30 Lightnings fought a battle over Cologne with 36 enemy fighters, of which ten were shot down. Seven U.S. fighters are missing.

The heavies bombed oil-storage facilities on the Danube at Regensburg, 60 miles north of Munich, and objectives near Crus, 50 miles northeast of Prague.

More than 1,000 RAF heavy bombers blasted Stuttgart and Nuremburg, electrical and engineering centers in the Reich, Thursday night. A lighter attack was made on Weisbaden in the Rhineland.

Bad weather curtailed operations by British-based U.S. heavies yesterday.

'Big Bertha' Weans a Baby

WITH U.S. THIRD ARMY, Oct. 20 (AP)—A German offspring of "Big Bertha," the gun which was used in the last war to shell Paris, has made its appearance on Lt. Gen. George S. Patton's front and has been lobbing 700-pound shells loosely over a wide area.

The big railway gun has been playing hide and seek in the area between Metz and Nancy, firing a few hours in one area and then a few hours in another for some weeks.

A censorship ban on news that the gun was operating was lifted today. Firing at a range of more than 30 miles, the gun is inaccurate in the extreme and the gunners are lucky if hits are scored within a mile of targets aimed at.

It is useful only for harassing fire against big targets like cities.

Three New Features Monday

The Stars and Stripes will present three new features to its readers in Monday's edition—a photoquiz contest, a crossword puzzle and our readers' answer to the question: "How do you explain the continued frenzy on the part of American girls for Frank Sinatra?"

Gale Blows Itself Out After Killing at Least 26

CHARLESTON, S.C., Oct. 20 (ANS)—The tropical hurricane which killed at least 26 persons and caused property damage in Florida and Cuba was diminishing in force today, although weather officials predicted flood tides in both Carolinas.

All warnings south of Savannah, Ga., were ordered lowered and hurricane flags were replaced by storm warnings from Savannah to Charleston. It was estimated that the wind inflicted $20,000,000 damage to Florida's citrus crop.

Corregidor Veterans Among Invaders at H-Hour of Revenge

GEN. MacARTHUR'S HQ IN THE PHILIPPINES, Oct. 20 (AP)—American troops were driving inland toward the fertile valleys of Leyte Island tonight in a powerfull shell- and bomb-prepared invasion which brought Gen. Douglas A. MacArthur, accompanied by every able-bodied survivor of Corregidor, back to the Philippines.

Operations are proceeding according to schedule tonight. The Japanese were caught strategically off guard by the attack.

MacArthur said, in a message to Gen. George C. Marshall, U.S. Army chief of staff, that his troops had sustained "extremely light losses," and that the enemy was taken unawares because he expected an attack farther to the south.

The attack left the Japanese forces on Mindanao—large island just south of Leyte—"no longer important" because they are practically cut off.

MACARTHUR

In one of the most dramatic strokes of the war, MacArthur thrust his advanced headquarters 600 miles north from Morotai, split the Japanese defenses in half and brought his forces within 415 miles of the Philippine capital, Manila.

The ground forces which poured ashore in the Gulf of Leyte from a huge convoy under the protection of a terrific naval and air bombardment knifed their way on to the east coast of Leyte Island and swiftly seized three strong beachheads along an 11-mile stretch.

While the American troops were pouring ashore from northern and southern attack forces under shattering fire from battleships, cruisers and destroyers, augmented by hundreds of Adm. William F. Halsey's fighters and bombers, rocket-firing ships were working close inshore, lending direct support to the infantry.

On D-Day-minus-three, a combat team landed on the northern tip of Dinagat Island and on the southern portion of Homohon Island bordering the entrance to Leyte Gulf, securing and capturing enemy installations.

Set Marker Beacons

These forces set small marker beacons as a guide for the convoy.

Prior to D-Day, minesweeping units and special naval demolition squads cleared the approaches to the objective area. Tons of steel from naval units blasted the landing areas in preliminary bombardment attacks yesterday and last night.

While his troops were thrusting into Leyte, MacArthur told the Filipino people in a broadcast that he had fulfilled his vow to return, made 2½ years ago, and that he had brought with him the Philippines president, Sergio Osmena, and his cabinet, who have already re-established their government on Philippine soil.

MacArthur called on the people to "rise and strike" their Japanese conquerors.

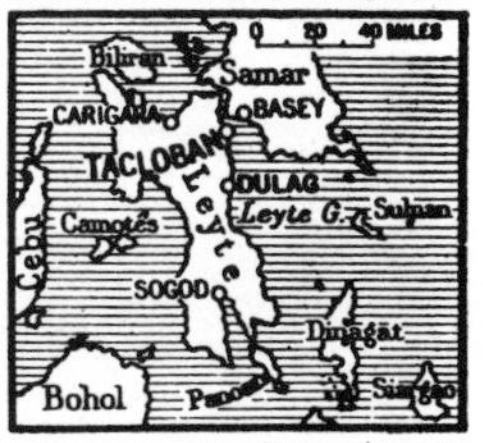

Stars and Stripes Map

One Jap Plane Rose to Battle In Philippines

By Dean Schedler

Associated Press War Correspondent

WITH MacARTHUR AT LEYTE, Oct. 20—Unopposed by Japan's Navy, American battleships and American and Australian cruisers laid a thunderous fire along the beaches as U.S. troops stormed ashore on this island in the central Philippines.

At H-Hour an enemy plane appeared, but strong anti-aircraft fire from the warships brought it down.

As the heavy naval fire raised billowing columns of smoke, carrier-based planes from Adm. William F. Halsey's Third Fleet and Vice-Adm. Thomas C. Kinkaid's Seventh Fleet bombed and strafed the beach. High overhead Hellcat Avengers patrolled the sky. It was only minutes before the few salvos from 16-inch guns increased into a continuous barrage which echoed and re-echoed across San Pedro Bay.

With brazen boldness the great battleships worked slowly along the shore, splitting the air with belching flame as the guns cracked round after round over the heads of the crouching infantrymen.

As we moved up to the entrance of Leyte Gulf, this huge convoy stretched across the Pacific as far as the eye could see. In it was every available man who was lifted from Corregidor 2½ years ago.

This was one of the most far-reaching amphibious operations of all time—moving 1,300 miles from the starting-point. This huge convoy was assembled at bases in Dutch New Guinea on the afternoon of Oct. 13 (Friday the 13th). Ships of every description moved slowly into position, and we advanced in strict radio silence and a stealthy blackout.

Ahead of us and in the center of the convoy were transports packed with hundreds of battle-rested jungle troops and equipment. Around them were landing craft of all descriptions and sizes.

5th and 8th Take Towns in Italy

ALLIED HQ, Italy, Oct. 20 (Reuter)—Eighth Army troops today smashed into Cesena, first big town up the Rimini-Bologna road, breaking through a stubborn defense.

On the Fifth Army front, American troops captured Lorenzone, 6½ miles from the Rimini-Bologna highway.

American troops attempting to drive northward on the Florence-Bologna road from Poggioli, nine miles from Bologna, met strong counter-attacks.

Death Sentence for Laval

A Marseilles court yesterday passed a sentence of death on Pierre Laval, in his absence, Algiers radio reported. The Vichy leader was accused of collaboration with the enemy.

No Jungle to Fight on Leyte

LEYTE ISLAND, Oct. 20 (AP)—For the first time since Gen. MacArthur started fighting his way back to the Philippines his army will have room to maneuver. Previously his troops have always had to fight a jungle campaign.

Leyte is the eighth largest Philippine island, and orderly rows of palm trees fringe the sandy beaches of the eastern coastline for 40 miles south of Tacloban.

Skirting the coast is an all-weather road joined at several points by lateral roads leading through a broad valley.

MacArthur's artillery will have wide fields of fire in the battle for the valley roads and for the island's half-dozen airfields, of which Tacloban, three miles from the town, is the most important.

Nature may take a hand in the battle. This is the beginning of the rainy season and near the end of the typhoons. Scores of rivers and streams criss-cross Leyte Valley.

ELECTION EXTRA

New York — London Edition — Paris

THE STARS AND STRIPES

Daily Newspaper of U.S. Armed Forces in the European Theater of Operations

VOL. 5 No. 6—1d. WEDNESDAY Nov. 8, 1944

ELECTION EXTRA

Roosevelt Wins

In War as in Peace—the Champ

Opposition Concedes After Early Returns In Record Balloting

Franklin D. Roosevelt's re-election to an unprecedented fourth term was proclaimed by the New York Times early this morning as the President swung into a substantial lead over Gov. Thomas E. Dewey in the four pivotal states of New York, Pennsylvania, Illinois and Massachusetts.

Almost at the same moment, with Mr. Roosevelt leading in 29 states on the basis of early returns, the New York Daily News, probably the President's bitterest opponent, conceded his re-election.

Nearly two hours earlier, Vice-President Henry A. Wallace announced to newsmen: "Roosevelt will occupy the White House until 1948."

Democratic National Chairman Robert Hannegan made it official a few minutes after the Times and Daily News by claiming victory for Mr. Roosevelt at 11.49 PM New York time (4.49 AM, BST).

There was no immediate comment from Gov. Dewey, listening to the returns at Republican headquarters in the Roosevelt Hotel, but a high-ranking Republican leader told Reuter:

"It now appears Roosevelt has won re-election."

Returns were far from complete, but Mr. Roosevelt early this morning was leading Gov. Dewey in upstate New York by some 31,000 to 27,000. None of these included New York City.

In Pennsylvania, where the President piled up a 115,000 plurality in seven-eighths of Philadelphia, 1,333 precincts out of 8,208 gave Mr. Roosevelt 409,390 to Dewey's 334,128.

One-fourth of Illinois gave the President 633,495 and Dewey 450,735. A substantial part of this came from Democratic Chicago.

Scant early returns from Massachusetts, with none of heavily Democratic Boston yet tabulated, gave Mr. Roosevelt 20,964 and 20,920.

At 5 AM (London time) this morning New York tabulations showed the Democratic standard-bearer leading incomplete returns from 32 states with 387 electoral votes, 105 more than the necessary majority for election.

The breakdown of the popular vote at that hour was: Roosevelt 11,795,000, or 54.7 per cent, and Dewey 5,347,000.

It was one of the heaviest votes in years, and United Press said there were indications it might equal or exceed the 1940 record polling of nearly 50,000,000 voters. Early and heavy voting was reported in the nation's industrial areas.

What influence the soldiers' vote had

(*Continued on page 4*)

GIs Crawl Through Mud To Vote In Holland

Shortly after midnight last night, David Anderson, American radio reporter, broadcast this picture of voting at the front in Holland:

"Just 20 minutes ago the polls closed here for the soldier vote. The task of assuring each man his democratic privilege was not easy. Officers crawled on their stomachs through rain-soaked peat and bog to accept the votes of doughboys in forward slit trenches. They reached into the jowls of tanks to take them from the hands of crew members. Tanks came from near and far with sealed ballots which will ultimately be opened in America."

Election Notes

Nutbush In First

FIRST returns in yesterday's election came from the tiny precinct of Nutbush, in Vance County, N.C., where every ballot had been counted by 10 AM. As usual, all 21 registered voters backed the Democratic candidate.

The village of Pratt City, Kan., polled 30 votes for Dewey against 27 for Roosevelt. Mashpee, Mass., recorded 51 for Dewey, 44 for Roosevelt. Chickasha, Okla., had 35 for Dewey, 23 for Roosevelt.

Mt. Washington, first Massachusetts town to report, gave Dewey 29, Roosevelt 8.

* * *

Mayor Fiorello LaGuardia of New York voted in Manhattan, and as he stood in line he saw a girl who had become tangled up in the booth's curtain. The Mayor hastily shouted instructions to her to extricate herself.

At the same time, President Roosevelt was voting at Hyde Park. He, too, got all tangled up with the curtain.

* * *

PARIS, Nov. 7 (AP)—The American election took top play in Paris newspapers today, most of them linking their stories with the government's invitation to President Roosevelt and Secretary of State Cordell Hull to visit Paris.

* * *

HQ, FIRST BOMBER DIVISION, Nov. 7—While a bunch of officers were shooting the Election Day breeze in the commissioned barber shop here, the barber—Sgt. R. D. Byrom, of Huntsville, Ala.—put in a couple of words on his special interest in the election. "You see, he said, "my full name is Roosevelt Dewey Byrom."

* * *

"ELECTION day dawned in a cold and cheerless drizzle on the Western Front," Larry Le Sueur, CBS reporter, told America in a broadcast yesterday from Holland. "The war in the West seems to have almost paused while you in America will decide the election. The doughboys themselves will be listening to election results on captured German radio sets.

"But most of the men who have been fighting all day will be asleep in their pup tents and in their water-logged foxholes.

"Gen. Eisenhower will get the election news at the front. 'Ike' seemed almost casual about the election when he left Supreme Headquarters today and visited

(*Continued on page 4*)

Allies, Nazis, Dutch Jam A Town, Nobody Fights

After carrying out naval maneuvers on land, British troops yesterday entered the Walcheren Island capital of Middelburg and found themselves in the swirling midst of a comic opera setting, where neither they nor the Germans could fight each other because the town was so packed with cheering Dutch civilians and troops that a shot might hit friend as easily as foe.

It was a situation that military strategists probably never conceived. While the British, after using boats and amphibious vehicles to cross the flooded fields outside the town, sought to restore order once they entered, Dutch refugees from other parts of the island and German troops milled about the streets in confusion. The Dutch welcomed the Allies with shouts, and the Germans, glum faced, were powerless to do anything but look on.

Middelburg, in the island's center, was estimated to contain almost double its 20,000 peacetime population. Amid the turmoil it was impossible to fight, though a few scattered clashes did occur. Reports said the Germans gave up easily, with about 2,000 prisoners already taken.

The First Army's battle for Vossenack, southeast of Aachen, was summed up in an American officer's report, as follows: "In the upper part of this town there are

(*Continued on page 4*)

Amnesty in France

The deGaulle government has pardoned all persons sentenced under military law before June 17, 1940, provided they worked in the Resistance Movement after that date, Paris radio reported yesterday.

Weather Halts Eighth Heavies

Adverse weather curtailed operations by the Eighth Air Force yesterday after a night in which RAF Lancasters bombed Coblenz and other objectives in western Germany.

However, Italy-based 15th Air Force Fortresses attacked the Vienna area yesterday for the sixth time in six days, while Liberators bombed the Brenner Pass.

Meanwhile, Lt. Col. Oris Johnson, who commands a Ninth Air Force night-fighter group of P61 Black Widows, disclosed yesterday that the Germans were sending up jet-fighters by night in increasing numbers.

"On recent nights we've counted 15 to 20 jet planes," he said. "They sometimes fly in formations of four, but often fly alone."

In approximately 560 sorties Monday Ninth fighter-bombers carried out several operations in close support of U.S. troops in the Aachen sector.

191 Jap Planes KOd at Luzon

American carrier-based planes sank one Japanese warship, damaged five others and destroyed 191 planes in surprise raids on Manila and southern Luzon Saturday, Adm. Chester W. Nimitz announced yesterday at Pearl Harbor.

One heavy cruiser was left burning and sinking, and a light cruiser and three destroyers were damaged.

According to Tokyo Radio, B29 Superforts flew over Tokyo yesterday but were driven off. The Japs said also that the Superforts had bombed the Volcanic Islands Sunday and that other U.S. planes raided the Bonin Islands.

New York Radio said yesterday that enemy opposition had ceased on Leyte Island in the Philippines.

Pledges Full Probe Of Moyne Murder

Declaring that Britain had suffered a heavy loss in the assassination at Cairo Monday of Lord Moyne, British resident minister in the Middle East, Prime Minister Churchill told the House of Commons yesterday that a full investigation of the two "foul assassins" would be made to determine the motive for the crime.

Lord Moyne died an hour after he had been shot. The two assassins were captured and nearly lynched.

Nebraska Dry Vote Just One Of Many Sidelight Issues

Stars and Stripes U.S. Bureau

NEW YORK, Nov. 7—While the Presidential contest held the center of the stage in the U.S. election today, the final vote tally will decide a number of other interesting issues in the wings.

Nebraska voted on a prohibition amendment to its Constitution which would make the state dry. Members of the State's 134th Infantry Regiment, now in France, have gone on record against the imposition of prohibition now, in their absence.

Three states—Arkansas, California and Florida—voted on virtually identical constitutional amendments aimed at the closed shop. They provide, in effect, that no worker should be compelled to join a union in order to get or hold a job. Both the AFL and CIO fought the amendments strenuously.

In the realm of personalities these were the feature state races today:

CALIFORNIA

The bid of Actress Helen Gahagan, wife of screen star Melvyn Douglas, for a seat in Congress from the 14th District. She is running as a Democrat and is opposed by William D. Campbell, Republican, former attorney of the Justice and Treasury departments and campaign manager for Gov. Earl Warren.

CONNECTICUT

Playwright Clare Booth Luce's quest of a second term in Congress from the Fourth District on the Republican ticket. Her Democratic opponent is a woman, Margaret E. Connors, 29, lawyer and former G-woman.

IOWA

White-haired Sen. Guy M. Gillette's contest for re-election—he is now the only Iowa Democrat in either the State or House. He is opposed by Gov. Bourke B. Hickenlooper, Republican.

KENTUCKY

The Republican effort to unseat Sen. Alben W. Barkley, Senate Democratic

(*Continued on page 4*)

Daily German Lesson
Wo ist der Weg nach der Stadt?
Vo ist der Vayk nakhh der Stahdt?
Where is the road to town?

New York — London Edition — Paris

THE STARS AND STRIPES

Daily Newspaper of U.S. Armed Forces in the European Theater of Operations

VOL. 5 No. 21—1d. SATURDAY, Nov. 25, 1944

Daily French Lesson
S'il vous plait, [illegible]
Seel voo play, [illegible]
Please show me

Report First Units Cross Rhine; Supers Hit Tokyo From Saipan

Arnold Says 'Battle for Japan' Is On

Superforts of the new 21st Bomber Command yesterday gave Tokyo its second raid of the war, opening up what was described officially as the "Battle for Japan" in a 1,500-mile flight from Saipan, in the Marianas, conquered on July 8.

"We took them by surprise again," said Brig. Gen. Emmett O'Donnell, who led the Superforts, upon his return to Saipan after the heaviest air blow yet hurled against Japan's war industry areas. "Certainly they weren't up to meet us in their fighters. It was one of the easiest missions I've been on." Anti-aircraft fire was meager and inaccurate, he said.

O'Donnell flew in the first Superfort over Tokyo, which was piloted by Maj. Robert Morgan, who flew the famous "Memphis Belle" while serving with a

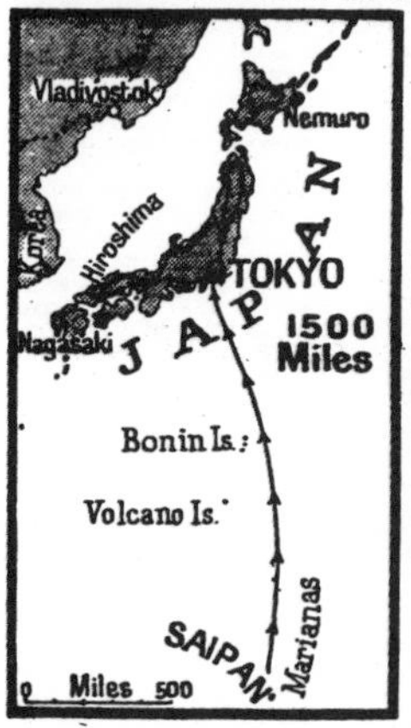

Fortress unit of the Eighth Air Force in Britain.

Important military objectives were hit, including the Nakajima aircraft factory, it was reported.

Yesterday's daylight strike against Tokyo was the first since April 18, 1942, when Mitchell bombers, under command of Jimmy Doolittle, took off from the carrier Hornet, since sunk, to rock the Japanese capital in one of the most elaborately planned surprises of the war. Doolittle, now a lieutenant general, commands the Eighth Air Force.

The Superforts took off at one-minute intervals at dawn and headed northwest in nine- and 12- plane formations. Some left from Isely airdrome, once the main Jap base in the Marianas but now only one of the series of Superfort bases already built or building on Saipan and near-by Guam and Timian Islands.

Gen. Henry H. Arnold, Army Air

(Continued on page 4)

Belfort Flight Cut Short for Nazi Officer

U.S. Army Signal Corps Photo

Trying to escape in a staff car when the French First Army took Belfort, this Nazi officer wound up in a ditch, wounded, and a prisoner of a French infantryman.

Canada Riots Protest Draft

OTTAWA, Nov. 24—Anti-conscription riots flared up in Quebec today as Prime Minister W. L. Mackenzie King struggled to keep his government intact in Canada's most critical cabinet crisis in 20 years.

The Prime Minister touched off the demonstrations yesterday when he announced the government's decision to proceed with partial conscription and to send overseas 16,000 Canadian soldiers—possibly including some conscripted Home Defense troops—as reinforcements during the next few months. Canada previously sent only volunteers overseas.

Gen. Andrew L. McNaughton, new Defense Minister, who took the floor in the House of Commons following the Prime Minister's announcement, said the move was necessary because efforts to raise sufficient volunteer reinforcements had not been adequate.

McNaughton explained, however, that he thought future reinforcement needs would be met on a voluntary basis. Some political observers believed this compromise offer on the conscription issue would enable the Liberal government to remain in power despite a Conservative Party motion for formation of a new government

Soon after the announcement C. G. Power, Air Minister, who opposed conscription for overseas service, resigned.

8th Army Drives Over Cosina River

Eighth Army troops have established a beachhead across the Cosina River along a two and a half-mile front and are pushing on towards Faenza, Allied Headquarters in Italy announced yesterday. The Germans reported the new situation critical, Reuter said.

British armor, rolling across five bridges, captured intact when the Cosina was breached, met fierce opposition from German Tiger tanks sent to wipe out the beachhead.

Black Market Feels Pinch As Freeze Grips Smokes

By Walter B. Smith
Stars and Stripes Staff Writer

LIVERPOOL, Nov. 24—The case of the missing cigarettes today had become so far-reaching in U.K. Western Base Section that even the operators in the once flourishing cigarette black market in Liverpool joined in the familiar chant—"Where are the butts?"

Meanwhile, thousands of cases of cigarettes stored in huge warehouses along Liverpool's 15-mile dock district were reported frozen this morning—presumably pending Gen. Eisenhower's investigation and completion of the new plan for Com Z distribution. Previously a large percentage of these bulk supplies had been earmarked for the Continent.

'Shipments Fairly Regular'

An officer at one of the largest depots in Western Base Section, unable to explain the shortage, said automatic shipments from the U.S. had been "fairly regular" of late, although he added that demand had "increased."

Sgt. Paul V. Carew, peace-time police lieutenant in South Orange, N.J., and now a special agent for Port Intelligence, told The Stars and Stripes that Liverpool black marketeers now had no more cigarettes than GI clerk typists.

He added that these operators were just as baffled by the shortage as were soldiers.

While port-supply officials here professed complete bewilderment as to the cause of the shortage, a thorough check of port police records proved conclusively that pilfering from the docks was not the answer.

11 of 12 Cases Recovered

Studying detailed theft reports, covering every PX ship which entered Liverpool in the last three months, this reporter discovered that loss of cigarettes through dock pilferage was only a fraction of one per cent.

The only incident of any size in the last eight months involved 12 cases of Lucky Strikes, totaling 120,000 cigarettes. Eleven of the cases were recovered. Even

(Continued on page 4)

Reds in Latvia Open New Push

Russian forces in Latvia, preceded by a gigantic artillery barrage, yesterday started a double offensive to wipe out the Nazi Northern Army Corps of an estimated 300,000 men.

Moscow said nothing about the new drive, but Berlin reported an all-out Soviet drive was under way, one force pushing ahead in the Auce area, about 55 miles southwest of Riga, and the other driving toward the Baltic port of Liepaja, 70 miles west of Auce.

The Germans admitted the Red Army had penetrated their lines in several points east of Liepaja.

Meanwhile, Stalin announced that Oesel Island, guarding the entrance to the Gulf of Riga, had been cleared of Germans, completing the liberation of all Estonian territory.

The new attack in the north was made without any slowing up of the giant attacks in the Balkans, where the entire German line from Czechoslovakia down to southern Hungary was being slowly forced back.

Heavy fighting continued around Budapest, where fresh German and Hungarian reserves were thrown into the line.

German V2 Factory Smashed by Forts

A V2 rocket components and assembly plant near Weimar, Germany, southeast of Leipzig, was almost destroyed Aug. 24 by Fortresses of the Eighth Air Force, it was disclosed yesterday. Approximately 130 heavies laid down a concentrated and accurate pattern of bombs.

Eighth aircraft were grounded yesterday by adverse weather.

Floods Help Foe Stiffen, Limit Gains

Advance U.S. and French reconnaissance units were reported yesterday, without verification, to have crossed the Rhine east of Strasbourg, which was entirely in Allied hands except for a small German bridgehead at the western end of the main Rhine bridge.

If the reports of the crossing are confirmed, these Allied troops will have been the first to cross the flood-swollen water barrier into the Reich.

American infantry had reached Strasbourg, where the Germans held perimeter positions around each of the three Rhine bridges, which were still intact. Germans holding out in forts around the city were restricting movement in and out by occasional mortar and machine-gun fire, and Siegfried Line guns were said to have shelled the center of the city. Troops entering the city found it lined with orderly crowds, cheering and waving flags.

A dispatch from Strasbourg said "the big push definitely is in high gear," and added that the roads into the city from the west were choked with hundreds of tanks and thousands of tons of war goods heading for the Rhine. More than 3,000 prisoners have been taken in Strasbourg, including two German generals.

Patton Across the Saar

A dispatch from the Third Army front said Lt. Gen. George S. Patton's troops had crossed the Saar River near [illegible], 26 miles south of Saarbruecken. Other troops on the left flank of these units were previously reported only 15 miles from Saarbruecken. The Saar had been described as one of the chief water barriers which the Germans would fight hard to hold.

Third Army forces kept up steady pressure along their 11-mile front inside Germany, with tank units making slow gains against innumerable tank obstacles. Patrols were reported to have entered Merzig, and fighting was going on in Tettingen, ten miles northwest. One of the five forts bypassed outside Metz was reported to have been taken, but the other four, manned by about 3,000 troops, still held out.

On the front inside Germany, enemy resistance against the Americans and British striking for the Ruhr industrial area was reported to have been stiffened greatly. Dispatches from the Ninth Army said the doughboys of Lt. Gen. William H. Simpson were now meeting the fiercest opposition. Despite enemy blows and mire-making rains, the Ninth captured the town of Pattern, three miles south of Julich, and repulsed counter-attacks near Gereonsweiler. Merzen-

(Continued on page 4)

GI Promises 'Justice' When We Get to Berlin

"There is nothing that will stop us now and we shall not stop before Berlin," declared an American doughboy yesterday over the Luxembourg radio in a message to German troops.

"You must understand that we are coming to weed out the evil among you and not to destroy you all," he said. "Justice is our motto, and that is what you will receive. Fanaticism for Hitler must be wiped out. If you understand that then we'll get along, but if you continue with this hopeless fight then you must surely take the consequences."

Jap Carrier Has Its Mortal Wound

A Jap carrier, already hit by U.S. planes, ploughs through waters off the Philippines, trying to avert further damage. The craft finally took one too many, heeled over and sank.

Witch on a Joy Stick

Ghost Disguised as Flying Fort Makes Perfect 3-Point Landing

29TH TACTICAL AIR FORCE HQ, Nov. 24 (UP)—A Flying Fortress, with its inboard engines out of action and the propellers feathered, made a perfect landing in a plowed field in Belgium—minus its crew.

The plane landed on a field near a British gun position guarding an Allied air base. Gunners rushed to see if they could help the crew, but found no one in or around the bomber.

Pfc John Wright, of Lake Placid, N.Y., received word at this headquarters from British liaison of a damaged U.S. plane landing. He notified a near-by fighter base, where an ambulance driven by Pfc Gilbert Simonsen, of Yankton, S.D., was dispatched to the scene.

Simonsen talked to Belgian farmers who saw the B17 land, but they insisted no one was in the plane when it came down.

U.S. officials believed the bomber landed under the control of its automatic pilot. Three parachutists were reported to have landed near by, but there have been no further reports of these three or any other possible parachute landings.

THE STARS AND STRIPES

MEDITERRANEAN

Vol. 2, No. 51, Saturday, November 25, 1944 — Printed In Italy — TWO LIRE

SUPER FORTS BOMB TOKYO

Allies Gain Possession Of Strasbourg

Grimmest Fighting Of Campaign Rages In Northern Sector

SHAEF, Nov. 24—All of the great city of Strasbourg except for a small bridgehead covering the main bridge over the Rhine River was reported in Allied hands tonight. A correspondent with the American 7th Army reported that reconnaissance elements had crossed the Rhine east of Strasbourg.

Earlier today it had been announced that French troops in Lorraine were fighting in the heart of the city while near the northern end of the 400-mile battleline British and American forces were locked with crack Nazi divisions in some of the bitterest struggles of the war.

A Paris radio report, without confirmation from front-line dispatches quoted the French War Minister to the effect that Strasbourg had been liberated. The broadcast said that General LeClerc's 2nd Armored Division, spearheading a drive from the northeast by the American 7th Army, had freed the key communications and industrial center and last major French city held by the Nazis.

Strasbourg was one of the key positions of the Maginot Line and its occupation would give Lt. Gen. Alexander M. Patch's 7th Army a kickoff point to move southward

(Continued on page 8)

Catroux New French Envoy To Russia

PARIS, Nov. 24—General Georges Catroux, who has been one of General Charles de Gaulle's staunchest lieutenants, has been appointed French Ambassador to the Soviet Union, the Provisional Government announced today.

General Catroux was governor general of Indo-China in 1940 when the Japanese demanded the right to send their troops into the country. He refused to accede to this request and was ousted by the Vichy Government. He went to England and joined the Free French movement. He led Free French forces, and his last job was Minister-Delegate for North African Affairs in the French Provisional Government.

On the French home front the purge of collaborators went on. Edouard Germonprez Carpenter was shot to death by a firing squad after being convicted of bearing arms against his country and giving information to the enemy, it was announced today. Evidence submitted before a military tribunal indicated he had been responsible for the death of some 30 Frenchmen during the German occupation.

Justin Bonnet and Jean Larue were executed at Angouleme yesterday after being found guilty of "intelligence with the enemy and treason." Emanuel Parbiere, a Vichy official, was sentenced to death for allowing the Gestapo to terrorize the region around Vichy under his control. Gabriel Bordeaux, who was also sentenced to death in Vichy some days ago, was executed there yesterday.

ROME SEES ITALIAN TROOPS

No Fascist Army, this! Detachments of some of the newly equipped and reorganized Italian units were in Rome yesterday. Equipped primarily with British equipment, they were greeted enthusiastically by Rome citizens. The troops had come from training camps in southern Italy.

(Staff Photo by Sgt. Grayson B. Tewksbury)

Thought Of Gals' West Point Frightens Folks In Pentagon

By Army News Service

WASHINGTON, Nov. 24—All five sides of the Pentagon building shuddered today when War Department officials were asked to comment on a bill providing for a woman's West Point, introduced by Rep. Eugene Cox (D., Ga.), International News Service reported.

A one-star general of the Army Service Forces which controls the Army's school and training programs, said simply, "It's a horrible thought, but don't quote me on that."

A West Pointer assigned to the schools and training program settled back thoughtfully and said that the idea had much to recommend it. "Imagine an annual Army-Navy basketball game with girls' rules." He imagined it would be "very interesting."

Officers of the Army's postwar planning group remarked, "here we sit day after day trying to plot a bright and happy future for everyone while Congressman Cox goes around scaring the suspenders off people."

The Army Service Forces opinion on the issue is that some other plan for the postwar future of Wacs and military minded misses will have to be worked out later.

"The Army maintains West Point to train leaders for troops over a period of years," an Army Service Forces general explained. "We don't need it to turn out second lieutenants. We can do that in a matter of months. Women are so bright that they can learn to type or work a teletype or take shorthand or anything else that they could conceivably be called upon to do in even less time what it takes to turn out a good second looey.

"Unless they plan to make women major generals and let them plan strategy there is no excuse for a woman's West Point. Unless we plan an Amazon society, the idea is pointless," he added.

Another Service Forces brasshat was fascinated by the domestic relations the problem raised.

"Don't women want husbands any more," he wondered, "or do they think that their husbands will

(Continued on page 8)

Keep National Guard Alive, Stimson Urges

WASHINGTON, Nov. 24 (ANS)—The War Department believes the National Guard should be continued in the postwar period as a component of the Reserve Army of the United States ready to serve anywhere.

Secretary of War Henry L. Stimson said today he had approved a report from the National Guard committee of the General Staff recommending that "we maintain as part of our peacetime military establishment a National Guard capable of immediate expansion to war strength."

The Secretary said: "It would be the mission of this reserve component in the event of a national emergency to furnish units fit for service anywhere in the world."

Basically the training would be pointed toward the defense of critical areas in the United States against land, seaborne or airborne invasion and assistance in covering mobilization and concentration of reserve forces, but the units, Stimson also said, would be capable of integration into groups.

He asserted that this conception of the new mission of the National Guard "would interfere in no way with the traditional mission of the National Guard of the states and territories," to function in the protection of life and property and the preservation of order under state authorities.

Planes Make Hop From Saipan Bases

WASHINGTON, Nov. 24—Tokyo, heart of the Japanese Empire, was bombed today by American Super Fortresses striking in probably the largest force ever to hit Japan either from land or sea. The giant B-29s gave Tokyo its second bombing of the war, the first since Gen. Jimmy Doolittle's heroic airmen chilled the Japanese people with their bolt out of the blue on April 18, 1942.

The War Department announced that Japan's capital city was rocked by B-29s that struck at daylight, coming in just at noon. They ranged widely, bombing other great Nipponese centers of Yokohama and Kobe.

The Super Forts came from Saipan Island in the Marianas, the first land-based armada to raid Tokyo.

They were the planes of the newly-established 21st Bomber Command under Brig. Gen. H. S. Hansell, Jr., and part of the 20th Air Force. The appointment of Lt. Gen. Millard F. Harmon as deputy commander of the 20th was announced soon after by the War Department. He will direct operations in the Pacific of both the China-based Bomber Command and the Marianas-based 21st.

The Forts soared into the air toward the Japanese capital from fields that American engineers have been constructing with Tokyo in mind ever since the Yanks crushed the Japanese defenders on Saipan.

Their targets included hydro-electric plants and dams, Tokyo's highly inflammable industrial district, shipyards and shipping and repair docks around Yokohama Bay.

Gen. Henry H. Arnold, commander of the Army Air Forces, said: "Tokyo's war industries have been badly hurt by a blow made possible by Americans who fought and died for the Marianas. The attack should be convincing proof that these far Pacific Islands captured by our Army and Navy at great

(Continued on page 8)

New Stars & Stripes Weekly Out Sunday

Beginning tomorrow, the Stars and Stripes family will be increased by the addition of "The Sunday Stars and Stripes," a 16-page tabloid which every Sunday will carry features, pictures and a brief summary of the news of the day.

Distribution of the newspaper will be identical with that of the daily paper, and circulation offices will be open Sundays, except that the Leghorn office will close at 3 PM.

Price of the tabloid will be two lire; front-line troops will receive their copies free of charge.

Red Army Strikes In Slovakia Offense

LONDON, Nov. 24 — General Ivan Y. Petrov's 4th Ukrainian Army was striking today in eastern Czechoslovakia with a power that looked like a full-scale offensive. The drive appeared to threaten the enemy in northern Hungary from the rear and raised the possibility of a junction with Marshal Rodion Malinovsky's 2nd Ukrainian Army fighting northeast of Budapest.

Petrov's forces began their drive on a 30-mile front west of Uzhorod, 170 miles northeast of Budapest. After clearing almost all of Ruthenia, easternmost province of Czechoslovakia, they have invaded the puppet Axis state of Slovakia, which was also part of Czechoslovakia formerly. The drive gained at least 10 miles in the first day.

Important news came tonight from Marshal Stalin who, in a special Order of the Day, announced that the island of Oesel in the Gulf of Riga had been cleared of Germans in a joint action by the Red Army and the Russian Baltic fleet. Possession of the island will now enable the Russians to use the

(Continued on page 8)

Soviet Press Continues Attack On Franco Spain

MOSCOW, Nov. 24 (UP)—The Red Army paper, Red Star, continued today the press attack against Francisco Franco's Spain. It laid down the proposition that preparations for a stable peace and postwar collaboration among the Allied powers should include help for the struggle of democratic elements in Spain.

Konstantin Gofman, Red Star writer, charged that Franco is trying to strengthen his ties with reactionary circles in France.

8th Smashes Across Cosina At Five Points

ADVANCED ALLIED FORCE HEADQUARTERS, Nov. 24—In a day of very bitter fighting, British troops of the 8th Army forced five bridgeheads over the Cosina River yesterday and drove to within three and a half miles of the important Forli-Bologna road junction of Faenza.

British infantry attacked across the Cosina River on a two and a half-mile front from Route 9 to the vicinity of the river bend. They crossed the river against fierce infantry opposition and strong enemy artillery, mortar and machine gun support.

A bridge at the river bend was captured intact and British tanks crossed the river to support the infantry.

The five bridgeheads were quickly consolidated and extended to a depth of 500 yards. The Germans reacted quickly and launched a number of tank-supported counterattacks, all of which were driven back by British infantry and armor.

Although the bridge across the Cosina to Pugna was found blown, the village was quickly enveloped into the British bridgehead along the north bank of the river.

On the 5th Army front sparring

(Continued on page 8)

THE STARS AND STRIPES
MEDITERRANEAN

Vol. 1, No. 137, Wednesday, December 6, 1944 — Printed In Italy — TWO LIRE

Guns Of 3rd Army Shell Saarbrucken, Now Six Miles Away

Americans In Saarlautern Clear Nazis From Town, Cross Saar Bridge

SHAEF, Dec. 5—Saarbrucken, industrial center of the great Saar Valley, was under Allied artillery fire today as 3rd Army troops pushed to within six miles of the city from the south.

Ten miles to the west, other 3rd Army forces cleared the remnants of the German garrison from the section of Saarlautern on the east bank of the Saar River. The main bridge spanning the Saar at Saarlautern still was under the fire of heavy German guns but at last reports still was in use.

The renewed 3rd Army push from the south was begun without preliminary artillery preparations before dawn yesterday and front-line dispatches said that the Germans were taken by surprise. Gains of up to two and one-half miles were registered along a ten-mile front and strategic heights were quickly seized.

Saaguemund and Forbach, to the southeast of Saarbrucken, also were brought under artillery fire from heights three miles south of Forbach.

Meanwhile, to the northeast of Aachen, American 9th Army forces fighting along the west bank of the flooded Roer River, quelled all organized resistance in Julich with the occupation of the huge sports arena near the city which the Nazis had converted into a fortress. The stadium controlled the approaches to one of the best fords on the Roer and American tanks were employed before the Nazis were driven out.

In the Duren sector to the south,

(Continued on page 8)

Red Army Drives To Isolate Budapest

LONDON, Dec. 5—The German position in Hungary continued to deteriorate today as Marshal Fedor Tolbukhin's 3rd Ukrainian Army advanced in its westward, northwestward and northward pushes from the west bank of the Danube.

Last night's Soviet communique reported that Tolbukhin's men had taken more than 100 additional inhabited places, including eight railway stations. In three days this group has taken more than 3,000 prisoners.

Front-line dispatches today reported that the Russians had advanced to within 30 miles of Budapest along the west bank of the Danube. It was said that if the advance continued at the present pace the Germans would be forced to clear out of the Hungarian capital before the weekend or face encirclement.

In Yugoslavia between the Danube and Sava Rivers, Yugoslav troops in cooperation with Soviet forces have driven up the Sava Valley from Belgrade to liberate the important communication center of Mitrovica, the Soviet communique announced. Mitrovica is 40 miles northwest of Belgrade and is a junction for roads to Budapest, Zagreb, Ljubljana and Italy.

The Germans said that they were "operating elastically" between the Danube and Lake Balaton or retreating. They said that they had abandoned the town of Siofck on the east shore of Lake Balaton, 60 miles southwest of Budapest.

A United Press dispatch from Sofia said that a special Bulgarian Army Corps commanded by General Stoycheff had joined Tolbukhin's 3rd Ukrainian Army. By this action, the dispatch said, the Bulgarians were securing for themselves a place among the United Nations.

NEW JOB

JOSEPH C. GREW

Grew Is Nominated To Stettinius' Post

WASHINGTON, Dec. 5 (UP)—President Roosevelt today nominated Joseph C. Grew, former Ambassador to Japan, as Undersecretary of State, succeeding the post occupied by Edward R. Stettinius, Jr., before becoming Secretary of State.

The President also named three new assistant secretaries of state: William C. Clayton, Texas cotton broker, who is leaving the Surplus War Property Administration; Archibald McLeish, poet who heads the Congressional Library, and Nelson A. Rockefeller, who has been Coordinator of Inter-American Affairs.

Mr. Roosevelt accepted the resignations of the three current assistant secretaries of state, Adolf Berle, Jr., G. Howland Shaw, and Breckinridge Long.

In the new State Department realignment, Clayton will handle foreign economic affairs, Rockefeller will be in charge of Inter-American Relations, which will be a continuation of his present job, and McLeish will handle public cultural relations.

Mr. Roosevelt also informed the Senate that he would soon nominate Norman Armour, former Ambassador to Argentina, to an "important diplomatic post abroad." The President added that other appointments strengthening the State Department would be made in the near future.

Berle will remain as head of the United States delegation to the current Civil Aviation meeting in Chicago which is expected to end tomorrow. In the future, Clayton will

(Continued on page 8)

Key City Of Ravenna Taken By Canadians

ADVANCED ALLIED FORCE HEADQUARTERS, Dec. 5—The historically important city of Ravenna, one of the 8th Army's prime objectives in its drive up the Po plain, fell to Canadian troops yesterday morning without a fight, according to a special announcement made here late this afternoon.

Exploiting their recent capture of Russi, units of the Princess Louise Dragoon Guards, in a brilliant encircling movement, outflanked the city from the north and forced the Germans to withdraw.

After reaching positions north of the city, the Canadians cut back sharply, severing the main coastal highway running up from Rimini and entering the city from the northeast.

Partisan Formations Reported Controlling Part Of Athens

LONDON, Dec. 5—Fierce fighting was in progress in Athens today, with Partisan formations said to be in virtual control of some districts, and strong formations of armed forces of the left reported moving toward the Greek capital from several directions.

Reports that the government of Premier Georges Papandreou resigned today were not confirmed.

In a stormy debate in the House of Commons, British Prime Minister Winston Churchill today gave the first official indication that civil war was actually in progress in Greece less than one month after the liberation of Athens. Churchill, in a lengthy statement following numerous demands by Labor members for immediate House discussion of the Greek crisis, deplored "the civil war which we are trying to stop," adding that British troops are acting only to prevent bloodshed. This statement was greeted by Labor cries of "Oh!" to which Churchill slowly and emphatically repeated, "To prevent bloodshed."

Maj. Gen. Ronald M. Scobie, British military commander in Greece, last night issued an ultimatum to the forces of ELAS, armed militia of the left-wing National Liberation Front, to evacuate a large area around Athens and the port of Piraeus by midnight Wednesday, or be regarded and treated as "enemies."

There was no indication, however, that the left-wing troops had intentions of leaving. Reuter's said that a whole ELAS division had now infiltrated into the capital. Severe armed clashes broke out again today in the center of Athens.

At one point in the city, followers of the rightist EDES organization barricaded themselves in the Metropolis Hotel and began firing on ELAS troops with pistols, rifles and hand grenades. The left forces counterattacked with heavy weapons.

A United Press dispatch late tonight estimated that thus far 143 persons have been killed and 250 wounded in clashes yesterday and during the night. Mortars, the re-

(Continued on page 8)

New China Cabinet Summoned In Crisis

CHUNGKING, Dec. 5 — Calling upon Free China to rally and annihilate the Japanese armies now only 250 miles from the capital, Generalissimo Chiang Kai-shek today summoned his newly-liberalized Cabinet to discuss the grave military situation.

The Generalissimo, describing the state of China's affairs as "extremely difficult," added, however, that the Japanese penetration into Kweichow Province toward Kweiyang was "within our anticipation," and preparations were being made to meet it.

Chiang called his Cabinet together shortly after announcing the appointment of T. V. Soong as President of the Executive Yuan (Yuan means branch of government). Most administrative duties now will fall upon Dr. Soong, brother of Mme. Chiang and a liberal.

While Chiang's Cabinet planned Free China's defenses, Japanese columns were moving deeper into Kweichow Province in the general direction of Chungking. They were 15 miles deeper today than yesterday. Advance elements battled near Tushan, about 75 miles southeast of Kweiyang.

Meanwhile, American commanders, concerned over Japanese advances which threatened to nullify all their efforts in China, were more than quadrupling the tonnage of air transport planes carrying supplies to Burma Road engineers hurrying to get the Road into operation and implement the embattled Chinese before the Japanese can cut the lifeline to Chungking.

An increase of 400 percent in the total tonnage was reported in the past month. The Air Transport

(Continued on page 2)

Daughter Of Mussolini Weds, Becomes Mother

ROME, Dec. 5—Edda Mussolini, daughter of Il Duce and widow of Count Galeazzo Ciano, was recently married in Switzerland to Marchese Emilio Pucci of Florence, it was learned here today. Roman gossip had it that Edda was in love with the Marchese long before Count Ciano, who had been Foreign Minister under Mussolini, was shot by the Fascists with whom he had worked.

It is believed that Pucci crossed the border with Edda last February when she fled to Switzerland. It is also said by well informed people that Edda gave birth to a son at about the date of the new marriage.

Meanwhile, units of the British 27th Lancers, pushing up from the north bank of the Fiumi Uniti Canal, entered the city from the south.

[A dispatch filed by Sgt. Stan Swinton, a Stars and Stripes correspondent with the 8th Army, said that not a shot was fired as 8th Army troops entered Ravenna. He reported the Germans began to pull out Sunday night when a Canadian armored unit which thrust across the Po Valley plain from the west, outflanked the city.

"Townspeople said the enemy completed his evacuation at 7 AM Monday. A British patrol crossed the Uniti River in assault boats before noon. Other units followed

at 2 PM. Mines were thickly sown in the streets and road blocks had been erected but there were no snipers or rearguards," Swinton stated.

After inspecting the city, Swinton wrote: "It has suffered moderately severe damage from shellfire and bombs. Many of the famous churches and land marks have suffered some damage."]

From their newly-won positions on the Ravenna-Russi road, 8th Army troops advanced northeast of Russi against light German opposition and captured the rail junction of Godo, one and a half miles northeast of the city.

A half-mile north of Russi, 8th

(Continued on page 8)

Statement By U. S. New Factor In Italy

ROME, Dec. 5—A formal statement by the United States Department of State today provided new ammunition to the leaders of the Socialist and Action parties in their opposition to a new government led by Ivanoe Bonomi, former Prime Minister. The statement came at a time when some sort of agreement was in the making.

The statement said:

"The position of this government has been consistently that the composition of the Italian Government is purely an Italian affair except in the case of appointments where important military factors are concerned. This government has not in any way intimated to the Italian Government that there would be any opposition on its part to Count Carlo Sforza.

"Since Italy is an area of combined responsibility we have reaffirmed to both the British and Italian Governments that we expect the Italians to work out their problems of government along democratic lines without influence from outside.

"This policy would apply to an even more pronounced degree with regard to governments of the United Nations in their liberated territories."

The leaders of the Christian Democrat, Liberal, Labor Democrat and Communist parties were in

(Continued on page 8)

It Ain't Artillery, Men, It's A Ruddy Earthquake!

By Sgt. JACK FOISIE
Staff Correspondent

WITH THE 5TH ARMY, Dec. 5—As if exploding artillery and bombs wasn't enough to worry a man up front, Mother Nature herself went on the warpath yesterday.

Two distinct earth tremors rocked the central sector astride Highway 65 yesterday—the worst shiver to strike the Apennines since 1929 when several buildings in Petramal toppled down, according to the 73-year-old Italian caretaker of the roads in this region. He could remember only one other damaging one, that in 1919.

Yesterday's shocks, the first occurring at 4:15 AM and the second about half an hour later awoke men who were sleeping in buildings, loosened plaster and rattled messkits but out in the field the men were more disturbed by harassing artillery and night bombers. Fifth Army engineers had received no reports of damage and in fact were entirely unaware that there had been an earthquake.

However, the caretaker, through interpreter T-5 John Chioda of Johnstown, Pa., seemed very excited about the event. He said that the tremors were frequent but seldom with the intensity of yesterday's. He also revealed that there were two small dormant volcanoes in the vicinity of Petramala, one named Culinelli and the other Fuoco Di Legno, which means "fire of wood."

The gas escaping from Culinelli, which takes its name from the early owner of a nearby house, could easily be lit with a match, while the rain water draining into the crater of Fuoco Di Legno starts boiling soon, the old man explained. However, there have been no active eruptions in his time.

THE STARS AND STRIPES

MEDITERRANEAN

Vol. 2, No. 53, Saturday, December 9, 1944 — Printed In Italy — TWO LIRE

Greek Strife Goes On; House Upholds Policy

U. S. Lands Division Aimed At Splitting Japanese On Leyte

Amphibious Attack Made By 77th In Surprise Philippines Action

LEYTE, Philippines, Dec. 8 — American troops in a surprise move aimed at splitting the Japanese defenses around the Ormoc section on Leyte Island have made an amphibious attack upon the beaches three miles south of Ormoc in the rear of the Yamashita Line, Gen. Douglas MacArthur's communique announced today.

Action flared up brightly in the central Philippines with the new American attack. Within two hours, a full division was put ashore. The Yanks met some opposition, particularly from the air, but pushed forward to secure the beachhead. The attacking troops were men of the 77th Division, making six divisions now pressing upon Ormoc.

Ending the three weeks' lull forced upon them by torrential rains and typhoons, MacArthur's men striking from the sea hit near the center of the Japanese defenses from the rear. The communique said the amphibious attack is separating the Nippon soldiers at Ormoc and in the valley to the north from those along the coast to the south.

Japanese planes, hitting the Yank convoy after the troops were ashore, sank a destroyer and a small transport.

Yank planes, however, caught another Japanese convoy approaching Ormoc behind the American. They bombed and strafed it until 13 Jap ships were sunk, and 62 defending planes shot down. It was estimated that 4,000 soldiers were lost aboard the 13 ships. The Yanks had five planes destroyed in the battle.

The action on the west coast of Leyte wasn't the only flareup on

(Continued on page 2)

B-29s Concentrate On Bonin Islands

WASHINGTON, Dec. 8 — Saipan's giant bombers were ranging the skies around the Japanese mainland again today and last night after being held up temporarily for a few days because of heavy weather. Daring reconnaissance planes plagued Tokyo, while in stronger force other B-29s struck at Iwo Jima in the Bonin Islands, 750 miles north of Saipan and about the same distance south of Japan.

The attack upon the Bonins was aimed at damaging airfields from which bold Nippon planes have sortied to Saipan to strike B-29 bases.

While details were not immediately available on the Bonin raid, communiques said the Super Forts were in goodly number. The shorter distance as compared with the Tokyo journeys enabled them to carry their full bombloads. Iwo Jima has been pounded frequently lately by various types of American planes, but this was the first B-29 raid.

Meanwhile, the Saipan command announced that two Super Forts on night weather reconnaissance flights over Tokyo dropped bombs upon the Nippon capital in separate strikes seven hours apart.

The first plane was commanded by Lt. Col. Robert K. Morgan, who led the first B-29 foray on Tokyo. He reported that Tokyo was brilliantly lighted, "just like flying over New York."

It was announced today also that American Super Fortresses attacking Manchuria on the preceding day hit an aircraft plant at Mukden and destroyed 26 enemy fighters, probably destroyed another 13 and damaged 24. One B-29 was lost.

3,000 Nazis Found Living in Big Caves

SHAEF, Dec. 8—More than 3,000 German civilians, who had disobeyed Nazi orders to evacuate to the interior of Germany, were found living in huge caves on the west bank of the Saar River, a correspondent with the 3rd Army disclosed yesterday.

The refugees, from eight villages, said they had been living in the caves with their cattle for a month despite Nazi threats to dynamite the entrance. The German threat was forestalled by the rapid advance of the 90th Infantry Division which overran the area.

The underground village was discovered when the American troops noticed smoke oozing from cracks in the side of the hill. The caves are located in property belonging to Frans von Papen, German diplomat.

Yanks Across Saar In 21-Mile Stretch

SHAEF, Dec. 8 — American 3rd Army forces driving on the great industrial city of Saarbrucken today were up to or across the Saar River along a stretch of 21 miles.

The thrust at the capital of the Saar Valley extended from north of the Siegfried Line stronghold of Merzig south and east to Furstenhausen. Troops of the 5th Division had entered this town which is less than three and one-half miles to the south of Saarbrucken.

Northwest of Saarlautern, the 90th Division had pushed a mile into the Pachtener Buchwald forest and at this point was eight miles inside the German frontier, the deepest penetration by Yank forces into the Saar Valley.

Meanwhile, the 35th Division secured a firm hold on the greater part of Saarguemines, ten miles to the southeast of Saarbrucken which still was in flames from the continuous artillery shelling and air assaults of the past several days.

Heavy tank battles were reported raging in the area of Rohrbach and Bitsche, eight miles southeast of Saarbrucken.

Farther to the east, elements of the 7th Army advancing northward on a 35-mile front entered Encshelberg, only seven miles from the border of the Reich and presented a threat to Nazi forces who might be forced back by the 3rd Army's frontal attack on the Saar.

Continued rains in the north made the 1st and 9th Army fronts along the Roer River to the northeast of Aachen a virtual quagmire and little change in position was reported along this approach to the Ruhr Valley.

The rains also broadened the

(Continued on page 8)

Commons Votes To Sustain Cabinet After Debate On Greek Issue

LONDON, Dec. 8—By the overwhelming confidence vote of 279 to 30, Prime Minister Winston Churchill crushed in the House of Commons today the most serious Labor challenge of his foreign policy since he took over Britain's leadership in 1940.

Angered by bitter Labor denunciations of his government's stand on Greece and other liberated countries in Europe, the stocky, 70-year-old Premier himself demanded a vote of confidence as justification for continuation of his policy.

Commons gave him that support — support which in Mr. Churchill's own words will mean that Britain "will persist in this policy of clearing Athens and the Athens region of all those who are rebels to the constituted authority of Greece."

The vote was taken tonight after a heated debate in which Labor members protested strongly against what they termed "the use of British troops to disarm the friends of democracy."

Opening today's historic debate, Labor member Seymour Cocks declared: "Today, on the sacred soil of Athens, in the shadow of the Acropolis, British soldiers and Greek patriots lie dead side by side, each with an Allied bullet in his heart. I ask that Parliament immediately put an end to this fratricidal strife."

He claimed that British policy had lately been inclined to support many old, worn-out regimes as against new, popular forces and asserted that Mr. Churchill had apparently vetoed a change in the present leadership of the Greek Government in much the same way as Hitler appoints Gauleiters for occupied territories.

"I think the House is entitled to some explanation," Mr. Cocks said.

In his reply to Labor criticism, Churchill said that the fact that the Greek guerrillas went into the mountains to fight the Germans did not qualify them to rule the country.

Amid some Labor interruptions, Churchill stated that to clamor to shoot everyone politically inconvenient was not democracy. He said he trusted the mass of people in almost every country, but not gangs of bandits who wanted to overturn the state authority by violence.

"During this war we have had to arm anyone who could shoot

(Continued on page 2)

Rains Drench Front In Record Downpour

WITH THE 5TH ARMY, Dec. 8 —The 5th Army front today experienced its heaviest rain of the year with a reported 2.4 inches drenching the front during the last 24 hours. Violent winds also swept across the fighting areas, but 5th Army engineers tonight reported only minor damage to roads and army installations.

The average autumn rainfall in the area of Italy in which most operations are going on is 18.4 inches. Already this autumn the area has had 25.9 inches of rainfall.

It's wet, and that's all brother!

8th Nears Faenza In Spite Of Weather

ADVANCED ALLIED FORCE HEADQUARTERS, Dec. 8 — British 8th Army troops, who crossed the Lamone River, southwest of Faenza, fought through steady rain and heavy morning fog yesterday to within three miles of the important Highway 9 road junction.

In the push, the British cleared scattered German outposts along the ridge to the northeast of the river and captured the small village of Castel Raniero.

North of Ravenna on the extreme right flank, other British units consolidated their positions along the east bank of the Lamone.

Other 8th Army elements captured Olmatello, less than a mile south of Castel Raniero, and Pideura, more than a mile and a half to the west. To the southwest, a sharp German counterattack on M. San Rinaldo, was repulsed yesterday with heavy losses to the enemy.

Eighth Army patrols, north of Ravenna, reported yesterday that the Germans are trying to establish defense positions in the marshland, south of the shallow inland sea, Valli Di Comacchio, approximately ten miles north of United Kingdom positions on the east bank of the Lamone River.

Artillery fire was exchanged along a wide stretch of the river, with British self-propelled guns setting fire yesterday to a number of enemy strongpoints on the far bank west of Russi.

Activity along the 5th Army front reached its lowest ebb in weeks yesterday, with Indian troops again registering the only gains of the day along the extreme east flank of the line.

Moving ahead against light German resistance, elements of an Indian division advanced 1,500 yards northeast of M. Giornetto to occupy M. Bitella. Farther west, other Indian troops made excellent progress during the day to

(Continued on page 8)

Fight Continues In Athens And Piraeus — Truce Moves Reported

ATHENS, Dec. 8 — Bitter and bloody fighting continued in Athens and Piraeus today, according to an official British communique, while the United Press reported that leaders of ELAS, armed force of the Greek Liberation Committee, and emissaries of the Greek Government had opened preliminary negotiations for a truce.

A communique from the headquarters of Lt. Gen. Ronald M. Scobie, British commander in Greece, said this afternoon that there was no sign of slackening of resistance in and around Athens, and that ELAS troops forced out of some sections of the city had begun to infiltrate again. A general strike was declared today in the harbor city of Salonika, 200 miles north of the Greek capital.

British field artillery joined tanks and paratroops today in their assault on ELAS hill positions overlooking Athens.

Troops of the insurgent Greek Liberation Army are still dug in firmly near the Stadium and Stadium Hill, and continued to hold their positions at the southern end of the ancient Acropolis despite yesterday's air attacks by RAF fighter planes.

Lt. Gen. Ronald M. Scobie's communique said today that fierce fighting continued in Athens and Piraeus but that some progress had been registered against stiff resistance. In the outskirts of the city and in Piraeus, "rebel troops" were reported to have taken up entrenched positions. Heavy ELAS mortar fire was directed against the Piraeus army barracks area, held by regular Greek forces.

British warships joined in the battle yesterday for the first time since fighting broke out last Sunday. A destroyer and two motor launches of the Royal Navy, anchored off Piraeus, attacked Lopos Kostello, a strongly garrisoned ELAS strongpoint. Fires were observed after the bombardment.

Yesterday's fighting centered on Arditos Hill, where Socrates was tried and sentenced more than

(Continued on page 8)

Jap Statement Implies Yank Airmen Executions

By Army News Service.

WASHINGTON, Dec. 8—Japan has formally notified the United States and Great Britain that it will "hold responsible" captured airmen who are "clearly found to have deliberately broken established practices of warfare."

The Japanese Government spokesman has announced that an implied threat on the day after the Third Anniversary of Pearl Harbor to execute American aviators who bomb Japan was made through the Swiss Legation at Tokyo, Dec. 3, in reply to Anglo-American inquiries of Sept. 6 and 26 regarding treatment of prisoners.

Sadao Iguchi, spokesman for the Japanese Government Board of Information, made the announcement, which was broadcast by Tokyo before Tokyo had broadcast the Pearl Harbor anniversary program during which it said: "The coming year is about to unfurl before us a total offensive for our nation"—that is a Japanese offensive.

No official comment was made here on the implicit Japanese threat that captured American airmen would be executed as were an unspecified number after the first aerial attack on Tokyo in April, 1942, but it was recalled that President Roosevelt has pledged that all Japanese responsible for such executions and for other violations of the Hague Convention will be brought to justice

Japan is not a subscriber to the Convention on the treatment of war prisoners.

Similar Japanese threats in the past have roused anger here and caused condemnation in Congress.

Now that Tokyo and industrial Japan generally have been brought under systematic attack by Super Fortresses, U. S. Army and Navy officials would not be surprised if captured aviators were executed. They have warned that the Japanese are barbarians who have re-

(Continued on page 8)

Medal Of Honor Winner Has Part In Pyle Movie

HOLLYWOOD, Dec. 8 (ANS)—The soldier who single-handedly wiped out three German machine gun nests during a busy afternoon near Oliveto, Italy, came here today to face the movie cameras so his feat will be part of the film story of U S. infantry in this war.

Cpl. James D. Slaton, 33, of Gulfport, Miss., will play the part of himself in Lester Cowan's "GI Joe" based on war correspondent Ernie Pyle's best seller, "Here Is Your War."

Cpl. Slaton has been awarded the Congressional Medal of Honor, the British Military Medal, the Russian Order of Patriotic Award and the Purple Heart.

De Gaulle Has Three Sessions With Stalin

MOSCOW, Dec. 8 — General Charles de Gaulle, head of the French Provisional Government, has had three talks with Marshal Joseph Stalin and has conferred repeatedly with Foreign Commissar V. M. Molotov. The United Press reported that the conversations are understood not to have gone beyond generalities and an exchange of views yet.

Attending the conferences are French Foreign Minister Georges Bidault, Soviet Ambassador to France, Alexander Bogomolov, French Ambassador to Russia, Roger Garreau and chief of the political section of the French Foreign Office, Maurice de Jean.

The Paris radio said today, according to Reuter's that General de Gaulle's Moscow visit is likely to be followed by a Russian military mission to Paris. This visit will be the prelude to the signing of a Franco-Russian treaty of alliance, it was believed.

In the course of his Moscow trip, General de Gaulle, accompanied by General Alphonse Pierre Juin, French chief of staff, inspected the Red Army Artillery School.

The General and his party also attended a concert and dance at the Red Army Club, where they and Molotov were greeted with prolonged applause.

Man Spricht Deutsch
Haende aus der Hosentasche.
Henda owss der Hosentashe.
Hands out of the pockets.

THE STARS AND STRIPES

Daily Newspaper of U.S. Armed Forces in the European Theater of Operations

Ici On Parle Français
Avez-vous autre chose?
AvAY voo otr shows?
Have you anything else?

Vol. 1—No. 138 | 1 Fr. | New York—PARIS—London | 1 Fr. | Tuesday, Dec. 12, 1944

2 Key Alsatian, Saar Cities Fall to Yanks; Mightiest Bomber Fleet Hits Reich

GI Handiwork On Siegfried Line

U.S. Army Signal Corps Photo

Huge columns of black smoke and debris fill the sky after Ninth Army engineers set off charges under a German pillbox in the Siegfried Line.

77th Div. Takes Ormoc, Dooms Leyte Garrison

The battle for the Philippines took a decisive turn yesterday as the veteran 77th Div. seized the Leyte port of Ormoc, the enemy's last seaport on the island where reinforcements and supplies could be brought in to aid their doomed garrison.

The fall of the port came late Sunday night after infantrymen, veterans of the Guam campaign, had worked a squeeze play on a Jap force south of Ormoc, Gen. MacArthur announced.

Late dispatches last night said that the U.S. Seventh Div., entrenched in the hills north of Ormoc, had engaged elements of the Jap garrison retreating from the captured harbor base. Gen. MacArthur predicted a link-up between the 7th, moving from the north, and the 77th, in Ormoc.

Seizure of Ormoc by the 77th followed closely the surprise landing last Thursday three miles south of the port.

American fighter planes smashing Jap troop concentrations and sup-

(Continued on Page 8)

End of Jap War In 1949 Seen

BOSTON, Dec. 11 (ANS).—The U.S. Navy estimates it will take five more years of fighting in the Pacific before the Japanese are defeated, Walker Mason, WPB regional director, told a labor conference yesterday.

He said that a European victory will "have absolutely no effect on arms and armament for the Navy, so great is the offensive program against Japan." He quoted the Navy as saying the astronomical amounts of ammunition that are being used in the Pacific war have just nicked the skin.

Bradley Lists 'Battle Orders' For GIs Dealing With Nazis

12th ARMY GROUP HQ.—"Stern courtesy and firmness tempered with strict justice" toward Germans was ordered yesterday by Lt. Gen. Omar N. Bradley, 12th Army Group commander for the "conquering" troops of the Ninth, First and Third Armies.

Seven "battle orders," issued in booklet form, govern conduct of Army personnel with German soldiers and civilians. In a letter to unit commanders, Gen. Bradley wrote that "this war is not a sporting proposition. We must not treat the Germans as we would our opponents in a football game after the final whistle. We do not want to play a return game next year or in 20 years."

In an introduction to what he called special "battle orders," Gen. Bradley wrote to his troops, "It is imperative that you do not allow yourselves to become friendly with Germans, but at the same time you must not persecute them. American soldiers can and have beaten German soldiers on the field of

(Continued on Page 8)

500 Italian-Based Heavies Assault Vienna Area

The mightiest heavy bomber fleet ever hurled against the Nazis by the Eighth Air Force—more than 1,600 Liberators and Flying Fortresses—thundered over the Reich yesterday, blasting railyards in the Frankfurt area with nearly 6,000 tons of explosives.

Escorted by 800 fighters, and flying in columns 300 miles long, the armada of heavies pounded the rail network behind the Rhine at Frankfurt, Hannau and Giessen, unloading its bombs through heavy, low-lying clouds which prevented observation of results of the raid.

500 15th AF Heavies Attack

At the same time, nearly 500 more Forts and Libs of the 15th Air Force, supported by 350 fighters, drove over the Alps to attack an ordnance depot and railyards at Vienna, an oil refinery 22 miles northwest of Vienna, and marshalling yards at Graz, 100 miles south of the Austrian capital.

Yesterday's record assault by Eighth heavies followed by a few hours an attack by an estimated 500 RAF Lancasters and Mosquitoes on the Ruhr industrial area at Osterfield, Heiderich and Bruckhausen.

Late reports last night indicated

(Continued on Page 8)

Julich Sportpalast Hit by U.S. Planes

WITH 29th CORPS, GERMANY, Dec. 11.—It took just 120 seconds to get quarter-ton bombs thudding into the enemy-held Julich Sportpalast after the 29th Div. had requested fighter-bomber support, it was revealed today.

Three flights of 29th TAC fighter-bombers were circling Schophoven, waiting for 30th Div. radio to approve another target, when the 29th Div. called the 29th Corps Air Support officer, Major D. R. McGovern, of Providence, R.I.

Maj. McGovern was about to call for fresh air support when the 30th Div. decided they didn't need the fighters. At a nod from McGovern, S. Sgt. Joseph A. Buckling, Jr., of Staunton, Ill., radioed the fighters over Schophoven to fly north and attack the Sportpalast.

Nazi Counter-Attacks Halted by 8th Army

ALLIED HQ, Rome, Dec. 11 (AP).—German counter-attacks against the Eighth Army bridgehead west of the River Lamone have been defeated decisively, today's communique reported.

House Votes 5th Star For 'General of Army'

WASHINGTON, Dec. 11—The House voted without dissent to put a new temporary five-star rank atop the Army and Navy to be known as "General of the Army" and "Admiral of the Fleet."

A House member said he believed the new top ranks will go to Gens. Marshall, Arnold, Eisenhower and MacArthur and Adms. King, Leahy, Nimitz and Halsey of the Navy. The Bill provides an annual base pay of $13,000.

Nazis Rush Aid To Stem Drive For Budapest

The Germans announced yesterday that fresh tank and SS units had been thrown into the battle for Budapest with orders to give not an inch of ground to the Red Army forces battering at the suburbs of the Hungarian capital.

Moscow dispatches, quoted by the Associated Press, said that Soviet forces were within four miles of Budapest on the north and south, while Red Army artillerymen were shelling the city from the east. The AP said there was no sign of any German withdrawal from the city, and supplies were rushed over the enemy's last highway into Budapest from Vienna.

After breaking through on the northern, eastern and southern approaches to the city the Soviets have maintained unflagging pressure on all sectors, keeping the entire German garrison in Budapest occupied. North of Budapest, Gen.

(Continued on Page 8)

Patterson Tells U.S. Drive Is 'Ahead Of Schedule'

American armies hammered at the great Ruhr and Saar industrial regions of Western Germany yesterday in fog, snow and rain while overhead the mightiest Allied air fleet ever sent against the Reich blasted railheads behind the bending German lines.

U.S. Third Army troops seized the key city of Sarreguemines in the Saar and U.S. Seventh Army troops to the east captured the northern Alsatian city of Hagenau without the expected house-to-house struggle, United Press front reports said last night.

The Stars and Stripes front dispatches revealed for the first time that Nazis were withdrawing their forces east of the River Roer as U.S. First Army troops smashed 2,000 yards eastward in a snowstorm to within a mile of the swollen river's western bank.

Waited for Supplies

In the United States, meanwhile, Undersecretary of War Robert Patterson disclosed that renewal of large-scale operations after the drive through France and Belgium—which were cleared "months ahead of schedule"—had to be deferred until supplies could be accumulated.

Patterson said Paris was taken by the Allies 60 days ahead of schedule, although the Allied forces had fallen behind the military time-table when they were penned on the Normandy Peninsula at the outset of the campaign. He discussed the time-table in an address prepared for radio broadcast em-

(Continued on Page 8)

Hacking at Siegfried Defenses

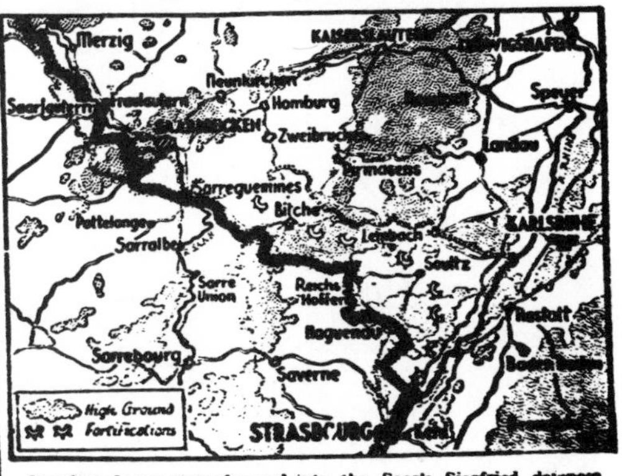

American forces surge forward into the Saar's Siegfried defenses from Metzig, in the north to Hagenau, which fell yesterday.

New York London Edition Paris

THE STARS AND STRIPES

Daily Newspaper of U.S. Armed Forces in the European Theater of Operations

VOL. 5 No. 39—1d. SATURDAY, Dec. 16, 1944

Daily German Lesson

Steigen Sie ein

Steygen Zee ain

Get in

Daily French Lesson

J'en voudrais un de plus

John voodRAY zan duh plew

I'd like one more

7th Smashes Into Germany

Churchill Tells Poles: OK Red Deal

Prime Minister Winston Churchill was sharply critical of the Polish government in a speech in the Commons yesterday in which he unreservedly backed Russia's claims to Polish territory and urged Poland to agree to them before the Russian armies penetrated the heart of Poland in their drive toward Germany.

Otherwise, he said, "misunderstanding between the advancing Russian armies and the Polish underground movement may take forms which will be most painful to all who have the permanent well-being of Poland" at heart.

Churchill termed the Russian proposals for new Polish frontiers "solid and satisfactory" and declared that Britain would back them "at the peace conference."

"If those areas around Lvov and the surrounding regions to the south known as the Curzon Line were joined to the Ukraine," he said, "Poland would gain in the north the whole of East Prussia west and south of Koenigsberg, including the great port of Danzig.

"Poland is free, so far as Great Britain and Russia are concerned, to extend at the expense of Germany in the west."

WASHINGTON, Dec. 15 (AP)—Prime Minister Churchill's statement to Commons on Poland caught Washington by surprise.

Sen. Robert A. Taft (R.-O) said, "It looks like the end of the Atlantic Charter and the return to power politics," and Sen. Claude Pepper (D.-Fla.), member of the Foreign Affairs Committee, said it posed the question of what part America was to play in European affairs. Sen. Warren R. Austin (R.-Vt.), another committee member, said boundary settlements should be postponed until the world peace organization was set up.

Churchill Wants Big 3 To Meet, But It's Dubious

Although Prime Minister Churchill yesterday demanded a meeting of Britain, Russia and the U.S. "at the earliest possible moment," an Associated Press dispatch from Washington indicated that such a meeting could not take place before February. It cited as reasons the facts that President Roosevelt had arranged for "the usual Christmas eve broadcast"; that he must submit his annual budget messages to Congress the first week in January; and that he must be in Washington for his fourth term inauguration Jan. 20.

Nazis Reported Seeking Peace Through Pope

NEW YORK, Dec. 15 (Reuter)—The New York Times in a dispatch from Rome today said: "The Germans in the last two weeks have been making efforts through the Vatican to get a more precise definition of the term 'unconditional surrender,' according to reports here. The Pope has been asked to ascertain whether the Allies will make any distinction between Nazis and the German people."

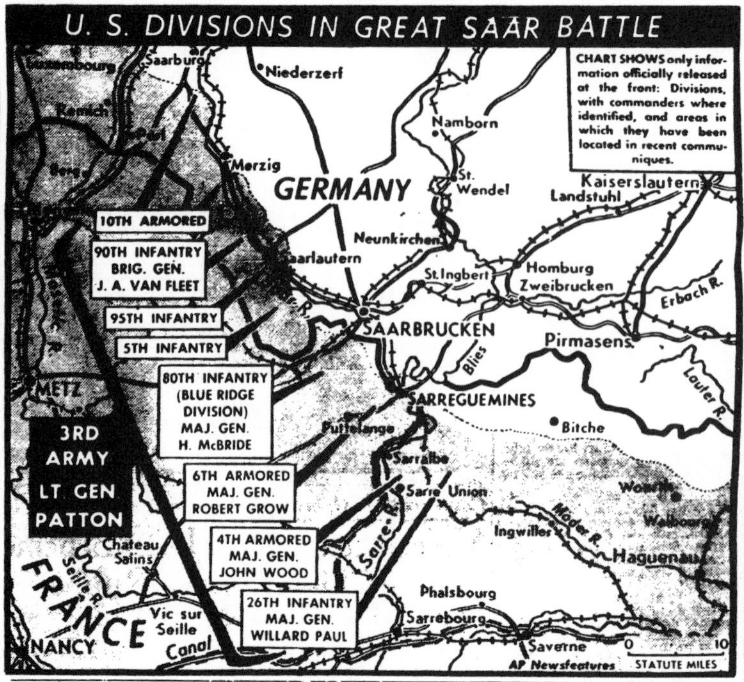

Yanks Span Lauter River On Border

Troops of three Seventh Army divisions entered Germany Friday, storming across the borderline Lauter River under fire from Siegfried Line guns, and gained two miles against stiff resistance to reach the town of Winden, 11 miles west of the Rhine near Karlsruhe—east of the Rhine—and 32 miles north of Strasbourg.

Breaching the Reich border exactly four months after their landing on the southern shores of France, now 400 miles behind them, Lt. Gen. Alexander M. Patch's men became the fourth American army to fight on German soil. The fifth Allied force already inside Germany is the British Second Army, which holds positions on the left flank of the U.S. Ninth.

Patch's troops first crossed the frontier near Wissembourg at 1.30 PM after two columns had swept around the Haguenau Forest and linked up for the thrust into Germany. Crack assault troops forced the Lauter and set up a bridgehead, which Friday night was under heavy mortar and machine-gun fire. The Siegfried defenses had received a "softening-up" bombardment from Allied medium bombers the day before. The Seventh has not yet reached the main Siegfried positions.

Farther east, the armor of another Seventh Army division thrust into the town of Lauterbourg, border town virtually on the Rhine where it forms the Franco-German frontier.

No major changes occurred on any of the other American fronts in Germany. The Third Army continued fighting hard in its Saar River bridgeheads, west of the Seventh's new gains, while the First split the Germans' only remaining bridgehead west of the Roer River when the Fifth Armored Division took Kufferath, three miles below Duren. Infantrymen of the 83rd Division moved up and consolidated the position.

All bridges over the Roer north of

(*Continued on page 4*)

91 Jap Planes Are Destroyed In Carriers' Raid on Luzon

Carrier-based planes from a U.S. naval task force, the first to appear east of the Philippines since last month, raided Japanese harbor installations and airfields on Luzon Wednesday, destroying 91 enemy planes—77 on the ground and 14 in the air—it was announced yesterday by Adm. Chester W. Nimitz.

While the raid was in progress, according to Jap Radio, a powerful Allied convoy passed through the central Philippines into the Sulu Sea.

"This is an important move by the enemy to turn the tide in the Philippines battle, extending his lines westward and maintaining the status quo in Leyte," the Jap broadcast said.

"There is a deep feeling that the Philippines battle is about to emerge from restricted localized fighting into a vast, extensive theater," it was added.

Catching the Japs by surprise the task-force planes—many of them carrying bombs and rockets—also damaged two Jap destroyers, a large cargo vessel and two oil tankers in Manila harbor.

Tokyo Radio said that 400 planes took part in the raids against Manila, Clark Field, Legaspi, Baogas and Lipa.

Superfortress raids on Tokyo also were reported by the Japs, but were not confirmed.

On Leyte, Gen. MacArthur announced that the 77th Division moved forward a mile north of Ormoc and captured the enemy's main supply depots.

650 Heavies Pound Reich

More than 650 Fortresses, escorted by upward of 550 Mustangs and Thunderbolts, resumed the offensive against German rail and industrial targets Friday.

The heavies struck at Hanover and Kassel, key points in Germany's battered rail routes to the Western Front. Kassel, a tank-production center, was last hit Dec. 4.

Eighth's losses were four bombers and two fighters. There was no enemy fighter opposition.

Italy-based 15th Air Force Forts and Libs also bombed rail facilities yesterday, pounding the yards at Innsbruck, northern terminus of the Brenner Pass, as well as strategic targets at Linz and Salzburg in Austria and Rosenheim and Amstetten in Germany.

May Reward Front Medics

WASHINGTON, Dec. 15—Secretary of War Henry L. Stimson said yesterday that the War Department was studying possible additional recognition for medical corps enlisted personnel serving with combat units, comparable to combat insignia and extra pay for expert infantrymen.

Meanwhile, Rep. Frances P. Bolton (R.-O.) proposed that holders of the medical corps Valor Badge be paid $10 extra monthly.

Stimson said any recognition of medics would have to be such that it would not impair their noncombatant status under the Geneva Convention.

He said the position of the medics from the standpoint of pay was not unfavorable because there was a larger proportion of technical ratings in medical units than in ordinary combat outfits.

WASHINGTON, Dec. 15—Secretary of War Stimson said today that the War Department was not considering any requests for lowering the minimum draft age from 18.

GIs Chew the Gum And Eschew the Scum

PARIS, Dec. 15 (UP)—Cries of "Any gum, Chum?" which greeted doughboys in Iceland, England, Morocco and France, will not be heard in Germany, for the Americans have taken steps to forestall any possible German appeals, according to reports from U.S.-held areas in the Reich.

Printed on many trucks, jeeps and tanks is the legend: "No gum, bums."

Infantry Lacks Replacements

WITH THE NINTH ARMY IN GERMANY, Dec. 15 (AP)—Already suffering from munition and tire shortages, American Western Front forces are now handicapped by a shortage of trained infantry replacements.

Instead of there being a steady flow of replacements from the U.S. men are being taken from divisions on quiet sectors to meet deficiencies of divisions suffering heavy battle casualties.

As yet, the replacement shortage has not seriously impaired the overall fighting efficiency of Gen. Eisenhower's forces, but it has caused unnecessary headaches to local commanders.

ROME, Dec. 15 (AP)—The U.S. Army announced today that 10,000 soldiers of specialized branches, including anti-aircraft gunners who are superfluous since the Luftwaffe's decline, will be retrained in Italy as infantrymen.

The programme is due to the requirements in Italy, where the terrain has thrown the bulk of the fighting on the infantry.

Blow It Out Here, Gents

Senate Cigarette Inquiry Opens in a Haze of Smoke

By Frederick C. Othman

United Press Staff Correspondent

WASHINGTON, Dec. 15—Smoke, curling up from crumbled butts in crystal ashtrays and puffs from 500 nostrils, billowed about Room 335 of the Senate Office Building, causing Sen. James M. Mead (D.-N.Y.) to sneeze.

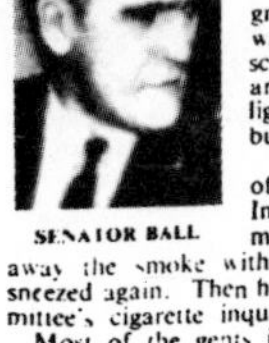

SENATOR BALL

The layers of gray haze fogged the wall mirror, obscured the windows and dimmed the light of the 100-bulb candelabra.

Mead—chairman of the Senate War Investigating Committee — fanned away the smoke with both hands and sneezed again. Then he opened the committee's cigarette inquiry.

Most of the gents in the room were presidents, vice-presidents and general managers of cigarette companies. Every one of them smoked cigarettes, mostly chain-fashion. Sen. Joseph Ball (R.-Minn.) also puffed a butt. This reporter, offered none of the precious cigarettes, puffed his pipe.

Mead and Sen. Homer Ferguson (R.-Mich.), another committee member, don't smoke.

The gathering got down to business.

Chiefs of the major tobacco companies observed there was nothing wrong with the cigarette situation that more cigarettes wouldn't cure. The other makers agreed.

The vice-president of the American Tobacco Co. said his firm was making 287 per cent more cigarettes than in 1935.

"Are those that never smoked before smoking now because cigarettes are hard to get?" asked Ferguson.

The makers believed that was correct.

Somebody brought in a lot of samples from Army rations. Ball eyed them longingly. But I am happy to report he did not swipe a single pack.

The hearing ended and the pretty secretary put down her cigarette and opened the window.

Greek Fighters Ask Regency

ATHENS, Dec. 15 (AP)—ELAS (resistance) leaders replied tonight to the British "lay down your arms" demand, stating they wanted assurances of amnesty for political prisoners, a representative government and a regency before they would order their followers to stop fighting.

Though sporadic, rain-soaked fighting continued throughout the day, receipt of the ELAS reply increased hopes that the undeclared civil war would end shortly.

Unofficial reports persisted that word was awaited from King George of the Hellenes—now in London—on the proposal that the Archbishop of Athens become temporary regent. The cleric was believed ready to attempt formation of a government acceptable to all concerned, pending a plebiscite to decide whether the nation should remain a monarchy or become a republic.

Ike, 6 Others Are Named To New 5-Star Rank

WASHINGTON, Dec. 15 (Reuter)—President Roosevelt today signed legislation creating the new five-star ranks of General of the Army and Admiral of the Fleet, and immediately nominated four generals and three admirals for appointment to the new ranks.

The five-star generals: George C. Marshall, chief of staff; Dwight D. Eisenhower,

GEN. MARSHALL MACARTHUR ADM. NIMITZ GEN. EISENHOWER

supreme commander in Europe; Douglas MacArthur, Southwest Pacific commander, and Henry H. Arnold, chief of the Army Air Forces.

Five-star admirals: William D. Leahy, chief of staff; Ernest J. King, commander-in-chief of the U.S. Fleet, and Chester W. Nimitz, Pacific Fleet commander-in-chief. Under the bill, one additional may be nominated.

Gen. John J. Pershing still technically outranks the newly-promoted with his title of General of the Armies.

Man Spricht Deutsch
Steigen Sie ein.
Steygen Zee ain.
Get in.

THE STARS AND STRIPES

Daily Newspaper of U.S. Armed Forces in the European Theater of Operations

Ici On Parle Français
Est-ce votre dernier prix?
Ess vutr dairnYAY pree?
Is that your lowest figure?

Vol. 1—No. 145 | 1 Fr. | New York—PARIS—London | 1 Fr. | Tuesday, Dec. 19, 1944

Crucial Battle On in West

Air Fights Drive Off Luftwaffe

The Luftwaffe roared over the U.S. lines again yesterday, braving bad weather and Ninth AF fighter-bombers to strike against American ground troops. An estimated 300 planes, supporting the counter-attacking Wehrmacht, concentrated on the U.S. First Army sector, and were finally beaten off with a loss of 45 planes by the Tactical Air Commands of the Ninth AF.

Incomplete figures last night indicated that the Ninth had hurled at least 450 fighter-bombers against the Luftwaffe and against Nazi armored columns and troop concentrations in the counter-attack zone. Preliminary estimates gave U.S. losses as seven planes.

Brig. Gen. Richard E. Nugent, chief of the 29th Tactical Air Command, said the aerial conflict raging over the area of the counter-attack surpassed the intensity of anything previously encountered by the Ninth AF on the Western Front or in North Africa.

Maj. Gen. Elwood R. Quesada's Ninth TAC, operating over the First Army front near Monschau and Prum, downed 33 planes. They were aided by fighter-bombers of the 29th TAC, which flew on both the First and Ninth Army sectors, destroying eight Nazi ME-109s and FW-190s at Duren, and smashing

(Continued on Page 8)

'Flip' Here

Col. Philip G. Cochran

Col. Philip G. Cochran, of Erie, Pa.—"Flip Corkin" of Milton Caniff's cartoon strip, "Terry and the Pirates"—is serving in the ETO as assistant G-3 (operations) of the First Allied Airborne Army, Lt. Gen. Lewis H. Brereton announced yesterday.

Cochran commanded the First Air Commando Task Force in the Burma invasion, led by the late British Maj. Gen. Orde Wingate.

Frauleins in the Front Lines

By Wade Jones
Stars and Stripes Staff Writer

WITH THE SEVENTH U.S. ARMY, Dec. 17.—There's either an acute manpower shortage in Germany, or else Wehrmacht female personnel, tired of fooling around with 4-Fs back home, have volunteered to work in the frontlines where men are men and women are glad of it.

Foxhole fraüleins, most of them working as clerks or stenographers, have recently been captured in positions as far forward as battalion CPs, according to Maj. Robert Herman, of Jacksonville, Fla., Seventh Army prisoner of war officer.

"There doesn't seem to be any sort of organization for these women and girls, such as our WAC," Maj. Herman said. "Some of them are wearing civilian clothes when captured and some have uniforms of a sort."

Although most of these Wehrmacht women, at least those in civvies, have the privilege, along with medical and Red Cross personnel, of returning through the lines to their own forces, none has done so here in the seventh Army sector.

B29s Rock War Plants At Hankow and Nagoya

NEW YORK, Dec. 18 (ANS).—Superfortresses, giving the Japanese little rest between raids, struck again yesterday at two vital sections of Jap war production. The 20th Air Force, flying from bases in China, blasted Hankow in daylight, while the 21st's B29s were hammering at Nagoya on the Jap mainland from bases on Saipan.

The B29 attacks were in line with the stepped-up schedule for bombing Japan which Gen. H. H. Arnold promised in Washington over the weekend.

The Nagoya raid was the second in five days on the heart of Japan's industrial area. The other attack was the first on Hankow, another munitions manufacturing city built up by the Japs since its occupation five years ago.

Mindoro Port Entered

ALLIED HQ, Philippines, Dec. 18.—American invasion forces now have the southern section of Mindoro Island completely in their hands. On Leyte other American troops fought some of the "blood-

(Continued on Page 8)

2 Slovak Forts Fall to Soviets

Russian troops, lashing out in a triple invasion of Czechoslovakia, captured two important mountain strongholds near the southern border yesterday while other Red Army forces already in Slovakia, drove to within 17 miles of Presov, important Hungarian-Slovak communications hub.

Little information was available last night on the success of the drives, reported briefly in Moscow dispatches, but the German radio said extremely heavy fighting had broken out along 135-miles of the Slovak southern border.

Two spearheads of the new Red drive were thrown across the border north of Budapest near Lucenc and Putnok. The other Soviet drive endangered German operations in eastern Czechoslovakia.

On the Budapest front, Russian infantry drove to within six miles of Budapest from the northeast yesterday.

Patrol Dons Long Johns For Use As Snow Suits

WITH SECOND INF. DIV., inside the Siegfried Line.—Ingenious Yanks pulled out their long winter underwear and used them for camouflage suits when snow caught troops without proper clothing.

"We painted our helmets white and put drawers and tops over our other clothing," Cpl. John K. Smith, of Louisville, explained. "It worked pretty good." Camouflage suits were later issued and the underwear returned to its accustomed use.

'All Now at Stake,' Nazi Troops Told; First Strikes Back

American First Army troops yesterday struck back at the mightiest enemy counter-offensive since D-Day. Spurred by the German High Command's proclamation that the Reich's "great hour" had arrived and that "everything is now at stake," Nazi armored and infantry columns smashed on along the old invasion route into Belgium and Luxembourg.

Associated Press front reports said that fierce battles were raging along the First Army front between the Monschau Forest and the Luxembourg-German border. In this sector what appeared to be one of the war's decisive battles was being fought under a security veil dropped by both the Allied and German High Commands.

Black-out on All Details

The situation on this front, Associated Press said, was so fluid that First Army and SHAEF decided to clamp a black-out on all detailed information on the extent of enemy advances and countermoves by the Americans. Such information, it was said, might aid the enemy in this crucial period.

The German communiqué, as reported by Reuter, indicated that while the Wehrmacht offensive was making progress, "details cannot be given until later, as doing so would be giving information to the surprised enemy."

Urged to give their all in "superhuman deeds for the Fuehrer," attacking Germans made gains in the Honsfeld area in Belgium, as well as at two points where they pushed into Luxembourg.

Field Marshal von Rundstedt, Germany's commander in the west, announced that the Reich's

(Continued on Page 8)

The Battle Area

Germany's most powerful counter-offensive since D-Day has smashed back into Belgium and Luxembourg at three points along the path of the German 1940 invasion.

Yanks, Crying in Rage, Tell How Nazis Killed Wounded

FRONT-LINE CLEARING STATION, BELGIUM, Dec. 18 (AP).—Muddy, shivering survivors, weeping with rage, told how German tankmen tried with machine guns to massacre 150 American prisoners standing in an open field.

"Those of us who played dead got away later," said T/5 William B. Summers, of Glenville, W. Va., "but we had to lie there and listen to German non-coms kill with pistols every one of our wounded men who groaned or tried to move."

"Those dirty —. I never heard of anything like it in my life. Damn them. Give me my rifle and put me in with the infantry. I want to go back and kill every one of those —."

Summers, who escaped with a gashed hand, was a member of an artillery observation battalion trapped at a road fork by a German armored column which had driven several miles into Belgium since the major Nazi offensive began yesterday.

Heavy guns on the enemy's Tiger tanks quickly shot up more than two-dozen American trucks and light armored vehicles. The captured Yanks were then led into a field, and as the German column moved past less than 50 yards away, Nazi gunners deliberately raked the defenseless group with machine guns and machine pistols.

Survivors expressed hope that a majority of the men had escaped with their lives by diving to the ground and lying still, but hours later fewer than a score had made their way back to their own positions.

Canadians in Italy Capture 1,100 Nazis

ROME, Dec. 18.—Canadian troops have captured more than 1,100 German prisoners since they opened their attack up the Bologna-Rimini highway two weeks ago, an official announcement said tonight.

New Zealand patrols on the Eighth Army front, feeling out enemy defenses north of captured Faenza, were turned back today after meeting powerful German forces near Bagna Cavallo. Other patrols crossed the Lamone River at two points between Faenza and Bagna Cavallo.

At Fifth Army advance headquarters, members of the House military affairs committee, after touring the Italian front, told newsmen today that they thought the war on the Italian front will continue longer than they expected it would when they left the U.S. a month ago.

Man Spricht Deutsch
Becilen Sie sich.
Beh-alice Zee sikh.
Hurry up.

THE STARS AND STRIPES

Daily Newspaper of U.S. Armed Forces in the European Theater of Operations

Ici On Parle Français
C'est dans mes moyens.
Say don may mwah-YAN.
I can afford it.

Vol. 1—No. 146 | 1 Fr. | New York—PARIS—London | 1 Fr. | Wednesday, Dec. 20, 1944

Nazis 20 Mi. Into Belgium

Tiny Unit Delays Tank Column 6 Hours

By Hal Boyle
Associated Press Correspondent

A BELGIAN VILLAGE UNDER GERMAN ATTACK, Dec. 19 (AP).—One lieutenant and two anti-tank gun crews knocked out four German Tiger "Royal" tanks yesterday in a flaming street battle which held up a Nazi armored column for six hours until American reinforcements arrived. The column was spearheading the counter offensive in that sector.

But for the battle wisdom of Lt. Jack Doherty, 27, of Latrobe, Pa., and the valor of his gun crews, this fight would have been lost before it was well started, and the speedy German column might have been miles inside the American lines shooting up rear area outfits.

Doherty and his men, supported only by a single company of doughboys who would have been powerless to take on the tanks alone, bore the brunt of the sledgehammer thrusts by the vanguard of the German armored smash.

"It was still dark when I sent one of my three-inch anti-tank guns across the stream at the edge of the town to try to hold the wooden bridge there," Doherty recalled. "We did hold it until daybreak, when machine-gunners drove us away, but we retook it by eight o'clock—and lost it again at nine. It was burning when we finally pulled back at noon.

"At ten o'clock, I got another of my guns up," Doherty continued. "Four Royal Tiger tanks came moving down the street. With their first shots each of my guns set one Tiger ablaze.

"Nobody came out of one tank, and only two crew men got out of the other. They ran into a house and climbed to the roof—so we shot the roof right out from under them."

Another German tank was hit by both guns simultaneously, and a fourth Tiger backed along the road like a blind, trapped beetle. During the fight, another Tiger had moved out and found a better corner.

"It had a better firing angle than we did—it could shoot at us, but we couldn't get back at it very well," Doherty said.

The Nazi monster tank knocked out Doherty's half-track and set his jeep on fire. Doherty ordered his men back. He managed to pull back one of the guns with the help of Sgt. Louis Celanto, New Haven, Conn., Cpl. Roy Ables, Cleveland, Tenn., the gunner, and the rest of the crew.

To protect them, the leading gun, commanded by Sgt. Martin Hauser, of Los Angeles, Calif., and Gun-

(Continued on Page 8)

No Great Damage In Drive Thus Far, Washington Says

Field Marshal von Rundstedt's mighty counter-offensive in the Ardennes, seemingly designed to split the Allied front in two, swept on yesterday under a news eclipse from which filtered only the fact that German armor had plunged 20 miles into Belgium.

As Nazis smashed through war-razed Belgian villages, other German forces defending the Saar and the Rhineland fought the U.S. Third and Seventh Armies to a standstill.

Frontline reports pictured blazing tank battles, exploding V-bombs and artillery and fleeing refugees, but the massive air battles of the first two days died away yesterday as swirling fog hampered Luftwaffe and Allied planes.

Before the fog rolled in, however, Ninth Air Force planes smashed 95 enemy tanks and damaged at least 26 more in support of American ground troops who lashed back to halt the breakthrough.

20 Miles from German Border

The news blackout on ground operations was lifted momentarily by reports of British Typhoon attacks on 20 German armored vehicles "west of St. Avelot." This Belgian town is 20 miles from the German border and due west of Malmedy.

It is eight miles south of Spa and 22 miles east southeast of Liege.

American lines appeared to be stabilizing along the front in Belgium, United Press front reports said, but in Luxembourg the situation was reported still fluid. Grim-faced doughboys took up positions in areas which only a few days before had been considered well in the rear.

At Washington, War Department authorities said the counter-offensive against the U.S. First Army had done no great damage yet and was designed primarily to boost German morale, United Press said. Officials were confident the Ger-

(Continued on Page 8)

5 Packs for All Is Butt Ration For Next Week

Com Z headquarters announced yesterday that the cigarette ration next week for all soldiers supplied by PXs would be five packs, providing "a uniform ration for all personnel in the ETO." The announcement added: "When stocks have reached the necessary level the normal ration of seven packs will be resumed."

Rear echelon troops here were cut from seven to five packs Nov. 6, and got none in the two weeks following Nov. 13. The ration for the last three weeks has been two packs, although PXs in the UK returned to five two weeks ago.

No official amplification has been made of the original statement that the cut was to allow combat men "their full ration." Members of the House Military Affairs Committee said in Paris Dec. 3 that high American officers told them there were plenty of cigarettes at European storage depots, but that lack of transportation, due to the need to keep supplies flowing to the front, caused the famine in rear areas.

B29s Keep Up Attacks on Jap Plane Industry

WASHINGTON, Dec. 19 (ANS)—China-based superforts bombed industrial targets on Kyushu Island again today in another blow at the roots of Japan's air power, the War Department announced in Washington today.

The big bombers of the 20th Air Force attacked Oura, whose big plane factory has been the target of three previous raids less than 24 hours after the same air force had blasted factories at Hankow, China, and 21st Air Force bombers from Saipan had blasted the Mitsubishi aircraft plants at Nagoya on Honshu Island.

Photographs showed that "damage was clearly extensive to the factory area with the precision bomb pattern sweeping from the edge of Nagoya Bay harbor directly across the plant district," a communiqué from Brig. Gen. Hansell's Saipan headquarters revealed.

In the Philippines, the retaking of Mindoro Island went ahead at full tilt without the slightest ground resistance from the Japs. U. S. commanders announced that at least 742 Jap planes had been put out of action in the last week.

Senio River Crossed By Indian Patrols

ROME, Dec. 19 (UP).—Indian patrols which crossed the Senio River today, three miles southwest of Route Nine, presumably withdrew after brief contact with the Germans in the day's only major action on the Italian front. The Germans counter-attacked on a small scale in the Naviglio bridgehead, but were repulsed.

North of Faenza, fierce counter-attacks with tank support forced the British back to the main Bologna highway, but northwest of Faenza the British continued to gain.

Armed Stag Line Greets GIs In Battle-Scarred Ballroom

By Allan Morrison
Stars and Stripes Staff Writer

WITH THE 95th DIV. IN SAARLAUTERN, Dec. 19.—Doughfeet of one platoon of the First Battalion 377th Inf. arranged and kept a bloody tryst in the long, shell-scarred ballroom of a hotel facing on the Goebbelsplatz in mid-Fraulautern, just across the river.

The infantry knew they had reached the outer ring of the Siegfried Line when they crossed the Saar after cleaning out this Nazi industrial center. And the deeper into the city the Americans pushed, the harder the fight became.

The tempo became red hot when the Yanks neared the Goebbelsplatz and the hotel adjoining it. The hotel was a large building and the fire that came from it told of troops inside with a fanatical conception of Patherland defense.

The observers sent back fire directions to the artillery and several missions were called. Concentra-

(Continued on Page 8)

Pocket Ships Hit By RAF at Gdynia

LONDON, Dec. 19.—An estimated 500 RAF Lancasters last night struck at the German-held Baltic port of Gdynia, with 2,500 tons of bombs. Chief targets were the German pocket battleships Scheer and Lutzen, and a number of Nazi submarines and destroyers.

The battleship Gneisenau, shattered into uselessness by previous air attacks, is also believed to be docked in the Polish port.

Word Goes Round 'n' Round—Town Goes

WITH THE FIFTH INF. DIV. IN GERMANY.—Sgt. Patrick Henry, of the third platoon of the Fifth Recon. Troop and Alderson, W. Va., co-operated with the rest of the Fifth Div. recently to adjust artillery fire on a company of Germans and raze the town of Frederichweiler near Saarbrucken.

It started when Henry from his observation post in the attic of a tall house in a town 2,000 meters from Frederichweiler, observed a company of Jerries in the woods between the towns. Henry shouted a fire direction to a GI on the next floor who passed it on to a Yank in another room who relayed it to a man on the ground floor who shouted it to a man at the door who passed it on to a soldier in the street who walked over to the recon car and told the radio operator. The radio operator sent it back to the liaison recon car at division headquarters. The radio operator in the recon at division glanced disagreeably at the rain outside and yelled his information to a soldier at the door of the command ... liaison section. This soldier told the man in the kitchen who yelled it down to a GI in the basement who told the recon liaison officer who got on the telephone and told division artillery.

Div. arty gave the mission over the phone to the 46th FA Bn. The 46th loosed a couple of rounds and Sgt. Henry adjusted it and gave "fire for effect," which passed back the same route as the original request. Germans started running out of the woods toward Frederichweiler as the guns zeroed in on them. So Henry, starting the chain of command again, adjusted the fire and killed Jerries as they ran into the town. Then, fearing he might have missed somebody, Henry called for a couple of concentrations on the town which left not a house unblasted.

Nazi Air Activity Hampered by Fog

Fog, blanketing most of the Western Front yesterday, sharply reduced Luftwaffe activity and held the tactical air war down to a minimum.

Approximately 200 sorties had been flown by Ninth AF fighter-bombers as night fell, ending the first day in which counter-attacking German forces have not been provided with strong Luftwaffe support.

A single sizable Nazi formation—70 planes—was hurled against a force of fighter-escorted RAF Lancasters smashing at the Trier area. In fierce dogfights, 11 Nazi planes were shot down with a loss of four Ninth AF Thunderbolts.

Man Spricht Deutsch
Ich habb's eilig.
Ish hahb's ailig.
I am in a hurry.

THE STARS AND STRIPES

Daily Newspaper of U.S. Armed Forces in the European Theater of Operations

Ici On Parle Français
Y a-t-il des droits de douane?
Yatee! day drwah duh doo-AN?
Does it pay duty?

Vol. No. 147 — 1 Fr. — New York—PARIS—London — 1 Fr. — Thursday, Dec. 21, 1944

Biggest Battle Since D-Day

Reich Hurls Its Best Men Into Attack

By Dan Regan
Stars and Stripes Staff Writer

WITH FIRST U.S. ARMY, Dec. 20.—It is apparent to observers at the front that the war might be won if the Allies can smash the current German counter-offensive—an assault designed to snatch victory or at least a favorable peace from what the Germans felt was an Allied steamroller.

The Nazis are using the best troops they have on the Western Front.

German officers are promising their men that they will spend New Year's Eve in Paris; that they will have Antwerp in five days; that Aachen will be given to Hitler for a Christmas present, and other such promises to hypo the Nazi soldiers into fanatical action.

The military consensus is that this offensive was planned and is being directed by "a soldier"—which means that apparently Von Rundstedt, and not Hitler's intuition, is at the helm.

Aim for Supply Dumps

One present aim of the Nazi spearhead will be to grab American supply dumps for the hoped-for German drive through Belgium and France.

These present German drives are salients composed of armored columns, tanks, trucks and armored infantry. The Germans are using the same technique we used in our recent armored spearheads across France with armored units dashing in several directions.

The aim of these spearheads appears to be to cut off our communications and harass our troops.

First Army forces are holding strongly along neighboring sectors of the drive, but the center still is fluid. It is difficult to spot the columns exactly since they are in

(Continued on Page 2)

Nazis Try Comeback Trail

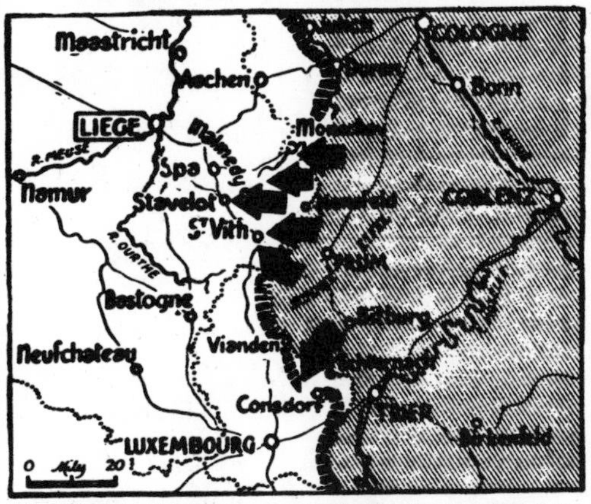

One thrust in the German counter-offensive has been halted at Monschau, but in Belgium and Luxembourg Panzer Divisions spear in the areas of Malmedy, Stavelot, St. Vith and Consdorf.

Headlines Grim Reminder To U.S. War Far from Over

By Carl Larsen
Stars and Stripes U.S. Bureau

NEW YORK, Dec. 20. — Germany's sudden shift to the offensive in Belgium, mounting American casualties on the Western Front and stepped-up draft requirements brought the nation a grim reminder today that the war in Europe is far from over.

The nation's newspapers used their boldest headline type to report the German threat. Editorial writers checked history books to draw parallels between the current Nazi drive and the Germans' final 1918 offensives under Ludendorff. However, no attempt was made to dismiss the threat lightly, although Washington officials said they were confident it ultimately would be checked.

Meanwhile, the War Department announced that the ground forces in western Europe suffered 57,775 casualties during November, including 8,250 dead, 43,330 wounded and 6,186 missing. The Western Front toll since D-Day is 258,124.

The War Department also dis-

(Continued on Page 2)

British Armada Is Under Nimitz

PEARL HARBOR, Dec. 20 (ANS).—Conferences between Adm. Chester W. Nimitz and the British Pacific fleet commander, Adm. Bruce Fraser, who arrived here with his staff yesterday from Australia, were begun today and their first act was to give Adm. Nimitz command of Fraser's British armada.

As the naval experts conferred, possibly on plans to increase British co-operation in the war against Japan, B29s, based on Saipan, were bombing Tokyo. It was the third superfort raid in the last three days on the Jap mainland.

In the Philippines, Yanks on Leyte seized a Jap airfield practically intact and captured Valencia, Jap headquarters on the island, then drove northward in an effort to engage the Japs fleeing into the dense mountains.

British Report Gains Along Faenza Front

ROME, Dec. 20 (UP).—British troops of the Eighth Army made limited gains today north and northeast of Faenza against strong resistance. Polish and Indian troops of the same army virtually cleared all organized enemy resistance south of the Senio River and west of the main Bologna-Rimini highway.

Zizzi Finds Zizzi, Seeks Other Zizzis

Cosmo Zizzi, a sergeant in a FA battalion, got a Christmas package addressed to Cosmo Zizzi. "Well," said Cosmo, "I ate contents of same."

"Later I look at the address," he continued. "It's meant for Cosmo Zizzi all right, but another one."

Cosmo wrote Cosmo explaining what had happened, and now, he says, "all is forgiven." The two Cosmo Zizzis are a couple of pals, happy to share the name of Zizzi.

But what they want to know now is, are there any more Cosmo Zizzis in the ETO? If so, maybe they could start a Cosmo Zizzi Club.

Germans' Assault On 60-Mile Front Is Halted in North

The security veil over the German counter-offensive was lifted partially yesterday to reveal the bloodiest battles since D-Day raging through eastern Belgium and Luxembourg where masses of men and armor were locked in one of the war's decisive struggles.

German armor smashed more than 20 miles into Belgium in the first 48 hours of the Nazi blitz, the like of which has not been seen in Europe since 1940. Exploding Saturday on a 60-mile front from the Monschau Forest to the German-Luxembourg frontier, the offensive penetrated U.S. First Army positions at four points by noon Monday.

Nazi armored strength in the drive was estimated at between five and six Panzer divisions, including an unstated number of SS Panzer divisions. Eight or nine infantry divisions were thrown into the assault, which obviously was planned to kick-off when murky weather would handicap superior Allied air power.

Panzer divisions encountered by Lt. Gen. Courtney H. Hodges' battling First Army men included units met and smashed at Caen. These had been re-fitted for battle.

It was predicted the Germans probably will continue to make progress. Counter-measures, it was said, cannot be prepared in a day and it was warned that immediate results cannot be expected.

Only in the north, in the Monschau Forest, has the drive been reported as brought to a halt. There, First Army men smashed enemy forces which entered the town of Monschau. Americans also managed to regain a portion of their old line east of the town where there were still enemy elements to be mopped up.

Feverish German activity was spotted behind the U.S. Ninth and Third Army lines, according to front reports.

Stars and Stripes Correspondent Jules Grad with Ninth Army reported that Ninth Air Force tactical commands Monday blasted the greatest concentration of German military transport seen since the Falaise Gap. He said trucks camouflaged with brown and green

(Continued on Page 2)

Foe Employing Tricks Aplenty

WITH THE FIRST U.S. ARMY, Dec. 20.—The counter-attacking Nazis were pulling every rabbit they had out of their helmets yesterday, using old and new ruses in an attempt to bewilder U.S. troops and infiltrate into American positions.

German vehicles were painted to look like those of U.S. units, and some were even emblazoned with white and yellow stars similar to those which distinguish Allied combat vehicles.

Captured U.S. tanks and equipment were being used by the Nazis. In one instance, Germans in an American tank pulled close to U.S. infantrymen and yelled in English:

"Come on over here."

When the GIs came over, they were mowed down by the Nazis.

Germans in civilian clothes, or wearing civilian garments over Wehrmacht uniforms were captured filtering into the U.S. lines on missions of sabotage and espionage.

Some Jerries were dressing in GI clothes, complete to U.S. dog-tags, in an effort to work their way back through the lines, using fifth-column tactics reminiscent of 1940.

B17s Bomb Nantes Again—This Time With Toys, Gifts

LONDON, Dec. 20.—Some 3,000 children will be guests of the 384th Bombardment Group, veteran Flying Fortress unit of the England-based Eighth AF, at a Christmas party in the war-blighted French city of Nantes.

Several B17s will take off with a cargo of presents for the children. The party will be held on New Year's Eve, France's traditional day for exchanging gifts, and the presents include candy, toys, toilet articles and clothing.

The gifts have come from the group's rations, from PX purchases, and from parcels requested from home. In addition, officers and EM contributed £160 to purchase more gifts for orphanages in Nantes.

Lt. Oscar Picard, of Linwood, Mass., said a party will be held for 300 children in one of Nantes' few undamaged orphanages, and another celebration will be held in the city's windowless market hall for 2,800 schoolchildren.

The 384th, commanded by Lt. Col. Theodore R. Milton, of Washington, D.C., in carrying out 240 operations over Europe, has hit targets at Nantes on several occasions.

Ici On Parle Français
Est-ce votre dernier prix?
Ess vutr dairnYAY pree?
Is that your lowest figure?

THE STARS AND STRIPES

Daily Newspaper of U.S. Armed Forces in the European Theater of Operations

ONE FRANC — ONE FRANC

Man Spricht Deutsch
Steigen Sie ein
Steygen Zee ain
Get in

Friday December 22, 1944 — New York—DIJON—Paris — Volume 1, Number 23

Nazis 30 Miles Inside Belgium

Japs Smashed On Leyte; MacArthur Men Mop Up

ALLIED PHILIPPINE HEADQUARTERS, Dec. 21—Leyte, first of the enslaved Philippine Islands to feel the touch of an American landing barge, was almost completely liberated tonight.

All organized resistance had ended and the Japs were being methodically hunted down and captured or exterminated, Gen. Douglas MacArthur's communique said. The battle is drawing rapidly to a close.

Enormous quantities of Japanese supplies of all types have been captured, it was reported. The supplies would have been sufficient to last the Japanese six months if their Yamashita Line had not broken and fallen apart under American attack.

Abandoning 1,541 dead, the Japanese forces faltered and fled. Small remnants in isolated pockets were putting up temporary resistance while scattered groups were trying to reach the north coast of Leyte.

No ground activity was reported on Mindoro, while on the main island of Luzon, to the north, Legaspi was bombed by heavy American planes. Large fires were started and heavy explosions were heard.

Conference On Leyte

PUFFING HIS CORN-COB PIPE, Gen. Douglas MacArthur confers with Sergio Osmena, president of the Philippines, as the last stage of the Leyte campaign draws to a close with the virtual ending of organized Jap resistance. "The new landing on Mindoro was a bold and decisive step, threatening the Japanese sea lanes," President Osmena declared today. "Americans have now crossed the Philippines from east to west."

78th Congress Adjourns After Hectic 2 Years

WASHINGTON, Dec. 21 — Although in disagreement with President Roosevelt on many domestic issues, the 78th Congress, which adjourned today, went along with him on all war measures and those which he proposed to implement the actual war effort.

Extension of lend-lease and the President's war-time powers was granted, although to the accompaniment of some requests for a check on lend-lease so that it would be ended as soon as possible after the war. Congress also approved participation in the UNRRA, or United Nations Relief and Rehabilitation Administration, which committed this country to paying the largest share of funds for the relief of countrys overrun by the Axis.

Service bills went through without trouble. Most notable of these were the measure for mustering out pay, with a maximum of 300 dollars, and the omnibus bill to aid veterans in the post-war world labelled the GI Bill of Rights, under which veterans may borrow money to purchase homes, businesses or farms, or to pursue schooling.

The 78th appropriated 182 billion dollars, but did not equal the record-breaking 77th Congress in that respect, although it did send the national debt to 260 billion.

Conflict with the President came on labor and tax measures. Congress overrode his veto of the 1943 tax bill, which was designed to put income taxes on a pay-as-you-go basis. The President argued that large taxpayers would benefit at the expense of the small. The Smith-Connally labor bill, which, it was hoped, would decrease strikes, was also passed over his veto.

Lupe Velez To Be Buried In Favorite Ermine Cape

BEVERLY HILLS, Dec. 21—The ermine-garbed body of Lupe Velez lay in state for three hours today before funeral services tomorrow and shipment to Mexico for burial. Her mother announced that, following the movie actress' request, she would be buried in her favorite full-length ermine cape.

Bonin Islands Bombed For 12 Days In Row

WASHINGTON, Dec. 21—American bombers have smashed at the Bonin Islands for the twelfth straight day, it was announced today.

The concentrated punishment of the islands, half-way between Saipan and Tokio, was regarded as a possible prelude to another amphibious operation that would place American forces within 750 miles of Japan.

While the Bonins were taking their pasting, Superfortresses swept over Mukden, Manchuria, for the second time this month. About 60 of the huge bombers hurled their cargo at industrial targets and railroads.

America's new aerial attacks were announced as a War Department official predicted that Japan may soon be cowering under the same trip-hammer blows that pulverized Cologne and other German cities.

Revealing the possibility of an all-out aerial blitz, he visualized fleets of a thousand or more bombers raging over Japan from medium, heavy and Superfortress bases that may be built on Mindoro, if it becomes strategically advisable.

From such bases, he pointed out, it would be possible to mount a vaster air offensive than was ever thought possible in the war in the Orient.

The imminent possibility of these huge attacks was made known as word came from Tokio that the Japanese are starting to consider the American air raids a grave menace. Radio Tokio announced that the Jap Diet, meeting for its 86th session Sunday, will give priority to a resolution urging a basic solution to the problems of evacuation and air attacks.

British Open 2 Burma Drives

NEW DELHI, India, Dec. 21—British troops opening up two new drives in Burma have slashed 15 and 18 miles respectively through strong Jap defenses and difficult country under strong Allied air support, front dispatches reported today.

Belgian, French Firms Get Mortar Contracts

WASHINGTON, Dec. 21—Belgian and French firms have contracted to manufacture 6,500,100 dollars worth of 60 and 81mm. mortars for the American Army to meet urgent needs for those weapons, according to the War Department.

This is part of the campaign to augment American production abroad and save both manpower and shipping. Fifteen continental firms now are manufacturing tires and tire caps, jeep batteries and parts and machine-guns. In addition captured German weapons and ammunition are being used against the enemy.

Drive Can't Be Stopped This Week, SHAEF Says

PARIS, Dec. 21—American fighting men struck back hard and halted Nazi thrusts on the flanks of Nazi Field Marshal Gerd von Runstedt's great offensive, it was disclosed officially today by Allied Supreme Headquarters, but in the center of the German drive advancing tank columns were reported to have cut swaths 30 miles into Belgium and three-quarters through the tiny Duchy of Luxembourg.

It was also admitted officially that the assault cannot be halted this week. It was pointed out that for the first time since the front was stabilized on the fringes of the Rhine, the war of movement, of sweeping armored thrusts and blazing tank battles, has reappeared.

American troops are declared to have checked a German thrust at Esternach, at the southern flank of the original 60-miles assault front, and at Monschau, on the northern end.

Other U.S. 1st Army troops recaptured the Belgian town of Stavelot, 10 miles south of Spa, and fought fiercely to retake the important center of Malmedy, into which the German had penetrated.

The German communique, reported by the United Press, claimed that Nazi advance elements had crossed the Liege-Bastogne-Arlon highway on a broad front, an advance of more than 30 miles into Belgium. A Reuters dispatch said it was claimed that the road had been cut 14 miles south of Liege, which would indicate that the German spearhead which first broke through to Stavelot had veered to the northwest. There was no confirmation of this report from any Allied source.

Stars and Stripes Correspondent Dan Regan, with the 1st Army, reported last night that the failure of German armored spearheads to capture U.S. gas dumps had slowed down the offensive. He said forces which broke through the American lines had seized many vehicles, but the gas to be siphoned out of them was estimated as sufficient to power German armor for only a single day.

The SHAEF communique today, which announced the recapture of Stavelot, admitted that German tanks reached Habiemont, which is 30 miles inside Belgium and 14 miles west of Malmedy. Paratroops were dropped southwest of Habiemont Monday night and Tuesday morning, the communique said.

Wednesday the Paris edition of Stars and Stripes, which reached the front today, carried a United Press story from Washington quoting unidentified War Department officials to the effect that this was an attack designed primarily to boost German morale. This brought wry smiles to the faces of the men who were facing the greatest German West Front drive since the fall of France.

The weather, meanwhile, re-

(Continued on page 4)

Germans Making All-Out Gamble, Stimson Says

WASHINGTON, Dec. 21 (UP)—Secretary of War Henry L. Stimson said today that the Germans in their counteroffensive against the U. S. 1st Army, have accepted the hazard of an all-out effort which, if it failed, may hasten the end of the war.

Stimson, in a press conference, said that the German drive was designed primarily to halt the American advance towards Cologne and the Saar basin. He declared the hazards were heightened for the Germans by the fact that they must also be prepared to meet the Soviet winter offensive, wherever it may strike.

Stimson pointed out that the counterattack came while Allied forces were being steadily reinforced and supported with a large movement of supplies and while the Germans were being subjected to steadily increasing winter aerial attacks.

"Under these conditions," he said, "the Nazi regime has a great deal to lose and might gain an extension of a few months' time before being called to the accounting for the misery they have inflicted on the world."

"I have not lost confidence in the wisdom, energy and aggressive fighting attitude of Gen. Eisenhower and his leaders," the secretary concluded.

Asks Competitive Tests For Vet Job Preference

WASHINGTON, Dec. 21 (ANS)—War veterans should be required to pass competitive tests before being entitled to preference for government jobs, the Civil Service Assembly committee said.

In a report to the Assembly, composed of government personnel administrators, the committee also recommended that veterans' preference policies should recognize the principle of open competition for public employment on the basis of merit and fitness and should not exclude the rising generation from opportunity for public employment.

Tiny Unit Delays Tanks 6 Hours

By HAL BOYLE
Associated Press Correspondent

A BELGIAN VILLAGE UNDER GERMAN ATTACK, Dec. 21 (AP)—One lieutenant and two anti-tank gun crews knocked out four German Tiger "Royal" tanks yesterday in a flaming street battle which held up a Nazi armored column for six hours until American reinforcements arrived. The column was spearheading the counter offensive in that sector.

But for the battle widson of Lt. Jack Doherty, 27, of Latrobe, Pa., and the valor of his gun crews, this fight would have been lost before it was well started, and the speedy German column might have been miles inside the American lines shooting up rear area outfits.

Doherty and his men, supported only by a single company of doughboys who would have been powerless to take on the tanks alone, bore the brunt of the sledgehammer thrusts by the vanguard of the German armored smash.

"It was still dark when I sent one of my three-inch anti-tank guns across the stream at the edge of the town to try to hold the wooden bridge there," Doherty recalled. "We did hold it until daybreak, when machine-gunners drove us away, but we retook it by eight o'clock—and lost it again at nine. It was burning when we finally pulled back at noon.

"At ten o'clock, I got another of my guns up," Doherty continued. "Four Royal Tiger tanks came moving down the street. With their first shots each of my guns set one Tiger ablaze.

"Nobody came out of one tank, and only two crew men got out of the other. They ran into a house and climbed to the roof—so we shot the roof right out from under them."

Another German tank was hit by both guns simultaneously, and a fourth Tiger backed along the road like a blind, trapped beetle. During the fight, another Tiger had moved out and found a better corner.

"It had a better firing angle than we did—it could shoot at us, but we couldn't get back at it very well," Doherty said.

The Nazi monster tank knocked out Doherty's halftrach and set his jeep on fire. Doherty ordered his men back. He managed to pull back one of the guns with the help of Sgt. Louis Celanto, New Haven, Conn., Cpl. Roy Ables, Cleveland, Tenn., the gunner, and the rest of the crew.

To protect them, the leading gun, commanded by Sgt. Martin Hauser, of Los Angeles, Calif., and Gun-

(Continued on page 4)

Man Spricht Deutsch
Sprechen Sie deutlicher.
Sprekhen Zee doytlikher.
Speak more distinctly.

THE STARS AND STRIPES

Daily Newspaper of U.S. Armed Forces in the European Theater of Operations

Ici On Parle Français
Aimez-vous les bonbons?
Ay May voo lay bono-bono?
Do you like candy?

Vol. No. 149 1 Fr. New York—PARIS—London 1 Fr. Saturday, Dec. 23, 1944

Foe 38 Miles from France

'Destroy Enemy Now'—Ike

Germans' Gamble Is Our Chance

From the front lines to the supply ports and from the highest general down through the ranks, the United States Army in Europe mobilized its entire reserves yesterday with a grim and confident determination to smash the German counter-offensive and the German Army.

In his third dramatic Order of the Day since the landings on June 6, Gen. Eisenhower said the Germans now were "gambling everything" and called upon every member of the Allied Expeditionary Force to rise "to new heights of courage, of resolution and of effort" to crush the enemy now.

"By rushing out from his fixed defenses, the enemy may give us the chance to turn his great gamble into his worst defeat," Eisenhower declared.

Not since the Falaise Gap, on the eve of the Allied victory in the Battle of France, has Eisenhower addressed his armies in an Order of the Day. He predicted a victory then, as he did in his D-Day message.

A tension comparable only to that of D-Day itself gripped the Army, from divisions in the line through the furthermost rear echelons.

Confidence, not gloom, marked the tension.

Brig. Gen. Ewart G. Plank, commander of Advance Section, Communications Zone, called upon the men of his command—the men who supply the materials and munitions for the armies—to redouble their efforts and pledged that not an

(Continued on Page 8)

SUPREME HEADQUARTERS
ALLIED EXPEDITIONARY FORCES

22 Dec. '44

ORDER OF THE DAY

TO EVERY MEMBER OF THE A.E.F.

The enemy is making his supreme effort to break out of the desperate plight into which you forced him by your brilliant victories of the summer and fall. He is fighting savagely to take back all that you have won and is using every treacherous trick to deceive and kill you. He is gambling everything, but already in this battle your gallantry has done much to foil his plans. In the face of your proven bravery and fortitude, he will completely fail.

But we cannot be content with his mere repulse.

By rushing out from his fixed defenses the enemy may give us the chance to turn his great gamble into his worst defeat. So I call upon every man, of all the Allies, to rise now to new heights of courage, of resolution and of effort. Let everyone hold before him a single thought—to destroy the enemy on the ground, in the air, everywhere—destroy him!

United in this determination and with unshakable faith in the cause for which we fight, we will, with God's help, go forward to our greatest victory.

Dwight D. Eisenhower

Anti-Spy Alert Is Stiffened; Paris 'Chutist Rumor Denied

U.S. Army and French authorities tightened their security restrictions yesterday following warnings from both the Provost Marshal and French radio that spies and saboteurs in Allied uniforms and civilian clothes were operating behind Allied lines.

Official sources denied yesterday that German paratroops have landed near Paris.

Associated Press reported that four German soldiers, wearing American uniforms and riding a jeep, were captured by six MPs in Belgium. The jeep packed enough dynamite to blow a strategic bridge and seriously hold up a Yank armored column moving to help block the German offensive.

The would-be saboteurs—three lieutenants and a sergeant—all

(Continued on Page 8)

New Red Drive Hinted in U.S.

WASHINGTON, Dec. 22 (AP).—A new Russian offensive in answer to rising Allied demands has definitely been promised and the starting date set, it was unofficially reported in the capital.

Soviet sources here said that this could not be confirmed officially but there is evidence the Allies are counting on a new winter drive by the Soviets. Informed sources said the projected drive will disclose the whereabouts of Red Army forces which last summer were fighting in the Baltic, Ukraine and White Russian fronts.

RUSSIAN GAINS IN SLOVAKIA

MOSCOW, Dec. 22 (AP).—German troops in Slovakia were feeling the sting of the Red Army lash today after the Russians had cut two important escape routes for Nazis trapped in the imperiled Czechoslovak rail city of Losonoc and had captured more than 30 towns and villages on the approaches to the city.

Moscow reported hearing German radio reports that more than 100,000 Russians had renewed the great offensive to encircle Budapest. It said hundreds of tanks and planes were thrown into an attempt to break through and that the Red Army had also resumed a great pincers movement on both sides of the city.

Two-Inch-High Banners Tell Home Front of Great Battle

By Carl Larsen
Stars and Stripes U.S. Bureau

NEW YORK, Dec. 22—With banner lines more than two inches high, newspaper accounts of the German counter-offensive for the past three days have startled U.S. readers, hitting them right between the eyes with such strongly-worded headlines as "Nazis Gained More in 3-Day Drive Than Allies Had Won in 3 Months."

Though a few editors even today approached the story from the angle of the New York World-Telegram's streamer, "Yank Rally Slows Nazis," most adopted a realistically tough policy like the Detroit Free Press: "Nazi Drive Grows in Fury: 45-Mile Gap Torn in U.S. Lines." The Buffalo Evening News banner warned (in its biggest type) "Nazis Gaining in Luxembourg; U.S. Loss Worst Since Baatan." The Chicago Sun's streamer said "Yanks Hit Back but Nazis Hurl 600 Tanks, 150,000 Men in Battle."

Other examples were: Chicago Tribune, "New German Drive Deepens Penetrations Into First Army Front"; St. Paul Pioneer Press, "Yanks Suffer Their Worst Losses of War and Inflict Heaviest"; Indianapolis Star, "Nazi Offensive Grows in Fury"; Oklahoma City Daily Oklahoman, "Nazis Swarm Through Gap in U.S. Lines"; St. Louis Globe Democrat, "Tanks Swarming Through Breach in U.S. Lines."

North Line Holds; Liege-Bastogne Highway Severed

Field Marshal von Rundstedt's plunging spearheads stabbed 40 miles into Belgium, but on the northern flanks of Germany's mightiest offensive of the war, the Nazi blitz came to a halt as Americans stood fast, Supreme Headquarters said last night.

Official battle reports, which lag 48 hours behind the situation at the blazing front, said enemy columns had reached the Belgian town of Laroche. This is 14 miles northwest of Bastogne, which the thrust outflanked on the north, and 11 miles northeast of Sedan. This placed them 38 miles from the French border.

American troops, responding to Gen. Eisenhower's call to crush Germany's desperate gamble—virtually unprecedented in modern history—were holding the charging line at several points.

Northern Stab Confined

SHAEF said U.S. troops had confined the northern Nazi stab to the area of St. Vith, Stavelot and Malmedy. The three Belgian towns were held by Americans up to noon Wednesday, the latest period covered by official reports.

In this whole sector, it was officially stated, the advance has been slowed. In the Monschau area, fighting diminished to only local actions and no substantial gains were made.

Germans were believed to be concentrating troops in this sector for another try.

The German DNB news agency, picked up by Reuter in London, last night dramatically interrupted its transmission from the Eastern front to flash the report that the Nazi winter offensive in the west has been slowed by flank attack by the U.S. Third Army, but there was no confirmation of this report from any Allied source.

On the southern flank where the drive had been halted as early as Tuesday, fighting had stabilized and all thrusts were checked in the areas of Dickweiler-Osweiler and

(Continued on Page 8)

Where German Columns Strike

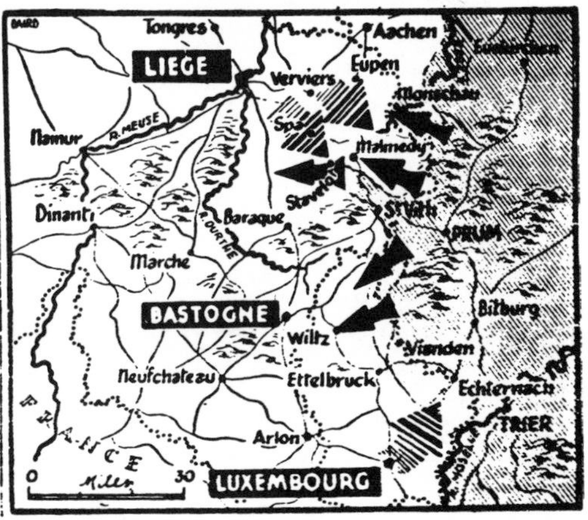

"...with unshakable faith in the cause for which we fight, we will, with God's help, go forward to our greatest victory."
Eisenhower's Order of the Day.

THE STARS AND STRIPES

Daily Newspaper of U.S. Armed Forces in the European Theater of Operations

"This is the battle in which the war probably will be won—by our side. Let's make sure it is the one."
A CO in France.

Vol. 1—No. 151 | 1Fr. | New York—PARIS—London | 1Fr. | Monday, Dec. 25, 1944

Yanks Stop Nazi Attack, Unleash Biggest Air Blow

Byrnes Acts To Spur U.S. War Output

Stars and Stripes U.S. Bureau

WASHINGTON, Dec. 24.—In one of the most drastic manpower moves of the war, the government yesterday served notice that materials, fuel and transportation would be denied businesses which defied manpower regulations.

Almost immediately after this announcement War Mobilization Chief James F. Byrnes ordered the nation's horse and dog racing tracks to shut down and stay closed until "war conditions permit reopening."

The actions capped a week of intensified endeavor to speed up the whole American war effort to a greater pace.

Had FDR's Support

Byrnes, acting with the President's approval on the racing ban, disclosed that he had requested Selective Service chief, Maj. Gen. Lewis B. Hershey, to have the nation's draft boards check on the classification of men known to be engaged in professional athletics who had been deferred because of failure to meet physical qualifications for the services, or who had

(Continued on Page 8)

Maj. Glenn Miller Lost On Flight from England

Maj. Glenn Miller, director of the USAAF band which has been playing in France, is reported missing while on a flight from England to Paris. The plane, in which he was a passenger, left England Dec. 15.

Maj. Miller lived at Tenafly, N.J., where his wife resides. No members of the band were with him.

Christmas Day—Puptent Version

Stars and Stripes Photo by Riordan

Pvt. Jack McDonald, of Chicago, decorates his Christmas tree outside his front-line home, but his weapons are ready.

'Christmas?' Asks Foxholer, —'Must Have Missed a Day'

By Bud Hutton
Stars and Stripes Staff Writer

WITH AMERICAN FORCES IN BELGIUM, Dec. 24.—They didn't even know what day it was.

They lay huddled in holes on a snow-covered hillside and peered down the slope to where the Germans were. When the 88s slammed into the hillside they crouched a little closer to the frozen earth. The cold ate through their clothing and made their lips grey. There was a six-day stubble of beard on their faces. Their hands were black with dirt worn into them, and from the powder of a lot of firing. They couldn't wash because there wasn't any water except in the little creek at the bottom of a hill, and even if they could have gotten

(Continued on Page 2)

Key Points Fall To Soviet Drive

BULLETIN

MOSCOW, Dec. 24 (Reuter).—Capture of Szekesfehervar and Bicske, strong points in the German defense of Budapest, was announced in an order of the day issued today by Marshal Stalin. Stalin said Soviet troops had broken through the enemy line of fortifications southwest of the Hungarian capital and had advanced up to 46 kilometers. Both captured towns are important communication centers.

In weather 18 degrees below freezing, Russian forces were battling against stern opposition toward the Baltic port of Libau along the Libau-Riga railroad in Latvia, according to German accounts yesterday.

The German news agency indicated that the first major battles of this winter offensive, on which Moscow so far has been silent, were being fought between Saldus, 57 miles northeast of Libau, and Mazeikiai, 52 miles southeast of Libau.

Bulge Stabilized; Columns Halted 29 Mi. from Sedan

WEST FRONT— Allied troops have stopped the German counter-offensive, Supreme Headquarters announced last night. SHAEF's Christmas Eve battle reports, 36 hours behind developments at the front, said the entire German salient was stabilized by Friday night and that the enemy made no farther advance.

AIR WAR— Led by history's greatest single bomber fleet, Allied air might rocked the stalled Wehrmacht with a series of sledge-hammer blows yesterday. More than 5,500 planes joined in the attack.

5,500 Planes Rock Enemy

The greatest force of heavy bombers ever mustered for a single mission by any air force—more than 2,000 Flying Fortresses and Liberators—ripped communication and supply centers of the German offensive in the most powerful of the day's air blows against Von Rundstedt's forces.

Thundering out in columns 400 miles long—so long that as the first bombers reached Germany, the last elements of the giant fleet were just taking off from their English bases—the heavies bombed a dozen road and rail junctions and supply centers from Euskir-

(Continued on Page 8)

German Wedge Split at St. Vith

Field Marshal von Rundstedt's counter-offensive, Germany's all-out effort to pull a stalemate out of impending defeat, was brought to a halt Friday night, SHAEF reported yesterday.

Nazi spearheads, aimed toward the Meuse Valley, were blocked as they stabbed 29 miles from Sedan in France after driving 40 miles through Luxembourg and Eastern Belgium.

Brightest official reports since the German offensive was sprung nine days ago said the bulge had been stabilized by Allied pressure on its flanks and center. As the

(Continued on Page 8)

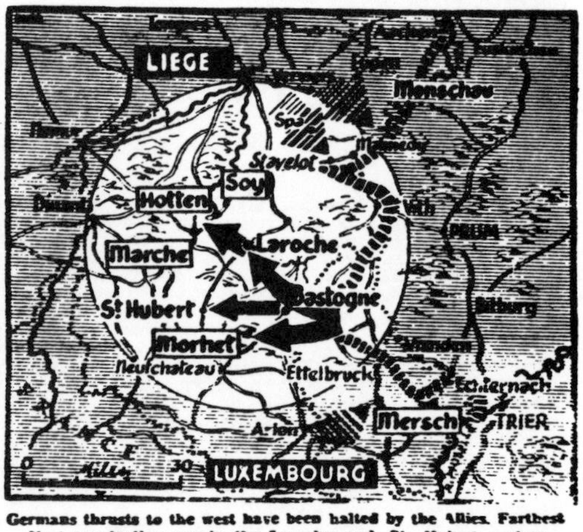

Germans thrusts to the west have been halted by the Allies. Farthest Nazi penetration was in the Laroche and St. Hubert sectors.

Acid-Throwing Nazi 'Chutists Hunt High Ranking U.S. Chiefs

By Jules B. Grad
Stars and Stripes Staff Writer

WITH U.S. FORCES, Belgium, Dec. 21 (Delayed).—German parachutists dropped behind U.S. lines to sabotage communications and kill high-ranking officers constitute a well-organized task force specially trained and equipped, a U.S. spokesman disclosed today.

They carry small phials of sulphuric acid which fit into match boxes and can be thrown in the faces of any who try to intercept them.

Their American uniforms were taken weeks ago from captured U.S. officers and men who were forced to strip to their underwear and then shot.

The parachutist force, equivalent to two battalions in strength, was specially organized to operate with the Nazi drive whenever it should start.

To organize it, the German High Command last October quietly withdrew all English-speaking soldiers from the Western, Russian and Italian fronts and sent them to a training center at Friedenthal, Berlin suburb.

THE STARS AND STRIPES

MEDITERRANEAN

Vol. 2, No. 42, Thursday, December 28, 1944 — ITALY EDITION * * TWO LIRE

Showdown Due In West; Greeks Accept Regency

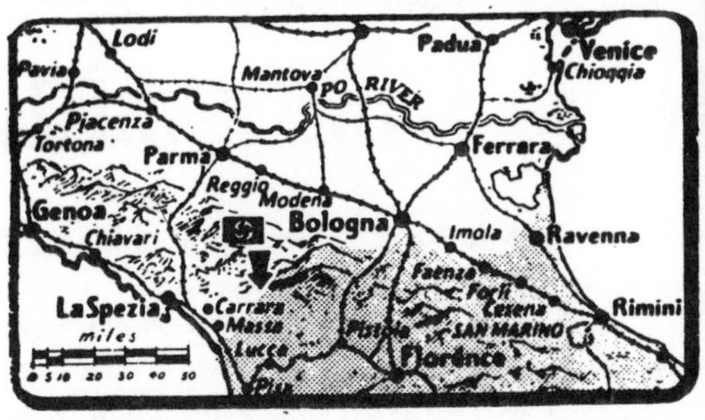

ENEMY ATTACKS against the 5th Army at the head of the Serchio River valley, and about 15 miles inland, were reported today.

Enemy Opens Drive On 5th Army Front

WITH THE 5TH ARMY, Dec. 27—For the first time in many weeks enemy activity flared up yesterday on the 5th Army front, as the Germans unleashed coordinated attacks of unrevealed strength at several points in the western sector.

In the West the Germans still hold the highest ground and they have strenuously opposed units of the 92nd Division who attempted to get more than a bare foothold on these Apennine slopes.

The location of their attacks, according to information thus far released, centers around the key road junction town of Gallicano at the head of the Serchio River Valley. Gallicano is about 15 miles inland from the sea and about 40 miles northeast of Leghorn, supply port for the 5th Army.

Elsewhere on the 5th Army front, the communique issued at Advanced Allied Force Headquarters said, things remained generally quiet with scattered patrol actions.

A number of German aircraft dropped anti-personnel bombs in the area of San Benedetto and Grizzana behind the 5th Army lines south of Bologna.

On the 8th Army front, Canadian troops continued to push ahead along the lateral road from Rossetta and cleared more fortified buildings along the east bank of the Senio River.

United Kingdom patrols were active northwest of Bagnacavallo and along the Senio, on the west bank of which the Germans were heard singing Christmas carols.

Supported by artillery, 8th Army troops continued to mop up enemy rearguards east of the Naviglio Canal between Bagnacavallo and Faenza, where the enemy is defending every building in an effort to hold his shrinking salient east of the Senio River.

Lloyd George Ends Parliament Service

LONDON, Dec. 27 (UP)—David Lloyd George, 81, "father" of the House of Commons and Prime Minister during World War I, disclosed today that he is retiring from Parliament on the advice of his doctor after 54 years of continuous service as member for Carnarvon.

His health has been somewhat impaired during recent years.

He was a struggling young lawyer, the son of an elementary school teacher when he won his first election in 1890 by 13 votes. He has never lost an election since.

Lloyd George was the man who inspired Britain's thought during the last war and who represented England in the Versailles peace conference. He was credited with building up Britain's munitions production and with instigating a single Allied command.

He married his secretary Frances Louis Stevenson last year.

It was recently reported he may be created an Earl in the New Year's honors list.

Free Ballot Will Decide Plan Of Rule

Prospects Brightened For Early Crisis Settlement

ATHENS, Dec. 27 — The representatives of all Greek factions, meeting for the second time today under the chairmanship of Archbishop Damaskinos, Primate of Greece, tonight unanimously agreed to the creation of a regency in place of the monarchy, until a free election can be held to determine what form of government the Greek people desire.

Archbishop Damaskinos will probably become regent, but will continue his chairmanship of the current negotiations.

This new development, which considerably brightened the prospects for an early settlement of the Greek civil war, came after Prime Minister Winston Churchill had assured Greek leaders here last night that Britain sought no advantages for herself in Greece.

Formation of a regency was one of the main demands of the guerrilla representatives. This afternoon, ELAS leaders put forth a number of proposals, which included a new cabinet, a governmental purge of Quisling elements, a free election, and the formation of a regency. Some of these proposals were still being considered late tonight.

The 70-year-old British Prime Minister, Foreign Secretary Anthony Eden and Field Marshal Sir Harold R. L. G. Alexander awaited the results after they had brought the leaders of the ELAS and the Greek government together yesterday.

The first meeting broke up late last night, after the British Premier's address, following which the opposing parties discussed the situation for several hours without coming to a definite solution. This morning, mortars and machine

(Continued on page 8)

Mother Kills Baby, It Looks Like Dad

LOS ANGELES, Dec. 27 (ANS) — Capt. Thad Brown of the Homicide Bureau said today that Mrs. Marian Johnson, 26, told police, "I threw my baby out of a window because he looked like my husband."

Mrs. Johnson was booked on suspicion of murder following the death plunge of her 3-week-old boy from the 11th floor of a downtown building. She declared her husband, Arnold Johnson, 33, an engraver at a Hollywood studio left her five months ago.

2 Red Armies Ready For Kill At Budapest

MOSCOW, Dec. 27 (UP)—After many weeks of fighting that has cost the Germans large losses in manpower and materials, Russian Armies operating around the Hungarian capital, Budapest, appear to be closing in for the kill today.

Soviet tank and infantry forces have completed their encirclement of Budapest, closing the escape corridor for many thousands of enemy troops.

The Russians have battled their way a mile and a half through the streets toward the heart of the city, smashing German resistance.

The Russians advanced into the city of Buda—west half of Budapest—capturing several communities within its limits, including Zugliget three and a half miles west of the Buda business district on the west bank of the Danube River.

Other Russian forces captured the great southwestern suburbs of Budafok, and Pilisvorosvar, five miles northwest of Budapest.

The shell-torn nine-mile Nazi escape corridor was sealed when Marshal Fedor Tolbukhin's 3rd Ukrainian Army advanced six miles and reached the Danube 19 miles northwest of Budapest.

These Russian forces captured 2,340 prisoners in the Budapest area on Monday, bringing the enemy's losses in these 5 days to a total of 21,808 killed and captured.

North of the Danube, Marshal Malinovsky's Army extended its wedge northeast of the Czech town of Sahy and smashed to within 91 miles northeast of Vienna by capturing the road junction of Rybnik.

Soviet troops advancing towards

(Continued on page 8)

Enemy Push Four Miles From Meuse

Spokesman Says Vital Supply Line Not In Danger

SHAEF, Dec. 27 — The great German counteroffensive on the Western Front which smashed to within four miles of the Meuse River below Namur in Belgium yesterday appeared to be nearing a decisive stage today.

Three full German armies, including two armored groups, were participating in the offensive which correspondents at Supreme Headquarters said was not merely a thrust to relieve Allied pressure on the Reich but an ambitious scheme to break through at the weak point in the Allied lines and roll up the whole Allied front in Belgium and Holland.

A Reuter's dispatch today said there was an immediate threat of the Germans reaching the Meuse in strength and trying to burst above it, but a SHAEF spokesman last night said that the strategic river line linking Allied supply lines to Liege had not yet been threatened "in any great strength."

In a review of several days action, the spokesman said that there had been little change since Sunday night when German troops had pushed to within four miles of the Belgian stronghold of Dinant on the Meuse and a second column had advanced to the town of Ciney in the same vicinity and 14 miles

(Continued on page 8)

UNRRA Taking Over Hospitals In Italy

WASHINGTON, Dec. 27—United Nations' Relief and Rehabilitation authorities will assume control of five camps and three hospitals for Greeks and Yugoslavs located in the "heel" of southeastern Italy on Jan. 1, the UNRRA announcement declared today.

A summary of UNRRA achievements during 1944 pointed out that the resolution which shaped the organization in November, 1943, has now developed a "mature" UNRRA.

Highlights of the summary include:

Regional administrative offices have been set up in London for European operations; in Sydney, Australia, for the Southwest Pacific, in Chungking, for the Far East.

A limited relief program is being set up in Italy.

A field office operating in Cairo is the base for a Balkan mission to Greece, Yugoslavia and Albania.

Missions have already gone to Ethiopia and Luxembourg.

Six middle Eastern refugee camps for Greeks and Yugoslavs have been operating under UNRRA supervision since May 1. Two reserve centers in Morocco and Algeria have also been established.

5th Army War Strictly Doughfoot Show

By Sgt. HAM WHITMAN

(This dispatch was written by the editor of Warweek, the weekly supplement published by the Paris edition of The Stars and Stripes. This is his story of the Italian Front as it compares to the Western Front.)

WITH THE 5TH ARMY, Dec. 27—Any Joe, crouched in a foxhole and looking toward the Po Valley, knows this is no cream-puff front. He may not know, however, just how it differs from war in northern France.

The first, and biggest, difference is that the northern Italian campaign is primarily an infantryman's war. On the French Front it is a team play, with armor, air force and artillery carrying as much of the load as do the foot sloggers.

Those divisions on the French Front have a break in terrain and they are able to send infantrymen into action, riding on tanks behind a barrage from the artillery and under the cover of the Air Force. That is they do when everything breaks right.

They don't have the heartbreaking mountain fighting in country which hampers the armor and under snow-charged icy fogs which blind bombardiers and artillery recon pilots alike.

This is the technique, worked out during last Summer's sweep across France.

In the main, the attack followed the road with motorized and lightly armored cavalry recon patrols jabbing toward the Germans along parallel roads. When the recon screen made contact, the heavier vehicles came up—each with a deck-load of doughboys. As the big tanks moved into position to blast the enemy strong-point, the infantry slipped to the ground, spread out and began filtering through on the flanks of the dug-in 88—or whatever the opposition turned out to be.

If the tank-infantry team found the going too tough, a radio car called on the Air Force for dive-bombers, or on the artillery-spotting planes to look the scene over and place fire where it was needed.

Often the spotter would find a concentration of German armor. When they did, and reported the

(Continued on Page 2)

German Planes Stage Brief Raid On Paris

PARIS, Dec. 27 (UP) — Enemy aircraft bombed Paris late Tuesday night the U. S. 9th Air Force announced today.

The raid was brief, and caused only slight damage and few casualties.

Bomb crashes startled the city shortly after 11 PM. Less than half an hour later the "all clear" was sounded. It was the first air raid alert the French capital has had since shortly after its liberation.

"The average replacement we are getting now is intelligent, well trained, has plenty of discipline."
—Lt. Col. J. T. Corley, 1st. Div.

THE STARS AND STRIPES

Daily Newspaper of U.S. Armed Forces in the European Theater of Operations

"If we fail to shatter the enemy's power now, the job will have to be done all over again within 20 years."
—Forrestal, Navy Secretary.

Vol. 1—No. 156 | 1 Fr. | New York—PARIS—London | 1 Fr. | Saturday, Dec. 30, 1944

Patton Retakes 13 Towns

Hammers Nazi Bulge from South As Air Power Cuts Enemy Lifeline

Master Race

Signal Corps Photo

Wearing a shelter-half and just about everything else he could carry on his short frame, this dejected German waits to be processed for a prison camp on the First Army Front.

9th Hits Bridges, Roads Behind Front

Tactical aircraft have cut all bridges, bombed all road bottlenecks behind the German advances and virtually completed the isolation of the battlefield from Wehrmacht supply installations, Ninth AF headquarters declared yesterday.

As fog again enveloped the front and hampered deployment of tactical air strength, the crucial importance for Allied forces of the five-day break in the weather was emphasized in figures released by the Ninth AF and the British Second TAF.

Since Von Rundstedt's offensive crossed the Belgian frontier Dec. 17, the Ninth AF alone has flown more than 10,000 sorties, despite a four-and-a-half-day air blackout because of heavy fog.

In the course of this onslaught the Ninth airmen knocked down 397 enemy planes, and destroyed or damaged 787 tanks and armored vehicles spearheading the offensive, almost 5,000 trucks and 1,700 railroad cars. In addition, concentrations of foot troops were strafed incessantly and supply lines battered.

Sorties Soar to 15,000

Since the counter-drives started, the Second TAF has flown approximately 6,200 sorties, to raise to well over 15,000 the tactical attacks on the German salient. The Tempests, Spitfires and Typhoons of the Second TAF have shot down 68 enemy planes and destroyed or damaged 709 armored and motor vehicles.

In addition ,the fighters escorting the heavies of the Eighth AF and the RAF, have inflicted heavy casualties on German vehicles and ground forces in the bulge, as well as on the Luftwaffe. The heavies themselves have flown close-behind-the-line support for the Allied armies, and have pounded rail and communication centers.

Since Von Rundstedt began his assault on Dec. 17, Ninth AF incomplete reports show 103 fighters and 44 bombers missing. During the past week, 50 heavy bombers and 60 fighters were lost from escorted Fortress and Liberators formations which totaled 9,590 sorties.

Stars and Stripes Map by Baird

Allied forces pound the tip of Von Rundstedt's giant spearhead into Belgium as Third Army forces push from the south.

Black-Market Net Snares 200 GIs, 2 Officers

Maj. Gen. Milton A. Reckord, ETO Provost Marshal, confirmed yesterday that 200 American EMs and two officers are under arrest on charges of selling cigarettes and other commodities, and said he thought those convicted should get the heaviest sentences possible.

Terming their actions "sabotage to the war effort and to soldiers at the front," he disclosed that they were rounded up in a drive which extended from Paris to Cherbourg by Army CID men and MPs. The drive against black-marketeers is continuing, he said.

Although the value of the cigarettes sold ran into thousands of dollars—one report put the figure at $200,000—Reckord agreed that black-market dealings, although considerable, could not have been the cause of the cigarette famine on the Continent.

Members of the House Military sub-Committee said in Paris Dec. 3 that high American officers told them that the famine was caused

(Continued on Page 8)

Tunnel Links Jap Islands

Tokyo radio announced yesterday that a tunnel had been completed between Honshu and Kyushu, the two principal Japanese home islands. It said that 130,000 men were employed two years in its construction.

Army Controls Ward's; Avery Raps Seizure

CHICAGO, Dec. 29 (ANS).—Montgomery Ward's properties in seven cities were under Army control today but the legality of the government seizure, remained unrecognized by Sewell Avery, 70-year-old chief of the nation-wide merchandising firm.

In challenging the President's authority to order the seizure, Avery said, "the company welcomes an opportunity to present its case to the courts." He told newsmen he would be in his office as usual today "unless I am thrown out."

Simultaneous with the seizure, the government acted to have the controversy with the company over non-compliance of War Labor Board directives settled in courts.

The President, in a statement accompanying the seizure order, termed Avery guilty of "consistent and wilful defiance" of WLB decisions. Avery retorted that Roosevelt's order was in violation of the Constitution and one which the company could not obey

After a conference with Maj. Gen. Joseph W. Byron, who has the title of "military manager of Montgomery Ward Inc.," Avery issued a statement asserting that the President had no power to seize a non-war business.

Today, government attorneys petitioned for an injunction to

(Continued on Page 3)

Fourth Armored Widens Path to Bastogne

Allied forces battled Field Marshal von Rundstedt's counter-offensive to a standstill while Lt. Gen. George S. Patton's U.S. Third Army hammered the deep German wedge from the south against the anvil of Allied might which is holding the north flank, official reports showed yesterday.

Battle reports yesterday, 24 to 30 hours behind events in the Battle of the Bulge, showed:

1. Third Army men seized 13 towns in attacks on a 35-mile front from Bastogne to the hinge of the Nazi wedge at Echternach.
2. Men and armor of the Third Army's Fourth Armored Div., which broke the siege of Bastogne, poured into the city and widened the corridor.
3. Allied air power has cut the main rail supply routes to the bulge from Germany by blowing up or damaging railway bridges in the rear.
4. While Von Rundstedt's drive is held momentarily in an Allied vise, there are indications that powerful German forces may launch a new assault.

American forces nipped the western tentacles of the Belgian salient between Rochefort and Celles where a Nazi force of regimental size was pocketed. Eastward, Von Rundstedt's forces pulled back into Germany and established defensive positions on the east side of Sauer

(Continued on Page 8)

Medic Captures 18 Nazis While Flat on His Back

WITH FOURTH INF. DIV., GERMANY.—It was all a misunderstanding, but when everything had quieted down Pvt. Robert J. Reynolds, Johnstown, N.Y. medic, had bagged 18 prisoners, and the

Germans were very pleased to be in a PW cage.

It started when a German threw down his pistol and raised hie hands as Reynolds approached. The Yank, however, was suspicious and tackled the Nazi with bare fists. Disturbed by this reaction, the German fought back. Other Germans crowded around. Finally the Nazis pinned down the medic's shoulders, and told him they wanted to surrender. So they marched back to the PW cage, feeling each had gotten the better of the bargain.

Nazi Offensive in Italy Loses Some of Its Dr...

ROME, Dec. 29.—Fighting has died down along the Serchio River near the west coast of Italy where the Germans launched a drive Allied Headquarters announced today. But it was disclosed that U. S. troops previously had been forced out of Gallicano, road and river town on the west bank of the Serchio.

The Fascist radio claimed that the Germans had seized the village of Fornaci, two miles south of Barga.

Ike Thanks Home Front

Gen. Eisenhower has thanked New York Manpower Commission's Regional Labor Committee for their message sent after his Dec. 22 Order of the Day calling for a supreme effort by Allied troops. The commission pledged that the home front would "rise to new heights of effort in bringing you the tools of war with which you are waging the fight."

The Supreme Commander replied: "Your heart-warming pledge has been published to our troops and will have a fine effect. None of us here has any doubt concerning the ability and readiness of all Americans at home to perform at top speed when they understand the need of their relatives and friends on the firing lines. My thanks to you and all those you represent for the promptness and decisiveness of your message."

34th Submarine Lost

WASHINGTON, Dec. 29 (ANS)—The U.S. Navy announced that the Sea Wolf, a 1,450-ton submarine commanded by Lt. Comdr. Albert M. Bontier, of White Plains, N.Y., is overdue on Pacific patrol and presumed lost with a crew of at least 62 men. The Navy said this was the 34th U.S. submarine lost from all causes in this war.

A Convoy From Bastogne:

Hurt GIs Want Paris 'Momma'

By Jimmie Cannon
Stars and Stripes Staff Writer

WITH AMERICAN FORCES —[illegible] shouted, but all you could hear was a smeared whisper through the bandages.

"I'll never forget that town," he muttered. "I left a piece of my nose in it."

The convoy of wounded came out of Bastogne in a slow trickle. The day was beautiful if you like Belgium in the winter time. The snow on the hills glittered in the sun, and the planes towed vapor trails across the big, clean sky.

The wounded sat stiffly in the trucks, and they rose tautly when they came to a rut in the frozen road. The dust of the road had made their hair gray, but it did not look strange because their faces were old with suffering and fatigue.

"We're all 4Fs in here," said Chicago to the guy who had climbed into the truck. "A healthy guy like you better look out. You'll get drafted."

Detroit's neck was swollen as he yelled, but his voice was still, small and remote.

"We were standing around a mess truck," he said, "waiting for some hot cakes when they let go with everything they had. We were in a field and they were up above us and all around us. What a going over they gave us!"

Pocono Mountains, who sat with a blanket over his head, said these hills reminded him of home.

"There was an outfit getting an awful going over in a little village", he said "We went across an open field and exposed ourselves to keep Jerry busy. He got too interested in us—those other guys got away.

"Give me Paris!" Brooklyn shouted. "Give me Paris and a nice Momma who'll wash and shave me and tuck me to sleep for 9,000,000 years."

They all laughed, but you couldn't tell they were laughing by looking at their faces.

"Find me a girl like that," said Illinois, "and I'll marry her myself."

"We are good in the hospital,"

(Continued on Page 8)

THE STARS AND STRIPES
MEDITERRANEAN

Vol. 2, No. 49, Friday, January 5, 1945 ITALY EDITION * * TWO LIRE

1st Army Opens Attack On Belgium Battlefront

Teams With 3rd In Drive To Eliminate Bulge; Artillery Battle Reported At Mulhouse

PARIS, Jan. 4 (UP)—The American 1st Army has opened the long awaited counteroffensive on the northern flank of the Belgian bulge, teaming with the 3rd Army in the south in a great drive against the 200,000 German defenders of the salient, it was announced at Allied Headquarters today.

(An announcement from BBC said the 1st Army had gained up to three and one-half miles in the first stages of the drive, launched in the St. Malmedy-Stavelot sector.)

Elsewhere, front dispatches said, in an obvious reference to the battle of the bulge, the American 1st and 3rd Armies stood less than 16 miles apart when the 1st went back over to the offensive for the first time since it was jolted loose from its Belgian-Luxembourg line by the German push beginning December 16.

Lt. Gen. Courtney Hodges sent his forces into action under low clouds which stripped the American forces of all direct air support, and at the same time permitted the Germans to shift their reserves inside the pocket without fear of attack from the air.

Heavy snow was reported falling all along the front this morning.

A SHAEF spokesman made it clear that this is a big Allied attempt to engage and destroy the 200,000 crack German troops and hundreds of tanks which Marshal von Rundstedt has drawn from Germany's last strategic reserves.

Third Army tanks were reported to be fighting their way through the Nazi forces in a four-column push. From Bastogne they drove up to five miles northeast of that town, reaching within five miles

(Continued on page 8)

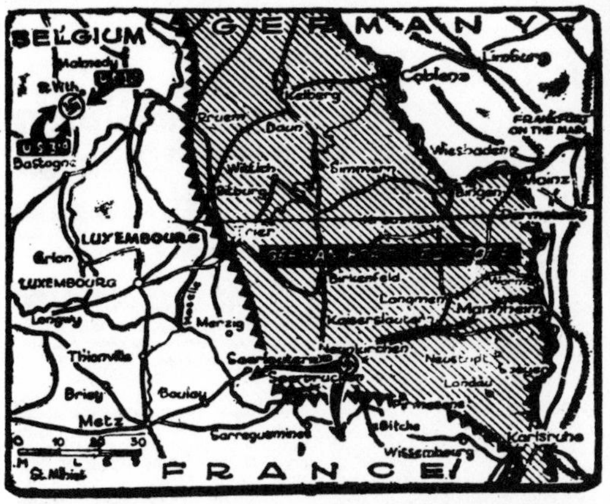

THE AMERICAN 1st Army has opened its long-awaited counterdrive on the northern flank of the Belgian bulge. The same bulge is being attacked from the south by the U. S. 3rd Army. On the southern end of the long West Front, the Germans are driving against the American 7th Army with some success.

New Landing Made On Mindoro Island

LEYTE, Jan. 4—American troops have made two new amphibious landings on Mindoro Island, one on the east coast on Monday, and one on the southwest coast on Tuesday, north of their present positions, it was revealed today.

Both landings were made without opposition, according to United Press.

The landings took place with the full support of heavy and medium bombers which, sweeping Japanese shipping off Luzon's west coast, sank or set afire one 7,000-ton transport, one 6,000-ton freighter, 21 smaller freighters and two large trawlers.

Simultaneously, medium and light bombers cut a wide path of destruction through southern Luzon, battering rail installations, reservoirs and barracks in the coastal area. Heavy bombers escorted by fighter planes hammered Clark Field on Monday, 47 miles northwest of Manila, shooting down 11 of 20 Japanese planes which attempted at interception.

There was no indication precisely where the New Mindoro landings have been made.

In a blow comparable to the devastating raids which preceeded

(Continued on page 8)

Turkey Announces Break With Tokyo

ANKARA, Jan. 4 (AP)—Turkey has decided to break off diplomatic and economic relations with Japan, it was announced tonight. Severance of relations is to become effective at midnight Saturday, January 6.

The Turkish Parliament voted to break unamiously after it had been made known that the United States and Great Britain wanted Turkey to take the step.

One of the first effects will be the expulsion of Japanese diplomatic and economic personnel who constituted an important enemy listening post.

The rupture will leave the Axis without a well-organized espionage system in the Middle East.

The break was announced in a surprise statement by Foreign Minister Hasan Saka in the National Assembly yesterday. In making the announcement, the Foreign Minister said that "naturally it will depend on the decision and attitude of other interested parties whether this severance of diplomatic relations will be transformed into a state of war."

Japanese agents known to be in Turkey are estimated at 20 by American Embassy sources. Since the rupture of relations between Turkey and Germany, the Japs have carried the full burden of Axis espionage in Turkey.

Sub Harder Lost

WASHINGTON, Jan. 4 (ANS)—The Navy has announced the loss of the submarine Harder and of three other craft. The Harder, holder of a Presidential Unit Citation for sinking thousands of tons of Japanese shipping, was the 35th U. S. submarine lost in this war.

Three Clashes Highlight 5th Army Front Activity

WITH THE 5TH ARMY, Jan. 4—While important but unspectacular operations against the Nazis continued today along most of the 5th Army Front in north Italy, Allied troops met the enemy in three main encounters:

(1) A German raid against English-held positions on the Mount del Verro Sillara ridge area, preceded by a rocket barrage, was repulsed. Another novel enemy tactic was the firing of huts and shelters in Allied outpost areas by the use of incendiary bullets.

(2) Northwest of Grizzano, South African troops clashed with the enemy in three areas. In the Gaggle region one sharp encounter took place inside a church with Allied troops using hand grenades to drive out two or three Germans who were hidden behind the altar.

(3) German night raiders were over the front lines last night dropping anti-personnel bombs. One plane is reported to have been shot down.

It was revealed today that in the recent Serchio Valley push, the drive was made by Wehrmacht troops which had passed through Italian Fascist troops holding defensive positions along that sector.

Advanced Allied Force Headquarters said that Canadian infantry and armor continued their charge up the marshy Adriatic coastal sector of the 8th Army front yesterday. They gained 3,000 yards against Tiger and Panther tanks brought up by Kesselring to support his infantrymen.

The area policed by the Canadians is northeast of Alfonsine on the Ravenna-Ferrara road.

After capturing Conventello, branching off coastal Highway 16 Canadians advanced toward San Alberto on the east side of the Vecchio ditch. Tankers are slogging some two miles from San Alberto, just before the great inland lagoon of Valli di Comacchio. These advances have carried the Canadians to points north of the Bologna meridian.

Enemy Relief Drive Gains In Hungary

Red Army Increases Holdings Inside Budapest

MOSCOW, Jan. 4 (UP)—A strong German counteroffensive from western Hungary, aimed at relieving the encircled Budapest garrison, gained ground today, but inside the Hungarian capital Soviet shock troops broke through to the Danube River and captured another 167 city blocks. They won the big central park in the eastern half of the city.

The Soviet command admitted that the Germans—at the cost of immense losses in men and materials—had recaptured several towns and villages on the south bank of the Danube, 31 miles northwest of Budapest, but said that the counteroffensive has been repelled.

A broadcast from Berlin said that the Germans have hurled thousands of men and tanks and hundreds of big guns into an effort to crack the steel ring around Budapest.

Sixty-one German tanks were destroyed yesterday, the majority southeast of the Czech town of Komaron, while the grim Budapest battle continued through the ninth day, with Russians appearing to hold half of the city, having won 962 blocks.

Nearly 50 miles northeast of Budapest, the Russians converged on the Czech rail city of Losong, taking Sacher, which is only one

(Continued on Page 3)

Heavies Set Record For Winter Bombing

LONDON, Jan. 4 — The 1,100 Flying Fortresses and Liberators of the 8th AAF, which smashed at road and rail centers in western Germany yesterday for the 12th day running—set a new record for sustained winter bombing.

The mission brought the heavies to within five days of all-time consecutive bombing record, 17 straight days in good summer weather.

During the past 12 days, 8th AAF planes have flown about 18,000 bomber and fighter sorties and dropped 26,000 tons of bombs.

Fighter pilots and bomber gunners have reported 386 German planes shot down during the period.

The targets yesterday included an unnamed communications center northwest of Karlsruhe, road junctions near the Belgian-German border and marshalling yards near Cologne and at Schafenburg and Fulda, both near Frankfort.

Alleged Nazi Agents Facing Army Court

NEW YORK, Jan. 4 — The trial of two alleged Nazi agents seized by the FBI after they were landed from a submarine on the Maine coast last Nov. 29 probably will be before a military tribunal.

President Roosevelt said yesterday he assumed that the two will be tried in the same manner as the eight German agents captured in 1942. The eight were tried in secret by a commission of Army officers which sentenced six to death and two to life imprisonment.

The prisoners, William C. Colepaugh, 26-year-old American, and Aric Gimpel, 37, native of Germany, are being held here by the FBI until a decision is reached on the type of charges to be preferred against them.

Yugoslavs Repulse Attacks In Bosnia

LONDON, Jan. 4 — Yugoslav troops repulsed German assaults from Bijeljina Polje in east Bosnia near the Slavonian border, killing 50 Germans and capturing 22, Marshal Tito's communique reported today.

In Croatia, in the sector north of Binac, four localities were liberated from the Germans after two days fighting. Enemy losses amount to over 300 German dead and 30 prisoners

Help For Veterans Theme Of Congress

WASHINGTON, Jan. 4 (ANS)—Proposals to aid returning soldiers predominated among the first bills introduced in the 79th Congress today and—while the proposals ranged from small claims to suggestions for overhauling government procedure—the "let's help the veterans' theme remained constant.

The first resolution introduced into the new House came from Rep. James Ludlow (D., Ind.). It asked that disability benefits be speeded for honorably discharged service personnel.

Another called for the government to match enlisted mens' savings dollar for dollar. A third asked cancellation up to 100 dollars of the amount of income tax owed by service men for the taxable year prior to their entering the service.

The tenor of the resolutions made it apparent that war legislation will be the main consideration of the Congress. Both houses, however, anxiously awaited President Roosevelt's annual message which will be delivered at a joint session Saturday.

The message is expected to beat

(Continued on Page 3)

Fair Enough

OMAHA — Nabbed for impersonating women at saloons, Edward Kinney said he gave mashers the eye, drank free.

THE STARS AND STRIPES

Daily Newspaper of U. S. Armed Forces in the European Theater of Operations

ONE FRANC

Man Spricht Deutsch

Sie können zu Fuss gehen.

Zee kennen tsoo Foose gayhen.

You can go on foot.

Volume 1, Number 30 — New York — STRASBOURG — Paris — Saturday, January 6, 1945

Monty Takes Northern Front Command

USAAF Flying Box Cars Make Saint Nick Look Pale

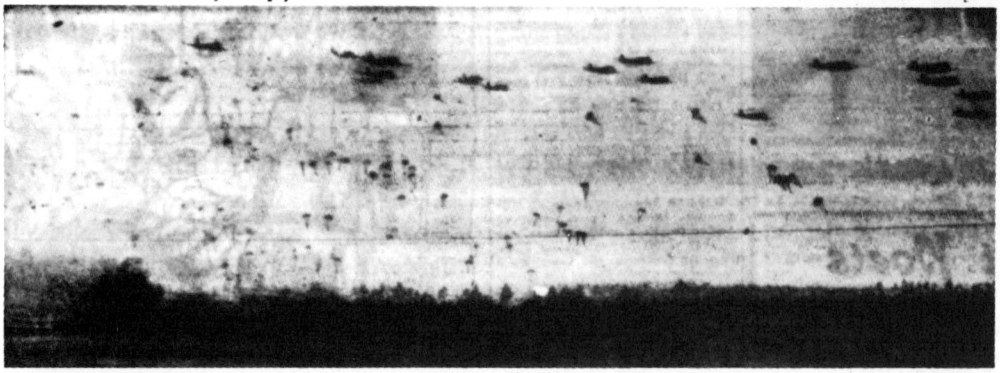

Christmas Day looked this way in Bastogne as C-47s dropped medical supplies and ammunition by parachutes to the beleagured garrison of 101st Airborne troops holding out against the Germans who in vain had tried to capture the stronghold. — Signal Corps Photo

Enemy Force Crosses Rhine; 'Bulge' Whittled

WITH THE U. S. 7TH ARMY, Jan. 5—German troops, 800 strong, today crossed the Rhine River above Strasbourg.

The crossing was made in the vicinity of Gambsheim, on the west bank of the river about 11 miles north of the Alsatian capital. Heavy fighting was in progress.

Field Marshal Sir Bernard Law Montgomery, Rommel's nemesis at El Alamein and Tunis, yesterday took over full command of all Allied armies north of the German salient in Belgium.

Official announcement of the change in the west front high command came from the headquarters of Gen. Dwight D. Eisenhower, Allied Supreme Commander. The accompanying statement said that the change was made because the German drive west had created a northern and a southern front within the former Allied west front.

In Washington, General George C. Marshall, U. S. chief of staff, declared that the Montgomery appointment had been made Dec. 17, at the start of the German offensive. Formerly chief of the 21st Army Group, including the British 2nd and the Canadian 1st Armies, the British Marshal has now had the U. S. 1st and 9th Armies added to his command.

Bradley Heads South

Lt. Gen. Omar N. Bradley, chief of the 12th Army Group, was named as Allied commander on the southern flank of von Rundstedt's bulge.

Slightly slowed by fog and bad weather, Marshal Montgomery's northern pincer on the German salient has made a general advance of three miles all along an approximate 21-mile front.

Backed by British tanks, the U. S. 1st Army has driven into the town of Arbrefontaine, some seven miles south-east of Stavelot.

The U. S. 3rd Army, on von Rundstedt's southern flank, has stood firm despite desperate German pressure. Correspondents reported that the enemy had thrown as many as 17 counterattacks against Lt. Gen. George S. Patton's troops in the last 24 hours in the Bastogne area.

Heaviest fighting of the day was reported from south of Rochefort, at the western tip of the German salient, where British troops have been making bloody and bitterly fought yard-by-yard advances against the enemy's 2nd Panzer division.

New Big Attack

South of the Saar and Palatinate borders, the Germans were reported in full-scale attack against the U. S. 7th Army. The enemy was said to have penetrated another two miles in a push toward the Saverne Gap, passage through the Vosges to Strasbourg on the Rhine.

Another 2,000 Allied heavy bombers have raided the Reich within the last 24 hours.

Operating from Britain in daylight, 1,000 8th USAAF Forts and Libs, supported by 800 Mustangs, attacked some 30 vital spots in the enemy's communication network for the western front from Cologne to Frankfurt. RAF Lancasters also made daylight raids on German rail yards at Ludwigshafen. Allied fighters ranged the battlefronts and British fighters attacked V-weapon launching sites in Holland.

Enemy Attempt To Relieve Buda Still Stymied

MOSCOW, Jan. 5—The strong German counteroffensive northwest of Budapest went into its fourth day today without the enemy being able to make any headway in the effort to relieve his trapped and steadily diminishing garrison in the Hungarian capital.

The Germans were reported using about seven panzer and two infantry divisions in these operations and have lost heavily in both men and materiel in the bitter battles in progress since Tuesday.

Russian troops have repelled all German efforts which have cost the enemy 51 tanks and 30 planes in the last 24 hours.

The fierce struggle within the Hungarian capital continued, with the Russians capturing another 300 blocks of buildings in the city and taking 2,300 more prisoners.

FDR Stays Mum On 'Big 3' Parley

WASHINGTON, Jan. 5—Despite repeated queries by correspondents, President Roosevelt at his press conference today refused to give any information or hints about his forthcoming meeting with Prime Minister Winston Churchill and Marshal Joseph Stalin.

Only positive news obtained about the scheduled »Big-Three« conference was an understanding that details of the meeting will not be available to the public until a week after it has taken place.

Wreck Kills Fifty

OGDEN, Utah—At least 50 persons were killed and 60 others injured in a New Year's Eve crash of a speeding Southern Pacific mail express and a slow-moving passenger train—both westbound — on the fog-shrouded causeway over the shallow waters of the Great Salt Lake.

101st AB Division General Says No 'Rescue' Took Place

To keep the record straight, Brig. Gen. Anthony G. McAuliffe emphatically asserted that his 101st Airborne Div. was not »rescued« at Bastogne.

Speaking at a press conference, the fighting general who made history by his epic reply of »Nuts!« to a German demand to surrender, declared:

»Anyone who says we were rescued or who thinks we needed rescue is all wrong. On Christmas night, I called my regimental commanders together and told them we now were ready for pursuit.«

That was the picture after a solid week of seige in which the Germans threw in everything they had against the surrounded 101st. McAuliffe revealed that the division had moved into Bastogne at a most inopportune time when their ranks were filled with several thousand reinforcements and when their supplies had run low. But, he pointed out, after a week the 101st had knocked out 144 German tanks, taken 75 prisoners and killed thousands of Nazis.

McAuliff's own story of how he replied »Nuts!« to the Germans who demanded his surrender was revealed in his dramatic Order of the Day:

»What's merry about all this, you ask? We're fighting—it's cold—we aren't home. But what has the proud Eagle Division accomplished with all its worthy comrades of the 10th Armored Division, the 705th TD Bn and all the rest? Just this: We have stopped cold everything that has been thrown at us from the north, east, south and west. We have identifications from four German Pz divisions, two German infantry divisions, and one German parachute division. These units, the last desperate German lunge, were headed straight west for key points. The Eagle Div. was hurriedly ordered to stem the advance.

Have Done Well

»How effectively this was done will be written in history: Not alone in our division's history, but in world history. The Germans actually did surround us, their radios blared our doom. Their commander demanded our surrender in the following impudent arrogance:

»Dec. 22, 1944. To the USA commander in the encircled town of Bastogne. The fortune of war is changing. This time the U.S. forces in and near Bastogne have been encircled by strong German armored units. More German armored units have crossed the river Ourthe near Ortheuville, have taken Marche, have reached Schubert by passing through Homores-Sibret-Tillet. Libramont is in German hands.

»There is only one possibility to save the encircled USA. troops from annihilation: That is, the honorable surrender of the encircled town. In order to think it over, a term of two hours will be granted, beginning with the presentation of this note.

Surrender Or Else

»If this proposal should be rejected, a German artillery corps and six heavy AA battalions are ready to annihilate the U.S. forces in and near Bastogne. The order for firing will be given immediately after this two-hour term.

»All these serious civilian losses caused by this artillery fire would not correspond with the well-known American humanity.

(Signed) The German commander.«

»The German commander received the following reply: 22 Dec. 44. To the German Commander: N-U-T-S (Signed) American Commander.«

Moscow Backs Poles in Lublin

MOSCOW, Jan. 5—The Soviet foreign office today announced recognition of the Polish provisional government in Lublin.

Formal exchange of ambassadors will be made between the two governments. It was understood that the Russian envoy has already left for his new post.

Great Britain and the United States have previously recognized the Polish government-in-exile in London as the legitimate regime of Poland. Russia has informed the U. S. of its decision to recognize the Lublin group and a U. S. State Department spokesman has declared that the U. S. will continue to recognize the London government.

The matter of recognition of the two Polish governments has split the Allies on policy regarding Poland. Britain and the U. S. back the Polish group in London, while Russia and France have given official nods to the Lublin regime.

New P.I. Landings

WASHINGTON, Jan. 5—U S forces today invaded another Philippine island.

The latest landings, reported in Gen. Douglas MacArthur's communique, were made without Jap opposition on the island of Marinduque, east of Mindoro and south of Luzon.

Germans Reach Wingen Vicinity Below Bitche

WITH THE 7TH ARMY, Jan. 5—German forces, increasing their efforts to break out of the bulge in our lines below Bitche, today reached vicinity Wingen, nine and one half miles below that fortress city after stepping up their artillery and mortar fire in the entire area.

Heavy fighting was reported in Philippsbourg and Berenthal, to the northwest. Both towns have changed hands several times since the Germans launched their large-scale attack on the 7th Army center New Year's Eve.

Enemy pressure at the southern tip of his six-mile deep wedge appeared to be an attempt to break out into the plains, some two miles away to the east and four miles distant on the west. Wingen lies astride Highway 45, strategic east-west route through the lower Vosges Mountains. It enters the Alsace plain about 11 miles north of Saverne.

The town of Reipertswiller, previously the southernmost tip of the German push, was cleaned up, relieving two American companies which had been temporarily cut off although they had as prisoners remnants of an entire German battalion together with the battalion CO.

At least one other point in the enemy salient, the Boche were attacking in two-company strength. So far, the hilly Vosges have prevented any extensive use of tanks by either side, although tank country is what the enemy is trying to reach.

The situation on the rest of the 7th Army front was relatively quiet today and last night. South of Wissembourg, the enemy threw in artillery concentrations. The French 1st Army sector had little activity.

ELAS Quits Fight

ATHENS, Jan. 5—All resistance by ELAS insurgent forces in Athens and the port of Pireaus ceased tonight.

There have been no reports concerning northern Greece, where civil clashes have also been going on between other ELAS units and government troops.

The recently-formed cabinet of General Nicholas Plastiras had made it clear earlier in the day that there will be no negotiations between government and ELAS groups until fighting ceased, as required by British truce terms.

Canadians Reach Marshes

ROME, Jan. 5—Canadian infantry, supported by British 8th Army tanks, today reached canals of the Comacchio Salt Marsh, south of Ferrara and the Po delta, after heavy clashes with German armored units.

Farther west in the Po valley, the 8th Army further reduced the enemy bridgehead east of the Senio River along the Faenza-Bologna road.

V-Weapon Awaited

WITH THE AMERICAN 7TH ARMY IN EASTERN FRANCE—German GI's anticipate the appearance of an improved jet-propulsion plane as the secret weapon which will turn the tide of war in their favor.

One prisoner said that he believes firmly in the promise of a new secret weapon which will eliminate Allied air superiority. The improved jet-propulsion job is elite, he said. Many of his comrades share this belief.

We shall be surprised, this prisoner predicts, by the large number of reorganized and newly organized divisions which stand ready in Germany to throw us back.

There's A Long Walk Ahead

WASHINGTON, Jan. 5—The War Department anticipates American soldiers will walk a considerable part of the road to Berlin and Tokio, having increased shoe requirements—for the first quarter of 1945.

About 150,000 more pairs of combat boots and service-type boots will be necessary over and beyond the amount used during each month of the last quarter of 1944.

The Quartermaster Corps is engaged in a vast shoe-rebuilding program in addition to its new procurements. Some 200,000 pairs are being fitted each month and issued for training purposes. In addition, the Corps recently fully-equipped and self-contained shoe repair unit which is about 13 tons lighter than the 33,000-pound tractor-trailer unit now in use.

The new unit is mounted on a two-wheel trailer less than half as long as the older model and weighs only 2,900 pounds. It may be towed by a jeep and is transportable in a plane or glider.

Man Spricht Deutsch
Kommen Sie heraus.
Kommen Zee herrowss.
Come out of there.

THE STARS AND STRIPES

Daily Newspaper of U.S. Armed Forces in the European Theater of Operations

Ici On Parle Français
Merci quand même.
MehrSEE kawn mehm.
Thanks just the same.

Vol. 1—No. 164 | 1 Fr. | New York—PARIS—London | 1 Fr. | Sunday, Jan. 7, 1945

'45 Can Be V-Year–FDR

Monty's Armies Drive 1,000 Yds. As 3rd Army Repels 6 More Attacks

Field Marshal Sir Bernard L. Montgomery's Anglo-American armies ploughed 1,000 yards deeper into the north flank of the frosty German salient yesterday as it became apparent that the time which Nazis hoped to gain by the Ardennes counter-offensive was running out in the hour-glass-shaped Belgian bulge.

Germans fell back doggedly under the powerful assault from the north. They forced U.S. Third Army troops on the south flank to pull back from Michamps, five miles northeast of Bastogne, to high ground two miles northeast of the siege city.

Lt. Gen. George S. Patton's forces smashed back six more counter-attacks between St. Hubert on the west end of the salient in Belgium to Wiltz in Luxembourg. The heaviest Nazi assault was launched by a battalion of infantry led by eight tanks north of Margaret, two miles northeast of Bastogne. American armored troops crushed the attack with tank and artillery fire.

Sporadic Forces Cross Rhine

Meanwhile, Field Marshal von Rundstedt's junior offensive in the Alsatian Rhineland continued to erupt at points north of Strasbourg as sporadic German forces boated across the Rhine. In northern Alsace, however, where Germans have driven a 10-mile bulge south of Bitche, the little offensive seemed to be running out of steam for the time being.

U. S. Seventh Army forces surrounded Wingen which the Germans took on the Sarre Union-Haguenau Road and recaptured Philippsbourg to the east.

The Alsace attack has none of the brilliance and careful planning of the Ardennes offensive. Germans were ordered out of their Siegfried pillboxes in the Palatinate to attack with only a few hours' notice and without definite objectives.

Yesterday's German communique spoke of Allied armored reinforcements being thrown into the Ardennes battle. It said that four British tank divisions were fighting on the north flank.

It was estimated yesterday that Von Rundstedt has lost about 100,000

(Continued on Page 8)

Yanks Capture Isle 20 Miles Off Luzon Tip

Stars and Stripes Map by Baird

Bombers Blast Manila; B29s Hit Targets Close to Tokyo

The American invasion of Marinduque Island in the Philippines, only 20 miles from the Luzon coast and 100 miles southwest of Manila, was made unopposed by units of the U.S. Sixth Army under Lt. Gen. Walter Krueger, it was announced yesterday. The landings on the 10-mile-square island were made on the southwest coast in the vicinity of Buenavista.

Heavy and medium bombers resumed the air attacks on Manila from American bases on Leyte and Mindoro.

Asia-based Superfortresses, of the

(Continued on Page 8)

GI Slain, 5 Held In Theft Ring

NINTH AIR SERVICE COMMAND HQ., France, Jan. 6.—A gang of AWOL American soldiers and French civilians dealing in stolen U.S. Army supplies has been broken up by Ninth Air Force Service Command MPs after a gun battle in which one soldier was killed and three wounded.

The gang's headquarters in Northern France was raided Thursday. Several thousands of dollars worth of rations, one jeep and two trucks were recovered.

While four soldiers were being questioned, a truck drove up. Sgt. Levi M. Dolloff, Needham, Mass., and Pvt. Albert DeWilde, Pineville, La., ordered the two men in the truck to dismount. Instead, the driver fired, wounding Dolloff. Another MP, Pvt. Frank J. Woods, New York City, killed the driver with a pistol. Woods was wounded in the exchange of fire. The driver's companion was hit by shots fired by Pfc Lawrence Allard, Attleboro, Mass.

Investigators said the soldiers made trips to Paris where, with forged requisitions, they drew 250 rations a day.

MESSAGE HIGHLIGHTS

1945 can see the final ending of the Nazi-Fascist reign of terror in Europe . . . the closing in of forces of retribution about Japan."

Adopt a "National Service Act as the most efficient and democratic way of insuring full production. . ."

A peace "which will secure so far as humanly possible the fulfillment of the principles of the Atlantic Charter. . ."

Renewed demand for "unconditional surrender" . . . but applied it only to . . "the armies of our enemies."

Power politics "must not be a controlling factor in international relations. . ."

". . . In Europe, we shall resume attack and, despite temporary setbacks here or there, we shall continue the attacks relentlessly. . ."

". . .Our Navy looks forward to any opportunity which the Lords of the Japanese Navy will give us. . ."

". . . Strenuous days of war ahead. . ."

P51s Streak Through Fog To Flush Out Tank Column

A handful of reconnaissance and fighter-bomber pilots flew through almost impossible weather Dec. 18, in the early stages of Von Rundstedt's offensive, to batter to a standstill a German armored column thrusting toward American oil-stores and communications, the Ninth AF disclosed yesterday.

A column of more than 200 tanks, armored cars and trucks, carrying elite troops of an SS division, was moving through virtually impenetrable fog when Maj. Gen. E. R. Quesada, Ninth TAC chief, in contact with First Army Hq., learned the Germans had driven through the Losheim gap and were racing toward Stavelot.

Two Mustangs, piloted by Capt. Richard H. Cassidy, of Nashville, Ark., and 2 Lt. Abraham Jaffe, of New York City, took off to find them. With visibility limited to only a few hundred feet they flew up and down valleys, sometimes less than 100 feet above the ground, finally spotting the armor moving west near Stavelot.

Cassidy and Jaffe reported to combat operations and fighter control, and Thunderbolts of the "Hell Hawks" group, carrying 500-pound bombs, roared toward the target guided by radio.

Seven flights took off, and by nightfall 126 armored vehicles and trucks were smouldering wrecks, with 40 more damaged.

Ssh! U.S.–'SS'

Sally's Sallies Suggest New Shoulder Patch For 30th Div.

WITH 30TH DIV.—The Joes of the 30th Div. have thrown one of "Sally's" sallies right back in the Nazi propaganda gal's face.

Sally had been saying in her nightly English language broadcasts that the 30th boys were "F. D.R.'s S.S. troops." The boys rather fancied the idea. They pointed out they really were Elite Troops, a chosen few, and top-notch fighters. Maj. E. L. Glaser, of Palm Beach, Fla., decided to adopt the designation and make a new division patch to go with it.

The result was a design, now under consideration at division headquarters, which combines the O and H of the 30th's Old Hickory with the two flashes of lightning which comprise the S.S. troopers' insignia—and to top it off, the President's well-known initials.

He Sleeps Alone

Snore Moves In—37 Exit

The Stars and Stripes London Bureau

LONDON, Jan. 6.—Because he snores offensively, constantly and uncontrollably, Pvt. Ramon Rodriguez, 35-year-old MP from Neptune, N.J. row sleeps alone in a 38-bed hut at an Air Transport Command station near here.

After nine months of sleeping outdoors "the great snore" was forced inside by the cold spell. When Rodriguez entered, 37 of his fellow MPs walked out.

"I guess I've had more shoes thrown at me than any man in the army," the ex-cab driver says. "Everyone likes me in the daytime, but at night I am all alone."

The Rodriguez snore, the other MPs declare, is something out of this world. Neither a gentle purring nor an occasional snort, his nocturnal nasal noises are purring nor an occasional snort, his nocturnal nasal noises are huge, rasping and incessant. Medical officers have told him they can do nothing about it.

"At my first station," the MP says, "we went out for battle drill and we all dug foxholes together. When I woke in the morning, everybody else had risen in the night and dug new holes far away."

Asks Laws To Harness Manpower

WASHINGTON, Jan. 6 (ANS).—President Roosevelt told the 79th Congress today that this year "can see the final ending of the Nazi-Fascist reign in Europe" as well as the "closing in of forces of retribution" on Japan.

It was the President's fourth wartime State of the Union message to Congress.

In the 8,000-word report, which was as much a report on the state of the world as on the state of the union, the Chief Executive declared that 1945 can be the greatest year of achievement in human history. To attain this he urged that Congress pass National Service legislation to bring the nation's war machine to capacity output and thus give the "supreme proof to all our fighting men that we are giving them what they are entitled to."

Pres. Roosevelt

He added that 1945 "can and must see the substantial beginning of the organization of a worded peace" for a future which "rings with notes of confidence."

He renewed the demand for "unconditional surrender" but applied it only to "the armies of our enemies" and that, he said, is the first step toward peace.

The President accorded recognition to differences which have arisen to plague the Allies and he pleaded for "understanding." The nearer we come to victory, he said, "the more we inevitably become

(Continued on Page 8)

ELAS Troops Leave Athens

Organized fighting between British forces and left-wing ELAS troops in Athens ended yesterday when ELAS insurgents withdrew from the Greek capital to mountains on the outskirts of the city, Reuter reported.

The end of more than a month of fighting came 24 hours after Gen. Nicholas Plastiras, leader of the 1923 Republican revolution, succeeded in forming a new Greek government with himself as premier besides holding four cabinet posts as Minister of War, Navy, Air and Merchant Marine.

British forces, aided by RAF Spitfires, meanwhile continued to harass remnants of ELAS troops in and around Athens. An armored sweep around the outskirts of the capital compelled several hundred ELAS troops to break up into small groups and head for the open countryside.

Convention Ban Urged To Ease Travel Burden

WASHINGTON, Jan. 6 (ANS)—James F. Byrnes proposed today the cancellation of all convention gatherings scheduled after Feb. 1 which are not "in the war interest." The ban proposed by the War Mobilization Director, with President Roosevelt's approval, would apply to conventions attended by more than 50 persons.

Man Spricht Deutsch
Machen Sie das Licht aus.
Makhen Zee das Leesht owss.
Put out the light.

THE STARS AND STRIPES

Daily Newspaper of U.S. Armed Forces in the European Theater of Operations

Ici On Parle Français
Vous êtes très aimable.
Voo zett treh zemmAHbl.
You are very kind.

Vol. 1—No. 166 | 1 Fr. | New York—PARIS—London | 1 Fr. | Tuesday, Jan. 9, 1945

Luzon Invaded, Japs Say

Allies Threaten Last Nazi Supply Line in Bulge

Foe Loses Initiative Near Rhine

Thousands of Von Rundstedt's picked troops faced entrapment in the Belgian bulge yesterday as Anglo-American troops, which already have cut the Laroche-St. Vith Highway, pushed southward through the snow toward the last remaining German supply line in the salient.

As the Allied vise tightened in Belgium, American and French troops in Alsace gained the initiative against diversionary attacks in the Rhineland. It was officially stated yesterday that the threat to Strasbourg is lessening.

The spreading battle on the north flank moved southward along a front of 26 miles from a point south of Marche to the Salm River. Infantry units closed up behind armor which had speared across the east-west highway running between Laroche and St. Vith.

Six Miles from Artery

United Press front reports placed advancing U.S. First Army tanks about six miles from the enemy's only remaining supply artery—the Houffalize-St. Vith road to the

(Continued on Page 8)

Death Dealt the Topkick Out

WITH U. S. TROOPS IN ALSACE, Jan. 8.—Bill Banderick was the first sergeant of Co. A—an old Army man. During 15 years he had trained all over the States, in Panama, and even with the British commandos in 1942.

Bill's CO yanked him out of the lines to give him a "48" to Paris. The guys in his outfit called him lucky.

It was his first pass since he'd been overseas, and he had a helluva time. He saw the Eiffel Tower and Notre Dame, Montmartre and the Champs-Elysees. He even did a little belated Christmas shopping for his wife and his two-year-old daughter.

Afterwards, he came back to the war.

At the Division CP, they looked at each other a little queerly when he said he was reporting back for duty to Co. A. Then they told him: There wasn't any more Co. A.

It had been cut off for two days, and everyone—except a few of the cooks and supply men—had been killed or captured.

Nazis Launch Counter-Attack Near Budapest

MOSCOW, Jan. 8 (AP).—German tank columns pushed on east and southeast of Esztergom today in a counter-thrust intended to ease the pressure on the decimated Nazi garrison in Budapest.

Esztergom, a road junction on the south bank of the Danube 20 miles north of Budapest, was lost to the Soviets yesterday in fighting which was marked by increased German armor and Luftwaffe support from Austrian bases. However, north of Esztergom, the Red Army drove westward 12 miles, endangering the Nazi right flank.

Soviet troops left piles of German dead and wrecked tanks in Esztergom.

In Budapest, Red forces captured the center of the city and now control half of the capital.

If the Russians maintain their drive along the northern bank of the Danube toward Bratislava, the German commander will have to choose whether to defend Budapest or Vienna. Defense of both appeared improbable.

The Nazis were also reported moving up sizable reinforcements in eastern Bosnia for a possible counter-offensive against Jugoslav patriots. Fierce fighting is reported on the Hans Pijesak-Vlasenica communication line.

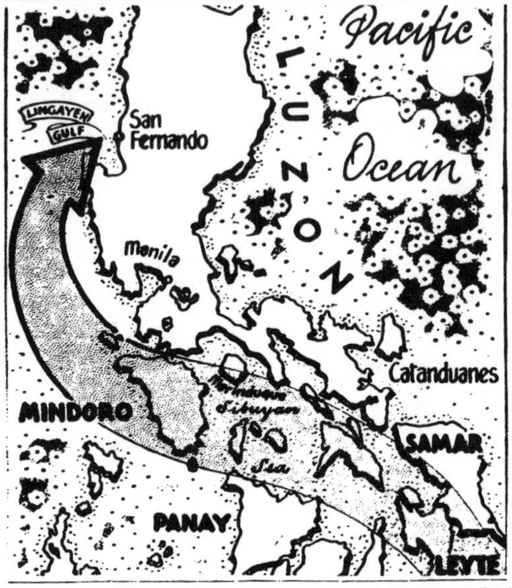

Stars and Stripes Map by Baird

Arrow Points to Reported Luzon Landing

U.S. Silent On Report Of Landing

Tokyo Radio reported yesterday that American troops had invaded Luzon Island in the Philippines. Landings were reported at San Fernando on the northeastern coast of the Lingayen Gulf.

Late last night Army and Navy communiques from the Pacific and Washington neither denied nor supported the Japanese claim. But the report was given credence by some observers who pointed out that in the past the Japs had always announced U.S. Pacific landings first.

A "huge invasion armada led by ten aircraft carriers" supported the operation against the largest of the Philippine islands, said the Tokyo radio. Manila is located on Luzon.

Tokyo Radio, quoting an eyewitness report for Domei News Agency, said American bombers opened an aerial assault at several points on the Lingayen Gulf Saturday morning. A naval task force appeared shortly after, steaming southward toward Damortis, 15 miles south of San Fernando, the report said. Damortis was one of the main landing points used by the Japanese when they invaded Luzon through Lingayen Gulf in Dec., 1941.

Carriers off Luzon

In Pearl Harbor, Adm. Nimitz, who declined any comment on the Japanese report, announced that a U.S. carrier fleet was in operation off Luzon. This would indicate that this fleet may be shielding the Lingayen operation from enemy naval attack from Formosa. Nimitz reported 27 Jap planes destroyed in air battles over Luzon.

If the Jap report proves true, American forces on Luzon have opened one of the most decisive battles of the Pacific war. It is from Luzon that American troops would "jump off" for the invasion of the China mainland, military observers claim.

A Reuter report from London, quoting a Japanese commentator, said that "the commander-in-chief of the Japanese forces on Luzon was expecting U.S. landing attempts at other points besides the Lingayen Gulf."

The Lingayen Gulf, about 100 air

(Continued on Page 8)

A Song of Love —Or— Can You Top It?

WITH 80TH DIV., Jan. 8.—How loving kindness changed the heart of a German canary is the new year's tallest combat yarn—and if you've got a taller one we'll take it all back. Ideal for telling the youngsters in 1950:

The 317th Inf's Chaplain, Harold O. Bomhoff, of Aberdeen, S. D. moved into a cold, abandoned, dirty old house. Deserted, it was, save for a sour-pussed, cheerless cross-eyed canary which glowered balefully at the chaplain and

whistled the Nazi "Horst Wessel Lied."

Did this turn the chaplain? No. He built a fire, fed the K-Ration cracker crumbs to his little feathered friend, and swears the grateful bird began to whistle "Yankee Doddle."

Yes, loving kindness does it . . .

Cassino to Rise Again

VATICAN CITY, Jan. 7 (AP).—Plans for the reconstruction of Monte Cassino Abbey, destroyed in the battle for Cassino last March, were announced here. Members of the Benedictine Order in the U.S. are collecting funds to finance the rebuilding.

Black Market GI Trial Today

Trials of two American officers and 182 EM accused of participating in large-scale black market sale of cigarettes are scheduled to begin today in Paris.

The courts-martial will be open to the public and speedy verdicts are expected. The Judge Advocate's office said yesterday that decisions on the first group to be tried may be expected tonight.

Maximum punishment possible is 30 years at hard labor and dishonorable discharges.

The accused soldiers were rounded up in a drive against black-market activities ranging from Cherbourg to Paris. Maj. Gen. Milton A. Reckord, ETO Provost Marshal, estimated that $200,000 worth of cigarettes had been sold by the ring.

Cherbourg-to-Paris Run Made by Baby Red Ball

A baby Red Ball Express is now running daily over the Cherbourg-Paris road network along which the original Red Ball Express hauled supplies.

The little Red Ball was inaugurated Dec. 13 and runs the 400 miles between freight points in Normandy and Paris. It is operated by the 3582nd Truck Co.

Admiral Says Buzz Bombs May Strike New York Soon

NEW YORK, Jan. 8 (ANS)—Adm. Jonas Ingram, commander-in-chief of the Atlantic Fleet, today warned that it was "possible and probable" that New York City or Washington will be hit by buzz bombs within the next 30 or 60 days.

Ingram said that he would take charge of the coastal defenses and he had moved "plenty of forces" to provide every possible precaution against the attack.

The attacks, Ingram pointed out, would come either from bombs launched from surface ships, submarines or long-range planes. He said that the bombs probably would be smaller than the V-1s or V-2s launched against Great Britain. He warned against panic and said the next alert would be the "real McCoy."

Ingram said that the Germans had 300 submarines "at least" in the Atlantic and the Navy was prepared to keep them from coming close enough to fire or to stop them before they fired many bombs. He said six or eight subs would be needed to bomb New York and that he thought some bombs would get through regardless of air coverage.

PW Exchange Ship

NEW YORK, Jan. 8 (ANS).—Third Naval District headquarters announced today that the exchange ship Gripsholm left yesterday for Marseilles carrying sick and wounded enemy prisoners of war and civilian nationals of Axis countries. The passengers will be repatriated in Switzerland.

FDR Visits Hull

WASHINGTON, Jan. 8 (ANS).—President Roosevelt visited Sunday with Cordell Hull and reported that the condition of the 73-year-old former Secretary of State was more improved than at any time since he entered the Naval hospital three months ago.

Correspondent Seeks Story And Finds It—He Made It

It was before the breakthrough at St. Lo. and T/4 Pat Hanna, of College Station, Tex., a correspondent for the orientation pamphlet, "Army Talks", was out looking for a story. He found it—in fact, he made it.

He decided to go out with a four-man patrol on reconnaissance near St. Lo. Armed with a carbine, he moved out with the patrol, and in quick succession:

Attacked two machine-gun nests and cleaned them out, killing nine Germans;

Cleared the enemy out of an OP and took two officer prisoners;

Sent the prisoners back under guard, and continued until he hit a mortar position, which he also cleared;

Ordered two men of the patrol to turn the captured mortars on a machine-gun nest on his flank, and led his squad as they infiltered into an enemy company CP;

Destroyed the company Hq. equipment and captured its personnel

Hanna never wrote the story. It was written for him in an official citation, and read when he was awarded the DSC yesterday in Paris. Brig. Gen. Oscar N. Solbert, head of ETO Special and Information Services, presented the medal.

M'Arthur Back on Luzon

THE STARS AND STRIPES

Daily Newspaper of U.S. Armed Forces in the European Theater of Operations

Vol. 1—No. 167 New York—PARIS—London Wednesday, Jan. 10, 1945

Ici On Parle Français

Il n'y a pas de quoi.
Eel nee ah pah duh kwah.
Don't mention it.

Foe Tanks Quit Bulge Tip; Vast Butt Theft Charged

4 Beachheads Secured by Mighty Army

BULLETIN

ALLIED HQ., Philippines, Jan. 9.—A "powerful invasion army" has secured four beachheads on northern Luzon, Gen. MacArthur announced tonight.

Landings under the support of a heavy naval and air bombardment took place along the eastern shores of the Lingayen Gulf in the vicinity of San Fernando and Damortis. Gen. MacArthur is on Luzon leading the operations personally, the announcement added.

WASHINGTON, Jan 9 (AP).—The War Department revealed today that Superfortresses attacked Japan and Formosa and carrier-based bombers hammered the coast of Luzon.

Co-ordinated raids by Brig. Gen. Haywood S. Hansell's 21st Bomber Command and Maj. Gen. Curtis Lemay's 20th Bomber Command blasted industrial targets.

The B29 assault lashed out from bases in China and the Marianas, striking hard at the Formosa staging point for Japan's reinforcements for the Philippines.

Aussies Take Over

Meanwhile, in Melbourne, it was announced that Australian and New Zealand soldiers have relieved sizable American ground forces which were pinning down bypassed Jap troops on New Guinea, New Britain and the Solomons.

Aussies have taken over from the Yanks in the Aitape-Wewak sector of British New Guinea and American garrisons in the Solomons have been replaced, including Empress Augusta bay, where the Yanks landed on Bougainville in November, 1943.

The change overs occurred last November, but because movements of the Americans had to be kept secret, Gen. MacArthur first disclosed them today.

World's Largest Bomber Being Developed in U.S.

DETROIT, Jan. 9 (Reuter).—General Motors revealed that the world's largest experimental bomber—Army's XB19A—has been under flight development for a year.

The bomber is built to carry an 18-ton bombload or 126 fully-armed men. The plane has a wingspread of 212 feet, compared with the B29's 141 feet. It has four liquid cooled Allison engines rated at 2,600 h.p. each.

You Pronounce It —Or— Can You Top this?

WITH 35th INF. DIV., Jan. 9.—When the sarge calls the roll, this man's name is a sneeze. Nobody knows how he passed the draft board. He's never been absent—if he has, nobody had time to write it down.

But it's written in his service record that he's the best cook they ever had. Besides being an accomplished barber and carpenter, he speaks nine languages, 16 South Pacific dialects and plays four or five musical instruments. Born in Bangkok, Siam, he attended University of California, and has travelled 'round the globe four times.

Friends call him "Leo" but, featured by Ripley as the longest in the world, here's his correct monicker:

Pvt. Llewsrsuirsszesszes Willsbisminizisstezni Hurwznssteizni. (We don't know what he wears for dog-tags).

Two Soldiers Get 50 Years In Mass Trial

By Ernest Leiser
Stars and Stripes Staff Writer

Two sentences of 50 years at hard labor and two others of 45 years were meted out by a Paris court-martial yesterday as the Army launched its mass-scale trial of 182 men and two officers accused of stealing cigarettes bound for the front and selling them on the black market.

Sitting in judgment on four enlisted men, the first of the group to be brought to trial, the nine-man court-martial sentenced all four after a session in which the Trial Judge Advocate called their actions "treason" against their fellow soldiers.

The convicted soldiers—all from Co. B, 716th Railway Operating Bn.—were S/Sgt. Alexander W. Fleming and T/4 William R. Smith, who were dishonorably discharged and given 50 years' imprisonment at hard labor; and Pvts. Arthur Nelson and William Davidson, who were given dishonorable discharges and 45 years at hard labor.

During a dramatic hearing, Maj. Carmon C Harris, Trial Judge Advocate, described a huge stream of cigarettes moving from the U.S., but dwindling almost to the vanishing point before reaching Paris. He indicated that pilfering of freight cars bound for the front lines was largely responsible for the shortage.

Lt. Harry W. Kine, Paris area PX official, testified that 77,000,000 packs of cigarettes a month were slated for delivery here, but that actually only 34,000,000 packs were available in September for continental distribution. Subsequent inventories revealed that only 11,000,000 packs reached their destination during a 30-day period—one pack out of every seven shipped from the U.S.

Defense attorneys denied the

(Continued on Page 8)

Danish Radio Station Blasted

COPENHAGEN, Jan. 9 (Reuter).—Danish radio reported today that violent bomb explosions destroyed DENKA, radio station at Valby, a suburb of Copenhagen.

On the Right Path—To the Reich

Doughs on a patrol near the German border cautiously peer over the brim of a hill to scout enemy gun positions. Man in foreground awaits word to move up.

3rd Armored Div. Yank KOs German Tank With Garand

By Pat Mitchell
Stars and Stripes Staff Writer

WITH THIRD ARMORED DIV., Jan. 9.—Pvt. Eugene Soto, of New York, destroyed a Tiger tank with an M1 during a Nazi counter-attack, it was revealed today.

Forty armored doughboys, an MG section and two rifle squads were holding a 300-yard section of line near Bizor, just east of Bastogne. Through the faint dawn-light T/Sgt. Robert Martin, of Mannington, W.Va., saw white-draped shapes moving up on his platoon's position.

"I let the nearest one have it," related Martin. "There were about 50 of them, followed by a Jerry Tiger tank."

Cpl. George E. Frank, a peep driver from Detroit, spoke up:

"I looked and saw this big Tiger about 50 yards away. He was firing point blank at our positions. Then Soto started shooting at the Tiger with his M1. He hit some inflammable material hanging on the side and the whole tank went up in flames. That's really some-

(Continued on Page 8)

British Troops Take Thebes, Fan North

ATHENS, Jan. 9 (ANS).—British-manned Shermans, supported by infantry, last night occupied Thebes and then sent a tank column fanning out north after being held temporarily by entrenched ELAS guerrillas.

Gen. Scobie, in a special order of the day to his troops, praised all ranks for "disregard of danger and restraint under provocation" which resulted in "complete expulsion of forces opposed to law and order with a minimum of damage caused to civilian population."

Not to Mention Payroll

Irishman's Yiddish Saves Day

WITH FOURTH INFANTRY DIV., Jan. 9.—Captured with a $5,600 payroll, Lt. William McConnell, of Utica, N.Y., raised hell in Yiddish, got the money back, and led a German platoon to disaster—all in one day's work during the recent counter-offensive.

He was alone when the infantry platoon, coming into the town, chased him through three floors of a hotel and took him prisoner. They also began sorting out his money. McConnell, an Irishman, remembered Yiddish he'd learned as a kid and made complaints the German sergeant seemed to understand. The money was returned, but worse doings followed.

They elected him as "cover" to lead them into town. He was ordered to walk toward a hotel which was the CP of Co. F, 12th Infantry Regiment.

As they neared the hotel, one of McConnell's buddies yelled: "Hey, Bill, are they your prisoners?"

"No," McConnell replied, "I'm their prisoner. Don't shoot . . . I mean, don't shoot me!"

Inside the hotel, Lt. John L. Leake, Keokuk, Iowa, and Lt. William Anderson, St. Paul, Minn., organized a duck-shooting party of their own.

"Pick 'em off one at a time, like in a gallery," was the order.

"It sounded like just one rifle," McConnell recounted. The entire German squad was killed. McConnell broke away, and 1/Sgt. Gervis Willis, Augusta, Ga., and Sgt. Norman Finan, Detroit, opened up on two other squads with a BAR.

When firing ceased there were 33 German dead and one prisoner—the sergeant who had rescued McConnell's $5,600.

German Armor Moving East, Reports State

The first signs that Von Rundstedt had begun to pull armor out of the western bulb of the bulge appeared yesterday as U.S. First Army infantry plodded relentlessly southward in Arctic-like storms toward the last German supply line in eastern Belgium. They followed in the wake of skidding tanks to within a mile of Laroche.

Twelve miles of icy hills and snowdrifted draws separated the southward-driving 83rd Div. infantrymen from the 101st Airborne positions, which form a horseshoe around Bastogne kicking into the bulge's south flank.

Reuter frontline reports stated that Von Rundstedt was trying to extricate his armor, leaving Wehrmacht infantry and Volksgrenadier divisions to hold the lines. United Press said remarkably light artillery and mortar fire in the British sector indicated a general German withdrawal from the north side of the bulge toward ridges protecting the last exit route through Houffalize.

British forces, pushing through heavy snowstorms southeast of Marche, found that Germans had withdrawn for a thousand yards on a three to four-thousand-yard front, UP said. Some British patrols in the softening western tip of the bulge probed a mile and one-half without contacting enemy troops.

Panzers Going East

The UP front report said two SS Panzer Divs., previously fighting in the tip of the bulge, were reported streaming eastward.

Three miles east of Laroche, however, other front-line reports described a big tank battle raging in a snowstorm at Samree. Nazi tanks, including several captured Shermans, were reported defending the town against advancing Second Armored Div. forces.

Second Armored tanks, and infantry of the 84th Div.'s 334th

(Continued on Page 8)

Robomb Scare In U.S. Decried

WASHINGTON, Jan. 9 (AP).—The Navy Department indicated last night it is not in complete accord with the view of Adm. Jonas Ingram that robot bomb attacks on the Atlantic coast were "probable" within the next 30 to 60 days.

"There is no more reason now to believe that Germany will attack with robot bombs than there was last November, when a joint Army-Navy statement considered such attacks 'entirely possible,' but did not extend the idea to probability," a Navy spokesman said.

On Monday, Ingram warned that bombs might be launched from surface ships, submarines or long-range planes and that he had moved "plenty of forces" to provide every possible precaution.

THE STARS AND STRIPES

MEDITERRANEAN

Vol. 2, No. 54, Thursday, January 11, 1945

ITALY EDITION * * TWO LIRE

Yanks Push For Manila

Great Tank Units Clash In Ardennes

U. S. Forces Enter Laroche On North Flank Of Bulge

SHAEF, Jan. 10—One of the great armored clashes of the Ardennes battle began its second day today as U. S. tanks and infantry entered the town of Laroche, on the northern flank of the German bulge.

At the western end of the salient in the Marche-Rochefort-St. Hubert area, large-scale but methodical German withdrawals were reported in what the Associated Press described as the start of an apparent last minute attempt to pull out from the closing Allied trap.

Field dispatches said that the Germans in the Laroche area were laying down a murderous fire on the advancing Americans, while other reports said the Nazis were using flying bombs in an effort to stem the American tide.

The Germans were still fighting hard to hold the line west of Bastogne, but the 101st Airborne Division stabbed a half-mile north to capture Reccogno, three miles northeast of Bastogne.

The 3rd Army advanced from a few yards to half a mile along a 20-mile front from north of Bastogne to east of Wiltz on the southern flank of the front.

Meanwhile, the 7th Army stiffened defenses and counterattacks were holding the Germans to a standstill in northeastern France on both sides of Bitche.

North of Strasbourg, Allied troops fought their way into Gambsheim and increased the pressure on the Nazi Rhine bridgehead in this sector.

The French 1st Army was pushed back from Boufshem, 17 miles south of Strasbourg by German attacks from the Colmar pocket but the enemy's ground gains were small.

MAIL CALL

A Letter From Mauldin About 'GI Joe'

Dear Editor:

The editorial writer in the New York Times who screamed about the over-use of the term, "GI Joe," should get a Pulitzer Prize or something.

The expression is a headline writer's joy and an advertiser's bread and butter—and it has become as nauseating as "Sammy" must have become to our guys in the last war, after the British hung that name on them.

"GI Joe" came into general use in the States about the same time I started drawing Joe and Willie in Stars and Stripes and I've thought of changing Joe's name to Aloysius or some damn thing several times since, because occa-

(Continued on Page 4)

5th Duels With Patrols While Sweating Out Cold

ADVANCED AFHQ, Jan. 10—Waiting for the bitter cold to lift in north Italy, the 5th and 8th Armies duelled with patrols and artillery in the midst of bitter cold today.

The 5th Army was still eight miles below Bologna. The 8th Army was six miles from Imola, where Field Marshal Albert Kesselring must divide his Wehrmacht forces against both armies.

On the 5th Army's right flank, six miles from Imola, an enemy patrol crossed the Senio River east of Rivola but was thrown back. A strong enemy patrol was repulsed near Highway 64, to the left of central 5th Army forces.

The 5th Army was five miles from Massa but farther inland, the Serchio Valley appeared to have been all but cleared of Krauts.

Gen. Nelson Named Deputy Of MTOUSA

AFHQ, Jan. 10—Maj. Gen. Otto L. Nelson, Jr., former Assistant Deputy Chief of Staff in the War Department, has been appointed Deputy Theater Commander, Mediterranean Theater of Operations, U. S. Army, it was announced officially here today.

On his arrival in Italy from the States this week, General Nelson was awarded the Distinguished Service Medal for his work as Assistant Deputy Chief of Staff to General George C. Marshall. The award was presented by Lt. Gen. Joseph T. McNarney, Deputy Supreme Allied Commander in the Mediterranean Theater, and commanding general of MTOUSA.

General Nelson was graduated from West Point in 1924 and served with the 17th Infantry at Fort Cook, Nebr., and later at Fort Leavenworth, Kans.

After a three-year tour of duty in Puerto Rico, he returned to West Point as an instructor. He is a graduate of both the Infantry School at Fort Benning, Ga., and the Command and General Staff School at Fort Leavenworth, Kan. He also holds degrees from Harvard University and Columbia University.

Red Army's Control Widens In Budapest

MOSCOW, Jan. 10 (AP)—Russians had control of some 2,300 of Budapest's 4,500 city blocks today. North of the Hungarian capital, Soviet salients were within 87 miles of Vienna, capital of the German province that used to be Austria.

Budapest fighting has so far cost Nazis forces 13,000 dead, more than 3[illegible],000 wounded, and 5,630 captured, Soviet estimates said.

Germany's counteroffensive had scored no additional gains, the communique indicated.

Norway Paratroops Re-Invade Homeland

LONDON, Jan. 10 (AP)—Norwegian paratroops have reinvaded their homeland and have cut the Germans' main railway line along which Nazi troops are being shipped from the north toward Germany in what a Norwegian Government spokesman described as a "good sized operation," it was announced here today.

How McArthur Made Landing

MACARTHUR'S HEADQUARTERS, Jan. 10 (AP)—Wearing his famous campaign hat and five stars on his collar, Gen. Douglas MacArthur returned to Luzon with his assault troops Tuesday morning.

Two torpedoes from a midget submarine missed his ship as the convoy headed for the landing.

General MacArthur then rode on the engine-box of a landing craft and waded knee-deep in water onto the soil of the Luzon that he had left nearly three years ago.

He hit shore about two hours after the first assault wave.

MacArthur talked with privates and generals alike, expressing himself as pleased with the way the operations were proceeding.

Shortly after his arrival, the general went into conference with aides and began to set in motion pre-landing strategy.

Showdown In Philippines Began With Luzon Action

By Sgt. JOE BAILY
(*Stars and Stripes Staff Writer*)

American troops have come back to Luzon and the long-awaited showdown battle of the Philippines has begun.

The U. S. landings yesterday on this main island of the Philippines, are but the opening phase of a battle for which fighting on Leyte, Mindoro and Samar was but preliminary skirmishing.

Even the naval clashes between almost the full might of the Jap Navy and the American Pacific Fleet served only to part the curtain.

Upon Luzon and around Manila, the enemy has been massing his strength. And the moves of General Douglas MacArthur, from the moment when he returned to the Philippines, have been directed toward Luzon. Establishing a foothold on Leyte was the first step. The building of a huge supply base there was to make ready for the Luzon battle.

The strike north up Samar, the daring sea voyage through the heart of the inner Philippines to Mindoro, the seizing of strategic Marinduque—all were aimed at flanking Manila Bay.

Most important of all throughout the preliminary campaigning the Yanks have been winning airfields to enable them to counter powerful Japanese air blows which are certain to come against the Americans pouring ashore on Luzon.

Within a few weeks of the Leyte landings, American planes were flying from fields taken from the Japs along the eastern fringe, or dug out of the worst mud and clay the Yanks had encountered in the Pacific. Rains and typhoons handicapped the land-based flights from Leyte, however and Leyte was too far from Luzon. And so the Mindoro landing was made to secure airfields within striking radius of the vital fields of Luzon clustered for the most part around Manila.

The Japs, from the first moment when General Douglas MacArthur and U. S. troops came ashore on Leyte, have been preparing to defend Luzon. Their garrison has been estimated at 150,000, and not many of these were sent to the nearby islands to defend them. The tiger stayed in his lair and

(Continued on Page 2)

Armored Units Strike Inland

MacArthur Says All Forces Making Gains Against Light Resistance

PEARL HARBOR, Jan. 10—Spearheaded by armored columns, American troops pushed inland today from the southern and eastern shores of Lingayen Gulf on Luzon Island and struck for Manila, 120 miles away over a low, dry country excellently suited for mechanized fighting.

Twenty-four hours after the first landings were made on the vital Philippines island against amazingly light opposition, 6th Army tanks were still pouring ashore over the same crescent of sand dunes which the Japanese invaders used three years ago, Associated Press reported.

General Douglas MacArthur established his headquarters along the gulf after wading ashore in the early waves. Field operations of 6th Army divisions were commanded by Lt. Gen. Walter Krueger.

An Associated Press dispatch pointed out that initial losses were light, although the Tokyo radio bragged that Luzon could be reached only at terrific cost.

The fighting region appeared to extend from the vicinity of Lingayen City on the southern shore of the gulf northeast to San Fabian.

Japanese defenses on the beaches proved inadequate. Some trenches were only a foot deep. The invasion was orderly, and there were no bloody battles on the beaches. At one point only 11 snipers could be found in an hour's search. At another, hundreds of Filipinos waving American flags came down to greet the doughboys, bearing gifts and shouting "victory."

A correspondent said the Americans were welcomed at the town of San Fabian, where one building

(Continued on page 8)

Largest Force Yet In Luzon Operation

WASHINGTON, Jan. 10 (AP) — American forces under General Douglas MacArthur have completed the largest amphibious operation of the Pacific war. More than 800 cargo and transport vessels escorted by hundreds of warships went in a great armada from Leyte through Surigao Straits, past the north coast of Mindanao, then southwest of Mindoro and west of Luzon and up to Lingayen Gulf.

The convoy was one-third larger than the force which invaded Leyte in October, the Associated Press reported. There were more than 2,500 landing craft in it. A pilot flying over the armada said that it stretched 100 miles along the China Sea. A correspondent said 50 percent more men went ashore in the first wave than landed at Leyte.

The American ships had to weather the most deadly air attacks that the Japanese could muster. The convoy was under enemy

(Continued on page 8)

B-29s Over Tokyo Add To Troubles Of Japs

WASHINGTON, Jan. 10 (UP) — Beset by Yank advances on Luzon, Japan battled flames today in Tokyo and counted up damage from yesterday's Super Fortress visits.

The B-29s which attacked Tokyo were making their first raid in force in two weeks. They found the skies clear and observed good results, the War Department announced. Other sky mammoths whipped from Asiatic bases to pummel military installations on Formosa. Japanese island stronghold which funnels planes, troops and supplies to invaded Luzon. In the first daylight raid by fleet units on enemy installations in the Kurile Islands, north of the Japanese mainland, Vice Admiral Frank Fletcher's North Pacific Fleet bombarded Suribachi on the east coast of Paramushiro for 20 minutes, destroying at least four large buildings and damaging 16 others.

Man Spricht Deutsch
Kennen Sie jene Frau?
Kennen Zee yehna Frow?
Do you know that woman?

THE STARS AND STRIPES

Daily Newspaper of U.S. Armed Forces in the European Theater of Operations

Ici On Parle Français
Où est la blanchisserie?
Oo ay lah blansh-ir-ree?
Where is the laundry?

Vol. 1—No. 169 | 1 Fr. | New York—PARIS—London | 1 Fr. | Friday, Jan. 12, 1945

Bulge Crumbles in West; Yanks 90 Mi. from Manila

30 Towns Captured On Luzon

Overrunning an airfield and about 30 towns and villages in their path, Sixth Army troops last night were swiftly driving inland on Luzon—reaching one point within 90 miles of Manila itself—while U.S. aircraft hammered at Jap reinforcements struggling north from the Philippine capital to meet the U.S. invaders, a report from Gen. MacArthur's headquarters said yesterday.

As the Americans poured armor and heavy artillery onto a 22-mile beachhead stretching from Lingayen to San Fabian, B29 Superfortresses, hitting at Japan's westernmost flank, were bombing Singapore in daylight, Tokyo Radio announced.

On Luzon, soldiers of Lt. Gen. Walter Krueger's Sixth Army were in possession of a hard-surfaced highway running along the shores of Lingayen Gulf through San Fabian, Maggaldan, Dagupan and Lingayen.

Airdrome Almost Undamaged

At Lingayen, engineers were extending the runways on the airdrome captured there almost undamaged. Another prize was Port Sual, ten miles northwest of Lingayen, where the navy was developing facilities for landing supplies.

Although no important Jap resistance has been met 48 hours after the landings, dispatches from Luzon said yesterday that somewhere on the central Luzon plains—between Lingayen and Manila—the biggest battle of the Pacific war may soon be waged.

As troops and equipment were

(Continued on Page 8)

Nazis Use Children As Saboteur Aides

WITH FIRST U.S. ARMY, Jan. 11.—First instances of the Nazis' use of children as saboteur aides was disclosed today with the arrest of five boys and one girl. Influenced by SS infantrymen, these adolescents, ranging in age from 12 to 17, attempted to sabotage American vehicles and communications.

Senator Asks Use of Force to Assure Peace

WASHINGTON, Jan. 11 (ANS). —Immediate assurance that the U.S. will meet with "instantaneous" force any effort of defeated Germany or Japan to rearm, was asked of Congress today by Sen. Arthur Vandenberg, (R-Mich.) of the Senate Foreign Relations Committee.

The Michigan Senator said that the nation ought to demand that all separate agreements on Europe's snarled political problems be put on a purely temporary basis and subject to review by a proposed international security organization. He called for the U.S. to "relight the torch" of the Atlantic Charter, asserting "we have not altered our original commitments to its principles."

Vandenberg's proposals brought from Sen. Connally, Foreign Relations Committee chairman (D-Tex.) a reply apparently typical of Democratic reaction. He indicated the belief that the problems involved in future world peace cannot be handled now. But must wait a definitive treaty of peace.

Vandenberg's Michigan colleague, Sen. Homer Ferguson, proposed that the Senate take the initiative in writing a "strong, effective foreign

(Continued on Page 8)

Line of the Bulge Moves Eastward

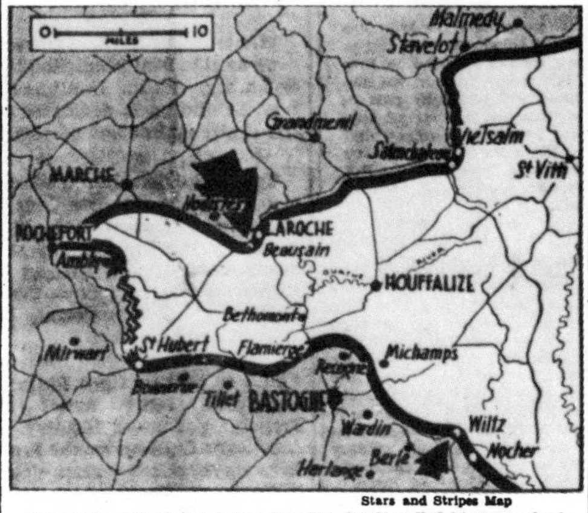

Stars and Stripes Map

This is the salient just before Von Rundstedt pulled his troops back beyond the River Ourthe between Laroche and Houffalize.

Nazis' Gap For Escape Now 8 Miles

The western half of the German salient in Belgium collapsed yesterday as Field Marshal von Rundstedt pulled back infantry and armor to positions east of the River Ourthe. Yesterday's German communique admitted the withdrawal. Reuter, from Stockholm, quoted a Berlin military spokesman as announcing that the winter offensive was over.

The gap between Field Marshal Sir Bernard L. Montgomery's forces on the north and Lt. Gen. Omar N. Bradley's troops on the south is now only eight miles, Reuter reported from the front last night. Through this gap, German armor and infantry are moving eastward in an orderly fashion, the Reuter report said.

The German communique said the city of St. Hubert, southwestern peg of the bulge, had been evacuated. Germans also apparently had evacuated the key road center of Laroche, on the north, according to front-line reports which said that Allied troops found the city virtually empty when they entered it yesterday morning.

Germans covered their withdrawal with dense fields of plastic mines which slowed Allied armor.

All reports indicated that the withdrawal was orderly and had not yet developed into the kind of retreat which the Allies could exploit.

Nazi Stand Expected

It was expected that Von Rundstedt would attempt to defend the still firm eastern half of the bulge on ridges between Houffalize and St. Vith.

British patrols ranged all the way through the forest of St. Hubert for four miles to the St. Hubert-Laroche highway and the vicinity

(Continued on Page 8)

5 More EM Get Stiff Terms For Cigarette Black Market

By Ernest Leiser
Stars and Stripes Staff Writer

Severe sentences were handed out again yesterday to the second group of soldiers court-martialed in the Army's mass prosecution of two officers and 182 men charged with the theft and black market sale of GI cigarettes.

Four prison terms of 40 years at hard labor and a fifth of 45 years were ordered for the five enlisted men tried during yesterday's hearings. All were dishonorably discharged.

The trials were highlighted by an acknowledgment made by Maj. Carmon C. Harris, the Judge Advocate prosecuting the cases, that the men accused "were just the ones who happened to get caught." He said that "those who have profited more have gone free" and asked the help of the "little culprits" in denouncing in open court those mainly responsible for the thefts.

Mild Punishment Refused

Sentences of 40 years were given T/4 Leonard P. French, of Houston, Tex.; Pfc. Thomas G. Harper, of Chicago; Pvt. Fred C. Jones, of Clarksburg, W. Va., and Pvt. Edward Wagner, of St. Paul, Minn. Sgt. Merel Young, of New York City, was given 45 years. All of the men were members of Co. "C", 716th Railway Operating Bn.

Capt. Robert Guthrie, handling the defense, pleaded in vain for a

(Continued on Page 8)

British and ELAS Near Agreement

British authorities and ELAS leaders have reached "a large measure of agreement over terms of a cease-fire order" at Athens, Army News Service reported yesterday.

The conference opened Wednesday and it was indicated the bloody 40-day-old Greek civil war would cease if an agreement could be reached on British terms.

Rockets Streak Ashore in Philippine Action

A barrage of rockets fired from an LCI streaks ashore to batter Japanese defenses as Americans invade the island of Mindoro in the Philippines.

Congress Gets 2 Bills For Medic Combat Pay

The Stars and Stripes U.S. Bureau

WASHINGTON, Jan. 11.—Two bills providing additional pay for enlisted medical personnel on duty in combat areas have been re-introduced into the 79th Congress. Both bills limit payments for combat service to six months after the cessation of hostilities.

Rep. Frances P. Bolton, (R-Ohio) has submitted a bill providing an additional $10 monthly to men awarded a proposed Medical Corps Valor Badge, while Rep. Richard F. Harris (D-Ariz.) sponsored a bill providing the same amount of extra pay to enlisted medics in combat areas with no valor badge required.

First Red Cross Girl Killed On Duty at Western Front

By Arthur White
Stars and Stripes Staff Writer

Ann Kathleen Cullen, of Larchmont, N.Y., the first American Red Cross girl to die through enemy action on the Western Front, was killed Dec. 20 when a German shell struck a U.S. hospital in Belgium.

She was the second American girl killed by enemy action in a hospital area here. 2/Lt. Frances Slanger, an Army nurse, lost her life Oct. 21 when German guns shelled her field hospital.

Member of a clubmobile group, "Katie" Cullen, 26, joined the ARC in June, 1943, and came to the Continent after a year's service in Britain.

She is buried in a military cemetery in Belgium.

Three other ARC girls, Catherine T. Gladding, of West Allenhurst, N.J.; Ann T. Knotts, of Sicily Island, La., and Anne Denney, of Dover, Del., narrowly escaped death when a German bomb demolished a Red Cross club in France. Soldiers dragged them from the wreckage, suffering from shock and bruises. They were given first aid and returned to duty.

Ann Kathleen Cullen

Man Spricht Deutsch
Treten Sie ab.
Treyten Zee up.
You are dismissed.

THE STARS AND STRIPES

Daily Newspaper of U.S. Armed Forces in the European Theater of Operations

Ici On Parle Français
Voulez-vous nettoyer le trottoir?
Voolay voo naytwayay luh trotwar?
Will you clean the sidewalk?

Vol. 1—No. 175 | 1 Fr. | New York—PARIS—London | 1 Fr. | Thursday, Jan. 18, 1945

Russians Seize Warsaw; Sweep to 15 Mi. of Reich

Allies Gain Ground; 1st, 3d Advance

Whiteclad Tommies pushed 1,000 yards into the fogbound Dutch triangle between the Maas and Roer Rivers and took the Dutch town of Gebroek yesterday in the first Allied assault since the Battle of the Bulge. U.S. First Army troops in the Ardennes smashed to within five miles of St. Vith and, according to Reuter, took Vielsalm.

On the dying salient's southern flank, U.S. Third Army troops trapped an undetermined number of Germans pocketed in Luxembourg near the Reich frontier. Other Third Army forces mopped up a Nazi pocket west of Houffalize, Reuter said.

The Allied attack in Holland was not a large operation, UP front reports said. German prisoners, the report said, could not understand how the British were able to attack in such terrible weather. Volunteer Dutch spread sand and cinders on slippery roads for Allied forces, the UP report said.

The British crossed the River Roode in two places and captured the village of Dieteren, nine miles north of Sittard.

Nazis Pour It On

In Alsace, U.S. Seventh Army troops battled mounting German pressure in the bulge south of Bitche and in the Rhine bridgehead north of Strasbourg.

The bulge yesterday was compressed into a lump extending about 50 miles across its base from the Monschau to the Echternach sectors, and about 12 miles at its widest point.

On the north, 30th Div. men pushed 3,500 yards to Recht, five miles northwest of St. Vith. The division averaged a gain of 2,500 yards all along its front.

On its left, First Div. forces plodded 1,500 to 2,000 yards through the deep snow south of Paymonville.

Between Vielsalm and Houffalize, Nazis launched four counter-thrusts against the 30th and the Third Armored Div., ploughing ahead in

(Continued on Page 4)

Where British Struck

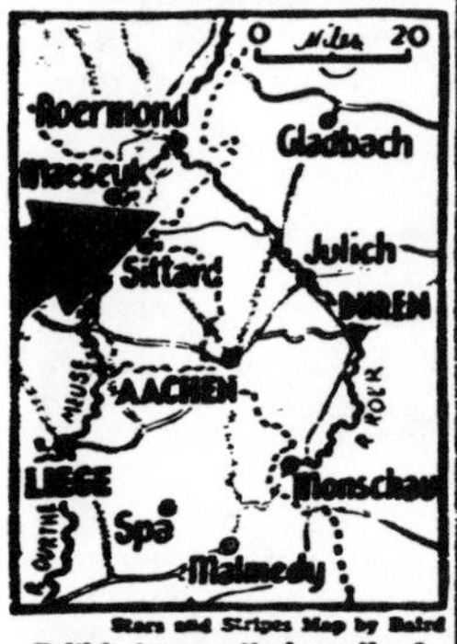

Stars and Stripes Map by Baird

British troops attack north of Sittard, Holland, on a front quiet for months.

Snow Capes for GIs on Western Front

Signal Corps Photo

Pvt. Frank J. Tryska, of New York City, left, and Sgt. Carl Pines, of Teaneck, N.J., right, wear the new issue snow cape as they start out on a patrolling mission in the First Army's Ardennes sector.

Five GIs Sentenced to Death In Black Market Gas Trials

Five American soldiers have been sentenced to death in the last ten days for desertion and for the theft and sale of Army gasoline on the Paris black market, the Seine Base Judge Advocate General revealed yesterday.

The men were rounded up and tried in an intensified prosecution of GI gasoline thieves in the ETO. Courts-martial gave two others life imprisonment and another 10 years. Four men have been acquitted.

Col. C. E. Brand, Staff JAG, disclosed that five more trials are now pending. He asserted that a considerable number of other men had been implicated by soldiers already tried.

Trial judge advocates said the soldiers, including men from combat units passing through Paris, would desert their outfits. They would buy, barter, or steal clothes from Frenchmen, and would go about the city as civilians. They lived in hotels or private homes, usually with women.

When they needed money, they would put on their uniforms, steal an Army truck, pull into QM depots, show a trip ticket or a forged requisition, load up with as many as 260 jerricans full of gas, and drive away. They sold the cans, and their contents for between 500 and 1,000 francs each.

Judge advocates said that two of the men, who operated for six weeks before they were captured, had made a total of nearly 800,000 francs from their black market sales.

Names of those tried and sentenced were withheld.

Heavies Blast German Fuel

Mighty forces of Eighth AF and RAF bombers yesterday punctuated Allied air chiefs' orders to destroy Germany's remaining oil reserves with a near-10,000-ton high-explosive exclamation point.

In a 24-hour period up to last night, the bulk of 2,500 Allied heavy bombers, escorted by more than 1,000 fighters, pounded synthetic oil refineries and storage depots in the Reich. Approximately 700 Eighth AF B17s and B24s led the attack yesterday with a raid on the Rhenania oil refinery, near battered Hamburg, and oil storage dumps and U-boat yards in the same area. In addition, the Eighth heavies hit marshalling yards at Paderborn and other transport facilities in northwest Germany. Ten bombers and five fighters are missing.

More than 1,200 British heavies had preceded the U. S. raids with sledge-hammer attacks Tuesday night on refineries at Brux, in

(Continued on Page 4)

Krakow Claimed Taken as Soviets Overrun Poland

Josef Stalin announced late yesterday that Warsaw had been liberated by Marshal Zhukov's First White Russian Army in co-ordinated smashes with two other powerful Red Armies moving westward toward the German border with speed that belittles the pace of any previous offensives launched by the Russians.

While Moscow was broadcasting news of the fall of the Polish capital, Lublin Radio claimed that Krakow, strongest German defense bastion in southern Poland, also had fallen to the Russian avalanche.

Punching gaping holes in the German line rapidly disintegrating before the massed impact of more than 2,000,000 Red Army soldiers, Marshal Koniev's First Ukrainian Army captured Czestochowa, 15 miles from the German-Silesian border.

Stalin also disclosed that Marshal Rokossovsky's Second White Russian Army had opened an offensive north of Warsaw across the Narew River, gaining more than 25 miles on a 62-mile front.

Last night Moscow shook under the massive victory salute of 40 salvos from 448 guns.

Order of Day Tells of Victory

Frontline dispatches said that Rokossovsky's and Zhukov's armies had opened their blitz breakthroughs by a devastating artillery barrage supported by powerful air support.

The first Order of the Day issued last night by Stalin said that Warsaw had been seized by a massed by-passing movement. One column poured across the Vistula, north of the city, another moved across the river on the south. The two columns then linked up.

The triumphant drive into the city was practically unopposed, with units of the Polish Liberation Army supporting the advance under direct command of Zhukov.

Berlin reports indicated that units of the First White Russian Army already had driven 35 miles west of Warsaw to Sochaczew, on the main rail and road route to Berlin.

Rokossovsky Joins Polish Offensive

In another Order of the Day, issued an hour after the Warsaw victory announcement, it was disclosed that the Second White Russian Army, under Rokossovsky, had joined the Polish offensive about 45 miles north of Warsaw. Rokossovsky struck across the Narew River toward the lower Vistula in the vicinity of Ciechanow.

This announcement answered the question of the whereabouts of Marshal Rokossovsky, whose previous army last year was given to the command of Zhukov.

The capture of the city of Czestochowa, last barrier in southwestern Poland, less than 15 miles from German Silesia, was the highlight of Stalin's third Order of the Day. Czestochowa is on the main rail line between Vienna and

(Continued on Page 4)

6 Weeks Out of States—He Kills 100 Nazis

By Ralph G. Martin
Stars and Stripes Staff Writer

WITH SEVENTH ARMY.—Only six weeks ago, he was downing ice-cream sodas back in Mt. Olive, N.C. Now, firing his machine-gun for the first time in combat, 20-year-old Pvt. Leon Outlaw Jr. protected the exposed flank of his regiment for five days and nights, killing at least 100 Germans, wounding many more and taking six prisoners who waved white socks.

For five rainy, snowy days and sleepless nights, Outlaw sat cramped in his foxhole, drinking melted snow, using his single blanket to cover his gun. He had only three K-rations—a fourth was slapped out of his hand by a piece of shrapnel.

In another foxhole, ten feet behind Outlaw, Sgt. Alphonse Myers, of Amsterdam, N.Y., kept his eyes glued to a pair of field glasses, directing and adjusting fire for Outlaw.

Outlaw usually waited until the Jerries came down the slope, 800 yards away, where there was no cover. Then he'd open up and cut them down.

But it was only after Outlaw started shooting up German command cars on a road 2,000 yards away that the Jerries started dropping the whole German artillery book on top of them.

Behind Outlaw, protecting the rear, were 17 deeply dug-in doughfeet. Several were wounded, one was killed.

Then came the payoff. Two German tanks rumbled up to within 900 yards of them, wandered around the area for more than two hours and then went away.

"I'll never be able to understand that," said Outlaw. "They could have come in and cleaned us out in a couple of minutes."

Myers' own communication with the rear was completely snafued. It might go on for five minutes and then not work for several hours. Meanwhile, bigger German patrols began com-

(Continued on Page 4)

Man Spricht Deutsch
Kennen Sie jene Frau?
Kennen Zee yehna Frow?
Do you know that woman?

THE STARS AND STRIPES

Daily Newspaper of U.S. Armed Forces in the European Theater of Operations

Ici On Parle Français
Où est la blanchisserie?
Oo ay lah blansh-ir-ree?
Where is the laundry?

Vol. 1—No. 169 | 1 Fr. | New York—PARIS—London | 1 Fr. | Friday, Jan. 12, 1945

Bulge Crumbles in West; Yanks 90 Mi. from Manila

30 Towns Captured On Luzon

Overrunning an airfield and about 30 towns and villages in their path, Sixth Army troops last night were swiftly driving inland on Luzon—reaching one point within 90 miles of Manila itself—while U.S. aircraft hammered at Jap reinforcements struggling north from the Philippine capital to meet the U.S. invaders, a report from Gen. MacArthur's headquarters said yesterday.

As the Americans poured armor and heavy artillery onto a 22-mile beachhead stretching from Lingayen to San Fabian, B29 Superfortresses, hitting at Japan's westernmost flank, were bombing Singapore in daylight, Tokyo Radio announced.

On Luzon, soldiers of Lt. Gen. Walter Krueger's Sixth Army were in possession of a hard-surfaced highway running along the shores of Lingayen Gulf through San Fabian, Maggaldan, Dagupan and Lingayen.

Airdrome Almost Undamaged

At Lingayen, engineers were extending the runways on the airdrome captured there almost undamaged. Another prize was Port Sual, ten miles northwest of Lingayen, where the navy was developing facilities for landing supplies.

Although no important Jap resistance has been met 48 hours after the landings, dispatches from Luzon said yesterday that somewhere on the central Luzon plains—between Lingayen and Manila—the biggest battle of the Pacific war may soon be waged.

As troops and equipment were

(Continued on Page 8)

Nazis Use Children As Saboteur Aides

WITH FIRST U.S. ARMY, Jan. 11.—First instances of the Nazis' use of children as saboteur aides was disclosed today with the arrest of five boys and one girl. Influenced by SS infantrymen, these adolescents, ranging in age from 12 to 17, attempted to sabotage American vehicles and communications.

Senator Asks Use of Force to Assure Peace

WASHINGTON, Jan. 11 (ANS).—Immediate assurance that the U.S. will meet with "instantaneous" force any effort of defeated Germany or Japan to rearm, was asked of Congress today by Sen. Arthur Vandenberg, (R-Mich.) of the Senate Foreign Relations Committee.

The Michigan Senator said that the nation ought to demand that all separate agreements on Europe's snarled political problems be put on a purely temporary basis and subject to review by a proposed international security organization. He called for the U.S. to "relight the torch" of the Atlantic Charter, asserting "we have not altered our original commitments to its principles."

Vandenberg's proposals brought from Sen. Connally, Foreign Relations Committee chairman (D-Tex.) a reply apparently typical of Democratic reaction. He indicated the belief that the problems involved in future world peace cannot be handled now. But must wait a definitive treaty of peace.

Vandenberg's Michigan colleague, Sen. Homer Ferguson, proposed that the Senate take the initiative in writing a "strong, effective foreign

(Continued on Page 8)

Line of the Bulge Moves Eastward

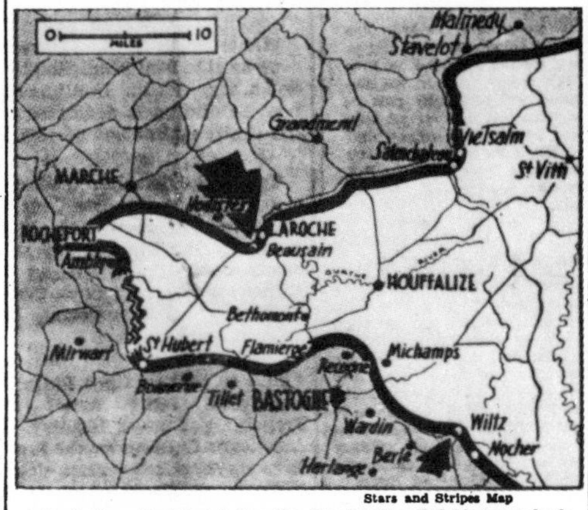

Stars and Stripes Map

This is the salient just before Von Rundstedt pulled his troops back beyond the River Ourthe between Laroche and Houffalize.

5 More EM Get Stiff Terms For Cigarette Black Market

By Ernest Leiser
Stars and Stripes Staff Writer

Severe sentences were handed out again yesterday to the second group of soldiers court-martialed in the Army's mass prosecution of two officers and 182 men charged with the theft and black market sale of GI cigarettes.

Four prison terms of 40 years at hard labor and a fifth of 45 years were ordered for the five enlisted men tried during yesterday's hearings. All were dishonorably discharged.

The trials were highlighted by an acknowledgment made by Maj. Carmon C. Harris, the Judge Advocate prosecuting the cases, that the men accused "were just the ones who happened to get caught." He said that "those who have profited more have gone free" and asked the help of the "little culprits" in denouncing in open court those mainly responsible for the thefts.

Mild Punishment Refused

Sentences of 40 years were given T/4 Leonard P. French, of Houston, Tex.; Pfc. Thomas G. Harper, of Chicago; Pvt. Fred C. Jones, of Clarksburg, W. Va., and Pvt. Edward Wagner, of St. Paul, Minn. Sgt. Merel Young, of New York City, was given 45 years. All of the men were members of Co. "C", 716th Railway Operating Bn.

Capt. Robert Guthrie, handling the defense, pleaded in vain for a

(Continued on Page 8)

British and ELAS Near Agreement

British authorities and ELAS leaders have reached "a large measure of agreement over terms of a cease-fire order" at Athens, Army News Service reported yesterday.

The conference opened Wednesday and it was indicated the bloody 40-day-old Greek civil war would cease if an agreement could be reached on British terms.

Nazis' Gap For Escape Now 8 Miles

The western half of the German salient in Belgium collapsed yesterday as Field Marshal von Rundstedt pulled back infantry and armor to positions east of the River Ourthe. Yesterday's German communique admitted the withdrawal. Reuter, from Stockholm, quoted a Berlin military spokesman as announcing that the winter offensive was over.

The gap between Field Marshal Sir Bernard L. Montgomery's forces on the north and Lt. Gen. Omar N. Bradley's troops on the south is now only eight miles, Reuter reported from the front last night. Through this gap, German armor and infantry are moving eastward in an orderly fashion, the Reuter report said.

The German communique said the city of St. Hubert, southwestern peg of the bulge, had been evacuated. Germans also apparently had evacuated the key road center of Laroche, on the north, according to front-line reports which said that Allied troops found the city virtually empty when they entered it yesterday morning.

Germans covered their withdrawal with dense fields of plastic mines which slowed Allied armor.

All reports indicated that the withdrawal was orderly and had not yet developed into the kind of retreat which the Allies could exploit.

Nazi Stand Expected

It was expected that Von Rundstedt would attempt to defend the still firm eastern half of the bulge on ridges between Houffalize and St. Vith.

British patrols ranged all the way through the forest of St. Hubert for four miles to the St. Hubert-Laroche highway and the vicinity

(Continued on Page 8)

Rockets Streak Ashore in Philippine Action

A barrage of rockets fired from an LCI streaks ashore to batter Japanese defenses as Americans invade the island of Mindoro in the Philippines.

Congress Gets 2 Bills For Medic Combat Pay

The Stars and Stripes U.S. Bureau

WASHINGTON, Jan. 11.—Two bills providing additional pay for enlisted medical personnel on duty in combat areas have been re-introduced into the 79th Congress. Both bills limit payments for combat service to six months after the cessation of hostilities.

Rep. Frances P. Bolton, (R-Ohio) has submitted a bill providing an additional $10 monthly to men awarded a proposed Medical Corps Valor Badge, while Rep. Richard F. Harris (D-Ariz.) sponsored a bill providing the same amount of extra pay to enlisted medics in combat areas with no valor badge required.

First Red Cross Girl Killed On Duty at Western Front

By Arthur White
Stars and Stripes Staff Writer

Ann Kathleen Cullen, of Larchmont, N.Y., the first American Red Cross girl to die through enemy action on the Western Front, was killed Dec. 20 when a German shell struck a U.S. hospital in Belgium.

She was the second American girl killed by enemy action in a hospital area here. 2/Lt. Frances Slanger, an Army nurse, lost her life Oct. 21 when German guns shelled her field hospital.

Member of a clubmobile group, "Katie" Cullen, 26, joined the ARC in June, 1943, and came to the Continent after a year's service in Britain.

She is buried in a military cemetery in Belgium.

Three other ARC girls, Catherine T. Gladding, of West Allenhurst, N.J.; Ann T. Knotts, of Sicily Island, La., and Anne Denney, of Dover, Del., narrowly escaped death when a German bomb demolished a Red Cross club in France. Soldiers dragged them from the wreckage, suffering from shock and bruises. They were given first aid and returned to duty.

Ann Kathleen Cullen

Man Spricht Deutsch
Treten Sie ab.
Treyten Zee up.
You are dismissed.

THE STARS AND STRIPES

Daily Newspaper of U.S. Armed Forces in the European Theater of Operations

Ici On Parle Français
Voulez-vous nettoyer le trottoir?
Voolay voo naytwayay luh trotwar
Will you clean the sidewalk?

Vol. 1—No. 175 | 1 Fr. | New York—PARIS—London | 1 Fr. | Thursday, Jan. 18, 1945

Russians Seize Warsaw; Sweep to 15 Mi. of Reich

Allies Gain Ground; 1st, 3d Advance

Whiteclad Tommies pushed 1,000 yards into the fogbound Dutch triangle between the Maas and Roer Rivers and took the Dutch town of Gebroek yesterday in the first Allied assault since the Battle of the Bulge. U.S. First Army troops in the Ardennes smashed to within five miles of St. Vith and, according to Reuter, took Vielsalm.

On the dying salient's southern flank, U.S. Third Army troops trapped an undetermined number of Germans pocketed in Luxembourg near the Reich frontier. Other Third Army forces mopped up a Nazi pocket west of Houffalize, Reuter said.

The Allied attack in Holland was not a large operation, UP front reports said. German prisoners, the report said, could not understand how the British were able to attack in such terrible weather. Volunteer Dutch spread sand and cinders on slippery roads for Allied forces, the UP report said.

The British crossed the River Roode in two places and captured the village of Dieteren, nine miles north of Sittard.

Nazis Pour It On

In Alsace, U.S. Seventh Army troops battled mounting German pressure in the bulge south of Bitche and in the Rhine bridgehead north of Strasbourg.

The bulge yesterday was compressed into a lump extending about 50 miles across its base from the Monschau to the Echternach sectors, and about 12 miles at its widest point.

On the north, 30th Div. men pushed 3,500 yards to Recht, five miles northwest of St. Vith. The division averaged a gain of 2,500 yards all along its front.

On its left, First Div. forces plodded 1,500 to 2,000 yards through the deep snow south of Faymonville.

Between Vielsalm and Houffalize, Nazis launched four counter-thrusts against the 30th and the Third Armored Div., ploughing ahead in

(Continued on Page 4)

Where British Struck

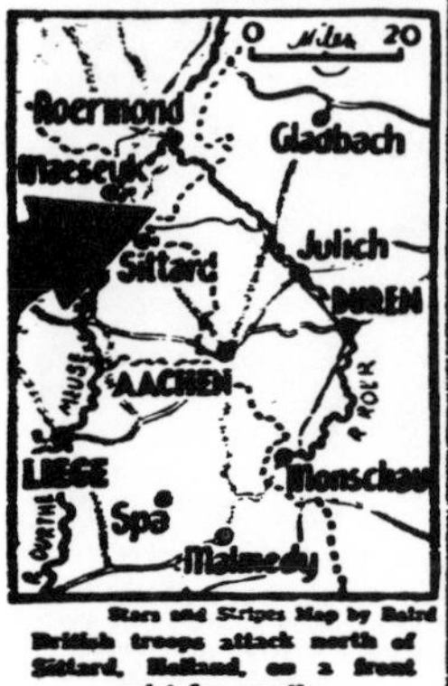

Stars and Stripes Map by Baird

British troops attack north of Sittard, Holland, on a front quiet for months.

Snow Capes for GIs on Western Front

Signal Corps Photo

Pvt. Frank J. Tryska, of New York City, left, and Sgt. Carl Pines, of Teaneck, N.J., right, wear the new issue snow cape as they start out on a patrolling mission in the First Army's Ardennes sector.

Five GIs Sentenced to Death In Black Market Gas Trials

Five American soldiers have been sentenced to death in the last ten days for desertion and for the theft and sale of Army gasoline on the Paris black market, the Seine Base Judge Advocate General revealed yesterday.

The men were rounded up and tried in an intensified prosecution of GI gasoline thieves in the ETO. Courts-martial gave two others life imprisonment and another 10 years. Four men have been acquitted.

Col. C. E. Brand, Staff JAG, disclosed that five more trials are now pending. He asserted that a considerable number of other men had been implicated by soldiers already tried.

Trial judge advocates said the soldiers, including men from combat units passing through Paris, would desert their outfits. They would buy, barter, or steal clothes from Frenchmen, and would go about the city as civilians. They lived in hotels or private homes, usually with women.

When they needed money, they would put on their uniforms, steal an Army truck, pull into QM depots, show a trip ticket or a forged requisition, load up with as many as 260 jerricans full of gas, and drive away. They sold the cans, and their contents for between 500 and 1,000 francs each.

Judge advocates said that two of the men, who operated for six weeks before they were captured, had made a total of nearly 800,000 francs from their black market sales.

Names of those tried and sentenced were withheld.

Heavies Blast German Fuel

Mighty forces of Eighth AF and RAF bombers yesterday punctuated Allied air chiefs' orders to destroy Germany's remaining oil reserves with a near-10,000-ton high-explosive exclamation point.

In a 24-hour period up to last night, the bulk of 2,500 Allied heavy bombers, escorted by more than 1,000 fighters, pounded synthetic oil refineries and storage depots in the Reich. Approximately 700 Eighth AF B17s and B24s led the attack yesterday with a raid on the Rhenania oil refinery, near battered Hamburg, and oil storage dumps and U-boat yards in the same area. In addition, the Eighth heavies hit marshalling yards at Paderborn and other transport facilities in northwest Germany. Ten bombers and five fighters are missing.

More than 1,200 British heavies had preceded the U. S. raids with sledge-hammer attacks Tuesday night on refineries at Brux, in

(Continued on Page 4)

Krakow Claimed Taken as Soviets Overrun Poland

Josef Stalin announced late yesterday that Warsaw had been liberated by Marshal Zhukov's First White Russian Army in co-ordinated smashes with two other powerful Red Armies moving westward toward the German border with speed that belittles the pace of any previous offensives launched by the Russians.

While Moscow was broadcasting news of the fall of the Polish capital, Lublin Radio claimed that Krakow, strongest German defense bastion in southern Poland, also had fallen to the Russian avalanche.

Punching gaping holes in the German line rapidly disintegrating before the massed impact of more than 2,000,000 Red Army soldiers, Marshal Koniev's First Ukrainian Army captured Czestochowa, 15 miles from the German-Silesian border.

Stalin also disclosed that Marshal Rokossovsky's Second White Russian Army had opened an offensive north of Warsaw across the Narew River, gaining more than 25 miles on a 62-mile front.

Last night Moscow shook under the massive victory salute of 40 salvos from 448 guns.

Order of Day Tells of Victory

Frontline dispatches said that Rokossovsky's and Zhukov's armies had opened their blitz breakthroughs by a devastating artillery barrage supported by powerful air support.

The first Order of the Day issued last night by Stalin said that Warsaw had been seized by a massed by-passing movement. One column poured across the Vistula, north of the city, another moved across the river on the south. The two columns then linked up.

The triumphant drive into the city was practically unopposed, with units of the Polish Liberation Army supporting the advance under direct command of Zhukov.

Berlin reports indicated that units of the First White Russian Army already had driven 35 miles west of Warsaw to Sochaczew, on the main rail and road route to Berlin.

Rokossovsky Joins Polish Offensive

In another Order of the Day, issued an hour after the Warsaw victory announcement, it was disclosed that the Second White Russian Army, under Rokossovsky, had joined the Polish offensive about 45 miles north of Warsaw. Rokossovsky struck across the Narew River toward the lower Vistula in the vicinity of Ciechanow.

This announcement answered the question of the whereabouts of Marshal Rokossovsky, whose previous army last year was given to the command of Zhukov.

The capture of the city of Czestochowa, last barrier in southwestern Poland, less than 15 miles from German Silesia, was the highlight of Stalin's third Order of the Day. Czestochowa is on the main rail line between Vienna and

(Continued on Page 4)

6 Weeks Out of States—He Kills 100 Nazis

By Ralph G. Martin
Stars and Stripes Staff Writer

WITH SEVENTH ARMY.—Only six weeks ago, he was downing ice-cream sodas back in Mt. Olive, N.C. Now, firing his machine-gun for the first time in combat, 20-year-old Pvt. Leon Outlaw Jr. protected the exposed flank of his regiment for five days and nights, killing at least 100 Germans, wounding many more and taking six prisoners who waved white socks.

For five rainy, snowy days and sleepless nights, Outlaw sat cramped in his foxhole, drinking melted snow, using his single blanket to cover his gun. He had only three K-rations—a fourth was slapped out of his hand by a piece of shrapnel.

In another foxhole, ten feet behind Outlaw, Sgt. Alphonse Myers, of Amsterdam, N.Y., kept his eyes glued to a pair of field glasses, directing and adjusting fire for Outlaw.

Outlaw usually waited until the Jerries came down the slope, 800 yards away, where there was no cover. Then he'd open up and cut them down.

But it was only after Outlaw started shooting up German command cars on a road 2,000 yards away that the Jerries started dropping the whole German artillery book on top of them.

Behind Outlaw, protecting the rear, were 17 deeply dug-in doughfeet. Several were wounded, one was killed.

Then came the payoff. Two German tanks rumbled up to within 900 yards of them, wandered around the area for more than two hours and then went away.

"I'll never be able to understand that," said Outlaw. "They could have come in and cleaned us out in a couple of minutes."

Myers' own communication with the rear was completely snafued. It might go on for five minutes and then not work for several hours. Meanwhile, bigger German patrols began com-

(Continued on Page 4)

THE STARS AND STRIPES
MEDITERRANEAN

Vol. 2, No. 59, Saturday, January 20, 1945 — Printed in Italy — TWO LIRE

Red Army Sweeping Poland; Lodz And Cracow Captured

Churchill's Policy Approved, 340-7, After Hot Debate

LONDON, Jan. 19—An attempt to express censure of Prime Minister Winston Churchill's interventionist policy in liberated lands was beaten overwhelmingly 340 to 7 in the House of Commons today, the Associated Press reported.

Bolstered by the vote of confidence, Prime Minister Churchill intends to put it squarely up to President Roosevelt and Marshal Stalin to join immediately in creating international machinery for dealing with problems arising in liberated lands.

This was revealed by Foreign Secretary Eden who dramatically brought to close the two-day war debate with the blunt demand that the House show whether "we have your support or not." He asserted he wanted to show the world that the Churchill Government was not "tottering."

Eden's call for a vote of confidence came over the protests of a small faction of Laborites who charged the government with putting them on the spot, since technically, the balloting was on war appropriations.

Some members announced flatly beforehand that while bitterly opposed to Mr. Churchill's policy, they would not vote against the government "to permit Tory hacks to say we voted against war credits," the Associated Press said.

The stocky, 70-year-old Prime Minister came in for some acid criticism from several members of the House, especially independents, Liberals and Laborites, of whom Aneurin Bevan, firebrand Laborite opponent of Mr. Churchill's Greek policies, was once again the most outspoken.

The House was thrown into an uproar as Bevan, who was elected to the Labor party's executive committee last December, castigated the Prime Minister, charging that "the picture of forces marching down on Athens to massacre some of the inhabitants is a characteristic piece of Churchillian rubbish."

Bevan claimed that the "Greek tragedy" was brought about because

(Continued on page 8)

Canadians Liquidate Enemy Bridgehead

ADVANCED ALLIED FORCE HEADQUARTERS, Jan. 19 — The small German bridgehead established south of the Senio River near Fusignano on Wednesday was erased yesterday after Canadian counterattacks, while the rest of the sleepy Italian front bristled with patrol actions.

It was reported today that units of the new Italian Army are in action on the 8th Army front.

Small 5th Army combat parties probed deep into enemy positions. One patrol pushed north toward Paroccia di Vignale, a village ten miles southeast of Bologna, and encountered tough opposition from a German battery set up in a church.

Other 5th Army patrols engaged the enemy in fire fights near Prada, left of Highway 65, and in the Mt. Grande area.

Enemy attacks against British outposts south of Cotignola, a town eight miles due north of Faenza, were beaten off with heavy losses.

The arrows tell the story on this map.

Sellout On Capitol's Hands—It's FDR's 4th Inauguration

By The United Press

WASHINGTON, Jan. 19—The White House is like a Broadway ticket broker's office after an overwhelming hit.

Everyone connected with the President's residence is being bombarded with requests for inauguration tickets.

Judging by the response, however, it would seem the President is surrounded only by "No-men" who are turning down literally thousands of bids from would-be spectators.

Unlike previous years, the 1945 inauguration of the President will be very simple and will cost the nation only 2,000 dollars.

There will be no special services at St. John's Episcopal Church and the President will review no Army parade. There will be no inaugural ball in the evening. Most conspicuous of all, the Capitol Plaza will be virtually deserted, swept clear by war of the 100,000, who stood there on March 4, 1933 and heard a youthful new president.

This is the inauguration day schedule:

In the morning there will be family prayers attended by the Cabinet, the Supreme Court and Congressional leaders.

At noon there will be the inaugu-

(Continued on page 8)

Stalin Says Air Attacks On Germany Aided Drive

LONDON, Jan. 19—Marshal Joseph Stalin paid tribute to the Allied air attacks on Germany as contributing to the success of the Russian armies smashing across Poland, a BBC correspondent in Moscow reported today.

The bombing of Reich industry had a direct influence on the Soviet successes, Marshal Stalin said.

Yanks Capture Town Nearer To Manila

LUZON, Philippines, Jan. 19—American troops driving down the central Luzon plain toward Manila have captured Paniqui, road junction 12 miles north of the important city of Tarlac, which is 65 miles above Manila, the Associated Press reported today.

Paniqui was captured by the eastern of two columns pushing down the main roads north of Manila. The western column was south of captured Camiling and about equal distance from Tarlac. Both were approximately 37 miles inland from Lingayen Gulf.

Their objective, beside Tarlac, was to strike for Clark Field, southwest of Tarlac and 47 miles north of Manila.

American fighter planes, operating from a Japanese-built airfield near Lingayen, were supporting the advance. Upon this airfield, 24 ... Douglas transports arrived from Mindoro, bringing the first air-borne freight to reach Luzon since the fall of Bataan.

The Americans were apparently not meeting much air opposition. ... W. Hutchinson, commander of a bomber wing, said that

(Continued on page 8)

MOSCOW, Jan. 19 — **Germany's eastern defenses crumbled tonight along a 400-mile front, from the Carpathians in southern Poland to the Baltic Sea in East Prussia, under the onslaught of four giant Red Army groups smashing westward along the rolling plains to Berlin.**

In five successive special Orders of the Day, Marshal Joseph Stalin, Supreme Commander of the Red Army, today celebrated what already appears to be one of the most victorious and most decisive days on the eastern front since the enemy was blasted from the gates of Moscow in the winter of 1941.

The day's biggest prize was the great industrial center of Lodz, 80 miles southwest of Warsaw. Poland's "second city," with its prewar population of 700,000 and great factories, fell to the onrushing armies of the 1st White Russian front, under Marshal Gregory Zhukov, after the greatest single advance of any Soviet campaign. Capture of the city was announced in Marshal Stalin's fifth triumphant victory order late tonight after the Germans had reported the Red Army battling in its streets.

Under the Germanic name of Litzmannstadt, Lodz was also known as one of Poland's great graveyards for thousands of Jews deported from the Reich.

FIVE ORDERS OF THE DAY

Within the space of only a few hours, Moscow announced these important gains:

1. A new offensive in the extreme south of Poland by General Ivan Y. Petrov's 4th Ukrainian Army group;
2. The capture of Cracow, fourth largest city in Poland and once the historical and intellectual center of the country;
3. Another offensive, this time in East Prussia, where troops of the 3rd White Russian front under the command of General Ivan D. Chernyakhovsky in five days captured 600 German towns and villages, doubled the area held by the Red Army, and advanced to within 15 miles of Insterburg, ten miles of Tilsit, and 65 miles of Koenigsberg;
4. The capture of a town only 98 miles southeast of Danzig, great Baltic seaport, and an advance to within two miles of the East Prussian border by the armies of the 2nd White Russian front under Marshal Konstantin Rokossovsky;
5. The liberation of Lodz, great industrial center only 250 miles west of Berlin, by Marshal Gregory Zhukov's 1st White Russian front, aided by Marshal Ivan Koniev's 1st Ukrainian Army group.

Cracow, great manufacturing center 50 miles from Silesia, historic burial place of Poland's kings and heroes, intellectual center

(Continued on page 8)

3rd Army In New Assault As British 2nd Advances

SHAEF, Jan. 19—As the British 2nd Army slogged ahead along the German-Dutch frontier in the southern Netherlands, powerful units of the American 3rd Army reached the German frontier in an attack begun in northern Luxembourg, three miles from the border.

Crossing the Sauer River in assault boats under cover of darkness early yesterday, Lt. Gen. George S. Patton's forces, estimated to number two divisions, struck out strongly against the southern corner of the Germans' flattened Ardennes bulge.

The German Overseas News Agency reported that the attack had been launched on an 18-mile front between Wiltz and Wallendorf. Very heavy and bitter fighting was reported to be taking place and some American gains were admitted by the Nazis.

Front-line dispatches from Allied correspondents reported that a firm bridgehead had been established across the Sauer and that Yank troops had entered Diekirch, a few miles west of Wallendorf.

Along the northern flank of the Ardennes salient, troops of the American 1st Army advanced from the northwest to within three miles of the Nazi pivot position at St. Vith. Other 1st Army elements pushed to within seven miles west of St. Vith in a two-mile advance that cleared two Belgian towns.

Meanwhile, in Alsace, German forces ... from their Rhine bridgehead eight miles north of Strasbourg and linked up with their forces further inland in northeastern Alsace, presumably to the north of the Hagenau forest. Reinforcements to strengthen the corridor were being rushed across the Rhine. It is not known whether any American forces were trapped by the breakthrough.

The British 2nd Army drive against the German bulge in the Geilenkirchen-Roermond area increased in scope and intensity as American artillery was thrown into the battle in support of the Tommies. Rising temperatures brought a thaw and armor was bogging down in the slush and mud.

British tanks and infantry had crossed the road from Sittard to Roermond in strength but stiff opposition was reported all along the five mile front.

The long dormant Nijmegen sector in The Netherlands flared into action late yesterday when a strong German patrol attacked a British outpost in the flooded area two miles north of Nijmegen. Instead of withdrawing, the enemy held its position overnight and was reported to have renewed the attack this morning.

Man Spricht Deutsch
Haben Sie Verbandszeug ?
Haben Zee Ferbahndszoyg ?
Have you a bandage ?

THE STARS AND STRIPES

Daily News paper of U.S. Armed Forces in the European Theater of Operations

Ici On Parle Français
On cherche la route à Liège.
Awn shersh la roo ta Li-AIJ.
I'm looking for the road to Liege

Vol. I—No. 1 | New York—LIEGE—London | Saturday, Jan. 20, 1945

Soviets Smash 20 Miles Into Reich

First Army Advancing On St. Vith

By Dan Regan
Stars and Stripes Staff Writer

WITH FIRST ARMY, Belgium, Jan. 19.—Infantry of the First Army drove within four miles of St. Vith today, as a high First Army staff officer said he believed the Germans would not make a determined stand this side of the Siegfried Line. He said the Germans were resisting the American advance in what might be termed «strong rear-guard action».

Good advances were made today all along the First Army front.

The 1st Division's 18th Inf. Regt. advanced 1,000 yards. The 1st Division's 16th Inf. pushed south of Faymonville 2,500 yards, entering Schoppen and cleaning it out.

The Germans apparently pulled out of a defile northeast of St. Vith last night as troops from the 23rd Inf. Regt. advanced 1,000 yards. Other units also entered Ebertange and pushed one-half a kilometer west of Montenau.

Mopping up Recht

Along the 30th Div. front, the 120th Inf. Regt. showed little change, but units were moving southeast of Recht which was being cleaned out today.

On the 75th Div. front, the 290th Inf. Regt. gained 3,000 yards southeast of Vielsalm as the 289th pushed 1,000 yards east of Salmchateau.

The front of the 83rd Div. also showed little change although patrols entered Bovigny and found no enemy.

The 3rd Armd. division's task forces gained important high ground overlooking the Ourthe River.

German prisoners taken by the First Army during the 24-hour period ending at midnight last Thursday totalled 251, making a grand total of 234,460 captured by the First Army since D-Day.

GERMANS ADVANCE IN ALSACE

PARIS, Jan. 19.—British troops advanced across the thawing Dutch panhandle on a front which had widened to five miles today to take the German border town of Hongen and on the Dutch town of Schilberg. Allied armor were meeting stiff resistance in the Dutch tow of Schilberg. Allied armor

(Continued on Page 4)

Army Casualties Total 330,912

WITH THE FIRST U.S. ARMY, BELGIUM, Jan. 19—The following figures were released today of U.S. Army casualties, including the air forces, from D-Day to January 1: killed in action, 54,562; wounded in action, 226,[illegible]; missing in action, 45,678.

These include American losses resulting from the Germans' December break-through which was estimated to have cost the Germans from 110,000 to 120,000 casualties, including 50,000 taken prisoner.

It was also revealed that the 106th Division was overrun by the Germans early in the break-through with a loss of [illegible] casualties, which include [illegible] killed, [illegible] wounded and [illegible] missing.

The Barbs of Wire and of Winter

Signal Corps Photo

In a raging blizzard, men of the 102nd Inf. Div. in Germany string barbed wire as a precautionary measure against enemy attack.

Calls Down Shells on Nazi Attack -- and on Himself

By Marshall Morgan
Stars and Stripes Special Writer

WITH SEVENTH ARMORED DIV.—«Regan, Dennis J., 2d Lt. missing in action»—that's the official report.

«Din,» a forward observer for the 440th Armored FA Battalion, was a man who laughed as much as anyone. He was also the sort of fellow who, at odd moments, would stroll away by himself, sit down somewhere and re-read his wife's letters, carefully folding out the creases.

That morning, Din was far forward with the infantry. The company he was supporting had been cut off, and was being smashed by artillery, mortar and small arms fire.

Din knew what the artillery's job was, in a case like that. He called for smoke.

As the white bursts mushroomed into a merciful screening cloud, first one battered platoon and then another limped through it and back toward the American lines.

The young lieutenant could have left, then. But he stayed, adjusting the smoke, multiplying it.

As soon as the Germans understood what was happening, they threw tanks and a frontal infantry assault against the dwindling pocket of American resistance.

Dennis Regan stayed on.

Back in the battalion fire direction center, exchanging glances, officers and

(Continued on Page 4)

Antwerp Dock Workers Threaten Strike for Coal

BRUSSELS, Jan. 19, (AP)—The newspaper, La Lanterne, said today that dockers in the port of Antwerp threatened to strike in protest against the lack of coal and butter.

Le Drapeau Rouge, communist newspaper, said the strike had already started and would continue 24 hours.

La Lanterne said, however, that Antwerp officials had persuaded the dockers to continue work and that Premier Hubert Pierlot had received a delegation.

New Fighter Plane Production

KANSAS CITY, Mo., Jan. 19 (Ans).—A new type of fighter plane, high on the Air Forces priority list, will go into production [illegible] a short time at the local plant of the North American Aviation Co., it was [illegible] here. No details of the new plane were released.

Com Z Men To Quit Desks For Infantry

By Ernest Leiser
Stars and Stripes Staff Writer

PARIS, Jan. 19.—In a sweeping move to replace some infantry losses, Com Z troops fit for frontline duty are being turned over to the Ground Forces Reinforcement Command and retrained as riflemen, Brig. Gen. Henry J. Matchett, ETO reinforcement chief, revealed today.

He declared that the number of physically fit rear echelon men transferred to combat divisions may reach 75 to 80 per cent of all able-bodied men in Com Z within the next few months. In their places will be put ex-combat

(Continued on Page 4)

Stars and Stripes in Liege

A new edition of **The Stars and Stripes**, published in Liege, comes to you today.

The Liege edition, which will be issued seven days a week, is established to serve expressly the men at the northern end of the Western Front and those behind that front. Its emphasis will be on news of particular interest to troops in this area, and it will be delivered more promptly than was possible for the Paris edition.

The Stars and Stripes in Liege is the sixth edition currently being published in Gen. Eisenhower's command. The others are at Paris, London, Strasbourg, Dijon and Marseilles.

Key Polish Cities Fall In Sweep

(Map on Page 3)

Spearheads of Marshal Koniev's First Ukrainian Army yesterday drove across the Reich frontier, stabbing 20 miles into German Silesia near Oppeln, according to German reports.

Marshal Stalin announced that five Red Armies had been thrown into the gigantic week-old winter offensive which has inundated three-fourths of Poland. From the Kremlin last night came an 11th order of the Day in 72 hours saluting the capture of Krakow, ancient capital of old Poland, and Lodz, the great industrial center. The orders also disclosed that the Fourth Ukrainian Army in Southern Poland had gained 50 miles in three days in a new offensive along the Carpathian mountains while the Third White Russian Army had broken through German defenses 12 miles south of Tilsit, in East Prussia, on a 36-mile front.

Numerous squadrons of German home guards were reported thrown into the fighting in the German Silesia sector.

Breach 37 Miles Wide

In announcing the offensive under Petrov in Southern Poland, Marshal Stalin revealed the drive was launched Jan. 5 from regions west of the Sanok River. In four days, the drive advanced 50 miles, opening a breach in the German lines 37 miles wide. After crossing the Wasloka and Dunapec Rivers, Petrov's army took Jaslo and Gorlice and 400 other inhabited places. Gorlice is 60 miles southeast of Krakow.

Berlin earlier had announced bitter fighting in the streets of Krakow but Moscow was silent until Stalin's announcement was made on the fall of the city. Russian tanks and advanced units of motorized infantry met increased resistance at the German Silesian frontier.

Lodz provides an important base for developing the Russian all-out offensive toward the heart of the Reich. It is a junction of highways and railways fanning out on the plain leading toward Germany, 65 miles away. Lodz had a pre-war population of over 600,000.

WARSAW REVIVING

MOSCOW, Jan. 19 (AP)—A red and white flag floated over Warsaw today as hundreds of Poles took up the gigantic task of bringing their ancient capital back to life.

Dispatches from the city told shocking stories of destruction. One correspondent called it «a desert of wreckage».

Warsaw has no more streets in the proper sense of theh word. But life returned quickly to the city to the tune of beating hammers and roaring tractors. Labor squads quickly threw crossings over blown up main bridges of the Vistula leading into Praga. «The streets are beoming unusually animated», a correspondent for Izvestia reported.

Brenner Pass Bombed

ROME, Jan. 19 (Reuter)—Patrols of the Fifth and Eighth Armies were active today probing enemy positions along the front. Bombers of the tactical air force attacked a number of bridges on the Brenner Pass.

Man Spricht Deutsch
Sind irgendwo Minen gelegt?
Sind eergendvo Meenen gelegt?
Are there any mines?

THE STARS AND STRIPES
Daily Newspaper of U.S. Armed Forces in the European Theater of Operations

Ici On Parle Français
Avez-vous vu des soldats russes?
Avay voo vew deh sohldah rews?
Have you seen Russian soldiers?

Vol. 1—No. 184 | 1 Fr. | New York—PARIS—London | 1 Fr. | Saturday, Jan. 27, 1945

Reds 91 Mi. From Berlin; Shut Ring Around Breslau

18,000 U.S. Soldiers AWOL in ETO

Upped Rate Linked to Theft Rise

Between 18,000 and 19,000 American soldiers—the equivalent of one and one half U.S. infantry divisions—are now AWOL in the ETO.

The Theater Provost Marshal, making this disclosure yesterday, said that the number of AWOLs is approximately twice as high as it was before the invasion.

Leading sources of the AWOLs are the Army's reinforcement depots. After them, the AGF, AAF, and Com Z have approximately equal proportions. The Provost Marshal emphasized, however, that the overall figures included a considerable number of "transient AWOLs" who were skipping channels and using their own methods to rejoin their units.

This, it was indicated, would account for an important number of the absences from reinforcement depots, and would greatly lessen the number of long-term AWOLs.

Lower Than World War I

The Provost Marshal declared, too, that the present figures, though high, are much lower than they were during the first World [illegible] plained by the larger number of troops in the ETO.

Simultaneously, Brig. Gen. Pleas B. Rogers, commanding Seine Base Section, declared that more than half of the men AWOL are mixed up in some way with black-market operations. Gen. Rogers revealed in an interview that the number of serious gasoline, cigarette and ration theft cases is on the increase, as are the numbers of men going AWOL.

The majority of the AWOLs find their way to Paris, Rogers said, and here, since they are not on any payroll, they have to rob their buddies or hold up somebody else to live.

It's No 'Witch Hunt'

Gen. Rogers made these statements in declaring that the Army was not conducting a "witch hunt," as he said many GIs feel, in its stringent prosecution of 716th Railway Bn. soldiers for the theft and sale of front-bound cigarettes. He said that these prosecutions represented part of a real effort to whip the rising crime problem, and added that no one, officer or enlisted man, will be spared in this drive.

He denied that any of the Army's commanders is "winking at these things," and said that "we don't look the other way, whether it's a corporal or a brigadier general." He cited the case of a brigadier general sent back to the States

(Continued on Page 8)

Merging Sight and Sound

Wounded Pair Conquer Helplessness

By Dave Gordon
Stars and Stripes Special Writer

203rd GEN. HOSP., Jan. 26.—The story of how a blind soldier and a buddy whose voice had been muted to a whisper merged the seeing eye and the speaking voice to call for aid after three days in a foxhole was told today at this hospital.

Pvt. John Lach, of Scranton, Pa., and his buddy were advancing with Co. K, 116th Inf., in German territory in the dawn of an early December day. Jerry artillery opened up. Shell fragments hit Lach in the right eye and his buddy in the throat. Concussion caused the loss of vision in Lach's left eye so that he was left completely blind.

Other GIs carried the two casualties to a nearby foxhole and said they would return. Rain began to fall and soon the bottom of the foxhole was a muddy pool. The two men could hear the whistling of shells and the rattle of machine guns.

The hours crawled by and no help came. Lach's buddy applied a dressing to Lach's eye and looked vainly for help. They divided a box of K-rations, their only food. The wind made them shiver.

Lach said he almost gave up hope. As time dragged on, their feet became swollen and numb. Hungry, wet, cold, suffering from their wounds, the men grew weaker. But on the afternoon of the third day Lach's buddy saw two GIs. He frantically nudged his companion, whispered what he saw and urged him to yell.

Lach summoned all his waning strength and shouted. "Medic, medic!"

His buddy watched the two GIs, filled with excitement. "Medic, medic!" Lach shouted again. This time he was heard and the two GIs cautiously approached the hole.

Subsequently the rescued men were evacuated but to different hospitals. By Dec. 28 Lach had recovered sight in his left eye.

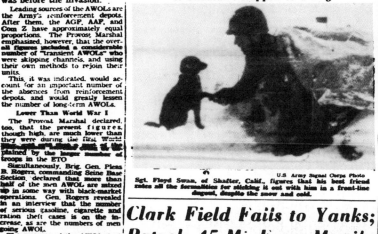

It Shouldn't Happen to a Dog

U.S. Army Signal Corps Photo

Sgt. Floyd Swan, of Shafter, Calif., figures that his best friend rates all the formalities for sticking it out with him in a front-line dugout, despite the snow and cold.

Clark Field Falls to Yanks; Patrols 45 Mi. From Manila

U.S. Sixth Army forces on Luzon have taken Clark Field and neighboring Fort Stotsenburg. After winning these successes, announced yesterday by Gen. Douglas MacArthur, the Yanks started clearing Japanese troops from near-by hills and sent patrols five miles southward to Angeles 45 miles north of Manila.

Clark Field was overrun so fast that the Japanese failed to put up any stiff resistance from defenses dug near the northern approaches. As the Yank patrols pushed on down the main highway to Manila, other Americans reached the highway town of Magalang 10 miles east of Clark. This means that two American divisions have troops on parallel highways which converge 15 miles to the south into a single road to Manila.

Push Toward Santa Cruz

Americans on the right flank were advancing down the west coast toward Santa Cruz, below Dasol Bay on the road leading to Bataan peninsula. Yank units on the left flank maintained heavy pressure on the Japanese around Rosario, and farther south San Manuel was entered against strong opposition.

American planes dropped 95 tons of bombs on the former U.S. naval base at Cavite, on Manila Bay, hammered enemy defenses on Corregidor and in Subic Bay, and sank a big Japanese tanker near Aparri. Other planes based in the Philippines continued to attack the Japanese naval base of Takao, on Formosa.

A U.S. naval task force, includ-

(Continued on Page 8)

Senate Group Bars Wallace

BULLETIN

The Stars and Stripes U.S. Bureau

WASHINGTON, Jan. 26.—The Senate Commerce Committee today rejected President Roosevelt's nomination of Henry A. Wallace to the twin jobs of Secretary of Commerce and Federal loan chief. The vote was 14 to 5.

The committee approved for submission to the Senate a bill which would strip the Commerce Department of its loan powers. Objections to Wallace's appointment have centered on the loan-power issue.

(Earlier details on Page 3.)

De Gaulle Asks Rhine Rule

After the war, French troops should be permanently installed on both banks of the Rhine, Gen. de Gaulle told an Allied press conference Thursday.

In addition, De Gaulle disclosed that France had not been invited to the "Big Three" conference.

Nazi Violations Cancel Truce at St. Nazaire

OUTSIDE ST. NAZAIRE, Jan 26.—The two-day extension of a truce to evacuate French civilians from the German pocket at St. Nazaire was cancelled by Allied Army authorities today when it became known the Germans had violated the truce.

The Jerries took advantage of the truce to forage for fuel in no-man's-land. Originally, approximately 12,000 civilians were to have been evacuated from the Nazi pocket.

Big Battle Still Rages For Posen

Red Army tank vanguards, stabbing irresistibly across the western Polish plains into the German province of Brandenburg, were reported within 91 miles of Berlin yesterday by a German News Agency broadcast. Other Soviet troops clamped steel pincers around Breslau, in German Silesia, and closed in on Posen from three sides.

By-passing Posen on the north and south, then racing 48 miles to the German-Polish frontier, Marshal Gregory Zhukov's First White Russian Army tank columns were engaged in furious battles for Driesen and Bentschen, German towns just over the border, the broadcast said.

Driesen is 91 miles east of the Reich capital and is on the south bank of the River Netze. The Germans, announcing the fighting at Driesen, claimed the entire Red Army column was "destroyed."

Resistance at Posen

In the area around Posen, the German High Command threw in powerful tank reserves in an effort to defend the city against the First White Russian Army. The Associated Press in London said that the Posen battle had been swaying back and forth for days, with Zhukov beating off German defensive counter-blows.

On the Upper Silesian front, Marshal Ivan Koniev's First Ukrainian Army closed the ring around Breslau, Germany's sixth largest city, a Moscow dispatch from United Press said.

Tanks under the command of Col. Gen. D. D. Lealushenko, Red Army liberator of Stalingrad, are leading the assault on the city from the northeast with the aid of artillery and aircraft.

On the Oder River 40 miles northeast of Breslau, some of the heaviest fighting of the day was reported. German reports said that Marshal Koniev's troops were smashing across the river near Beuthen, one of Upper Silesia's largest towns and an important coal center. Hindenburg, another coal town, three miles from the

(Continued on Page 8)

Seventh Army Forces Nazis Back in Alsace

Counter-attacking, U.S. Seventh Army troops smashed the enemy back against his Moder River bridgehead southwest of Haguenau yesterday, stalling temporarily, the Nazi offensive in northern Alsace between the Eifel Mountains and the Rhine.

Northward along the Roer River in Germany, U.S. Ninth Army's 102nd Inf. Div. made a local attack, took the Nazi town of Brachelen and drove the Germans to the river's east bank.

In the Ardennes, U.S. First Army tanks and infantry cleared four more Belgian towns as they struggled through the snowdrifts toward the pre-breakthrough line. Driving into the center of the withered salient, U.S. Third Army men thrust to within two miles of the German-Luxembourg frontier.

Main Nazi Effort

It was disclosed yesterday that Nazi forces attacking on the northern Alsace Plain included the Sixth SS Mountain Div., the 21st Panzer Div., the Tenth SS Div., the 25th Panzergrenadier Div. and the Seventh Parachute Div.

The Sixth Mountain had been moved down from Norway to fight in the salient south of Bitche and had been fairly well roughed up there by Seventh Army men.

The German attack in northern Alsace, which now constitutes the main Nazi effort in the west, had gained two bridgeheads across the Moder, which winds across the plain from east to west between the Eifel to a point east of Haguenau.

Lt. Gen. Alexander M. Patch's

(Continued on Page 8)

Eisenhower, Stalin Reported In 'Contact' for First Time

The Stars and Stripes U.S. Bureau

NEW YORK, Jan. 26.—Merrill Mueller, NBC news reporter, broadcast today that Gen. Eisenhower had just "established contact" with Josef Stalin for the first time. An NBC press commentary said interpretatively that "for the first time in this war there is a cohesive plan of action between the Russian and western fronts."

(No confirmation or comment was obtainable at SHAEF last night. Merrill Mueller left France for the U.S. about a week ago.)

LONDON, Jan. 26 (UP).—Before D-Day, Gen. Eisenhower indicated that operational co-ordination with the Russians would be effected when the military situation warranted.

If the "contact" mentioned in the broadcast by Merrill Mueller means close military liaison—a point which is necessarily clouded by censorship—it would appear to indicate that the Supreme Commander is convinced the time has come for a co-ordinated two-way squeeze play on Germany possibly an all-out Allied offensive to bring pressure on the western front equivalent to that which the Reds are applying along the Oder line.

Man Spricht Deutsch
Zweelf Jahre Nazi-Regime.
Tsweiff Yaahre Nazi-Regime.
Twelve years of Nazism.

THE STARS AND STRIPES

Daily Newspaper of U.S. Armed Forces in the European Theater of Operations

Ici On Parle Français
Avez-vous une allumette?
A-vay-voo oon al-loom-et?
Have you a match?

Vol. 1—No. 187 | 1 Fr. | New York—PARIS—London | 1 Fr. | Tuesday, Jan. 30, 1945

Relentless Surge of the Russian Tidal Wave Shown Day by Day

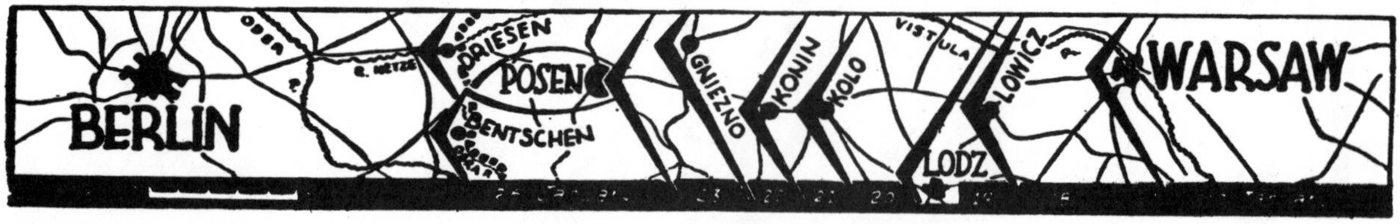

Berlin in Peril, Nazis Say

3rd Crosses Our River Into Reich at 2 Points

U.S. Third Army infantry plunged across the Our River into Germany yesterday and the First Army widened its attack in the snows of eastern Belgium with a new assault east of Malmedy.

In the Alsatian Rhineland, Franco-American troops of Gen. De Montsabert's French Second Corps advanced to within a kilometer of Colmar, key strongpoint in the Germans' trans-Rhine salient between Strasbourg and Mulhouse.

From Third Army, Stars and Stripes Correspondent James Cannon reports that two crossings were made on the Our, which forms the Luxembourg-German border. The doughs made one crossing in the vicinity of Peterskirche and Oberhausen, but the location of the second was not immediately reported.

First Div. Attacks

Stars and Stripes Correspondent Dan Regan with First Army said that the First Div. kicked off at 20 minutes past midnight yesterday and nine hours later the Third Bn. of its 26th Regt. took Bullingen, 10 miles east of Malmedy. Other First Army infantry, attacking six miles to the south, pressed east of St. Vith for gains up to 3,000 yards.

Along the German-Dutch borderlands, British Second Army troops were clearing enemy pockets between Heinzberg and Roermond as the Tommies closed up along the Roer and Wurm Rivers. The British operation in this sector is virtually completed.

All along the front from eastern Holland to the Saar the Allies were moving up against Germany's natural and artificial barriers—the Roer River, north of Aachen, and the Siegfried Line to the south.

Regan said First Army forces were within six miles of the Sieg-

(Continued on Page 8)

Hopkins Here In Pre-Big 3 Meeting Tour

Harry L. Hopkins, President Roosevelt's No. 1 adviser, is making a swift tour of Europe in advance of the "Big Three" conferences, it was revealed yesterday.

Hopkins spent five days in London and three in Paris. He told correspondents he might also get to Moscow, but pointed out that flying to the [illegible] was difficult in winter. He emphasized that Soviet leaders knew of his trip.

Harry Hopkins

An indication of the scope of the forthcoming Big Three talks was seen by civilian correspondents in Paris in the nature of Hopkins' talks with Gen. Charles de Gaulle, although French sources said the President's emissary did not invite the French leader to join in the talks.

Hopkins, in his Paris talks, was understood to have received the broad outlines of French desires in the settlement of such questions as controls to be placed on the Ruhr and Rhine industrial basins, territorial changes, and post-war trade facilities intended to rehabilitate France's industry, transportation and agricultural resources.

A tight censorship veiled Hopkins' presence in Europe until Paris radio let it slip out through a misunderstanding. The visit was supposed to be a complete secret in order to protect persons other than himself, Hopkins told correspandents earlier.

Subasic Told to Form New Jugoslav Regime

LONDON, Jan. 29 (Reuter).—Prime Minister Dr. Ivan Subasic of Jugoslavia today handed his resignation from the Cabinet to King Peter, who accepted it and at the same time charged Subasic with the task of forming a new government.

(An article giving the background of the Jugoslavian crisis, will be found on Page 2.)

Red Soldiers on the Move

Infantrymen of Marshal Rodion Malinovsky's Third Ukrainian Army leap from their dugouts to attack a German position shown smoking in the background. Picture received from Moscow by radio.

Jitters Bordering on Panic Reported Gripping Germany

By Carl Larsen
Stars and Stripes Staff Writer

NEW YORK, Jan. 29.—News and radio reports reaching here from inside Germany today presented a picture of jitters amounting almost to panic, with huge disorganized flights of civilians from the eastern Reich and hints of local outbreaks against the Nazis.

The German radio itself spoke of difficulties in handling thousands fleeing from Berlin, and there was even a report that the German General Staff had advised Hitler to sue for peace.

A neutral diplomat arriving in Stockholm from Berlin told a London Daily Mail correspondent that Adolf Hitler has refused the general staff's recommendation that he ask for an armistice. The Stockholm dispatch said the general staff is no longer holding itself responsible for a situation beyond its control.

Observers warned that such reports should be taken with caution, since Germany's propaganda

(Continued on Page 8)

New Lightnings Carry 4,000 Lb. Bomb Load

BURBANK, Calif., Jan. 29 (AP).—The newest model of the Lightning fighter-bomber, known as the P38L or "On to Tokyo" model, can carry a bomb load of 4,000 pounds, the Lockheed Aircraft Corp. has disclosed with army approval.

The new model, which is the 18th version of the Lightning in six years travels more than 425 MPH, has a range of more than 3,000 miles and a service ceiling exceeding 40,000 feet.

RedArmies Slash Deep Into Reich

With Posen and Breslau encircled, three Red Army spearheads slashed deep into Germany yesterday, reaching a point only 85 miles from the great port of Stettin as German radio told Berlin citizens that the capital may have to be yielded to the Russians.

Sweeping west from captured Bromberg, the northern wing of Marshal Gregory Zhukov's First White Russian Army cut the Berlin-Frankfort-Danzig railway by encircling the Pomeranian rail junction of Scheidemuhl, then sweeping 30 miles past the border to an undisclosed point 85 miles from Stettin. This report came from the official Soviet News Agency.

Marshal Stalin announced in an Order of the Day that Zhukov's forces had captured Driesen, Woldenberg, Schonlanke, Lukas and Kreus, all German strongpoints along the German frontier.

Nazis Admit Desperation

A great Zukhov tank force blasted its way into the area north of Kreuz, also on the Danzig-Berlin railway, 110 miles northeast of Berlin. Further south violent tank battles for the German town of Bentschen raged into the fourth day. The Germans admitted that the Reds had succeeded in breaching the Kreuz-Bentschen line.

German radio, admitting the Wehrmacht was "fighting with sheer desperation," fixed the most dangerous Red Army penetration in the Scheidemuhl zone, where Zhukov's forces, if they continue their present pace, may reach Stettin in a few days and cut off another chunk of the north-

(Continued on Page 8)

80,000 Troops In U.S. Switched To the Infantry

WASHINGTON, Jan. 29 (ANS).—The War Department today emphasized the need for more infantrymen with the announcement that 55,000 men from the Air Forces and 25,000 from service units had been transferred to the ground forces.

The announcement said that the troops would be given six weeks special training at camps in the U.S. to fit them for service with ground commands. The WD emphasized that with approaching victory the mission of the infantry is becoming more important since the culminating factor of all successfull wars is infantry action.

Noncoms, it was said, will be given an additional six weeks training to qualify them for infantry duty commensurate with their grade.

Man and Machine Team Up to Help Clear the Enemy From Belgian Soil

U.S. Army Signal Corps Photo

With tanks backing them up, armored infantrymen prepare to fight their way forward with the Third Army in the Belgian zone.

S & S for the Front
Don't shortstop
this newspaper
behind the line.

LIEGE EDITION
THE STARS AND STRIPES
Daily News paper of U.S. Armed Forces in the European Theater of Operations
Vol. I—No. 18 Tuesday, Feb. 6, 1945

S & S for the Front
The Joe at the front
wants to read
this paper too.

Zhukov Across Oder River, Nazis Admit; 30 Mi. to Go

Bridgeheads Forced On 100-Mi. Line

Red Army tank spearheads, grinding northwest around the battles raging for the key "Berlin Bulge" cities of Frankfurt and Kuestrin, yesterday drove into the northern "elbow" of the Oder River to reach a point slightly more than 30 miles northeast of Berlin.

Along the Oder in Silesia, the Germans claimed that the Soviets had opened the "second phase" of the winter offensive.

With long-range guns pouring an endless barrage of steel onto German fortifications on the west bank, Marshal Gregory Zhukov's troops probed for weak points on the Oder River line as assault troops, according to enemy reports, held a half-dozen bridgeheads across the river on a 100-mile front from south of Frankfurt north to a point near Kuestrin.

German Radio said that Zhukov was massing thousands of troops between Frankfurt and Kuestrin, building up for a "frontal assault" on the German capital while armored forces were being moved into the Oder "Elbow" where an effort will be made to outflank Berlin from the north.

Violent armored clashes at Kienitz, on the west bank of the Oder 23 miles northwest of Kuestrin, were reported last night by the Germans.

Marshal Ivan Koniev's troops, possibly throwing the "left-hook", gained 14 miles in a push west from an Oder bridgehead at Brieg, German official reports said last night, describing the attack as the beginning of the "second phase of Marshal Stalin's winter offensive."

DNB said Koniev had concentrated powerful tank and infantry formations in the Brieg area between Berlin and Oppeln. Heavy battles were reported in progress for the communications town of Grottkau, 28 miles northwest of Oppeln on the west bank of the Oder.

In East Prussia fighting has reached the decisive stage as Red Army troops, tightening the noose around the Prussian province, captured Landsberg and Bartenstein, two of the last four big cities still in German hands.

Koenigsberg was in flames as Soviet troops threw overwhelming forces at three defense points ringing the city against stiff German resistance, according to Moscow dispatches.

Fighting in the area around Danzig was in progress for three communications towns on the Danzig-Berlin railway but thaw and rain appeared to have slowed the tempo of the Red advance.

News of Zhukov's thrust toward Stettin was not mentioned in last night's Moscow communique.

NAZI ROBOMBS FOR BERLIN?

LONDON, Feb. 5 (AP)—Reports that the Germans had been building flying bomb ramps 50 miles west of and facing Berlin, for use against the capital if it falls to the Russians, were received in London today from German underground sources.

Yanks Free North Half Of Manila

The Stars and Stripes flew over the northern half of Manila, capital of the Philippines, yesterday as American soldiers drove in from three directions bent on completing the liberation of the almost encircled city.

The Yanks were closing in from the north, south and east to trap the garrison in a squeeze play under which the Japanese had almost no hope of making a successful stand.

First entry into Manila was made Saturday night by the veteran motorized First Cav. Div., which had raced 140 miles in 60 hours to avenge the capture in 1942 of its former commander, Lt. Gen. Jonathan M. Wainwright, now believed to be a prisoner of war in Japan.

Meet Only Sniper Fire

While the Japanese garrison blasted installations in the southern half of the capital, the First Cav. and 37th Inf. Div. pressed through the northern and eastern sections of Manila toward the heart of the city. They encountered little more than sniper fire.

The enemy faced a new threat from the south, where men of the 511th Reg. of the 11th Airborne Div. made a surprise landing on Taygay Ridge, 32 miles southwest of the capital. Latest official reports put them 18 miles from the city, but they were almost certain to have outstripped the official communiques.

Gen. MacArthur, who vowed he would return after he had been ordered to leave Bataan in 1942, was unable to enter his prewar headquarters with the first U.S. spearhead. A blasted bridge barred his way and he had to turn back to take another route.

The long-awaited American return to Manila climaxed a sensational contest between the First Cav. and 37th Inf. which, despite official efforts at caution, had virtually become a footrace. Though the cavalrymen won, entering the city from the east after carrying out an encircling maneuver, the doughboys arrived a few hours later from the north.

Manila, known to tourists as the Pearl of the Orient, will be the largest city yet liberated by the Americans in their drive against the Japanese.

Entry into the capital was made just 26 days after MacArthur and his men

(Continued on Page 4)

FDR Hails Manila Fall As Warning to All Foes

WASHINGTON, Feb. 5 (AP)—The American entry into Manila was hailed by President Roosevelt in a message which he sent to Sergio Osmena, President of the Philippines.

"Let the Japanese and other enemies of peaceful nations take warning from the great events in your country," Mr. Roosevelt said. "Their world of treachery, aggression and enslavement cannot survive in a struggle against our world of freedom and peace."

The president also told Osmena: "The American people rejoice with me in the liberation of your capital."

Manila—Luzon Goal Accomplished

Here's aerial view of Manila, northern half of which is now held by Americans, with Pasig River in foreground.

Tank Crashes Gate, Frees 3,700 Starving Prisoners

MANILA, Feb. 5.—An American tank crashed through the gate of Santo Tomas University and liberated 3,700 civilian internees, mostly Americans, who for more than two years suffered there in dread Japanese imprisonment.

Unbounded joy, verging almost on hysteria, greeted the liberators even as they fought from room to room and killed Japanese defenders.

In short order the American flag was hoisted over the building for the first time since Jan. 3, 1942. Men, women and children, even the doughboys, wept unashamedly and hugged each other in happiness.

But it was a grim reunion. The internees, hollow-eyed from malnutrition, unashamedly asked for food. They reported that for the past five months they had been starving to death. From a daily diet of 1,400 calories in 1942 the meals had deteriorated to 750, one prisoner said.

The most moving union was that of Frank Hewlett, UP Manila bureau manager, and his wife Virginia with whom he had parted on New Year's Eve in 1942 to go to Bataan with MacArthur while she stayed as a hospital nurse.

"I found her there today," he wrote. "Her weight dropped to 80 pounds."

Robert Crabb, UP Manila reporter, who

(Continued on Page 4)

U.S. Planes Down Japs at 5-1 Ratio

WASHINGTON, Feb. 5 (ANS)—The Navy disclosed today that the Naval and Marine airmen had destroyed 9,819 Japanese aircraft in the first three years of war while losing 1,882 of their own—a ratio of more than 5.2 to 1.

The figures included only planes shot from the air or destroyed on the ground. They did not include Japanese or U.S. losses from anti-aircraft fire or operational accidents. The score in 1942 was 1,134 to 384, a ratio of 3-1; in 1943, 2,212 to 351, or 6.3-1; and last year 6,473 to 1,147 or 5.7-1.

Despite heavy losses, however, the Japanese are believed to have a substantial air force and to be maintaining production at a higher level than losses. Some estimates place Japanese plane production as high as 1,000 to 1,500 a month. However, Superfortress raids on the Jap homeland undoubtedly have impaired the enemy's aircraft output.

A favorable factor from the U.S. point of view is that at least 65 per cent of the Navy and Marine fliers downed are rescued. No figures are available on Japanese rescues but it is known that the enemy, holding life cheap, doesn't concern himself as much with picking up "dunked" pilots as does our Navy.

500,000 Tons Rained On Reich in 3 Years

NEW YORK, Feb. 5 (ANS)—Teamwork between the U.S. Eighth AF and the RAF was assigned as the basic factor in the effective bombing of Germany in a transcribed overseas broadcast last night by Lt. Gen. James H. Doolittle, Eighth AF commander.

He reported that 500,000 tons of bombs had been dropped and 12,000 of his aircraft destroyed in three years since the two air forces joined.

Gains Scored Beyond Roer By 78th, 9th

By Russell Jones
Stars and Stripes Staff Writer

WITH FIRST ARMY, Feb. 5—Tanks working with doughs of the 78th Inf. Div. pushed forward up to a mile and a half today in the forested waterway system of the eastern Siegfried defenses to capture Strauch and Steckenborn, within two miles of Rurstausee. Rurstausee is the northernmost of the great lakes formed by dams in the Urft River before it empties into the Roer River to the west.

The Ninth Inf. Div., which yesterday had troops along the shores of the southern lake, Urtstausee, put patrols this morning across Urfttalsperre Dam, which forms the large lake of the same name. (A Stars and Stripes dispatch from SHAEF later said that the Ninth's 47th Inf. Reg. captured the dam, to gain control of the southern bank of the lake.)

Nazis Counter-Attack

Farther south, the Second Inf. Div. was hit by strong counter-attacks at Hellenthal, three miles southwest of Schleiden.

Armored elements, together with the 309th and 311th Inf. of the 78th, moved forward half a mile before 0600 and by 1400 hours had pushed up to a mile more. The 309th advanced farther into the

(Continued on Page 4)

Poles to Govern E. Prussia

The president of the Lublin National Council, now located in Warsaw, announced yesterday that Poland would assume control of civil administration in Silesia and East Prussia immediately. He also said there was no basis for rapprochement between the Poles in London and the Warsaw government.

New York — London Edition — Paris
THE STARS AND STRIPES
Daily Newspaper of the Armed Forces in the European Theater of Operations
TUESDAY, Feb. 13, 1945

Daily German Lesson
Der sieg ist unser
Deir zeeg is oonser
The victory is ours

Daily French Lesson
Vous etes tres belle
Voo zet tray bell
You are very beautiful

Big 3 Agree on Occupation, Plan World Security Group

They Plan So It Won't Happen Again

This photograph taken at the scene of the historic Crimea Conference at Yalta, near Sevastopol, shows the Big Three and members of their staff at their deliberations in the conference room. Seated, left to right: Marshal Stalin; Ivan M. Maisky, Deputy Commissar for Foreign Affairs; Unidentified, Adm. William D. Leahy, Chief of Staff to the President; U.S. Secretary of State Edward R. Stettinius Jr.; Harry Hopkins, special assistant to the President; Pres. Roosevelt, Sir Alexander Cadogan, Permanent Undersecretary of State for Foreign Affairs; Unidentified, and Prime Minister Churchill.

Tell German People 'Defeat Costlier By Hopeless Resistance'

President Roosevelt, Prime Minister Churchill and Marshal Stalin last night announced the results of their eight-day conference in the Crimea, issuing a joint communique that revealed close agreement in plans for the final defeat of Nazi Germany, its occupation and control, for an international organization to maintain peace and security, and for joint action in dealing with the political and economic problems of European countries liberated from the Nazi yoke.

The three Allied heads summed up their plans as a reaffirmation of their "common determination to maintain and strengthen in the peace to come that unity of purpose and of action which has made victory possible and certain for the United Nations in this war."

The talks were held at Yalta, near Sevastopol, in the Crimea.

Meetings of the military staffs of the three powers, the communique declared, resulted in closer co-ordination of the military effort of the U.S., Britain and Russia than ever before and promised even more powerful blows to be launched by land and air against Germany from East, West, North and South.

"Nazi Germany is doomed," the statement read. "The German people will only make the cost of their defeat heavier to themselves by attempting to continue a hopeless resistance."

Common policies for enforcing unconditional surrender, terms which by necessity will not be made known until the final defeat of Germany, have been agreed upon, but the communique said only that the three powers will each share in the occupation of Germany, with a Central Control Commission, consisting of the Supreme Commanders of the three powers, operating with headquarters in Berlin.

France, too, may share in the occupation. The Big Three has agreed to invite the French to take a zone of occupation and join the Control Commission.

Germany will be stripped of militarism and Nazism; all German military equipment will be removed or destroyed; industry that could be used for military purposes will be eliminated or controlled; the German general staff will be broken up; war criminals will be brought to swift justice, and Germany will have to make compensation for the damage it has wrought in Europe. A Commission for the Compensation of Damage will be set up, with headquarters in Moscow.

However, the three leaders declared that it is not their purpose to "destroy the people of Germany but only when Nazism and militarism have been extirpated will there be hope for a decent life for Germans and a place for them in the comity of nations."

The Crimean agreement calls for the "earliest possible" establishment of an international organization to maintain peace and security, which would prevent aggression and remove the causes of war through close and permanent collaboration. The peace organization would be cast from the mould made at Dumbarton Oaks.

A conference of the United Nations to

(Continued on back page)

FDR Asks U.S. Join In World Money Group

WASHINGTON, Feb. 12—Declaring that world political collaboration as set forth in the Dumbarton Oaks proposals was not in itself enough to weld international security, President Roosevelt, in a message to Congress today, urged "prompt action" in authorizing American participation in the international economic organization proposed at the Bretton Woods financial conference.

In his first major public statement since leaving for the Big Three conference, Mr. Roosevelt declared that "it is time for the United States to take the lead in establishing the principle of economic co-operation as a foundation for expanded world trade."

The President described the Bretton Woods plan, which calls for an international bank and an international monetary fund, as the "cornerstone of international economic co-operation," just as the Dumbarton Oaks plan is the "cornerstone for international political co-operation."

Mr. Roosevelt promised further recommendations, ranging from control of cartels to legislation allowing the U.S. to lend money directly to stimulate trade, and once more called for repeal of the Johnson Act, which prohibits lending to countries in default on war debts.

Vignette of Peace

Picks Up Pins (Sob!) and Quits

HOLLYWOOD, Feb. 12 (ANS)—News from the movie capital today sounded its usual familiar themes—the annual "Oscar" derby, divorce, marriage, bundles from heaven, ad infinitum—but it was left for a young starlet to sound the most depressing note of the day.

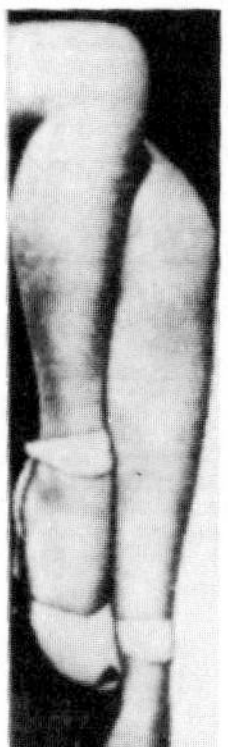

THOSE LEGS

Ramsay Ames announced she was through posing for leg art—and strong men wept. (See accompanying photo.)

This may not be earth-shaking news, but its repercussions may be felt around the world. (See accompanying photo.)

For the photographed charms of Miss Ames, when clad in as little as possible, have served as a morale booster for thousands of GIs in camps and battle zones from here to China and back again. (See accompanying photo.)

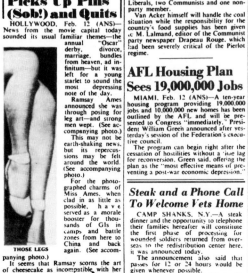

It seems that Ramsay scorns the art of cheesecake as incompatible with her desires to be the intellectual type. After 958 sittings for pin-up purposes (she supplied the statistics herself) she's going dramatic on us. (See accompanying photo.)

Canadians Take Cleve, Fight for Roads to Ruhr

Two key German communications centers fell yesterday to Allied troops as the U.S. 3rd Army captured all but a few houses in Prum, 10 miles inside the Reich from the Belgian border, and Scottish troops of the Canadian 1st Army took Cleve, hub of railways and roads leading to the industrial Ruhr.

The two towns, which served as bastions of the West Wall, were largely ruined, Prum from artillery barrages preceding the entry of doughboys of the 4th Division, and Cleve from all-out assaults by tanks and flamethrowers which wiped out the last fanatical resistance. Cleve was the largest city taken in side Germany by Canadian 1st Army forces.

A Scottish colonel who led the armored sweep through Cleve said all the Allied troops had been pulled back from the town at 4 AM yesterday. Half an hour later the tanks roared in, blasting and searing the last hold-out points. Scottish infantry followed up the armor.

Described as 'Naval' Battle

North of Cleve, Canadian troops were engaged in what was described as a minor naval engagement as they went forward in amphibious vehicles from "island to island" to take small villages abandoned by the Germans along the flooded south bank of the Rhine in Holland.

Striking southeast from Cleve, Canadian troops swept along the road to Goch, joining British forces rolling down from near-by Matterborn heights in the face of artillery and mortar fire. The enemy was said to be rushing more artillery and heavy weapons into the area in an effort to stem the push.

Following the Germans' blasting of the floodgates of the main dam checking the Roer River, activity on the 1st Army front has subsided somewhat. Troops of the 78th Infantry Division were trying to take the half of the Schwammanauel dam still in German hands. Patrols which sought to cross the swollen Roer farther north in the Duren area found

(Continued on back page)

Belgium Gets New Cabinet

BRUSSELS, Feb. 12 (UP)—Premier Achille Van Acker will ask for a vote of confidence from the Belgian Parliament on Wednesday, when he will submit the proposed policy of his newly named Cabinet, whose chief task will be providing coal and food for an already impatient population, it was reported today.

Foreign Minister Paul Henri Spaak is the only member of the fallen Pierlot government to be included in the new Cabinet, made up of six members of the Catholic party, five Socialists, four Liberals, two Communists and one nonparty member.

Van Acker himself will handle the coal situation while the responsibility for the country's food supplies has been given to M. Lalmand, editor of the Communist party newspaper Drapeau Rouge, which had been severely critical of the Pierlot regime.

AFL Housing Plan Sees 19,000,000 Jobs

MIAMI, Feb. 12 (ANS)—A ten-year housing program providing 19,000,000 jobs and 10,000,000 new homes has been outlined by the AFL and will be presented to Congress "immediately." President William Green announced after yesterday's session of the Federation's executive council.

The program can begin right after the cessation of hostilities without a time lag for reconversion, Green said, offering the plan as the "most effective means of preventing a post-war economic depression."

Steak and a Phone Call To Welcome Vets Home

CAMP SHANKS, N.Y.—A steak dinner and the opportunity to telephone their families hereafter will constitute the first phase of processing for wounded soldiers returned from overseas to the redistribution center here, it was announced today.

The announcement also said that passes for 12 or 24 hours would be given whenever possible.

Wounded veterans brought directly here from transports will remain approximately 72 hours before being sent to general hospitals located as near as possible to their homes.

Greeks May Vote on King

ATHENS, Feb. 12 (UP)—Agreement has been reached on all points discussed in the peace negotiations between the Greek government and EAM delegates, it was announced officially today.

Though the terms will not be made public until final documents have been drawn up, it was understood the government had promised to hold a plebiscite on the question of the monarchy and to hold a general election this year.

Under the agreement the EAM will not be represented in the government and its military formation, the ELAS, will be disarmed by March 15. A law providing for an amnesty for political offenses will be promulgated as soon as possible.

Vignette of War

Sufferin' Cats, Some Me(ow)nu!

PARIS, Feb. 12 (Reuter)—Paris police stations have become miniature "Scotland Yards" as the gendarmes try to keep tabby on the dwindling feline population of the capital, whose hungry inhabitants have accounted for an estimated 30,000 since the city was liberated, it was reported today.

30 SHILLINGS PER

Every day between 200 and 300 cats are reported missing to the police by their owners. With the animals bringing $5 each on the market —$2.50 for the meat and $2.50 for the fur—Paris is experiencing what amounts to a systematic cat-hunt. Some enterprising Parisians, otherwise unemployed, were said to be dangling baited fishlines from upper-story windows, getting a daily catch of two or three.

Russians Aim To Split Nazi Berlin Front

Marshal Koniev's Red Army troops, driving northward parallel to the Oder river in one of the greatest encircling movements of the war, last night were reported across the Bober River at two points in the Bunzlau area, about 75 miles northeast of Dresden and a little over 100 miles southeast of Berlin.

There was no official confirmation of reports that Koniev's forces had crossed the Bober, but Marshal Stalin announced that they had reached the river and captured Bunzlau.

Koniev's 1st Ukrainian Army, after breaking out of its bridgehead across the Oder at Steinau, apparently had two objectives.

The northern spearhead was pushing

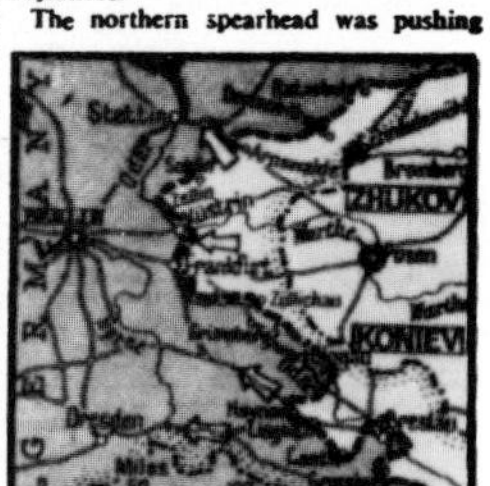

along the southern route to the German capital to cut behind the main Nazi defense line facing Marshal Zhukov's forces in front of Berlin.

The largest body of German troops defending Berlin is massed on the bank of the Oder east and southeast of the Reich capital and an encircling movement subjecting them to attacks from both sides could bring about a complete collapse on the Eastern Front.

This northern thrust, advancing at a rate of about 20 miles a day, was reported by German Radio to have penetrated "some 12 miles north of Sagan," considerably less than 100 miles from Berlin and about 30 miles from a junction with Zhukov's southern flank.

Koniev's left spearhead was driving west through Bunzlau toward Dresden and Leipzig and soon may engulf huge areas of southeastern and central Germany.

There was little doubt that Koniev's troops, after overrunning Silesia, had completely shattered German defense positions below Berlin exactly one month after breaking out of their Vistula bridge-

(Continued on back page)

USMR Casualties 6,017

WASHINGTON, Feb. 12 (AP)—U.S. Merchant Marine casualties from Sept. 27, 1941, to Jan. 31, 1945, numbered 6,017, the Navy announced tonight. The casualties included 755 dead, 4,683 missing and 579 prisoners of war. During January this year casualties totaled 64, resulting directly from enemy action.

THE STARS AND STRIPES
MEDITERRANEAN

Vol. 1, No. 187, Wednesday, February 14, 1945 · Printed in Italy · TWO LIRE

Budapest Captured; 6-Week Siege Ends With 110,000 Taken

Gen. Wildenbruck, Nazi Commander, Prisoner; Koniev Advances

MOSCOW, Feb. 13 — After more than six weeks of siege and bitter street fighting to parallel Stalingrad, the Hungarian capital of Budapest was cleared of all German officers and men, Marshal Stalin announced tonight in an Order of the Day.

Budapest, with a prewar population of almost 1,200,000, is the largest city the Red Army has captured. Warsaw had a larger prewar population, but it was a wrecked, decimated city when the Russians seized it.

To signalize the victory in Budapest, which was credited jointly to Marshal Rodion Malinovsky's 2nd Ukrainian Army Group and Marshal Feodor Tolbukhin's 3rd Ukrainian Army Group, Stalin ordered the firing of 24 salvos by 324 guns, a salute reserved for the biggest triumphs.

Stalin's announcement came a few hours after the German announcement that Budapest had been evacuated. But the Nazi report of evacuation had no facts to support it. Budapest was completely cut off 47 days ago, and the Red Army has been clearing the city street by street.

In the period of the siege, the Red Army has captured 110,000 officers and men, including Col. Gen. Peter Wildenbruck, commander of the garrison, and his staff.

Marshal Ivan Koniev's hard-driving 1st Ukrainian Army Group blasted the Germans' Bober River Line today and pressed on toward the province of Saxony, with Dresden less than 75 miles away. Ahead were objectives of tremendous importance—the north-south railroads and highways that have enabled the Nazis to keep their front from being splintered in two.

While Koniev's troops were push-

(Continued on page 8)

Conference News Delayed By Nazis

LONDON, Feb. 13—News of the decisions of the Big Three Crimea Conference was withheld from the German public by Nazi radios and newspapers until late this morning although batteries of American radio stations on the western front and BBC broadcast the communique in German throughout the night.

The Allied stations told the Germens all the details of the conference and repeated over and over again the warning that the cost of defeat would be only more heavy if the German people continued their hopeless resistance.

Once the German propagandists decided to tell their people of the conference, however, they pulled out all the stops.

The Nazi radio poured out a terrific tirade today against the Big Three agreement, terming it, according to the Associated Press, as "the hate program of Yalta" and "a crime on mankind and humanity," a "crime" which was blamed directly on "the Jew, the wandering Jew."

German newspaper readers, according to the United Press, had the conference analyzed for them under the headline: "Germany has to be exterminated."

The official DNB analysis which comes complete with headlines—and woe betide any editor who alters them — summarized the Crimea statement as "the Program of the Haters of Yalta," and then offered

(Continued on page 2)

Dakar Will Become French Naval Base

PARIS, Feb. 13 (AP) — The French Government announced today that it would build Dakar, West Africa, into a huge naval air base to protect the empire's lifelines and as a contribution to "collective security."

The Council of Ministers approved the plan at a session during which Gen. Charles de Gaulle said he was notified last night by the American, British and Russian Ambassadors of the decisions of the Crimea Conference.

The emphasis on collective security strengthened the belief that France plans to make Dakar an international base and place it eventually at the disposal of the United Nations Security Council.

Canadians In New Gains Beyond Cleve

SHAEF, Feb. 13 (AP)—The Canadian 1st Army threw more zip into its drive around the northern end of the Siegfried Line today and pressed eastward from captured Cleve.

One hundred miles to the south, Lt. Gen. George S. Patton's companion drive into Germany paused to mop up Prum and general quiet was reported along the Roer River flood front, held by the American 1st and 9th Armies.

The German army radio said today that Gen. Dwight D. Eisen-

hower was massing equipment for river-crossing along the western front in preparation for a drive to the Rhine.

"From hour to hour we expect a full-scale Allied offensive to roll into the Rhine plain," the broadcast said. "The stupendous forces massed west of Dueren and Junich are to carry our enemies to the Rhine.

Two cores of surprisingly strong

(Continued on page 8)

World Hails Decisions Announced By Big 3

The decisions taken at the Crimea Conference for speeding victory and securing a permanent peace were hailed throughout the world of the United Nations today as a charter of hope for the tortured earth. A dissenting opinion came from Berlin where the Big Three agreement was termed "a psalm of hate written by arrogant authors."

The most momentous document of our time, released to the world on Monday night at 9:30 PM (Rome time), constituted an all-embracing program for hastening military victory over Germany and for solving the political and economic ills that have plagued a sickened Europe for generations.

In their eight days of consultation in the former Czar Nicholas' palace in balmy Yalta, President Roosevelt, Prime Minister Churchill and Marshal Stalin dealt with all the hard problems and found precise solutions. Their declaration, the world agreed, was not couched in the generalizations of conventional diplomacy but in terms as exact as the calibration of a fine weapon.

The military plans, which the world—and the enemy—will discover in good season, look to coordinated blows by all the Allies "from east, west, north and south," until unconditional surrender is achieved. The general staffs of the Big Three met continuously throughout the conference and arrived at the closest coordination of the war. While nothing was said officially about the war in the Pacific, it was believed that Russia's future role against Japan was discussed.

To prevent another European war, the Big Three laid down a detailed program for the dismemberment of Germany's war potential, its general staff, the Nazi party and every vestige of the Nazi idea. Full agreement was reached on plans for the occupation of defeated Germany, with a role in this task reserved for France. The question of reparations was also examined, and agreement reached.

To secure the peace, the conferees decided to follow through with the foundation laid at Dumbarton Oaks. To this end a United Nations meeting was called for April 25, 1945. The thorny problem of voting procedures was solved. The Foreign Ministers agreed to meet in the major capitals for periodic consultations.

The breadth and vision of the Crimea decisions made almost certain that few stumbling blocks to victory and peace remained on the political level, it was agreed. The unanimity with which the members of the United States Senate greeted the announcement was assurance that this time America would give its full support and cooperation to a new and better world order.

Moscow

MOSCOW, Feb. 13 (AP)—Pravda set the keynote of Soviet reaction to the Crimea Conference today with a bold editorial declaration that "the Crimean Conference has proved that the alliance of the three big powers possesses not only an historical yesterday and a victorious today, but also a great tomorrow."

Pravda ordinarily does not publish on Tuesday, but came out today in honor of the conference.

"The conference will go down in history as an example of real democratic cooperation," it said.

The editorial assured the Russians that the conference not only decided Hitler's defeat but "elaborated the conditions which will make it impossible for a repetition of German military aggression."

Pravda points out that Marshal Stalin, President Roosevelt and Prime Minister Churchill have not planned the extermination of the German people, but have seen to it that Nazism and Fascism will die and not reappear.

Izvestia called the conference "a unanimous solution" of many questions.

"Hitlerite Germany is doomed."

(Continued on page 2)

London

LONDON, Feb. 13—The British press this morning hailed the Crimea agreement as a straight-from-the-shoulder declaration that goes further then mere words and binds the United States with Great Britain and Russia in solving post-war Europe's political problems, the Associated Press reports.

The London Times declared that the "sacred obligations" of unity which the three powers impose upon themselves in the Crimea communique was the most important feature of this "great and heartening document."

"The world will seize at once upon the hope," the Times continued, "which the conference offers that the greatest of all stumbling blocks to inter-Allied understanding is rolled away by the unanimity reached between the three great powers on Poland. The date of the meeting and its relation to the march of military events invest the proceedings with immediate authority over the whole future of Europe which has not been equalled on any previous occasion."

The Manchester Guardian said the results of the Yalta meeting "justify nearly all our hopes Certainly on the immediate political questions of the war, Russia has shown herself willing to move a long way toward meeting the western Allies' point of view."

The London Daily Telegraph said, "Nothing has been shirked. No difficulties have been ignored. In the long communique there are no loose ends."

The Yorkshire Post described the statement as "the most hopeful document that has been produced in the present century. We can breathe more freely."

The eight days of the conference will "remold the European world," the Daily Mail said, and the Daily

(Continued on page 2)

Washington

WASHINGTON, Feb. 13—Optimism for the future was reflected throughout the United States today as Americans devoted their thoughts and conversations to the plans and policies drafted by President Roosevelt, Prime Minister Churchill and Marshal Stalin at their eight-day Crimea conference.

Senators and Congressmen of both parties expressed jubilation at the terms outlined in the Big Three communique and unqualified praise came from the great newspapers of the country.

Sen. Tom Connally (D., Texas), chairman of the Foreign Relations Committee which will be responsible for the peace treaty, said that the agreement would advise the people of the world "that both in war and peace, the Allies are working in a spirit of harmony and unity to accomplish the high objectives of the war and the peace machinery to follow."

Sen. Alben Barkley (D., Ky.), Democratic floor leader, called the agreement a "source of great gratification to me and, I am sure, to all peace-loving peoples of the world."

Sen. Wallace H. White Jr., (R., Me.), minority leader, lauded the "forthright terms" of the pact and declared, "I feel that great work has been done."

Chairman Andrew J. May (D., Ky.), of the House Military Affairs Committee said that the proposed destruction of German militarism is "the only thing that will meet the demands of people throughout the world. Nobody will be satisfied with anything else."

Chairman Sol Bloom (D., N. Y.), of the House Foreign Affairs Committee said that if the Allies were falling back on the Atlantic Charter "they have a pretty good basis to work from."

From the New York Herald Tribune came the comment that "those all over the world who have been looking to the conference for mutual understanding, for clarity of purpose and for concrete decision amid the tempestuous issues of the war's great climax have not been disappointed.

"Every line of the remarkable document is indistinct with the knowledge that in this moment unity is more important than argument, and that to set a firm course in some positive direction is infinitely better than any amount of fine-spun debate over what the course should be."

The New York Times declared: "Even a first glance gives assurance that, though they may disappoint

(Continued on page 2)

Meeting Bolsters Belief Russia Will Fight Japan

WASHINGTON, Feb. 13 — The belief that President Roosevelt and Prime Minister Churchill had reached an agreement with Marshal Stalin for eventual Russian participation in the war with Japan gained headway in Congress today, according to the Associated Press.

The belief, was predicted on three results of the Crimea Conference. One was the announcement that a "very close partnership had been established between the three general staffs."

The second was that April 25, the date selected for the meeting of United Nations diplomats in San Francisco to begin the formation of a world security organization, is the date when Russia must announce her intentions concerning an extension of the non-aggression pact with Japan. April 25 is the fourth anniversary of the effective date of the five-year treaty and by that date the Soviets must either denounce the treaty or allow it to become effective automatically for another five years, the AP said.

The third straw in the wind, according to the United Press, is that Marshal Stalin had agreed to include China as one of the sponsors of the San Francisco conference.

Sen. Tom Connally (D., Tex.), chairman of the Senate Foreign Relations Committee, said he held a strong belief that Marshal Stalin may have told Mr. Roosevelt and Mr. Churchill that Russia will join in the fight against Japan.

MALTA, Feb. 13 (AP) — Plans for stepping up the war against Japan, as well as finishing off the conflict in Europe, were discussed on this war-torn Mediterranean Island by President Roosevelt, Prime Minister Churchill and members of their staffs before they flew off to their Crimea meeting with Marshal Stalin.

This information came from a high ranking American officer and constituted the only mention of Japan in connection with the Big Three meeting.

Chinese Circles Welcome Big Three Pronouncement

CHUNGKING, Feb. 13 (AP)—Chinese circles today welcomed the Big Three pronouncement as indication of a future accord on Far Eastern questions and the eventual entry of Russia in the war against Japan.

It was generally believed here that in essentials the plan for destruction of German militarism would serve as a basis for a similar accord for extirpation of Japanese militarism.

THE STARS AND STRIPES
MEDITERRANEAN

Vol. 2, No. 63, Saturday, February 17, 1945 Printed in Italy TWO LIRE

Giant Task Force Rocks Tokyo

HELLCATS OFF TO CRACK AT JAPS

Navy Hellcats, buzzing bearers of death and destruction for the Japanese, are shown here springing from a task force carrier in the Pacific. With their companion Helldivers and torpedo Avengers, the Hellcats of Vice Admiral Marc A. Mitscher's Task Force 58 carried out the first seaborne assault upon Tokyo and vicinity. (U. S. Navy Photo)

1,500 Planes Lash Capital Nine Hours

PACIFIC FLEET HEADQUARTERS, Guam, Feb. 16—An American naval task force, the mightiest armada of battleships and carriers ever assembled, stood offshore at Tokyo today, deep in Japan's home waters, and sent 1,500 Hellcats, Helldivers and Avengers in wave after wave over the heart of the Japanese nation.

For nine hours, from dawn to early afternoon, the carrier planes of Task Force 58, commanded by Vice Admiral Marc A. Mitscher, ranged over Tokyo and vicinity, dealing death and destruction, hitting Japan's most vital targets and terrorizing its people.

At last reports the Tokyo radio, which was screaming forth all day about the raids, said that the American fleet was still operating in Tokyo waters. The Japanese looked for another attack tomorrow.

A B-29 reconnaissance pilot, Lt. David McMillan of San Francisco, who circled over the panic-stricken city while the raids were under way, brought back the report that smoke was rising 7,000 feet and spreading from Tokyo to Yokohama.

The first announcement of the historic assault came in a communique from Admiral Chester W. Nimitz, tersely reporting that a powerful task force of the Pacific Fleet was attacking military targets, air bases and aircraft in and around Tokyo in a long-planned seaborne offensive against "the heart of the enemy's homeland."

Coordinated with it was an assault by surface units and island-based aircraft upon Iwo Jima in the Volcano group, 700 miles south of Japan. This task force was reported to have about 30 warships and carriers. The Japanese said the Americans were laying down a naval barrage upon strategic little Iwo Jima and also blasting the adjoining Bonin islands.

Pacific Fleet Headquarters did not give any indication of the purpose of the great naval assaults. The Associated Press commented that they could easily be intended to cover new amphibious landing operations within the inner defense ring of Japan's island guards.

A Tokyo radio commentator speculated that the barrage upon Iwo Jima may mean an imminent American landing there.

The approach of the fleet so near

(Continued on page 2)

SEADOG

MARC A. MITSCHER
. . . commands task force . . .

Mitscher Warships Mightiest Yet Afloat

PACIFIC FLEET HQ., Guam, Feb. 16—When Task Force 58, largest war fleet in history, rode restlessly at anchor in an American naval base a few days ago, and its grim, grizzled admiral awaited anxiously the word to put to sea for the first seaborne strike at Tokyo, an Associated Press correspondent looked out upon the great array of naval might and wrote this:

"The task force is so large that it is difficult for the mind to grasp this fantastic mixture of large and small fighting ships and all the auxiliary vessels needed to keep them armed, fueled and supplied.

"The fleet that will soon steam toward Tokyo in quest of a fight will be the greatest ever known to man. It will include the largest and newest American carriers, battleships, light carriers, jeep carriers, cruisers and destroyers."

That fleet, when it finally steamed out of the harbor Tokyo-bound, took hours assembling and made a great column in the Pacific 200 miles long.

The admiral was out on the deck of his flagship. He was the veteran Vice Admiral Marc A. Mitscher, about to add new laurels to his legendary career in the Pacific.

The armada was bound upon the greatest adventures of all for the Pacific Fleet. Admiral Chester W. Nimitz, the fleet's commander, could announce today: "This operation has long been planned and the opportunity to accomplish it fulfills a deeply cherished desire of every officer and man of the Pacific Fleet."

When the Hellcats, Avengers and Helldivers of Task Force 58 struck targets in the vital heart of Japan, many of their pilots, like their admiral commander, were fortified by

(Continued on page 2)

Koniev Throws Armor Toward Reich Capital

By The Associated Press

MOSCOW, Feb. 16—Marshal Ivan Koniev hurled the main weight of his 1st Ukrainian Army in "the direction of Berlin" today in a raging battle near the east bank of the Spree, last important river guarding the southeastern gateways to the capital.

He permitted Red Army correspondents to hint that the Neisse River line was shattered by the armored columns bearing down upon the stretch of the Spree at Cottbus, 60 miles southeast of Berlin.

This communication center controls the Berlin route from the south side of the lake country extending to the suburbs of the capital.

The Russian communique announced that Koniev had reached the Bober River at a new point west of Grunberg and captured an additional 50 communities, including the important junction town of Rothenberg, a few miles south of the Oder.

Fierce actions also were being fought by Koniev's armor in the vicinity of Forst and Guben, on the Neisse south of its confluence with the Oder near Furstenberg.

If the Soviet press hints are borne out, however, this pair of strongholds may be already bypassed and outflanked, following yesterday's capture of Sommerfeld, Sorau and Grunberg, southeast of Berlin.

Koniev seemed to hold Berlin's destiny in his hands, at least for the moment, as his columns fanned out over rain-soaked southeastern Brandenburg and overran makeshift enemy defense zones.

His flank now solidly linked with Koniev's, Marshal George Zhukov was reported to have increased the attacks on Furstenberg as a preliminary in an attempt to break past

(Continued on page 8)

Press Meet Abroad Scheduled By FDR

WASHINGTON, Feb. 16—A group of White House correspondents have left here by plane to cover a press conference "somewhere overseas" with President Roosevelt on the Big Three meeting, Reuter's reported.

A news dispatch from Paris said that Mr. Roosevelt is preparing to receive the White House newsmen before his return to America.

Reuter's said that the President will limit his interview to American correspondents, and that the White House policy was believed to have been influenced by widespread press criticism in the United States that Prime Minister Churchill has "scooped" the American press repeatedly on reports of these conferences and other major war developments in his addresses in the House of Commons.

Canadian 1st Army Seizes Huisberden

SHAEF, Feb. 16—Canadian and Scottish troops of the Canadian 1st Army strengthened their hold along the west bank of the Rhine at the ferry crossing to Emmerich today and moved along the Kalfach River three miles to the south to take the village of Huisberden.

Meanwhile, other elements of Lt. Gen. H. D. G. Crerar's forces, encountering heavy artillery and mortar fire advanced south from Cleve along three highways leading to Calcar, Goch and Udem. Allied troops were last reported two and one-half miles from Calcar, three miles from Goch and five miles from Udem.

Nearer the Maas, to the west, strong forces of the Canadian 1st extended their bridgehead across the Niers River along a five-mile front, extending all the way up to Kessel, four miles northwest of Goch.

Kessel was taken yesterday by Scottish troops who built a bridge over the Niers to replace the one destroyed by the Germans, and threatened to outflank Goch from the west if British troops north of that highway center were held up by stubborn resistance.

A thick mist hung over the battlefield and restricted the tactical air support which has been blast-

(Continued on page 8)

Adolf Orders More Death Decrees For Non-Fanatics

LONDON Feb. 16 (UP)—A German news agency dispatch broadcast by Radio Berlin revealed today that Adolf Hitler has had to order special courts martial set up in Germany empowered to deal out death penalties against Germans who try "to shirk their duty."

The issuance of the decree by the Reich Ministry of Justice appeared to be an indirect admission that the Nazis are dealing with increasing attempts by their own people to quit resistance.

The publication of the decree was followed by a long broadcast from Berlin describing in detail the plans that have been made for the defense of Berlin—a job which has been turned over to Propaganda Minister Joseph Goebbels.

The plan anticipated among other things a breakdown in the normal administration services and said that when that happens, Berliners can "turn to the already established Nazi party offices."

Army rations would be the last ditch source of food, it was said.

BBC correspondent Paul Winterton, in a radio broadcast from Moscow, said the reports from Silesia told how Adolf Hitler had visited a border town a few days before it was overrun by the Russians and urged the Nazis to become guerrillas but that his plea had found negligible response.

Bill To Study Chaplin Deportation Introduced

WASHINGTON, Feb. 16 (AP) — Sen. William Langer (R., N. D.), introduced legislation yesterday directing the U. S. Attorney General to investigate Charles Chaplin to determine whether the British actor should be deported as an undesirable alien.

Langer contended that Chaplin should be deported on the basis of the actor's own evidence in the court action brought by Joan Berry, who charged that Chaplin is the father of her child. Chaplin was acquitted.

5th Yields Ground On Coastal Sector

ADVANCED ALLIED FORCE HEADQUARTERS, Feb. 16—Despite unusually light enemy artillery fire, German pressure along the 5th Army's coastal sector yesterday forced our troops to withdraw to the southern slopes of Mt. Canale, a 1,200-foot ridge bordering the narrow coastal plain about four miles from the sea.

This position, according to today's communique, was held prior to a recent attack by our forces, indicating the Krauts may have occupied ground in addition to regaining what they lost during the recent Allied attacks.

Little contact was reported elsewhere along the 5th Army line although several Kraut infiltration attempts were repulsed. German installations north of Bologna received a pounding from our aircraft and artillery.

The belief that the Krauts have been forced to economize on the use of shells was advanced by some officer observers, a Stars and Stripes correspondent with the 5th Army wrote. Loss of German coal resources in upper Silesia, vital to the manufacture of synthetic oil, may be curtailing the transportation of ammunition to the front lines, it was said.

THE STARS AND STRIPES

MEDITERRANEAN

Vol. 2, No. 87, Monday, February 19, 1945 — ITALY EDITION * * TWO LIRE

Yanks Land On Corregidor; Iwo Jima Attacks Continue

Soviets Aim At Berlin's South Flank

Nazis Rush Reserves To Spree Salient

MOSCOW, Feb. 18 (AP)—Marshal Ivan Koniev's Army, which has broken more enemy river lines than any other in the Red Army, were fighting today to hold and expand their marshy foothold in southeast Brandenburg, preparatory to a new thrust soon against Berlin's south flank, Associated Press reports.

More German reserves moved into the crucial salient east of the Spree Lakes and south of the Od r bend, where Koniev's armored vanguards have temporarily dug in.

Fickle weather, which turned the German countryside into a sea of mud the middle of last week, might again produce a hard frost, but for the moment the Russian transport columns, shifting their supply bases 50 to 80 miles forward, are seriously hampered.

Into the bulge driven into Brandenburg by Koniev's tank-led flying columns after the Oder breakthrough, rifle divisions poured steadily and mopped up a number of bypassed German garrisons.

Stiff fighting was going on along much of the 70 miles of the winding Neisse River from where it falls into the Oder near Wellmitz to the uplands of Saxony, but scant information reached Moscow of the latest developments.

More than 85 miles from the nearest point of this "Berlin direction" front, Koniev's siege of Breslau methodically continued and southward, another 23 miles one of his task forces attacked the outskirts of Strehlen on the major Silesia-Moravia railway.

Breslau, with most of its civilian population reported evacuated before Koniev closed in, has been strongly manned by the Wehrmacht and its fortifications have been strengthened for a long siege.

Breslau is the Nazis' largest "kessel" (cauldron) left in Silesia. With Koniev's attention centered on reaching the heart of the Reich, it might take as long to reduce Breslau as Marshals Rodion Malinovsky and Feodor Tolbukhin required for winning the six and one-half weeks battle for Budapest.

In the north the Red Armies scored big gains over the week-end. Driving to split the shrinking East

(Continued on Page 8)

Ickes Asks To Develop Postwar Power Projects

WASHINGTON, Feb. 18 (ANS)—Secretary of Interior Harold L. Ickes asked Saturday for the postwar job of developing giant water and power projects for the nation, Associated Press reported. Ickes wrote President Roosevelt that he has the organization for the job in the Interior Department. The program would employ at least 125.000.000 men annually. Ickes said. A bill incorporating the plan has been presented to a group of western senators.

Advocates of postwar power development by the Interior Department are opposed by a group favoring new units along the line of the autonomous Tennessee Valley Authority headed by D. E. Lilienthal. AP

Silence Veils Task Force

GUAM, Feb. 18—Battleships and cruisers of the 5th Fleet are continuing the bombardment of Iwo Jima, invasion-menaced island 750 miles south of Tokyo, Adm. Chester W. Nimitz announced today, Associated Press reported.

Task Force 58's actions offshore at Tokyo, however, were shrouded in radio silence, and apparently Vice Adm. Marc A. Mitscher's planes did not raid the Nippon capital today.

The communique made no mention of Japanese reports that Iwo Jima already had been invaded.

But Tokyo radio repeated its claim.

Admiral Nimitz made it clear that enemy resistance on Iwo Jima still is strong, despite the withering shelling and 71 days of previous air attacks.

The Japanese Radio, besides reporting landings, said that the bombarding fleet was supplemented by another huge fleet coming up from the rear, possibly an invasion armada.

Eloquent Jap claims that heavy losses were inflicted on the attacking fleet were denied in the Admiral's disclosure that just one of the bombarding warships was damaged by "shore gunfire." He did not give the ship's category.

Any landings on Iwo Jima would put the Americans for the first time on Japanese soil administered as part of the Tokyo prefecture, Associated Press pointed out.

Operations of the Mitscher task force were secret today. Admiral Nimitz's communique said no details were available on the results of the Friday and Saturday carrier raids on the Tokyo area. No men-

(Continued on Page 8)

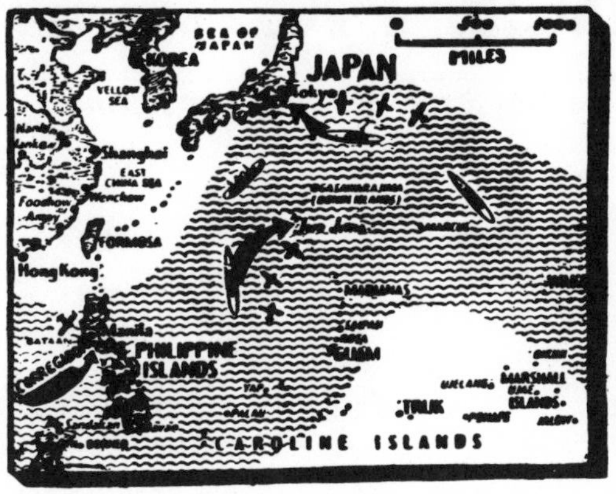

Goch, German Road Fort, Under Siege From 3 Sides

PARIS, Feb. 18 (AP)—British troops camped firmly today on the escarpments of the Siegfried Line's pivotal road bastion of Goch as Allied troops were converging in a semi-circle around the enemy city.

Scottish troops broke through for a 1,500-yard advance on the Allied right flank, enveloping the town of Afferden as artillery explosions screened the 17-mile front between the Maas and the Rhine.

The Allied thrusts on Goch grew in intensity under the fire of Field Marshal Sir Bernard L. Montgomery's array of guns and the enemy has had no time to coordinate any plan of counterattack to halt them.

He continued to counterattack savagely in any sector where it appeared an Allied breakthrough was imminent. By this method, the Germans regained no ground, but suffered heavy casualties.

The Canadians looked down today upon the dust that remains of Goch, the enemy's Siegfried Line defense hub, from firmly-held heights.

Welsh troops broke up repeated enemy kickbacks pushed down the Cleve-Goch road, but north and south of Calcar extremely bitter fighting was in progress.

The enemy counterattacked heavily in the Moyland sector, just north of Calcar on the main artery to Cleve, and furious fighting is now raging. The troops have almost cleaned out Moyland woods to the south and control heights which overlook the roads into Calcar.

Except for the Goch-Geldern

(Continued on Page 8)

Section Of Cassino To Stay As Shrine

AFHQ. MEDITERRANEAN, Feb. 18 — Two-thirds of Cassino, Italy's most bombed and shell-shattered town, will be left in ruins as a shrine of World War II. Colonel Jenny, peacetime New York consulting engineer, now Director of the Allied Commission for Public Works, announced today.

Trapped Japs Told To Quit

MANILA, Feb. 18—American troops have landed on Corregidor, "The Rock" fortress in the mouth of Manila Bay, have seized its decisive points, and its complete capture is assured, Gen. Douglas MacArthur announced today.

Paratroopers and doughboys made the landings with "light casualties" following a coordinated bombardment by warships of the U. S. 7th Fleet and planes of the Far Eastern Air Force.

The Corregidor assault was followed by an ultimatum delivered by Maj. Gen. Oscar Griswold, 14th Corps commander, demanding the immediate surrender of the trapped Japanese garrison. General Griswold's ultimatum said:

"Your situation is hopeless and your defeat inevitable. We offer you an honorable surrender. If you decide to accept, raise a large Filipino flag over the flag you are now flying and send an unarmed emissary with a white flag to our lines. This to be done within four hours or I am coming in.

"In the event that you do not accept my offer, we expect that in conformity with the true spirit of the Bushido and Samurai code you will permit all civilians .. be evacuated without delay in order to prevent innocent blood being shed."

The Japanese radio sent out a reply, United Press reported, but it was unintelligible, while this morning the Japs hoisted a Red Cross flag, but it was uncertain what this meant.

When no definite answer was received after the four-hour expiration, American tanks and guns renewed the assault upon the old walled city in South Manila.

The Corregidor landings came after Rear Admiral Arthur Struble's 7th Fleet units steamed from Olongapo Naval Base in Subic Bay north of Bataan and stood four

(Continued on Page 8)

Fifth Army Patrols Prowl Mine-Filled No Man's Land

By Sgt. JACK FOISIE
(Stars and Stripes Staff Writer)

WITH THE 5TH ARMY, Feb. 18—Almost five months of stalemated war have caused the Apennine No Man's land to become probably the most treacherous front of any in the world.

Time is what the Germans needed to lay an elaborate system of mines and booby traps tied in to their interlocking machinegun positions and other strongpoints—and the winter lull has given them that time.

Mines are the question mark facing every patrol that heads out into the gap between friend and foe. Combat patrols may have the exact information of their objective—how many enemy hold it, with how many guns and how much supporting fire — but if whether the approaches to the objective are mined, that is not often known. Most of the time it is unknown.

With more than five year of experience behind them, the Wehrmacht has developed new twists in mine warfare, so devilish that observers are beginning to compare its ruthlessness with that of gas in the last war. For instance, one recent patrol touched off some Schu mines. Schu is the name of the inventor. The mines in turn set off flares, exposing the party in the midst of the mine field to the fire of the alerted machineguns.

Today's on record background tells of another instance where a lonely Italian mountain hut near Abetaia, north of Pistoria, was found booby trapped. Such is Teutonic thoroughness!

Schu mines seem to have generally replaced the famed S mine, better known as Jumping Betsy, as an antipersonnel device, but frontliners warn that there are still plenty of Jumping Bets, only the Nazis have taken out the jump and they explode on contact.

All this is to set the stage for today's communique which announced without fanfare that "activity on the fronts of 5th and 8th Armies continues to be limited to patrolling."

15th AAF Bombs Austria For 6th Consecutive Day

MAAF HQ., Feb. 18 — Escorted Flying Forts of the 15th AAF today attacked communications targets at Linz, Austria, 95 miles west of Vienna. It was the second consecutive day of attacks on the Linz targets and the sixth consecutive day that the heavy bombers have penetrated Austria. Due to heavy clouds, the bombing was by instrument and no results were observed.

Mitchell medium bombers of MATAF today attacked two bridges on the Brenner Pass line, while fighter bombers carried out scattered attacks on rail lines throughout northern Italy.

Argentina Warns Nazis On Holding Repatriates

WASHINGTON, Feb. 18 — The Argentine Government last night warned Germany that if she insists on defying safe conduct to Argentine repatriates from Germany it will be considered as an a. of hostility.

Evening papers here consider it as a possible preliminary to a declaration of war, according to Reuter's. The warning was given in a note delivered today through the Swedish Legation.

The note is a reply to one from Germany which said that if Great Britain did not authorize the repatriation of members of the German exchange group, already evacuated from Argentina and now in Portugal, Germany would deny safe conduct to an equal number of Argentine repatriates now in Sweden.

Argentina declares that she will not consent to her repatriates being kept as hostages as a method of "extortion." Included in the group are seven Argentine diplomats.

Ici On Parle Français

Avez-vous autre chose?
Avay voo otre shows?
Have you anything else?

LIEGE EDITION

THE STARS AND STRIPES

Daily News paper of U.S. Armed Forces in the European Theater of Operations

Vol. I—No. 32 Tuesday, Feb. 20, 1945

Man Spricht Deutsch

Der Rueckzug ist abgeschnitten.
Dir Rewktzoog ist abgeschnitten.
The roads to the rear are cut.

Marines Fight On Iwo Jima

Yanks Duplicate This Scene 750 Miles From Japan

This Pacific landing scene was duplicated yesterday when Fourth and Fifth Marine Divs. invaded Iwo Jima, tiny island air base 750 miles south of Tokyo. The landing followed 72 days' air bombing and ten days' naval shelling. Initial opposition was strong.

Resistance Heavy As Veteran Units Drive on Airfield

U.S. PACIFIC FLEET HQ., Feb. 19 (ANS).—American Marines, fighting within 750 miles of Tokyo, stormed ashore on Iwo Jima today, quickly established a secure beachhead and drove to the edge of one of the tiny island's three important airfields, Adm. Chester W. Nimitz announced.

At first Japanese resistance was light, but counter-fire from enemy artillery and mortars steadily increased as the Marines went forward, smashing against Jap troops entrenched on ridges and scorching them out of pillboxes with flame-throwers.

The landing followed the most intensive softening up campaign in the Pacific war. The operation cut in half the distance separating American ground forces from the Japanese homeland. The closest previous approach to Japan was made by American forces which took the Marianas Islands, 1,500 miles south of Tokyo.

Men of the oldest U.S. ampibious unit—the veteran Marine Fifth Corps, including the Fourth and Fifth Divs.—swarmed ashore in hundreds of rocket-firing landing craft at 0900 hours, after Iwo had been bombarded for three days by American warships. Carrier and land-based bombers also hit the island, which had been subject to air attack for 72 consecutive days.

More than 800 U.S. vessels were involved in the operation. Fifth Fleet warships which poured devastating fire into the eight-square-mile island included new 45,000-ton battleships.

The Marines established a three-mile beachhead to an average depth of 500 yards. Then they drove inland to the southern end of Suribach airfield and penetrated defenses east of the field.

Vice Adm. Richmond K. Turner, directs

(Continued on Page 4)

Reds Reach Guben Area

Soviet assault columns from the south reached the area of Guben, important road junction 65 miles southeast of Berlin, the Germans reported last night, adding that the Nazi high command had launched an all-out hid to stop the Red Army winter offensive.

On the East Prussian battlefield, the late Gen. Ivan Cherniakovsky's army yesterday captured seven places south of Koenigsberg in a battle of annihilation against remnants of 20 German divisions cut off from land contact with the rest of the Reich.

The first indication that the Russians had driven far beyond their last known positions near Sommerfeld came from a Berlin military spokesman, who said the town of Guben had been recaptured by the Germans.

First Indication

Neither side had previously reported Soviet seizure of Guben, and this was the first statement that the Red Army had penetrated as far as the town.

A Reuter military analyst stated last night that "should Moscow confirm the fact that Koniev has reached Guben and the east bank of the Neisse, nearly 45 miles beyond the Oder, Guderian's Berlin defense armies massed before Zhukov's forces to the east will be faced with an imminent blow at their southern flank."

The German Overseas News Agency reported the Russians had established a bridgehead across the Oder south of Krossen, about 70 miles southeast of Berlin.

Vital Sector

Guben, apex of the defense triangle southeast of the Reich capital, lies in what now is the most vital sector of the Eastern Front to the Germans.

(Continued on Page 4)

Senator Urges Death For Hitler, Associates

WASHINGTON, Feb. 19 (ANS)—Execution of Adolf Hitler and "his immediate war criminals," after the European war ends and assignment of "several millions of Germans" to "rebuild the Europe they have destroyed," was advocated today by Sen. Joseph Ball, (R-Minn.)

"Germany must be looked upon as an aggressor and not a normal belligerent in the old sense of the word," he said on the University of Chicago Round Table broadcast.

Cherniakovsky, Russian General, Is Killed in Battle

Gen. Cherniakovsky

MOSCOW, Feb. 19 (AP)—The Soviet Union tonight mourned the death of Gen. Ivan Danilovitch Cherniakovsky, 37, former commander of the Third White Russian Army who died of a head wound while directing the current East Prussian drive toward the Baltic.

Cherniakovsky, youngest Russian Army group commander, was the liberator of Lithuania and his men were the first to enter Germany. His forces are now surrounding Koenigsberg, capital of East Prussia.

that a monument would be erected to

From Vilna, Lithuania, came word the handsome, broad-shouldered Jewish officer. A state funeral will be held at Vilna.

In Moscow, it was reported that Cherniakovsky had been slated for promotion to marshal.

Leaders of the Soviet government and the Communist party declared that Russia had lost "one of the best leaders of the Red Army."

The son of a railroad worker, Cherniakovsky was noted for his modesty. Most of his travelling at the front was done in an American jeep, and he often took the wheel himself if the driver had had a hard day.

1st Canadians Fight in Goch

Canadian First Army units were engaged in savage house-to-house fighting for Goch, Siegfried Line communications hub at the northern tip of the Western Front, yesterday as Third Army bit two chunks off the enemy's Our River salient between Prum and Echternach.

The Seventh Army was officially reported to be fighting on German soil for the first time since its withdrawal from the Reich early in January.

Scattered enemy artillery and mortar fire was reported in several sectors of the Ninth Army front, with the heaviest concentrations falling on the towns of Flossdorf, Linnich and Roerdorf, all on the bank of the Roer River.

The Roer itself was still four feet, five inches flooded. Its current still averaged six miles an hour, which was considered excessive.

There was relative quiet along the British Second and French First Army fronts.

Caen of the North

Scottish troops of the Canadian First met machine gun and mortar fire from the pillbox cellars of innocent-appearing dwellings in Goch as they fought their way from the northeast and northwest into the "Caen of the north," which had a pre-war population of about 14,000. Casulties on this front were reported to

(Continued on Page 4)

10,000 Germans Hold Out in Crete

ATHENS, Feb. 19 (AP)—Approximately 10,000 Germans are living on borrowed time in a concentration camp of their own devising along a sliver of Crete coast, and the Allied command is leaving them alone to let hunger decide when they will surrender.

A force of German troops, estimated at 10,000 and about 4,000 Italians, still hold a 35-mile stretch of coast in Canea Province, but they are almost as helpless as if they were in a prisoner camp. They are completely cut off and have no hope of replenishing their food supply, which will probably run out within two months.

To make sure none of the enemy escapes, tough Cretan Andartes sit quietly on the hills surrounding the German perimeter, raining bullets on all who try to make a break.

Fleet Attack Costs Japs 509 Planes

U.S. PACIFIC FLEET HQ., Guam, Feb. 19 (ANS)—Fleet Adm. Chester W. Nimitz, making his first report on results of the 1,500 carrier-plane attacks against Tokyo and Yokohama Friday and Saturday, disclosed today that at least 509 Japanese planes were destroyed, four warships and ten freighters sunk, and war plants and military installations severely damaged.

Forty-nine U.S. planes and 33 to 40 fliers were lost. None of the ships in the huge naval task force was damaged by enemy action.

(In Washington, the War Department announced that Marianas-based Superfortresses attacked industrial plants in the Tokyo area yesterday. India-based B-29s struck rail centers in Malaya.)

Nimitz said the carrier planes won a "decisive" victory in their two-day raid. They approached the enemy coast under cover of darkness and bad weather, which hampered Japanese air defenses. The attack caught the enemy by surprise, Nimitz claimed.

Other details disclosed by Nimitz were that a Jap escort carrier was set afire and went down near Yokohama, while an enemy destroyer and two escort destroyers were sunk. More than 20 other vessels were damaged.

U.S. airmen shot down 332 Jap planes and destroyed 177 on the ground the first day. Enemy air losses the second day were not disclosed, but they probably topped 150.

(Reuter reported that the attacks on aircraft plants included one against the Tama factory, about eight miles from the Imperial Palace grounds in Tokyo. Many airfields were hit.)

The Farmer's Daughter —Latest War Version

LONDON, Feb. 19 (Reuter)—Here's the latest version of the old one about the farmer's daughter.

Flying Officer J.P. Crisp, a RAF radio operator, bailed out of his night bomber and fell halfway through the roof of a Belgian farmhouse. He wiggled through the roof into the room below. In the room was the farmer's daughter and she hadn't been expecting callers. She screamed.

"Her two brothers ran into the room when she screamed," said Crisp, "and the family soon got the situation straight."

Churchill Is Home

LONDON, Feb. 19 (AP)—Prime Minister Churchill has returned safely to England from the Big Three conference at Yalta.

1,100 Forts, Libs Hit Western Reich

SHAEF, Feb. 19—Rail centers and industrial areas in western Germany were high priority targets for the Eighth AF yesterday as bombs from more than 1,100 Forts and Liberators hit marshalling yards and factories in Munster, Osnabruck, Rhiene and Siegen. Approximately 2,500 tons of bombs were dropped.

The 500 Mustangs and Thunderbolts, which flew escort, strafed German transport on the railway networks in the Ruhr, and an estimated 123 locomotives were destroyed or damaged by the fighters. Pilots reported the largest congestions of enemy trains were in the Hanover, Brunswick and Magdeburg areas.

One hundred thirty-one Ninth TAC Thunderbolts destroyed and damaged 217 railcars and locomotives, 20 motor transports and three bridges in the Cologne, Duren, Euskirchen and Grevenbroich areas.

Twenty-ninth TAC had six planes up. One of them was lost flying a weather mission over the Rhine.

Two Ninth TAC pilots, 1/Lt. Donald E. Miller, of Buffalo, and 2/Lt. Irwin Simpson, of Punxsutawney, Pa., scored hits on a highway overpass west of Cologne, crashing it in on a train. In the eastern outskirts of Euskirchen, a rail bridge, already bombed by B26s, was finished off by 1/Lt. John G. Dixon, of Athens, Pa.

1/Lt. Harold J. Buelow, of Dubuque, Iowa, dropped two rockets on what he thought was a concealed locomotive, and destroyed a steamshovel.

THE STARS AND STRIPES

MIDDLE EAST

VOL. III No. 8 | CAIRO | FOUR CENTS | FEBRUARY 23, 1945

Roosevelt Meets Churchill, Mid-East Sovereigns in Historic Egypt Talks

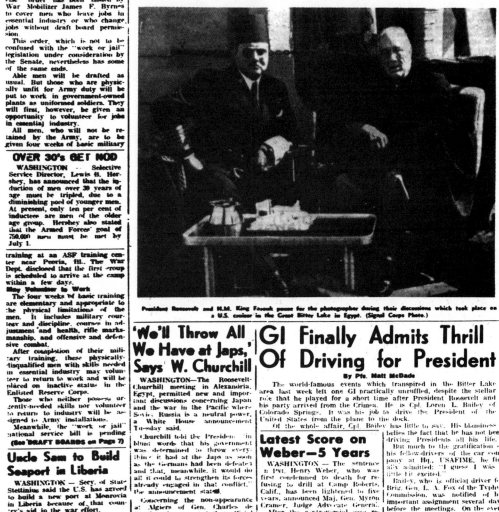

President Roosevelt and H.M. King Farouk pause for the photographer during their discussions which took place on a U.S. cruiser in the Great Bitter Lake in Egypt. (Signal Corps Photo.)

Sees King Farouk, Ibn Saud, Negus On Cruiser in Suez

President Roosevelt and Prime Minister Churchill flew to Egypt following the Crimea Conference, here met the leaders of four Middle Eastern countries in historic discussions concerning the relation of the U.S. and Britain with the Middle East and also conferred themselves again on the prosecution of the war against Japan, it was revealed Tuesday.

In a crowded week that saw the greatest assembly of world leaders in Egypt since the Cairo Conference in October of 1943—

1. President Roosevelt, on board a U.S. cruiser in the Great Bitter Lake, received H.M. King Farouk; Haile Selassie, Emperor of Ethiopia; and King Abdul Aziz Ibn Saud of Saudi Arabia in conferences that lasted two days.

2. The President's cruiser moved to Alexandria harbor where Prime Minister Churchill came aboard for meetings that had been arranged before they left Yalta to discuss the war in the Far East which could not be touched on at the Crimea Conference. Secy. of State Stettinius and Ambassador to London John G. Winant conferred with the President the same day, having flown from Moscow and London to meet him in Alexandria.

3. Prime Minister Churchill came to Cairo where he held talks with King Farouk and Chukri El Kuwatli Bey, president of Syria, then proceeding to Auberge du Lac, Fayoum, where he visited King Ibn Saud encamped there.

Details of what was discussed with the Middle Eastern leaders was not made known except in the case of Emperor Haile Selassie with whom the President is said to have stressed communications between the two countries, particularly by air.

The White House also announced that the discussions with King Farouk touched on export of long-staple Egyptian cotton and post-war tourist trade.

(See ROOSEVELT on Page 7)

Draft Boards Turn Guns on 'Job Hoppers'

WASHINGTON — A "work or else" order has been issued by War Mobilizer James F. Byrnes to cover men who leave jobs in essential industry or who change jobs without draft board permission.

This order, which is not to be confused with the "work or jail" legislation under consideration by the Senate, nevertheless has some of the same ends.

Able men will be drafted as usual. But those who are physically unfit for Army duty will be put to work in government-owned plants as uniformed soldiers. They will first, however, be given an opportunity to volunteer for jobs in essential industry.

All men, who will not be retained by the Army, are to be given four weeks of basic military training at an ASF training center near Peoria, Ill.. The War Dept. disclosed that the first group is scheduled to arrive at the camp within a few days.

May Volunteer to Work

The four weeks of basic training are elementary and appropriate to the physical limitations of the men. It includes military courtesy and discipline, courses in adjustment and health, rifle marksmanship, and offensive and defensive combat.

After completion of their military training, these physically-disqualified men with skills needed in essential industry may volunteer to return to work and will be placed on inactive status in the Enlisted Reserve Corps.

Those who neither possess urgently-needed skills nor volunteer to return to industry will be assigned to Army installations.

Meanwhile, the "work or jail" national service bill is pending

(See DRAFT BOARDS on Page 7)

OVER 30's GET NOD

WASHINGTON — Selective Service Director, Lewis B. Hershey, has announced that the induction of men over 30 years of age must be tripled, due to a diminishing pool of younger men. At present, only ten per cent of inductees are men of the older age group. Hershey also stated that the Armed Forces' goal of 750,000 men must be met by July 1.

Uncle Sam to Build Seaport in Liberia

WASHINGTON — Secy. of State Stettinius said the U.S. has agreed to build a new port at Monrovia in Liberia because of that country's aid in the war effort.

Stettinius visited Liberia last week on his way home from the Crimea Conference.

His statement, released by the State Dept., said Liberia had played "an honorable part in the war effort by creating air bases and increasing production."

In return, the U.S. has provided Lend-Lease and agreed to build a new port, it was added.

DSM FOR NEGRO GENERAL

WASHINGTON—Brig. Gen. Benjamin Davis has been awarded the Distinguished Service Medal for "wise advise and counsel ... on matters pertaining to Negro troops."

Gen. Davis, who is the first Negro to receive this award, worked his way up through the ranks during 46 years of Army service. He is currently serving in ETO

'We'll Throw All We Have at Japs,' Says W. Churchill

WASHINGTON—The Roosevelt-Churchill meeting in Alexandria, Egypt, permitted new and important discussions concerning Japan and the war in the Pacific where Soviet Russia is a neutral power, a White House announcement Tuesday said.

Churchill told the President "in blunt words that his government was determined to throw everything it had at the Japs as soon as the Germans had been defeated and that, meanwhile, it would do all it could to strengthen its forces already engaged in that conflict," the announcement stated.

Concerning the non-appearance at Algiers of Gen. Charles de Gaulle who reported that official business would not permit him to meet the President Roosevelt said:

"Questions of mutual interest and importance to France and the United States are pending. I wanted very much to see the General before leaving for home."

It was revealed that the President did stop in Algiers, however, conferring with Ambassadors Jefferson Caffery from Paris and Alexander Kirk from Rome.

Would Hike Overseas Pay

WASHINGTON — Representative Sparkman (Dem., Ala.) proposed that members of the armed forces be granted a five per cent increase in pay for each year after the first year of overseas service.

The increase would be in addition to the present increase for overseas duty.

GI Finally Admits Thrill Of Driving for President

By Pfc. Matt McDade

The world-famous events which transpired in the Bitter Lake area last week left one GI practically unruffled, despite the stellar role that he played for a short time after President Roosevelt and his party arrived from the Crimea. He is Cpl. Loren L. Bailey of Colorado Springs. It was his job to drive the President of the United States from the plane to the dock.

Of the whole affair, Cpl. Bailey has little to say. His blandness belies the fact that he has not been driving Presidents all his life.

But much to the gratification of his fellow-drivers of the car company at Hq., USAFIME, he finally admitted: "I guess I was a little bit excited."

Bailey, who is official driver for Brig. Gen. L. A. Fox of the Typhus Commission, was notified of his important assignment several days before the meetings. On the evening before the President's arrival, the GI drivers headed out for the Middle East airbase under cover-of-night secrecy. Bailey drove the sleek, black limosine — a Chrysler Crown Imperial 8 — to the destination.

Gets Briefed

Upon his arrival, he was thoroughly interrogated and briefed in his duties — coached in his behavior from the moment the President approached the car until he left it at the dock. And on the following day, there were two dry-runs. Cars were lined up on the field, planes were simulated by chalk marks and the fleet of cars swept to the quay, escorted by MP motorcycle patrols. Everything was carried out to the letter, without of course the stars of the show.

(See UP FRONT on Page 10)

Latest Score on Weber—5 Years

WASHINGTON — The sentence of Pvt. Henry Weber, who was first condemned to death for refusing to drill at Camp Roberts, Calif., has been lightened to five years, announced Maj. Gen. Myron Cramer, Judge Advocate General.

After the controversial case received nationwide publicity and protest, the court martial death sentence was reconsidered and reduced to life. Now, the Board of Review has reduced it further "in order to equalize the sentence in accordance with the WD policy.

M.E. as Crucible for U.S. Foreign Policy

WASHINGTON — Senator Burton (Rep., Ohio) suggested this week that North Africa and the Middle East be used as a "proving ground for a constructive and vigorous foreign policy in the interest of American agriculture, labor and industry."

He said experience gained there in coordination of civilian and military agencies and local governments is "of unique value."

782,180

WASHINGTON — The United States passed through its 1,168th day of war on Feb. 17, a period twice as long as America's participation in World War I. In similar comparison, U.S. battle casualties, which have now reached a total of 782,180, are more than double those suffered in the first world war.

The Army's over-all losses are 693,342, of which 394,487 were lost on the Western Front between D-Day and February 7. The Army's ground losses in January on this front were 8,868 killed, 41,325 wounded and 11,789 missing.

Total losses for the Navy are 88,838.

It was also revealed that the Army's strength reached 8,100,000 this month, as compared to nation's total armed strength in World War I, when only 4,355,000 men were in service.

NANCY EDITION
Volume 1, Number 38
Sunday, March 4, 1945

THE STARS AND STRIPES
Daily Newspaper of U. S. Armed Forces in the European Theater of Operations

Ici On Parle Francais
Cela coûte trois francs le mètre.
Sla koot trwa fron luh metr.
It costs three francs a meter.

9th Meets British; Ruhr Bombardment Starts

Fleeing Nazis Strafed Along Rhine by 9th AF

Germans Destroying Supplies, Fearing 1st-9th Trap

Planes of the 9th AF flew over 1,300 sorties yesterday to bomb and strafe German troops and supplies moving across the Rhine in anything that would float. Pilots reported numerous barges sunk and huge fires started among supply dumps.

Having blown numerous bridges to forestall Allied crossings, the Germans were evidently relying heavily on barges to supply and reinforce troops still holding on the west side of the Rhine.

The 29th TAC, flying with the 9th Army, sent 31 barges to the river bottom and damaged ten more. Docks at Wessel were also shattered by the 29th, whose planes ranged up and down both sides of the river to attack all forms of transport.

Similar reports of destruction came from the 2d TAC, which said that great fires were blazing last night on the western side of the Rhine as the Germans were setting undamaged supplies afire and falling back in the face of a possible 1st-9th Army trap.

Railroad Traffic Stopped

Second TAC pilots said that all German rail traffic west of the Rhine had ceased.

Planes of the 19th TAC, hampered by cloud and iceing conditions, compiled 529 sorties ahead of the 3d Army in the Bitburg and Trier areas.

Luftwaffe opposition was ineffective along the Rhine front.

The 8th AF yesterday sent more than 1,100 Forts and Liberators to bomb oil refineries and industrial plants in the Brunswick and Misburg areas, oil plants at Magdeburg and Ruhland, rail yards at Chemnitz and other targets.

On the 6th Army Group front, the 1st TAF reported a successful P-47 raid on three German trains in the Kaiserlautern - Mannheim area during a day in which approximately 600 sorties were flown.

'Don't Flee Homes,' Ike Tells Germans

Gen. Eisenhower yesterday told German civilians west of the Rhine to stay where they are, for every attempt at evacuation means immediate danger of death from Allied artillery and air bombardment. Instructions were broadcast over the Luxembourg Radio, Reuter reported.

Declaring that "There is no security east of the Rhine," Gen. Eisenhower told the Germans that henceforth all roads to the Rhine and its crossings will be overcrowded with fleeing Nazi troops and will be kept under artillery and air bombardment. He urged the civilians to avoid a "senseless bloodbath."

Berlin Reports Red Drive Within Sight of Baltic

Berlin radio reported yesterday that Soviet troops in eastern Pomerania were within sight of the Baltic after a drive which cut off large German forces in Danzig and the Polish Corridor from all land communications with Germany.

Marshal Stalin announced last night that Marshal Konstantin Rokossovsky's troops had captured the towns of Rummelsberg and Pollnow, important communications centers and German strongpoints in Pomerania.

Fall of the towns strengthened the base of Marshal Rokossovsky's drive toward the sea. Pollnow is 22 miles and Rummelsberg about 30 miles from the sea.

German reports said that Rokossovsky's advanced forces had cut across the Danzig-Stettin railroad and highway just east of Koeslin, with only four miles to go before reaching the Baltic.

Reich City That Once Fostered Goebbels Is Ghostly in Silence

By BUD HUTTON
Staff Correspondent

MUENCHEN-GLADBACH, March 3—In the streets where Joseph Paul Goebbels spent a loud-mouthed boyhood and grew up hating even the kids he went to school with, there isn't a sound.

In one of the biggest Nazi cities yet captured on the West Front the silence is worse than the noise the shells made yesterday. It's worse because there are people here, and one might expect the noises people make in living. This is the town in which Joseph Goebbels grew up. That in itself is enough to expect noise. But there isn't any.

The sound of the fighting is gone. The weary, muddy doughs of the 29th Inf. Div. have killed or captured the last German who would fight.

They swept past a big castle-like affair called Schloss-Rheydt, which was the castle the Nazis told the people to give Goebbels, their native son, "out of gratitude."

In the cellar of the police station, old Johann (he was afraid of using his last name—still afraid of the Gestapo) and his daughter Maria sat and talked about Joseph Goebbels.

Johann, 59, was born here, and he remembers the kid with the beady eyes and the big mouth. Johann grinned and made a motion with his hands to show Pvt. Walter Wolf of Garfield, N. J., who

(Continued on page 8)

The Squeeze on the Rhine

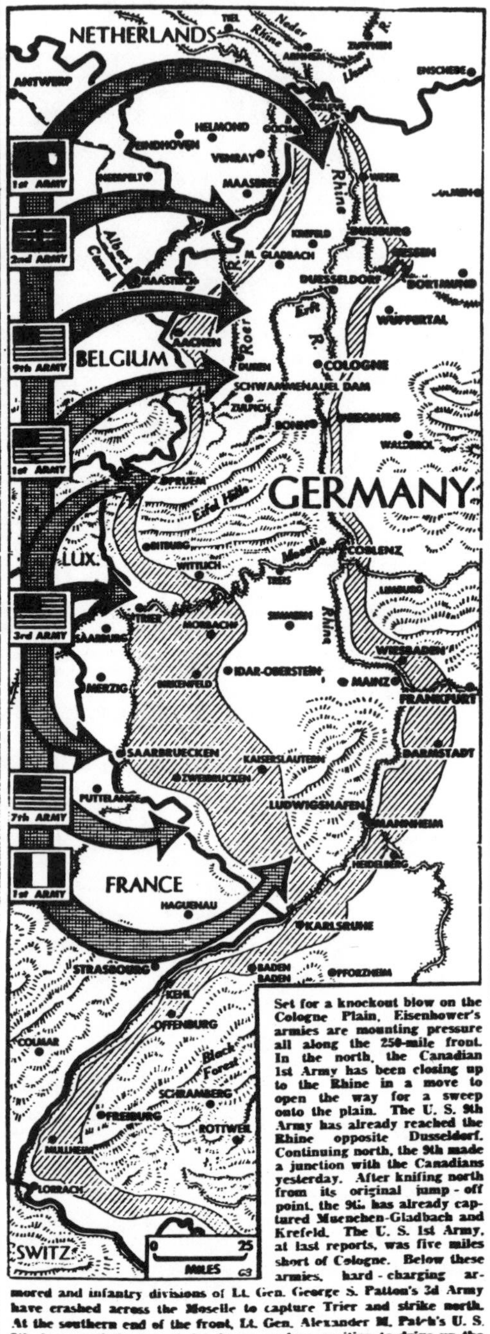

Set for a knockout blow on the Cologne Plain, Eisenhower's armies are mounting pressure all along the 250-mile front. In the north, the Canadian 1st Army has been closing up to the Rhine in a move to open the way for a sweep onto the plain. The U. S. 9th Army has already reached the Rhine opposite Dusseldorf. Continuing north, the 9th made a junction with the Canadians yesterday. After knifing north from its original jump-off point, the 9th has already captured Muenchen-Gladbach and Krefeld. The U. S. 1st Army, at last reports, was five miles short of Cologne. Below these armies, hard-charging armored and infantry divisions of Lt. Gen. George S. Patton's 3d Army have crashed across the Moselle to capture Trier and strike north. At the southern end of the front, Lt. Gen. Alexander M. Patch's U. S. 7th Army and the French 1st Army are in a position to drive up the Rhine Valley.

Germans Blow Up Rhine Spans as Two Armies Link

By ROBERT L. MOORA
Staff Correspondent

TWELFTH ARMY GROUP HQ., March 3—The American and British drive to the Rhine converged in the northern Cologne plain today as elements of the 17th Cav. Squadron of the 9th Army's 16th Corps made contact with British troops from the Canadian 1st Army high above Dusseldorf.

Meanwhile, the big guns of the 9th Army sounded the death knell of the German Ruhr industry with the opening barrage of artillery fire from captured positions on the west bank of the Rhine River.

BULLETIN

WITH THE U. S. 7TH ARMY, March 4 (Sunday) (Reuter)—The U. S. 7th Army today resumed the attack after a week's lull, taking high ground along the Saar southeast of Saarbrucken and clearing several more blocks in Forbach. There were no other details.

American forces were firmly established on the Rhine both north and south of Neuss, the Dusseldorf suburb on the west bank. The town of Neuss itself was almost cleared, according to reports tonight, by men of the 83d Inf. Div., who entered the town in the dark hours of yesterday morning.

Armor Rolls North

The 83d held positions south of Dusseldorf, while the 2d Armored Div., having reached the Rhine north of the big Ruhr city,

(Continued on page 8)

3d Army Mop-Up Nets 4,600 Nazis

By a Staff Correspondent

WITH THE 3D ARMY, March 3—Troops of the 3d Army yesterday captured an estimated 4,600 German soldiers in mop-up operations along a 45-mile front which netted the Patton men 13 towns captured in an advance better than three miles.

In the area northwest of Trier and north of the Moselle River, 2d Cav. and elements of the 76th Inf. Div. cleaned out German stragglers while other 76th Div. troops made contact with 10th Armored doughs in the vicinity of Trier.

The 80th Div. captured Hitenbach, seven miles northwest of Bitburg, after a short push while the 6th Cav. Group advanced one mile east to reach heights overlooking the Nims River, ten miles northwest of Bitburg.

The 6th Armored Div. gained a mile and a half eastward along a four-mile front, also reaching the Nims River's high west bank.

Farther north the 87th Div. drove a mile east and cleaned out 62 pillboxes. The 87th reached a point eight miles northeast of Prum.

Man Spricht Deutsch
Eroberer, nicht Unterdruecker.
Eroberer, nicht Oonterdreucher.
Conquerors, not oppressors.

PARIS EDITION
THE STARS AND STRIPES
Daily Newspaper of U.S. Armed Forces in the European Theater of Operations

Ici On Parle Français
J'ai fini.
Jay feenee.
I have finished.

Vol. 1—No. 223 · 1 Fr. · 1 Fr. · Wednesday, March 7, 1945

Cologne Falls

Red Army Plunges to OderMouth

The Stars and Stripes London Bureau

LONDON, March 6.—Marshal Gregory Zhukov's Red Army troops, exploiting their gains in northern Pomerania, yesterday reached the mouth of the Oder River.

Cammin, on the Oder, two miles from the Baltic and 40 miles from the German V-weapon experimental station at Peenemunde, was captured as Soviet long-range artillery began the first phase of the battle for the port of Stettin.

Graudenz Captured

Capture of Cammin was announced by Marshal Stalin, who reported also that Marshal Konstantin Rokossovsky's forces, after two weeks of hard fighting, had captured Graudenz, a powerful German strongpoint in Poland, 60 miles south of Danzig.

More than 5,000 prisoners, including the commander of the garrison, Maj. Gen. Fritsche, and his staff, were taken prisoner.

Stalin's announcement that Zhukov's forces had taken Cammin came shortly after German reports that Russian forces in 48 hours had seized a 75-mile stretch of the Baltic coast and cleared most of Pomerania between the Oder and the Danzig pocket.

The Soviet communique reported that Zhukov's forces had fought their way into more than 500 towns and villages, and that Rokossovsky's men had captured more than 70 places below Danzig.

Within Artillery Range

Below Stettin, the Germans reported, Zhukov's forces reached the Oder at several points and the city was said to be within easy range of heavy artillery both from the north and south.

Below his northern position, Zhukov was reported by the Germans to have massed seven armies—five infantry and two tank—for a frontal attack on Berlin. When Stettin has been taken, it is believed Zhukov will concentrate on Berlin and leave the mopping-up operations in the north to Rokossovsky's troops.

Moscow dispatches indicated that Marshal Zhukov's army would play one part in a giant pincer movement around Berlin, with Koniev's forces taking care of the southern half of the maneuver.

Overseas Airmail Cut—V-Mail Still Flown

WASHINGTON, March 6 (ANS).—Army Postal Service to-day said airmail service to troops overseas has been curtailed because of insufficient cargo space on aircraft.

Use of airmail stamps, therefore, does not guarantee that letters will go by air. Only V-mail is assured of air transportation.

Crowds Battle Police in Rome; Crisis Looms

ROME, March 6 (Reuter)—A political demonstration against the escape of Gen. Mario Roatta, accused Fascist, degenerated today into a violent battle with police. One woman was killed and several persons were wounded.

[The Associated Press reported a political crisis threatens the Bonomi government on the heels of the Roatta escape. The government, apparently trying to ease tension, announced dismissal of Taddo Orlando, Carabinieri chief and former army general on Roatta's staff.

[Roatta escaped from a hospital Sunday night. He was defendant in a trial accusing him of having committed various Fascist crimes. Jugoslavia, the AP said, also wants to try him as a war criminal.

[The Spanish Embassy denied a report Roatta had found refuge there.]

Sponsored by Unions

The demonstration, sponsored by trade unions and opposition political parties, formed at the Colosseum. After some speech-making, the crowd poured into the Piazza Quirinal outside the Royal Palace.

When mounted Carabinieri rode through the crowd, angry demonstrators struck at the horses. While the Carabinieri tried to clear the square, a grenade exploded opposite a police station. Police then fired 30 or 40 shots, felling at least three persons who were taken to hospitals.

[The AP said it was not clear whether the dead woman was killed by a shot or by the explosion.]

Cooking With Gas on Iwo

IWO JIMA, March 6 (ANS).—U.S. Marines were cooking with gas today, thanks to the cooperation of the Mt. Suribachi volcano, which bubbled into action and enabled the leathernecks to have hot rations for the first time in several days.

During the night the 560-foot cone began erupting hot sulphurous steam from hundreds of little fissures on the northern slope. No flame or lava flow was detected.

"It didn't take the boys long to get wise," said Capt. E. R. McCarthy, of Medford, Mass., commanding officer of a weapons company. "They began shoving cans of rations into the cracks and in 15 minutes took them out piping hot."

McCarthy said many Japs were

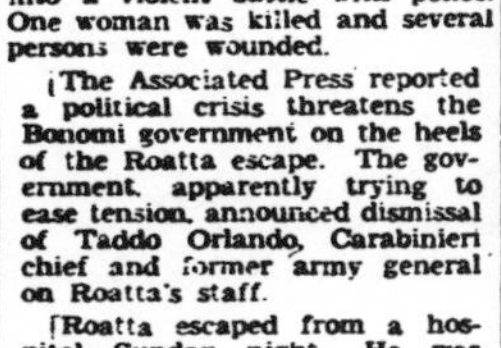

seen scuttling out of volcano caves and speculated the sulphur fumes might have driven them into the open.

First Army Takes City 24 Hours After Entry

By Dan Regan
Stars and Stripes Staff Writer

WITH THE FIRST ARMY, March 6.—Cologne has fallen to the American First Army, it was officially announced at Lt. Gen. Courtney S. Hodges' headquarters tonight.

Although there was still some sporadic firing from isolated enemy machine-gun nests, the bulk of the city's defenders were pulling out southwards toward Bonn on a highway along the river banks. There they faced the Ninth Inf. Div., last reported nearing Bonn.

Stars and Stripes Map by Baird

U.S. First Army's Third Armored, 104th and Eighth Inf. Divs. yesterday took Cologne, capital of the Rhine.

Cologne had a pre-war population of 768,426 inhabitants, ranking in size behind Berlin, Hamburg and Munich.

[Some frontline dispatches said that 150,000 inhabitants were found in the city.]

The Reich's fourth largest city fell to Yank doughboys a little more than 24 hours after the Third Armored Div. entered the Rhine capital from the northwest, to be joined by the 104th Inf. Div.

Elements of the divisions worked side by side within Cologne and by nightfall had pushed to the Rhine River.

The Eighth Inf. Div. broke into the city from the southwest.

Cathedral Still Stands

From within 50 yards of the cathedral, Cologne's most noted landmark, the structure appeared to be only slightly damaged, Andy Rooney, S and S correspondent, reported. Like St. Paul's in London, the surrounding buildings are in ruins. There have been hits on the north wing of the cathedral, one of the world's most famed, but the great spires are still intact. There is no glass in the windows.

Engineers flowed into Cologne as soon as the city's areas were cleared, said Rooney. Maj. Stewart R. Smith, of Springfield, Mass., assistant engineering officer for the Third Armored, said he was in town to get the water system running, "so the general and his boys can have a bath."

Cologne's electric power and water systems are in operation, but there is no public transit.

Most civilians in Cologne are either very old or very young, Rooney observed. A band of seven boys of 13 said they had lived in cellars because the Germans had ordered that they be evacuated, possibly for military service.

'Key' Houses for Defense

Instead of the strong house-to-house fighting which had been expected in Cologne, which has been compared physically to Stalingrad, the Germans were using a defense system of "key" houses. They held one house until flushed out, then withdrew to another a few blocks beyond and repeated the technique.

A huge pile of rubble was seen accumulated at the end of the Hohenzollern Bridge. Aerial photos

(Continued on Page 8)

Drama of Death and Victory In Shadow of the Cathedral

By Andy Rooney
Stars and Stripes Staff Writer

COLOGNE, March 6.—Three American soldiers, perhaps the last to give their lives in the battle for this huge Rhine city, died in a Sherman tank tonight at the northwest corner of the great Cologne cathedral.

Five tanks of a six-tank task force, ordered to advance through the murderous crossfire of Cologne's streets, pushed past the cathedral, past the smoking Sherman, past the three newly-dead Americans and to the Rhine river, 200 yards away.

The fight for Cologne was won.

The Third Armd. Div. tanks were commanded by Lt. Col. C. L. Miller. On board one M4 was 1 Lt. Ferdinand Ledoux.

At the corner of the cathedral, just short of the river, the lead tank stopped and Ledoux got out to direct the following tanks.

From beyond the far side of the cathedral, hidden behind brick rubble, the 88 of a German Mark IV opened up and bored a hole through the gun turret of the lead tank. The driver was killed instantly and two other men were trapped in the burning tank.

Miller and Ledoux ran back to the tank. With the assistant driver,

(Continued on Page 8)

3 COs Cleared In 716th Trials

Three company commanders of the 716th Railway Operating Battalion—Capts. Samuel S. Gillespie, Harold G. Gould and Meander E. Peterson—were acquitted yesterday by a Paris court martial of charges of neglect of duty in black-market offenses in their units. The prosecution contended that their failure to discover and prevent black-marketing in their outfits constituted neglect.

They were the last of eight officers of the battalion tried. Two others were acquitted previously, and three convicted and sentenced to prison terms. Sixty-two EMs still await trial.

Nazis Say Reds 10 Mi. Beyond Oder, 28 from Berlin

New York — London Edition — Paris
THE STARS AND STRIPES
Daily Newspaper of U.S. Armed Forces in the European Theater of Operations
Vol. 5 No. 108—1d. FRIDAY, MARCH 9, 1945

Daily French Lesson
Quelle heure est-il?
Kel ur ay-t eel?
What time is it?

1st Crosses Rhine

Report Big Battle Rages At Kustrin

A great Russian drive toward Berlin appeared to be in full swing last night as German commentators—in reports so far unconfirmed by Moscow—admitted that Marshal Zhukov's Red Army troops had sliced through Nazi defenses on the Berlin side of the Oder River to a depth of ten miles and reached the town of Seelow, only 28 miles due east of Hitler's capital.

This and other disclosures about activity on the Kustrin-Frankfurt front along the Oder indicated that the long-expected assault was well under way. These Nazi reports were not confirmed by the Soviets but it is usual practice for the Russians to keep silent in the early stages of any large-scale movement..

After early statements that fighting between Kustrin and Frankfurt had assumed proportions greater than of local importance, the Germans announced that Zhukov's forces had broken out of their Goeritz bridgehead six miles south of Kustrin and penetrated to Seelow, ten miles west of the Oder.

'Steadily Recapturing Ground'

"German troops are steadily recapturing the ground in counter-attacks," one German commentator stated. Another said Zhukov was pouring reinforcements into the battle.

German News Agency said terrific fighting was raging in Berlin's forefield and indicated the ferocity of the battle with the claim that some localities changed hands every hour.

The Russians also were reported to have captured Rathstock, west of the Oder on the Kustrin-Frankfurt road, as well as Klessin, in the Oder loop to the southeast. The Germans claimed to have re-entered Rathstock and said that in Klessin "the remnants of the Russian defenders were crushed."

Northwest of Kustrin, Zhukov was said to have intensified his attacks near Zehden and plunged forward to Niederwutzen, 31 miles northeast of Berlin.

Attacking Near Manschow

The Russians also were reported attacking near Manschow, five miles southwest of Kustrin; Lebus, five miles north of Frankfurt; and at Kietz, two miles southwest of Kustrin on the main Kustrin-Berlin highway which appeared to have been cut.

These reports did not make it clear whether all the places mentioned were in one large bridgehead or whether each represented a separate thrust across the Oder River.

Farther north along the Oder, Zhukov's right wing troops driving toward Stettin were reported to have reached Altdamm, a suburb only four miles from the city. Soviet forces were said to be closing in from the northeast, east and south and to hold nearly all the east bank of the mouth of the Oder.

The channel was under Zhukov's guns, and Stettin as an operational port has ceased to exist.

Shift in Fighting Appears

The heaviest fighting along the Baltic appeared to have shifted to Marshal Rokossovsky's front farther east where German forces trapped on the Pomeranian coast were counter-attacking strongly in an attempt to break out to the west.

On Rokossovsky's right flank, Soviet troops were reported within 13 miles of Danzig on the southwest and 21 miles on the southeast.

Both of these offensive wedges have reached the outer defenses of the port, the Germans acknowledged.

In the Polish Corridor, Marshal Stalin in an Order of the Day announced that Rokossovsky's forces had captured the railway towns of Buetow and Koscierzyna, 31 miles southwest of Danzig.

Other elements of Rokossovsky's army were reported by the Germans to be nearing Stolp, 40 miles east of the Koeslin area where his forces reached the Baltic.

The Tiger Has Teeth and He Bites

Keystone Photos

This is the type of armored opposition doughs have to slug it out with on the Western Front, one of the Nazi iron monsters that are causing so much bitter discussion in military circles, especially in foxhole forums. In the top photo the camera stares into the muzzle of a 15-inch howitzer mounted on a Tiger tank chassis, captured by the 9th Army. Below, a U.S. soldier checks up on specifications of the shell fired by this behemoth.

Build a Bridgehead South of Cologne; Opposition Is Slight

Lt. Gen. Courtney H. Hodges's 1st Army troops have crossed the Rhine, breaking the last great natural barrier on the Western Front in a drive apparently co-ordinated with the German-reported renewed Russian offensive toward Berlin.

Victors of Aachen and Cologne, the 1st Army sent a special task force across the Rhine at 4:30 PM Wednesday and established a solid bridgehead on the river's east bank opposite Remagen, 12 miles south of Bonn and 23 miles north of Coblenz, a Reuter dispatch said.

Although the Rhine at this point is almost a half-mile wide and the opposite shore rises to cliffs below the small town of Erpel, the Americans met but little opposition as the German defenses collapsed under the attack. Big enemy supply and munition dumps have already been captured.

With the initial bridgehead already firm, more troops were being rushed across the Rhine.

Moving at Lightning Speed

The war in the West was moving with lightning speed. The Rhine was crossed only 13 days after the opening of the drive to cross the Roer and two days after the fall of Cologne, Germany's fourth city.

Completely confused by the rapidity of the American thrusts, the Germans could muster only light artillery and mortar fire against the Rhine crossing site during the first 24 hours, dispatches said.

How the crossing was accomplished was not explained. A railway bridge crosses the Rhine to Erpel, but there was no report whether it was still standing.

While part of the 1st Army was already across the Rhine, other troops were slicing up the Germans still left on the west bank. Paris radio said Bonn had been captured, but latest official accounts said only half of the city had been cleared by doughboys of the 1st Division.

Battle for Bonn Harder

The battle for Bonn was harder than that for Cologne, dispatches said. The Germans rocketed the town, it was reported, and killed many civilians. The road northward from Bonn to Cologne has been cut.

A partial security blackout was still in effect on the 1st Army's front, and all units of the 9th Army, to the north, went on the secret list as they closed up to the Rhine, reports said. The only one mentioned in dispatches was the 35th Infantry Division, which was still engaged along with the Canadian 1st Army in battering down the Germans' Wesel bridgehead.

Artillery of the 4th Armored Division, which was disclosed early yesterday to have reached the Rhine northwest of Coblenz on Wednesday afternoon, was reported to be shelling Germans ferrying

(*Continued on back page*)

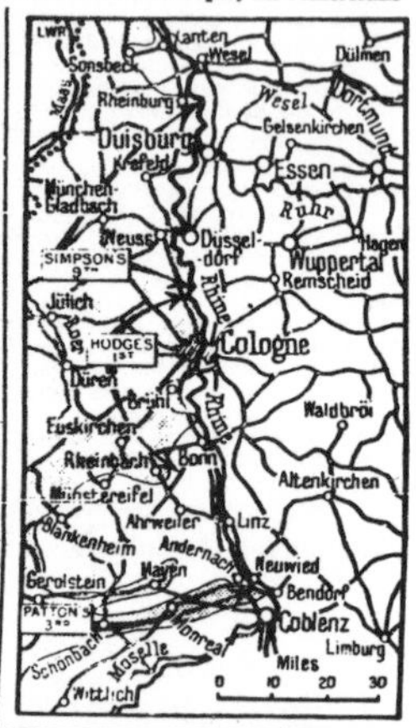

3,000 U.S., RAF Heavies Blast Nazis Near East, West Fronts

Allied bombers again centered on targets near both fronts in Germany yesterday when heavies of the 8th and 15th Air Forces and the RAF, some 3,000 in all, struck at Nazi communications and oil refineries close to the Rhine on the Western Front and near Berlin and Budapest on the Eastern Front.

The 8th, getting away a tremendous force of 1,350 Fortresses and Liberators, its biggest since the massive three-way, low-level assault on Feb. 22, hit oil plants and rails in a concentrated area of western Germany stretching from Essen, 15 miles east of Gen. Simpson's 9th Army, south to Giessen, 50 miles east of Coblenz.

15th Also Co-ordinates

The 15th, also dispatching a strong force of Forts and Libs, aimed its attack in direct co-ordination with the Red Army, striking at railways in Hegyeshalom, 70 miles from the Soviet lines in the Budapest area.

The day's offensive got its start with the all-night activities of the RAF, which let loose 1,250 planes to hit oil refineries at Hamburg and Heide, the rail and industrial town of Dessau, just south of Berlin, and Berlin itself, which took a pounding for the 16th night in a row.

Dessau, said to be an important supply center for the Russian front, was the chief target, and the RAF's heavies rained more than 500,000 incendiaries on the town, which houses several Junker aircraft factories. Thirty-eight RAF planes are missing from the operations.

Oil Targets for 8th

Oil targets for the 8th consisted of six benzol and synthetic oil plants in the Gelsenkirchen and Dortmund areas, just east of Essen. Rail yards were attacked at Essen; at Siegen, 40 miles east of Cologne; at Betzdorf and Dillenburg, in the Siegen sector; and at Giessen. One bomber failed to return from the raids.

Bombardiers had to use instruments because of the continuing heavy clouds, but there was no enemy air opposition and flak was extremely light, the weakest show by enemy gunners some crews had ever seen over the Ruhr.

Tito Heads New Jugoslav Government

A new Jugoslav government has been formed, with Marshal Tito as Premier and Minister of National Defense and Dr. Milan Subasitch as Foreign Minister, Moscow Radio announced yesterday.

The new regime is the result of the agreement reached recently at Moscow between Tito and Subasitch, former Prime Minister of the Royal Jugoslav government in exile in London.

The Marshal Studies a Map—Berlin?

Associated Press Photo

Marshal Zhukov, reported by the Germans to have opened the final drive on Berlin, lays his battle plans, poring over maps with two staff officers.

New American Tank Named 'Gen. Pershing'

WASHINGTON, Mar. 8 (ANS)—America's new battle tank with a 90mm. gun described by Under Secretary of War Robert Patterson as the answer to Germany's Tiger tank has been named the "General Pershing."

150,000 Lose Homes in Flood

PORTSMOUTH, O., Mar. 8 (AP)—The unrelenting struggle against the greatest flood to have struck the Ohio River valley since 1937 appeared today to have been won as the huge water crests headed downstream, but more than 150,000 persons were reported homeless and approximately ten killed by the raging waters.

This city continued today to be the scene of the stiffest fight against the rising waters. State guardsmen and civilian volunteers piled up thousands of sandbags on the floodwall in an effort to impede an overflow. The waters have already reached the level of the bags.

Louisville residents began a calm evacuation of the river areas as the river inched towards a 47-foot crest. In the Pittsburgh area, the Monongahela and Alleghany Rivers, swollen to a crest of 33 feet, dropped steadily today to 29 feet. Many of the area's factories, however, remained shut with more than 25,000 employes idle.

Drunk and Disorderly

Civilians Looted Cologne

By Hal Boyle
Associated Press Correspondent

COLOGNE, Mar. 8 (AP)—Civilians reacted to the capture of Cologne with an exuberance which in many instances bordered on the carnival spirit.

In the cobblestoned area along the Rhine drunken German men and women today staggered along the streets, waving wine bottles and offering drinks to American soldiers. The soldiers, who are prohibited from fraternizing with civilians, are usually greeted with chilly suspicion.

While some Germans walked toward the suburbs in orderly manner, pushing hand-carts containing piles of houshold belongings, others raided stores, carrying away boxes of cheese, cases of liquor and clothing.

"Warehouses here were well stored with food, good cheese and other things that the people have not had in any quantity, though they certainly don't seem underfed," an officer said. The inhabitants were indifferent to occasional Nazi shellfire across the Rhine, he said, but were afraid of the bombings.

Discussing civilian looting, he said: "We arrested all the policemen, and that's one of our troubles—their uniforms were only a shade different from the regular German Army uniforms and we were going too fast to stop to match the colors."

The Germans in Cologne were the "most obnoxious we have yet met in Germany," the officer said. "Some living in the better districts of Cologne don't seem to realize they have been conquered. The more you see these people the more you realize there's a good deal of resistance left in Germany."

THE STARS AND STRIPES

AFRICA-MIDDLE EAST

VOL. III No. 12 | CAIRO | FOUR CENTS | MARCH 23, 1945

Have You Mailed Your Contribution for the GI Memorial Home?

Our appeal for funds that will help to build a home for the widow and eight kiddies of Pfc. Privett, recently killed in France, has already been answered by a number of warm-hearted GIs and officers.

There hasn't been sufficient time yet to receive any mail response from the outlying sections of the command but we're hoping to give you a healthy financial report next week.

If you haven't sent in your donation yet, please do it now. Send it anyway you wish but we'd suggest a money-order (no matter how small), made payable to Mrs. Rachel Privett, Blytheville, Ark., in care of the Publications Officer, AMET.

New Draft Call For Older Men

WASHINGTON — The increased drafting of men of 30 and over from essential jobs was foreseen this week by Selective Service as it was forced to defer some 145,000 younger men in five vital war industries.

A critical manpower shortage in such essential war industries as steel, coal mining, transportation, copper, lead and zinc mining, and synthetic rubber prompted a complete reversal of Selective Service's earlier ruling that not more than 30 per cent of younger workers in the 18 to 29 age group could retain draft deferments because of essential jobs.

Local draft boards were ordered to use their own judgment in administering the new policy.

It is expected that the limit of deferments for men under 30 will go as high as 90 per cent for some operations, comparing with the present 30 per cent limit.

At the same time, a joint Army-Navy statement warned that all men in the 18 to 20 age group who are drafted during the next three months will be assigned to the Army as combat replacements with few exceptions.

Practically the only exceptions will be future radio technicians and air crew members.

The Navy's quota during this period will be filled from draftees 21 through 37, while any others remaining will go into the Army.

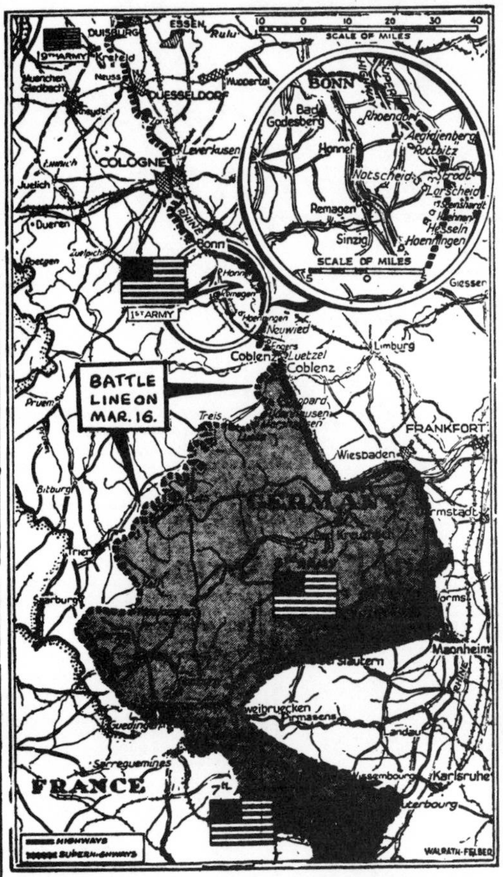

Gen. Patton's armored sweep south of the Moselle brought the Third Army to the west banks of the Rhine's elbow where Coblenz, Mainz, Worms, Ludwigshaven and Kaiserslautern are either taken or being entered. Gen. Patch's Seventh Army pierced the Siegfried defenss of the Saar, captured Saarbruecken, and swung northward to link up with the Third. The Patton-Patch vise is rapidly closing on thousands of Nazis trapped west of the Rhine. Meanwhile Gen. Hodges is pouring more guns and tanks into the bridgehead for a possible breakthrough to the Ruhr Plain. (New York Times Map.)

Patton, Patch Grind Nazis in Rhine Vise, Ludwigshaven Taken

Focus of western front action this week shifted from the U.S. First Army's growing bridgehead and swung southward to the swift-moving armored spearheads of Patton's Third and Patch's Seventh which swept through Siegfried fortifications and linked up in a pincer move toward the Rhine.

Patton's spectacular lunge to the Coblenz sector of the Rhine several weeks ago was equalled by his quick thrust from the southern bank of the Moselle River to the Rhine with six armored divisions providing the high-powered punch for his numerous infantry divisions.

The Third Army's tank-tipped spearheads fanned out from the Moselle, and from north to south each attacking force headed for a keystone of the river defense system. The northernmost unit captured Coblenz, a bit southward one division drove into Mainz, farther south the Fourth Armored Division advanced 13 miles in 12 hours to take the medieval city of Worms while the troops forming the bottom of Patton's salient stormed Kaiserslautern.

As the augmented forces of the U.S. Third swept to the elbow of the Rhine, Patch's Seventh Army troops burst into the Saar region and swung northernmost of American armies on the western front, entered Bitche, strongpoint of the last enemy foothold in France, breached the dragon's teeth of the Siegfried defenses, took Saarbruecken and sent one arm hooking north to a link-up with the Third Army.

Ludwigshaven Falls Easily

About 12 miles west of Kaiserslautern, Patton and Patch locked forces and sealed off the rich coal deposits and steel mills of the Saar Valley. There remained to be mopped up a huge V-pocket whose base on the Rhine extends from Ludwigshaven to the east-bank city of Karlsruhe. Trapped in this vise-like grip are thousands of Nazis who were caught on the west bank of the Rhine with their bridges down.

When the two armies eliminate this enemy pocket in the Saar, the Allies will have wiped out the last vestige of German holdings on the right side of the Rhine

(See PATTON on Page 2)

Super-Bombs Pound Reich

Air assaults continued unabated against German industry and communications last week with the RAF's new 10-ton super-bomb (11 tons, according to American short-ton standards) playing a noteworthy role.

These world's heavyweight champions knocked out a huge chunk of the vital Berlin-Ruhr railway viaduct on Wednesday. Reconnaissance photographs later showed that the viaduct had collapsed into the Ruhr River either because of a direct hit or because the bomb exploded in the river bed and undermined the foundation piers.

Berlin Churned Again

The super-bombs even had an effect on RAF crews. One squadron leader said that the explosion caused a pain in his spine that lasted more than a minute, feeling as if he had been hit severely in the back. "My Lancaster," he added, "bounced up well over 500 feet after release of the big load."

More than 1,300 Eighth USAAF heavy bombers accompanied by 700 Mustangs conducted a powerful daylight raid against Berlin on Sunday, striking communications inside the German capital and suburban armament works. Nearly 1,000 bombers pin-pointed Schlesischer depot and the north station freight yards, both within two miles of Berlin's heart.

VFW Stumps for 18-Month Rotation

WASHINGTON — Veterans of Foreign Wars renewed its plea for rotation or furloughs to provide 30 days leave in the U.S. for all soldiers having 18 months or more of foreign service.

In a letter to Secy. Stimson, the VFW said it recognized the difficulties but "surely there are enough replacements and transportation to grant relief to personnel who have been in continuous service and much of it in combat for three years or more."

It specifically mentioned the 25th Division fighting in the Pacific since Pearl Harbor.

The War Dept. said about 30,000 troops are returned to the U.S. monthly on furlough and rotation programs and that some members of divisions overseas for long periods are brought back even though the division itself remains abroad.

PEACE FEELERS EXPECTED

LONDON — Allied diplomats believe that a wave of German peace feelers will strike neutral European capitals soon.

UNINVITED GUEST

HICKORY, N.C. — Dawn was breaking on the Western Front and Sgt. Robert Adams of Hickory shouted to awaken the unknown companion with whom he'd shared a foxhole. There was instant response. It was a "kamerad."

MRS. MacARTHUR IN MANILA

MANILA— Mrs. Douglas MacArthur, the general's wife, and their son, Arthur, 7, have returned here by boat from Australia.

Negro Infantrymen Go Into Action In Mixed Combat Units on Rhine

PARIS — For the first time in American history, White and Negro troops are fighting side by side in battle. A front-line dispatch to 'Stars and Stripes' disclosed this week that mixed Infantry companies were being used in the 1st and 7th armies.

Many Negro service and supply troops volunteered for combat after Lt. Gen. John C. Lee told them:

"It is planned to assign you without regard to race or color to units where your assistance is most needed. Your comrades at the front are anxious to share the glory of pictory with you. Your relatives and friends are urging that you be granted this privilege.

"The Supreme Commander is confident that many of you will take advantage of the opportunity to carry on in keeping with the glorious record of colored troops in former wars."

Flood of Volunteers

The first quota was set at 2,300. This quota was quickly exceeded and hundreds of others were rejected. Four Negro first sergeants took breaks to private to qualify for the necessary refresher training course.

Sentiments of the Negro troops was summed up by Pfc. Leroy Kemp of Atlantic City. He said, "We're all in this together now. Most of the Negro troops in service outfits have been giving lots of sweat. Now we'll mix some blood with it."

839,589

WASHINGTON — The over-all casualties for the Army and Navy have now reached 839,589, a week's increase of 15,956, announced War Secy. Stimson last week.

He also revealed that U.S. ground casualties on the Western Front dropped to 34,468 in February, the smallest number in three months.

A breakdown of total Armed Forces' casualties shows:

Killed	180,671
Wounded	492,209
Missing	100,139
Captured	66,570
Total	839,589

'Just Send Medal by Mail,' Asks Widow of Pilot

NEWARK, N.J. — "Since he is not alive to receive it, all meaning of the medal is gone for me."

These were the pathetic words contained in a letter received from a fighter pilot's wife in declining an invitation to attend ceremonies for the posthumous award of an Air Medal to her husband, killed in action in the Southwest Pacific.

Maj. Arthur J. Lonegran, public relations officer who received the young mother's letter, said he had obtained her permission to release it to the press. The widow, however asked that no names, or the pilot's home city be revealed since her husband's invalid mother had not been informed of his death because the family feared the shock would be too great.

In declining to attend the presentation ceremonies here, the widow said, "I am used to the Government leaving things at my door: the telegram and the Purple Heart, so I won't mind the Air Medal coming through the mail.

"I would like to have it, you see, because of my son," she added. "He's never seen his father, but still there's so much I want him to know of his Dad. I guess the only way to start is to show off his father's medals to him.

"I wish I could tell him his father died to save him from being drawn into a third world war. I'll just have to tell him about his father as a civilian young man, just out of college with life ahead of him, dying before he had a chance to live for what he was fighting for."

Lonegran presented the medal to the young mother at her home.

PARIS EDITION

Man Spricht Deutsch
Blockleiter of Nazi Organizations
SA—Sturm-Abteilungen.
Nazi Stormtroopers.

THE STARS AND STRIPES

Daily Newspaper of U.S. Armed Forces in the European Theater of Operations

Ici On Parle Français
Ceci se fait en une minute.
Suscee suh fay on ewn meeneut.
This is done in a minute.

Vol. 1—No. 241 | 1 Fr. | 1 Fr. | Sunday, March 25, 1945

Rhine Crossed in North By Three Allied Armies

Where Allied Armies Stormed Across Rhine

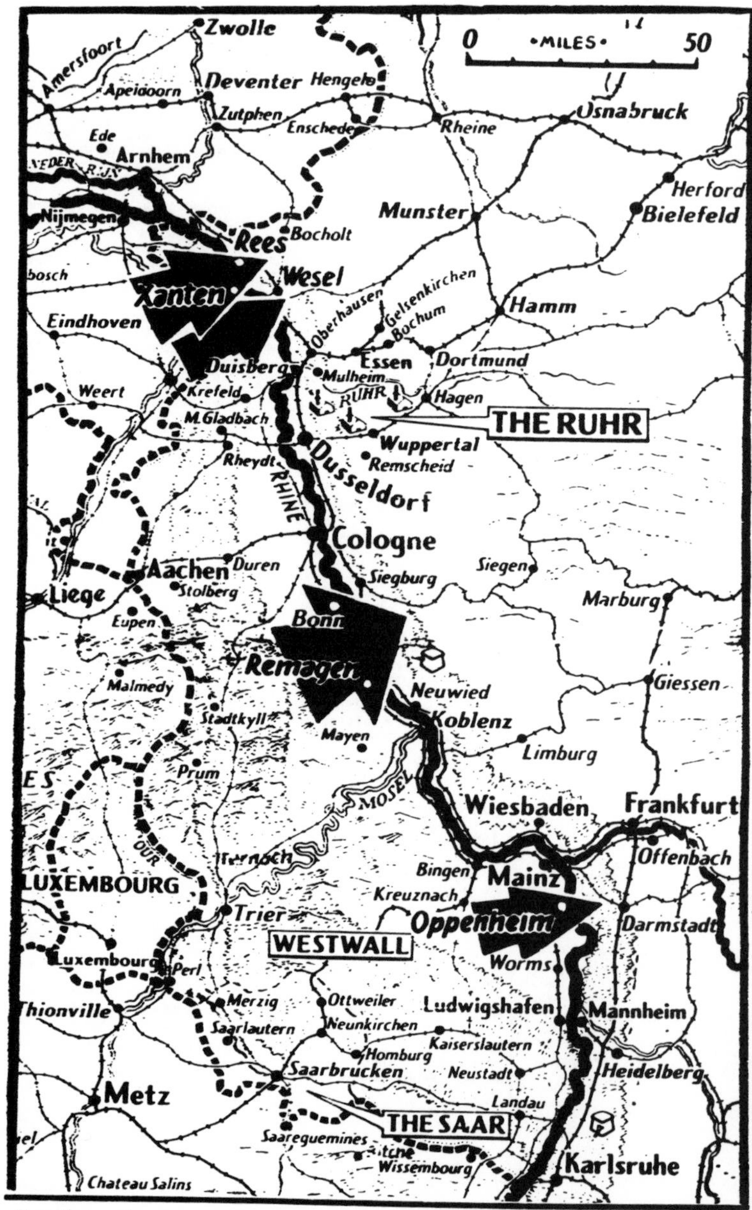

PM Map

Five Allied armies are across the Rhine today on a 125-mile front. In the north, the British Second Army has bridgeheads north and south of Wesel. Below Wesel, U.S. Ninth Army troops are four miles beyond the river. Inland, the First Allied Airborne Army, dropped yesterday morning, is fighting to link up with bridgehead forces. To the south, the First Army's Remagen bridgehead has swelled to 33 by 10 miles, and between Mainz and Worms the Third Army is pumping troops and supplies into its bridgehead won Thursday.

Airborne Troops, 9th, British Strike

By Robert L. Moora
Stars and Stripes Staff Writer

The Allies hurled three armies across the northern Rhine River yesterday, one of them by air, to open the grand offensive to win the war in Europe.

American, British and Canadian troops, crossing at night with the aid of the U.S. and Royal Navies and in the wake of the greatest softening-up aerial offensive in history, stormed onto the east bank of the river at scattered points along a 25,000-yard front just above the Ruhr. Within 24 hours they had secured strong bridgeheads, had thrown pontoon bridges across and were in control of the east bank at one point for a distance of more than 12 miles.

As daylight came, long columns of troop-carrying aircraft and towplanes, 3,000 strong, roared over the area to deliver thousands of paratroops and glider troops behind the enemy's riverfront defenses. By afternoon ground and airborne forces had linked.

From dawn until dusk, Allied air forces, using every plane they could get into the air, brought to a smashing climax the program of devastation they had carried on day after day across northwest Germany. Bombers and fighters blasted railways, road networks, airfields and supply points and rained bombs and bullets on enemy troops facing the attackers.

It was a combined operation second only to the Normandy assault itself.

Field Marshal Sir Bernard Montgomery, commanding the 21st Army Group, launched the offensive shortly after 9 PM

Turn to Pages 4 and 5 for Airborne Operation Pictures

Friday. From the west bank, which had been shrouded by a 66-mile-long smokescreen for days, American troops of Lt. Gen. William H. Simpson's Ninth Army and British and Canadian troops of the British Second Army crossed the river in assault craft of every type used in previous river crossings—and, in addition, small naval craft brought overland for the task.

Their attacks were north and south of Wesel, a city of 24,000 peacetime population on the east bank only a dozen miles north of the congested factory districts of the Ruhr Valley.

Headquarters of 21st Army Group announced late last night that the Allies were in control of the east bank for a distance of

(Continued on Page 8)

An Air View, Start to Finish

All Was Clockwork As Carriers Swept In

By Russell Jones
Stars and Stripes Staff Writer

WITH 436th CARRIER GP., Over Wesel, March 24.—The paratroops had hit their dropping zone almost an hour before the first glider-tows swept over. All that could be seen were the burning wrecks of planes which had swung back toward friendly territory west of the Rhine, and the multicolored patches of 'chutes hanging in the trees and crumpled against the ground on the east side.

The carrier planes—the RAF Lancasters and Halifaxes, pulling giant Horsa gliders, and the C47s of the Ninth Troop Carrier Command, with their twin-towed CG4s seemed as slow as freight trains as they plowed northeast from their assembly point near Brussels. When they neared the landing zone, they were in rigid formation, the RAF on the left and the Americans on the right.

Our group commander, Col. Adriel N. Williams, of Shelbyville, Ky., had taken the first ship off on schedule and the operation had run like clockwork—the assembly points were hit on the second—and 1/Lt. D. F. Rhoades ("Dusty," naturally), of Maryland, Wis., had our plane in the glider run exactly on time.

Despite the fighters which were constantly sweeping the ground looking for gun emplacements, flak and small-arms fire came up from the area northeast of Wesel. Rhoades and his co-pilot, 2 Lt. C. W. Alderdyce, of Toledo, Ohio were

(Continued on Page 8)

Final Edition

LIEGE EDITION
THE STARS AND STRIPES
Daily News paper of U.S. Armed Forces in the European Theater of Operations
Vol. I—No. 67
Tuesday, March 27, 1945

Final Edition

First Armor Breaks Loose; Seventh Army Over Rhine

3rd Drive For Vienna Reported

German sources reported yesterday that the Soviet high command unleashed a third offensive yesterday in the drive for Vienna. North of the Danube, according to the German News Agency, men of Marshal Rodion Malinovsky's Second Ukrainian Army struck across the Hron River 50 miles north of Budapest—and an even one hundred miles east of the Austrian capital.

Col. Ernst Von Hammer of German News Agency said they succeeded in establishing a narrow bridgehead southwest of Leva, 50 miles above Budapest, on the edge of the strip of country that Hungary took from Slovakia in 1938.

Even as Berlin was describing the third push toward Vienna—matching the two drives south of the Danube by Marshal Feodor Tolbukhin and other elements of Malinovsky's group Marshal Stalin announced the capture of Papa in Hungary, 38 miles east of the Austrian border; Devecser, 15 miles south of Papa, and Banska-Bystrica in Czechoslovakia 70 miles north of Budapest.

At Papa, Tolbukhin's Russians were within 59 miles of Bratislava and 75 miles of Vienna—and in position to strike from a new direction toward the northwestern Hungary rail center of Gyor, already within artillery range of other Tolbukhin columns.

Malinovsky's new attack north of the Danube advanced the Russians into territory from which they had been thrown back at the end of the Winter campaign. At that time Malinovsky advanced as far as Komarom, 28 miles beyond the Hron but was thrown back to the river.

300 Heavies Paste Oil, Arms Plants

While Ninth AF yesterday continued to fly cover for Allied armies and hammer enemy defenses and communications along the Western Front, American Flying Fortresses shifted to two vital targets in central Germany.

More than 300 Eighth AF heavies, with an escort of 450 Mustangs, hit a synthetic oil plant at Zeitz and a factory at Plauen where the Germans have been turning out armored vehicles and self-propelled guns.

Zeitz is about 20 miles south of Leipzig. Plauen is approximately 50 miles below Zeitz. The targets were bombed visually and without opposition from the Luftwaffe.

Ninth AF flew more than 1.800 sorties troop concentrations ahead of advancing First Army troops.

Ninth AF flew more than 1.800 sorties while Fifteenth AF flew more than 2 500 sorties against four Nazi airfields in Czechoslovakia and Brenner Pass targets. RAF Mosquitoes maintained nightly attacks on Berlin and made offensive patrols against German supplies off Norway.

Lloyd George Dead

LLANYSTUMDWY, North Wales, Mar. 26 (AP).—David Lloyd George former prime minister of England, died tonight.

Frankfurt-on-Main Deserted

Germany's ninth largest city and one-time financial capital of Europe yesterday was reported to be virtually deserted when Third Army troops entered the city. The pre-war population of Frankfurt was 550,000.

Tokyo Reports:

Yanks Try New Landing 325 Miles From Japan

GUAM, Mar. 26 (ANS)—Domei News Agency today reported that American troops, supported by an intensive bombardment from a large carrier and battleship task force, are "attempting" landings on the Okinawa group in the Ryukyu chain only 325 miles south of Kyushu in the Japanese homeland. This was not confimed by U.S. officials.

Tokyo said an aerial bombardment of several Ryukyu islands including Okinawa itself and of airbases in the southern Japanese home islands of Kyushu, Shikoku and Honshu preceded the reported landings.

Okinawa was bombarded three times Saturday by U.S. battleships, possibly some of the biggest and newest 16-inch-gun battlewagons in Vice Adm. Raymond A. Spruance's Fifth Fleet, the Japanese added.

Adm. Nimitz has announced only that Minami Daito, 250 miles east of Okinawa, was shelled.

Domei's broadcast, made in English and recorded by the FCC reported that landings were attempted on Toka Sima and Aka Jima, small islands west of the

(Continued on page 4).

65,000 Doughs From AF, CZ

Approximately 65.000 soldiers have been withdrawn from Com-Z and Air Force units and retrained as infantrymen, ETOUSA HQ announced yesterday. An additional 42.000 will be withdrawn "in the near future" for similar training and reassignment, it said.

Civilian volunteer workers, reclassified ex-combat soldiers and Wacs are on duty in many rear-echelon posts formerly held by soldiers designated for combat duty. The Army now employs 175.000 French, British, Dutch, Belgian and Luxembourg civilians in jobs ranging from typist to stevedore.

Also helping to relieve the manpower situation are 7.500 Wacs assigned to duties requiring special skills. Thousands of additional Wacs are being requested from the states.

Many civilian volunteers are persons driven from their homes by the war, who in several cases are organized into mobile labor units for rebuilding bridges and roads and working in clothing and salvage depots.

Churchill Returns

LONDON, Mar. 26 (AP).—Winston Churchill has returned to Britain following his visit to the battlefront, it was announced tonight.

Frankfurt Entered By Third; Hodges Advances 22 Miles

Lt. Gen. Courtney H. Hodges' First U.S. Army tanks broke loose from the Remagen bridgehead yesterday to burst the German defenses in at least three places. One armored colum advanced at least 22 miles.

Far to the south, Lt. Gen. Alexander M. Patch's Seventh U.S. Army crossed the Rhine River. Meanwhile, a columl of the Third Army's Fourth Armd. Div., commanded by Brig. Gen. William H. Hoge, entered Frankfurt-on-Main, Germany's ninth largest city with a pre-war population of 550,000. The Americans found the city virtually deserted.

The Seventh Army crossing of the Rhine—which the Germans said was in the vicinity of Karlsruhe—was made without air or artillery report. It put elements of four American armies east of the Rhine.

One First Army column—part of one of the largest tank concentrations in history—sped 22 miles southeast from the southern end of the bridgehead to capture Limburg, on the Lahn River 20 miles northwest of Frankfurt. This armor was reported still moving late yesterday while two other armored forces plunged through other gaps in the German defenses east of Remagen.

North of the Ruhr, the British Second Army was reported to have driven almost 18 miles east of the Rhine. Just to the south, below Wesel, the Ninth U.S. Army consolidated a bridgehead ten miles wide and ten miles deep.

One unidentified First Army force, drove 15 miles to reach the town of Standt, three miles east of the Ruhr-Frankfurt super-highway. A second steel shaft hit the outskirts of Altenkirchen, in the center of the First Army bridgehead 20 miles east of Bad Godesberg.

Working with the 99th Inf. Div., advanced elements of this armored column bypassed the city and sped on.

First Army infantry advanced generally from three to seven miles yesterday all along their front, establishing a 30 mile line running 15 to 20 miles east of the Rhine.

Meanwhile, far to the southeast, the Third Army's Fourth Armd. Div., commanded by Brig. Gen. William C. Hoge, was across the Main River 23 miles southeast of Frankfurt. It was on a rolling plain 230 miles from Berlin and 270 miles from the Russian front.

The Fourth Armd. crossed the Main on a bridge captured intact at the southern outskirst of Aschaffenburg.

In the First Army sector, motorized

(Continued on Page 4)

Nazi Nurse Seeks Aid for 6,500 in Mine

By George Dorsey
Stars and Stripes Staff Writer

WITH THE NINTH ARMY ACROSS THE RHINE, Mar. 26—The sallow, tired German nurse sat in the low-ceilinged kitchen of a house just behind our lines and told her story of misery, danger and death.

The Jewish master sergeant, Bernard Bernkof, a 313th Infantry soldier from Camden, N.J., listened carefully and patiently translated her words.

Her name was Anna Heiss, 30, and she still wore her soiled German Red Cross uniform. A nurse's cap topped straggling brown hair which framed a plain but not unattractive face.

It happened in a workers' colony in Wehofen, a northern suburb of Duisburg, and it began with the great preparation bombardment that American artillery laid down prior to the Ninth Army's Rhine crossings. The barrage took the people by surprise and, as they rushed to the mine shaft designated as a shelter, some were cut down by the onslaught of shells. About 6.500 persons, including 1.000 children, reached the refuge and crowded into three short subterranean passageways.

They were still there today, said nurse Anna Heiss, after three waterless, foodless days and nights. So terrible was their plight—there were no toilets nor

(Continued on page 4).

It'll Be Movie of the Year

NEW YORK, Mar. 26—The New York Sun reported today that the War Department has prepared a special film which has been sent under seal to every part of the world where U.S. troops are stationed, and which explains plans for soldiers' discharges or Pacific service after Germany's defeat.

"Within a few hours after the cessation of hostilities in Europe," said the Sun's special dispatch from Washington, "Every U.S. man on every fighting front in the world will be fully informed of the details of the Army's plans concerning his own personal future."

The film explains how an individual's status is determined, it was said. It will not be possible for the individual to determine in all cases whether he will be discharged or sent to the Pacific, but it will be possible to calculate his own standing on the basis of the point system, in relation to the other men in his outfit, according to the report.

"If he is to go to the Pacific," the Sun said, "he will understand why certain groups and units must be sent directly with no opportunity for even a brief home leave. If he is to be discharged, he will see clearly why it may be many months before he can actually be sent to the U.S."

U.S. Saboteurs Drop To Sweden by Error

STOCKHOLM, Mar. 26 (AP).—Five American saboteurs dropped into Sweden instead of Norway Saturday, a Swedish press report said today.

The report said that on early Sunday, Swedes found quantities of munitions and explosives which had been parachuted onto a frozen lake and in the neighborhood five men hiding in the belief they were in Norway.

THE STARS AND STRIPES
MEDITERRANEAN

Vol. 2, No. 118, Tuesday, March 27, 1945 ITALY EDITION * * TWO LIRE

U. S. 3rd Enters Frankfurt; Allies Open 200-Mile Front

Red Armies Near Austria In Fast Drive

Border Only 30 Miles Distant In Push On Bratislava

MOSCOW, Mar. 26—The Red Army intensified its drive toward Bratislava and Vienna today with advance units reaching within 30 miles of the Austrian frontier. Two Soviet Army Groups were smashing at German defenses in western Hungary south of the Danube on a wide front.

The 3rd Army Group, commanded by Marshal Feodor Tolbukhin, was advancing at the rate of about 12 miles a day west of the northern tip of Lake Balaton, while the left wing of the 2nd Ukrainian Army Group, led by Marshal Rodion Malinovsky, moved westward just below the Danube.

Tolbukhin's troops captured the junctions of Papa and Devecser, Stalin announced in a second Order of the Day. Papa is 31 miles east of the Austrian border and 74 miles southeast of Vienna. At Papa, Soviet forces were 25 miles northeast of the German bastion of Gyor.

Malinovsky's right wing captured Banska Bystrica, 80 miles north of Budapest, Stalin announced in his first Order. Capture of the city, once a center of Patriot resistance to the Germans, meant the Russians had established a large bridgehead on the west bank of the Hron River.

In the far north around the Baltic two more Red Army Groups were fighting to reduce the last German strongholds in that area.

The 2nd White Russian Armies, commanded by Marshal Konstantin

(Continued on Page 8)

15th AAF Supports Red Army Advance

MAAF HQ., Mar. 26 — Fifteenth Air Force heavy bombers, their campaign against German oil targets virtually completed, today threw their weight in support of Russian forces advancing in Austria and Hungary, bombing communications behind enemy lines.

Long-range Mustangs had a successful strafing day in the Vienna area and in Czechoslovakia. Early reports indicated that the P-51s destroyed 31 locomotives. They also knocked down an FW-190, while other Mustangs, escorting the bombers, shot down four FWs near Lake Balaton. Lightnings dive-bombed a rail bridge in Austria on the main line from Vienna to Linz. Hits were reported on abutments and approaches.

Among the targets hit by the heavies were the railyards at Szombathely, in Hungary; Bruck, 22 miles southeast of Vienna; Strasshof, 18 miles east of Vienna and Wiener Neustadt, 30 miles southwest of Vienna.

U-Boats Hit

LONDON, Mar. 26 (AP)—Royal Air Force planes made effective attacks last night on six U-boats, 12 freighters and three armed escorts in western Norwegian waters. Eight of the ships attacked received direct hits

9th Threatens Duisburg, Biggest Inland Port

SHAEF, Mar. 26—The U. S. 3rd Army, commanded by Lt. Gen. George S. Patton, has entered the great industrial city of Frankfurt-on-Main, a late United Press dispatch said tonight. The city, which had a prewar population of 500,000, is 17 miles east of the Rhine. It was enveloped from west, south and east, as the 3rd Army, spearheaded by the crack 4th Armored Division, pushed beyond captured Darmstadt and entered Hanau and Aschaffenburg. Hanau is 10 miles east of Frankfurt and Aschaffenburg is on the right bank of the Main River 26 miles southeast of Frankfurt. At Hanau the 3rd controlled seven miles of the south bank of the Main River. Elements of the 3rd have advanced to within 250 miles of Berlin.

The great Allied offensive east of the Rhine appeared to be gaining momentum. A late BBC report said the U. S. 1st Army had broken over the road leading to Frankfurt and that two columns were striking rapidly due east. The report said one column had pushed on 22 miles and the second had chalked up a gain of 15 miles. One wing of the 1st earlier was reported opposite Coblenz which fell to the 3rd Army.

While the 3rd and 1st Armies continued their march through Germany, the U. S. 9th, British 2nd and 1st Allied Airborne Armies were expanding their bridgehead in the Westphalian plains north of the Ruhr. The five armies were pressing the Krauts back over a front 200 miles long.

Allied tanks were streaming across

(Continued on Page 8)

'Ike' At Bridgehead, Sets Berlin As Goal

WITH U. S. 1st ARMY, Mar. 26—General Dwight D. Eisenhower, Supreme Allied Commander, left little doubt today that the current Allied offensive east of the Rhine is the straw designed to break the Wehrmacht's back.

Commending the 1st Army for its action at the Remagen bridgehead, the general said:

"I expect them to lick everybody they come up against. They did it all the way across France and I see no reason why they should stop on the road to Berlin."

David Lloyd George Dies In Wales At 82

CRICCIETH, Wales, Mar. 26 — David Lloyd George, 82-year-old British statesman and World War I Prime Minister, died at his home in Wales today after a long illness.

The statesman began his career in British politics in 1890 when he was elected to Parliament by a majority of 18 votes. Before the start of the last war he was Chancellor of the Exchequer. In December, 1916, he was named Premier—a position he held until his resignation in 1922.

He was given an earldom in King George's New Year honors list this year.

Extend TD In U. S. To 45 Days

Here's good news for those of you sweating out TD—and better yet, for troops currently in the U. S. under the War Department's Temporary Duty policy.

Effective March 14, the period of time authorized overseas personnel returned to the States on Temporary Duty is increased to 45 days. Previously, a 30-day leave had been authorized.

The 15-day extension, which applies to all future returnees, is applicable as well to men now in the States on TD. Those men will be notified automatically of their 15-day extension.

The new policy does not apply, however, to troops now at U. S. ports awaiting return to this theater, or those already in transit on their return to active duty.

It's Rough, A Glider Landing In Germany

Some Get In Safely; Some Are Coffins

By Sgt. ED CLARK
(Stars and Stripes Writer)

WITH THE 17TH AIRBORNE DIVISION, Mar. 24 (Delayed)—It's hard to adequately describe a glider landing, particularly when it's made in the heart of enemy territory with fighting on all about. Too much happens too fast.

Some lucky gliders and their crews made it without a scratch. Many others, riddled by artillery and small arms fire as they hit the ground, become charred and burned out funeral pyres.

Lying on their bellies near what remained of their gliders, while machinegun, mortar and small arms fire rakes the farmyard landing fields, the lucky ones can briefly see what happens or has happened to their less fortunate comrades. What they see is not pleasant. To the left, one glider ripped with ack-ack fire, crashed nose deep into the loamy earth. Not a man comes out.

In a few seconds the fire started by tracers roars through the fabric. The framework crumbles over and what used to be a glider joins the rest of the smoldering and charred wrecks.

Other gliders come winging dangerously close to the ships and men already on the ground. The new arrivals smash through fences, wheel through wires, crash into grounded ships. One loses a wing as it collides with a telephone pole.

Men who are unhurt tumble out of the last ships. There are a few calls for medics, but there is not much that can be done about them. Despite the losses, the number of glider troops on the field and those nearby is gradually increasing.

Those who have made it now have the job of trying to reach

Ack-Ack Guns Take Their Toll

their pre-arranged assembly point. Most of the men belly-crawl toward what they think is the right road. Some, not so wary, stand up and try to run for it. They were wrong and paid for their error with death by snipers' bullets at the road.

Those still left check with others, ask for this or that and they want to know where Capt. Jones is, and "if Joe Blow made it OK."

They start to flush the Krauts out of the farmhouse strongpoints and the nearby gun positions. Many prisoners are taken. Many Krauts are killed but sniper fire continues. Finding them is like finding a needle in a haystack which is probably where they are. There are a lot of chutes down

(Continued on Page 8)

Patrols Again Take Spotlight In Italy

ADVANCED AFHQ, Mar. 26 — Activity along the 5th and 8th Army fronts was confined to patrol skirmishes and very light artillery fire, today's communique reported.

Troops on the 5th Army's central sector repulsed several German patrols, killing 11 of the enemy in one engagement. Three more Krauts were killed when their attempted ambush was detected by Allied troops. In the Serchio Valley, another enemy party was driven off.

Along the 8th Army front, an enemy patrol of 40 men attacked Allied positions near Faenza, but was driven off by small arms, mortar and artillery fire. South of Route 9, Allied troops successfully attacked an enemy strongpoint house at Tebano.

Airborne Head

SHAEF, Mar. 26—Maj. Gen. Matthew B. Ridgeway, who as commanding general of the U. S. 82nd Airborne Division led his outfit in the Normandy landings, was identified today as being in command of the XVIII Airborne Corps in the 21st Army Group sector east of the Rhine.

U.S. 1st, 9th Armies Forge Ring Around Industrial Ruhr

NANCY EDITION
Volume 1, Number 67
Monday, April 2, 1945

THE STARS AND STRIPES
Daily Newspaper of U.S. Armed Forces in the European Theater of Operations

Man Spricht Deutsch
Blacklist of Nazi Organizations
NS Deutscher Studentenbund.
Nazi students' league.

Yanks Invade Ryukyus

10 Nazi Divisions Trapped; Planes Fuel U. S. Tanks

A steel band of American armor was riveted around the Ruhr at 3:30 p.m. yesterday when the U. S. 9th Army's 2d Armored Div. linked up with the U. S. 1st Army at Lippstadt, 20 miles southwest of Paderborn.

The Ruhr encirclement was completed by Lt. Gen. William H. Simpson's 9th army tanks driving east along the northern fringes of the great industrial pulse of Germany and forces of Lt. Gen. Courtney H. Hodges' 1st Army pushing north.

It meant that Nazi Germany had lost the last industrial area from which its war machine could be fed. Gen. Eisenhower had predicted at the outset of the offensive that organized resistance could not long continue in the Reich once the Ruhr was lost.

On the southern flank of the great, fluid front, Lt. Gen. Alexander M. Patch jr. shot infantry and armor of his 7th Army south in a new thrust which gained up to 18 miles.

Tanks 70 Miles Past Rhine

Meanwhile United Press frontline reports said the week's most sensational breakout occurred during the past 12 hours on Field Marshal Sir Bernard L. Montgomery's front with hundreds of tanks streaming east and northeast far beyond any previous positions reached.

Driving ahead under security silence, some tank forces were officially reported 70 miles east of the Rhine in the vicinity of Muenster and Rheine, the latter a

(Continued on page 8)

Daylight Saving Comes to the ETO

ETO clocks jumped forward one hour this morning as double summer time went into effect in France, Britain, Belgium, the Netherlands, Luxembourg, and western occupied Germany.

With the introduction of double summer time, the legal time is now two hours ahead of Greenwich time. Clocks in the U. S. are also being set one hour ahead, and the five-hour difference remains.

Air Strikes Aid Drives of 3d, 7th

More than 100 B-26 Mauraders of the 1st TAF bombed barracks areas and supply depots yesterday in the vicinity of Stuttgart, while 12th TAC P-47s attacked enemy strongpoints, gun positions, and fortified buildings ahead of the 3d and 7th Armies. Particularly heavy blows were directed at Aschaffenburg, where street fighting is stilll in progress, and at Koenigshofen, 50 miles farther into Germany.

Counting up the results of nearly 1,000 sorties, 1st TAF reported 198 fortified buildings destroyed and 118 more damaged; 30 locomotives blasted and 63 damaged;; 122 railway cars disabled and 364 damaged, and 122 motor transports disabled and 204 damaged.

RAF pilots bombed the rocket coast of Holand and predicted there would be a marked "diminution" of V-1 and V-2 launchings from the Netherlands coast.

Meanwhile Mediterranean-based 15th AF Mustangs and Lightnings celebrated their first anniversary by shooting down 335 enemy planes in a "typical Hollywood version of an air battle," according to Lt. Col. Fred C. Stofel, leader of the 31st Group.

Six Divisions Hit Okinawa Isle In Greatest Pacific Operation

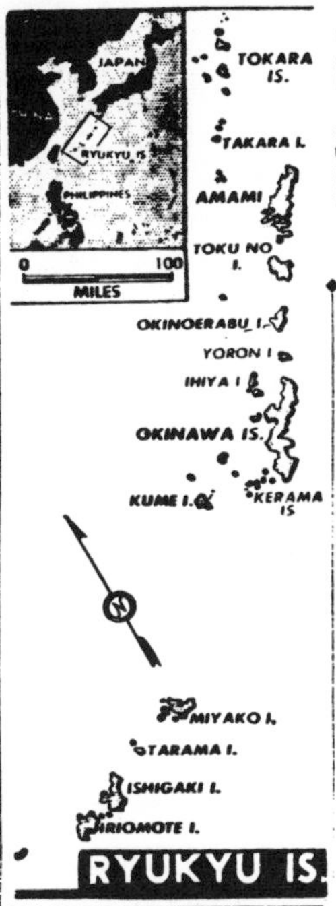

GUAM, April 1 (ANS)—The New U. S. 10th Army landed today on Okinawa Island, in the Ryukyu chain 325 miles southwest of the Japanese homeland, in the largest amphibious operation of the Pacific war.

The Americans have expanded their beachhead to three miles deep at several points, it was officially announced tonight. Sporadic mortar and artillery fire fell on the beachhead during the day. Heavy warships continued to shell the Jap installations on the island.

Adm. Chester W. Nimitz, commander-in-chief of the Pacific Fleet, personally read the communique announcing that the invasion had been carried out by the U. S. 24th Army Corps and the Marine 3d Amphibious Corps, which together form the 10th Army.

At least a dozen towns and villages fell to American forces advancing inland along a seven-and-a-half-mile line in the southern part of Okinawa, the Associated Press reported.

The place chosen for the landing indicated that the American forces also intended to drive eastward across the island, cutting off the well-populated and industrial southern third from the mountainous northern section.

The soldiers and Marines went ashore in great strength

(Continued on page 8)

B-29s Hit Tokyo

BULLETIN

WASHINGTON, April 1 (Reuter)—Military targets in Tokyo have been raided again by large Force bomber command. The raid announced today by 20th Air force bomber command. The raid was made in the early morning hours by bombers based in the Marianas.

Soviets Capture Sopron, 33 Miles East of Vienna

Red Army forces rolling forward in Hungary yesterday captured the German stronghold of Sopron, 33 miles southeast of Vienna and 19 miles from the Austrian city of Wiener-Neustadt, an important center of German aircraft production.

Marshal Stalin announced the fall of Sopron to the northern forces of Marshal Feodor Tolbukhin's 3d Ukranian Army, some units of which already have invaded Austria. Other forces of the 3d, driving for the Austrian communications center of Graz, were reported last at the Austrian Hungarian border.

Marshal Rodion Malinovsky's 2d Ukrainian Army, advancing toward Vienna from the east, captured the Slovakian town of Svenc, about 15 miles from Bratislava and 47 from Vienna, Stalin announced. The 2d also took Trnava and Hlohovec.

The Soviet forces at Sopron were three miles from the Austrian border. Their operations, and those inside Austria, were supported by U. S. heavy bombers of the 15th AF, which flew from Italy to attack the Maribor rail bridge, in Yugoslavia about 35 miles below Graz, and the St. Polten railyards, 35 miles west of Vienna.

Marshal Stalin also announced last night that troops of Marshal Ivan Koniev's 1st Ukrainian Army had captured the city of Glogau, in Silesia 55 miles northwest of Breslau, and taken more than 8,000 German troops. Glogau, a by-passed German strongpoint, had been under attack for weeks.

Finds Paradise: Pop. 35 Gals

BOCA RATON, Fla., April 1 (ANS)—The War Department released today the story of the adventures of an Army Air Force officer who drifted for 16 days on a life raft in the South Pacific with little to eat, and then landed on a tropical paradise populated by 35 women and an island chieftan.

Capt. Balfour C. Gibson of Berkeley, Calif., was permitted to tell the account publicly—and to explain things privately to his wife, Anita—more than a year after the experience.

When his B-17 was shot down by the Japanese, Gibson and his crew survived by eating mouldy K-rations, sharks and sea gulls.

On the 17th day they sighted a string of seven small islands, he said and found them populated by friendly natives, mostly women.

Because of the food shortage, he said, each crewman was assigned to a separate island. On Gibson's were the chief and five pretty girls and women who stuffed him with chicken, lobster and other dainties. His landing weight of 110 pounds increased to 160. Gibson may want to forget that tranquil setting some day, but his wife, although taking it as one of the fortunes of war, may not let him.

Yanks on Okinawa Meet Little Trouble

WITH THE U. S. 10TH ARMY ON OKINAWA, April 1 (AP)—Streaming ashore directly in the face of a rising sun, thousands of American troops quickly established beachheads today on this island, "front porch of the Japanese homeland."

A terrific naval bombardment had torn holes in a sea wall, permitting entry of tanks and other armored vehicles. Troops drove inland rapidly against scant initial opposition.

This afternoon, waves of troops were digging in for the night, while landing craft poured more men and supplies into the coral approaches. Americans camped in a small farm area.

Supers Plaster Nagoya Again

GUAM, April 1 (ANS)—Marianas-based Superfortresses returned yesterday to the Japanese homeland island of Honshu and attacked Nagoya, Japan's biggest aircraft production center.

Report Nazis Murder 8 Danes

LONDON, April, 1 (Reuter)—Eight imprisoned Danish patriots were executed by Germans on Wednesday and Thursday, it was learned here today. Danish quarters here said that executions are against International Law and must be considered as murder of Danish prisoners of war. All who have assisted in them will be prosecuted, they said.

Tea and Crumpets Are German Trap For Wary Troopers

WITH THE 17TH AIRBORNE DIV. EAST OF THE RHINE, April 1—The soundness of the Army's non-fraternization policy was proved to the satisfaction of three air-doughs of the 17th Airborne Div. who became suspicious of a German invitation to tea and cakes.

The men, members of the 194th Glider Inf., had just finished clearing their third house when they were offered the invitation.

They posted a fourth man outside the house to cover them. He noticed the 12-year-old youngster of the house slipping out to warn Nazi soldiers hiding in a haystack.

The ensuing fight resulted in liquidation of the tea party.

GERMANY EDITION
Thursday, April 5, 1945
Volume 1, Number 1

THE STARS AND STRIPES
Daily Newspaper of U.S. Armed Forces in the European Theater of Operations

Third Clears Kassel as French Enter Karlsruhe

Fighter-Bombers Smash a Retreating German Truck Column

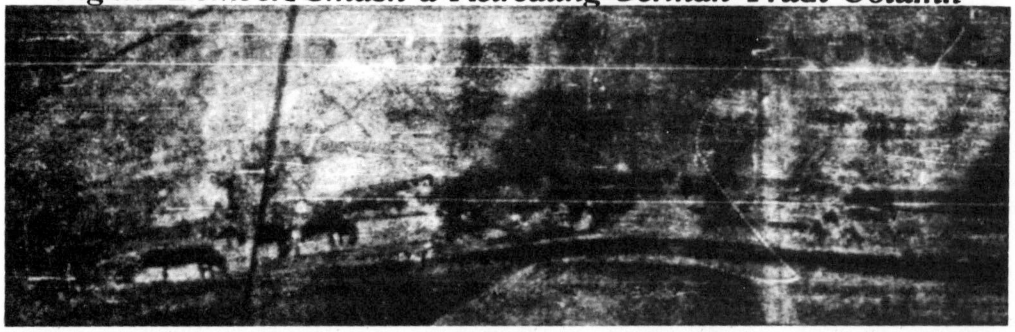

A German convoy under attack northwest of Giessen by fighter-bombers of XIX Tactical Air Command. Two trucks are burning at center.

Yanks Split Main Island In Ryukyus

GUAM, April 4 — Marines and soldiers of the U. S. Tenth Army, battling on the Ryukyu Island chain less than 325 miles south of Japan, have split Okinawa—the main island of the chain—after a swift push against scattered Japanese resistance.

It was believed that the bulk of the Japanese garrison on Okinawa—estimated to number 60,000 to 80,000 men—had been driven into the hills north of the Marine-Army spearhead by the ten-day bombardement that preceded the U. S. landings.

Casualties so far have been low and Adm. Nimitz'e Pacific fleet headquarters said that the victory of cutting the island is two had been accomplished ten days ahead of schedule.

U. S. carrier planes and battleships continued to support the American advance today with powerful bombardments of Jap positions around the ports on the southern part of the island.

Main objective of the U. S. operation is to secure the fine fleet anchorage of Nakagushuku Bay, a few miles south of Tobara and less than a mile from the American spearheads.

The Okinawa operation was called the "greatest invasion of the Pacific war" by Adm. Nimitz' headquarters. It also put into action the new U. S. Tenth Army and the Marine Third Amphibious Corps, numbering more than 100,000 men.

Front dispatches said that the Yanks had already captured four

(Continued on Page 4)

They Saw It Happen — On Columbia, Not Rhine

RUFUS, Ore., Apr. 4 — It was no surprise to residents of this Columbia River hamlet that the Yanks were able to bridge the Rhine in nine hours—and even less in some spots.

For months they watched Army engineers build bridges and push them across the Columbia in practice for the operation.

Bratislava Falls as Reds Reach Suburbs of Vienna

Bratislava, the capital of Slovakia and the last big obstacle to the Red Army's drive from the east on Vienna, fell yesterday to Marshal Rodion Malinovksy's Second Ukrainian Army, Marshal Stalin announced in an order of the day.

The Third Ukrainian Army, under Marshal Feodor Tolbukhin, drove to the Viennese suburbs from the south, after its capture on Tuesday of Wiener-Neustadt, industrial city 25 miles south of the Austrian capital.

Tolbukhin's infantry was following up tank spearheads which had put a quarter-circle of steel around Vienna to the south and southeast. Yesterday they overran a 20-mile stretch of the rail line leading from Vienna to Italy, while on Tolbukhin's far southern wing Russian and Bulgarian troops crossed into Yugoslavia.

Although the Russians had bypassed Bratislava on the north, its capture opened a pathway some 30 miles straight west to Vienna through the Bratislava Gap, a stretch of low land between the north bank of the Danube and the Carpathian foothills.

Bratislava, which had a pre-war population of 100,000, was taken by storm, Stalin announced. It was an important industrial city and Danubian port.

Kiel U-Boat Yards Ripped by Heavies

One thousand Allied heavy bombers yesterday hit what the Nazis have left of Germany, and early this morning German radio warnings revealed that allied air fleets again were over German targets.

The major attacks yesterday were concentrated against U-boat yards at Kiel and nearby airfields. Fifteen German aircraft were downed during the trip, while nine Allied bombers were later reported missing.

This morning's Nazi broadcast indicated that the enemy feared attacks in the Hamburg, Leipzig and Brandenburg areas and particularly on Berlin, which had been visited by RAF Mosquitoes Tuesday night.

S&S Publishes in Germany

This is he first edition of The Stars and Stripes to be published in Germany — in this or any other war.

Three years ago less twelve days, the first Stars and Stripes of this war was published. That was in London, April 17, 1942.

Since then, 20 new editions have been started. These papers have followed the American Armies in their advance on Germany until The Stars and Stripes is now in Pfungstadt, 20 miles south of Frankfurt.

This edition won't be good. We are wrestling with strange equipment, much of it with key parts missing. The dispossessed civilians helping this GI staff speak a dozen languages, none of them English. We are short of materials, we haven't yet liberated an engraving plant and, damn it, we can't find the Mauldin cartoons. We're doing our best and if you never get to read this, that wasn't enough.

However, we are going to press thanks to the help of a lot of GIs in a lot units in the Third and Seventh Armies and the Ninth Air Force. Ninth Troop Carrier Command, for one, sent an advance party of five (with jeep) as close to the front as a C47 could go; they were put up and chowed by the Fifth Inf. Div.,

(Continued on Page 4)

Army to Boost Furloughs Home, VFW Chief Says

WASHINGTON, Apr. 4 (ANS)—Jean A. Brunner, commander-in-chief of the Veterans of Foreign Wars, said today that information supplied by the Army indicated that furloughs home for combat troops would be stepped up greatly after Germany's defeat.

He said that Maj. Gen. J. A. Ulio, adjutant general, has advised the VFW that 40,000 to 50,000 line soldiers were being sent home each month and that the rate would be definitely increased "during the months ahead."

Brunner, however, cautioned families "not to expect wholesale shipments of men back to the U. S. when V-E day arrives," and he added: "We must take into consideration the future conduct of the war against Japan and the vast problem of policing conquered Germany."

He said that Ulio, in a letter replying to a VFW request that 30-day furloughs be given combat troops with 18 months or more service overseas, reported that the War Department would expand its rotation furlough plan "when military needs permit."

Ulio pointed out that the shortage of qualified replacements was the greatest factor barring increased rotation. Other limiting factors, he said, are restricted shipping space, the necessity to continue a steady increase in overseas strength and the "pace and vicissitudes of war."

Work Farms or Starve, Allies Warn Germans

SHAEF, April 4— German farmers were told in a broadcast from here last night that the nation would face wholesale starvation unless they stayed at work.

"Remember," the farmers were told, "for years Germany has relied on plundered food from occupied countries."

The message followed an earlier "the German government has "the German government has ceased to exercise affective control over wide areas."

7th Gaining Despite Stiff Nazi Defense

General Eisenhower's armies yesterday tore new holes in the German last-ditch defenses of the inner Reich, with Lt. Gen. George S. Patton's Third Army shooting some seven columns of heavy forces beyond Kassel, which was cleared in the afternoon, and Gen. Jean de Lattry de Tassigny's First French Army bursting into Karlsruhe to highlight the day.

One of Patton's columns, the Fourth Armd. Div., cleared Gotha, a little over 25 miles from Weimar, home of the Nazi-destroyed German republic which was set up after the last war. Meanwhile, the Sixth Armd. Div. swept within four miles southwest of Muhlhausen, with its advance units last reported to be 145 miles from Berlin. The 11th Armd. Div. was reported at Suhl, 20 miles to the south.

Third Army tanks and troops now have cracked through the Thuringen forests and once more are on the open plain leading to Berlin.

Opposition Increases

Resistance against Lt. Gen. Alexander M. Patch's Seventh Army piled up somewhat yesterday, as the Nazis sought to hold open possible escape routes for German forces seeking to wind up the second World War in the Bavarian mountains. Opposition was especially strong at Heilbronn and toward Uffenheim.

Two regiments of the 42nd (Rainbow) Div. were making good prodress in Wurzburg, which was last reported more than half-cleared. The Nazis were dug in on the east bank of the Main river north of the city, although resistance in the built up area was said to be comparatively moderate.

Some of the toughest fighting on the western front confronted Seventh Army troops as they closed a ring around Heilbronn and made new crossings of both the Neckar and Main rivers. In the vicinity of Neckargartasch, where part of the 39th Inf. of the 100th Div. crossed earlier against initial light resistance, an enemy counterattack regained some ground. The Nazis lost it again, however, despite

(Continued on Page 4)

Eisenhower Praises Ruhr Encirclement

SHAEF, Apr. 4 — General Eisenhower yesterday issued the following order of the day:

"The encirclement of the Ruhr by a wide pincer movement has cut off the whole of Army Group B and parts of Army Group H, thus forming a large pocket of enemy troops whose fate is sealed and who are ripe for annihilation.

"The most vital industrial area is denied to the German war potential. This magnificent feat of arms will bring the war more rapidly to a close. It will long be remembered in history as an outstanding battle—the Battle of the Ruhr."

THE STARS AND STRIPES
MEDITERRANEAN

Vol. 1, No. 224, Friday, April 6, 1945 — Printed in Italy — TWO LIRE

USSR Denounces Jap Treaty

Allies Gain In West; Soviets At Vienna

Armies Drive Near Bremen, Hanover; U. S. 3rd Fans Out

SHAEF, April 5—The U. S. 3rd Army drove north into Muhlhausen on the broad plain southwest of Berlin and southward to within 40 miles of the Czech frontier today, while American and British forces in northwest Germany advanced within 25 miles of Hanover and 38 miles of Bremen.

Allied pilots, returning from an almost continuous stream of air assaults in front of rapidly advancing ground forces, reported the Germans were beginning to evacuate both Hanover and Bremen and appeared to be moving equipment and troops from Hamburg, which is now less than 100 miles from Allied spearheads.

As Lt. Gen. George S. Patton's armor fanned out in central Germany, with the north prong heading toward the town of Nordhausen, an announcement from Field Marshal Bernard L. Montgomery's 21st Army Group located the British 7th Armored Division three miles south of Diepholtz or 38 miles southwest of Bremen on the main Munster-Bremen highway.

The announcement lifted a security blackout which had obscured the 7th Armored Division's exact operations for more than 24 hours. It was made shortly after the British 2nd Army and the U. S. 9th Army linked up on the bank of the Weser River at the outskirts of Minden. Some elements of these armies were reported across the river and about 25 miles short of Hanover.

The U. S. 3rd Army, encountering relatively little organized resistance, was advancing so rapidly in so many directions that news from

(Continued on page 8)

Hungary Liberated, Moscow Announces

MOSCOW, April 5—All of Hungary has been liberated.

The Red Army cleared the last remnants of German troops clinging to the fringes of the country by clearing the southwestern area, last night's Soviet communique announced. The northwestern sector adjoining Austria was freed the day before yesterday.

The Nazi-controlled puppet government of Ferenc Szalasi, which set up shop in Budapest last fall when Admiral Nicholas Horthy was prevented by the Nazis from carrying out a plan to make peace with the Allies, has not been heard from. It moved to Sopron on the western border of Hungary before Budapest was encircled. It has probably taken refuge somewhere in Austria or Germany.

Eisenhower Doubts Definite Surrender

WASHINGTON, April 5—"It is probable that there will never be a clean-cut military surrender of forces on the western front," General Dwight D. Eisenhower has told President Roosevelt in a letter dated March 31, according to Reuter's correspondent here.

General Eisenhower is quoted as believing that "this would lead into forms of [German] guerrilla warfare which would require for its suppression a very large number of troops."

"It is, of course, always possible that there might be in Germany a sudden upsurge of popular resentment against the war which would lead to much easier pacification than that described above," the letter goes on to say, according to the text so far available.

"My opinion is based upon supposition that our experience to date provides our best basis of future prediction."

In his letter to the President, General Eisenhower outlined what

(Continued on page 8)

Red Army Battles Way Through Last Defenses Of Capital

MOSCOW, April 5 — The battle for Vienna itself began today. The Red Army drove almost flush with the city limits; Russian shellfire poured into the final defense zone of the Austrian capital.

Marshal Feodor Tolbukhin's 3rd Ukrainian Armies crashed through the outer defenses skirting the southern suburbs of the city and reached to within three miles of the city boundaries early this morning.

From the east, Marshal Rodion Malinovsky's forces raced toward Vienna after capturing Bratislava, Czechoslovak city (in "Slovakia") on the north bank of the Danube. These Russian troops were believed to be less than 25 miles east of Vienna early today and were driving ahead rapidly after smashing the defenses of what Marshal Stalin called "the mighty strongpoint of Bratislava."

The left wing of Malinovsky's armies, fighting toward Vienna from the southeast on the south bank of the Danube, captured the junction of Bruck, 18 miles from the capital, Marshal Stalin tonight announced in his first Order of the Day.

On the other side of the Danube, Malinovsky's forces took Malacky in Czechoslovakia near the Austrian border. In the high Carpathians, the Russians, in cooperation with Rumanian troops, seized Previdza and Banovce, northeast of Bratislava, Stalin announced.

In a second Order of the Day, Stalin disclosed that General Andrei I. Yeremenko, hero of Stalingrad and the Crimea, had replaced General Ivan Petrov as commander of the 4th Ukrainian Armies. This order reported the capture by these armies of Ruzomberek, in western

(Continued on page 8)

Note Says Tokyo Helped Nazis In War On Russia

LONDON, April 5—In a sensational note which accused the Japanese of helping Germany in its war against Russia, the Soviet Government today served notice that it was denouncing the Japanese-Soviet neutrality pact.

Following strict diplomatic procedure, Foreign Commissar V. M. Molotov handed a note to Japanese Ambassador Sato at 3 PM, declaring that it would not renew the treaty dated April 13, 1941.

The treaty does not expire until April 13, 1946, but under its terms it would be renewed automatically unless either party denounced it a year before its expiration. The meticulous Moscow Government, in its official statement today, said that the denunciation will take effect on April 13.

The Russians, though they pursued formal diplomatic procedure, minced no words in telling the Japanese why they were denouncing the treaty. They reminded the Tokyo Government that this pact was signed before the German attack on the Soviet Union, and before Japan began its war on the U. S. and Britain.

The situation has changed radically, the official announcement said. Not only is Japan, Germany's ally, helping Germany in its fight against Russia, but Japan is waging war against the Soviet Government's Allies. Therefore, the Japanese were told, the pact has lost its mean-

(Continued on page 2)

BOWS OUT

KUNIAKI KOISO

Jap Cabinet Quits; Losses Are Blamed

WASHINGTON, April 5—Premier Kuniaki Koiso of Japan, the "Tiger of Korea," and his Cabinet resigned en bloc today, and the senior Japanese statesmen decided to recommend Admiral Baron Kantaro Suzuki, president of the Privy Council, to succeed him. The admiral afterwards saw the Japanese Emperor who instructed him to form a new Cabinet.

After an extraordinary meeting at Koiso's official residence, the "Tiger" proceeded to the Imperial Palace and at 1030 hours tendered the collective resignation of his Cabinet to Emperor Hirohito.

The Tokyo radio announced the resignation and broadcast a statement by Koiso that "the Cabinet has decided to resign en bloc in order to open the way for a far more powerful administration."

The "gravity of the situation," the announcement admitted, was the fundamental cause of the resignation.

Prominent among the war leaders who have opposed Koiso's administration lately is General Jiro Minami, who became president of the recently formed Political Association of Great Japan, the party which superseded the long-dominant Imperial Rule Assistance As-

(Continued on page 8)

Yanks On Okinawa 4 Miles From Naha

GUAM, April 5—Marines and infantrymen of the U. S. 10th Army on Okinawa, driving to within four miles of Naha, capital city, were reported by Admiral Chester W. Nimitz today to have taken 80 square miles of the island.

As men of the 77th Division moved toward Naha, largest city in the Ryukyus, the Japanese were still offering only scattered resistance. Their artillery fire, however, was increasing in volume. American field officers expected to encounter the enemy in strength in front of the vital city.

Along the eastern coast, at Nakagusuku Bay, once a large Japanese fleet anchorage, doughboys of the 7th Division consolidated the positions they won when they cut across the island. By nightfall yesterday the Americans held about 15 miles of shoreline there, the northern end of which was occupied by the Marines of the 3rd Amphibious Corps.

The scattered and ineffectual Japanese defense of Okinawa has enabled the Americans to exceed their invasion schedule and pile up supplies and ammunition ashore to meet the expected stiffening of enemy resistance.

The Okinawa townspeople were reported to have been apathetic. Naval patrols on the east coast picked up two boatloads of civilians trying to escape from the island.

An Associated Press correspondent said that more than 1,000 dirty, mis-

(Continued on page 2)

Officials Seeking Policy Agreements In Preparation For Conference At S. F.

WASHINGTON, April 5 (UP)—High U. S. officials are working at top speed to settle recent Big Three difficulties before the San Francisco conference opens on April 25, well-informed circles here said today.

They are confident of reaching satisfactory solutions and certain that serious breach in the wartime partnership is not in prospect.

The U. S. officials base their confidence on the three points outlined by the Secretary of State, Edward R. Stettinius Jr., in his Chicago address last night:

1. The ability in the past three years of the United States to overcome other far more serious difficulties and dangers.

2. The determination of the United States and each of its Allies to cement in peace the partnership born in wartime.

3. The fact that the extent of the Big Three agreement is far wider and more fundamental than the extent of their differences.

Mr. Stettinius told the Chicago Council of Foreign Relations:

"We face difficulties and dangers whose magnitude it is hardly possible to overestimate. Very active efforts are being made by the United States to resolve the temporary difficulties of a political nature that have recently arisen in connection with the San Francisco conference."

Stettinius said that, because of those efforts, he could not discuss the difficulties which involve Poland, Russia's bid for two autonomous republics, and the Soviet Government's decision not to send its Foreign Minister.

The Secretary of State set the course for U. S. postwar policy by asserting that it would be based on two "hard facts":

First, "If we are to prevent disaster and another war for the United States we must find a means to act effectively with other nations to prevent aggression anywhere in the world."

Second, "We cannot have prosperity in the United States if the rest of the world is sunk in depression and poverty."

To these he added two "realities":

First, "After two World Wars and a terrible worldwide depression, all within the space of 25 years, we are convinced that political isolationism and nationalism are utterly unrealistic and can only lead on to complete disaster for our country and for the world."

Second, "Economic warfare, depressions, hunger, poverty and despair—these are the conditions that undermine democracy and block its development, that breed tyrants and aggressors, and turn nations one

(Continued on page 2)

Russia OKs Change In 'Oaks' Proposal

WASHINGTON, April 5 (AP)—Russia has agreed to accept a change in the Dumbarton Oaks world security proposals, so as to include a resolution that would recognize previous bilateral treaties of mutual assistance, it was learned today. The resolution, it was said, would meet some French demands.

Coupled with other diplomatic developments, the Russian attitude was seen helping to clear the atmosphere for the San Francisco meeting April 25

Adequate Meat Supplies Year After V-E Day Seen

WASHINGTON, April 5 (AP) — An estimate that world meat demand and supply may "strike a balance" within one year after the end of the European war was given to the Senate food-investigating committee today by Lt. Col. Ralph W. Olmstead, chairman of the War Food Administration's allocations committee.

He testified that there is a present deficit of 6,200,000,000 pounds, or 15 percent of standard requirements.

EXTRA

PARIS EDITION

THE STARS AND STRIPES

Daily Newspaper of U.S. Armed Forces in the European Theater of Operations

EXTRA

Vol. 1—No. 260 1 Fr. 1 Fr. Friday, April 13, 1945

ROOSEVELT DIES

FRANKLIN DELANO ROOSEVELT

Cerebral Hemorrhage Is Fatal at Warm Springs

WASHINGTON, April 12.—President Franklin Delano Roosevelt died unexpectedly this afternoon at Warm Springs, Ga., of a cerebral hemorrhage. He was 63 years old.

The 32nd President of the United States, the only Chief Executive in the country's history to be elected four times, died at his winter cottage at 1:53 P.M., Georgia time (8:53 P.M., Paris time).

His death was announced at the White House by Mrs. Eleanor Roosevelt, and other members of his family were called to the capital. A Cabinet meeting was called while Vice-President Harry S. Truman was notified.

The President complained of a very severe headache this morning while an artist was sketching him. In a few minutes, Mr. Roosevelt lost consciousness.

The President had been under the care of Rear Adm. Ross T. McIntyre, his personal physician, for ten days.

The President had carried the burden of the nation's problems longer than any other President in history, and had led the nation at a time of its greatest crises, including the depression that rocked the world after 1929, and the greatest war in history.

The message announcing his death and sent to his four sons in service by Mrs. Roosevelt was: "The President slept away this afternoon. He did his job to the end as he would want to do. Bless you and all our love, Mother."

Funeral Saturday

Funeral services will be held Saturday in the East Room of the White House. Burial will be at Hyde Park Sunday afternoon. The exact time has not yet been decided.

Roosevelt died in the bedroom of his little white bungalow atop Pine Mountain, where he had been visiting for twenty years to take treatment for infantile paralysis, with which he was stricken in 1921.

Only two persons are believed to have been in the cottage at the time of his

(Continued on Page 8)

Truman New President; Faces War, Peace Task

WASHINGTON, April 12.—Vice-President Harry S. Truman, once a Missouri farmboy, was sworn in as the 33rd President of the United States today a few hours after the death of President Roosevelt.

Truman, a FA captain in World War I and a Missouri county judge in 1934, becomes

President Truman's first act after he had been sworn in was to announce that the San Francisco conference would go on as scheduled.

the leader of the nation through the most momentous days in its history.

He will be confronted not only by the problems of winning final victory in a two-front war, but by the gigantic task of working to ensure a lasting peace and directing the transition of America from a war to peace-time economy.

Truman is the seventh man to succeed to the Presidency through the death of an incumbent. He came into prominence when as U.S. senator from Missouri he made a 35,000-mile trip across America to inspect defense plants and Army installations. His report to Congress on the waste he found resulted in the formation of the Truman Committee.

Truman was born at Lamar, Mo., May 8, 1884. When Harry was four his parents moved to a farm near Independence.

HARRY S. TRUMAN

His weak eyes—he wears steel rimmed glasses—cost him an appointment to West Point.

Then he returned to his mother's farm and stayed there for ten years. His mother, now 91, says he could plow the straightest row of corn she ever saw.

Friends say he still lives the simple life of a farmer, rises early and is as homespun as an old shoe. He is modest, an average-looking man with thin lips, glasses, flatly-combed gray hair and a pleasant Missouri twang. He is still a member of the First Baptist Church of Grandview, Mo.

Truman's sole business venture after the war—a haberdashery shop on Kansas City's 12th Street

(Continued on Page 4)

The Soldiers' Loss

The death of President Franklin Delano Roosevelt comes as a personal shock to millions of fighting men.

We have lost at once a great leader and a sincere friend.

As Commander-in-Chief of America's military forces, Mr. Roosevelt has in a few short years welded the manpower and resources of the United States into the greatest fighting machine in world history.

It is a tragedy that he could not have lived to see his work fulfilled in complete victory.

As soldiers, we salute the passing of a great leader and we pledge to our new Commander-in-Chief, Harry S. Truman, continued allegiance to our cause and the promise that we will carry on the fight to final triumph.

Ninth Spans Elbe, 100 Mi. from Reds

Lt. Gen. William H. Simpson's U.S. Ninth Army crossed the Elbe River, last water barrier before Berlin, S & S Correspondent Wade Jones reported from the front last night.

A Reuter flash from Ninth Army placed Gen. Simpson's columns 57 miles from Berlin. There were no further details on the Elbe crossing.

Less than 50 miles southward, armor of Lt. Gen. George S. Patton's U.S. Third Army broke out of the Erfurt sector and drove 46 miles across the Thuringian plain.

The Allied high command dropped a security veil over forward elements of both the Ninth and Third Armies. It was apparent, however, that the new breakthroughs were moving with the speed and power of the dashes out of the Rhine bridgeheads.

Armored lunges by the two armies cut the Nazi corridor remaining between Allied and Russian armies to less than 100 miles and extended a huge pincers whose prongs were from 57 to 70 miles from the German capital.

It was evident from German radio that the new thrusts have

(Continued on Page 4)

9th AF Blasts Parked Planes

P47 Thunderbolts of the Ninth AF destroyed 147 German planes yesterday including 74 of about 360 parked on two airfields near Leipzig. The Eighth AF was grounded for the first time in ten days.

Ninth bombers and fighter-bombers also hit a large ordnance depot, transportation lines, and headquarters of a Wehrmacht general. The latter target was marked by U.S. artillery smoke shells.

First TAF P47s attacked marshalling yards and airfields, destroying 42 German planes on the ground and four in the air

THE STARS AND STRIPES
MEDITERRANEAN

Vol. 2, No. 71, Saturday, April 14, 1945 — Printed in Italy — TWO LIRE

Passing Of Good Neighbor Mourned Throughout World

Push-Off For Berlin Near As Allies Race Through Germany

SHAEF, April 13 — Allied armies raced on, one to two miles an hour, across the German Reich today, capturing upward of 100 cities and towns and cagging between 40,000 and 50,000 Nazi prisoners.

SHAEF announced the U. S. 9th Army had built up a six-mile front on the east bank of the Elbe and a final push-off for Berlin, 60 miles away, was expected hourly.

Late tonight, the BBC said 9th Army elements were within 50 miles of the capital, and the Associated Press said the 9th Army's 83rd Infantry Division is at Barby on the Elbe, south of Magdeburg.

The Berlin radio told its people that American tanks may reach the Nazi capital's outskirts within three days.

Patrols were moving almost within sight of Leipzig, the big rail, commercial and university center 100 miles south of the Nazi capital. The U. S. 1st Army was less than 17 miles to the northwest, and the U. S. 3rd Army was within 24 miles from the southwest. American armor was skirting Halle, the rail center 20 miles northwest.

In Holland, German resistance appeared crumbling fast before a new Canadian offensive that pushed across the IJssel River and stormed Arnhem, where fighting has been in progress for a week. In northwest Germany, the Germans were falling back along a line from Emden to east of Bremen.

In Washington, high Army officials handed the U. S. Senate Military Affairs Committee a statement that all organized fighting in Germany would end within a few days. Names of the Army officials were not disclosed.

In London, delegates to the British Dominions Conference predicted all organized resistance would end by the last of May, except for some pockets, the most substantial one being in Norway. Observers in both Washington and London expected a juncture of American and Russian forces,

(Continued on page 8)

NEW HAND ON THE WHEEL

PRESIDENT HARRY S. TRUMAN

Nation Backs Up Truman As He Tackles Tough Job

WASHINGTON, April 13 (AP)—A dazed and questioning world today watched President Harry S. Truman pick up the war and peace plans that slipped yesterday from the lifeless fingers of President Franklin D. Roosevelt.

President Truman arrived at the White House today at 9 AM. Solemn groups which had gathered near his residence and in the vicinity of the executive mansion watched him as he made the trip from his modest apartment.

The White House, announcing that the President would not officially see the press until Monday, reported that Mr. Truman would meet at 11 AM with Admiral William D. Leahy, Mr. Roosevelt's military adviser; Admiral Ernest J. King, General George C. Marshall, Secretary of War Henry L. Stimson and Secretary of the Navy James V. Forrestal.

The new President proclaimed tomorrow as a day of mourning throughout the nation.

The White House announced tonight that President Truman will make a short speech to both Houses of Congress on Monday. He will later broadcast a brief message to the armed forces on Tuesday night over short wave.

These prospects loomed: Further military talks and a conference with Secretary of State Edward R. Stettinius Jr., on the pressing complications of the world situation.

These transcended such important questions as the likelihood that Mr. Truman will want to meet as soon as possible with Prime Minister Winston Churchill, whom he knows slightly, and Premier Stalin, whom he knows not at all.

But there remained a thousand questions that only time could answer. Some of these were:

Will President Truman continue definitely, without alteration, Mr. Roosevelt's foreign policy?

Can he acquire background to meet soon such pressing issues as those raised in connection with the new coalition government for Po-

(Continued on page 5)

Men At Fronts, Civilians Grieved By Tragic News

A shocked world bowed its head in sorrow yesterday as news of the sudden death of President Franklin Delano Roosevelt on Thursday afternoon spread across the seas and to the far corners of the globe.

Americans were overcome with a sadness such as the nation as a whole has seldom known. In other lands, too, emotions of loss and sadness were shared everywhere as commoner, statesman and king joined in mourning the departed American leader.

In Washington, the new President of the United States, Harry Shippe Truman, spent his first full day on the biggest and toughest job in America with a heavy heart. He began immediately to carry out the plans laid down by his former chief.

Back home, the nation went into mourning, with all official entertainments canceled and with flags flying at half mast everywhere. Throughout the world where Americans in uniform were fighting and working, periods of mourning were begun.

The heart of America was muted. On the fighting fronts American soldiers—who had received the tragic news with stunned surprise—drove the more vigorously into the battle. Soldiers and sailors, many of whom could scarcely remember any other President, paused for a moment to hear the news and to express their sense of personal loss.

Messages of deepest sorrow and sympathy poured into the White House from farmers, schoolboys, girls, factory workers, servicemen and political leaders from every corner of the nation. The messages came from all the United Nations and the neutrals.

Prime Minister Winston Churchill and Marshal Joseph Stalin, the two men with whom President Roosevelt collaborated to chart a blueprint for victory and enduring peace, sent messages to President Truman and to Mrs. Roosevelt. Pope Pius XII, King George VI and countless other temporal and spiritual leaders expressed their sorrow.

For the first time in its history, the House of Commons in London adjourned in deference to the head of another state. Churchill spoke

(Continued on page 2)

Great Leader Lost, Gen. Marshall Says

WASHINGTON, April 13 (ANS)—General of the Army George C. Marshall, Chief of Staff, in a special message to Army personnel on the death of the President, said today "We have lost a great leader."

Secretary of War Henry L. Stimson, Navy Secretary James V. Forrestal and Fleet Admiral Ernest J. King also mourned Roosevelt as a friend and leader.

General Marshall's statement added: "His far-seeing wisdom in military counsel has been a constant source of courage to all of us who have worked side by side with him from the dark days of the war's beginning.

"No tribute from the Army could be so eloquent as the hourly record of victories of the past few weeks."

Mr. Stimson said:

"We have lost a great President and great Commander in Chief. Throughout these years of crisis when the nation was plunged into war by powerful enemies, the faith and dauntless courage of Franklin Roosevelt have never faltered nor has the broad vision with which he supported his military commanders ever failed. He believed unswervingly that the right and strength of free nations would triumph over the evils of despotism. The American people have upheld his faith. The friendly warmth of his spirit has been an inspiration to soldiers of all ranks. Encouragement in dark days was a reward in the time of victory. We shall do

(Continued on page 5)

5th, 8th Moving Ahead In Northern Italy Battles

By ED HILL
Staff Correspondent

WITH THE 15TH ARMY GROUP, April 13—Allied troops hammered both flanks of the Italian front yesterday, scoring significant gains in the Adriatic sector and continuing their drive up the Ligurian Highway toward La Spezia.

Biggest gains on the 8th Army front were in the vicinity of Massa Lombarda which we captured late last night. Our troops pushed on to take San Patrizio, three miles to the north, plus the bridgehead town of Mordano.

Resistance south of Lake Comacchio, where units of the 8th Army had landed behind German forward positions on Wednesday, was described as "partially disorganized" in the official communique issued at the headquarters of General Mark W. Clark.

British troops in this sector were beyond captured Menate and Longastrino. They were reported halfway to Bastia, some six miles due west of Menate and four miles southeast of Argenta on Highway 16, the main route to Ferrara. The Reno River parallels the highway at Bastia.

Farther south, 8th Army forces met stiffer German opposition, and fierce fighting continued in all three Santerno River bridgeheads. The Germans threw in Tiger tanks in a desperate effort to halt the drive, but counterattacks were beaten off and the bridgeheads steadily expanded.

An important advance was reported from the upper Santerno Valley, where Italian troops of the 8th Army and Partisans pushed up to 4,000 yards along both sides of the valley, following the capture of Tossignano. Tossignano lies on a secondary road approximately seven miles south of Imola, situated on

(Continued on page 8)

Fight In Reich May End In Few Days, Army Says

WASHINGTON, April 13 (AP)—High Army officials told Senators today that the end of organized fighting in Germany probably will come within a few days.

Describing the pell-mell dash of the U. S. Armies across Germany, general staff officers expressed the opinion to members of the Senate Military Committee that a collapse of Nazi arms is imminent.

Those who attended the conference said that the Army chiefs were so sure of the results that orders have been drawn up drastically reducing shipments of durable equipment to Europe in preparation to reversing the flow to the Pacific.

Allied Nations Leaders Pay Roosevelt Tribute

WASHINGTON, April 13 — To Mrs. Roosevelt and President Truman, American military leaders and a nation in deepest sorrow and mourning the world today paid tribute to Franklin Delano Roosevelt.

The leaders of Allied nations, stunned and saddened at the loss of their great good friend, sent messages of unqualified praise of Mr. Roosevelt's work, his wisdom, courage and achievements.

From **WINSTON CHURCHILL**, to Mrs. Roosevelt: "I send my most profound sympathy in your grievous loss. It is also the loss of the British nation and of the cause of freedom in every land. I feel so deeply for you all. As for myself, I have lost a dear and cherished friendship which was forged in the fire of war. I trust you may find consolation in the glory of his name and the magnitude of his work."

MARSHAL JOSEPH STALIN addressed separate messages to Mrs. Roosevelt and President Truman. His telegram to Mrs. Roosevelt read: "Please accept my sincere condolences on the occasion of the death of your husband and the expression of my sincere sympathy for your great sorrow. The Soviet people highly valued Roosevelt as a great organizer in the struggle of freedom-loving nations against the common enemy and the leader in the cause ensuring security for the whole world."

Stalin's message to the new President was: "The government of the Soviet Union expresses its sincere sympathy to the American people for their great loss and the conviction that the policy of friendship between the great powers who have shouldered the main burden against the common enemy will continue to develop in the future."

GENERALISSIMO CHIANG KAI-SHEK sent condolences to Mrs. Roosevelt and said the news was

(Continued on page 2)

THE STARS AND STRIPES
MEDITERRANEAN

Vol. 1, No. 231, Tuesday, April 17, 1945 Printed In Italy TWO LIRE

All-Out Italy Push Under Way

Five More Miles To Cut Reich In Two

Units Of U. S. 3rd Near Czech Border; 7th In Nuremberg

SHAEF, April 16—The U. S. 3rd Army had but five miles to go tonight to reach the Czechoslovakian border and cut Germany in two.

Armored columns rolled into the town of Hof, midway between Bayreuth and Plausen, against relatively little resistance as the southern wing of the 85-mile Allied line in central Germany continued to surge forward. The advance cut the last direct road of any kind between the central German cities of Berlin, Dresden and Leipzig and the south German cities of Nuremberg and Munich.

Tonight only by crossing western Czechoslovakia could the Germans move from the northern part of their own country to their reported hide-outs in the south Bavarian mountains.

Late in the day, Lt. Gen. Alexander Patch's 7th Army entered the outskirts of Nuremberg, the south German city that Hitler made into a Nazi political center.

Fall of Nuremberg would be a severe blow to German morale, since the city had become a Nazi shrine. All Nazi party conventions since Hitler came to power were held there.

U. S. 3rd Army forces were within 45 miles of Dresden. Other American troops surrounded Leipzig and Halle, fought at the outskirts of Chemnitz, and in the streets of Magdeburg. To the north, the British 2nd Army battled SS troops in Bremen streets and engaged German troops in a major battle at Ulzen, midway between the Weser and Elbe Rivers.

Throughout the day German artillery shelled U. S. 9th Army troops assembling on the Elbe's east bank for the final push to Berlin, 45 miles away.

SHAEF announced that all bridgeheads, except the one the 2nd Armored Division had to relinquish yesterday, were being held.

Just south of the 9th Army, columns of the U. S. 1st Army pushed far beyond Leipzig. They reached the Mulde River at two points—

(Continued on page 8)

TOO CLOSE FOR COMFORT

Men of the 10th Mountain Division hit the ground as a German mortar shell lands nearby during the opening of the 5th Army offensive. (Staff Photo by Pvt. Joe Redmond)

Truman Links His Aims With Ideals Of Roosevelt

WASHINGTON, April 16 (UP)—President Harry S. Truman today addressed a joint session of Congress with a "win the war" and "win the peace" statement on the new Administration's policies.

In his first appearance before Congress, the new President assured the world that he would support and defend President Roosevelt's ideals "with all my strength and all my heart."

"Our demand," he declared in a portion of his address devoted to immediate war aims, "has been and remains unconditional surrender."

"Both Germany and Japan can be certain beyond a shadow of doubt that America will continue to fight for freedom until no vestige of resistance remains," he said. He commented that "we are deeply conscious of the fact that much hard fighting is still ahead of us."

Congress gave a terrific ovation to Mr. Truman. The galleries were filled to capacity and the entire diplomatic corps listened to his 15-minute statement.

"It is with a heavy heart that I stand before you in Congress," he said. "At times like this, words are inadequate.

"Yesterday we laid at rest the mortal remains of President Roosevelt and the most eloquent tribute would be reverent silence.

"Yet, in this decisive hour our silence might be misunderstood and might be of comfort to our enemies. A tragic fate has thrust upon us grave responsibilities, but we must carry on. Our departed leader never looked backward, he always looked forward and moved forward. That is what he would want us to do and that is what America will do.

"So much blood has already been shed for our cherished ideals that we dare not permit even a momentary pause in our hard fight for victory.

"Today the entire world is looking to America for enlightened leadership to peace and progress. Such leadership requires vision, courage and tolerance, and can be provided only by a united nation deeply devoted to its highest ideals.

"To settle for merely another temporary respite would be sure to jeopardize future security of all the world. We will not traffic with

(Continued on page 2)

Big Red Army Push Started, Hitler Says

LONDON, April 16—The Red Army has begun its all-out push on Berlin, the Nazi High Command announced today. Lending credence to the report, not yet confirmed in Moscow, was an urgent order of the day issued today by Adolf Hitler to his armies on the east front.

"For the last time," Hitler's order began, "the Jewish Bolshevist arch enemy has hurled his masses into attack. He is trying to pulverize Germany and exterminate our people."

Then Hitler went on to describe in scarifying terms what a victorious Red Army would do to Germans, and he laid emphasis on the fate in store for German women, maidens and children.

In an obvious effort to get the Wehrmacht and Volkssturm to fight, Hitler's order painted not only his version of horrors to come, if the Russians were successful, but promised that fresh men and material

(Continued on page 8)

26 Kraut Divisions Are Seen Destined For Final Defeat

By ED HILL
Staff Correspondent

WITH THE 15TH ARMY GROUP, April 16—Two Allied armies threw their full weight against the Germans in the Po Valley today, keeping the Yalta promise of an assault from the south, in a combined all-out offensive aimed at total destruction of an estimated 26 Nazi divisions in northern Italy.

Vastly superior in the air, bolstered by a favorable margin of tanks and heavy guns, battlewise troops of the International 15th Army Group struck hard in a blow designed to destroy or capture the Nazis before they could withdraw beyond the Po River, their next natural defense line.

Field Marshal Sir Harold R. L. G. Alexander, Supreme Allied Commander of the Mediterranean Theater, and General Mark W. Clark, commanding the 15th Army Group, issued Orders of the Day revealing the start of the long-awaited spring drive. They predicted that the assault might produce the final defeat of the disintegrating Wehrmacht.

"Final victory is near," Marshal Alexander told the troops. "The German forces are now very groggy and only need one mighty punch to knock them out for good. The moment has now come for us to take the field for the last battle which will end the war in Europe."

General Clark called on the fighting men to give "the full measure of your devotion to your countries and to the Allied cause."

"Hit them with all you've got," he said. "And with God's help we will have a decisive and perhaps a final victory."

The Army commanders—Lt. Gen. Lucian K. Truscott Jr., of the 5th and Lt. Gen. Richard L. McCreery of the 8th—also urged utter destruction of the enemy in Orders of the Day read to units under their command.

The tension apparent along the entire Italian front for nearly one week was released early today when 5th Army forces jumped off against

(Continued on page 8)

MTO's Topmost Leaders Signal 'All-Out' Drive

AFHQ, April 16—That the Allied offensive against the Germans in north Italy has reached the "all-out" level of intensity was signalized here today by a series of four Orders of the Day issued by the Mediterranean Theater's topmost commanders.

The Orders came from Field Marshal Sir Harold R. L. G. Alexander, Supreme Allied Commander of this theater; from General Mark W Clark, commanding the 15th Army Group; from Lt. Gen. Lucian K. Truscott Jr., commanding the 5th Army; and from Lt. Gen. Sir Richard L. McCreery, commanding the British 8th Army.

The text of Marshal Alexander's Order, directed to soldiers, sailors, and airmen of the Allied forces in this theater, follows:

"Final victory is near. The German forces are now very groggy and only need one mighty punch to knock them out for good. The moment has now come for us to take the field for the last battle which will end the war in Europe. You know what our comrades in the west and in the east are doing on the battlefields. It is now our turn to play our decisive part. It will not be a walk-over; a mortally wounded beast can still be very dangerous. You must be prepared for a hard and bitter fight; but the end is quite certain—there is not the slightest shadow of doubt about that. You, who have won every battle you have fought, are going to win this last one.

"Forward, then, into battle—with confidence, faith and determination to see it through to the end. Godspeed and good luck to you all."

The text of General Clark's Order of the Day to his troops follows:

"Fifteenth Army Group is resuming the offensive with the object of

(Continued on page 2)

British Complaints Make U. S. Discard Burma Film

LONDON, April 16 (AP) — A U. S.-made film of the Burma campaign, directed by Col. Frank Capra and produced at the special request of Admiral Lord Louis Mountbatten has been scrapped following complaints by British military authorities that the film was "completely unfair" to British troops and "suggests that most of the Burma fighting has been done by United States troops."

Ground forces in Burma are predominately British, authorities said.

10th Mountain Battles Grimly To Clear Ridge

By Sgt. STAN SWINTON
Staff Correspondent

WITH U. S. FORCES ATTACKING WEST OF HIGHWAY 64, April 15 (Delayed)—The 5th Army's wild central front exploded into full-scale action today as mountain-wise troops of the 10th Division fought the toughest infantry battles in their combat experience to clear the two-mile length of jagged Raffeno ridge.

By dusk tonight the mountaineers had seized Rocca di Roffeno, bare-crested 2,889-foot pyramid four miles west of Highway 64; Hill 903, a 2,934-foot knob 1,500 yards to the northwest, and Hill 913, the 2,970-foot peak 1,500 yards farther west which dominates the entire ridge line.

The wrecked villages of Torre Iussi, Le Ville, Roffeno Misiolo and Casigno, all located in the green valley south of Roffeno ridge—which was a strongpoint-dotted no man's land until this morning—have been cleared.

It has been a grim battle from the start, despite the support of massed artillery which threw more than 30,000 shells up to 1800 hours and despite day-long assistance from fighter-bombers. German infantrymen, who refuse to be driven from their shell and bomb-ripped strongpoints, are contesting every advance with intense small arms and mortar fire despite the eerie silence of their own artillery.

Fields of Teller mines, laced by high and low trip wires, have slowed up the advance. Casualties among engineers clearing them have been bloody—50 percent in one operation—and limited armor support to direct fire missions.

A few Germans have surrendered —18 came out behind a white flag

(Continued on page 2)

THE STARS AND STRIPES

AFRICA-MIDDLE EAST

VOL. III No. 16 | CAIRO | FOUR CENTS | APRIL 20, 1945

...Yet Shall He Live...

A New York State policeman stands guard at the grave of President Roosevelt following burial. (OWI Radiophoto)

Roosevelt Laid to Rest in Beloved Rose Garden of Hyde Park Ancestral Home

HYDE PARK — On a bright spring Sunday morning Franklin D. Roosevelt was laid to rest in the soil of the Hudson River home where, in retirement, he had hoped to relish his well-loved role of "country squire."

The 31st President of the United States lies in a hemlock-hedged rose garden between the house he was born in and the Library which houses his state papers and which he had aready given to the nation.

Mrs. Roosevelt and their only two children to be present at the funeral and burial services, Elliott and Anna, stood at the foot of the grave facing the Rev. Anthony, rector of the church at Hyde Park where the President had been senior warden for many years.

Behind her stood the wives of the four Roosevelt sons and behind them President and Mrs. Harry S. Truman.

Eldest Son Too Late

Others in the garden included members of the Roosevelt cabinet, the Supreme Court, Congressional leaders and war advisers, the White House staff, Sir Anthony Eden, Britain's Foreign Secretary who represented Prime Minister Churchill, Canada's Prime Minister MacKenzie King, Gov. Thomas E. Dewey of New York who had opposed President Roosevelt in the 1944 campaign, Bernard Baruch, the British Amassador Lord Halifax and the Earl of Athlone, the Governor General of Canada, on whose Campobello Island the Roosevelt's long have had a home.

Marine Col. James Roosevelt, the eldest of the four sons, arrived in New York after a ten-thousand-mile flight from Manila 90 minutes too late for his father's burial.

Bombers, fighters and training planes of the Air Forces the President had done so much to build up circled overhead. An honor guard lined the hemlock hedge around the quarter-acre garden

"I am the resurrection and the life," began Dr. Anthony from the Episcopal Church's traditional Burial of the Dead. "He that believeth in me, though he were dead,

(See HYDE PARK on Page 12)

Text of Truman's Message To the Fighting Forces

WASHINGTON—President Truman called on America's fighting forces to march with him down the road to victory laid out by the late Franklin D. Roosevelt. He spoke from the small reception room on the lower level of the White House, a room used for years by President Roosevelt for his famous "fireside chats."

His speech, carried by shortwave around the globe, follows:

"To the Armed Forces of the United States throughout the world:

"After the tragic news of the death of out late commander-in-chief it was my duty to speak promptly to the Congress and the Armed Forces of the United States

"Yesterday, I addressed the Congress. Now I speak to you.

"I am especially anxious to talk to you for I know that all of you felt a tremendous shock as we did at home when our commander-in-chief fell.

"Friend of Services" Lost

"All of us have lost a great leader, a far-sighted statesman and a real friend of democracy. You have lost a hard-hitting chief and an old friend of the services.

"Our hearts are heavy. However, the cause which claimed Roosevelt also claims us. He never faltered. Nor will we.

"I have done as you do in the field when the commander falls. My duties and responsibilities are clear. I have assumed them. These duties will be carried on in keeping with our American tradition.

"As a veteran of the first World War I have seen death on the battlefield. When I fought in France with the 35th Division I saw good officers and men fall and be replaced.

"I know that this is also true of the officers and men of the other services, the Navy, the Marine Corps, the Coast Guard and Merchant Marine.

Debt To Fighting Men

"I know the strain, the mud, the misery, the utter weariness of the soldier in the field. And I know, too, his courage, his stamina and his faith in his comrades, his country and himself.

"We are depending on each and every one of you.

"Yesterday, I said to the Congress and I repeat it now:

"'Our debt to the heroic men and valiant women in the service of our country can never be repaid. They have earned our undying gratitude. America will never forget their sacrifices. Because of these sacrifices the dawn of justice and freedom throughout the world slowly casts its gleam across

(See TRUMAN on Page 12)

899,390

WASHINGTON—Casualty figures for the U.S. armed forces have reached 899,390, of which 196,669 have lost their lives, the War Dept. revealed.

The Army's share of the dead is 159,267 and the Navy's including Marines and Coast Guard is 37,402.

12-PAGE EDITION

To provide adequate news coverage of the death of the President, Stars and Stripes has increased its size to 12 pages, and omitted all regular features.

Yanks are Across Elbe After Bitter Fighting

Tank-powered advances by the western Allies ripped deeper into the half-conquered Reich this week with the Ninth Army carving a costly Elbe bridgehead within 51 miles of Berlin and the pace of Eisenhower's armies being slowed: 1) because of stretched supply lines; 2) because of last-ditch resistance in the besieged cities of Bremen, Madgeburg, Dessau, Halle, Leipzig, Chemnitz and Nurenberg.

Advances made by the four American armies on the eastern perimeter (no news has yet been released on Gerow's Fifteenth) were bold, dashing strokes on the map. The array of armies is now one interlocked frontline force overrunning the shattered Wehrmacht.

At the northern end the Canadians pressed a V-shaped drive against Holland's North Sea coast. A little to the east the British are hammering a fan of spearheads straight northward, one outside Oldenburg, another into Bremen, a zy-passing third within 18 miles of Hamburg.

Facing Berlin the U.S. Ninth Army swept to the Elbe and spread out along its west bank from Magdeburg up 65 miles to Wittenburg, with an 8 by 10 mile bridgehead below Magdeburg. Hodges' First Army is stalled in its advance to the Elbe by the obstacle cities of Dessau, Halle and Leipzig. It is reported that Third Army tanks slashed across the border of Czechoslovakia and bisected the Reich while the Seventh in the south penetrated Nurenberg.

Battle for Magdeburg

With an all-out assault coordinated with the air arm, Gen. Simpson made the first real attempt to seize Magdeburg last week although he had reached it the week before. Ninth Army infantrymen stalked through the trees rimming the city while tanks raced forward after the second refusal of 36-year-old Nazi General Regner to accept an ultimatum for surrender.

According to UP correspondent Robert Vermillion, the Second Armored and Thirtieth Infantry Divisions cleared the western sector of the Elbe-divided city in a battle of "men against boys". Americans fought for six hours through the rubbled streets against the fanatical resistance of 14 to 18-year-old members of the Hitler Jugend who manned the road-blocks and building stumps.

After a four-day silence was lifted on the Ninth Army's Second

(See YANKS ACROSS on Page 12)

Nine Red Armies Drive on Berlin, Report Germans

While a strict security blackout blankets the entire Oder front, the all-out Russian drive to reach Berlin and link-up with the Americans is furiously underway, according to the Germans.

For the past six days, Radio Berlin has crackled constantly with reports of the big offensive, which it alleges is clutching at Berlin from the northeast, east and southeast. According to German estimates, the Russians are throwing nine armies, including 2,500,000 men, toward the German capital.

Driving south from Wriezen and west from Seelow, forward Russian units have purportedly advanced within 17 miles of Greater Berlin.

Moscow is completely silent. But one Red army dispatch from the Oder front tended to substantiate week-long German reports. It stated that Russian troops are within eyesight of burning Berlin. There was no elaboration on the brief message.

In Moscow itself, there is an air of great expectancy and good-natured betting over who will arrive in Berlin first—the Russians or the Americans.

Solid Wall

The Germans declared that Red army units have merged Oder bridgeheads east of the capital into one solid 45-mile wall, all but isolating Frankfurt. Breaks through defenses west of Kuestrin and north of Wriezen were admitted.

The Nazis said that the Red Army opened initial attacks last Saturday with a terrifying barrage of 6-inch artillery guns near

(See RED ARMIES on Page 12)

Jap Bullet Confirms 'Hunch'; Ernie Pyle Killed in Action

WASHINGTON—Just as he said he would be, Ernie Pyle has been killed in action.

America's best-loved and most widely-read war correspondent was killed instantly by Japanese machine gun fire Tuesday on Ie Shima, a small, Japanese-held island off Okinawa.

He had been standing beside the regimental commander of headquarters troops of the 77th Army Division; so he died as he had lived these past years—with the foot soldier whose curse of battle's dirt and grime he had shared in Africa, Sicily, Italy, France and Germany.

The slight, balding fellow whose millions of readers well knew he was haunted by a premonition of death, had gone to the Pacific with the Navy two months ago after a brief rest in the States from his years in Europe. He had landed with one of the first waves of Marines on Okinawa. But by a cun-

(See ERNIE PYLE on Page 12)

Man Spricht Deutsch
Treten Sie ab.
Trayten Zee up.
You are dismissed.

PARIS EDITION
THE STARS AND STRIPES
Daily Newspaper of U.S. Armed Forces in the European Theater of Operations

Ici On Parle Français
Dépêchez-vous!
Day-pesh-ay-voo!
Hurry up!

Vol. 1—No. 270 | 1 Fr. | 1 Fr. | Monday, April 23, 1945

Street Battles Raging Inside Blazing Berlin

Allies Drive On German Stronghold

Three American Armies, pushing to the south, were driving full on Hitler's National Redoubt in Southern Germany yesterday. On the central front, link up between Russians who have outflanked Berlin and Potsdam and U.S. forces was reported imminent by Press Association dispatches.

In the north, Field Marshal Sir Bernard L. Montgomery's British and Canadian armies tightened the squeeze on areas of enemy defenses in western Holland and around the North Sea ports of Bremen and Hamburg.

Drive On Focal Points

It was evident from all reports that the Allies were driving to stamp out the north and south focal points of German resistance which would be left when the Reich is cut in half by the linkup.

War correspondents with Lt. Gen. William H. Simpson's U.S. Ninth Army were told yesterday that the junction would not be officially disclosed when it occurred.

Instead, Reuter reported, it would be announced by the governments of the United States, Great Britain and the Soviet Union as a United Nations announcement.

Reports that the linkup had been made by patrols somewhere east of the Elbe persisted, but were not confirmed by any authoritative source.

An American radio correspondent speaking from Gen. Omar N. Brad-

(Continued on Page 8)

DutchStarving, Deaths on Rise

SOMEWHERE IN FREE NETHERLANDS, April 22 (UP).—Three and a half-million Hollanders still in German-occupied territory face starvation unless relief comes within two weeks, according to military government officials.

A statement based on reports smuggled through the German lines reveals that people in the industrial areas of Amsterdam, Rotterdam, The Hague and Utrecht have been living since midwinter on a weekly ration consisting of four ounces of potatoes and four ounces of bread. Food from which these rations are drawn is expected to be exhausted by May 1.

Reports of deaths in western Holland are pouring in so fast that it has become impossible to keep an accurate record. Military officials say there is not a single child under one year left alive.

12 Nationalities Form Allied Armies in Italy

ROME, April 22.—Allied troops fighting in Italy probably constitute the greatest array of nationalities ever welded into a united striking force. They include:

Poles, Italians, Jugoslavs, American whites and Negroes, Brazilians, British, New Zealanders, South Africans, Ghurkas, Greeks, Zionists and French.

Nazis in Italy Flee Toward Po River Line

ROME, April 22 (UP).—German forces in eastern Italy today were in full flight toward the Po River as the entire Adriatic flank of their trans-peninsula line gave way under the pounding of the Allied Fifth and Eighth Armies.

Latest reports to AFHQ, admittedly hours behind the actual situation, said U.S. Fifth Army infantry and South African tankmen were 20 miles northwest of Bologna, capture of which yesterday caused the collapse of Nazi Col. Gen. Heinrich von Vietinghoff's eastern line.

Strafe Retreating Nazis

Although no towns were named in today's communique, a 20-mile dash from Bologna to the northwest would place the Allies within two miles of Modena, key junction on the ancient Via Emilia leading to the upper Po Valley. The enemy was forced to use this and other secondary roads since the direct route northeast through Ferrara is threatened by Eighth Army troops driving from the east.

Allied aircraft were strafing and bombing the long columns of enemy armor, transport and marching men as they clogged the roads leading to the Po River, where they are expected to wheel and put up a fight. Ahead of them, other Allied planes bombed bridges and ferries across the river.

Drive on Ferrara

Behind the retreating Germans came Allied infantry and tanks, smashing rearguards in their race to catch up with the main body of the enemy.

The Eighth Army's thrust toward Ferrara was still meeting some opposition, but last reports placed Allied troops within seven miles of the city and moving ahead steadily. Ferrara, which lies five miles south of the Po River, is the hub of the intricate road and rail network between Bologna and the Po.

Separatists, Students Clash in Palermo Riot

ROME, April 22 (Reuter).—Thousands of students were stoned by Sicilian separatists today in Palermo as they demonstrated in favor of retention of Trieste by Italy.

The students forced a police cordon around the building housing separatist headquarters, evicted the occupants and hoisted the Italian flag.

Soviet Troops 4 Miles From Unter Den Linden

Russian troops fighting inside Berlin yesterday were only four miles from Unter Den Linden, in the heart of the city, the German High Command reported as Soviet guns poured explosives into the capital's burning streets. After a night in which Russian heavy bombers roared over the Nazi capital, setting 50 large fires, thousands of Soviet artillery pieces ranging from siege guns to mortars pounded Berlin's crumbling remains, dispatches reaching Moscow said.

Russian troops in Berlin, by German admission, were fighting four miles east of Unter den Linden, in the city's heart.

From the east, northeast and southeast, the Russians were said to be driving toward the city's heart, and the Germans reported bitter fighting in the Lichtenberg area, four miles east of the city's center, and at Niederschoenhausen, four miles north of the center. Lichtenberg is five miles inside greater Berlin and Niederschoenhausen is three miles inside.

Unofficial frontline dispatches partly confirmed Nazi reports that the Russians were advancing across the ringbahn circular railway which runs around Berlin's administrative center. One dispatch said the Reds were driving along Landsberger and Frankfurter Allee, main highways, in a converging movement toward the city's heart.

Soviet dispatches told of fanatical German resistance in the blazing streets. The Nazis were throwing in all kinds of forces—detachments with both officers and enlisted men in the ranks, units

(Continued on Page 8)

Freed S & S Writer Describes Eastward Surge of Ex-PWs

This is the second of four articles by Sgt. Thomas Hoge, Stars and Stripes correspondent who was captured by the Germans after he participated in the Holland airborne operation last September. He escaped to Russian lines and is now in Italy.

By Tom Hoge

SOMEWHERE IN POLAND, EN ROUTE TO RUSSIA, March 5 (Delayed).—Swarming out of eastern Germany through Poland, and advancing in ever larger hordes towards the Russian border for the last six weeks, has progressed one of the strangest pilgrimages of all time.

By Bicycle, Horse, Foot They Surge Eastward

GIs—thousands of them—along with legions of French, Italians and Jugoslavs, all liberated from Nazi prison camps by the Russian advance, are moving by bicycle, horseback and on foot in a vast surge eastward, striving to find a way to their homelands.

The pace is slow and painful across frozen plains and through devastated villages. Strafing planes are a continual threat along the open stretches, and snipers vary the monotony in the towns.

The wanderers live an existence that runs from rags to riches.

In German-evacuated Landsberg, GIs given the run of the town by the Russian garrison, slept in lofty luxury flats, between silk sheets, and munched anchovy sandwiches as they wandered through the panelled suites in search of souvenirs.

In Poland's threadbare Sagen, bled white after five years of Ger-

(Continued on Page 8)

$200,000 Price Put On 'Queens' by Hitler

LONDON, April 22 (UP).—Adolf Hitler offered $200,000 and highest Reich honors to the U-boat crew which could sink one or both of Britain's great liners—the Queen Mary and the Queen Elizabeth—according to the London Daily Express. In five and a half years the ships have transported more than a million troops.

Russians Ring Berlin, Occupy Half of Capital

Man Spricht Deutsch
Was verstecken Sie da?
Vahs ferstecken Zee da?
What are you hiding there?

PARIS EDITION
THE STARS AND STRIPES
Daily Newspaper of U.S. Armed Forces in the European Theater of Operations

Today's Russian Lesson
Ya a-mee-ree-ka-neets.
I am an American.

Vol. 1—No. 273 | 1 Fr. | 1 Fr. | Thursday, April 26, 1945

Reich Army Smashed, Allied Chiefs Proclaim

The disintegration of the German army as a unified fighting force was announced by Supreme Headquarters yesterday as the British smashed into Bremen in the north and American tanks rolled toward the National Redoubt in the south, reaching points 18 miles from the Austrian border.

On the central sector, UP frontline reports said, a linkup of American and Russian forces was expected yesterday. Detailed instructions were issued to line units for the junction as the world's two biggest military forces moved together, crushing between them the remnant of what once was the world's strongest military machine.

The Supreme Headquarters announcement said that the German Army has ceased to exist as an integrated fighting force and that Hitler's government now controls only a few pockets of resistance in the Reich

Allies Sealing Off Redoubt

Three Allied armies, advancing along a 200-mile arc from the Rhine to the Czech frontier, were sealing off the Redoubt from the north and west. Allied air power struck at railyards at Berchtesgaden, gateway to the Bavarian fortress, and hammered the mighty Skoda munitions plant at Pilsen, Czechoslovakia, to isolate the Redoubt battlefield.

The Stars and Stripes Patrick Mitchell said the 11th Armd. Div. of Lt. Gen George S. Patton's U.S. Third Army rammed 15 miles southeast in a drive paralleling the Czech border to reach a point 18 miles from pre-war Austria. On the western curve of the arc, forces of Gen. Jean de Lattre de Tassigny's French First Army crossed the Rhine at Kembs, in southern Alsace, and reached the Swiss frontier.

In the center of the drive, the 12th Armd. Div. of Lt. Gen. Alexander M Patch's U.S. Seventh Army fanned out from its Danube River bridgehead and reached the autobahn to Augsburg at a point 20 miles east of Ulm.

Luxembourg radio reported Seventh Army forces had entered Augsburg, 50 miles from Munich,

(Continued on Page 8)

Red Army Holds Half Of Capital

Encirclement of doomed Berlin was announced last night by Marshal Stalin.

In an order of the day, Stalin said that forces under Marshal Gregory Zhukov and Marshal Ivan Koniev had linked up northwest of Potsdam, some 15 miles southwest of the German capital's center.

As the Russians thus cut off the city from outside aid and prevented the flight of trapped Nazi officials, Soviet tanks and infantrymen were little more than a mile from Unter den Linden and Moscow radio said more than half the total area of greater Berlin had been captured.

According to Nazi propagandists, Hitler still was in the city, which frontline reports described as a blazing bulk of smashed buildings.

The Germans claimed a three-mile escape gap to the west of the doomed capital still remained between Span-

(Continued on Page 8)

Berlin Ex-Mayor Seized

WITH FIRST U.S. ARMY, April 25 (Reuter).—A former mayor of Berlin, fleeing through the corridor between Russian and American troops, was captured today by the Second U.S. Infantry Division.

Baseball Czar Post Goes to Sen. Chandler

CLEVELAND, April 25—Sen. Albert B. "Happy" Chandler (D-Ky) yesterday was unanimously elected to succeed the late Judge Kenesaw Mountain Landis as high commissioner of baseball. He signed a seven-year contract at $50,000 a year.

(For complete details see page 6)

Some Soldiers, In Four Years, To Be Released

WASHINGTON, April 25 (AP).—The Army plans to start releasing some men this summer who will have been in uniform four to five years, it was learned today

This release policy, which may preclude any marked cut in draft calls after June 30, was disclosed in official but publicity-shy quarters today. The Army yesterday formally announced plans to honor discharge requests of enlisted men 42 and over

By next month a considerable number of Uncle Sam's "emergency soldiers" will have spent five years in the service. Vigorous recruiting began in May 1940 and Selective Service began drafting in November of that year

The policy of discharging veterans of four and five years' service is expected to get under way around

(Continued on Page 8)

Dr. Butler, 83, Resigns As Columbia President

NEW YORK, April 25 (ANS)—Dr Nicholas Murray Butler, 83, one of the nation's foremost educators, has resigned as president of Columbia University. His resignation is effective Oct 1, the 44th anniversary of his presidency

United Nations Parley Opens, Seeks League to Guard Peace

SAN FRANCISCO, April 25.—An historic effort to create world machinery to prevent war began this afternoon in the San Francisco Opera House, where delegates from 46 United Nations gathered in the midst of the bloodiest war civilization has ever known.

Despite the dispute between the U.S and Britain, on one hand, and Russia, on the other, on the Polish question, the conference opened on a harmonious note. Secretary of State Edward R. Stettinius Jr. announced that the U.S., Russia, Britain and China had agreed to support specific proposals that international differences be settled "with due regard for the principles of justice and international law."

Stettinius, head of the American

(Continued on Page 3)

Officer Faces Trial on Drugs

An American officer will be tried by court martial in Paris next month on a charge of selling penicillin in the black market, it was learned at the office of the Judge Advocate according to United Press

The officer, unidentified, is said to be a doctor who sold the tubes at $80 each to French civilians. A penicillin tube brings $500 in the black market

The French government revealed that penicillin is being sold on the black market at 300 times its normal price, and threatened "unusually severe measures against the culprit." The French are beginning to manufacture their own penicillin, after receiving U.S. Army supplies.

Britain to Get U.S. Wines

LONDON, April 25 (INS).—Agencies have made arrangements to market American wines in Britain

Fifth, Eighth Armies Gain From Po River Bridgehead

ROME, April 25 (UP)—From a 50-mile bridgehead on the north bank of the Po River Allied Fifth and Eighth Army troops today were driving toward Verona and the Brenner Pass backdoor to Hitler's Bavarian redoubt.

It became increasingly apparent as the Allies fanned out through the rolling Po Valley that the Nazi high command in Italy, already groggy from the loss of a third of its fighting strength, was trying desperately to pull as many troops as it could through the Alps. Enemy columns clogging the roads to the northeast were under constant attack from Allied aircraft, which have so far destroyed 4,000 vehicles and killed hundreds of German soldiers.

Objectives in the advance beyond the Po for troops sweeping into

(Continued on Page 8)

PARIS EDITION

THE STARS AND STRIPES

Daily Newspaper of U.S. Armed Forces in the European Theater of Operations

Man Spricht Deutsch
Ruehrt Euch nicht vom Platz.
Rewrt Oych nisht fom Plahtz.
Don't make a move.

Today's Russian Lesson
G-deh sahl-da-tih?
Where are the soldiers?

Vol. 1—No. 275 | 1 Fr. | 1 Fr. | Saturday, April 28, 1945

1st ARMY YANKS LINK WITH REDS

American First Army infantrymen and Russian troops have linked in the heart of Germany, cutting the Reich in two. The junction, announced simultaneously at 1800 yesterday in Washington, London and Moscow, was firmly established at 1600 Thursday at Torgau, Germany, on the Elbe River, 28 miles northeast of Leipzig.

The Americans' first contact with the Russians took place Wednesday afternoon at 1332, when 1/Lt. Albert L. Kotzebue, of Houston, Tex., led a four-man patrol of the U.S. 69th Inf. Div. to the Elbe, The Stars and Stripes' Andy Rooney reported.

1/Lt. William Robertson, of Los Angeles, later was sent to the Russian lines, where he arranged for Maj. Gen. E. F. Reinhardt, 69th Div. commander, to meet the commander of the 58th Russian Guards Div. of Marshal Ivan S. Koniev's First Ukrainian Army. The two commanders met at Torgau, Thursday, at 1600 hours. The mutual exchange of Allied prisoners of war was discussed.

Stars and Stripes Photos by Riordan

American and Russian soldiers drink a toast after meeting on the west bank of the Elbe. **(Other linkup pictures, pages 4 and 5.)**

Lt. Kotzebue's patrol was made up of members of the 69th Inf. Div.'s 273rd Regt. The first Russians contacted were assigned to the 173rd Inf. Regt. of the 58th Russian Guards Div.

Reuter reported that other junctions with the Russians were expected along Lt. Gen. Courtney Hodges' U.S. First Army front "in the near future." Reconnaissance pilots, it was said, have reported Red Army armored columns racing toward the First Army sector.

Were 2,200 Miles Apart

The linkup came in the 41st month of America's war against Germany, after the forces of Gen. Eisenhower and Marshal Stalin had swept toward each other across some 2,200 miles of Nazi-occupied Europe.

Overnight, the fighting men who slugged 700 miles eastward from the bloody beaches of Normandy and 800 miles from the tip of the Brest peninsula and those who smashed the 1,400 miles westward from Stalingrad have eliminated the western and eastern fronts as such.

In their places have come the northern and southern fronts, each curving powerfully around the last enemy-held sectors of Germany and the occupied countries from which the enemy has not yet been pried loose.

In the south, the Russians, Amer-

(Continued on Page 8)

Berlin's Fall Imminent; 3rd Slashes Into Austria

Capital Making Its Last Stand

Berlin's defenders yesterday were making their last stand in deep underground shelters, public buildings and homes, subway stations and ruined streets as the Red Army tightened its grip on the encircled capital and stormed its remaining bastions.

Front reports indicated that Soviet columns had overrun virtually

(Continued on Page 8)

Nazis Crumble On Danube Line

German defense bastions in the north and south were crumbling yesterday as the West Front was dissolved by the junction of American and Russian armies.

All Bremen, with the exception of the lower docks, fell to the British Second Army under Lt. Gen. Sir Miles Dempsey. In the south, the enemy's Danubian defense line

(Continued on Page 8)

When Good Soldiers Meet:

Trading Day Along the Elbe

By Andy Rooney
Stars and Stripes Staff Writer

WITH KONIEV's UKRAINIAN ARMY, April 26 (Delayed).—There was a mad scene of jubilant celebration on the east and west banks of the Elbe at Torgau today, as infantrymen of Lt. Gen. Courtney H. Hodges' First U.S. Army swapped K rations for vodka with soldiers of Marshal Koniev's First Ukrainian Army and congratulated each other, despite the language barrier, on the linkup, which means the defeat of the German Army as a fighting unit.

Men of the 69th Inf. Div. sat on the banks of the Elbe in warm sunshine today, with no enemy in front of them or behind them, and drank wine, cognac and vodka while they watched their new Russian friends and listened to them as they played accordions and sang Russian songs.

Russian sodiers, strong and young looking, built a little heavier and shorter than most Americans, inspected American equipment and Americans took the chance to fire the Russian automatic rifle. When the day was over many a U.S. soldier walked back to his jeep in Russian boots while the Russian soldier he traded with fought with the straps on his newly acquired GI shoes.

The Russian uniform consists of high, fitted leather boots, not unlike the German officer's. His pants are built like riding breeches of a light cotton material. His blouse is a tunic that buttons to the neck and his cap resembles an overseas cap spread farther apart at the top than the American one. Many

(Continued on Page 5)

THE STARS AND STRIPES

MEDITERRANEAN

Vol. 2, No. 147. Monday, April 30, 1945 — ITALY EDITION * * TWO LIRE

MUSSOLINI EXECUTED

5th Enters Milan; 7th In Munich

Brazilians Take Nazi Division

(BULLETIN) WITH THE 15TH ARMY GROUP, April 29 — The 56th London Division of the British 8th Army, headed by the famous 169th Queens Brigade, has entered Venice.

The 2nd New Zealand Division has reached the the Piave River, scene of Italy's greatest victory in World War I.

WITH THE 15TH ARMY GROUP, April 29 — Organized German resistance in Italy was crumbling today under the paralyzing blows of two Allied Armies, gathering momentum for the knockout punch and there were signs that the complete disintegration of the German Armies had begun.

Dramatic developments were disclosed in tonight's communique

Milan has been entered by 5th Army troops.

Negotiations were in progress for the surrender of the Liguarian Army, formerly commanded by Marshal Rodolfo Graziani, now a prisoner and under Allied military control.

The 148th German Infantry Division surrendered to the Brazilian Expeditionary Force delivering up

(Continued on Page 8)

Patriots Claim Fall Of Treviso, Turin

ROME, April 29 — Radio Milan from all indications firmly in the hands of Italian Patriots, claimed the liberation of Turin and of the province of Treviso, in northeast Italy today Reuter's reported

The radio announcement said that Turin had been liberated by the Partisans and all its military barracks occupied

General Mark W Clark 15th Army Group Commander, broadcast the following instructions to the Partisans:

"You must by all means prevent the Germans from carrying out the destruction of industrial plants and machinery", General Clark said "On this task depends the future of Italy

The signal for a general rising of North Italian Partisans was given by Field Marshal Sir Harold R. L. G. Alexander, Allied commander in chief in Italy through the National Liberation Committee the Milan Radio disclosed.

Himmler Statement Hints Hitler Death

SAN FRANCISCO, April 29 (UP) — The possibility that Heinrich Himmler may have killed Hitler, as cynical evidence to the Allies of his "good faith" in desiring to surrender Germany, was suggested in diplomatic quarters here today.

A high British source revealed first evidence in what was regarded in San Francisco as a desperate attempt by Himmler to save his own skin. These quarters assert that Himmler advised the Allies through Stockholm that Hitler "may not live another 24 hours."

The timing of the message was such that many believe Hitler may already be dead at the hands of his once trusted lieutenant."

Berlin 90 Percent In Russian Hands

MOSCOW, April 29 — The Red Army is now battling for a May Day victory in Berlin — '90 percent of which according to United Press is in Russian hands.

With less than 24 hours to go before the eve of the great Soviet holiday, Marshals Gregory Zhukov and Ivan Koniev have launched a crushing all-out assault on the center of the city where the Germans are now hemmed into an area roughly covering the oldest part of the Reich capital.

The Moabit section of Berlin, northwest of the Wilhelmstrasse, fell to the Red Army tonight, according to the Soviet communique.

The German High Command, gambling everything on the possibility of a last-minute 'split' developing between the West and East Front Allies, has withdrawn its troops facing U. S. forces on the

(Continued on Page 8)

Yanks Push Into Shrine Of Nazism

SHAEF, April 29 — Munich, fourth largest city of Germany and birthplace of Nazism, was entered by troops of the 6th Army Group tonight. Entry into the great Bavarian city after a 20-mile advance from the west, was made by elements of Lt. Gen. Alexander M. Patch's U. S. 7th Army from the north and southwest.

Initial dispatches did not tell of any fighting within the city which for the past two days had been wracked by unrest and revolt.

Earlier today American armies had been reported converging on the city in an 80-mile arc extending from the northeast to the southwest, and dispatches tonight told of the liberation by the U. S. 3rd Army of 27,000 Allied prisoners of war from a camp at Moosburg on the Isar River, 27 miles northeast of Munich. A great number of those freed prisoners were reported to be American airmen.

There has been no indication yet that Allied Armies have reached the most notorious of German concentration camps at Dachau, eight miles northwest of Munich.

The situation within Munich remained uncertain following an apparent attempt yesterday by a group identifying itself as the "Free Bavarian Movement" and led by General Ritter von Epp, Hitler's 75-year-old commissioner for Bavaria, to take over the city's government.

Reuter's reported that a radio using the city's wave length had told of revolt within the city, and had called upon the advancing Allies to bomb Field Marshal Albert C. Kesselring's headquarters near Munich.

Later, Reuter's said, the south

(Continued on Page 8)

Patriots Also Kill Aides, Mistress

ROME, April 29—Benito Mussolini has been executed by Italian Patriots, Radio Milan, voice of the Committee of National Liberation of Northern Italy, said today.

The Radio said Mussolini was executed last night along with a number of his henchmen and his mistress.

Two British war correspondents, Christopher Lumby, of the London Times, and Stephen Barber, of the London News Chronicle, who went into Milan in advance of Allied troops, reported today that they had personally seen the bodies of Mussolini and 17 of his henchmen on display in the Piazza Loreto. They said that crowds of Italians swarmed to view the bodies, and revile them.

BENITO MUSSOLINI
Reviled In Death

The correspondents reported that Mussolini and others, after having been captured near Lake Como were taken to the village of Giuliano di Mezzegra nearby. There they were tried and executed at 1630 hours on Saturday, April 28. Their bodies were carried in trucks to Milan for public display on the same spot where just a year ago 15 Patriots were executed.

Rome newspapers, like Il Giornale del Mattino and Libera Stampa, spread the news in bold, black headlines. Over all Rome quickly the report travelled, and crowds gathered around every newstand and great excitement stirred the people. At a rally being held near Piazza Venezia in honor of the northern Patriots, loud cheering greeted the announcement.

Radio Milan did not give details of the executions, nor of the summary trial which must have preceded them. Italians in Rome believed Mussolini and his followers were stood against a wall and shot by a firing squad of Partisans.

Among the others mentioned as executed were Alessandro Pavolini, Carlo Scorza, Fernando Messasona, Goffredo Coppola, Nicola Bombacci and Claretta Petacci, mistress of Mussolini.

Pavolini was probably the chief Fascist among them. He was once Mussolini's propaganda minister. As one of a group of seven in the Fascist Grand Council, he used

(Continued on Page 8)

Truman To Tell When Nazis Fall

WASHINGTON, April 29 — Official confirmation of a German collapse "when and if it comes—will be proclaimed in person by President Harry S. Truman in a message over all radio networks, Stephen T Early, presidential secretary, announced last night.

Early's announcement was made after the nation had broken out in a pandemonium of joy and exultation over a false report from San Francisco that Germany had surrendered

Meanwhile Secretary of State Edward R Stettinius Jr. and Russian Commissar for Foreign Affairs V. M. Molotov met in a surprise session late yesterday to consider the contents of a note from Marshal Stalin to President Truman and Prime Minister Churchill.

The note, according to a Reuter's dispatch, recommended that the offer of Heinrich Himmler, chief of all Nazi defenses, to surrender Germany to the U. S. and Great Britain, be rejected.

That such an offer had been made was "confirmed in responsible Soviet quarters," Tass, the Soviet news agency, said it had been "authorized to state.

Reports from Washington and London that said that Himmler's offer had been turned down because only unconditional surrender to all three major powers would be acceptable

The Soviet view, according to Reuter's, as expressed in Marshal Stalin's note was that Himmler might not have sufficient authority to make such an offer and that no surrender talks should be started before Nazi armed might is completely annihilated.

The Russians, Reuter's reported, are said to be determined that the Nazis should not have the slightest justification or the appearance of justification for a repetition of German propaganda after World War I that Germany could have fought on but agreed to give up.

The peace story which originated in San Francisco yesterday touched off celebrations which did not end until long after President Truman announced that rumors about the end of the war in Europe were groundless.

Radio networks throughout the

(Continued on Page 8)

Nazi Civilians Get Diet One-Third of GIs

SHAEF, April 29—German civilians will be allowed a diet about one-third that of American soldiers and slightly more than half the standard for liberated Europe it was announced here today, according to Reuter's

The majority of Germans will be allowed 1,150 calories daily as compared with the 4,000 daily of American soldiers and with the consumption of between 2,500 and 3,000 in the U. S. and the 2,000 which is the standard of the liberated countries.

GERMANY EDITION
Tuesday, May 1, 1945
Dry Run

THE STARS AND STRIPES
Daily Newspaper of U.S. Armed Forces in the European Theater of Operations

Divisions CPs! Pass along this copy of The Stars and Stripes. Others enjoy readig it, too.

Hitler Dead, Germans Claim; Seventh Army Seizes Munich

New Gains Are Made In Redoubt

Munich, capital of Bavaria and home of the Nazi movement, today was completely in the hands of 7th Army troops.

Far to the north, troops of the U.S. 2nd Armored Div. linked up with British units under Field Marshal Bernard L. Montgomery's command, pushing east from their Elbe River bridgehead in a move to clear the Baltic coastal plain and seal off Denmark from the greater Reich.

Allied gains along the southern base of the front, from Lake Constance to the junction of the German, Austrian and Czech borders, chipped new areas from the presumed Nazi bastion in the mountains of Central Europe.

New Border Crossing

Associated Press reports said armored elements of the 3d Army had broken across the Austrian border north of the Danube at a new point near Kappel and had raced to within 37 miles of a junction with Soviet troops at Linz. Previous reports had placed the nearest 3d Army column 83 miles from the Russians.

By yesterday afternoon, British 2d Army forces had joined their Elbe bridgeheads into a solid foothold 30 miles long and 12 miles deep. Armored elements in the northwest of this front, probing toward the port of Hamburg, entered Stade, 15 miles west of the port. Beyond Hamburg, units were reported within 18 miles of Lubeck, on an inlet of the Baltic Sea.

Gains in Bavaria

Munich was cleared yesterday after troops of at least three divisions—the 3d, 42d and 45th—overran the city. Southeast of Munich, elements of the 3d and 42d were across the Isar River, driving into the last enemy-held sector of Bavaria. Twenty miles below the city, doughs of the 36th Div., renewing operations at the fringes of the Austrian mountain area, entered Koenigsdorf.

Devers Lauds Munich Victory

SIXTH ARMY GROUP HQ.— With the capture of Munich completed, Gen. Jacob L. Devers, commander of the 6th Army Group, today issued a statement congratulating troops of the 7th Army on their victory. The statement said:

"Under the brilliant army leadership of Gen. Patch, the 7th U.S. Army has marched triumphantly 900 road miles from the beaches of southern France and has now captured this great military prize.

"The significance of the conquest of Munich birthplace and 'capital' of the Nazi movement and the cultural center of Germany, as well as one of its most important industrial and railroad centers, cannot be at once evaluated; it may well affect the final stages of the war to a degree second only to the fall of Berlin."

SO SORRY

NIAGARA FALLS, N. Y., (ANS) —Mrs. Julie Abaron reported to police that she was beaten on a street near her home by a man who apologized, saying he had mistaken her for his wife.

Nazi Capital in Its Last Days

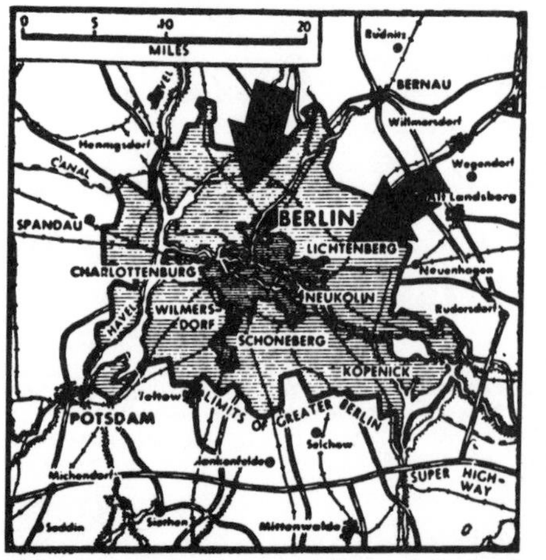

As the final battle for Berlin raged toward its conclusion, the Nazis announced the death of Hitler in the dwindling pocket at the heart of the capital.

Allies Advance On Trento and Brenner Pass

Allied troops advanced on Trento and the Brenner Pass yesterday to threaten retreat routes for German troops remaining in northwesten Italy after a declaration from Gen. Mark Clark, 15th Army Group commander, that enemy military power in Italy has practically ceased.

Clark declared that the Germans could no longer effectively resist the allied armies, which have already torn to pieces 25 enemy divisions and taken more than 120,000 prisoners. "Scattered fighting may continue as remants of the German armies are mopped up," he added.

Allied armies were sweeping toward both corners of the north Italian plain and forcing bypassed Germans to surrender. Turin has been taken by the Nisei 442nd Combat Regt.

IVY LEAF CG PROMOTED

WITH THE 4TH INF. DIV.— Harold W. Blakeley, of Washington, D.C., CG of the 4th Inf. Div., has been promoted to major general.

Soviets Storm Final Pocket In Nazi Capital

Soviet tommy-gunners charged over piles of German dead tonight in hand-to-hand fighting for the last remnants of Berlin, as the Nazi High command confessed that a reduced garrison had been backed into a "very narrow space."

The German communique said that superior Russian forces were hurling ceaseless attacks at the defenders, jammed into a small area in the heart of the city. Red artillery and rolling air assaults contributed heavily to the battering handed the last Berlin die-hards.

Soviet troops fought from building to building in the Wilhelmstrasse and along Unter den Linden. Already, with 95 percent of the capital in their hands, the Reds had hoisted the Red banner over the Reichstag building in the Brandenburg section. The central postoffice and Heinrich Himmler's Ministry of International Affairs have also been occupied.

MOSCOW BLACKOUT ENDS

MOSCOW (Reuter) — Moscow's blackout has Been lifted.

Doenitz, As New Chief, Will Continue War

Adolf Hitler, for 12 years the master of Germany and the man who set out to conquer the world, died yesterday afternoon, the German radio at Hamburg announced. Declaring that Grand Admiral Karl Doenitz, commander of the German Navy, was Hitler's successor, the radio stated:

"It is reported from Der Fuehrer's headquarters that Der Fuehrer, Adolf Hitler, has fallen this afternoon at his command post in the Reich Chancellery, fighting to the last breath against Bolshevism and for Germany."

The announcement did not explain how Hitler, who was 56 years old 12 days ago, had "fallen." Russian forces in recent days have been battling toward the massive Chancellery which Hitler built in the Wilhelmstrasse, in the center of Berlin.

The broadcast reported that on April 13 Hitler named Doenitz as his successor. Then Doenitz came on the program with a fiery promise to keep up what he termed "the struggle against Bolshevism." He said the Germans would fight American and British forces to the extent that they hindered his fight against Russia.

There was no indication as to the whereabouts of Heinrich Himmler, Gestapo chief and leader of the German home defense forces, who has been reported offering to surrender. Neither was there any word of Propaganda Minister Paul Joseph Goebbels or other Hitler henchmen.

The announcement of Hitler's death was preceded by the playing of solemn Wagnerian music, including "Twilight of the Gods." The southern German radio kept up a program of light music all through the program from the north, indicating that communication is broken down between the two German pockets.

Doenitz came on the air immediately after the brief announcement of Hitler's death, saying:

"German man and women, soldiers of the German Wehrmacht:

"Our Fuehrer, Adolf Hitler, has fallen. The German people bow in deepest mourning and veneration.

"My first task is to save the German people from destruction by Bolshevism. If only for this task, the struggle will continue.

"Adolf Hitler recognised beforehand the terrible dangerof Bolshevism and devoted his life to fighting it. At the end of this, his battle, he stands as a hero in the battle of the capital of the Reich.

'We Shall Fight'

"The Fuehrer has appointed me as his successor. Fully conscious of the responsibility, I take over the leadership of the German people at this fateful hour.

"It is my first task to save the German people from destruction by Bolshevists, and it is only to achieve this that the fight continues.

"As long as the British and the Americans hamper us from reaching this end, we shall fight to defend ourselves against them as well. The British and Americans are not fighting for their own interests, but for the spreading of Bolshevism."

Doenitz, whose appointment came as a surprise, called on the German people to help him to the utmost and urged them to keep order and discipline. Only by complete fulfillment of every German's duty, he said, could the country avoid collapse.

The 50-year-old Doenitz, regarded as the Nazis' top man in the navy, has always been held high in Hitler's esteem and has been classified as a fervent party man from the outset of the Nazi movement. He led the Atlantic submarine wolf packs before he became navy chief two years ago. He was confined in

Werewolves May Turn Into North Polar Bears

LONDON (UP)—Wolves or polar bears? The German Werewolf Station, even more hysterical than usual with the Russians in Berlin, says the werewolves will never lay down their arms "even if we have to fight at the North Pole."

Service Casualties Jump to 929,313

WASHINGTON (ANS)—Army and Navy combat casualties since the beginning of the war now total 929,373.

Secretary of War Henry L. Stimson placed Army losses at 829,001, on the basis of names received here through April 14, and the latest report from the Navy added 100,372 names to the list. The total represented an increase of 16,895 casualties since last week's report.

A breakdown of Army casualties, with corresponding figures for the preceding week, showed killed, 166,104 and 162,505; wounded, 507,018 and 496,803; missing 82,671 and 83,926; prisoners, 73,208 and 70,636.

Nazis Digging Sewers 'Sir' Jewish Foremen

LONDON, (UP)—Cologne's former Nazi overseers are now digging shewers while the Jews whom they baited are helping to run the city.

The civilian population is being fed captured Wehrmacht stores. Everyone has to work for his rations.

Very few Nazis have complained of the humiliation of sewer digging.

Catching Up With the SS

Yanks Free 32,000 at Dachau Death Camp

DACHAU, Germany, April 29 (Delayed) (AP)—The infamous Dachau prison camp and 32,000 inmates have been liberated by the 42d and and 45th Divs.

Two columns of infantry riding trucks and bulldozers rolled down from the northwest and completely surprised the SS guards in the extermination camp shortly after lunch hour. Scores of SSers were taken prisoner and dozens slain as doughboys, in tearful rage at the camp's horrors, went through the SS barracks spraying lead from machine guns.

"Trusties" working outside the barbed wire enclosure — Poles French and Russians — seized SS weapons and swiftly exacted full revenge from their tormentors.

Fifty boxcars loaded with bodies were found on a siding at the camp. Implements of torture were strewn about, and there were fully equipped torture chambers. A gas chamber and enormous cremating ovens were also a part of the camp.

Retreating Germans shelled both the camp and the city of Dachau, resulting in considerable damage.

Famous Inmates Gone

It was learned from officials that several famous prisoners—including Marshal Stalin's son; Kurt Schuschnigg, former Austrian chancellor; Prince Xavier de Bourbon-Parme; Pastor Niemoeller, and the Prince of Liechtenstein — had been removed to a new hideout a few days ago. The hideout is believed to be in the Tyrol.

One of the remaining prisoners claimed to be the son of Leon Blum, former premier of France.

Prisoners with access to records and familiar with the camp's inner workings said that 9,000 prisoners had died of hunger or disease or been shot during the past three months, and 4,000 more perished during the cold winter months.

Typhus was reported prevalent in the camp, and the locality's water supply was said to be contaminated from 6,000 graves on high ground which drains into the Amper River, on which Dachau is situated.

American liberators of the camp were told that the week before a French general had been slain by an SS guard, who shot him in the back as the general, believing he was to be evacuated, was walking toward a truck.

GERMANY EDITION
Volume 1, No. 27
Tuesday, May 1, 1945

THE STARS AND STRIPES

Daily Newspaper of U.S. Armed Forces in the European Theater of Operations

Russian Lesson
Da.
Yes.

Munich Falls to 7th

Himmler Sends New Bid

Peace Offer To 3 Allies Is on Way

LONDON, April 30 (Reuter)—Count Folke Bernadotte, Swedish intermediary, again has seen Heinrich Himmler, German Gestapo leader, and is believed to be on his way back to Stockholm with the German reply to the Allied demand for unconditional surrender to the three major powers—the U.S., Britain and Russia.

According to the Stockholm radio, Bernadotte, who carried the original Himmler offer to surrender only to the U.S. and Britain, met Himmler last night in the south Danish town of Aabenraa and received from him a new offer of Germany's unconditional surrender addressed to Russia, as well as the U.S. and Britain.

Bernadotte, a nephew of the King of Sweden, is expected back in Stockholm in a few hours and will turn over the reply to the Allied ministers there, who in turn will relay it to their capitals.

Churchill in London

Prime Minister Churchill returned to London from the country today, and a meeting of the War Cabinet will consider any reply from Himmler as soon as it arrives. It will be considered simultaneously at Washington and Moscow.

If all three Allies consider that the offer goes far enough, it is probable that the next step will be an "instrument of surrender," signed by the German leaders, including war chiefs. The Allies have declared that the only surrender they will accept is that of the German high command.

Unless Himmler's reply incorporates an agreement of the lead-

(Continued on Page 4)

Germans Agree To Leave PWs in Abandoned Camps

LONDON, April 30 (Reuter)—The following message issued today by Supreme Headquarters is being broadcast tonight in English and German by the BBC's European service:

"German authorities have offered to leave behind all prisoners of war of the Allied nations in camps which they abandon in the face of the Allies' advance. The governments of the United States, Great Britain, the USSR and France have accepted this offer.

"It has not been possible for German authorities to transmit this information to all their commanders in the field. It is therefore broadcast in this manner so that all German commanders concerned may know of this agreement.

"The Supreme Commander expects that all German commanders shall carry out their part of this agreement and will hold them strictly responsible for any violation thereof."

Two More Linkups Made, and More Coming

U. S. 1st Army troops linked up again with the Russians at Wittenberg yesterday, while the 9th Army, from its bridgehead at Barby, met the Russians northwest of Wittenberg. In the north, the British 2d Army deepened its bridgehead across the Elbe and the Russians captured Greifswalde. —S and S Map by Brown

Tanks Roll Down Unter Den Linden

Soviet tanks were reported rolling through the Tiergarten and down Unter den Linden three abreast last night, blasting the remaining core of resistance in the German capital in an all-out attempt to complete capture of the city in time for Moscow's May Day.

Soviet forces battling in the central Brandenburg section hoisted the Red flag on the Reichstag building. The Central Postoffice, Heinrich Himmler's Ministry of International Affairs and 200 city blocks in the center of Berlin have been occupied.

Bombers and artillery crews were smashing Germans out of their last remaining strongpoints in the heart of the city. Nazi attempts to withstand the stepped-up Soviet assault with specially recruited battalions of German women and parachutists served only to make enemy losses higher.

Meantime, Marshal Stalin's order of the day from Moscow indicated large advances for Marshal Konstantin Rokossovsky's 2d White Russian Army, driving westward toward Rostock.

Griefswald, on the Baltic coast 50 miles east of Rostock and 20 miles west of Anklam, whose capture was announced Sunday, fell to the White Russian troops.

Hospital Ship Damaged By Jap Suicide Pilot

OKINAWA, April 30 (AP)—A Japanese suicide pilot dived upon the fully lighted and unescorted American hospital ship Comfort, bound for rear areas with a full load of Okinawa battle casualties. The raid, announced yesterday by Admiral Nimitz's headquarters on Guam, occurred on April 6, and caused slight damage to the vessel.

Yanks Seize Dachau Camp, Most Notorious in Germany

DACHAU, Germany, April 29 (Delayed) (AP)—The infamous Dachau prison camp and 32,000 inmates have been liberated by the 42d and 45th Divs.

Two columns of infantry riding trucks and bulldozers rolled down from the northwest and completely surprised the SS guards in the extermination camp shortly after lunch hour. Scores of SSers were taken prisoner and dozens slain as doughboys, in tearful rage at the camp's horrors, went through the SS barracks spraying lead from machine guns.

"Trusties" working outside the barbed wire enclosure — Poles, French and Russians — seized SS weapons and swiftly exacted full revenge from their tormentors.

Fifty boxcars loaded with bodies were found on a siding at the camp. Implements of torture were strewn about, and there were fully equipped torture chambers. A gas chamber and enormous cremating ovens were also a part of the camp.

Retreating Germans shelled both the camp and the city of Dachau, resulting in considerable damage.

Famous Inmates Gone

It was learned from officials that several famous prisoners—including Marshal Stalin's son; Kurt Schuschnigg, former Austrian chancellor; Prince Xavier de Bourbon-Parme; Pastor Niemoeller, and the Prince of Liechtenstein — had been removed to a new hideout a few days ago. The hideout is believed to be in the Tyrol.

One of the remaining prisoners claimed to be the son of Leon Blum, former premier of France.

(Continued on Page 4)

3d Gains in East; Ninth Meets Reds

Munich, capital of Bavaria and home of the Nazi movement, fell yesterday to the 7th Army, according to Reuter reports, as troops of the 1st and 9th armies established new linkups with Russian forces along the Elbe.

Reduction of the enemy's stronghold in the southeast continued, with 3d Army troops crossing the Isar River, southern branch of the Danube, at three places, squeezing the enemy into the lower corner of Bavaria.

In the north, British 2d Army forces, following their kick-off across the Elbe south of Hamburg, were reported to have expanded their double bridgehead to a maximum penetration of six miles.

Munich, with a prewar population of 829,000, was the third largest city in Germany, following Berlin and Hamburg.

Last night's 7th Army communique placed three divisions inside Munich but did not claim its capture. Units of the 3d and 42d Divs. had pushed in from the west and northwest, while troops of the 45th Div. had driven into the center of the city, after seizing all the Weisenfeld airports in the northern part of the city.

In the 7th Army's southwest sec-

(Continued on Page 4)

Italy Nazis Done—Clark

ALLIED HQ., Italy, April 30 (Reuter)—German military power in Italy has practically ceased, Gen. Mark Clark, 15th Army Group commander, said today.

He declared the Germans could no longer effectively resist the Allied armies. Twenty-five German divisions have been torn to pieces. Prisoners now total more than 120,000.

Clark said, "Scattered fighting may continue as remnants of the German armies are mopped up."

Meanwhile Allied armies were sweeping toward both corners of the north Italian plain and forcing bypassed Germans to surrender.

Turin has been captured by the Nisei 442d Combat Regt. The capital of Piedmont was reported Friday to have been freed by patriots. Americans and South Africans also have taken Treviso, north of Venice, and are heading for Udine on the way to Trieste.

Venice, which the British 8th Army entered Sunday, was occupied by 13th Corps troops pushing on 20 miles northeast to the Piave River which was crossed by the New Zealanders. Less than 50 miles remained between them and Marshal Tito's Yugoslav forces which have broken into Trieste.

The U. S. 5th Army, driving toward the Brenner Pass, was meeting resistance north of Lake Garda.

GERMANY EDITION
Volume 1, No. 28
Wednesday, May 2, 1945

THE STARS AND STRIPES

Daily Newspaper of U.S. Armed Forces in the European Theater of Operations

KAPUTT

HITLER DEAD

Adolf Hitler, for 12 years the master of Germany and the man who set out to conquer the world, died yesterday afternoon, the German radio at Hamburg announced last night. Declaring that Grand Admiral Karl Doenitz, commander-in-chief of the German Navy, was Hitler's successor, the radio stated:

"It is reported from Der Fuehrer's headquarters that Der Fuehrer, Adolf Hitler, has fallen this afternoon at his command post in the Reich Chancellery, fighting to the last breath against Bolshevism and for Germany."

Death Is Not Explained

The announcement did not explain how Hitler, who was 56 years old 12 days ago, had "fallen." Russian forces in recent days have been battling toward the massive Chancellery that Hitler built in the Wilhelmstrasse, in the center of Berlin.

The broadcast reported that on April 13 Hitler named Doenitz as his successor. Then Doenitz came on the program with a fiery promise to keep up what he termed "the struggle against Bolshevism." He said the Germans would fight American and British forces to the extent that they hindered his fight against Russia.

There was no indication as to the whereabouts of Hein-

(Continued on Page 4)

7th Clears Munich

Yank Armor Across Elbe

Munich, capital of Bavaria and home of the Nazi movement, today was completely in the hands of 7th Army troops.

Far to the north, troops of the U.S. 2d Armored Div. linked up with British units under Field Marshal Bernard L. Montgomery's command, pushing east from their Elbe River bridgehead in a move to clear the Baltic coastal plain and seal off Denmark from the greater Reich.

Allied gains along the southern base of the front, from Lake Constance to the junction of the German, Austrian and Czech borders,

(Continued on Page 2)

Reds Gain on Baltic, Race Into Moravia

MOSCOW, May 1 (Reuter)—Capture of Stralsund, on the Baltic Sea opposite the island naval base of Ruegen, was announced tonight in an order of the day from Marshal Stalin.

Marshal Rokossovsky's 2d White Russian Army had also advanced to within 30 miles of Rostock, and Gemmin, Malchin, Waren and Wesenberg, important communications centers, have fallen.

On the southern front, the Soviet offensive in Czechoslovakia advanced swiftly following capture of Moravska-Ostrava in the north. Collapse of the whole area back to Prague, the Czech capital, was indicated.

The battle of Berlin had developed into a gigantic mopping-up operation. Though some Germans were still fighting frantically, the Nazi defense was broken and many Volkssturm units were laying down their arms, sometimes lining whole streets with white flags.

Against this, however, some SS battalions had made suicide pacts to go down with the buildings they were defending.

Col. Gen. Berzarin, Soviet commandant in Berlin, is re-establishing normal life in occupied areas. Some factories have been reopened, and power stations and water works will be in operation Thursday. Twenty hospitals have been opened.

Marshal Zhukov's forces had taken 14,000 prisoners in Berlin, while Marshal Rokossovsky was credited with 8,000.

—EXTRA—

THE STARS AND STRIPES

MEDITERRANEAN

Vol. 2, No. 150, Thursday, May 3, 1945 FREE EDITION

Nazi Armies In Italy Surrender

By SGT. HOWARD TAUBMAN

AFHQ, May 2—The German armies in Italy and in part of Austria have surrendered—completely and unconditionally.

The long, bitter, back-breaking campaign of Italy has been crowned with victory. In the theater where the western Allies made their first breach in Adolf Hitler's Fortress Europe, the fighting has ended with the surrender of an entire front.

This front covers not only the rest of Italy but the western area of Austria. The Germans defending the Austrian provinces of Voralberg, Tyrol, Salzburg and part of Carinthia and Syria have surrendered to the Allied might of the Mediterranean Theater.

This means that vital cities like Innsbruck and Salzburg are ours without a fight. It means that Allied forces take over Austrian territory within ten miles of Berchtesgaden, where Hitler built what he thought was a personal fortress so deep in the fastnesses of the Alps that it would take years to approach it.

It means that the bankruptcy of German aggressive policy and German arms has caused an old line Prussian military leader like Col. Gen. Heinrich von Vietinghoff and a convinced Nazi like SS General Karl Wolff, the two commanders on this front who have surrendered, to ignore Hitler's and Himmler's injunction —to fight to the end.

It means that other fronts where the Germans have any sort of sizable formations may follow suit. It may be that here, in Italy, where the Allies have done their hardest and most sustained fighting, the way has been shown to German commanders how to end the useless slaughter at once.

But above all else, the surrender in Italy means that the valorous fighters of the 5th and 8th Armies who fought their way up the entire length of the relentless Apennines, need not begin the heart-breaking task of conquering the mountains that lead to the Brenner Pass and into Austria.

It means, too, that the fliers of the Mediterranean Allied Air Forces need not go plunging into the flak alleys around Brenner Pass or in the other narrow passages among the Alps where the Germans defended

(Continued on Page 8)

GERMANY EDITION
Volume 1, No. 31
Saturday, May 5, 1945

THE STARS AND STRIPES
Daily Newspaper of U. S. Armed Forces in the European Theater of Operations

Germans Surrender In Holland, Denmark; 7th and 5th Link Up

Armies Join On Border At Brenner

The northern and southern operations of the Allied armies in Europe were joined into a single front yesterday, when troops of the 7th Army's 103d Div. raced through the Brenner Pass into Italy, to link up with advance units of the 5th Army, moving north from the Adige valley.

Virtually encircling the last remaining areas of German resistance in Central Europe, the linkup, coming after the surrender of the Nazis' southwestern command, reduced the operations of the western Allies to the clearing of pockets in the mountainous fringes of Austria and Czechoslovakia.

As the entire roof of the redoubt caved in, 7th Army men of the 3d Div. stormed through to clear Berchtesgaden, Hitler's mountain retreat in the Bavarian appendix. Salzburg, one of the presumed Nazi strongholds in Austria, fell. Innsbruck, capital of the Austrian Tyrol, was captured.

Organized resistance in the southwest sector of the 7th Army front was officially said to have collapsed along a stretch of 70 miles in western Austria. Troops of the 103d

(Continued on Page 4)

Rhodes Raiders Eliminate Guns

CAIRO, May 4 (Reuter)—A surprise blow against German garrisons in the Dodecanese Islands was struck in four daring assaults early Wednesday when Allied raiding forces liquidated three Nazi gun positions and destroyed ammunition stocks.

Greek raiders, under Greek and British naval officers, landed under cover of darkness and attacked enemy forces on Rudimania, a small island west of Rhodes, and at Chimarasse, Noti and Foca on Rhodes itself. Today's naval communique said that in addition to elimination of gun positions, the raiders destroyed all ammunition, vehicles, stores, huts and tents, setting jetties and other stores on fire.

Dwindling Fragments of the Once Mighty Nazi Empire

With the surrender of German forces in Denmark and Holland, ending resistance in the white areas in the northwest, the only serious fighting by the Nazis is in Czechoslovakia, where the Russians are advancing on Prague, and in Austria, where the Americans are within five miles of Linz. The dotted area of Austria indicates the territory surrendered to the armies in Italy. —S and S Map by Brown

Reds Open Up Roads To Prague

What may prove to be the last battles on the old Russian-German front are being fought in central Czechoslovakia, where forces commanded by Marshal Malinovsky and General Eremenko are exerting increasing pressure on the enemy and opening up roads to Prague.

The last German hopes of effective resistance on all other sectors were ending with the Red armies now linked with the Allies across a broad front. Soviet forces were shovelling back German troops in the Magdeburg pocket west of Berlin, heralding an extension of the linkup from the Baltic to the gates of Dresden, the last large German city still in enemy hands.

Berlin Streets Blocked

Reports from Berlin yesterday described conditions within the devastated city. The main streets were blocked and made impassable by bomb craters and debris. Some had collapsed into the underground subway. Hitler's Chancellery and Goering's Air Ministry were burning ruins.

The Red Army chose its first post-Nazi mayor of the Berlin district. He is Paul Laecke, described as a "non-party man", who was appointed to administer civil affairs in the Friedricheberg district. Laecke had been mayor of the district from 1907 to 1934.

Rangoon Captured Intact; Japs Unable to Defend It

Rangoon, Burma's great port city and capital, was seized by British 14th Army troops before its installations could be destroyed, and its inner harbor is expected to be open for Allied shipping in a few days, Reuter reported last night.

A special Southeast Asia Command communique said: "In a series of battles of great intensity, the Japanese armies in Burma have been so decisively defeated that they were unable to defend the port."

An American brigade was a part of the forces which moved on Rangoon from the north.

Meanwhile, Gen. MacArthur announced from Manila that Borneo invasion forces had advanced to within a few hundred yards of the Tarakan airfield, and that Australians had entered Lingkas, principal city of Tarakan Island.

On the Philippines front, it was reported that the U. S. 24th Div. had smashed through Japanese defenses and penetrated into Davao, enemy stronghold on Mindanao.

(Continued on Page 4)

Nazis Cede All Land in Northwest

Capitulation of enemy forces in northwest Germany, Holland, Denmark, including Heligoland and the Frisian Islands, has been announced by SHAEF, the Associated Press reported last night, and surrender will become effective at 0800 this morning.

The surrender was reported to Gen. Eisenhower by Field Marshal Montgomery, 21st Army Group commander. No dispatches named a German commander as actually surrendering to Montgomery, but it is known that Nazi troops in northwest Germany are commanded by Gen. Ernst von Busch.

In Denmark, the Danish Freedom Council said Gen. Lindemann had issued an order of the day yesterday directing his troops to fight to the last man. Whether he had later surrendered was not clear.

The AP quoted Gen. Eisenhower as saying: "German forces on the Western Front disintegrated today.

(Continued on Page 4)

Prison Where Hitler Wrote Book Overrun

By a Staff Correspondent

WITH THE 103D DIV.—When Landsberg fell to this division several days ago, they found cold looking gray stone walls crowned by onion-shaped towers. This was the fortress in which Adolf Hitler, Rudolf Hess and Maurice Grebel were imprisoned after the abortive Munich beer hall putsch in 1923. Cell No. 7 is marked with a plaque which says: "Here the dishonorable system imprisoned Germany's greatest son from Nov. 11, 1923, to Dec. 24, 1924. During this time, Adolf Hitler wrote the book of the National Socialist revolution, Mein Kampf."

Sgt. Howard Brown, of Detroit, and Sgt. Arthur Kopf, of Hackensack, N. J., talked to Landsberg's English-speaking jailer, who told them he was tickled to see the Americans come. He was anti-Nazi himself, he said.

GERMANY EDITION
Volume 1, No. 34
Tuesday, May 8, 1945

THE STARS AND STRIPES

Daily Newspaper of U.S. Armed Forces in the European Theater of Operations

EXTRA

NAZIS QUIT!

Doenitz Gives Order

Unconditional surrender of all German forces was announced yesterday by the German radio at Flensburg.

Grand Adm. Doenitz, successor to Hitler, ordered the surrender and the German High Command declared it effective, the German announcement said.

There was no immediate announcement from the capitals of the Allied powers, but Associated Press and Reuter correspondents assigned to SHAEF stated unofficially that the Germans had surrendered unconditionally to the western Allies and Russia at 0241 Monday (ETO time).

High German officers formally surrendered the German forces at a meeting in the big red schoolhouse which is Gen. Eisenhower's headquarters, the AP and Reuter reported.

Although there was no Allied announcement, the British Ministry of Information said that today (Tuesday) would be considered as V-E Day.

Not waiting for formal confirmation of the peace news, New York and battered London, beflagged as never before, began celebrations.

(Continued on Page 4)

VE-DAY

New York · London Edition · Paris

THE STARS AND STRIPES

Daily Newspaper of U.S. Armed Forces in the European Theater of Operations

Vol. 5 No. 158—1d. TUESDAY, MAY 8, 1945 ★

VE-DAY

GERMANY QUITS

Today, May 8, is VE-Day, and will be officially proclaimed so by the leaders of the Big Three in simultaneous declarations in Washington, London and Moscow.

This was announced last night following unofficial celebrations yesterday afternoon throughout the world, inspired by a broadcast by Germany's new Foreign Minister that the Wehrmacht High Command had ordered its armed forces to surrender unconditionally, and by press reports, unconfirmed by SHAEF, that the Reich's capitulation to the Allies and Soviets had been signed early yesterday morning at Rheims, France, at a schoolhouse serving as Gen. Eisenhower's HQ.

Following publication yesterday afternoon of an Associated Press dispatch datelined Rheims and reporting that the surrender terms were signed by Lt. Gen. Walter Bedell Smith, Gen. Eisenhower's chief of staff; Russian Gen. Ivan A. Suslapatov and French Gen. Francois Sevez, for the Allies and Russia, and Col. Gen. Gustav Jodl, new Wehrmacht chief of staff, for the Germans, the British Ministry of Information announced in London that today would be treated as VE-Day, ending the war five years, eight months and seven days after the Nazis invaded Poland on Sept. 1, 1939.

Prime Minister Churchill will broadcast the proclamation to the British at 3 PM in London today. Since the announcement will be made simultaneously by the Big Three leaders, this means that the statements by President Truman and Marshal Stalin will be broadcast from Washington and Moscow at 9 AM and 4 PM respectively.

Breaking by The Associated Press of the story on the surrender negotiations created a furore, coming soon after Flensburg Radio, on the Danish-German border, carried the broadcast announcing Germany's unconditional surrender.

SHAEF authorized correspondents there to state that, as of 4:45 PM yesterday, it had not made anywhere any official statement for publication up to that hour concerning the complete surrender of all the German armed forces in Europe, and that no story to that effect had been authorized. United Press and International News Service said dispatches from their Paris bureaus told of the suspension by Allied military authorities of the Associated Press filing of news dispatches from the ETO because of its Rheims dispatch.

Lack of direct confirmation for the Rheims story—though there was no outright denial of the details—created considerable confusion before the Ministry of Information announcement was released. The Columbia Broadcasting System's chief correspondent in London reported in a broadcast to New York that both Truman and Churchill were prepared to issue their proclamation last night, but that Marshal Stalin was not ready to do so, with the result that all three had agreed to postpone the announcements until they could be made at the same time.

In Washington yesterday afternoon President Truman announced, through his press secretary Jonathan Daniels, that he had agreed with London and

(Continued on back page)

U.S. Really Let Go With Yells At (Unofficial) Peace News

NEW YORK, May 7—Clouds of torn paper and ticker tape swirled down on screaming crowds packed in the streets of New York this morning within a few minutes after news had been received that Germany had surrendered unconditionally.

Office girls opened windows and emptied wastebaskets. Bits of paper fluttered in clouds all over Manhatten and settled in a thick carpet on the damp streets.

Some offices closed as soon as word was received from Associated Press at 9:35 AM and employes joined the thousands milling through the thoroughfares.

City authorities said the crowds, estimated at 1,000,000 persons, were "bigger than 1918." The streets were knee deep in paper, all phones were dead and traffic was diverted.

In the Hudson River liners and tugs let loose their sirens, adding to the noise of planes that dipped crazily over the city. The whole city was gripped by the spirit of celebration.

In Times Square cheers rang out and couples danced through a blizzard of confetti. Service men of many nations mingled in the packed victory throng.

Outside one Broadway hotel, a group of Americans, British and Canadian servicemen formed a grinning line, while a long string of girls marched past placing congratulatory kisses on their lipstick-covered faces.

In the financial district, coatless and hatless men and women filled the narrow streets, their yells accompanied by the ceaseless honking of automobile horns.

New York newspapers rushed out with extras based on the AP dispatch. The Journal-American carried a banner in type three and-one-half inches deep "It's VE-Day." The Sun had a two-line banner

(Continued on page 3)

London Shouts 'It's All Over'

News of Germany's final capitulation yesterday hit streets jammed with thousands of Londoners—and Americans—milling around in excited groups, cramming sidewalks until they flowed over into the streets, still awaiting the official word on the surrender but satisfied that the Hun had quit.

Whitehall crowds reached Times Square proportions as expectant mobs stopped nearly all sidewalk traffic in an effort to get close to the Ministry of Health building where Prime Minister Churchill was expected to speak from a flag-decked balcony. Eventually, they rolled out onto the street and traffic there came to a standstill, except for a beer truck which clattered down the street, draped with Aussies singing Tipperary at the tops of their voices.

Even the bobbies were not their unruffled selves, as they shrugged their shoulders, doffed their hats and mopped their brows after attempting to handle the growing mobs. One even got mixed up trying to give a GI directions to Piccadilly.

Piccadilly, of course, was packed—mostly with GIs—and dominated by a carnival spirit, with all the hurdy-

(Continued on page 3)

THEY SIGNED: Associated Press reported that among those who signed the terms by which Germany surrendered unconditionally to the Allies were Lt. Gen. Walter B. Smith, Gen. Eisenhower's chief of staff (left), and Col. Gen. Gustav Jodl, the Wehrmacht's new chief of staff.

Passes, Furloughs Extended 48 Hours

Effective with the official announcement of VE-Day today, passes and furloughs of all military personnel in the U.K. are extended for 48 hours, U.K. Base AG announced yesterday.

Neutral Swiss Rejoice

BERN, May 7—All church bells in Switzerland were rung for a quarter of an hour following news of the unconditional surrender by the Germans. And although there was no planned victory celebration, the neutral Swiss, who never made any secret of their Allied sympathies, greeted the end of the war in Europe with cheers and rejoicing.

THE STARS AND STRIPES
MEDITERRANEAN

Vol. 1, No. 249, Friday, May 11, 1945 | Printed In Italy | TWO LIRE

85 Points Key To Discharges

WASHINGTON, May 10 (ANS)—The War Department disclosed today how many points toward discharge will be given for each of the four factors on which discharges will be based for the 1,300,000 men to be released from the Army in the next 12 months.

Any soldier in any branch of the service who has 85 points or more and any Wac who has 44 points or more, will be eligible for discharge and the first of such service personnel will start moving to separation centers next week.

But the minimum number of points needed for discharge—"the critical score," as the Army calls it—will probably be lower than that. Just exactly what the critical score will be will not be announced for about six weeks.

Here's how the points will be awarded:

One point for each month of service since Sept. 16, 1940.

One point for each month overseas since that date.

Five points for each medal and battle participation star.

Twelve points for each child under 18 up to the limit of three children.

Only time served, medals won and children born up to Saturday, May 12, can be counted. But awards earned before that date although not actually received until later may be counted, as also may children born before then even though the soldier may not hear of the birth until later.

The critical score, which is the lowest number of points a man can have and still get out, will be different for the air forces than it is for the ground and service forces. A third critical score will be established for Wacs.

It was emphasized that the mere fact that a man has enough points to equal or exceed the critical score will not automatically guarantee him discharge.

The Department said enlisted men with the highest point totals will become eligible for release from the Army "except where considerations of military necessity make it impossible to let them go until qualified replacements can be obtained." This exception applies particularly to men possessing special skills required in the war against Japan and men in units which will move toward the Pacific so quickly that there will be no chance to replace them until they reach the new theater.

To make sure any such cases represent "military necessity," a board of "selected mature officers" will be established in each theater to pass on cases where men having

(Continued on page 8)

20,000 Nazis Quit In Channel Isles; Prague Liberated

LONDON, May 10—It was VE-Day-plus-three today, but some final acts of the war were being played out in various parts of Europe.

The Channel Islands were freed today, with about 20,000 German troops surrendering to an Allied task force. The French port of Dunkirk was liberated, following yesterday's freeing of Lorient and St. Nazaire. A German garrison of about 10,000 gave up at Dunkirk.

In an Order of the Day last night, Marshal Stalin announced that Prague, capital of Czechoslovakia, had been liberated by fast-moving tanks of Marshal Ivan Koniev's 1st Ukrainian Armies. Thus the Patriots, who had been battling Germans to the last in Prague, had possession of their capital.

A regular Soviet communique was issued last night. It told of the surrender of German forces in the pocket of Latvia, where German troops have been cut off for months. On the Vistula estuary, and in other areas near the Baltic, other German troops surrendered.

There remained nests of resistance in Czechoslovakia, where German troops refused to surrender to the Russians and were retreating hastily to the west and southwest.

Copenhagen, capital of Denmark, was formally handed over to the Allies by the Germans last night. Vice Admiral Reginald V. Holt, who represented the Allies, immediately handed back the port to Denmark. Two British cruisers and four destroyers arrived yesterday afternoon, and they accepted surrender of units of the German fleet.

The liberation of Denmark was underlined by the formal opening of the Riksdag (the Danish Parliament) by King Christian.

The liberation of Oslo, capital of Norway, was also an accomplished fact. British troops were flown into the city today to accept the surrender of the German garrison.

In Austria Soviet troops occupied the second largest city, Graz, which had remained in German hands until the end. The Russians took several other towns, and linked up with American troops about 30 miles from Linz.

The Germans were surrendering grimly and dejectedly. A mass of 60,000 gave up in Austria to the U. S. 3rd Army. An AP reporter described the scene:

"They came wearing the dejection on their faces that only beaten men can assume. The weight of six years of war was on their faces, and hopeless despair was in their eyes.

"Patton's army met the Germans

(Continued on page 8)

Government Ends Curfew, Race Ban

WASHINGTON, May 10 — The midnight curfew and the ban on horse racing were lifted today, and the Government promised civilians a slightly increased supply of gasoline and limited quantities of new electric refrigerators, radios, washing machines and even passenger automobiles.

In a report to President Truman, War Mobilization Director Fred M. Vinson said that economic reconversion to a civilian scale will begin immediately, and that cuts in war production of from 10 to 15 percent will be effected during the next six months.

He emphasized, however, that the nation has a big job ahead to defeat the Japanese. Rationing will continue. And even in 1946, at least two-thirds of the nation's production will be for war use.

He said there would still be no new nylon or silk stockings, and that food and fuel supplies would continue tight. He said also that the Government would retain its control over prices, wages, building, transportation, production and manpower.

At a news conference preceding release of the report, Vinson announced lifting of the midnight curfew and of the ban on horse racing, the two most criticized war restrictions. Entertainment places in New York and Chicago said they planned to resume after-midnight hours shortly. Several racing tracks planned to resume racing within the next few weeks.

The "brownout," another much-criticized restriction, was lifted Tuesday.

The Office of Defense Transportation lifted its regulations on regular motor and rail transportation for horses and dogs to and from race tracks, but continued its

(Continued on page 8)

All To See Victory Film, 'Two Down, One To Go'

HQ MTOUSA, May 10—The film, "Two Down and One to Go," was released for theater-wide showing at 1800 hours today. The signal to commence showing of the film was received from the War Department yesterday, and was transmitted to all major and independent commands within this Theater.

The War Department has directed that every member of the U. S. Army shall see the film.

Major and independent commands within this theater have a "Two Down and One to Go" officer who has prepared a thorough plan to show the film to all personnel within his organization.

Distribution of prints of the film from Hq MTOUSA, including flights by official couriers, was begun May 7.

Army Explains Methods Of Redeploying Forces

WASHINGTON, May 10 (ANS) — Approximately 2,837,000 troops will be moved out of Europe within nine months, the Army disclosed today. Within 12 months 3,100,000 troops are expected to be out of Europe, leaving only an occupation force estimated at 400,000.

The majority of these soldiers will come to the U. S. for redeployment to the Pacific area, or for discharge from the Army. Others will be routed direct to the Pacific.

Maj. Gen. Charles P. Gross, chief of the Army Transportation Corps, outlined this schedule for the movement of troops from overseas theaters:

Approximately 845,000 men, or an average of slightly more than 280,000 a month, will be withdrawn during the first three months following VE-Day;

Approximately 1,185,000, or an average of 395,000 a month, will be moved out during the second three months; and

About 807,000, or 269,000 a month will be shifted during the third three months

After that, redeployment will be carried on until only an occupation force of some 400,000 is left, General Gross said. All troops destined to be brought out under the redeployment program should leave Europe within a year. After the last World War, it required ten months to evacuate two million troops.

More than 400 converted cargo ships and 800 transport planes will be used to move troops. Gross said that by using captured enemy passenger ships, the movement of troops may be speeded up by as much as 60,000 men during the second three months of redeployment, and by 117,000 during the third quarter.

Within a week after arriving in this country, General Somervell estimated, soldiers should reach home for furloughs or permanent release, as the case may be. Furloughed men, on completion of leaves, will go to personnel centers, will be formed into groups and sent to assembly points for reassignments and special training.

Jap Targets Rocked By 400 Super Forts

GUAM, May 10—Super Fortresses pounded Japan today in the heaviest raids of the Pacific war. More than 400 sky giants ranged over the Japanese homeland, some of them bombing industrial and military targets on the southern tip of Honshu on Japan's Inland Sea, some continuing the relentless blows at Kyushu.

The 20th Air Force said that a huge force of B-29s attacked Japan's critical aviation fuel supplies. Another force bombed the airfields in Kyushu from which Japanese planes have been flying to attack Allied shipping off Okinawa.

Lt. Gen. Barney M. Giles, commander of U. S. Army Air Forces under Admiral Chester W. Nimitz, said Japan will soon be rocked by round-the-clock bombing such as annihilated Germany's heavy industries. He promised that a heavier weight of bombs would be dropped on Japan than on the Reich.

Adverse weather continued to hamper operations on Okinawa. Admiral Nimitz placed American casualties there through Monday at 16,452. Japanese casualties for the same period are 36,535. American losses include 2,107 soldiers and 577 Marines killed.

Vandenberg Plan Adopted In Move To Widen Power Of 'Oaks' Assembly

SAN FRANCISCO, May 10—With many of the leading delegates at the World Security Conference here either already departed or soon to leave, the United Nations were reported by OWI today to have reached a substantial—although not complete—agreement on some of the most difficult problems confronting the committees and commissions.

Anthony Eden, British Foreign Minister, has been asked by Prime Minister Winston Churchill to return to London. Associated Press understood. Vyacheslav M. Molotov, Russian's Foreign Commissar, left today—and the fact that the other two members of the Yalta Declaration's commission on the Polish question are to leave today was seen by some as indicating an early settlement of that issue. The other two members are W. Averell Harriman and Sir Archibald Clark-Kerr, U. S. and British Ambassadors, respectively, to Moscow.

In the first formal action by any committee, a committee dealing with powers of the General Assembly has agreed that that body shall have the right to recommend measures "for peaceful adjustment of any situation" endangering friendly relations among nations. The AP said the language approved was substantially that drafted by Sen. Arthur H. Vandenberg (R., Mich.) of the U. S. delegation.

Final agreements on trusteeships and on fitting regional blocs of nations into the world organization have yet to be reached.

France and Russia have each submitted proposals which, while far from identical, are alike in that the Security Council would have veto power over any steps taken by regional blocs, except for steps aimed at nations which are or were aggressors in the present war. Five Latin American nations — Chile, Colombia, Costa Rica, Ecuador, and Peru—want the regional blocs empowered to act virtually independently of any world-scale decisions. The U. S. delegation is said to favor such independence, but only until such a time as the new world organization is "activized" as a functioning body.

The Big Five are reported nearer in accord than ever in the matter of Pacific island trusteeships, although continued discussions may result from a clause sponsored by China. It calls for an end to discriminatory practices based on racial or related grounds, and if adopted would oblige trustee powers to revise many such practices now in effect.

Our First Weather Tip: Doff Those Long Undies!

ROME, May 10—Among other things, the end of the war means that you can talk freely about weather while it's going on. So here's the first weather report Stars and Stripes ever has published:

Fair today over the Po Valley and coastal plains; partly cloudy with scattered showers this afternoon over the Apennines. Today's maximum temperature in Rome will be 88 degrees Fahrenheit. Yesterday's maximum and minimum Rome temperatures were 86 and 52 degrees. Rainfall, niente.

Peace, it's wonderful!

Today's German Lesson
Er ist geflüchtet
Err ist geflewchtet
He has fled

New York — London Edition — Paris

THE STARS AND STRIPES

Daily Newspaper of U.S. Armed Forces in the European Theater of Operations

Vol. 5 No. 163—1d. TUESDAY, MAY 15, 1945

Today's Russian Lesson
A-PA-snost!
Danger!

Doolittle Ordered to New Job: Kepner to Head 8th

500 B29s Set Nagoya Ablaze

No Details of Position Disclosed

Lt Gen James H Doolittle, commander of the 8th Air Force since Jan 6, 1944 is returning to Washington for a new assignment and has been succeeded by Maj Gen. William F Kepner formerly head of the 8th's 2nd Air Division it was announced officially last night.

What Doolittle's new job will be was not indicated in the announcement, which merely said he would report to Army Air Forces HQ. However, it appeared likely that he would now be called upon to play some part in the steadily mounting air war against Japan, whose capital received its first American blow from Mitchell bombers which he led from the aircraft carrier Hornet on Apr 18, 1942.

Subsequently he headed the Army Air Forces in the North African expedition before taking over command of the 8th which, with its combat role in the ETO at an end, will now be available for operations in the Pacific.

In a press conference last Friday Doolittle said that, apart from those who will remain in the ETO as the "air army of occupation" and others who will be returned to the U.S. as a reserve, the 8th's personnel would be sent directly to the Pacific as conditions permit.

Both he and his companion at the press conference, Maj Gen Orvil A. Anderson, former deputy commander of operations, who had already been posted to a new, undisclosed assignment, forecast that Japan would be hit, if necessary, by as many as 2,000 Superforts in a single raid and that the increasing use of B29s would convert the B17s and B24s, which the 8th used in its strategic bombing of targets in Europe, into virtually medium bombers. However, Doolittle said, the same pattern that knocked out Germany—weakening the enemy from the air to enable occupation by ground troops—would be followed in the war against Japan.

Kepner formerly commanded the 2nd Division of the 8th AF and prior to that headed the 8th Fighter Command. He is a native of Kokomo, Ind.

The new 8th commander has served with the Marines, Infantry, Cavalry and Air Corps and has had periods of detached duty with the Navy.

Eden Leaves Frisco, Talks With Truman

WASHINGTON, May 14 (AP)—British Foreign Secretary Anthony Eden, who arrived here today by plane from San Francisco on his way to London, had an afternoon appointment with President Truman at the White House, where he was expected to discuss arrangements for an early conference between the Big Three.

In San Francisco, meanwhile, the exodus of leading delegates was expected to grow, with Prime Minister Mackenzie King of Canada planning to leave today to prepare for a general election in the Dominion. Georges Bidault, leader of the French delegation, is also planning to leave.

Stars and Stripes Photo by Cordaro

WACs mark third Anniversary parading in London

Queen Calls on WACs

By A. Victor Lasky

Stars and Stripes Staff Writer

Queen Elizabeth stepped up to the WAC PX counter in London yesterday. Pfc Francis T Stewart, of Torrington, Conn., smiled and handed Her Majesty a carton containing several weeks' supply of rations, mainly cosmetics.

"We thought since cosmetics are so hard to get in England, the Queen would appreciate what we gave her," Pfc Stewart, still a little incredulous at seeing royalty in the PX, said later.

Queen Elizabeth, who has a daughter serving in the British forces, was paying an informal call to the WAC billets at 38 Upper Grosvenor St.

Greeted by Brig. Gen E F Koenig, CG of U.K. Base, and Capt Georgina B Watson, Coventry, Ga., CO of the WAC Detachment, Her Majesty was shown around by 1 Sgt. Gertrude Regner, Milwaukee, Wis.

The visit was part of U.K.-wide ceremonies honoring the third anniversary of the Women's Army Corps. Earlier in the day London's WACs paraded before Gen. Koenig in Hyde Park. In Birmingham on Sunday the 6888th Negro WAC Postal Battalion represented the U.S. in a four-mile victory parade.

A WAC dance last night officially opened a new clubroom at 37 Park St., London, for all U.S. Army personnel.

Interested in WACs' Wardrobe

The Queen not only was visibly impressed with the ample PX stores lying on the shelves, but showed great interest in the varied wardrobe of the WAC. Several WACs modeled.

"How lovely," Her Majesty commented when examining the new WAC off-duty dress.

The WACs were equally impressed. "She is beautiful," murmured Pfc Jean Matthews, of Glen Alden, Del., who works in the U.K. finance office. "What a lovely complexion she has," said M. Sgt. Dolores Frost, of Hamilton, Mont.

Their Pallas Athene insignia glistening, the WACs stood by their beds as the Queen quietly walked about and talked to the girls. Feeling the mattress of one sack, she said, "Must be good to get into at the end of a long, hard day."

At the conclusion of her tour the Queen inspected the WAC guard of honor on the outside of the billet. A member of the guard was Pfc Marian Jean Brody, Cleveland, Ohio, who had taken the day off from punching a teletype machine. All Jean could say was, "Isn't she sweet?"

Ike Scores 'Friendly' Treatment of Nazis

Drastic measures have been ordered to insure that Nazis and high German officials are not treated on a "friendly enemy" basis, Gen Eisenhower announced at SHAEF yesterday. He said he had read press accounts where senior U.S. officers had been involved in such incidents, that he regretted these "errors" and that the persons concerned "will be personally made acquainted with the expressions of my definite disapproval."

The Supreme Commander did not mention any specific incidents, but Reuter said it was believed that he probably referred to the circumstances of the surrender of Reichsmarshal Hermann Wilhelm Goering when, according to dispatches, Brig. Gen. Robert J Stack, assistant commander of the 36th Division, shook hands with the Luftwaffe chief after taking him captive and later accompanied him and his family to a castle occupied by Goering's acquaintances.

Goering will be the first Nazi leader to be brought to trial by the Allied War Crimes Commission, which has already examined charges against him by both Czechoslovakia and Poland and moved that he be tried, Luxemburg radio said yesterday. The Czechs hold Goering responsible for the infamous Lidice slaughter, where the village was completely wiped out as a reprisal measure by the Germans, for the deaths of thousands of Czechs in concentration camps, and for the murder of Czech students in demonstrations in 1939, the broadcast said. The Poles charged that Goering laid the plans for the deportation of hundreds of thousands of foreign workers to Germany.

Will be Tried With Goering

Walther Darre, Nazi Food Minister, who has also been captured, will be tried with Goering, the broadcast said, adding that Polish and Czech representatives will act as prosecutors.

SHAEF had no information regarding the reported incidents of preferential treatment to certain Germans. Paris Radio carried reports, otherwise unconfirmed, that an unidentified high-ranking American officer had dinner with Goering after the latter's capture.

The text of Eisenhower's statement follows:

"My attention has been called to press reports of instances of senior United States officers treating Nazi and high German officials as a 'friendly enemy.'

"Any such instance has been in direct violation of my express and long-standing orders.

"Drastic measures have been set in motion to assure the termination of these errors forthwith. Moreover, any past instances of this nature are by no means indicative of the attitude of this Army, but are the results of the faulty judgment of the individuals concerned who will be personally acquainted with the expressions of my definite disapproval.

"In the name of this great force and in my own I regret these occurrences."

Soviet Awaits End in Redoubt

RADSTADT, Austria, May 14—Three Allied armies—the U.S. 7th from the west, the British 8th from the south and Soviet troops from the east—today linked up near Berchtesgaden as Moscow saluted the near collapse of the last German resistance in the Bavarian redoubt.

The Russians announced that on all sectors of the Eastern Front more than 1,000,000 German holdout troops, most of them in Czechoslovakia and Austria, had surrendered since last Wednesday.

The Allies' greatest problem was said to be the handling of hundreds of thousands of German prisoners. Lack of planning and agreement in advance as to their disposition has complicated the task, according to an Associated Press dispatch from 12th Army Group HQ.

Biggest Raid Yet Drops 3,500 Tons

The greatest Superfort fleet of the war—described officially as "well over 500" planes—dropped more than 3,500 tons of fire bombs on the great Japanese industrial city of Nagoya in daylight yesterday as Tokyo Radio reported the continuation of attacks by carrier-based planes on other vital targets on the Jap home islands.

The B29 force, which flew a 3,300-mile round-trip to drop a total of 1,165,000 six pound incendiaries on a nine-square-mile area of the industrial center, was so large that the first Superfort had turned for home 90 minutes before the last plane started from its Marianas base.

It would take more than 1,000 Flying Forts and Liberators to carry an equal bomb load.

One of the principal targets yesterday was believed to have been the famous Mitsubishi aircraft plants. The planes rendezvoused off the Japanese coast and went in at medium altitude, attacking in columns of squadrons of 11 planes each. Weather conditions were not good, but bombing was visual.

Call Raid "Unqualified Success"

The returning crews described the raid as an unqualified success, and said anti-aircraft fire was not troublesome, fighter opposition was timid and losses light. One crew member from one of the last planes over the area said smoke was rising up to 18,000 feet.

The Japanese claimed most of the fires had been extinguished five hours later, and claimed eight bombers shot down and nine others heavily damaged. There was no official report on losses.

Nagoya, Japan's third largest city with a population of 1,300,000—one-quarter of which is believed engaged in plane production—was last bombed on Mar. 19 when more than three square miles were reported destroyed.

The B29s struck as Tokyo was reporting the continuation of attacks by carrier planes against targets on the islands of Kyushu, southern Honshu and Shikoku. Honshu is the main Jap home island on which Tokyo is located. Shikoku is a smaller island between Honshu and Kyushu, the most southerly one of the group.

Believed From Task Forces

These planes, Tokyo said, were "believed to be operating from two task forces." They also claimed to have attacked these task forces and to have sunk one U.S. aircraft-carrier and damaged two others.

The massive air attacks coincided with sharp Japanese setbacks on other fronts of the vast Pacific battlefield.

On Okinawa, U.S. Marines reached the edge of the business district of Naha, capital of the island, and were battling to cross the Asato River to complete the capture of the city. The Japanese were fighting desperately, however, and fighting had been deadlocked for about 24 hours. The Japs attempted to land a force behind the American lines, but the seaborne land-

(Continued on back page)

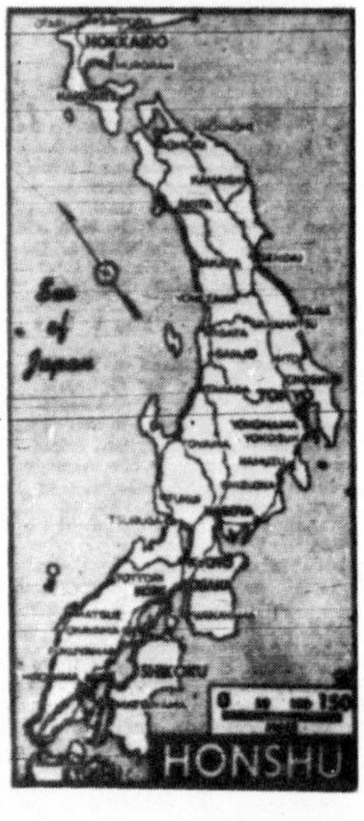

But Failed

Nazis Tried to Bomb N.Y.

(The following story was written by a Stars and Stripes correspondent who was on TD with the N.Y. Bureau in November 1944. It was withheld by The Stars and Stripes until after Germany's fall.)

By Andy Rooney

Stars and Stripes Staff Writer

A German attempt to bomb New York City was made last Election Day, Nov. 7, according to sources considered reliable.

The bomb, presumably a jet- or rocket-propelled projectile, was reported to have been launched from the deck of a German submarine lying off the Atlantic coast. The attempt failed when the V-bomb either fell short of New York or was shot down by fighter pilots alerted to watch for such projectiles.

Soldier operators at Mitchell Field said they detected the projectile on its course toward the city and decided that it had dropped into the sea.

No confirmation or denial of the story was given by tight-lipped Mitchell Field G2 officers to a Stars and Stripes reporter at the time. In Washington, on the following day, Nov. 8, high-ranking officials in the War Department refused to comment.

Later that day, a joint statement was issued by the Army and Navy warning the people along the Atlantic coast that a German V-bomb attack on the United States was "entirely possible."

The official statement said that the robots might be launched from long-range bombers guided across the Atlantic by radio control from submarines.

Soon afterward, strong fighter reinforcements were moved into the Atlantic coastal area.

Rear Adm. Jonas Ingram, soon after his appointment as Commander-in-Chief of the Atlantic Fleet, told a press conference on Jan. 8, 1945, that "it is possible and probable the Germans will attempt to launch bombs against New York or Washington within the next 30 to 60 days."

He said the opinion was based on his own experience with the enemy and not on intelligence reports. He added: "There is no reason for anyone to become alarmed. Effective steps have been taken to meet this threat."

The same day the Navy Department said "There is no more reason now to believe Germany will attack with robot bombs than there was Nov. 7, 1944."

Truman Invites Iraq Regent

BAGHDAD, May 14 (Reuter)—President Truman has confirmed the late President Roosevelt's invitation to Emir Abdul Illah, Regent of Iraq, to visit the U.S. and the royal party will arrive in Washington on May 26, it was announced today.

Lt. Gen. James H. Doolittle
He'll Get New Assignment . . .

Maj. Gen. William E. Kepner
He's new boss of 8th . . .

PACIFIC EDITION

THE STARS AND STRIPES

U. S. Armed Forces Daily — In The Pacific Ocean Areas

Vol. 1, No. 4 — Thursday, May 17, 1945 — Two Cents Per Copy

Nagoya Blazing Ruin

Richardson Previews 'Stars And Stripes'

FIRST ISSUE—Lt. Gen. Robert C. Richardson, Jr., CG, U.S. Army Forces, POA, is shown in the composing room of The Honolulu Advertiser just before the first issue of "The Stars and Stripes" went to press. Looking over the metal forms and layout sheet with the General are the managing editor, Sgt. Charles Avedon of Los Angeles, center, and the make-up editor, Sgt. Walter P. Wachter of Farrell, Pa.

(U. S. Signal Corps Photo)

General & GIs Welcome Army Daily For POA

"It's here, but I still can't believe it!"

The Pacific Edition—The Stars And Stripes, made possible by the personal efforts of Lt. Gen. Robert C. Richardson, Jr., still was being greeted today, fourth day of publication, with a mixture of pride and typical GI skepticism among news-hungry Army fighting men of the Pacific Ocean Areas.

Stars And Stripes made its bow in POA on Monday, May 14, when General Richardson came down to The Advertiser Building in Honolulu to see GI newsmen put the first edition on the presses.

Talks With GI Staff

He talked with the soldier editors, reporters and print shop workers, said:

"You men have done an excellent job in putting out this newspaper in the short space of time you had."

General Richardson himself was chief of the War Department Bu-

Continued on Back Page

Bombed Flattop Saved In Epic Fight Off Japan

By ALVIN S. McCOY
(Representing the Combined American Press)

ABOARD U.S.S. SANTA FE IN WESTERN PACIFIC, March 19 (Delayed) — (UP) — Japanese bombs struck the huge Essex class carrier, the U.S.S. Franklin, March 19 off the southern coast of Japan, causing one of the heaviest losses of life in our naval history when the carrier's own bombs and 100 octane gasoline blasted the ship for hours.

Official losses will be announced by the Navy Department. (Unofficial figures showed 949 dead, more than 221 wounded.)

Scenes of indescribable horror took place on the big flattop. Men were blown off the flight deck into the sea, burned to a crisp on the hangar deck, or trapped in compartments below and suffocated by smoke. Scores drowned. Other scores were torn by shrapnel.

At Breakfast, Saved

I was the only war correspondent aboard and survived only because I was below decks at breakfast at the time.

The rescue of the crippled carrier, towed flaming from the very shores of Japan, will be an epic

Continued on Back Page

Million Fire Bombs Hit Arms Center

GUAM, May 17 (ANS)—**Nagoya, city of 1,500,000 and one of Nippon's vital aircraft and munitions centers, is now the most heavily bombed spot in Japan. After the strike by more than 500 Superfortresses on Thursday (Guam time) 16 square miles of Nagoya were in flames.**

The B-29s struck shortly after midnight, dropping more than one million firebombs from a medium altitude. They were aided by the light of fires started in Monday's strike.

Japanese broadcasts reported that 12 hours later, 40 fighter planes from Iwo Jima strafed the Fujisawa district on the southern outskirts of metropolitan Tokyo.

3,500 Tons Dropped

The B-29s dropped more than 3,500 tons of firebombs on the target area, which was the only section on Nagoya not previously hit in the past three incendiary raids.

Fires were left roaring along the waterfront, reported Lt. George Walker, Superfort navigator, of Boston, Mass.

"I don't believe there's much left of the city," added Sgt. Ray Karpowicz, radioman from Madison, Ill., who has been on 14 Nagoya raids.

Returning crewmen reported antiaircraft fire was meager and the few interceptor planes were not anxious to fight. There was no report of any B-29s lost.

Bombers Go In Low

The silvery fleets of Superfortresses went in lower today than on Monday, apparently to cross up Japanese antiaircraft gunners. The bombers, some manned by veterans of European air war who are being transferred to Pacific to give Japan a taste of what they gave the Nazis, took off from bases on Guam, Saipan, and Tinian.

"We were over the target early but even then large fires were burning in the southern part of the city," reported T/W.C. Loehner, Milwaukee, Wis., instrument specialist. "We started a few dandy blazes ourselves by the time we left Nagoya. Smoke was billowing thousands of feet into the air."

The target area included the Mitsubishi aircraft assembly plant, which has been called the world's largest.

Also attacked today were small

Continued on Back Page

Troops Aiming Final Drive At Okinawa Line

GUAM, (UP)—Doughboys and Marines of the U.S. 10th Army, massed along the Naha-Yonabaru line of southern Okinawa, sent patrols into both key towns Thursday preparatory to what may be the final lunge for control of the island only 300 miles from southern Japan.

The Japanese were resisting furiously in well established defense positions.

One of the Army's Regiments was within 200 yards of Shuri in the center of the line where enemy resistance appeared to be strongest and was blocking a swing down the island on both the western and eastern flanks.

Tanks Gain 800 Yards

On the eastern flank, tanks pushed 800 yards closer to Yonabaru while on the west, 6th Marine Division patrols probed into the streets of Naha, wrecked capital city of the island.

It was estimated that 30,000 fanatically fighting Japs still are ahead of the Americans.

American forces were killing Japs at the rate of one a minute in the bitter climactic fighting. A Pacific Fleet communique announced that 46,505 Japs had been killed and 1,038 taken prisoner through Tuesday.

Our Losses Now 20,950

American casualties for the first 44 days of the Okinawa campaign through Monday totalled 20,950—3,781 dead, 17,009 wounded, and 156 missing.

Japanese forces staged a counterattack against the 1st Marine Division north of Takamotoji Monday. After the attack was repulsed, 585 Jap dead were counted and it was estimated that 446 more enemy troops had been killed.

Late News

U. S. Guns Stop Yugoslav Partisans

TRIESTE (UP)—American troops halted Yugoslav soldiers at gunpoint in the disputed Italian border area near Gorizia Thursday and confiscated loot from Partisans moving from the west side of the Isonzo river.

The Americans threw up road blocks, halted and searched all Yugoslav soldiers and Italian Partisan followers, and, backed by machine guns and anti-tank batteries, seized a considerable quantity of property apparently stolen from Italian soil during recent wholesale looting west of the Isonzo river.

Most of the looters were members of the Italian Communist brigade operating under Marshal Tito's Yugoslav Partisan banner, but a number of Yugoslavs also were halted.

Baron, Refugee From Nazis, In Army

DETROIT (AP)—The former Baron Egon Karl von Mauchenheim, 32-year-old refugee from Nazi Germany whose fight against deportation was carried to Congress, will be inducted into the Army May 25, his draft board announced.

Early in the war von Mauchenheim was ruled unacceptable for service because of his alien status. The board said the Army reversed its position a year ago and von Mauchenheim is now up for induction with other men of his age.

Continued On Back Page

First Dischargees In POA Head Home Within A Month

By CPL. JOHN L. DUKE
Stars And Stripes Staff Writer

Lt Gen. Robert C. Richardson, Jr. Commanding General, U S Army Forces, Pacific Ocean Areas, announced today that within a month, the first group of POA soldiers to be released under the Army's readjustment program will be on their way back to home and civvies.

Most of these men have had combat experience, but are presently stationed on Oahu.

CPBC's Personnel Center will be the gathering place for the first men to be released. Thereafter, each base command will operate its own center. Speedy transportation is promised and men will be formed into "Reception Station Groups" to be based on home areas of the dischargees. It will be the usual policy to discharge men at the separation center nearest their homes, but they can be released elsewhere if desired.

Since men will be in geographical groups the number for which transportation must be provided can be radioed to the Coast in advance and trains made ready so there will be no delay at the port of debarkation.

A. G. Makes Decision

Further clarification of the points system of release reveals several things hasty readers of the points plan may have overlooked. Most important is the fact all men will go back to the Mainland as "readjustment groups." They might be reassigned to other military duties in some instances.

The POA Adjutant General's office will decide whether a man possesses an "essential" skill which makes it imperative to retain him in service, regardless of whether he has sufficient points for release.

Continued on Back Page

Ex-Vichy Boss Petain Passes Buck to Laval

PARIS (UP)—**Marshal Henri Philippe Petain, under questioning for two hours Wednesday in connection with alleged collaboration with Germany, sought to place full responsibility on former Premier Pierre Laval, it was reported.**

The aged, former French chief of state who headed the **Vichy government during the occupation,** appeared tired during **preliminary** questioning but retained **full command of his faculties and remembered names and dates without** difficulty.

Asked by the **president of the** preliminary investigation commission why he appointed the **Laval** government if he disliked the collaborationist premier, **Petain was** said to have replied:

"I hoped he would **improve.**"

During questioning **on French** relations with **Spain, Petain** reportedly made **unfavorable** comments about **Generalissimo Francisco Franco.**

PACIFIC EDITION
THE STARS AND STRIPES
U. S. Armed Forces Daily — In The Pacific Ocean Areas

Vol. 1, No. 8 — Tuesday, May 22, 1945 — Two Cents A Copy

1st Army To Pacific

Yanks Inch Forward In Shuri Duel

GUAM (AP) — American infantrymen and Marines fought toward the battered fortress city of Shuri from three sides against fierce Japanese resistance as Yank patrols entered Yonabaru and bloody enemy counterattacks were beaten back by determined marines.

An estimated 500 Japanese, some of them wearing American marine uniforms and carrying U. S. weapons, counterattacked fiercely against the 4th regiment, 6th Marine division, on Sugar Loaf Hill.

Leave 200 Dead

Two hundred dead Japanese were found after the attack was repulsed, and at least 100 others were believed killed.

Marine casualties also were heavy.

Pfc. Paul R. Hunter of Lake Worth, Fla. commented after looking over one slope where about 30 Marines and 15 Japanese lay dead. "That's the first time I have ever seen a hill with more Marine bodies than Jap bodies."

About 35 enemy planes made the first strong Japanese air attack on Okinawa shipping in several days, Adm. Nimitz reported.

They damaged five light vessels in low-level sweeps, he said. Twenty-six were shot down.

Across the island, the 381st Regiment of the 9th Infantry division sent two patrols into Yonabaru, meeting negligible resistance.

The 77th division, in the center of the line, caught the enemy off balance with a surprise pre-dawn attack and within an hour and a quarter had captured the town of Taila, 500 yards from Shuri.

Near Malaybaylay

MANILA (INS)— Infantrymen of the 31st division advanced to within one mile of Malaybaylay, capital of Bukidnon province, and reached the edge of the airdrome adjacent to the city.

Continued on Back Page

Lend-Lease At 39 Billion; Reds Get 5th

WASHINGTON (AP)—Lend-lease aid to all Allies from the U. S., through March 31 amounted to $38,971,797.00, President Truman anounced in the 19th report on lend-lease operations.

The report, transmitted to Congress, revealed that total lend-lease shipments to Russia for the period covered by the report were $8,410,000,000, with $3,285,000,000 sent in the past year. Included were 13,300 airplanes, "more than to any other ally," 6,800 tanks and 312,000 tons of explosives.

The $38,971,797,000 is exclusive of consignments valued at $874,383,000 to commanding generals for transfer in the field to lend-lease countries. Most of the latter were turned over to the French forces in North Africa and to China.

Actual exports totalled $29,310,457,000. In addition to the shipments to Russia, Britain received $12,775,392,000; Africa, the Middle East and Mediterranean area $3,313,058,000; China and India $2,023,339,000; Australia and New Zealand $1,257,089,000;

Continued on Back Page

By Courtesy Of . . . Two doughboys gaze proudly at this bold billboard, high in the hills of northern Bataan. The cocky but justified proclamation is on Highway 7, scene of bitter fighting.

U. S. Army Photo

Bulletins

Forts Bomb Southern Honshu Again

SAN FRANCISCO (AP)— Japanese domestic broadcasts reported three American superforts bombed southern Honshu, including the city of Nagoya and the Hammatu area. The transmissions were recorded by FCC.

One of the B-29s struck at the eastern section of Nagoya, the enemy report said, while the others penetrated the area of the Enshu straits to the southeast.

Japs Release PW Supplies To Russians

WASHINGTON (UP)— A shipment of 1,500 tons of supplies for Allied prisoners of war held by Japan has been sent to Vladivostok, Russian Far East port, the American Red Cross announced.

The supplies, including food and medical aids, valued at $1,154,275 were dispatched from a west coast port on a Russian ship.

Nearly 700 tons of supplies, previously sent, are still in storage at Vladivostok pending negotiations with the Japanese government to distribute them.

Continued on Back Page

ETO Veterans Aim At Japan

By SGT. MILTON LEHMAN
Stars and Stripes Staff Writer

NEW YORK—The First Army is on its way to the Pacific theater . . . and Tokyo.

The War Department announced Tuesday that the Army was being transferred to the war against Japan, the first army to be moved from the European to the Pacific theater.

Spearheaded Normandy Invasion

The action brings to the war on Japan the army which spearheaded the Normandy invasion, took the brunt of the Ardennes offensive, and has been in the forefront of virtually the entire Western Front drive.

For the First Army, this is the way it began:

"SHAEF, June 6—The invasion of Europe from the west has begun. In the gray light of a summer dawn, Gen. Dwight D. Eisenhower threw his great Anglo-American force into action today for the liberation of the continent. The spearhead of attack was an Army group commanded by Gen. Sir Bernard L. Montgomery, and comprising troops of the United States, Britain and Canada."

"SHAEF, August 10 — The American First Army continued its eastward sweep today while German broadcasts say "the battle of Paris is on."

"WITH THE AMERICAN FIRST ARMY, Dec. 17 — The German counter-offensive that started yesterday moved forward several miles into our lines today and with increased power. It looks like the real thing."

"SHAEF, March 6—Cologne, fourth largest city in Germany, fell today to the American First Army.

"SHAEF, March 8—Elements of the United States First Army held a bridgehead on the east bank of the Rhine after crossing yesterday at Remagen in a manner not yet revealed."

"SHAEF, April 25—Elements of the U. S. First Army and the First Ukrainian Army made contact at 4:40 p. m. today on a demolished bridge over the Elbe River at Torgau."

On May 8 came the surrender, and on May 22 the American

Continued on Back Page

Coalition Ends; Britain To Go To Polls Soon

LONDON, (AP)- The British Labor Party adopted a 12-point program aimed at establishment of "a socialist commonwealth of Great Britain."

The move came as Prime Minister Churchill, faced by a decision of the Labor Party to withdraw from the coalition government, was expected to ask King George VI to dissolve parliament and thereby precipitate Britain's first general election in 10 years. The decision to withdraw from the coalition government was made Monday.

The 1,100 labor party delegates, meeting at Blackpool at the party's national convention, gave swift approval to the platform which virtually meant the opening of the political campaign.

Election In July

Political circles predicted that Parliament would be given about three weeks to wind up its affairs and that the election would be fixed for July 5, provided Churchill acts by Thursday. If he delays until May 30, the alternate date for the election probably will be July 11.

The developments brought from the London press, which has been urging an early "Big Three" conference to settle the Polish issue and other European problems, the assertion that such a meeting now is out of the question until late July or August.

Japan To Jail Anyone Giving Peace Speech

SAN FRANCISCO (AP) — A high Japanese official admitted growing peace agitation in the homeland and called for the arrest of any person making speeches "that might cause disorder in the national unity," the Domei news agency said.

The official, Procurator-General Naruyuki Nakano, was quoted as declaring Monday morning that "the growing critical situation of the war" has led to a tendency toward peace [illegible].

The broadcast, intercepted by FCC, quoted Nakano as admitting [illegible] economic conditions "allow for no optimism."

Fighting Men With Tender Hearts

GIs Play Nurse To Oki's Orphans

(Editor's Note: A fortnight ago Bill Land, one of our battlefront reporters, learned that he was a father. Back to us by radio came this story of Oki's orphans. Unable to go home to see his own daughter in Baton Rouge, La., Bill let himself go on Oki's orphans—being left to die by the Sons of Heaven. But the GIs wouldn't let the kids die . . . And how do you like Oki Sally's green camouflaged diapers?)

By PFC. WILLIAM LAND

OKINAWA—Here's a story you could call "The Children's Hour." Ever since I got that radio about my new baby daughter I've had in mind writing a children's story, especially since the material is so plentiful.

It is said that there are more children on Okinawa than there are goats, and, brother, that is some statement.

Very rarely does one see a woman who isn't carrying either a born or unborn child around and most of the time its both.

Set Up Orphanage

"Barefoot and pregnant" seems the fashion in Okinawa society.

For doughboys and leathernecks, the care of children started on the first day of the inva-

Continued on Back Page

Future Aggie Champ GIs look out for Okinawa children, even to teaching them age-old American games. Pfc. James Murdock, Laurinburg, N. C., instructs an Okie child how to shoot marbles while the boy's mother, and Pfc. J. R. Brook, Fort Smith, Ark., look on.

Photo by Pfc. Bill Land

GERMANY EDITION
Volume 1, Number 21
Friday, May 25, 1945

THE STARS AND STRIPES

Daily Newspaper of U.S. Armed Forces in the European Theater of Operations

4,500 Tons of Fire Bombs Hit Tokyo

Okinawa Jap Attack Shattered

PEARL HARBOR, May 24 (UP)—American troops today gained up to 2,000 yards in a new drive to encircle the bitterly defended town of Shuri in southern Okinawa, but three other divisions were reported virtually stalemated in a frontal assault on Shuri's powerful defenses.

One division hurled back counter-attacking Japs after an all-day battle in which the enemy penetrated 600 yards into the American lines.

On Okinawa, Marine divisions in the west and the Army in the east formed a new trap around the inland cities and the 30,000 remaining defenders.

One column went across the Asato River deep into the ruins of Naha and another knifed southwest toward the rear approaches to Shuri. Army forces drove 2,000 yards into the Jap flank and captured the east coast port of Yonabaru.

Naha may fall without a major battle, frontline reports said. Patrols which pushed across the Asato River spearheading the Marines' main crossing discovered no mines or prepared positions. There is a probability that the Jap garrison has gone underground to draw the main Marine force into a trap.

Superforts Can Bomb Japan from These Bases

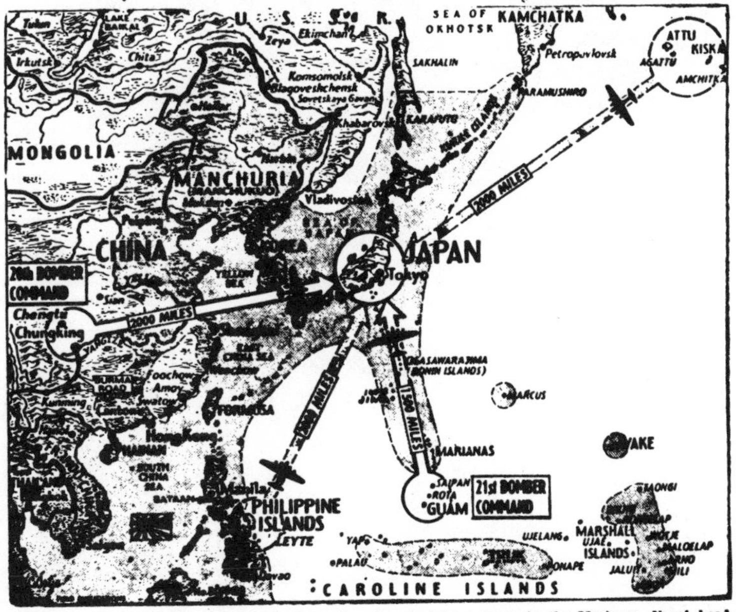

The bulk of B-29 assaults against Japan have been launched from bases in the Marianas. Naval headquarters figures indicate that a single island in the group can accommodate 800 planes. Prospective new take-off points are Iwo Jima, 750 miles from Tokyo, and Okinawa, 320 miles from the southernmost tip of the Jap islands.

B-29 Strike Heaviest of Pacific War

GUAM, May 24—The biggest single air blow of the Pacific war was struck early today by a fleet of more than 550 Marianas-based Superfortresses which dropped 4,500 tons of fire bombs on densely populated Tokyo.

Tokyo's waterfront, railway yards and aircraft-parts shops south of the Imperial Palace were blanketed with incendiaries which touched off great fires visible for 200 miles.

A brilliant moon and a ring of oil fires illuminated the target area, in the Shinagawa industrial section. That area of Japan's capital is inhabited by more than 750,000 persons, and is crowded with highly inflammable shops making precision parts for the Japanese Air Force.

Crews of the American planes reported that the weather was perfect for bombing. The sky was cloudless and all targets were bombed visually.

Jap Fighters Cautious

Japanese anti-aircraft gunners sent up fire that was moderate to intense. Enemy fighters were up, but they were scattered and apparently not over-aggressive.

About 750,000 fire bombs were dropped by the Superforts, which were returning to Tokyo in force for the first time in more than two weeks.

The 550 Superforts, the greatest fleet ever sent aloft, formed a sky train 200 miles long. Losses were reported to have been unexpectedly light.

Radio Tokyo reported that some fires still were burning in Tokyo three hours after the American attack. The Japanese also said that the Singaku Temple, symbol of Japanese chivalry, had been destroyed. The temple is less than two and a half miles south of the Imperial Palace.

Japs Report New Allied Task Force In Okinawa Area

LONDON, May 24 (Reuter)—Tokyo Radio reported today that a new Allied task force had steamed into Okinawa waters, bringing to 400 the number of Allied warships in this area halfway between Formosa and the Japanese mainland.

The report threw into sharp relief two circumstances which are causing Tokyo to expect serious developments in the Pacific war:

(1) News that the Chinese are clearing approaches to the great port of Foochow, captured on Friday and separated from the task forces by only 500 miles of sea.

(2) Japanese hints of a new counteroffensive in southwest China.

Meanwhile Tokyo radio also reported without confirmation a raid by 28 B-24s on Jap installations in Singapore.

Discussing the action Tokyo believes imminent, Domei, the Jap news agency, said the China counteroffensive would be linked with an American assault on the Japanese mainland.

AF Veteran Clark Gable Back at His Civilian Job

HOLLYWOOD, May 24 (ANS)—Looking a little older but still the same forceful actor, Clark Gable donned make-up and returned to the cameras yesterday after an absence of three and a half years on war duty.

In his first picture, an adventure story, Gable plays a merchant mariner opposite Greer Garson.

Bevin Outlines Labor's Goals

LONDON, May 24—Britain, preparing for its first general election in 10 years, today was studying the Labor Party program offered by Ernest Bevin, minister of labor in Prime Minister Churchill's retiring government.

Bevin's program included these planks:

1—The British Government must be at the center of a great Empire and Commonwealth.

2—The aim of the government must be agreements between the United States, Britain and Russia.

3—Britain must never play off small states against big states.

4—The problems of Europe must be settled around the conference table.

After Churchill resigned yesterday, thus disbanding the coalition government he formed in 1940, King George VI announced that Parliament would be dissolved by royal proclamation on June 15. The general election will follow in 17 days.

Gendarmes Curb Paris Night Life

PARIS, May 24 (INS) — Paris city authorities have decreed an 11 p. m. closing time for most bars and cabarets. The drive, which is backed up by Paris Police patrols, is aimed at reducing debauchery and helping to eliminate the black market.

Lt. Col. K. G. Pavey, Deputy Provost Marshal of the Paris Seine Section, said yesterday he had no knowledge of the campaign.

New Trieste Note Is Reported Sent By Tito to Allies

ROME, May 24 (UP)—Allied officials indicated today that a new note on Trieste which might aid settlement of the problem had been received from Marshal Tito.

In London, official circles reported that the dispute was still in progress despite some reports that Tito had agreed to Allied military control of the disputed areas, if Yugoslav Army units were permitted to remain.

One of the major difficulties in the dispute is said to be Tito's desire to leave Yugoslav personnel in the key position in the Italian Province of Venezia Giulia.

Junction Near On Mindanao

MANILA, May 24 (UP)—Converging American troops in north central Mindanao today were only eight miles from a junction that would split the island and put the Japs in a critical position for further defense.

Only light resistance was encountered by troops which struck 10 miles north to capture Dalwangan. Kalasungay, a half mile north of Malaybalay, also was captured by a column that pushed on beyond Maluko. The Japs were reported retiring to the hills for a last stand.

(Continued on Page 4)

Perkins, Biddle, Wickard Out in Cabinet Reshuffle

WASHINGTON, May 24 (AP)—Reshuffle of President Harry S. Truman's cabinet today found four new faces added to six holdovers from the Roosevelt regime. New Secretaries of Agriculture and Labor and a new Attorney General were named, following earlier designation of a new Postmaster General. Each appointment is effective June 30.

Political observes noted that the new selections had given the West added representation and lowered the average age. A somewhat "liberal tinge" was regarded as preserved.

As Attorney General to replace Francis Biddle, 59, Mr. Truman named 45-year-old T. C. Clark, of Dallas, Tex., assistant Attorney General. As Secretary of Labor, the President replaced the country's only woman cabinet member, 63-year-old Frances Perkins, with Federal Judge Lewis B. Schwellenbach of Washington, 50, an ex-Senator and close friend of Truman.

Rep. Clinton P. Anderson, (D-N.M.), who like Schwellenbach, supported most Roosevelt measures, become Secretary of Agriculture in place of Claude Wickard, 52. Anderson is chairman of the House committee investigating food supplies.

The appointments followed earlier designation of Robert Hannegan, 41, to replace 59-year-old Postmaster General Frank Walker.

Syria Protests French Action

Syria and Lebanon took their troubles with France to the United Nations conference in San Francisco yesterday, and there accused the French of "resorting to brute" force by sending troops into The Levant.

The Syrian premier, Faris El Khour, acting as spokesman for both nations, said France had refused to withdraw her garrisons until the two governments signed a treaty granting France extensive cultural, strategic and economic advantages.

A spokesman for the French delegation at San Francisco said that France must maintain her dominant position in The Levant or some other great power would replace her.

Dispatches from Damascus, Syria, reported that French troops in Syria were confined to their barracks, as strikes and riots spread. Lebanon was quieter, though students in Beyrouth held orderly demonstrations.

GERMANY EDITION
Volume 1, Number 57
Thursday, May 31, 1945

THE STARS AND STRIPES

Daily Newspaper of U.S. Armed Forces in the European Theater of Operations

FRISCO CONFERENCE
Secretary of State Stettinius reports to the armed forces on the San Francisco conference. See Page 2.

MacArthur Hits at Last Luzon Japs

Two American divisions have joined forces in northern Luzon to drive into the Cagayan Valley in an attempt to crush the last major Japanese garrison in the Philippines, the United Press reported last night.

The 25th and 32nd Divs. linked up along Villa Verde trail near captured Santa Fe after wiping out the last organized enemy resistance in the mountains to the east of the valley. The newly won area is only 35 miles from the Lingayen beaches where Gen. MacArthur's forces invaded Luzon last Jan. 9. It has been the scene of the bitterest fighting of the entire Luzon campaign.

Ahead of the two divisions in Cagayan Valley lay an estimated 30,000 Japanese, the only sizeable force left in the Philippines.

Dam Seized Intact

In the hills northwest of Manila, troops of the U. S. 38th Div. captured Wawa Montalaban dam, last of three sources of Manila's water supply held by the Japanese. The dam was seized intact with all its machinery workable, although suffering from lack of maintenance.

Philippine-based heavy bombers fired industrial plants and wrecked rail facilities, on Formosa and destroyed considerable railway equipment along the French Indo-China coast.

Meanwhile, Chungking reported that Chinese forces operating in the Indo-China corridor southwest of captured Nanning were nearing Suilu.

Envoy's Talks Please USSR

MOSCOW, May 30 (AP)—Harry Hopkins, President Truman's special envoy to the Kremlin, has had most satisfactory discussions with Russian leaders, according to informed diplomatic circles here. The conversations touched every phase of world problems, particularly Russo-American relations.

Moscow political spokemen said it was unlikely that any news or announcement of the discussions would be made public until Hopkins returns to Washington and reports to the President.

Gen. Knudsen to Retire From Army This Week

WASHINGTON, May 30 (AP).—Lt. Gen. William S. Knudsen, former president of the General Motors Corporation, will retire Friday as one of the War Department's chief production experts, it was announced today.

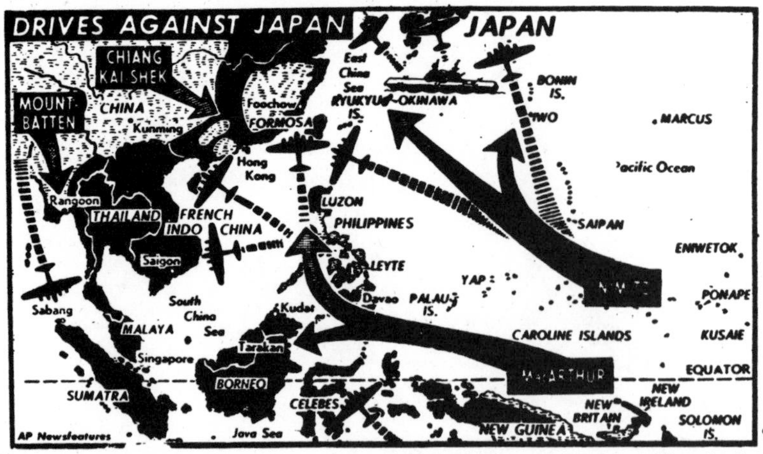

Coordinated blows, struck by land, sea and air, pierce the wide-ranged Japanese holdings in the Pacific and on the Asiatic continent.

Syria Oil Line Factor in Fight

While continued fighting in the Damascus area further aggravated the critical Syrian situation, United Press correspondent Joseph Grigg indicated from Paris that oil was at the bottom of French-Arab conflict in the Near East.

Quoting "sources close to the government," Grigg said that France was determined in the solution of the Syria-Lebanon crisis to safeguard at all costs her economic and strategic interests in the Levant, chiefly the Mosul pipeline from Iraq to the Mediterranean. This oil line, terminating at Tripoli, is the main source for refueling the French Mediterranean fleet, Grigg said.

He listed other French interests as naval bases and airfields which France plans to use as major points on the supply line to the Far East, and the French universities in Syria and Lebanon.

United Press dispatches from the scene of trouble reported that shelling continued in Damascus until 10 p.m. last night, and, "according to reliable reports," one French plane dropped a couple of bombs and strafed the city.

Honolulu Trial Deferred Again

WASHINGTON, May 30 (ANS)—The Senate Judiciary Committee approved today legislation further deferring courts martial for the Pearl Harbor disaster of Dec. 7, 1941.

A resolution introduced by Sen. Homer Ferguson (R-Mich.) postpones until Dec. 7 of this year the statute of limitations authorizing such prosecutions.

Big 5 Defeated at Frisco; Assembly's Power Widened

SAN FRANCISCO, May 30 (Reuter)—Twenty-seven small nations yesterday overrode Big Five opposition to a proposal giving the general assembly of the projected world organization the right to discuss any matter within the sphere of international relations.

The small nations won a necessary two-thirds majority decision in the committee on political and security functions. The proposal was based on an Australian suggestion supported by Belgium.

Opposition was voiced by delegates of the United Kingdom, Russia, France, China and the United States on the grounds that an amended version of Dumbarton Oaks proposals sufficiently extended the powers of the assembly. Siding with the Big Five were White Russia, Czechoslovakia, Honduras, the Ukraine, South Africa and Jugoslavia.

Speeches favoring the proposal were made by delegates of Egypt, Mexico, Colombia and Iran, in addition to those of Australia and Belgium.

Lord Haw-Haw's Quarrel with Wife Brought Capture

LUNEBURG, May 30 (AP)—A quarrel between William Joyce, the Nazi radio's Lord Haw-Haw, and his wife indirectly led to their capture, a senior British Intelligence Officer revealed today.

The officer said Joyce's wife had been arrested approximately the same time as her husband, and not several days before, as was previously reported.

Joyce had been strolling through the woods after a spat with his wife in their home at Kuffermuhle, near Flensburg when he ran into two British officers who were gathering firewood. The officers recognized his voice and one of them shot him through the thigh when he made a move to draw a gun.

Patton and Doolittle To Visit Los Angeles

LOS ANGELES, May 30 (ANS)—Gen. George S. Patton and Lt. Gen. James H. Doolittle will be guests at a celebration here June 9 and 10, Mayor Fletcher Bowron announced.

The mayor said he was informed by Gen. George C. Marshall, Army Chief of Staff, that Patton will fly here directly from Germany. It will be a homecoming for both. Patton's home town is nearby San Gabriel.

Doolittle once attended high school here.

Soviets Draft Boys For Army Training

MOSCOW, May 30 (AP)—Russia will mobilize all 15 and 16 year old youths for Army training beginning June 5, the Kremlin announced today.

Lt. Gen. Pronin, Chief of Russia's General Defense Training, said, "Military training in the present period should be conducted on even a higher level than in the days of war. The peaceful state into which our country has entered should not lessen our attention to the problem of defense."

Naha Falls; Japs' Line Gives Way

GUAM, May 30 (ANS)—The entire western side of the Jap lines on Okinawa collapsed yesterday as U. S. Marines took all of Naha and broke through formidable defenses to reach Shuri Castle.

A climactic American assault to crush completely southern Okinawa's "Little Siegfried Line," stretching from Naha on the west coast to Yonabaru on the east, appeared to be under way.

North and northeast of Shuri, two U. S. infantry divisions and one Marine division were heavily engaged against tank-supported Japs, who apparently were fighting to cover an enemy withdrawal from Shuri. All day Japanese vehicles and troops moved southward from Shuri, their routes covered by American artillery.

Naha, the capital of the Ryukyu Islands, fell to Sixth Div. Marines who previously had brought under control all of the city north of the harbor.

Brig. Gen. William T. Clement, assistant commander of the Sixth Marine Div., said that Naha (population, 66,000) was the largest city ever captured by Marines in the corps' 169-year history.

Naval gunfire and artillery fire had reduced the city to complete rubble. Not one building was standing, and a few dead civilians were the only trace of the capital's pre-invasion population.

The First Marine Div.'s drive to Shuri Castle was so swift that the Yanks surprised Japs swimming in the moat surrounding the fortress.

Hitler's Aide Key Witness

Adolf Hitler's former confidential secretary, Chreste Schroeder, has been taken into custody by the American Seventh Army near Berchtesgaden, according to the United Press. The arrest was made, the UP said, to ensure his presence as a star witness at the coming trials of Nazi war criminals.

In another report on the looming trials, the London Daily Express said that archives of the German foreign ministry and other Nazi state papers had been captured intact and would play a large role in the prosecution of Nazi leaders.

The documents were taken by the U. S. First Army in the Harz Mountains of central Germany, where they were sent for safe keeping when the Red Army first menaced Berlin. The London daily said that 30 railway cars full of files had been brought to London and were being examined by American and British experts.

Wind Spreads Fire Through Yokohama War Industries

GUAM, May 30 (AP)—Members of Superfortress crews who participated in Tuesday's great daylight fire-bomb raid on Yokohama reported today that destruction wrought on the Japanese port city went beyond that dealt out in previous attacks on enemy industrial areas.

The airmen told of seeing great clouds of black smoke, like that from burning oil, rising to a height of four miles over the inflammable commercial area of the city's south end. A strong wind appeared to be spreading the flames through automotive, aircraft and rubber plants.

The B-29s flew through intense flak to strike at their targets. Mustang fighters from Iwo Jima, which escorted the Superforts, shot down 26 of 140 interceptors, scored 10 more probables and damaged 18. Three American fighters were lost, but one of the pilots was rescued.

The Japanese reported that they had shot down 20 B-29s and 21 Mustangs, but actually only two of the big bombers were lost. This was far lower than losses for the two recent large-scale attacks on Tokyo.

Japanese government officials, acknowledging "considerable" damage to Yokohama, said that 60,000 homes had been wrecked and 250,000 civilians made homeless. The raid virtually isolated Yokohama from the rest of Japan, they said.

The enemy report came on the heels of a 21st Bomber Command announcement that 51 square miles—nearly half—of Tokyo had been destroyed in 24 major B-29 raids. It was confirmed that many buildings within Emperor Hirohito's Imperial Palace grounds and adjacent areas had been destroyed. However, Hirohito's own residence appeared undamaged.

Maj. Gen. Curtis LeMay, chief of the 21st Bomber Command, said that, from Hirohito's scorched palace, a scene of terrible desolation now stretches for miles, with only the jagged stumps of buildings standing. LeMay said that if the Japanese kept on with the war, "I promise that they have nothing more to look forward to than the complete destruction of their cities."

The Japanese news agency reported that Viscount Kikujiro Ishii, member of the Privy Council and dean of Japan's diplomatic service, was presumed to have died as a result of the American air attack on Tokyo last Friday.

Pacific Edition

THE STARS AND STRIPES

U. S. Armed Forces Daily — In The Pacific Ocean Areas

Vol. 1, No. 17 — Friday, June 1, 1945 — Two Cents A Copy

Pacific Army Doubling; More 'Air' Is Promised

War Crimes Trials Open In Germany

By JOHN B. McDERMOTT
United Press War Correspondent

AHRWEILER, Germany—A witness testified at the murder trial of three Germans that he saw German civilians shoot and beat an American flyer to death when he parachuted into the Reich from a crippled bomber last August.

The testimony was given as the first trial of German civilians in American-occupied territory opened Friday before a military commission in the tiny courtroom of the Ahrweiler city hall. The Germans were charged with war criminality and pleaded innocent.

Eye Witness Testifies

Accused of murdering the American flyer whose identity never was established were Peter Kohn, a crane operator from the town of Priest; Matthias Gierens, a Priest railway worker, and Mathias Gierens, a blacksmith and rural policeman.

A handful of German civilians attended the public hearing at which the charges were read and testimony was heard.

The chief prosecution witness, Nicholas Nospes, 74, said he saw the airman shot in cold blood and then clubbed mercilessly while he still bled from his bullet wounds.

Cripple Fires Shots

Nospes said townsfolk rushed to the scene and Peter Back, a semi-

(Continued on Back Page)

"Fresh, spirited American troops, flushed with victory, are bringing in thousands of hungry, ragged, battle weary prisoners." (News item.)

This drawing won for Sgt. Bill Mauldin, Stars and Stripes famed combat cartoonist, the 1944 Pulitzer Prize for cartoons. It is reprinted here by permission of United Features Syndicate.

Truman Bares Military Policy For Jap Defeat

WASHINGTON (UP)—The American army in the Pacific will be more than doubled, President Truman told Congress in a special message Friday.

He said the overseas force for the Pacific would be larger than the 3,500,000 men who fought in Europe.

In a 9,000-word mesage he appealed not only to Congress but to the nation not to let down with a false feeling that the job of winning the war is about done.

Increasing Air Blows Pledged

The President threatened Japan with steadily increasing American air power and urged Japanese civilians to leave their cities "if they wish to save their lives."

Mr. Truman said American military policy for the defeat of Japan includes:

(1) "Pinning down Japanese forces where they now are and keeping them divided so they can be destroyed piece by piece."

(2) "Concentrating overwhelming power on each segment we attack."

(3) "Using ships, aircraft, armor, artillery and other materials in massive concentrations so we can gain victory with the smallest possible loss of life."

(4) "Applying relentless and increasing pressure to the enemy by sea, air and land so he cannot rest, reorganize or regroup his battered forces and dwindling supplies to meet our next attack."

Surender Only Jap Hope

Mr. Truman said if the Japs insist on continuing resistance "beyond the point of reason, their country will suffer the same destruction as Germany. Our blows will destroy their whole modern industrial plant and the organization they have built up during the past century and now are devoting to a hopeless cause."

"We have no desire nor intention to destroy or enslave the Japanese people," he said. "But only surrender will prevent the kind of ruin they have seen come to Germany as a result of continued useless resistance."

Puts Grenade Beneath Foot To Save Pals

WASHINGTON (ANS). The Army told the story of a Tennessee infantryman who saved his own life and those of two buddies by stamping a Japanese grenade into the ground and holding it down with his foot as it exploded.

The hero is 31-year-old Pfc Dora Wilcox, Stelmo, Tenn., rifleman whose foot was shattered by the blast. Wilcox is now receiving treatment at Letterman General hospital, San Francisco.

Wilcox, along with other men of the 32nd division, had just completed a three-day forced march to a ridge on Leyte, from which they could cover strategic Ormoc road. The Japanese discovered them and began hurling grenades. One dropped into the foxhole where Wilcox and two other infantrymen were lying.

Without hesitating, Wilcox stamped the grenade into the ground and as it exploded he slumped back. His foot was smashed but his buddies were unharmed.

2 Nosy Kids Foil Pennsy Jail Break

PITTSBURGH (ANS) — Two small boys thwarted a prison break at Western penitentiary.

George Gregor, 5, and his brother Paul, 6, discovered a 35-foot tunnel which had been dug under the wall of the big house.

Eight feet underground and two feet in diameter the tunnel had been completed and escape by one or more prisoners awaited only the propitious moment, Warden Stanley Ashe said.

The tunnel was discovered as the brothers were at play near the prison walls.

MILWAUKEE, WISC., (ANS) — You can't blame William Gersheker, director of Marquette university's band for feeling hurt. He received a form letter from the city's noise abatement committee, asking cooperation in eliminating "unnecessary din."

Gadget Cures Britain's Fogs; Shortens War

LONDON (UP) — The famed English "pea soup" fog, a terrific obstacle to Allied aerial operations against Germany, was overcome by a high-secret British invention called Fido which may have shortened the war by two years, it was disclosed Thursday.

Fido, which stands for "Fog Investigation and Dispersal Operations," consisted of a series of pipes, laid in a rectangle on British airdromes, through which an intense wall of flame could be thrown up, evaporating the moisture and dispersing the fog.

The device could be turned on and off quickly—just before planes were scheduled to take off and just before they returned from their bombing missions.

Air Vice Marshal Bennett said that Fido "may have saved the war from going on another couple of years," which he said might have been the case had Field Marshal Gerd von Rundstedt's Ardennes offensive succeeded last December.

Fire Raging Unchecked In Bomb-Soaked Osaka

GUAM (UP)—Fires still raged out of control in Osaka, Japan's greatest industrial center, Friday, more than five hours after some 450 Superforts, escorted by 150 Mustang fighters, poured 3,200 tons of fire bombs into the city.

Returning airmen said smoke rose to a height of five miles over the city, almost covering some of the Superforts and their escorts.

The huge 600-plane armada was over the city above an overcast but one pilot said he saw flames engulfing the dock area with a wind fanning the blaze toward the city. Another said, "It's a cinch we gave them a fiery bath."

A "Milk Run"

Because of the overcast skies, pilots returning to Marianas bases said the Osaka assault was almost a "milk run" compared with previous big attacks on the Japanese homeland. The raiders reached the target easily but some of the squadrons were forced to bomb by instruments.

"We were flying at about 21,000 feet and the smoke rolled up above us," said Sgt. Robert Rucker, Grantsville, W. Va., a gunner on one of the bombers. "We must have started a hell of a fire down there."

Lt. Wayne Underwood, Chaffee, Mo., said the smoke was "amazing. It must have been 25,000 feet high. We were able to bomb visually when the weather opened up momentarily and I could see the Osaka docks below. Then I never was in such smoke."

Smoke Hampers Jap Defense

Pilots said Japanese ground defenses apparently were hampered by the overcast and the smoke. Some fighters buzzed around the Superfort formations, but generally they kept out of the way, content to call altitudes to the ground defenses to guide the anti-aircraft gunners.

The Osaka attack came as the 21st Bomber Command reported that a "principal portion" of Yo-

(Continued on Back Page)

ANNIVERSARY

Lt. Gen. Robert C. Richardson, Jr., Friday observed his second anniversary as CG of Army Forces in this sector of the Pacific.

When the general arrived on Oahu in mid-1943, the defense of the Hawaiian Islands and the West Coast of the U. S. was a major concern. Today the war has moved a long way west in the 20-million-square-mile area now under the CG's command.

See Last-Ditch Fight By 20,000 Japs Trapped In Oki Pocket

OKINAWA—Tenth army troops completely surrounded Shuri Friday in a muddy advance southwest of the citadel as the toll of enemy killed in the campaign mounted to 61,519.

The 96th Infantry division rolled westward to make contact with the 1st marines only 800 yards southwest of Shuri. The advance trapped an estimated 1,000 Japanese still holding out in the fortified city's northern sector, United Press reported.

Col. Louis Ely of the Tenth army staff said the Japanese probably have more than 20,000 troops equipped and still ready to fight a last-ditch battle for Okinawa in the dwindling 32-square mile pocket at the south end of the island. This pocket already was in the process of being chopped up by southward American drives.

Ely predicted that the Japanese may have a difficult time holding longer defense lines in the south, the first of which might develop along the high ground running inland from the south bank of Naha harbor slightly southeastward to Inasomi village, thence due east to Baten harbor on the Chinen peninsula.

From the mouth of Naha harbor to Baten harbor the line runs 10,000 yards and the 7th division already threatens its eastern flank and holds high ground dominating it.

The 7th already was within two miles of the south coast.

Reports from the front indicated that complete conquest of Okinawa may take another two weeks or more. In fighting in the first two months of the campaign, American forces have killed Jap defenders at a rate of more than 1,000 a day. A Pacific fleet communique announced that 61,519 Japanese dead had been counted through Wednesday and another 1,253 Japanese are held as prisoners of war.

The Americans still fought mud and muck in their advances nearly as hard as they fought Japs. Continuing rains and electrical storms kept the battle area a sea of mud.

Marines of the 6th division on the west coast pushed southeast from Naha city and held a line south of Kobakura village in their push toward the Kokuba pier.

S & S Weatherman . . .
LONDON and VICINITY
Moderate S.W. winds. Cool. Probable scattered showers.
MIDLANDS and E. ANGLIA
Fair and cool. Probable rain toward evening.

New York — London Edition — Paris

THE STARS AND STRIPES

Daily Newspaper of U.S. Armed Forces in the European Theater of Operations
Vol. 5 No. 183—1d. THURSDAY, JUNE 7, 1945

. . . Predicts for Today
W. ENGLAND and WALES
Probable rain. Unsettled.
SCOTLAND
Unsettled. Cool. Rain.

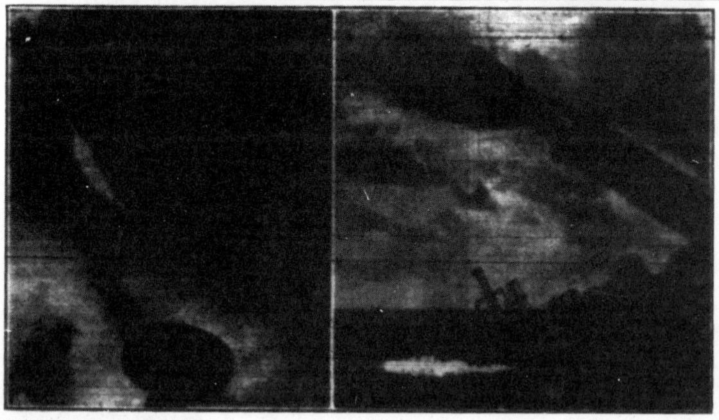

Keystone Photo

SUICIDE, INC.: Here are two illustrations on why Jap bomber pilots don't have to be voluntary suicides to make the long descent to their ancestors. U.S. Navy ack-ack guns send them along whether they like it or not. Left, a flaming bomber plunges into the sea after pom-poms zeroed in, and right, another hits the water off the stern of an Essex-class carrier.

Okinawa V-Day Believed at Hand

A strict security silence blacked out official news of ground operations on Okinawa yesterday as Japanese Radio reported that Jap units "now firmly entrenched in new positions" were locked in fierce fighting with "numerically superior" American forces.

Adm. Nimitz' communique failed to mention land activity on the island and this ommission was interpreted by correspondents as indicating that a special communique was in the offing announcing Okinawa's capture.

A Reuter dispatch said "the official announcement of the end of the ten-week old Okinawa campaign is expected at any hour."

Last official reports of American progress on Okinawa said U.S. troops controlled half of Naha airfield, largest air base in the Ryukyus chain of islands and the biggest prize of the Okinawa campaign. The Japs yesterday admitted a new landing on Oroku Peninsula, south of Naha, by marines of the 6th Division.

Farther east, American forces were pushing toward the southern tip of the island to split the Jap garrison. Only one-thirteenth of Okinawa remained in Jap hands. More than 62,000 enemy troops already have been killed in the campaign and those remaining will be exterminated or stage the first mass surrender of the Pacific war. Frontline reports, Reuter said, mentioned a big increase in the number of suicides among the Japs.

Japs Report More Raids

The Japanese yesterday reported more raids by carrier-based planes against "suicide" plane fields on the home island of Kyushu and said these attacks were paving the way for an imminent Allied invasion of the Jap mainland.

"The moment of a battle of decision on our own soil is rapidly approaching," a Tokyo newspaper warned. Japanese News Agency claimed that elaborate underground fortifications were being constructed to counter the coming attack.

Meanwhile, it was announced that Tuesday's big fire bomb raid on Kobe, Japan's sixth largest city and one of her most important ports, was one of the most successful carried out. Fires roared through the important seaport for six hours, reports said.

Eight Superforts were lost in the attack, and at least one fell to a Jap "suicide" pilot who deliberately rammed a B29 over the target.

In the Philippines, a showdown battle for northern Luzon was believed near as American units, advancing along the roads to Cagayan Valley, captured Aritao village, 30 miles south of the Jap base of Bayombong. At Aritao, U.S. troops encountered the first prepared Jap defense line.

In China, Generalissimo Chiang Kai Shek's forces were reported to have captured Liuchow, on Japan's supply corridor to Indo-China. Liuchow, which was taken by the Japs last October, formerly was a forward base for the U.S. 14th Air Force.

Syria Orders French to Get Out, Stay Out

Syria told the French in no uncertain terms yesterday to get out and stay out of the country, even while dispatches from Damascus reported that British troops had been called out to keep Syrians from looting French homes.

The "get going" demand came from President Shukri Bey El Kuwaitly, who told a United Press correspondent, "This generation of Syrians will not tolerate seeing one Frenchman walk again through the streets of Syria. They will have no communities in our towns unless there are among them people who wish to live in constant risk of their lives."

The French, he said, "have gone absolutely mad. They have killed, robbed and humiliated us for 25 years. Now, thanks to the U.S. and Britain, a bloody massacre and a long war have been averted. Syria and the Lebanon are determined to get rid of the French."

At Cairo, the Arab League Council was still in secret session debating the Syrian situation.

The Syrians were reported to have called on British troops to put down looting by Syrians of French homes. This looting was said to be in retaliation for French looting of Syrian homes, and one report said the British had recovered some loot from French troops moving out of Damascus.

With the Levant otherwise quiet, acting Premier Mardam Bey announced yesterday in Damascus that Syria wanted the French Generals Paul Beynet and Oliva Roget tried as war criminals for last week's outbreak.

Roget was reported last night as having arrived in France for a meeting with French Chief of State Gen. de Gaulle. Paris radio earlier had denied reports of his dismissal.

Jap Suicide-Plane Menace Is Discounted by Mitscher

WASHINGTON, June 6 (ANS)—Only one per cent of the Japanese suicide planes reach their targets, Vice Adm. Marc A. Mitscher told a press conference yesterday. He added that 1,600 enemy aircraft had been shot down over Okinawa alone.

Mitscher told newsmen that the suicide plane menace was not "too serious" but conceded that the Navy had suffered a good many casualties on smaller ships. Stating that he believed the menace could be virtually eliminated through redesign of equipment aboard ships, Mitscher asserted, however, that no one was particularly concerned about it.

MITSCHER

Mitscher said no large warships had been lost to suicide attacks in the entire Okinawa campaign.

Meanwhile, observers here believed that reports from the Pacific of a superior new Japanese plane manned by highly competent pilots indicated that the enemy was drawing on his last air resources.

Report Reds Seek Control of Half of Reich

Moscow newspapers were reported yesterday by Tass (Soviet News Agency) to have published maps showing the Russian zone of occupation in Germany, despite the fact that no exact definition of those zones has been announced officially as yet by any of the four major occupying powers.

Details accompanying the maps indicated that Russia would control about half the total area of Germany. They showed Russia taking over everything east of a line running from Lubeck to where Schleswig-Holstein and Mecklenburg meet, thence along the western border of Mecklenburg to Hanover, along the eastern border of Hanover to Brunswick, along the western border of Saxony to Anhalt, along the western border of Thuringia to the Bavarian border, and along the northern border of Bavaria to the 1937 Czechoslovak frontier.

Some of the territory shown in the maps is presently occupied by U.S. and British troops. Dispatches indicated that Marshal Gregory Zhukov, Russian member of the Allied Control Council, had refused to discuss further occupational problems at the council's first meeting in Berlin Tuesday until these troops had been removed from the Russian zone.

Taking Over U.S. Territory

Meanwhile, British troops were reported from Dusseldorf as taking over that part of the Ruhr originally occupied by U.S. forces. Lt. Gen. Leonard T. Gerow's 15th Army, it was said, will have relinquished by June 15 roughly half the Rhineland territory it has occupied for some two months.

The area being taken over by the British comprises about 5,000 square miles and includes the cities of Dusseldorf, Essen, Wuppertal, Cologne and Bonn, occupied by Maj. Gen. Ernest N. Harmon's 22nd Corps consisting of the 17th Airborne and 94th Infantry divisions. Harmon is to be given another assignment, it was reported, but the disposition of the Corps troops was not disclosed.

When this withdrawal is completed, the 15th Army will be left occupying only the sector south of Bonn down through the Saar Basin and, according to reports, will consist only of the 23rd Corps.

Meanwhile, arrival in Vienna of U.S., British and French military missions indicated early steps to place Austria under a four-power control reported to be similar in scope to the control of Germany.

British Wives Going to Reich

BRITISH 2ND ARMY HQ, June 6—Wives of British troops occupying Germany probably will be living with their husbands by the end of this year, according to British Cabinet plans approved by the Army.

When the plan goes into effect, every married man may ask permission for his wife to join him in Germany. Permission will be granted on two grounds—the man's length of service overseas, and length of time he is likely to continue serving overseas.

In the interim, leaves among 2nd Army men are being increased to nine days every three months or 12 days every four months. Camps are being developed on the Belgian coast, in Brussels and at a number of French centers where the troops may meet their wives during the short leaves.

Suit for Vet Out, Draft Men Told

NEW YORK, June 6 (ANS)—Selective Service has not the authority to institute legal action on behalf of veterans, U.S. District Attorney Miles C. McDonald, of Brooklyn, today informed New York City Draft Director Col. Arthur V. McDermott.

McDermott had asked that the federal attorney undertake court action to determine the right of an honorably discharged war veteran to be retained in his old job even if an employer must lay off workers of greater seniority to keep the veteran.

McDonald explained the veteran involved in such case must bring suit himself. Abraham Fishgold, of Brooklyn, the veteran concerned in the case cited by McDermott, declared that he would file suit himself.

Fishgold, inducted in May, 1943, and discharged in August, 1944, had been employed as a welder at the Sullivan Drydock and Repair Corp., Brooklyn. He was reinstated in the job after discharge but was laid off from time to time when local 13 of the Industrial Union of Marine and Shipbuilding Workers (CIO), which has a contract with the Sullivan Corp., protested that workers of greater seniority than Fishgold should be given preference.

Take '2nd Honeymoon' Sonja Henie Tells GIs

PARIS, June 6—Sonja Henie today advocated a "second honeymoon" for all GIs when they return from overseas.

This would erase in anyone's mind, the movie star said, the misapprehension that the GI has been unduly influenced by French or British or any other European girls.

A few days with their American wives and sweethearts also will dispel any ideas that servicemen may have that things have changed at home, said the blonde skater, who is touring American hospitals in France.

Plane Flying 18 WACs Is Missing in Africa

WASHINGTON, June 6 (AP)—The War Department announced today that an Army transport plane carrying 18 WACs and a crew of three had been missing for a week on a 766-mile flight in Africa.

Reveal Parliament Hid an Arms Plant

For more than 2½ years, a munitions factory—one of the "top secrets" of the war—has been working at full pressure beneath the British Houses of Parliament.

Existence of the factory, which employs some 150 men and women, has just been disclosed. The plant is still producing.

Special cranes lowered large machine tools into the vault beneath the central lobby. With them, weapons to repel flying bombs were made while London was subjected to attacks. Work did not stop once during the air raids.

Smoke Obscures Miami

MIAMI, June 6 (ANS)—Florida's burning everglades last night covered Miami and surrounding areas with thick yellow smoke. It was impossible to see the tops of taller buildings here.

PWs Here Go Direct to U.S.

All freed PWs now in the U.K. on leave or furlough from Lucky Strike RAMP Camp No. 1, Normandy Base Section, will not have to return to Lucky Strike even if their papers order them to do so, U.K. Base Headquarters announced yesterday. Instead, they will be given orders returning them to the U.S. from a port in the U.K., the announcement added.

Such men will, upon expiration of their furloughs, report to the Adjutant General, U.K. Base, in Room 514, 47 Grosvenor Sq., London, where orders will be issued returning them to the U.S. The announcement advised men whose leaves have already expired and who have orders issued by U.K. AG directing their return to Lucky Strike, to disregard these orders and report to 47 Grosvenor for new orders sending them directly to the States.

States Suit 'Em Fine

British Kids Shun Return

KANSAS CITY, June 6 (AP)—Five British children, who were evacuated to America in 1940, do not want to return to England, according to their hosts, the Theodore Barties, of Kansas City, and the Lewis Oswalls, of Hutchinson, Kan.

Bartie said that his young guests, Jennifer and Dennis Brown, 14 and 11, had acquired a love of farm life and a definite American accent and that they had begged their parents to come to Kansas.

The children who found a haven from the blitz with the Oswalds—Nigel, Patricia and Jacqueline Fletcher, are the children of a London caterer and his wife.

They have become so much a part of the local American community that Nigel is now an Eagle Scout and Jacqueline's entry recently took first prize and junior championship honors in a livestock show.

Brazil Declares War on Japan

RIO DE JANEIRO, June 6 (Reuter)—The Brazilian foreign minister announced today that a state of war now existed between Brazil and Japan. Diplomatic relations between the two nations were severed on January 28, 1942. Brazilian forces served in the Allied campaign in Italy.

Laval Still Untagged As a War Criminal

Pierre Laval has not been classified officially as a war criminal, Richard K. Law, British Foreign Office spokesman told the House of Commons yesterday.

"To be that," Law declared, "he would have to be nominated by the French government. And so far he has not been so nominated."

Varga Girl Set Free to Roam

Court Restores Esquire's Rights to Mails

WASHINGTON, June 5 (ANS)—The U.S. Court of Appeals yesterday upheld Esquire Magazine's second-class mailing privileges, giving the Varga Girl a clean bill of health.

The attempt of the Postoffice Department to force the magazine hew to its own concept of morality was denounced by the court, which said that censorship, freedom of the press and freedom of competitive enterprise were at stake.

Postmaster General Frank C. Walker, who will be replaced July 1 by Democratic National Chairman Robert E. Hannegan, had suspended Esquire's second-class mailing privileges. Walker held that the magazine's Varga Girl drawings and other material were morally substandard, and a district court later upheld his ruling.

In reversing the latter decision, the Court of Appeals said: "We hope this is the last time a government agency will attempt to compel "acceptance of its literary or moral standards relating to material admittedly not obscene."

The court remarked on the "mental confusion which always accompanies such censorship," and said three questions were involved:

1—When is a scantily-clad woman art and when is she improper?

2—Where is the dividing line between refined humor and low comedy?

3—How far would the Postmaster General go in reforming periodical literature if he were given a free hand?

The court didn't try to answer the first two questions but with a rare sense of humor had this to say about No. 3:

"We believe postoffice officials should experience a feeling of relief if they are limited to the more prosaic functions of seeing to it that 'Neither snow nor rain nor heat nor gloom of night stays these couriers from the swift completion of their appointed rounds.'"

Justice Thurman Arnold wrote the decision.

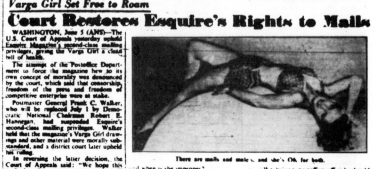

There are mails and males, and she's OK for both.

SOUTHERN GERMANY EDITION
Saturday, June 9, 1945
Volume 1, Number 28

THE STARS AND STRIPES

Daily Newspaper of U.S. Armed Forces in the European Theater of Operations

The Weather

Today: Partly cloudy, few scattered showers; highest temperature 78.

Tomorrow: Fair.

2 Landings Made on Mindanao

U.S. Forces Press Drive on Cagayan Valley Foe

MANILA, June 8—American troops were driving rapidly inland today from two new beachheads on Mindanao Island, while far to the north other forces were closing in upon the last Japanese defenses in the Cagayan Valley of Luzon Island.

Gen. Douglas MacArthur announced the new landings on Mindanao yesterday. They were made at Cape San Augustin, at the tip of Mindanao, and on little Balut Island, which guards the entrance to Davao Gulf.

Japanese supply dumps and radio transmitters in the area were destroyed, and destroyers supported the landings against opposition that was officially described as negligible.

Bayombong Taken

Infantrymen closing in upon the Japanese in the Cagayan Valley of northern Luzon captured Bayombong, which had a pre-war population of 12,000 and was an important enemy supply base. There was almost no fighting in Bayombong itself, although, in the seven-mile drive to it from Bambang, American troops killed 119 Japanese and knocked out two flame-throwing tanks. They were believed to have been the first ever encountered in the Southwest Pacific.

It was revealed that Gen. Joseph W. Stilwell, chief of the Army's Ground Forces and a foremost expert on fighting the Japanese, had conferred with MacArthur and his staff.

Allied planes hammered Japanese bases in Java and along the China coast. International News Service quoted "high authorities" that 80 per cent of the strategic island of Formosa had been knocked out as an enemy military stronghold.

Pick-a-Back Flying Bomb

OKINAWA, June 4 (AP) (Delayed)—A new Japanese weapon being used against U.S. forces fighting on Okinawa is the "Baka" bomb. It is a glider with a 10-foot wingspan and a heavy charge of explosive that is carried to the target area by a mother ship. Then, it is cut loose and a suicide pilot tries to guide it to the target.

It's the Raw Salad That Causes Trouble

BURTON COGGLES, Lincolnshire, England, June 8 (INS)—The good women of this tiny village of 160 inhabitants yesterday offered the world a nine-point program to keep peace—in the home.

Here is their recipe for making a husband happy:

1. Feed him well. 2. Never clean his shoes and don't shout at him. 3. Don't try too much raw vegetable salad on him. 4. Pull together. 5. Give and take. 6. But never argue with him. 7. Let him think he is your ideal. 8. Serve him a large slice of tolerance, a good layer of love, a dash of patience and a sprinkling of humor. 9. Dress nicely.

Stilwell Visits Fighting Fronts On Luzon Island

MANILA, June 8 (Reuter)—Gen. Joseph Stilwell, chief of the Army's Ground Forces, visited the fighting fronts on northern Luzon Island yesterday.

He inspected strong Japanese emplacements in Balete Pass and the ground over which the 25th. Div. fought into Sante Fe to join the 32nd Div.

Stilwell, who chatted in fluent Chinese with Chinese guerillas attached to the 25th Div., said that the terrain of northern Luzon "seems as tough as anything can be."

"In Burma," he said, "it was thick, impenetrable jungle; here it is cliffs and the worst sort of mountain terrain."

It was "Vinegar Joe" Stilwell's first trip to the Pacific since he was called from command of U.S. forces in the China-Burma-India Theater and put in charge of the Ground Forces. Military observers said then that he had been given the job because of his knowledge of the Japanese and his long experience in the Pacific. He had fought in the CBI since the first days of the war.

House Votes Approval Of Bretton Woods Accord

WASHINGTON, June 8 (AP)—The House overwhelmingly approved the Bretton Woods monetary agreements yesterday, and sent them on to the Senate, where a vigorous fight against ratification was expected.

Sweatin' It Out — *By Mauldin*

"If ya see Willie, tell him Joe's lookin' fer him. He swiped my razor."

The great era of respectability has come to the ETO and to Joe and Willie, Bill Mauldin's unshaven infantrymen, whose ironic comments on brass, fresh second lieutenants, 88s, foxholes, girls and off-limit signs made GIs chuckle and approve on all fronts.

Gone are the unshaven faces. Joe and Willie have banished the whiskers and are now seeing how the other half lives. Thus, "Up Front With Mauldin" takes its place in history and in its place is "Sweatin' It Out."

Joe and Willie seem quite unconcerned that their doings won Bill the Pulitzer Prize and the Legion of Merit. They are counting their points, learning how it feels to live above the ground, listening to future barflies tell how the war against the Nazis was won, and getting away from eating out of cans.

Please don't disappear, Joe and Willie. There is still plenty of horse sense needed to [illegible] pompous fools and fed [illegible] of an inflated sense of importance, and to soften the spit-and-polish of life.

Reds Yield On Vetoes At Frisco

Deadlock Ends As Russia Agrees to Drop Stand

SAN FRANCISCO, June 8 (Reuter)—In a major concession that ends the deadlock at the United Nations Security Conference, Russia has agreed that no nation represented on the proposed security council should have the right to veto discussions on a dispute brought before it.

The original Russian view, which was opposed by a majority at the conference, was felt to be uncompromising and unreasonable, insisting as it did that one nation had a veto power. However, it was always recognized that the motives behind this stand were anxiety as to her own security and remnants of suspicion of future actions of some nations.

Reds Conciliatory

Marshal Stalin has now recognized the sincerity of the nations which wish to be Russia's friends, not only by the abandonment of the veto claim but by positive instructions to the Soviet delegates here to show a more conciliatory attitude to insure the success of the conference.

As an example of the new Russian attitude of cooperation, a Soviet delegate said: "If a point is proven to us with which we disagree and we are not feel that it is [illegible] agree."

Moscow thus has made a momentous gesture that will do much to restore confidence on all sides. As a result, an easing of the situation between the Soviet Union and other nations on other international matters is now expected by the delegates.

Chutists Work To Rescue Trio In Shangri La

HOLLANDIA, Dutch New Guinea, June 8 (AP)—Paratroopers, dropped as the first persons from the outside world into Dutch New Guinea's hidden valley of Shangri La, are striving to rescue a Wac and two Army airmen whose plane crashed into the mountains May 13 and killed 21 other occupants.

One group of paratroopers is trying to clear enough space for a glider to land, while another seeks to bring the trio out of the jungle on foot. The rescuers at first had trouble with the strange, tall, spear-wielding natives, 50,000 of whom live in the valley, but solved that problem by producing salt, basic item of friendship in New Guinea.

The remote valley was explored in part by the National Geographic Society but the explorers never reached Shangri La. It is 150 miles west of Hollandia.

The lieutenant, sergeant and Wac corporal who survived the crash with slight burns and shock have been kept alive by field rations and medical supplies dropped by parachute and they have a walkie-talkie radio also dropped to them. In constant touch with circling planes, they report, "We're all right—just keep sending us supplies."

By radio, the survivors took part in funeral services for those who died in the crash. Catholic and Protestant services were solemnized in a plane and 20 wooden crosses were dropped with one wooden Star of David to mark the grave of a Jewish Wac sergeant.

'Death Factory' Boss Seized

MOSCOW, June 8 (AP)—The arrest of Paul Hoffman, head of the notorious Maidanek "death factory" concentration camp in Poland, was reported today by the Tass News Agency. Tass said Hoffman was taken into custody by Polish police.

Big 3 Meeting In Near Future, Truman Says

WASHINGTON, June 8 (ANS)—President Truman said yesterday that he expects the next Big Three meeting to be held within 40 days.

The President added that he had rejected French and Russian proposals for a Big Five conference to discuss the strife in the Levant states and other Near East problems. The Near East situation, he told a press conference, he thought would be settled in the near future.

The only meeting he contemplates, Mr. Truman told his press conference, is a discussion with Prime Minister Churchill, Marshal Stalin and himself.

President Truman at the same time disclosed that he had turned down requests by labor leaders for immediate relaxation of wage controls. He said that the Little Steel Wage Formula would stand, at least pending a thorough study to be made later of wage and commodity-price schedules.

The President's announcement on wage controls came only a short time after AFL President William Green and CIO President Philip Murray called at the White House to press for a quick revision of the Little Steel Formula.

'Black Market' GIs Will Fight in Pacific

PARIS, June 8 (UP)—Members of the 716th Railway Operating Bn. who were court martialed for selling Army cigarettes to the black market several months ago will be sent to the Pacific, the Judge Advocate Generals office has announced.

The 115 men given clemency by Gen. Eisenhower and formed into a special combat unit after the courts martial, which sentenced some men to as much as 50 years at hard labor, had arrived on the Western Front just before V-E Day.

Umberto's Wife Hikes To Italy to Join Him

TURIN, Italy, June 8 (AP)—The Princess of Piedmont, wife of Crown Prince Umberto, Lieutenant General of the Realm, and sister of King Leopold of the Belgians, has returned to Italy after hiking part of the way back from Switzerland, where she has been living with her four children for the past few years.

After a ten-day stay at the palace at Racconigi, south of Turin, she left today for Rome to rejoin her husband, whom she has not seen for 18 months.

The princess hiked from Switzerland to Aosta with a pack on her back. Since Aosta was behind the French lines, she waited there to see AMG officials, and finally received permission to go to Racconigi.

American officers asked her about Italy, but she replied: "I have been out of the country so long that you know more about Italy than I do."

British Deny Blame in Syria

LONDON, June 8 (AP)—A Foreign Office spokesman firmly denied today that the British were in any way responsible for the disturbances which precipitated the French crisis in Syria.

The commentator told a press conference that all British military and civilian personnel had been working in the closest possible cooperation under the British commander in chief and the British minister in the Levant.

Their efforts, he explained, had been directed "not to stirring up trouble between the French and Syrians," toward reducing friction and "assuaging and bridging differences."

3 Months More

Luftwaffe Had Bombers Ready To Raid U. S., Says Seversky

By RICHARD LEWIS, Staff Writer

SHAEF, June 8—The German Luftwaffe was on the verge of bombing U.S. East Coast ports with a new long-range bomber, the ME-264, but could not solve special fuel problems in time, it was revealed here today by Alexander de Seversky, War Dept. consultant assigned to the AAF.

Seversky said he learned of the scheme in an interview with ex-Reich Marshal Hermann Goering, who said his Luftwaffe needed only three more months to iron out fuel problems for the trans-Atlantic bomber.

Seversky described the ME-264 as a four-engined jet bomber with auxiliary propellers to help in the take-off. Its bomb load was small—two to three tons—but the Germans planned to use large numbers for intensive bombing.

German scientific development in the air, especially in jet and rocket propulsion, is being put at the disposal of the Allies in the war against Japan by German scientists, who wish to see years of research bear fruit, he said.

Seversky said he did not foresee V-bombing of Japan on the scale of the German robot attacks against Britain. Bombers could do the job more efficiently, he believes.

He predicted faster-than-sound air travel for the post-war future. He said the most efficient cruising speed for aircraft would be 1,000 miles per hour—a speed which will be common for aircraft which now are breaking through the speed of sound.

German Jet Producer Gives Up With Designs

PARIS, June 8—Heinrich B. Oelerich, inventor, designer and producer of German jet planes and F[illegible]0, and ME 1[illegible], and 110, has turned himself over to the 5th Inf. Div. in Germany and offered his designs and improvements to the American Army Com Z has announced.

The German inventor offered designs and improvements for planes, motorcycles, tanks, and a new type of artillery shell. He was directing the evacuation of a plant producing jet planes from Czechoslovakia to the Tyrol when the war ended.

S & S Weatherman . . .
LONDON and VICINITY
MIDLANDS and E. ANGLIA
Cloudy. Rain. Cool.

New York — London Edition — Paris

THE STARS AND STRIPES

Daily Newspaper of U.S. Armed Forces in the European Theater of Operations

Vol. 5 No. [illegible] — TUESDAY, JUNE 12, 1945

. . . Prediction for Today
W. ENGLAND, WALES [illegible]
SCOTLAND
Cloudy. Rain. Cool.

Borneo Invaded by Australians

Japs Pushed Back Against Okinawa Tip

The rapidly dwindling Jap garrison on Okinawa brought all its remaining artillery into play yesterday in an effort to halt a large-scale American attack against the heavily-fortified Yaeju-Dake escarpment, but Japanese News Agency indicated that further withdrawals toward the southern tip of the island were being made.

The Japs were using heavy artillery at point-blank range in their attempt to slow down the U.S. 10th Army, but marines and infantrymen made gains all along the line.

Flame-throwing tanks led the ground charges while aircraft rocketed, strafed and bombed enemy forces and their well-protected gun positions.

On the west coast, marines of the 1st Division drove through the town of Itoman and attacked Junishi Ridge, the western end of the escarpment.

More than 30 Mustang fighter planes, led by two Superforts, carried the air blitz against the Jap home islands through its fifth consecutive day, strafing airfields in the Tokyo and Yokohama areas, the Japanese reported.

Reconnaissance photos of Sunday's B29 attack showed that the Hitachi engineering works and the adjacent rail yards at Sukagawa were struck by 820 high-explosive bombs. Results at the four other targets hit in the five-way raid were reported to have been good.

As Japan smoldered from its worst weekend of the war, Tokyo radio warned of more and bigger raids to come, declaring that from 700 to 800 Superforts, along with Liberators, Mitchells and Marauders, had been massed within range of the home islands.

The Japs said ten U.S. airfields were in use on Okinawa and the neighboring island of Ie, and that Libs, B26s and B25s from these bases already had struck Japan.

Maj. Gen. Curtis Lemay, 21st Bomber Command chief, announced yesterday that Superforts flew 54 missions in May for a new monthly record.

A total of 3,785 sorties was flown in May and 1,700 more in the first nine days of June. Forty B29s were lost in May and 21 in the nine days of June.

Lemay's report said that 36.19 square miles of urban areas in four Jap cities were destroyed in May, bringing the total areas burned out in Japan to 92.61 square miles.

On Luzon, U.S. forces captured the highway junction of Bagabag and isolated a large body of enemy troops in the mountains east of the Cagayan Valley.

Tax, Price Cuts For France GIs

(See Editorial, Page 2)

PARIS, June 11 (Reuter)—American and British troops in France may soon be supplied with vouchers exempting them from paying luxury taxes on purchases of souvenirs and may be able to buy other commodities at substantially reduced prices, the French Finance Ministry disclosed yesterday, adding that the nearly-completed plan would call for as much as an 80 per cent reduction on such luxury articles as perfumes and silks.

The plan was worked out by Finance Minister Rene Pleven in agreement with U.S. authorities with whom he recently discussed it in Washington.

French economists, meanwhile, termed The Stars and Stripes' campaign for a change in the franc-dollar exchange rate "inopportune and irresponsible," maintaining that purchasing power of Allied troops in France "cannot be the governing factor in the complicated machinery of international exchange."

Associated Press Photo

C.O.D. OKINAWA: U.S. Navy LSMs etch the sky off Okinawa with flame-tipped rockets sent against Jap installations.

A Hidden Flame of Sabotage

Hitler Youths Still Carrying Torch for Nazism in Berlin

By Eddy Gilmore
Associated Press Correspondent

BERLIN, June 11 (AP)—The spirit of Nazism is alive in Berlin. Houses have been fired by Hitler Youths, and at least two Russian officers have been killed by snipers.

These cohorts of Hitler are performing just as the Russians predicted they would—carrying on operations behind the backs of the Allies, committing sabotage and spreading the seeds of distrust whenever they can.

I have talked to about 50 Germans in Berlin and, with the exception of Lord Mayor Arthur Werner and his proven anti-Fascist Town Council, very few showed any sense of guilt or shame about the war.

They were quick to argue that Germany was not to blame, though grudgingly admitting she had a lot to do with starting it.

Condemning Hitler publicly is popular, but the childishness of the tactic is apparent when Berliners automatically wait for applause for saying nasty things about the Fuehrer.

Anti-Semitism, arrogance and cunning are still noticeable characteristics here.

A young German in civilian clothes—obviously fresh out of the Wehrmacht or the SS—told me: "Germany has always been misunderstood. Look at all this destruction. Why do this to one of the great centers of world culture? I hope you will pardon me, but your American aviators were slightly barbaric. I can't see any other point to such wanton destruction. Just look at our monuments of beauty and culture—all ruined."

An Allied visitor is amazed at the way most Berliners have reacted to their defeat. Definitely, they expect to do business at the same old stand in the same old way.

City of London To Honor Ike

Gen. Eisenhower arrived in London last night on the eve of ceremonies in which the City of London will pay homage to the Supreme Commander by offering him the "honorary freedom of the City."

Eisenhower flew from France in his new plane, a C54 Skymaster, named "Sunflower" in honor of his home state, Kansas. He was accompanied by several members of his staff. A ten-car cavalcade took him and his party from the suburban airport where they landed to a hotel in London's West End.

Britain's leaders, led by Prime Minister Churchill, will take part today in the ancient ceremony. Eisenhower will drive in an open carriage from Temple Bar on Fleet St. to the Guildhall in the City, where the pomp and ritual of presenting the Supreme Commander with a "token" sword of honor will take place.

Quarrel Keeps Jap Diet In Session Another Day

Six hours of argument resulting from a member's disagreement with statements by Japanese Premier Adm. Kantaro Suzuki during the special session of the Diet (Parliament) called to approve extraordinary war measures forced the legislators to extend their meeting for still another day, Tokyo Radio reported yesterday.

A Parliamentary committee was reported to have ironed out differences between the legislators and the Cabinet and the proposals—which would give Suzuki dictatorial powers—will now come before a plenary session, Tokyo said.

Japs May Yield Key Link In China Airfield Chain

CHUNGKING, June 11 (UP)—Indications are growing that the Japanese are withdrawing from Kweilin, one of the three main keys in the enemy's network of air bases in southeastern China. Chinese forces reached a point only ten miles north-west of the city yesterday and fighting is now going on, according to reports here.

Also Land on Isle; Opposition Light

Australian troops under command of Gen. MacArthur invaded the Japanese-held island of Borneo early Sunday morning, it was officially announced yesterday. Frontline dispatches reported that the invading forces in the first 36 hours pushed 2½ miles inland from two beachheads in Brunei Bay against scattered enemy opposition.

Other Australian forces landed on Labuan Island at the north end of Brunei Bay and captured the city and airfield of Labuan.

The landings, made simultaneously on Labuan and at Brooketon and Maura, inside Brunei Bay on the western coast of Borneo, were first reported by the Japanese and later confirmed by MacArthur and by Australia's acting prime minister, Joseph B. Chifley.

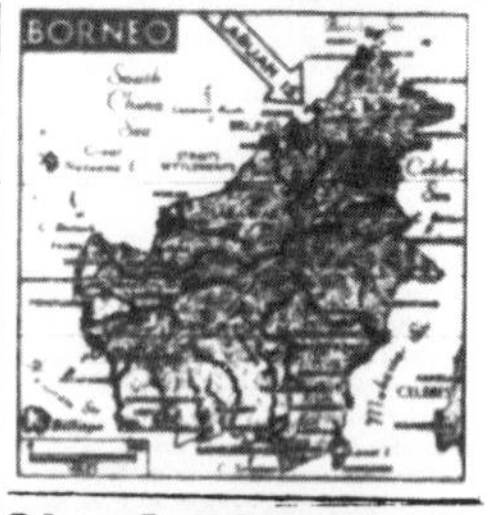

Warships of the U.S. 7th Fleet and the Australian Navy, as well as bombers and fighters of the 13th Air Force supported the landings. The naval and air bombardment leveled the enemy's beach defenses and the assault troops swept ashore with only light casualties.

The landings, 800 miles north of Singapore and 600 miles east of Indo-China, followed the invasion a month ago of Tarakan Island, 600 miles to the east by sea on the opposite side of Borneo. The Japs apparently were taken by surprise and were unprepared to put up effective resistance.

MacArthur visited the beachhead a few hours after the troops had landed. He was accompanied by Gen. George C. Kenney, Allied air forces commander in the Pacific, and Lt. Gen. Sir Leslie Morshead, senior Australian commander.

United Press reported MacArthur as saying that Japan, with the Australians firmly grasping footholds in Borneo, had definitely lost the strategic battle of the Southwest Pacific.

The Brunei area is rich in oil, rubber, lumber, coal and other resources. Brunei Bay offers an excellent anchorage.

The establishment of air and naval facilities in North Borneo, combined with those of the Philippines, will complete a string of [illegible] from Singapore [illegible].

With bases at Brunei and Tarakan, the Allies are in the geographic center of the enemy-occupied areas of Bali, the Celebes, Java, Sumatra, Malaya and Indo-China.

Enemy shipping in the South China Sea has already been practically destroyed by planes from the Philippines, and with these new bases the Allies will be able to hammer overland communication lines in Indo-China and Malaya.

Yugoslav Troops Leave Trieste as AMG Moves In

TRIESTE, June 11 (UP)—Hundreds of Yugoslav troops began moving out of Trieste today, following the agreement reached over the week end between the U.S., Britain and Yugoslavia which placed the Adriatic port and disputed areas under the control of the Allied military government. Britain is expected to operate the ports of Trieste and Pola.

The Allied government, which will work along with civilian administration already organized by Marshal Tito, is preparing to bring in food supplies for the population.

108,240 Dead Japs in Burma

ADVANCED HQ, Burma, June 11 (Reuter)—It is estimated that 108,240 Japanese have been killed in Burma since Feb. 1, 1944.

Need 500,000 To Invade Japan

OKINAWA, June 11—It will take at least 500,000 men to invade Japan and if the Japanese carry their resistance into Manchuria the Pacific war could easily last two years after the fall of Japan proper, Gen. Joseph W. Stilwell, Army Ground Forces commander, declared here today. Stilwell has been at the front for several days, watching the tactics of troops whose training is his responsibility.

"We would be foolish to start to invade Japan with anything less," he said. "When you have to attack an enemy you're not exactly sure about you want to take along a full load. Well, I think we should take along a full load.

"Even after Honshu Island and Tokyo fall, it is quite possible we will have to fight the Japs in Manchuria. If that happens the war could easily last as long as two years in the provinces north of the Yellow River."

The former American commander in China still can see no reason to expect a Japanese crack-up. "I can't see that when they are so tenacious individually," he said, "that we can expect a crack in morale in the mass."

Asked how much help could be expected from China, Stilwell smiled, shook his head and said: "I have to keep off that subject by order."

—Vignette of War—

Norway Still Full of Nazis

OSLO, June 11 (UP)—Norway wants to be rid of the Germans—and the commonest question asked today is, "When are they going to go?"

It is a strange situation where there are still thousands more fully-armed Germans than there are Allied troops. Only 48,000 of the 400,000 Germans still in Norway have been disarmed.

The most recent official statement on the subject said merely that it was impossible to forecast when the Germans would leave.

They are still running more special military services than the Allies. Many telephone calls from Oslo still go through the German military exchange. If a teleprinter circuit is required, British officers order the Germans to lead them there. "It will be done," the Germans reply, and soon it is—with German operators at both ends of the line.

Allied planes still use the German weather service and fly into the country on a German beam.

When the question of German "freedom" arises, Allied military officials point out that German troops in Norway are not prisoners of war, but only members of a surrendered army, according to the Geneva Convention.

RAF to Discharge 300,000

About one-third of the approximately 1,000,000 men and women of the Royal Air Force will be discharged from active duty, beginning June 18, in the next 12 months, an Air Ministry spokesman announced yesterday.

More men will be sent to the Far East and about 100,000 will be retrained this year for the war against Japan, he declared. A large influx of RAF recruits will make up for the loss of personnel by discharge.

Iwo Jima Escaped Its Bombs

U.S. Plane Bags 'Ghost' B29

IWO JIMA, June 11 (Reuter)—Soldiers manning this outpost, which is now a way-station on the Superfortress run between the Marianas and Japan, watched grimly fascinated as an American P61 night-fighter chased a bomb-laden "ghost" B29 twice over the island and shot it down into the sea.

A direct flak hit over Osaka killed the pilot, knocked out the radio equipment and slammed the bomb doors shut, preventing the release of the bomb load. The crippled plane was flown to Iwo Jima, far behind the rest of the formation, by the co-pilot, who had been wounded.

On the way it was picked up by a patrolling Black Widow night fighter piloted by Lt. Arthur Shepherd. He guided the flak-battered B29 and at the same time flashed radio warnings to other planes to keep clear.

Since the big craft's instrument panel was shot away and the nose badly damaged, a landing was impossible and a crash-landing would have exploded the bombs. Consequently, the co-pilot gave the bail-out order.

With only the dead pilot aboard, the crippled Superfort started an unguided flight. The Black Widow followed.

Firing all eight guns, Shepherd poured bursts into the bomber's engines. The left outside engine caught fire but still the ship flew on.

Reduced power on one side swung the bomber over this island. Onlookers held their breath until it cleared the island and then saw the fighter give the bomber everything it had—some 546 rounds of machine-gun bullets and 320 rounds of cannon-fire, finally bringing the ghost ship down.

Planet Photo

WHERE HUMPTY DUMPTY-ED: Hitler's famed "West Wall" is being dismantled by the Germans, who thought it impregnable. At Scheveningen, Holland, a fashionable seaside resort whose promenade was surrounded by massive concrete walls, topped with glass spikes and lined with anti-tank traps and mines, Germans are shown removing detonators from "potato masher" hand grenades found in one of the emplacements.

THE STARS AND STRIPES
MEDITERRANEAN

Vol. 2, No. 14, Friday, June 22, 1945 | Printed In Italy | TWO LIRE

82-Day Okinawa Battle Over

Frisco Conference To Close Tuesday With Truman Talk

Charter Draft Requires Only Few Changes For Completion

SAN FRANCISCO, June 21—The United Nations Conference, which has been in session here since April 24 to draw up a new world charter, will adjourn next Tuesday with its task done even beyond optimistic expectations.

President Truman will address the conference next Tuesday before its adjournment, Secretary of State Edward R. Stettinius Jr., announced last night.

"We can set this date," Stettinius said, "with entire confidence, since the charter will be in draft form today, and only technical and formal steps remain to complete our great enterprise." It was hoped that the conference could end Saturday, Stettinius said, but the delay was unavoidable because several delegations had asked for postponement and time was needed to complete technical details.

The President will arrive Monday from Washington state, where he is visiting. Before his speech on Tuesday, the delegates of 50 nations will sign the charter. This task will begin on Monday afternoon, and the ceremony, which will be filmed, will take eight hours.

The conference proceeded at full blast yesterday, with these accomplishments most important:

1. Unanimous approval was voted at a public commission meeting of the committee decision reached on the most troublesome conference problem—the voting procedures in the Security Council.

2. The last outstanding problem was cleared up. It concerned the extent of the discussion and recommendatory powers of the General Assembly.

Adoption of the Yalta formula for the Security Council was accompanied by many solemn speeches on the harmony and faith existing among the United Nations.

In the main, delegates who spoke before the commission represented countries which had been most vigorous in their opposition to the formula—an opposition based on the premise that it grants excessive power to the five permanent members of the Council.

All expressed their confidence that the permanent members would not misuse that power. Their position was perhaps summed up best by Peter Fraser, Prime Minister of New Zealand, who said that although he regarded the formula as a "defect" in the charter, the work of the conference must be judged

(Continued on page 8)

Gen. Nelson Appointed MTOUSA Chief Of Staff

AFHQ, June 21—Maj. Gen. Otto L. Nelson Jr., Deputy Commander, MTOUSA, today was named Chief of Staff of MTOUSA by Gen. Joseph T. McNarney, Deputy Supreme Allied Commander of MTO and commander of MTOUSA.

He succeeds Maj. Gen. George D. Pence as Chief of Staff. General Pence has left the theater for a new assignment, an AFHQ statement said. General Nelson will continue his duties as Deputy MTOUSA Commander.

AFHQ also announced the appointment of Col. Kenneth D. McKenzie as chief of transportation of MTOUSA, succeeding Col. Edward H. Lastayo.

Hitler And Goering Old Drug Addicts

SHAEF, June 21—Hitler had taken strychinine for energy during the latter years of his life, Dr. Karl Brandt, physician in the Fuehrer's entourage, revealed to intelligence officers today.

The doctor also disclosed that Herman Goering was a confirmed drug addict. Without these drugs, Goering would have become a raving lunatic. In captivity, he was receiving now a diminishing supply currently estimated at about 18 pills daily, a SHAEF spokesman said.

Reich On Her Knees, Not Out, Says Monty

21ST ARMY GROUP HQ., June 21 (Reuter's)—Field Marshal Bernard L. Montgomery said last night that Germany was not down but only on her knees. The next two or three months, he said would be a testing period.

German SS troops were likely to be kept in prison cages for 20 years, he said. Members of the German general staff, he added, would be taken from Germany and isolated in small colonies where they would be kept in prison communities for an indefinite time. The exile was to prevent the German general staff from hatching future plots, he said.

When Montgomery was asked about Germany's immediate future, he said the Allies would have to keep close watch on a million trained German soldiers who would soon be demobilized in Germany.

Wives of men in occupation forces situated in Germany would be unable to live there for the present owing to the lack of accomodations, Montgomery said. This applied to all British officials living in Germany irrespective of rank.

Nazi Industrialists In Plot, Says Solon

WASHINGTON, June 21 (UP)—Sen. Harley M. Kilgore (D., W. Va.), recently returned from Germany, charged today that Nazi industrialists have prepared detailed plans to rearm Germany and finance Nazi underground activities.

The allegation is based on hitherto undisclosed documents.

"Masquerading as neutral businessmen, without political allegiance, they have already conceived vicious plans for a third attempt at world conquest," Kilgore said.

He said that hearings will be opened tomorrow before the Senate Military Affairs Subcommittee.

Kilgore's report cited meetings of leading German industrialists in the latter part of 1944 at which they warned that Germany had lost the war.

The report said they tried to disassociate themselves from the Nazi party, strengthen economic contacts with foreign firms "individually and without any suspicion," and cloak their future activities under the guise of non-military research.

The documents revealed that research offices were to be established in large cities and small villages whose existence was to be known to only a few in each industry and by the chief of the Nazi party. "As soon as the party is strong enough to re-establish control over Germany, the industrialists will be paid for their effort and cooperation by concessions and orders," one document revealed.

12 Polish Leaders Ruled Diversionists By Soviet Tribunal

Prison Sentences Range From Four Months To Ten Years

MOSCOW, June 21—Twelve of the 16 Polish underground army leaders today were found guilty of "diversionist activities" behind the Red Army line and given sentences ranging from four months to 10 years.

(Reuter's quoted the sentences as reading "deprivation of freedom," rather than prison terms.)

The 10-year sentence was given to General Leopold Okulicki, charged by the prosecution as being the ringleader of the accused. Other sentences were:

Jan Jankowski, eight years; Adam Bein and Stanislaw Juskowitz, five years; K. V. Puzhak, 18 months; Kasimir S. Baginski, one year; Alexander Zwecziwersky, eight months; Eugene Czarnowski, six months; Stanislaw Merzuva, O. F. Stupulkowski, J. S. Hatsenski and F. A. Urbanski, four months each.

Three of the 16 defendants were acquitted and another, Soviet dispatches said, was ill and would stand trial later.

Diplomatic observers and correspondents who had been invited to the trial by the Soviet government agreed that the Russian prosecution had been lenient in not asking the death penalty. The prosecution earlier said that Russia would not ask for death for the accused because "they were no longer dangerous to the Soviet Union."

The Associated Press and Reuter's said one of the important effects of the trials would be a factor in the expected reorganization of the Polish provisional government and a likelihood that it would eventually be recognized by the United States and Great Britain.

The end of the trial also meant total "embarrassment" for the London Polish Government in Exile, which gave orders, the accused admitted, for failure to disband the Polish Home Army in the rear of the Red Army, and other anti-Soviet directives, observers said.

General Okulicki, whose forehead glistened with beads of perspiration as he took the stand in his own defense, pleaded for mercy on the grounds that he was "politically and morally responsible for the action of the underground army, but legally not guilty."

He said that there is no proof

(Continued on page 8)

Nimitz Reports Victory; 87,343 Japanese Killed

GUAM, June 21—The battle of Okinawa is over. In a special communique, Fleet Admiral Chester W. Nimitz today announced the successful completion of the 82-day campaign in which almost 90,000 enemy troops were killed or captured.

The announcement of the end of one of the bitterest and longest campaigns of the Pacific war came within an hour after General Joseph W. Stilwell was named to take over command of the 10th U. S. Army in future operations.

General Stilwell succeeds Lt. Gen. Simon Bolivar Buckner Jr., who was killed several days ago by Japanese shellfire in a forward OP on Okinawa.

The text of Admiral Nimitz' brief communique read:

"After 82 days of fighting, the battle of Okinawa has been won. Organized resistance ceased on June 21. Enemy garrisons in two small pockets are being mopped up."

Earlier, a communique from Admiral Nimitz' headquarters said that the remaining pockets were being pressed from all sides by forces supported by flamethrowers and tanks. Resistance still encountered came mostly from snipers hiding behind rocks and in the tall grass.

The communique said 87,343 Japanese have been killed so far on Okinawa, while 2,565 have been taken prisoners.

Meanwhile, Australian 9th Division troops made a third landing on Borneo, this time at Mampakul about 20 miles west of last Sunday's landing at Weston.

Land troops, supported by artillery fire from Labuan island in Brunei Bay, stormed ashore against no opposition, a communique said.

The new landing gives the Australians control of shores bordering both entrances into the important Brunei Bay.

In the Philippines, U. S. troops on Luzon advanced another seven miles into the Cagayan valley and liberated Ilagan, capital of a northern Luzon province, encountering only scattered resistance.

General Douglas MacArthur's communique said heavy bombers and fighters again bombed the Balikpapan oil area along the Borneo east coast and struck at Japheld airfields in all parts of Borneo.

The Tokyo radio reported 300 Allied planes attacked Wake island early in the day, but no confirmation of this was contained in today's communiques.

GUAM, June 21—U. S. forces are still fighting the Japanese on Saipan island after nearly a year of U. S. occupation, Admiral Nimitz said today.

Since May 27, U. S. forces in night skirmishes have killed 44 Japs on the island and captured 13 others, he said. In addition, 43 Japs have surrendered during that period.

U. S. forces took the island July 8, 1944.

10TH ARMY CHIEF

GENERAL STILWELL

Chinese Threaten Liuchow Air Base

CHUNGKING, June 21—Veteran Chinese troops pushed through Japanese defenses to within three miles of the one-time U. S. air base at Liuchow and to within six miles of Liuchow itself, the high command announced today.

Assault columns captured a strategic highway junction southwest of the city, while other Chinese troops engaged the Japanese in a fierce battle for the city itself, the announcement said.

In Burma, Allied forces occupied Paukkaung, 22 miles east of Prome, which had been abandoned by the Japanese in their retreat eastward. The Allies also occupied Enyinmakhaung, a village 36 miles southeast of Prome.

CHUNGKING, June 21—A new tactical headquarters will be established shortly by U. S. Army forces in China, Lt. Gen. Albert C. Wedemeyer's headquarters announced today.

The new location, as yet unannounced, will serve as General Wedemeyer's field headquarters.

'The Voice' Bags GI Cheers But Nary A Swooning Wac

By Sgt. BOB FLEISHER
Staff Correspondent

ROME, June 21—In the words of an old Roman named Julius Caeser, it was a simple case of "I came, I saw, I conquered" for the first Frank Sinatra show in Italy tonight.

They "came" to the Summer Festival at the Rome Rest Center; they "saw" about 2,000 GIs, Wacs and civilian guests; and they "conquered" nearly everybody in sight. Whatever may have been the pre-performance audience temper it was all with the "Voice" the gags and the dances before the show was ten minutes old.

Thirty minutes before Master of Ceremonies Phil Silvers stepped on to the stage at 8:30, chairs and tables around the dance floor were at a premium and the space in front of the microphone was jammed with GIs sitting on the cement floor.

It was definitely a holiday crowd with gags about swooning and bobby sox crowding each other for space.

"Let her faint. It's good for her in the fresh air," one soldier advised his friend who was lucky enough to have a date.

While Sinatra was definitely the big attraction as far as most of the audience was concerned, he is not by any means a one man show.

Phil Silvers, an old gag man from way back, had no trouble getting his laughs—by himself or with

(Continued on page 8)

Ex-Prisoner Of Nazis Forms Norway Cabinet

OSLO, June 21—Norway's "strong man," 46-year-old Laborite Einar Gerhardsen, who spent years in German concentration camps, today completed the formation of a new Norwegian cabinet.

It includes two Communists and members of the resistance movement, but retains the political complexion of the refugee government which had a majority of Labor when it resigned after returning to the liberated homeland.

Gerhardsen was Mayor of Oslo when the Nazis invaded the country. He returned to Norway a few days before liberation from more than three years in Nazi concentration camps and prisons.

S & S Weatherman . . .
LONDON, MIDLANDS, WALES, SCOTLAND.
Cloudy. Occasional rain. Cool.

New York — London Edition — Paris

THE STARS AND STRIPES

Daily Newspaper of U.S. Armed Forces in the European Theater of Operations

Vol. 5 No. 212—1d. — WEDNESDAY, JULY 11, 1945

. . . Predicts for Today
GENERAL FORECAST.
Cloudy with occasional rain throughout British Isles.

1,000 Planes Over Tokyo 8 Hrs.

Mightiest Men o' War In Big Strike

WASHINGTON, July 10 (UP)—America's newest and mightiest ships of war are among those riding in the huge 3rd Fleet carrier task force now bombarding Tokyo and daring the enemy to come out and fight.

The greatest is the battleship Iowa of at least 45,000 tons. First of the six ships laid down in the Iowa class, the Iowa, with a main armament of nine 16-inch guns, was completed in 1942. At least three others of this class have been completed.

Three other battleships named by Adm. Nimitz as participating in the blow were the South Dakota, Indiana and Massachusetts. They are all of the new Indiana class, of 35,000 tons. Completed in 1941, these ships also carry a main armament of nine 16-inch guns. As in the case of the Iowa, further armament has been added since they were completed.

The South Dakota is the most famous of the battleships in the task force. In the drawn-out battle of the Solomons it shot down 32 attacking planes while protecting a carrier.

Carriers in the task force represent two of America's most numerous class of flat tops. One is the Essex, of 27,000 tons. These have an announced capacity of 100 planes each and very probably more. They have an announced speed of 35 knots.

The Independence and San Jacinto are of the nine-ship Independence class of 10,000 tons. Light, fast carriers, they are unofficially reported to carry between 50 and 60 planes.

Three of the four cruisers were completed only last year. Most powerful is the Chicago, with nine eight-inch guns and four aircraft. She was completed in 1944, one of the Baltimore class of heavily-armored heavy cruisers. The San Juan, of 6,000 tons, is of the San Diego class of light cruisers. She was completed in 1941 and carries 16 five-inch guns.

The Springfield and Atlanta, both completed in 1944, are of the 10,000-ton Cleveland class of light cruisers. They have a main battery of 12 six-inch guns and carry four aircraft each.

Navy Accounts System Scored

WASHINGTON, July 10 (ANS)—A House Naval Subcommittee today questioned the effectiveness of the Navy's cost accounting system in determining to what extent the citizen is being protected in the use of his tax dollar.

After a lengthy review of personnel and cost procedures at dry-docks, shipyards, air facilities and other shore installations, the committee, headed by Rep. Lyndon B. Johnson (D-Tex.), asserted:

"It is apparent that the Undersecretary of the Navy does not have adequate means for measuring the relative efficiency of operation of the Navy's industrial establishments and effective utilization of manpower."

It cited as an example the fact that 12 months elapsed between the completion of a ship and the date when final figures on it became available.

The committee also charged inadequate attention to the problems of its 500,000 civilian employes.

Board to Run Farben Plants

FRANKFURT, Germany, July 10—An advisory board has been appointed to control and direct the recently-seized I. G. Farbenindustrie, the U.S. Group Control Council announced yesterday.

Associated Press Photo

DRAMA ON CARRIER DECK: Shrapnel and debris fly through the air after explosion of a bomb dropped accidentally by a Navy torpedo bomber as it taxied along the flight deck of a carrier in the Pacific. The man lying on the edge of the deck is hit and died a few minutes later. The two men on the right are wounded and about to fall.

Grew Says U.S. Got Unofficial 'Peace Feelers'

WASHINGTON, July 10 (AP)—The Japanese know beyond question that their defeat is certain and they are using "purported peace feelers" in an attempt to stir dissension among the Allies with the objective of attaining a peace short of unconditional surrender, Acting Secretary of State Joseph C. Grew said today.

Grew emphasized that the U.S. had received "no peace offers from the Jap government either through official or unofficial channels."

He said conversations relating to peace had been reported to the State Department from various parts of the world, but in no case had the approach been made by a person who could speak authoritatively for the Japanese government.

"The policy of this government is and will continue to be unconditional surrender. . . . That is the best comment I can make upon peace feelers and rumors of peace feelers of whatever origin," he said.

Quit Now or Be Grab Bag, Japs Told

WASHINGTON, July 10 (ANS)—The OWI today broadcast to Japan an argument by columnist David Lawrence for unconditional surrender before the political and international situation in the Far East becomes complicated by the demands of other powers.

Lawrence was replying to a recent Tokyo broadcast by Adm. Kichisaburo Nomura, last Japanese ambassador to the U.S. Nomura referred to Lawrence's writings on casualties and said that the Allies' unconditional surrender policy would cost them higher casualties.

The Lawrence answer said in part: "Japan's only chance for survival as an economic factor in the world lies in surrender, not a year or two hence, after Allied losses have been heavy, but now, in the next 30 to 60 days, before the political and international situation in the Far East grows complicated by the demands of other powers than the U.S."

Berlin Food Problem Is Solved by 3 Allies

BERLIN, July 10 (AP)—The three Allied powers have amicably solved the problem of feeding nearly 3,000,000 Berlin civilians, it was announced officially tonight.

The official statement said that Soviet Marshal Zhukov, British Lt. Gen. Sir Ronald Weeks and U.S. Lt. Gen. Lucius D. Clay decided that Berlin's food supplies would come from "contributions from all Allied occupation zones in Germany."

The three officers, who met in Berlin, also took steps to solve the coal problem of the German capital along the same lines.

They also arranged for the French representative to participate tomorrow in the first meeting of Berlin's Inter-Allied Joint Command.

In effect the Soviet position was vindicated by today's decisions after failure among the same three representatives to agree last Saturday. Presumably British and American transport systems will bring considerable stocks of food and coal into their Berlin sectors from western occupation zones. The Anglo-American demand had been for all Berlin to be supplied from the Soviet-held hinterland.

The British and Americans are believed to be able to meet the food problem in a matter of days—safely before the small reserves in their sectors are exhausted.

Charges Reich Plans New War

WASHINGTON, July 10 (ANS)—The Germans remain the major threat to world peace and already have "set in motion" plans for a third attempt to enslave the world, the Senate Subcommittee on War Mobilization asserted last night.

"Germany today is better prepared to implement her plot for world conquest than she was at the end of World War I," the group headed by Sen. Harley M. Kilgore (D-W. Va.) said in a preliminary report to the Senate Military Affairs Committee.

The committee said that despite strategic bombing many of Germany's major war industries still were intact. It listed Germany's major war-making resources as the world's third strongest industrial economy, tremendous industrial recuperative power, a world-wide network of economic and political reserves and a science of aggression perfected by her leading industrialists.

Armless, Legless Vet to Walk on Artificial Limbs

BATTLE CREEK, Mich., July 10 (ANS)—Armless and legless, the first such battle casualty of the war, M/Sgt. Fredrick Hensel, of Corbin, Ky., is recovering at Percy Jones General Hospital and doctors say he'll walk again on artificial legs and also will be able to use artificial arms.

Hensel had both legs above the knees and his left arm above the elbow blown off on Okinawa June 2 when he stepped on a Japanese land mine. Despite desperate efforts by doctors to save his mangled right forearm, that, too, was amputated while he was en route to the States.

Hospital officials said there had been another such case in the Army during the war, but he wasn't a battle casualty. He was an Army pilot who lost parts of all four limbs due to freezing after a plane crash in New England.

Hensel, meanwhile, drawled: "I make a good picture for propaganda against the next war."

Powers Row on Vienna

Disagreement still exists among the major powers over the occupation zones for Vienna, a British Foreign Office commentator disclosed yesterday. He declined to indicate what the stumbling-block was, but said the disagreement had delayed activation of an Allied control commission for Austria.

Bare 15th Army HQ Ship Sinking

SHAEF, July 10—The British troopship Empire Javelin, bringing the main body of U.S. 15th Army HQ across the English Channel, was sunk in mid-passage by a torpedo or mine Dec. 28 with a loss of 13 soldiers, it was disclosed here today in publication of a part of 15th Army's history. Twenty others were injured.

The survivors of the stricken ship, totaling 1,483 officers and EM, were transferred to the French frigate L'Escarmouche, which had drawn up alongside.

The entire complement of survivors jumped from the Javelin to the decks of L'Escarmouche in 55 minutes. A few minutes after the transfer was completed an explosion shook the Javelin which sank sternwards into the Channel.

Transatlantic Calls Halted for a Time

Acceptance of requests for transatlantic calls from the U.K. by U.S. Army personnel has been discontinued indefinitely due to the heavy backlog of such calls, the British GPO announced yesterday.

Commercial calls will continue to be accepted and as soon as the arrears have been cleared social calls will be resumed it was said.

Commercial calls are only those between business firms in England and the U.S. All personnel calls are rated as social.

Other Ships By Hundreds Bomb Isles

More than 1,000 carrier-based planes from Adm. William F. Halsey's massive 3rd Fleet, supplemented by hundreds of 5th and 7th Air Force fighters and bombers from Iwo Jima and Okinawa, hammered the Japanese home islands for more than eight hours yesterday in the greatest air attack of the Pacific war.

The assault, which Tokyo Radio said was the "first step" toward an invasion of the home islands, began at dawn when the first fighters, fighter-bombers and dive-bombers roared off the flat tops of Vice Adm. John S. McCain's task force, believed to be cruising some 200 miles southeast of the main Jap island of Honshu.

Hour after hour the assault went on, with planes shuttling back and forth between carriers and targets, most of which were located in Tokyo and the Kanto district around the capital. As many as 700 planes were over Tokyo at one time, reports stated.

The carrier planes concentrated their attacks on Tokyo and an estimated 80 airfields in the Kanto district around the capital. Kanto, the plain area around Tokyo, is the site of Japan's greatest single concentration of airfields and aircraft installations.

Perfect Weather Over Targets

Weather over the targets was perfect, with visibility unlimited. Pilots returning from early strikes said anti-aircraft fire was scanty and caused little trouble. No fighter opposition was encountered, and one United Press dispatch stated that the task force had broken radio silence to challenge the Japs to come out and fight.

Planes roamed the skies at will doing reconnaissance work and taking pictures to aid later attacks.

It was not clear from dispatches whether the assault had ended at dusk. U.S. military experts predicted that the assault would continue for at least two or three more days.

Adm. Nimitz announced at 9.30 AM that the carrier-plane raids were in progress and in an unprecedented statement identified 26 of the warships participating in the operation. Nimitz also listed the flag officers directing the attacks.

This was the first time the Navy had named the components of a fleet while they were still in action.

The Japanese said ten carriers were being used. At least ten would be necessary to launch 1,000 planes.

The first carrier-plane attack followed the big 3,500-ton incendiary and high-explosive raid by between 500 and 550 Superforts on five widely-scattered cities. One of the targets was Sendai, 190 miles north of Tokyo, and the 3,960-mile trip there and back was the longest mission flown by the B29s from their bases in the Marianas.

B29s, Mustangs Join Attack

A small force of Superforts and several hundred Mustang fighter-bombers joined in the attack yesterday and straightened out some of the kinks in the Kinki district near Osaka just before noon.

Later in the afternoon 30 Liberators, 30 Mitchells and 70 fighters raided targets on the southern Jap island of Kyushu.

Nimitz made the first official announcement that Liberators and Mitchells had attacked the Japanese islands when he disclosed that they had struck Omura airfield on Kyushu July 5. He did not say where these planes were based, but they were presumed to be on Okinawa.

Coinciding with these attacks, the War Department announced yesterday that the hundred thousandth ton of bombs hit Japan on July 4 and that "Japan has already been hit as hard from the air as Germany itself when our forces invaded the Continent."

In Borneo, Dutch East Indies troops made two new landings on the north side of Balikpapan Bay and were mopping up Jap troops in the area. Australian troops continued to push north beyond Manggar airfield. The Japs were leaving road blocks of blazing oil drums in the Aussies' path to hinder their advance into the Sambodja oilfields.

Army Backs Doctor's Barring Of Hospital Aid to Marine Vet

WASHINGTON, July 10 (ANS)—Walter Reed Hospital authorities said today that investigation absolved Capt. John A. Nesbitt of blame in his refusal to admit a 22-year-old marine for treatment after the veteran had suffered a battle-fatigue collapse at a Fourth of July fireworks display.

The ex-marine, Wallace Reid, had fallen to the ground after hearing explosions and tried to dig a foxhole in the pavement.

Sobbing uncontrollably and near unconsciousness, he was taken to the Army hospital in a private automobile, where Nesbitt, the medical officer on duty, gave him a brief examination and sent the car to a civilian hospital.

Spokesmen at the hospital said that Nesbitt had acted according to regulations. Had Reid required emergency treatment, the spokesmen said, he would have been admitted.

Meanwhile, Rep. Bertrand D. Gearhart (R-Cal.) told the House that he considered it "outrageous" for the Army hospital to turn away a veteran in need of immediate treatment.

Gearhart said it was his understanding that Reid did need immediate care and that he had been turned away simply on "legalistic grounds" involving a marine entering an Army hospital.

Gearhart repeated his earlier demand that the House Military Affairs Committee investigate the matter.

The hospital spokesman said reports of the affair had been "exaggerated" and that Nesbitt's judgment was borne out by the fact that Reid was discharged from Mount Alto hospital after spending a night there.

Allied Status for Italy Urged by House Group

WASHINGTON, July 10 (AP)—The House Foreign Affairs Committee voted today to authorize President Truman to invite Italy into the United Nations.

The committee took this action by approving a resolution requesting the President to use his good offices to that end.

Italy is now treated diplomatically as a co-belligerent, which leaves it short of full Allied status.

Two Cents A Copy

Pacific Edition
THE STARS AND STRIPES
U. S. Armed Forces Daily In The Pacific Ocean Areas

20 Sen A Copy In The Ryukyus

Vol. 1. No. 53 Friday, July 13, 1945

Typhoon Hits U. S. Fleet

Report Japs Saving Planes For Invasion

GUAM (AP)—Virtually unopposed air blows by around 700 B-29s, heavy and medium bombers, fighters and long range search planes across a 770-mile arc of Japan, extending north and south of Tokyo, were announced Friday.

As enemy homeland factories and railroads were wrecked and even the smallest shipping sunk offshore, Brig. Gen. David F. Hutchison of the Far East air force told the Associated Press at Okinawa that Japan obviously was hoarding planes to use in suicide tactics when Yank infantrymen storm Nippon's invasion beaches.

Rear Adm. D. C. Ramsey, new chief of staff of the 5th fleet, estimated Japan might have 9,000 planes available and probably could throw about 4,000 into the battle over Japan.

450-Mile Area Fired

United Press reported that jellied gasoline flames, whipped by a Pacific gale flared over a 450-mile strip of the homeland as Gen. George Kenney, commander of the Far East air force, grimly warned the Japs to get set for 'round-the-clock, blasting in the near future.

The fires were started by five fleets of Superforts totalling 500 to 550 planes which hit the homeland in the 38th consecutive day of aerial attacks.

Kenney, commander of three air forces, all based within striking distance of Japan, promised to attack from "10 feet to 10,000" with fire bombs and explosives and fighters and bombers 24 hours a day. His statement came after it was announced that the 7th AAF, heretofore a Central Pacific outfit, has been added to the 5th and 13th AAFs in the FEAAF.

Domei, the Japanese news agency, said the 24-hour attacks already are a reality. The Japs said the Superforts, which have been pounding Japan steadily for months, have shifted their concentration from major cities to smaller war centers, and their next and probably final phase before invasion will be attacks on railway and highway communications.

A Japanese broadcast said the latest Superfort raid hit seven cities—Ogaki, Ichinomiya, Kagamigahara, Tsuruga, Utsonomiya, Tsurumi and Koriyama.

The Japs admitted that flames were still raging out of control hours after the strike at some points.

Official American announce-

(Continued on Back Page)

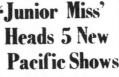

LOVE PWs—Mrs. Fae Burns, 19 (above), and Mrs. Lenora Hodgson, 26, face trial at Seattle, Wash., where they are charged with aiding escape of Italian prisoners of war. They say they love and will marry the men after they are divorced. Mrs. Burns, whose husband is in the Pacific, is the mother of two children.

British Loose Sumatra Blow

CALCUTTA (AP) — British fleet units have bombarded the strategic Nicobar islands while carrier planes attacked airfields in northwest Sumatra, southeast Asia command heaquarters announced Friday in a special communique.

From July 5 to 10 British minesweepers swept the approaches Malacca strait, which lies between Sumatra and the great naval base of Singapore, without sighting a Japanese vessel.

While fleet units attacked the Nicobars, planes laid explosives on the islands. The Nicobars lie 200 miles northwest of Sumatra, rich Dutch oil producing island, and about 900 miles from Singapore. They are 400-mile west of the Kra peninsula of Malaya, linking Singapore to the mainland.

Japanese broadcasts, first to tell of the attacks on the Nicobars, speculated that a landing attempt would be made.

Diana Lewis Hurt

WAUKESHA, Wis. (ANS)—Diana Lewis, actress wife of screen star William Powell, is recovering in Veterans Hospital here from minor head injuries received when the automobile in which she was riding collided with another car.

'Junior Miss' Heads 5 New Pacific Shows

By T/5 GEO. S. TALMAGE
Stars and Stripes Staff Writer

Five new USO-Camp Shows have arrived on Oahu.

Casts of the three-act comedy, "Junior Miss", three hospital shows, and a musical group reported to Honolulu's Registration Division for finger-printing Thursday before embarking on a six-month tour of the Hawaiian and forward area circuit. Fifteen girls and 17 men are in the troupes.

In the cast of "Junior Miss" are three vets of World War I—Brandon Peters, Alex Campbell, and Paul Kirk Giles—and a vet of World War II, Jay Eldrige, discharged from the Navy for wounds received when his ship was torpedoed off Casablanca. Four more men and six girls complete the cast.

Not Abbreviated

"We're putting on the same three-act production which played at the Lyceum Theatre in New York for a year and a half," Peters, manager of the troupe, said. "It is not an abbreviated version."

One of their cast, Elizabeth Keen, was in New Guinea with the "Over 21" troupe.

"I got back as quickly as I could," she said. "Service audiences are wonderful and responsive. Besides," she added, "I like to be in uniform, too."

Cowboy Phil and his three Golden West girls, Abbie, Gay and Tina, are here to entertain men in the hospital wards.

Western Flavor

"We sing and play cowboy, Western and old-time songs," said the tall cowpuncher, "and there's dancing, too."

Two more hospital shows, "Mystery and Melody" and

(Continued on Back Page)

Cpl. Jim Newman Alive 12th Day

FORT WORTH, Tex. (UP)—Cpl. Jim Newman completed his twelfth day on borrowed time Thursday and his mother said the young soldier was "eating well and is about the same."

Corporal Jim, 25, was sent home by Army doctors at Santa Fe, N. M., who gave him two days to live and, at the outside, no more than one chance in a thousand to recover from the effects of three years in a Japanese prison camp.

Mrs. O. F. Newman, Corporal Jim's mother, said her son is being given no solid foods and no medicine. He is clinging to life on a diet of vitamin pills, orange juice, grape juice and milk.

Seize Nazi Property

LONDON (UP)—The Berlin radio said Friday that the city council has decreed that the property of all Nazis, and anyone who aided them, will be confiscated in Berlin.

21 Halsey Ships Hurt; Most Back In Action

GUAM (AP)—A raging typhoon lashed Adm. William F. (Bull) Halsey's Third fleet with 138 mile an hour winds last June 5, tore the bow off the cruiser Pittsburgh and damaged at least 20 other warships, Adm Chester W. Nimitz announced after virtually every damaged ship was back in action.

At least four of the damaged ships, the battleship Massachusetts and Indiana, the carrier San Jacinto, and the destroyer John Rodgers, participated in last Tuesday's 1,000-plane carrier strike at Tokyo.

The typhoon damaged more ships than the Japanese navy has been able to do in action in any single battle. Nimitz said no ships were sunk.

Pittsburgh Being Refitted

The cruiser Pittsburgh, which miraculously stayed afloat, is being refitted for action. Presumably some additional ships, not identified, were damaged and have not returned to sea.

A thunderous sea ripped off 104 feet of the Pittsburgh's prow "and tossed it aside as though it were a match box to wallow in the storm," AP Correspondent Robbin Coons reported.

Sealed bulkheads kept the Pittsburgh afloat and the cruiser, normally capable of 33 knots, lumbered back to Guam at nine knots. The bow was taken in tow and brought back to port.

Towering seas crushed 25 feet of the carrier Hornet's flight deck and badly damaged several destroyers.

Flipped Like Beanbags

Planes on one small escort carrier "were flipped around like beanbags, tossed into the air end over end and piled in a jumbled heap of wreckage."

Ships which suffered damage and have returned to action include Essex class carriers Hornet and Bennington; the fast battleships Massachusetts, Indiana and Alabama; the Independence class cruiser-type carriers San Jacinto and Belleau Wood; destroyers John Rodgers and Blu; escort carrier Bougainville.

Three other cruisers and seven destroyers which suffered minor damage also have been repaired and returned to action.

Last December 18 another typhoon struck the Third Fleet between the Philippines and the Marianas and three destroyers capsized and were lost in the violent seas.

Pistol Packin' Marlene Returns From Europe

NEW YORK (ANS)—Marlene Dietrich who left Hollywood 11 months ago to entertain servicemen in Europe, came back from Paris Friday by plane, the best looking pistol packing mama customs officials had seen in some time.

Temporarily they had to confiscate several souvenirs which grateful men had given her—a pair of Luger pistols and three other German guns

New Artillery Has Less Kick Than .22 Rifle

WASHINGTON (ANS) — The Army disclosed performance details on its new kickless cannon which fires artillery shells with less recoil than a .22 rifle.

The two guns, 57 and 75 millimeter, were battle tested in Europe and now are being turned against the Japanese "with much success" the Army said.

The 57 mm. rifle, which can be fired from the shoulder or from a small tripod, weighs only 45 pounds yet can toss a regular shell weighing about three pounds for two miles.

The 75 mm. rifle, weighing 110 pounds (a regular field artillery piece weighs more than one ton) throws a 14-pound shell more than four miles.

Gen. Courtney Hodges, First Army commander, hit a three-foot-square target at 800 yards the first time he fired the 57 mm. gun shoulder style.

Although the guns resemble rocket weapons, they are rifled which increases accuracy and they fire standard artillery ammunition rather than rocket projectiles. The recoil is absorbed by allowing the counterbalancing portion of the propellant gases to escape through openings in the breech.

It's Friday, 13th At Hoodoo Ranch

MONTICELLO, Utah (ANS) — Owners of the Hoodoo Ranch aren't exactly superstitious but all employees, three cowhands and a choreboy, have Friday off with pay to avoid a repetition of the last Friday the 13th.

Nobody had ever paid much attention to the name of the place — least of all Rancher John Baker and his wife, until last April 13, a Friday.

First, one of the cowhands asked another to pull his aching tooth after breakfast. The other complied, broke the tooth and received a fragment of it in his eye.

A third cowboy was harnessing a work horse. The animal bolted, bouncing a metal piece of the harness in the cowboy's face and knocking out several teeth.

Rancher Baker offered to take the boys to town for medical attention and pulled his watch from his pocket to check the time. The time piece caught, then dislodged, striking him in the face. A few minutes later he broke his thumb while changing his trousers.

Mrs Baker decided to go to town with the others. While straining to hook a wartime girdle, she sprained her wrist.

Out in the barn the choreboy didn't like something about a cow's demeanor. Lifting his foot to kick the animal, he fell backwards and landed on a sizeable spike driven into the floor.

In the doctor's office Baker thumbed through a calendar until he found today's date. Then and there the staff was promised the holiday—with pay.

More than 60,000 soldiers in the Mediterranean Theater attend educational courses given by the Armed Forces Institute.

'Finishing School' For Infantry

How Do You Know A Jap's Dead?

By PFC. TOM GRAY
Stars and Stripes Staff Writer

"Hey, Sarge, how do you know if a Jap's dead or playing possum?" The young replacement seemed embarrassed at his own ignorance.

"They can fool you," conceded the sergeant, late of the Palaus. "I almost passed by six of 'em once. They were sprawled like deaders, but I noticed one's skin was shiny. A dead Jap won't sweat, so his skin won't shine. I shot this one and he jumped—so I shot the rest of 'em.

"That's another thing. If they jump when you shoot 'em, they were alive, so shoot again to make sure."

Typical Lesson

This is a typical session of an Army "finishing school," where battle-wise cadre noncoms awaiting rotation at replacement depots, and fresh-from-the states replacements discuss ways and means of finishing the Jap.

The "school" operates on no schedule. It holds classes during any 10 minute break, or whenever a rookie has a question to ask. Nothing is SOP, and nobody has to pay attention. But the rookies listen to every word.

At every session, comes the inevitable question, "Do you take time to aim?"

An ex-platoon sergeant answers this one. "Sometimes Lots of times though, you shoot from the hip. That's why you're taught hip firing here."

Don't Know Weapons

"Too many of you replacements don't know your weapons," said another noncom. "I've seen service and artillery troops sent to me as infantry replacements. Some of 'em couldn't load an M1.

"Every GI should at least be familiarized with all the infantry weapons, no matter what his job is. Anything can happen in combat, and usually does."

"On Iwo," a rifle sergeant said, "we actually had to hold classes in loading and unload-

(Continued on Page Four)

S & S Weatherman . . .
Clear
Maximum Temperature 88

Germany Edition
THE STARS AND STRIPES
Daily Newspaper of U.S. Armed Forces in the European Theater of Operations

Non-Fraternization
GIs take brass to task. See Mail Call, Page 2, for discussion.

Volume 1, Number 103 | Monday, July 16, 1945 | 20 Pfennig

Truman Arrives at Potsdam

3 New Ships Bombard Japan

3rd Fleet Hits Islands Again From Air, Sea

GUAM, July 15—America's newest and most powerful battleships, the 45,000-tonners Iowa, Missouri and Wisconsin, today added their fire-power to the shelling of Japan.

Their 16-inch guns—nine of them to each battlewagon—bombarded the important steel center and port of Muroran on the southeast coast of Hokkaido, the island north of Honshu.

At the same time more than 1,000 carrier planes renewed their attacks on Hokkaido and Honshu.

The twin blow by sea and air was a continuation of the Third Fleet's latest strike at Japan, which started yesterday with a heavy bombardment some 200 miles south of where the warships operated today.

Fleet Floats At Will

The bombardments apparently were carried out by two separate task forces of the Third Fleet ranging just about wherever they pleased along the Japanese coast.

The big battleships which, with other craft, composed the bombardment group in action today, are the newest, fastest, biggest and mightiest afloat. Their 45,000-tons displacement becomes 52,000 tons under full load. Each is 860 fleet long.

In addition to the nine 16-inch guns, they have 20 five-inch and scores of automatic medium and light anti-aircraft weapons. Each carries four or more planes launched by catapult to observe and correct fire during bombardments.

(An International News Service correspondent aboard the battleship South Dakota said that in yester-

(Continued on Page 8)

But What If It Hits?

SAN FRANCISCO, July 15 (ANS)—Tokyo Radio offered the Japanese small consolation today as U. S. warships ranged the coast. Speaking of the naval bombardment, the radio said: "Unless a bullseye is scored on a shelter there is nothing to fear."

Any Gripes, Boss? Just Write Mail Call

The Stars and Stripes has a new reader, the Boss himself, President Truman.

True, he has special cables from the Pacific, and we guess he has other sources of information on things back home—but he can't get Li'l Abner anywhere else in the ETO.

Furthermore, if he has any complaints, Mail Call is open to anybody, including the Commander-in-Chief.

Three Strong Points Taken on Luzon

MANILA, July 15 (ANS)—The capture of three key strongpoints in northern Luzon from Japanese remnants still strongly resisting was announced today at Gen. MacArthur's headquarters.

The Sixth Inf. Div. has taken Kiangan, which until six weeks ago was known as enemy army headquarters. In the high Cordilleras, guerrillas seized Bontoc, capitol of Luzon's mountain province.

Italy Declares War on Japan, Seeks to Join United Nations

ROME, July 15 (UP)—Italy entered the war against Japan today in a frank bid to gain a place in the ranks of the United Nations.

The declaration of war was voted unanimously by the Italian cabinet Friday. It was announced by the foreign office Saturday night and went into effect today.

(In Washington, Ambassador Alberto Tarchiani said that the Italian fleet would be placed immediately at the disposal of the Allies and probably would be routed through the Suez Canal for Pacific duty.

(He said that Italy expected to recruit a corps of ground troops for service against Japan and said Italian air force units also might be used.)

Hope for Bid

The foreign office said that the cabinet hoped the war declaration would help Italy gain the right of entry into the United Nations.

According to the announcement, Italy has considered its relations with Japan broken since September, 1943, when the Japs "interned all Italian diplomats in concentration camps both in Japan and in temporarily-occupied territories."

The foreign office cited the declaration as Italy's proof, on the eve of the Potsdam Conference, of her "resolute will to fight regimes of aggression and militarist imperialism wherever they may be."

Power of I.G. Farben Amazes Investigators

HOECHST, Germany, July 15 (AP) Findings from records of the I. G. Farbenindustrie, giant German industrial monopoly, proved so startling that a brigadier general, whose name cannot be disclosed, is flying to Washington today.

"It is one of the most amazing stories in modern times," Col. Edwin Pillsbury, who directed the seizure of 24 Farben plants, said. "The manner in which Farben agents gained control over certain industries and carried on a dominating role in the world's chemical industry is almost unbelievable," he declared.

In Pillsbury's opinion, the German war machine would have collapsed without Farbenindustrie.

Balikpapan Harbor Opened to Shipping

MANILA, July 15 (ANS)—Balikpapan harbor, greatest oil port of Borneo, was open to allied shipping today while Australian amphibious forces pushed 14 miles up the east coast of Balikpapan Bay and seized a former Japanese seaplane base.

The enemy did not resist the new landing. Some naval supplies were captured by the Australians, but the base itself had been demolished by the retiring Japanese.

Big 3 Parleys Are Expected To Start Today

POTSDAM, July 15 (AP)—President Truman arrived at the Big Three conference area by plane at 4:15 p.m., Berlin time today.

POTSDAM, July 15—President Truman, Prime Minister Churchill and Generalissimo Stalin will begin their first conference tomorrow either in the Sans Souci Palace built by Frederick the Great or Kaiser Wilhelm's former palace, according to the best information available today in this heavily-guarded residential Suburb of Berlin.

Potsdam is so alive with U.S., British and Russian military sentries, posted at close intervals and intermingled with Secret service, Scotland Yard and NKVD operatives, that the historic meeting place is completely inaccessible. Although the movements of the leaders of the three nations have been freely advertised, a veil of secrecy blankets this entire area on the eve of the conference.

President Truman's quarters during the parley will be a 30-room house once inhabited by German civilians. The house, about a 10-minute drive from the actual meeting place, was stripped of its furnishings during the war but has been refurnished since by the Russians.

Speculation as to the subjects to be discussed by the Big Three ranged from a possible Russian declaration of war on Japan to straightening out of matters connected with the joint occupation of Germany and Berlin.

An AP correspondent described the conference as "the Versailles of 1919 and the Teheran of 1943 rolled into one."

"A full dress peace conference supposedly is sure to come later, but the voices of decision regarding the European peace are Russian, American and British, and they will be heard during the next few days," he wrote.

London Storm Kills 2

LONDON, July 15 (Reuter)—A lightning and rain storm believed to be the worst since 1927 caused at least two deaths here last night and considerable damage.

Truman Hailed in Antwerp Before Flight to Potsdam

BRUSSELS, July 15—President Truman embarked by plane for Potsdam this afternoon, two and a half minutes ahead of schedule after thousands of liberated Belgians had turned out in their Sunday best to speed him on to his conference with Prime Minister Churchill and Premier Stalin.

Truman's reception began about 7 a.m. today, when he was cheered aboard the cruiser Augusta by Belgians and Hollanders lining the south banks of the Scheldt Estuary and those crowding the dikes on flooded Walcheren Island. The President appeared on deck wearing a grey tweed suit and a grey hat. He took special interest in Walcheren's broken dikes, and could see the residents waving huge flags in welcome.

No Cheers From PWs

At one turn in the Scheldt Estuary, however, there were no cheers from persons who watched the Augusta make its way toward Antwerp. These were thousands of German PWs, cooped behind barbed wire.

Mr. Truman left the Augusta at Antwerp about 11 a.m., thus becom-

(Continued on Page 8)

Allied Chiefs Gather by Air

Although it had not been announced by press time last night, all the chief participants in the Big Three conference probably have arrived at Potsdam.

Planes were whizzing all over Europe yesterday, carrying the conferees.

President Truman and his party flew from Antwerp in a fleet of C-47s. The President arrived at Potsdam at 4:15.

Prime Minister Churchill boarded a plane at Bordeaux for a nonstop flight to Berlin.

Generalissimo Stalin and Foreign Minister Vyacheslav Molotov left Moscow.

Foreign Minister Anthony Eden and Clement Attlee took off from London. Attlee, the Labor Party leader, will attend the conference with Churchill so that he will be acquainted with Big Three decisions if his party wins the British election and he becomes the next prime minister.

S & S Weatherman . . .
ENGLAND, WALES, S. SCOTLAND
Mod. N.W. Winds. Mostly Fair and Cool.

New York — London Edition — Paris

THE STARS AND STRIPES

Daily Newspaper of U.S. Armed Forces in the European Theater of Operations

Vol. 5 No. 2[illegible]—[illegible] — SATURDAY, JULY 28, 1945

. . . Prediction for Today
GENERAL FORECAST
All of U.K.,
Cool. Little Change.

Japan Spurns Ultimatum; U.S. Warns New Targets

STEEL CURTAIN GUARDS TASK FORCE: This fleet battleship protecting a carrier task force in the Pacific hurls a heavy anti-aircraft barrage to halt a Japanese bomber trying a suicide dive on one of the carriers in the group.

Attlee Names Cabinet; Bevin Foreign Secretary

Britain's new Prime Minister, Clement R. Attlee, last night announced the leading members of the new government which he had pledged will win the Pacific war, co-operate with Russia and the U.S. in building the peace and put through the socialistic domestic program of his Labor Party.

Ernest Bevin, tough-minded trade union leader who mobilized Britain for war as Minister of Labor, was named to take over the post of Foreign Secretary, formerly held by Anthony Eden.

Hugh Dalton, who was in Churchill's War Cabinet as President of the Board of Trade, was named Chancellor of the Exchequer.

Sir Stafford Cripps becomes President of the Board of Trade; Herbert Morrison, Lord President of the Council; Arthur Greenwood, Lord Privy Seal, and Sir William Jowitt, Lord Chancellor.

Churchill's future role was uncertain. He was re-elected to his seat in the House of Commons and the Times commented that "he will make a formidable and dominating figure on the front opposition bench, and his presence there will be an effective assurance to the public that he is still active in the service of the state."

Eden May Lead Party

But there was speculation, too, that he would turn over the Conservative party leadership to Eden and retire to write his memoirs.

The new Parliament will meet Aug. 1, but it will not officially be opened for business until the "address from the throne" is read Aug. 8 and debated in both the House of Lords and the Commons. This speech, prepared by Attlee, will outline the proposals of the new Left-wing government.

The impact of the Labor victory is expected to be felt politically by many governments which leaned heavily on British Conservative support.

While Attlee pledged the prosecution of the Pacific war as the new government's first task, he also said, "We are embarked on a great adventure of democracy, freedom and social justice."

Attlee was prepared to take office with the intention of nationalizing every basic industry—railroads and other transport, coal mines and heavy industries—in the United Kingdom, making the Bank of England public property and ultimately nationalizing the land. Attlee hopes, by putting them into the hands of the people, to make them stronger and more productive.

Labor Triumph Blow to Franco

MADRID, July 27 (AP)—Labor's victory in Britain was interpreted in Spain today generally as a defeat for the Falangists and Chief of State Francisco Franco.

"Britain's going Bolshevik," an official of the Falangist press censorship said when the full scope of the Labor victory became apparent. "Now we have nothing between us and Russia save the Americas, and they are withdrawing."

This comment was not typically Spanish reaction, but was typical of the reaction of Falangists and their fellow travelers in Franco's officialdom. The working classes were frankly delighted.

The Falangist press censorship agreed the public should be told the election had nothing to do with Spain and concerned only Britain's internal affairs. Another angle which will be developed is that Britain voted labor to obtain social benefits which the Falange is giving to Spain.

German Social Democrats Find 'New Hope' in Results

BERLIN, July 27 (AP)—The leaders of Germany's Social Democrat Party discussed today whether to send a congratulatory message to British laborites, as a first step in establishing friendly relations with the new British government.

The chairman of the party's central committee, Erich Gnaffke, said the British election results had given "new hope" to the Social Democrats in Germany and that they believed they would receive more sympathy and help from Attlee's administration than they had expected from Churchill's conservative regime.

U.S. Flag for St. Marylebone

In appreciation for the friendly spirit in which its citizens accepted the problems occasioned by a large influx of American troops, Col. Donald S. McConnaughy, U.K. Base Deputy Commander, presented an American flag to the Borough of St. Marylebone in colorful ceremonies Thursday at the Town Hall.

Charter OK Seen Imminent

WASHINGTON, July 27 (Reuter)—Ratification by the Senate of the United Nations charter is virtually assured late tomorrow or on Monday.

Sen. Alben Barkley, majority leader, announced that the Senate would meet in night session tonight and begin work two hours earlier than usual tomorrow. Night sessions are rare in the history of the Senate, being called only on measures of major importance.

Eighty-year-old Sen. Arthur Capper (R.-Kans.), who voted against the League of Nations in 1919, reversed his position and told the Senate the United Nations organization to keep the peace "will work."

He told his colleagues on the fourth day of debate on the charter that it has a greater chance of success than the old League ever had.

This, he said, is because of the realization that unless the Big Five powers, particularly the Big Three, work together in the post-war world, "the prospects of avoiding World War III are slender indeed."

Capper explained his vote of 1919 by saying the Versailles Peace Treaty and the League held no guarantee of American sovereignty. The new charter possesses such a guarantee, he declared.

Workers Told To Evacuate Doomed Cities

Thousands of leaflets were showered down on 11 of Japan's arms and ammunition production centers last night (Japanese time) warning them that they were next on the list for destruction from the air and that Superforts of the 20th Air Force would raid four of them in the next few days.

In an unprecedented pre-bombing warning, Maj. Gen. Curtis Lemay, commander of the 20th AF, advised the 890,000 residents of the 11 cities to flee and to "restore peace by demanding new and good leaders who will end the war."

The warning contained in 60,000 leaflets later was repeated in broadcasts from American-held Saipan, punctuating announcements of Allied demands for surrender.

The leaflets said the Air Force was determined to destroy all the tools "the military clique" was using to prolong "this useless war," but that the Americans did not wish to injure innocent people, and warned them "to evacuate the cities named and save your lives."

The targets scheduled for attack were Ichinomiya, Tsu, Ujiyamada, Nagaoka, Nishinomiya, Aomori, Ogaki, and Koriyama, all transport, munitions and industrial centers on Honshu island; Uwajima, a war industry city of Shikoku; Kurume, a rail and manufacturing center on Kyushu, and Hakodate, a manufacturing city on Hokkaido.

Won't Come Out and Fight

Some time within the next few days a "normal force" of B29s will strike four or more of these cities, it was stated.

"The Japanese have refused to come out and fight. We have been roaming their air at will, burning down cities. Now we are telling their citizens what towns we are going to burn down," Lemay said.

Gen. MacArthur announced, meanwhile, that 300 bombers and fighters from Okinawa gave Shanghai its fourth pounding in a week on Wednesday. Other Libs attacked the air center at Tsuki, on Kyushu. The enemy's hoarded fighters came to intercept the bombers and seven out of 30 were shot down. One B24 was lost.

Adm. Nimitz' communique reported bomb and rocket attacks on Anami Island in the Ryukyus, but did not mention Adm. William F. Halsey's 3rd Fleet.

There was no further word about a Japanese report of a landing by American troops on Pulgt Island off Malay Peninsula.

Jap troops on Borneo were reported withdrawing toward the Samarinda oilfields north of Balikpapan.

Chinese Fight for Kweilin, Site of Big Air Base

CHUNGKING, July 27 (Reuter)—Chinese troops have reached the western suburbs of Kweilin, Japanese base in Kwangsi province, where fighting is now raging, a Chinese high command communique reported today. Kweilin is one of the most important air bases in southern China.

It had previously been disclosed that the seventh of the American air bases captured by the Japanese had reverted to Chinese-American control with the capture of Nanyung, 125 miles northeast of Canton.

War Has Cost U.S. 325 Billion So Far

WASHINGTON, July 27 (INS)—World War II has already cost the U.S. $325,000,000,000, or nine times the amount spent to finance all of World War I. This was disclosed in the annual report of outgoing Secretary of the Treasury Henry Morgenthau.

U.S. to Step Up Direct Sailings To the Pacific

WASHINGTON, July 27 (AP)—The timetable for the defeat of Japan has been moved forward and more American soldiers will be sent directly from Europe to the Pacific than was originally expected, Maj. Gen. John M. Franklin said today.

Franklin, acting chief of transportation for the Army Service Forces, told the Senate War Investigating committee that the rate of return of troops to the U.S. would be reduced in August and the succeeding months.

"Our military timetable for the defeat of Japan has been moved forward as a result of our recent air, sea and ground successes, and top priority must be given to the movement of forces and supplies needed by Gen. MacArthur and Adm. Nimitz," he testified.

"It is changes of this type in the calendar of military operations which makes it impossible to forecast with exactness any plans of military transportation on a long-range basis."

Franklin was called to give the Army's version of the redeployment situation after Col. J. Munroe Johnson, director of defense transportation, had told the committee that the Army drafted a ten-month troop movement program and later increased it without consulting him.

British Navy's Role Defended

WASHINGTON, July 27 (Reuter)—A British naval spokesman today described as "very surprising" Wednesday's statement by Sen. Thomas Hart (R.-Conn.), former commander of the U.S. Asiatic fleet, that the Royal Navy had failed to operate effectively in the Indian Ocean and had made no effective contribution to Adm. Nimitz's current operations against Japan. "As far as the Indian Ocean is concerned, the senator apparently forgot that the British forces started amphibious operations 15 months ago, operations which culminated in the complete reconquest of Burma and the destruction of the largest single force of Japanese ever," the spokesman said.

"As far as British usefulness to Adm. Nimitz is concerned, it only needs to be pointed out that the decision to employ British vessels was reached by the combined chiefs of staff—a decision they presumably did not reach lightheartedly.

"Furthermore, Adm. Nimitz himself was largely instrumental in planning with Adm. Sir Bruce Fraser, British C.-in-C., Pacific, British participation and has officially put on record his appreciation of the Royal Navy's efforts."

WD Denies Planes Spared Farben Because of Cartel

WASHINGTON, July 27 (ANS)—A War Department spokesman said yesterday that Allied air forces did not bomb I. G. Farbenindustrie's main plant at Frankfurt intensively because "it never was a prime industrial target."

The Farben plant Frankfurt was only the main office building and as such was not manufacturing articles of war that could be used against the Allies, he said.

The Australian Senate recently took official notice of reports that the Allies did not bomb the Farben Frankfurt plant because of the company's cartel agreements with English and American industrialists.

Denying the accusation, the War Department spokesman said Farben's large manufacturing plants in Germany were bombed repeatedly. "The main industrial plants at Ludwigshaven, Oppau and Leuna were subjected to concentrated bombing and severely damaged," he said. "The former was attacked 119 times and the latter 22 times by the RAF and 8th Air Force."

Coffin Nails

RANGOON, July 27 (Reuter)—Cigarettes which exploded when they were half smoked were among the booby-traps left behind by the Japanese in Burma, an Indian Army observer said today.

Broadcast Says Foe Will Fight 'To Bitter End'

Japan will "ignore" the three-power warning to "surrender or be destroyed," issued at Potsdam on Thursday, and "will prosecute the war of greater East Asia to the bitter end in accordance with her fixed policy," Domei, the Japanese news agency, declared yesterday, but officials in Washington classed the proclamation as the most important statement to the Japanese people since the war began and predicted that it would shorten the Pacific conflict.

The news agency broadcast, recorded in San Francisco, said it had been learned "authoritatively" that the ultimatum would be rejected and it was generally believed that a member of the Jap cabinet had supplied the information.

In another broadcast, it was announced that the cabinet had met at Premier Suzuki's home to hear a report from Foreign Minister Shigenori Togo on the surrender demand.

In Washington, legislators, who have been most outspoken in demanding a definition of unconditional surrender, approved the Potsdam statement.

Congrat the President

Sen. Kenneth S. Wherry (R.-Neb.), who only a few days ago demanded a blueprint of what the U.S. would accept from Japan, and Sen. Homer E. Capehart (R.-Ind.), another who insisted on more precise conditions, congratulated President Truman.

"I believe it is a step in the right direction and that something will come of it," Wherry said.

Meanwhile, Rep. Sam Rayburn, speaker of the House, said in Denison, Tex., that peace overtures have been made by Japan, but that there were military matters involved with which he was unfamiliar.

Diplomatic sources considered it significant that the three signers of the proclamation—President Truman, former British Prime Minister Churchill and Generalissimo Chiang Kai-shek—did not mention the Japanese emperor and placed all the blame for Japan's crimes on her war lords.

Popular Revolution Possible

A Reuter report stated that students of Japanese affairs did not exclude the possibility of a popular revolution, led by the emperor, to overthrow the war leaders.

Meanwhile, U.S. radio transmitters on Saipan bombarded the Japs with the Potsdam declaration. It also was planned, reports said, to scatter leaflets throughout the home islands defining the terms.

Peace overtures from Japanese forces in China also were admitted last night by Gen. Okamura, Jap commander in south China.

Since the Soviet Union is not at war with Japan, Russia played no part in issuing the proclamation. Moscow newspapers, however, played the ultimatum prominently. No comment was made.

Sen. Alexander Wiley (R.-Wis.) yesterday urged Russia to enter the Pacific war and said "Russia's mere entrance into the war would be sufficient to make the Japanese throw in the sponge without a single additional Russian or American boy dying."

Big 3 Parley Resumes Today With Attlee in Churchill Role

POTSDAM, July 27 (AP)—The Potsdam conference of the Big Three will be resumed tomorrow. It was learned definitely tonight that Prime Minister Clement R. Attlee, Sir Edward Bridges, secretary of the war cabinet, and Gen. Sir Hastings Ismay are returning tomorrow afternoon.

Winston Churchill and Anthony Eden, former Foreign Secretary, it is reported, are not returning, and no word has been received as to whether they will or not.

Meanwhile the Big Two—President Truman and Marshal Stalin—marked time here today.

The President was presumably using the day to rest up for final conference sessions and continue discussions with his staff on policies still to be decided.

There was no further information on the U.S., British and Chinese ultimatum to Japan. The fact that the proclamation was issued from Potsdam indicated that Premier Stalin at least must have been informed of its contents and that an ultimatum was to be made.

Whether he concurred in its issue is not known. There is also no information to indicate that he was requested to join in the signatures.

The President was at Frankfurt when news of the Labor Party's victory came in yesterday. There was no comment from him or from his delegation. Silence likewise reigned at Stalin's HQ.

Washington dispatches disclosed that two administration economic experts, Judge Samuel I. Rosenman, special counsel to President Truman, and Oscar Cox, deputy administrator of the Foreign Economic Administration, had left New York for Potsdam.

Their departure re-emphasized the concern felt by the Allies over conditions in Europe. Rosenman was the author of a report prepared last spring on measures required for the restoration of Europe.

An indication that the Big Three may be encountering difficulty in formulating a common policy toward Germany was contained in a statement made in Frankfurt today by Secretary of War Henry L. Stimson, who said that "the government leaders at Potsdam were working on discrepancies between American and Russian zones for governing Germany."

BRUSSELS, July 27 (Reuter)—The U.S. cruisers Augusta and Philadelphia which brought President Truman to Europe left Antwerp today for an unknown destination.

STEPS DOWN: Winston Churchill leaves 10 Downing St. yesterday after a farewell meeting with members of his former cabinet.

Two Cents A Copy

THE STARS AND STRIPES

U. S. Armed Forces Daily In The Middle Pacific

20 Sen A Copy In The Ryukyus

Vol. 1, No. 69 ★★ Wednesday, August 1, 194

Japs Put U. S. PWs In Target Areas; Record Fleet Of 800 Superforts Drop 6,000-Ton Load On Four Jap Cities

GUAM, Thursday (AP)—A record aerial armada of 800 Superforts, carrying 6,000 tons of incendiary and high explosive bombs, probably the greatest bomb load ever carried on a single mission, executed the sentence of death by fire on four Japanese cities early Thursday (Japan time).

Taking off from Marianas bases late on the 38th anniversary of the Air forces, the giant bombers struck savagely soon after midnight at the war centers of Mito, Hochioji, Nagaoka and Toyama, all on Honshu, and petroleum installations at Kawasaka near Tokyo. This greatest of all bombing missions came barely 24 hours after more than 1,000,000 Japanese were warned to evacuate 12 cities or be destroyed.

Transportation Centers

All four cities are important transportation centers with a total population of around 210,000. The raid was announced in the first communique issued by the U.S. Army Strategic Air forces, the Pacific, commanded by Gen. Spaatz.

The take off came nine months to the day after the Superfort "Tokyo Rose" made the first flight over the Japanese capital.

Meanwhile, it was announced in a United Press Dispatch that land-based planes and one submarine shelled Japan as Adm. Halsey's Third fleet remained under a security blackout.

Japanese Imperial headquarters conceded that American carrier planes and land-based bombers caused "considerable damage" to Japanese cities, factories and shipping in attacks during the last month. The Japs claimed, however, that damage to air bases and military installations was slight and said the Japanese army and navy steadily are strengthening preparations to meet an "enemy invasion."

Radio Tokyo reported that 20 Mustangs bombed, rocketed and machine-gunned air bases and transportation facilities in the Osaka-Kobe area for 50 minutes

(Continued on Back Page)

WASHINGTON (UP)—The State department Wednesday revealed that the Japanese government is following a policy of moving American prisoner-of-war and civilian internment camps into strategic areas subject to Allied bombardment.

Some camps already have been hit by American bombs and high casualties are certain.

In disclosing the diabolical scheme—a desperate attempt to stop the destruction of their cities and industries—the State department said that the U. S. must continue the methodical bombing and shelling of Japan.

Military men bitterly denounced the Japanese move and promised revenge, but none indicated a belief that the bombing schedule for Japan should change.

Airmen Cautioned

Military men said American airmen will continue to be briefed carefully on the known location of all prison camps and will do their utmost to avoid them, but necessary risks must be taken rather than let a key Japanese arsenal or other objectives go unscathed.

The U. S. has protested for at least a year the Japanese practice of using American prisoners, in effect, as hostages. The only result has been non-committal "so sorry" replies.

The State department announcement of the Japanese practice told a sad story of unsuccessful attempts to persuade Japan to abide by the rules covering prisoners of war as laid down by the Geneva convention. It indicated that the department has abandoned hope that the Jap-

(Continued On Page Four)

Big 3 Meet Ends; Result Still Secret

POTSDAM (AP)—The Big Big Three came to the end early Wednesday night of their historic sessions upon which the future peace of the world may possibly hinge.

Formal adjournment of the meeting awaited conclusion of a last plenary session among President Truman, Prime Minister Attlee and Premier Stalin.

A joint communique announcing the conference end was expected hourly.

(Armed officers are guarding the broadcasting station at Potsdam to prevent paemature disclosure of the communique, the American broadcasting company reported.)

Hint Russian Step

(A London Daily Express dispatch from Berlin speculated that the communique may announce that Russia considers herself at war with Japan.)

President Truman will fly to England Thursday to meet King George VI at luncheon aboard the British Battleship Renown at Plymouth. He will sail from Plymouth to the U.S.

An official spokesman confirmed that the parley was nearing an end. Correspondents were packed and ready to leave on short notice with the presidential party.

Await Phraseology

Completion of the drafting in final phraseology of the involved Big Three agreements in two languages, English and Russian, was believed to be the main task remaining. Principles of these agreements already have been decided.

A spokesman said "a great deal of progress was made" by the three leaders at a three and a half hour meeting Tuesday.

The conference's survival of the defeat of the government of Prime Minister Churchill, apparently demonstrated the solid foundation for decisions which had been reached.

Phoney Veteran Given Jail Term

NEW YORK (ANS)—Leon Zeid, 28, former yacht club steward at suburban Larchmont, N.Y. was sentenced in federal court to a three-month jail term for illegally wearing an honorable discharge lapel emblem.

Assistant U.S. Attorney Gerald V. Clark said it was the first prosecution of its kind in the country.

Zeid was accused of acquiring his yacht club job by representing himself as an honorably discharged veteran, even though he had never been in the armed forces. U.S. Attorney John F. X. McGohey said other such cases would be vigorously prosecuted to protect the rights of honorably discharged servicemen.

War Dept. Postpones Critical Score Again

WASHINGTON (AP)—The War Department Tuesday postponed announcement of a new point score for discharging troops under the redeployment plan.

Early in June after the present interim 85 point discharge score had been fixed the department promised that its permanent "critical" score of points for release would be given out during July.

TAIL STINGER—T/Sgt. Ben Kuroki peers out of his tail gunner's position on a B-29. AAF Photo by Sgt. L. L. Sharpe

B-29 Gunner Pleases Mama, Helps Build Fire In Yokohama

By S/SGT. JOHN ADVENT
Stars and Stripes Correspondent

TINIAN—"I didn't think of it as my parents' birthplace—it's just another enemy country to me," said T/Sgt. Ben Kuroki, believed to be the first American of Japanese ancestry to bomb Japan.

The 27-year-old tail gunner from Hershey, Neb., flew 30 missions against the Nazis before volunteering for combat in the Pacific.

During one of his 27 Pacific air-strikes, T/Sgt. Kuroki watched Yokohama, his mother's home town, go up in smoke. Now he's anxious to bomb Kagoshima, because "dad will get a kick out of it. He was born there."

'We All Feel The Same'

"My father, mother, brothers and I all feel the same," he said. "We don't give a damn what happens to Japan or the Japanese. We are Americans."

Now with the 313th Bomb wing, Kuroki formerly was a B-24 gunner with Brig. Gen. Ted Timberlake's "Flying Circus" of the 8th Air force. He flew against the Axis over Tunisia, Sicily, Italy, France, and Germany, and took part in the famous raids

(Continued on Back Page)

Charter Row Hits Senate

WASHINGTON (ANS)— Senatorial unity on the United Nations Charter broke wide open over a proposal that President Truman appoint a Security Council delegate without letting Congress define his authority.

Chairman Tom Connally (D-Tex.) of the Foreign Relations committee stirred the storm with an announcement that he had asked the State department to determine if any legislation is needed to cover the appointment of Edward R. Stettinius to the post.

The reaction to Connally's personal view that there is no need for a bill—to which might be attached a limitation on authority to vote for the use of American troops — was vigorous and prompt.

Sen. Arthur Vandenberg (R-Mich.) who served with Connally as a delegate to the San Francisco conference made it plain he thinks Congress should set up the office and define its powers.

Birthday Promise: 1,200-Plane Raid

GUAM (AP)—The Superfort, now such a master of the sky over Japan that it warns in advance the city it is going to hit, "soon" will attack during a

Pictures of AAF Pacific Action . . . . on Page 5.

single raid with 1,200 planes carrying up to 8,000 tons of bombs, a high official promised Wednesday on the 38th birthday of the Army Air force.

Thirty-eight years ago a dubious Army assigned one captain and two enlisted men to "study the flying machine and the possibility of adopting it to military purposes." They decided that the machine, previously a victim of skepticism and doubt, could be adapted.

From the decision of these three men, less than four decades ago, has emerged the Air force of today.

'Top Level' Dispute Reported Over Need For 7,000,000 GIs

WASHINGTON (ANS)—A top-level disagreement on the number of soldiers required to defeat Japan was reported Tuesday by Associated Press, which said some officials contend the Army High Command doesn't need the 7,000,000-man force it plans to use.

These officials were quoted by the AP as saying the Army and Navy in their eagerness to have a sufficiency have actually amassed and are holding too much war materiel to the detriment of the civilian economy in the reconversion period.

The News agency said the comments were made by certain officials in civilian war agencies on the understanding names would be withheld.

Procurement Improving

"The Army has been conservative in seeing that it has plenty to meet military eventualities," said one top administration figure, according to the AP. "However, its planning procurement is much better than it was a year ago.

"The military is bound to be conservative because an officer will never be criticized for having too much and will be criticized plenty if he hasn't got enough."

This official added, "A 7,000,000-man Army seems to be a helluva big Army for the one-front war." AP said.

"Civilians don't tell Gen. Marshal what he needs to beat Japan nor do they tell Adm. King how big a Navy he needs," he continued. "Nevertheless this view is widely held and I think there will be increasing pressure on the Army to release more men."

Gen. Jacob Devers, commanding Army Ground forces, said last week the Army planned to use a 7,000,000-man force to shatter Japan with one great blow rather than wage Pacific war in piecemeal efforts."

Jackie Coogan To Get Discharge On Points

INDIANAPOLIS (UP) — Lt. Jackie Coogan, former child movie star, is en route to the Santa Ana, Calif., separation center for release from the Army.

The "Kid" is being released under the Army point system. He was the first pilot to set a glider down behind Jap lines in airborne operations in north central Burma last year.

LCTs Traverse 5,000 Miles Of Ocean Under Own Power

By SP2/c M. B. GODCHAUX

A PHILIPPINE BASE — With 5,000 miles of blue Pacific behind, a "cockleshell convoy" of LCTs was at anchor here after one of the most remarkable voyages of World war II.

The Landing Craft, Tanks, sailed here under their own power from Pearl harbor because larger craft—aboard which LCTs usually ride pick-a-back during long voyages—were not available.

"It was a good deal like going to sea in a wash basin," said Ensign Carl R. Forsberg of Sacramento, Calif., who skippered one of the LCTs and admitted being "nervous as hell."

Long Trips Unheard-Of

Tough customer though it is in a landing, the LCT never was designed for deep sea cruising, Forsberg explained, and 5,000-mile voyages in the craft were unheard-of.

"We put ourselves together at Pearl," the ensign explained, and meant it literally, for his LCT was shipped from the U.S. in three parts and was assembled in Hawaii. "Then we loaded all the food, water and fuel that could be stowed, and set sail. Our crews numbered two officers and 14 enlisted men.

Displacing only 130 tons and drawing barely two feet of water, the LCTs bobbed about like corks on the long Pacific rollers. Sometimes waves would pitch a craft as much as 90-degrees off course

(Continued on Back Page)

S & S Weatherman . . . .
LONDON, E. ENGLAND, and E. MIDLANDS
Unsettled, Cloudy, Warm.
W. MIDLANDS, S. WALES
Fair, Warm.

New York London Edition Paris

THE STARS AND STRIPES

Daily Newspaper of U.S. Forces in the European Theater

Vol. 5 No. 284—1d. THURSDAY, AUGUST 2, 1945

. . . Predicts for Today
N. ENGLAND, S. SCOTLAND
Cloudy with Probable Rain.

800 B29s Strike Mightiest Blow

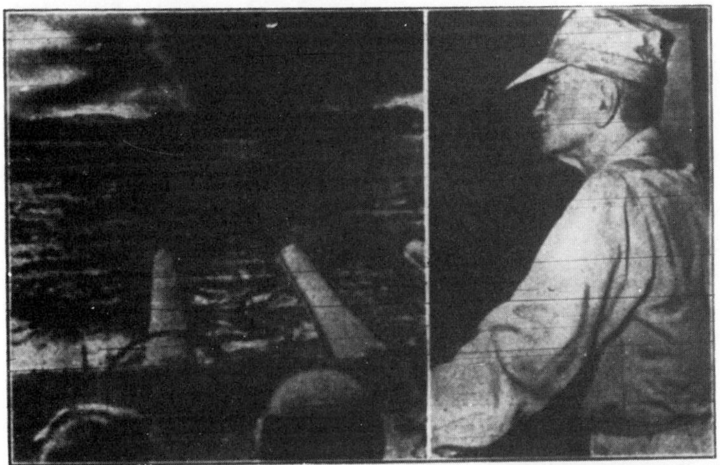

NAVY BIG GUNS: Gun crewmen of the battleship U.S.S. Massachusetts watch smoke belch from the Japanese city of Kamaishi, on northeast Honshu, after the ship rammed home a salvo of 16-inch steel. Right, Adm. William F. Halsey, boss of the rampaging 3rd Fleet, looks for new fields to conquer from the deck of his flagship.

'Jap Fleet Wiped Out As a Fighting Force'

WASHINGTON, Aug. 1—Japan's fleet has been "wiped out as a fighting force," and the Japanese people can escape utter destruction only by "immediate surrender," Undersecretary of Navy Artemus L. Gates announced last night.

"The Japs do not have a single battleship left in operation," Gates declared in a radio broadcast. "The Japs probably still have two to three carriers that may be operational, but they are no longer a serious threat. If the Jap fleet has three cruisers left that can still steam I'd be very much surprised. They may have 15 to 20 destroyers and some submarines.

"The strikes of our carrier-borne planes last Wednesday and Thursday were aimed at the remaining warships, camouflaged and tied up at docks and buoys from Kure to Kobe. We knew what ships we wanted to hit. We found every one of them and every one was damaged.

"On Saturday and Sunday we went back to finish the job. We did. The battleship Haruna was left beached and burning. The battleships Ise and Hyuga were apparently resting in the mud. We knocked out three cruisers and put two more carriers out of operation.

Free to Roam Coast at Will

"Our ships are free to roam the enemy coast at will, shelling harbors, rail lines and vital installations. For Japan, the only escape now from utter destruction is immediate surrender," Gates declared.

Meanwhile, official communiques issued during July showed that the month's combined carrier and land-based plane attacks cost the enemy at least 1,546 ships and small craft sunk or damaged in home waters and more than 1,300 aircraft destroyed or wrecked, with results still incomplete.

Adm. William F. Halsey's 3rd Fleet planes, including some 250 British aircraft, accounted for most of these enemy ships and aircraft, including 99 warships.

Land-based planes of Adm. Nimitz' command sank 85 vessels, mostly freighters and cargo ships, damaged 176 and destroyed or damaged 53 planes.

The Far East Army Air Forces accounted for 250 ships and small craft totalling 250,000 tons after they started operations from Okinawa early in the month, Gen. MacArthur announced.

List of Specialists Due for Cut Soon

Stars and Stripes Paris Bureau

PARIS, Aug. 1—Theater Service Forces disclosed today that in the next two months certain Army specialists, such as clerk-typists, probably will be removed from the category of critical specialists in the ETO.

In June, clerk-typists, stenographers and various other specialists were classified as critical, or ineligible, for discharge under the point system in this theater. The rule did not apply to critical specialists in organizations being redeployed. When a specialist with a point-score of 85 or more is released from the critical list, he again will become eligible for discharge.

TSF said that the Army is training low-score men as replacements for specialists.

Japs Keep PWs Near Targets

WASHINGTON, Aug. 1 (AP)—The Japanese persist in trying to protect their target areas from bombing by putting prisoner of war camps near them, the State Department declared yesterday.

While denouncing this practice, the State Department said that it was trying to verify a Tokyo radio report that a PW camp was hit during the bombing of Kawasaki, Southeast Tokyo, resulting in casualties among American prisoners.

The department further announced that the Swiss Government had been asked to verify the incident, and the next-of-kin would be notified as soon as information was received.

Although the Japs were not a party to the Geneva Convention covering the treatment of PWs, they had agreed to conform with the law prohibiting the use of prisoners to protect certain areas.

Million GIs to Quit ETO By Jan. '46

WASHINGTON, Aug. 1 (ANS)—A million American troops will leave Europe for this country in the remaining five months of 1945. This was reported yesterday by Maj. Gen. C. P. Gross, Army chief of transportation, who said it would leave almost 900,000 to be moved during the following four months to complete redeployment from Europe by May, 1946.

Gross estimated that total embarkation from Europe will number 800,000 men by the end of July. That total includes thousands who will make the voyage direct to the Pacific theater, as well as those coming home. Embarkation by July 13 totaled over 635,000, of whom 532,250 had arrived in the U.S. on that date, 407,978 by ship and 124,280 by plane.

Going to the Dogs? Not The Legion Membership

INDIANAPOLIS, Aug. 1 (ANS)—American Legion headquarters disclosed yesterday that Fighting Dogs, veterans of the K-9 Corps, had been ruled ineligible for membership.

The matter was raised when the Charles Roth post at Oak Park, Ill., inducted Jack von Lustig Bennett, an honorably discharged K-9. The national judge advocate, in ruling the dog ineligible, stood pat on Webster's Dictionary definition of a "person."

Petain Defense Offers Letter From Leahy

PARIS, Aug. 1—Marshal Henri Philippe Petain, on trial here on charges of high treason against France, threw a virtual bombshell into the courtroom today when his attorneys introduced a letter from Adm. William D. Leahy, President Truman's personal chief of staff and former U.S. ambassador to Vichy, which stated that the aged Marshal's "principal concern was the welfare and protection of the helpless people of France."

(Two American Congressmen who attended today's proceedings as observers announced they would press for an immediate investigation into Leahy's letter. Members of the House Judiciary Committee, Reps. Michael A. Feighan (D.-Ohio) and James G. Fulton (R.-Pa.) said they wanted to know whether the letter had been cleared properly through State Department channels and whether it could be considered as representing an official viewpoint of the U.S. Government.)

Dated June 22, 1945, and addressed to Petain in answer to a letter of June 13 from Petain's attorneys, Leahy's letter read:

He Couldn't Become Involved

"It is impossible for me as Chief of Staff to become involved in the internal controversy in France in which you find yourself enmeshed. My knowledge of your personal and official attitude toward the Axis powers is strictly limited to the period of January, 1941, to April, 1942, when I had the honor of being U.S. Ambassador to France.

"During that period, I held your personal friendship and your devotion to the welfare of the French people in high regard. You often expressed to me the fervent hope that the Nazi invader would be destroyed.

"During that period, you did on occasion at my request take action in opposition to the desires of the Axis and favorable to the Allied cause. . . . When you failed to accept my recommendation to oppose the Axis powers by refusing their demands, your stated reason was that such positive action by you would result in additional oppression of your people by the invaders.

"However, I must in all honesty repeat my personal opinion expressed to you at the time that positive refusal to make any concessions to Axis demands, while it might have brought immediate increased hardships to your people, would in the long run have been advantageous to France."

At the end of the French translation of the letter, Judge Pierre Mongibeaux remarked, "There's one sentence against Petain in that letter." The defense protested and Mongibeaux did not repeat or explain his remark.

A Tired and Dirty Laval Returns to Paris for Trial

PARIS, Aug. 1—Pierre Laval, tired, dirty and paunchy, was brought back by plane to Paris this afternoon to stand trial on charges of collaboration with the Nazis.

As soon as his plane landed at Le Bourget airfield he was whisked off to a cell at Fresnes prison. He had been brought back from Innsbruck, Austria, where the U.S. 65th Division had turned him over to French officials after his flight from Spain yesterday.

6,000 Tons of Fire, Explosive Bombs Rip 5 Jap Targets

A record aerial armada of approximately 800 Superforts early today (Japanese time) dumped 6,000 tons of incendiary and high explosive bombs—probably the greatest load of destruction ever carried on a single mission—on four Jap cities and a petroleum center near Tokyo.

Taking off from their Marianas bases late on the 38th anniversary of the Army Air Forces, the giant bombers struck soon after midnight at the war centers of Mito, Hachioji, Nagaoka and Toyama, all important transport cities with a total population of about 240,000.

Oil installations at Kawasaki, near Tokyo, were the fifth target in the massive assault.

The takeoff for this greatest bombing mission to date came barely 24 hours after 1,300,000 persons had been warned to evacuate 12 cities or be wiped out.

All of the cities pounded in today's raid were warned on Tuesday to expect a visit from the B29s within 72 hours. Nagaoka also was among the cities notified on July 27 that they were high on the list scheduled for destruction. The 20th Air Force now has raided ten of the 19 cities given pre-bombing warnings.

Tokyo Radio announced that about 160 fighters and medium bombers from Okinawa attacked military targets on Kyushu.

Adm. Nimitz' communique stated that bad weather had turned the 3rd Fleet carrier planes away from targets in the Tokyo area and that they had attacked the Maizuru naval base on western Honshu instead, sinking a destroyer, damaging another and a light cruiser, and destroying or damaging 89 planes.

Chinese Take Supply Base, Drive Toward Lingling

CHUNGKING, Aug. 1 (AP)—Chinese troops have captured the bomb-battered Japanese supply base of Pingio in South Central China's Kwangsi Province, and have hurled a new spearhead at the old "flying tigers" airfield at Lingling, 370 miles southeast of Chungking, the Chinese high command announced.

Pingio was taken last Friday by Chinese troops who have been pushing for a month towards this highway center from Liuchow, 74 miles southwest.

Wife No. 1 Received Captain's Dough as He Courted WAC

CHICAGO, Aug. 1 (ANS)—Mrs. Ruth Schultz, the wife Capt. Carl Schultz said he believed was dead when he sought to marry WAC Sgt. Kamella Koutouvaris in Berlin last week, today said she received a $150 money order from him about that time.

The pretty 23-year-old brunette, mother of two children, made this disclosure when informed the Army's case against her husband may hinge on whether he cancelled her allotment at the time he claimed he heard of her death last May.

"He sure did cancel it," she said. "It was the last of May that he wrote and said he was trying to get my allotment increased. He said, though, that it was 'all bawled up' over there and that he believed he'd just send me money orders in letters so that I'd be sure to get all he wanted to send me."

Mrs. Schultz said she received a letter two weeks later containing a money order for $150. Two more money orders were subsequently received she said—one for $170 in June and another for $150 last week.

Truman, King Meet Today Off British Coast

President Truman is scheduled to reach England by plane this morning to meet King George. The President will arrive from Potsdam, where the Big Three conference ended last night.

Details of the unprecedented meeting, which were released by the British, said the President would land at an unspecified airport and proceed to the U.S.S. Augusta at Plymouth. The King—who normally remains at Buckingham Palace to receive visitors—left London for Plymouth last night. The meeting will take place aboard the British ship H.M.S. Renown, where the President and King are to have lunch together.

The Big Three session yesterday afternoon, first session held in three days because of Premier Stalin's illness, was a "fruitful" one, it was [illegible] much of the final work was disposed of rapidly and smoothly.

No official information was available as to when the communique summarizing achievements of the conference would be released, although most reports estimated it would be issued simultaneously Thursday night or Friday in Washington, London and Moscow.

The meeting between the President and the King will be brief, according to plans, with Mr. Truman not expected to stay overnight in England. After the rendezvous at sea, the President will return to the Augusta, and later the King will board the American cruiser to bid the President farewell.

Mr. Truman will be accompanied by Secretary of State James F. Byrnes and Adm. William D. Leahy, his personal chief of staff. The British Ambassador to Washington, Lord Halifax, who returned to England from the U.S. Monday, will accompany the King.

100 Wounded Still In ETO Hospitals

PARIS, Aug. 1—The chief surgeon's office announced yesterday that only 100 American wounded soldiers are still in hospitals in Europe. These men are suffering from such serious wounds that they cannot be moved. All other American wounded either have been returned to duty or transferred to hospitals in the U.S.

Air Force Show Cancelled

Due to unsatisfactory weather conditions, the proposed 8th Air Force formation flying demonstration, which was to be held over London and other parts of England and the Continent yesterday, in connection with the observance of U.S. Army Air Forces Day, was cancelled.

Commons Breaks Out in Song As New Parliament Convenes

At the first meeting of Britain's new Parliament yesterday the House of Commons rang out with "The Red Flag," sung by Government members of the victorious Labor Party.

Rendition of the popular revolutionary song, frequently sung at international labor gatherings, followed quickly after Conservative Party members had greeted the entrance of Winston Churchill with a lusty version of, "For he's a jolly good fellow," and had loudly cheered the former Prime Minister. Opening business of the new House was the re-election of the speaker, Col. Clifton Brown, member of the Conservative Party.

The Labor Party's victory was interpreted yesterday by Prof. Harold J. Laski, chairman of the party's national executive committee, as the era of the common man. Interviewed by an Associated Press reporter Laski declared the election has as much social and economic significance as the emergence of the middle class in England in the 1830s.

"This is the arrival of the people in power," he said. "We are now prepared to give the little man—within the framework of the British constitution—all the progressive change he requires."

Speaking on foreign policy Laski stated, "Our first great task is the utter defeat of the Japanese." Referring particularly to Spain, he declared democracy and fascism could not live side by side.

First step in the party's domestic program would be nationalization of the Bank of England, he asserted. Next in order would be public ownership of coal mines, followed by transport, iron and steel.

RUSSIA ENTERS PACIFIC WAR

SOUTHERN FRANCE EDITION
THE STARS AND STRIPES
Daily Newspaper of U.S. Armed Forces in the European Theater
Vol. 1—No. 149 Thursday, August 9, 1945 ONE FRANC

Molotov Cites Causes to Japs

Soviet Foreign Commissar Vyacheslav Molotov, in a statement to the Japanese government announcing Russia's declaration of war, said the Japanese request that the Soviet government mediate in the Far Eastern war "loses all basis" in the face of Japan's rejection of the Allied ultimatum to surrender unconditionally issued from Potsdam July 26.

The statement, which Molotov handed to Japanese Ambassador Sato for transmission to the Japanese government, follows:

"After the defeat and capitulation of Hitlerite Germany, Japan became the only great power that still stood for the continuation of the war. The demand of the three powers, U.S.A., Great Britain and China on July 26 on the unconditional surrender of the Japanese Armed Forces was rejected by Japan. And thus the proposal of the Japanese government to the Soviet Union on mediation in the war in the Far East loses all basis.

Mr Molotov

"Taking into consideration the refusal of Japan to capitulate, the Allies submitted the proposal to the Soviet government to join the war against Japanese aggression, and thus shorten the duration of the war, reduce the number of victims and facilitate speedy restoration of universal peace.

"Loyal to its Allied duty, the Soviet government has accepted the proposal of the Allies and has joined in the declaration of the Allied powers of July 26.

"They consider that this policy is the only means able to bring

(Continued on Page 8)

Russo-Jap Pact Voided Last April 5

The Russo-Japanese neutrality pact was signed April 13, 1941, two months after Germany invaded the Soviet Union and almost eight months before Japan declared war on the U.S. and Britain. It was repudiated by Russia April 5 this year.

In his note to the Japanese ambassador in Moscow, announcing Russia's repudiation of the pact, Foreign Commissar Vyacheslav Molotov reminded Japan that these events (her aggression) had changed relations between the Russians and the Japanese. The note said:

"Germany has attacked the Soviet Union and Japan, Germany's ally, has been lending assistance to the latter in her war against the Soviet Union. Furthermore, Japan is waging war against the U.S. and Britain, who are allies of the Soviet Union.

"Under such circumstances the neutrality pact between Japan

(Continued on Page 8)

1,500,000 REDS WAIT ON BORDER FOR FIRST BLOW

Perhaps as many as 1,500,000 specially trained Red Army soldiers, backed by all the necessary machines of war, stand ready on the Russo-Manchurian border to strike the first blow in the Soviet Union's war against Japan.

From Vladivostok, which possibly will become an active center of Russian operations in the Far East, Niigata, the "back door" to Tokyo, is only 525 miles across the Sea of Japan. Military experts have long considered an invasion of the main enemy home island of Honshu via this route a distinct probability once the Soviets entered the Pacific war.

An even shorter, but less advantageous, invasion route is from Siberia's Kamchatka Peninsula through the Jap-held Kurile Islands, which have been hit repeatedly by U.S. bombers from the

(Continued on Page 8)

Rain, Hail Lash Staging Areas

Rain measuring an inch within the last 48 hours brought mud to the "dust bowls" of Marseille's staging area, while hail at Calas flattened tents.

Marignane Airfield weather forecaster Sgt. Max G. Zywiak, of Utica, N.Y., predicted there would be no more dust storms "for at least a month."

The rain was accompanied by a ten degree slump in temperature, the maximum for Tuesday being 86, while the Wednesday maximum was 76. Sgt. Zywiak predicted showers and 80 temperature for today.

Potsdam Proposal Accepted

Russia has declared war on Japan.

The news was announced last night by Radio Moscow and in Washington by President Truman.

The Russian declaration, a Moscow report said, was in response to a proposal made by the U.S. and Britain at the recent Big Three Conference in Potsdam.

Russia had received requests from Tokyo to act as mediator in the Far Eastern conflict, the statement continued, but rejected them in view of Japan's failure to act on the U.S.-British-Chinese ultimatum delivered from Potsdam last week.

Reporters Summoned

President Truman issued the momentous statement to a hurriedly summoned conference. The President said he had only a simple statement to make but it was so important he could not delay it.

Then with a broad smile, the President declared: "Russia has declared war on Japan. That is all."

The Russian declaration of war upon Japan came 125 days after the Soviet Union denounced her neutrality pact with the Japanese, an act which was regarded at the time as a final step toward Russia's entry into the Pacific war and which precipitated the fall of the Koiso cabinet in Tokyo.

The disclosure that the Soviet Union had at last thrown her enormous strength alongside the U.S. and Britain and against the enemy in the Pacific had not been unexpected. When it would come, however, had been a matter of conjecture for months.

Reuter reported that the Russian statement said that on Aug. 8, Russian Foreign Secretary V. M. Molotov received British Ambassador Sir Archibald Clark-Kerr, U.S. Ambassador W. Averell Harriman and Chinese Ambassador Wing Shih Chien and told them of the decision of the Soviet government to declare on Aug. 9 a war between the Soviet Union and Japan. The ambassadors expressed satisfaction with the declaration of the Soviet government, the statement added.

Official Washington at once took this development along

(Continued on Page 8)

Atom Razes 4 Sq. Miles

GUAM, Aug. 8—Four and one-tenth square miles of Hiroshima—60 percent of the built-up area—were obliterated and the rest of the city was badly damaged Sunday by the atomic bomb, Gen. Carl A. Spaatz, USAAF commander, announced today on the basis of reconnaissance photos.

Japanese broadcasts went even farther, admitting: "Practically all living things . . . were literally seared to death by the tremendous heat and pressure engendered by the blast."

Protesting that "this atrocious bomb" violated international law, the enemy gave details reconnaissance pictures could not obtain on the "disastrous ruin that struck the city."

". . . The destructive power of the bomb is indescribable . . . The dead are simply uncountable . . . It is impossible to distinguish the men from the women . . ."

Spaatz served notice more planes were ready to fly against Japan with atomic bombs.

He refused to disclose how the bomb was carried, dropped and detonated, from what altitude it was loosed or its size.

History's first atomic bomb was dropped into the center of Hiroshima, on Honshu Island southwest of Tokyo, at 9:15 AM Sunday. Col. Paul W Tibbets Jr., of Miami, Fla., pilot of the atom-carrying Superfortress, apparently had not been restricted to any particular target. He picked Hiroshima "because it was clear there."

Immediately after "atoms away" the Superfort made its getaway.

The launching plane was at least ten miles away when the explosion came. A flare "bright as the sun" dazzled the airmen despite their smoked glasses.

A gigantic column of smoke, black and dusty at its base but whitening at its top, mushroomed 40,000 feet—into the stratosphere—and continued boiling up for three or four minutes.

Soong-Stalin Resume Talks

LONDON, Aug. 8 (UP)—Russo-Chinese talks, interrupted last month by the Potsdam Big Three Conference, were resumed last night when Premier Stalin received Chinese Premier T. V. Soong for further conversations, Moscow radio announced today.

Soviet Foreign Commissar Molotov and Wong Shih Chien, China's new foreign minister, were present at the talks.

U.S. Ambassador Averell Harriman, British Ambassador Sir Archibald Clark-Kerr and French Ambassador Gen. Georges Catroux welcomed the Chinese delegation on their arrival yesterday.

Two Cents A Copy

THE STARS AND STRIPES

U. S. Armed Forces Daily — In The Middle Pacific

20 Sen A Copy In The Ryukyus

Vol. 1, No. 76 ★★ Thursday, August 9, 1945

Reds Storm Manchuria; Atom Razes Nagasaki

Bomb Hits 11th Largest Enemy City

GUAM (UP)—Preliminary reports indicated that the second atomic bomb to be dropped on Japan all but obliterated Nagasaki, a major naval base and Japan's 11th largest city, during the noon rush hour Thursday.

Crew members of the Superfortress which loosed the terrifying bomb on Nagasaki watched the earth-shaking explosion and flashed back to Gen. Carl A. Spaatz, commander of the Strategic Air Forces, that results were "good."

"No further details will be available until the mission returns," Spaatz said in a brief communique.

Blown Off Map

But, to all hands, that brief report—"results good"—indicated that Nagasaki, a city of 252,630 persons, virtually had been blown off the map of Japan by an explosion equal to that which leveled four and one-tenth square miles of Hiroshima.

Powerless to halt the atomic bombings, Japan cried out in "horror" against them, indirectly pleading for withdrawal of the weapon in the name of humanity and fair play.

"Men, women and children, the sick, cripples and helpless—the bomb has no mercy in whom it kills," a Tokyo broadcast said. "From earlier reports, we are certain Hiroshima was subjected to the most inhuman and barbaric act yet reported in the annals of America."

More Than One

The Associated Press reported that more than one bomb may have been dropped in this second attack and it might have been of a different size than the one which devastated Hiroshima.

The carefully worded communique, saying only that the second use of the atomic bomb had occurred, left to speculation all other details.

Radio Tokyo was silent on the results of the Nagasaki attack.

(Continued on Back Page)

Truman Address

WASHINGTON (AP)—President Truman reports to the nation Thursday night on the war situation. His half-hour address over all radio networks will begin at 4:30 (HWT).

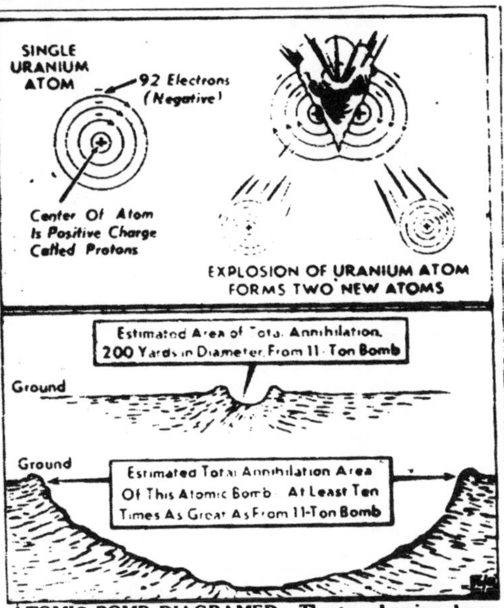

ATOMIC BOMB DIAGRAMED—The top drawing shows in its most rudimentary form the uranium atom, used in the new atomic bomb. The 92 electrons are held in their orbit by the attraction of the positive electrical force in the center, called protons. When this atom explodes (top right) it divides into two complete atoms of different chemical element. Lower drawing shows a rough estimated comparison between the complete demolition area of an 11-ton British "earthquake" bomb and the new atomic bomb. (AP WIREPHOTO SKETCH)

Russians Cross North Border On Wide Front

LONDON (UP)—Moscow's first official communique said the Far Eastern Russian forces crossed the Manchurian border in the area of Trans-Baikalia, with several towns and villages captured in the first move of Russia's war against Japan.

The communique said the Red troops were breaking through strong concrete defenses in the northwest corner of Manchuria in the Khabarovsk sector and added that the Russians had advanced nine and one-third miles in their head-on collision with the Japanese.

More than 1,000,000 Russians were engaged directly or indirectly in the battle.

13-Mile Gain

The Russians gained about 10 miles across the Amur river and, at other points, made as much as 13 miles. Just east of Lake Baikal they captured two towns. Lake Nomohan in the northern region was the scene of heavy Red-Japanese fighting points. Heavy resistance was being encountered in the area east of Lake Baikal.

Tokyo broadcasts said Russian forces crossed into Manchuria from the east along a 300-mile stretch of the Siberian border from Hungchung, 80 miles west of Vladivostok, to Hutou, 250 miles north of Vladivostok.

Nearer To Tokyo

Russia's great Far Eastern air base and naval center of Vladivostok is only 650 miles northwest of Tokyo, 250 miles closer than American-held Okinawa.

In the west, Tokyo said, Russian forces attacked along the border at Manchouli, 50 miles east of the border of outer Mongolia.

Japanese imperial headquarters announced, "Garrison forces of Japan in Manchukuo engaged the invaders for self-defense and fighting is in progress." Another Japanese broadcast said there was "sharp fighting" in all areas.

The Japs said Red bombers, moving in ahead of the ground forces, bombed communications centers at Hailan, Harbin, Chiamussu and Kirin in Manchuria, and Rashin and Genzan in northern Korea.

Reds Didn't Hesitate

Russia exploded the first Far Eastern offensive of this war only a few minutes after her declaration of war against Japan took effect at midnight Wednesday. The Japs said the assault began at 12:10 a. m. Thursday, Russian time.

The Japanese reports of the operations indicated that the offensive is taking the shape of giant pincers in the east and west, aimed perhaps at cutting Manchuria in half.

Japan moved swiftly to rally its puppet forces in Manchuria and Tokyo. The Manchurian government proclaimed a defense decree for the entire nation against the "Soviet army's unlawful invasion." An extraordi-

(Continued on Back Page)

Leaflets Urge Japs Revolt, Sue For Peace

MANILA (UP) — Millions of leaflets asking the people of Japan to revolt against their leaders and sue for peace before their country is destroyed were dropped on the enemy homeland Thursday.

The leaflet barrage coincided with the Russian entry into the war and the dropping of the second atomic bomb on Japan.

Allied propagandists believed Japan now might be ripe for surrender. Russian Foreign Commissar Molotov revealed that the Japs had peace in mind as long ago as June and that Emperor Hirohito even sent a personal request to Moscow seeking a possible negative peace.

But the Allies, Russia now included, will accept only unconditional surrender.

The leaflets, only slightly larger than postcards, were secretly printed by Gen MacArthur's psychological warfare branch in anticipation of the Russian declaration of war.

They showed giant American and Russian soldiers clasping hands over the Jap home islands.

OWI URGES SURRENDER

New warnings to Japan to surrender before the country is destroyed by atomic bombing are being broadcast to the enemy homeland by OWI Pacific stations coupled with announcement of Russia's entry into the war.

The new series of special warnings regarding the atomic bombs started Wednesday night from Honolulu, San Francisco and Saipan stations and were continued five times hourly.

Third Fleet Strikes, Sends 1,500 Planes Against Foe

GUAM (UP)— Halsey's great Third fleet sailed into Japanese home waters again Thursday, unleashing 1,500 planes against dwindling centers of enemy resistance as the Japs reported a new strike by 100 Superfortresses against Tokyo.

Simultaneously, Gen. Spaatz announced the most complete devastation ever brought to any Jap city by high explosive bombs was accomplished at Toyama in northern Honshu a week ago.

Japanese broadcasts said a fleet of Superforts in the late afternoon attacked industrial targets around the metropolitan area. American warships earlier thrust to within 10 to 20 miles of the Jap coast and shelled Kamaishi, a steel center in northeast Honshu, while hundreds of carrier planes ranged over a 700-mile stretch of central Japan throughout the day.

New Target Tokyo

Tokyo identified the Superforts' targets as the industrial heart of Tokyo.

Spaatz said photos of Toyama showed 99.5 per cent destruction accomplished there on Aug 2. It was one of four cities and an oil refinery hit by 800 Superforts on that date.

Lt. Gen. Nathan F. Twining, commander of the 20th AAF, said Wednesdays task forces, totaling 400 Superforts on three missions, accomplished "good to excellent" results.

Halsey's new blow against Honshu coinciding with the Russian declaration of war, broke an 11-day news blackout covering operations of the Third fleet.

Continue Most of Day

Tokyo broadcasts, reporting that the attacks still were continuing nine hours after they started at dawn, indicated that the great force of Hellcats, Corsairs, Helldivers and Avengers

(Continued on Back Page)

Petain Judge Called Unfair

PARIS (UP) — Marshal Petain's top military advisers in the Vichy regime testified Wednesday that the old marshal never believed in a German victory, approved plans for a secret mobilization of the French Army and supplied military information to Britain while pretending to cooperate with the Germans.

Gen. Jacques Campet, for three years chief of Petain's military household in Vichy, and Air Force Gen. Jean Bergeret, were the latest to testify in the long procession of defense witnesses.

There was some doubt that their testimony that he played a double game in Vichy for four years would win an acquittal for Petain. Those who have watched the trial for 15 days note an obvious hostility among the jurors toward defense witnesses. Defense Counsel Payen has complained repeatedly that Judge Pierre Mongibeaux showed prejudice in favor of prosecution witnesses.

Public opinion polls show the French man-in-the-street is even more convinced of Petain's guilt than he was last September. A survey by the French Institute of Public Opinion showed 76 per cent in favor of conviction, 15 per cent for acquittal. Now 37 per cent favor a death sentence, compared to 32 per cent last September.

Powerful Jap Group Calls Hurried Session

SAN FRANCISCO (UP) — Tokyo radio said Thursday that the Japan Political association called an "emergency meeting" for Thursday afternoon and held an "important conference" relating to the rapidly changing war situation.

The association president, Gen. Jiro Minami, requested an audience with Premier Kantaro Suzuki.

The action of the powerful Political association, coming close on the heels of the Russian declaration of war and American use of the atomic bomb, could foreshadow another governmental shakeup or some action toward surrender.

Maj. Dick Bong Buried In Tiny Rural Cemetery

POPLAR, Wis. (ANS)— Maj. Richard A. Bong, at 24, America's greatest wartime aviator, was buried Wednesday afternoon in a tiny rural cemetery two miles from the farm on which he lived before the war.

Interment of the ace who was killed Monday at Burbank, Calif., in the explosion of a jet propelled plane he was testing, followed simple Lutheran funeral rites at Concordia church at Superior.

Bombing Date Set Year Ago

GUAM (ANS) – Brig. Thomas L. Farrell, Albany, disclosed that Aug 5, the U. S date for dropping the first atomic bomb on the enemy, was set "well over a year ago."

Farrell, aide to Maj. Gen. Leslie Groves, Pasadena, Calif., veteran Army construction engineer who was in charge of the bomb development program, said at a news conference the goal was set in order to lay out a schedule for completing the huge project.

'Golden Gate Sept. 8,' New GI Victory Cry

GUAM (ANS) — With Russian entry into the war, down came the signs here that said "The Golden Gate by '48" and up went a new slogan:

"The Golden Gate By Sept. 8."

East coasters competed with:

"Old Gotham, Here I Come, At The Latest by December One."

Yield or Face Atomic Ruin, Truman Tells Japs

S & S Weatherman . . .
LONDON and S.E. ENGLAND: Mainly Cloudy, Occasional Rain; Rather Cool.

New York — London Edition — Paris

THE STARS AND STRIPES

Daily Newspaper of U.S. Forces in the European Theater

Vol. 5 No. 22[illegible]—1d. FRIDAY, AUGUST 10, 1945

. . . Predicts for Today
FURTHER OUTLOOK: Cloudy; Local Rain in S.E. England at first. Rather Cool.

Reds 14 Miles Into Manchuria; 3rd Fleet, Planes Strike Honshu

Jap Raiders Sent Up for First Time

Airfields, war plants and shipping in the northern Honshu area of Japan were under their second straight day of attack today (Friday) by U.S. and British carrier planes and guns of Adm. William F. Halsey's 3rd Fleet, Adm. Nimitz announced at Guam. Twelve hundred planes were engaged in the operations, reports said.

Yesterday's blows were struck against Kamaishi, first city to be blasted when Halsey opened his campaign against Japan proper a month ago. Tokyo first reported yesterday's strike, marking Halsey's return to action off Japan after a nine-day lull enforced by weather. Nimitz confirmed today that battleships, cruisers and destroyers had bombarded Kamaishi yesterday, but did not specify any new targets in today's attack.

Dispatches from correspondents with the fleet said many Jap planes were fired on the ground, two ships were sunk and six damaged. Kamaishi, a steel center, is on Honshu's east coast 275 miles north of Tokyo. It was previously hit July 14.

For the first time since Halsey began parading his ships up and down Japan's coast, the enemy sent out planes to attack. But, dispatches said, they did not go to work with the same zeal as the Kamikaze Corps pilots had done off Okinawa. None of the plans came very near, reporters said. Two were shot down. No damage was done to the fleet.

Yesterday's announcement followed Navy disclosure at Washington on Wednesday that Halsey's fleet would soon strike again. The fleet had had to call off its blows against Japan while riding out typhoons in the area, with the result that the Japanese coast had a nine-day rest.

Halsey's return to action, one correspondent reported, was probably the noisiest of any naval operation, for the ships held daily anti-aircraft practice, firing at sleeve targets towed by carrier planes.

Manchuria Put On War Basis

NEW YORK, Aug. 9 (Reuter)—The Manchurian puppet government has decreed a state of emergency for the entire country against the Soviet Army's "unlawful invasion," Tokyo Radio announced today, as Japan's totalitarian party leaders discussed counter-measures to meet the sudden developments in the war situation.

Tokyo stated an "extraordinary" meeting of the Manchurian government was called this morning, and that totalitarian leaders are meeting again tomorrow to decide on a policy to be submitted to the Japanese Government and the high command.

Hours before Russia announced its declaration of war, the Japanese-operated Hongkong radio asserted that the Soviet Union was "too busy" to join the conflict against Japan. An English-language enemy broadcast spoke highly of the "unshakable friendship of the Soviet Union toward Japan."

After all-day warnings by the Japanese Domei News Agency that an important announcement was coming through, the Mutual Broadcasting System reported that the Jap announcement was merely a formal statement that Russia had entered the war.

Ex-CO of 10th Denies Guards Beat Prisoners

CHICAGO, Aug 9—Col. James A. Kilian, of Highland Park, Ill., who commanded the Army's 10th Replacement Depot in England for more than two years, denied reports that American prisoners in the depot guardhouse were beaten by their guards, according to a dispatch to the Chicago Tribune.

"Those reports are absolutely false," said Kilian at Camp Jackson, S.C., where he was stationed. "No such beatings ever occurred. My officers had specific instructions not to impose any punishment without my knowledge or authorization."

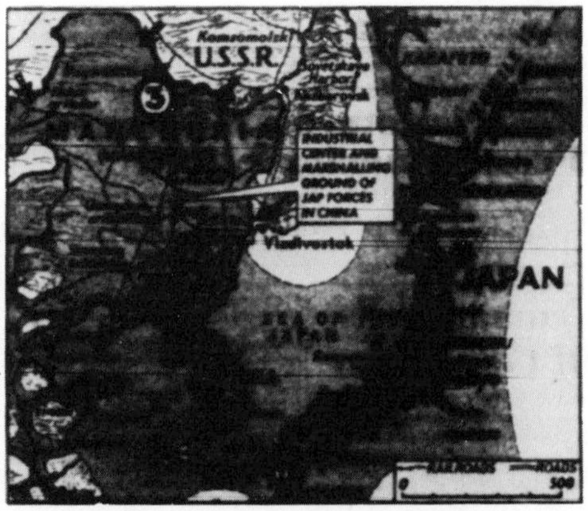

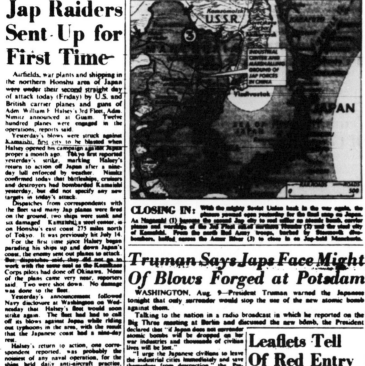

CLOSING IN: With the mighty Soviet Union back in the war again, the pincers yawned open yesterday for the final snap on Japan. As Nagasaki (1) became the second Jap city to suffer an atomic bomb, carrier planes and warships of the 3rd Fleet raked northern Honshu (2) and the steel city of Kamaishi. From the north Red Army troops, backed by Stormovik dive-bombers, knifed across the Amur River (3) to close in on Jap-held Manchuria.

Truman Says Japs Face Might Of Blows Forged at Potsdam

WASHINGTON, Aug. 9—President Truman warned the Japanese tonight that only surrender would stop the use of the new atomic bomb against them.

Talking to the nation in a radio broadcast in which he reported on the Big Three meeting at Berlin and discussed the new bomb, the President declared that "if Japan does not surrender atomic bombs will be dropped on her war industries and thousands of civilian lives will be lost."

"I urge the Japanese civilians to leave the industrial cities immediately and save themselves from destruction," the President said.

The President revealed that Russia had decided at the Berlin conference to enter the war against Japan and had made the decision before she had learned about the new atomic bomb.

This secret decision—made known yesterday when the President and the Russians announced it—was the only secret arrangement, other than current military arrangements, made at the Berlin meeting, the President said.

Grateful that the U.S. had been spared the ravages of war he had seen in Europe, the President declared, "we must do all we can to spare her from the ravages of any future breach of the peace."

"That is why," he said, "though the U.S. wants no territory or profit or selfish advantage out of this war, we are going to maintain the military bases necessary for the complete protection of our interests and of world peace. Bases which our military experts deem to be essential for our protection, and which are not now in our possession, we will acquire. We will acquire them by arrangements consistent with the United Nations charter."

Mr. Truman revealed that the Council of Foreign Ministers of the Big Five set up at the Berlin meeting—the U.S., Britain, Russia, China and France—would be the "continuous meeting ground" on which common understanding on the peace settlements would be reached.

This council, he said, would not "dictate" any peace terms, but would apply the principles of the United Nations

(Continued on page 3)

Leaflets Tell Of Red Entry

MANILA, Aug. 9—Millions of leaflets, prepared four months ago on a gamble by Gen. MacArthur's Psychological Warfare Division, were showered on Japan today telling the Japanese people that "the Red Army strikes."

Flying its first mission in support of its new Soviet allies, the Far East Air Forces bombarded the home islands with postcard-size leaflets picturing giant American and Russian soldiers clasping hands over Japan and warning the Japanese to surrender and avoid utter destruction.

At the same time, MacArthur's HQ was putting into effect prepared plans for liaison between the Russian armies and American forces in the Pacific.

"I am delighted at the Russian declaration of war against Japan," MacArthur stated. "This will make possible a great pincer movement which cannot fail to end in the destruction of the enemy.

"In Europe, Russia was on the Eastern Front and the Allies on the West. Now the Allies are on the East and the Russians on the West—but the result will be the same."

It was believed that the liaison and operational plans now being rushed into effect were made here with the knowledge that Russia would soon join the war. However, Brig. Gen. Bonner F. Fellers, PWD officer, said the advance preparation of leaflets was a gamble.

Second Atomic Raid Wrecks Nagasaki

Japan got the works yesterday as the American-British-Soviet commands opened up by land.

Soviet soldiers scored a nine- to 14-mile gain over the border into Manchuria, Stalin announced in his first communique of the Pacific war.

A Superfort mission from the Marianas atom-bombed Nagasaki, getting "good results" and leaving Hiroshima-rivaling clouds of ruin hovering over the Kyushu port, principal POE for the Emperor's Asia-bound forces. Other B29s struck at Amagasaki, 47 per cent of which had already been razed in a July 20 raid. Air Force HQ at Guam announced that Toyama, one of Japan's warned cities, had been 99.5 per cent destroyed in the Aug. 2 raid by 800 B29s.

Adm. Halsey's 3rd Fleet and swarms of U.S. and British carrier planes, 1,200 strong, showed up again off Japan's coast, lambasting the steel city of Kamaishi and airfields near by.

Japs Reel as Allies Hit From All Sides

Russian forces smashed into Manchuria yesterday on a "broad front" and advanced from nine and a half to 14 miles at several points, Generalissimo Stalin announced last night in his first communique of the Soviet war against Japan.

Stalin's communique was broadcast by Moscow exactly 24 hours after the announcement yesterday that as from midnight the USSR would be at war with Japan.

Red Army troops, Stalin stated, crossed the frontier from Outer Mongolia at Manchouli on the northwest tip of Manchuria. Other forces thrust westward from the old Siberian maritime provinces at Khabarovsk, on the opposite tip to the northeast.

About 85 miles south of Manchouli, on the Outer Mongolian border—territory technically Chinese but under Communist rule for a number of years—the swift-striking Red Army crossed the border in the vicinity of Lake Buir Nor and captured Jinjinsume and Hoshusume.

Japanese Imperial Headquarters announced yesterday that Soviet forces also had slashed into Manchuria at "several points" along a mountainous 300-mile front extending southward from Hutou to Hunchun. Hutou is 350 miles east and Hunchun 280 miles southeast of Harbin, key Japanese industrial and communications center regarded as the primary objective of the Red Army's double thrust.

Stalin also announced that the Red Air Force had attacked the main Manchurian railway junctions of Harbin, Changchun and Kirin and the port of Seishin, also called Rashin, in Korea.

In the northwestern area around Manchouli, Russian troops overcame fierce enemy resistance, stormed the Manchuro-Dalaimor area fortified by the Japanese and occupied the towns and railway stations of Manchouli and Dalaimor.

On the northeastern frontier Soviet forces fought their way across the Amur and Ussuri Rivers to capture Fuyuan and other populated places.

Constellation Zips Again

PARIS, Aug. 9—A C69 Constellation plane, which last week flew non-stop from New York to Paris in 14 hours and 12 minutes, arrived at Orly Field today nine hours and 22 minutes after taking off from Stephensville, Newfoundland.

Nagasaki is Blasted In 2nd Atomic Blow

Marianas-based Superforts have atom-bombed another Japanese city—Nagasaki, a port on the west coast of Japan's [illegible] Kyushu and the chief embarkation point for enemy troops headed toward the Asiatic mainland—and struck with nearly 500 tons of demolition bombs at Amagasaki, near Osaka on Honshu, 20th Air Force HQ announced at Guam early today.

It was not clear whether one or more atom bombs had been hurled at Nagasaki. A communique from Gen. Carl A. Spaatz, Strategic Air Forces chief in the Pacific, merely said: "The second use of the atomic bomb occurred at noon Aug. 9 at Nagasaki. Crew members reported good results. No further details will be available until the mission returns."

Nagasaki is Japan's 12th largest city, although its population is about 250,000, less than that of Hiroshima, 60 per cent of which was destroyed in the first atom bomb attack. Nagasaki covers an area of 12 square miles and is one of Japan's most densely populated centers.

More than 47 per cent of Amagasaki had been destroyed in a raid on July 20, reconnaissance reports said, before a force of about 80 B29s struck there again early today (Friday, Far Eastern Time). Amagasaki is one of Japan's principal centers for storing aviation gasoline.

Spaatz revealed that atom bombing is not the only means by which American airmen can wipe out Jap cities. He reported that Toyama, one of the cities warned in pre-attack leaflets raids, had been 99.5 per cent destroyed in the Aug. 2 blow by 800 Superforts.

Reports of previous attacks on warned Japanese cities showed that six of those on Honshu had been 50 per cent knocked out.

Tokyo reported that about 100 Superforts had raided the capital area yesterday and that 300 other planes were active over the mainland, but these claims were not confirmed from U.S. sources. There were no Tokyo announcements up to last night concerning the Nagasaki atom bomb raid. Enemy broadcasts said Allied planes were over Hiroshima again, but did not say for what purpose.

Okinawa-Based B29s To Bear 15-Ton Bomb Load Each Trip

OKINAWA, Aug. 9 (AP)—Eighth Air Force Superforts based on Okinawa will be able to carry a 15-ton bomb load in every strike they take at Japan, Lt. Gen. James H. Doolittle said today.

Such a load will be 50 per cent greater than those carried by Marianas-based B29s, which must fly 1,000 miles or more to attack the enemy's homeland.

Okinawa is 400 miles fro mthe mainland and about 700 from Tokyo. Nearness to their targets and some technical changes permit the increased bomb load.

No Special Session

BONHAM, Tex., Aug. 9 (AP)—Speaker Sam Rayburn (D.-Tex.) said today he saw no immediate need for recalling Congress into session because of Russia's entry into the war with Japan.

Russia Gains a Voice in the Far East's Future

WASHINGTON, Aug. 9 (AP)—By going to war against Japan Russia has claimed a seat at the Pacific peace table, and Washington speculated today on the far-reaching diplomatic and territorial implications brought about by her presence there.

By the declaration of war against Japan, Russia became a partner with Britain, the U.S. and China in settlements which will determine, among other things, which strategic islands in the Pacific the Americans will continue to hold after the fighting ends.

The assumption in diplomatic quarters here is that when the Soviets finally agreed to enter the conflict against Japan they automatically accepted the terms of the Cairo agreement made in November, 1943, by the late President Roosevelt, Prime Minister Churchill and Generalissimo Chiang Kai-shek. And the belief has been strengthened by authentic disclosures that Stalin told Mr Roosevelt and Churchill at Yalta that he would enter the Pacific war but did not set a specific date.

The disposition of islands such as Iwo Jima and Okinawa were not mentioned in the Cairo plan, in which the three powers then fighting Japan denounced all territorial expansion for themselves. It was agreed that Japan should be stripped of all Pacific islands she had seized or occupied since 1914, and that territories stolen, such as Manchuria and Formosa, would be restored to China. The three powers also agreed that "in due course Korea shall become free and independent."

American political quarters however have speculated that Russia might want anything from part of Manchuria to all of Korea. And the Soviet voice will also be heard in the post-war disposition of Hongkong and Singapore, where the British had important pre-war holdings.

ALLIES OKAY JAPS' OFFER

SOUTHERN FRANCE EDITION

EXTRA **THE STARS AND STRIPES** EXTRA

Daily Newspaper of U.S. Armed Forces in the European Theater

Vol. 1—No. 152 Saturday, August 11, 1945 ONE FRANC

Emperor Must Be Controlled By Allies, Byrnes Tells Foe

WASHINGTON, Aug. 11 (AP)—The U.S. has agreed to accept Japanese surrender provided the supreme commanders of the Allied Powers rule Japan through the authority of the Emperor.

In a reply made to Japan's offer to surrender made through the Swiss government, Secretary of State James F. Byrnes said the U.S. would accept the surrender if Hirohito would be made subject to the supreme commanders' orders.

This also represented the viewpoints of the United Kingdom, the Soviet Union and China, Byrnes told the Japanese through the Swiss embassy.

(The Washington announcement apparently did not mean the war actually was over. The Japanese would have to reply favorably to the Allied interpretation of the Emperor's status following capitulation before the surrender could be considered accepted.

(What the Japanese reaction to the Allied note would be was open to question.

(Presumably a delay of several hours at least could be expected before the Japanese action would become known. The Allied message would have to be transmitted to Japan through diplomatic channels, and the Japanese reply thereto would come back through the same channels.)

The Japanese surrender offer, first announced in a Domei news agency broadcast Friday morning, was sent to neutral Sweden and Switzerland for transmission to the U.S., Britain, Russia and China.

While Big Four officials awaited official receipt of the offer, long-distance telephone consultations were begun on the basis of the Domei broadcast, which said the Japanese were ready to accept the Potsdam surrender ultimatum of July 26 "with the understanding that said declaration does not comprise any demand which prejudices the prerogatives of His Majesty as sovereign ruler."

Decision for the peace offer was ascribed to the "gracious command" of the Emperor, who, the broadcast said, "is ever anxious to enhance the cause of world peace."

The Emperor, the offer stated, wished to end hostilities quickly "with a view of saving mankind from calamities to be imposed upon them by further continuation of the war."

The Domei text also said that the Japanese government had asked the Russians to mediate several weeks ago—an effort mentioned by Soviet Foreign Minister Vyacheslav Molotov in the Russian declaration of war on Japan—and that the attempt had failed.

In requesting that the Emperor's status be unchanged, the surrender offer concluded, "The Japanese government hope sincerely that this understanding is warranted and desire keenly that an explicit indication to that effect will be speedily forthcoming."

Reds Invade Korea, S. Sakhalin—Tokyo

The Japanese surrender offer yesterday came as the Red Army drove into Korea and the southern half of Sakhalin Island in new offensives and gained nine to 15 miles in Manchuria, the enemy reported.

A Japanese communique said the Soviet push into Korea—guaranteed its freedom by the Cairo declaration—was made near Keiko, in the northeast corner of the Peninsula. The drive into the lower half of Sakhalin—the part owned by Japan—was carried out near Buika, the enemy said.

Moscow remained silent on the Korea and Sakhalin offensives, but detailed successes by the Red Army all along the wide Manchurian front.

On the eastern flank, Soviet soldiers forded the Amur and Ussuri Rivers from the Khabarovsk area, some 375 miles northeast of Vladisvostok. The Jap stronghold of Juyuan was captured after the Russians had broken through "a reinforced concrete defense zone."

Some 600 miles across the plains of Manchuria the second prong of the Red pincers was closing on the big industrial center of Harbin. Thrusting southeastward along the southern branch of the trans-Siberian railway, the Soviets captured the major rail towns of Manchouli and Chalainor, cutting the railroad.

CASUALTIES UP 7,489 LAST WEEK

WASHINGTON, Aug. 10 (ANS)—Combat casualties reported by the armed forces reached 1,068,216 yesterday, an increase of 7,489 in a week

JAP CITY ONLY 5 PCT. INTACT

GUAM, Aug. 10 (ANS)—Toyama, on the Japan Sea 160 miles northwest of Tokyo, is the most devastated city in Japan, the 20th AF announced. The city of 127,000 is 95.5 percent destroyed. Toyama was one of the forewarned cities hit by a record force of 820 Superforts on Aug. 2.

As the result of other raids the 20th listed the following damage to built-up areas in other Jap cities:

Nagaoka, an important north central Honshu machine tool center, 65.5 percent; Hachioji, a railway hub controlling all Tokyo traffic, 56 percent; and Mito, an industrial rail city near Tokyo, 61.3 percent.

Three oil centers at Kawasaki in Tokyo Bay were described as 35 to 49 percent crippled.

It's Going 'Through Channels'

Berne Awaiting Jap Note; Diplomatic Route Traced

BERNE, Aug. 10 (By Telephone)—The Japanese surrender offer, which Domei News Agency said had been addressed to the Swiss government for transmission to the U.S., Britain, China and Russia, had not been received by American diplomatic officials here at 5 PM yesterday.

George Tait, first secretary of the U.S. legation in Berne, said he was "standing by and waiting" for receipt of the note from the Swiss Foreign Office on the basis of what he had heard over the radio.

According to Tait, the normal procedure in a case such as this would be:

The Swiss minister in Tokyo would be handed the note for transmittal to the Swiss Foreign Office in Berne, which, in turn, would immediately notify both the U.S. and Japanese legations there of receipt of the communication.

Then the note would follow one of two paths to Washington. It could be forwarded directly to the State Department by American diplomatic officials, or it could be sent by the Swiss Foreign Office to the Swiss legation in Washington for presentation to the State Department.

Barring unforeseen transmission or technical difficulties, Tait said, the note could be forwarded to Washington and a reply sent to Tokyo, via Berne, in a matter of a "very few hours"

U.S. Ship Lost Off Philippines

WASHINGTON, Aug. 11 (ANS)—The destroyer escort Underhill has been sunk in Philippine waters with the loss of 112 men, the Navy announced today.

American submarines operating in Far Eastern waters have sunk 13 more Japanese ships, including a light cruiser.

OKINAWA B29s HAUL 15 TONS

OKINAWA, Aug. 11 (ANS)—Superfortresses based on Okinawa will be able to carry a 15-ton bomb load on every strike they make on Japan, Lt. Gen. James H. Doolittle disclosed as he welcomed the B29s of his Eighth AF to their new base here.

S & S Weatherman . . .
Cloudy
Maximum Temperature 74
Detailed Weather on Page 8

Germany Edition
THE STARS AND STRIPES
Daily Newspaper of U.S. Armed Forces in the European Theater

USO Shows
Soldiers continue to be vocal about them. See B Bag, Page 2.

Volume 1, Number 132 | Tuesday, August 14, 1945 | 20 Pfennigs

Allied Blows Continue as World Waits

Fleet Blasts Tokyo Region; U.S. Ship Hit

GUAM, Aug. 13—Adm. William F. Halsey hurled more than 1,000 carrier planes of his Third Fleet at the Tokyo area today and all other American commanders in the Pacific made it clear that they were continuing to fight as the surrender negotiations lagged.

The Japanese, on their part, torpedoed and damaged "a major U. S. war vessel" anchored in Buckner Bay at Okinawa yesterday, Adm. Nimitz announced. No further details were disclosed except that the plane which launched the torpedo got away. Another enemy torpedo plane was shot down near the Third Fleet this morning and other attacking aircraft were driven off.

Japs Claim Carrier

(A Domei broadcast said that the warship hit at Okinawa was a large aircraft carrier and claimed it was sunk.)

The American and British carrier planes started their attack at dawn. Their targets were 60 to 70 airfields on the Kanto Plain surrounding Tokyo and various military installations and arsenals.

Far East Air Forces planes from Okinawa, whose daily assaults have been made by 400 to 500 planes, also continued their forays. Over the weekend they had sunk or damaged 51 Japanese ships and fired and blasted factories, warehouses, barracks and railroad yards and bridges on Kyushu Island.

A spokesman for Gen. Mac-

(Continued on Page 8)

Mop-up in Philippines Nets 3,138 Jap Dead

MANILA, Aug. 13 (ANS)—The American mop-up campaign in the Philippines yielded 3,738 additional Japanese dead and 485 captives last week, Gen. MacArthur's communique reported today. Enemy casualties for the entire campaign reached 447,155. Last week's operations cost Americans 41 killed and 88 wounded.

At It Again

Adm. Halsey: his Third Fleet resumes attacks on Japan.

Medic Badge Pay Approved

WASHINGTON, Aug. 13 (ANS)—Holders of the Combat Medic Badge will get an extra 10 dollars a month pay starting with the payday at the end of this month, the Army said today.

A bill passed by Congress and signed by President Truman in July provided for payment of the extra 10 dollars to all Medical Department EM and officers assigned or attached to combat infantry outfits. The pay starts as of Aug. 1, when the bill became effective.

Earlier this year Congress had approved a Combat Medic Badge and award of the emblem started March 1. The badge itself carried no extra pay, so even men who have had the badge since March 1 will receive additional pay only from Aug. 1.

Victory May Shove U.S. Clocks Back

WASHINGTON, Aug. 13 (ANS)—War time is expected to be an early casualty of peace. The clocks may go back one hour soon after Congress reconvenes and has time to adopt a resolution.

The stepped up schedule has not been popular with the legislators. Chairman Clarence Cannon (D-Mo.) of the House Appropriations Committee said recently that he wanted to end it as soon as conditions premitted.

3 Red Armies Deep in Korea, Manchuria

MOSCOW, Aug. 13—Fresh gains up to 21 miles carried three Red armies deep into Manchuria and Korea today, while still another Russian force was reported by the Japanese to have launched a new offensive across Chinese Inner Mongolia toward the Yellow Sea.

Headquarters of the enemy Kwantung Army in Manchuria claimed the latest Soviet drive had started in Outer Mongolia and was aimed at reaching the ocean, possibly by way of Peiping, the ancient capital of China. Such an operation, if successful, might split the estimated 1,500,000 Japanese troops on the Asiatic mainland into two huge pockets.

Capitalizing on their surprise seizure of the big enemy naval base of Rashin and the nearby port of Yuki in Korea yesterday, Soviet amphibious troops of the First Far Eastern Army immediately began pushing down the peninsula's coastal highway along the Sea of Japan. At some points, they were as much as 22 miles into Korea after storming ashore some 90 miles southwest of Vladivostok.

Land at Night

The landings were made at night under the protective guns of Adm. Ivan Yemashov's Soviet Pacific Fleet during a storm so severe the Japanese believed an amphibious operation impossible. Dispatches from Korea said the enemy garrisons fled in panic, abandoning supplies and equipment as well as several "fishing boats" which had been plying Soviet waters.

By Japanese report, Russian troops also were invading the lower part of Sakhalin Island, of which Russia owns the northern half and Japan the southern.

On the mainland, tank-led cavalrymen of Marshal Rodion Y. Malinovsky's Trans-Baikal Army were well over the great Khingan Mountains and were hurling the Japanese back onto the plains of Central Manchuria, where the enemy would have virtually no defense against the swiftly-moving Russian armored units.

Point to Harbin

Driving down the railroad from captured Hailar, this force was approximately 245 miles northwest of the metropolis of Harbin.

At the same time, Malinovsky's southern wing developed a new threat to the Japanese by breaking off toward Mukden, an early B-29 target and site of numerous camps where U. S., British, Australian, New Zealand and Canadian troops are confined.

The First Far Eastern Army, smashing inland from the Siberian maritime province of Primorye, rolled up advances of nine to 21 miles in its offensive through the rugged Chan Kwantai Range, some 175 miles southeast of Harbin.

Slightly less than 300 miles due north of Harbin the Second Far Eastern Army was approaching the Little Khingan Mountains after capturing a town 50 miles southeast of the big Siberian border town of Blagoveschensk.

Worried

Chiang Kai-shek: Jap guns in Communist hands cause him concern.

China Fears A Civil War

CHUNGKING, Aug. 13—Talk of a possible civil war or revolution in China was heard here last night, an American radio correspondent reported, after Chinese Communist troops in the north reportedly had accepted the surrender of some Japanese and Chinese puppet units.

Reports trickling through a strict Chungking censorship said that Gen. Chu Teh, commander-in-chief of the Chinese Communist forces, had ordered his troops to accept the Japanese surrender and seize Japanese arms. An Associated Press correspondent said there were indications the Communists planned to occupy as many points and seize all the military supplies they could.

The Alleged Communist action led to an order by Generalissimo Chiang Kai-shek, calling upon all chinese troops to "stand by for further instructions from the National Military Council and hold themselves in readiness to execute such terms of the surrender as the Allies may decide upon." He said the U. S., Britain, Russia and China were conferring "on questions related to the Japanese surrender with the view of arriving at a joint decision."

Fighting, however, continued in southwestern China. A Chungking communique announced that Chinese troops had recaptured the important rail center of Chuanhsien, 69 miles northeast of the Kwangsi province capital of Kweilin.

Japs Received Terms Late, Tokyo Claims

WASHINGTON, Aug. 13—Continued silence from Japan on the latest Allied surrender terms led to some letdown today in the capital's eager expectancy, but officials still seemed hopeful of a speedy end to the war.

A late Domei broadcast said that the official text of the terms was received in Tokyo from Switzerland only today. This, if true, might account for the delay in reply.

The broadcast made no other comment, and the reason for the reported delay in transmission was not apparent. The Japanese ambassador in Berne received the document Saturday night.

The tone of Japanese home broadcasts seemed significant to some observers. The press and radio, possibly seeking to steel the uninformed millions for imminent surrender, erupted with appeals for staunch loyalty to the emperor—who could retain his throne under the surrender but would be subject to the authority of the Allied Supreme Commander.

One Domei news agency broadcast said the press stressed that "unswerving loyalty" to Emperor Hirohito "is the only factor which will save the nation from the worst crisis with which it ever has been confronted."

Denounces America

For foreign consumption, however, Tokyo Radio had only the news that the emperor received Foreign Minister Shigenori Togo in a second audience, and a 15-minute denunciation of American war aims by an unidentified commentator.

The official Japanese reply to the four-power surrender demand would be transmitted to the U. S. and China through Switzerland and to Russia and Britain through Sweden, but the first disclosure of it could be expected from Tokyo Radio, which similarly revealed the original surrender offer Friday

(Continued on Page 8)

Papen to Play Trial Roles Of Star Witness, Defendant

WIESBADEN, Aug. 13 (AP)—Franz von Papen, front man for German aggressors in two wars, will play a dual role in the first war criminal trials next month. The dapper Junker diplomat will appear as a star witness and as a defendant when the trials open here before an international tribunal.

The link between Germany's two unsuccessful attempts at world conquest, Papan is believed to hold the inner secrets of Nazi foreign policy. It is these secrets which the war crimes court will attempt to wrest from him.

Appearing at the same time will be Joachim von Ribbentrop, Nazi foreign minister and confidant of Hitler. The former champagne salesman will be pressed to unfold other secrets of the Nazi foreign office.

Also slated for first-act appearances before the court are Field Marshal Hermann Goering and Generals Wilhelm Keitel and Gustav Jodl. Julius Streicher, Robert Ley, Nazi Labor Front chief, and Arthur Seyss-Inquart, Austrian Quisling, are scheduled among the first defendants.

Special precautions have been taken to prevent suicide by any of the defendants, all of whom have been transferred to Nuremberg in preparation for the trials. Conviction of these leaders would set the stage for trials of the lesser Nazis now in Allied custody.

Ike Ordered Halt at Elbe To Assault Redoubt in South

MOSCOW, Aug. 13 (AP)—Gen. Eisenhower said today that he had ordered U. S. troops smashing across Germany last spring to stop at the Elbe River because he wanted to break up Hitler's national redoubt in the south—and not because the Red Army or Premier Stalin had requested it.

In an interview, the former Supreme Allied Commander declared there had been complete coordination with the Russians. He said he told his commanders weeks ahead of time to pull up at the Elbe at certain places and to turn southward at others with all possible speed. He added it had never been his plan to stop at any military or political zone.

As long ago as January of this year, Eisenhower revealed, U. S. Ambassador to Russia W. Averell Harriman and Maj. Gen. J. Russell Deane, chief of the U. S. military mission to the USSR, worked out a plan of cooperation and collaboration with the Red Army.

His talks with Stalin during his current visit to Moscow, made at the suggestion of the Soviet government indicated that one of Russia's paramount desires was for lasting friendship with the U. S., Eisenhower said. While he asserted that he was unable to reveal the subject of conversations with the premier, he said he was markedly impressed with Stalin's absolute sincerity.

THE STARS AND STRIPES
AFRICA-MIDDLE EAST
CAIRO   Wednesday, August 15, 1945   FREE

EXTRA

IT'S ALL OVER!

Truman Announces Japs' Unconditional Surrender

WASHINGTON, Aug. 15 (Army News Service)—Japan has officially accepted the Allied terms for unconditional surrender without qualification, President Truman announced Tuesday, at 1900 hours.

The surrender will be accepted by General MacArthur when arrangements can be completed. The terms provide that authority of the Emperor shall be subject to the Supreme Commander of the Allied Powers with the Emperor issuing such orders as the Supreme Commander requires.

Gen. MacArthur will be Allied Supreme Commander in Japan.

Other terms as set forth in the Potsdam Declaration call for elimination of authority and influence of those "who have deceived and misled people of Japan into embarking on world conquest," occupation by Allies of designated points in Japanese territory, limiting of Japanese sovereignity to four main home islands, complete disarmament of all Jap military forces, removal of all obstacles to revival of "democratic tendencies" among Japanese people, and withdrawal of Allied occupation forces as soon as their objectives have been accomplished and responsible Japanese Government has been established.

The Japanese reply stated:

"With reference to the announcement of August 10 regarding the acceptance of the provisions of the Potsdam Declaration and the reply of the governments of the United States, Great Britain, the Soviet Union and China sent by the Secy. of State James F. Byrnes on August 11, the Japanese government has the honor to reply to the governments of the four powers as follows:

"His Majesty the Emperor has issued an imperial rescript regarding Japan's acceptance of the provisions of the Potsdam Declaration. The Emperor is prepared to authorize and ensure the signature by his government and his imperial headquarters of the necessary terms for carrying out the provisions of Potsdam.

"His Majesty the Emperor is also prepared to issue this communications to all military, naval and air authorities to issue to all forces under their control wherever located to cease active resistance and to surrender arms.

PRES. HARRY S. TRUMAN
Commander in Chief

ADM. CHESTER W. NIMITZ
USN Commander in Chief

GEN. DOUGLAS A. MacARTHUR
Supreme Allied Commander

GEN. CARL A. SPAATZ
Pacific AF Commander

'VICTORY' SHELLS KILL GIs

OKINAWA — At least six men were killed and 30 injured by falling ack ack shell fragments and bullets Friday night when U.S. troops on Okinawa touched off a spectacular display of rockets, ack ack and flares in premature celebration of the end of the war. To quell the half-hour demonstration, island commanders ordered the air raid alert sounded, then warned the men by radio to cease firing.

U.S. OFFERS JAPS SHIP

WASHINGTON — The United States has offered to transfer to Japan immediately an 11,758-ton ship to replace the Japanese relief vessel, Awa Maru, sunk accidentally by an American submarine. The government notes that the ship is not offered as indemnity.

TOVARICH, MAC!

BERLIN — The streets and cabarets of Berlin echoed with friendly greetings of "Tovarich" this week as Soviet soldiers and American GIs hailed Russia's declaration of war. In jammed night spots, they clinked glasses in toasts to comradeship.

ORIENTAL OPTIMISM

SAN FRANCISCO — The unpredictable Japanese looked up out of the rubble this week and decided that they'd found another benefit from air raids, adding to a recent interesting statement that they were getting a lot of scrap iron. The raids, chants Radio Tokyo, "are making possible extensive replanning of Japanese cities" —which were apparently a mess to begin with.

POPE DENIES BOMB STORY

ROME — Pope Pius is quoted by American newsmen as denying that anyone had been authorized to express the Vatican views on the use of the atomic bomb against Japan. Previously a Vatican City dispatch had quoted "an authoritative Vatican source" as making a statement to the effect that the Vatican was against the use of the atomic bomb. The Pope told the correspondent that the statement was completely unauthorized.

EXTRA

New York — London Edition — Paris

THE STARS AND STRIPES

Daily Newspaper of U.S. Forces in the European Theater

★★ Vol. 5 No. 242—1d. WEDNESDAY, AUGUST 15, 1945

EXTRA

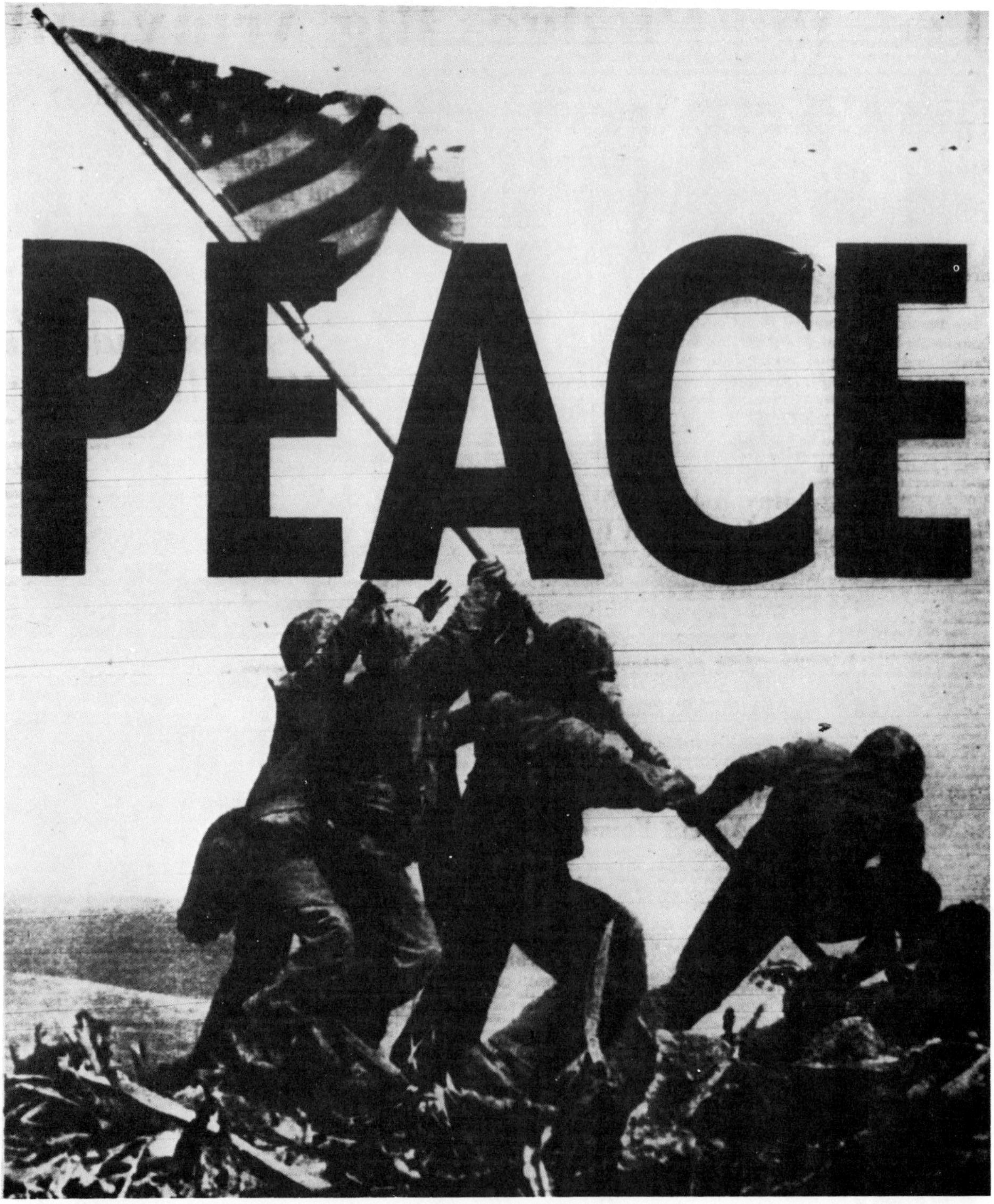

Japan has surrendered unconditionally. President Truman announced at midnight last night (British time). Gen. Douglas MacArthur has been named Supreme Allied Commander to receive the formal surrender as soon as arrangements can be made. Allied forces have been ordered to cease offensive action and the Japanese have been ordered by the President to cease all fighting immediately. The President said that between 5,000,000 and 5,500,000 men would be demobilized in the next year to 18 months.

The surrender of Japan came 93 days after the fall of Nazi Germany.

THE STARS AND STRIPES
MEDITERRANEAN
Vol. 2, No. 57, Thursday, August 16, 1945 Printed In Italy TWO LIRE

MacArthur Summons Japs To Sign Surrender In Manila

All World Rejoices Over Peace

Entire Nation Celebrates; D. C. Has Its Biggest Fete Of All Time

As the news that fighting has ended spread throughout the world, the peoples of the earth lifted up their heads again and rejoiced.

The rejoicing, according to the temperaments of the individuals and their communities, was either devotional or boisterous. But the celebration of the end of the war was on a scale that dwarfed even the spontaneous enthusiasm that marked the observance of the armistice in 1918.

In the U. S., a carnival spirit spread through big cities, towns and villages. Broadway and Main Streets all over America joined in the festivities. Americans crowded restaurants and bars. They thronged the streets. They met in their own homes and gave profound thanks that there would be no more loss of precious American blood.

Times Square, bellwether for American celebrations, was a solid mass of humanity. There were dancing and shouting in the streets. People blew horns, and wore gay paper hats. Servicemen kissed and hugged strange girls. There were no strangers in America. Everybody talked to everybody else; all of America was brother.

Washington, the nation's capital, had its wildest celebration in history. Restaurants and theaters emptied immediately after the announcement at 7 PM (Eastern War Time), and hordes of celebrants jammed downtown streets.

The MP guard around the White House was increased as a mass of people thronged around the fence. President Truman received a demonstration that lasted for many minutes when he went out on the White House portico to speak

(Continued on page 3)

DEATH PENALTY

MARSHAL HENRI PETAIN

Petain Sentenced To Die For Treason

PARIS, Aug. 15 — Convicted of treason, Marshal Henri Philippe Petain, discredited leader of the discredited Vichy state, today was sentenced to death before the firing squad.

The verdict was reached at 4:20 AM. — a few hours before dawn — by a jury of 12 resistance party members and 12 former senators and deputies who had deliberated a little less than seven hours.

Dazed, seemingly uncomprehending, the pale, whitehaired, 89-year-old Petain showed virtually no emotion when sentence was imposed by Pierre Mongibeaux, the presiding judge. Nor was there any demonstration in the courtroom.

Docilely, he permitted himself to be conducted to his cell after Mongibeaux intoned the traditional

(Continued on page 8)

President Given Great Public Ovation After Telling News

WASHINGTON, Aug. 15—One of the greatest displays of exuberance ever to greet an American President met President Truman last night when he told the huge crowd waiting expectantly outside the White House—

"This is the day we have been looking for since Dec. 7, 1941. This is the day when fascists and police governments cease to exist in the world."

The President proclaimed Wednesday and Thursday as legal holidays. All Federal workers were to receive the days off, and the President said any war workers remaining on the job during the two-day holiday would be paid overtime wages.

President Truman addressed the crowd outside the White House shortly after the historic two-minute news conference at which he announced Japan's surrender. Thousands of men, women and children had waited outside the White House for hours to receive the dramatic announcement.

With Mrs. Truman standing at her husband's left and a few White House intimates around him, the President waved to the cheering crowd, and then stepped to the microphone linked with the public address system rigged up for the occasion.

"This is a great day," he began. "This is the day we have been looking for since Dec. 7, 1941. This is the day when fascist and police governments cease to exist in the world. This is the day for democracy. It is the day when we can start the real task—the implementation of free government in the world.

"We face a real emergency. I know we can meet it. We face the greatest task ever faced—the great-

(Continued on page 3)

Nip War Minister Commits Hara-Kiri

By Sgt. JOE BAILY
Staff Correspondent

The dawn of the first day of peace after eight tragic years of war brought momentous aftermaths to the Japanese capitulation.

In stricken Japan, the Emperor made an unprecedented speech informing his people of the defeat, the cabinet of Premier Kantaro Suzuki collapsed and War Minister Korechika Anami committed hara-kiri.

KORECHIKA ANAMI

In the triumphant Allied capitals, the victors—setting in motion the war-end machinery — made plans for binding up wounds and steering the now fully-freed world into new courses of civilized living.

From the Philippines, General Douglas MacArthur, the newly-designated Supreme Allied Commander, called upon Japan to begin arrangements at once for the formal signing of the surrender by sending representatives to him to receive instructions. His message, transmitted by radio to Tokyo, followed within a few short hours President Truman's order to Japan to cease hostilities.

Guns the world over were silent for the first time since the Japanese Armies, crossing the Marco Polo Bridge at Peiping, China, in July, 1937, touched off the spark plug that raged into a conflagration.

The bells rang out everywhere, and free men rejoiced. Gala celebrations stirred the Allied capitals, and every Allied city and town. But the bells were tolling, too, for those who died in the eight war years, for the maimed, the starved and the homeless. And through their rejoicing the free men looked with sober eyes to the future, and resolved solemnly that this would be the last war of all.

Japan was a beaten and battered nation. Her Emperor said she was quitting the war because of the terrible potentialities of the atom bomb, which he described as "a new and most cruel bomb, the power of which to do damage is indeed incalculable."

Japan's cities were in ashes, her people in terror, her dream

(Continued on page 8)

Peace Will Speed Discharges

5 Million To Get Out In 12-18 Months

WASHINGTON, Aug. 15 — Release from the Army of 5,000,000 to 5,500,000 men during the next 12 to 18 months was predicted by President Truman last night after he announced Japan's capitulation.

Exact figures, he said, were unavailable, but "it is apparent that we can release as many men as can be brought home by the means available during the next year."

Selective Service inductions, he announced, would be reduced immediately from 80,000 to 50,000 a month to provide only enough replacements for occupational armies. Men under 26 years of age, he said, could probably fill the new quotas.

The Navy announced today its plan to demobilize 1,500,000 to 2,500,000 Naval personnel in the next 12 to 18 months, with 327,000 scheduled for immediate release.

The Navy's point system gives credit for age, length of service and dependency as follows: one-half point for each year of age; one-half point for each full month of active duty since Sept. 1, 1939; and 10 points for a dependent (no additional credit if more than one.) Eligibility for release is set at 44 points for enlisted men, 29 for Waves, 49 for officers, and 35 for Wave officers.

An announcement from the Marine Corps released today said its demobilization plan will be identical with that of the Army.

Congressmen called for complete halt to inductions, and Chairman Andrew J. May (D. Ky.), of the House Military Affairs Committee, said he would discuss with the President the possibility of an immediate proclamation ending the national emergency.

The proclamation, he explained, would mark the beginning of the "plus six months" period mentioned in the Selective Service Act. All inducted men, he said, would be discharged from the Army not later than six months after the proclamation became effective.

Chairman May said he would introduce legislation as soon as Congress reconvenes next month to end all draft calls. Yesterday, Sen. William Langer (R., N.D.),

(Continued on page 6)

MTO Redeployment Plan Pushed Up

By Sgt. DAVE ANDERSON
Staff Correspondent

CASERTA, Aug. 15—VJ-Day will speed up redeployment in this theater by at least one month, redeployment experts predicted today.

Under the speedup, the redeployers are shooting at Jan. 1 as their target for clearing the theater of all except occupation troops. A month ago, General Joseph T. McNarney, deputy supreme Allied commander, had said that MTO troops "should be redeployed by early 1946." As things look now MTOUSA hopes to beat that forecast.

By the end of September most of the men who now have 85 points and more will be on their way home, redeployment officers declared. They qualified that prediction, however, by adding "—if there are no changes in the present scoring of the point system." By that time the theater, they believe, will have dipped into 89-

(Continued on page 6)

Text Of Emperor's Talk On Japanese Surrender

WASHINGTON, Aug. 15—Here is the text of the dramatic surrender speech made by Emperor Hirohito today to the people of Japan—marking the first time in history that a Japanese Emperor has spoken over the air waves to the nation:

"To our good and loyal subjects:

"After pondering deeply on the general trend of the world and actual conditions obtaining in our empire today, we have decided to effect settlement of the present situation by resorting to extraordinary measures.

"We have ordered our Government to communicate to the governments of the United States, Great Britain, China and the Soviet Union that our empire accepts the provisions of their joint declaration.

"To strive for the common prosperity and happiness of all nations, as well as for the security and well-being of our subjects, is the solemn obligation which has been handed down by our imperial ancestors, and which lie close to our hearts.

"Indeed, we declared war on America and Britain out of our sincere desire to ensure Japan's self-preservation and stabilization of East Asia, it being far from our thoughts either to infringe upon the sovereignty of other nations or to embark upon territorial aggrandizement.

"But now the war has lasted for

(Continued on page 8)

Germany Edition
THE STARS AND STRIPES
Daily Newspaper of U.S. Armed Forces in the European Theater

Volume 1, Number 147 | Wednesday, August 29, 1945 | 20 Pfennigs

S & S Weatherman . . .
Partly Clou y
Maximum Temperature 80

Inside Index

First American Troops Land in Japan

Talk of Cut In Points Still Astir

WASHINGTON, Aug. 28—A War Department spokesman said today that a reduction of the critical score for army discharges will be announced shortly after Sept. 1, the International News Service reported.

INS said the critical score would be dropped first to 80 points and later to 75 points.

"We will progressively lower the point system and bring back combat troops as speedily as possible," the spokesman was quoted as saying.

(Editor's Note—This is the 37th in a series of stories quoting unidentified sources in the War Department about changes in the point score. Any one of them may be right. The last informed speculation, which usually means guesswork, said that the score would be reduced to 75.)

Stars and Stripes publishes these stories on the theory that they're news, but warns against acceptance of them as gospel truth.)

President Voices Motives

President Truman, meanwhile, gave his reasons for favoring continuation of the draft for men 18 to 25 years old and for opposing a declaration that the war emergency had ended. Such a declaration would automatically halt inductions.

His views were set forth in letters to chairman Elbert Thomas (D-Utah) of the Senate Military Affairs Committee and Chairman Andrew J. May (D-Ky.) of the House Military Committee. The House group was called together today to consider the draft and the redeployment program.

Mr. Truman said he wished it were possible for him to recommend "that the drafting of men be stopped altogether and at once."

"But," he added, "sharing the deep feeling of our people that those veterans who have given long and arduous service must be returned to their homes with all pos-

(Continued on Page 8)

Mountbatten's Forces, Japs Sign Local Peace Treaty

RANGOON, Aug. 28—Preliminaries for peace in Southeast Asia and the Indies were signed here today by a representative of Count Terauchi, Japanese commander in the theater.

Described as a local agreement between the Allied and Japanese theater commanders, the terms smooth the way for the Allies pending the signature of the over-all Japanese surrender aboard the U.S. battleship Missouri in Tokyo Bay next Sunday.

British authorities ordered the Japanese commander to keep a rendezvous off Penang at the head of Malacca Strait leading to Singapore to arrange for the surrender of the former enemy submarine base at Penang.

The Japanese also were instructed to allow entry of Allied ships into Japanese-controlled waters and to permit mine sweeping operations.

The negotiations were said to include plans for Adm. Lord Louis Mountbatten's entry into Singapore, probably early in September.

Lt. Gen. Numata, Count Terauchi's Chief of Staff, and Lt. Gen. A. M. Browning, Adm. Mountbatten's Chief of Staff, signed the agreement in the presence of representatives of the U. S., the Netherlands, China, France and Australia.

Jap Ultra-Patriots Save Face by Death

SAN FRANCISCO, Aug. 28 (AP)—Thirty-six members of Japanese "ultrapatriotic" organizations already have committed hara-kiri, the Domei News Agency announced today.

Ten killed themselves near the Atagoyama shrine, 12 before the Imperial Palace and 14 near the Yogami parade ground.

Allied Fleet Sails Into Tokyo Bay

GUAM, Aug. 28—American occupation troops landed in Japan today and an occupation fleet sailed into Tokyo Bay.

A group of 150 U.S. technical specialists landing at Atsugi airport, 20 miles from Tokyo, in 48 heavily-armed transport planes, found the Japanese co-operative—"polite as pie," said one report to Okinawa. They invited the crews to six-course dinners.

The Americans immediately set to work to make arrangements for the arrival of the main occupation forces Thursday, headed by Gen. MacArthur.

Crash Kills 20

The only mishap was an accident on Okinawa involving an American transport bound for Atsugi Airfield. An NBC correspondent said the crash killed about 20 Americans and destroyed valuable communications equipment. The broadcaster reported that those killed were veterans in the communications field, and that the mishap had caused some delay in obtaining necessary information from Japan.

Reports from Manila said that while 300 aerial transports would leave Okinawa daily, once the occupation program got in full sway, it might be as long as five months before U. S. forces in northern Japan reach their maximum strength.

Observers here considered it unlikely there would be any immediate march on Tokyo once the Americans went shore on Honshu in large numbers.

10,000 to Land

Meanwhile, Adm. Nimitz disclosed that virtually the entire strength of the four U. S. fleets and three amphibious forces in the Pacific would be employed to put Allied occupation troops in Japan and then "control the coastal waters" there for an indefinite period after that.

The combined amphibious forces, which will begin operations Thursday by landing 10,000 U. S. marines and sailors at the Yokosuka Naval

(Continued on Page 8)

Jap Suiciders Won't Give Up

NEW YORK, Aug. 28 (ANS)—The Moscow radio reported last night that Japanese suicide garrisons were refusing to surrender to Soviet troops despite the capitulation of Kwantung Army forces totaling nearly 500,000 men.

"These squads consist of the most depraved men of the Japanese Army and are imbued by implacable hatred toward Russians," Moscow said. "Suicide garrisons and single Japanese troops belonging to these suicide units literally have to be blown to bits by Soviet troops."

Sub Entered Bergen Twice

LONDON, Aug. 28 (AP)—The same British submarine twice during the war penetrated the heavily defended port of Bergen, Norway, under the very noses of the Germans, blasting a 7,000-ton merchant vessel, a floating dock and other harbor installations.

The craft which carried out these daring missions was revealed today as a four-man submarine carrying attachable explosive charges.

It first entered Bergen harbor in April, 1944, with Lt. M. H. Shean in command, and laid a charge under the merchant ship Marenfels. The resulting explosion sank the ship.

Again in September, 1944, the same craft, this time with Lt. H. P. Westmacott in command, slipped into Bergen harbor in extremely heavy weather, through 30 miles of island passages, mine fields and other defenses.

French Meat Ration Up

PARIS, Aug. 28 (Reuter) — The French meat ration for September will be increased from three to five ounces weekly, it was announced today. Heavy workers and young people between 16 and 21 will receive eight ounces.

Sailor Arrested After 5 Blazes Fire Europa

LONDON, Aug. 28 (UP)—A U.S. sailor was arrested in Bremerhaven after five fires broke out simultaneously on the former German luxury liner Europa, which was being prepared there for use as a troop transport, it was reported today by The Daily Mail.

Doubled Navy and Marine watch parties had kept close check on the ship, which has a large amount of wood construction, and found that the fires had started in bored-out holes stuffed with paper and oil waste.

Gen. Wainwright Flies to Chungking

CHUNGKING, Aug. 28 (UP)—Lt. Gen. Jonathan Wainwright, American commander of Bataan and Corregidor when the Philippines fell to the Japanese, arrived here today by plane with a group of British and Dutch senior officers liberated from a Manchurian prison camp.

The officers were released from a camp at Sian, 100 miles north of Mukden, by American paratroops and Red Army ground forces last week.

Location of Graves May Be Obtair ed

PARIS, Aug. 28 — Location of graves of American military personnel buried in the ETO may now be obtained from the Theater Graves Registration Service headquarters at TSFET Rear, APO 887, it was announced today.

Requests for information should include the name, rank, serial number and last organization of the deceased. All U. S. miliary cemeteries permit the placing of flowers on graves and the taking of photographs. The Army cannot arrange to have flowers put on graves or furnish pictures, however.

Persons now buried in Germany will be reinterred in military cemeteries in Allied territory.

Heidelberg Train Busy

HEIDELBERG, Aug. 28—Approximately 25,000 civilians are being hauled each day on the electric railway running between Heidelberg and Mannheim.

Yanks on Passes to Paris Tipped Off on Tax Refunds

PARIS, Aug. 28 (S & S)—"Getting proper receipts from French business firms when purchasing gifts to be mailed home means money in the pocket to all GIs and officers stationed in France," according to Lt. Robert L. Michaelson, of Alexandria, Minn., who is on duty at the Central Registration Bureau, 11 Rue Scribe, Paris.

Refunds totalling more than 1,000,000 francs have been made to 120,000 American soldiers at the bureau on gift purchases during the past ten days, in accordance with the French government's recent decision to return luxury taxes to U. S. Army personnel, Michaelson said.

The rebate supplements the French government's cash gift to soldiers amounting to 850 francs per soldier per month.

Most of the refunds thus far have been made on perfume purchases, Michaelson said, pointing out that on this item alone soldiers are entitled to a 33 per cent return on the sale price. Other tax free items include jewelry, silks, cosmetics and three dimensional pictures. Certain high priced handbags also are included.

According to Michaelson, a "GI or an officer, to be eligible for a refund must present to the bureau a bill of sale made out in ink or indelible pencil showing the firm's letterhead, the item purchased, the amount paid and the store's certified number, given each firm by the French government. In addition, all gifts for which refunds are asked, must be mailed at the bureau, which is open daily from 9 a.m. to 5 p.m."

Purchases made at Army PX stores are not eligible for tax refunds as no taxes are charged on items sold through those channels.

Italian Idle May Go To Jobs in Russia

MOSCOW, Aug. 28 (AP) — An agreement between Russia and Italy whereby some of Italy's 2,000,000 unemployed would be moved to jobs in the Soviet Union is now under discussion, Giuseppe di Vittorio, general secretary of the Italian General Confederation of Labor, disclosed today.

Di Vittorio is here as the head of an Italian trade delegation discussing Italy's labor problems with Soviet Labor unions.

Nazis' Mistresses to Testify

NUREMBERG, Aug. 28 (AP) — The mistresses of several Nazi leaders have been brought here as witnesses against their former lovers in the War Crimes trials, it was disclosed yesterday by Col. John H. Amen, head prosecutor of Supreme Court Justice Robert Jackson's interrogation section.

Shanghai Gains Freedom

CHUNGKING, Aug. 28 (ANS)—Shanghai, greatest city of China, has reverted to Chinese control after eight years of Japanese occupation, a dispatch from the city indicated last night.

Tokyo radio reported airborne troops of Generalissimo Chiang Kai-shek's armies and "part of the U. S. Air Forces in China" began landing in the Shanghai area this morning. Landings were made peacefully in accordance with arrangements made with the Japanese commander, the broadcast said.

The first dispatch from Shanghai since the Japanese occupied the great port in 1937 said underground forces of the Chinese National Government had taken over the Japanese.

By VERN HAUGLAND

OVER SHANGHAI, Aug. 28 (Delayed) (AP)—We "buzzed" Shanghai for almost an hour in a Flying Fortress shortly after sunrise today and found the city decked with Chinese, American and British flags.

Although we droned repeatedly over the city at levels as low as 300 feet, not a single anti-aircraft gun opened up. About 40 Japanese fighters, apparently undamaged but with engines hooded as though decommissioned, were parked at the edge of the airdrome.

This beautiful city has virtually escaped damage. Few factories were bombed—we counted less than half a dozen—and they were by no means completely wrecked.

Two Cents A Copy

THE STARS AND STRIPES

U. S. Armed Forces Daily In The Middle Pacific

20 Sen A Copy In The Ryukyus

Vol. 1, No. 96 ★★ Saturday, September 1, 1945

Surrender Stage Is Set

Luxury Life May Entice Volunteers

WASHINGTON (ANS) — The armed services are seeking to encourage volunteer enlistments with a program of inducements and at the same time went down the line for continuation of the draft.

Navy and Marine Corps officers told the House Military Committee that those services do not believe recruitment alone will keep them up to needed strength service. Witnesses suggested, however, that if volunteering exceeds expectations, draft calls could be trimmed.

The program of inducements was offered by a joint Army-Navy board to the House Committee, several of whose members had indicated a desire to go on a straight volunteer basis for occupation armies and eliminate the draft entirely. There was talk within the committee of asking President Truman to explain to the nation why he thinks the draft is still necessary.

Full Scale Drive

As the Navy set in motion a full scale recruitment drive, the joint report urged these benefits for volunteers:

1—Increased pay for overseas duty beginning with 20 per cent and increasing five per cent yearly to a maximum of 35 per cent above continental duty pay.

2—Increase the number of non-commissioned grades and ratings.

3—Continuation of free postage.

4—Assurance of mustering out pay for men discharged and a bonus on reenlistment.

Other Benefits

5—An option for Army men regarding payment to them of money in lieu of quarters.

6—Transportation costs for reenlistment furloughs.

7—A guarantee of most benefits now accorded to inductees.

The military committee also heard that the nation's shortage of doctors is to be alleviated soon. Officers said 13,000 of the Army's 45,000 physicians will be discharged by Feb. 1.

Navy witnesses reported that 1,000 of that service's 14,000 doc-

(Continued on Back Page)

Ft. Ord To Send Stream Of AGF Replacements

FORT ORD, Calif. (ANS)—The Army Ground Forces Replacement Depot here will continue to send a constant stream of replacements to the Pacific to relieve high-point combat veterans, Brig. Gen. Benjamin C. Lockwood, Jr., the commanding general, has announced.

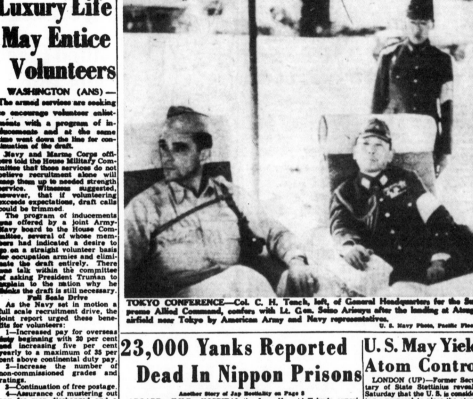

TOKYO CONFERENCE—Col. C. H. Tench, left, of General Headquarters for the Supreme Allied Command, confers with Lt. Gen. Seizo Arisuye after the landing at Atsugi airfield near Tokyo by American Army and Navy representatives.

U. S. Navy Photo, Pacific Fleet

23,000 Yanks Reported Dead In Nippon Prisons

Another Story of Jap Bestiality on Page 8

ABOARD THE HOSPITAL SHIP BENEVOLENCE IN TOKYO BAY (UP)—Survivors of Japanese prisoner camps Saturday described torture, neglect, brutality and sadistic "medical experiments" by the Japs.

An American doctor said this resulted in at least 23,000 dead among 30,000 American troops in the Far East.

Dr. Mack Leonard Gottlieb who was captured on Guam in 1941 described a burn treatment which consisted of pouring a small amount of incense-like powder into wounds and lighting it.

The treatment usually resulted in second degree burns.

He said two deaths occurred in the Shinagawa camp as the result of infection after burnings.

Gottlieb said a Jap medical officer—a Lt. Tokuda, later a captain—experimented with various injections, one consisting of pumping nicotinic acid into the spine, resulting in excruciating pain and vomiting.

Patients Became Worse

Dr. Harold W. Keschner was forced to do laboratory work for the Japs. He said Tokuda experimented particulary on tuberculosis cases. He said he was ordered to drain bile from gall bladders of patients suffering from amoebic dysentery, and mix it with caprilic acid. The mixture then was mixed and injected into tubercular patients.

Keschner said, as might have been expected, the patients became worse and that some slight cases developed enormous lung cavitites and others died much sooner than if the disease had been allowed to run its normal course.

Lt. Cmdr. Arno Town of New York City, medical officer aboard the Benevolence, said about 50 per cent of the prisoners thus far hospitalized suffered from tuberculosis and that about 50 per cent of all liberated prisoners require hospitalization.

Dr. Gottlieb said one of the most inhuman Jap practices was the mental torture of repeating the phrase, "Atone Chiisai Hako" meaning "very soon all of you will be in a small box."

Work Or Die

He was referring to the Jap practices of cremating the dead and putting the ashes in a small box. He said the Japs repeated this phrase constantly and told the prisoners, "You'll work for Japan or die."

He said prisoners and Allied doctors caring for the sick were placed on reduced rations since it was presumed they were not working.

Gottlieb said the Japs' idea of a full ration would be laughable if it weren't so heartbreaking.

Chief machinist's mate Alfred

(Continued on Page Four)

U. S. May Yield Atom Control

LONDON (UP)—Former Secretary of State Stettinius revealed Saturday that the U. S. is considering a proposal to place the atomic bomb secret with the World Security Council to enforce permanent peace.

Stettinius, now chief of the American delegate executive committee of the United Nations Preparatory Commission, said control of the world's newest and deadliest weapon might pass on to the world police organization.

He said this decision is being studied by the executive legislative branches of the government in Washington.

His remarks at a press conference seemed contradictory to official American and British statements saying that the atomic bomb would remain a secret at least for the present.

Frank Craven Dead; Stage, Screen Actor

BEVERELY HILLS, Calif. (AP)—Frank Craven, 70, veteran playwright, stage and screen actor, died at his home here Saturday after several months illness.

Steel Grip Tightens On Tokyo Area

YOKOHAMA (AP) — American troops Saturday extended their steel grip along both sides of Tokyo Bay area, the stage on which will be played out Sunday the greatest military pageant of the century—the final and formal surrender of the Japanese empire.

(In Washington, it was announced from the White House that the surrender ceremonies will go on the air—at 4 p.m. Saturday, Hawaii time.

(President Truman will broadcast a nine-minute speech immediately preceding the ceremonies, after which the broadcast will be switched back to the surrender scene for brief addresses by Gen. MacArthur and Adm. Nimitz. The president's speech will begin at

Last of the actors to take their places for the surrender drama were the Eighth Army men of Lt. Gen. Robert L. Eichelberger, scheduled to begin their mass landings in the Tokyo Bay sector by nightfall. (A radio report said the landings already had begun.)

As a backdrop, there was the black horror endured by prisoners of war, who poured from their stockades of death and degradation with blood-freezing accounts of the wanton cruelties inflicted upon them in the years when Japan was riding the crest of conquest.

Now, as the gaunt Lt. Gen. Jonathan Wainwright remarked, "the shoe is on the other foot."

He and his staff who survived the forced march of the Philippines and the evil years behind enemy wire arrived to witness the Japanese surrender signatures aboard the battleship Missouri.

Gen. MacArthur laid his plans at a private conference Friday night with Adms. Nimitz and Halsey and Gens. Spaatz and Kenney in Yokohama's New Grand Hotel.

MacArthur warmly greeted Gen. Wainwright, the man in whose command he left the losing battle of Bataan in March, 1942, when he was sent to Australia to organize the long trek back to victory. Wainwright made a brief broadcast to the people of the U. S., expressing his gratitude for their "generous understanding of my dire misfortune" at Corregidor.

Japanese imperial headquarters made one half-hearted attempt to postpone the national ignominy a little longer by asking MacArthur for further conferences on surrender terms, but it was declared at his headquarters that the ceremony would proceed as scheduled.

Already on hand were the rep-

(Continued on Back Page)

Settlement Seen 'Certainty' For Chinese-Yenan Confab

CHUNGKING (UP)—Conferences between Communist leader Mao Tze-Tung and national government leaders are expected to continue until the middle of next week when comprehensive settlements ending the threat of civil war will be reached, the Central News Agency reported Saturday.

Central reported that the fourth conference was held Friday with the military side of the issue coming under close study.

Central said "well informed observers" thought a complete settlement was a "certainty."

It was reported that Russia is "watching with interest and concern the negotiations between Chiang Kai-shek and the leader of the Chinese Communist party" and said, "it is imperative that China take the road of unity without delay."

("The Japanese are still hoping that dissension in China will prevail and are doing their utmost to provoke a rift," the broadcast, recorded by United Press, said "They are still powerful and exert a strong influence in the country.)

("They even went so far as to ask the supreme Allied commander, Gen. MacArthur, to allow Japanese residents to remain in China and permit them to keep arms allegedly in defense against marauders. We do not doubt that the supreme commander will reject the request. But the implications are obvious.")

Nearly twice as much money is in circulation in $1,000 bills as in $500 bills.

Gen. Wainwright's Wife Hears His Broadcast

NEW YORK (ANS)—Mrs. Jonathan Wainwright, wife of the hero of Corregidor, heard her husband's voice Friday for the first time in nearly four years, NBC reported. She was listening when Wainwright broadcast from U. S Army studios of Radio Tokyo to the U. S.

Jap Guards In Filth-Littered PW Camp Feast On K Rations

By S/SGT. JOHN W. THORBURN
Stars and Stripes Staff Writer

YOKOHAMA—A K ration menu ticketed for Allied prisoners of war and dropped by U.S. "biscuit bombers" over the Kawasaki Concentration Camp provided a feast for the Japanese prison guards.

The rations, along with civilian and service publications, including Stars and Stripes, squarely hit the mark—but they arrived several hours after the prisoners had been evacuated.

Nipponese guards, sporting billiard ball haircuts, and looking fat and 4-F, squatted around long wooden tables enjoying the K rations and curiously eyeing pictures in the newspapers in picnic style.

The camp, littered with filth, had once been utilized as a flophouse hotel. It was two blocks from a war plant between Tokyo and Yokohama, and housed 200 Allied prisoners whose lives would have hung on a thread had the war plant been bombed.

Candy bars enclosed in the K rations went over big with the Japs. They told interpreters they "like these best." Puffing on American cigarets, a Jap made the comment, "Ah, those American cigarets."

A moment later, looking at a cheesecake picture on the back page of The Stars and Stripes, he again made the sage observation, "Ah, those American girls."

The Japs were all bows and smiles. They quickly made it known that the prisoners had not minded internment, and had been cooperative, never having to be punished.

The poor state of the prisoners' health, the miserable conditions in the camp and the stories told by the prisoners hardly agreed with the Jap version, however.

S & S Weatherman . . .
LONDON, SOUTHERN ENG., and S. WALES
Mainly Fair, with possible local Showers, Warm.

New York — London Edition — Paris

THE STARS AND STRIPES

Newspaper of U.S. Armed Forces in the European Theater

Vol. 5 No. 258—1d. MONDAY, SEPTEMBER 3 1945

. . . Predicts for Today
NORTHERN ENG., N. WALES, S. SCOTLAND
Fair and Warm.

20-Minute Signing Ends History's Bloodiest War

M'Arthur May Enter Enemy Capital Today

ABOARD THE USS MISSOURI IN TOKYO BAY, Sept. 2—Virtually six years to the day after its inception, the costliest and bloodiest war in world history came to a close today aboard this mighty 45,000-ton flagship of the U.S. 3rd Fleet.

Formal finis to World War II, which Hitler launched on Sept. 1, 1939, by sending his legions into Poland, came during a 20-minute ceremony starting at 10:30 AM (2:30 AM British time), when the surrender document was signed.

At that hour New York was alive with Saturday night joy seekers, London was asleep, Moscow was greeting the dawn and Tokyo lay under a mid-morning overcast.

Although various parts of the Japanese empire were occupied and more were being occupied last night, Tokyo, the capital city, was not yet occupied. But Gen. Douglas MacArthur, according to various reports, was expected to enter that city tomorrow to confer with Japanese representatives on the entry of Allied troops. The victory march into Tokyo was expected to take place within a week or ten days.

Two nervous Japanese statesmen formally and unconditionally surrendered all remnants of their stolen empire by signing the paper before a group of Allied leaders—most of them Americans who had converted the Pearl Harbor defeat into a smashing victory after some three years and nine months of fighting.

In the midst of high-ranking United Nations delegates assembled on the gallery deck of the Missouri stood Lt. Gen. Jonathan M. Wainwright, hero of Corregidor; Lt. Gen. Archibald Percival, Britain's defender of Singapore, and other recently-released prisoners of the Japanese who were invited to witness the historic ceremony.

They watched the 11-man Japanese delegation climb to the deck and stop ten paces from a long green covered table on which the surrender documents were placed.

Opposite them were bemedalled officers representing eight nations—each row six men deep. To the right of the Japs were lined America's fighting leaders in 21 rows, four deep.

In an electric silence, Foreign Minister Mamoru Shigemitsu, wearing a wrinkled silk morning coat and top hat, leaned heavily on his cane to favor his lame leg as the ceremony began. With him were four civilians, three top-hatted and one in a rumpled white suit. Others in the Jap party were in uniform.

Shigemitsu signed first for Japan. His cane fell and clattered to the blue-painted deck when he seated himself at the table. He took off his top hat, tinkered with his pen, then firmly affixed his signature.

The document, making Japan's 70,000,000 people—from Emperor Hirohito down—subject to the authority of Gen. MacArthur as Supreme Allied Military Commander, was about 12 by 18 inches in size. Shigemitsu signed the American copy first, then the duplicate to be retained by Japan.

Gen. Yoshijiro Umezu, chief of the Japanese General Staff, followed him, resolutely scrawling his name as though in a great hurry. If the moment was bitter for the 63-year-old conqueror of Manchukuo and leader of the expeditionary forces in North China, his inscrutable face and correct manner did not betray it.

A Japanese colonel was seen to wipe tears from his eyes. All the Japanese looked tense and weary.

MacArthur was next to sign on behalf of all the victorious nations.

"Will Gen. Wainwright and Gen. Per-

(Continued on back page)

Corregidor Conqueror Gives Up

The surrender of Lt. Gen. Tomoyuki Yamashita, Japanese commander in the Philippines, and the capitulation of Truk, most powerful enemy bastion east of Tokyo, yesterday highlighted the piecemeal collapse of the Emperor's Pacific Empire.

In northern Luzon, Yamashita, conqueror of Corregidor and the "Tiger of Malaya," walked three miles from his mountain command post to give himself up to the U.S. 32nd Div. He left immediately by plane for Baguio, Philippines summer capital, for surrender formalities.

The surrender of Truk in the Carolines was accepted by Vice Adm. George D. Murray aboard the cruiser Portland. Naval headquarters at Guam said the surrender was made without incident.

Capitulation of Truk, where the Jap garrison was believed to number 50,000 men, eliminated the most powerful of Japan's by-passed strongholds.

Formal surrender of Jap forces in China was set for Thursday in Nanking. Gen. Ho Ying-Chin, commander of China's field forces, will head the Chinese delegation.

The formal capitulation of Jap forces in New Guinea, New Britain, New Ireland and the Solomons is expected in a few days, Melbourne Radio said last night. It was estimated that 86,000 Japanese are in these areas.

New York radio, meanwhile, stated that

(Continued on back page)

History Comes From Inkpot

TOKYO BAY, Sept. 2 (ANS)—These were the signers of the Japanese surrender document in the order in which they signed:

Mamoru Shigemitsu, Japanese Foreign Minister.

Gen. Yoshijiro Umezu, Japanese Imperial General Staff chief.

Gen. Douglas MacArthur, Allied Supreme Commander, on behalf of all the Allies.

Adm. Chester W. Nimitz for the U.S.

Gen. Hsu Yung-chang for China.

Adm. Sir Bruce Fraser for the United Kingdom.

Lt. Gen. Derevyanko for Russia.

Gen. Sir Thomas Blamey for Australia.

Col. Lawrence Moore-Cosgrave for Canada.

Gen. Jacques LeClerc for France.

Adm. Helfrich for the Netherlands.

Air Vice Marshal Isitt for New Zealand.

Keystone and Associated Press radiophotos

LAST CURTAIN: Flush with victory, Gen. Douglas MacArthur reaches the long-awaited day as he conducts formal surrender of the Japs aboard the USS Missouri in Tokyo Bay. Still wearing his famed cap and with the collar of his khaki shirt open (top photo), he signs the document, witnessed by liberated leaders Lt. Gen. Jonathan Wainwright and Gen. Sir Archibald Percival. Then, hands thrust nonchalantly into his pockets (lower), he watches Jap Foreign Minister Mamoru Shigemitsu sign the surrender instrument.

Stalin Sees Score to Settle With Japanese

By the United Press

Russia has a "special account to settle with Japan," Premier Stalin declared yesterday in a broadcast speech on the occasion of the Japanese surrender.

He added that Japan's unconditional surrender "means that Southern Sakhalin and the Kuriles will pass to the Soviet Union, and will no longer serve as a means of isolating the Soviet Union from the (Pacific) Ocean and as a base for a Jap attack on our Far East."

Reviewing Russian-Japanese history, Stalin pointed out that the Japanese attacked Port Arthur in 1904 while negotiations between Russia and Japan were still in progress, a trick she repeated at Pearl Harbor in 1941.

"It is well known that Russia suffered defeat and that Japan took advantage of the Czarist defeat to wrest southern Sakhalin from Russia and to strengthen her hold over the Kurile Islands, and thus lock our country from all outlets to the ocean in the east."

"For 40 years we men of the older generation," he concluded, "have waited for this day."

Truman, In Message to Forces, Pledges to Speed Their Return

WASHINGTON, Sept. 2 (UP)—President Truman told members of the U.S. armed forces in a broadcast schedule for tonight that the great majority of them will return to civil life as soon as ships and planes can get them home.

"I think I know the American soldier and sailor," the President said. "He does not want gratitude or sympathy. He had a job to do. He did not like it. But he did it. And how he did it. Now he wants to come back home and start again the life he loves, a life of peace and quiet, the life of a civilian.

"But he wants to know that he can come back to a good life. He wants to know that his children will not have to go back to the life of the fox hole and the bomber, the battleship and the submarine. I speak on behalf of all your countrymen when I pledge you that we shall do everything in our power to make those wishes come true."

"For some of you," President Truman said, "I am sorry to say military service must continue for a time. We must keep an occupation force in the Pacific to clean out the militarism of Japan, just as we are cleaning out the militarism of Germany. The United Nations are determined that never again shall either of these countries be able to attack its peaceful neighbors.

"But the great majority of you will be

(Continued on back page)

Lease Debts Not Canceled

WASHINGTON, Sept. 2 (AP)—Secretary of State James F. Byrnes said yesterday that the U.S. has not canceled lend-lease obligations of other nations.

They will not be asked to pay in dollars because they have no dollar credits.

It seemed probable that they would be requested to pay in the form of lowered trade restrictions. This may particularly apply to the British, whose economic representatives will arrive next week to discuss possible Lend-Lease substitutes.

Byrnes made it clear in a formal statement that President Truman's report to Congress saying that the $42,000,000,000 of lend-lease might as well be "written off" did not mean that there would be no settlement by means other than cash.

Japan Agrees To Do This . .

Article by article, here is what Japan agreed to do under the terms of surrender:

1—Accept all provisions of the Potsdam Declaration.

2—Surrender unconditionally all armed forces.

3—Cease hostilities forthwith and preserve and save from damage all ships, aircraft and military and civil property.

4—Command Imperial General Headquarters to issue orders to all field commanders everywhere to surrender their forces unconditionally.

5—See that all civil, military and naval officials obey and enforce all orders of the Allied Supreme Commander.

6—Carry out in good faith under Allied direction the Potsdam Declaration, under which free institutions may be established leading to the restoration of sovereignty.

7—Liberate all Allied war prisoners and civilian internees and see that they arrive safely at debarkation points.

8—Acknowledge that the authority of the Emperor and the Japanese government is subject to the will of the Supreme Commander.

Truman Backs Army-Navy Merger

Vast Plan To Rebuild Is Outlined

WASHINGTON, Sept. 6 (INS)—President Truman put before Congress today a legislative and executive program designed to meet the aftermath of the war. The comprehensive pattern for reconstruction in effect told the American people how to "achieve the highest standard of life known to history."

The 15,000-word message, which described the needs of labor, industry, agriculture and national defense, was read to the hastily reconvened House and Senate. The President did not appear himself.

His program for national defense and world security included a promise of immediate action "during the current session of Congress" on unification of the armed services in a single Department of Defense, which also would control the use and development of atomic energy.

Would Continue Draft

He also reiterated his proposal for universal training and continuation of the draft for men aged 18 to 25 for a two-year period.

Forecasting "a great deal of inevitable unemployment during reconversion," Mr. Truman said his answer to the problem was "to achieve as full peacetime production and employment as possible in the most efficient and speedy manner."

His program for the attainment of that goal included these aspects:

1. Demobilization as soon as possible.
2. Immediate settlement of war contracts.
3. Removal of all possible wartime government controls of industry.
4. Retention of rent and price ceilings until fair competition can work to prevent inflation.
5. Holding wages in line where increases would encourage inflationary price rises.
6. Prevention of any rapid decrease in wages or purchasing power.

He urged Congress to give the quickest possible approval to his interim plans to help Britain and other Allies out of their lend-lease

(Continued on Page 8)

This S and S Is Uncensored

PARIS, Sept. 6—U. S. military press censorship ended in Europe today and this is the first uncensored edition of The Stars and Stripes in its history.

Wind-up of American military censorship, which went into effect at the beginning of the war, followed by a few hours the end of French press censorship at midnight Wednesday. There is now no press censorship in France.

German publications in the U. S. zone of occupation in Germany will, however, continue to be censored by UFSET's information control division. This does not apply to the two editions of The Stars and Stripes published in Germany or other American or Allied publications distributed there.

The end of military censorship brought widespread unemployment to the remnant of U. S. officer-censor detachments which at one time numbered 170 in the European Theater. Censors will be redeployed or reassigned, some to public relations jobs.

Senators Vote Inquiry Of Pearl Harbor Blow

WASHINGTON, Sept. 6—The Senate late today voted unanimously for a joint congressional inquiry into the Pearl Harbor disaster.

The vote came on a resolution introduced by Senate Majority Leader Alben W. Barkley of Kentucky. The resolution now goes to the House for concurrence.

SOUTHERN GERMANY EDITION

THE STARS AND STRIPES

Newspaper of U.S. Armed Forces in the European Theater

Volume 1, Number 123 | 20 Pfennig | Friday, September 7, 1945

The Weather

Today: Partly cloudy. Maximum temperature 75.
Tomorrow: Unchanged.

70s to Quit Europe Before End of Year

Little Left After Atomic Bomb Hit Nagasaki

This photograph was taken while rescue groups were at work following the atomic bomb raid on Nagasaki Aug. 9, according to the Japanese sources which supplied the picture. Buildings over a wide area were levelled by the blast and the toll of dead is still mounting.

Men 35 Also Will Go; 1,300,000 to Ship Out In Next Four Months

By ROBERT J. DONOVAN, Staff Writer

PARIS, Sept. 6—All men with 70 or more points, on the basis of the revised adjusted service rating score, and a limited number with fewer than 70 points will leave Europe for the U.S. before Christmas, Brig. Gen. George S. Eyster, deputy assistant chief of staff of USFET G-3, announced today. All troops eligible for discharge for age also will be home or on the way home before Dec. 25, he said. The total number of troops to be shipped out of the theater between now and Dec. 31, Eyster revealed, will be 1,300,000.

Because of the inevitable lapse of time between the moment a soldier first sees his name on shipping orders and his arrival home, it is "problematical" how many high-pointers and over-age men will be in their homes Christmas Day, Eyster said.

Generally speaking, he said, to be home by Christmas a soldier should be in transit from his station in the ET to the assembly area by Thanksgiving. Most of those who do not find themselves on the way until after Thanksgiving will have a pretty tight squeeze making it by Christmas Day, he indicated.

'Close-Out Force' Is Sought

Eyster announced that the ET was negotiating with the War Department for retention in this theater for six months after Jan. 1 of a "close-out force" of as many as 300,000 men to liquidate the American military establishment in Europe. This force would be in addition to the army of occupation, which will number about 400,000.

The point-score levels of troops to be assigned to the army of occupation and to the close-out forces have not been decided, Eyster said. It is as yet no hard-and-fast rule that men with 45 or fewer points will be in the army of occupation, but it is probable that they will be, he said. The dividing line, he explained, may be at a point-level higher than 45, if it is found that there are not enough 45-pointers available.

Eyster, reviewing the entire redeployment situation, disclosed that Army plans provided for movement of 1,300,000 troops out of the ET between Sept. 1 and Dec. 31. The September shipping schedule has been boosted to the record figure of 410,000, Eyster said. Indications were that October, November and December shipments would run to about 300,000 a month.

One reason for the prospective decline from the September level is that the service under which a considerable number of high-point men have been flown home each month will be abandoned on Sept. 30, after which all high-pointers will return home by water. Eyster said he believed the Air Transport Command planes used for that purpose would be transferred to the Pacific to fly men home from the Orient. Flying conditions in the Atlantic, he pointed out, are unfavorable in winter.

TSF Shipments Will Be Heavy

Eyster disclosed that beginning the latter part of September and continuing throughout October, shipping quotas for Theater Service Forces, including headquarters in Paris, will be "very heavy." Until now the lion's share of shipping space has been going to field troops, with 14 divisions scheduled to depart this month.

Observing with a smile that soldiers are not fond of "repple depples" and casual companies, Eyster said that so far as possible all troops, even headquarters and service troops, would be sent home in regular units and that the number going through repple depples would be held to a minimum. Regular units leaving for the U. S. will be allowed to travel over-strength to absorb home-bound men from other units, he said. Thus, a man from a quartermaster outfit might go home with a medical outfit.

Eyster reiterated previous official statements that all men with 85 or more points on the basis of either the V-E Day or V-J Day computation, would leave the ET by Oct. 31.

Army Won't Wait for Lower Score

The Army, he said, will not wait until the critical score has been lowered again before it begins to send home men with fewer than 80 points. As soon as 80-pointers are out of the way men in the seventies will be called. The critical score, Eyster pointed out, did not determine who may be shipped out of the theater, but, rather, who may be discharged upon return to the U. S., he said. The War Department will lower the critical score as rapidly as it can handle returning men at separation stations. Men sent home with points below the critical score will be subject to further duty in the U. S. until the critical score drops to their level, Eyster said.

The general said many men with low scores had been "lucky" in getting home because they happened to be in the process of being redeployed when the Japanese war ended, terminating shipments from the ET to the Pacific. Low-point men still remaining in assembly and staging areas are being withdrawn and assigned to duties in Europe, and

(Continued on Page 8)

U.S. Recon. Force Enters Tokyo; Whole Division Follows Tonight

YOKOHAMA, Sept. 6—Reconnaissance troops of the U. S. Army moved through Tokyo's streets today to prepare the way for the 1st Cav. Div., which will formally occupy the imperial city Saturday, beginning at 6 a.m. (11 o'clock tonight, Central European Summer Time) Gen. MacArthur was expected to enter Tokyo with the main cavalry forces and, in that belief, the famous old 7th Cav. Regt. started selecting an honor guard to escort him. Troops who entered the city today were detailed to choose buildings for the permanent occupation.

Thirty-five to 40 square miles of Tokyo's more than 200 square miles will be taken under military control by 1st Cav. Div. troops in the initial occupation Saturday. Japan's Domei news agency said 8,000 officers and men will comprise units entering Tokyo at that time.

Secret Police to Help

Domei's broadcast said that when MacArthur's headquarters move in, his troops will be stationed at 3rd Regt. headquarters at Azabu and also at Yoyegi parade grounds.

Augmenting of both Tokyo and Yokohama civilian police by carefully selected members of the former Kimpei-Tai, Japan's secret police, was announced by U. S. 8th Army headquarters.

Only a few of these recruits will be armed, headquarters said, although all are empowered to arrest Japanese civilians.

Japan's Diet, radio and press continued to publicize a variety of opinions on causes of the nation's defeat. The newspaper Asahi blamed struggles between the army and navy and between the Cabinet and militarists over control of the country.

Cost Over 5 Million Casualties

A government spokesman told the Imperial Diet that the war had cost their Army and Navy a total of 5,085,000 casualties.

The losses included 310,000 army dead and 157,365 navy dead. Allied air raids killed 241,309 and injured 313,041, the spokesman said. In Tokyo alone, 88,250 were killed.

Despite these losses, the official told the Diet that Japan's armed strength at the war's end was nearly three times what it was at the start of the war.

Vienna Council Will Meet Soon

VIENNA, Sept. 6 (Reuter)—Deputies of the American, British, Russian and French commanders in chief in Austria have agreed that the first official meeting of the Allied Control Commission in Vienna will take place "at an early date," probably Sept. 11, it was disclosed today.

Establishment of the commission in Vienna was discussed when all four Allied commanders met here last month.

Meanwhile, British authorities said that despite efforts of the Allies the food situation in Vienna was so serious that it would be a major problem to be taken at the forthcoming meeting of foreign ministers in London.

Hines Is Nominated As Panama Envoy

WASHINGTON, Sept. 6 (ANS)—President Truman yesterday sent to the Senate his formal nomination of Brig. Gen. Frank Hines, former Veterans Administrator, to be Ambassador to Panama.

The President also nominated Lt. Gen. Raymond A. Wheeler to be Chief of Army Engineers, succeeding Lt. Gen. Eugene Reybold, and Maj. Gen. Robert W Crawford to be president of the Mississippi River Commission, replacing Brig. Gen. Max C. Tyler.

Nazi Butcher Seized in Japan

SAN FRANCISCO, Sept. 6 (AP)—The "Butcher of Warsaw", Joseph Meisinger, has been captured in Japan, according to a broadcast today from Tokyo.

The Weather Today
SHANGHAI & VICINITY
Fair
CHUNGKING & VICINITY
Cloudy
KUNMING & VICINITY
Clearing

CHINA EDITION
THE STARS AND STRIPES
Newspaper of U.S. Armed Forces
In The China Theater
Vol. 1—No. 8
Two Cents U.S.
CN$10
SATURDAY, OCT. 6, 1945

Chinowledge
Chinese girls have the most beautiful legs the world has ever seen.

Chiang Troops Tighten Grip On Kunming

By HARRY PURCELL
(Staff Correspondent)

KUNMING, Oct. 5—A statement issued last night from the headquarters of Lt. Gen. Tu Li-ming, new commanding general in the Kunming defense forces, said all resistance to the reorganization of the Yunnan Provincial Government is ended.

At least three American soldiers were wounded by stray bullets in the disorders, involving the private army of General Lung Yun, who was relieved of his post as Governor of Yunnan, and Government forces, Reuter's said.

Martial law was proclaimed in the city after sniping and sharp street clashes had brought about a virtual siege.

MOTOR FIRE HEARD

It is understood that the fighting broke out because two regiments of General Lung Yun's private army were not informed that their general was being relieved of his position.

The last apparent skirmish took place Wednesday night in the vicinity of the West Gate, the China end of the Burma Road. The crump of mortars could be heard and the path of tracer bullets observed.

Nationalist troops still patrol the streets of the city and the adjacent highways.

An official statement released by the SOS Headquarters follows:

AURAND IN COMMAND

"Maj. Gen. H. S. Aurand, Senior U. S. Armed Forces Commander in the Kunming District, assumed emergency command of all U.S. Armed Forces in that area at 5.45 a.m. on Oct. 3, 1945, "for protection of American lives and property."

This action was taken as a result of the visit of two staff officers of Lt. Gen. Tu. These officers brought, with them a letter from Gen. Tu which stated Generalissimo Chiang Kai-shek had ordered reorganization of the Yunnan Provincial Government and that during this reorganization, 'in order to prevent any likely disorders' certain precautionary measures were to be taken by all persons in the Province.

Armed US Junk Fought Navy's Final Battle

SHANGHAI, Oct. 5—(UP)—The United States Navy's last surface engagement of World War II was won off the China coast by a handful of Yanks aboard a pair of ancient junks.

The battle occurred Aug. 20—five days after the Japanese

surrender—when one Army captain, two Marine officers, one Navy lieutenant and four Navy enlisted men conquered a heavily armed Jap army junk, killed 43 Japanese and took 39 prisoners, all but four of whom were wounded.

The Navy's first battle under sail since Civil War days took place on the night of Aug. 19 when Lt. Livingston "Swede" Swentzel, jr., led a little two-junk flotilla out of a coastal town near Hainan, Shanghai bound.

Commanding the second junk was Marine Lt. Stewart L. Pittman. Aboard Swentzel's junk were Capt. Austin B. Cox, an army air-ground support officer whose necessity to reach Shanghai was one of the reasons for the voyage; Capt. Pat O'Neill, U.S. Marine Corps Reserve and Seaman First Class James R. Reid.

With Pittman were three enlisted men—Gunners Mate William K. Barrett, Gunners Mate Floyd Rose and Motor Machinists Mate David A. Baker.

The morning of the 20th, while tacking north against a heavy wind, the tiny task-force suddenly confronted a big menacing junk.

The Americans spotted a gleaming .75 howitzer which immediately belched smoke and fire, making a direct hit about 10 feet above the deck. The blast killed a pair of Chinese tommy-gunners and knocked out a third and sprayed Captain Cox with fragments.

When the junks were less than 100 yards apart, Reid got a rocket off which exploded squarely on the deck of the Jap ship. Swentzel said: "You could see pieces of junk and pieces of Japs flying in all directions."

Soon after that the Nips gave up, hoisting a dirty skivvy shirt on a bayonet in token of surrender. The Americans, who came alongside and boarded found the ship a terrific shambles. The ship was loaded with Jap ammunition.

3,400,000 Home By June

NEW YORK, Oct. 5—(UP)—The United States Army will return 1,800,000 more troops from Europe by end of March and 1,600,000 from the Pacific by end of June, Col. E.C.R. Lasher, second zone transportation officer of the Army Transportation Corps said last night.

He added that 400,000 German and Italian prisoners of war will be sent back to Europe in lots of 500 by March.

Lasher also disclosed that organized troop movements within the United States alone will involve 1,250,000 men per month.

Japanese Cabinet Quits In Face Of Mac's Orders

TOKYO, Oct. 5—(UP)—The Japanese cabinet, headed by Prince General Naruhika Higashi-Kuni, resigned today.

The premier submitted his resignation to Emperor Hirohito after a brief cabinet meeting late this morning.

Higashi-Kuni formed the cabinet shortly after Japan's surrender. He had succeeded Premier Baron Admiral Kantaro Suzuki.

The cabinet resignation followed by a few hours Gen. Douglas D. MacArthur's order ousting the Japanese Home Minister and every Japanese police chief from office, and ordering the release of political prisoners.

MacArthur's orders, which also demanded abolition of the notorious "thought police" and an end to all other measures restricting Japanese freedom of thought and action, set a deadline of next Wednesday for compliance.

MOVE RUMORED

There had been rumors for some days that the cabinet might resign in face of the increasingly stern controls ordered by the Supreme commander of Allied occupation forces.

Observers are watching with interest the results of the cabinet resignation and release of some 3,000 political prisoners of liberal and leftist leanings.

Communist leaders, who comprise a large number of the political prisoners to be released, have openly declared their intention to lead a revolution for overthrow of the Emperor and the Japanese feudal system.

AVOID CIVIL STRIFE

It is presumed that the cabinet accepted as a direct reproof MacArthur's latest directives. United States counter-intelligence officers told the United Press that MacArthur gave the Japanese government an unmistakable indication of his desires and ample time to comply. His orders were issued only when the Japanese indicated they had no intention of carrying out reforms voluntarily.

Detroit Wins 2nd Game 4-1

BRIGGS STADIUM, Detroit, Oct. 5—A pair of ex-service-men—Hank Greenberg and Virgil Trucks—teamed up yesterday to lead the Detroit Tigers to a 4-1 victory over the Chicago Cubs and even the Series at one game each.

While Trucks took care of the throwing, Big Hank took care of the hitting. With the score tied one-all in the fifth and two men on base, Greenberg leaned on one of Hank Wyse's twisters sending it high up in the stands in left center field. That was all Trucks and the Tigers needed.

It was only fitting that Trucks and Greenberg should come through. They were the central figures in the victory over the Browns that gave the Tigers the pennant last Sunday.

Trucks, only three days out of the Navy, started and was relieved in the sixth after giving up only three hits. All Greenberg did was unload his speciality, a home run, in the top of the ninth with the bases loaded. It was enough to topple the Brownies, 6-3.

And yesterday this duo was just as effective. Except for some slow fielding by Roger Cramer on Bill Nicholson's single in the fourth, Trucks would have had a shutout. Phil Cavarretta had doubled and when Cramer played Nicholson's drive the long way home, Cavarretta scored.

Pregame betting was 8-5 that Wyse, a 22-game winner for Chicago this season, would

(Continued on Page 3)

Palace Back In Bounds

SHANGHAI, Oct. 5—The Palace Hotel restaurant is back in bounds. Army officials announced yesterday that sanitary conditions in the restaurant kitchen, which resulted in an "out-of-bounds" listing last week, had been corrected.

Nazi Accused Of Setting Savage Dogs On Prisoners

LUNEBURG, GERMANY, Oct. 5—(AP)—Josef Kramer, former master of two concentration camps who said reports of mass killings and deaths at Auschwitz were "untrue from beginning to end", was accused at his trial here of lining up selected victims at the edge of a flaming funeral pit, commanding savage dogs to force some into the fire and machinegunning the rest.

Prosecutor Thomas M. Backhouse read to a military court trying Kramer and 44 others as war criminals for murder and mistreatment of concentration camp inmates, an affidavit by Regina Rosenthal, Polish Jewess interned successively at Auschwitz and Belsen, both of which Kramer commanded.

"While at Auschwitz I saw about 200 people around a ditch in which a big fire was burning," she said in her statement. "Lager Commandant Kramer was behind them with a machinegun and some dogs. When he pointed to a man, the dogs would attack and the man was either killed or fell into the fire. Kramer then machine-gunned the others."

The prisoners in the dock, particularly the women, appeared amused each time one of their number was mentioned by name in an affidavit which named some new brutality or murder charged by a former inmate.

World War II Vets Bid To Boss VFW

CHICAGO, Oct. 5 (ANS)—World War II veterans made a bid today to begin taking over leadership of Veterans of Foreign Wars.

At least one candidate, Edward Hellar, 20, Mitchell, Ohio, among the youngest men at the 46th National Encampment, was openly out for the post of junior vice commander-in-chief of the organization, heretofore run by veterans of World War I and previous wars.

Russians Serve Notice

MOSCOW, Oct. 5—(AP)—Pravda, the organ of the Communist Party, declared in an editorial today that "times were gone forever" when Pacific affairs could be settled without Soviet participation.

Famed Pearl Of Asia Found In Marseilles Toilet Drain Pipe

PARIS, Oct. 5—(UP)—The fabulous Pearl of Asia largest in the world and formerly owned by Kuan Lung, 18th Century Emperor of China—is on sale here for $500,000 after being discovered in its wartime hiding place in the toilet drain pipe of a Marseilles boarding hosue.

Yvon Colette, an almost equally fabulous character, has been charged with stealing the pearl and is awaiting trial. He contended he nabbed the jewel to keep it from Nazi Marshal Hermann Goering and intended to present it to Gen. Charles de Gaulle.

According to the authorities, the pearl was seized in April, 1944, by four self-styled S.S. men who burst into the room where French experts were examining it. These so-called SS men were believed to have been Colette and an accomplice.

After the Allied landings in Normandy, Colette tried vainly to sell the gem. During the liberation of Paris he sent his wife to the country to hide the jewel in an oak tree. He later removed it to the boarding house in which it has been found.

The 605-carat, three-inch, pear-shaped jewel, mounted in delicate rose quartz, has an Arabian Nights history.

It was found in the Persian Gulf in 1628 and later was placed in a sarcophagus with Emperor Kuan Lung.